Blackstone's Statutes Series

Employment Law in Context

Text and Materials

Third Edition

David Cabrelli

University of Edinburgh

David Cabrelli is Senior Lecturer in Commercial Law at the University of Edinburgh and a solicitor (non-practising) in Scotland. David's research interests lie in the field of labour law, particularly the common law, and statutory regulation, of the contract of employment. He has published papers in a number of leading academic journals in the field of labour law, and his research has been cited by the UK Supreme Court, the Hong Kong High Court, the Supreme Court of Australia, the Law Commission, and the Scottish Law Commission.

OXFORD
UNIVERSITY PRESS

OXFORD
UNIVERSITY PRESS

Great Clarendon Street, Oxford, OX2 6DP,
United Kingdom

Oxford University Press is a department of the University of Oxford.
It furthers the University's objective of excellence in research, scholarship,
and education by publishing worldwide. Oxford is a registered trade mark of
Oxford University Press in the UK and in certain other countries

© Oxford University Press 2018

The moral rights of the author have been asserted

First edition 2014
Second edition 2016
Impression: 2

Public sector information reproduced under Open Government Licence v3.0
(http://www.nationalarchives.gov.uk/doc/open-government-licence/open-government-licence.htm)

Published in the United States of America by Oxford University Press
198 Madison Avenue, New York, NY 10016, United States of America

British Library Cataloguing in Publication Data
Data available

Library of Congress Control Number: 2017964397

ISBN 978-0-19-881314-9

Printed in Great Britain by
Bell & Bain Ltd., Glasgow

This book is dedicated to my mother, Rosanna Cabrelli

■ PREFACE TO THIRD EDITION

The interval between the second and third editions of this work was rudely punctuated by the monumental decision of the British people to exit from the European Union ('EU'). As a result, this third edition will seek to cover the potential impact of the phenomenon dubbed 'Brexit' on employment law, insofar as that is possible at the time of writing. This endeavour is far from an exact science, given the fluidity of the terms of the European Union Withdrawal Bill and the negotiations between the EU and the UK, as well as the mass of speculation and counter-speculation in the media and various social media outlets about the possibility of a fixed-term post-Brexit transitional period. Although the period from the EU referendum to date can be characterized as something of a 'phoney war' for labour and employment law, it would be short-sighted to dismiss the coming of a major storm or hurricane in the area of employment law; for that reason, this new edition suggests where reforms of the existing framework can be expected, whether of a deregulatory hue or not.

Alongside Brexit, there have been other notable developments. The increase in 'gig economy' working and the deployment of zero-hours contracts by employers in the UK labour market has generated a welter of case law at the level of the employment tribunals and the Employment Appeal Tribunal ('EAT'). The likelihood is that the Court of Appeal and UK Supreme Court will be called upon to pronounce on the employment status of such workers in the near future. Motivated by concerns about the precariousness of atypical work in general and the need to balance the adverse effects of such working practices against the demand in the economy for flexible working, a review process chaired by Matthew Taylor issued a report entitled 'Good Work' in July 2017. A number of recommendations were made to improve the lives of working people and the third edition of this book is peppered throughout with references to, and critiques of, the various suggestions that were made. The UK Government announced in the Autumn Budget in late November 2017 that it would be digesting the various recommendations proposed by the Taylor Review and legislative reform is expected in 2018.

Turning away from Brexit, the gig economy, zero-hours, and atypical working patterns, there has been very little legislative activity in the field of labour and employment law since the publication of the second edition, but the usual flurry of case law at the level of the 'EAT', the Court of Appeal, and the UK Supreme Court has served up much to discuss and a few surprises to boot. For example, no up-to-date discussion of recent developments in employment law can be completed without some coverage of the central decision of the UK Supreme Court in *R (on the application of UNISON) v Lord Chancellor*. In this case, the employment tribunal fees regime was quashed on the basis that it amounted to an infringement of the common law right to access the courts and justice. As such, the requirement for employee claimants to pay fees to present a complaint to an employment tribunal and to have a hearing, has been abolished. The annual leave and holiday pay 'saga' continues to be a rich source of case law, with decisions such as *British Gas Trading Ltd v Lock (No. 2)*, *Dudley Metropolitan Borough Council v Willetts*, *Sobczyszyn v Szkola Podstawowa w Rzeplinie*, and *The Sash Window Workshop Ltd v King*. The question of employment status has thrown up important decisions from the Court of Appeal in *Secretary of State for Justice v Windle* and *Pimlico Plumbers Ltd v Smith*. Meanwhile, discrimination law continues to be characterized by its usual frenetic pace of change, with a number of decisions from the Court of Justice of the European Union, the UK Supreme Court, the Court of Appeal, and the EAT over the past two years, such as *Achbita v G4S Secure Solutions NV*,

Bougnaoui v Micropole SA, Essop v Home Office (UK Border Agency), Education, Children's Services and Skills v Interim Executive Board of Al-Hijrah School, Taiwo v Olaigbe, Lee v McArthur, Wasteney v East London NHS Foundation Trust, Chief Constable of West Midlands Police v Harrod, Perera de Souza v Vinci Construction (UK) Ltd, Banaszczyk v Booker Ltd, FirstGroup Ltd v Paulley, O'Brien v Bolton St Catherine's Academy, and *Griffiths v Secretary of State for Work and Pensions,* amongst many others.

I owe a great debt to a number of people who have assisted in some shape or form in the production of this work or have explored some of the ideas imparted in the third edition of this book. First, I would like to highlight Laura Bremner for special praise, who provided editorial assistance in the review of the chapters for this third edition. Thanks also go to my former students, Laura Fairgrieve, Alexandra Mitrea, and Fraser McDonald for their invaluable research assistance. Professor Douglas Brodie, Dr Rebecca Zahn, Lorna Richardson, and Laura Macgregor continue to be excellent sounding boards for discussion of the various labour law and employment law issues which arise from time to time, as well as helpful sources of support. I would also offer my thanks to the anonymous reviewers of draft chapters of this book. Finally, I would like to thank the editors at Oxford University Press, and in particular Felicity Boughton and Kimberley Payne, who were extremely patient, as well as the University of Edinburgh for its collegiate environment and research support.

I have sought to bring the law in this work up to date to 12 December 2017, but some subsequent developments have been included where necessary or appropriate.

David Cabrelli
Edinburgh
12 December 2017

■ LATE NEWS

In the recent decision of the Supreme Court in *Reilly v Sandwell MBC*[1] Baroness Hale made remarks to the effect that the range of reasonable responses text is ripe for a rigorous review by the Supreme Court. In fact, Lady Hale doubted whether it was an appropriate test and seemed to be inviting practising lawyers to bring a case before the Supreme Court where a definitive ruling could be made on its continued validity.

In April 2018, by a majority of 3 (Lady Hale, Lady Black, and Lord Wilson) to 2 (Lord Lloyd-Jones and Lord Briggs), the UK Supreme Court decided the case of *Newcastle upon Tyne NHS Foundation Trust v Haywood* [2018] UKSC 22. A common law implied term in law was recognized by the majority to the effect that a written notice of termination will take effect where the recipient actually reads the communication or ought to have had a reasonable opportunity of doing so. The alternatives, which were rejected by the majority of the Justices of the Supreme Court, were that the written notice terminating the contract of employment was effective from the moment it would have been delivered in the ordinary course, or when it was in fact delivered to the recipient. As such, the moment of termination is prolonged until the notice comes to the attention of the recipient or ought to have done so. This decision has the effect of aligning the legal position at common law and under the statutory unfair dismissal regime in *Gisda Cyf v Barrett* [2010] UKSC 41, [2010] ICR 1475, on which see sections 15.2.1 and 16.2.3.

■ *Reilly v Sandwell MBC* [2018] UKSC 16, paras 32–35

Lady Hale:

The case might have presented an opportunity for this court to consider two points of law of general public importance which have not been raised at this level before. The first is whether a dismissal based on an employee's "conduct" can ever be fair if that conduct is not in breach of the employee's contract of employment. Can there be "conduct" within the meaning of section 98(2)(b) which is not contractual misconduct? Can conduct which is not contractual misconduct be "some other substantial reason of a kind such as to justify the dismissal" within the meaning of section 98(1)(b) ? It is not difficult to think of arguments on either side of this question but we have not heard them—we were only asked to decide whether there was a duty to disclose and there clearly was. Nor have we heard any argument on whether the approach to be taken by a tribunal to an employer's decisions, both as to the facts under section 98(1) to (3) of the [ERA] and as to whether the decision to dismiss was reasonable or unreasonable under section 98(4), first laid down by the Employment Appeal Tribunal in *British Homes Stores Ltd v Burchell (Note)* [1978] ICR 303 and definitively endorsed by the Court of Appeal in *Post Office v Foley*, is correct. As Lord Wilson points out, in para 20 above, the three requirements set out in *Burchell* are directed to the first part of the inquiry, under section 98(1) to (3), and do not fit well into the inquiry mandated by section 98(4). The meaning of section 98(4) was rightly described by Sedley LJ, in *Orr v Milton Keynes Council* [2011] ICR 704, at para 11, as "both problematical and contentious". He referred to the "cogently reasoned" decision of the Employment Appeal Tribunal (Morison J presiding) in *Haddon v Van den Burgh Foods* [1999] ICR 1150, which was overruled by the Court of Appeal in *Foley*. Even in relation

---

[1] [2018] UKSC 16, 14 March 2018.

to the first part of the inquiry, as to the reason for the dismissal, the *Burchell* approach can lead to dismissals which were in fact fair being treated as unfair and dismissals which were in fact unfair being treated as fair. Once again, it is not difficult to think of arguments on either side of this question but we have not heard them. There may be very good reasons why no-one has challenged the *Burchell* test before us. First, it has been applied by Employment Tribunals, in the thousands of cases which come before them, for 40 years now. It remains binding upon them and on the Employment Appeal Tribunal and Court of Appeal. Destabilizing the position without a very good reason would be irresponsible. Second, Parliament has had the opportunity to clarify the approach which is intended, should it consider that *Burchell* is wrong, and it has not done so. Third, those who are experienced in the field, whether acting for employees or employers, may consider that the approach is correct and does not lead to injustice in practice. It follows that the law remains as it has been for the last 40 years and I express no view about whether that is correct.[2]

---

[2] Sourced from BAILII available at http://www.bailii.org/cgi-bin/format.cgi?doc=/uk/cases/ UKSC/2018/16.html&query=(reilly)+AND+(v)+AND+(sandwell) (last visited 26 April 2018).

■ GUIDE TO THE BOOK

There are several carefully selected learning features to help you make the most of your textbook. This guided tour shows you how to utilize them to reinforce your study and to put employment law in context for yourself.

> Hypothetical A
>
> Having incorporated Danny's Demolishers Ltd ('DD'), Danny
> employees on permanent full-time contracts. One of the emplo
> works for DD on a demolition site in Crewe. After three years
> cides to terminate AP's contract of employment and dismiss hin
> DD does not comply with the ACAS Code of Practice 1 on Disc
> Procedures. AP presents a complaint of unfair dismissal to the I
> cessful. The ET calculates AP's compensatory award for unfair
> decides to award a compensatory uplift of the full 25 per cent ir
> to adhere to the ACAS Code of Practice. Therefore, AP's final a
> £9,534 + (25 per cent × £9,534) = £2,383.50.

Hypotheticals

The fictional case study of Danny's Demolishers Ltd. forms an integral part of your learning. It follows the life cycle of an employer, using hypothetical scenarios to examine activities including hiring staff, varying contractual terms, modifying work hours, allegedly discriminating between staff, making staff redundant, outsourcing, and finally going into liquidation.

Its practice-oriented approach will encourage you to apply relevant cases and legislation to real-life scenarios and allow you to consider the best course of action for each situation.

> ■ S. and B. Webb, *Industrial Democracy* (London, Longmans,
>
> Whenever the economic conditions of the parties are unequal, legal freedo
> enables the superior in strategic strength to dictate the terms.
>
> ■ M. Weber, *Economy and Society: An Outline of Interpretive*
> Roth and C. Wittich (New York, Bedminster Press, 1968) 729
>
> [The right of a prospective employee to decide the basis and terms of his co
> resent the slightest freedom in the determination of his own conditions of
> guarantee him any influence in the process.

Extracts

Primary case and statutory material—together with carefully selected extracts from journals and academic texts—is consistently interwoven within the text to place important issues in context. Each extract is highlighted within a shaded box to ensure easy reference during study and revision.

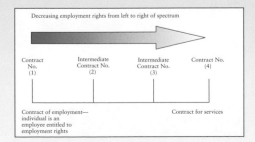

Figures and tables

Pictorial representation complements the description of key employment law data, concepts, and processes to support your understanding of the complexities of this rich subject.

Reflection points

1. In light of the earlier extracts from Brodie and Collins, do yo[u]
   able for the implied terms to become entrenched so that the[y]
   displacement by express terms? Give reasons for your answer[.]
2. Consider whether the implied terms ought to be able to displa[ce]
   are the impediments confronting such a development?
3. Are you of the view that it is desirable for the implied terms t[o]
   the statutory 'worker' contract? Give reasons for your answer[.]
4. What are the advantages and disadvantages of conceptualizi[ng]
   the contract of employment in terms of an abstract organizing

Reflection points

In-chapter reflection points will further your critical engagement with the issues at stake and provide you with ample material to discuss in seminars.

ACAS the Advisory, Conciliation and Arbitration Service.

Additional adoption leave additional statutory leave available to parents of adopted children.

Additional maternity leave additional statutory leave available to mothers of children.

Adoption leave statutory leave available to parents of adopted children.

Glossary terms

The detailed glossary provides invaluable support for understanding complex employment law terminology and is a helpful resource when it comes to revision time.

[135] *Hall v Woolston Hall Leisure* [2001] 1 WLR
[136] *Wheeler v Quality Deep Ltd* [2005] ICR 265[,]
[137] [2008] ICR 1423, 1431C–H per Pill LJ.
[138] For example, see *Connolly v Whitestone Solic*[itors]
[139] [2005] ICR 231.
[140] *Hounga v Allen* [2014] UKSC 47, [2014] 1 W[LR]

Footnotes

Used throughout the text, footnotes elaborate on the discussion within the text, often bringing your attention to useful online sources and material.

For additional reading on identifying and classifying the contract of employment, visit the Online Resources for this book at www.oup.com/uk/cabrelli3e/

Additional reading

Within each chapter section, there are reminders directing you to further reading recommendations provided on the online resources to direct your further study.

■ GUIDE TO THE ONLINE RESOURCES

www.oup.com/uk/cabrelli3e/
Employment Law in Context is accompanied by open-access online resources offering ready-to-use teaching and learning resources.

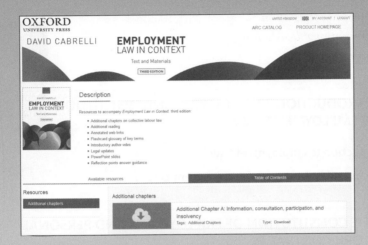

Additional chapters on collective labour law

The hard-copy book chapters cover individual labour law, which forms the basis of most standard undergraduate employment law courses. Four additional chapters are available for students wanting access to material on collective labour law. For more detail about these chapters see pages 835 to 840.

Reflection points answer guidance

Enhance your critical engagement skills by comparing your own responses to key reflection points in the book with the author's answer guidance.

Additional reading

Within each chapter section in the book, there are reminders directing you to further reading recommendations provided on the online resources. These will provide you with useful guidance for taking your study even further.

Annotated web links

The author has carefully selected web links to direct you to the most useful and reliable online information, allowing you to be focused and efficient with your research.

Flashcard glossary

Test yourself on the complex terminology of employment law with this series of interactive flashcards.

Introductory author video

Meet the author as he introduces the book and the running case study, setting the scene for your studies.

CONTENTS IN BRIEF

CONTENTS IN FULL

PART VII BUSINESS REORGANIZATIONS, CONSULTATION, AND INSOLVENCY

PART VIII COLLECTIVE LABOUR LAW

■ TABLE OF CASES

Cases in **bold type** are quoted in part or in full. Further references may occur on the same page. *n* = footnote.

■ TABLE OF PRIMARY LEGISLATION

Legislation in **bold type** is quoted in part or in full. Further references may occur on the same page. *n* = footnote.

■ TABLE OF SECONDARY LEGISLATION AND CODES

Legislation in **bold type** is quoted in part or in full. Further references may occur on the same page. *n* = footnote.

Statutory (and other) codes

■ TABLE OF EUROPEAN LEGISLATION

Legislation in **bold type** is quoted in part or in full. Further references may occur on the same page. *n* = footnote.

TABLE OF INTERNATIONAL LEGISLATION

Legislation in **bold type** is quoted in part or in full. Further references may occur on the same page. *n* = footnote.

■ ACKNOWLEDGEMENTS

Grateful acknowledgement is made to all of the authors and publishers of copyright material which appears in this book, and in particular to the following for permission to reprint material from the sources indicated.

This book contains public sector information licensed under the Open Government Licence v3.0., on which, see http://www.nationalarchives.gov.uk/doc/open-government-licence/open-government-licence.htm. Crown Copyright material is reproduced with the permission of the Controller, HMSO (under the terms of the Click Use licence).

Content from the Office of National Statistics is reproduced without adaptation and licensed under the Open Government Licence v.3.0. http://www.ons.gov.uk/ons/site-information/information/creative-commons-license/index.html.

Content from the Low Pay Commission is reproduced without adaptation and licensed under the Open Government Licence v.3.0. http://www.ons.gov.uk/ons/site-information/information/creative-commons-license/index.html.

Only European Community legislation as printed in the Official Journal of the European Union is deemed to be authentic.

Bloomsbury Publishing PLC: extracts from B. Langille, 'Labour Law's Back Pages' in G. Davidov and B. Langille (eds), *Boundaries and Frontiers of Labour Law* (Hart, 2006). Table 2.1 reproduced from G. S. Morris, 'The Development of Statutory Employment Rights in Britain and Enforcement Mechanisms' in L. Dickens (ed), *Making Employment Rights Effective* (Hart, 2012); and Table 11.1 reproduced from B. Hepple, *Equality: The New Legal Framework*, 2nd edition (Hart, 2014).

Cambridge Law Journal and the authors: Figure 15.4 reproduced from C. Barnard and L. Merrett, 'Winners and Losers: *Edwards* and the Unfair Law of Dismissal', *Cambridge Law Journal*, 72 (2) (Cambridge University Press, 2013).

Incorporated Council of Law Reporting: extracts from the *Law Reports: Queen's Bench Division (QB), the Law Reports: Appeal Cases (AC), the Weekly Law Reports (WLR) and the Industrial Cases Reports (ICR).*

Oxford University Press and the authors and sponsoring societies: extracts from H. Collins, *Employment Law* (2nd edn, Oxford University Press, 2010); H. Collins, *Justice in Dismissal* (Oxford University Press, 1992); G. Davidov and B. Langille (eds), *The Idea of Labour Law* (Oxford University Press, 2011); S. Fredman, *Discrimination Law*, 2nd edn, Oxford University Press, 2011); M. Freedland, *The Personal Employment Contract* (Oxford University Press, 2003); M. Hall and P. Edwards, 'Reforming the Statutory Redundancy Consultation Procedure' in *Industrial Law Journal*, 28 (4) (Oxford University Press, 1999); R. Wintemute, *Sexual Orientation and Human Rights Framework* (Clarendon Press/Oxford University Press, 1997). Figure 19.1 reproduced from C. Barnard, *EU Employment Law*, (4th edn, Oxford University Press, 2012); and Figures 16.1 and 16.2 reproduced from D. Brown, S. Forshaw, A. Korn, J. Palca,

G. Mansfield, and J. Bowers, *Blackstone's Employment Law Practice 2010* (Oxford University Press, 2010).

Palgrave MacMillan: extracts from S. Honeyball, *Great Debates: Employment Law* (Palgrave Macmillan, 2011). Reproduced with permission of Palgrave Macmillan.

Every effort has been made to trace and contact copyright holders prior to going to press, but this has not been possible in every case. If notified, the publisher will undertake to rectify any errors or omissions at the earliest opportunity.

PART I
INTRODUCTION AND SOURCES AND INSTITUTIONS OF EMPLOYMENT LAW

CHAPTER ONE

INTRODUCTION TO EMPLOYMENT LAW

1.1 GENERAL INTRODUCTION

In this chapter we provide an overview of the fundamental goals of this book. Readers are introduced to the running case study feature which is used throughout the text to explain concepts and rules of employment law.[1] The chapter then moves on to explore general academic and policy debates in employment/labour law and places those issues in context. This will entail an exposition of the general contextual background to labour law and an examination of the distinctiveness of the subject. The justifications for intervention in the employment relationship and labour relations are also addressed. The impact which progressive changes in economic and industrial relations systems and structures have had on labour laws and institutions will be examined. Finally, we will consider the important 'legal origins' theory which postulates that labour laws grounded in the common law tradition are more flexible and efficient than those found in civilian law jurisdictions.

1.1.1 The approach of this book

This textbook is primarily intended to give an account of the current laws relating to the regulation of the workplace, employment, and industrial relations. It seeks to comprehensively cover the subject of individual employment law and collective labour law[2] in the UK in an accessible, engaging, and highly contextual format. The principal focus is on drawing a clear dividing line between:

(1) an initial explanation of the issues and problems which confront policy-makers,[3] judges, and legislators entrusted with the task of crafting, reforming, applying, and interpreting labour laws; and

---

[1] The expressions 'employment law' and 'labour law' will be used interchangeably in this book.

[2] The expression 'collective labour law' is adopted here as a reference to the labour laws regulating the constitution, status, listing, independence, and recognition of trade unions, the relationship between trade union members and their trade union, the protection of trade union members in employment, the regulation of collective bargaining, and the law of industrial action, on which, see Chapters B–D of the Online Resources.

[3] For a general discussion in the UK Parliament of the policy issues, see Hansard, at cols 1246–70, 12 September 2013, available at http://www.publications.parliament.uk/pa/cm201314/cmhansrd/cm130912/debtext/130912–0003.htm (last visited 18 October 2017).

(2) an account of the substance of the applicable UK labour laws designed to deal with those issues.

The treatment of (1) will involve an evaluation of the social, historical, and political context within which these policy considerations operate, together with an analysis of the economics of labour law intervention. The text also furnishes an academic treatment of the subject by bringing key scholarly debates to the attention of students. The contextual approach is pursued by drawing on extracts from case reports, articles in legal, economic, industrial relations, and human resources management journals, as well as reports and codes of practice of institutions central to the disciplines of labour law and industrial relations, e.g. the Advisory, Conciliation and Arbitration Service ('ACAS'), the Equality and Human Rights Commission ('EHRC'), and the Central Arbitration Committee ('CAC'). Excerpts are also taken from key academic articles and reports which are central to employment/labour law scholarship and thinking in its current state. Relevant statistics[4] are cited from time to time in order to fortify points made throughout the text. Further, reference is made to extracts from newspapers and internet sites in order to provide reports on stories that contextualize the subject-matter and give examples of the consequences of employment law and policies in practice.

Therefore, the five objectives of this text are as follows:

(1) to present the subject in a manner which etches a clear boundary line between the contextual and the substantive;

(2) to explore the issues which confront policy-makers, judges, and legislators in the field of labour law, employment, and the labour market;

(3) to introduce undergraduate and postgraduate students to some of the central contributions made to labour law scholarship;

(4) to offer suggestions as to how labour law might develop in the future; and

(5) to articulate the written material in an engaging format which attracts and maintains the attention of students, inviting them to think critically about the subject.

A preliminary flavour of the matters that the subject of labour law comprises is provided in the following extract, which is taken from an influential text written by the late Lord Wedderburn:

■ Lord Wedderburn, *The Worker and the Law: Text and Materials,* 3rd edition (London, Penguin Books, 1986) 13

It may be useful at this stage to indicate the main areas that fall within the province of labour law . . . They are:

(1) The employment relationship between [employee] and employer . . . [including] the concept of 'the employee' . . .; the nature of the individual contract of employment; and the problems of job security connected with its termination.

(2) The area of collective bargaining between trade unions and employers; legal encouragement of, support for, or obstacles to, collective organization and negotiation; and the legal effect of the collective agreement;

(3) Parliamentary provision by statute of a 'floor of rights' for individual employees, and the interpretations of it, from . . . rights in respect of job security (especially unfair dismissal and redundancy) and matters such as equal pay, [anti-]discrimination [provisions] and [the] protection of wages.

---

[4] For example, sourced from the website of the Office for National Statistics, available at http://www.ons.gov.uk/ons/index.html (last visited 18 October 2017).

(4) Strikes, lock-outs and industrial action generally; the interplay of Parliament's statutes and the judges' decisions, and the role of the State in industrial conflict.

(5) The status of trade unions, the right of union members, and the role of the trade union movement.[5]

The relationship between the employee, the employer, and the trade union as regards (1), (2), (3), and (5) is depicted in Figure 1.1.

This book is divided into eight parts and covers each of the five principal areas outlined in the extract at various points. In this first part, we set out the structure of the book and the sources and institutions of labour law. Part II goes on to examine the employment relationship and the constitution, classification, and identification of the employment contract and other personal work contracts. In Part III, we focus on the content, performance, structure, variation, and suspension of the common law employment contract. In Part IV, we take our first foray into the province of individual statutory employment rights. This involves consideration of the statutory regulation of the wage–work bargain and working time. Statutory measures that are intended to strike a balance between work and family life are also explored in Part IV. In Part V, our attention turns to a comprehensive and detailed analysis of employment equality law, including the statutory rules against discriminatory conduct in the workplace. Meanwhile, Part VI explores the common law and statutory controls on the employer's power of dismissal. Part VII concentrates on the measures designed to regulate collective redundancies, reorganizations, and business transfers, to promote workplace representational participation and consultation, and to protect employees in the event of the insolvency of their employers. Finally, Part VIII can be found on the Online Resources and evaluates the area of collective labour law, including the law of trade unions and industrial action.

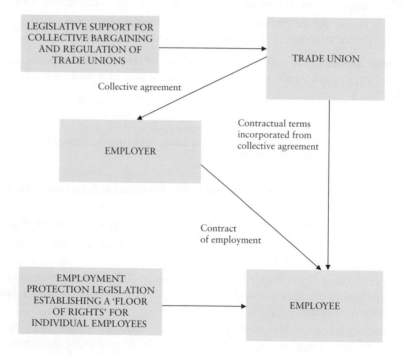

Figure 1.1 *Relationship between employee, employer, and trade unions*

---

[5] Writer's annotations appear in square brackets throughout this chapter.

1.1.2 The running case study feature

One of the primary aims of this text is to communicate the subject of employment law in an accessible, engaging, relevant, and contextual manner. The text seeks to achieve this ambition through the use of a running case study feature which is centred on the business of an employer called 'Danny's Demolishers Ltd' ('DD'). This running case study is encountered throughout the book via the medium of hypothetical scenarios. It is designed to illustrate key concepts, as well as to explain how certain rules of employment law operate in practice. As a subject, labour law lends itself to exploration and explanation from the perspective of the life-cycle of a company's business, from incorporation through to expansion, growth, and finally liquidation. This is the trajectory which the employer, DD, will follow.

We now turn to provide some basic information about DD. DD is a company incorporated in England and Wales by Danny Dandie and his brother Robin, with its registered office in Macclesfield, Cheshire. As the unimaginative title suggests, DD is a business engaged in the demolition and construction trade. From humble beginnings, consisting solely of Danny and Robin, the company grows into a regional powerhouse in the northwest of England. After a period of time, DD moves into the northeast of England and eventually becomes a national player. A long period of consolidation follows, whereupon, in Chapter A of the Online Resources, the company takes the fateful decision to expand into Italy by acquiring a large Milanese demolition company called ZAB SpA. This international acquisition turns out to be a disaster. Unfortunately, DD enters into liquidation and is ultimately wound up in the final chapter.

As the various hypothetical scenarios in this book will demonstrate, DD undertakes the following activities throughout its life-cycle which are relevant to our understanding of employment law:

- it hires employees, self-employed contractors, casual workers, 'zero-hours' workers, 'gig economy' workers, immigrant workers, barristers, and agency workers;[6]
- it enters into, and subsequently varies, contractual terms and conditions with its employees and workers, and provides them with access to its confidential information and intellectual property;[7]
- it modifies the hours of work of its employees and provides accommodation, tips, and bonuses to some of its workers in lieu of pay;[8]
- it allegedly treats some of its workers differently, depending on whether they are female or male, British or foreign nationals, disabled or able-bodied;[9]
- it allegedly discriminates against its part-time and fixed-term staff;[10]
- it dismisses individual members of staff, makes others redundant, and explores possible alternatives to redundancies where possible;[11]
- it disposes of parts of its business in Essex and Yorkshire to third-party purchasers, outsources some of its support functions to third-party contractors, and makes large numbers of its employees redundant;[12] and
- it expands its field of business operations by acquiring an Italian demolition/construction company and ultimately enters into liquidation.[13]

---

[6] See Chapters 3 and 4.   [7] See Chapters 5, 6, and 7.   [8] See Chapters 8 and 9.
[9] See Chapters 10, 11, 12, and 14.
[10] See Chapter 13. The regulation of part-time work and fixed-term employment is addressed in Chapter 13 in the context of Part V of the book on the topic of equality law, rather than Chapter 4. The grounds for this decision are that (a) it was thought necessary to first introduce readers to the idea of comparators and comparison exercises, which are considered in Chapter 10, and (b) the majority of part-timers and fixed-termers are female, and many of the cases on part-time and fixed-term work involve indirect sex discrimination.   [11] See Chapters 14, 15, 16, 17, and 18.
[12] See Chapters 19 and 20.   [13] See Chapter A of the Online Resources.

It is recognized that the adoption of a running case study feature is not a traditional way of approaching legal study, teaching, and learning. Therefore, the hypothetical scenarios have been designed in a 'light-touch' manner so as not to distract students from an engagement with the legal issues and extracts explored in the text. The case study will work best if students put themselves in the place of the characters in the hypotheticals and ask how they would respond to the issues raised. Sometimes, students will find that their solutions will differ from the legal position. This should prompt students to consider the justifications for the regulatory approach adopted by the law and whether the law is fit for purpose or requires a measure of reassessment and reform.

1.2 INTRODUCTION TO KEY ISSUES AND THEMES IN EMPLOYMENT LAW

In this section, we pose some elementary questions about the subject of labour law. The first issue we address is whether labour law has a valid claim to be treated as a self-contained discipline and what distinguishes it from other branches of the law. We also explore the role of this area of law and the arguments in favour of the introduction and preservation of such laws. We will then move on to address a central area of controversy, which is whether such laws stifle or stimulate economic growth.

1.2.1 What is labour law, what are its distinguishing features, and what are the justifications for its introduction and preservation as an independent discipline?

Approximately 32.21 million[14] out of 65 million people living in the UK are in employment. Most of those workers rely on their job as their main source of income. Employment takes up a significant part of the average worker's average day and week. A great deal of satisfaction is derived from work and an individual's occupation is also the principal means of marking out his/her social status. Work also provides a measure of predictability, routine, and structure to an individual's life. These facts have not escaped the judiciary:

■ *Johnson v Unisys Ltd* [2003] 1 AC 518, 539B–C and 549C

Lord Hoffmann:

. . . over the last 30 years or so . . . [i]t has been recognised that a person's employment is usually one of the most important things in his or her life. It gives not only a livelihood but an occupation, an identity and a sense of self-esteem . . .

Lord Millett:

. . . It is generally recognised today that 'work is one of the defining features of people's lives' . . . [15]

---

[14] See Office for National Statistics, *Labour Market Statistics* (January 2018), available at https://www.ons.gov.uk/employmentandlabourmarket/peopleinwork/employmentandemployeetypes/bulletins/uklabourmarket/january2018 (last visited 9 February 2018).

[15] See also D. Brodie, 'Legal Coherence and the Employment Revolution' (2001) 117 *Law Quarterly Review* 604, 604–5.

In light of the central importance of employment to the lives of countless individuals, a fundamental preliminary question we must ask ourselves is whether there is in fact such a thing as employment 'law'. Taking into account the fact that the two principal sources of employment law are the common law and legislation, one would be forgiven for thinking that there is nothing special about the subject that sets it apart from other areas of law. However, there is powerful force in the argument that the role and objectives of employment law are so distinctive that its treatment as an autonomous field of study is wholly warranted.[16] For example, the judiciary have noted that the employment relationship differs from a commercial relationship, and that the employment contract and law cannot be equated to commercial contracts and law:

■ *Johnson v Unisys Ltd* [2003] 1 AC 518, 532F–539C

Lord Steyn:

It is no longer right to equate a contract of employment with commercial contracts. One possible way of describing a contract of employment in modern terms is as a relational contract . . .

Lord Hoffmann:

At common law the contract of employment was regarded by the courts as a contract like any other. The parties were free to negotiate whatever terms they liked and no terms would be implied unless they satisfied the strict test of necessity applied to a commercial contract. Freedom of contract meant that the stronger party, usually the employer, was free to impose his terms upon the weaker. But over the last 30 years or so, the nature of the contract of employment has been transformed . . . [and t]he law has changed to recognise this social reality . . .

■ *Autoclenz Ltd v Belcher* [2011] ICR 1157, 1168E–G

Lord Clarke:

. . . The critical difference between this type of case and the ordinary commercial dispute is identified by Aikens LJ . . . as follows:

'. . . the circumstances in which contracts relating to work or services are concluded are often very different from those in which commercial contracts between parties of equal bargaining power are agreed. I accept that, frequently, organisations which are offering work or requiring services to be provided by individuals are in a position to dictate the written terms which the other party has to accept.'

---

[16] See the discussion in M. Freedland, 'Otto-Kahn-Freund, the Contract of Employment and the Autonomy of Labour Law' in A. Bogg et al. (eds), *The Autonomy of Labour Law* (Oxford, Hart, 2015) 29; H. Collins, 'Contractual Autonomy' in A. Bogg et al. (eds), *The Autonomy of Labour Law* (Oxford, Hart, 2015) 45; G. Davidov, *A Purposive Approach to Labour Law* (Oxford, OUP, 2016) Chapters 2–5, D. Brodie, 'The Autonomy of the Common Law of the Contract of Employment from the General Law of Contract' in M. Freedland et al. (eds), *The Contract of Employment* (Oxford, OUP, 2016) 124; G. Davidov, 'Articulating the Idea of Labour Law: Why and How?' (2012) 3 *European Labour Law Journal* 130; G. Davidov, 'Notes, Debates and Communications: The (Changing?) Idea of Labour Law' (2007) 146 *International Labour Review* 311; and G. Davidov, 'Setting Labour Law's Coverage: Between Universalism and Selectivity' (2014) 34 *Oxford Journal of Legal Studies* 543, 547–9.

Further, employment law is a dynamic and challenging area of law:

■ *R (on the application of UNISON) v Lord Chancellor* [2017] 3 WLR 409, 422G–H

Lord Reed:

. . . it is necessary to bear in mind that it is generally difficult to predict with confidence that a[n
employment law] claim will succeed . . . [as] employment law is characterised by a relatively high
level of complexity and technicality.

An additional noteworthy point is that since employment law comprises elements of
contract, tort, constitutional, criminal, and commercial law, any claim in favour of its autonomy and independence as a field of enquiry must invoke its conceptual and normative
coherence and distinctive intellectual tradition. In the following extract, Langille searches
for labour law's 'constituting narrative':

■ B. Langille, 'Labour Law's Back Pages' in G. Davidov and B. Langille (eds),
Boundaries and Frontiers of Labour Law (Oxford, Hart Publishing, 2006) 14–17

One way of approaching . . . labour law as a separate legal subject matter is to think along the following lines. If one examines the typical North American law school curriculum it is not hard to see
that it reveals a basic structure based upon some very basic legal distinctions which can be easily
mapped. We start with the familiar if controversial division between public law (state–citizen relationships) and private law (citizen–citizen relationships). Thus criminal law and constitutional law
fall on the public side, and tort, contract and property on the private law side. And within private
law we have other familiar distinctions—the law of property (what people own) and the law of obligations (what people owe each other). And within the law of obligations we have the distinction
between obligations voluntarily assumed (contract) and those involuntarily imposed (tort). And so
on. But there is another truth revealed in the stricture of the standard curriculum. This is that law
school courses are considered to be suitable for singling out as separate subject matters because
they have a coherence and severability from the rest of the law. This coherence is often in virtue
of the rationality given to their subject matter not simply by the logic of the conceptual map just
outlined, and upon which they can be located, but in virtue of the conceptual coherence, or basic
grammar, of individual legal concepts themselves. So, the coherence of tort law, for example, is
provided with the inner logic or rationality of the legal concept of tort itself. This is what makes
tort law tort law, provides its internal organisational structure, and its distinctiveness from the rest
of the law—something separate from contract, or unjust enrichment, or tax law for that matter.
And the fundamental normative (that is, moral) underpinnings appropriate to tort (say, corrective
justice) give it a claim to our resources, intellectual and otherwise. But it will be quickly observed
that while this can be said of some of the law's categories it is not true of all. Many other topics in
the law school curriculum—say family law and labour law, but also trade law and environmental
law—do not have whatever coherence they have in virtue of a defining legal concept. Their claim
to coherence must be and is based upon another mode of thinking, one which is at once also
intuitively obvious but also more complex, difficult, and controversial. Rather than start with the
law or a legal concept (as with tort or contract—or trusts, by way of another example) these other
sorts of subject matters start with reality, ie by looking out of the window and seeing what goes
on in the real world. Subjects like labour law take a dimension of human life such as work, or the
family, or trade between nations, and then draw together all of the law which applies to that aspect
of life. But while this may be a useful and necessary intellectual game to play it is also a dangerous
one, for how is one to know whether one has carved up reality 'at the joint' as it were. How do we

know we have a coherent and appropriate subject if we obtain it by simply looking at life without a guiding legal framework to tell us where to carve? On this approach one could (and some actually have) come up with [useless] categories such as 'swimming pool law' . . . The thinking is—here is a part of reality, swimming pools, and we should draw together all of the law which applies to them . . . and write a text, or offer a course, to satisfy our need to address all of these issues comprehensively. But there is the rub—what would it mean to address these issues 'comprehensively', that is beyond merely listing, comprehensively, other legal categories which may bear upon this aspect of reality? This is a good and difficult question . . . Comprehensiveness is not enough . . . When will it be the case that we have hit upon a useful category? What informs our judgement of 'usefulness'? It must be something more than comprehensiveness—it must be some notion of 'coherence'. But, as we have noted, coherence here cannot mean what it means in the case of tort or contract law . . . It must be a different idea of coherence, and I believe that our notion of coherence has two dimensions. First, it must be the case that there is something compelling, or deeply interesting, about this particular part of reality, something which makes it normatively salient and not simply another grain of sand on a very large empirical beach. It must be, in a word, important. Secondly, it must also be the case that when we carve reality at this point and address all the law applicable, the whole is greater than the sum of the parts. That is, it must be the case that in studying all of the various aspects of the law which bear upon, inform, structure this part of our lives, we see them as part of a larger structure. That is we see in each aspect of the law something which would be missed if we did not see them as connected to the other parts of a larger whole. In short, there must be a benefit to be obtained from an overview of all of the law which bears upon our chosen category in the form of insight which would be lost if we did not carve reality here and if we did not attempt to provide a surview or account of it as a whole. This is not to say that there is only one way to carve reality. Rather it is to say, by way of an example, that while the contract of employment may usefully be seen as part of contract law, it is also usefully seen as a key part of labour law because something is gained when it is seen as a building block of this cross-cutting category, that is, when it is seen in the light of the other legal elements of the package of law regulating, say for now, work. To put it another way, there is a package here which needs to be seen and understood as a package. There is a positive way of putting this. In order to say that we have found an appropriate subject matter of the sort in which coherence is generated in this way, it must be true that we are able to construct a compelling story (or narrative), both conceptually and normatively, of all the law appropriate to this subject matter as a subject matter, that is, of what it is (and is not), why it is important, and therefore why we should worry about it. If such a constituting narrative is available and compelling then we have a viable subject matter—and not something to be relegated to the garbage can along with swimming pool law. Such a narrative provides the organising conceptual structure and framework for the field . . . as well as an account of its normative importance. When such narratives are successful, as labour law's has been, they are not so much what people have in mind when they think about the question 'what is labour law?' as the background condition that makes that question possible. It tells us that there is such a subject which one can worry about. So, such frameworks are often implicit and unarticulated, but are understood and deployed by every well-educated labour lawyer—in the most mundane of activities (answering questions such as 'should I read this case?', 'is it of relevance to my field?') to the construction of the most complicated legal arguments . . .

As for the basic question posed by Langille in the extract, 'what is labour law?', the answer is inextricably bound up with the various rationales in favour of regulatory interference into the central institution which is the target of regulation by employment law: the contract of employment. A number of justifications have been, and are, cited in favour of legal intervention in the field of employment. The traditional approach was to stress the role of labour laws in correcting *the imbalance in bargaining power inherent within the employment relationship.*[17] As such, the mission of labour law was to override the freedom of contract doctrine to some extent by protecting employees and workers on the ground that they suffer from an inequality of power in the contractual bargaining process:

■ **S. and B. Webb,** *Industrial Democracy* **(London, Longmans, Green, 1920) 217**

Whenever the economic conditions of the parties are unequal, legal freedom of contract merely enables the superior in strategic strength to dictate the terms.

■ **M. Weber,** *Economy and Society: An Outline of Interpretive Sociology,* **eds. G. Roth and C. Wittich (New York, Bedminster Press, 1968) 729**

[The right of a prospective employee to decide the basis and terms of his contract does not] represent the slightest freedom in the determination of his own conditions of work and it does not guarantee him any influence in the process.

■ *R (on the application of UNISON) v Lord Chancellor* **[2017] 3 WLR 409, 417E–F**

Lord Reed:

Relationships between employers and employees are generally characterised by an imbalance of economic power. Recognising the vulnerability of employees to exploitation, discrimination, and other undesirable practices, and the social problems which can result, Parliament has long intervened in those relationships so as to confer statutory rights on employees, rather than leaving their rights to be determined by freedom of contract. In more recent times, further measures have also been adopted under legislation . . .

In recent times, the vulnerability of workers has arguably risen as a result of the growth of the 'gig economy' and 'crowdwork', where sophisticated technology platforms and apps are used to enable individuals to find users of their services at minimal cost.[18] The UK Office of Tax Simplification has defined the 'gig' economy as 'an environment in which temporary positions are common and organisations contract with independent workers for short-term or on-demand engagements':[19] this is a modern phenomenon to which we will return in this book, since its labour law ramifications have not yet been fully worked out.

---

[17] See *Autoclenz Ltd v Belcher* [2011] ICR 1157, 1168E–G per Lord Clarke for the judicial recognition of the significance of this power imbalance.

[18] See J Prassl, *Humans as a Service* (Oxford, OUP, 2018); V. De Stefano, 'Crowdsourcing, the Gig-Economy, and the Law' (2016) 37 *Comparative Labor Law & Policy Journal* 461; V. De Stefano, 'The Rise of the Just-in-Time Workforce: On-Demand Work, Crowdwork and Labor Protection in the Gig-Economy' (2016) 37 *Comparative Labor Law & Policy Journal* 471; J. Prassl and M. Risak, 'Uber, Taskrabbit, & Co: Platforms as Employers? Rethinking the Legal Analysis of Crowdwork' (2016) 37 *Comparative Labor Law & Policy Journal* 619; B. Rogers, 'Employment Rights in the Platform Economy: Getting Back to Basics' (2016) 10 *Harvard Law & Policy Review* 479.

[19] See https://www.gov.uk/government/uploads/system/uploads/attachment_data/file/573483/OTS_Gig_economy_Focus_paper_Nov16_final.pdf (last visited 18 October 2017).

The common law is underpinned by a belief in the equality of legal persons, i.e. that all are equal before the law. However, in the context of labour relations, adopting a form of myopia to the inevitable divergences in the power of management and labour is not necessarily a desirable approach. Although freedom of contract is a sacred doctrine which lies at the foundation of the liberal philosophy underpinning the common law, there has been a realization on the part of Parliament that liberty and neutrality can only be meaningfully preserved if steps are taken to redress the bargaining inequalities inherent within the employment contract. Whilst the common law by and large clings to the idea of freedom of contract, legislation over the past 50 years has intruded into the employment relationship by nudging the power balance in a pro-employee direction:

■ **P. Davies and M. Freedland (eds),** *Kahn-Freund's Labour and the Law* **(London, Stevens & Sons, 1983) 14–18**

The principal purpose of labour law, then, is to regulate, to support and to restrain the power of management and the power of organised labour . . . The individual employee or worker . . . has normally no social power, because it is only in the most exceptional cases that, as an individual, he has any bargaining power at all . . . Typically, the worker as an individual has to accept the conditions which the employer offers . . . [As such,] the relation between an employer and an isolated employee or worker is typically a relation between a bearer of power and one who is not a bearer of power. In its inception it is an act of submission, in its operation it is a condition of subordination, however much the submission and the subordination may be concealed by that indispensable figment of the legal mind known as the 'contract of employment'. The main object of labour law has always been, and we venture to say will always be, to be a countervailing force to counteract the inequality of bargaining power which is inherent and must be inherent in the employment relationship. Most of what we call [employment protection] legislation . . . is an attempt to infuse law into a relation of command and subordination . . . There can be no employment relationship without a power to command and a duty to obey, that is without this element of subordination in which lawyers rightly see the hallmark of the 'contract of employment'. However, the power to command and the duty to obey can be regulated . . . [As such,] the law limits the range of the worker's duty of obedience and enlarges the range of his freedom. This, without any doubt, was the original and for many decades the primary function of labour law.[20]

Kahn-Freund makes the point that labour legislation has interfered in the employment relationship, e.g. to regulate terms and conditions of employment, furnish rules on the hiring and dismissal of employees, and regulate the basic work–wage bargain, i.e. the exchange of the worker's services in return for remuneration. However, the law has also been traditionally concerned with the provision of indirect 'auxiliary support'[21] for the one-time endemic social practice of collective bargaining. Prior to the 1980s, the prevailing industrial relations philosophy was 'collective laissez-faire',[22] also known as 'voluntarism'. This

---

[20] For an economic account of why labour laws are necessary in order to address inequalities of bargaining power, see B. E. Kaufman, 'Labor Law and Employment Regulation: Neoclassical and Institutional Perspectives' in K. Dau-Schmidt, S. D. Harris, and O. Lobel (eds), *Labor and Employment Law and Economics* (Cheltenham, Edward Elgar, 2009) 1, 30–6.

[21] See A. Bogg, *The Democratic Aspects of Trade Union Recognition* (Oxford, Hart Publishing, 2009) 3.

[22] See O. Kahn-Freund, 'Legal Framework' in A. Flanders and H. Clegg (eds), *The System of Industrial Relations in Great Britain* (Oxford, Basil Blackwell, 1954) 42, 53. The most powerful exposition of the virtues of collective bargaining is found in O. Kahn-Freund, 'Labour Law' in *Law and Opinion in England in the 20th Century* (London, Stevens, 1959).

philosophy emphasized the desirability of collective bargaining[23] between an employer or employer's association[24] and an independent trade union recognized by the employer. The principal feature of that system was that trade unions (on behalf of their worker members) and employers or employers' associations would negotiate and conclude collective agreements which would include various provisions dealing directly with the protection and rights of employees, e.g. pay, working conditions, holidays, dismissal procedures, procedures applicable in the event of economic reorganizations, such as redundancies, redeployments, and variations in job requirements, etc. It was the collective social power which the forces of labour could muster by banding together in trade unions, backed up by the credible threat of industrial action through strikes, which routinely brought employers to the negotiating table and served to offset the inevitable weaknesses in the bargaining positions of individual employees. This approach was characterized by voluntarism, i.e. the absence of any State or legal compulsion on employers or trade unions to engage in collective bargaining, and the only statutory intervention in the field of employment was designed to support the collective laissez-faire industrial relations[25] system.[26] These legal 'props' were adopted to reinforce this widespread social practice of collective bargaining.

However, in the contemporary context, the concern with the correction of inequalities in bargaining power via the prophylactic of labour laws or the social practice of collective bargaining has lost much of its force.[27] Economists have attacked the notion that legal intervention is required to offset the unequal exchange of resources between the employee and the employer:

■ H. Spector, 'Philosophical Foundations of Labour Law' (2006) 33 *Florida State University Law Review* 1119, 1133

It might be thought that inequality of bargaining power can also prevent workers from obtaining fair contract terms, such as health and safety conditions or protection against wrongful discharge. The point would be that such terms could not be agreed on voluntarily by employers and employees because employers have greater bargaining power than employees. Unequal bargaining power could also warrant regulation of the employment contract. But, as Duncan Kennedy argues, 'even a monopolist has an interest in providing contract terms if buyers will pay him their cost, plus as much in profit as he can make for alternate uses of his capital'. Monopolists do not affect contract terms but adjust quantity and price. Accordingly, asymmetrical bargaining power does not prevent the free negotiation of any term or condition that the employee is prepared to pay for. Ian Ayres and Stewart Schwab extend this thesis to the labor monopsonist: '[I]n a well functioning employment market, employers will provide all benefits and protections that employees are willing to pay for.' Therefore, the argument of unequal bargaining power cannot justify nonprice compulsory terms in employment contracts. While monopsony-related considerations can justify wage regulations, they are irrelevant for justifying regulation of employment contract terms.

---

[23] Collective bargaining can be divided into enterprise-level collective bargaining, which takes place between a trade union and an employer generally, plant-level collective bargaining conducted between a trade union and an employer, which is applicable at a particular site or sites only, or sectoral collective bargaining conducted between a trade union and employers or employers' associations, which would govern the workplace conditions of all employees falling within a particular industry sector (e.g. the aviation industry) throughout the UK.   [24] Such as the Confederation of British Industry ('CBI').

[25] For the relationship between labour law and industrial relations as a branch of sociology, see B. E. Kaufman, 'History of the British Industrial Relations Field Reconsidered: Getting from the Webbs to the New Employment Relations Paradigm' (2014) 52 *British Journal of Industrial Relations* 1, 4.

[26] See A. Flanders, 'The Tradition of Voluntarism' (1974) 12 *British Journal of Industrial Relations* 352.

[27] For the demise of labour law as a contextual discipline—in terms of the traditional tendency to approach the subject from an industrial relations and economics perspective—and the emergence of a more individualist, doctrinal, take on the subject, see H. Collins, 'The Productive Disintegration of Labour Law' (1997) 26 *Industrial Law Journal* 295.

Another powerful critique of the 'inequality of bargaining power' justification for labour law centres on its lack of analytical precision. For example, consumers suffer from unequal bargaining power in the contracting process, but by no means can we claim that consumer law is best viewed as a subset of labour law. The notion of 'inequality of bargaining power' as the moral foundation for employment laws has also come in for criticism from labour law scholars themselves. For example, Langille has argued that it is outmoded as a justification and fails to assist us in identifying who should be covered and protected by labour laws.[28] Therefore, we find that the premise of the correction of imbalances in bargaining strength between the worker and the employer has given way to

(1) the *regulation of labour market failures and the achievement of efficient labour markets*,[29] and

(2) the *realization of social justice through the repulsion of the 'economic logic of the commodification of labour'*,[30]

as the principal justifications in favour of employment protection laws. Justification (1) links labour law closely to the functioning of the labour market and anchors it firmly within a market-driven ideology, whereas justification (2) clings more faithfully to the traditional social objectives of labour law, i.e. the redistribution of wealth, resources, and power away from the employer (i.e. management and shareholders) to the employee as a form of social equality.[31] Consider the following extract:

■ **H. Collins, 'Theories of Rights as Justifications' in G. Davidov and B. Langille (eds), *The Idea of Labour Law* (Oxford, OUP, 2011) 137**

An investigation of the idea of labour law calls for a theory. Such a theory must address the moral, political, and legal force of labour law. Ideally, the theory should justify the existence and weight of such typical rules and principles of labour law as minimum wages, safety regulations, maximum hours of work, the outlawing of discrimination against particular groups, and the recognition of a trade union for the purposes of collective bargaining. Given the general commitment in liberal societies to respect for freedom of the individual and a free market, labour law requires a theory of why such mandatory constraints should exist. There is no shortage of theories of this kind. Historically, it is possible to detect two predominant strands of justification. One strand appeals to efficiency or welfare considerations, in order to justify rules that address market failures caused by transaction costs and asymmetric information, problems arising in the governance of contracts of employment such as coercion and opportunism, and more generally the desirability of promoting productive efficiency and competitiveness through a well-coordinated and flexible division of labour. From this perspective, labour law addresses the idiosyncratic problems that arise in relation

---

[28] B. Langille, 'Labour Law's Theory of Justice' in G. Davidov and B. Langille (eds), *The Idea of Labour Law* (Oxford, OUP, 2011) 105–10. For a persuasive response to these criticisms, see R. Dukes, *The Labour Constitution* (Oxford, OUP, 2014) 211–21.

[29] The main exponents of this approach are Deakin, Wilkinson, Mitchell, and Arup, on which, see S. Deakin and F. Wilkinson, *The Law of the Labour Market: Industrialization, Employment, and Legal Evolution* (Oxford, OUP, 2005) 5–35; R. Mitchell and C. Arup, 'Labour Law and Labour Market Regulation' in C. Arup et al. (eds), *Labour Law and Labour Market Regulation* (Sydney, Federation Press, 2006) 3; P. Davies and M. Freedland, *Labour Law: Text and Materials*, 2nd edition (London, Weidenfeld and Nicholson, 1984) 1–11; and A. Hyde, 'What is Labour Law?' in G. Davidov and B. Langille (eds), *Boundaries and Frontiers of Labour Law* (Oxford, Hart Publishing, 2006) 37. For a discussion and critique, see R. Dukes, *The Labour Constitution: The Enduring Idea of Labour Law* (Oxford, OUP, 2014) 92–122 and 194–221; G. Davidov, 'Setting Labour Law's Coverage: Between Universalism and Selectivity' (2014) 34 *Oxford Journal of Legal Studies* 543, 547–9.

[30] See H. Collins, *Employment Law*, 2nd edition (Oxford, OUP, 2010) 5.

[31] See S. R. Bagenstos, 'Employment Law and Social Equality' (2013) 112 *Michigan Law Review* 225.

to contracts of employment through a mixture of special contract law and market regulation. The other predominant strand of justification for labour law appeals to considerations of a fair distribution of wealth, power, and other goods in a society. On this view, the principal aim of labour law is to steer towards a particular conception of social justice, such as a more egalitarian society, and the norms of labour law are required primarily for the instrumental purpose of securing that goal. This second strand of justification tends to support the practice of collective bargaining and the imposition of basic labour standards such as a minimum wage, because these interventions in the labour market are calculated to improve the position of poorer and weaker members of the society. In diverse combinations and variations, most labour lawyers have either explicitly or implicitly traditionally relied on these two kinds of competing and to some extent antagonistic justifications—efficiency and social justice—to explain the normative foundations of labour law.[32]

This change in emphasis in the currency of the competing justifications for employment laws has coincided with vast changes in the UK labour market over the past 30–40 years. This period witnessed a sea-change in the organization of work,[33] the industrial relations landscape, and the industrial base of the UK economy, in particular:

(1) the change in the UK from a manufacturing-based economy to a service-based economy; together with

(2) the transformative effects of globalization;

(3) the adjustments to the labour market wrought by the increasing pace of technological change and the development of new flexible modes of production;[34] and

(4) the rapid process of deunionization,[35] i.e. the decline in trade union membership from 13.2 million members in 1979 to just 6.2 million members in 2016;[36] and

(5) the steady departure from the traditional employer-employee model towards (a) growing self-employment, as typified by the 'gig economy' and crowdwork phenomenon and (b) the sharing or parcelling out of managerial functions (such as hiring, firing, receiving the individual's labour and providing work and pay) amongst a number of distinct (in law) legal persons, where that role was traditionally carried out by one legal entity as employer.[37]

---

[32] See also H. Collins, 'Justifications and Techniques of Legal Regulation of the Employment Relation' in H. Collins, P. Davies, and R. Rideout (eds), *Legal Regulation of the Employment Relation* (London, Kluwer, 2000) 4 and 26; B. Hepple, 'Factors Influencing the Making of Labour Law' in G. Davidov and B. Langille (eds), *The Idea of Labour Law* (Oxford, OUP, 2011) 32–4; B. Hepple, *Labour Laws and Global Trade* (Oxford, Hart Publishing, 2005) 262; and S. Deakin and F. Wilkinson, 'Labour Law and Economic Theory: A Reappraisal' in H. Collins, P. Davies, and R. Rideout (eds), *Legal Regulation of the Employment Relation* (London, Kluwer, 2000) 42–7.

[33] See M. Weiss, 'Re-Inventing Labour Law?' in G. Davidov and B. Langille (eds), *The Idea of Labour Law* (Oxford, OUP, 2011) 45–6.

[34] For example, outsourcing, franchising, teleworking, sub-contracting, etc., on which, see H. Collins, 'Independent Contractors and the Challenge of Vertical Disintegration to Employment Protection Laws' (1990) 10 *Oxford Journal of Legal Studies* 353.

[35] On the decline in trade union membership in the UK and internationally, see A. Charlwood, 'The New Generation of Trade Union Leaders and Prospects for Union Revitalisation' (2004) 42 *British Journal of Industrial Relations* 379; D. Blanchflower, 'International Patterns of Union Membership' (2007) 45 *British Journal of Industrial Relations* 1; and J. T. Addison, A. Bryson, P. Teixeira, and A. Pahnke, 'Slip Sliding Away: Further Union Decline in Germany and Britain' (2011) 58 *Scottish Journal of Political Economy* 490.

[36] See the 2016/17 Annual Report of the Certification Officer, available at https://www.gov.uk/government/uploads/system/uploads/attachment_data/file/629399/Cert_Off_Ann_Rep_2016–2017.pdf at page 26 (last visited 18 October 2017); Department for Business, Energy and Industrial Strategy, *Trade Union Membership 2016* (May 2017), available at https://www.gov.uk/government/uploads/system/uploads/attachment_data/file/616966/trade-union-membership-statistical-bulletin-2016-rev.pdf at page 5 (last visited 18 October 2017).   [37] J. Prassl, *The Concept of the Employer* (Oxford, OUP, 2015).

A major consequence of this reduction in trade union membership has been the demise of the voluntarist industrial relations system of 'collective laissez-faire' described earlier, accompanied by a rapid diminution in the percentage of workers in the UK that are covered by collective agreements:[38] a process that is referred to as decollectivization. The European Union and successive UK Governments have adjusted to these processes of deunionization and decollectivization by increasing the number and variety of statutory employment rights afforded to workers and employees in an individual capacity: phenomena often referred to as 'juridification' and 'individualization'. The knock-on effect of this transformation in the economic and industrial relations landscape has been the emergence of new modes of conceptual thinking:

■ J. Fudge, 'Labour as a "Fictive Commodity"' in G. Davidov and B. Langille (eds), *The Idea of Labour Law* (Oxford, OUP, 2011) 124

From a labour lawyer's perspective, the most important shift in the discipline has been away from collective bargaining towards individualization, whether in the form of the contract of employment, human rights and anti-discrimination law, or employment standards . . . In official accounts of labour law, redistribution and protection have given way to competition and flexibility. Forms of work outside of the standard employment relationship have proliferated and the scope of collective bargaining has contracted in most developed economies. These empirical changes have resulted in a conceptual and normative crisis in labour law, and a concomitant loss of prestige. Labour law's crisis both reflects and is part of a broader conceptual and normative shift within society and the academy. In economics, the neo classical vision of Friedrich Von Hayek and Milton Friedman eclipsed the institutional approach of John Maynard Keynes and John Kenneth Galbraith, and social democracy was dislodged by neo-liberalism and the third way in politics. In the academy, work and class gave way to identity and social movements in sociology, and in political science and political theory recognition and identity trumped redistribution as the prevailing normative discourse. The predominant normative concern shifted away from redistribution from capital to labour to promoting horizontal equity within the workforce. At the same time, vertical inequality increased to levels not seen since before the Second World War in the dominant developed countries.

Labour laws grounded in one, some, or all, of the justifications for interference in the employment relationship, i.e.

(1) the *correction of imbalances in bargaining power inherent within the employment relationship*;

(2) the *regulation of labour market failures and the achievement of efficient labour markets*; and

(3) the *realization of social justice through the repulsion of the 'economic logic of the commodification of labour'*,

operate in a manner which interferes in the bureaucratic power of the employer to allocate, assign, and direct labour as a kind of property right—such power being referred to as the 'managerial prerogative'[39]—in two ways.

[38] See Department for Business, Energy and Industrial Strategy, *Trade Union Membership 2016* (May 2017), available at https://www.gov.uk/government/uploads/system/uploads/attachment_data/file/616966/trade-union-membership-statistical-bulletin-2016-rev.pdf at pages 22 and 36 (last visited 18 October 2017); W. Brown, 'The Contraction of Collective Bargaining in Britain' (1993) 31(2) *British Journal of Industrial Relations* 189.

[39] H. Collins, 'Market Power, Bureaucratic Power, and the Contract of Employment' (1986) 15 *Industrial Law Journal* 1. See Chapter 5, section 5.1.1.

First, labour laws secure a measure of *procedural* and *substantive* justice in favour of employees, i.e. they confer a series of *procedural* and *substantive* rights:

■ **B. Langille, 'Labour Law's Back Pages' in G. Davidov and B. Langille (eds), *Boundaries and Frontiers of Labour Law* (Oxford, Hart Publishing, 2006) 20**

[Labour] law protects those in need of protection in the market place. The first mode of intervention is procedural. If the problem is that we are not securing justice for employees through this contractual bargaining relationship, because of inequality of bargaining power on the part of employees, then we must simply adopt the procedural device of turning up the bargaining power on the side of the employee. Our primary mechanism for achieving this is through the device of collective bargaining. Here we permit workers to secure whatever additional substantive rights and benefits they can in the contracting process by making available to them whatever increases in bargaining power will accrue through collective representation by [trade] unions . . . The accepted wisdom is that collective bargaining is entirely procedural in the sense that the substance of the bargain to be is still left open to the parties to determine through the exercise of their now restructured bargaining power relationship. The employer's freedom *to* contract with whom it wishes is taken away, and it is compelled to bargain with the collective representative. But the employer's freedom *of* contract is maintained . . . But labour law consists in more than simply procedural intervention through collective bargaining. There is a second response to our problem of securing justice in employment relationships. This second response is substantive in nature. The logic here is as follows. If our problem is that we will not secure justice in employment relationships because these relationships are analysed in contractual terms, and employees suffer from inequality of bargaining power in the negotiation of such contracts, then we should simply rewrite the resulting bargain. This we do via human rights codes, employment [protection] legislation, occupational health and safety regulation, and so on.[40]

Whilst labour laws offer such procedural and substantive protection, the tendency is for legal rules to take the latter form, rather than the former: the procedural protections have steadily decreased over the past 40–50 years, as has the ability of workers and trade unions to harness them.

Secondly, labour laws consist of commands directed to adjudicators to examine the decisions and actions of employers, which, absent the same, would otherwise be subject to the employer's untrammelled managerial prerogative. These commands enjoin courts and tribunals to evaluate managerial behaviour according to precisely drawn *rules* or more open-textured *standards of review*, e.g. notions such as 'reasonableness', 'rationality', or 'proportionality'. These *rules* and *standards of review* signal the law's expectations about acceptable managerial conduct in a particular context, e.g. recruitment and selection, suspension, variation of contractual terms, dismissal, redundancy, general treatment of employees, etc., and will be articulated at a particular intensity, which will vary according to the context. As such, these rules and standards of review represent the evaluative criteria against which the actions and decision-making of employers are judged.[41]

The earlier discussion about the goals of labour law and the rationales for its existence leads us on neatly to consider a deeply contested issue. It is often questioned whether

---

[40] See also B. Langille, 'Core Labour Rights: The True Story (Reply to Alston)' (2005) 16 *European Journal of International Law* 409, 428–30.

[41] See D. Cabrelli, 'Rules and Standards in the Workplace: A Perspective from the Field of Labour Law' (2011) 31 *Legal Studies* 21; D. Cabrelli, 'The Hierarchy of Differing Behavioural Standards of Review in Labour Law' (2011) 40 *Industrial Law Journal* 146.

labour laws have a benign effect on economic efficiency and the property rights of employers, or whether they produce adverse economic consequences. As such, in pursuing equity via labour laws, is there an inevitable trade-off with efficiency? The politically influential neoliberal philosophy[42] responds to this question in the affirmative, since it characterizes employment protection laws as a burden on business, impeding the efficient operation of the marketplace and generating negative effects on economic growth. For example, scholars argue that firms located in jurisdictions with flexible labour markets and less rigid unfair dismissal laws generate higher stock market returns: since the likelihood of being fired is greater in the absence of job security protections such as unfair dismissal laws, employees invest greater effort and achieve higher satisfaction in their jobs.[43] For the same reason, there is evidence which demonstrates that one outcome of increased employment protection legislation is a reduction in worker effort in their jobs, together with higher absences, in comparison with workers with more limited employment protection laws, such as casual workers, temporary workers, and other atypical workers.[44] This perception of labour laws as a cost on business is reflected at a grass-roots level, where we encounter a consistent tendency amongst businesses in the UK to perceive labour law regulation as burdensome.[45] These assumptions about employment law also lay behind the Coalition Government's 'Employment Law Red Tape Challenge'.[46] This was an initiative intended to consult business about the necessity and appropriateness of existing labour regulations and ways in which they could be simplified, better implemented, and enforced.

However, there is an alternative narrative which classes employment laws as positive factors contributing to an increase in productive output: this suggests that an alignment between equity and efficiency is not impossible. For example, there is evidence to suggest that protective employment laws do not have any negative effects on equality,[47] productivity, or unemployment,[48] and that they may have a positive impact

[42] See F. A. Hayek, *The Constitution of Liberty* (London and New York, Routledge Classics, 2006); R. Plant, *The Neo-liberal State* (Oxford, OUP, 2010).

[43] A. Edmans, L. Li, and C. Zhang, 'Employee Satisfaction, Labor Market Flexibility, and Stock Returns Around the World', European Corporate Governance Institute (ECGI)—Finance Working Paper Series No. 433/2014, available at http://papers.ssrn.com/sol3/papers.cfm?abstract_id=2461003 (last visited 19 October 2017).

[44] See S. Bradley, C. Green, and G. Leeves, 'Employment Protection, Threat and Incentive Effects on Worker Absence' (2014) 52 *British Journal of Industrial Relations* 333.

[45] See E. Jordan, A. P. Thomas, J. W. Kitching, and R. A. Blackburn, *Employer Perceptions and the Impact of Employment Regulation*, Report for Department for Business, Innovation and Skills, Employment Relations Research Series 123 (March 2013), available at https://www.gov.uk/government/publications/a-research-paper-on-employer-perceptions-and-the-impact-of-employment-regulation at page 37 (last visited 19 October 2017); F. Peck, G. Mulvey, K. Jackson, and J. Jackson, *Business Perceptions of Regulatory Burden*, Report for Department for Business, Innovation and Skills (May 2012), available at https://www.gov.uk/government/uploads/system/uploads/attachment_data/file/31595/12–913-business-perceptions-of-regulatory-burden.pdf at pages 57–9 (last visited 19 October 2017); and J. Purcell, 'Management and Employment Rights' in L. Dickens (ed.), *Making Employment Rights Effective* (Oxford, Hart Publishing, 2012) 159–60.

[46] See http://www.redtapechallenge.cabinetoffice.gov.uk/themehome/employment-related-law/ (last visited 19 October 2017).

[47] S. Deakin, J. Malmberg, and P. Sarkar, 'How Do Labour Laws Affect Unemployment and the Labour Share of National Income? The Experience of Six OECD Countries, 1970–2010' (2014) 153 *International Labour Review* 1.

[48] S. Avdagic, 'Does Deregulation Work? Reassessing the Unemployment Effects of Employment Protection' (2015) 53 *British Journal of Industrial Relations* 6; S. Deakin, C. Fenwick, and P. Sarkar, 'Labour Law and Inclusive Development: The Economic Effects of Industrial Relations Laws in Middle-Income Countries' in M. Schmiegelow and H. Schmiegelow (eds), *Institutional Competition between Common Law and Civil Law* (Heidelberg, Germany, Springer-Verlag, 2014) 185; and S. Deakin, J. Malmberg, and P. Sarkar, 'How Do Labour Laws Affect Unemployment and the Labour Share of National Income? The Experience of Six OECD Countries, 1970–2010' (2014) 153 *International Labour Review* 1.

on innovation[49] and productivity,[50] perhaps owing to the 'efficiency wage' theory,[51] i.e. the idea that better-paid and happier employees, enjoying higher contractual benefits, secure in employment without fear of dismissal, and treated well and appreciated by their employers in the workplace,[52] equate to higher productivity and firm value. The various arguments are summarized in the following extracts:

■ S. Deakin, 'The Contribution of Labour Law to Economic and Human Development' in G. Davidov and B. Langille (eds.), *The Idea of Labour Law* (Oxford, OUP, 2011) 156–61

For the past two decades the debate over law and development has been dominated by the view, generally referred to as the 'Washington consensus', that countries should adapt their institutions to a global template based on constitutional guarantees for private property, a minimalist state, and the liberalization of trade and capital flows. In the context of labour law, the Washington consensus proceeded on the basis that 'laws created to protect workers often hurt them'. This approach was used in numerous countries to resist calls for the extension of labour laws and to initiate programmes of deregulation . . . Within contemporary social and economic theory three distinct positions on the role of labour law with relation to labour markets can be identified, which may be characterized respectively as *neoclassical*, *new-institutional*, and *systemic* . . . The neoclassical view sees labour law regulation as an external intervention in, or interference with, the market. As such, it is liable to distort the operation of supply and demand. The result will be to reduce economic growth in various ways. This is the standard neoclassical view of, for example, minimum wage regulation . . . The basic claim of the neoclassical approach is that autonomous decision-making by individual agents (workers and employers) can lead to an outcome which is in the interests of society as a whole. Regulation is seen as the expression of sectional, collective interests. Labour laws enacted with a redistributive end in mind can be seen as involving a trade-off between equity and efficiency. Thus countries which maintain extensive labour law regulations are effectively making a choice which implies lower growth and reduced development, in favour of certain social goals such as a more egalitarian income distribution. The view that labour regulation has a *market-limiting* function is not confined to neoclassical economics. Non-economic justifications for labour law which view protective legislation as 'decommodifying' labour relations take a similar position but, more or less explicitly, view the trade-off between efficiency and equity which this involves in a different, more positive light . . . Neoclassical models . . . are based on the assumption that, in general, markets tend to self-adjust. Thus, in the absence of labour law regulation, the labour market is in equilibrium. This position is challenged by new-institutionalist perspectives

[49] V. Acharya, R. Baghai-Wadji, and K. Subramanian, 'Labor Laws and Innovation' (2013) 56 *Journal of Law and Economics* 997; V. Acharya, R. Baghai-Wadji, and K. Subramanian, 'Wrongful Discharge Laws and Innovation', NBER Working Paper No. 18516, available at http://www.nber.org/papers/w18516 (last visited 19 October 2017); H. Zhou, R. Decker, and A. Kleinknecht, 'Flexible Labour and Innovation Performance: Evidence from Longitudinal Firm-Level Data' (2011) 20 *Industrial and Corporate Change* 941; G. Manso, 'Motivating Innovation' (2011) 66 *Journal of Finance* 1823; F. Belloc, 'Law, Finance and Innovation: The Dark Side of Shareholder Protection' (2013) 37 *Cambridge Journal of Economics* 863.

[50] R. Freeman and J. Medoff, *What Do Unions Do?* (New York, Basic Books, 1984); R. Vergeer and A. Kleinknecht, 'Do Labour Market Reforms Reduce Labour Productivity Growth? A Panel Data Analysis of 20 OECD Countries (1960–2004) (2014) 154 *International Labour Review* 365. For a discussion, see S. Deakin, 'Labor and Employment Laws' in P. Cane and H. Kritzer (eds), *The Oxford Handbook of Empirical Legal Research* (Oxford, OUP, 2010) 308, 314.

[51] G. Akerlof and J. Yellen, *Efficiency Wage Models of the Labour Market* (Cambridge, CUP, 1986); C. Shapiro and J. Stiglitz, 'Equilibrium Unemployment as a Worker Discipline Device' (1984) 74 *American Economic Review* 433.

[52] See A. Grant and F. Gino, 'A Little Thanks Goes a Long Way: Explaining Why Gratitude Expressions Motivate Prosocial Behavior' (2010) 98 *Journal of Personal Social Psychology* 946.

which view unregulated labour markets as affected by imperfections of various kinds, including transaction costs, information asymmetries and externalities. The presence of imperfections can give rise to an efficiency-based case for intervention . . . [and the new institutionalist economic approach emphasizes] the 'market-correcting' role of labour law; that is, its use as a mechanism for correcting the effects of market failures . . . The basic claim of new institutionalist approaches is that autonomous decision making by economic agents may lead to societally beneficial outcomes, but only under certain conditions, and that regulation may be needed to bring these outcomes about or to adjust for their absence. To the extent that markets are not perfectly competitive, relevant information concerning prices and quality is not costlessly available, and the factors of production are not completely mobile, there is scope for intervention on efficiency grounds. The suggestion that labour law regulations act upon markets which are already at the equilibrium point is seen as implausible. To this extent, new institutionalist perspectives offer a refutation of neoclassical arguments for deregulation . . . New institutionalist approaches use abstract economic-theoretical insights to generate a potential case for the efficiency-enhancing effects of labour law rules in a relatively narrow range of contexts.

■ S. Deakin and Z. Adams, 'Corporate Governance and Employment Relations' in G. Davidov, J. Gordon, and W. Ringe (eds), *The Oxford Handbook of Corporate Law and Governance* (Oxford, OUP, 2018), 1055

A body of work is beginning to look at the relationship between employment protection laws (EPL) and innovation. There are two possible routes by which they might be related. One possibility is that EPL, by raising dismissal costs, provides incentives for firms to move to, or remain on, a 'high road' to competitive success, based on continuous product and process innovation, as the condition of being able to maintain a credible commitment to job security. This also implies a greater commitment by firms to training and upgrading of the labour force. A second possible route depends on the effect of EPL in reducing the downside costs to employees of risk taking of the kind associated with high-innovation practices. If employees are confident that their knowledge and know-how will not be appropriated ex post by the employer, through dismissal, they are more likely to contribute their skills and knowledge to the development of innovative products and processes.

These differing accounts of the relative efficiency of labour laws are a rich source of debate amongst economists.[53] For example, economists adhering to the neoclassical account who favour deregulatory agendas would disagree with Deakin and Adams and emphasize the sclerotic effect of labour laws on a country's economic development. Classical economists also reject the argument that labour regulation is necessary in order to remedy labour market failures. Meanwhile, new institutional economists ('NIEs')[54] take the opposite view and advocate the line that labour laws must be introduced and maintained to offset the inevitable failures in the capitalist market system, i.e. to correct market failures. Their approach points to the adverse effects of unregulated capitalism on third parties such as the forces of labour—referred to as 'externalities' in the economic literature—and the inequalities between employer and employee in the level and

---

[53] See S. Deakin, 'The Law and Economics of Employment Protection Legislation' in C. Estlund and M. Wachter (eds), *Research Handbook on the Economics of Labor and Employment Law* (Cheltenham, Edward Elgar, 2012) 330.

[54] See R. Richter, 'The New Institutionalist Economics: Its Start, Its Meaning, Its Prospects' (2005) 6 *European Business Organization Law Review* 161.

sophistication of knowledge and information—known as 'information asymmetries' by economists.[55] The more advantageous position enjoyed by employers in the contracting process as a result of their greater bargaining power operates to convince NIEs of the merits of labour regulation to achieve a more equitable balance between the interests of capital and labour. To that extent, the argument that unregulated labour markets are required in order to achieve higher economic growth, productivity, and more efficient labour markets is rejected. Instead, NIEs recognize that the basic institutions of private law, such as property law and contract law, have been battered by the common law judiciary over a significant period of time into a shape favouring the employer's interests and function to produce market failures, thus demanding a measure of correction via the prophylactic of employment laws.[56]

This highly topical debate between neoclassical and NIEs about the consequences of labour laws also links in with another influential theory. This is a theory which postulates that the legal origins of a jurisdiction's legal system are also determinative of the regulatory style and rigidity of its labour laws. This account is referred to as the 'legal origins' hypothesis. It predicts that legal systems grounded in the common law tradition will tend to support labour markets and will have lower levels of employment protection, with higher labour force participation and lower unemployment. This can be contrasted with civilian systems which the legal origins hypothesis asserts are characterized by higher labour market rigidities, with a tendency to control and restrain labour markets. As such, the theory claims that the economic performance and labour markets of common law jurisdictions such as the UK and US are more efficient than those with civilian foundations. Support for the 'legal origins' theory was produced by the labour regulation index created by Botero et al., which coded the labour laws of 85 developed and developing countries:

■ **J. C. Botero, S. Djankov, R. La Porta, F. Lopez-De-Silanes, and A. Shleifer, 'The Regulation of Labor' (2004) 119 *Quarterly Journal of Economics* 1339, 1378–80**

There are three broad theories of government regulation of labor. Efficiency theories hold that regulations adjust to efficiently address the problems of market failure. Political theories contend that regulations are used by political leaders to benefit themselves and their allies. Legal theories hold that the patterns of regulation are shaped by each country's legal tradition, which is to a significant extent determined by transplantation of a few legal systems. We examined the regulation of labor markets in 85 countries through the lens of these theories. As we indicated, the efficiency theory is difficult to reject, but we do not find much support for conventional versions. In particular, we find that heavier regulation of labor has adverse consequences for labor force participation and unemployment, especially of the young. There is some support for the view that countries with a

---

[55] For exhaustive accounts of the market failures which are addressed by labour laws, see A. Hyde, 'What is Labour Law?' in G. Davidov and B. Langille (eds), *Boundaries and Frontiers of Labour Law* (Oxford, Hart Publishing, 2006) 54–8; B. E. Kaufman, 'Labor Law and Employment Regulation: Neoclassical and Institutional Perspectives' in K. Dau-Schmidt, S. D. Harris, and O. Lobel (eds), *Labor and Employment Law and Economics* (Cheltenham, Edward Elgar, 2009) 1, 14–17; S. Deakin and F. Wilkinson, 'Labour Law and Economic Theory: A Reappraisal' in H. Collins, P. Davies, and R. Rideout (eds), *Legal Regulation of the Employment Relation* (London, Kluwer, 2000) 29; and H. Collins, 'Justifications and Techniques of Legal Regulation of the Employment Relation' also in Collins, Davies, and Rideout (2000) 1.

[56] See S. Deakin, J. Malmberg, and P. Sarkar, 'How Do Labour Laws Affect Unemployment and the Labour Share of National Income? The Experience of Six OECD Countries, 1970–2010' (2014) 153 *International Labour Review* 1, 4; C. Mummé, 'Property in Labor and the Limits of Contracting' in U. Mattei and J. D. Haskell (eds), *Research Handbook on Political Economy and Law* (Cheltenham, Edward Elgar, 2015) 400.

longer history of leftist governments have more extensive regulation of labor, consistent with the political theory. There is, finally, strong evidence that the origin of a country's laws is an important determinant of its regulatory approach, in labor as well as in other markets. Moreover, legal origin does not appear to be a proxy for social democracy—its explanatory power is both independent and significantly larger. This evidence is broadly consistent with the legal theory, according to which patterns of regulation across countries are shaped largely by transplanted legal structures . . . [Therefore,] the main factor explaining labor laws in our data is legal origin . . . The bottom line of this research is the centrality of institutional transplantation: countries have regulatory styles that are pervasive across activities and shaped by the origin of their laws.[57]

The index compiled by Botero et al. is perhaps the least influential of those constructed. The Organisation for Economic Co-operation and Development ('OECD') has also produced an index which assesses the strictness of employment protection legislation in each of its 34 member countries.[58] Meanwhile, the World Bank's *Doing Business* report,[59] which codes countries for the rigidity of their employment laws, is by far the most widely recognized. Each of these indices share in common two implicit assumptions about the effects of labour laws: first, that employment protection legislation is a burden on business insofar as it impedes the flexibility of labour markets and enables the labour force to extract anti-competitive rents; secondly, that the legal origins of a country determine the efficiency of its labour laws. These assumptions are being challenged by some law and economics scholars, who have questioned the methodological approaches adopted by Botero et al.[60] This debate is significant for the UK, since the international statistics demonstrate that UK labour laws are some of the most flexible in the world.[61] Of course, this chimes with the 'legal origins' theory, but acts as a counter-narrative to that promoted by Government and British industry, namely that UK employment laws are too rigid, technical, and detailed, and exert negative effects on the ability of British firms to compete internationally.

Reflection points

1. See the articles by H. Collins, 'The Productive Disintegration of Labour Laws' (1997) 26 *Industrial Law Journal* 295, and A. Aviles, 'The 'Externalisation' of Labour Law' (2009) 148 *International Labour Review* 47, which chart the fragmentation of labour laws. In light of the discussion in this chapter, do you believe that there are convincing reasons to distinguish labour law from private law and public law and to treat it as an independent field of enquiry? Give reasons for your answer.

---

[57] See also S. Deakin, P. Lele, and M. Siems, 'The Evolution of Labour Law: Calibrating and Comparing Regulatory Regimes' (2007) 146 *International Labour Review* 133; J. Armour, S. Deakin, P. Lele, and M. Siems, 'How Do Legal Rules Evolve? Evidence from a Cross-Country Comparison of Shareholder, Creditor and Worker Protection' (2009) 57 *American Journal of Comparative Law* 579.

[58] See http://www.oecd.org/employment/emp/oecdindicatorsofemploymentprotection.htm (last visited 19 October 2017).

[59] See http://www.doingbusiness.org/data/exploretopics/employing-workers (last visited 19 October 2017).

[60] See S. Deakin, 'Legal Origin, Juridical Form and Industrialization in Historical Perspective: The Case of the Employment Contract and the Joint-Stock Company' (2009) 7 *Socio-Economic Review* 35.

[61] See http://www.oecd.org/employment/emp/oecdindicatorsofemploymentprotection.htm (last visited 19 October 2017).

2. In light of prevailing attitudes amongst employers that employment regulation is burdensome and a barrier to business, are you convinced by the justifications in favour of the introduction and maintenance of labour laws? If not, why not? If so, why?

3. See P. Skedinger, *Employment Protection Legislation: Evolution, Effects, Winners and Losers* (Cheltenham, Edward Elgar, 2010). Do you subscribe to the view that labour laws are inefficient and serve to suppress economic growth? Give reasons for your answer.

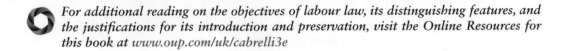

For additional reading on the objectives of labour law, its distinguishing features, and the justifications for its introduction and preservation, visit the Online Resources for this book at www.oup.com/uk/cabrelli3e

CHAPTER TWO

SOURCES AND INSTITUTIONS
OF EMPLOYMENT LAW

2.1 INTRODUCTION TO THE SOURCES AND INSTITUTIONS OF EMPLOYMENT LAW

This chapter is primarily intended to examine the principal sources and institutions of labour law in the UK. The relationship between the common law and employment protection legislation will first be reviewed. We will then move on to address the significance of codes of practice. A brief exploration of the importance and extent of European Union ('EU') competence in the field of social policy will then follow, including the potential implications of Brexit, before our attention turns to informal sources of regulation and the institutional framework of employment law, e.g. the importance of the specialist tribunal system and the courts. Finally, consideration will be given to the importance of human rights and the role of international labour standards.

2.1.1 The relationship between the common law and statutory employment rights: 'oil and water'?

The common law and statute are undoubtedly the most important formal sources of labour law in the UK. First, the common law regulates the contract of employment entered into between the employee and the employer by supplying the rules for its formation, identification/classification, interpretation, suspension, variation, transformation, and termination. It also influences the structure and performance of the contract by imposing implied obligations on the contracting parties. Secondly, employment protection legislation operates as a mandatory 'floor of rights', conferring inderogable minimum entitlements in favour of employees. Statute has intervened to regulate the employment relationship in a myriad of ways and contexts. For example, statute controls the content of the basic wage–work bargain struck between employee and employer, and the duration of the employee's working time, as well as the proscription of the prejudicial treatment of the employee based on personal factors such as sex, race, disability, etc. Legislation also regulates the dismissal of employees and industrial action.[1]

A key issue is how well these two sources of labour law mix.[2] Bearing in mind that novel statutory concepts need to be construed and applied, to what extent should the techniques and vocabulary of the common law perform any role in this process? This is a policy issue which will sometimes need to be addressed by the judiciary. In *Bournemouth University Higher Education Corp. v Buckland*,[3] the nature of the relationship between the common law of the contract of employment and employment protection legislation was described in terms of the superimposition of the latter over the former:

■ *Bournemouth University Higher Education Corp. v Buckland*
[2010] ICR 908, 913G

> *Sedley LJ:*
>
> Modern employment law is a hybrid of contract and status. The way Parliament has done this is to graft statutory protections on to the stem of the common law contract.

The danger is that the interface between employment legislation and the common law evolves in an unclear and unhappy manner so that they are incapable of mutual co-existence, instead resulting in an inability to mix, akin to 'oil and water'.[4] The common law regulation of the employment relationship which defers to the doctrine of freedom of contract has—somewhat counter-intuitively, in light of the intention to break from the common law approach—exerted something of a talismanic grip upon the interpretation and application of employment protection legislation. In other words, the common law, and contract law generally, has been marshalled by the courts in a number of instances to infuse meaning into statutory concepts. This is despite the fact that there

---

[1] See Chapters 8–14, 16–20, and Chapters B, C, and D of the Online Resources.

[2] See J. Riley, 'Uneasy or Accommodating Bedfellows? Common Law and Statute in Employment Regulation', Phillipa Weeks Lecture in Labour Law, Canberra, ACT, Presentation (September 2013), available from SSRN at http://papers.ssrn.com/sol3/papers.cfm?abstract_id=2356032 (last visited 30 November 2017).

[3] [2010] ICR 908.

[4] J. Beatson, 'Has the Common Law a Future?' (1997) 56(2) *Cambridge Law Journal* 291, 301; A. Burrows, 'The Relationship between Common Law and Statute in the Law of Obligations' (2012) 128 *Law Quarterly Review* 232; B. Hepple, *Rights at Work: Global, European and British Perspectives* (London, Thomson/Sweet & Maxwell, 2005) 52 and 65; and A. Bogg, 'Common Law and Statute in the Law of Employment' (2016) 69 *Current Legal Problems* 67, 87.

may be little to suggest from the text of the statute that Parliament had intended such an approach to be adopted:

■ S. Anderman, 'The Interpretation of Protective Employment Statutes and Contracts of Employment' (2000) 29 *Industrial Law Journal* 223, 224

In the case of claims based on statute, however, the courts have experienced difficulties of a more systemic nature in deciding what weight to give the contract of employment in interpreting statutory provisions. The root cause of these difficulties has been a judicial tendency to refrain from treating statutory employment protections as an independent layer of regulation subject to its own values and assumptions even when regulating contractual employment relations. Thus, even where the protective statutory provisions call for a test in which the terms of the contract are only part of the factual matrix, judges have applied a 'contractual' test, by treating the terms of the contract as the decisive factor in interpreting the statute. Some of these provisions such as 'place of work' and 'kind of work' in the definition of redundancy [in section 139(1)(b) of the Employment Rights Act 1996 ('ERA')] do not even mention the contract of employment. Others such as 'continuous service' [in section 210 of the ERA], 'employee' [in section 230 of the ERA and section 295 of the Trade Union and Labour Relations (Consolidation) Act 1992 ('TULRCA')] and 'dismissal' [in section 95 of the ERA] explicitly refer to the contract of employment in their definitions but call for a finding which may or may not reflect the express terms of an agreement reached between the parties. A number of such cases of exaggerated contractual interpretation of statutory provisions have been noted and corrected by the judiciary but these judicial efforts at self correction have been piecemeal and make no acknowledgment of a pattern.[5]

As noted in the Anderman extract, the law of unfair dismissal contained in Part X of the ERA is a prime example of a piece of legislation where the common law has been harnessed to fashion the normative content of protective statutory provisions, rather than treating the latter as an autonomous self-contained body of regulation.[6] For example, section 95(1) of the ERA provides three definitions of 'dismissal' for the purposes of the unfair dismissal regime in Part X of the ERA. Section 95(1)(c) of the ERA lays down one instance of a 'dismissal', referred to in shorthand as a 'constructive dismissal'. This statutory measure provides that an employee will have been constructively dismissed where the employee terminates 'the contract under which he is employed (with or without notice) in circumstances in which he is entitled to terminate it without notice by reason of the employer's conduct'. In *Western Excavating (ECC) Ltd v Sharp*[7] and *Bournemouth University Higher Education Corp. v Buckland*,[8] the judiciary decided that an employee is constructively dismissed where the employer has committed a repudiatory breach of the contract of employment going to the root of that contract. Here we can see that the statutory concept of constructive dismissal has been construed in a manner which relies on traditional contract law doctrine (i.e. the common law of repudiatory breach) to inject it with a measure of substance and workable content.

---

[5] Writer's annotations appear in square brackets throughout this chapter. See also A. C. L. Davies, 'The Relationship Between the Contract of Employment and Statute' in M. Freedland et al. (eds), *The Contract of Employment* (Oxford, OUP, 2016) 75–80; M. Freedland, *The Personal Employment Contract* (Oxford, OUP, 2003) 10–12, 155–6, 189, and 339–44; M. Freedland and N. Kountouris, *The Legal Construction of Personal Work Relations* (Oxford, OUP, 2011) 101; L. Barmes, 'Common Law Implied Terms and Behavioural Standards at Work' (2007) 36 *Industrial Law Journal* 35, 37–8; T. Kerr, 'Contract Doesn't Live Here Any More?' (1984) 47 *Modern Law Review* 30; S. Honeyball, 'Employment Law and the Primacy of Contract' (1989) 18 *Industrial Law Journal* 97, 105–8; S. Honeyball and D. Pearce, 'Contract, Employment and the Contract of Employment' (2006) 35 *Industrial Law Journal* 30; and P. Elias, B. Napier, and P. Wallington, *Labour Law: Cases and Materials* (London, Butterworths, 1980) 526–7.
[6] See Chapter 16.   [7] [1978] QB 761, [1978] IRLR 27.   [8] [2010] IRLR 445.

There are many other examples of the propensity of the judiciary to cling to common law concepts when applying statutory employment protection regimes. These include the deference of employment protection legislation to the common law tests for the establishment of 'employee' status[9] and the one-time dominance of the 'contract' test in determining whether an employee had been made redundant for the purposes of section 139(1)(b) of the ERA.[10] One can also cite the continued relevance of the contract law doctrines of frustration[11] and illegality[12] of contract in the context of reaching a decision whether an employee has been 'dismissed' for the purposes of section 95(1) of the ERA, or whether an individual is working on the basis of a contract of employment or not as the case may be.

Nevertheless, it should be stressed that the traffic has not all been one-way. Employment protection legislation has itself acted as a powerful influence, generating movements in the common law of the contract of employment.[13] It has been judicially recognized that the common law develops 'sometimes by analogy with statutory rights'.[14] Hence, a kind of 'feedback' loop has been generated. For example, the development of the crucially important implied contractual term of mutual trust and confidence[15] can be attributed to the judicial construction of the normative content of the statutory unfair dismissal regime. Despite the fact that the implied term forms part of the common law, as was explained by Lord Nicholls in the House of Lords decision in *Eastwood v Magnox Electric plc*,[16] it emerged from the welter of cases which considered the definition of constructive dismissal in section 95(1)(c) of the ERA. There have also been circumstances in which the judiciary have used the existence of statutory employment protection legislation to justify their refusal to extend the scope of common law employment rights. The classic examples are the decisions of the House of Lords in *Johnson v Unisys Ltd*[17] and of the Supreme Court in *Edwards v Chesterfield Royal Hospital NHS Foundation Trust*,[18] where it was held that the statutory unfair dismissal regime precluded the Court from recognizing a common law employment right to damages in respect of the manner of an employee's dismissal.

Another arena in which statute and the common law have come into contact is in the context of 'contracting out'. Here, the question is to what extent an employee's statutory employment protection rights are to be treated as inderogable, i.e. incapable of exclusion or limitation in the employee's employment contract. Alternatively, should they be permissive and susceptible to disapplication by agreement? From the employer's perspective, it will be argued that an employer and employee ought to be permitted to agree (via the medium of an express term in the contract of employment) to disapply or restrict the operation of statutory employment rights.[19] However, the opposite view is that Parliament has chosen to enact a statutory regime which is designed to protect employees from arbitrary, unfair, or unjust treatment on the basis that they labour under unequal bargaining power. Therefore, as a matter of public policy, it should not be possible for

---

[9] See Chapter 3, section 3.2.1.

[10] *Nelson v BBC* [1977] IRLR 148 (CA) and *Nelson v BBC (No. 2)* [1979] IRLR 346, which has now been abandoned in favour of a 'causation' test in the decision of the House of Lords in *Murray v Foyle Meats* [1999] IRLR 562, on which, see Chapter 18, section 18.2.2.3.

[11] For example, *Sharp & Co. Ltd v McMillan* [1998] IRLR 632; *Hare v Murphy Brothers Ltd* [1974] ICR 603 (CA); and *FC Shepherd & Co. Ltd v Jerrom* [1986] IRLR 358 (CA).

[12] See Chapter 3, section 3.3.

[13] M. Freedland, *The Personal Employment Contract* (Oxford, OUP, 2003) 339.

[14] *Johnson v Unisys Ltd* [2001] UKHL 13, [2003] 1 AC 518, 539C per Lord Hoffmann.

[15] See Chapter 6, sections 6.2.4 and 6.3.3, and Chapter 7, section 7.4.

[16] [2004] IRLR 733, 735 at paras 4–7.   [17] [2001] UKHL 13, [2003] 1 AC 518.

[18] [2011] UKSC 58, [2012] 2 WLR 55. See Chapter 15, section 15.3.1.

[19] Alternatively, the employer will argue that there ought to be no impediment to an employee waiving these rights or acknowledging that he/she will not seek to rely on them.

an employer and employee to agree to subvert that protective regime. This is the argument which has prevailed and various provisions of employment protection legislation effectively convert the statutory rights into a mandatory 'floor' of protection.[20] These provisions can only be waived or excluded in exceptional circumstances, e.g. where an employee settles a claim by following a prescribed statutory procedure with the benefit of professional advice about his/her legal rights and signs a settlement agreement[21] or enters into a COT3 agreement.[22]

Therefore, legislation tightly controls the circumstances in which an employee will be entitled to waive his/her statutory rights. As such, one might argue that statutory employment rights amount to inderogable law.[23] However, that would be wide of the mark. It is sometimes possible for an employing entity to structure the personal work relationship with an individual in a way which operates to indirectly deprive the latter of any employment protection rights. This can be achieved by ensuring that the individual is treated as a self-employed independent contractor, performing personal services under a contract for services, rather than under a contract of employment. Since the benefit of the majority of statutory employment rights are afforded to 'employees' only, the effect of such a contractual arrangement is that the employing entity is able to indirectly derogate from the operation of protective legislation. Of course, this simple way of denying employment rights is controversial, and as demonstrated by the recent spate in 'gig economy' cases, it is less likely to be accepted by the courts. As we will see later in Chapter 3, the courts and tribunals are alive to sham transactions which are specifically drawn up in writing by the employer in a manner that deliberately seeks to establish a type of relationship which does not exist in reality.

2.2 FORMAL AND INFORMAL SOURCES OF EMPLOYMENT LAW

UK employment law consists of a disparate variety and range of formal and informal sources. The latter, which are voluntary, once amounted to the most central source of labour law, given the collective laissez-faire tradition of voluntary collective bargaining

---

[20] See section 203(1) of the ERA; section 288 of TULRCA; section 49 of the National Minimum Wage Act 1998; sections 142–144 of the EA; regulation 35 of the Working Time Regulations 1998 (SI 1998/1833); regulations 40 and 41 of the Transnational Information and Consultation of Employees Regulations 1999 (SI 1999/3323); regulation 9 of the Part-Time Workers (Prevention of Less Favourable Treatment) Regulations 2000 (SI 2000/1551); regulation 10 of the Fixed-Term Employees (Prevention of Less Favourable Treatment) Regulations 2002 (SI 2002/2034); regulations 39 and 40 of the Information and Consultation of Employees Regulations 2004 (SI 2004/3426); regulation 18 of the Transfer of Undertakings (Protection of Employment) Regulations 2006 (SI 2006/246); and regulation 15 of the Agency Workers Regulations 2010 (SI 2010/93).

[21] See section 288(2A) and (2B) of TULRCA; section 203(2)(f) and (3) of the ERA; section 49(3) and (4) of the National Minimum Wage Act 1998; the Employment Code of Practice (Settlement Agreements) Order 2013 (SI 2013/1665); and the Advisory, Conciliation and Arbitration Service ('**ACAS**') Code of Practice on Settlement Agreements (under section 111A of the ERA), available at http://www.acas.org.uk/media/pdf/n/o/Acas-response-to-Settlement-Agreements-Code-June-2013.pdf (last visited 30 November 2017).

[22] This is an agreement concluded with the involvement of an ACAS conciliation officer under section 18 of the Employment Tribunals Act 1996 ('ETA').

[23] For a discussion of the distinction between inderogable and derogable employment rights, see O. Kahn-Freund, 'A Note on Status and Contract in British Labour Law' (1967) 30 *Modern Law Review* 635; B. Rudden, 'Ius Cogens, Ius Dispositivum' (1980) 11 *Cambrian Law Review* 87; Lord Wedderburn, 'Inderogability, Collective Agreements and Community Law' (1992) 21 *Industrial Law Journal* 245; and M. Freedland, 'Ius Cogens, Ius Dispositivum, and the Law of Personal Work Contracts' in P. Birks and A. Pretto (eds), *Themes in Comparative Law* (Oxford, OUP, 2002) 165.

which we discussed in Chapter 1.[24] However, formal sources, such as the common law and statutory employment protection rights, have overtaken voluntary and informal sources in importance and now supply the lion's share of the norms which impact on employees in the workplace. The effect of all these sources is that, when evaluating a legal question, it is not enough for a lawyer to simply search for the law in a single place.[25] For example, where a claim is made that an employee's dismissal constitutes discriminatory treatment on the basis of her sex, the common law of wrongful dismissal will need to be consulted, as will the statutory rules on unfair dismissal and sex discrimination found in the ERA and the EA. The lawyer must also consider the terms of the Code of Practice 1 on Disciplinary and Grievance Procedures[26] issued by ACAS and the Code of Practice on Employment[27] promulgated by the Equality and Human Rights Commission ('EHRC').[28] Turning to informal sources of law, the contents of voluntary collective agreements entered into between employers and trade unions are also relevant as they may contain provisions regulating dismissals or discriminatory conduct. The claim is also impacted upon by EU law and the European rules which prohibit sex discrimination in the workplace—at the very least, pending Brexit and any subsequent transitional arrangements agreed between the EU and UK. Article 14 of the European Convention on Human Rights ('ECHR') which prohibits discrimination and was incorporated into UK law by the Human Rights Act 1998 ('HRA') in October 2000 will also merit attention. As such, we can see how this somewhat straightforward example serves to underscore the existence of a great variety of sources which will come into play in resolving a legal issue. With these thoughts in mind, we now move on to address the common law as a formal source of law.

2.2.1 Common law

The first formal source which we consider is the common law. The common law is situated at the very heart of individual employment law and collective labour law. It infuses employment law with its traditional regard for the underlying liberal values of party autonomy, individualism, protection of property rights,[29] respect for freedom of contract, the freedom to quit, and the freedom to trade. The judiciary have tended to cleave to these axiomatic values in handing down judgments in employment law cases. These judgments have accumulated over time to form precedents and reinforce further the saliency of these doctrines.[30] As such, it has been difficult for judges to resist the temptation to depart from these default values. The focus on protecting the employer's property

---

[24] See Chapter 1, section 1.2.1.

[25] These sources will also influence and shape the content and application of each other in a sophisticated way. Furthermore, although an informal source of employment law such as a collective agreement may not be legally binding, it may be crowned with the success of legal enforceability if it is incorporated into an employee's individual contract of employment.

[26] See http://www.acas.org.uk/?articleid=2174 (last visited 30 November 2017) for the full version of the ACAS Code.

[27] See https://www.equalityhumanrights.com/sites/default/files/employercode.pdf (last visited 30 November 2017).

[28] These statutory codes of practice amount to formal sources of 'soft' law inasmuch as they are admissible in evidence before an employment tribunal ('ET') or in criminal, or civil, proceedings in court. If an employer fails to adhere to them, this must be taken into account by a court or tribunal in any case in which it appears to the court or tribunal to be relevant, on which, see section 207(2) and (3) of TULRCA, section 15(4) of the Equality Act 2006, and section 2.2.3.

[29] See *National Union of Rail, Maritime & Transport Workers v Serco; ASLEF v London & Birmingham Railway Ltd* [2011] ICR 848, 854A per Elias LJ; C. Mummé, 'Property in Labor and the Limits of Contract' in U. Mattei and J. Haskell (eds), *The Research Handbook on Political Economy and Law* (Cheltenham, Edward Elgar, 2015) 400.

[30] See D. Renton, *Struck out* (London, Pluto Press, 2012) 115–27.

and contractual rights from outside interference from the interests of labour has generated the perception that the common law is the 'enemy of social justice . . . [with] deep
roots'.[31] Consider the following extract:

■ **A. Davies, 'Judicial Self-Restraint in Labour Law' (2009) 38** *Industrial Law*
Journal **278, 287–8**

> The judicial role has long been a matter of debate in labour law. There is a tendency among labour
> lawyers to regard the courts with suspicion. The perception is that the judges are hostile to the
> interests of workers, and particularly to the collective interests of workers in trade unions, and that
> they favour the interests of employers . . . The labour law literature approaches this set of issues us-
> ing a more or less explicitly political vocabulary. The less explicit version of the argument is that the
> courts have a particular 'common law mindset' that favours individualism and freedom of contract.
> This does not sit comfortably with labour law's traditional emphasis on collective action and on
> redressing inequalities of bargaining power in contractual relationships. The more explicitly politi-
> cal version of the argument is that for reasons of class and background, the judges simply favour
> the interests of capital over those of labour.

The extract from Davies yields the important observation that labour lawyers have
been traditionally cautious about the prospects of success in the courts, given the (assumed) inclination of the judiciary to prefer the interests of employers over those of
workers.[32]

At the level of individual employment law, the majority of employment rights with a
common law or statutory source are conferred in favour of employees in an employment
relationship. In turn, this is established if there is a contract of employment in place with
an employer. The principles applied to ascertain whether such a contract exists are supplied by the common law of the contract of employment. Therefore, the common law is
responsible for the rules on the formation, identification, and classification of a contract
as an employment contract. The common law also governs the content, performance, and
structure of the contract of employment.[33] It does this by prescribing implied contractual
terms which subject the employer and employee to certain core obligations, e.g. duties
of care and trust and confidence on the part of the employer and duties of care, fidelity,
and loyalty on the part of the employee.[34] If those obligations are breached, the innocent
party has a remedy in damages and may also be entitled to terminate the employment
contract depending on the gravity of the breach, i.e. if it is repudiatory. Moreover, if the
employer intends to vary, suspend, or terminate the employment contract, norms laid
down by the common law must also be taken into account. Sometimes, they must be
considered alongside detailed statutory regulation, e.g. the control of the termination of

---

[31] K. D. Ewing, 'The Sense of Measure: Old Wine in New Bottles, or New Wine in Old Bottles, or New
Wine in New Bottles?' in E. Christodoulidis and R. Dukes, 'Dialogue & Debate: Labour, Constitution and
A Sense of Measure: A Debate with Alain Supiot' (2010) 19 *Social & Legal Studies* 217, 234.

[32] See also H. Arthurs, 'The Constitutionalization of Employment Relations: Multiple Models, Pernicious Problems' (2010) 19 *Social & Legal Studies* 403, 405–6.

[33] See Chapter 3, section 3.2.1. Interestingly, these common law tests are derived from the nineteenth-
century law of master and servant, which was a status-based relationship pre-dating the modern incarnation of the employment relationship in a contractual form, on which, see S. Deakin and F. Wilkinson, *The
Law of the Labour Market: Industrialization, Employment, and Legal Evolution* (Oxford, OUP, 2005); S.
Deakin, 'Legal Origin, Juridical Form and Industrialization in Historical Perspective: The Case of the Em-
ployment Contract and the Joint-Stock Company' (2009) 7 *Socio-Economic Review* 35; and B. Veneziani,
'The Evolution of the Contract of Employment' in B. Hepple (ed.), *The Making of Labour Law in Europe*
(Oxford, Hart Publishing, 2010) 31.   [34] See Chapter 6, sections 6.2 and 6.3.

the employment contract by the unfair dismissal and redundancy regimes in Parts X and XI of the ERA.

Turning to the field of collective labour law, this is also an area where the common law has exerted a degree of influence. The primary example is the law of industrial action. It is impossible to fully understand the legislative intervention into the law regulating workplace strikes without an appreciation of the underlying common law rules on the economic torts. The rules in TULRCA which confer statutory immunities from liability in tort owe their existence to the common law economic torts, which the trade unions would otherwise commit in their absence.[35] In the area of collective labour law, the common law also provides the principles governing the rights of trade union members vis-à-vis the trade union.

2.2.2 Employment protection legislation

It is an astonishing fact that any account of UK labour law prior to the enactment of the Contract of Employment Act 1963 (now repealed) would have made scant reference to legislation as a source of the law. Legislation affecting the workplace before 1963 was principally concerned with the regulation of trade unions, wage protection, the protection of the physical safety of workers, or women and children in particular.[36] In fact, the main sources of workplace norms were the common law and the informal collective agreements struck between trade unions and employers or employers' associations pursuant to the voluntarist system of industrial relations. However, since 1963, the volume of legislation has grown exponentially to overshadow collective agreements in terms of their significance for employment law. In fact, this phenomenon has been so widespread that some commentators have debated whether a continuing role for trade unions can ever exist in the teeth of an increased volume of individual employment legislation:[37]

■ G. S. Morris, 'The Development of Statutory Employment Rights in Britain and Enforcement Mechanisms' in L. Dickens (ed.), *Making Employment Rights Effective* (Oxford, Hart Publishing, 2012) 8–10

The residual role of statute as a source of regulation has been transformed over the past 50 years. The process began modestly, with the introduction of the right to a written statement of employment terms and minimum notice periods in 1963. 1965 saw the introduction of statutory redundancy payments for no-fault economic job loss, followed by a broader range of individual rights in 1971, most notably the right not to be unfairly dismissed. The 1970s also brought the right to equal pay for men and women and individual rights in the areas of sex and race discrimination; maternity; and membership and non-membership of, and participation in, trade unions. The 1979–97 Conservative governments sought to deregulate the labour market both by weakening trade unions and relaxing or removing statutory standards; the powers of the long-standing wages councils, for example, were curtailed and eventually abolished. However, there were limits

[35] In recent times, the content of the ECHR has had some effect on this complex interaction between the common law and the statutory immunities, particularly Article 11, on which, see section 2.4.1 and Chapter D of the Online Resources.

[36] The Trade Union Act 1871 (34 & 35 Vict. C. 31), the Truck Act 1831 (1 & 2 Will. 4, c. 37), the Factory and Workshop Act 1901 (1 Edw. 7, c. 22), the Coal Mines Act 1911 (1 & 2 Geo. 5, c. 50), and the Employment of Children Act 1903 (3 Edw. 7, c. 45). Some legislation provided auxiliary support for the informal system of collective laissez-faire, but did not seek to regulate or supplant it and, on occasion, legislation existed which would govern spheres of activity not traditionally covered by collective agreements.

[37] M. O'Sullivan, T. Turner, and J. Wallace, 'Is Individual Employment Law Displacing the Role of Trade Unions?' (2015) 44 *Industrial Law Journal* 222.

to the deregulatory strategy: obligations resulting from membership of the European Community (now the European Union) required new or extended statutory rights, such as rights on transfer of a business and a broader scope for equal pay. Protection against disability discrimination was introduced following domestic pressure. The advent of a Labour government in 1997 brought more fundamental reforms, the most notable being the introduction of a national minimum wage to which the trade union movement had dropped its historical opposition. Further EU obligations also produced important changes, particularly general restrictions on working time; rights for part-time workers and those working under fixed-term contracts; rights to non-discrimination on a much wider range of grounds, including age; and 'family-friendly' rights. New rights for agency workers, again required by EU law, were introduced by the Conservative–Liberal Coalition Government which took office in 2010. The major areas covered by the multiplicity of statutory rights which now govern the employment relationship include those listed in [Table 2.1] below. The significance of statutory rights as a source of employment protection in Britain was enhanced by the radical decline in the coverage of collective bargaining since the early 1980s . . . The proportion of employees covered by collective agreements fell from 64 per cent in 1984 to 41 per cent by 1998 in workplaces with 25 or more employees . . . Collective bargaining is now largely confined to the public sector . . . Moreover the range of issues over which bargaining took place has also shrunk . . . Thus, far from being an adjunct to collective bargaining, statutory minimum standards are now for many workers the main source of protection in relation to fundamental terms, such as pay, hours and holidays. They are also particularly important in relation to discipline, termination of employment and equality . . . There are certain important features of statutory employment rights which are [important, including] . . . the technical complexity of many of these rights, which can make it difficult for workers who have no access to specialist advice to claim them and potentially poses problems for employers seeking clarity about their obligations. Moreover, the incremental approach to legislation has meant that rights are located in a wide variety of statutes and secondary legislation rather than being collected in a single document [e.g. an exhaustive Labour Code]; indeed the relevant provisions governing a specific right may themselves be scattered among different legislative instruments.

The principal statutes in the field of labour law are the ERA, TULRCA, and the EA. Each of these legislative measures is a consolidating statute and collectively they are responsible for the vast majority of the rights conferred in favour of employees under employment law. Other pieces of primary legislation include the National Minimum Wage Act 1998. As noted in the extract from Morris, employment law is an area which has been heavily influenced by developments emanating from the EU. Such provisions have generally been transposed into UK law by subordinate legislation, e.g. the Working Time Regulations 1998,[38] the Transnational Information and Consultation of Employees Regulations 1999,[39] the Part-Time Workers (Prevention of Less Favourable Treatment) Regulations 2000,[40] the Fixed-Term Employees (Prevention of Less Favourable Treatment) Regulations 2002,[41] the Information and Consultation of Employees Regulations 2004,[42] the Transfer of Undertakings (Protection of Employment) Regulations 2006,[43] and the Agency Workers Regulations 2010.[44] As such, when the UK Leaves the EU, there will no longer be any legal requirement to continue to recognize the employment rights conferred by the aforementioned subordinate legislation, and the effect is that they are liable to future repeal or modification should Parliament decide to do so.

[38] SI 1998/1833. See Chapter 8.   [39] SI 1999/3323. See Chapter A of the Online Resources.
[40] SI 2000/1551. See Chapter 13.   [41] SI 2002/2034. See Chapter 13.
[42] SI 2004/3426. See Chapter A of the Online Resources.
[43] SI 2006/246. See Chapter 19.   [44] SI 2010/93. See Chapter 4.

Table 2.1 *Statutory rights governing the employment relationship*

(1) Statutory employment rights in place in 1997 include:
— a minimum period of notice of termination;
— a statement of the principal terms and conditions of the contract of employment and of discipline and dismissal procedures;
— an itemised pay statement;
— a statement of the reason for dismissal;
— protection against unfair dismissal;
— protection against discrimination on grounds of race, sex and disability;
— time off work for ante-natal care;
— maternity leave and pay;
— return to work after leave for childbirth;
— time off work for various public and trade union duties;
— equal pay and other contractual terms as between men and women;
— redundancy payments;
— protection against dismissal or action short of dismissal on grounds of trade union membership, non-membership or union activity;
— preservation of acquired rights on the transfer of undertakings.

(2) Statutory employment rights introduced since 1997 include:
— the national minimum wage;
— protection against dismissal or detriment for 'whistleblowing';
— the right to be accompanied in grievance and disciplinary hearings;
— statutory limits on working time;
— paid annual leave;
— parental leave;
— time off for family emergencies;
— the right to request flexible working;
— paternity leave and pay;
— adoption leave and pay;
— equal treatment for part-time workers;
— protection for fixed-term employees;
— protection against discrimination on grounds of age, religion or belief and sexual orientation.

(3) Statutory employment rights introduced since 2010 include:
— protection for agency workers.

Source: G. S. Morris, 'The Development of Statutory Employment Rights in Britain and Enforcement Mechanisms' in L. Dickens (ed.), *Making Employment Rights Effective* (Oxford, Hart Publishing, 2012) 7, 9.

2.2.3 Codes of practice

Codes of practice issued under statutory authority serve as useful indicators of good practice in certain employment relations contexts. They are not only designed to be reflective of existing good practice, but also to be sufficiently flexible that they respond to developments at the grass-roots level. The most high-profile codes of practice are the Code of Practice 1 on Disciplinary and Grievance Procedures[45] issued by

---

[45] See http://www.acas.org.uk/?articleid=2174 (last visited 1 December 2017) for the full version of the ACAS Code.

ACAS[46] and the Codes of Practice on Employment[47] and Equal Pay,[48] both promulgated by the EHRC under section 14 of the Equality Act 2006. These statutory codes of practice are often supplemented by non-statutory guidance.[49] Other bodies and persons involved in the promulgation of codes include the Health and Safety Executive ('HSE'),[50] and the Secretary of State, e.g. the Codes of Practice on Picketing,[51] Access and Unfair Practices during Recognition and Derecognition Ballots,[52] and Industrial Action Ballots and Notice to Employers.[53] The provisions of section 207 of TULRCA govern the consequences of a failure by an employer to adhere to the terms of a code of practice:

Section 207 Effect of failure to comply with Code

(1) A failure on the part of any person to observe any provision of a Code of Practice issued [by ACAS or the Secretary of State] shall not of itself render him liable to any proceedings.

(2) In any proceedings before an [ET] or the Central Arbitration Committee [('CAC')] any Code of Practice issued under this Chapter by ACAS shall be admissible in evidence, and any provision of the Code which appears to the [ET or CAC] to be relevant to any question arising in the proceedings shall be taken into account in determining that question.

(3) In any proceedings before a court or [ET or CAC] any Code of Practice issued under this Chapter by the Secretary of State shall be admissible in evidence, and any provision of the Code which appears to the court, [ET or CAC] to be relevant to any question arising in the proceedings shall be taken into account in determining that question.[54]

The effect of these provisions is that non-adherence to a code of practice on the part of the employer may have a serious impact on the outcome of any claim brought against it.[55] Although a procedural flaw in adherence will not always give rise to liability on the part of the employer,[56] this will be the consequence in the vast majority of cases, since a tribunal or court will often look unfavourably on non-compliance. Moreover, an unreasonable failure to comply with the provisions of the ACAS Code of Practice 1 on Disciplinary and Grievance Procedures or codes of practice issued by the Secretary of State may be taken into account by an ET, if it considers it just and equitable in all the circumstances to do so, as a means of increasing any compensation award against the employer by no more than 25 per cent.[57] This is illustrated in the following Hypothetical A.

---

[46] See also section 199(1) of TULRCA and the Code of Practice on Time Off for Trade Union Duties and Activities, available at http://www.acas.org.uk/index.aspx?articleid=2391 (last visited 1 December 2017).

[47] See https://www.equalityhumanrights.com/sites/default/files/employercode.pdf (last visited 1 December 2017).

[48] See https://www.equalityhumanrights.com/sites/default/files/equalpaycode.pdf (last visited 1 December 2017).

[49] For example, see ACAS's non-statutory guide on the ACAS Code of Practice 1 on Disciplinary and Grievance Procedures, namely 'Discipline and Grievances at Work', available at http://www.acas.org.uk/index.aspx?articleid=2179 (last visited 1 December 2017).

[50] See http://www.hse.gov.uk/pubns/books/index-cop.htm (last visited 1 December 2017).

[51] See https://www.gov.uk/government/publications/code-of-practice-picketing (last visited 1 December 2017).

[52] See https://www.gov.uk/government/publications/code-of-practice-access-and-unfair-practices-during-recognition-and-derecognition-ballots (last visited 1 December 2017).

[53] See https://www.gov.uk/government/publications/code-of-practice-industrial-action-ballots-and-notice-to-employers (last visited 1 December 2017).

[54] For broadly equivalent provisions in the case of codes of practice issued by the EHRC, see section 15(4) of the Equality Act 2006; in the case of the HSE, see sections 16 and 17 of the Health and Safety at Work Act 1974.

[55] See *Lock v Cardiff Railway Co. Ltd* [1998] IRLR 358 (EAT); *West Midlands Co-operative Society Ltd v Tipton* [1986] AC 536.   [56] See *Buzoli v Food Partners Ltd* [2013] All ER (D) 340 (February).

[57] See section 207A(1) and (2) of, and Schedule A2 to, TULRCA.

Hypothetical A

Having incorporated Danny's Demolishers Ltd ('DD'), Danny appoints a number of employees on permanent full-time contracts. One of the employees Arnold Price ('AP') works for DD on a demolition site in Crewe. After three years of employment, DD decides to terminate AP's contract of employment and dismiss him with immediate effect. DD does not comply with the ACAS Code of Practice 1 on Disciplinary and Grievance Procedures. AP presents a complaint of unfair dismissal to the ET and his claim is successful. The ET calculates AP's compensatory award for unfair dismissal as £9,534 and decides to award a compensatory uplift of the full 25 per cent in respect of DD's failure to adhere to the ACAS Code of Practice. Therefore, AP's final award is £11,917.50, i.e. £9,534 + (25 per cent × £9,534) = £2,383.50.

2.2.4 EU law and social policy

The impetus for the Treaty of Rome and the creation of the European Economic Community in the 1950s was primarily economic, namely the emergence of an integrated market for the exchange of goods, services, labour, and capital. Few efforts were made at the outset to promulgate measures addressing the adverse social consequences of this integrationist economic policy. The only exceptions were the Articles in the Treaty of Rome relating to the free movement of workers and equal pay between the sexes for equal work.[58] The original disinclination to treat the European project as one concerned with the creation of a pan-European labour law code can be explained by the existence of a deep-seated view that social policy was a key area of regulation which ought to remain firmly entrenched within the sovereignty of Member States. As such, the social policy agenda was subordinated to the economic objectives of the European project. Further, the diverse industrial relations traditions of each Member State could also be cited as a key factor militating against the institution of a European labour law regime. Other reasons for the subordination of social objectives to the economic integrationist approach are explored in the following extract from Barnard and Deakin:

■ C. Barnard and S. Deakin, 'In Search of Coherence: Social Policy, the Single Market and Fundamental Rights' (2000) 31(4) *Industrial Relations Journal* 331, 332

> Nearly all matters relating to labour legislation . . . were left within the competence of the individual member states. The decision to do this was based on a mixture of beliefs: scepticism towards market-failure type arguments for harmonisation; optimism concerning the capacity of the common market to generate convergence on wages and incomes of its own accord; and confidence in the strength of political pressures within member states for the maintenance of effective labour standards and welfare state systems. These beliefs were made explicit in the Ohlin report of ILO experts and in the Spaak report of foreign ministers which paved the way for the Treaty of Rome . . . As a result, the Treaty contained few social policy measures of any significance.

[58] In fact, the latter was motivated more by economic than social considerations, on which see Chapter 11, section 11.1.1.

However, with the advent of the Social Action Programmes, the Social Chapter and Agreement on Social Policy, an identifiable central role for European social policy and labour law emerged:[59]

■ **P. Syrpis, *EU Intervention in Domestic Labour Law* (Oxford, OUP, 2007) 1**

> The EU has profoundly affected the nature of UK labour law. Labour lawyers in the UK have long been aware of the need to monitor developments at the European level. They have become used to the range of ways in which the EU acts, and have spent time and energy poring over the pronouncements of the European courts. The nature of EU intervention has changed significantly with time . . .

■ **P. L. Davies, 'The Emergence of European Labour Law' in W. McCarthy (ed.), *Legal Intervention in Industrial Relations* (Oxford, Blackwell Business, 1992) 313, 313–14**

> The contrast between the late [1960s] and the present day is, of course, a startling one . . . Those in the UK committed to a role for the law in the fields of employment protection, equality and the promotion of industrial democracy today often seem to place their hopes entirely on [EU], rather than UK, developments, with the [European Union Charter of Fundamental Rights ('EUCFR')] standing as a particularly powerful symbol of the [EU]'s potential in these fields . . .

Whilst it is true that domestic trade unions and labour lawyers have historically invested great hope in the power of the European Social Model ('ESM') to effect social policy changes for the benefit of workers, the current level of legislative (in)activity on the part of the EU is such that the European social policy agenda can be described as stagnant at best. This is partly attributable to the financial crisis which occurred during the period between 2008 and 2009 and the euro and sovereign debt crises which had a tendency to flare up on an ongoing basis during the period from 2010 to 2015, but it can also be explained as a by-product of a pervasive ideological outlook that treats labour laws as an impediment to economic growth and job creation.[60] This process of stagnation has caused some commentators to lament the demise of the ESM,[61] although others are slightly more optimistic, pointing to the trajectory of the ESM in the past, and its inherent ability to regenerate itself after it had seemed dead and buried.[62]

---

[59] See C. Barnard, *EU Employment Law* (Oxford, OUP, 2012) 8–28; S. Simitis and A. Lyon-Caen, 'Community Labour Law: A Critical Introduction to its History' in P. Davies, A. Lyon-Caen, S. Sciarra, and S. Simitis (eds), *European Community Labour Law: Principles and Perspectives* (Oxford, Clarendon Press, 1996) 1; and see the various chapters by A. Supiot, F. Hendrickx, A. Bogg, and R. Dukes in N. Countouris and M. Freedland (eds), *Resocialising Europe in a Time of Crisis* (Cambridge, CUP, 2013).

[60] C. Crouch, 'Entrenching Neo-Liberalism: The Current Agenda of European Social Policy' in N. Countouris and M. Freedland (eds), *Resocialising Europe in a Time of Crisis* (Cambridge, CUP, 2013) 36; J. Fudge, 'The Way Forward for Social Europe: How Do We Get There from Here?' (2014) 77 *Modern Law Review* 808, 813–14.

[61] J. Fudge, 'The Way Forward for Social Europe: How Do We Get There from Here?' (2014) 77 *Modern Law Review* 808.

[62] C. Barnard, 'EU Employment Law and the European Social Model: The Past, the Present and the Future' (2014) 67 *Current Legal Problems* 199.

Of course, since 2015, there has been the no little matter of Brexit. At the present time, the exact post-Brexit relationship between the UK and EU remains unclear, but what is uncontested is that the UK will no longer be bound to implement future EU social policy Directives. In addition, the domestic courts will not be bound by the decisions of the European Court of Justice ('ECJ').[63] As for decisions of the ECJ prior to Brexit, these are likely to attract the status of decisions of the UK Supreme Court. The EU Withdrawal Act 2018 (or 2019) ('EUWA') will repeal the European Communities Act 1972 upon which many statutory employment rights (derived from EU law) are based. As such, in order to preserve such EU-derived statutory labour laws, the EUWA will (re-)incorporate them into domestic law. Post-Brexit, Parliament will be at liberty to remove or modify statutory employment protection rights that are historically derived from EU law. In fact, in the opinion of the author, at the very least, the following are susceptible to such excision or dilution:

- the protections for part-time, fixed-term, and agency workers we discuss in Chapters 4 and 13; and

- the protections on collective redundancies considered in Chapter 20.

Since the majority of UK employment protection legislation explored in this book is derived from European Directives,[64] we are dealing with a substantial body of EU-derived labour law that is being re-incorporated into UK law as a result of the EUWA. But until Brexit day, whenever that may be, students of labour law will have to understand and grapple with the relevant EU-derived statutory employment protection laws. It is for this reason that we cover EU law in detail in this book.

Article 151 of the Treaty on the Functioning of the European Union ('TFEU')[65] articulates the objectives of the EU in the social policy field. These are identified as the promotion of employment, improved living and working conditions, so as to make possible their harmonization while improvements are being maintained, proper social protection, dialogue between management and labour, the development of human resources with a view to lasting high employment, and the combating of (social) exclusion. A more cynical perspective on the idealistic tone of Article 151, however, would attribute European employment laws to a desire to avoid a 'race to the bottom' amongst the Member States in employment protection laws, i.e. Member States engaging in (de)regulatory competition by a never-ending lowering of social standards.[66] One of the attractions of harmonizing social protection measures is that it operates as a means of imposing broadly similar labour costs on Member States.

Although key aspects of social policy and labour regulation fall outside the competence of the EU and are reserved to the Member States—such as the regulation of pay,[67] minimum wages and the wage–work bargain, freedom of association, strikes, and industrial

---

[63] The ECJ has been renamed the Court of Justice of the European Union ('**CJEU**') with effect from December 2009, and the abbreviations 'ECJ' and 'CJEU' will be used interchangeably in this book.

[64] For example: (1) rules on the particulars of the terms of the employment contract, on which, see Chapter 5, section 5.2.1; (2) rules prescribing limitations on weekly working time and conferring annual leave, on which, see Chapter 8, section 8.3; (3) policies designed to promote the reconciliation of family and working life, on which, see Chapter 9; (4) employment equality laws, on which, see Chapters 10–12; (5) the principles adopted to protect part-time and fixed-term workers, on which, see Chapter 13; (6) the equal pay laws, on which, see Chapter 14; (7) the procedural protections afforded to workers selected for redundancy, on which, see Chapter 20; and (8) the rights conferred on employees in the context of the transfer of the business of their employer, on which, see Chapter 19.

[65] OJ 2012 C326/47 of 26 October 2012, available at http://eur-lex.europa.eu/legal-content/en/TXT/?uri=CELEX:12012E/TXT (last visited 4 December 2017).

[66] See P. Syrpis, *EU Intervention in Domestic Labour Law* (Oxford, OUP, 2007) 37–8; S. Deakin and F. Wilkinson, 'Rights vs. Efficiency? The Economic Case for Transnational Labour Standards' (1994) 23 *Industrial Law Journal* 289, 295–6.

[67] Of course, the major exception to this is Article 157 of the TFEU which provides for equal pay for equal work between the sexes.

action[68]—the following articles of the TFEU prescribe the fields of activity where it has the power to act:

Article 18

... any discrimination on grounds of nationality shall be prohibited. The European Parliament and the Council ... may adopt rules designed to prohibit such discrimination.

Article 19

1. ... the Council ... may take appropriate action to combat discrimination based on sex, racial or ethnic origin, religion or belief, disability, age or sexual orientation ...

Article 153

1. ... the Union shall support and complement the activities of the Member States in the following fields:
   (a) improvement in particular of the working environment to protect workers' health and safety;
   (b) working conditions;
   (c) social security and social protection of workers;
   (d) protection of workers where their employment contract is terminated;
   (e) the information and consultation of workers;
   (f) representation and collective defence of the interests of workers and employers, including co-determination ...;
   (g) conditions of employment for third-country nationals legally residing in Union territory;
   (h) the integration of persons excluded from the labour market ...;
   (i) equality between men and women with regard to labour market opportunities and treatment at work;
   (j) the combating of social exclusion ...

Article 157

1. Each Member State shall ensure that the principle of equal pay for male and female workers for equal work or work of equal value is applied. For the purpose of this Article, 'pay' means the ordinary basic or minimum wage or salary and any other consideration, whether in cash or in kind, which the worker receives directly or indirectly, in respect of his employment, from his employer.

The objectives specified in Article 153(1)(c), (d), (f), and (g) must be passed unanimously by the European Council of Ministers.[69] This allows a Member State to veto measures designed to harmonize social security regulation, laws regulating the dismissal of employees, worker representational participation, and trade union representation. As for legislative measures brought into force under the policy fields enumerated in Article 153(1) (a), (b), (e), (h), (i), and (j), these can be passed by a majority of the Member States.[70]

---

[68] However, the right to freedom of association, strikes and industrial action are enshrined in Articles 12 and 28 of the EUCFR, on which, see later.

[69] See Article 153(2) of the TFEU.

[70] In an effort to avoid resistance from Member States determined to wield their veto to scupper a legislative initiative, a number of Directives which perhaps ought to have been approved under Article 153(1) (c), (d), (f), or (g) instead have been based on Article 153(1)(a) or (b), e.g. the Working Time Directive 2003/88/EC (OJ 2003 L299/9) ('WTD').

Article 153(2) stipulates that a European Directive is the legislative instrument of choice to give effect to the fields of activity specified in Article 153(1). Indeed, all of the European legislative interventions in labour law have been by Directive. This has been the preferred means of legal intervention owing to the fact that Directives are an eminently flexible mode of effecting changes in social policy. That is attributable to the nature of a European Directive, which is essentially an instrument directing a Member State to transpose its provisions into its national legal order. As such, a Directive is an unsuitable instrument where the intention is to rigorously approximate the national labour laws and social policies of the Member States.[71]

Since a Directive is not addressed to legal persons as such, but to Member States only, its provisions are not legally enforceable by private legal persons against each other, i.e. it does not have *direct horizontal effect*. However, where the State fails to transpose the requirements of a Directive into its national law within the timescale specified in that Directive, its provisions may be enforced by an employee or worker against a public body or an 'emanation of the State' to secure compensation: this is referred to as *vertical direct effect*. Further, owing to the fact that the national courts and ETs are 'emanations of the State', they are under an obligation to construe national law in compliance with European law.[72] Therefore, the provisions of a Directive are said to have *indirect horizontal effect*, enabling a court or tribunal to apply them as an interpretive aid in the context of national law.

It should be stressed that the contents of Directives are minimum requirements which may be improved upon by the national legislation of the Member States. For example, Article 7 of the WTD prescribes that every worker is entitled to four weeks of paid annual leave in every leave year. This can be contrasted with regulation 13(1) of the Working Time Regulations 1998[73] which increases this to 28 days' paid annual leave in any one leave year.[74]

At this juncture in our analysis of the importance of EU law to the development of labour law, it is opportune to consider the role played by the EUCFR.[75] In order to appreciate the role of the EUCFR, it is useful to consider the position prior to its adoption. From the 1970s, the ECJ began to 'discover' unwritten principles referred to as 'fundamental principles of European law'.[76] Where there was a patent inconsistency between these fundamental principles and the domestic legal provisions of the Member States, the ECJ would apply the former to disapply the latter. The creation and content of the EUCFR can be thought of as a political attempt to consolidate and codify these fundamental principles in a single instrument.[77] The effect of Article 6(1) of the Treaty on the

---

[71] Instead, Directives are an effective means of instituting specific changes in national labour laws of the Member States in order to deliver the incremental convergence of national systems, e.g. via 'framework' Directives such as the 'framework' PTWD, FTWD, and the Framework Equality Directive 2000/78/EC (OJ [2000] L303/16).

[72] *Pfeiffer v Deutsches Rotes Kreuz Kreisverband Waldshut eV* [2005] ICR 1307, 1360D–E. More stringently, the court or tribunal may strike down provisions of national law where they do not conform to fundamental principles of EU law, such as the principle of equality and non-discrimination, on which, see *Defrenne v SABENA (No. 3)* C-149/77 [1978] ECR 1365, 1378; *Mangold v Helm* Case C-144/04 [2006] IRLR 143; *Seda Kücükdeveci v Swedex GmbH & Co. KG* C-555/07 [2011] 2 CMLR 703 ('*Kücükdeveci*'); and Chapter 10, section 10.2.1.

[73] SI 1998/1833.   [74] This is sometimes referred to as 'gold-plating'.

[75] Pronounced on 7 December 2000 in Nice (OJ 2000 C 364/1) and a second time in Strasbourg on 12 December 2007 (OJ 2007 C 303/1) and also published in OJ 2010 C 83/389. See T. Hervey and J. Kenner (eds), *Economic and Social Rights under the European Charter of Fundamental Rights: A Legal Perspective* (Oxford, Hart Publishing, 2003). The predecessor of the EUCFR was the Community Charter of the Fundamental Social Rights of Workers of 1989.

[76] See Case 4/73 *Nold v Commission* [1974] ECR 491, para 13.

[77] Some cynics have argued that its creation was an attempt by the Member States to *constrain* the activities of the ECJ.

European Union ('TEU') is that the EUCFR is treated as having the same legal force as the TEU and the TFEU. However, that is subject to the proviso that the EUCFR does not enlarge the competence of the EU to act in the field of social policy. The EUCFR has vertical direct effect inasmuch as Article 51(1) stipulates that its provisions are addressed to the various institutions and bodies of the EU and the Member States when implementing EU law.

The relevance of the EUCFR to employment law lies in the extent to which it confers social and economic rights. For example, several Articles of the EUCFR are peppered with references to absolute rights conferred in favour of workers, in particular Articles 4, 12, 21, 23, 27, 28, 30,[78] 31, and 33.[79] One might quibble that these social norms enshrined in the EUCFR are too open-textured to be justiciable. However, as noted by Advocate-General Bot in his opinion in the case of *Kücükdeveci*,[80] the significance of the EUCFR for workers' rights does indeed lie in its direct justiciability between private legal persons, i.e. its *horizontal direct effect*, particularly where the relevant Charter right is the distillation of jurisprudence pertaining to an area of labour law that explicitly falls within the competence of the EU, e.g. the spheres of operation laid down in Articles 18, 19, 153, and 157 of the TFEU. For example, in *Benkharbouche v Embassy of the Republic of Sudan*[81]—a case about an employer's State immunity and whether it extended to employment claims of race discrimination, unfair dismissal, and failures to pay the national minimum wage or comply with the WTR—it was held that Article 47 of the EUCFR, which confers a right to an effective remedy and a fair trial, could be relied upon by the employee claimant to displace the relevant provisions of the State Immunity Act 1978 as regards the employment law claims in respect of which the EU had competence, e.g. the race discrimination and working time claims. In such a context, Article 47 of the EUCFR had horizontal direct effect and so could be enforced by the employees directly against the employer.

Finally, it ought to be stressed that, in *Kücükdeveci*, the EUCFR played a central role as an interpretive aid,[82] i.e. as an instrument to be consulted by the Grand Chamber of the CJEU in construing provisions of national law of a Member State transposing EU law.[83] This interpretive function is a central element of the softer role played by the EUCFR.

2.2.5 Collective agreements

In Chapter 1, we considered the extract from Langille, who stressed the key role of collective bargaining in affording workers a measure of procedural justice.[84] Rather than

---

[78] Article 30 confers protection on workers against unjustified dismissal. It has been held that this right in the EUCFR cannot be used by an employee to challenge his/her dismissal or eligibility criteria or qualifying thresholds applied under domestic unfair dismissal laws, since dismissals and unfair dismissal laws fall outside the scope of EU labour laws: *Nisttahuz Poclava v Ariza Toledano* [2015] IRLR 403.

[79] These are the Articles (1) prohibiting slavery and forced labour, (2) conferring a right to freedom of assembly and association, (3) conferring the freedom to choose an occupation and the right to engage in work, (4) prohibiting discrimination based on a number of protected grounds, (5) conferring a right to equality between women and men, (6) conferring a right to information and consultation, (7) conferring a right to collective bargaining and action, (8) conferring a right to justified dismissal, (9) conferring a right to fair and just working conditions, and (10) conferring a right to family and professional life.

[80] [2010] ECR I-365, [2010] IRLR 346, 355.

[81] [2017] 3 WLR 957. See also *Dansk Industri v Rasmussen's Estate* [2016] 3 CMLR 27.

[82] Whilst Protocol 30 of the TFEU expressly provides the UK with an opt-out from the EUCFR to the extent that it cannot be used by the CJEU to disapply any provision of the laws or practices of the UK, there is no doubt that its content is of interpretive value even where cases are brought in the context of UK law, on which, see *British Airways plc v Williams* [2012] ICR 847, 878A. See also *R v Secretary of State for Home Department* [2013] EWHC 3453 (Admin); P. Koutrakos, 'Does the United Kingdom Have a General Opt out from the EU Charter of Fundamental Rights?' (2014) 39 *European Law Review* 1.

[83] [2010] ECR I-365, [2010] IRLR 346, 358.   [84] See Chapter 1, section 1.2.1.

individual employment rights mediated via the common law or employment protection legislation, the process of collective bargaining was the traditional method of offsetting the inherent disparity in bargaining power between the forces of capital and labour. The outcome of the process of collective bargaining is the collective agreement, which performs two functions:

■ P. Davies and M. Freedland (eds), *Kahn-Freund's Labour and the Law* (London, Stevens & Sons, 1983) 154–5

A collective agreement is an industrial peace treaty [i.e. the 'contractual function'] and at the same time a source of rules for terms and conditions of employment, for the distribution of work and for the stability of jobs [i.e. the 'normative function']. Its two functions express the principal expectations of the two sides, and it is through reconciling their expectations that a system of industrial relations is able to achieve that balance of power which is one of its main objectives. What can the law do to protect these expectations? To the two social functions of a collective agreement there correspond two actual or potential legal characteristics. The agreement may be, and in many countries is, a contract between those who made it, i.e. between an employer or employers or their association or associations on the one side and a trade union or unions on the other. At the same time the agreement is also potentially, and in many countries actually, a legal code. In this country it is generally neither a legally enforceable contract, nor (exceptions apart) a legally enforceable code. But its terms normally become, through voluntary incorporation, enforceable terms of the contracts of employment. The contractual function is mainly, but not exclusively, sub-servient to the maintenance of industrial peace . . . The normative, i.e. the codifying and rule-making function, of a collective agreement serves to ensure that the agreed conditions are applied in the plant, enterprise or industry to which the agreement refers, i.e. applied by individual employers and workers. Many of them prescribe the terms of the individual employment relationship, others the conditions under which that relationship may or may not be created . . .[85]

The process of collective bargaining in the UK is characterized by a lack of legal compulsion. First, employers are not legally required to engage in collective bargaining.[86] Secondly, when they do, there is no legal obligation to enter into a collective agreement as part of that process. Moreover, it is not mandatory for an employer to recognize a trade union, although the statutory recognition process contained in Schedule A1 to TULRCA may be deployed by a trade union.[87] Further, collective agreements do not need to cover certain prescribed matters by law. Unlike many Continental jurisdictions, statute specifically provides that collective agreements are presumed not to be legally binding or enforceable.[88] Where they are unequivocally stated to be legally binding, it is by no means the case that they will be treated as regulating the terms of individual contracts of employment of member employees. For example, the common law has developed rules which require the term of the collective agreement to be apt for incorporation into the individual contracts of employees.[89]

---

[85] See also Lord Wedderburn, *The Worker and the Law: Text and Materials*, 3rd edition (London, Penguin Books, 1986) 318–54.

[86] However, see the decision of the European Court of Human Rights in *Demir and Baykara v Turkey* [2009] IRLR 766; see also K. D. Ewing and J. Hendy, 'The Dramatic Implications of *Demir and Baykara*' (2010) 39 *Industrial Law Journal* 1, which suggests that the right to collective bargaining is an essential right protected by Article 11 of the ECHR.   [87] See Chapter C of the Online Resources.

[88] See section 179(1) of TULRCA.   [89] See Chapter 5, section 5.2.1.

2.3 INSTITUTIONS OF EMPLOYMENT LAW

In this section, we move our attention away from the sources of employment law towards the central institutions which are relevant to a proper understanding of the UK system of labour law. In particular, we focus on the specialist tribunals instituted to resolve labour disputes, i.e. the ET and the Employment Appeal Tribunal ('EAT'). We then turn to examine the roles of the EHRC, ACAS, the Certification Officer, and the CAC.

2.3.1 The ET and EAT

One would be forgiven for thinking that one of the most significant outcomes of the Donovan Commission was the establishment of the independent ET system.[90] However, that is incorrect. Instead, the ET was preceded by the Industrial Tribunal ('IT') which was established by the Industrial Training Act 1964. The IT had jurisdiction to hear appeals from Industrial Training Boards which dealt with decisions regarding the provision of grants to employers for the purposes of staff training. The IT's jurisdiction was extended by the Redundancy Payments Act 1965 to the resolution of disputes between employers and employees in relation to redundancy payments. Therefore, by the time the Donovan Commission produced its report in 1968, the ITs were already a, albeit small, part of the fabric for the resolution of labour disputes. However, what the Donovan Commission did do was extend that jurisdiction to all disputes between an employer and employee in relation to the contract of employment or statutory employment claims.[91] This was partly motivated by a desire to (a) keep the courts out of struggles between the forces of labour and capital (which are often political in nature),[92] and (b) institute a specialist body staffed by persons with the requisite expertise to resolve labour disputes in an efficient and less formal manner than the courts:

■ *Report of the Royal Commission on Trade Unions and Employers' Associations 1965–1968* (London, HMSO, Cmnd 3623) 157, para 578

> . . . it is one of the principal purposes to provide for the parties an easily accessible, speedy, informal and inexpensive procedure for the settlement of their disputes . . . This makes it desirable to concentrate in one tribunal all cases arising from the contract of employment and from statutory rights arising from the employment relationship.

The present jurisdiction of the ETs by and large covers the resolution of claims relating to statutory employment rights. As such, common law claims continue to be heard by the courts. However, there is one exception to this split between ETs adjudicating statutory employment disputes and the courts resolving common law claims: any common law contract claim in respect of arrears of wages or damages for wrongful dismissal up to

---

[90] A little-known fact is that it took two years of deliberations for the idea of a statutory employment right to a fair dismissal (now found in Part X of the ERA) to be proposed to the Donovan Commission, on which, see D. Renton, *Struck out* (London, Pluto Press, 2012) 29–31. In light of the fact that the unfair dismissal jurisdiction is one of the enduring legacies of the Donovan Commission, this is somewhat ironic.

[91] See *Report of the Royal Commission on Trade Unions and Employers' Associations 1965–1968* (London, HMSO, Cmnd 3623) para 573.

[92] The common law courts have traditionally been thought of as unsympathetic to the claims of employees. There is an influential view that leaving disputes to the courts raises questions about the legitimacy of their role.

the value of £25,000 falls within the purview of the ETs.[93] Hence, an employee present-ing a statutory unfair dismissal claim to the ET is also entitled to sue under the common law for arrears of wages, breach of notice period, or damages for wrongful dismissal in the same proceedings, provided that the value of the latter is less than £25,000. The fact that the ETs deal with breach of contract claims is borne out by the statistics shown in Table 2.2.

ETs sit in a range of locations throughout the UK. Subsequent to the comprehensive review conducted by Underhill J in 2011–12,[94] the rules of procedure governing the ETs are now prescribed in the Employment Tribunals (Constitution and Rules of Procedure) Regulations 2013 ('ETCRoPR').[95] Alongside the Employment Tribunals and the Employ-ment Appeal Tribunal Fees Order 2013,[96] the ETCRoPR[97] include various mechanisms which enable ETs to deter, prevent, discourage, or screen out weak, vexatious, scandal-ous, or frivolous claims:

(1) The ET has power to strike out a claim at a preliminary hearing on the basis of a number of grounds, including that it is scandalous, vexatious, or has no reasonable prospect of success.[98]

(2) At a preliminary hearing, the ET may also order a claimant to pay a deposit of up to £1,000 as a condition of continuing to advance a claim, where it is of the view that any specific allegation or argument in the claim has little reasonable prospect of success.[99]

(3) Costs orders, preparation time, and wasted costs orders are also possible pursuant to the provisions of the ETCRoPR.[100] A costs order enjoins the unsuccessful party to pay the legal costs of the other side or to reimburse the other side in respect of his/her own in-house preparation time if he/she is not legally represented. This is subject to a £20,000 maximum.[101] A wasted costs order is an order compelling a paid representa-tive to pay costs where his/her conduct has resulted in wasted time.

(4) Between July 2013 and July 2017, claimants were obliged to pay fees to lodge a claim with the ET or EAT. Fees were payable by the claimant when the claim was made and to enable his/her case to go to a hearing. As noted by Mangan, the 'ethos behind the introduction of fees for launching claims [wa]s: those who use government services should pay for them'.[102] The fees were controversial because statistical evidence dem-onstrated that they had been fixed too high and the number of claims reaching ETs had fallen off a cliff. The fees regime was challenged on a variety of legal grounds,[103] but the main argument that was ultimately successful before the Supreme Court was that it breached the common law right[104] to access the courts and operated as a bar-rier to justice:

---

[93] Employment Tribunals Extension of Jurisdiction (England and Wales) Order 1994 (SI 1994/1623) and Employment Tribunals Extension of Jurisdiction (Scotland) Order 1994 (SI 1994/1624).

[94] See BIS Consultation Paper, *Employment Tribunal Rules: Review by Mr Justice Underhill* (September 2012), available at https://www.gov.uk/government/consultations/employment-tribunal-rules-review-by-mr-justice-underhill (last visited 1 December 2017).

[95] SI 2013/1237.   [96] SI 2013/1893.   [97] SI 2013/1237.

[98] See paras 37 and 53 of Schedule 1 to ETCRoPR. On strike-out generally, see *Tayside Public Transport Co. Ltd v Reilly* [2012] IRLR 755.   [99] See paras 39 and 53 of Schedule 1 to ETCRoPR.

[100] See paras 74–84 of Schedule 1 to ETCRoPR.   [101] See para 78 of Schedule 1 to ETCRoPR.

[102] D. Mangan, 'Employment Tribunal Reforms to Boost the Economy' (2013) 42 *Industrial Law Journal* 409, 414.

[103] Assaults on the legality of the fees regime ranged from it (i) breaching the principle of effectiveness in EU law, (ii) breaching the principle of equivalence in EU law, (iii) breaching the public sector equality duty enshrined in section 149 of the EA, and (iv) amounting to indirectly discriminatory treatment based on sex/gender.

[104] See the discussion in A. Adams and J. Prassl, 'Vexatious Claims: Challenging the Case for Employ-ment Tribunal Fees' (2017) 80 *Modern Law Review* 412.

Table 2.2 *Quarterly total number of employment tribunal receipts by jurisdiction, January 2013 to September 2017*

Financial year		Total Claims Accepted	Total Jurisdictional Complaints	Average Jurisdictional Compliant per claim	Age discrimination	Breach of Contract	Disability discrimination	Equal Pay	National Minimum Wage	Part-time Workers regulation	Race Discrimination
2013	Jan to March	63,715	121,219	1.9	810	7,804	1,811	7,928	122	204	1,240
	April to June	44,334	76,476	1.7	621	6,297	1,801	8,091	108	447	1,089
	July to Sept	39,660	69,209	1.7	524	5,465	1,619	6,877	78	469	973
	Oct to Dec	10,842	24,431	2.3	248	2,486	807	998	36	151	500
2014	Jan to March	10,967	23,852	2.2	601	2,514	969	1,236	37	96	502
	April to June	8,533	18,353	2.2	393	1,945	673	1,997	46	132	430
	July to Sept	13,609	27,926	2.1	256	2,319	828	2,506	38	86	457
	Oct to Dec	18,831	42,725	2.3	220	2,037	824	1,758	42	45	471
2015	Jan to March	20,335	40,962	2.0	218	1,949	781	3,360	35	41	500
	April to June	12,744	27,439	2.2	428	2,161	878	2,410	89	82	643
	July to Sept	23,069	55,526	2.4	11,574	2,183	888	12,239	52	46	485
	Oct to Dec	17,920	30,754	1.7	434	2,385	838	1,744	34	36	460
2016	Jan to March	29,298	64,360	2.2	200	2,550	866	670	64	51	414
	April to June	15,844	39,833	2.5	5,739	1,980	902	5,335	23	35	743
	July to Sept	31,545	43,913	1.4	1,299	2,009	946	2,500	50	24	537
	Oct to Dec	9,935	19,780	2.0	260	2,000	992	1,168	63	32	488
2017	Jan to March	31,152	40,420	1.3	330	1,945	954	1,464	88	283	472
	April to June	13,759	36,465	2.7	5,642	2,121	978	6,333	61	111	702

Source: Reproduced from Table C2 of the Tribunals and gender recognition certificate statistics quarterly—July to September 2017 at https://www.gov.uk/government/statistics/tribunals-and-gender-recognition-certificate-statistics-quarterly-july-to-september-2017.

Note
Data may not match the main tribunals' tables due to it being extracted at different times.

■ *R (on the application of UNISON) v Lord Chancellor* [2017] 3 WLR 409, 432A–440G

Lord Reed:

It may be helpful to begin by explaining briefly the importance of the rule of law, and the role of access to the courts in maintaining the rule of law. It may also be helpful to explain why the idea that bringing a claim before a court or a tribunal is a purely private activity, and the related idea that such claims provide no broader social benefit, are demonstrably untenable . . . Courts exist in order to ensure that the laws made by Parliament, and the common law created by the courts themselves, are applied and enforced . . . In order for the courts to perform that role, people must in principle have unimpeded access to them. Without such access, laws are liable to become a dead letter, the work done by Parliament may be rendered nugatory, and the democratic election of Members of Parliament may become a meaningless charade . . . Access to the courts is not, therefore, of value only to the particular individuals involved. That is most obviously true of cases which establish principles of general importance. When, for example, Mrs Donoghue won her appeal to the House of Lords (*Donoghue v Stevenson* [1932] AC 562), the decision established that producers of consumer goods are under a duty to take care for the health and safety of consumers of those goods . . . To say that it was of no value to anyone other than Mrs Donoghue and the lawyers and judges involved in the case would be absurd . . . Every day in the courts and tribunals of this country, the names of people who brought cases in the past live on as shorthand for the legal rules and principles which their case established . . . When Parliament passes laws creating employment rights, for example, it does so not merely in order to confer benefits on individual employees, but because it has decided that it is in the public interests that those rights should be given effect. It does not envisage that every case of a breach of those rights will result in a claim before the ET. But the possibility of claims being brought by employees whose rights are infringed must exist, if employment relationships are to be based on respect for those rights. Equally, although it is often desirable that claims arising out of alleged breaches of employment rights should be resolved by negotiation or mediation, those procedures can only work fairly and properly if they are backed up by the knowledge on both sides that a fair and just system of adjudication will be available if they fail . . . It is thus the claims which are brought before an ET which enable legislation to have the deterrent effect and other effects which Parliament intended, provide authoritative guidance as to its meaning and application, and underpin alternative methods of dispute resolution . . . It is therefore necessary to consider, first, whether the Fees Order effectively prevents some persons from having access to justice . . . In order for the fees to be lawful, they have to be set at a level that everyone can afford, taking into account the availability of full or partial remission. The evidence now before the court, considered realistically and as a whole, leads to the conclusion that that requirement is not met. In the first place . . . 'it is clear that there has been a sharp, substantial and sustained fall in the volume of case receipts as a result of the introduction of fees' . . . The fall in the number of claims has in any event been so sharp, so substantial, and so sustained as to warrant the conclusion that a significant number of people who would otherwise have brought claims have found the fees to be unaffordable . . . Secondly . . . around 10% of the claimants, whose claims were notified to Acas but did not result either in a settlement or in a claim before an ET, said that they did not bring proceedings because they could not afford the fees . . . The question whether fees effectively prevent access to justice must be decided according to the likely impact of the fees on behaviour in the real world. Fees must therefore be affordable not in a theoretical sense, but in the sense that they can *reasonably* be afforded. Where households on low to middle incomes can only afford fees by sacrificing the ordinary and reasonable expenditure required to maintain what would generally be regarded as an acceptable standard of living, the fees cannot be regarded as affordable. Thirdly, the conclusion is strengthened by consideration of the hypothetical examples which provide some indication of the impact of the fees on claimants in low to middle income households . . . the fundamental problem is the assumption that the right of access to courts and tribunals can lawfully be made subject to impositions which low to middle income households can only meet by sacrificing ordinary and reasonable expenditure for substantial periods of time . . . For all these reasons, the [fees regime] effectively prevents access to justice, and is therefore unlawful . . .

Unlike the formality of a court, and consistent with the message of access to justice that can be drawn from the extract just quoted, the parties do not require to be represented in the ET by qualified solicitors, barristers, or advocates. In practice, however, they often are.[105] However, legal aid is not available.[106] It is also rare for an ET to award costs or expenses, except in relation to frivolous claims. Section 4 of the Employment Tribunals Act 1996 ('ETA') governs the composition of ETs. The general position is that the ET comprises three persons. The first is referred to as the employment judge and is usually a qualified solicitor, barrister, or advocate. The other two 'wing' members are lay participants with expertise in industrial matters, duly appointed from both sides of industry, i.e. employers' organizations and trade unions/other organizations representing employees.[107] The inclusion of the latter is consistent with the original conception of the ETs as 'industrial juries', i.e. the ET, staffed with two laypersons experienced in industrial relations and a legally qualified employment judge, can draw on its own expertise of workplace relations to decide whether the claimant's claim ought to succeed.[108] However, there are exceptions to the inclusion of lay participants. For example, in claims presented to the ET relating to unfair dismissal, unauthorized deductions from wages, unpaid holiday pay, failures to inform and consult in respect of transfers of undertakings under the Transfer of Undertakings (Protection of Employment) Regulations 2006,[109] and a variety of other claims, the employment judge may sit alone.[110]

A party may appeal on a point of law from an ET to the EAT.[111] There are a variety of bases on which an appellant will succeed in an appeal on a point of law. First, an appeal will be allowed if the appellant is able to show that the ET misdirected itself in law, misunderstood the law, or failed to apply the law correctly.[112] Alternatively, an appeal will succeed if the appellant convinces the EAT that a finding of fact made by the ET was 'perverse' in the sense that it could not be supported by any evidence at all, i.e. there is an overwhelming case that it was a finding 'which no reasonable tribunal, on a proper appreciation of the evidence and the law, would have reached'.[113] As such, if the EAT merely has grave doubts about the findings of the ET, this is insufficient to satisfy the requisite standard of 'perversity'. Another basis for a successful appeal is inadequate reasoning on the part of the ET.[114] Finally, a substantiated allegation of bias or procedural impropriety on the part of the ET is another ground for success.[115]

The EAT sits in London and in Edinburgh. Its rules of procedure are laid down in the Employment Appeal Tribunal Rules 1993.[116] The EAT is composed of judges of the High Court, one judge from the Court of Session in Scotland, and, once again, lay members with expertise in industrial matters from both sides of industry.[117] The general rule is that

---

[105] For a detailed analysis of the formal and informal representation of claimants and employers, see P. Urwin, F. Buscha, and P. L. Latreille, 'Representation in UK Employment Tribunals: Analysis of the 2003 and 2008 Survey of Employment Tribunal Applications' (2014) 52 *British Journal of Industrial Relations* 158.

[106] Scotland is an exception.   [107] Section 4(1) of the ETA.

[108] *Priddle v Dibble* [1978] ICR 149, 152 per Bristow J; *British Telecommunications plc v Sheridan* [1990] ILR 27, 30 per Lord Donaldson MR.   [109] SI 2006/246.

[110] See section 4(2) and (3) of the ETA. The list of claims in which an employment judge may sit alone has been extended since 1993, on which, see S. Corby and P. L. Latreille, 'Tripartite Adjudication: An Endangered Species' (2012) 43 *Industrial Relations Journal* 94; B. Hepple, 'Back to the Future: Employment Law under the Coalition Government' (2013) 42 *Industrial Law Journal* 203, 212–13.

[111] Section 21 of the ETA. It is not always straightforward to distinguish between a point of law and a point of fact masquerading as a point of law.

[112] *Watling v William Bird & Son Contractors* [1976] 11 ITR 70.

[113] *Yeboah v Crofton* [2002] IRLR 634, 643 per Mummery LJ.

[114] *Meek v City of Birmingham DC* [1987] IRLR 250.

[115] *Lodwick v Southwark London Borough Council* [2004] IRLR 544. There is a debate as to whether excessive delay exists as a stand-alone basis for an appeal: see the decision of the Court of Appeal in *Bangs v Connex South Eastern Ltd* [2005] 2 All ER 316.

[116] SI 1993/2854.   [117] Section 22 of the ETA.

proceedings before the EAT are to be heard by a judge sitting alone.[118] Nevertheless, a judge of the EAT has the power to direct that proceedings should be heard with members.[119] Unlike the ET, legal aid is available. Awards of costs and expenses are unusual, except in relation to frivolous claims. The powers of the EAT match those of the High Court and the ETs in relation to the examination of witnesses.

A number of criticisms can be made of the ET system. First, there is the charge that it fails to live up to the expectations of the Donovan Commission. For example, a succession of reforms over the years have chipped away at the informality of the system to the point that ETs and the EAT now mimic very closely the practices of the courts. This legalistic approach has been persuasively attributed to 'isomorphism',[120] i.e. the tendency of tribunals to evolve and become assimilated with the court system. Studies have also revealed that the ET system has a tendency to generate barriers to justice for vulnerable workers who are not trade union members and cannot afford legal advice.[121] Meanwhile, the employer's perspective is captured in the Beecroft Report, which characterized the ET system as 'expensive, time consuming and personally stressful [to employers]',[122] i.e. the exact opposite of the 'speedy [and] inexpensive procedure' for the settlement of disputes which the Donovan Commission had intended. Beecroft also raised concerns about the number of misconceived claims raised, and appeals pursued, by employees, as well as the inconsistency of judicial decisions and the complexity and detailed technicality of the procedural rules.[123] Nevertheless, these criticisms have been subjected to a pointed rebuttal in the Court of Appeal:

■ Gayle v Sandwell & West Birmingham Hospitals NHS Trust [2011] EWCA Civ 924 at paras 9–22

Lord Justice Mummery:

. . . [various] comments have been made in recent public discussions and consultations about the workings of the ET system generally. Some of the criticisms are justified, others need correction and all of them must be seen in their proper perspective. The ETs are under enormous pressure in these difficult economic times. Their caseload has increased by over 50% in one year, which comes as no surprise at a time of high unemployment. The cases have become more complex with the legislative expansion of employment protection since the tribunal system was first established. They take longer to process. It is not proper for me to comment on proposed reforms of substantive employment law. That is a controversial policy area for public debate and Parliamentary action. Procedural efficiency and justice are, however, of direct concern to the judiciary: the courts and the tribunals are equipped with wide discretionary powers to ensure that cases are dealt with justly. One area of debate is about cases of little or no merit, but considerable nuisance value. All are agreed that they should be cleared out of the system as soon as possible. They should not be allowed to take up a disproportionate amount of time in the ET or cause the other party to incur irrecoverable legal costs and loss of valuable working time. As for procedural justice and efficiency generally I would make the following points with particular reference to the EAT's comments on what happened in this case. First, Ms Gayle's litigation has now reached the third level of decision. That is not typical: most employment disputes do not even go one round,

---

[118] Section 28(2) of the ETA.   [119] Section 28(3), (4), (6), and (7) of the ETA.

[120] See S. Corby and P. L. Latreille, 'Employment Tribunals and the Civil Courts: Isomorphism Exemplified' (2012) 42 *Industrial Law Journal* 387.

[121] N. Busby and M. McDermont, 'Workers, Marginalised Voices and the Employment Tribunal System: Some Preliminary Findings' (2012) 41 *Industrial Law Journal* 166.

[122] See http://www.telegraph.co.uk/news/politics/9280473/Controversial-Beecroft-Report-on-employment-law-published-ahead-of-schedule-after-leak.html at page 13 (last visited 4 December 2017).

[123] See *ibid.*, page 13.

because they are settled through the good sense of the parties or thanks to the good offices of ACAS. When they are contested the vast majority of cases only go one round. Secondly, this case is based on events of nearly five years ago. Most cases are in fact finally decided at the level of the ET within months, not years, of the relevant events. Thirdly, the hearing of this case in the ET lasted nearly three weeks at the end of 2008 and beginning of 2009[, but] most cases in the ET take only a day or two, not weeks as here. Fourthly, the EAT heard the appeal a year later. Most ET decisions are not appealed. Appeals, which are limited to points of law, are as of right, though the preliminary procedure devised in the EAT and streamlined over the years usually sifts out the hopeless points at an early stage and without a contested hearing. Fifthly, an appeal to this court on a point of law may only be brought with permission . . . Rightly or wrongly many other appeals are treated as having greater priority and there are not enough judges in this court to hear and decide them all expeditiously. The important point is that most employment cases never reach a full court hearing. The hopeless ones are sifted out by a single Lord Justice at the permission stage . . . Sixthly, in every case the parties, who both think that they have a good case, are entitled to expect that their case will be dealt with justly. That takes time, care and patience, as well as considerable practical experience and specialist knowledge. It takes much longer than most people begin to appreciate to perform properly the most vital function in the whole civil justice and tribunal system. Establishing the facts soundly in every case at first instance is, in practice, of far greater practical importance than the limited corrective powers exercisable by the appellate courts in the relatively small proportion of cases that reach them. In the ET the issues have to be identified. In a case like this a mass of conflicting evidence is produced. It has to be assimilated, organised, analysed and assessed by the ET. There were nearly a dozen witnesses in this case. The ET then had to listen to competing legal arguments and detailed submissions from the parties. It had to consider and write up the decision with its detailed findings and reasoned conclusions. Seventhly, as for those who complain about the time taken and the legal costs and other expenses and losses incurred, I think that they would want the hearings to be conducted in the interests of justice to both sides. I have seen very few constructive suggestions for practical improvements. If workers are given rights, there must be properly qualified, impartial and independent tribunals to adjudicate on them in accordance with a fair procedure. If workers are not given the necessary means for the just adjudication of their claims, procedures of a more rough and ready non-judicial kind may be used. The alternative procedures would probably not be impartial, independent or just, and are unlikely to do much for public order, social harmony or national prosperity. Eighthly, the ETs continue to make good progress in managing cases efficiently and justly to ensure that the oral hearing concentrates on what really matters without wasting time and money on what does not matter or is only marginally relevant. If the ETs are firm and fair in their management of cases pre-hearing and in the conduct of the hearing the EAT and this court should, wherever legally possible, back up their case management decisions and rulings. Lastly, the parties and their advisers themselves have duties to discharge, personal and professional responsibilities in the preparation and presentation of the cases in the tribunals. They must keep a proper sense of proportion in the issues raised for decision, in the selection of legal points worth taking and of relevance in the quantity and quality of the evidence that they need to call. Contrary to the way that some observers see it and the way that some participants do it, justice in the tribunals (and in the courts) is not a war, or a battle, or a game. It is not a talent contest for spotting the winner and awarding a prize: it is (or certainly should be) a reasonable, sensible and civilised way of sorting out disputes that the parties have unfortunately been unable to sort out themselves. In my view, some (though by no means the majority) of the shortcomings identified by critics are not in the system itself, or in the tribunals, or in their practice and procedure, but in the attitudes and approaches of some litigants to the process of reasonable resolution of conflict.[124]

---

[124] Sourced from BAILII at http://www.bailii.org/cgi-bin/markup.cgi?doc=/ew/cases/EWCA/Civ/2011/924.html&query=gayle+and+v+and+sandwell&method=boolean (last visited 4 December 2017).

On the points raised by Lord Justice Mummery in the extract, it is a matter of note that an ET now has an additional power to order an employer to pay a financial penalty of a sum between £100 and £5,000 where it loses a claim and there are aggravating features.[125] There are also powers[126] which deal with the enforcement of tribunal awards[127] and empower enforcement officers to issue penalty notices if a tribunal award remains unpaid after an officer has issued a 28-day warning notice.

2.3.2 The courts

Despite the importance of the ET and EAT in the resolution of employment disputes, the ordinary courts continue to exercise a fundamental role in contemporary labour law. First, as noted earlier, the courts have jurisdiction to hear common law tortious/delictual claims and contract claims, e.g. in relation to personal injury or an alleged breach of a term of an employee's contract of employment. Common law adjudication is particularly important in respect of claims relating to the formation, identification/classification, interpretation, content, performance, variation, suspension, and termination of a contract of employment.[128] Further, certain classes of public servants who hold an office, rather than an employment contract, will be obliged to advance a judicial review claim in public law in the courts if they wish to challenge some aspect of their working life.[129] Secondly, the courts will have jurisdiction to resolve and hear questions of employment law where an appeal is made from the EAT, i.e. where section 37 of the ETA applies:

> **Section 37 Appeals from appeal tribunal**
>
> (1) ... an appeal on any question of law lies from any decision or order of the [EAT] to the [Court of Appeal in the case of proceedings in England and Wales, and the Court of Session in the case of proceedings in Scotland ('relevant appeal courts')] with the leave of the [EAT] or of the relevant appeal court.

An appeal on a point of law may also be made from the Court of Appeal or the Inner House of the Court of Session to the UK Supreme Court. Decisions of the Court of Appeal bind the EAT and the ETs, whilst the EAT is not bound by its own decisions as they are of persuasive value only. However, the previous decisions of the EAT are of precedential value for the ETs.[130]

2.3.3 The EHRC

The EHRC was established by section 1 of the Equality Act 2006 and replaced the Disability Rights Commission, the Equal Opportunities Commission, and the Commission for Racial Equality, which were disbanded in 2007. It is charged with the promotion of the

---

[125] Section 12A of the ETA.   [126] This inserts sections 37A–37Q into the ETA.

[127] D. Mangan, 'Assessing Employment Tribunal Awards' (2014) 43 *Industrial Law Journal* 212, 213–14.

[128] Whilst there has been an element of statutory interference in respect of the termination of the employment contract via the medium of the statutory unfair dismissal regime and such claims must be heard by ETs, common law adjudication still commands an element of importance.

[129] For example, see the high-profile judicial review case of *R (on the application of Shoesmith) v OFSTED* [2011] ICR 1195 decided by the Court of Appeal in relation to the dismissal of the Director of Children's Services (Ms Sharon Shoesmith) subsequent to the death of 'Baby P'. For discussion of public office-holders, see L. Rodgers, 'Public Employment and Access to Justice in Employment Law' (2014) 43 *Industrial Law Journal* 373; L. Rodgers, 'The Interpretation of Article 6 ECHR and Access to Justice for Public Employees' (2015) 40 *European Law Review* 563.

[130] This rule also applies to bind ETs sitting in England and Wales where the decision is of a Scottish division of the EAT: *Davidson v City Electrical Factors Ltd* [1998] IRLR 435 per Morison J (P).

proscription of discrimination in the workplace based on each of the protected characteristics laid down in section 4 of the Equality Act 2010 ('EA'), namely sex, race, age, sexual orientation, disability, religion or belief, gender reassignment, marriage and civil partnership, and pregnancy and maternity.[131] The following are its express statutory objectives:

Section 3 General duty

The [EHRC] shall exercise its functions under this Part with a view to encouraging and supporting the development of a society in which—

(a) people's ability to achieve their potential is not limited by prejudice or discrimination,

(b) there is respect for and protection of each individual's human rights,

(c) there is respect for the dignity and worth of each individual,

(d) each individual has an equal opportunity to participate in society, and

(e) there is mutual respect between groups based on understanding and valuing of diversity and on shared respect for equality and human rights.

The Equality Act 2006 confers two principal powers on the EHRC:[132] first, there is the power to conduct an inquiry;[133] and secondly, the power to undertake formal investigations.[134] The EHRC has a restricted power to conduct an inquiry: it can only do so in relation to its statutory duties in sections 8 and 9 of the 2006 Act to promote equality and diversity and the importance of human rights. The result of an inquiry is a report and recommendations, which are not legally binding. As for its power of investigation, section 20(2) provides that the EHRC may only do so where it suspects that the person concerned may have committed an unlawful act:

■ **B. Hepple, 'Agency Enforcement of Workplace Equality' in L. Dickens (ed.),** *Making Employment Rights Effective* **(Oxford, Hart Publishing, 2012) 56**

[Section 20(2) of the Equality Act 2006] sets a 'threshold test' of 'reasonable belief'. This seems to codify the case law . . . but it has been argued that only if the [EHRC]'s decision to investigate is irrational or strongly disproportionate should a court intervene . . . a single complaint of unlawful conduct is unlikely to suffice as the basis for initiating an investigation, but a series of complaints over time might be sufficient. The suspicion may (but need not) be based on matters arising in the course of an inquiry.

If the EHRC exercises its power of investigation, any investigation is limited to whether the relevant person has committed an unlawful act, has complied with a requirement imposed by any unlawful act notice under section 21 of the Equality Act 2006, or has complied with any undertaking given under section 23 of the 2006 Act. The outcome of an investigation may be the issuance of an unlawful act notice[135] or an action plan.[136]

---

[131] See Chapter 11.

[132] See C. O'Cinneide, 'The Commission for Equality and Human Rights: A New Institution for New and Uncertain Times' (2007) 36 *Industrial Law Journal* 141; B. Hepple, *Equality: The New Legal Framework*, 2nd edition (Oxford, Hart Publishing, 2014) 177–91; B. Hepple, 'Agency Enforcement of Workplace Equality' in L. Dickens (ed.), *Making Employment Rights Effective* (Oxford, Hart Publishing, 2012) 55–62; and B. Hepple, 'Enforcing Equality Law: Two Steps Forward and Two Steps Backwards for Reflexive Regulation' (2011) 40 *Industrial Law Journal* 315.

[133] Section 16 of the Equality Act 2006.　　[134] Section 20 of the Equality Act 2006.

[135] Section 21 of the Equality Act 2006.　　[136] Section 22 of the Equality Act 2006.

2.3.4 **ACAS**

ACAS is a body independent of Government established on a statutory footing by section 247 of TULRCA. It is subject to the direction of a Council, composed of a chairman and between nine and 15 ordinary members appointed by the Secretary of State.[137] Its primary function is dictated by statute, namely the promotion of the improvement of industrial relations.[138] It discharges this obligation by providing conciliation and arbitration services in respect of *individual* and *collective* workplace disputes. Much of its work is directed at keeping employment disputes out of the ET if at all possible by encouraging settlements via the 'cost-effective filter[s]'[139] of conciliation or arbitration.

Turning first to individual workplace disputes, where these concern claims of unfair dismissal, discrimination, equal pay, and the denial of various statutory employment protection rights under the ERA, TULRCA, the WTR, and other legislation, sections 18 and 18C of the ETA subjects ACAS to a statutory obligation to get involved in proceedings *once such a claim has been lodged with the ET*.[140] Where such a claim has been presented by an employee claimant to an ET and a copy of it has been sent to an ACAS conciliation officer, the conciliation officer is obliged to step in to endeavour to promote a settlement between the parties without it being determined by the ET in two circumstances:[141] first, where the conciliation officer is requested to do so by the employee claimant and the respondent employer; and second, in the absence of such a request, where the conciliation officer considers that he/she has a reasonable prospect of success in promoting such a settlement. In all cases, the conciliation officer must have regard to the desirability of encouraging the use of the employer's grievance procedures for the purposes of securing a settlement to a dispute.[142] Moreover, discussions between a conciliation officer and the parties are treated as confidential and are generally not admissible in evidence in any proceedings before an ET.[143] Where a settlement is reached, the parties will record this in a COT3 settlement agreement.

ACAS's statutory duty in sections 18 and 18C of the ETA can be distinguished from its post-claim individual conciliation services (discussed in the preceding paragraph) by the fact that the former is triggered *in advance of a prospective employee claimant lodging an employment claim with the ET*: as such, it is a *pre-claim* conciliation service.[144] The provisions of sections 18A and 18B of the ETA force a prospective employee claimant to provide prescribed information to ACAS about his/her intended claim under the auspices of an ACAS conciliation officer. Once ACAS receives the requisite information from the prospective claimant, a conciliation officer must endeavour to promote a settlement between the claimant and the respondent employer within a limited period of time.[145] However, it should be stressed that the employee claimant's obligation is limited to notification in the prescribed manner, and there is no superadded obligation to submit to mandatory conciliation if the employee does not wish to do so.[146] If the conciliation officer is of the view that a settlement is not possible or the prescribed period expires without the conclusion of a settlement, he/she must issue a certificate in the prescribed manner to the prospective employee claimant to that effect.[147] Without that certificate,

---

[137] Section 248 of TULRCA.   [138] Section 209(1) of TULRCA.

[139] L. Dickens, 'ETs and ADR' in L. Dickens (ed.), *Making Employment Rights Effective* (Oxford, Hart Publishing, 2012) 44.   [140] Sections 18(1), (1A), and 18C(1) of the ETA.

[141] Section 18C(1) of the ETA.   [142] Section 18(6) of the ETA.   [143] Section 18(7) of the ETA.

[144] Section 18A(1) of the ETA. See D. Mangan, 'Employment Tribunal Reforms to Boost the Economy' (2013) 42 *Industrial Law Journal* 409, 413–14.

[145] Section 18A(3) of the ETA. The prescribed period is one calendar month in terms of para 6 of Schedule 1 to the Employment Tribunals (Early Conciliation: Exemptions and Rules of Procedure) Regulations 2014 (SI 2014/254).

[146] B. Hepple, 'Back to the Future: Employment Law under the Coalition Government' (2013) 42 *Industrial Law Journal* 203, 218.   [147] Section 18A(4) of the ETA.

the employee claimant is prevented from instituting ET proceedings to progress his/her claim.[148] Whilst there are certain limited exemptions prescribed in regulation 3 of, and the Early Conciliation Rules of Procedure contained in the Schedule to, the Employment Tribunals (Early Conciliation: Exemptions and Rules of Procedure) Regulations 2014, the decision of the EAT in *Cranwell v Cullen*[149] reminds us that an ET will have no option but to reject a claim where an employee claimant fails to notify ACAS as required, since there is no exemption for general unfairness. As for the impact of the pre-claim conciliation procedure,[150] ACAS statistics for the period from April 2017 to June 2017 indicate that 19 per cent of cases resulted in a successful COT3 settlement, an additional 64 per cent of employee claimants decided not to take their claim further, and only the remaining 17 per cent actually progressed to an ET claim.[151]

Another part of ACAS's remit is to offer conciliation in collective disputes. Where a trade dispute exists or is apprehended and one or more of the parties to that dispute so requests or otherwise of its own accord, ACAS may offer conciliation or mediation[152] services. Alternatively, it may refer the matter on to a qualified third party, with a view to securing a settlement.[153] The definition of 'trade dispute' here is broader than that in play for the purposes of industrial action in section 244(1) of TULRCA.[154] ACAS is specifically enjoined to have regard to the desirability of encouraging the parties in dispute to use any agreed negotiation or settlement procedures. The evidence suggests that ACAS resolves a marginally higher proportion of collective disputes than individual disputes by conciliation: 92 per cent of collective disputes in comparison with 72.6 per cent of individual disputes.[155]

Notwithstanding the high success rate of ACAS in reaching settlement of collective disputes through the process of conciliation, there will be instances in which arbitration may be more appropriate.[156] Section 212 of TULRCA enables one or more of the parties to an actual or anticipated collective dispute to voluntarily refer that dispute to ACAS for arbitration. However, it is an absolute requirement that all of the parties in dispute consent to such a referral and that ACAS applies its mind to whether the dispute would likely be settled by conciliation instead.[157] ACAS must also reject a referral to arbitration if the parties have not adhered to agreed procedures for the negotiation or the settlement of disputes or there is no special reason justifying arbitration as an alternative to those procedures.[158] The arbitration process differs from that prescribed

---

[148] Section 18A(8) of the ETA. For a trenchant critique of this pre-claim conciliation procedure, see D. Renton, *Struck out* (London, Pluto Press, 2012) 139–40.

[149] (UKEATPAS/0046/14/SM, 20 March 2015). See also the effect of the minor error in the employment tribunal claim form in *Giny v SNA Transport Ltd* (UKEAT/0317/16/RN, 22 May 2017).

[150] See ACAS Paper at http://m.acas.org.uk/media/pdf/2/t/Evaluation-of-Acas-conciliation-in-Employment-Tribunal-applications-2016.pdf and http://www.acas.org.uk/media/pdf/5/9/Acas-Early-Conciliation-decision-making.pdf (last visited 29 November 2017).

[151] See Table 2 of ACAS's Early Conciliation statistics available at http://www.acas.org.uk/index.aspx?articleid=6057 (last visited 29 November 2017).

[152] On mediation, see T. Bennett, 'The Role of Mediation: A Critical Analysis of the Changing Nature of Dispute Resolution in the Workplace' (2012) 41 *Industrial Law Journal* 479.

[153] Section 201(1) and (2) of TULRCA.

[154] See Chapter D of the Online Resources. A 'trade dispute' is a dispute between employers and workers, or between workers and workers, which is connected with one of more of the following: employment terms and conditions; physical work conditions; engagement or re-engagement, or termination or suspension of employment or the duties of employment, of one or more workers; the allocation of work or duties of employment; disciplinary matters; the membership or non-membership of a trade union on the part of a worker; facilities for trade unions' officials; and various negotiation and consultation machinery.

[155] See Annual Report 2016/17, available at http://www.acas.org.uk/media/pdf/e/s/Acas-annual-report-2016–2017.pdf at pages 26 and 32 (last visited 4 December 2017).

[156] Section 212A of TULRCA also lays down a voluntary scheme for the arbitration of individual disputes relating to unfair dismissal and flexible working claims.

[157] Section 212(2) of TULRCA.   [158] Section 212(3) of TULRCA.

by the Arbitration Act 1996 or the Arbitration (Scotland) Act 2010.[159] The procedure for the arbitration is set by the parties and although the award of the arbitrator is not legally binding, it is uncommon for the parties not to adhere to its terms. Most collective disputes are referred to a single arbitrator for resolution, without legal representation on the part of the parties, and the arbitrator's award may be published if ACAS and the parties agree.[160]

Apart from its statutory duties to furnish machinery for the resolution of individual and collective workplace disputes by conciliation, mediation, or arbitration, ACAS also conducts a range of other functions. For example, it provides information and advisory services in relation to industrial relations pursuant to section 213 of TULRCA. Moreover, it has the statutory power to conduct inquiries into any question relating to industrial relations generally or in relation to any particular industry or undertaking or undertakings.[161] As noted earlier,[162] the issuance of codes of practice is another power vested in ACAS. Codes of practice lay down practical guidance for the purpose of promoting the improvement of industrial relations or for purposes connected with trade union learning representatives,[163] e.g. the Code of Practice on Time Off for Trade Union Duties and Activities.[164] Finally, ACAS is also involved in the disclosure of information and consultation pursuant to the Information and Consultation of Employees Regulations 2004 ('I&C Regs')[165] and the Transnational Information and Consultation of Employees Regulations 1999 ('TICE').[166]

2.3.5 The Certification Officer

The Certification Officer ('CO') is a central figure in the field of collective labour law and the regulation of trade unions in TULRCA.[167] In terms of section 254 of TULRCA, the CO is an independent officer and must be appointed by the Secretary of State after consultation with ACAS. The CO's principal function is to maintain a list of trade unions and employers' associations in terms of sections 2 and 123 of TULRCA, and to evaluate whether a trade union ought to be considered 'independent' under section 6 of TULRCA. The CO's role also ranges from addressing whether a trade union's name ought to be removed from the official list[168] to collating and processing annual returns received from trade unions.[169] The CO also has judicial responsibilities, e.g. a statutory power to investigate the financial affairs of trade unions by virtue of section 37A of TULRCA, and jurisdiction to hear complaints in respect of trade union elections[170] and complaints from members of a trade union that the latter has applied its funds in breach of the statutory rules on the use of political funds.[171] Moreover, in terms of sections 98 and 103 of TULRCA, the CO has the responsibility for ensuring that the statutory procedures for amalgamations, transfers of engagements, and trade union changes of name are complied with, and for dealing with complaints by members about the conduct of merger ballots.

---

[159] Section 212(5) of TULRCA.   [160] Section 212(4)(b) of TULRCA.

[161] Section 214(1) of TULRCA. ACAS has the power to publish the findings of such an inquiry: section 214(2) of TULRCA.

[162] See section 2.2.3.   [163] Section 199(1) of TULRCA.

[164] See section 199(2) of TULRCA and http://www.acas.org.uk/media/pdf/n/k/Acas_Code_of_Practice_Part-3-accessible-version-July-2011.pdf (last visited 4 December 2017).

[165] SI 2004/3426. See Chapter A of the Online Resources, section 1.3.

[166] SI 1999/3323. See Chapter A of the Online Resources, section 1.2.

[167] See Chapter B of the Online Resources. See also G. Lockwood, 'The Administration of Union Business: The Role of the Certification Officer' (2006) 37 *Industrial Relations Journal* 209; D. Cockburn, 'The Certification Officer' in L. Dickens and A. Neal (eds), *The Changing Institutional Face of British Employment Relations* (The Hague, Kluwer, 2006) 91 and S. Cavalier and R. Arthur, 'A Discussion of the Certification Officer Reforms' (2016) 45 *Industrial Law Journal* 363.

[168] Sections 4 and 125 of TULRCA.   [169] Section 32 of TULRCA.

[170] Section 54 of TULRCA.   [171] Section 72A of TULRCA.

An annual report is produced by the CO relating its activities throughout the year, which contains useful statistics concerning the number, independence, and financial affairs of trade unions.[172] Section 256 of TULRCA empowers the CO to regulate procedures to be followed on any application or complaint made to him/her or where the CO's approval is sought with respect to any matter.

2.3.6 The CAC

Section 259 establishes the Central Arbitration Committee ('CAC').[173] It is a body wholly independent of ACAS and Government that is engaged in the resolution of industrial relations disputes through the process of arbitration. The CAC sits in London and consists of a chairperson, deputy chairpersons (there are currently nine deputies), and members appointed by the Secretary of State who are experienced in industrial relations, both from the employers' and workers' side of industry.[174] A member is appointed for an initial term of five years, which may be renewed.[175] The principal kinds of matters with which the CAC is involved include applications for the statutory recognition and derecognition of trade unions under Schedule A1 to TULRCA,[176] dealing with disputes in relation to the disclosure of information for the purposes of collective bargaining,[177] applications and complaints under the I&C Regs,[178] the operation of European Works Councils under TICE,[179] and various disputes relating to the provision of information, consultation, and worker participation in the case of European companies,[180] cooperative societies,[181] and cross-border mergers.[182] There is also statutory machinery in section 212 of TULRCA enabling ACAS to remit a trade dispute to the CAC for settlement by arbitration where this is requested by one or more of the parties to the dispute and all the parties consent to the same.

The general proceedings of the CAC are regulated by section 263 of TULRCA. Here, it is stipulated that the CAC shall be composed of the chairperson or a deputy chairperson and such other members as the chairperson or deputy may direct. The CAC also has the power to call in the aid of an assessor if it considers it expedient to do so.[183] Proceedings of the CAC may be conducted in public or in private, and where it is not possible to reach a unanimous decision, the chairperson or deputy has a casting vote with the same full powers of an umpire or oversman.[184] However, in the case of applications for statutory recognition or derecognition of a trade union, a distinctive set of proceedings are

---

[172] Section 258 of TULRCA. See https://www.gov.uk/government/publications/annual-report-of-the-certification-officer-2016–2017 (last visited 4 December 2017).

[173] See https://www.gov.uk/government/organisations/central-arbitration-committee/about/membership (last visited 4 December 2017); S. Gouldstone and G. Morris, 'The Central Arbitration Committee' in L. Dickens and A. Neal (eds), *The Changing Institutional Face of British Employment Relations* (The Hague, Kluwer, 2006) 79.

[174] Section 260 of TULRCA.   [175] Section 261(2) of TULRCA.

[176] There were 66 applications for trade union recognition and no applications for derecognition between 1 April 2016 and 31 March 2017: see pages 2 and 10 of the CAC Annual Report 2016–17, available at https://www.gov.uk/government/uploads/system/uploads/attachment_data/file/629689/CAC_Annual_Report_2016–17.pdf (last visited 4 December 2017).   [177] See section 183 of TULRCA.

[178] Page 14 of the CAC Annual Report 2016–17 reveals that the CAC received four applications under the I&C Regs in that period: see https://www.gov.uk/government/uploads/system/uploads/attachment_data/file/629689/CAC_Annual_Report_2016–17.pdf (last visited 4 December 2017).

[179] Page 14 of the CAC Annual Report 2016–17 reveals that the CAC received three complaints under TICE in that period: see https://www.gov.uk/government/uploads/system/uploads/attachment_data/file/629689/CAC_Annual_Report_2016–17.pdf (last visited 4 December 2017).

[180] See the European Public Limited-Liability Company (Employee Involvement) (Great Britain) Regulations 2009 (SI 2009/2401).

[181] See the European Cooperative Society Regulations 2006 (SI 2006/2078).

[182] See the Companies (Cross-Border Mergers) Regulations 2007 (SI 2007/2974).

[183] Section 263(2) of TULRCA.   [184] Section 263(3) and (4) of TULRCA.

prescribed by statute. Paragraph 171 of Schedule A1 to TULRCA sets the scene for the CAC's proceedings in such trade union recognition and derecognition applications to the extent that it directs that it 'must have regard to the object of encouraging and promoting fair and efficient practices and arrangements in the workplace'. Further, section 264 provides that the chairperson must establish a panel consisting of three persons, namely the chairperson him/herself or a deputy chairperson, a member of the CAC whose experience is as a representative of employers, and another member of the CAC whose experience is as a representative of workers. Like the general procedure, the panel may sit in public or in private, and in the event that it is not possible for it to reach a unanimous decision, the majority opinion will prevail.[185] If there is no majority view, the chairperson will have the power to decide.[186]

2.4 HUMAN RIGHTS LAW AND INTERNATIONAL LABOUR STANDARDS

In this section, we consider those instruments and international legal standards to which the UK is subject which have a bearing on the development of employment law. In particular, the socio-economic rights found in the ECHR are addressed, as are the labour standards promulgated by the International Labour Organization ('ILO').

2.4.1 Labour rights as human rights

Since the coming into force of the HRA 1998, the ECHR has formed part of UK law. The ECHR consists of civil and political rights, as well as socio-economic rights. The most relevant ECHR rights in the context of labour law are Articles 6, 8, and 11. These articles confer a right to a fair trial, a right to privacy and a family life, and freedom of assembly and association. As for the basic architecture of the HRA, section 1 incorporates the ECHR into domestic law. Section 2 of the HRA goes on to specifically direct that a court or tribunal must take into account the jurisprudence and judgments of the European Court of Human Rights ('ECtHR') so far as is possible when it is required to determine the application of the ECHR rights in a domestic dispute.[187] In section 3 of the HRA it is provided that primary and subordinate legislation of the UK Parliament must be read and given effect in a way which is compatible with the ECHR rights. Where it is not possible for a court to read down primary legislation in accordance with the ECHR rights, section 4 of the HRA enjoins it to make a 'declaration of incompatibility'. However, a declaration of incompatibility does not affect the legal validity of that primary legislation, i.e. it is still in full force and effect, albeit inconsistent with the ECHR.

One of the key debates at the time the HRA came into force[188] was whether it had horizontal effect, since section 6 of the HRA seems to impose a duty on public authorities only to act in accordance with the ECHR. It was questioned whether private parties would be required to act in a way which did not infringe the ECHR rights or whether the application of ECHR rights was restricted to vertical relations between the State and private parties. The general weight of opinion pointed to indirect horizontal

---

[185] Section 263A(4) and (5) of TULRCA.   [186] Section 263A(6) of TULRCA.
[187] See *Ghaidan v Godin-Mendoza* [2004] 2 AC 557.
[188] See Sir W. Wade, 'Horizons of Horizontality' (2000) 116 *Law Quarterly Review* 217; Sir R. Buxton, 'The Human Rights Act and Private Law' (2000) 116 *Law Quarterly Review* 48; and D. Pannick and A. Lester, 'The Impact of the Human Rights Act on Private Law: The Knight's Move' (2000) 116 *Law Quarterly Review* 380.

effect[189] and, in 2004, the impact of the HRA on private employers was specifically addressed by the Court of Appeal in the case of *X v Y*.[190] In *X v Y*,[191] Mummery LJ clarified that, as public authorities, courts, ETs, and the EAT have an obligation under section 3 of the HRA to interpret labour legislation in a way which is compatible with the ECHR rights, and that no distinction should be drawn between public authority and private sector employers.[192] This is particularly the case where the State has a positive duty to secure enjoyment of the relevant ECHR rights between private persons, which is the case in respect of Articles 6, 8, and 11 of the ECHR which have had some impact on labour law in the UK.[193] As a result, it is now clear that the ECHR rights have indirect horizontal effect and apply in the context of the relationship between private employers and employees.

What is clear is that the impact of the HRA on the development of employment law has been modest at best to date.[194] After 15 years, in the absence of the emergence of what Fredman and Davies have referred to as a 'human rights culture',[195] there are few signs that the ECHR has had any major effect on substantive and procedural labour law in the UK. As we will see, this is despite recent step changes in the approach of the ECtHR as evidenced by the cases of *Demir and Baykara v Turkey*,[196] *Enerji Yapi-Yol Sen*,[197] *Danilenkov v Russia*,[198] *Pay v UK*,[199] *Wilson v UK*,[200] *Eweida v UK*,[201] *Redfearn v UK*,[202] and *Barbulescu v Romania*[203] and the decisions of the domestic courts in a slew of recent key cases, e.g. *R (on the application of G) v Governors of X School*,[204] *X v Y*,[205]

---

[189] See H. L. MacQueen and D. Brodie, 'Private Rights, Private Law and the Private Domain' in A. Boyle, C. Himsworth, A. Loux, and H. L. MacQueen (eds), *Human Rights and Scots Law* (Oxford, Hart Publishing, 2002) 141.

[190] *X v Y* [2004] IRLR 625.   [191] *ibid*.   [192] *ibid*., 630–2 per Mummery LJ.

[193] *ibid*., 633 per Mummery LJ, and *Copsey v WWB Devon Clays Ltd* [2005] IRLR 811, 815 per Mummery LJ.

[194] For a review of the perceived advantages and disadvantages which the discourse of human rights might have for the interests of workers, see H. Collins, 'Theories of Rights as Justifications' in G. Davidov and B. Langille (eds), *The Idea of Labour Law* (Oxford, OUP, 2011) 139; K. D. Ewing, 'The Human Rights Act and Labour Law' (1998) 27 *Industrial Law Journal* 275; H. Arthurs, 'The Constitution-alization of Employment Relations: Multiple Models, Pernicious Problems' (2010) 19 *Social & Legal Studies* 403; C. Fenwick and T. Novitz, 'Conclusion: Regulating to Protect Workers' Human Rights' in C. Fenwick and T. Novitz (eds), *Human Rights at Work: Perspectives on Law and Regulation* (Oxford, Hart Publishing, 2010) 587–8; V. Mantouvalou, 'Are Labour Rights Human Rights?' (2012) 3 *European Labour Law Journal* 151; K. Kolben, 'Labor Rights as Human Rights' (2009) 50 *Virginia Journal of International Law* 450, 461–2; J. Fudge, 'The New Discourse of Labor Rights: From Social to Fundamental Rights' (2007) 29 *Comparative Labour Law and Policy Journal* 29, 29–32; P. Alston, 'Labour Rights as Human Rights: The Not So Happy State of the Art' in P. Alston (ed.), *Labour Rights as Human Rights* (Oxford, OUP, 2005) 1, 4–5; J. Fudge, 'Constitutionalizing Labour Rights in Europe' in T. Campbell, K. D. Ewing, and A. Tomkins (eds), *The Legal Protection of Human Rights: Sceptical Essays* (Oxford, OUP, 2011) 244; M. Pearson, 'Offensive Expression and the Workplace' (2014) 43 *Industrial Law Journal* 429; V. Mantouvalou, *The Right to Work: Legal and Philosophical Perspectives* (Oxford, Hart Publishing, 2015); H. Collins and V. Mantouvalou, 'Human Rights and the Contract of Employment' in M. Freedland et al. (eds), *The Contract of Employment* (Oxford, OUP, 2016) 188; J. Atkinson, 'Human Rights as Foundations for Labour Rights?' in H. Collins, G. Lester, and V. Mantouvalou (eds), *The Philosophical Foundations of Labour Law* (Oxford, OUP, 2018) and P. Collins, 'The Inadequate Protection of Human Rights in Unfair Dismissal Law' (2018) 47 *Industrial Law Journal* (forthcoming).

[195] S. Fredman, *Human Rights Transformed* (Oxford, OUP, 2008); A. Davies, 'Workers' Human Rights in English Law' in C. Fenwick and T. Novitz (eds), *Human Rights at Work: Perspectives on Law and Regulation* (Oxford, Hart Publishing, 2010) 183–4.

[196] [2009] IRLR 766 (ECtHR). See K. D. Ewing and J. Hendy, 'The Dramatic Implications of *Demir and Baykara*' (2010) 39 *Industrial Law Journal* 1, and Chapter C of the Online Resources.

[197] Application No. 68959/01, judgment dated 21 April 2009 (ECtHR). See Chapter D of the Online Resources.   [198] Application No. 67336/01, 30 July 2009 (ECtHR).

[199] [2009] IRLR 139 (ECtHR).   [200] (2002) 35 EHRR 20. See Chapter D of the Online Resources.

[201] [2013] IRLR 231.   [202] [2013] IRLR 51. See Chapter 16, section 16.2.1.1.

[203] [2017] IRLR 1032.   [204] [2011] UKSC 30, [2011] 3 WLR 237. See Chapter 17, section 17.2.1.4.

[205] [2004] IRLR 625. See Chapter 16, section 16.2.4.3.2.

and *National Union of Rail, Maritime & Transport Workers v Serco; ASLEF v London & Birmingham Railway Ltd.*[206]

2.4.2 International labour standards

The ILO was established in 1919 after the First World War[207] with the express goal of alleviating labour conditions and standards in the international arena: this is captured in the refrain that 'labour is not a commodity'.[208] Since then, the ILO has promulgated 189 international labour Conventions, which are binding on the Member States that have ratified them.[209] Ratification, however, is not effective to render a Convention part of UK domestic law, since it will not be accorded such status unless it is transposed into legislation. Standard-setting at the ILO level is divided between Conventions and Recommendations. The latter are not legally binding, have a lesser status than Conventions, and are generally adopted in respect of 'issues that [a]re not considered suitable for treatment by means of a Convention'.[210] As such, Recommendations furnish guidance to Member States, rather than affirm matters of principle. At present, there are 186 Member States[211] and the UK has ratified 87 ILO Conventions.[212] There are eight instruments promulgated by the ILO which 'constitute the core ILO human rights standards, and form the basis of the Declaration of Fundamental Rights and Principles adopted . . . in 1998'.[213] These are ILO Convention 87 on freedom of association,[214] ILO Convention 98 on the right to organize and collective bargaining,[215] ILO Conventions 29 and 105 on abolishing forced labour,[216] ILO Conventions 138 and 182 on abolishing child labour,[217] ILO Convention 100 on equal pay,[218] and ILO Convention 111 on discrimination in employment and occupation.[219]

One of the purposes of international labour standards is to tackle the adverse effects of globalization and trade liberalization on the workplace. The ILO has the capacity to act as a guarantor of fair play in international markets by harmonizing labour standards and thus disincentivizing States from introducing abusive labour practices that generate unfair competitive advantages by undercutting their competitors:

---

[206] [2011] ICR 848. See Chapter D of the Online Resources.

[207] See T. Ramm, 'Epilogue: The New Ordering of Labour Law 1918–45' in B. Hepple (ed.), *The Making of Labour Law in Europe* (Oxford, Hart Publishing, 2010) 277.

[208] See the Preamble to the ILO Declaration of Philadelphia of 1944, available at http://blue.lim.ilo.org/cariblex/pdfs/ILO_dec_philadelphia.pdf (last visited 4 December 2017).

[209] Article 19(5)(d) of the ILO Constitution, available at http://www.ilo.org/dyn/normlex/en/f?p=1000:62:1193311024488183::NO:62:P62_LIST_ENTRIE_ID:2453907:NO#A19 (last visited 4 December 2017).

[210] B. Creighton, 'The Future of Labour Law: Is There a Role for International Labour Standards?' in C. Barnard, S. Deakin, and G. Morris (eds), *The Future of Labour Law: Liber Amicorum Bob Hepple QC* (Oxford, Hart Publishing, 2004) 253, 269.

[211] See http://www.ilo.org/dyn/normlex/en/f?p=1000:1:0::NO::: (last visited 4 December 2017).

[212] See http://www.ilo.org/dyn/normlex/en/f?p=1000:11200:0::NO:11200:P11200_COUNTRY_ID:102651 (last visited 4 December 2017).

[213] B. Creighton, 'The Future of Labour Law: Is There a Role for International Labour Standards?' in C. Barnard, S. Deakin, and G. Morris (eds), *The Future of Labour Law: Liber Amicorum Bob Hepple QC* (Oxford, Hart Publishing, 2004) 253, 255. See also B. Hepple, 'The WTO as a Mechanism for Labour Regulation' in B. Bercusson and C. Estlund (eds), *Regulating Labour in the Wake of Globalisation* (Oxford, Hart Publishing, 2008) 164.

[214] ILO Convention 87 (Freedom of Association and Protection of the Right to Organise Convention, 1948).

[215] ILO Convention 98 (Right to Organise and Collective Bargaining Convention, 1949).

[216] ILO Convention 29 (Forced Labour Convention, 1930) and ILO Convention 105 (Abolition of Forced Labour Convention, 1957).

[217] ILO Convention 138 (Minimum Age Convention, 1973) and ILO Convention 182 (Worst Forms of Child Labour Convention, 1999).

[218] ILO Convention 100 (Equal Remuneration Convention, 1951).

[219] ILO Convention 111 (Discrimination (Employment and Occupation) Convention, 1958).

■ **S. Deakin and F. Wilkinson, 'Rights vs. Efficiency? The Economic Case for Transnational Labour Standards' (1994) 23 *Industrial Law Journal* 289, 301**

[This is] the idea that harmonization is needed to establish a *level playing field* between member states by establishing *parity of costs* imposed by [labour] legislation on employers. Alternatively, harmonization is seen as providing a minimal *floor of rights* to prevent destructive competition . . . [there is also] a third possibility, namely that standards operate as *guarantors of economic participation and development.*

However, there are several formidable obstacles to the ILO performing the role of an international policeman of the workplace. First, supervision of compliance with ILO standards is conducted primarily by the Member States engaging in reporting, rather than via formal enforcement mechanisms. For this reason, the ILO's international labour standards are often characterized as nothing more than paper tigers, such is their lack of teeth: 'Many . . . believe that the ILO, while useful in setting standards, can be ignored because it has little ability to enforce those standards.'[220] Another difficulty is that Member States are reluctant to support the adoption of labour standards in their own jurisdictions or those of developing countries where labour laws are weak and their corporations are in the habit of doing business. In a similar vein, the ILO often finds itself powerless in the face of transnational corporations which have the 'capacity to direct investment from countries that adhere to relatively high labour standards to countries that do not'.[221] The cumulative effect is that ILO standards only have an indirect, rather than direct, impact on UK labour law where the UK has not ratified and transposed that standard domestically. This indirect effect is particularly evident where ILO principles are used as an interpretive aid by the ECJ or the ECtHR. Here, the ILO standard effectively functions to inform the content of EU law or the scope of a human right in the ECHR. Examples of this phenomenon include the decisions of the ECJ and CJEU in *Schultz-Hoff*[222] and *KHS AG v Schulte*,[223] in which it was held that the WTD must be construed in light of the ILO Convention on the Hours of Work Industry Convention of 1919[224] and ILO Convention 132 of 24 June 1970 concerning Annual Holidays with Pay (Revised).[225] Likewise, in *Demir and Baykara v Turkey*,[226] the ECtHR referred to ILO Convention 87 on freedom of association[227] and ILO Convention 98 on the right to organize and collective bargaining,[228] in order to reach the conclusion that Article 11 of the ECHR included a right to collective bargaining. Fundamentally, these decisions demonstrate that ILO principles act as a key indicator of what is considered acceptable and appropriate in international circles.

---

[220] J. Atleson, 'The Voyage of the Neptune Jade: Transnational Labour Solidarity and the Obstacles of Domestic Law' in J. Conaghan, R. M. Fischl, and K. Klare (eds), *Labour Law in an Era of Globalization* (Oxford, OUP, 2004) 381.

[221] B. Creighton, 'The Future of Labour Law: Is There a Role for International Labour Standards?' in C. Barnard, S. Deakin, and G. Morris (eds), *The Future of Labour Law: Liber Amicorum Bob Hepple QC* (Oxford, Hart Publishing, 2004) 253, 264.

[222] [2009] IRLR 214, 239.   [223] [2012] IRLR 156, 168, and 170.

[224] See http://www.ilo.org/dyn/normlex/en/f?p=1000:12100:0::NO::P12100_ILO_CODE:C001 (last visited 4 December 2017).

[225] See http://www.ilo.org/dyn/normlex/en/f?p=1000:12100:0::NO::P12100_INSTRUMENT_ID: 312277 (last visited 4 December 2017).   [226] [2009] IRLR 766 (ECtHR).

[227] ILO Convention 87 (Freedom of Association and Protection of the Right to Organise Convention, 1948).

[228] ILO Convention 98 (Right to Organise and Collective Bargaining Convention, 1949).

Reflection points

1. What are the pros and cons of resolving disputes between employers and employees in specialist tribunals, rather than the courts?

2. Are you convinced that the UK Government is correct in thinking that ACAS should play a more prominent role in the resolution of disputes between employers and employees? Give reasons for your answer.

3. To what extent do you think human rights and international labour standards should have a role to play in interpreting, applying, and developing common law and statutory employment protection rights? Give reasons for your answer.

 For additional reading on the sources and institutions of employment law, visit the Online Resources for this book at www.oup.com/uk/cabrelli3e/

PART II
THE CONSTITUTION OF EMPLOYMENT AND PERSONAL WORK CONTRACTS

CHAPTER THREE

THE EMPLOYMENT RELATIONSHIP AND THE CONTRACT OF EMPLOYMENT

3.1 ANALYSIS OF THE EMPLOYMENT RELATIONSHIP AND THE CONTRACT OF EMPLOYMENT

In this chapter, we address the various tests that are adopted by the courts and tribunals to distinguish between the contract of employment and the contract for services. We move on to consider the statutory concept of continuous employment. This is an important issue because an individual may be required to establish a period of continuous employment based on a contract of employment to avail him/herself of certain statutory employment protection rights. Finally, we turn to the effect of an illegal contract of employment. Where an individual meets the tests for the establishment of a contract of employment and has the requisite continuity of employment to be entitled to various common law or statutory employment rights, public policy and, in particular, the doctrine of illegality may nonetheless operate to deprive him/her of such protection. In such a case, the illegality rules function to negate the existence of the employment contract *ab initio*, i.e. from the very beginning as if it never existed.

The tests for the binary divide between the contract of employment and the contract for services are essentially applied as a means of identifying the employment status of an individual who is providing services to a third party and also to classify the nature of their contractual relationship. The basic question is whether that individual is an employee. The status of that individual will not necessarily be an issue where he/she is content in the working relationship and has no quarrel with the employing entity. However, it will become an acute point of focus when there is a dispute concerning:

(1) whether he/she has satisfied the qualifying criteria for access to common law or statutory employment rights;

(2) his/her income tax and social security status;

(3) whether the employing entity is vicariously liable for torts committed by the individual in the course of his/her employment; or

(4) whether the employing entity owns intellectual property rights created in the course of his/her employment for the purposes of section 39 of the Patents Act 1977 and section 11 of the Copyright, Designs and Patents Act 1988.

The matter of the employment status of such an individual can often be fractious owing to the fact that the law makes a number of options available to individuals and enterprises when they wish to enter into a contract to supply and acquire labour:

(1) the parties may co-ordinate their relationship as a contract of sale, e.g. where a party commissions an artist to paint a picture; or

(2) the relationship may be arranged as a contract for services whereby the individual is paid a fee to perform a particular task for the enterprise on a one-off or ongoing basis, e.g. where a professional consultant is paid a retainer for an indefinite or definite period; or

(3) the parties may structure the arrangement as a contract of service, i.e. a contract of employment, in terms of which the individual is hired to perform work for an indefinite or periodic term.

Although each of these options share the common feature that they are contractual arrangements, the content of those contracts prescribed by law differs to a marked degree. As such, the nature and substance of the norms binding the parties and the applicable regulatory regime imposed by law will depend on which of those contracts they have chosen to govern their relationship.

You might think that it should not be too difficult to characterize a particular relationship between an individual and enterprise in terms of one of the three contracts we have identified. However, the multitude of case law on the topic demonstrates otherwise. In fact, it is important to appreciate the depth of the complexity involved, when you come to answer problem or essay-type exam questions. Matters are further confounded by the fact that the doctrine of freedom of contract—which is so central to the liberal common law tradition—legitimizes the diverse variety and range of contractual arrangements which may be adopted by individuals and enterprises to capture their relationship.

3.1.1 Contextual introduction to the employment relationship

The contract of employment is one of the most pivotal legal institutions developed by the common law. It has been described as the 'cornerstone of the edifice' of employment law.[1] Common law and statutory employment rights[2] are conferred on individuals in accordance with the discipline which we call 'employment' or 'labour' law if they are performing work for an enterprise based on a contract of employment. As such, the employment contract is the rock around which the relational scope of employment laws is configured and, in view of the prominence given to the employment contract in any discussion of employment law, you would be forgiven for thinking that this had always been the case. However, the situation is not so straightforward. An examination of the historical context reveals that the importance of the law of contract, and in particular the law of the contract of employment, is a comparatively recent development in the regulation of the

---

[1] O. Kahn-Freund, 'Legal Framework' in A. Flanders and H. Clegg (eds), *The System of Industrial Relations in Great Britain* (Oxford, Basil Blackwell, 1954) 45.

[2] Also included are rights won by trade unions in collective agreements concluded with employers or employers' associations.

employment relationship. Consider, e.g., the eighteenth and early nineteenth centuries. At that time, the relationship between a hirer and a supplier of labour was governed by the 'master and servant regime', rather than the law of contract. This was a status-based relationship. A series of Master and Servant Acts were passed from 1747 until their repeal with the introduction of the Employers and Workmen Act 1875.[3] This statutory master and servant regime established a framework through which the working relationship was channelled, including the rights of the parties, which were heavily weighted in favour of the employer, with a multitude of co-relative duties imposed on the servant. It represented a sort of extension of the economic and social relations within the household, whereby the servant subordinated himself to the direction of the master. The master had the power to co-ordinate the activities and work patterns of the servant. If the workman absented himself from work or was guilty of indiscipline, the ultimate sanction afforded to the employer by virtue of the Master and Servant legislation was the imprisonment of the employee.

It is only towards the middle of the twentieth century that one can meaningfully talk of a uniformly applicable contract of employment regulating the employment relationship. This evolved out of the pre-existing master and servant model.[4] During the nineteenth century, the nexus between white-collar, professional workers and the employer had come to be treated by the courts as one grounded on a contractual footing. This relationship was ultimately crafted into the particular form of the contract of employment which we now recognize today. With the repeal of the Master and Servant Acts in 1875, the incarnation of the contract of employment, which had been adopted by the common law as regards such white-collar and professional workers, slowly but surely came to be applied to blue-collar, industrial, and manual workers. As such, uniformity and homogeneity were introduced across the entire range of workers irrespective of the class of work which they performed.

The nature of the relationship between an individual supplier of labour and an enterprise developed into a question of the distinction between the contract of employment and the contract for services. The universal reliance on contract was coupled with the traditional common law respect for the efficiency secured by the doctrine of freedom of contract. As a result, the parties were afforded the power to draw up all sorts of contracts tailored to their own specific requirements. The dominance of the contract of employment reached its heights in the early and mid-twentieth century. It largely coincided with a period where it suited management to hire labour on the basis of what has been referred to as the 'typical working' or 'standard employment' relationship, i.e. a full-time contract with a single employer to perform personal services for an indefinite period at the employer's premises irrespective of whether the employer had sufficient work to provide the employee or not. This is associated with the 'Fordist' model of production.[5] Over time, the common law adapted to the reality of the typical working relationship by imposing a more evenly balanced set of implied obligations on the employer and employee, leading to the emergence of the 'mutual' or 'reciprocal' contract of employment.[6]

The division between the contract of employment/service and the contract for services is the emblematic regulatory device deployed to decide whether an individual supplier of labour is entitled to the protection of employment laws. Traditionally, the dichotomy

---

[3] S. Deakin and F. Wilkinson, *The Law of the Labour Market: Industrialization, Employment, and Legal Evolution* (Oxford, OUP, 2005) 61–74.

[4] *ibid.*, 74–86; O. Kahn-Freund, 'The Contract of Employment: Blackstone's Neglected Child' (1977) 93 *Law Quarterly Review* 508.

[5] A. Supiot, *Beyond Employment: Changes in Work and the Future of Labour Law in Europe* (Oxford, OUP, 2001) 1 and J. Fudge, 'The Future of the Standard Employment Relationship: Labour Law, New Institutional Economics and Old "Power Resource Theory"' (2017) *Journal of Industrial Relations* 374 and see Chapter 4, section 4.1.1.

[6] See Chapter 5, section 5.1.1.

between the contract of service and the contract for services was designed to mirror the fault-line between:

(1) dependent and independent labour;

(2) subordinate and non-subordinate relationships; and

(3) employment and self-employment.[7]

As such, if an individual is classified as performing services on the basis of a contract of employment, the implication is that he/she is a dependent employee in a position of subordination vis-à-vis the employer. Consider the following basic illustrations.

Hypothetical A

Having incorporated Danny's Demolishers Ltd ('DD') to run his business, Danny is delighted to learn that he has been chosen by Cheshire East Council ('CEC') to demolish a derelict building situated in Macclesfield. The building is to be developed by CEC into residential flats for council tenants. Danny decides to hire five individuals on six-month fixed-term contracts to undertake the demolition work. The individuals appointed are Charles Ferdinand, Owen Smith, David Dent, Michael Franks, and John Doyle. Each of these individuals pays PAYE and National Insurance contributions, which are deducted by DD from their monthly wage. None of them performs any work for any other organization. Although there is no written contract of employment in place, they are obliged to comply with the direct instructions of DD in relation to the performance of the work at the Macclesfield site and to provide their services personally. Given their dependence on DD for a livelihood and their position of subordination vis-à-vis DD, it is more likely than not that Ferdinand, Smith, Dent, Franks, and Doyle are employees engaged on the basis of an employment contract.

Hypothetical B

Not long after securing the Macclesfield contract, Danny's Demolishers Ltd ('DD') is appointed by a house builder to demolish a factory in Stockport. The demolition works are complex and DD takes the decision to hire specialist structural engineers to assist in the process. Having interviewed Mark Anderson and Thomas Timson, DD enters into a contract with them at a fee of £10,000 each (inclusive of VAT) for their specialist engineering services. The contract provides that the engineers are to attend the factory when called upon to do so by DD and that they are bound to provide specialist advice to DD about structural engineering issues involved in the demolition works. They are entitled to refuse to attend if they are engaged in work for other clients, but they must provide a minimum of 55 hours of work for DD at the factory. Considering the independence which Anderson and Timson enjoy in the performance of their work and the fact that they are paid a fee, rather than a wage or salary, the likelihood is that they would be classified as self-employed independent contractors engaged on the basis of a contract for services.

---

[7] It should be noted that the extent to which notions of dependence or subordination continue to serve as a useful point of reference in evaluating whether an individual is deserving of the protection of employment laws is open to question: see M. Freedland and N. Kountouris, *The Legal Construction of Personal Work Relations* (Oxford, OUP, 2011) 437. Cf. the view of the Court of Justice of the European Union in *Holterman Ferho Exploitatie BV v Spies von Büllesheim* [2016] IRLR 140, 153, that an employment contract 'presupposes a relationship of subordination . . .'.

Although the choice of form in which the parties contract for the supply of labour ultimately comes down to an assessment of which side of the binary divide the contract falls down—i.e. (1) a contract of employment, or (2) self-employment on the basis of a contract for services—this should not cloud us from the reality that the contractual arrangements struck by individuals and hirers come in many shapes and sizes.[8] This freedom afforded to hirers of labour to choose from a diverse range of contractual structures enables them to 'demutualize' the risks and costs associated with a working relationship by hiving them off on to the shoulders of the individual supplier of labour.[9] Consider, for example, the relentless rise of the 'gig economy'. The Office of Tax Simplification in the UK defines the 'gig' economy[10] as 'an environment in which temporary positions are common and organisations contract with independent workers for short-term or on-demand engagements'.[11] Individuals selling their services are matched with buyers via a technological intermediated interface such as an app or internet platform operated and co-ordinated by companies such as Uber, Deliveroo, etc. and the individuals provide their services to third parties via these apps. Although the technological and operational functions of the companies in the gig economy will share many common features, the contractual structures adopted by each of these companies will differ,[12] which only goes to accentuate the point that companies and other business organizations benefit from freedom of contract.

The broader issue is that conferring a freedom upon employers to choose a form of contract in preference to the contract of employment gives them the power to indirectly contract out of labour laws:

■ H. Collins, *Employment Law*, 2nd edition (Oxford, OUP, 2010) 36–42

Freedom of contract permits the employer to acquire labour through an enormous variety of contractual relations. An employer may hire one worker on a contract that pays the worker by the hour or week for performing services according to the instructions of the managers, and hire another worker to perform tasks in return for payment for each piece of work completed. Although these workers may in fact be performing exactly the same range of tasks, the contractual framework differs, which produces significant consequences for the parties . . .

The variety of patterns of working relation presents two kinds of problem for any attempted legal regulation. In the first place, as a central instance of the need for reflexivity in employment law, general legal regulation has to cope with the diversity of contractual arrangements. A minimum wage law that specifies a minimum payment for an hour's work, for instance, can apply straightforwardly to an employee paid by the hour for work, but how might it apply to piecework, commission on sales, salaried workers who receive a fixed wage regardless of hours worked, or the

---

[8] P. Davies and M. Freedland, *Labour Law: Text and Materials*, 2nd edition (London, Weidenfeld and Nicholson, 1984) 81.

[9] M. Freedland and N. Kountouris, *The Legal Construction of Personal Work Relations* (Oxford, OUP, 2011) 440; N. Kountouris and M. Freedland (eds), *Resocialising Europe in a Time of Crisis* (Cambridge, CUP, 2013).

[10] For some of the academic literature, see J Prassl, *Humans as a Service* (Oxford, OUP, 2018); V. De Stefano, 'Crowdsourcing, the Gig-Economy, and the Law' (2016) 37 *Comparative Labor Law & Policy Journal* 461; V. De Stefano, 'The Rise of the Just-in-Time Workforce: On-Demand Work, Crowdwork and Labor Protection in the Gig-Economy' (2016) 37 *Comparative Labor Law & Policy Journal* 471; J. Prassl and M. Risak, 'Uber, Taskrabbit, & Co: Platforms as Employers? Rethinking the Legal Analysis of Crowdwork' (2016) 37 *Comparative Labor Law & Policy Journal* 619; B. Rogers, 'Employment Rights in the Platform Economy: Getting Back to Basics' (2016) 10 *Harvard Law & Policy Review* 479.

[11] See https://www.gov.uk/government/uploads/system/uploads/attachment_data/file/573483/OTS_Gig_economy_Focus_paper_Nov16_final.pdf at page 1 (last visited 18 November 2017).

[12] For example, contrast the contractual patterns found in *Uber BV v Aslam and Farrer* [2018] IRLR 97 and *IWGB v RooFoods Ltd (t/a Deliveroo)* [2018] IRLR 84.

tips given to waiters in restaurants by customers in addition to any wages from the owner of the restaurant? . . . The second problem concerns the scope of employment regulation. In order to determine the application of any statutory or analogous regulation of contracts for the performance of work, the regulation has to determine the types of contract to which it applies. For example, legislation that mandates a minimum wage has to identify the types of contract that concern wages as opposed to fees or other species of payment for services; and legislation that grants workers a right not to be unfairly dismissed has similarly to determine its field of application. Given the enormous variety and subtle differences between contracts for the performance of work, the scope of regulation or what is sometimes called the 'personal scope of labour law' is frequently hard to determine. The difficulty lies both in deciding what kinds of contract should be covered in view of the policy objectives of the regulation, and then in implementing that decision through clear legal rules that determine the scope of the regulation . . .

As contracts for the performance of work have splintered into a huge variety of non-standard employment relations [e.g. temp work, casual work, agency work, fixed-term work, etc.], the scope of employment law becomes indistinct, because each legal regulation applies to a different subset of non-standard contracts and employment-like relationships. As well as causing compliance problems owing to regulatory complexity, the indeterminate scope of employment law raises questions about the underlying purposes of this branch of the law and whether it constitutes a coherent whole. Calls have been made to reconfigure the scope of employment law around other concepts such as contracts for the personal performance of work. Yet as long as employers can use their freedom of contract to construct any type of contract for the performance of work that achieves the flexibility and efficiency they seek, rather than being confined to a limited range of types of contract, any coherence and transparency in the legal test for determining the proper scope of employment law will prove elusive.[13]

Collins identifies two of the key questions that the adoption of the contractual paradigm causes us to pose, namely:

(1) how should employment law approach the classification of the great diversity of contractual structures for the supply of labour deployed by individuals and enterprises; and

(2) what should be the relational scope of employment law, i.e. to what kinds of contracts and relationships should employment law apply as a means of conferring common law and statutory employment protection rights?

Collins makes the fundamental point that the existing conceptual apparatus applied by the common law in order to identify those individuals covered by employment laws—namely the binary division between the contract of employment and the self-employed contract for services—may be inadequate in light of the contortions its exercise often produces.[14] Further, part of the difficulty in identifying the criteria for distinguishing between the two contracts lies in the fact that the distinction must be drawn for an inordinate range of purposes, from the law of employment, the law of vicarious liability, intellectual property ownership,[15] social security law, to income tax law.[16] As we will see in Chapter 4, the UK Parliament has sought to address some of the difficulties encountered by the existence of a wide range of contractual arrangements for the personal

---

[14] Indeed, Freedland has questioned whether the distinction between the contract of service and the contract for services was ever clear in conceptual terms, and he has likened the search for the distinguishing criteria to the quest for the Philosopher's Stone: M. Freedland, *The Personal Employment Contract* (Oxford, OUP, 2003) 22.

[15] Section 39 of the Patents Act 1977 and section 11 of the Copyright, Designs, and Patents Act 1988.

[16] See S. Honeyball, *Great Debates in Employment Law* (Basingstoke, Palgrave Macmillan, 2011) 18–30; M. Freedland, 'Rethinking the Personal Work Contract' (2005) 58 *Current Legal Problems* 517, 526.

performance of work by offering a more modest measure of statutory employment protection to individuals who are providing personal services on the basis of contracts other than the contract for employment. Yet that response has been incomplete, which begs the question whether the institutional backcloth of the contract of employment—and the law of contract generally—is really equipped to cope with the regulation of the individual supply of labour.[17] The suitability of the law of the contract of employment is also open to question in light of the growing incidence of self-employment, casualization, and flexibilization of the labour market, with the exponential surge in the atypical working relationships[18] adverted to in the extract from Collins, e.g. zero-hours, agency, casual and 'gig economy' workers.[19] Owing to the nature of the tests crafted by the judiciary for the identification of a contract of employment, such atypical workers often fall outside the relational scope of employment laws. Indeed, some have called for the construct of the contract of employment to be abandoned completely.[20]

There is also the argument that the construct of the contract of employment is not a particularly 'contractual' concept at all.[21] There are three particular justifications for this claim.

(1) The ability of the employer to contract out of many statutory employment protection rights is expressly excluded.[22] Absent the ability to contract out of such rights, the contention is that it makes little sense to treat the contract of employment as truly contractual in any meaningful sense. In the memorable words of Lord Diplock, employment protection legislation has drawn the relationship between employer and employee 'out of the field of contract and into that of status'.[23] This represents something of a reversal of the 19th century transition from 'status' to 'contract' discussed earlier.

(2) There is also the charge that if the employment relationship is truly based on a contractual structure, then it is incomprehensible why some of the obligations of the employer and employee continue in effect notwithstanding that the employment contract has been terminated.[24] In fact, some norms implied by employment law also apply prior to the formation of the employment contract[25] to exercise constraints over the conduct of *prospective* employers and employees, as well as the obligations owed by the latter to their *existing* employers.

---

[17] See M. Freedland and N. Kountouris *The Legal Construction of Personal Work Relations* (Oxford, OUP, 2011) 310–12.

[18] An atypical working relationship is one in which at least one of the following six variables is missing: (1) a full-time contract (2) with a single employer (3) for an indefinite period of time (4) to perform personal services (5) at the employer's premises (6) irrespective of whether the employer has sufficient to work to provide the employee or not. For a statistical evaluation of this growth in atypical working, see W. Brown and D. Marsden, 'Individualization and Growing Diversity of Employment Relationships' in D. Marsden (ed.), *Employment in the Lean Years: Policy and Prospects for the Next Decade* (Oxford, OUP, 2011) 73, 75.

[19] See the discussion in M. J. Walton, 'The Shifting Nature of Work and Its Implications' (2016) 45 *Industrial Law Journal* 111, 113 ff.

[20] See Chapter 3, section 3.1.2; B. Hepple, 'Restructuring Employment Rights' (1986) 15 *Industrial Law Journal* 69; and Lord Wedderburn, 'From Here to Autonomy?' (1987) 16 *Industrial Law Journal* 1, 5–7.

[21] See M. Freedland and N. Kountouris, *The Legal Construction of Personal Work Relations* (Oxford, OUP, 2011) 310–12.

[22] See e.g. section 203(1) of the Employment Rights Act 1996 ('ERA'); section 288(1) of the Trade Union and Labour Relations (Consolidation) Act 1992; section 49(1) of the National Minimum Wage Act 1998; regulation 35(1) of the Working Time Regulations 1998 (SI 1998/1833); and section 144(1) and (2) of the Equality Act 2010.

[23] *Ford v Warwickshire County Council* [1983] 2 AC 71, 79C.

[24] For example, the implied term in law imposing a duty on the employer to exercise reasonable care in producing a reference for a former employee: *Spring v Guardian Assurance plc* [1995] 2 AC 296. Likewise, in the case of the implied term in law imposing a duty of fidelity and loyalty on the employee not to disclose or exploit the trade secrets of the employer post-employment: *Faccenda Chicken Ltd v Fowler* [1987] Ch 117.

[25] See the implied term of mutual trust and confidence which can apply in the context of a pre-employment 'forward' contract: *Tullett Prebon plc v BGC Brokers LP* [2011] EWCA Civ 131, [2011] IRLR 420.

(3) The common law of the contract of employment also exhibits clear ruptures from traditional contract law doctrine in a variety of ways,[26] e.g. in a departure from contractual orthodoxy:[27]

(a) the implied terms which supply the content of the employment contract do not necessarily always give way to the express terms;[28]

(b) adherence to the obligations imposed by the express terms of the employment contract may constitute a breach of contract in certain circumstances, e.g. 'work-to-rule' practices were held unlawful in *Secretary of State for Employment v ASLEF (No. 2)*;[29] and

(c) the breach of a term of an employer's disciplinary procedure that is incorporated into an employee's contract of employment will not give rise to a damages remedy.[30]

This has led many commentators and judges to categorize employment as a relationship which is more fittingly conceived of as a mixture of status and contract, whereby 'contracts in the employment sphere occupy an intermediate position between these two poles'.[31] The point being made here is that the content and substance of a true status-based relationship is inderogable and not subject to the exigencies of the freedom of contract doctrine:

■ *Buckland v Bournemouth University Higher Education Corp.* [2010] EWCA Civ 121, [2011] QB 323, 331G

Lord Justice Sedley:

Modern employment law is a hybrid of contract and status. The way Parliament has achieved this is to graft statutory protections on to the stem of the common law contract.

However, there is a powerful response to the contention that the employment relationship comprises a blend of status and contract. The point is illustrated by the following excerpt from the judgment of Mr Justice Bristow:

■ *Tomlinson v Dick Evans 'U' Drive Ltd* [1978] ICR 639, 642G–643A

Mr Justice Bristow:

It is said that . . . the result of the employment legislation is to give the employee a protected status. While it may be a convenient shorthand to say that the effect of the employment legislation is that the law is moving away from contract in this field and towards status, it is misleading if such shorthand tends to disguise the fact that it is the employee's situation as a party to a contract of employment which is the subject of protection by the legislation which it did not enjoy under the common law. Unless he was a party to a contract of employment, the statute cannot and does not give him a right not to be unfairly dismissed, or to the right to receive a redundancy payment.

---

[26] See M. Freedland, 'The Obligation to Work and to Pay for Work' (1977) *Current Legal Problems* 175.

[27] *BP Refinery (Westenport) Pty Ltd v Shire of Hastings* (1977) 52 AJLR 20, 26 per Lord Simon of Glaisdale; *Philips Electronique Grand Public SA and another v British Sky Broadcasting Ltd* [1995] EMLR 472, 481–483 per Sir Tom Bingham MR.

[28] See Chapter 7, section 7.4.2, and *Johnstone v Bloomsbury Health Authority* [1992] QB 333, 350C–F per Sir Nicolas Browne-Wilkinson V-C, which was expressly endorsed by Lords Hoffmann and Steyn in *Johnson v Unisys Ltd* [2003] 1 AC 518 (HL), 539 at para 37 per Lord Hoffmann and in *Barber v Somerset County Council* [2004] 2 All ER 385, 397e–g at para 24 per Lords Steyn and Rodger.

[29] [1972] 2 WLR 1370. See Chapter 6, section 6.3.2.

[30] See Chapter 15, section 15.3.1, and *Edwards v Chesterfield Royal Hospital NHS Foundation Trust* [2011] UKSC 58, [2012] 2 AC 22.

[31] A. Davies, 'Employment Law' in E. Simpson and M. Stewart (eds), *Sham Transactions* (Oxford, OUP, 2013) 188.

The fundamental point being made in this passage is that whilst the common law and statutory employment protection legislation function to impose norms into the employment relationship to bind the employer and the employee, such norms will only be imposed as a matter of law if the parties *have first voluntarily entered into a contract of employment*. Without this *antecedent consensual agreement*, there is no foundation upon which those statutorily prescribed and common law norms can be built. As such, mandatory employment protection norms can be avoided by the parties drawing up their relationship on some contractual basis other than that of a contract of employment.[32] The employment relationship can be contrasted with a true status relationship, a 'characteristic feature of [which] . . . is its legally imposed condition which cannot be got rid of at the mere will of the parties without the interposition of some agent of the State, administrative, legislative or judicial'.[33] Essentially, this represents the difference between *ius dispositivum* (i.e. derogable law) and *ius cogens* (i.e. mandatory/inderogable law), a distinction which is prevalent in civil law legal systems,[34] but is alien to British employment law.

Notwithstanding the critiques of the construct of the contract of employment, there are certain scholars who are sceptical about the practicability of breaking employment law away from the contractual model. Such scholars counsel against discarding the contract of employment on the ground that the common law and Parliament are indelibly wedded to its continued recognition and deployment as the paradigmatic central organizing concept for the employment relationship. Furthermore, so long as freedom of contract is embraced as an axiomatic principle of the law, employers cannot be precluded from selecting the arrangements they make for the provision of labour from the diverse variety of available forms of contractual structure. Thus, if the concern is about the contractual model excluding individuals from the purview of employment protection laws, a response which is much less radical than dispensing with the regulatory device of the contract of employment is available, namely that employment laws instead be conferred upon a much wider class of working individuals on the basis of an enlarged contractual concept. All of this leads us to question the distinction between the relative approaches to a contractual and non-contractual model, which takes us neatly on to section 3.1.2 where we examine the policy options available to a legislature or law-maker in designing a system of employment law.

Reflection points

1. In light of the earlier discussion, what are the advantages and disadvantages of constructing employment law around the central concept of the contract of employment?

2. The distinction between the contract of service and the contract for services can result in over-inclusivity as well as under-inclusivity when a finding is made that an individual is engaged under the former contract. Consider the implications of this statement.

3. What do you think are the principal reasons that we permit individuals and employing enterprises to adopt a variety of contractual structures in order to capture their relationship? Give reasons for your answer.

[32] This is a common feature of the case law and amounts to an indirect form of contracting out of employment laws.

[33] R. H. Graveson, 'The Movement from Status to Contract' (1941) 4 *Modern Law Review* 261, 270. See also the historical discussion in M. Freedland and N. Kountouris, 'Towards a Comparative Theory of the Contractual Construction of Personal Work Relations in Europe' (2008) 37 *Industrial Law Journal* 49, 57–9 and C. Mummé, 'From Control Through Command to the Control of Discretion: Labour Time, Labour Property and the Tools of Managerial Control in Early Twentieth Century Ontario' (2016) 45 *Industrial Law Journal* 176, 182–188.

[34] O. Kahn-Freund, 'A Note on Status and Contract in British Labour Law' (1967) 30 *Modern Law Review* 635, 635–42; M. Freedland, 'The Legal Structure of the Contract of Employment' in M. Freedland et al. (eds), *The Contract of Employment* (Oxford, OUP, 2016) 34–8; and M. Freedland, 'The Exchange Principle and the Wage-Work Bargain' in M. Freedland et al. (eds), *The Contract of Employment* (Oxford, OUP, 2016) 68.

For additional reading on the employment relationship, visit the Online Resources for this book at www.oup.com/uk/cabrelli3e/

3.1.2 Designing an employment law system around a central organizing concept: the policy options

We now consider the policy options available to a jurisdiction in designing the nature and shape of the central organizing concept to be applied for the purposes of classifying the status of an individual supplier of labour. In doing so, we will make passing references to jurisdictions other than England and Wales, and Scotland, in order to underscore certain points from time to time throughout the text. The relational scope of labour laws—i.e. the degree to which *fewer or more* individual suppliers of services are consciously included within the remit of employment protection laws—is a question of regulatory strategy, conditioned by multifarious factors, e.g. social and economic policy, as well as historical and political factors. Two key policy choices present themselves:

(1) first, policy-makers may decide to regulate the employment relationship around a contractual model; or

(2) secondly, there is the alternative scheme whereby a purely non-contractual model is adopted.

The option of a contractual model is intersected at two other levels by two distinct considerations, which may be referred to as the (a) 'breadth' and (b) 'literal/contextual' factors. These two factors also determine whether *fewer or more* individual service providers performing work on the basis of a contractual relationship—ranging from the contract of employment at one end to the contract for services at the other—are duly covered by the protection of employment laws.

Turning first to the contractual model, in such a system, the classification of an individual provider of services would be governed by the existence of some form of contract. Of course, traditionally in the UK, the contract of service/employment has been the central paradigm contractual form applied to perform this task and confer common law and statutory employment rights. However, it is by no means the only possibility: in certain jurisdictions, a closed list of differing contractual concepts may be applied instead to regulate the relationship between an enterprise and individual provider of services.[35] For example, French and Italian law adopt this approach. Here, the law prescribes a 'menu' of contractual forms, which are clearly defined, and the parties are compelled to choose one from that 'approved list'. Each contractual concept affords fewer or more employment rights to such individuals depending on where it falls on a notional sliding scale, consisting of an employment contract at one extreme and another defined personal services contract at the other, with a cluster of personal service contracts lying in between. The greater the level of dependence and subordination of the individual vis-à-vis the enterprise inherent within the contractual concept, the more employment protection the law will offer. Ultimately, such a model entails a deliberate choice on the part of a legal system that individual workers engaged in a contractual relationship with an enterprise other than on the basis of a contract of employment are sufficiently similar to the latter that they are deserving of a measure of, if not identical, employment protection laws.

---

[13] See also the discussions in E. Albin and J. Prassl, 'Fragmenting Work, Fragmented Regulation' in M. Freedland et al. (eds), *The Contract of Employment* (Oxford, OUP, 2016) 209; J. Riley, 'The Definition of the Contract of Employment and its Differentiation from Other Contracts and Other Work Relations' in M. Freedland et al. (2016) 321; and J. Prassl and E. Albin, 'Employees, Employers, and Beyond' also in M. Freedland et al. (2016) 341. Writer's annotations appear in square brackets throughout this chapter.

[35] See H. Collins, *Employment Law*, 2nd edition (Oxford, OUP, 2010) 38.

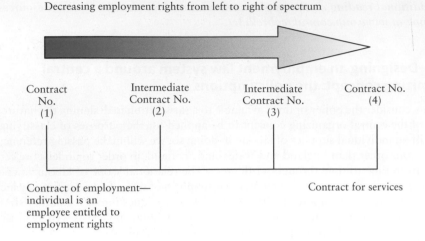

Figure 3.1   *Classificatory spectrum of personal work contracts*

This arrangement can be conceived of in terms of a notional classificatory spectrum representing the extent of the individual's economic dependence, which is directly proportionate to the employment rights they receive. Figure 3.1 and the following Hypothetical C provide a very loosely based illustration of how a legal system might put into practice such a *regulatory contractual model*.

Hypothetical C

A period of substantial growth has impelled Danny's Demolishers Ltd ('DD') to expand its workforce to service the growing number of orders received from clients. In particular, one client has placed an order and around ten workers will be needed for six months to demolish the relevant site. However, Danny is reluctant to hire more employees to perform that order owing to the perceived expense associated with employment laws. For that reason, he telephones his solicitor seeking guidance about how he can hire 'flexible workers' who would still remain under his control and direction. The solicitor suggests that DD could take on casual workers ('CWs') to perform the work required by the order. Here, a contract would be put in place with those workers containing a clause which states that they are not permitted to perform work for any other business and entitling them to bring along a substitute individual to provide the services to DD when the hired worker is unavailable or unwilling to work. Another option the solicitor proposes is for DD to hire self-employed independent contractors ('SEICs') on the basis of a contract for services which would feature a term stipulating that DD would simply be one of the clients of those individual workers.

If we plot an employee, the CWs, and the SEICs against the classificatory spectrum shown in Figure 3.1, the employee would clearly occupy the territory up to the left-hand boundary of the spectrum at Contract No. 1. Meanwhile, the CWs would be found at either of the intermediate contract types at Contract No. 2 or 3 in Figure 3.1:

• owing to the lack of consistent personal service afforded by the existence of the substitution clause in the contract struck between the CWs and DD; and

• on the basis of the level of economic dependence of the CWs on DD by virtue of the contractual term precluding them from working for another employer or organization.

Finally, the SEICs would fall into Contract No. 4 at the right-hand boundary of the spectrum in Figure 3.1, since the contractual term permitting them to provide services to other organizations is suggestive of a distinct lack of economic dependence on DD. For that reason, we can conclude that the SEICs probably fall outside the remit of employment laws.

Having introduced the possible approaches a legal system might apply in constructing the applicable central organizing contractual concept or concepts, we now turn to the first of the cross-cutting issues which a jurisdiction must also consider. This is the question of the *breadth* of that contractual concept. To some extent, this overlaps with our discussion relating to the notional classificatory spectrum. However, it goes further. A deeper consideration of the appropriate breadth of operation of employment laws reveals that the exact location of the outer left-hand boundary in Figure 3.1 is by no means fixed. For example, Hepple has suggested that the outer rim ought to be stretched in a leftwards direction from the 'contract of employment' at Contract No. 1, so that the law confers employment rights in favour of a wider class of individuals supplying labour to a hirer on the basis of a contract:

■ B. Hepple, 'Restructuring Employment Rights' (1986) 15 *Industrial Law Journal* 69, 74

> The contract of service should be replaced by a broad definition of an 'employment relationship' between the worker and the undertaking by which he is employed. That relationship would of course, be based upon voluntary agreement between the worker and the undertaking to work in return for pay. The insistence on agreement makes it appropriate to describe this as a 'contract' rather than a 'status,' but it would be a 'contract' of a new kind, one that encompassed both the intermittent exchange of work for remuneration, and the single continuous contract.

A similar approach is suggested by Collins, who advocates the adoption of a legal presumption that a contract of employment will be deemed to exist where a worker is engaged in the performance of services for another pursuant to any form of contractual arrangement.[36] Alternatively, Langstaff has suggested focusing on 'arrangements', which seems somewhat similar to the 'contractual' approach and Hepple's reliance on 'agreement'.[37] Meanwhile, Freedland originally favoured[38] a more nuanced and refined approach, whilst also advocating that the boundary of the outer tier at Contract No. 1 (Figure 3.1) be moved further to the left so as to be configured around the 'personal employment contract'.[39]

Not only is the question of the relational scope of employment laws shaped by the breadth of the chosen central organizing contractual concept, but the approach it takes to the existence of that concept through the process of adjudication in individual cases is also paramount. This second cross-cutting consideration is particularly relevant since no special form is required to create a contract for the provision of services, which can

[36] H. Collins, 'Independent Contractors and the Challenge of Vertical Disintegration to Employment Protection Laws' (1990) 10 *Oxford Journal of Legal Studies* 353, 378–9.

[37] Sir Brian Langstaff, 'Changing Times, Changing Relationships at Work . . . Changing Law?' (2016) 45 *Industrial Law Journal* 131, 142.

[38] It should be stressed, however, that Freedland's thinking has shifted towards a model less wedded to the contractual schema, e.g. see M. Freedland and N. Kountouris, 'Towards a Comparative Theory of the Contractual Construction of Personal Work Relations in Europe' (2008) 37 *Industrial Law Journal* 49; and M. Freedland and N. Kountouris, *The Legal Construction of Personal Work Relations* (Oxford, OUP, 2011).

[39] M. Freedland, *The Personal Employment Contract* (Oxford, OUP, 2003) 28–31. The expression the 'personal employment contract' is a reference to the contract of employment and the semi-dependent workers' contract.

be constituted in writing, orally, or by the conduct of the parties. Here, we address the 'literal/contextual' consideration which we put forward as an important factor. For instance, in contrast with a *contextual* or *factual* evaluation of a contract, a *literal* appraisal of a contract will often result in *fewer*, rather than *more*, individual suppliers of services being included within the scope of employment protection laws. Jurisdictions preferring a literal approach will generally defer to the express wishes of the contracting parties. This is perfectly rational as it can be justified on the ground that it enables a court to reflect the true intentions of the parties, consistent with the degree of respect afforded by the law of contract to autonomy, consent, and intention. However, contracts for the supply of services are 'contracts of adhesion' in the sense that they are usually prepared by enterprises that enjoy greater bargaining power than the individuals concerned and are presented to them on a 'take it or leave it' basis.[40] They will often contain clauses denying the individual the benefit of employment status. As such, where a literal assessment is preferred by a jurisdiction's judiciary, this functions to legitimize the enterprise's inherent capacity to frustrate the operation of employment protection laws. The *literal* approach has been traditionally associated with common law jurisdictions:

■ *Express & Echo Publications Ltd v Tanton* [1999] ICR 693, 697F–H

Peter Gibson LJ:

Clause 3.3 to my mind vividly illustrates the difficulty in approaching the identification of the terms of the agreement by concentrating on what actually occurred rather than looking at the obligations by which the parties were bound. Of course, it is important that the industrial tribunal should be alert in this area of the law to look at the reality of any obligations. If the obligation is a sham it will want to say so. But to concentrate on what actually occurred may not elucidate the full terms of the contract. If a term is not enforced that does not justify a conclusion that such a term is not part of the agreement.[41]

However, there are signs that the position is now changing by virtue of the decisions of the Supreme Court in *Autoclenz Ltd v Belcher*[42] and the House of Lords in *Carmichael v National Power plc*.[43] It is now clear that the courts are less reluctant to:

• reclassify contracts as contracts of employment when they are in fact a sham and fail to reflect what was actually agreed between the parties or their true intentions;[44] or

• classify contracts in accordance with the surrounding circumstances, oral exchanges, and how the parties conducted themselves subsequent to contractual formation.

The latter will be relevant where it appears from the terms of the contract and/or from what the parties said or did that such documents were not intended to constitute an exclusive memorial of the parties' agreement.[45]

---

[40] See H. Collins, *Employment Law*, 2nd edition (Oxford, OUP, 2010) 6–8; H. Collins, *Regulating Contracts* (Oxford, OUP, 1999) 228–36; F. Kessler 'Contracts of Adhesion: Some Thoughts about Freedom of Contract' (1943) 43 *Columbia Law Review* 629; P. Davies and M. Freedland, *Kahn-Freund's Labour and the Law* (London, Stevens & Sons, 1983) 31; and T. Rakoff, 'Contracts of Adhesion: An Essay in Reconstruction' (1983) 96 *Harvard Law Review* 1174.

[41] See also *Staffordshire Sentinel Newspapers Ltd v Potter* [2004] IRLR 752, 753 per Judge Peter Clark.

[42] [2011] UKSC 41, [2011] 4 All ER 745, [2011] ICR 1157.   [43] [1999] 1 WLR 2042.

[44] *Autoclenz Ltd v Belcher* [2011] ICR 1157, 1163C–D and 1167A–1168H per Lord Clarke. For example, see *Boss Projects LLP v Bragg* (UKEAT/0330/13/SM, 6 November 2013).

[45] [1999] 1 WLR 2042, 2047B–D, 2049C–D, and 2051A–C per Lord Irvine of Lairg QC and Lord Hoffmann. The force of this approach will be greater where the nature of the work is unusual, the arrangement is ad hoc and informal and a variety of circumstances and factors have to be taken into account, and/or there has been a conscious modification of the basis of the employee's employment.

The predominant 'literal/contextual' approach in the UK can be contrasted with the 'contrasting mindset'[46] at play in EU Continental jurisdictions such as France. Here, the emphasis is on the *contextual* and *factual* reality of the parties' relationship. Rather than placing emphasis on the terms of the parties' written agreement, such jurisdictions curtail the ability of enterprises to avoid the operation of employment laws by careful contracting. Instead, the courts will routinely look behind the contractual documentation and apply a more *contextual* approach to identify the nature of the working relationship. If the *factual* reality fails to accord with the documentation and is consistent with the existence of a contract of employment, the courts will characterize the engagement as an employment contract, notwithstanding any term of the documentation rejecting such a connection. Since the enterprise invariably wields greater bargaining power than the individual service provider and has the upper hand in framing the terms of the contractual documentation, the adoption of a *contextual* approach by a legal system amounts to a policy decision to recognize a much wider relational scope to its employment laws than that associated with the *literal* assessment.

If we now turn to the other major policy option available to a jurisdiction, namely the non-contractual model, the outcome of its application is that relationships which cannot be fitted into the contractual analysis may nonetheless fall within the relational scope of employment laws. According to such a non-contractual scheme, whether an individual is entitled to the benefit of employment protection laws would not be governed by the existence of a particular form or forms of contract—such as the contract of employment. Instead the focus would be on the relational character of the arrangement, duly divorced from the lexicon of contract. This would include consideration of factors such as the exchange of services for remuneration and the existence of subordination, domination, direction, supervision, and/or control of the individual supplier of labour. For example, Rideout has argued that '[o]nly by an open admission of a status of employment can the law hope to keep pace with the practicality of the industrial scene . . . [and that s]tatus alone is the real guarantee of the workers' rights and there is no reason why, having built on the wrong foundation [of the contract of employment] 150 years ago, the law should not now reappraise its attitude'.[47] Likewise, Supiot's vision involves offering the protection of employment laws to individuals providing personal services and in an economically dependent position vis-à-vis the enterprise. This radical approach would afford employment rights to a broad variety of individuals, predicated on their labour force membership status.[48] Another suggestion has been put forward by Freedland and Kountouris whereby employment laws would be arranged around a central organizing concept of the 'personal work relation'. This emphasis on 'personal work' entails a conscious 'move into the sphere of "the personal contract for services" and of relations of "personal self-employment" . . . only the first of which has traditionally or classically been regarded as the proper sphere of employment law'.[49] However, the drawback of grounding employment law on the foundation of a 'relationship' or notions of 'work relations' is that such concepts often mask the fact that the criteria for their establishment will likely mimic those which we apply to identify an employment contract alongside perhaps the addition of 'dependency' and/or 'subordination'. Consider the following extract:

[46] See M. Freedland and N. Kountouris, 'Towards a Comparative Theory of the Contractual Construction of Personal Work Relations in Europe' (2008) 37 *Industrial Law Journal* 49, 66.

[47] R. W. Rideout, 'The Contract of Employment' (1966) 19 *Current Legal Problems* 111, 127.

[48] A. Supiot, *Beyond Employment: Changes in Work and the Future of Labour Law in Europe* (Oxford, OUP, 2001) 219–22.

[49] M. Freedland and N. Kountouris, *The Legal Construction of Personal Work Relations* (Oxford, OUP, 2011) 434.

■ Sir Brian Langstaff, 'Changing Times, Changing Relationships at
Work . . . Changing Law?' (2016) 45 *Industrial Law Journal* 131, 142

What of abandonment of the contractual concept? If it were to be abandoned what would replace it? Primacy could be given to 'the employment relationship' rather than the need for contract. But when discussing this with European Labour Court Judges, it is apparent that each EU Jurisdiction adopts a similar approach—the cardinal features of the employment relationship are those identified by Arden LJ in *Halawi* [v *WDFG UK (t/a World Duty Free)* [2015] IRLR 50, i.e. whether, on the one hand, the person concerned performed services for and under the direction of another person in return for which he or she received remuneration or, on the other hand, he or she was an independent provider of services who was not in a relationship of subordination with the person who received the services]. They might add 'economic dependence' to our UK List but that concept taken in isolation is apt to include relationships which no one would recognise as requiring the same degree of protection. The farmer who will sell his produce to anyone, but who enjoys a contract by which 80% of it is taken by Tesco, is economically dependent, but no one would regard him as a worker for, or employee of, Tesco.

Finally, there is a completely different non-contractual model through which the relational scope of employment laws could be channelled, namely through the prism of constitutionalized employment rights. The transformative potential of classifying employment rights as constitutional rights is grounded in the ability to entrench those rights so that they are rendered mandatory/inderogable and furnished to workers generally. Under such a scheme, employment rights are not dependent on the existence of a contract. As such, when they clash or come into contact with the rights or freedoms of employers implied by the common law or employment protection legislation, the latter will give way to the constitutionally guaranteed employment rights. Moreover, the express disapplication or waiver of these rights is precluded. One of the other appeals of conferring employment rights through constitutional means lies in its capacity to reclaim the workplace from the orthodox neo-liberal practice of subjecting it to the laws of the free market and globalization,[50] with its emphasis on sacrificing employment laws on the altar of economic efficiency, competitiveness, and flexibility.[51] To that extent, the rhetoric that employment rights *are* constitutional rights is an important means by which proponents of social justice seek to recalibrate the balance of power between labour and the now extremely mobile forces of capital.[52]

This is the formulation adopted in South Africa. Sections 18 and 23(1) of the South African Constitution confer a constitutionalized labour right to 'freedom of association' and 'fair labour practices' on 'everyone'. Although a diverse range of individual and collective labour rights are afforded to *workers* and trade unions in section 23(2), (4), and (5) of the Constitution, this should not detract from the symbolic character associated with

---

[50] For an introduction to neo-liberalist thought, see R. Plant, *The Neo-Liberal State* (Oxford, OUP, 2010).

[51] R. Dukes, 'Constitutionalising Employment Relations: Sinzheimer, Kahn-Freund and the Role of Labour Law' (2008) 35 *Journal of Law and Society* 341, 341–2, and 361–2; H. Arthurs, 'The Constitutionalization of Employment Relations: Multiple Models, Pernicious Problems' (2010) 19 *Social & Legal Studies* 403, 404; J. Fudge, 'The New Discourse of Labor Rights: From Social to Fundamental Rights' (2007) 29 *Comparative Labor Law and Policy Journal* 29, 29–32; and P. Alston, 'Labour Rights as Human Rights: The Not So Happy State of the Art' in P. Alston (ed.), *Labour Rights as Human Rights* (Oxford, OUP, 2005) 1, 4–5.

[52] Lord Wedderburn, 'Labour Law 2008: 40 Years On' (2007) 36 *Industrial Law Journal* 397, 404; H. Arthurs, 'The Constitutionalization of Employment Relations: Multiple Models, Pernicious Problems' (2010) 19 *Social & Legal Studies* 403, 405–15.

labour rights being conferred in the abstract upon 'everyone', rather than an 'employee' or 'worker'. This amounts to the conscious deliverance of employment rights from the otherwise all-pervasive contractual framework, resulting in a much broader relational scope of employment laws. However, it should be stressed that constitutionalizing employment rights is not an entirely benign endeavour without its attendant risks. There is the danger that labour law could disappear as a rational discipline, its uniform fabric ruptured by constitutional law. Indeed, this 'decompartmentalization' of employment law is a real concern in South Africa, where scholars have articulated the fear that labour law as an autonomous body of learning is in grave peril of becoming extinct and generally subsumed by the burgeoning discipline of constitutional law.[53]

On a more profound note, it should be stressed that a policy designed to establish a broad relational scope of employment laws can be something of a double-edged sword. It gives rise to an anxiety that employment law might lose its 'normative edge' and stray beyond its legitimate boundaries by affording rights to individual suppliers of labour who are not necessarily deserving of employment protection:

■ M. Freedland, 'From the Contract of Employment to the Personal Work Nexus' (2006) 35 *Industrial Law Journal* 1, 28–9

The anxiety to which I refer . . . is a fear that, as one extends the frontiers of [employment] law to include contracts or relationships formerly regarded as outside the territory, because they are more in the nature of business contracts or relationships with independent contractors, so one risks foregoing the normative claim for [employment] law to constitute an autonomous legal domain within which inequality of bargaining power between worker and employer may be taken for granted, and where protection of the worker against unfair exploitation is therefore a paramount and systemic rationale for law-making and for adjudication. This fear has, however, generally been a rather muted one, if only because the discussion has mainly concentrated upon modest or intermediate extensions of the personal scope of employment law, which can be envisaged as reaching out to working people who, although deemed independent, are, in reality, at least semi-dependent upon employing enterprises, and as vulnerable to exploitation as workers in the 'employee' category.

This muted anxiety becomes the more strident as we further extend the personal scope of employment law . . . It becomes hard to see how the normative edge of [employment] law can fail to be blunted by the [enlargement of the] framework of analysis. Two alternative particular dangers present themselves . . . Either the worker-protective envelope of [employment] law will fail to 'stick' at the entrepreneurial margins to which the 'family of personal work contracts' theory seeks to pin them or, on the other hand, the inclusionary category will prevail but at the cost of a normatively crippling compromise with the economic and social neutrality of general private contract and commercial law.[54]

The enlargement of the relational scope of employment laws—with more, rather than fewer, individuals falling within the purview of common law and statutory employment protection laws—also has implications for the unemployed. The danger is that an ever-growing gulf will emerge between the privileged individual employee as a supplier of labour, on the one hand, and the disadvantaged unemployed, bereft of any employment

---

[53] S. Van Eck, 'Constitutionalisation of South African Labour Law' in C. Fenwick and T. Novitz (eds), *Human Rights at Work: Perspectives on Law and Regulation* (Oxford, Hart Publishing, 2010) 290.

[54] See also B. Langille, 'Labour Law's Theory of Justice' in G. Davidov and B. Langille (eds), *The Idea of Labour Law* (Oxford, OUP, 2011) 107–9; M. Freedland and N. Kountouris, *The Legal Construction of Personal Work Relations* (Oxford, OUP, 2011) 437–9; G. Davidov, 'Setting Labour Law's Coverage: Between Universalism and Selectivity' (2014) 34 *Oxford Journal of Legal Studies* 543, 566.

or employment protection, on the other hand. The potential for such segmentation to take root with the attendant social, political, and economic costs is a matter of concern not to be taken lightly.[55]

Reflection points

1. In your opinion, what is the appropriate relational scope of employment laws? Give reasons for your answer.

2. Which of the *literal* or *contextual* approaches to the evaluation and classification of a contract do you prefer?

3. In your opinion, should the contractual model be abandoned in favour of a more relational rather than contractual construct? What are the potential disadvantages of adopting a more inclusive relational construct as the central organizing concept for the purposes of employment law?

 For additional reading on the policy options, visit the Online Resources for this book at www.oup.com/uk/cabrelli3e/

3.2 IDENTIFYING AND CLASSIFYING THE CONTRACT OF EMPLOYMENT

The preceding discussion noted the prevailing judicial policy in the UK towards the determination of the category of individuals eligible to claim common law and statutory employment rights. This entails assessing whether such individuals have entered into a contract of service/employment or a contract for services with a hirer of their labour. The common law has traditionally conceptualized matters in terms of which side of this binary divide an individual falls. However, for the reasons outlined, this is a somewhat crude approach somewhat removed from reality. Instead, it is perhaps better to think of an individual supplier of labour as falling somewhere within a classificatory spectrum, with the contract of employment at one end and the contract for services at the other. Throughout an individual's working life with an enterprise, he/she may travel along the spectrum from the contract for services to the contract of employment (or in the opposite direction), and such a process may be negotiated in a smooth movement or a jagged progression or 'jump' from one camp to the other. The separation between the contract of service and contract for services is also particularly fraught, since 'two individuals may be engaged in discharging absolutely identical functions for the same employer but, nevertheless, the legal classification of the contracts under which they are engaged may not be the same'.[56]

---

[55] A. Davies, 'Identifying "Exploitative Compromises": The Role of Labour Law in Resolving Disputes Between Workers' (2012) 65 *Current Legal Problems* 269; A. Davies, '"Half a Person": A Legal Perspective on Organizing and Representing "Non-Standard" Workers' in A. Bogg and T. Novitz (eds), *Voices at Work* (Oxford, OUP, 2014) 122.

[56] D. Brodie, *The Employment Contract: Legal Principles, Drafting, and Interpretation* (Oxford, OUP, 2005) 1. The extent to which employment law should continue to conceive of the employer functions as exercisable by a single entity has recently been questioned by Prassl: J. Prassl, *The Concept of the Employer* (Oxford, OUP, 2015); J. Prassl, 'The Notion of the Employer' (2013) 129 *Law Quarterly Review* 380; E. McGaughey, 'Social Rights and the Function of Employing Entities' (2017) 37 *Oxford Journal of Legal Studies* 482.

The judiciary have devised several tests to identify the contract of service and to distinguish it from the contract for services. This forms the primary focus of this section. If the prevailing judicial policy is to draw the tests for the identification of the contract of employment too narrowly, the danger is that this will afford employers much greater leeway to indirectly contract out of employment protection laws. Conversely, if the courts develop criteria that are too broad, there is scope for the anxiety identified by Freedland in section 3.1.2 to materialize, undermining the legitimacy of employment law as an autonomous discipline.

3.2.1 The tests

There are numerous reported cases that address the employment status of individuals. In fact, this is one of the key areas for employment litigation since so many employment laws and rights revolve around the existence of employment status. In this section, we have attempted to carefully limit our discussion of the tests for the establishment of the employment contract to those reported decisions that underscore certain central points about the nature of those tests (or indicators of employment status) that are routinely applied by the courts. We also take account of recent key decisions in the narrative where appropriate in order to underline modern trends in the structure of contracts for the personal supply of labour.

The starting point for our discussion is section 230(1) and (2) of the ERA. This provides a definition of an 'employee' for the purposes of the employment protection rights conferred under that statute:

> ### Section 230 Employees, workers etc.
>
> (1) In this Act 'employee' means an individual who has entered into or works under (or, where the employment has ceased, worked under) a contract of employment.
>
> (2) In this Act 'contract of employment' means a contract of service or apprenticeship, whether express or implied, and (if it is express) whether oral or in writing.[57]

Of course—bar the trite observation that a contract of some kind, express or implied, oral or in writing, must be in place[58]—this statutory definition does not take us much further forward. In response, the tribunals and courts have relied on the tests developed by the common law to identify the hallmarks of a contract of service. Here, we encounter our very first example of the symbiotic relationship between statutory employment protection rights and the common law of the contract of employment, which we highlighted in Chapter 2.[59]

Before we embark on an exposition of the common law tests, it is worthwhile first identifying whether the classification exercise is a question of fact or law. This matters, since if the issue is one of law, the decision of an employment tribunal may be appealed to the Employment Appeal Tribunal ('EAT')[60] and upwards to the Court of Appeal and the Supreme Court, but not so if it is a matter of fact:

---

[57] Similar provisions are found in section 295(1) of the Trade Union and Labour Relations (Consolidation) Act 1992 and various other pieces of primary and secondary legislation which confer statutory employment protection rights.

[58] For example, the absence of a contract will be fatal to a claimant's argument that he/she is an employee, e.g. a volunteer (*X v Mid Sussex Citizens Advice Bureau* [2013] 1 All ER 1038), or an office-holder: *Sharpe v Bishop of Worcester* [2015] IRLR 663 and *Gilham v MoJ* [2017] IRLR 23.

[59] See Chapter 2, sections 2.1.1 and 2.2.1.   [60] Section 21(1) of the ETA.

■ *O'Kelly v Trusthouse Forte* [1984] QB 90, 124A–C

Sir John Donaldson MR:

The test to be applied in identifying whether a contract is one of employment or for services is a pure question of law and so is its application to the facts. But it is for the tribunal of fact not only to find those facts but to assess them qualitatively and within limits, which are indefinable in the abstract, those findings and that assessment will dictate the correct legal answer. In the familiar phrase 'it is all a question of fact and degree.' It is only if the weight given to a particular factor shows a self-misdirection in law that an appellate court with a limited jurisdiction can interfere. It is difficult to demonstrate such a misdirection and, to the extent that it is not done, the issue is one of fact.

This approach was refined by Lord Griffiths in the Privy Council in the case of *Lee Ting Sang v Chung Chi-Keung*.[61] Here, it was held that, in a routine case, the classification of a contract as a contract of service or a contract for services will be a question of fact rather than law for the employment tribunal or trial court to ascertain:

■ *Lee Ting Sang v Chung Chi-Keung* [1990] 2 AC 374, 385E–F

Lord Griffiths:

... The decision will depend upon the evaluation of many facts and there will be many borderline cases in which similarly instructed minds may come to different conclusions. It is in such situations that an appeal court must not interfere and it is in this sense that the decision is said to be one of fact.

As such, pursuant to the approach in *Lee Ting Sang v Chung Chi-Keung*, the position now seems to be that the test for distinguishing a contract of employment from a contract for services is a question of law, but that the application of the test, or tests, in a particular case is a question of fact.[62]

We now move on to consider the tests developed by the common law to identify the contract of employment.[63] First, we address the 'control test'. This is the most venerable test, stretching back to the 1880s[64] when the impact of workmen's compensation and social insurance legislation compelled the courts to develop a yardstick which would enable them to distinguish between manual and non-manual workers. The modern exposition of the control test is as follows:

---

[61] [1990] 2 AC 374.

[62] See G. Pitt, 'Law, Fact and Casual Workers' (1985) 101 *Law Quarterly Review* 217; G. Pitt, 'Deciding Who is an Employee—Fact or Law?' (1990) 19 *Industrial Law Journal* 252; and S. Honeyball, *Great Debates in Employment Law* (Basingstoke, Palgrave Macmillan, 2011) 13–18.

[63] These tests owe much of their origin to the specific nature and content of the contract of employment, i.e. its 'personal/relational' and 'mutual/reciprocal' nature, as well as the inherent 'authority/power relation', which are ideas we will explore in more depth in Chapter 5, section 5.1.1. Suffice to say at this juncture that the personal nature of the employment contract manifests itself in the 'personal service' test, its mutual/reciprocal nature in the 'mutuality of obligation' test, and the authority/power relation in the 'control' test.

[64] *Yewens v Nokes* (1880) 6 QBD 330.

■ *Ready Mixed Concrete (South East) Ltd v Minister of Pensions and National Insurance* [1968] 2 QB 497, 515C–517B

Mackenna J:

I must now consider what is meant by a contract of service.

A contract of service exists if these three conditions are fulfilled. (i) The servant agrees that, in consideration of a wage or other remuneration, he will provide his own work and skill in the performance of some service for his master, (ii) He agrees, expressly or impliedly, that in the performance of that service he will be subject to the other's control in a sufficient degree to make that other master, (iii) The other provisions of the contract are consistent with its being a contract of service. I need say little about (i) and (ii).

As to (i). There must be a wage or other remuneration. Otherwise there will be no consideration, and without consideration no contract of any kind. The servant must be obliged to provide his own work and skill. Freedom to do a job either by one's own hands or by another's is inconsistent with a contract of service, though a limited or occasional power of delegation may not be . . .

As to (ii). Control includes the power of deciding the thing to be done, the way in which it shall be done, the means to be employed in doing it, the time when and the place where it shall be done. All these aspects of control must be considered in deciding whether the right exists in a sufficient degree to make one party the master and the other his servant. The right need not be unrestricted . . .

To find where the right resides one must look first to the express terms of the contract, and if they deal fully with the matter one may look no further. If the contract does not expressly provide which party shall have the right, the question must be answered in the ordinary way by implication . . .

An obligation to do work subject to the other party's control is a necessary, though not always a sufficient, condition of a contract of service. If the provisions of the contract as a whole are inconsistent with its being a contract of service, it will be some other kind of contract, and the person doing the work will not be a servant. The judge's task is to classify the contract (a task like that of distinguishing a contract of sale from one of work and labour). He may, in performing it, take into account other matters besides control.

The upshot is that the absence of managerial control will be fatal to the existence of an employment contract. A related question concerns whether a minimal level of control on the part of management is also sufficient to deny employment status. In *White v Troutbeck SA*,[65] the issue for resolution was whether certain caretakers/managers of a house and small farm estate who lived there rent-free were employees and entitled to unfair dismissal rights under the ERA. The putative employer was largely an absentee landlord and exercised a low level of actual day-to-day control over the activities of the claimants. In the employment tribunal, the low level of actual control was held to preclude the existence of a contract of employment. This was notwithstanding that the written documentation entered into between the claimants and the enterprise contained a reference to 'this employment agreement'. The decision of the employment tribunal was overruled by the EAT and in the Court of Appeal, Lord Justice Mummery agreed with the EAT, holding that a much broader evaluation of the agreement between the parties and the surrounding circumstances should be adopted. As such, the absence of actual hands-on day-to-day control will not be determinative. Instead, it is more important to evaluate whether the putative employer has the 'power to exercise control', rather than whether it exercises actual control.

Notwithstanding that it harbours the attraction of simplicity, as a stand-alone single test, the notion of control is clearly inadequate in the modern industrial context. This is

---

[65] [2013] IRLR 949.

particularly true in the case of 'persons possessed of a high degree of professional skill and expertise, such as surgeons and civil engineers'.[66] The courts have recognized that 'the test of control is . . . not as determinative as used to be thought to be the case',[67] and that such skilled employees 'may nevertheless be employed . . . notwithstanding that their employers can, in the nature of things, exercise extremely little, if any, control over the way in which such skill is used'.[68] The following passage from Kahn-Freund articulates the classic critique of the control test as the sole touchstone of employment status:

■ O. Kahn-Freund, 'Servants and Independent Contractors' (1951) 14 *Modern Law Review* 504, 505–6

The traditional test was that a person working for another was regarded as a servant if he was 'subject to the command of the master as to the manner in which he shall do his work', but if the so-called 'master' was only in a position to determine the 'what' and not the 'how' of the services, the substance of the obligation but not the manner of its performance, then the person doing the work was said to be not a servant but an independent contractor, and his contract one for work and labour and not of employment. This distinction was based upon the social conditions of an earlier age: it assumed that the employer of labour was able to direct and instruct the labourer as to the technical methods he should use in performing his work. It reflects a state of society in which the ownership of the means of production coincided with the possession of technical knowledge and skill and in which that knowledge and skill was largely acquired by being handed down from one generation to the next by oral tradition and not by being systematically imparted in institutions of learning from universities down to technical schools. The control test postulates a combination of managerial and technical functions in the person of the employer, *i.e.*, what to modern eyes appears as an imperfect division of labour. The technical and economic develop- ments of all industrial societies have nullified these assumptions. The rule respondeat superior (and, one may add, the whole body of principles governing the contract of employment) 'applies even though the work which the servant is employed to do is of a skilful or technical character, as to the method of performing which the employer himself is ignorant'. To say of the captain of a ship, the pilot of an aeroplane, the driver of a railway engine, of a motor vehicle, or of a crane that the employer 'controls' the performance of his work is unrealistic and almost grotesque. But one need not think of situations in which the employee is physically removed from his employer's premises: a skilled engineer or toolmaker, draftsman or accountant may as often as not have been engaged just because he possesses that technical knowledge which the employer lacks. If in such a case the employee relied on the employer's instructions 'how to do his work' he would be breaking his contract and possibly be liable to summary dismissal for having misrepresented his skill. No wonder that the Courts found it increasingly difficult to cope with the cases before them by using a legal rule which, as legal rules so often do, had survived the social conditions from which it had been an abstraction.

In response to the flaws inherent in the control test, the courts developed various alterna- tives. The most prominent were the 'integration' and 'economic/business reality' tests. The 'integration' test simply asked whether the individual was an integral part of the business or organization of the enterprise. If he/she was 'part and parcel' of the organiza- tion, then this was a factor tending to show that he/she was an employee.[69]

---

[66] *Whittaker v Minister of Pensions and National Insurance* [1967] 1 QB 156, 167A per Mocatta J.
[67] *ibid.*, 167B per Mocatta J.   [68] *ibid.*, 167A per Mocatta J.
[69] *Stevenson, Jordan & Harrison Ltd v Macdonald & Evans* [1952] 1 TLR 101.

Hypothetical D

Jack Oldman has a contract with Danny's Demolishers Ltd ('DD') whereby he attends DD's various premises throughout the southeast of England to fix and repair various problems with the plumbing as and when they arise. He wears the branded uniform of DD, takes lunch with individuals directly employed by DD in the staff canteens of the various premises operated by DD, and drives a van laid out in the branding and logo of DD. Jack has never thought about his employment status, but the issue comes up when he discusses his position with a representative of a trade union recognized by DD. If we apply the integration test, the branded uniform, Jack's use of canteen facilities, and the layout of the van, all suggest that he forms an integral part of DD and, as such, that he is an employee.

Nonetheless, as noted by McKenna J in *Ready Mixed Concrete (South East) Ltd v Minister of Pensions and National Insurance*,[70] the difficulty with this 'part and parcel' approach as a single test lies in its intrinsic vagueness. As for the 'economic/business reality' test, this entailed enquiring whether the performance of the work was undertaken by the individual 'in business on his own account'[71] having assumed a sufficient level of financial risk.

Hypothetical E

Jack Oldman has a contract with Danny's Demolishers Ltd ('DD') whereby he attends DD's various premises throughout the southeast of England to fix and repair various problems with the plumbing as and when they arise. He wears his own uniform, drives his own van, and provides and uses his own tools. He has clients other than DD. Jack has never thought about his employment status, but the issue comes up when he discusses his position with a representative of a trade union recognized by DD. If we apply the economic reality test, the fact that Jack has his own clients and provides his own uniform, van, and tools suggests that he is running a business on his own account and, as such, that he is not an employee of DD.

Whilst simply asking whether the individual was running a business was reassuringly straightforward, this test also suffered from deficiencies if applied as a single determinative criterion:

(1) it broke down as a suitable measure of an individual's status where that individual was carrying on a vocation or profession, e.g. not all self-employed professionals are involved in the running of a business;[72] and

---

[70] *Ready Mixed Concrete (South East) Ltd v Minister of Pensions and National Insurance* [1968] 2 QB 497, 524B per McKenna J.

[71] *Market Investigations Ltd v Minister of Social Security* [1969] 2 QB 173, 184G–H per Cooke J.

[72] The Court of Appeal has held that equity partners and fixed-share partners in a limited liability partnership ('LLP') are unlikely to be classified as employees, since they each contribute capital to the LLP, have a prospect of a share in the profits and in the surplus assets on a winding up of the firm, and a voice in relation to the management of the LLP: *Tiffin v Lester Aldridge LLP* [2012] 1 WLR 1887.

(2) it is not wholly clear whether there is any discernible or material difference in asking whether someone is working on their own account or not and enquiring whether that person is self-employed or an employee. Both sets of questions seem to amount to the same thing, leading to an undesirable degree of circularity.

In the passage from *Ready Mixed Concrete*, the point is made that there must be an exchange of work for remuneration in order for a contract to be classifiable as a contract of employment. This means that the putative employer and employee must enter into a wage–work bargain, whereby the latter undertakes work for the former and the former, rather than a third party, must actually pay[73] the employee in exchange.[74] As such, 'it would . . .be an unusual case where a contract of service is found to exist when the worker takes the economic risk and is paid exclusively by third parties'.[75] However, such a basic exchange of wages for work, i.e. the work–wage bargain, is insufficient of itself to establish employment status. The notion that the employment contract was a mutual and reciprocal contract of an indefinite nature took hold in the 1960s and 1970s. This development occurred against the backdrop of the growth in statutory employment protection legislation and the judicial categorization of the wage–work bargain struck between the employer and employee as the expression of the requisite exchange of consideration.[76] The doctrine of consideration subsequently manifested itself in the extremely important 'mutuality of obligation' test[77] applied for the purposes of identifying a continuous contract of employment:[78]

■ S. Deakin and F. Wilkinson, *The Law of the Labour Market: Industrialization, Employment, and Legal Evolution* (Oxford, OUP, 2005) 306–7

The development of a relational model of the employment contract under the influence of collective bargaining and protective legislation created its own reaction: the greater the emphasis placed by the courts upon reciprocity between employer and employee, the more problematic it became to apply the employment model to casual or irregular forms of work. The result was the 'mutuality of obligation' test for determining employee status: according to this test, in order for the court to find a contract of employment, it is necessary not just to show that there has been an exchange of work for wages, but that, in addition, there has been an exchange of mutual undertakings to be available for [a minimum or reasonable amount of] work over a period of time, on the employee's part, and to make [a minimum or reasonable amount of] work available

---

[73] Alternatively, that it is intended that the putative employer pay the putative employee or that the former is supposed to pay the latter: see *Secretary of State for Business, Innovation and Skills v Knight* [2014] IRLR 605; *Stack v Ajar-Tec Ltd* [2015] IRLR 474.

[74] However, contrast this orthodoxy with the decisions of the EAT in *Secretary of State for Business, Innovation and Skills v Knight* [2014] IRLR 605, where it was held that a majority shareholder of the putative employer who had not been paid by the putative employer for two years could nevertheless qualify as an employee since there was no need for consideration for an individual to be classified as an employee, and the Court of Appeal in *Stack v Ajar-Tec Ltd* [2015] IRLR 474, where an individual director and shareholder of a company was treated as an employee of that company notwithstanding that the parties had not expressly agreed a term regarding payment, since a term that the individual would be paid a reasonable rate was implied. See also *Department for Employment and Learning v Morgan* [2016] IRLR 350 for a similar decision.

[75] *Stringfellow Restaurants Ltd v Quashie* [2013] IRLR 99, 106 per Elias LJ.

[76] That much is apparent from the extract taken from McKenna J's judgment in *Ready Mixed Concrete (South East) Ltd v Minister of Pensions and National Insurance* [1968] 2 QB 497, 515E–F per McKenna J.

[77] See *O'Kelly v Trusthouse Forte* [1984] QB 90; *Nethermere (St Neots) Ltd v Gardiner* [1984] ICR 612; *McLeod v Hellyer Brothers Ltd* [1987] IRLR 232; *Clark v Oxfordshire Health Authority* [1998] IRLR 125, 128 at para 22 per Sir Christopher Slade; and *Carmichael v National Power plc* [1999] 1 WLR 2042.

[78] H. Collins, 'Employment Rights of Casual Workers' (2000) 29 *Industrial Law Journal* 73, 76.

[and pay for it], on the employer's. The background to the rise of the mutuality test is the now near-universal adoption of the contract of employment as the gateway to statutory rights . . . It is arguable that the mutuality of obligations test only has a tenuous connection to mainstream contract law. Although the test has antecedents in nineteenth century decisions on mutuality and the definition, for master and servant purposes, of 'exclusive service', its modern use appears to date from the period in the 1970s when the courts first undertook the task of interpreting and applying the newly created body of statutory employment protection rights. In so far as the new legislation provided employees with legal expectations of continuing income and employment in the event of interruptions to work on the grounds of lay-off, illness and maternity, as well as compensation for redundancy for unfair dismissal, it assumed a normal pattern of continuous and regular employment. The rise of the mutuality test reflects the difficulty which the courts have had in applying these rights to the growing number of employment relationships which were, by their nature, discontinuous and irregular, in particular those involving outworking, task contracts and frequent re-hirings. Like control, integration and economic reality before it, it emerged in a particular statutory and social context of employment law (see Table [3.1]). Within this context, the principal significance of the mutuality test has been to revive old notions of subordination and control in a new form. The essence of the test is that unless the worker agrees to be available for [a minimum or reasonable amount of] work on a continuing basis, and in this extended sense *at the disposal of the employer*, the agreement is said to lack the necessary mutuality of obligation. What counts here is not reciprocity in exchange as such, but a particular form of mutuality under which the worker must cede autonomy to the employer over the timing and physical location of the work in order to count as an employee. Thus in the employment sphere, 'mutuality of obligation' does not bear its normal meaning in contract law. A contract to work in return for pay will not lack 'mutuality' in the sense of the reciprocal promises needed for consideration as one of the elements in the formation of a contract. However, if the judgments of the Court of Appeal in *O'Kelly v Trusthouse Forte plc* are to be believed, such an arrangement, without more, will not be a contract of employment.

Table 3.1 *The genealogy of the tests for identifying the contract of employment*

Test	Period of pre-eminence	Initial statutory context	Function
Control	1890s–1920s	Early workmen's compensation and social insurance legislation	Enabling the courts to draw a distinction between manual and non-manual or managerial labour in the application of social legislation
Integration	1930s–1940s	Advanced workmen's compensation and social legislation	Providing an explanation for the inclusion in the 'employee' category of middle-class and managerial employees
Economic reality	1940s–1970s	Advanced social insurance and income tax legislation	Applying a purposive test to the binary divide between employees and the self-employed
Mutuality of obligation	1980s–2000s	Employment protection legislation	Reflecting judicial scepticism concerning the application of employee status to casual, agency, and freelance workers

It is common for atypical workers, such as casual workers, 'zero-hours' contract workers, task contract workers, agency workers, and homeworkers to have entered into a contract which expressly refutes the existence of such mutual commitments. For example, the contract of a zero-hours contract worker will provide that the individual has no guaranteed hours of work and that he/she agrees to be potentially available for work, although is not obliged to accept it. As such, it is unusual for such atypical workers to be classified as employees in the tribunals and courts.[79] In the extract from Deakin and Wilkinson, the point is made that the emergence of the mutuality of obligation test in the 1970s and 1980s effectively operates to leave a whole host of such atypical workers outside the relational scope of employment laws. This feeds into the debate surrounding the current controversy over the status and abuse of zero-hours contract workers[80] and 'gig economy' workers. Such workers find it extremely difficult to satisfy the mutuality of obligation test, which is a point that has been picked up in a slew of reports and reviews surrounding the rights of workers operating in the 'gig economy', such as the House of Commons Work and Pensions Committee 13th Report of Session 2016/17 on Self-Employment and the Gig Economy,[81] the House of Commons Select Committee on Business, Energy and Industrial Skills' Future World of Work and Rights of Workers Inquiry,[82] the Department for Business, Innovation and Skills' Employment Status Review,[83] the Office of Tax Simplification's Employment Status Report,[84] and of course, the Taylor Review.[85] HMRC has also produced an employment toolkit for casual workers to check their status.[86]

The leading authority on the mutuality of obligation test is *Carmichael v National Power plc*.[87] Here, the issue for determination was whether two tour guides of a power station who had entered into a contract 'on a casual as required basis', whereby they were offered, and performed, work as and when it arose, should be classified as employees. In rejecting the contention that the tour guides were employees, the House of Lords expounded the notion that mutuality of obligation amounted to one of the irreducible minimum factors inherent in a contract of employment. As such, its absence in the case at hand precluded the existence of an employment contract. Likewise, the same point was made in the decision of the Court of Appeal in *Montgomery v Johnson Underwood*.[88]

---

[79] For example, see *Saha v Viewpoint Field Services Ltd* (UKEAT/0116/13/DM, 20 February 2014). However, it is not impossible. For example, for two cases where a zero-hours contract worker was in fact treated as an employee, see *St Ives Plymouth Ltd v Haggerty* [2008] All ER (D) 317 (May) and *Pulse Healthcare Ltd v Carewatch Care Services Ltd* (UKEAT/0123/12/BA, 6 August 2012).

[80] Sections 27A–27B of the ERA ban exclusivity clauses in zero-hours contracts, i.e. express terms which prevent the individual zero-hours contract worker from working for a third party. Paradoxically, the effect of this ban is to render it even more unlikely that a zero-hours contract worker will qualify as an employee.

[81] See *Self-Employment and the Gig Economy*, available at https://publications.parliament.uk/pa/cm201617/cmselect/cmworpen/847/847.pdf (last visited 19 November 2017).

[82] See *The Future World of Work and Rights of Workers Inquiry*, available at https://www.parliament.uk/business/committees/committees-a-z/commons-select/business-energy-industrial-strategy/inquiries/parliament-2015/the-future-world-of-work-and-rights-of-workers-16–17/ (last visited 19 November 2017).

[83] Employment Status Review, available at https://www.gov.uk/government/uploads/system/uploads/attachment_data/file/585383/employment-status-review-2015.pdf (last visited 19 November 2017).

[84] See *Employment Status Report*, available at https://www.gov.uk/government/uploads/system/uploads/attachment_data/file/537432/OTS_Employment_Status_report_March_2016_u.pdf (last visited 19 November 2017).

[85] See *Good Work: The Taylor Review of Modern Working Practices* (July 2017), available at https://www.gov.uk/government/uploads/system/uploads/attachment_data/file/627671/good-work-taylor-review-modern-working-practices-rg.pdf (last visited 19 November 2017).

[86] See *Check Employment Status for Tax*, available at https://www.gov.uk/guidance/check-employment-status-for-tax (last visited 19 November 2017).

[87] [1999] 1 WLR 2042, 2047B per Lord Irvine.   [88] [2001] ICR 819, 831B–C per Buckley J.

In *Montgomery*, in holding that an agency worker was not an employee, the existence of a sufficient degree of control (i.e. the control test) was also cited as an additional irreducible minimum criterion.

Although it is undoubtedly the law that mutuality of obligation is an essential criterion for the establishment of employment status, scholars have questioned the high standing that it has been afforded by the courts. For example, Countouris has argued that the 'time might have come for English law to reassess the function of mutuality of obligations . . . [whereby] the concept ought to embrace a more sober demeanour in which fewer, and arguably clearer, functions are assigned to it'.[89] In fact, insofar as the common law treats mutuality of obligation as necessary in order to articulate and reflect the stability, continuity, and relationality of the contractual employment relationship, it is not entirely clear why such a device is treated as a prerequisite for employment when one considers that an implied default rule is prescribed by the common law that the contract of employment is indefinite in nature.[90]

In *Express & Echo Publications v Tanton*[91]—a case concerning the status of a delivery driver—the requirement for personal service on the part of the individual supplier of labour was also added as an irreducible minimum requirement for the establishment of employment status. Thus, we find that the basic ingredients for a contract of service are threefold: mutuality of obligation, control, and personal service. The absence of any one of these factors is fatal to the existence of an employment contract. As for the element of personal service, in *Express & Echo Publications v Tanton* the effect of a 'substitution' or 'delegation' clause in a contract was considered. This is a clause permitting an individual supplier of labour A to send along another person B to perform the services personally if A were 'unable or unwilling' to do so. *Staffordshire Sentinel Newspapers Ltd v Potter*[92] is another case to have addressed such clauses. Here, it was held that the irreducible minimum of personal service was missing since a substitution clause gave the individual supplier of labour A an unfettered power to send along a substitute B. Meanwhile, in *McFarlane v Glasgow City Council*,[93] it was held that a contract did not cease to be a contract for personal service simply because there was a clause empowering A to substitute or delegate in a limited sense.[94] Here, the substitution clause provided that if the qualified gym instructor were 'unable'—rather than 'unable or unwilling' (as in *Express & Echo Publications v Tanton*)—to take a class, she would be required to arrange for a replacement from a register of coaches maintained by the employer. Since the employer effectively had a power of veto over any substitute worker put forward by the gym instructor where she was unable to work, she was held to be an employee.

What is particularly interesting about the historical judicial approach to these substitution clauses is the extent to which it provided substantial leeway for employers to dislodge the necessary personal service required to establish a contract of service. The use of such a clause gives rise to 'disguised employment', i.e. the employer disguising what is in reality employment as a contract for services. The following excerpt from *Staffordshire Sentinel Newspapers Ltd v Potter*[95] illustrates the reluctance of the judiciary to consult the factual matrix behind the contractual documentation, which of course, would be drawn up by the employer:

---

[89] N. Countouris, 'Uses and Misuses of "Mutuality of Obligations" and the Autonomy of Labour Law' in A. Bogg, C. Costello, A. C. L. Davies, and J. Prassl (eds), *The Autonomy of Labour Law* (Oxford, Hart Publishing, 2015) 187.

[90] *De Stempel v Dunkels* [1938] 1 All ER 238, 246G–H, and 259 per Greer LJ and Scott LJ; *McClelland v Northern Ireland General Health Services Board* [1957] 1 WLR 594; and *Richardson v Koefod* [1969] 1 WLR 1812, 1816C–F per Lord Denning MR.

[91] [1999] ICR 693, 699G per Peter Gibson LJ.   [92] [2004] IRLR 752.   [93] [2001] IRLR 7.

[94] This is consistent with the judgment of Mackenna J in *Ready Mixed Concrete (South East) Ltd v Minister of Pensions and National Insurance* [1968] 2 QB 497, 515E.

[95] [2004] IRLR 752.

■ *Staffordshire Sentinel Newspapers Ltd v Potter* (UKEAT/0022/04/DM, 18 March 2004)

> *His Honour Judge Peter Clark:*
>
> We accept [counsel for the employer's] analysis of these two cases, *Tanton* and *McFarlane*. They are not inconsistent with each other as a matter of principle, indeed they are entirely consistent. The critical question is what is the relevant contractual term? Where there is no clear express term in writing then it may be necessary to look at the overall factual matrix in order to discern that term—see *Carmichael v National Power plc* [2000] IRLR 43. However, where the term is clear from the contractual document that course is unnecessary, subject to variation of the term or where it can be said to be a sham, to use Peter Gibson LJ's expression in *Tanton*.[96]

It should be stressed that if each of the three basic elements of mutuality of obligation, control, and personal service is present, this does not automatically compel a tribunal or court to treat the individual as an employee. Instead, the judiciary will often look for the existence of additional factors before finding that a contract of employment is in place:

■ *Ready Mixed Concrete (South East) Ltd v Minister of Pensions and National Insurance* [1968] 2 QB 497, 516–17B

> *Mackenna J:*
>
> The third and negative condition [of a contract of service] is for my purpose the important one, and I shall try with the help of five examples to explain what I mean by provisions inconsistent with the nature of a contract of service.
>
> (i) A contract obliges one party to build for the other, providing at his own expense the necessary plant and materials. This is not a contract of service, even though the builder may be obliged to use his own labour only and to accept a high degree of control: it is a building contract. It is not a contract to serve another for a wage, but a contract to produce a thing (or a result) for a price.
>
> (ii) A contract obliges one party to carry another's goods, providing at his own expense everything needed for performance. This is not a contract of service, even though the carrier may be obliged to drive the vehicle himself and to accept the other's control over his performance: it is a contract of carriage.
>
> (iii) A contract obliges a labourer to work for a builder, providing some simple tools, and to accept the builder's control. Notwithstanding the obligation to provide the tools, the contract is one of service. That obligation is not inconsistent with the nature of a contract of service. It is not a sufficiently important matter to affect the substance of the contract.
>
> (iv) A contract obliges one party to work for the other, accepting his control, and to provide his own transport. This is still a contract of service. The obligation to provide his own transport does not affect the substance. Transport in this example is incidental to the main purpose of the contract. Transport in the second example was the essential part of the performance.
>
> (v) The same instrument provides that one party shall work for the other subject to the other's control, and also that he shall sell him his land. The first part of the instrument is no less a contract of service because the second part imposes obligations of a different kind . . .

---

[96] Sourced from BAILII at http://www.bailii.org/cgi-bin/markup.cgi?doc=/uk/cases/UKEAT/2004/0022_04_1803.html&query=staffordshire+and+sentinel+and+newspapers+and+ltd.+and+v+and+potter&method=boolean (last visited 19 November 2017).

This extract shows that, in addition to the three elementary requirements of mutuality of obligation, control, and personal service, the courts will apply a multifactorial approach involving consideration of a constellation of factors. The more affirmative the responses produced to the following questions, the more likely it is that the individual will be classified as an employee:

- Has the individual made no investment of capital in his/her work and does the individual suffer no risk of loss in his/her work?
- Does the individual pay income tax and National Insurance contributions as an employee instead of VAT on the provision of his/her services?
- Does the enterprise supply tools, uniforms, stationery, equipment, or materials to the individual?
- Is the individual paid a wage or salary instead of a fee, commission, or royalties?
- Is the individual subject to the enterprise's disciplinary or grievance procedures?

Where these questions are posed, but the answers are evenly balanced, the court may have regard to the label the parties have attached to their relationship to break the deadlock.[97] For example, in *Stringfellow Restaurants Ltd v Quashie*,[98] the Court of Appeal was called upon to decide whether a lap dancer was an employee or an independent contractor. Having held that there was substantial control but no wage–work bargain—the putative employer did not engage and pay the claimant to dance for clients, but instead afforded her the opportunity to dance for clients, whereupon the claimant would be paid exclusively by these clients—Lord Justice Elias remarked that 'it is legitimate for a court to have regard to the way in which the parties have chosen to categorise the relationship, and in a case where the position is uncertain, it can be decisive'.[99]

Traditionally, it was very difficult to satisfy the court that a written term of a contract was a 'sham'. The sham test[100] required a claimant to show that both parties had included a written term in their contract with the explicit intention of painting a 'false picture as to the true nature of their respective obligations',[101] i.e. that there was a mutual intention to deceive the outside world. However, in an extremely progressive decision, which has wide-ranging implications for the classification and content of the contract of employment, Lord Clarke in the Supreme Court in *Autoclenz Ltd v Belcher*[102] extended the reach of the 'sham' doctrine. It should be understood that this decision came some time after 'mutuality of obligation' had been cemented by the House of Lords in *Carmichael v National Power*[103] as a necessary, but not sufficient, condition for the establishment of a contract of employment. The effect of *Autoclenz Ltd v Belcher* is that there is now greater scope for individual workers to invoke the 'sham' doctrine as a means of persuading a tribunal or court that the terms of written contractual documentation regulating employment status should be overlooked and the contract classified as one of employment:

---

[97] *Massey v Crown Life Assurance* [1978] ICR 590, 594 per Lord Denning MR.

[98] [2013] IRLR 99.   [99] *ibid.*, 106.

[100] *Snook v London and West Riding Investments Ltd* [1967] 2 QB 786; *Consistent Group Ltd v Kalwak* [2008] EWCA Civ 430, [2008] IRLR 505. See A. Davies, 'Sensible Thinking about Sham Transactions: *Protectacoat Firthglow Ltd v Szilagyi*' (2009) 38 *Industrial Law Journal* 318 and A. Bogg, 'Sham Self-Employment in the Court of Appeal' (2010) 126 *Law Quarterly Review* 166.

[101] *Autoclenz Ltd v Belcher* [2011] ICR 1157, 1166G–H per Lord Clarke. See J. McClelland, 'A Purposive Approach to Employment Protection or a Missed Opportunity?' (2012) 75 *Modern Law Review* 427; A. Bogg, 'Sham Self-Employment in the Supreme Court' (2012) 41 *Industrial Law Journal* 328; and A. Davies, 'Employment Law' in E. Simpson and M. Stewart (eds), *Sham Transactions* (Oxford, OUP, 2013) 176.

[102] [2011] ICR 1157.   [103] [1999] 1 WLR 2042.

■ *Autoclenz Ltd v Belcher* [2011] ICR 1157, 1168

[The headnote to the case sets forth the facts as follows:] The claimants carried out car cleaning services on behalf of the respondent company. In order to obtain the work, they were required to sign contracts which stated that they were subcontractors, and not employees, that they had to provide their own materials, that they were not obliged to provide services to the company, nor was the company obliged to offer work to them, and that they could provide suitably qualified substitutes to carry out the work on their behalf.

Lord Clarke:

Aikens LJ [in the Court of Appeal decision] stressed at paras 90–92 the importance of identifying what were the actual legal obligations of the parties. He expressly agreed with Smith LJ's analysis of the legal position in [*Protectacoat Firthglow Ltd v Szilagyi* [2009] IRLR 365] and in paras 47–53 in this case. In addition, he correctly warned against focusing on the 'true intentions' or 'true expectations' of the parties because of the risk of concentrating too much on what were the private intentions of the parties. He added:

'What the parties privately intended or expected (either before or after the contract was agreed) *may* be evidence of what, objectively discerned, was actually agreed between the parties . . . But ultimately what matters is only what was agreed, either as set out in the written terms or, if it is alleged those terms are not accurate, what is proved to be their actual agreement at the time the contract was concluded. I accept, of course, that the agreement may not be express; it may be implied. But the court or tribunal's task is still to ascertain what was agreed.'

I agree.

At para 103 Sedley LJ said that he was entirely content to adopt the reasoning of Aikens LJ:

'recognising as it does that while employment is a matter of contract, the factual matrix in which the contract is cast is not ordinarily the same as that of an arm's length commercial contract.'

I agree.

The critical difference between this type of case and the ordinary commercial dispute is identified by Aikens LJ in para 92 as follows:

'. . . the circumstances in which contracts relating to work or services are concluded are often very different from those in which commercial contracts between parties of equal bargaining power are agreed. I accept that, frequently, organisations which are offering work or requiring services to be provided by individuals are in a position to dictate the written terms which the other party has to accept. In practice, in this area of the law, it may be more common for a court or tribunal to have to investigate allegations that the written contract does not represent the actual terms agreed and the court or tribunal must be realistic and worldly wise when it does so.'

So the relative bargaining power of the parties must be taken into account in deciding whether the terms of any written agreement in truth represent what was agreed and the true agreement will often have to be gleaned from all the circumstances of the case, of which the written agreement is only a part. This may be described as a purposive approach to the problem. If so, I am content with that description.

A note of caution ought to be struck about the breadth of the decision in *Autoclenz*. Although it undoubtedly adopts a liberal approach to the application of the 'sham' doctrine, its impact may perhaps turn out to be less radical than initially thought for the following reasons:

(1) The final passage in the extract from *Autoclenz* should not be read as saying that inequality of bargaining power per se will function to compel the court to characterize a contract as one of employment. Many contracts for the personal performance of work are typified by a disequilibrium in bargaining power. Of itself, such disparity

in power will be insufficient justification to treat a contract as a sham.[104] Instead, inequality of bargaining power must be accompanied by contractual terms imposed by the enterprise which fail to reflect the reality of the situation and the true agreement of the parties considered objectively in the round having evaluated 'all the relevant evidence'.

(2) It is not enough for the individual claimant simply to point towards a degree of divergence between the written terms of the contract of employment and the actual practice of the parties. The passage from *Autoclenz* advises the judiciary to be alive to the possibility that the rights conferred by the written contract are genuine notwithstanding that they have not been exercised in practice, e.g. a substitution clause.

The existence of these two factors limits the scope of operation of the 'sham' doctrine. In fact, it is entirely possible that they will be deployed by the judiciary in the future to blunt the impact and normative edge of the decision in *Autoclenz*. The history of the common law is littered with examples of judicial retrenchment following a decision by an appellate court that appeared to have far-reaching and transformative implications for an area of law.

Having addressed the various tests for the identification and classification of the employment contract, consider the following Hypothetical F. Do you think that Keith Marshall is an employee?

Hypothetical F

Keith Marshall has an open-ended contract with Danny's Demolishers Ltd ('DD') whereby he is obliged to attend DD's premises throughout the southeast of England to fix and repair various problems with the plumbing as and when they arise. He is under an absolute obligation to be at DD's premises—location to be notified by DD from time to time—from 10am to 5pm each day in the working week. He wears his own uniform, drives his own van, and provides and uses his own tools. He has clients other than DD, but when at work for DD, DD exercises actual day-to-day control over the provision of Keith's services, instructing when and where he is to work. The contract includes a clause which provides that Keith may send along a substitute to perform services in his stead, but only if he is unable to work. Keith pays income tax and National Insurance contributions as a self-employed contractor, i.e. no PAYE is deducted from the sums he is paid by DD and VAT is payable on the fee he charges DD. Keith is subject to DD's disciplinary and grievance procedure.

As for the reform of the rules on employment status, the Taylor Review[105] has recommended that several changes be made to simplify and improve the existing law to ensure that its defects are addressed. For example, Taylor has suggested that the burden of proving that an individual is not an employee be shifted to the employer.[106] The current law

---

[104] Moreover, such a proposition would jar against the weight of prior authorities which have comprehensively held that inequality of bargaining power is not a proper basis to evaluate the substantive fairness of a contract. See *Pao On v Lau Yiu Long* [1980] AC 614 (PC); *National Westminster Bank plc v Morgan* [1985] 1 All ER 821 (HL); and J. McClelland, 'A Purposive Approach to Employment Protection or a Missed Opportunity?' (2012) 75 *Modern Law Review* 427. See also J. Riley, 'The Definition of the Contract of Employment and its Differentiation from Other Contracts and Other Work Relations' in M. Freedland et al. (eds), *The Contract of Employment* (Oxford, OUP, 2016) 332–3.

[105] See *Good Work: The Taylor Review of Modern Working Practices* (July 2017), available at https://www.gov.uk/government/uploads/system/uploads/attachment_data/file/627671/good-work-taylor-review-modern-working-practices-rg.pdf (last visited 19 November 2017).   [106] *ibid.*, page 62.

prescribes that the onus is on the individual to prove that he/she is an employee and this recommendation seems sensible and practicable. Another proposal is that legislation, backed by detailed guidance, ought to clearly, simply, and definitively set out the tests for employment status.[107] Whilst clarity, accessibility, and simplicity are admirable goals, it is doubtful whether legislation can capture and cater for the variety of complex factual situations which may present themselves before an employment tribunal or court. It presupposes that the reduction of such multifaceted fact patterns to clear outcomes with the application of carefully chosen evaluative criteria is a distinct possibility that can be easily achieved. However, this is a forlorn aspiration and assumes a level of sophistication in the applicable tests which is unrealistic. Setting out the tests for the establishment of employment status may also lead to ossification whereby the evaluative criteria become stale and unable to respond adequately to changes in underlying social and economic conditions. The chosen tests must also be sufficiently flexible to frustrate employers in any attempts to adopt evasive action and it may be the case that a statutory statement will achieve the exact opposite effect.

3.2.2 Continuity of employment

In order to benefit from the protection of certain statutory employment rights, an employee must have a sufficient period of continuous employment. For example, in the case of the statutory right not to be unfairly dismissed in terms of Part X of the ERA, the employee must have been continuously employed for a period of not less than two years ending with the effective date of termination of the employment contract.[108] In this instance, the two-year period is known as the 'qualifying threshold'. Continuous employment is defined in sections 210 and 211 of the ERA:

> **Section 210 Introductory . . .**
>
> (3) In computing an employee's period of continuous employment for the purposes of any provision of this Act, any question—
>
>   (a) whether the employee's employment is of a kind counting towards a period of continuous employment, or
>
>   (b) whether periods (consecutive or otherwise) are to be treated as forming a single period of continuous employment,
>
>   shall be determined week by week; but where it is necessary to compute the length of an employee's period of employment it shall be computed in months and years of twelve months in accordance with section 211.
>
> (4) . . . a week which does not count in computing the length of a period of continuous employment breaks continuity of employment.
>
> (5) A person's employment during any period shall, unless the contrary is shown, be presumed to have been continuous.
>
> **Section 211 Period of continuous employment**
>
> (1) An employee's period of continuous employment for the purposes of any provision of this Act—
>
>   (a) . . . begins with the day on which the employee starts work, and
>
>   (b) ends with the day by reference to which the length of the employee's period of continuous employment is to be ascertained for the purposes of the provision . . .

---

[107] *ibid.*, page 35.   [108] Section 108(1) of the ERA.

The presumption in section 210(3) is that an employee's period of continuous employ-ment will be calculated working week by working week. The clock starts ticking when the employee 'starts work',[109] and so the period spent working during an initial proba-tionary period counts towards continuity of employment. Meanwhile, section 210(4) states that the accumulation of continuity of employment will be broken if the employee has a gap of a working week or more which fails to count towards a qualifying period.[110] This is subject to section 212 which stipulates that gaps of a week or part of a week be-tween periods of continuous employment—owing to the fact that no contract of employ-ment is in effect—may be bridged in certain circumstances:[111]

Section 212 Weeks counting in computing period

(1) Any week during the whole or part of which an employee's relations with his employer are gov-erned by a contract of employment counts in computing the employee's period of employment . . .

(3) . . . any week (not within subsection (1)) during the whole or part of which an employee is—

    (a) incapable of work in consequence of sickness or injury,

    (b) absent from work on account of a temporary cessation of work, or

    (c) absent from work in circumstances such that, by arrangement or custom,[112] he is regarded as continuing in the employment of his employer for any purpose, counts in computing the employee's period of employment.

(4) Not more than twenty-six weeks count under subsection (3)(a) between any periods falling under subsection (1).

Where an individual is engaged on a series of individual contracts of employment with intervening gaps, he/she may not need to rely on section 212 to bridge those gaps and take advantage of an unbroken period of continuous employment. Despite the breaks where he/she is not working, this seamless continuity may be secured where the indi-vidual engagements can be aggregated and treated by the common law as a 'global' or 'umbrella' contract of employment. This is achieved through the intercession of the 'mu-tuality of obligation' test, which operates at two levels:

(1) The first level is the basic wage–work bargain between the employer and the employee, in terms of which the employer provides a reasonable and minimum amount of work and pays for it, and the employee performs the reasonable and minimum amount of work offered by the employer: this is the *exchange* element.

(2) The second level entails the exchange of mutual promises, whereby the employer makes an ongoing commitment to provide a reasonable and minimum amount of

---

[109] This is a matter of interpreting the terms of the contract of employment, which may entail a purpo-sive construction: see *Boufoy-Bastick v University of the West Indies* [2015] IRLR 1014.

[110] For example, in *Booth v USA* [1999] IRLR 16, the employer engaged the employees on the basis of a series of fixed-term contracts of employment but with gaps of about two weeks in between each con-tract. It was held that this deliberate choice on the part of the employer broke the continuity of employ-ment of the employees. However, a gap of a working week between two jobs at two different premises of the employer (Sheffield and Blackpool) may be bridged where an agreement is made in one week to begin work in the next: *Welton v Deluxe Retail (t/a Madhouse)* [2013] IRLR 166.

[111] The Taylor Review has recommended that this be increased to one month: See *Good Work: The Taylor Review of Modern Working Practices* (July 2017), available at https://www.gov.uk/government/uploads/system/uploads/attachment_data/file/627671/good-work-taylor-review-modern-working-prac-tices-rg.pdf (last visited 19 November 2017) 45.

[112] See *Booth v USA* [1999] IRLR 16 and *Curr v Marks & Spencer* [2002] EWCA Civ 1852, [2003] ICR 443 for the interpretation of the words 'arrangement or custom'.

work in the future and to pay for it with a corresponding obligation imposed on the employee to perform that reasonable and minimum amount of work when offered in the future: this is the *reciprocity* element.[113]

It is the second level which operates to connect a chain of individual contracts of employment interrupted by breaks into a 'global' or 'umbrella' contract of employment.[114] As such, it is only where a 'global' or 'umbrella' contract of employment is *absent* owing to the inability of an employee to satisfy the second level of the mutuality of obligation test[115] that section 212 assumes relevance. Although it does not serve to create a global continuous employment contract during the gaps when the individual is not working, section 212 offers the potential to link the separate contracts of employment into a continuous period of employment via a statutory fiction. For example, in *Cornwall County Council v Prater*,[116] Mrs Prater was engaged by the council's Education Out of School Service to give tuition to pupils referred by the Service as the need arose. This was arranged on the basis of a series of single discrete engagements of varying durations. The teaching was conducted at the home of the pupils concerned. There was no continuous contract of employment and the council had no obligation to allocate pupils to Mrs Prater. There were a number of gaps between the individual engagements and the arrangement lasted for ten years. Although there was no continuous global contract of employment in existence for the ten-year period, the Court of Appeal held that there was sufficient mutuality of obligation at the first level to treat each individual hiring as a contract of employment. Section 212 then operated as a statutory bridge to establish a continuous employment relationship linking up each of the individual employment contracts.[117]

Section 212(3) will operate where the break in the individual contracts of employment is attributable to the sickness or injury of the employee, a temporary cessation of work, or there is an arrangement or custom in place that the break is to be ignored. It is the question of what constitutes a 'temporary cessation of work' in section 212(3)(b) which has generated by far the most case law. Here, we should note that the claimant must show that there has been a 'cessation' of work—rather than an absence—which is 'temporary' for section 212(3)(b) to be satisfied. The word 'temporary' symbolizes a relatively short cessation, e.g. owing to a shortage of work, fire, or explosion.[118] The evaluation of whether a cessation is temporary is made on a retrospective[119] basis:

■ *Ford v Warwickshire County Council* [1983] 2 AC 71, 83G–84A

Lord Diplock:

. . . it is in the sense of 'transient,' i.e. lasting only for a relatively short time, that the word 'temporary' is used in [section 212(3)]. So, the continuity of employment for the purposes of the [ERA] . . . is not broken unless and until, looking backwards from the date of the expiry of the . . . contract on

---

[113] See the excellent analysis by Judge David Richardson in *Drake v Ipsos Mori UK Ltd* [2012] IRLR 973, 976–8 which follows this two-dimensional approach to the 'mutuality of obligation' test.

[114] See M. Freedland, *The Personal Employment Contract* (Oxford, OUP, 2003) 88–92; A. C. L. Davies, 'The Contract for Intermittent Employment' (2007) 36 *Industrial Law Journal* 102, 103; and Chapter 6, section 6.2.1.

[115] For example, see *Hellyer Bros Ltd v McLeod* [1987] 1 WLR 728, [1987] ICR 526, where the Court of Appeal held that deep-sea trawlermen were not engaged on the basis of a global employment contract.

[116] [2006] EWCA Civ 102, [2006] 2 All ER 1013, [2006] ICR 731.

[117] See A. Davies, 'Casual Workers and Continuity of Employment' (2006) 35 *Industrial Law Journal* 196.

[118] *Fitzgerald v Hall Russell & Co.* [1970] AC 984 (HL), 1002H per Lord Upjohn.

[119] *ibid.*, 1003G per Lord Upjohn.

which the employee's claim is based, there is to be found between one . . . contract and its immediate predecessor an interval that cannot be characterised as short relatively to the combined duration of the two . . . contracts. Whether it can be so characterised is a question of fact and degree and so is for decision by an industrial tribunal rather than by the Employment Appeal Tribunal or an appellate court of law.

In *Ford*, the approach taken was to compare the length of the period out of work with the length of the periods in work on either side. Since the duration of the gap was longer than the length of the periods in work, this was held to be fatal to the operation of section 212(3).[120] This approach may be appropriate where the length of the periods in employment are regular, but may be of less assistance where they are irregular and fluctuate.[121] For example, in *Flack v Kodak Ltd*,[122] applying *Fitzgerald v Hall Russell & Co.*,[123] the Court of Appeal adopted a broader interpretation to the effect that, where the periods in employment fluctuate, the length and numbers of the breaks out of work should be considered in light of the overall length of the period of employment.

Turning now to the meaning of the expression 'cessation of work', *Byrne v Birmingham City District Council*[124] concerned an individual who featured within the employer's pool of casual labour. The employer would allocate work to one of the individuals within that pool on an intermittent basis. The Court of Appeal held that the 'expression "cessation of work" must denote that some "quantum of work" had for the time being ceased to exist, and, therefore, was no longer available to the employers to give to the employee'.[125] Owing to the fact that the gaps in the individual's engagements could not be attributed to a diminution in the quantum of work the employer had available—the work had simply been assigned to another individual within the pool—the work which the employer had to offer had not ceased to exist and so the 'cessation of work' test was not met. Whilst clearly reasoned, the stance adopted in *Byrne* appears to conflict with the speech of Lord Upjohn in *Fitzgerald v Hall Russell & Co.*,[126] where he said 'the words "absent from work on account of a temporary cessation of work" mean that [the employee] was laid off or dismissed because his employer had no longer work available for him personally any longer'.[127] By fixing the enquiry on whether the work available for the employee to perform personally had ceased, rather than the work the employer had to offer generally, *Byrne* is arguably inconsistent with *Fitzgerald*. Since the latter is of higher authority, it is suggested that it ought to attract greater weight.

---

[120] See also *Berwick Salmon Fisheries v Rutherford* [1991] IRLR 203. However, in *Hussain v Acorn Independent College Ltd* [2011] IRLR 463, applying *Ford*, the EAT held that the interval of the employer's summer holidays in between a temporary fixed-term contract of a length of approximately two-and-a-half months and a permanent contract of approximately nine-and-a-quarter months (which was terminated by the employer) was a temporary cessation for the purposes of section 212(3)(b) of the ERA. The fact that there was a difference in the nature of the contracts on either side of the gap (i.e. one was a fixed-term contract and the other a permanent contract) was irrelevant.

[121] *Sillars v Charrington Fuels Ltd* [1989] ICR 475.

[122] [1987] 1 WLR 31, 36E–36H per Woolf LJ.

[123] [1970] AC 984 (HL), 1003G per Lord Upjohn.

[124] [1987] ICR 519.   [125] *ibid.*, 525E–F per Purchas LJ.   [126] [1970] AC 984 (HL).

[127] *ibid.*, 1002H per Lord Upjohn. Interestingly, it is not necessary that the employer at either end of the temporary cessation of work is identical, so long as one is associated with the other: *Holt v EB Security Ltd* (UKEAT/0558/11/CEA, 13 July 2012). See also *Da Silva Junior v Composite Mouldings & Design* [2009] ICR 419.

Reflection points

1. If the three irreducible minimum criteria of control, mutuality of obligation, and personal service are present in a working relationship, is the tribunal or court *obliged* to make a finding that a contract of employment exists?

2. In your opinion, is the sham doctrine expounded in *Autoclenz Ltd v Belcher* [2011] ICR 1157 a viable and logical basis for characterizing what appears to be a written contract for services as a contract of employment?

 For additional reading on identifying and classifying the contract of employment, visit the Online Resources for this book at *www.oup.com/uk/cabrelli3e/*

3.3 ILLEGALITY OF THE CONTRACT OF EMPLOYMENT

This section analyses the common law doctrine of illegality of a contract of employment. Where a contract of employment is deemed to have been illegal or contrary to public policy, it is treated as void *ab initio*, i.e. as if it never existed at all. The leading case of *Hall v Woolston Hall Leisure*[128] demonstrates that the common law doctrine of illegality forges a distinction between:

(1) a contract which was illegal in its purpose or objective *when it was formed*, whereby the employee intends to enter into the contract in order to commit unlawful activities;[129]

(2) a contract which is *expressly or implicitly prohibited by statute*;[130] and

(3) the illegal *performance* of a legal contract.[131]

Consider the following Hypothetical G.

Hypothetical G

David Crouch is a foreign national who has worked for Danny's Demolishers Ltd ('DD') for three years as a contracts manager on the basis of a permanent contract of employment. Prior to the commencement of his contract of employment, David applied to work in the UK on the basis of a UK Tier 2 work permit. However, his application was rejected, since he was unable to satisfy the UK Visa Bureau that he had passed a Higher National Diploma (HND) qualification that was relevant to his employment with DD. When asked by DD whether he had a work permit, David replied that he did not, but DD hired him nonetheless. After a period of three years, DD dismisses David on the ground that he was working illegally in the UK. In order to claim unfair dismissal under section 94 of the ERA, David must satisfy the employment tribunal that he was an employee.

---

[128] [2001] 1 WLR 225, 236B–D per Peter Gibson LJ.
[129] *St John Shipping Corp. v Joseph Bank Ltd* [1957] 1 QB 267, 283 per Devlin J.
[130] *ibid.*, 283 per Devlin J.
[131] *Ashmore, Benson Ltd v Dawson Ltd* [1973] 1 WLR 828, 833 per Lord Denning MR.

In such a case, there is nothing illegal about the purpose of the contract of employment. For example, the contract of employment does not entail engaging in prostitution, which would be unlawful.[132] Moreover, there is no intention on the part of the employee to enter into the contract in order to commit an illegal act, e.g. where an employee is hired as a 'hitman' or smuggler. As Brodie has noted, '[i]t is uncommon for an employment contract to be held unlawful on the basis that it had been formed for an illegal purpose'.[133] Moreover, there is nothing in David's contract of employment enjoining him to provide the services of a contracts manager which can be said to expressly or implicitly contravene a particular piece of legislation. Instead, the issue for determination in Hypothetical G—and the matter for determination in the lion's share of the reported cases concerning the purported illegality of a contract of employment—is whether there has been illegality in the performance of the contract, in that it has been performed in contravention of statute or common law.

Like David's circumstances in Hypothetical G, a great number of cases on illegality of the contract of employment involve facts whereby the *employer* was in breach of immigration legislation by hiring the employee or involved in tax fraud. *Wheeler v Quality Deep Ltd*[134] is an example of the latter. Here, the question is whether the employee should be deprived of a statutory employment right based on the illegality of the *employer's* performance of the contract:

■ *Wheeler v Quality Deep Ltd* [2005] ICR 265, 270C–H

[The headnote to the case sets forth the facts as follows:] The employee, of Thai origin and with a limited knowledge of English was employed . . . as a cook at a Thai restaurant. On her complaint of unfair dismissal, the employment tribunal found that. . . no deductions for income tax or national insurance contributions had been made by the employer, that the only two payslips the employee could produce wrongly showed payment of a gross amount of £72 per week, and that the employee had not received any tax coding or had any correspondence with the revenue. The . . . Court of Appeal [held that the contract of employment was not illegal].

Lord Justice Hooper:

. . . one of the difficulties with the employment tribunal's decision is that it does not distinguish between illegality of a contract and illegality in the performance of a legal contract . . .

I turn briefly to the law. There was no dispute that the only principles relevant to the resolution of this case in this court are those set out in *Hall v Woolston Hall Leisure Ltd* [2001] ICR 99 . . . Peter Gibson LJ said, at p 110, para 38:

'In cases where the contract of employment is neither entered into for an illegal purpose nor prohibited by statute, the illegal performance of the contract will not render the contract unenforceable unless in addition to knowledge of the facts which make the performance illegal the employee actively participates in the illegal performance. It is a question of fact in each case whether there has been a sufficient degree of participation by the employee . . .'

It follows that the employment tribunal had to be satisfied that the performance of the contract was illegal, that the employee knew of the facts which made the performance illegal and actively

---

[132] However, where part of an employee's duties involves hiring prostitutes for clients of his/her employer, this will not render the contract of employment illegal since the very purpose of that contract was not to undertake that illegal or immoral act. Instead, something more will be necessary to enable a party to demonstrate that the employee has engaged in illegal performance of what is in fact a legal contract: see *Coral Leisure Group Ltd v Barnett* [1981] IRLR 204.

[133] D. Brodie, *The Employment Contract: Legal Principles, Drafting, and Interpretation* (Oxford, OUP, 2005) 43–4. Freedland and Kountouris have referred to the distinction drawn in the case law between contracts illegally 'formed' and 'performed' as nothing more than 'casuistry': M. Freedland and N. Kountouris, *The Legal Construction of Personal Work Relations* (Oxford, OUP, 2011) 148.

[134] [2005] ICR 265.

participated in the illegal performance. Not only did the employment tribunal not apply the right test it did not make the necessary findings. The only finding which comes anywhere near the necessary findings is the enigmatic finding: 'Between them Mr and Mrs Wheeler must have known something was wrong. They would have made a choice to acquiesce.' That is clearly not sufficient . . .

As such, where there has been illegality in performance by the employer, there must be some evidence of collusion on the part of the employee for the contract to be declared illegal. This involves two components for an 'illegal performance' claim to be met:

(1) 'knowledge'; and

(2) 'active participation'.

The extent of the employee's active engagement in the illegal performance of the contract with the employer will be a matter of fact and degree.[135] However, the proper approach to be applied to the state of knowledge of the employee is slightly trickier. The traditional approach in contract law is to apply a test of objectivity. However, in *Wheeler v Quality Deep Ltd*, Hooper LJ appeared to suggest that the state of knowledge of the employee as to the illegality of the performance is a subjective test, i.e. if the employee believed that the performance of his/her obligations under the contract of employment was in breach of law, the contract would be illegal. Otherwise, it would not.[136] Support for this proposition is provided by the decision of the Court of Appeal in *Enfield Technical Services Ltd v Payne*.[137] Here, it was held that the 'knowledge' criterion will be met where there is an explicit or implicit misrepresentation by the employee that he/she is performing his/her obligations lawfully, or he/she attempts to conceal the true unlawful nature of such performance. The effect of this approach is rather unusual. That is to say that the greater the level of ignorance displayed by the employee as to the lawfulness or otherwise of the performance of his/her obligations, the less likely it is that the contract of employment will be held illegal.[138]

Where the employer has not been engaged in illegal performance of the contract, we must turn to *Vakante v Addey and Stanhope School (No. 2)*[139] for guidance. Here, Mummery LJ stated that, in such a case, the contract of employment will be treated as void, without the need to establish (1) knowledge or (2) active participation. Instead, the courts will apply the 'inextricable link' test, i.e. whether there is a sufficiently close connection between the illegality (e.g. immigration offences) and the employee's employment law claim, or whether the illegality 'merely provided the setting or context in which that [breach of employment law] was committed, and to allow [the employee] to recover . . . would not amount to the court condoning what it otherwise condemns'.[140] Illegality of performance on the part of the employee is particularly relevant where it is alleged the employee has been working in breach of immigration laws:

■ *Vakante v Addey and Stanhope School (No. 2)* [2005] ICR 231, 240H

[The headnote to the case sets forth the facts as follows:] An asylum-seeker, was given limited leave to remain in the United Kingdom on condition he did not obtain employment without permission from the Home Office. In breach of that condition he obtained employment with the . . . employer. He was subsequently dismissed and made a complaint of unlawful race discrimination . . .

---

[135] *Hall v Woolston Hall Leisure* [2001] 1 WLR 225, 236B–D per Peter Gibson LJ.
[136] *Wheeler v Quality Deep Ltd* [2005] ICR 265, 276B–C.
[137] [2008] ICR 1423, 1431C–H per Pill LJ.
[138] For example, see *Connolly v Whitestone Solicitors* (UKEAT/0445/10/ZT, 24 June 2011).
[139] [2005] ICR 231.
[140] *Hounga v Allen* [2014] UKSC 47, [2014] 1 WLR 2889, 2912B–C per Lord Hughes.

Mummery LJ:

The application of the *Hall* approach to this case is comparatively straightforward. This case is clearly different from *Hall* [2001] ICR 99 and similar cases, in which (a) the illegal conduct was that of the employer in the performance of the contract; and (b) the involvement of the [employee] was one of awareness of the employer's illegal conduct and in deriving benefit from it. It is not a case where the [employee] has been working in good faith in the belief that it was lawful for him to work . . .

As for the illegal conduct here: (a) it was that of the [employee]; (b) it was criminal; (c) it went far beyond the manner in which one party performed what was otherwise a lawful employment contract; (d) it went to the basic content of an employment situation—work; (e) the duty not to discriminate arises from an employment situation which, without a permit, was unlawful from top to bottom and from beginning to end.

It was not a case of innocent oversight or an acceptable misunderstanding. The [employee] had been clearly informed in writing of the true position. Instead of making an application for a work permit, he obtained work with the employer by making a false statement. The [employee] was solely responsible for his illegal conduct in working for the employer and creating an unlawful situation, on which he had to rely in order to establish that there was a duty not to discriminate against him. The fact that he had previously obtained employment and might, or would, have obtained a work permit if he had applied for it is not a defence to a criminal offence committed by him and is irrelevant to the illegal nature of his conduct at the material time.

I agree with the employment tribunal that the complaints by the [employee] of his discriminatory treatment in employment are so inextricably bound with the illegality of conduct in obtaining and continuing that employment with the employer that, if it were to permit him to recover compensation for discrimination, the tribunal would appear to condone his illegal conduct.

In contrast to *Vakante*, applying the inextricable link test, the Supreme Court reached a different result in *Hounga v Allen*.[141] *Hounga* was a very disturbing case concerning a 16-year-old Nigerian female who had come to the UK to work as a domestic servant. Mrs Allen and her family had trafficked Hounga from Nigeria to work exclusively for them in England. Hounga continued to remain in the UK and work when her temporary work visa expired (which had been obtained on a dishonest basis by both Allen and Hounga). Miss Hounga suffered physical, verbal, and emotional abuse, and race discrimination. However, her claims for unfair dismissal, breach of contract, unlawful deductions from wages under Part II of the ERA, and for race discrimination, were barred by the Court of Appeal owing to the illegality of the contract of employment.[142] The Supreme Court reversed the decision of the Court of Appeal, the majority of the Justices holding that there was an insufficiently close link between the immigration offences and the discrimination perpetrated. Instead, the illegality was simply the context within which the discrimination took place. Lords Wilson and Kerr and Lady Hale went even further,[143] arriving at the conclusion that the public policy behind the illegality defence—that the integrity of the legal system should be preserved by ensuring that no person should profit from his/her own criminal, wrongful or illegal actions—was outweighed by the public policy consideration of preventing human trafficking and protecting Hounga as a victim.[144]

Hounga has been approved in academic circles on the ground that, by removing the harshness in-built within the illegality defence, the approach adopted by the Supreme

---

[141] [2014] UKSC 47, [2014] 1 WLR 2889.

[142] [2012] EWCA Civ 609, [2012] IRLR 685.

[143] Lord Hughes was not convinced: [2014] UKSC 47, [2014] 1 WLR 2889, 2912C–D.

[144] For a similar case where the strictness of the illegality defence was softened, see *Blue Chip Trading v Helbawi* [2009] IRLR 128.

Court functions to target the hardships experienced by vulnerable migrant workers. However, there is an argument that the exact test governing the illegality defence in discrimination claims has been left unresolved, e.g. whether the 'inextricable link' defence or a test entailing the balancing of policy considerations takes precedence.[145] Bogg and Green have persuasively argued that what ought to be adopted is a 'composite test, requiring there to be an inextricable link before the court moves to consider the public policy reasons for and against permitting illegality to be operative'.[146] The approach in *Hounga* has been endorsed by a 6:3 majority of the Supreme Court in *Patel v Mirza*.[147] Here, delivering the leading judgment, Lord Toulson expressed the opinion that the courts should weigh the relative seriousness of the wrongdoing associated with the illegality against the policy underpinning the prohibition and then balance that with the fairness of denying the claimant any relief.

Reflection points

1. In your opinion, is it logical for the law to distinguish between (1) a contract which is illegal in its purpose or objective when it was formed and (2) the illegal performance of a legal contract? Give reasons for your answer.

2. Do you agree with the decision of the Supreme Court in *Hounga v Allen* [2014] 1 WLR 2889? If so, why? If not, why not?

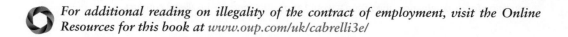

For additional reading on illegality of the contract of employment, visit the Online Resources for this book at www.oup.com/uk/cabrelli3e/

---

[145] See J. Goudkamp and M. Zou, 'The Defence of Illegality in Tort Law: Beyond Judicial Redemption?' (2015) 74 *Cambridge Law Journal* 13, 15.

[146] See A. Bogg and S. Green, 'Rights are Not Just for the Virtuous: What *Hounga* Means for the Illegality Defence in the Discrimination Torts' (2015) 44 *Industrial Law Journal* 101. See also the discussion of *Hounga* in E. Lim, 'Attribution and the Illegality Defence' (2016) 79 *Modern Law Review* 476, 483–7.

[147] [2017] AC 467. For commentary, see J. Goudkamp, 'The end of an era? Illegality in private law in the Supreme Court' (2017) 133 *Law Quarterly Review* 14.

CHAPTER FOUR

ALTERNATIVE PERSONAL WORK CONTRACTS AND RELATIONS

4.1 INTRODUCTION TO ATYPICAL WORKING AND LABOUR MARKET FLEXIBILITY

When an individual is providing a personal service to an enterprise, he/she may be working or employed for legal purposes on the basis of one of the following four contract types:

(1) a contract of employment/service;

(2) a 'worker' contract;

(3) a 'contract personally to do work'; or

(4) a contract for services, i.e. as an independent self-employed contractor in business on his/her own account.

This chapter is divided into two sections. First, we will study in depth the two statutory constructs that have been carefully formulated by the UK Parliament as a repository for the conferral of certain statutory employment rights, namely (2) the 'worker' contract and (3) the 'contract personally to do work'. These two alternative personal work contracts are intermediate contract types, lying somewhere between (1) the contract of employment and (4) the contract for services. Secondly, we address the related, albeit separate, question of the legal status of agency workers. We enquire as to whether the Agency Workers Regulations 2010[1] address the disadvantages experienced by this section of the UK workforce. The examination of the legal regulation of the two alternative personal work contracts and agency workers is conducted within the wider theme of labour market flexibility and atypical work.

---

[1] SI 2010/93.

4.1.1 The incidence and nature of atypical working relationships and the possible policy responses

One of the effects of deindustrialization, the general demise of the manufacturing industry in the UK, the emergence of a service-based economy, and the disappearance of the once-pervasive 'Fordist'[2] model of production has been a rise in the demand for labour markets which are more responsive to oscillations in managerial requirements for labour, i.e. 'labour market flexibility'. The Fordist model entailed wholly integrated processes of production at the level of a single firm. The firm acted as a single employer to a multitude of workers, discharging each level of the production process in-house and hiring labour on an indefinite standard employment relationship.[3] However, in the recent past, the once vertically integrated firm has broken down into separate production processes dispersed amongst a number of disparate enterprises. This phenomenon is referred to as 'vertical disintegration'.[4] We have witnessed the growing trend for firms to engage in 'outsourcing',[5] whereby responsibility for the performance of various internal functions is contracted out by the firm to third parties. As part of the outsourcing process, the third-party contractor may accept some of the employees of the firm into their employment. Alternatively, the third-party contractor may hire fresh labour, freelancers, or agency staff to enable it to perform the contractual obligations it owes to the firm. Completely separate from outsourcing is the situation where the firm hires flexible labour directly itself, e.g. where it engages fixed-term temps, casual labour on the basis of zero-hours contracts, agency staff, etc. What is particularly clear is that there is a large degree of heterogeneity[6] in the forms of non-standard or atypical working, which are protean:

■ S. Fredman, 'Labour Law in Flux: The Changing Composition of the Workforce' (1997) 26 *Industrial Law Journal* 337, 338–9

> . . . flexibility can be numerical or functional. Numerical flexibility involves adjusting labour inputs to meet fluctuations in the employers' needs, usually by utilising part-time, temporary and casual workers, or altering the working time patterns of shift or full-time workers. At its most intense, numerical flexibility includes 'distancing strategies' whereby the employer contracts out work rather than using its own workforce. Functional flexibility relates not to changes in the numbers of

---

[2] This has been defined as 'a large industrial business engaging in mass production based on a narrow specialization of jobs and competencies and pyramidal management (hierarchical structure of labour, separation between product design and manufacture)' in A. Supiot, *Beyond Employment: Changes in Work and the Future of Labour Law in Europe* (Oxford, OUP, 2001) 1.

[3] The orthodox account is that the number of standard employment contracts is diminishing, being displaced with, and replaced by, precarious atypical personal work contracts—see G. Standing, *The Precariat: The New Dangerous Class* (London, Bloomsbury, 2011) and D. Weil, *The Fissured Workplace* (Harvard, Harvard University Press, 2014)—and that its ultimate demise is predicted. However, for a sceptical counterpoint, see Z. Adams and S. Deakin, 'Institutional Solutions to Precariousness and Inequality in Labour Markets' (2014) 52 *British Journal of Industrial Relations* 779 and S. Deakin, 'The Standard Employment Relationship in Europe: Recent Developments and Future Prognosis' (2014) 5 *Soziales Recht* 89.

[4] H. Collins, 'Independent Contractors and the Challenge of Vertical Disintegration to Employment Protection Laws' (1990) 10 *Oxford Journal of Legal Studies* 353; H. Collins, 'Contractual Autonomy' in A. Bogg, C. Costello, A. C. L. Davies, and J. Prassl (eds), *The Autonomy of Labour Law* (Oxford, Hart Publishing, 2015) 55; and M. Freedland, *The Personal Employment Contract* (Oxford, OUP, 2003) 22.

[5] See H. Collins, 'Independent Contractors and the Challenge of Vertical Disintegration to Employment Protection Laws' (1990) 10 *Oxford Journal of Legal Studies* 353; S. Deakin and F. Wilkinson, *The Law of the Labour Market: Industrialization, Employment, and Legal Evolution* (Oxford, OUP, 2005) 314.

[6] See L. Hipp, J. Bernhardt, and J. Allmendinger, 'Institutions and the Prevalence of Nonstandard Employment' (2015) 13 *Socio-Economic Review* 351.

workers, but in their tasks: it consists in the ability of the employer to require employees to adjust their skills to match the demands of changes in workload, production methods and technology. Although functional flexibility creates pressure on traditional contractual notions, it is in respect of numerical flexibility and distancing strategies that labour law has faced its major challenge. The advantages of numerical flexibility to employers are self evident: the use of casual, part-time and temporary workers permits employers to match staffing levels to peaks in demand and non-wage costs such as national insurance payments are low. The advantages for the employer, however, inevitably translate into detriments for flexible workers. Atypical[7] workers have a particularly high incidence of low pay.[8]

The growth in the fragmentation of work, flexibilization, and atypical[9] working arrangements is wholly consistent with the policy drive for 'managerial adaptability'.[10] Although most recent controversies have centred around zero-hours[11] and 'gig economy'/'crowdwork' workers[12] in particular, research has indicated that the future 'spread of atypical working is . . . inevitable'.[13] Statistics cited by the Taylor review were to the effect that the numbers of atypical workers in the UK labour market (illustrated in Table 4.1), were modest, but a by-product of this spreading out process is likely to be an acceleration in the emergence of new flexible forms of work in the future.

Successive UK Governments have distanced themselves from policies that preclude employers from adopting atypical workers on flexible contracts.[14] However, whilst recognizing that employers should have the ability to hire flexible labour through contracts which cannot be characterized as contracts of employment, a series of responses have been elicited from UK Governments, who have been particularly alert to the attendant social and economic risks associated with the growing trend to deploy atypical working arrangements. In particular, Governments have been anxious to prevent the emergence

---

[7] An atypical working relation is one in which one or more of the following six variables is missing: (1) a full-time contract (2) with a single employer (3) for an indefinite period of time (4) to perform personal services (5) at the employer's premises, (6) irrespective of whether the employer has sufficient work to provide the employee or not.

[8] See also H. Collins, 'Regulating the Employment Relation for Competitiveness' (2001) 30 *Industrial Law Journal* 17; H. Collins, 'Flexibility and Stability of Expectations in the Contract of Employment' (2006) 4 *Socio-Economic Review* 139.

[9] See the discussion in J. Prassl and E. Albin, 'Work, Regulation and Social Exclusion' in M. Freedland et al. (eds), *The Contract of Employment* (Oxford, OUP, 2016) 209.

[10] P. Davies and M. Freedland, *Towards a Flexible Labour Market: Labour Legislation and Regulation since the 1990s* (Oxford, OUP, 2007) 20–4.

[11] For discussion of the growth in zero-hours contracts in the UK, see J. Kenner, 'Inverting the Flexicurity Paradigm: The United Kingdom and Zero Hours Contracts' in E. Ales, O. Deinert, and J. Kenner (eds), *Core and Contingent Work in the European Union: A Comparative Analysis* (Oxford, Hart, 2017) 153.

[12] See J Prassl, *Humans as a Service* (Oxford, OUP, 2018); V. De Stefano, 'Crowdsourcing, the Gig-Economy, and the Law' (2016) 37 *Comparative Labor Law & Policy Journal* 461; V. De Stefano, 'The Rise of the Just-in-Time Workforce: On-Demand Work, Crowdwork and Labor Protection in the Gig-Economy' (2016) 37 *Comparative Labor Law & Policy Journal* 471; J. Prassl and M. Risak, 'Uber, Taskrabbit, & Co: Platforms as Employers? Rethinking the Legal Analysis of Crowdwork' (2016) 37 *Comparative Labor Law & Policy Journal* 619; B. Rogers, 'Employment Rights in the Platform Economy: Getting Back to Basics' (2016) 10 *Harvard Law & Policy Review* 479.

[13] A Ludera-Ruszel, 'Typical or Atypical: Reflections on the Atypical Forms of Employment Illustrated with the Example of a Fixed-Term Employment Contract—A Comparative Study of Selected European Countries' (2016) 37 *Comparative Labor Law & Policy Journal* 407, 443.

[14] Such a restrictive approach would curtail the freedom of choice of employers, e.g. by compelling them to select a contract for the hiring of labour from a statutorily prescribed 'menu' of contractual forms: see Chapter 3, section 3.1.2, and H. Collins, *Employment Law*, 2nd edition (Oxford, OUP, 2010) 38 for further details.

Table 4.1 *Numbers of atypical workers in the UK*

Category	Numbers in the UK	Percentage of UK Labour Market (approximate)
All employees/workers (including self-employed)	32.21 million people in employment[1]	100%
Employees/workers (excluding self-employed)	27.235 million[1]	84.55%
Self-employed	4.77 million[1]	14.81%
Agency workers	800,000 to 1.2 million[2]	3.73%
Zero-hours contract workers	900,000[3]	2.8%
'Gig economy' workers	1.3 million[3]	4.04%

Notes

1 See Office of National Statistics, *Labour Market Statistic Bulletin* (January 2018) 1 and Table 3, available at https://www.ons.gov.uk/employmentandlabourmarket/peopleinwork/employmentandemployeetypes/bulletins/uklabourmarket/january2018 (last visited 10 February 2018).

2 See *Good Work: The Taylor Review of Modern Working Practices*, July 2017 at 24, available at https://www.gov.uk/government/uploads/system/uploads/attachment_data/file/627671/good-work-taylor-review-modern-working-practices-rg.pdf (last visited 19 November 2017). See also the statistics in W. Brown and D. Marsden, 'Individualization and Growing Diversity of Employment Relationships' in D. Marsden (ed.), *Employment in the Lean Years: Policy and Prospects for the Next Decade* (Oxford, OUP, 2011) 73, 75.

3 See *Good Work: The Taylor Review of Modern Working Practices*, July 2017 at 25.

of a two-tier labour force. This entails full-time permanent individuals working on the basis of a contract of employment enjoying job security and employment rights at one extreme, and vulnerable atypical workers[15] operating without any security of employment and outside the relational scope of protective employment laws at the other:

■ M. Walton, 'The Shifting Nature of Work and its Implications' (2016) 45 *Industrial Law Journal* 111, 113-27

[Atypical precarious working] relationships may be divided into two general groups. The first is a group of arrangements which constitute an employment contract but do not bear the aforementioned features of the standard employment contract. This group includes part-time, short-term or project-specific work, [zero-hours contract workers] as well as casual employment. The second group exists outside of the contract of employment entirely. Independent contracting (including outsourcing, insourcing and subcontracting), labour hire agreements, franchises, bailment and self-employment fall within this category. Other arrangements are blurred within or between those categories, such as workers deemed to be employees or becoming corporations which are in turn hired as employees. 'Sham' arrangements with clauses that clearly state the relationship is not one of employment, which are designed by employers to evade the responsibilities attendant upon that arrangement, are also difficult to categorise . . . For some classes of worker, the new arrangements have meant high mobility between workplaces and a competitive power in securing wages. For others, the [growth in atypical work] has resulted in flat or declining real wages,

---

[15] See L. Rodgers, *Labour Law, Vulnerability and the Regulation of Precarious Work* (Cheltenham, Edward Elgar, 2016) for an extensive discussion of the nature of the vulnerabilities experienced by precarious atypical workers.

reduced social protection, weakened political influence and a diminishing capacity to defend their own interests. Although flexibility may benefit a worker who can operate successfully as a 'free agent in a boundary-less workplace', it also effectively passes economic pressures or risks down to 'the parties least able to resist or counteract them', driving labour market polarisation. At its best, therefore, the contemporary working environment can reward flexibility, skill and entrepreneurial self-marketing which may benefit some workers. However, at its worst, the contemporary employment landscape potentially creates enclaves of workers who do not have access to ongoing or permanent work, have limited bargaining power and may even be trapped performing 'unpleasant and lowly paid labour without a right to complain or an expectation of improvement'. This disparity exposes the potential existence of a 'dual labour market', where workers are separated into primary and secondary markets. Broadly speaking, those engaged in the primary market have job security and the potential for advancement whereas those in the secondary market are engaged in work that is characterised by instability and few promotional opportunities.

The policy responses adopted to inhibit the development of a segmented two-tier labour market,[16] and to afford atypical workers a measure of social protection, are traditionally assumed to be limited to one or more of the following four techniques:

(1) careful recalibration of the location of the threshold at which one finds the binary divide between the contract of employment and the contract for services;

(2) the legal recognition of a new contract type (or types) lying in an intermediate position somewhere between the contract of employment and the contract for services, which entails the rejection of the binary '"all or nothing" approach'[17] which often generates under-inclusion;

(3) the separate regulation of distinct forms of atypical work, such as part-time, fixed-term, agency, or zero-hours work, protecting workers engaged on such contracts from less favourable treatment; and

(4) the rejection of the contractual model and its replacement with a legally recognized personal work relationship or personal work relationships.[18]

In the UK, option (2) has been the principal domestic technique adopted to stymie the evolution of a two-tier labour market. Meanwhile (3) has been a secondary approach, primarily adopted by the EU and thus, indirectly by the UK as a result, e.g. the Part-Time Workers (Prevention of Less Favourable Treatment) Regulations ('PTWR'),[19] the Fixed-Term Employees (Prevention of Less Favourable Treatment) Regulations ('FTER'),[20] the Agency Workers Regulations 2010 and section 27A of the Employment Rights Act 1996 ('ERA').[21] There is also some evidence of the adoption of option (1) at the margins. Technique (4) involves a departure from the contractual model and envisages employment

---

[16] See V. De Stefano, 'A Tale of Oversimplification and Deregulation: The Mainstream Approach to Labour Market Segmentation and Recent Responses to the Crisis in European Countries' (2014) 43 *Industrial Law Journal* 253.

[17] G. Davidov, M. Freedland, and N. Kountouris, 'The Subjects of Labor Law: "Employees and other Workers"' in M. W. Finkin and G. Mundlak (eds), *Comparative Labor Law* (Cheltenham, Edward Elgar, 2015) 115, 128.

[18] See M. Freedland and N. Kountouris, 'The Legal Characterization of Personal Work Relations and the Idea of Labour Law' in G. Davidov and B Langille (eds), *The Idea of Labour Law* (Oxford, OUP, 2011) 202.

[19] SI 2000/1551. See Chapter 13.   [20] SI 2002/2034. See Chapter 13.

[21] SI 2010/93. See section 4.3.2.

laws with a broader coverage based on relational, rather than contractual, considerations.[22] This policy response has been rejected by UK Governments.[23]

Having adopted option (2) as its main regulatory technique, the UK Parliament has furnished statutory recognition to two intermediate categories of personal work contract which lie between the contract of service and the contract for services:

- the statutory 'worker' contract; and
- the 'contract personally to do work', which is sometimes referred to as the 'employed person' category.

Persons engaged by an enterprise to provide labour on the basis of these two contracts are provided with more limited statutory employment protection than an employee, with the statutory 'worker' entitled to a greater range of rights than the 'contract personally to do work'/'employed person'. Notably, both categories are inclusive of individuals employed under contracts which fail to qualify as a contract of employment:

■ M. Freedland, *The Personal Employment Contract* (Oxford, OUP, 2003) 23–5

The actual response to the perceived need to redraw the boundaries of employment legislation has been a rather different one. It has consisted neither in expanding the concept of the contract of employment, nor in adopting the 'employment relationship' method of defining the boundary, but instead in using two contractual categories which are wider and more inclusive than that of the contract of employment, those of the 'employed person' and the 'worker' . . . These categories which have been increasingly used in recent employment legislation seem to be intermediate ones which include some but not all contracts for services. They are tending towards the identification of an intermediate category of semi-dependent employment contract; but their relationship to the contract for services and to each other is not yet fully clear. The first of those two categories, that of the ['contract personally to do work'] has been used in the successive measures against discrimination in the field of employment. This has been a long-standing exception to the confinement of individual employment legislation to workers with contracts of employment [and is now found in section 83(2)(a) of the Equality Act 2010]. For the [employment and equal pay provisions of the Equality Act 2010] are all applied to employment under a [contract of employment, a contract of apprenticeship or a *contract personally to do work*]. This is therefore a contractually defined category which by definition extends beyond contracts of employment. However, it does not extend to all contracts for services, but only those which are for the execution of work or labour *personally*. Not all contracts for services are for the personal execution of work in that statutory sense; some contracts for services fall outside that category because they do not essentially require or contemplate performance by the contractor himself or herself. This is a point of the utmost importance; the restriction to personal execution of work excludes many self-employed people from the category of persons employed . . . From the mid-1980s onwards . . . it became increasingly common for employment legislation to be applied to 'workers', which was a category of persons employed under a rather differently defined set of contracts. This . . . extend[s] only to contracts where the sta-

---

[22] B. Hepple, 'Restructuring Employment Rights' (1986) 15 *Industrial Law Journal* 69.

[23] The UK approach can be contrasted with German law, namely section 12a of the *Tarifvertragsgesetz* of 1974, on which, see M. Weiss, 'Re-Inventing Labour Law?' in G. Davidov and B. Langille (eds), *The Idea of Labour Law* (Oxford, OUP, 2011) 48–9. In Germany, the policy preference has been to pursue an elaborate amalgam of techniques (2) and (4). This involves the recognition of a category of relationship situated somewhere in between the contract of employment and the contract for services, namely the 'employee-like person' (*arbeitnehmerähnliche Person*), who is self-employed and economically dependent on the hirer of his/her labour. For further discussion, see G. Davidov, M. Freedland, and N. Kountouris, 'The Subjects of Labor Law: "Employees and other Workers"' in M. W. Finkin and G. Mundlak (eds), *Comparative Labor Law* (Cheltenham, Edward Elgar, 2015) 115, 127–9.

tus of the party contracting to receive or purchase the services 'is not by virtue of the contract that of a client or customer of any profession or business undertaking carried on by the individual'. It is convenient to think of this as the *profession or business to client or customer exception*. This formula was used to identify the personal scope of. . . some of the employment law measures introduced after 1997, in particular, the National Minimum Wage Act 1998 and the Working Time Regulations 1998. The aim of using this 'worker' formula seems to have been that of identifying a contractual category of semi-dependent workers more precisely than the ['contract personally to do work'] formula used in the [Equality Act 2010]. The requirement of personal execution of work went some way towards this, excluding contractors who employed or subcontracted with other people to carry out the work in question, but it was evidently felt that some further or clearer confinement of the category was necessary before it could safely or appropriately be used to designate the personal scope of the new statutory employment rights which were being introduced. This explains the introduction of the customer or client to business or profession exception. The category of 'worker' is often referred to as excluding the 'genuinely self-employed', and those who describe it as such seem to regard the exception as accomplishing that exclusion. That seems to be because the exception imports a restriction of *capacity*, in addition to a requirement of performance in person; it excludes the contractor who may carry out the work in question *in person*, but who does so in a business-person to customer capacity, or in a professional practitioner to client capacity. The exclusion of those working in what is perceived as an independent business or professional capacity thus ensures that the 'worker' formula is confined to those with contracts for dependent or semi-dependent employment, and does not extend to all contracts for services.[24]

This extract from Freedland clarifies that a clear distinction may be drawn between the statutory concept of 'worker' and the 'contract personally to do work' on the basis that the former are not engaged in an independent business, whereas the latter may be. We find, therefore, that the concept of 'workers' would seem to share a number of affinities with the contract of employment. Not only must both the individual carrying out work as a 'worker' or under the contract of employment provide the services personally— rather than having the power to subcontract the personal services out—but both concepts also involve the individual being economically dependent on the enterprise. In fact, commentators such as Davidov have stressed the potential significance of the notion of 'dependency' for the purposes of establishing a 'worker' contract.[25] Davidov distinguishes dependency from subordination, describing the latter as the 'social condition of being under the control of another (to some extent), of having a boss that you have to answer to, of lacking the ability to influence the way the work is performed and choose the work to be performed'.[26]

■ G. Davidov, 'Setting Labour Law's Coverage: Between Universalism and Selectivity' (2014) 34 *Oxford Journal of Legal Studies* 543, 559–61

A simple (but in my view powerful) way to understand intermediate groups is by distinguishing between two characteristics of employment relationships: subordination and dependency. These two concepts are often treated interchangeably, but they refer to different vulnerabilities, each justifying separate parts of labour law. Subordination points attention to being under

---

[24] Writer's annotations appear in square brackets throughout this chapter.

[25] G. Davidov, 'Who is a Worker?' (2005) 34 *Industrial Law Journal* 57.

[26] *ibid.*, 62. However, the distinction between 'subordination' and 'economic dependency' is not always appreciated in the case law and the two ideas are sometimes conflated, e.g. see the EAT decisions in *James v Redcats (Brands) Ltd* [2007] ICR 1006, 1017D per Elias J, and *Bates van Winkelhof Clyde & Co. LLP* [2012] IRLR 548.

the control of an employer—being in a relationship characterized by democratic deficits. It can explain the need for regulations setting maximum hours or protecting workers' privacy, for example. Dependency refers to being dependent on a specific employer for economic as well as social and psychological needs—and as a result, inability to spread risks. It can sometimes exist in work relations not characterized by subordination, that is, even if the worker has a large degree of control over his or her time and is not subject to instructions of the employer/client. Dependency can justify regulations setting minimum wages or allowing collective bargaining, for example. Most people who work for others are under both subordination and dependency, and it is convenient to refer to them as 'employees'. But increasingly there are also people who are dependent on others but are not subordinated to them; consider, for example, people who have some characteristics of a small business, but have only one major 'client' (such as a truck owner-operator working mainly for one company, or a 'freelance' journalist working mainly for one newspaper). The 'client' in such cases should be responsible in some respects under labour law. The term 'dependent contractor' is thus most fitting, in my view, for the intermediate group. The 'worker' category developed in recent years in UK law can serve the same goals, if interpreted accordingly.[27]

In this extract, Davidov clearly takes the view that the economic dependency of the individual on the enterprise is the principal requirement for the purposes of the identification of a 'worker' contract, rather than subordination. This can be contrasted with Brodie's view that the touchstone of the 'worker' contract is whether the individual concerned is running a business or not,[28] i.e. whether the hirer of his/her labour is a client or customer.

However, the focus on the relative dependency of the individual for the purposes of the identification of a business has led commentators such as Deakin to question whether there is any clear daylight separating the concepts of 'worker' and 'employee'. In turn, this compels us to consider the legitimacy of, and necessity for, the former concept.[29] Brodie has also criticized the formulation that prioritizes dependency as the crucial factor for the purposes of establishing a 'worker' contract. This is on the ground that it is illogical to assert that an individual running a business cannot be economically dependent on a particular client.[30] Consistent with this, the courts have decided that over-analysis of the degree of dependence of the individual ought to be avoided as the means of distinguishing between a 'worker' and an 'employee'.[31] This recognizes that a genuinely self-employed independent contractor operating a business as a sole trader may be just as economically dependent on a contractor for his/her livelihood as an individual working under a contract of employment or a 'worker' contract. In other words, the absence of economic dependency cannot be equiparated with the running of a business. As such, the recent judicial trend has been to acknowledge that there is no single test that can be mechanically deployed to distinguish between the concepts of 'worker', 'contract personally to do work', the 'employee', and the 'genuinely self-employed'. Instead, each of these categories has differing, albeit similar, criteria for their identification, which must be applied in order to determine whether they exist or not. It is to those criteria that we turn in section 4.2.

---

[27] See also G. Davidov, 'The Goals of Regulating Work: Between Universalism and Selectivity' (2014) 64 *University of Toronto Law Journal* 1.

[28] D. Brodie, 'Employees, Workers, and the Self-Employed' (2005) 34 *Industrial Law Journal* 253.

[29] S. Deakin and F. Wilkinson, *The Law of the Labour Market: Industrialization, Employment, and Legal Evolution* (Oxford, OUP, 2005) 312–13.

[30] D. Brodie, 'Employees, Workers, and the Self-Employed' (2005) 34 *Industrial Law Journal* 253.

[31] *James v Redcats (Brands) Ltd* [2007] ICR 1006, 1017D per Elias J.

Reflection points

1. Do you agree with the parliamentary policy response of crafting intermediate categories between the contract of service and the contract for services in order to afford a measure of statutory employment protection to atypical workers incapable of satisfying the definition of 'employee'?

2. In policy terms, what would be the effect of assimilating the 'worker' and 'contract personally to do work' categories, bearing in mind that individuals falling within the latter concept are entitled to the protection of equality laws, whereas 'workers' are entitled to a broader range of employment laws, including equality laws?

 For additional reading on the incidence and nature of atypical working relationships and the possible policy responses, visit the Online Resources for this book at www.oup.com/uk/cabrelli3e/

4.2 THE 'WORKER' CONTRACT AND THE 'CONTRACT PERSONALLY TO DO WORK'

We now turn in this section to an in-depth examination of the two intermediate categories recognized by statute for the personal performance of work. It should be stressed that, when an individual is providing a personal service to an enterprise, he/she may be working or employed under (1) a contract of employment, (2) a 'worker' contract, (3) a 'contract personally to do work', or (4) a contract for services.[32] Categories (2) and (3) are statutory creatures, whereas (1) and (4) have long been recognized by the common law. The common law and statutory employment rights enjoyed by each of these categories of individual are illustrated in Figure 4.1, Figure 4.2, Figure 4.3, and Figure 4.4.

As such, we can see that the range of employment rights reduces as we move along from categories (1) to (4). In section 4.2.1, we examine the 'worker' contract.

4.2.1 The 'worker' contract

The logical place to begin our analysis of the statutory 'worker' contract is the definition in section 230(3)(b) of the ERA:[33]

> *Section 230 Employees, workers etc.*
>
> (1) In this Act, 'worker' . . . means an individual who has entered into or works under (or, where the employment has ceased, worked under)—
>
>   (a) a contract of employment, or

---

[32] For written examples of these contracts, see the Online Resources.

[33] Section 296(1)(b) of the Trade Union and Labour Relations (Consolidation) Act 1992 ('TULRCA'), section 54(3) of the National Minimum Wage Act 1998 ('NMWA') (section 28 of the NMWA creates a presumption that an individual qualifies as a worker entitled to be paid the national minimum wage by reversing the **burden of proof**), and regulation 2(1) of the Working Time Regulations 1998 (SI 1998/1833) provide for definitions that are similar to that contained in section 230(3) of the ERA. Likewise, see regulation 1(2) of the Part-Time Workers (Prevention of Less Favourable Treatment) Regulations 2000 (SI 2000/1551) in respect of the statutory protection of part-time workers and section 88 of the Pensions Act 2008 which enjoins an employer to auto-enrol workers into a pension scheme.

(b) any other contract, whether express or implied and (if it is express) whether oral or in writing, whereby the individual undertakes to do or perform personally any work or services for another party to the contract whose status is not by virtue of the contract that of a client or customer of any profession or business undertaking carried on by the individual.

Figure 4.1 *Common law and statutory employment rights conferred on employees working under a contract of employment*

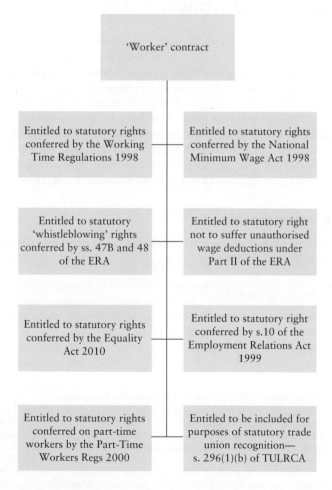

Figure 4.2 *Common law and statutory employment rights conferred on 'workers'*

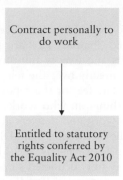

Figure 4.3 *Common law and statutory employment rights conferred on individuals engaged on the basis of a 'contract personally to do work'*

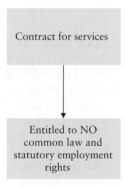

Figure 4.4 *Common law and statutory employment rights conferred on 'independent contractors' engaged on the basis of a contract for services*

From that statutory definition, it is clear that a 'worker' contract comprises at least three elements, namely:

(1) a contract;

(2) a degree of personal service on the part of the individual providing the services; and

(3) the hirer of the individual's labour must not be the latter's client or customer.

To that can be added a fourth ingredient established by the case law, namely 'mutuality of obligation'. See Figure 4.5 for each of the elements of the 'worker' contract, which depicts the common law criterion of 'mutuality of obligation' at the top tier and the statutory criteria at the bottom.

We now go through each of these four factors in light of the following hypothetical.

Hypothetical A

Danny's Demolishers Ltd ('DD') is in the process of undertaking demolition works on a site situated in Maidstone which is owned by Kent County Council ('KCC'). Unfortunately, there have been complications involved in the demolition process. As such, DD instructs a structural engineer named Miriam Dunwoody at a firm of structural engineers called Dunwoody, Marsh & Chaloner LLP to produce a report on the state of part of the building. Dunwoody, Marsh & Chaloner LLP are an independent firm of structural engineers with hundreds of clients and twenty full-time structural engineer employees. Unusually, DD instructs Miriam directly over the telephone, rather than through Dunwoody, Marsh & Chaloner LLP. The fee for the report is agreed at £10,000. Miriam's qualified understudy, Chloe Worthington, who works full-time for Dunwoody, Marsh & Chaloner LLP, undertakes the work and delivers and signs off on the report within one month of Miriam receiving the instruction from DD. There is no paperwork clarifying the nature of the relationship between DD and Miriam. DD pays Miriam £8,000 only. Miriam claims that DD unlawfully deducted sums from the agreed fee of £10,000 without her authorization in contravention of Part II of the ERA. The statutory right not to suffer an unauthorized deduction from earnings in Part II of the ERA is conferred in favour of a 'worker' only.

In the case of Hypothetical A, turning to the first element in Figure 4.5, it is essential that there is a contract in place between the parties, e.g. in *Sharpe v The Bishop of Worcester*,[34] it was held that a Church of England rector holding a statutory office could not be a 'worker' since he had not entered into any contract with the diocese. The fact that there is no written contract between DD and Miriam in Hypothetical A has no bearing on matters: section 230(3)(b) provides that a contract may arise through implication. As such, the key issue is whether there is consideration passing between DD and Miriam, and offer and acceptance. These factors are surely present in the case of Hypothetical A since there is clearly an exchange of services for remuneration.

Closely linked to the first element (the requirement for the existence of *a contract*)[35] is the second element in Figure 4.5: the requirement imposed by case law that a degree of

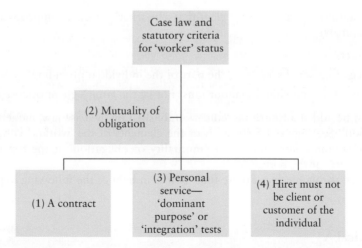

Figure 4.5 *Case law and statutory criteria for the identification of the 'worker' contract*

---

[34] [2015] IRLR 663. See also *Gilham v MoJ* [2017] IRLR 23 in the case of a district judge.
[35] Each of the four criteria in Figure 4.5 for the establishment of 'worker' status are shown in italic text.

mutuality of obligation must be present in the relationship between the individual and the enterprise.[36] However, unlike the incarnation of the mutuality of obligation test applicable in the context of determining the existence of a contract of employment, it was held in *James v Redcats*[37] that the absence of mutual commitments between the parties to provide and perform work whilst the individual is not working has no bearing on his/her status whilst he/she is actually performing the work. As such, it is with the first of the two levels of the mutuality of obligation test that we are concerned in the context of the 'worker' contract, i.e. at the level of the basic wage–work bargain agreed by the parties in terms of which the enterprise obliges itself to provide work and pay for it and the individual service provider undertakes him/herself to perform the work offered by the former.[38] So long as that wage–work bargain has been struck, the basic elements of consideration are present for the recognition of the 'worker' contract. It is inconsequential whether there are undertakings exchanged between the parties to continue to perform and provide a minimum or reasonable amount of work in the future *in between periods of the performance of the work*.[39] As such, whilst he/she is working, the requisite mutuality of obligation is present and the worker is entitled to avail him/herself of each of the employment rights listed in Figure 4.1. A good illustration of this point is the decision of the Court of Appeal in *Pimlico Plumbers Ltd v Smith*,[40] which concerned the status of a plumber called Mr Smith. Mr Smith had a contractual obligation to work a minimum 40-hour week, but there was no legal obligation on Pimlico to provide him with work. Mr Smith was also free to refuse any particular work assignment on any particular date if he was unable or unwilling for any reason to do so, but obviously he could not refuse all assignments offered since he had an obligation to work a minimum 40-hour week. It was held that although there was insufficient mutuality of obligation to treat Smith as an employee working for Pimlico on the basis of a contract of employment, he was required to be available for work throughout the working week and so satisfied the incarnation of the test of mutuality of obligation in the case of the 'worker' contract. As such, whilst he was working, he was a 'worker' and entitled to holiday pay. Applying all this to Hypothetical A, Miriam had assumed an obligation to perform the work in relation to the preparation of the report when DD had provided the work pursuant to its instructions. Therefore, whilst Miriam was actually working, the necessary mutuality of obligation was present.

Turning now to the third of the elements listed, it is beneficial if we address that factor in conjunction with the fourth element, given the overlap between these two categories. First, with regard to the third factor of *personal service*, the courts and tribunals have adopted two alternative tests, namely the 'integration' and the 'dominant purpose' tests. Both these criteria entail a consideration of the relationship between the individual and the enterprise in light of all the circumstances of the case; this proposition flows from the fact that mutuality of obligation is required in order to establish a 'worker' contract, i.e. the personal performance of work. In *James v Redcats (Brands) Ltd*,[41] Elias J judged that the correct approach was for tribunals to distinguish between a 'worker' and a 'contract for services' by applying the 'dominant purpose' test:

---

[36] *Byrne Bros (Formwork) Ltd v Baird* [2002] ICR 667, 680H per Mr Recorder Underhill QC.

[37] *James v Redcats (Brands) Ltd* [2007] ICR 1006, 1022C–1025C per Elias J (President).

[38] The term 'mutuality' in this sense denotes the presence of consideration at the first level, rather than the specific notion of 'mutuality' utilized, in a separate context, to draw a distinction between contracts of employment and contracts for services giving rise to self-employment, on which, see Chapter 3, section 3.2.2.

[39] See *Singh v Members of the Management Committee of the Bristol Sikh Temple* [2012] All ER (D) 68 (May).

[40] [2017] ICR 657.   [41] [2007] ICR 1006.

■ *James v Redcats (Brands) Ltd* [2007] ICR 1006, 1017D–1020G

Mr Justice Elias (President):

What the courts must essentially try to do here, it seems to me, is to determine whether the essence of the relationship is that of a worker or somebody who is employed, albeit in a small way, in a business undertaking . . . In [addressing] that [issue] I think that . . . [the courts must ask] whether the 'dominant purpose' of the contract is the provision of personal services or whether that is an ancillary or incidental feature. It is only if it is the dominant purpose that the definition is engaged . . . the dominant purpose test is really an attempt to identify the essential nature of the contract. Is it in essence to be located in the field of dependent work relationships, or is it in essence a contract between two independent business undertakings? An alternative way of putting it may be to say that the courts are seeking to discover whether the obligation for personal service is the dominant feature of the contractual arrangement or not. If it is, then the contract lies in the employment field; if it is not—if, for example, the dominant feature of the contract is a particular outcome or objective—and the obligation to provide personal service is an incidental or secondary consideration, it will lie in the business field. This is not to suggest that a tribunal will be in error in failing specifically to apply the 'dominant purpose' or indeed any other test. The appropriate classification will in every case depend upon a careful analysis of all the elements of the relationship, as Mr Recorder Underhill QC pointed out in *Byrne Bros (Formwork) Ltd v Baird* [2002] ICR 667. It is a fact sensitive issue, and there is no shortcut to a considered assessment of all relevant factors. However, in some cases the application of the 'dominant purpose' test may help tribunals to decide which side of the boundary a particular case lies.

The *Redcats* extract yields the proposition that the 'dominant purpose' test is concerned with an evaluation of the degree of personal service inherent within the relationship between the individual and the enterprise. This assists in determining whether (a) the individual is running a business or not and (b) the client/customer exception in section 230(3)(b) has been engaged.[42] As such, *Redcats* treats the 'dominant purpose' test as a proxy for the fourth element (*that the hirer must not be the individual's client or customer*) in section 230(3)(b) of the ERA, since in 'practice the application of the dominant purpose test has the effect of excluding . . . those found to be in business on their own account'.[43]

The 'dominant purpose' test can be contrasted with the alternative 'integration' test, propounded in *Cotswold Developments Construction Ltd v Williams*.[44] This test asks whether the purported worker:

(1) actively markets his/her services as an independent person to the world in general (in which case he/she would have clients or customers and is unlikely to be a 'worker'); or

(2) is recruited by the other party to work for it as an integral part of its operations.

[42] M. Freedland and N. Kountouris, *The Legal Construction of Personal Work Relations* (Oxford, OUP, 2011) 281. However, it should be stressed that (a) whether the individual is running a business or not and (b) the client/customer exception criteria, should not be equated or conflated, since where the client/customer exception is satisfied an individual nonetheless may not be treated as a worker, e.g. where the individual is clearly carrying on a profession or business undertaking in the sense that he/she is actively marketing his/her services as an independent person to the world in general and picking up or attempting to pick up work where available from a variety of sources: *MacAlinden v Lazarov* (UKEAT/0453/13/JOJ, 17 October 2014).

[43] *James v Redcats (Brands) Ltd* [2007] ICR 1006, 1019H per Elias J (President). Where the terms of the contract expressly provide that the individual is not a worker and is working in business on his/her own account, this will not be conclusive of the issue: *Boss Projects LLP v Bragg* (UKEAT/0330/13/SM, 6 November 2013).   [44] [2006] IRLR 181.

Like the 'dominant purpose' criterion, the 'integration' test acts as a proxy for the fourth element (*that the hirer must not be the individual's client or customer*) in section 230(3)(b) of the ERA.

In *Hospital Medical Group Ltd v Westwood*,[45] the Court of Appeal preferred the 'integration' test and used it to hold that Dr Westwood—a general practitioner with his own medical practice in Cheshire—was nonetheless acting in a worker capacity when he was undertaking hair restoration procedures for the Hospital Medical Group. Dr Westwood's arrangement with the Hospital Medical Group was exclusive, he was integrated into their operations, and he did not actively market his hair restoration services to the world. Dr Westwood's working arrangements can be contrasted with those of Dr Suhail in *Suhail v Barking Havering & Redbridge NHS Trust*.[46] In *Suhail*, there was no doubt that Dr Suhail had the freedom to work as often as he liked and for whomsoever he chose, i.e. there was no exclusivity and those hiring his services were clearly his clients or customers. As such, the EAT ruled that Dr Suhail was not a worker.

What is particularly noteworthy about *Hospital Medical Group Ltd v Westwood* is Maurice Kay LJ's judgment. Here, his Lordship remarked that neither the 'integration' nor the 'dominant purpose' tests will be determinative in identifying whether the third and fourth elements (*personal service* and *that the hirer must not be the individual's client or customer*) in section 230(3)(b) of the ERA have been established, but remarked that the former criterion will usually be preferable. The significance of Maurice Kay LJ's judgment lies in the way in which it was endorsed by Baroness Hale in the Supreme Court in *Bates van Winkelhof v Clyde and Co. LLP*:[47]

■ *Hospital Medical Group Ltd v Westwood* [2013] ICR 415, 426C–427D

Maurice Kay LJ:

In *James v Redcats (Brands) Ltd* [2007] ICR 1006 . . . Elias J (President) agreed that Langstaff J's formulation [of the 'integration' test in *Cotswold Developments Construction Ltd v Williams* [2006] IRLR 181] 'will often assist in providing the answer'. However, he . . . was not suggesting that such a test would provide the solution as a matter of universal application. Yet again, it is a question of deploying appropriate tools in relation to specific factual matrices. The striking thing about the judgments in *Cotswold* and *Redcats* is that neither propounds a test of universal application. Langstaff J's 'integration' test was considered by him, at para 53, to be demonstrative 'in most cases' and Elias J said, at para 68, that the 'dominant purpose' test 'may help' tribunals 'in some cases'. In my judgment, both were wise to eschew a more prescriptive approach which would gloss the words of the statute . . . If Parliament had intended to provide for an excluded category defined as those in business on their own account, it would have said so, rather than providing a more nuanced exception . . . I do not consider that there is a single key with which to unlock the words of the statute in every case. On the other hand, I agree with Langstaff J that his 'integration' test will often be appropriate, as it is here.

■ *Bates van Winkelhof v Clyde & Co. LLP* [2014] 1 WLR 2047, 2058D–G

Lady Hale:

Maurice Kay LJ pointed out . . . [in *Hospital Medical Group Ltd v Westwood*] . . . that neither the *Cotswold* 'integration' test nor the *Redcats* 'dominant purpose' test purported to lay down a test of general application. In his view they were wise 'to eschew a more prescriptive approach which

---

[45] [2013] ICR 415.   [46] (UKEAT/0536/13/RN, 11 June 2015).   [47] [2014] 1 WLR 2047.

would gloss the words of the statute'. Judge Peter Clark in the appeal tribunal had taken the view that Dr Westwood was a limb (b) worker because he had agreed to provide his services as a hair restoration surgeon exclusively to HMG, he did not offer that service to the world in general, and he was recruited by HMG to work as an integral part of its operations. That was the right approach. The fact that Dr Westwood was in business on his own account was not conclusive because the definition also required that the other party to the contract was not his client or customer and HMG was neither . . . I agree with Maurice Kay LJ [in *Hospital Medical Group Ltd v Westwood*] that there is not 'a single key to unlock the words of the statute in every case'. There can be no substitute for applying the words of the statute to the facts of the individual case.

In *Hospital Medical Group Ltd v Westwood* and *Bates van Winkelhof v Clyde and Co. LLP*, both Maurice Kay LJ and Baroness Hale support the argument that there can be no universal test to identify an individual as a 'worker'. Nonetheless, it is acknowledged that in the particular case of *Westwood* the integration test provided assistance in coming to the correct conclusion that the self-employed individual was in fact a 'worker'.[48] The 'integration' test and the 'dominant purpose' test still remain important alongside consideration of the relevant factual matrix. However, as each of Maurice Kay in *Westwood*, Mr Justice Elias in *Redcats*, and Baroness Hale in *van Winkelhof* readily accept, the identification of a worker is in every case a fact-sensitive issue. There is no substitute for a frank consideration of all the relevant factors impacting on the relationship between the individual and the employing entity in light of both tests and any other relevant circumstances.

In the same vein as the case law addressing whether an individual is working on the basis of a contract of employment,[49] in approaching the requirement for the third element of *personal service* in the context of the 'worker' contract, the judiciary have had cause to grapple with clauses inserted into written contracts purporting to enable individuals to substitute their performance with that of another. The use of such 'substitution' clauses has been particularly pronounced in the case of contracts signed by (i) 'gig economy' workers, as shown by the facts of *Uber BV v Aslam*[50] and *IWGB v RooFoods Ltd (t/a Deliveroo)*,[51] and (ii) labour-only subcontractors working on a construction site, e.g. contracted bricklayers. In *Byrne Brothers (Formwork) Ltd v Baird*,[52] although anxious not to create a general rule, Mr Recorder Underhill QC remarked that '[s]elf-employed labour-only subcontractors in the construction industry are . . . a good example of the kind of worker who may well not be carrying on a business undertaking in the sense of the definition . . . and for whom the 'intermediate category' [of the 'worker' contract] was designed'.[53] In an attempt to preclude the establishment of 'worker' status in the case of hired contract bricklayers, in *Redrow Homes (Yorkshire) Ltd v Wright*,[54] the hirer included a provision in Mr Wright's contract to the effect that 'the contractor must at all times provide sufficient labour'. The Court of Appeal rejected the hirer's argument that such a clause did not impose an obligation on Mr Wright to personally perform the work. Since the contract provided that the contractors were to perform personally and be paid

---

[48] See also *Pimlico Plumbers Ltd v Smith* [2017] ICR 657, 682E–G per Sir Terence Etherton MR where the Court of Appeal also adopted the integration test as a proxy for the fourth element, i.e. whether *the hirer was the individual's client or customer*.

[49] See Chapter 3, section 3.2.1.

[50] [2018] IRLR 97, 99 and 111 at paras 11 and 118. For commentary on the employment tribunal decision, see M. Freedland and N. Kountouris, 'Some Reflections on the "Personal Scope" of Collective Labour Law' (2017) 46 *Industrial Law Journal* 52, 68–70.

[51] [2018] IRLR 84, 88, 89, 90, and 92–93 at paras 54, 59, 76–86, and 98–104.

[52] [2002] ICR 667.   [53] *ibid.*, 678C.   [54] [2004] EWCA Civ 469, [2004] ICR 1126.

individually, and that they had the capacity to undertake work they were contractually required to perform, it was held that they were workers.[55]

Redcats[56] is another case concerning the judicial treatment of substitution clauses, albeit the individual was a contract parcel courier rather than a bricklayer. In effect, the hirer attempted to introduce a form of substitution clause into the parcel courier's contract which would confer an unfettered right of substitution in the latter's favour. However, that attempt failed. The parcel courier's contract contained a clause to the effect that she had the right to find an alternative courier if she were 'unable to work' through illness or childcare duties. Borrowing from the analysis of the EAT in *MacFarlane v Glasgow City Council*,[57] Elias J drew a distinction between the phrases 'unable' and 'unable or unwilling' to provide work where they feature in contractual documentation. Elias J remarked '[i]f I need not perform the work when I am unwilling, then there is never any obligation of any kind to perform it[, so i]t is entirely my will and therefore my choice . . . [b]ut if I can only be relieved of the duty when I am unable, then I must do the work personally if I am able'.[58] On that basis, the substitution clause enabling the parcel courier to call on another to perform the work when she was unable to do so was insufficient to dislodge the requisite degree of personal service necessary for the establishment of a 'worker' contract[59] and there was no unfettered right of substitution provided to the individuals. A similar result was reached in *Pimlico Plumbers Ltd v Smith*.[60]

As for the potential for the courts to invoke substitution clauses as a means of recharacterizing the relationship between individuals and the hirers of their labour, akin to their appearance in contracts of employment, *Uber BV v Aslam*[61] demonstrates how these will be subject to the 'sham' doctrine enunciated in *Autoclenz Ltd v Belcher*[62] in the context of cases determining whether an individual is a 'worker'. In *Uber BV v Aslam* the EAT was prepared to reclassify what appeared to be an agency relationship as a 'worker' relationship. The effect here is to override the contractual terms—such as the substitution clause—by reference to the factual reality. This has the impact of recategorizing the relationship from one that is ostensibly commercial to a 'worker' arrangement. The courts may also essentially 'ignore' the substitution clause on the ground that there was never any contractual intention on the part of either party for it to be used.[63]

If we now apply the jurisprudence on the third and fourth factors (*personal service* and *that the hirer must not be the individual's client or customer*) in Figure 4.5 to Hypothetical A, then we find that Miriam does not qualify as a worker. First, turning to the third factor and using the 'dominant purpose' test in this case, the obligation of personal service is not the dominant purpose of the contract entered into between Miriam and DD; instead, the dominant purpose of the contractual arrangement between Miriam

---

[55] The case of *Redrow Homes (Yorkshire) Ltd v Buckborough* [2009] IRLR 34 demonstrates how Redrow subsequently modified its standard terms and conditions for the hire of contract bricklayers in response to its defeat in the Court of Appeal in *Redrow Homes (Yorkshire) Ltd v Wright*.

[56] *James v Redcats (Brands) Ltd* [2007] ICR 1006.   [57] [2001] IRLR 7.

[58] *James v Redcats (Brands) Ltd* [2007] ICR 1006, 1014H–1015A.

[59] See also *Parkes v Yorkshire Window Co. Ltd* [2010] All ER (D) 108 (August) where an individual did not have an unfettered right to provide a substitute and was held to be a 'worker'. *Redcats* and *Parkes* can be contrasted with *Community Dental Centres Ltd v Sultan-Darmon* [2010] IRLR 1024, where a substitution clause afforded a dentist an unfettered right to provide a substitute and so he was not treated as a 'worker'. See also *Premier Groundworks v Jozsa* (UKEAT/0494/08/DM, 17 March 2009), where it was held that a groundwork services contractor was not a 'worker' since the substitution clause afforded him an unfettered right to delegate performance of the work to a third party so long as the hirer was notified in advance and the substitute was sufficiently capable, experienced, and as qualified as the individual.

[60] [2017] ICR 657.

[61] [2018] IRLR 97, 109–12 at paras 92–115. See also *Redrow Homes (Yorkshire) Ltd v Buckborough* [2009] IRLR 34; and Chapter 3, section 3.2.1.

[62] [2011] UKSC 41, [2011] ICR 1157.

[63] See *Boss Projects LLP v Bragg* (UKEAT/0330/13/SM, 6 November 2013).

and DD is the completion of the report on the condition of the building at Maidstone. If we apply the 'integration' test, we reach the same result, since Miriam is engaged in the active marketing of her services as an independent qualified person to the world in general. As for Chloe, there is no contract struck between her and DD, and as such the first element in Figure 4.5 requiring a basic contract is missing. Secondly, in relation to the customer or client exception in section 230(3)(b) of the ERA, the evidence suggests that Miriam is in fact operating a business and marketing her services generally. For that reason, she cannot be engaged on the basis of a 'worker' contract. Therefore, her claim under Part II of the ERA for an unauthorized deduction from wages would be unsuccessful and she would need to challenge the £2,000 shortfall by some other legal means.

The final part of the jigsaw in Figure 4.5 is the status of the element of *subordination*. The effect of the decision of the Court of Appeal in *Bates van Winkelhof v Clyde & Co. LLP*[64] had been to add this as a fifth element necessary for the establishment of the 'worker' contract. The factor of 'subordination' enjoined an individual to show that he/she was subordinate to the hirer of his labour in the sense of some subservience to the direction of the hirer in return for the receipt of remuneration. The question in *Bates van Winkelhof v Clyde & Co. LLP* was whether a partner of a limited liability partnership could be a 'worker', which was answered in the Court of Appeal in the negative owing to the absence of 'subordination'. The requirement for 'subordination' derives from European law, and in particular the decisions of the Supreme Court in *Jivraj v Hashwani*[65] and of the European Court of Justice ('ECJ' or 'CJEU') in *Allonby v Accrington and Rossendale College*.[66] In fact, both *Jivraj v Hashwani*[67] and *Allonby v Accrington and Rossendale College*[68] are cases concerning the relational scope of equality law and equal pay law and the meaning of the expression 'contract personally to do work' in section 83(2)(a) of the Equality Act 2010,[69] rather than the 'worker' contract. For that reason, it is arguable that to transplant the requirement for subordination into the criteria necessary for the establishment of 'worker' status was inappropriate, unnecessary, and illogical. Unsurprisingly, the decision of the Court of Appeal in *Bates van Winkelhof v Clyde & Co. LLP* was reversed by the Supreme Court.[70] As such, the partner in the LLP was treated as a worker and the law has been reformulated to remove the requirement for subordination. The end result is that the anxiety that the 'worker' and the 'contract personally to do work' categories could be conflated has been dampened to some extent:

■ *Bates van Winkelhof v Clyde & Co. LLP* [2014] 1 WLR 2047, 2058G–2059B

Baroness Hale:

I agree with Maurice Kay LJ that there is not 'a single key to unlock the words of the statute in every case'. There can be no substitute for applying the words of the statute to the facts of the individual case. There will be cases where that is not easy to do. But in my view they are not solved by adding some mystery ingredient of 'subordination' to the concept of employee and worker. The experienced employment judges who have considered this problem have all recognised that there is no magic test other than the words of the statute themselves. As Elias J recognised in the *Redcats* case [2007] ICR 1006, a small business may be genuinely an independent business but be completely

---

[64] [2013] ICR 883.
[65] [2011] UCSC 40, [2011] 1 WLR 1872.   [66] [2004] ECR I-873, [2004] ICR 1328.
[67] [2011] UCSC 40, [2011] 1 WLR 1872.   [68] [2004] ECR I-873, [2004] ICR 1328.
[69] See Chapter 4, section 4.2.2.
[70] For discussion of the UK Supreme Court decision, see J. Prassl, 'Members, Partners, Employees, Workers? Partnership Law and Employment Status Revisited. *Clyde & Co LLP v Bates van Winkelhof*' (2014) 43 *Industrial Law Journal* 495; and E. Berry, 'When is a Partner/LLP Member Not a Partner/LLP Member? The Interface with Employment and Worker Status' (2017) 46 *Industrial Law Journal* 309.

dependent on and subordinate to the demands of a key customer (the position of those small factories making goods exclusively for the 'St Michael' brand in the past comes to mind). Equally, as Maurice Kay LJ recognised in *Westwood*'s case [2013] ICR 415, one may be a professional person with a high degree of autonomy as to how the work is performed and more than one string to one's bow, and still be so closely integrated into the other party's operation as to fall within the definition. As the case of the controlling shareholder in a company who is also employed as chief executive shows, one can effectively be one's own boss and still be a 'worker'. While subordination may sometimes be an aid to distinguishing workers from other self-employed people, it is not a freestanding and universal characteristic of being a worker.

The Taylor Review[71] was particularly alive to the problematic and haphazard judicial development of the criteria for the establishment of the 'worker' contract. In response to these difficulties, Taylor made a host of recommendations, which have been considered by the House of Commons Work and Pensions and Business, Energy and Industrial Strategy Committees.[72] First, it is suggested that the 'worker' concept be renamed 'dependent contractors'.[73] Of itself, apart from introducing a measure of terminological clarity, it is unclear what else such a reform is likely to achieve. Taylor also proposes that the various tests for worker status be clarified and codified.[74] Whilst striving for greater clarity is always an admirable goal, bitter experience has shown how this is much easier said than done in this field of activity. As for codification of the tests for 'worker' status, there is a danger that the legislation becomes subject to ossification and that the statutory criteria are bypassed by changes in underlying social, economic, and political conditions to such an extent that they become irrelevant. In this way, any statutory tests would have to be kept under constant review. Taylor also recommends that the onus of proving that an individual is not a worker be shifted to the hirer of the individual's labour.[75] It is also suggested that workers be issued with a statement of the main particulars of their contract from day one:[76] at present, this is a statutory requirement for employees only.[77] Finally, the difficulties experienced in the case law as a result of the use of substitution clauses has also prompted Taylor to recommend that the 'personal service' requirement be removed and that increased relevance be afforded to the 'control' test for worker status.[78] This seems somewhat surprising for two reasons: first, inasmuch as removing 'personal service' would include a greater number of individuals within the protective cloak of employment law, but would have the bizarre effect of enabling legal persons other than natural persons to qualify as workers—which surely cannot be the intention; secondly, it is odd in light of the fact that neither 'control' nor 'subordination' are criteria for an

---

[71] See *Good Work: The Taylor Review of Modern Working Practices* (July 2017), available at https://www.gov.uk/government/uploads/system/uploads/attachment_data/file/627671/good-work-taylor-review-modern-working-practices-rg.pdf (last visited 19 November 2017).

[72] See *A Framework for Modern Employment*, available at https://www.parliament.uk/business/committees/committees-a-z/commons-select/work-and-pensions-committee/news-parliament-2017/future-of-work-report-17-19/ (last visited 4 December 2017).

[73] See *Good Work: The Taylor Review of Modern Working Practices* (July 2017), available at https://www.gov.uk/government/uploads/system/uploads/attachment_data/file/627671/good-work-taylor-review-modern-working-practices-rg.pdf at page 35 (last visited 19 November 2017).

[74] See *ibid*., page 36.   [75] See *ibid*., page 62.   [76] See *ibid*., page 38.

[77] See chapter 5, section 5.2.1. However, the employer has two months to issue such a statement to an employee, whereas the proposal here is that it would be a 'day one' right.

[78] See *Good Work: The Taylor Review of Modern Working Practices* (July 2017), available at https://www.gov.uk/government/uploads/system/uploads/attachment_data/file/627671/good-work-taylor-review-modern-working-practices-rg.pdf at page 36 (last visited 19 November 2017). For criticism, see K. Bates, A. Bogg and T. Novitz, '"Voice" and "Choice" in Modern Working Practices: Problems with the Taylor Review' (2018) 47 *Industrial Law Journal* 46.

individual to qualify as a 'worker'. It also has the counter-intuitive effect of nudging the 'worker' and 'contract personally to do work' categories ever closer together, albeit that personal service would continue to be a requirement for the establishment of the latter but not the former under Taylor's proposals.

Reflection points

1. In your opinion, are the 'dominant purpose' or 'integration' tests both convincing means of distinguishing between the 'worker' contract and the contract for services? Give reasons for your answer.

2. Do you agree with the point (made in *James v Redcats (Brands) Ltd*) that a distinction can be, and ought to be, drawn between the notions of (a) running a business and 'economic dependency', and (b) 'subordination' and 'economic dependency'?

3. Are you convinced by the distinction crafted in *James v Redcats (Brands) Ltd* between 'unable' and 'unable or unwilling' substitution clauses? Give reasons for your answer.

4. To what extent is it necessary for the criterion of 'subordination' to play a role in identifying the existence of a 'worker' contract? Do you agree with Baroness Hale's approach in the decision of the Supreme Court in *Bates van Winkelhof v Clyde & Co. LLP* in this regard?

4.2.2 The 'contract personally to do work'

Prior to the Supreme Court's decision in *Jivraj v Hashwani*,[79] it had been thought that the definition of the 'contract personally to do work' in section 83(2)(a) of the Equality Act 2010 was sufficiently broad to encompass individuals operating in a business or professional capacity, such as architects, solicitors, accountants, plumbers, electricians, consultants, etc:

Section 83 Interpretation and exceptions

(2) 'Employment' [in Part 5 of this Act] means—

   (a) employment under a contract of employment, a contract of apprenticeship or a contract personally to do work;

However, since *Jivraj*, the understanding that all self-employed professionals invariably fall within the section 83(2)(a) definition must be contested.[80] That is despite the fact that there is nothing in the wording of section 83(2)(a) of the Equality Act 2010 to suggest that someone with a contract personally to do work is unable to bring a claim under that statute if the other party is one of his/her professional clients. In fact, it would now appear that the four elements shown in Figure 4.6 must feature in the relationship between the individual service provider and the relevant enterprise.

Turning to the first requirement for *a contract*,[81] the same points made in the case of the 'worker' contract also apply here. For example, it has been held by the Supreme

---

[79] [2011] UCSC 40, [2011] 1 WLR 1872.
[80] See *Windle v Secretary of State for Justice* [2015] ICR 156.
[81] Each of the four criteria for the establishment of the 'contract personally to do work' in Figure 4.6 are shown in italic text.

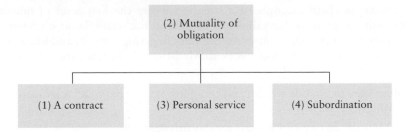

Figure 4.6 *Case law and statutory criteria for the identification of the 'contract personally to do work'*

Court that a volunteer without a legally binding contract will not be engaged on the basis of a 'contract personally to do work'.[82] As such, somewhat controversially, volunteers do not fall within the protective coverage of the anti-discrimination provisions in the Equality Act 2010. Secondly, the criterion of *mutuality of obligation* was added by case law. Mutuality of obligation here is not a reference to any requirement for the existence of mutual commitments between the parties to provide and perform work whilst the individual is not working, but instead is simply a reference to the elementary wage–work bargain.[83] A strong inference that mutuality—in the sense of the wage–work bargain—is required can be drawn from the decision of the Court of Appeal in *Mingeley v Pennock (t/a Amber Cars)*:[84]

■ *Mingeley v Pennock (t/a Amber Cars)* [2004] EWCA Civ 328, [2004] ICR 727, 733H–734

[The headnote to the case sets forth the facts as follows:] [Mingeley] was a taxi driver who owned his own vehicle and paid [Amber Cars], the operators of a taxi service, £75 per week for a radio and access to their computer system, which allocated calls from customers to a fleet of drivers. Though under his contract with [Amber Cars] [Mingeley] could not work for any other operator and was required to wear [Amber Cars'] uniform and adhere to [Amber Cars'] scale of charges, he was not obliged to work any particular hours, or at all, and he kept all the fare money. [Mingeley] made a complaint to the employment tribunal that [Amber Cars] had discriminated against him on grounds of his race.

Maurice Kay LJ:

. . . on the plain words of [section 83(2)(a) of the Equality Act 2010] and the authorities to which I have referred, the employment tribunal was correct to conclude that, in order to bring himself within [section 83(2)(a)], Mr Mingeley had to establish that his contract with Amber Cars placed him under an obligation 'personally to [do] work . . .'. As the tribunal found, there was no evidence that he was ever under such an obligation. He was free to work or not to work at his own whim or fancy. His obligation was to pay Amber Cars £75 per week and, if he chose to work, then to do so within the requirements of the arrangement. However, the absence from the contract of an obligation to work places him beyond the reach of [section 83(2)(a)].

---

[82] *X v Mid Sussex Citizens Advice Bureau* [2013] 1 All ER 1038.
[83] For example, see *Windle v Secretary of State for Justice* [2015] ICR 156.
[84] [2004] ICR 727. See also *Halawi v World Duty Free* [2015] 3 All ER 543.

Mingeley is an excellent example of a situation where the first level of mutuality of obligation—the wage–work bargain—will be absent. For example, at no point did Mr Mingeley ever owe any obligation to Amber Cars to perform work, and likewise Amber Cars had no obligation to provide work to Mr Mingeley. Instead, the only obligations which arose were:

- for Amber Cars to provide a radio and computer system and to allocate incoming calls to Mr Mingeley; and

- for Mr Mingeley to pay £75 a week for this privilege.

As such, no wage–work bargain was ever struck and so there was no mutuality of obligation.[85]

It is the third requirement that the individual be engaged in the provision of a *personal service* which gave rise to the 'dominant purpose' test that we considered earlier in the context of the 'worker' category. The dominant purpose test was established in cases such as *Mirror Newspapers Ltd v Gunning*[86] and *Mingeley v Pennock (t/a Amber Cars)*.[87] Owing to the fact that we addressed the dominant purpose test in detail in Chapter 4, section 4.1.1, we propose to skip this element and focus on the fourth factor of *subordination* instead. In the Supreme Court decision in *Jivraj v Hashwani*,[88] Lord Clarke ruled that the words 'employment under . . . a contract personally to do any work' in section 83(2)(a) of the Equality Act 2010 require the individual to be in a relationship of subordination with the enterprise. The inclusion of the words 'employment under' in section 83(2)(a) of the Equality Act 2010 suggested to Lord Clarke that Parliament intended to confine the statutory creature of the 'contract personally to do work' to the province of employment, rather than extend it to the commercial field, e.g. the contract for services entered into by the plumber or electrician. As such, when searching for the existence of a contract personally to do work for the purposes of section 83(2)(a) of the Equality Act 2010, *Jivraj* enjoins courts and tribunals to focus on 'whether, on the one hand, the person concerned performs services for and under the direction of [the hirer] in return for which he or she receives remuneration, or, on the other hand, he or she is an independent provider of services who is not in a relationship of subordination with [the hirer]'.[89] Applying that analysis, the Supreme Court held that the role of an arbitrator appointed privately to resolve a commercial dispute between two contracting parties could not naturally be considered to be in a relationship of subordination with the parties who received his services and was not one of employment under a contract personally to do work.[90] Instead, the arbitrator was an independent service provider.[91] Similarly, in *Halawi v World Duty Free*,[92] the Court of Appeal held that a beauty consultant selling cosmetic products through her own limited company at a duty-free shop operated by WDF at Heathrow airport could not raise a discrimination claim against WDF. Lady Justice Arden in the Court of Appeal ruled that there was a want of subordination and the beauty consultant could not be engaged on the basis of a contract personally to do

---

[85] However, contrast the decision in *Mingeley* with *Muschett v HM Prison Service* [2010] IRLR 451 which appears to conflate the 'contract personally to do work' and the 'contract for services', which is incorrect: M. Freedland, *The Personal Employment Contract* (Oxford: OUP, 2003) 24. Many (if not all) contracts of the latter type will amount to the former, but not all contracts of the former type will fall within the latter.

[86] [1986] 1 WLR 546, approved by the House of Lords in *Kelly v Northern Ireland Housing Executive* [1999] 1 AC 428 and the Court of Appeal in *Legal Services Commission v Patterson* [2003] EWCA Civ 1558. See *Halawi v World Duty Free* [2015] 3 All ER 543 for circumstances in which the individual's contractual power to send along a substitute worker in her stead was held to be incompatible with the personal performance of her services.   [87] [2004] EWCA Civ 328, [2004] ICR 727.

[88] [2011] UKSC 40, [2011] 1 WLR 1872, 1887C–H per Lord Clarke.

[89] *ibid.*, 1886E–F per Lord Clarke.   [90] *ibid.*, 1882H–1883B per Lord Clarke.

[91] *ibid.*, 1888C–1889E per Lord Clarke.   [92] [2015] 3 All ER 543.

work with WDF, since she 'was not subject to WDF's control in the way she carried out her work [and] independence was not a necessary feature of her work'.[93]

Five points flowing from this idea of 'subordination' deserve our attention.

(1) First, there is the nature of the interaction between the 'dominant purpose' and subordination factors, which to some extent overlap with each other. In *Jivraj*, Lord Clarke clarified the proper relationship between them in the following manner:

■ *Jivraj v Hashwani* [2011] 1 WLR 1872, 1887H–1888B

Lord Clarke:

[Although] dominant purpose cannot be the sole test . . . it may well be relevant in arriving at the correct conclusion on the facts of a particular case. After all, if the dominant purpose of the contract is the execution of personal work, it seems likely that the relationship will be, in the words of *Allonby* [2004] ICR 1328, para 67, a case in which the person concerned performs services for and under the direction of the other party to the contract in return for remuneration as opposed to an independent provider of services who is not in a relationship of subordination with him or it.

As such, both tests are of equal importance for the purposes of evaluating the status of an individual and whether he/she qualifies as a contractor personally doing work.[94]

(2) Secondly, there is the question whether there is any relationship between the subordination test and the mutuality of obligation test for employment that we discussed in detail in Chapter 3. At first glance, the two concepts seem mutually exclusive and wholly unrelated, so the response would be in the negative. In fact, the former would appear much more onerous than the former for an individual to establish.[95] However, in *Windle v Secretary of State for Justice*,[96] Lord Justice Underhill in the Court of Appeal opined that the idea of mutuality of obligation as applied for the purposes of establishing employment status could prove useful in determining whether an individual is subordinate to a hirer of his/her labour:

■ *Secretary of State for Justice v Windle* [2016] ICR 721, 731B–D

Lord Justice Underhill:

. . . the ultimate question must be the nature of the relationship during the period that the work is being done. But it does not follow that the absence of mutuality of obligation outside that period may not influence, or shed light on, the character of the relationship within it. It seems to me a matter of common sense and common experience that the fact that a person supplying services is only doing so on an assignment-by-assignment basis may tend to indicate a degree of independence, or lack of subordination, in the relationship while at work which is incompatible with [the contract personally to do work] status . . . Of course it will not always do so [and] its relevance will depend on the particular facts of the case; but to exclude consideration of it in limine runs counter to the repeated message of the authorities that it is necessary to consider all the circumstances.

---

[93] *ibid.*, 554g–h at para 44.
[94] See also the discussion in *CVS Solicitors LLP v Van Der Borgh* (UKEAT/0591/11/JOJ, 16 April 2012).
[95] See H. Dhorajiwala, '*Secretary of State for Justice v Windle*: The Expanding Frontiers of Mutuality of Obligation' (2017) 46 *Industrial Law Journal* 268.   [96] [2016] ICR 721.

For the reason that *Windle* appears to generate a degree of convergence between the contract of employment and the contract personally to do work, it is highly controversial. It has been criticized by Prassl for the reason that the categories of the contract of employment and the contract personally to do work are not simply degrees of employment, but rather *differences in kind*. As such, the notion that any weight should be attached to the mutuality of obligation test adopted for the purposes of the classification of a contract as a contract of employment is dismissed by Prassl.[97]

(3) In policy terms, and in parallel with the recognition of mutuality of obligation in *Windle* as a proxy for 'subordination', the most significant effect of the imposition of the requirement for subordination is the restriction of the relational scope of the category of the 'contract personally to do work'. Lord Clarke himself recognized this point when he remarked that it would be surprising if a 'customer who engages a person on a one-off contract as, say, a plumber, w[ere held to be] subject to the whole gamut of discrimination legislation'.[98] This reining in of the boundaries of the relational scope would appear contrary to the prevailing parliamentary policy of affording equality and anti-discrimination rights to a wider class of individuals than the 'worker' category. In effect, it has the somewhat counter-intuitive effect of relegating the importance and impact of the equality legislation.

(4) In light of Baroness Hale's rejection of 'subordination' in *van Winkelhof*[99] as an instrument that can assist in differentiating between 'workers' and self-employed independent contractors, academic commentators have rightly questioned whether 'subordination' serves any useful function in the context of the contract personally to do work. For example, Prassl has remarked that the *van Winkelhof* decision 'provides fertile ground for arguments challenging the Supreme Court's earlier decision in *Jivraj v Hashwani*, which had drastically curtailed the personal scope of discrimination law in the employment context [by adopting the subordination test].'[100] It is difficult to disagree with that statement, *Windle* notwithstanding.

(5) Finally, although the subordination test heralded in *Jivraj* shares many commonalities with the 'control' test we addressed in Chapter 3,[101] the exact content and nature of that concept remains elusive. For example, is it really coterminous with the 'control' test which is one of the defining attributes of the contract of employment,[102] and how does it correspond to the notions of economic dependency, labour disadvantage, and vulnerability (if at all)? Consider the following extracts from McCrudden, and Freedland and Kountouris:

■ C. McCrudden, 'Two Views of Subordination: The Personal Scope of Employment Discrimination Law in *Jivraj v Hishwani*' (2012) 41 *Industrial Law Journal* 30, 51

The application of [the notion of subordination] calls for the exercise of considerable judgement as to who is 'subordinate', and to whom. No doubt, in the future, there will be considerable debate as to what 'subordination' involves, such as how far it extends beyond the 'control' test, applied by

---

[97] J. Prassl, 'Who is a Worker?' (2017) 133 *Law Quarterly Review* 366, 369.

[98] [2011] UKSC 40, [2011] 1 WLR 1872, 1889F per Lord Clarke.

[99] *Bates van Winkelhof v Clyde & Co. LLP* [2014] 1 WLR 2047, 2058G–2059B.

[100] J. Prassl, 'Members, Partners, Employees, Workers? Partnership Law and Employment Status Revisited: *Clyde & Co. LLP v Bates van Winkelhof*' (2014) 43 *Industrial Law Journal* 495, 503.

[101] See Chapter 3, section 3.2.1.

[102] In *Halawi v World Duty Free* [2015] 3 All ER 543, 544f–i, Lady Justice Arden does appear to equate 'subordination' with 'control' and a lack of independence.

the Supreme Court in *Jivraj*, to also include 'economic dependency'. So too, there is the potential for debate as to whether the emerging domestic concept of subordination is the same as European civil-law ideas of subordination, which it will be for the CJEU to interpret. The European concept of subordination may, or may not, be coterminous with the older British concept of subordination. All this is for the future and the outcome of these debates is uncertain. Although the Supreme Court's anti-subordination approach is uncertain, we can at least say that it is different from the [US] approach . . . Under the US approach, an anti-subordination approach is part of a general anti-discrimination perspective and focuses on status-based social stratification, in the context of a history of particular 'historically oppressed group[s]', such as those of a particular race, gender, religion, etc. The UK Supreme Court's approach, and this echoes accurately the approach adopted by the ECJ, adopts a different (and perhaps older) conception of vulnerability and social stratification, where the oppression arises from the subordination inherent in the labour context, rather than focusing on the subordination of particular status-based groups.

■ **M. Freedland and N. Kountouris, 'Employment Equality and Personal Work Relations: A Critique of *Jivraj v Hashwani*' (2012) 41 *Industrial Law Journal* 56, 65**

Perhaps at a deeper level intentionally, Professor McCrudden . . . adduces the analogy of the 'subordination approach' to discrimination law, an approach of which we were not ourselves fully aware. For, as he so clearly explains, that latter approach deploys a notion of 'subordination' which is almost synonymous with that of 'disadvantage' or 'vulnerability'. This notion of 'subordination' seems to us wholly different from the narrowly technical notion of subordination which is used to distinguish between dependent and independent personal work relations in the framing and application of employment law. If there was a historical time at which the narrow technical-legal notion of subordination operated as a satisfactory proxy for the broader normative notion of disadvantage or vulnerability, we feel sure that this time is long since passed. So far is that equation from now being a valid one that we feel that the 'subordination approach' to discrimination law in general which Professor McCrudden has identified actually argues against the 'subordination approach' to employment discrimination law in particular which the Supreme Court took in this case. The fact that the 'subordination approach' embraced by the Supreme Court in *Jivraj* is developed by reference to the one developed by the ECJ in *Allonby*—which one might regard as broader than the one traditionally superseding the English law notion of contract of service—is more of a Pyrrhic victory than a glass half full. It still in our view represents the entrenchment of the binary divide between employment and self-employment, and as such provides an inadequate central organising concept not just for employment discrimination law but also, as we argue elsewhere, for labour or employment law at large.

There is a strong argument that the impact of *Jivraj* and *Windle* is to edge the concept of the 'contract personally to do work' ever closer to the contract of employment category to the point at which they may have become indistinguishable. It would seem that both now comprise at least the following tests:

(1) control/subordination;

(2) mutuality of obligation as a result of *Windle*, in the sense that there must be mutual undertakings exchanged between the parties to continue to perform and provide a minimum or reasonable amount of work and pay for it in the future; and

(3) an obligation to provide personal service which is either the sole or dominant feature of the contract.

This 'empty box' phenomenon is explored in the following extract from Freedland and Kountouris:

M. Freedland and N. Kountouris, 'Employment Equality and Personal Work Relations: A Critique of *Jivraj v Hashwani*' (2012) 41 *Industrial Law Journal* 56, 58

The Supreme Court, on the other hand, treated the notion of 'employment under' such a contract as imposing a crucial restriction upon this relational descriptor, confining it to relations of 'employment' in the sense of relations of subordinate employment taking place under the direction of the employer. In the Supreme Court, it was acknowledged 'that there is an element of circularity in that approach'; but might it not be argued that there is an element not merely of circularity but also of illogicality in that approach? The illogicality would be of the following kind. Subordinate employment taking place under the direction of the employer is, for English law, the generic identifier or defining attribute of the contract of employment (including for this purpose the contract of apprenticeship). This would suggest that, if that particular restrictive effect is accorded to the notion of 'employment under', there is logically no such thing as employment under a contract *other than* a contract of employment or apprenticeship. The notion of 'employment under a contract personally to do work' where that contract is *not* a contract of employment or apprenticeship is thereby emptied of all content; the legislator has on that view simply evoked a logically non-meaningful category or empty box.

Reflection points

1. Do you agree that a distinction ought to be drawn between the first level of 'mutuality of obligation' in terms of the basic wage–work bargain for the purposes of the 'worker' contract and the 'contract personally to do work', on the one hand, and the second level of 'mutuality of obligation' in terms of a set of ongoing mutual commitments to provide and pay for work and perform it for the purposes of identifying the contract of employment, on the other? Consider the implications if both levels of 'mutuality of obligation' had to be satisfied in order to establish the 'worker' contract and the 'contract personally to do work'. Would such an approach be conceptually and practically sound?

2. Do you agree that the 'subordination' factor ought to be necessary in order to establish the existence of a 'contract personally to do work'? Give reasons for your answer.

Now consider Hypothetical B.

Hypothetical B

Danny's Demolishers Ltd ('DD') approaches an Asian barrister Abdul Khan to advise it on a dispute it has with a former landlord in respect of an office in Warrington. Having had an initial meeting with the barrister to consider preliminary matters, DD decides to appoint another barrister instead. Abdul suspects that the failure to appoint him was motivated by racial discrimination. In your opinion, in light of the relevant tests, would Abdul Khan qualify as a 'worker' or be engaged on the basis of a 'contract personally to do work'? Give reasons for your answer.

4.3 AGENCY WORK

Agency work is a highly flexible mode of labour supply involving a triangular relationship: an 'employment business' or 'agency' places the agency worker on assignment with an end-user undertaking/hirer, which engages him/her temporarily while paying the agency a fee. In turn, the agency remunerates the agency worker, as illustrated in Figure 4.7.[103]

The archetypal triangular relationship involves the employment of a dual contractual structure. The agency and the hirer conclude a contract whereby the former agrees to supply labour to the latter in return for the payment of a fee ('Contract No. 1'); the agency and the agency worker enter into a contract in terms of which the latter agrees to perform personal services for a hirer identified by the agency under the supervision and control of such hirer in return for payment ('Contract No. 2'). Rather than paying the agency worker directly, it is standard practice for the hirer to tender payment of a fee to the agency under the terms of Contract No. 1. The agency deducts a percentage from that sum and remits the balance to the agency worker in conformance with Contract No. 2. Furthermore, Contract No. 2 will invariably stipulate that it is not a contract of service.

In the summer of 2017, the Taylor review estimated that there were between approximately 800,000 and 1.2 million agency workers in the UK,[104] amounting to approximately 4 per cent of the entire British workforce. The length of the average assignment is less

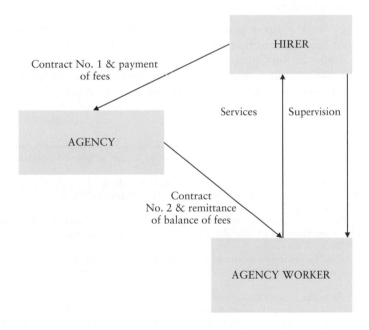

Figure 4.7 *Basic triangular employment relationship*

[103] See also in the Explanatory Memorandum to the Agency Workers Regulations 2010, available at http://www.legislation.gov.uk/uksi/2010/93/pdfs/uksiem_20100093_en.pdf diagram at page 11 (last visited 5 December 2017).

[104] See *Good Work: The Taylor Review of Modern Working Practices* (July 2017), available at https://www.gov.uk/government/uploads/system/uploads/attachment_data/file/627671/good-work-taylor-review-modern-working-practices-rg.pdf at page 24 (last visited 19 November 2017). However, much depends on what criteria are adopted to define what is intended by the words 'agency worker'.

than three months in the case of approximately 60 per cent of all agency workers.[105] In the case of some employers, their total staff consists of up to 40 per cent non-employees, including temporary agency workers.[106]

From the agency worker's perspective, part of the attraction in being hired to work in this manner is the flexibility which it involves.[107] Moreover, it is often said that agency work is a useful stepping stone to a permanent employment contract.[108] Meanwhile, for the hirer, the advantages of the tripartite agency arrangement are manifold:

(1) the engagement of agency workers enables the hirer to arrange short-term replacement cover for staff absences or workers on long-term leave, or to cover a position before a permanent recruitment is appointed;[109]

(2) agency workers are often engaged in order to satisfy seasonal or cyclical fluctuations in customer demands;[110]

(3) the hirer can avoid counting the agency workers in its overall employee headcount when reporting to the financial markets, which functions to make it look like a lean employer;[111]

(4) the hirer is relieved of the requirement to perform payroll administration in respect of the agency workers, which is undertaken by the agency on its behalf;

(5) hirers enjoy low exit costs owing to the lack of dismissal protection laws applicable to agency workers and the challenges they face in unionizing themselves; and

(6) the arrangement is inherently more flexible than engaging workers on the basis of a contract of employment.[112]

However, agency work is open to the accusation that it is an exploitative way of hiring labour. It has been claimed that agency workers fall into the category of 'vulnerable workers'. The Trades Union Congress ('TUC') established a Commission on Vulnerable Employment in 2007.[113] The conditions of agency workers were analysed and the TUC came to the conclusion that 'the law is not strong enough to prevent mistreatment'.[114]

---

[105] See the Explanatory Memorandum to the Agency Workers Regulations 2010, available at http://www.legislation.gov.uk/uksi/2010/93/pdfs/uksiem_20100093_en.pdf at pages 13 and 14 (last visited 5 December 2017).

[106] See P. Leighton, M. Syrett, R. Hecker, and P. Holland, *Out of the Shadows: Managing Self-Employed, Agency and Outsourced Workers* (London, Butterworth Heinemann, 2007); P. Leighton and M. Wynn, 'Temporary Agency Working: Is the Law on the Turn?' (2008) 29(1) *Company Lawyer* 7.

[107] S. McKay, 'Employer Motivations for Using Agency Labour: Hard Work, Hidden Lives—The Full Report of the TUC Commission on Vulnerable Employment' (2008) 37 *Industrial Law Journal* 296, 297.

[108] For the evidence substantiating this assertion, see D. Storrie, *Temporary Agency Work in the EU* (European Foundation for the Improvement of Living and Working Conditions, 2006), available at http://www.eurofound.europa.eu/pubdocs/2002/02/en/1/ef0202en.pdf at pages 59–62 (last visited 5 December 2017).

[109] M. Cully, S. Woodland, A. O'Reilly, and G. Dix, *Britain at Work, as Depicted by the 1998 Workplace Employee Relations Survey* (London, Routledge, 1999); S. Houseman, A. Kalleberg, and G. Erickcek, 'The Role of Temporary Agency Employment in Tight Labor Markets' (2003) 57 *Industrial & Labor Relations Review* 105, 106–7.

[110] J. Purcell, K. Purcell, and S. Tailby, 'Temporary Work Agencies: Here Today, Gone Tomorrow?' (2004) 42 *British Journal of Industrial Relations* 705, 712; C. Forde and G. Slater, 'Agency Working in Britain: Character, Consequences and Regulation' (2004) 42 *British Journal of Industrial Relations* 249, 252–3.

[111] J. Purcell, K. Purcell, and S. Tailby, 'Temporary Work Agencies: Here Today, Gone Tomorrow?' (2004) 42 *British Journal of Industrial Relations* 705, 710.

[112] G. Davidov, 'Joint Employer Status in Triangular Employment Relationships' (2004) 42 *British Journal of Industrial Relations* 727, 728.

[113] See S. McKay, 'Employer Motivations for Using Agency Labour: Hard Work, Hidden Lives—The Full Report of the TUC Commission on Vulnerable Employment' (2008) 37 *Industrial Law Journal* 296.

[114] See *ibid.*, 299.

These findings suggested that it was imperative that the conditions of agency workers be improved. A few years later, the Agency Workers Regulations 2010 ('the Regulations')[115] were introduced to afford agency workers equal treatment rights. With this contextual background in mind, we now move on to examine the employment status of agency workers under the common law and the equal treatment model promulgated in the Regulations.

4.3.1 The common law status of agency workers

Since the establishment of a contract of employment entails the identification of a bilateral exchange between two parties, it does not readily fit the tripartite or multilateral arrangements involved in agency employment. There are two difficulties that arise when pressing ordinary contractual principles into service in the context of such a triangular relationship:

(1) the first concerns the requirement to establish mutuality of obligation; and

(2) the second relates to the partitioning of the control of the agency worker between the hirer and the agency.

The first issue amounts to a significant barrier to a finding of employment status, since the agency will tend not to contractually undertake to provide work to the agency worker on an ongoing basis but instead offer engagements when they are available. Likewise there will be no ongoing contractual obligation imposed on the agency worker to accept or perform prospective work sourced by the agency.[116] As such, the 'irreducible minimum obligation' of mutuality is absent, rendering the finding of a 'global' or 'umbrella' contract highly unlikely.[117] Turning to the second difficulty, it is a feature of the tripartite agency arrangement that the hirer enjoys *operational* control in the sense that it has responsibility for the supervision of the tasks performed. However, the agency exercises *transactional and quality* control whereby it remunerates and selects, vets, and prepares the worker for the assignments concerned. The interpositioning of the agency between the agency worker and the hirer means that the control function is divided between the agency and hirer where it would ordinarily be unified under one employing entity.[118] The end result is that it is near impossible for the agency worker to satisfy the basic ingredient of control required in order to establish a contract of employment with the agency or the hirer.[119]

Unsurprisingly, the judiciary have struggled to classify the agency arrangement as a contract of employment. As a result, agency workers in low-end jobs are left vulnerable vis-à-vis both the agency and the hirer, because they are unable to avail themselves of certain basic common law and statutory employment rights. Although agency workers fall within the statutory definition of a 'contract worker' in section 41 of the Equality Act

[115] SI 2010/93.

[116] For a finding of lack of mutuality of obligation leading to no 'global' contract, see *Dacas v Brook Street Bureau (UK) Ltd* [2004] EWCA Civ 217, [2004] ICR 1437, 1455C–G per Mummery LJ.

[117] 'An umbrella contract is one which obliges one party to offer and the other to accept employment [and t]he key obligation on the worker under the contract is to enter into employment contracts': D. Brodie, *The Contract of Employment* (Edinburgh, Thomson/W. Green, Scottish Universities Law Institute, 2008) 50.

[118] For a solution to this problem where different entities share managerial functions traditionally carried out by a single employer, see J. Prassl, *The Concept of the Employer* (Oxford, OUP, 2015) 42–54 and 224–5; E. McGaughey, 'Social Rights and the Function of Employing Entities' (2017) 37 *Oxford Journal of Legal Studies* 482; and J. Prassl and E. Albin, 'Employees, Employers, and Beyond' in M. Freedland et al. (eds), *The Contract of Employment* (Oxford, OUP, 2016) 353–7.

[119] *Dacas v Brook Street Bureau (UK) Ltd* [2004] ICR 1437, 1451B–D, and 1459H–1460B per Mummery and Munby LJJ.

2010 and section 34 of the National Minimum Wage Act 1998,[120] the desire of agency workers to claim employment status in order to benefit from the statutory unfair dismissal and redundancy regimes in Parts X and XI of the ERA has often been frustrated. Fundamentally, the key questions for resolution in the decided cases have been 'is the agency worker employed?', and 'if so, who is the employer—the agency, the hirer, or neither?' If it is the latter and the agency worker finds him/herself in a 'black hole', can this ever be justifiable in policy terms?[121]

In some of the earliest common law decisions, the courts entertained the possibility that an agency worker might be in an employment relationship with the employment agency.[122] However, this approach did not last. Subsequent cases witnessed a dynamic of retrenchment on the part of the judiciary, who attached far greater weight to the irreducible minimum requirements for mutuality of obligations between the agency and the worker, and sufficient control exercised by the agency over the worker.[123] The requirement to establish both of these two factors[124] has made successful litigation against agencies a bleak prospect since it is difficult for individuals to set up an umbrella employment contract with the agency.

This judicial approach indirectly incentivized agency workers to attempt to establish employment with the hirer. At first glance, this might seem a forlorn prospect, since there will normally be no express written agreement between the hirer and the agency worker (see Figure 4.7); instead, Contract No. 1 is formed between the agency and the hirer and Contract No. 2 is concluded between the agency and the agency worker. Nevertheless, there is undoubtedly a personal relationship between the agency worker and the hirer. It is the nature of that relationship that has beguiled the judiciary, compelling them to consider 'whether that work is provided pursuant to a contractual obligation'.[125]

In a series of cases, namely *Frank v Reuters*,[126] *Dacas v Brook Street Bureau (UK) Ltd*,[127] and *Cable & Wireless plc v Muscat*,[128] the idea evolved that it might be possible for an agency worker to set up an implied contract[129] with the hirer rather than the agency. For example, in *Dacas*, clearly motivated by policy considerations, the Court of Appeal lamented the absurdity of the no-man's land in which agency workers found themselves. Sedley LJ (and Mummery LJ in agreement) took the view that it was 'simply not credible' that Mrs Dacas was employed by nobody: '[O]nce arrangements like these had been in place for a year or more, I would have thought that the same inexorable inference (that there was a contract of employment) would have arisen.'[130] In adopting this position, the Court of Appeal held that it was *necessary* in such circumstances to imply

---

[120] See also regulation 36 of the Working Time Regulations 1998 (SI 1998/1833) ('WTR') which applies the employment rights in the WTR to agency workers vis-à-vis the agency or the hirer, depending on which of those two parties is responsible for tendering payment. Health and safety law also applies in the context of agency arrangements: section 3(1) of the Health and Safety at Work etc. Act 1974 imposes a duty on the hirer to protect the health and safety of agency workers present on its premises, notwithstanding that they are not in the hirer's employment. See also *McTigue v University Hospital Bristol NHS Foundation Trust* [2016] IRLR 742.

[121] The agency is treated as the employer of the agency worker for the purposes of income tax and National Insurance legislation: sections 44–46 of the Income Tax (Earnings and Pensions) Act 2003. However, this is not taken into account for the purposes of the common law status of the agency worker: see *McMeechan v Secretary of State for Employment* [1997] ICR 549, 561E–G per Waite LJ.

[122] *McMeechan v Secretary of State for Employment* [1997] ICR 549.

[123] *Montgomery v Johnson Underwood Ltd and another* [2001] ICR 819, 824B–826B per Buckley J; *Dacas v Brook Street Bureau (UK) Ltd* [2004] ICR 1437, 1455C–G per Mummery LJ.

[124] *Dacas v Brook Street Bureau (UK) Ltd* [2004] ICR 1437, 1454 per Mummery LJ; *Bunce v Postworth Ltd (t/a Skyblue)* [2005] IRLR 557, 561 per Keene LJ. See also E. Brown, 'Protecting Agency Workers: Implied Contract or Legislation?' (2008) 37 *Industrial Law Journal* 178, 179.

[125] *James v Greenwich London Borough Council* [2007] ICR 577, 583 per Elias J (P).

[126] [2003] ICR 1166.   [127] [2004] ICR 1437.   [128] [2006] ICR 975.

[129] In accordance with section 230(2) of the ERA.   [130] [2004] ICR 1437, 1458H.

a contract of employment. Likewise, in *Cable & Wireless plc v Muscat*,[131] the Court of Appeal expressly upheld the reasoning of the majority in *Dacas*,[132] finding that it was *necessary* to imply a contract of employment between the agency worker and the hirer in order to give business reality to the relationship.[133]

However, as with many policy-driven judgments, this logical and sensible approach was achieved at the expense of doctrinal coherence. By emasculating the 'black hole' within which agency workers found themselves, the Court of Appeal clashed with established doctrine by ignoring the absence of mutuality of obligation and control exerted by the hirer over the agency worker. Moreover, confronted by the existence of two perfectly valid written contracts (Contract No. 1 and Contract No. 2),[134] it was stretching matters to contend that the stringent necessity test in *The Aramis*,[135] which is needed for the implication of a contract, had been satisfied. *The Aramis* directs that an inference of an implied contract arising by conduct will only be drawn where it is necessary to do so, which is a particularly high test.[136] The tripartite agency working arrangement will often preclude an inference of implication, since the classic tests of mutuality of obligation and control for the establishment of an employment contract will not be met. Furthermore, the existence of the two contracts is evidence of a clear intention not to enter into an employment contract.[137]

Nonetheless, this traditional conceptualization of the necessity test conflicts with the more relaxed line of thought developed by the Court of Appeal in *Frank v Reuters*,[138] *Dacas v Brook Street Bureau (UK) Ltd*,[139] and *Cable & Wireless plc v Muscat*.[140] The subsequent number of cases which sought to challenge the approach of the Court of Appeal[141] reflects the degree of uneasiness felt by legal practitioners about the sacrifice of legal principle on the altar of policy.[142] Ultimately, the Court of Appeal had the opportunity to revisit its previous decisions in the case of *James v Greenwich London Borough Council*.[143]

Prior to its decision in *James v Greenwich Council*, there was a heightened expectation that the Court of Appeal would use the case as an opportunity to deal with some of the criticisms levelled at its previous pronouncements on the subject. That is exactly what happened. It was held that the common law principle of necessity for the implication of a contract, as outlined in *The Aramis*, ought to be applied in preference to the usual criteria for the identification of a contract of employment (i.e. control, personal service, and mutuality of obligation), and, in some very extreme cases, by exposing sham arrangements.[144] The upshot of the application of the necessity test is that the existence of

---

[131] [2006] ICR 975.   [132] *Cable & Wireless plc v Muscat* [2006] ICR 975, 985B per Smith LJ.
[133] *ibid.*, 990C–E per Smith LJ.   [134] See Figure 4.7.   [135] [1989] 1 Lloyd's Rep 213.
[136] *ibid.*, 224 per Bingham LJ.
[137] F. Reynold, 'The Status of Agency Workers: A Question of Legal Principle' (2006) 35 *Industrial Law Journal* 320, 323.
[138] [2003] ICR 1166.   [139] [2004] ICR 1437.   [140] [2006] ICR 975.
[141] *Cairns v Visteon UK Ltd* [2007] ICR 616; *Mr A J Craigie v London Borough of Haringey* (UKE-AT/0556/06/JOJ, 12 January 2007); *Secretary of State for Trade and Industry v Mr E Alade, P J Personnel Ltd (in liquidation)* (UKEAT/0591/06/ZT, 16 February 2007).
[142] See M. Wynn and P. Leighton, 'Will the Real Employer Please Stand up? Agencies, Client Companies and the Employment Status of the Temporary Agency Worker' (2006) 35 *Industrial Law Journal* 301; F. Reynold, 'The Status of Agency Workers: A Question of Legal Principle' (2006) 35 *Industrial Law Journal* 320.
[143] [2008] ICR 545.
[144] *James v Greenwich London Borough Council* [2008] ICR 545, 558. In arriving at such a conclusion, Mummery LJ confirmed Elias J's observations in the EAT in *James v Greenwich London Borough Council* [2007] ICR 577, where four propositions were propounded: (1) a tribunal must not simply focus on the express contractual arrangements, but must consider the possibility of an implied contract based on conduct; (2) the basis for implication of a contract is necessity, in line with *The Aramis* decision; (3) a contract can be implied where the express contracts are a sham; and (4) absent a sham, it will be appropriate to imply a contract if the express contract no longer adequately reflects reality.

the two valid express contracts between the hirer and the agency and the agency and the agency worker will foreclose any need to imply a third contract between the hirer and the agency worker in the vast majority of cases. Ultimately, by following the narrow incarnation of the necessity test set down in *The Aramis*[145] at the expense of the more liberal approach in *Dacas*, the Court of Appeal acknowledged that orthodox doctrinal criteria such as contractual intention and freedom of contract ought to be afforded priority over policy considerations. The overall effect is that only in rare cases will an agency worker be treated as an employee of the hirer. For example, in *Smith v Carillion (JM) Ltd*,[146] the Court of Appeal held that an agency worker was not the employee of the hirer notwithstanding that he was clearly integrated into the operations of the hirer and the placement with the hirer was envisaged to be for a reasonably lengthy period of time.

In arriving at its conclusion in *James v Greenwich Council*, the Court of Appeal laid bare the difficult policy issues arising in this context and called on Parliament to act in order to confront these matters. It also recognized the inherent limitations of the common law as an instrument for social and economic reform:

■ *James v Greenwich London Borough Council* [2008] EWCA Civ 35, [2008] ICR 545, 559B–560A

Mummery LJ:

Through their decisions adjudicating on legal disputes courts and tribunals are builders in the law. They are not architects of economic and social policy. As they must operate within the legal architecture created by others, they cannot confer the right not to be unfairly dismissed on a worker who is without a contract of employment. The courts and tribunals are fully aware of the current controversy about the absence of job protection for agency workers, who do not have an express or implied contract of employment. While this appeal and this judgment were pending articles appeared in the newspapers under such headlines as 'The slow death of the real job is pulling society apart', 'Agency workers could get full-time rights' and 'Temps may get full work rights under EU law' . . . The courts and tribunals are also well aware of the nature of the arguments for and against a change in the law, but it is not for them to express views about a change or to initiate change. This is a matter of controversial social and economic policy for debate in and decision by Parliament informed by discussions between the interested parties, the Department for Business and Enterprise, the TUC, the CBI and other employers' organisations and the European institutions and governments of member states. The questions for discussion, negotiation and decision are not legal questions susceptible to adjudication or appropriate for comment by a court or tribunal. The questions are outside their province and competence. On the one hand, there are arguments for a flexible labour market in the interests of a competitive economy and of full employment. There is a real need to hire temporary workers from agencies at short notice for extra busy periods or special projects. If this is made less attractive or more costly, job losses may follow and more work may be added to the burden borne by long term employees. On the other hand, a significant

---

[145] What is particularly striking is how the deployment of the necessity test for the purposes of the implication of an employment contract was held to operate in one direction only, so as to protect the hirer from burdensome and unforeseen potential employment liabilities on the basis that its agency workers might be employees and be entitled to unfair dismissal protection. Indeed, there 'seems to be little or no perception . . . that the implication of a contract of employment might be judged to be "necessary" in the very different sense that any other legal construction would deprive the worker of a legally protected status vis-à-vis the [hir]er, and might deprive the worker of a legally protected status vis-à-vis any of the persons or enterprises involved in the set of arrangements under which he or she works': M. Freedland and N. Kountouris, *The Legal Construction of Personal Work Relations* (Oxford, OUP, 2011) 166.

[146] [2015] IRLR 467.

move in the direction of the casualisation of labour and the growth of a two-tier workforce, one tier enjoying significant statutory protection, the other tier in a legal no man's land being neither employed nor self-employed, vulnerable, but enjoying little or no protection, may create social injustice and a festering sense of grievance which would not be satisfactory in the interests of an efficient workforce, a competitive economy, a healthy society or anything else . . . Policy decisions have to be taken by others about what changes (if any) to make, what rights to confer on whom, what qualifying periods to set and so on.

Shortly after the decision of the Court of Appeal was handed down in *James v Greenwich Council*, a breakthrough was reached at the European level, culminating in the adoption of the Agency Workers' Directive ('the Directive').[147] The Directive applies an equal treatment model similar to that found in the Part-time Workers Directive[148] and the Fixed-Term Workers Directive.[149] This is achieved by guaranteeing the agency worker parity of pay with a permanent worker recruited directly by the hirer.[150] The UK adopted the Regulations[151] in order to transpose the Directive and the former came into force in October 2011. Although only introduced into UK law comparatively recently, like the PTWR and the FTER, it is debatable whether the Regulations will survive for long after Brexit. We now turn to an examination of the Regulations.

4.3.2 The effect of the Agency Workers Regulations 2010

The definition of 'agency worker', found in regulations 2 and 3, governs the relational scope of the Regulations. These provisions cover individuals supplying labour via an agency on a temporary basis to, and under the supervision and direction of, a hirer,[152] where that individual has entered into a contract with the agency which qualifies as (a) a contract of employment with the agency or (b) a contract with the agency to perform work or services personally. Since the agency worker must be working on a temporary basis, agency workers who have worked, or are working, for a hirer on an open-ended contract concluded with the agency are somewhat controversially excluded from the protections conferred in the Regulations.[153] Regulation 3(2) exempts individuals who are running their own business from the protective coverage of the Regulations, i.e. where the status of the agency or hirer, by virtue of the contract entered into with the individual, is of a client or customer of a profession or business undertaking carried on by the individual. It is noteworthy that this 'client/customer exception' in regulation 3(2) adopts the same wording found in section 230(3)(b) of the ERA, section 54(3) of the NMWA, and regulation 2(1) of the Working Time Regulations 1998.[154] For that reason, it is suggested that the criteria applicable in Figure 4.5 are to be transposed from the law interpreting the 'worker' contract to cast light on the meaning of regulation 3(2). As such, if the obligation of personal service is not the dominant purpose of the contract between the agency worker and the agency, or the former is not integrated into the operations of the

---

[147] Directive 2008/104/EC (OJ 2008 L 327/9). See L. Zappala, 'The Temporary Agency Workers' Directive: An Impossible Political Agreement?' [2003] 32 *Industrial Law Journal* 317.

[148] Directive 97/81/EC (OJ 1998 L14/9). See Chapter 13, section 13.2.1.

[149] Directive 99/70/EC (OJ 1999 L175/43). See Chapter 13, section 13.2.2.

[150] Article 5.   [151] SI 2010/93.

[152] Regulation 2 defines a hirer as 'a person engaged in economic activity, public or private, whether or not operating for profit, to whom individuals are supplied, to work temporarily for and under the supervision and direction of that person'.

[153] *Moran v Ideal Cleaning Services Ltd* [2014] ICR 442.   [154] SI 1998/1833.

latter, the probability is that the former will be treated as running his/her own business venture, thus precluding the operation of the Regulations.[155]

It should be stressed that there are certain 'day one' rights enjoyed by the agency worker:

(1) he/she is entitled to access any shared facilities that comparable permanent employees or workers of the hirer can access;[156]

(2) he/she must be afforded the same opportunity to apply for relevant vacancies as comparable permanent employees or workers.[157] It should be stressed that this does not translate into an entitlement to apply for a vacancy, be interviewed, or secure a preference for a vacancy in priority to such a permanent employee or worker.[158]

However, the fundamental right conferred upon agency workers—parity of pay/equal treatment—finds its expression in the more restrictive regulations 5 and 6 of the Regulations. Regulation 5(1) directs that an agency worker has the right to the same basic working and employment conditions as a comparable permanent employee or 'worker' employed by the hirer.[159] Regulation 6(1) defines the relevant terms and conditions[160] of the agency worker, which must be equivalent to those of the permanent employee or worker of the hirer, and generally we find that these are pay-related, namely terms and conditions relating to:

• pay;
• the duration of working time;
• night work;
• rest periods;
• rest breaks; and
• annual leave.

From the agency worker's perspective, 'pay' is defined rather narrowly as 'any sums payable to a worker of the hirer in connection with the worker's employment, including any fee, bonus, commission, holiday pay or other emolument referable to the employment, whether payable under contract or otherwise'. The restricted nature of this definition is particularly clear when one compares the definition of 'pay' with the breadth of interpretation afforded to that word in the jurisprudence interpreting Article 157 of the Treaty on the Functioning of the European Union ('TFEU').[161] Indeed, regulation 6(3) expressly excludes, inter alia, the following from the operation of the Regulations: occupational sick pay; pension payments; compensation payments for loss of office; maternity, paternity or adoption leave payments; redundancy payments; bonus payments not referable to the amount or quality of work undertaken by the worker (e.g. payments attributable to the annual turnover or profits of the hirer); statutory guarantee payments; and

---

[155] It is unclear whether this accords with the Directive, since in the decision of the CJEU in *Betriebsrat der Ruhrlandklinik gGmbH v Ruhrlandklinik gGmbH* [2017] IRLR 194, it was held that the Directive applies not only to workers who have concluded a contract of employment with a temporary-work agency, but also to those who have an 'employment relationship' with such an undertaking. It also ruled that the legal characterization under national law is not decisive.
[156] Regulation 12.   [157] Regulation 13.   [158] *Coles v Ministry of Defence* [2015] IRLR 872.
[159] *Amissah v Trainpeople.Co.UK Ltd* [2017] IRLR 318 addresses the calculation of compensation in accordance with regulation 5 where there is no parity of pay.
[160] The limitation of the equal treatment model in the Regulations to the basic pay-related conditions of the agency worker can be contrasted with the regime adopted at European level in relation to other atypical workers, such as part-time and fixed-term workers, on which, see Chapter 13. Furthermore, unlike regulation 8 of the FTER, there is nothing in the Regulations preventing the successive deployment of temporary agency work contracts.   [161] See Chapter 14, section 14.2.1.1, for a fuller discussion.

out-of-pocket expenses. The absence of terms prescribing periods of notice for termination of the agency work contract is surprising, since it means that agency workers can be dismissed with no notice if they do not qualify as employees. The inclusion of bonuses as 'pay' is something of a headache for employers, bearing in mind that many sectors of the economy provide for discretionary bonuses for their permanent staff based on their personal performance and it is not wholly predictable how such entitlements can be transposed into a meaningful comparable term applicable to temporary agency workers.

What also remains unsettled is whether the words '[same] relevant terms and conditions' in regulations 5(3) and 6 demand a 'term-by-term' or 'overall package' comparison.[162] For example, if the contractual term that prescribes the pay of the hirer's permanent employee reveals that it is higher in comparison with the term confirming the pay of the agency worker, it remains unclear whether that is sufficient to breach the agency worker's right to equal treatment in circumstances where other contractual terms of the agency worker mean that his/her pay package is more favourable overall. Consider the following hypothetical, to which the correct answer is presently uncertain.

Hypothetical C

Danny's Demolishers Ltd ('DD') hires an agency worker Stephanie Wiggins on a 12-month fixed-term contract as a highly specialist IT consultant via an agency called Employment Bureau Solutions ('EBS'). EBS pays Stephanie £13 per hour, which is £5 per hour less than Fritz Schmidt, who is directly employed by DD as its senior IT manager. However, a term of Stephanie's contract with EBS entitles her to a guaranteed Christmas bonus of £20,000 per annum in recognition of her productivity during the previous year. Meanwhile, Fritz's employment contract with DD does not provide for a Christmas bonus. If Stefanie complains that she is being paid less than Fritz, will her guaranteed bonus be taken into account for the purposes of the 'parity of pay'/equal treatment model in the Regulations?

The characteristics and qualities of the comparator permanent employee of the hirer are set out in regulation 5(3) and (4). It is provided that the permanent employee must be engaged in the same or broadly similar work as the agency worker. It is recognized that there may be no comparable employee working at the same 'establishment' as the agency worker, and in such circumstances another permanent employee or worker based at another 'establishment' of the hirer satisfying the requisite provisions may be invoked as a comparator. However, there are a number of issues here which remain unclear:

(1) there is no definition of 'establishment' in the Regulations, rendering this concept somewhat opaque;

(2) as matters stand, there is the potential for the hirer to subvert the operation of the Regulations by hiring a 'token' permanent employee or worker on low pay to perform the same, or a broadly similar, role as the agency worker;[163]

---

[162] See the case of *Hayward v Cammell Laird Shipbuilders Ltd* [1988] AC 894 and Chapter 14, section 14.2.1.1, for the resolution of this issue in the context of UK equal pay law. However, the decision of the EAT in *Kocur v Angerd Staffing Solutions Ltd.* (UKEAT/0181/17/BA, 23 February 2018) suggests that the words 'the same' in Regulations 5(3) and 6 do not preclude an agency worker from receiving a higher rate of pay than a directly employed recruit.

[163] See the case of *Pickstone v Freemans plc* [1989] AC 66 and Chapter 14, section 14.2.2, for the 'token man' phenomenon in the context of UK equal pay law.

(3) whether the agency worker is permitted to invoke a hypothetical permanent employee or worker as a comparator where no real comparator is available is left unresolved,[164] which issue will be particularly significant where the other staff of the hirer performing the same role as the agency worker are also agency workers.[165]

Regulation 5(1) refers to an initial qualifying period and regulation 7 prescribes that the agency worker's right to equal treatment is only activated once he/she has worked in the same role with the same hirer for at least 12 continuous calendar weeks. This severely curtails the effect of the Regulations, as it is open to hirers to avoid the Regulations by terminating an assignment prior to the 12-week qualifying period. Coupled with the fact that agency work assignments often last for less than 12 weeks, this means that approximately 55 per cent of agency workers in the UK will be ineligible to claim the equal treatment rights in the Regulations.[166] However, there is a specific, albeit narrow, anti-avoidance mechanism in regulation 9. Regulation 9 will treat an agency worker as having completed the 12-week qualifying period if he/she would have completed it but for the structure of the assignments of the agency worker, e.g. where the hirer transfers the agency worker into a new role or work specification. If the agency worker completes two or more assignments with the end-user, having performed two or more different roles, regulation 9 will apply.

Another deficiency with the Regulations is that they fail to clarify whether the agency worker is an employee of the agency or the hirer. As such, the Regulations defer this central matter to the common law and so the approach in *James* is left undisturbed, despite Lord Justice Mummery's aspiration that Parliament would take the opportunity to address the matter.

Reflection points

1. In your view, is the danger of the emergence of a 'two-tier workforce' a sufficiently material consideration to justify the extension of common law and statutory employment protection rights to agency workers? Give reasons for your answer.

2. Assume that your answer to question 1 is affirmative. Are you of the opinion that the current legal regulation of agency work strikes an appropriate balance between the agency worker's need for protection and the needs of employment agencies and hirers for a flexible labour market in the service of an efficient, productive economy?

3. Do you believe it to be appropriate that the necessity test in *The Aramis*, which was developed in the field of commercial relations, should be applied in order to determine whether an agency worker is in an employment relationship with a hirer? In order to assist you in answering this question, read the articles by F. Reynold, 'The Status of Agency Workers: A Question of Legal Principle' (2006) 35 *Industrial Law Journal* 320, and M. Wynn and P. Leighton, 'Agency Workers, Employment Rights and the Ebb and Flow of Freedom of Contract' (2009) 72 *Modern Law Review* 91, 96–9.

[164] See the discussion in R. Horton and N. Kountouris, 'The Temporary Agency Work Directive: Another Broken Promise?' (2009) 38 *Industrial Law Journal* 329, 333–4.

[165] On one reading of the Regulations, hypothetical comparators are precluded, since otherwise the implicit acknowledgement in regulation 5(4)(b) that an agency worker may be permitted to invoke a comparable employee from another establishment of the hirer would be redundant.

[166] See Department for Business, Enterprise and Regulatory Reform, *Agency Working in the UK: A Review of the Evidence* (October 2008), available at http://webarchive.nationalarchives.gov.uk/20090609003228/http://www.berr.gov.uk/files/file48720.pdf Table 2.1 at page 6 (last visited 5 December 2017).

4. Are you of the view that Mummery LJ's call for Parliament to address the difficult social and economic policy considerations raised by agency work is adequately answered by the reforms introduced by the Regulations?

 For additional reading on agency workers, visit the Online Resources for this book at www.oup.com/uk/cabrelli3e/

4.4 FINAL EVALUATION OF THE LAW OF ALTERNATIVE PERSONAL WORK CONTRACTS AND RELATIONS

The desire to avoid the emergence of a two-tier labour force is one of the key judicial and parliamentary policy considerations underpinning the current condition of the relational scope of employment laws. In order to ensure that this objective does not clash with the labour market flexibility agenda, successive UK Governments have sought to confer common law and statutory employment protection rights upon a broader class of individual suppliers of services without disturbing the freedom of enterprises to adopt a diverse array of contractual arrangements for the provision of labour. Such has been the manner in which a careful balance between these competing policy concerns has been struck.

However, some fear that this extension of employment laws calls into question the legitimacy of employment law as a coherent autonomous discipline—that the greater the number of atypical workers brought within its frame of reference, the more the edges between 'employment' and 'commercial' arrangements become frayed:[167]

■ M. Weiss, 'Re-Inventing Labour Law?' in G. Davidov and B. Langille (eds), *The Idea of Labour Law* (Oxford, OUP, 2011) 48–9

De-legitimacy of labour law definitely would be the result if one would follow the suggestions of those who plead for inclusion of all relationships which are characterized by inequality of bargaining power. In my view these suggestions ignore not only the specific character of the employment relationship as indicated above but also the interrelationship of individual and collective mechanisms as means of protection. The changes of the employment reality as sketched above force labour law to be adapted to the new employment reality. But labour law is not to be misunderstood as a tool to compensate the position of the weaker party everywhere. There are different subsystems in society for which legal progress has developed specific instruments which are shaped according to the needs within the respective subsystem, be it family law, consumer protection law or whatever. This progress is not to be reversed but has to be adapted to changes of reality. For labour law this means that it has to respond to the new realities in the area of employment in its broadest sense but not to expand in overarching categories for all the miseries of the world. Then it would lose its function.[168]

---

[167] See P. Davies and M. Freedland, 'Employees, Workers, and the Autonomy of Labour Law' in H. Collins, P. Davies, and R. Rideout (eds), *Legal Regulation of the Employment Relation* (London, Kluwer, 2000) 267, 268–74; C. Summers, 'Similarities and Differences between Employment Contracts and Civil or Commercial Contracts' (2001) 17 *International Journal of Comparative Labour Law and Industrial Relations* 5.

[168] Of course, Weiss's sentiments here share many affinities with Freedland's 'anxiety' referred to in Chapter 3, section 3.1.2.

Perhaps the judiciary were implicitly aware of these concerns, since their somewhat conservative approach in cases such as *Jivraj v Hishwani* has functioned to narrow the impact of the intermediate 'contract personally to do work' statutory concept.[169] Furthermore, there is also some evidence that the Government's enthusiasm for expanding the relational scope of employment laws is limited: section 23 of the Employment Relations Act 1999 confers a radical power upon the Secretary of State to make an order which has the effect of extending statutory employment rights under the ERA or TULRCA to individuals 'who are of a specified description' but who do not qualify as employees or a statutory 'worker'. It is quite telling that this far-reaching statutory provision has never been invoked—once again, an omission which may be explained by a deep-seated reluctance to overstretch the reach of employment laws. Another rationale for such hesitancy may be the void one encounters when it comes to identifying the content of such non-employment relationships, i.e. the implied obligations impressed upon the parties privy to the statutory 'worker' contract or the 'contract personally to do work'.[170] The striking absence of behavioural norms calls into question the viability of these non-employment concepts and leaves open the important issue of the normative content of these statutorily crafted alternative personal work contracts.[171]

---

[169] But cf. *Bates van Winkelhof v Clyde & Co. LLP* [2014] 1 WLR 2047, where a more progressive approach was taken by the Supreme Court to the intermediate statutory construct of 'worker'.

[170] At best, what we do know is that the worker contract is terminable by the employer on reasonable notice: *McCarthy v Blue Sword Construction Ltd* (EAT/1223/03/DM, 14 July 2003). As such, it seems clear that the unrestricted reasonable notice rule referred to in Chapter 15, section 15.1.1, also applies in the case of the 'worker' contract.

[171] This is a matter to which we will return in Chapter 7, section 7.4.3.

PART III
THE CONTENT OF THE PERSONAL EMPLOYMENT CONTRACT

CHAPTER FIVE

THE NATURE AND CONTENT OF THE PERSONAL EMPLOYMENT CONTRACT

5.1 THE NATURE AND CONTENT OF THE PERSONAL CONTRACT OF EMPLOYMENT

This chapter takes as its starting point the idea that the employment relationship is constructed against the backcloth of a contract, namely the contract of employment. In Chapters 3 and 4, we sought to differentiate that contract from other similar contracts which can be adopted by individuals to provide personal services to employing entities and enterprises. By distinguishing the contract of employment from alternative personal work contracts, a variety of factors were identified as being of import, such as personal service and mutuality/reciprocity. These factors feed back into the *nature* and *content* of the contract of employment and it is with these matters that this chapter is concerned. Therefore, after first reflecting on the nature of the employment contract, we will then go on to consider its substance/content. We will note that the contract of employment is primarily a repository for the rights and obligations of the employer and employee, a point whose relevance will become particularly apparent in Chapter 6 when the implied terms of the employment contract are dissected in detail. In discussing the content of the contract, we will be introduced to the statutory duty of an employer to provide the employee with a statement of the main particulars of employment and consider whether this statement is exhaustive of the terms and conditions of the contract of employment. Finally, in analysing the employment contract's content, our focus will shift to the importance of express terms, the express or implied incorporation of provisions of an external document (e.g. from a collective agreement or workplace procedure, handbook, or policy) into the contract of employment, the custom and practice of the workplace, imposed terms, and implied terms.

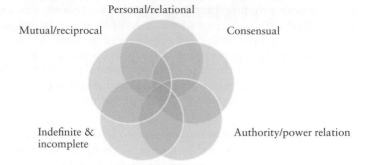

Figure 5.1 *Shaping the contract of employment*

5.1.1 The contract of employment: some context

A variety of interlocking features shape the nature of the contract of employment and ultimately serve to influence its content and substance. These are recurring features that we will regularly encounter throughout the discussion of various legal institutions in this book. In short, the contract of employment is characterized by its personal/relational, consensual, mutual/reciprocal, indefinite, and incomplete nature, as well as the authority or power relation which lies at its centre. We can consider how these features interlock by looking at Figure 5.1.

We now explore each of these central features in turn.

(1) For the reasons discussed in Chapter 3, the contract of employment is inherently *personal and relational*. Personal service is required for its constitution and the discontinuance of personal service by virtue of the death[1] or incapacity[2] of the employee will lead to its automatic termination at common law. Moreover, a contract whereby company A undertakes to provide services to company B cannot be an employment contract, since the former is not an individual and so there are no personal services in issue. Further, as the case of *Nokes v Doncaster Amalgamated Collieries Ltd*[3] clarifies, the contract is personal to the parties involving *delectus personae* and cannot be transferred by the employer to a purported transferee employer without the consent of the employee. It has also been recognized that the contract is relational in that it establishes a relationship between two parties, the significance of which lies in what that means for the rules on the classification, duration, content, performance, and termination of employment.[4]

(2) This notion of consent links in with the second distinguishing feature of the contract of employment, namely its *consensual nature*. Since the relationship between the employee and the employer is consensual and based on a contract, the areas of contract law in which the role of mutual consent is stressed apply with equal force to the common law of the contract of employment, e.g. with regard to the express terms of the contract, the rules on the implication of terms in fact, and the variation of contractual terms.

---

[1] *Stubbs v The Holywell Railway Co.* (1867) LR 2 Exch 311; *Farrow v Wilson* (1869) LR 4 CP 744, 766 per Willes J; and *Ranger v Brown* [1978] ICR 603, 605G per Phillips J.
[2] *Condor v Barron Knights Ltd* [1966] 1 WLR 87.   [3] [1940] AC 1014.
[4] See D. Brodie, 'How Relational is the Employment Contract?' (2011) 40 *Industrial Law Journal* 232; H. Collins, 'The Contract of Employment in 3D' in D. Campbell, L. Mulcahy, and S. Wheeler (eds), *Changing Concepts of Contract* (Basingstoke, Palgrave MacMillan, 2013) 65; D. Brodie, 'Relational Contracts' in M. Freedland et al. (eds), *The Contract of Employment* (Oxford, OUP, 2016) 145.

(3) The analysis in previous chapters on the classification of a contract as a contract of employment invoked the significance of the concept of *mutuality/reciprocity*. This feature feeds through into the nature and substance of the contract of employment, which will become particularly apparent in Chapter 6 when the mutual/reciprocal nature of the implied terms of the contract of employment is laid bare. In this context, this concept functions 'to ensure an adequate and reasonable degree of mutuality or reciprocity between the rights and obligations of the [employee] and those of the [employer]'.[5]

(4) The default model of the contract of employment prescribes that it is *indefinite in duration*. Deakin and Wilkinson[6] have shown how the presumption which prevailed in the eighteenth and early nineteenth centuries that the employment contract was for an annual hiring had begun to wane by the mid-nineteenth century with the advent of a modern industrial society. Any last vestiges of its existence were finally swept away by the decision of the Court of Appeal in *Richardson v Koefod*[7] which adopted a presumption in favour of the open-ended employment contract.[8] At around the same time as the demise of the presumption in favour of an annual hiring and the emergence of the indefinite employment contract, the 'unrestricted reasonable notice rule'[9] began to evolve. Therefore, the notion that the contract of employment was indefinite in duration acted as a catalyst for the development of the rule that it could be terminated by the employer or employee on providing reasonable notice.[10]

Like many other open-ended contracts, the contract of employment is *incomplete* in nature. However, the employment contract possesses certain attributes which are unique in that this incompleteness is particularly pronounced. This is partly attributable to it being 'incomplete by design',[11] in the sense that the employer deliberately casts the express terms of the contract at a high level of generality. This ensures a large degree of flexibility and discretion in the employer's enforcement and power of decision-making:

■ **W. Brown and D. Rea, 'The Changing Nature of the Employment Contract'**
(1995) 42 *Scottish Journal of Political Economy* **363, 363–4**

II The Incomplete Nature of the Employment Contract

All economic interaction is mediated by a process of contracting. A contract is a set of rules which defines the mutual obligations and rights which are necessary to govern an exchange. A normal sales contract is a 'complete contract' because there is an *ex ante* agreement on a set of rules which comprehensively defines the rights and responsibilities of both parties for the whole life of the exchange. This is possible because the exchange is relatively simple and predictable. The employment contract, by contrast, is 'incomplete'. There are both *ex ante* and *ex post* agreements and

---

[5] M. Freedland, *The Personal Employment Contract* (Oxford, OUP, 2003) 129.

[6] See S. Deakin and F. Wilkinson, *The Law of the Labour Market: Industrialization, Employment, and Legal Evolution* (Oxford, OUP, 2005) 44–5 and 78–9; S. Jacoby, 'The Duration of Indefinite Employment Contracts in the United States and England: An Historical Analysis' (1982) 5 *Comparative Labor Law* 85.

[7] [1969] 1 WLR 1812.

[8] For a comprehensive discussion, see N. Countouris, 'The Contract of Employment as an Expression of Continuing Obligations' in M. Freedland et al. (eds), *The Contract of Employment* (Oxford, OUP, 2016) 395–9; and D. Cabrelli, 'Duration, Lawful Termination, and Frustration of the Employment Contract' in M. Freedland et al. (eds), *The Contract of Employment* (Oxford, OUP, 2016) 517–21.

[9] See Chapter 15, section 15.1.1.

[10] This can be contrasted with the evolution of the 'employment-at-will' contract in the USA around about the same time, which provided for lawful termination on summary, rather than reasonable, notice.

[11] H. Collins, *Employment Law*, 2nd edition (Oxford, OUP, 2010) 10.

rules. The *ex ante* agreements fail to cover all relevant future rights, responsibilities and contingencies because the parties expect that, once employment has got under way, and gaps in the contract are discovered, they will amend and adapt the contract *ex post*. The incompleteness of the employment contract reflects the fact that there is a high level of uncertainty about the future conduct of exchange . . . This uncertainty arises from two distinct features of employment . . . First, its nature is such that it is difficult and usually undesirable to specify the precise conduct of the task that will be required; it can be left to subsequent supervision . . . the second feature is the long[-]term nature of most employment. It is not possible to formulate a contingent contract covering an entire tenure of employment, so hiring is done on the basis that future terms may be varied, whether by collective bargaining or by management edict . . . The incomplete nature of the employment contract makes it inherently controversial. There is a high degree of interdependency between employer and employee, and the simple fact that so much may be renegotiable, from the conduct of today's work to the development of a lifetime's career, means there are always potentially conflicting interests, as well as shared ones. Frequent incremental adjustment offers recurrent opportunities for employees to perceive themselves as unfairly treated which, in turn, has implications for their motivation and productivity. The content and interpretation of the incomplete employment contract depends heavily upon the power relationship between the employer and either the employee or the employee's trade union organisation. The power relationship can be conceived in terms of the level of uncertainty that each side can, in a controlled way, subject the other to, as a proportion of other uncertainties faced . . . [12]

(5) The Brown and Rea extract exposes the undoubted link between the incompleteness of the contract and final feature of the employment contract: the *asymmetrical authority/power relation*. This is something more than the 'inequality of bargaining power' inherent in the employment relationship which is cited as the principal justification for employment protection laws.[13] Instead, the idea of asymmetrical authority/power relation is connected to the important edifice of the 'managerial prerogative' which is descriptive of the employer's general power to assign tasks and functions to the employee, and to direct and allocate methods and patterns of working, as it sees fit:

■ H. Simon, 'A Formal Theory of the Employment Relationship' (1951) 19 *Econometrica* 293, 293–4

1. The Concept of Authority

The authority relationship that exists between an employer and an employee, a relationship created by the employment contract, will play a central role in our theory. What is the nature of this relationship? We will call our employer *B* (for 'boss'), and our employee *W* (for 'worker'). The collection of specific actions that *W* performs on the job (typing and filing certain letters, laying bricks, or what not) we will call his behavior. We will consider the set of all possible behavior patterns of *W* and we will let *x* designate an element of this set. A particular *x* might then represent a given set of tasks, performed at a particular rate of working, a particular level of accuracy, and so forth. We will say that *B* exercises *authority* over *W* if *W* permits *B* to select *x*. That is, *W* accepts authority

---

[12] Writer's annotations appear in square brackets throughout this chapter. See also O. Hart and J. Moore, 'Foundations of Incomplete Contracts' (1999) 66 *Review of Economic Studies* 115.

[13] See Chapter 1, section 1.2.1.

when his behavior is determined by B's decision. In general, W will accept authority only if x_o, the x chosen by B, is restricted to some given subset (W's 'area of acceptance') of all the possible values. This is the definition of authority that is most generally employed in modern administrative theory.

2. The Employment Contract

We will say that W enters into an employment contract with B when the former agrees to accept the authority of the latter and the latter agrees to pay the former a stated wage (w). This contract differs fundamentally from a sales contract—the kind of contract that is assumed in ordinary formulations of price theory. In the sales contract each party promises a specific consideration in return for the consideration promised by the other. The buyer (like B) promises to pay a stated sum of money; but the seller (unlike W) promises in return a specified quantity of a completely specified commodity. Moreover, the seller is not interested in the way in which his commodity is used once it is sold, while the worker is interested in what the entrepreneur will want him to do (what x will be chosen by B).

The authority and power of the employer translates into the submission and subordination of the employee. Hence the managerial prerogative is relied upon by the employer to co-ordinate labour.

We have now developed an understanding of the interconnected nature of the contract as demonstrated in Figure 5.1, and so we will now move on to consider its substance and content. In line with the notion that the employment contract is 'incomplete' in that the rights, obligations, and powers of the parties are not fully articulated in the written agreement, we can perhaps think of it as an 'empty box'. If we enquire how, and with what, that box is filled, we find that it is multilayered with a plethora of sources:

■ **S. Deakin and F. Wilkinson, 'Labour Law and Economic Theory: A Reappraisal' in H. Collins, P. Davies, and R. Rideout (eds), *Legal Regulation of the Employment Relation* (London, Kluwer, 2000) 45–6**

The 'incompleteness' of the contract of employment is widely recognised to be the consequence of its long-term orientation and the extreme degree of uncertainty over future performance which this induces. In the case of most contracts of employment, it is unclear when the employment relationship is to end; the precise content of the employee's obligation to work is rarely specified; and the intensity of work effort is left unstated. These elements are normally left to be worked out as the relationship proceeds; but they are subject to normative influences which range from implicit understandings to workplace rules ('custom and practice') and more formal, third party regulation. It is not simply a matter of fairness, but it is also economically efficient for private ordering to be supplemented by labour law regulation in this way. The normative framework supplied by labour law may therefore be not just an important means of reducing transaction costs, but also of promoting co-operation based on *trust* . . . most systems of labour law supply to the employment relationship a set of standardised terms, some of which are optional in the nature of default rules and others of which are mandatory. In many cases, these legal norms operate alongside (and in some cases concretise) a body of formal and informal rules which are derived from external or extra-legal sources, such as a collective agreement, or exceptionally, are agreed by the individual parties themselves or which derive from custom and practice. At some risk of over-generalisation, we may define the distinctive features of this regulatory framework as twofold: the employment contract (1) underpins the employer's power of direction, the 'managerial prerogative', while at the same time (2) granting the employee certain expectations of continuing employment and income security.

Thus, the content of the contract of employment comprises norms which govern the behaviour of the employer and the employee. Each of the norms belongs to one of a series of different sources which freely interact with each other rather than being neatly compartmentalized in separate 'walled-off' sections of the 'empty box'. Furthermore, cross-fertilization between the norms is a frequent phenomenon. The extract from Deakin and Wilkinson reveals some of the sources of those norms to be:

(1) the bureaucratic power of the employer to co-ordinate patterns of work through the medium of the managerial prerogative;

(2) the express terms of the contract agreed between the parties, including the contents of an incorporated peripheral document such as a collective agreement, works rule-book, staff handbook/manual, or procedure/policy;

(3) the 'custom and practice' of the workplace;

(4) employment protection legislation/regulation (including imposed terms);

(5) the implied terms of the contract specific to the parties' relationship, i.e. implied terms in fact; and

(6) the standardized default terms of the contract, i.e. the implied terms in law.

Each of these sources can also be divided according to the identity of the entity responsible for their promulgation and the features identified earlier can be linked to those sources. For example, (1) is a source of norms for which the *employer* is responsible, whereas the *employer and/or the employee* are responsible (or presumed to be responsible) for each of the sources (2), (3), and (5). Meanwhile (4) is attributable to *Parliament* and (6) have been developed and fashioned by *the judiciary*.

Turning to the connection between sources (1)–(6) and the five features discussed earlier which comprise the nature of the employment contract, the relationship can be depicted in Table 5.1. Table 5.1 also shows the division between the different sources of the norms comprising the content of the contract of employment and the identity of the body or bodies responsible for them.

In this chapter, our focus will turn to sources (2)–(5). Meanwhile, source (6) is the subject of Chapters 6 and 7. As for source (1), its relatively ad hoc and employer-specific nature renders it outside the scope of legal study and instead industrial relations studies can be consulted in order to shed further light on it. A final point to make is that there is an undoubted fluidity in the importance of the sources, which is determined to some extent by prevailing social and economic orthodoxies, the bargaining strength of the employees,

Table 5.1 *Relationship between the sources of workplace norms and five features comprising the nature of the personal employment contract*

Source	Feature/Nature	Responsibility
1. Managerial prerogative	Personal/relational, indefinite, incomplete and authority/power relation	Employer
2. Express terms	Personal/relational, consensual, indefinite, incomplete and authority/power relation	Employer and employee
3. Custom & practice	Personal/relational, consensual, indefinite and incomplete	Employer or employee
4. Labour legislation/ regulation	Personal/relational, indefinite, incomplete and authority/power relation	Parliament
5. Implied terms in fact	Personal/relational, consensual, indefinite and incomplete	Employer and employee
6. Implied terms	Personal/relational, mutual, indefinite, incomplete and authority/power relation	Judiciary

the nature of the employer, and the work performed, including whether a trade union has been recognized.

 For additional reading on the nature and content of the contract of employment, visit the Online Resources for this book at www.oup.com/uk/cabrelli3e/

5.2 FILLING IN THE CONTENT OF THE PERSONAL CONTRACT OF EMPLOYMENT: EXPRESS, IMPOSED, AND IMPLIED TERMS, AND CUSTOM AND PRACTICE

In this section, we take as our focus the express terms, external documents incorporated into the contract of employment, imposed terms, and implied terms in fact.

5.2.1 Express terms

The express terms are the starting point for our discussion of the content of the contract of employment. Where an express term gives rise to an obligation, its breach will sound an action in damages: an order of specific performance or injunctive relief is rarely granted.[14] The express terms may be set out in writing, agreed orally, or established by conduct. However, written express terms are by far the most important, particularly since the introduction of the Contract of Employment Act 1963, which is the statutory predecessor of Part I of the Employment Rights Act 1996 ('ERA'). Part I of the ERA requires the employer to supply the employee with a 'written statement of [the] particulars of employment' not later than two months after the beginning of employment. The parliamentary objective here is to 'ensure that employers ma[k]e essential contractual information available to their employees without impinging on the autonomy of the parties to conclude their own contractual bargain'.[15] The content of the written statement may be embodied in the form of a contract of employment or letter of engagement,[16] but must be set out in a single document and include the following particulars:

Section 1 Statement of initial employment particulars

(3) The statement shall contain particulars of—

   (a) the names of the employer and employee,

   (b) the date when the employment began, and

   (c) the date on which the employee's period of continuous employment began (taking into account any employment with a previous employer which counts towards that period).

(4) The statement shall also contain particulars, as at a specified date not more than seven days before the statement (or the instalment containing them) is given, of—

   (a) the scale or rate of remuneration or the method of calculating remuneration,

   (b) the intervals at which remuneration is paid (that is, weekly, monthly or other specified intervals),

---

[14] See Chapter 15, section 15.3.2.

[15] J. Kenner, 'Statement or Contract: Some Reflections on the EC Employer Information (Contract or Employment Relationship) Directive after *Kampelmann*' (1999) 28 *Industrial Law Journal* 205, 205; P. Leighton and S. Dumville, 'From Statement to Contract' (1977) 6 *Industrial Law Journal* 133.

[16] Sections 7A and 7B of the ERA.

(c) any terms and conditions relating to hours of work (including any terms and conditions relating to normal working hours),

(d) any terms and conditions relating to any of the following—

(i) entitlement to holidays, including public holidays, and holiday pay (the particulars given being sufficient to enable the employee's entitlement, including any entitlement to accrued holiday pay on the termination of employment, to be precisely calculated),

(ii) incapacity for work due to sickness or injury, including any provision for sick pay, and

(iii) pensions and pension schemes,

(e) the length of notice which the employee is obliged to give and entitled to receive to terminate his contract of employment,

(f) the title of the job which the employee is employed to do or a brief description of the work for which he is employed,

(g) where the employment is not intended to be permanent, the period for which it is expected to continue or, if it is for a fixed term, the date when it is to end,

(h) either the place of work or, where the employee is required or permitted to work at various places, an indication of that and of the address of the employer,

(j) any collective agreements which directly affect the terms and conditions of the employment including, where the employer is not a party, the persons by whom they were made, and

(k) where the employee is required to work outside the United Kingdom for a period of more than one month—

(i) the period for which he is to work outside the United Kingdom,

(ii) the currency in which remuneration is to be paid while he is working outside the United Kingdom,

(iii) any additional remuneration payable to him, and any benefits to be provided to or in respect of him, by reason of his being required to work outside the United Kingdom, and

(iv) any terms and conditions relating to his return to the United Kingdom . . .

Section 3 Note about disciplinary procedures and pensions

(1) A statement under section 1 shall include a note—

(a) specifying any disciplinary rules applicable to the employee or referring the employee to the provisions of a document specifying such rules which is reasonably accessible to the employee,

(aa) specifying any procedure applicable to the taking of disciplinary decisions relating to the employee, or to a decision to dismiss the employee, or referring the employee to the provisions of a document specifying such a procedure which is reasonably accessible to the employee,

(b) specifying (by description or otherwise)—

(i) a person to whom the employee can apply if dissatisfied with any disciplinary decision relating to him or any decision to dismiss him, and

(ii) a person to whom the employee can apply for the purpose of seeking redress of any grievance relating to his employment, and the manner in which any such application should be made, and

(c) where there are further steps consequent on any such application, explaining those steps or referring to the provisions of a document explaining them which is reasonably accessible to the employee.

(2) Subsection (1) does not apply to rules, disciplinary decisions, decisions to dismiss grievances or procedures relating to health or safety at work.

These statutory provisions have been shaped and supplemented by the European Directive 91/533/EEC[17] on an employer's obligation to inform employees of the essential aspects of the contract or employment relationship in writing.[18] Like the position in European law,[19] the written statement of particulars is of probative value, i.e. it furnishes 'strong prima facie evidence'[20] of the express terms of the contract of employment. Indeed, it has been held that the written statement of particulars may even constitute the contract of employment itself where it has been signed by the employee.[21] This can be contrasted with its status where the employee has signed to acknowledge the fact that he/she is in receipt of the written statement: in such a case, the statement will be probative only.[22] Where no such statutory statement is furnished by the employer or the statement given is incomplete or fails to comply with the statutory requirements, section 11 of the ERA directs that an employee may present a complaint to an employment tribunal. The remedy available to the employee is particularly weak, since it merely entails a determination by the tribunal as to what particulars ought to have been included or referred to in a, or the, statement and gives rise to no compensation. For example, in *Harðarson v Askar Capital hf*,[23] it was held that an employer's failure to update the remuneration terms of an employee's employment contract in writing did not render a reduction in an employee's salary ineffective as a matter of law.

Not only do the written express terms of the contract of employment form a central part of the content of the contract, but so do the provisions of collateral agreements or documents which have been incorporated therein.[24] In such a case, the specific content of those outside documents which have been expressly incorporated will constitute express terms and form part of the contract of employment. For example, a collective bargain agreed between a trade union and an employer, a staff handbook, or a policy or procedure of the employer may be expressly incorporated in full or in part.[25] A breach of a provision of that document which can be construed as imposing an obligation on the employer will give rise to damages in breach of contract.

We start our discussion here by first considering the incorporation of the contents of a collective agreement. The character of the content of the collective agreement is closely related to its social purposes. A collective agreement performs two social functions in the sense that it governs the *collective* relationship between the employer and the trade

---

[17] Directive 91/533/EEC (OJ 1991 L288/32).

[18] *ibid.*, Article 2(1).

[19] *Kampelmann v Landschaftsverband Westfalen-Lippe* [1997] ECR I–6907, [1998] 2 CMLR 131, [1998] IRLR 333.

[20] *System Floors (UK) Ltd v Daniel* [1982] ICR 54, 58A per Browne-Wilkinson J; *Glendale Managed Services v Graham* [2003] EWCA Civ 773, [2003] IRLR 465.

[21] *Gascol Conversions Ltd v Mercer* [1974] ICR 420.

[22] *System Floors (UK) Ltd v Daniel* [1982] ICR 54; *Robertson v British Gas Corp.* [1983] ICR 351.

[23] [2013] IRLR 475.

[24] For a review of the nature of the express terms of the employment contracts of UK employees and the extent to which they incorporate the terms of collective agreements, see W. Brown, S. Deakin, D. Nash, and S. Oxenbridge, 'The Employment Contract: From Collective Procedures to Individual Rights' (2000) 38 *British Journal of Industrial Relations* 611.

[25] For a collective agreement, see *National Coal Board v Galley* [1958] 1 All ER 91 and *Robertson v British Gas Corp.* [1983] ICR 351.

union and also operates as a possible source of rules which bind *individual* employees and employers;[26] this collective/individual dichotomy is plainly visible in the nature of its content. The latter function is only 'possible' insofar as those employment rules are treated as contractually enforceable.[27] Here, there is a hurdle, since the general rule embodied in section 179 of the Trade Union and Labour Relations (Consolidation) Act 1992 ('TULRCA') is that collective agreements are *not* legally binding, unless the parties include a provision stating that they intend the agreement to be a legally enforceable contract.[28] Therefore, between the trade union and the employer, the agreement has no legal standing in the absence of written stipulation to that effect, the latter being particularly unusual. Even where the agreement is so binding, this does not have any bearing on the legal enforceability of the agreement vis-à-vis the employee and the employer: unless an agency relationship arises whereby the trade union is deemed to be an agent of the employee member and entitled to bargain on his/her behalf,[29] the employee is treated as a third party and not privy to the collective agreement.

Thus, the failsafe way for a collective agreement or part of it to be made contractual is for it to be expressly incorporated[30] into the employee's contract of employment.[31] The contractual status of the collective agreement vis-à-vis the trade union and the employer is of no consequence in such circumstances, since an express incorporation will be valid notwithstanding that the trade union and the employer have stipulated in the collective agreement that it is binding in honour only.[32]

In the absence of the express incorporation of a collective agreement, it is open to the courts to incorporate a collective agreement or a part thereof by implication. On the basis that collective agreements amount to 'crystallised custom'[33] and serve to 'convert formal into factual freedom of contract as between employer and workman, by raising the latter to a level of equality of bargaining power',[34] Kahn-Freund was of the view that implied incorporation should be embraced by the judiciary as a matter of course:

■ O. Kahn-Freund, 'Collective Agreements' (1941) 4 *Modern Law Review* 225, 226–7

> Although English law has not so far taken cognisance of the normative function of collective industrial rules, it may soon be found that the present state of the law is unsatisfactory and that the individual contract of employment should not be allowed to derogate from the terms of the collective bargain to the detriment of the employee. It will then be necessary to reflect upon the ways

---

[26] See Chapter 2, section 2.1.5; Chapter C, section 2.1.1, of the Online Resources; and P. Davies and M. Freedland (eds), *Kahn-Freund's Labour and the Law* (London, Stevens & Sons, 1983) 154.

[27] Please consult the Online Resources for an illustration of a collective agreement.

[28] See Chapter C, section 2.2.2, of the Online Resources.

[29] This will be rare, since union membership of itself will not give rise to such an agency relationship: *Burton Group v Smith* [1977] IRLR 351.

[30] Section 1(4)(j) of the ERA acts as a 'prompt' to the parties to entertain the possibility of express incorporation, since it enjoins the employer to specify in the statutory written statement whether a collective agreement is in force.

[31] For example, as in *NCB v Galley* [1958] 1 All ER 91. Once a provision of a collective agreement has been incorporated into an individual contract of employment, it is able to survive the demise of the collective agreement: *NCB v NUM* [1986] ICR 736. However, in order to be expressly incorporated, the term in the collective agreement must be brought to the notice of the parties: *Worrall v Wilmott Dixon Partnership* (UKEAT/0521/09/DM, 9 July 2010).

[32] *Marley v Forward Trust Group Ltd* [1986] ICR 891.

[33] P. Davies and M. Freedland (eds), *Kahn-Freund's Labour and the Law* (London, Stevens & Sons, 1983) 168.

[34] O. Kahn-Freund, 'Collective Agreements under Wartime Legislation' (1943) 6 *Modern Law Review* 112, 117.

in which the normative function of collective agreements can be made legally effective . . . In order to achieve its social purpose, the collective bargain must not impair the validity of the contract of employment, the *vinculum obligationis* as between employer and employee must remain intact, but the contract must be deemed to have been concluded upon the terms of the collective bargain. This is a characteristic shared by collective wage and labour agreements with other legal rules protecting the socially weaker against the socially stronger party to a contract (housing legislation, etc.).

Kahn-Freund's approach of 'readily inferred implied incorporation' did not find favour with the judiciary; instead, they adopted, and continue to adopt, a cautious approach and insist on the existence of an intention to incorporate before they will entertain the possibility of implied incorporation. For example, in *Alexander v Standard Telephones Ltd (No. 2)*,[35] the court stipulated that one must be able to 'extract . . . a recognisable contractual intent as between the individual employee and his employer'.[36] Establishing such intent amounts to a high hurdle[37] and is evaluated on the basis of an objective standard of scrutiny.[38] For example, if implied incorporation would potentially lead to 'anarchy' or have 'disastrous consequences'[39] for the employer, this will militate against a finding that there is the requisite intention. Moreover, the employee's membership or non-membership of the trade union responsible for the negotiation of the collective agreement will be irrelevant for the purposes of determining whether there should be implied incorporation.[40] Further, the intention of the trade union and the employer or employers' association in negotiating and concluding the collective agreement will be relevant for the purposes of contractual incorporation. Therefore, if there was an understanding that individual employee members might specifically incorporate particular provisions of the collective agreement into their contract of employment, this will be taken into account.[41]

Not all provisions of a collective agreement relate to substantive conditions of employment such as hours of work, rates of pay, rest breaks, etc. Instead, some are purely procedural inasmuch as they establish machinery for conciliation, the resolution of disputes, decisions or conduct to be taken, or simply amount to an agreement that is specific to the trade union and the employer or employers' association. If the part of the collective agreement which the employee seeks to incorporate falls within the scope of the latter, then it is unlikely that it will be capable of implied incorporation.[42] Furthermore, the content and character of the collective agreement will be had regard to in determining whether implied incorporation is permitted.[43] Likewise, the balance between collective and individual content will be a relevant factor,[44] and it has been held that if a part of a collective agreement concerns or regulates the individual employment relationship, then that may well be sufficient to evince the requisite intention to incorporate.[45] Ultimately, whether implied incorporation ought to proceed is a highly fact-dependent enquiry.

It should be stressed that the establishment of the requisite intention that a particular provision of a collective agreement be incorporated is not of itself sufficient for incorporation to be effected. Closely connected to the idea that there must be an intention to incorporate and reflective of the dual collective and individual functions of a collective

---

[35] [1991] IRLR 286.   [36] *ibid.*, 292.
[37] See *George v Ministry of Justice* [2013] EWCA Civ 324.
[38] *Malone v British Airways plc* [2010] EWCA Civ 1225, [2011] ICR 125, 141D per Smith LJ.
[39] *ibid.*, 140A–141B per Smith LJ.   [40] *Hamilton v Futura Floors Ltd* [1990] IRLR 478.
[41] *Lee v GEC Plassey Telecommunications* [1993] IRLR 383, 391–2 per Mr Justice Connell. One might argue that this rule of law is rather odd, given that the touchstone of implied incorporation is reliant on the intention of a party not privy to the contract of employment in question, namely the trade union.
[42] *Young v Canadian Northern Railway Co.* [1931] AC 83.
[43] *Lee v GEC Plassey Telecommunications* [1993] IRLR 383, 391–2 per Mr Justice Connell.
[44] *Alexander v Standard Telephones Ltd (No. 2)* [1991] IRLR 286.
[45] *NCB v NUM* [1986] ICR 736, 773D–H per Scott J.

agreement, it is also necessary to show that the particular term in question is *apt* for incorporation.[46] Unfortunately, no clear juridical test has been developed to establish what is or is not apt, but two points emerge clearly from the jurisprudence.

(1) A distinction—which is not often easy to draw in practice at the borderlines—is made between *collective or procedural* matters regulated by the collective agreement (such as redundancy planning,[47] enhanced redundancy payment provisions, redundancy selection procedures,[48] or conciliation and dispute resolution procedures)[49] and *individual* matters specified in the collective agreement which are referable to the employment relationship or regulate working conditions (e.g. provisions fixing rates of pay, hours of work, or absence management provisions).[50] Only the latter are apt for incorporation,[51] which is rooted in the idea that underpinning the notion of 'aptness' is whether the provisions 'were intended to be legally enforceable by an individual employee against his employer'.[52]

(2) The provision in the collective agreement may be couched in language which is inherently vague or ambiguous, or establish a general framework for discussion,[53] or may amount to an expression of policy, objective, or aspiration, in which case it will not be apt for incorporation.[54] It had been thought that an objective test was applicable in order to determine whether a provision is apt for incorporation. However, in *Malone v British Airways plc*,[55] it is arguable that the Court of Appeal applied a more subjective standard of scrutiny from the viewpoint of the employer, which affords the latter an additional means of avoiding incorporation:

■ R. Russell, '*Malone v British Airways plc*: Protection of Managerial Prerogative' (2011) 40 *Industrial Law Journal* 207, 208

. . . the Court of Appeal's decision turned on the 'disastrous consequences' for BA that would follow were incorporation to be allowed. The Court of Appeal appears to have interpreted 'aptness' (which questions whether a term is in keeping with that which might be found in an employment contract) as 'appropriateness' (which considers whether it is desirable that a term be incorporated). This subtle shift in emphasis introduces subjective notions of desirability into the test of aptness and inevitably begs the question: by whose standards is aptness to be judged? It also risks entrenching the use of the aptness test 'as a filter to ensure that the employer has actually consented to the collectively agreed form having normative effect, as opposed to determining whether or not the term was sufficiently "individualised"'.[56]

---

[46] *Alexander v Standard Telephones Ltd (No. 2)* [1991] IRLR 286.

[47] *British Leyland (UK) Ltd v McQuilken* [1978] IRLR 245.

[48] *Alexander v Standard Telephones Ltd (No. 2)* [1991] IRLR 286. It is provisions relating to redundancy which have generated the most difficulty for the courts in applying the 'aptness' criterion, e.g. *Allen v TRW Systems Ltd* [2013] ICR D13.   [49] *NCB v NUM* [1986] ICR 736.

[50] *Sparks v Department for Transport* [2016] IRLR 519. Other distinctions drawn in the case law are whether the provisions were 'substantive' or 'procedural', or couched in language that is 'obligatory' or 'aspirational': *Chakrabarty v Ipswich Hospital NHS Trust* [2014] EWHC 2735 (QB) at para 130 per Mrs Justice Simler.

[51] *NCB v NUM* [1986] ICR 736, 772–3 per Scott J; *Kaur v MG Rover Group Ltd* [2005] ICR 625; and *Malone v British Airways plc* [2010] EWCA Civ 1225, [2011] ICR 125, 136B–H per Smith LJ.

[52] *George v Ministry of Justice* [2013] EWCA Civ 324 at para 47 per Rimer LJ.

[53] *Sparks v Department for Transport* [2016] IRLR 519.

[54] *NCB v NUM* [1986] ICR 736, 772–3 per Scott J; *Kaur v MG Rover Group Ltd* [2005] ICR 625, 630F, and 635F per Keene LJ; *Malone v British Airways plc* [2010] EWCA Civ 1225, [2011] ICR 125, 136B–H per Smith LJ; and *George v Ministry of Justice* [2013] EWCA Civ 324.

[55] Contrast this with the more objective evaluation adopted by Mr Justice Globe in *Sparks v Department for Transport* [2015] IRLR 641, 648–9.

[56] See also F. Reynold and J. Hendy, 'Reserving the Right to Change Terms and Conditions: How Far Can the Employer Go?' (2012) 41 *Industrial Law Journal* 79, 87–92.

Having addressed the incorporation of collective agreements into employment contracts, we now consider the scope for the terms of other documents purporting to govern the employment relationship to be treated as legally enforceable. Three obvious candidates are the *employer's works rulebook* which communicates instructions to employees as to how they should perform their work, the *employer's staff handbook or manual* which is a source of information for the employees in respect of the employer's objectives and policies, and the *employer's written policies or procedures*.[57] There is no general rule that works rulebooks,[58] staff handbooks,[59] and policies or procedures,[60] of themselves, are contractually binding. However, as regards the latter, Lord Dyson in *Edwards v Chesterfield Royal Hospital NHS Foundation Trust*[61] does seem to suggest that there is a presumption of sorts that disciplinary and grievance procedures will be readily clothed with contractual force.[62] The same point can be made in respect of the incorporation of staff handbooks.[63] From the perspective of the employer, it is perhaps beneficial that the provisions of such documents are not given contractual effect, since it means that the unilateral modification of these documents does not amount to a breach of contract[64] and an employee's refusal to abide by the new rule or change in policy will amount to a breach of his/her implied duty to obey reasonable orders.[65]

Like collective agreements, provisions of these documents may become legally binding if they are (a) incorporated into the individual contracts of employment of employees expressly or by implication and (b) apt for incorporation. As such, the principles governing the incorporation of such documents are the same as those applicable for collective agreements. However, the case law does suggest that the incorporation of provisions from collective agreements will be entertained less readily by the courts and tribunals[66] than incorporation from staff handbooks or policies/procedures. Moreover, the aptness criterion will be relaxed in the case of such staff handbooks or policies/procedures.

An example of the ease with which the courts will expressly incorporate a provision of a staff handbook is provided by the case of *Keeley v Fosroc International*.[67] Here, an employee's contract of employment expressly incorporated, by reference, the employers'

---

[57] For examples of these external materials, please consult the Online Resources. The policies or procedures of the employer sometimes form an integral part of the staff handbook or manual. Section 3(1) of the ERA prompts the employer and the employee to refer in the employment contract to disciplinary and grievance procedures applicable to employment.

[58] *Secretary of State for Employment v ASLEF (No. 2)* [1972] 2 WLR 1370.

[59] However, the fact that a handbook contains a statement that it is not contractual is not necessarily conclusive: *Peries v Wirefast Ltd* (UKEAT/0245/06/DA, 14 September 2006).

[60] *Grant v South-West Trains Ltd* [1998] IRLR 188; cf. *Secretary of State for Scotland v Taylor* [1997] IRLR 608. Where the terms of the disciplinary procedure were agreed between the employer and the employee in *Hussain v Surrey and Sussex Healthcare NHS Trust* [2011] EWHC 1670 (QB), [2011] All ER (D) 91 (July), it was held that there is no single test for determining whether the parties intended the provisions to be contractual, but that the following considerations would be taken into account, namely (a) the importance of the provision to the contractual working relationship, (b) the level of details prescribed by the provision, (c) the certainty of what the provision required, (d) the context of the provision, and (e) whether the provision was workable. These tests were applied more generally in *Sparks v Department for Transport* [2016] IRLR 519, 523 per McCombe LJ.

[61] [2011] UKSC 58, [2012] 2 WLR 55.

[62] *ibid.*, 66F–H. For a powerful critique of the reasoning for this assertion, see A. Bogg, 'Express Disciplinary Procedures in the Contract of Employment: Parliamentary Intention and the Supreme Court' (2015) 131 *Law Quarterly Review* 15.

[63] *Keeley v Fosroc International* [2006] EWCA Civ 1277, [2006] IRLR 961.

[64] For example, see *Dryden v Greater Glasgow Health Board* [1992] IRLR 469.

[65] See Chapter 6, section 6.3.1.

[66] For example, see the different results reached in *Cabinet Office v Beavan* [2014] IRLR 434, *Anderson v London and Fire Emergency Planning Authority* [2013] IRLR 459, and *Thorne v House of Commons Commission* [2014] IRLR 260.   [67] [2006] EWCA Civ 1277, [2006] IRLR 961.

staff handbook, 'Policies for People'. The latter included the following statement in the redundancy section of that handbook:

> Those employees with two or more years' continuous service are entitled to receive an enhanced redundancy payment from the company, which is paid tax free to a limit of £30,000. Details will be discussed during both collective and individual consultation.

The Court of Appeal held that the employee was entitled to an enhanced redundancy package in terms of the handbook and the failure of the employer to provide such enhanced payments amounted to a breach of contract. By virtue of the application of ordinary contractual principles, such a contractual breach will entitle the employee to a damages remedy. However, a note of caution should be struck, since a major exception applies where the external document incorporated is a disciplinary policy or procedure of the employer. In the case of *Edwards v Chesterfield Royal Hospital NHS Foundation Trust*,[68] the Supreme Court held that where there is a defect in the employer's adherence to an expressly incorporated disciplinary procedure, unless expressly agreed to the contrary, the employee will not be permitted to avail him/herself of a damages remedy *where the claim relates to the manner of the employee's dismissal*:

■ *Edwards v Chesterfield Royal Hospital NHS Foundation Trust* [2011] UKSC 58, [2012] 2 WLR 55, 68H–69C at paras 38–39

Lord Dyson:

. . . if provisions about disciplinary procedure are incorporated as express terms into an employment contract, they are not ordinary contractual terms agreed by parties to a contract in the usual way . . . The question remains whether, if provisions about disciplinary procedure are incorporated into a contract of employment, they are intended to be actionable at common law giving rise to claims for damages in the ordinary courts. Parliament intended such provisions to apply to contracts of employment, inter alia, in order to protect employees from unfair dismissal and to enhance their right not to be unfairly dismissed. It has specified the consequences of a failure to comply with such provisions in unfair dismissal proceedings. It could not have intended that the inclusion of these provisions in a contract would also give rise to a common law claim for damages for all the reasons given by the House of Lords in *Johnson v Unisys Ltd* for not extending the implied term of trust and confidence to a claim for damages for unfair manner of dismissal. It is necessarily to be inferred from this statutory background that, unless they otherwise expressly agree, the parties to an employment contract do not intend that a failure to comply with contractually binding disciplinary procedures will give rise to a common law claim for damages . . .[69]

However, in such circumstances, the employee is not barred from seeking an injunction.[70] A final point to make is that logic dictates that the decision in *Edwards* should also apply in the case of a disciplinary procedure impliedly incorporated into the contract of employment, i.e. an employee will have no right to a damages remedy where his/her claim concerns the manner of his/her dismissal flowing from an irregularity in the application of an impliedly incorporated disciplinary procedure.[71]

---

[68] [2011] UKSC 58, [2012] 2 WLR 55.

[69] See also [2011] UKSC 58, [2012] 2 WLR 55, 82G at para 94 per Lord Mance.

[70] For example, see *Chhabra v West London Mental Health NHS Trust* [2014] ICR 194. For a critique of this decision, see Chapter 15, section 15.3.1.

[71] In the case of *Hussain v Surrey and Sussex Healthcare NHS Trust* [2011] EWHC 1670 (QB), [2011] All ER (D) 91 (July), decided prior to *Edwards*, it was held that the terms of a disciplinary procedure which had been impliedly incorporated into a doctor's employment contract had been breached, thus amounting to a breach of contract. Subsequent to *Edwards*, it is submitted that the only appropriate remedy would be an injunction.

Turning on that note to the implied incorporation of external documents, we consider the case of *Briscoe v Lubrizol*.[72] Here, the Court of Appeal accepted an employee's argument that a reference in the statutory written statement of the main particulars of his employment to an income-protection scheme—whose provisions were detailed in the employer's staff handbook and an insurance policy between the employer and an insurer—were incorporated into his contract of employment. In doing so, Potter LJ expressed the following opinion:

■ *Briscoe v Lubrizol* [2002] EWCA Civ 508, at para 14

Lord Justice Potter:

It is of course frequently the case that details of an employee's contract and the benefit to which he is entitled by virtue of his employment are largely to be found in a handbook of the kind supplied to the claimant in this case. For this purpose, and depending upon the circumstances, incorporation by express reference in the statutory particulars of employment will not usually be required by the court. Again, it is frequently the case that, in the employment context, the language of a handbook, while couched in terms of information and explanation, will be construed as giving rise to binding legal obligations as between employer and employee.[73]

Once a court is satisfied that a provision of the works rulebook, staff handbook, or policy has been expressly or impliedly incorporated, it must also be apt for incorporation in order to attract full legal force and effect. For example, in *Keeley v Fosroc International*,[74] the Court of Appeal ruled that an enhanced redundancy scheme contained in a staff handbook expressly incorporated into a contract of employment was apt for incorporation since it was articulated in terms of an entitlement in favour of the employee; likewise in *Harlow v Artemis International Corp. Ltd*,[75] where an employee's contract expressly incorporated 'all ... terms and conditions ... as detailed in the staff handbook as issued to you, and subject to its most recent update'. The staff handbook, which had originally been printed as a manual in hard-copy form, was made accessible as a series of policies on a staff intranet site using (and known as) Lotus Notes. The Lotus Notes contained a redundancy policy which provided for an enhanced redundancy package and the employee claimed that he was entitled to an enhanced redundancy payment in terms of that policy. The employer resisted this on the ground that the staff handbook did not include the redundancy policy and that, if it did, the latter was not apt for incorporation. Mr Justice McCombe in the High Court agreed with the employee that the redundancy policy formed part of the staff handbook since the employer's staff had at all material times regarded the employer's policies and procedures on the intranet site as the 'staff handbook' after the discontinuation of the printed publication. Further, it was held that the redundancy policy was apt for incorporation by virtue of the fact it was kept with other policies that must have had contractual effect, such as sickness and holiday pay, and contained an express statement of the manner of calculation. The fact that the employer's past practice on the payment of an enhanced redundancy package had been variable was of no consequence. In making this decision, Mr Justice McCombe advanced

---

[72] [2002] EWCA Civ 508, [2002] IRLR 607.

[73] Sourced from BAILII at http://www.bailii.org/cgi-bin/markup.cgi?doc=/ew/cases/EWCA/Civ/2002/508.html&query=briscoe+and+v+and+lubrizol&method=boolean (last visited 12 October 2017).

[74] [2006] EWCA Civ 1277, [2006] IRLR 961.

[75] [2008] IRLR 629. See also *MoD v Carr* (UKEAT/0291/09/LA, 18 November 2010). Contrast these cases with *Carter v Ludwig Institute for Cancer Research* [2007] EWHC 1672 (QB) where an enhanced redundancy payment in the General Medical Council's staff code was not apt for incorporation on the basis that the research scientist was not an employee of the General Medical Council.

the following view on the appropriate approach to be taken to the task of interpretation of an external handbook or policy:

■ *Harlow v Artemis International Corp. Ltd* [2008] EWHC 1126 (QB) at para 28

Mr Justice McCombe:

The fact of the matter is that employment contracts today, such as Mr Harlow's in this case, consist of all sorts of materials put together by human resources officers, rather than lawyers, and are designed to be read in an informal and commonsense manner in the context of a relationship affecting ordinary people in their everyday lives. Close arguments arising out of nuance of language, possibly of moment in more formal contracts, seem to me to be singularly inappropriate in such a context, unless it is made clear in the document that an important point of distinction is being made.[76]

In *Sparks v Department for Transport*,[77] an absence management procedure in a staff handbook was also held to be apt for incorporation even though Lord Justice McCombe recognized that such provisions were generally matters of guidance and good practice. He remarked that specific absence management provisions can be clothed with contractual force where their placement in the handbook suggests that they were motivated by a desire to confer an entitlement in favour of the employees.

A final point to make is that collective agreements and other external materials such as works rules, staff handbooks, and employer policies may be implied into the contract of employment by 'custom and practice'.[78] We now turn to this 'uncrystallized' source of workplace norms.

5.2.2 **Custom and practice**

Although the space within which custom and practice may operate has been crowded out by the exponential increase in significance of the express terms and external documents such as collective agreements and staff handbooks, it nonetheless continues to be a relevant source of workplace norms. There is no precise definition in the case law of custom and practice, but some useful guidance is provided in the following extracts:

■ W. Brown, 'A Consideration of "Custom and Practice"' (1972) 10 *British Journal of Industrial Relations* 42, 48–61

A [custom and practice] rule . . . arises from informal processes . . . [Custom and practice] rules . . . [are] those transactional rules of job regulation which arise, not from any explicit and formal negotiation, but from a process whereby managerial error or omission establishes a practice that workers see as legitimate to defend. Besides being a type of job regulation rules, [custom and practice] is used as a claim and an excuse in circumstances where powerful work-forces interact with unco-ordinated managements . . . Whatever it is called, the phenomenon is evident in most of industry. In some industries it provides the basis and origin of the bulk of rules of job regulation. It does not just augment formally negotiated rules; it supplants them. Even many ostensibly

---

[76] Sourced from BAILII at http://www.bailii.org/cgi-bin/markup.cgi?doc=/ew/cases/EWHC/QB/2008/1126.html&query=harlow+and+v+and+artemis&method=boolean (last visited 12 October 2017). For a similar approach, see *Anderson v London Fire and Emergency Planning Authority* [2013] EWCA Civ 321, [2013] IRLR 459.   [77] [2016] IRLR 519.

[78] For example, in *Henry v London General Transport Services Ltd* [2002] ICR 910.

solid formal agreements are no more than the temporary recording of the current state of [custom and practice] rules. Once signed, these agreements may become battered by managerial deviation and worker pressure and finally dissolve into the broad flux of [custom and practice]. If, in much of industry, [custom and practice] is king, its reign is curiously blind. Its rules do not emerge from any of the conscious bargaining processes with which industrial relations theories have concerned themselves. They do not arise from intention, deliberation or conspiracy. They are the product of management error and worker power.

■ D. Brodie, 'Reflecting the Dynamics of Employment Relations: Terms Implied from Custom and Practice and the *Albion* Case' (2004) 33 *Industrial Law Journal* 159, 159–60

. . . the parties may come to behave in a way that is not provided for in the contract (albeit no breach occurs). This may well happen as the result of a unilateral introduction (more or less formally) of a policy or practice by the employer. For example, the contract may provide for Statutory Sick Pay but the employer may pay the normal amount of wages during periods of absence due to illness. Similarly the contract may provide that the amount of any redundancy payment should be in line with the statutory entitlement; the employer may elect to pay on an uncapped basis.

The Brodie extract singles out custom and practice which emanates from the unilateral actions or practices of an employer ('single employer custom and practice'). This can be contrasted with 'industry-wide custom and practice' or general trade usage. The law crafts a distinction between these two sources of custom and practice, and it is generally less onerous for an employee to establish the latter than the former since the requisite criteria which are necessary to establish it can be more easily inferred. It is generally accepted that a party seeking to rely on an industry-wide custom and practice must show that it is reasonable, notorious, and certain.[79] It has been said that 'notoriety is no more than widespread knowledge and understanding [of the custom]; certainty relates to the nature of the arrangement',[80] and as for what is reasonable, this 'must be approached in the round'.[81] An example of a trade custom which has satisfied the reasonable, notorious, and certain test includes the practice of making deductions from employees' wages for shoddy work in the weaving industry in Lancashire in *Sagar v H Ridehalgh & Son Ltd*.[82] Conversely, in *Solectron Scotland Ltd v Roper*,[83] it was held that the employer had failed to establish a custom and practice which dislodged a predecessor employer's contractual enhanced redundancy payment scheme, since the practice it relied upon was neither certain (different terms were set for each redundancy exercise), nor reasonable (since it depended upon the will of the employer), nor notorious (since there was no consistent application of any of the terms). Where the reasonable, notorious, and certain test is satisfied, it is entirely inconsequential that the employee is unaware of the trade custom since he/she is deemed to have been aware of it when he/she entered into employment with the employer.[84]

---

[79] *Devonald v Rosser & Sons* [1906] 2 KB 728 at paras 743–4 per Farwell J.
[80] *Garratt v Mirror Group Newspapers Ltd* [2011] IRLR 591, 598 at para 42 per Lord Justice Leveson.
[81] *ibid.*, 598 at para 43 per Lord Justice Leveson.
[82] [1931] 1 Ch 310. If you entered employment in that trade you were taken to be aware of the custom.
[83] [2004] IRLR 4.
[84] *Strathlorne Steamship Co. v Baird & Sons* 1916 SC (HL) 134, 136 per Lord Chancellor Buckmaster; *Sagar v H Ridehalgh & Son Ltd* [1931] 1 Ch 310.

The position is slightly more complex when we consider whether an established single employer custom and practice has achieved contractual status, since additional considerations arise. At the policy level, on the one hand, what we find is that the courts have been anxious not to tie down an employer to a practice which has been entirely gratuitous on its part (e.g. an *ex gratia* bonus or enhanced redundancy payment)[85] or to commit the employer to a contractual obligation by virtue of engaging in a mere repeated pattern of behaviour without more.[86] However, on the other hand, the judiciary have been keen to protect and enforce the reasonable expectations of employees where they have been stoked or encouraged by an employer regularly engaging in a particular practice. This trade-off is an ever-present undercurrent in the case law and is generally resolved by the requirement that there be some form of communication of the practice by the employer to the employee before the necessary contractual status is arrived at.

Another matter concerns the interaction between the custom and practice and an express term of the employment contract. Contractual orthodoxy dictates that an express term supersedes a custom and practice. However, as is recognized in the Brown extract, a point in time may come when the behaviour of the employer becomes so entrenched or 'battered' into a regular pattern that it is completely inconsistent with an express term. Examples of the circumstances in which this might take place are provided in the extract from Brodie. What takes precedence and, if it is to be the custom and practice, what is the juridical basis for that result? What is now fairly clear is that the custom and practice 'trumps' the express term in such a situation, and some scholars argue that the ascription of legal status to the custom and practice can be grounded in the law of unilateral contract. Here the argument runs that the unilateral contract is set up by an employer unilaterally undertaking to be bound by the practice and the employee accepting that undertaking by continuing to work for the employer.[87] Whilst extremely attractive, the jury is still out on whether this is the best explanation, since there is a paucity of jurisprudence in the case law setting out a plausible legal basis as to why the express term will be supplanted by a single employer custom and practice. Matters are further complicated here by the rule that the custom and practice will take precedence even where it is rooted in the employer's mistaken belief that the employees had secured an express contractual right to the benefits associated with the custom and practice in the past.[88]

Ultimately, in the context of a single employer custom and practice, the principal question is whether the courts 'are able to infer from regular application of the practice that the parties must be taken to have accepted that the practice has crystallised into contractual rights'.[89] As a proposition, that is helpful, but it fails to supply any practical guidance. For example, in *Duke v Reliance Systems Ltd*,[90] the question was whether a normal retirement age of 60 amounted to a unilateral custom and practice of the employer. The EAT rejected the contention that a single employer custom and practice had been established since there was no evidence that the policy *at the very least* had been drawn to the attention of the employees or followed without exception for a substantial period of time.[91] Thus, a repeated pattern of behaviour on the part of the employer for a quiet life without more is insufficient to establish a single employer custom and practice.[92] In the

---

[85] *Grieve v Imperial Tobacco*, Guardian, 30 April 1963.

[86] *Quinn v Calder Industrial Materials Ltd* [1996] IRLR 126; *Strathlorne Steamship Co. v Baird & Sons* 1916 SC (HL) 134; *Campbell v Union Carbide Ltd* (EAT/0341/01, 15 March 2002), [2002] All ER (D) 143 (September); and *Pellowe v Pendragon plc* (UKEAT/804/98/0106, 1 October 1998).

[87] D. Brodie, 'Reflecting the Dynamics of Employment Relations: Terms Implied from Custom and Practice and the *Albion* Case' (2004) 33 *Industrial Law Journal* 159, 162–3; D. Brodie, *The Employment Contract: Legal Principles, Drafting, and Interpretation* (Oxford, OUP, 2005) 153.

[88] *CSC Computer Sciences Ltd v McAlinden* [2013] EWCA Civ 1435.

[89] *Solectron Scotland Ltd v Roper* [2004] IRLR 4, 6 per Elias J.   [90] [1982] ICR 449.

[91] *ibid.*, 452G per Browne-Wilkinson J.

[92] For example, *Express and Star v Bunday* [1987] ICR 58.

subsequent case of *Quinn v Calder Industrial Materials Ltd*,[93] in rejecting the argument that a single employer custom and practice gave rise to a contractual right to an enhanced redundancy payment, Lord Coulsfield in the Court of Session explored the mechanics of how the employer ought to draw the practice to the employee's attention:

■ *Quinn v Calder Industrial Materials Ltd* [1996] IRLR 126, 128

Lord Coulsfield:

In a case such as the present, the factors to which Browne-Wilkinson J referred [in *Duke v Reliance Systems Ltd*] are likely to be among the most important circumstances to be taken into account, but they have to be taken into account along with all the other circumstances of the case. Thus, for example, in our view, the question is not whether the period for which a policy has been followed is 'substantial' in some abstract sense, but whether, in relation to the other circumstances, it is sufficient to support the inference that that policy has achieved the status of a contractual term. Again, with regard to communication, the question seems to us to be not so much whether the policy has been made or become known directly to the employees or through intermediaries, but whether the circumstances in which it was made or has become known support the inference that the employers intended to become contractually bound by it.

Quinn was followed by the decision of Peter Gibson LJ in the Court of Appeal in *Albion Automotive Ltd v Walker*[94] and by *Park Cakes Ltd v Shumba*,[95] both of which also concerned whether a unilateral management policy to make enhanced redundancy payments attracted contractual status. In holding that the employees had established a contractual right to an enhanced redundancy payment, Underhill LJ in *Park Cakes* adopted a multi-factorial approach which ought to be applied in the context of an analysis of a single employer custom and practice:

■ *Park Cakes Ltd v Shumba* [2013] EWCA Civ 974 at paras 34–36

Lord Justice Underhill:

. . . the essential object is to ascertain what the parties must have, or must be taken to have, understood from each other's conduct and words, applying ordinary contractual principles: the terminology of 'custom and practice' should not be allowed to obscure that enquiry.

Taking that approach, the essential question in a case of the present kind must be whether, by his conduct in making available a particular benefit to employees over a period, in the context of all the surrounding circumstances, the employer has evinced to the relevant employees an intention that they should enjoy that benefit as of right. If so, the benefit forms part of the remuneration which is offered to the employee for his work (or, perhaps more accurately in most cases, his willingness to work), and the employee works on that basis . . . It follows that the focus must be on what the employer has communicated to the employees. What he may have personally understood or intended is irrelevant except to the extent that the employees are, or should reasonably have been, aware of it.

In considering what, objectively, employees should reasonably have understood about whether a particular benefit is conferred as of right, it is, as I have said, necessary to take account of all the circumstances known, or which should reasonably have been known, to them. I do not propose to attempt a comprehensive list of the circumstances which may be relevant, but in a case concerning enhanced redundancy benefits they will typically include the following:

(a) *On how many occasions, and over how long a period, the benefits in question have been paid.*
   Obviously, but subject to the other considerations identified below, the more often enhanced

---

[93] [1996] IRLR 126.   [94] [2002] EWCA Civ 946.   [95] [2013] IRLR 800.

benefits have been paid, and the longer the period over which they have been paid, the more likely it is that employees will reasonably understand them to be being paid as of right.

(b) *Whether the benefits are always the same.* If, while an employer may invariably make enhanced redundancy payments, he nevertheless varies the amounts or the terms of payment, that is inconsistent with an acknowledgment of legal obligation; if there is a legal right it must in principle be certain. Of course a late departure from a practice which has already become contractual cannot affect legal rights (see *Solectron*); but any inconsistency during the period relied on as establishing the custom is likely to be fatal. It is, however, possible that in a particular case the evidence may show that the employer has bound himself to a minimum level of benefit even though he has from time to time paid more on a discretionary basis.

(c) *The extent to which the enhanced benefits are publicised generally.* Where the availability of enhanced redundancy benefits is published to the workforce generally, that will tend to convey that they are paid as a matter of obligation, though I am not to be taken as saying that it is conclusive, and much will depend on the circumstances and on how the employer expresses himself. It should also be borne in mind that 'publication' may take many forms. In some circumstances publication to a trade union, or perhaps to a large group of employees, may constitute publication to the workforce as a whole. Employment tribunals should be able to judge whether, as a matter of industrial reality, the employer has conducted himself so as to create . . . 'widespread knowledge and understanding' on the part of employees that they are legally entitled to the enhanced benefits.

(d) *How the terms are described.* If an employer clearly and consistently describes his enhanced redundancy terms in language that makes clear that they are offered as a matter of discretion— e.g. by describing them as *ex gratia*—it is hard to see how the employees or their representatives could reasonably understand them to be contractual, however regularly they may be paid. A statement that the payments are made as a matter of 'policy' may, though again much depends on the context, point in the same direction. Conversely, the language of 'entitlement' points to legal obligation.

(e) *What is said in the express contract.* As a matter of ordinary contractual principles, no term should be implied, whether by custom or otherwise, which is inconsistent with the express terms of the contract, at least unless an intention to vary can be understood.

(f) *Equivocalness.* The burden of establishing that a practice has become contractual is on the employee, and he will not be able to discharge it if the employer's practice is, viewed objectively, equally explicable on the basis that it is pursued as a matter of discretion rather than legal obligation.[96]

Although the judiciary in some of the post-*Albion Automotive* decisions considering single employer custom and practice appear to have restricted themselves to consideration of whether the practice was reasonable, notorious, and certain,[97] it is now more common to find engagement with the criteria in *Park Cakes*.[98] However, as noted by Lord

---

[96] Sourced from BAILII at http://www.bailii.org/cgi-bin/markup.cgi?doc=/ew/cases/EWCA/Civ/2013/974.html&query=park+and+cakes+and+ltd.+and+v+and+shumba&method=boolean (last visited 12 October 2017).

[97] For example, *Henry v London General Transport Services Ltd* [2002] ICR 910; *Solectron Scotland Ltd v Roper* [2004] IRLR 4; *Rutherford v Seymour Pierce* [2010] IRLR 606; and *Garratt v Mirror Group Newspapers Ltd* [2011] IRLR 591, 597–8 where Lord Justice Leveson was equally content to analyse whether a custom and practice had been established by operation of the reasonable, notorious, and certain test or the more detailed approach in *Albion Automotive Ltd v Walker*.

[98] For example, see *CSC Computer Sciences Ltd v McAlinden* [2013] EWCA Civ 1435 at para 11 per Underhill LJ; *Peacock Stores v Peregrine* (UKEAT/0315/13/SM, 25 March 2014) at paras 20–3 per Mr Justice Langstaff.

Justice Leveson in *Garratt v Mirror Group Newspapers Ltd*,[99] there is undoubtedly an element of overlap between the traditional 'reasonable, notorious, and certain' criteria and the criteria applicable in the case of the multi-factorial approach adopted in *Albion Automotive* and *Park Cakes*. Moreover, the Court of Appeal in *Park Cakes* and *Albion Automotive* expressly said that they did not intend to lay down an exhaustive list of relevant factors.[100]

5.2.3 Imposed terms

Through the medium of employment protection legislation, Parliament has intervened to introduce terms directly into the contract of employment. Such contractual terms are often referred to as 'statutorily imposed terms' and cover a variety of situations. They are distinct from 'statutory employment protection rights' generally[101] and, by virtue of being contractual, they give rise to damages if they are breached. Moreover, there are various restrictions on contracting out of these imposed terms *in pejus*, i.e. by qualifying or limiting the scope of the employment protection afforded by the term:[102]

■ **Equality Act 2010**

Section 66 Sex equality clause

(1) If the terms of A's work do not (by whatever means) include a sex equality clause, they are to be treated as including one.

(2) A sex equality clause is a provision that has the following effect—

   (a) if a term of A's is less favourable to A than a corresponding term of B's is to B, A's term is modified so as not to be less favourable;

   (b) if A does not have a term which corresponds to a term of B's that benefits B, A's terms are modified so as to include such a term.

■ **Working Time Regulations 1998 (SI 1998/1833)**

Regulation 4 Maximum weekly working time

(1) Unless his employer has first obtained the worker's agreement in writing to perform such work, a worker's working time, including overtime, in any reference period which is applicable in his case shall not exceed an average of 48 hours for each seven days.[103]

---

[99] [2011] IRLR 591, 597.

[100] *Allen v TRW Systems Ltd* [2013] ICR D13. See also *Peacock Stores v Peregrine* (UKEAT/0315/13/SM, 25 March 2014) at para 20 per Mr Justice Langstaff.

[101] Statutory employment protection rights represent an enormous proportion of employment law, which will be analysed throughout most, if not all, of the chapters in this work.

[102] For example, see section 144 of the Equality Act 2010, regulation 35 of the Working Time Regulations 1998 (SI 1998/1833), and section 49 of the National Minimum Wage Act 1998. For a comprehensive discussion, see A. C. L. Davies, 'Terms Inserted into the Contract of Employment by Legislation' in M. Freedland et al. (eds), *The Contract of Employment* (Oxford, OUP, 2016) 427.

[103] In *Barber v RJB Mining (UK) Ltd* [1999] ICR 679, the High Court decided that regulation 4(1) of the Working Time Regulations was an imposed term incorporated into all contracts of employment.

■ **National Minimum Wage Act 1998**

> *Section 17 Non-compliance: worker entitled to additional remuneration*
>
> (1) If a worker who qualifies for the national minimum wage is remunerated for any pay reference period by his employer at a rate which is less than the national minimum wage, the worker shall . . . be taken to be entitled under his contract to be paid, as additional remuneration in respect of that period . . . [104]

5.2.4 Implied terms: implied terms 'in fact' and implied terms 'in law'

The common law recognizes two kinds of implied terms. First, terms will be implied into a contract of employment where a purely factual enquiry reveals that it is necessary to do so in order to give business efficacy to the transaction as must have been intended at all events by both the contracting parties.[105] This 'business efficacy' test is supplemented by the 'officious bystander' construct.[106] Here, one must enquire whether the term suggested is so obvious as to go without saying, so that if an officious bystander had suggested it to the contracting parties when they concluded their contract, they would have both approved of the term without hesitation. If a term is implied as a consequence of the operation of the 'business efficacy' and 'officious bystander' tests, this term is referred to as an implied term in fact and the term applies to the contract between the employer and employee only. Therefore, it is not of universal application to contracts of a particular class or type, but specific to the contract at hand between the relevant contracting parties. The justification for inserting implied terms in fact into the contract of the parties is that they are required in order to make the contract 'work'.[107]

An implied term in fact can be contrasted with an implied term in law. It is implied terms in law with which Chapter 6 is concerned. Implied terms in law are imposed 'from the outside' by reference to the parties' presumed intentions and apply to all contracts of a particular type, e.g. a contract for the sale and purchase of goods, a contract of agency, and a contract of employment. Where the common law establishes that an implied term in law should be recognized in the case of a contract of employment, that term will be imported into every employment contract concluded between an employer and employee, rather than simply being included in a contract of employment concluded between two particular contracting parties. The test for implying a term in law into a contract of employment is predicated on 'necessity', i.e. it must be a 'necessary incident'[108] of the employment relationship based on 'wider considerations'[109] or 'general considerations' of policy.

The distinction between an implied term in fact and an implied term in law is illustrated in Hypotheticals A and B.

---

[104] Another example of an imposed term is the statutory right to minimum periods of notice of termination of employment in terms of sections 86–91 of the ERA.

[105] *The Moorcock* (1889) LR 14 PD 64 and *Marks & Spencer plc v BNP Paribas Securities Services Trust Co. (Jersey) Ltd* [2015] UKSC 72, [2015] 3 WLR 1843.

[106] *Shirlaw v Southern Foundries (1926) Ltd* [1939] 2 KB 206.

[107] For the distinction between implied terms 'in law' and implied terms 'in fact', see *Liverpool County Council v Irwin* [1977] AC 239, 254F–255C and 265C–269B per Lords Wilberforce and Edmund-Davies. For implied terms in fact, see *Equitable Life Assurance Society v Hyman* [2002] 1 AC 408; and *Marks & Spencer plc v BNP Paribas Securities Services Trust Co. (Jersey) Ltd* [2015] UKSC 72, [2015] 3 WLR 1843.

[108] *Lister v Romford Ice and Cold Storage Co. Ltd* [1957] AC 555, 576 per Viscount Simonds; *Liverpool City Council v Irwin* [1977] AC 239, 254F–255C per Lord Wilberforce; and *Scally v Southern Health and Social Services Board* [1992] 1 AC 294, 306G–307F at para 12 per Lord Bridge.

[109] *Scally v Southern Health and Social Services Board* [1992] 1 AC 294, 306G–307F at para 12 per Lord Bridge.

Hypothetical A

Danny's Demolishers Ltd ('the Employer') decides to appoint an individual as a sales and marketing assistant to be based at premises in Oxford. This role involves the individual making regular visits to past clients of the Employer by car, as well as potential clients in the public sector. The majority of the individual's time is engaged in travelling by car to and from the sites of these past and potential clients.

After a year or so, the individual appointed resigns and the Employer readvertises the sales and marketing assistant post. Owen Jones ('the Employee') who has considerable experience in sales and marketing is appointed as a replacement. At his interview, the Employer explains to the Employee that the post is identical to that undertaken by the previous employee. Therefore, it will entail a significant amount of time in a car on the road. The Employee explains that he does not own a motor vehicle. The Employer informs him that this should not be a problem.

The Employee arrives at the premises of the Employer on his agreed start date and is handed ten files with addresses and details of past and potential clients. He is asked to go off to meet these clients forthwith to discuss potential demolition deals. From a review of the files, the Employee notes that the addresses of each of these clients are over 150 miles away from the Employer's premises. He starts to panic as there is no transport made available to enable him to travel.

The difficulty encountered by the Employee on his first day at work is that the Employer does not appear to have made transport available to enable him to visit the clients. In these circumstances, the law would intervene to furnish a degree of clarity with regard to the obligations of the Employer. It is likely that the common law would imply a term in fact into the Employee's employment contract to the effect that the Employer is obliged to furnish the Employee with a company car in order to enable him to reach the premises of the Employer's past and potential clients on the basis of the 'business efficacy' and 'officious bystander' tests. This is so obvious as to go without saying, so that the Employer and Employee would have approved this term if it had been suggested by an officious bystander at the inception of their relationship. Such an implied term in fact is necessary so that the employment contract can be rendered 'workable'.

In order to contrast the implied term in fact with an implied term in law, let us consider Hypothetical B.

Hypothetical B

The Employer would like to reduce the travelling costs associated with the Employee's post. The decision is taken to reduce the amount of time the Employee spends travelling by 60 per cent so that the majority of the Employee's time will now be spent at the Employer's premises at Oxford. The Employer would like the Employee to conduct meetings with past and potential clients at the Oxford premises by using electronic media such as Skype and video conferencing. The Employee is extremely resistant to the proposed changes to his working pattern as he has no idea how to use the technologies the Employer has suggested.

It is part of the managerial prerogative to decide (a) how work available is to be allocated and (b) the arrangements by which that work is to be done. Therefore, the Employer has the right to enforce changes to the Employee's role. However, the common law has recognized that a measure of control should be placed on the untrammelled power of the Employer to direct labour as it sees fit. One way it has done so is to imply a term in law which imposes a duty on the Employer to provide all necessary support and training where it is proposing to effect a change in the Employee's method of work.[110] By the same token, the common law recognizes an implied term in law obliging employees to adapt to new working patterns in relation to the discharge of their existing job and role.[111] As such, the Employee cannot take the support and training yet continue to adopt an intransigent attitude to the new pattern of working. This implied term of adaptation is effective to impress a duty on the Employee which fits 'hand in glove' with the Employer's obligation of support and training. A final point to stress is that such implied terms do not emerge as a consequence of the 'business efficacy' and 'officious bystander' tests; instead, they are implied as a necessary legal incident of all contracts of employment. The significance of this point is that the implied terms in law imposing obligations on the Employer and Employee apply to all employment contracts, rather than being restricted to the Employer and Employee's contract only. It is with implied terms in law to which our consideration will turn in Chapter 6.

Reflection points

1. Consult the sample collective agreement on the Online Resources. To what extent do you believe that it is possible to divide the collective from the individual content of that agreement? What bearing does your answer have on the rule that a provision of a collective agreement must be apt for incorporation into the contract of employment?

2. Distinguish a trade custom from a single employer custom and practice. Are you convinced that the legal distinction between these two typologies of custom and practice is necessary, and to what extent are you of the view that the legal tests for ascribing contractual status to these two forms of custom and practice are truly distinct?

 For additional reading on the terms of the contract of employment (express, imposed, and implied terms, and custom and practice), visit the Online Resources for this book at www.oup.com/uk/cabrelli3e/

---

[110] *Cresswell v Board of Inland Revenue* [1984] ICR 508.
[111] *ibid.*

CHAPTER SIX

THE IMPLIED TERMS OF THE PERSONAL EMPLOYMENT CONTRACT

6.1 THE ROLE PLAYED BY THE IMPLIED TERMS

In this chapter, we examine the implied terms in law of the contract of employment. We will note how the principal judicial technique with regard to the implied terms in law has been to carefully craft duties on employers and corresponding rights on employees alongside terms imposing obligations on employees and conferring rights in favour of employers. In doing so, we will identify certain themes and ideas which cut across the span of the implied terms, whether looked at from the perspective of the employee's or employer's obligations, e.g. the contribution made by the notions of the wage–work bargain, mutuality/reciprocity, fidelity, loyalty, care, co-operation, trust, confidence, and good faith.

6.1.1 The function of terms implied in law

Akin to other nominate contracts,[1] the law prescribes a suite of standardized implied terms which serve to interpret and rationalize the internal structure and normative content of the contract of employment. The implication of terms into the contract of employment represents one of the most telling contributions the common law has made to employment law in the UK. Such terms can be equated to a default 'operating system'[2] and have been developed incrementally through an iterative process of common law adjudication, representing the judicial conceptualization of the employment relationship. The number, scope, and content of implied terms has ebbed and flowed over time, duly characterized by bursts of activity alongside checks on expansion. Whilst the traditional orientation of the implied terms was employer-protective in the sense of shoring up the managerial prerogative, there is little doubt that the past half-century has witnessed a remarkable spate of judicial innovation resulting in a more pro-employee framework.[3] The general importance of that phenomenon to the evolution of employment law should not be understated.

When we enquire about the *function or role* of the implied terms in law, we must also engage in the identification of the underlying *policy justifications* for their emergence. The judiciary's subjective motivations for the formulation of the implied terms are not always clear in their judgments. At one level, we can take the judicially declared rationales for implying the implied terms in law at face value. Therefore, we would encounter the observations that the common law will imply terms in a well-defined category of contract such as employment as a 'necessary incident'[4] of the employment relationship based on 'wider considerations' or 'general considerations'. In other words, the test for implying terms is fashioned by policy considerations, predicated on 'necessity, not reasonableness'.[5] This suggests that the incorporation of implied terms in law into the employment contract will be undertaken by the courts 'from outside' as a matter of policy and that such implied terms in law 'become so fundamental as to amount to general norms for a wide range of personal work or employment contracts, or even for the totality of personal work or employment contracts'.[6] Nevertheless, the fact that certain factors peculiar to the employment contract necessitate the implication of contractual terms from the standpoint of policy does not really take us any further forward. Apart from the fact that the terminology of 'wider' or 'general' considerations reveals very little, we are also none the wiser as to the nature of the relevant policy considerations, which remain firmly concealed.

In order to shed more light on the processes in which the judiciary are engaged when they draw up implied terms, it is helpful to consult the academic literature. Commenting on Freedland's analysis[7] of the implied terms within the context of an assessment of the

---

[1] For example, implied terms of the contract for the sale of goods are provided for in sections 12–15 of the Sale of Goods Act 1979. See S. Smith, *Contract Theory* (Oxford, OUP, 2004) 307–14.

[2] H. Collins, 'Justifications and Techniques of Legal Regulation of the Employment Relation' in H. Collins, P. Davies, and R. Rideout (eds), *Legal Regulation of the Employment Relation* (London, Kluwer, 2000) 26.

[3] M. Freedland and N. Kountouris, *The Legal Construction of Personal Work Relations* (Oxford, OUP, 2011) 183–4.

[4] *Lister v Romford Ice and Cold Storage Co. Ltd* [1957] AC 555, 576 per Viscount Simonds; *Liverpool City Council v Irwin* [1977] AC 239, 254F–255C per Lord Wilberforce; and *Scally v Southern Health and Social Services Board* [1992] 1 AC 294, 306G–307F at para 12 per Lord Bridge.

[5] *Scally v Southern Health and Social Services Board* [1992] 1 AC 294, 306G–307F at para 12 per Lord Bridge; *Spring v Guardian Assurance plc* [1995] 2 AC 296, 339H–340A, and 354B per Lords Slynn and Woolf respectively; *Johnson v Unisys Ltd* [2001] UKHL 13, [2003] 1 AC 518, 539B per Lord Hoffmann; *Reid v Rush and Tompkins Group plc* [1990] 1 WLR 212, 220A per Gibson LJ; and *Tai Hing Cotton Mill Ltd v Liu Chong Hing Bank Ltd* [1986] AC 80, 104H–105C per Scarman LJ.

[6] M. Freedland, *The Personal Employment Contract* (Oxford, OUP, 2003) 122.

[7] *ibid.*, 119–27.

features of standard-form employment contracts, Collins has identified three roles which may be performed by implied terms in law:

(1) a *traditional 'gap-filling' function* whereby lacunae in the contract of employment—which is naturally 'incomplete by design'[8]—are plugged;

(2) an *interpretative role* in furnishing guiding principles for the interpretation of written express terms; and

(3) a *regulatory function* in operating as mandatory norms which police and constrain the exercise of powers conferred by express contractual terms:

■ H. Collins, 'Legal Responses to the Standard Form Contract of Employment' (2007) 36 *Industrial Law Journal* 2, 7–10

In the context of either oral contracts of employment or perfunctory written documents, implied terms performed an important gap-filling role. Gaps in the contractual agreement could be closed by terms implied in fact according to the presumed intentions of the parties, by reference to the customs of the trade or the workplace, and by terms implied by law into every contract of employment. In the context of nearly comprehensive standard form contracts, however, few gaps need to be filled . . . [and] the gap-filling role of implied terms inevitably ceases to be a vital source for the completion of the terms of the employment relation. Yet discussions about implied terms remain at the forefront of employment law discourses. Employment lawyers appear to use implied terms for two new purposes. The first comprises an aid to construction of the express terms, and the second, which is a more radical adaptation, is to use implied terms to control the content of express terms.

A. An Aid to Construction

[I]n recent litigation, terms implied into every contract of employment as default rules, often described as terms implied by law, seem to have developed a new role. Their function in legal reasoning is to establish a particular context for interpretation . . . [and] in order to ensure that contracts have commercial efficacy and do not lead to absurd results, a court should protect the reasonable expectations of the parties, and the implied terms can be used to articulate those reasonable expectations. It follows that implied terms, particularly those implied by law as the standard incidents of the contract of employment, now perform the function of providing part of the context in which meaning is attributed to the words and phrases used in the standard form contract by supplying a set of presumptions about the probable content of the implicit meanings of the express terms of the contract. For this purpose, no doubt, the obligation to perform in good faith (or mutual trust and confidence) provides the crucial overarching principle of interpretation: this implied term means that the explicit obligations in the standard form contract should be interpreted in a way which accords with the principle of good faith, and that principle can be further elucidated as a set of reasonable expectations on the part of employer and employee, which themselves are articulated by terms implied by law . . . This change in the function of terms implied by law—from gap-filling of incomplete, informal contracts to presumptions of interpretation for written documents—is indirectly acknowledged by Professor Freedland . . . Terms implied by law can serve both functions, but my suggestion is that they serve predominantly the role of presumptions of interpretation or guiding principles about the context.

---

[8] See Chapter 5, section 5.1.1; H. Collins, *Regulating Contracts* (Oxford, OUP, 1999) 160–1; H. Collins, *Employment Law*, 2nd edition (Oxford, OUP, 2010) 9–11; S. Deakin and F. Wilkinson, 'Labour Law and Economic Theory: A Reappraisal' in H. Collins, P. Davies, and R. Rideout (eds), *Legal Regulation of the Employment Relation* (Kluwer, London, 2000) 42–7; O. Hart and J. Moore, 'Foundations of Incomplete Contracts' (1999) 66 *Review of Economic Studies* 115; and I. Ayres and R. Gartner, 'Filling Gaps in Incomplete Contracts: An Economic Theory of Default Rules' (1990) 99 *Yale Law Journal* 87.

B. Mandatory Norms

The social practice of the widespread use of standard form contracts issued by an employer may also explain the motivation for the increasing speculation regarding the legal heresy of 'mandatory implied terms'. It is trite law that implied terms may always be overridden or excluded by express terms in the contract, subject only to legislative intervention . . . It is surprising that there have been tentative suggestions that terms implied by law, or at least some of them, should be regarded as to some extent mandatory norms, or rules that cannot be excluded or modified by express terms . . . There is clearly a temptation here to use terms implied in law as a device to try to rebalance a standard form contract produced by the employer . . . This temptation should be resisted. This line of reasoning has much in common with the earlier attempt in consumer contract cases to discover certain fundamental obligations that were effectively impossible to exclude by express terms of the contract. Those judicial interventions were met with the social practice of increasingly sophisticated and comprehensive terms in standard form contracts that stripped consumers of their rights acquired under implied terms. Not only did the judicial intervention prove ineffective, but it also created a serious problem of coherence in the law of contract, which was eventually resolved by discarding the doctrine of 'fundamental breach'. Without making implied terms mandatory in law, it did not make doctrinal sense to say that sufficiently explicit terms in standard form contracts were incapable of excluding them. If this technique of rebalancing standard form contracts by implied terms became accepted, similar problems of ineffectiveness and doctrinal incoherence would be encountered. This rebalancing through implied terms can only be achieved coherently and effectively in the more limited context of explicit discretionary powers conferred on management, following the lead of Browne-Wilkinson LJ in *Johns[t]on[e] v Bloomsbury Health Authority* [[1991] ICR 269, CA].[9]

It is self-evident that Collins prefers the approach which characterizes implied terms as providing a tool-kit for the construction of express terms, i.e. role (2).[10] He rejects the notion that the implied terms function, or ought to function, to disapply express terms, bearing in mind the contractual orthodoxy that implied terms always give way to express terms. Collins's approach can be contrasted with that of Freedland. Although Freedland employs the language of 'interpretation and construction'[11] to describe the task undertaken by the implied terms, it is clear that he perceives the implied terms to be performing an additional regulatory function in restraining powers conferred on a contracting party by the express terms, i.e. role (3).

As a description of the present state of the law, for reasons which will become clear,[12] this writer tends towards Freedland's view that implied terms are best understood as doctrines which amount to a complex mixture of regulatory techniques and principles designed to guide the performance and content of employment contracts, i.e. a mixture of roles (2) and (3).[13] This combined approach is achieved primarily by articulating open-textured standards about the behaviour of the employer and employee. In other words, it can be said that the implied terms in law operate to signpost expectations about managerial and employee behaviour, whose content includes broadly expressed evaluative criteria against which the conduct of the contracting parties is to be assessed. To that extent, the implied terms are deployed as a means of projecting a particular vision of the

---

[9] Writer's annotations appear in square brackets throughout this chapter.

[10] However, in more recent writings, Collins's view seems to have changed: H. Collins, 'Implied Terms in the Contract of Employment' in M. Freedland et al. (eds), *The Contract of Employment* (Oxford, OUP, 2016) 489–90.

[11] M. Freedland, *The Personal Employment Contract* (Oxford, OUP, 2003) 127.

[12] See Chapter 7, section 7.4.

[13] M. Freedland and N. Kountouris, *The Legal Construction of Personal Work Relations* (Oxford, OUP, 2011) 180.

employment relationship containing various underlying assumptions, amounting to an elaborate form of judicial legislation.

Having explored the grounds for the conviction that the implied terms perform a complex amalgam of interpretation and regulation of the express terms, i.e. roles (2) and (3), we return to analyse the policy justifications in favour of their formulation. In the following Freedland extract, the justifications cited for the implied terms are referred to as 'principles'. Nonetheless, it is sufficiently clear that Freedland is referring to the policy considerations or collective goals which the judiciary are implicitly seeking to promote:

■ **M. Freedland, *The Personal Employment Contract* (Oxford, OUP, 2003) 127–8**

. . . the whole process of interpretation and construction of personal work or employment contracts is informed by a set of approaches or principles. These can be regarded as the *structural principles* or *guiding principles* which are provided by the law of personal work or employment contracts for the interpretation and construction of the content of personal work or employment contracts . . . There is a core group of three such principles which tend slightly more towards the purely interpretative, derive mainly from adjudication rather than legislation, and which can be seen as quite closely tied to a broad organizing notion of mutuality of obligation. These are the principles of:

   (1)   mutuality and reciprocity,

   (2)   care and co-operation, and

   (3)   trust and confidence.

We can then see in the course of emergence two further, and rather more obviously regulatory, principles, which are in the course of being internalized into the adjudicative process. These are the principles of:

   (4)   loyalty and freedom of economic activity, and

   (5)   fair management and performance . . .

The argument which we advance is that the five principles serve to identify the main goals or values which courts and tribunals pursue when interpreting and construing the content of personal work or employment contracts, and when, therefore, declaring and developing the common law concerning the content of those contracts.[14]

It is submitted that the 'five principles' identified provide explanatory force for the policies underpinning the implied terms. The realization that the implied terms are intended to promote these five values will become apparent when we turn to a detailed consideration of the legal position in sections 6.2 and 6.3 of this chapter. However, before we embark on a detailed scrutiny of the implied terms, we first address the role of the common law in shaping the modern face of the employment relationship in section 6.1.2.

Reflection points

1. Which of the 'gap-filling', 'interpretative', or 'regulatory' functions do you believe the implied terms should seek to play? Give reasons for your answer.

2. Now consider whether it is possible for the implied terms to perform one or more of these functions.

3. Do you think that it is logical for implied terms to restrain or override express terms? In order to respond to this question, read Chapter 7, sections 7.4.1 and 7.4.2, regarding the future direction of the implied terms. Give reasons for your answer.

---

[14] See also M. Freedland, 'The Legal Structure of the Contract of Employment' in M. Freedland et al. (eds), *The Contract of Employment* (Oxford, OUP, 2016) 39–45.

6.1.2 The role of the common law and the changing face of the employment relationship

The expansion of the common law implied terms has coincided with a sea-change in the judicial conceptualization of the employment relationship. With the obsolescence of 'master and servant' law,[15] individual employment rights have burgeoned somewhat over the past 40 years. This growth in employment rights has been principally channelled through the promulgation of worker-protective legislation. As for the part played by the common law, traditionally, the judiciary adopted a conservative neoclassical laissez-faire approach to the law of the contract of employment and invoked a fiction that the contract was like any other commercial contract with both of the parties operating at an equal level of bargaining strength. Indeed, recent judicial dicta have acknowledged that the traditional common law stance was to protect the employer's private law rights from outside interference.[16] However, the position of the judiciary has undergone a radical transformation in recent times[17] and there is now recognition that the contract should be perceived in something more than purely economic terms. The realization that the contract of employment gives rise to a social relationship characterized by a 'disparity of power'[18] has heralded an expansion of the common law. The implied terms of the contract of employment have been in the vanguard of that 'revolution', as a basis for reflecting the wider contemporary standards of society, transcending mere concerns about the financial interests or welfare of employees:[19]

Johnson v Unisys Ltd [2003] 1 AC 518, 539A–D

Lord Hoffmann:

At common law the contract of employment was regarded by the courts as a contract like any other. The parties were free to negotiate whatever terms they liked and no terms would be implied unless they satisfied the strict test of necessity applied to a commercial contract. Freedom of contract meant that the stronger party, usually the employer, was free to impose his terms upon the weaker. But over the last 30 years or so, the nature of the contract of employment has been transformed. It has been recognised that a person's employment is usually one of the most important things in his or her life. It gives not only a livelihood but an occupation, an identity and a sense of self-esteem. The law has changed to recognise this social reality. Most of the changes have been made by Parliament . . . And the common law has adapted itself to the new attitudes, proceeding sometimes by analogy with statutory rights. The contribution of the common law to the employment revolution has been by the evolution of implied terms in the contract of employment. The most far reaching is the implied term of trust and confidence. But there have been others . . .

In the *Johnson* extract, Lord Hoffmann made the point that individual employment rights instantiated through the common law implied terms have recently expanded

---

[15] *Malik v BCCI* [1998] AC 20, 45H–46A per Lord Steyn.

[16] *National Union of Rail, Maritime & Transport Workers v Serco; ASLEF v London & Birmingham Railway Ltd* [2011] EWCA Civ 226, [2011] IRLR 399, 402 per Elias LJ. See also C. Mummé, 'Property in Labor and the Limits of Contract' in U. Mattei and J. Haskell (eds), *The Research Handbook on Political Economy and Law* (Cheltenham, Edward Elgar, 2015) 400.

[17] *Spring v Guardian Assurance plc* [1995] 2 AC 296, 335 per Lord Slynn of Hadley; *Johnson v Unisys Ltd* [2001] UKHL 13, [2003] 1 AC 518, 527E–F per Lord Steyn.

[18] *Malik v BCCI* [1998] AC 20, 37G per Lord Nicholls; *Gisda Cyf v Barratt* [2010] UKSC 41, [2010] 4 All ER 851, 862e–f per Lord Kerr; *R (on the application of UNISON) v Lord Chancellor* [2017] 3 WLR 409, 417E-F per Lord Reed.

[19] D. Brodie, 'Legal Coherence and the Employment Revolution' (2001) 117 *Law Quarterly Review* 604.

by analogy with statutory rights and legislative policy.[20] The implied term of mutual trust and confidence is paradigmatic of this phenomenon, since it emerged from the statutory concept of constructive dismissal in section 95(1)(c) of the ERA.[21] However, the interplay between the common law and statute has not been in only one direction, since the common law has also operated to promote statutory employment rights and policy.[22]

Falling firmly within the province of contract law, the implied terms are naturally derogable.[23] Therefore, they give way to express terms, duly reflecting the 'will theory' of contract law inherent within common law reasoning which posits that courts should defer to the expressed intentions of the contracting parties.[24] In light of this fact, it is something of a paradox that the judiciary elected to adopt the implied terms of the contract of employment as the instrument to project a modern vision of the employment relationship and to forge the behavioural standards against which the conduct of the contracting parties will be judged. However, such a rationalization of the position fails to factor into the equation the implied term of mutual trust and confidence. As will become apparent, in its orientation, the implied term of mutual trust and confidence has marched along an altogether different path from the other implied terms. In effect, the implied term of mutual trust and confidence has been fashioned in a way which serves to constrain the exercise of express terms in a highly worker-protective manner. Therefore, whilst not going so far as to say that the implied term of mutual trust and confidence is an implied mandatory norm which functions to displace an express term, the scope of discretion afforded to a contracting party by an express term is somewhat curtailed. Many employment relationships are relationships of domination in which the employee is vulnerable and highly dependent on the employer, with the latter enjoying a higher degree of bargaining strength and able to subject the employee to the arbitrary exercise of the managerial prerogative.[25] In light of that fact, there was perhaps something of a subconscious change of mindset on the part of the judiciary in the 1970s that a common law implied term in the guise of the trust and confidence term ought to be developed in order to address this potential abuse of managerial power. This is essentially the phenomenon being described by the Law Lords in the earlier excerpt from *Johnson*.

A final point worth stressing is that the subsistence of the implied terms is not necessarily co-terminous with the employment relationship.[26] This is reflective of the fact that the employment relationship and the contract of employment do not necessarily co-exist simultaneously.[27] For example, some of the implied terms will apply prior to the inception

---

[20] *Johnson v Unisys Ltd* [2003] 1 AC 518, 539 at para 37. See also *Eastwood v Magnox Electric plc* [2005] 1 AC 503, 524 at paras 12–14 per Lord Nicholls.

[21] See *Eastwood v Magnox Electric plc* [2005] 1 AC 503, 521–2 per Lord Nicholls.

[22] On the interaction between common law and statute, see Chapter 2, section 2.1.1.

[23] *Malik v BCCI* [1998] AC 20, 45D–E per Lord Steyn; *Johnson v Unisys Ltd* [2003] 1 AC 518, 539F and 536A–B per Lords Hoffmann and Steyn; H. Collins, 'Legal Responses to the Standard Form Contract of Employment' (2007) 36 *Industrial Law Journal* 2, 10; and D. Cabrelli, 'The Implied Duty of Mutual Trust and Confidence: An Emerging Overarching Principle?' (2005) 34 *Industrial Law Journal* 284, 290–6. For a contrary view, see D. Brodie, 'Beyond Exchange: The New Contract of Employment' (1998) 27 *Industrial Law Journal* 79, 82–6; D. Brodie, *The Employment Contract: Legal Principles, Drafting, and Interpretation* (Oxford, OUP, 2005) 78–80 and 185–6; and M. Freedland, *The Personal Employment Contract* (Oxford, OUP, 2003) 164.

[24] A. Bogg, 'Good Faith in the Contract of Employment: A Case of the English Reserve?' (2011) 32 *Comparative Labor Law & Policy Journal* 729, 753–5.

[25] See F. Lovett, *A General Theory of Domination and Justice* (Oxford, OUP, 2010) 38–41; P. Pettit, *On the People's Terms: A Republican Theory and Model of Democracy* (Cambridge, CUP, 2012).

[26] S. Honeyball and D. Pearce, 'Contract, Employment and the Contract of Employment' (2006) 35 *Industrial Law Journal* 30.

[27] For example, see *Société Générale (London Branch) v Geys* [2012] UKSC 63, [2013] 1 AC 523, 554f, 555a, and 562d per Lord Wilson.

of the employment relationship[28] to exercise constraints over the conduct of employers and employees, while others will continue in effect notwithstanding that the employment relationship has been terminated.[29] However, none of them operates to constrain the power of dismissal.[30]

For additional reading on the implied terms of the personal contract of employment, visit the Online Resources for this book at www.oup.com/uk/cabrelli3e/

6.2 DUTIES OF EMPLOYERS

The implied terms in law can be conceptualized as imposing (1) duties on employers which operate to confer rights on employees and (2) obligations on employees which entail corresponding rights in favour of employers (see Figures 6.1 and 6.2). They are also expressed at a high level of generality, i.e. as open-textured standards, and it is through them that the law's expectations regarding the behavioural standards of the contracting parties are channelled.[31] A final point to note is that the implied terms are both proscriptive and prescriptive of managerial conduct and the actions of the employee. Indeed, some of the implied terms themselves entail a proscriptive and prescriptive element.[32] Our discussion will begin by examining the implied terms which impose obligations on the employer (see Figure 6.1).

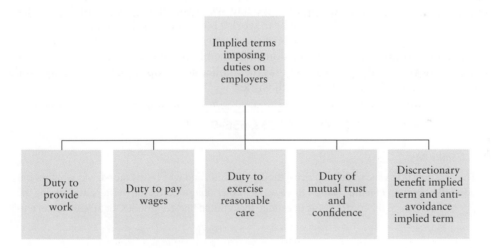

Figure 6.1 *Implied terms imposing duties on employers*

---

[28] Implied term of mutual trust and confidence: *Tullett Prebon plc v BGC Brokers LP* [2011] EWCA Civ 131, [2011] IRLR 420.

[29] Duty to exercise reasonable care: *Spring v Guardian Assurance plc* [1995] 2 AC 296; duty of fidelity: *Faccenda Chicken Ltd v Fowler* [1987] Ch 117.

[30] See *Johnson v Unisys Ltd* [2003] 1 AC 518; *Reda v Flag Ltd* [2002] UKPC 38, [2002] IRLR 747.

[31] L. Barmes, 'Common Law Implied Terms and Behavioural Standards at Work' (2007) 36 *Industrial Law Journal* 35.

[32] For example, the implied term of mutual trust and confidence, on which, see D. Cabrelli, 'The Implied Duty of Mutual Trust and Confidence: An Emerging Overarching Principle?' (2005) 34 *Industrial Law Journal* 284, 299–300.

6.2.1 **Duty to provide work**

In section 6.1.1, we drew attention to the fact that the fostering of mutuality and reciprocity between the employer and the employee can be conceived as one of the five policy goals which the implied terms seek to promote. Moreover, in Chapters 3 and 5 we identified mutuality/reciprocity of obligation as an essential organizing lynchpin of the employment relationship and noted that it was a key factor adopted by the common law to distinguish between the contract of employment and the contract for services.[33] As Freedland has noted, the concept of mutuality/reciprocity is present in the contract of employment at two levels:

(1) the basic wage–work bargain struck between the employer and the employee, in terms of which the employer provides a minimum or reasonable amount of work to the employee and pays for it and the employee performs the minimum or reasonable amount of work offered by the employer; and

(2) the mutual promises whereby there is an ongoing commitment on the part of the employer to provide work to the employee in the future and to pay for it with a corresponding undertaking by the employee to perform that work when offered in the future. It is this second level that serves to link together a chain of wage–work bargains into an 'umbrella' contract of employment.[34]

One would expect that this connection between the wage–work bargain and the notion of mutuality/reciprocity would translate directly into the content of the implied terms. As such, one might anticipate the implied terms conferring a universal right to work in favour of the employee with a corresponding duty to provide work on the part of the employer.[35] However, that is not what we find when we examine the case law. Instead, somewhat counter-intuitively, the right to work[36] is conspicuous by its absence: 'The normal interpretation placed on contracts of employment by courts is that the employer does not promise to provide work to be done, but merely promises to pay wages.'[37] Indeed, the starting point is the proposition that the implied terms do not impose a duty on the employer to provide an employee with work:

Turner v Sawdon & Co. [1901] 2 KB 653, 656–9

A L Smith MR:

The real question which the [employee] thought to raise, and which was raised, was whether beyond the question of remuneration there was a further obligation on the masters that, during the period over which the contract was to extend, they should find continuous, or at least some, em-

---

[33] See Chapter 3, section 3.2.1, and Chapter 5, section 5.1.1.

[34] M. Freedland, *The Personal Employment Contract* (Oxford, OUP, 2003) 88–92; A. C. L. Davies, 'The Contract for Intermittent Employment' (2007) 36 *Industrial Law Journal* 102, 103.

[35] Here, when we refer to 'a right to work', we are using that phrase in the sense of the employee having a right to be provided with work whilst employed, rather than in terms of an individual having a human right to work, a right to be hired as an employee, or an employee having an entitlement to be continuously employed free from dismissal. For a comprehensive survey of the potential theoretical meanings of a right to work, see V. Mantouvalou (ed.), *The Right to Work: Legal and Philosophical Perspectives* (Oxford, Hart Publishing, 2015).

[36] The common law right to work has also been associated with Lord Denning's attempts to break the 'closed shop' by guaranteeing an employee's right to work in a job without trade union interference: see A. Bogg, 'Only Fools and Horses: Some Sceptical Reflections on the Right to Work' in V. Mantouvalou (ed.), *The Right to Work: Legal and Philosophical Perspectives* (Oxford, Hart Publishing, 2015) 173–6.

[37] H. Collins, 'Progress towards the Right to Work in the United Kingdom' in V. Mantouvalou (ed.), *The Right to Work: Legal and Philosophical Perspectives* (Oxford, Hart Publishing, 2015) 236.

ployment for the [employee]. In my opinion such an action is unique—that is an action in which it is shewn that the master is willing to pay the wages of his servant, but is sued for damages because the servant is not given employment . . . It is within the province of the master to say that he will go on paying the wages, but that he is under no obligation to provide work. The obligation suggested is said to arise out of the undertaking to engage and employ the [employee] as their representative salesman. It is said that if the salesman is not given employment which allows him to go on the market his hand is not kept in practice, and he will not be so efficient a salesman at the end of the term. To read in an obligation of that sort would be to convert the retainer at fixed wages into a contract to keep the servant in the service of his employer in such a manner as to enable the former to become au fait at his work. In my opinion, no such obligation arose under this contract, and it is a mistake to stretch the words of the contract so as to include in what is a mere retainer an obligation to employ the [employee] continuously for the term of his service . . .

Where the general rule applies, the contract of employment is construed so that the existence of an implied duty to provide work is precluded. Here, the consideration moving from the employer to the employee is restricted to the payment of the remuneration agreed.

One can conceive of three justifications for the approach adopted by the common law. The first is predicated on basic economics:

■ B. Hepple, 'A Right to Work?' (1981) 10 *Industrial Law Journal* 65, 75

The present policy of the law is in general to allow a degree of managerial freedom to pay wages and not to provide work, a policy which might be thought essential in a market economy where the demand for work is subject to fluctuations and technical reorganisation is a matter of economic necessity.

Such a justification can be rationalized as a form of economic pragmatism, affording an employer a degree of flexibility in how it co-ordinates work patterns. This can be contrasted with the second rationale, which is more doctrinal in nature:

■ B. Hepple, 'The Right to Work at One's Job' (1974) 37 *Modern Law Review* 681, 685

There are very good reasons for thinking that a 'right to work at one's job' is not compatible with other common law rules. At best, the right would be to work out any notice which the worker may be given. It is not possible to reconcile this, as a general proposition, with the rule that an employee cannot keep the contract alive against his employer's will by refusing to accept wages in lieu of notice. It would be a meaningless right because the employer could avoid it by summarily terminating the contract.

As for the third explanation for the absence of an implied right to work, this is rooted in the implied default rule that the contract of employment is open-ended, of indefinite duration.[38] In light of the judicial recognition of this implied default rule in the nineteenth

---

[38] See Chapter 5, section 5.1.1; *De Stempel v Dunkels* [1938] 1 All ER 238 (CA), 246G–H and 259 per Greer and Scott LJJ; *McClelland v Northern Ireland General Health Services Board* [1957] 1 WLR 594 (HL); and *Richardson v Koefod* [1969] 1 WLR 1812 (CA), 1816C–F per Lord Denning MR.

century, it was felt to be unrealistic to legally hold an employer to an obligation to continuously supply work to the employee. As such, the common law was adapted to shelter employers from breach of contract claims where their staff were left sitting idle, albeit being paid.[39]

Nevertheless, since the decision in *Turner*, the courts have recognized a number of exceptions to the general rule. In those specific situations, the employee has an implied right to be given work if the employer has work available to be done.[40] Here, it is acknowledged that the employee's interest in the employer's business extends beyond the payment of salary or wages which trumps the three justifications which we identified earlier. Thus the consideration moving from the employer to the employee extends to an obligation to permit the employee to do the work as well as the payment of the remuneration agreed.[41] For example, workers on commission and employees who have bargained for publicity as part of their employment have an implied right to work.[42] To those exceptions, we can add piece workers, where there is an implied undertaking that they will be supplied with a reasonable amount of work in order to enjoy a certain level of earnings.[43] However, these exceptions are particularly narrow and merely serve to reinforce the general rule.

We can see that there has been a greater willingness on the part of the judiciary to protect and maintain firm-specific and task-specific skills of employees which are unique, particularly where such activities must be frequently exercised, lest the employee become deskilled.[44] In light of the subsequent disapproval of the general rule in *Turner*, this is perhaps unsurprising.[45] There is an understanding that the skilled employee ought to be afforded the opportunity to maintain and develop skill levels. As noted by Lord Justice Morritt in *William Hill Organisation Ltd v Tucker*,[46] this entails an intricate factual enquiry into the terms of the employee's contract in light of the surrounding circumstances, including whether the employee's post is specific and unique.[47] In such circumstances, it has been held that an employee will have the right to be provided with work where there is work available to be done. Examples of posts where an obligation to supply work has been established in light of the contractual scheme pertaining to that employee include the senior dealer working in the spread betting business in *William Hill Organisation Ltd v Tucker*,[48] the chartered accountant in *Provident Financial Group and Whitegates Estate Agency v Hayward*,[49] the chief engineer in *Breach v Epsylon Industries Ltd*,[50] and the sales director in *Bosworth v Angus Jowett & Co. Ltd*.[51] These cases can be contrasted with *Christie v Johnston Carmichael*,[52] where it was held that there was nothing special about the employee's occupation as a chartered tax adviser. This can be attributed to the fact that a number of other employees performed the same task and there was no evidence that the employee would be deskilled as he had the ability to keep

---

[39] *Turner v Sawdon & Co.* [1901] 2 KB 653 (CA) 656–9 per A L Smith MR.

[40] Therefore, where one of the exceptions applies and the employee has an implied right to work, the employer does not have an obligation to find work *if there is none available to be done*.

[41] *William Hill Organisation Ltd v Tucker* [1999] ICR 291, 301E per Morritt LJ.

[42] See *Turner v Goldsmith* [1891] 1 QB 544; *Herbert Clayton and Jack Waller Ltd v Oliver* [1930] AC 209.

[43] *Devonald v Rosser & Sons* [1906] 2 KB 728. See H. Collins, 'Progress towards the Right to Work in the United Kingdom' in V. Mantouvalou, *The Right to Work: Legal and Philosophical Perspectives* (Oxford, Hart Publishing, 2015) 239.

[44] *Collier v Sunday Referee Publishing Co. Ltd* [1940] 2 KB 647; *William Hill Organisation Ltd v Tucker* [1999] ICR 291.

[45] *Re Rubel Bronze and Metal Co. Ltd* [1918] 1 KB 315, 324 per McCardie J.

[46] [1999] ICR 291, 300C–E.

[47] This approach provides support for the contention that the implied terms in law function as an aid to the interpretation of the express terms of the contract of employment.

[48] [1999] ICR 291, 300C–E.   [49] [1989] 3 All ER 298.   [50] [1976] ICR 316.

[51] [1977] IRLR 374.   [52] [2010] IRLR 1016.

himself up to date. Therefore, *Christie* shows that sufficient space continues to exist for the general rule to operate.

The exact juridical nature of the rule that certain employment contracts, skilled workers, or jobs of a higher status attract a right to work is unclear. For example, is this right conferred via another distinct implied term or on some other basis? In the following extract, Collins explores this dimension:

■ **H. Collins, 'Progress towards the Right to Work in the United Kingdom' in V. Mantouvalou (ed.),** *The Right to Work: Legal and Philosophical Perspectives* **(Oxford, Hart Publishing, 2015) 241**

[The case law] suggests that some jobs may have special features that entitle the employee to expect work of a particular kind actually to be offered. Those jobs are presumably relatively high status positions; the job of 'sub-editor' is described as an 'office'. Freedland doubts whether it is satisfactory to identify jobs where the employer is under an obligation to provide work to be performed on the basis of 'this rather suspect typology of contracts and of workers'. He argues instead that the issue should be regarded rather as whether the employer has misused its managerial powers so as to violate the implied term of mutual trust and confidence. In the *Collier* case, for instance, Freedland suggests that the employers may have hoped that the employee would resign in response to the absence of work, thereby avoiding any obligation to pay wages for the remainder of the fixed-term contract. But it is hard to describe the employer's behaviour in this case as an abuse of managerial power, for it consisted only in continuing to pay wages when the editor was redundant. Another solution is to recognise, using the vehicle of an implied term, that at least in some jobs the performance of work of the particular kind promised will be important to the employee for reasons of gaining experience, know-how and fulfilment, and that deprivation of that opportunity (even though wages are being paid) would constitute a breach of that implied term. For example, if a person were appointed to be the Vinerian Professor of English Law at the University of Oxford, but then was instructed not to perform any of the duties of the post such as giving lectures, it could be argued that the University would have committed a breach of an implied term of the contract that the professor should be able to profess her field of expertise.

Where an employee falls within one of the exceptions, a related issue is whether an employer is entitled to withhold the provision of work by inserting an express provision in the contract of employment. A **suspension clause** and a **garden leave clause** are the most obvious examples of such an express term. These clauses are very similar in that they both empower the employer to hold back work from the employee subject to the continued receipt of all contractual benefits, including salary. However, they may be distinguished by the fact that the former is commonly invoked by the employer in the context of an allegation of misconduct or impropriety against the employee, whereas the latter is engaged subsequent to the employee or employer serving notice of termination of the contract of employment. Furthermore, given the potential for managerial abuse of the garden leave clause, the courts will police them rigorously, on the same basis as post-termination of employment restrictive covenants:

■ *Christie v Johnston Carmichael* **[2010] IRLR 1016 at para 38**

Lady Smith:

The expression 'garden leave' is commonly used to refer to circumstances where either the employer or (more often) the employee gives notice but the employer does not want the employee to attend work during the notice period. It is also frequently the case that the employer does not want the employee to work for a competitor during that period. During the notice period, the contract of employment remains in place. The employee is, accordingly, bound by its terms which will usually include confidentiality clauses and will always include the implied duties of fidelity and trust and confidence. That means, for instance, that an employee is bound to refrain from taking any action directed towards diverting existing business away from his employer or directed towards building up clientele for a business which he either intends to start himself or to start working for once he is free to do so.[53]

■ *J M Finn & Co. Ltd v Holliday* [2013] EWHC 3450 (QB) at paras 61–62

Mrs Justice Simler DBE:

. . . an injunction sought to aid or enforce a garden leave clause must be justified on similar grounds as a restrictive covenant. This means that the [employer] must demonstrate a legitimate interest to protect and must show that the injunction sought extends no further than is reasonably necessary to protect that legitimate interest. The grant of an injunction is a discretionary remedy, and may be refused if in fact the [employer] will suffer no damage (or because of delay). Finally, there is greater flexibility in cutting down the terms of the restriction when dealing with garden leave than when dealing with the terms of a restrictive covenant. The court accordingly has the flexibility to grant an injunction for less than the full notice period if that is the extent of the period in respect of which it can be justified. In this case, the legitimate interest sought to be protected is customer or client connection.[54]

An employee's implied right to work is sufficiently weighty to compel the employer to furnish work in the absence of an express garden leave clause.[55] The foundation for that approach was laid bare by the Court of Appeal and the EAT in the following extracts:

■ *Provident Financial Group and Whitegates Estate Agency v Hayward* [1989] ICR 160, 165E–F

Lord Justice Dillon:

The practice of long periods of 'garden leave' is obviously capable of abuse. It is a weapon in the hands of the employers to ensure that an ambitious and able executive will not give notice if he is going to be unable to work at all for anyone for a long period of notice. Any executive who gives notice and leaves his employment is very likely to take fresh employment with someone in the same line of business, not through any desire to act unfairly or to cheat the former employer but to get the best advantage of his own personal expertise.[56]

Of course, if the employee is not highly skilled, he/she has no implied right to work and so the employer would be able to exercise garden leave, irrespective of whether an

---

[53] Sourced from BAILII available at http://www.bailii.org/cgi-bin/markup.cgi?doc=/uk/cases/UKE-AT/2010/0064_09_2707.html&query=johnston+and+carmichael&method=Boolean (last visited 13 November 2017). See also *Ashcourt Rowan Financial Planning Ltd v Hall* [2013] IRLR 637, 643 per Andrew Smith J.

[54] Sourced from BAILII available at http://www.bailii.org/cgi-bin/markup.cgi?doc=/ew/cases/EWHC/QB/2013/3450.html&query=j+and+m+and+finn&method=boolean (last visited 13 November 2017).

[55] *William Hill Organisation Ltd v Tucker* [1999] ICR 291, 301F–G per Lord Justice Morritt.

[56] See also *J M Finn & Co. Ltd v Holliday* [2013] EWHC 3450 (QB) at para 60 where Mrs Justice Simler DBE makes the same point.

express clause to that effect had been inserted in his/her written employment contract.[57]

Meanwhile, in the converse situation where the employee falls within one of the exceptions to the general rule and a garden leave clause has been included in the written contract of employment, it has been decided that the latter is sufficient to dislodge the employee's implied right to work:[58]

■ *William Hill Organisation Ltd v Tucker* [1999] ICR 291, 301F

Lord Justice Morritt:

[I]n practice, an employer will need to stipulate for an express power to send his employee on garden leave in all cases in which the contract imposes on him an obligation to permit the employee to do the work.

This is a fairly unequivocal statement inasmuch as it suggests that a garden leave clause is necessary *in all conceivable circumstances or cases* where the construction of the employment contract confers an implied right to work in favour of an employee.[59] However, as subsequent case law has revealed, that is not necessarily the case. For example, in *SG & R Valuation Service v Boudrais*[60] and *Standard Life Health Care Ltd v Gorman*,[61] it was held that the employees concerned had an implied right to work as they fell within one of the recognized exceptions to the general rule. However, since the employees had breached the contract of employment such that they had rendered it impossible or reasonably impracticable for the employer to provide work, the employer was held to be entitled to compel the employees to take garden leave—despite the absence of a garden leave clause. In such a case, the employee had shown that he/she was not ready and willing to work:

■ *Standard Life Health Care Ltd v Gorman* [2009] EWCA Civ 1292 at para 27

Lord Justice Waller:

It seems to me strongly arguable that in the circumstances of a case such as this, where the employer discovers that the employee has been in serious breach of duty and in breach of his duty of good faith, and then discovers that the employee is tied effectively to a rival already, and as here registered as an agent of a rival, then the employer has, even if he keeps the contract alive, no obligation to provide work; that obligation to provide work being interdependent with the obligation of the employee to act loyally.[62]

---

[57] For example, *Christie v Johnston Carmichael* [2010] IRLR 1016.

[58] However, in such a case, the clause will be ineffective if the employer is in repudiatory breach of contract and the employee will be entitled to treat him/herself as constructively dismissed: *JM Finn & Co. Ltd v Holliday* [2013] EWHC 3450 (QB).

[59] Moreover, insofar as this statement can be taken to imply that a garden leave clause affords an employer an unfettered discretion, one should exercise caution, since it is reasonably clear that the implied term of mutual trust and confidence will operate to constrain the manner in which such a clause is exercised: *TFS Derivatives Ltd v Morgan* [2005] IRLR 246. In addition, the restraint of trade doctrine will also apply, since the employee's freedom to trade is being curtailed during the operation of a garden leave clause, on which, see *JM Finn & Co. Ltd v Holliday* [2014] IRLR 102. Thus the view that the rise in the number of garden leave clauses in employment contracts is explicable on the basis that they are a more reliable substitute for a post-termination restrictive covenant is misguided, on which, see *Credit Suisse Management Ltd v Armstrong* [1996] ICR 882, 892 per Neill LJ.

[60] [2008] IRLR 770.   [61] [2010] IRLR 233.

[62] Sourced from BAILII available at http://www.bailii.org/cgi-bin/markup.cgi?doc=/ew/cases/EWCA/Civ/2009/1292.html&query=standard+and+life+and+health+and+care+and+limited+and+v+and+gorman&method=boolean (last visited 13 November 2017).

Whilst this may be an attractive proposition, it remains controversial, particularly where the employer has decided not to accept the employee's repudiatory breach of contract and terminate the contract of employment. The difficulty with this line of reasoning is that the employer could conceivably invoke any current or ongoing repudiatory breach of contract committed by the employee, as a pretext to displace the employee's implied right to work and place him/her on garden leave in the absence of a garden leave clause. In fact, in Scots law, the approach in *Standard Life Health Care* has been rejected[63] and whether it is compatible with the approach adopted by the EAT in *Atkinson v Community Gateway Association*[64] is doubtful. Although not concerned with garden leave or the right to work, *Atkinson* is an authority for the proposition that an employee is entitled to accept the employer's repudiatory breach (in defectively conducting a disciplinary hearing involving allegations against the employee) and terminate the employment contract even though the employee himself was in anterior repudiatory breach.

6.2.2 Duty to pay wages

The policy objective of mutuality/reciprocity is also identifiable as the basis for the implied term that imposes a duty on an employer to pay wages.[65] This is particularly clear when one recognizes that the duty to pay wages is part of the basic exchange transaction inherent within the employment relationship, i.e. the wage–work bargain.[66] One might conceive of wages as being payable by the employer for the completion of work on the part of the employee, which is captured in the maxim of 'no work, no pay'[67] or, more evocatively, 'the consideration for work is wages, and the consideration for wages is work'.[68] For example, in *Browning v Crumlin Valley Collieries Ltd*,[69] it was held that an employer may legally withhold wages where it was required to close down a mine which was dangerous, through no fault of its own, in order to effect repairs. During the period of closure, the Court of Appeal ruled that the employees had not worked and so were not entitled to remuneration. This doctrine is also consistent with the traditional approach of the common law which developed a presumption to the effect that contracts of employment were entire rather than divisible. This presumption[70] posited that if an employee engaged on the basis of an annual hiring[71] failed to perform the work over the entire length of that contract, the 'entire contracts' doctrine functioned to deny the employee any part of the agreed remuneration.[72] Alongside the drastic sanction of dismissal, the employer's right to withhold the payment of wages on the basis of the 'entire contracts' doctrine represented a highly effective instrument of maintaining discipline amongst its workforce.[73] Nonetheless, the purchase of this doctrine/presumption has receded to the point of extinction as a result of three developments:

---

[63] *McNeill v Aberdeen City Council (No. 2)* [2015] ICR 27. See section 6.3.3.

[64] [2015] ICR 1.

[65] The implication of a duty to pay wages is as far as it goes here; the common law recognizes no implied contractual right to an ongoing or annual pay increase: *Thorne v House of Commons Commission* [2014] IRLR 260. Contrast this decision with *Cabinet Office v Beavan* [2014] IRLR 434.

[66] See M. Freedland, 'The Obligation to Work and to Pay for Work' (1977) *Current Legal Problems* 175, 179–80 and M. Freedland, 'The Exchange Principle and the Wage-Work Bargain' in M. Freedland et al. (eds), *The Contract of Employment* (Oxford, OUP, 2016) 52.

[67] *Luke v Stoke-on-Trent City Council* [2007] ICR 1678, 1685E per Lord Justice Mummery.

[68] *Browning v Crumlin Valley Collieries Ltd* [1926] 1 KB 522, 528 per Lord Justice Greer.

[69] [1926] 1 KB 522.   [70] The force of this presumption had began to wane by the 1840s.

[71] Prior to the middle of the nineteenth century, the common law generally assumed an annual hiring unless specified to the contrary, on which, see S. Jacoby, 'The Duration of Indefinite Employment Contracts in the United States and England: An Historical Analysis' (1982) 5 *Comparative Labor Law* 85, 90–1; S. Deakin and F. Wilkinson, *The Law of the Labour Market: Industrialization, Employment, and Legal Evolution* (Oxford, OUP, 2005) 44–5 and 78–9.   [72] *Cutter v Powell* (1795) 6 TR 320.

[73] H. Collins, *Employment Law*, 2nd edition (Oxford, OUP, 2010) 163.

(1) the decision in *Richardson v Koefod*[74] essentially consigned the common law presumption in favour of an annual hiring to oblivion, ushering in a fresh presumption in favour of the 'indefinite' employment contract;[75]

(2) section 2 of the Apportionment Act 1870 provides that periodical payments in the nature of income are considered as accruing from day to day; and

(3) since the emergence of the doctrine of substantial performance in cases such as *Taylor v East Midlands Offender Employment*[76] and *Cooper v Isle of Wight College*,[77] it is clear that the common law now treats contracts of employment as divisible so that the link between the duration of the contract and remuneration has been severed.

The end result is that payment must be made notwithstanding that the employee has terminated the contract or ceased to perform the work prior to the expiry of the agreed duration.[78]

With the erosion of the entire contracts doctrine, there has been a tendency on the part of the courts to treat the readiness and willingness of the employee to work, rather than the completion of the work itself, as the consideration for the payment of remuneration.[79] According to this formula, the employee is entitled to payment notwithstanding that no work is actually undertaken and the employee is unable to work.[80] The jural co-relative of such an implied duty is that an employee has the right to be remunerated in full if he/she is willing to work, even if he/she is actually undertaking no such work and the employer has no work to offer the employee. As such, where an employee is not willing to work, he/she will forfeit the right to payment of wages or salary.[81] Interestingly, the policy goals of fostering mutuality/reciprocity also lie at the heart of this change in approach. For example, mutuality of obligation was at the forefront of the decision of the Court of Appeal in *Devonald v Rosser & Sons*.[82] Here, tinplate piece-rate workers were held entitled to security of earnings during the 28-day notice period where the employer had closed the tinplate works owing to a downturn in trade. It was held that the allocation of risk ought to be struck in a manner which ensured that the employer bore the financial consequences of the period of unavailability of work from the date of closure of the tinplate works to the date of expiry of the notice period.

This reformulation of what constitutes the consideration for wages is reflective of a more profound change at a judicial level. It signals the willingness of the courts to acknowledge that the employment contract is something more than an exchange transaction and that, instead, it is a relational contract:

---

[74] [1969] 1 WLR 1812. See G. Williams, 'Partial Performance of Entire Contracts' (1941) 57 *Law Quarterly Review* 373; P. Elias, B. Napier, and P. Wallington, *Labour Law: Cases and Materials* (London, Butterworths, 1980) 435–6.

[75] See Chapter 5, section 5.1.1.   [76] [2000] IRLR 760.

[77] [2008] IRLR 124. See also *Hartley v King Edward VI College* [2017] 1 WLR 2110 and *Amey v Peter Symonds College* [2014] IRLR 206, where the Supreme Court and High Court ruled that 1/365th rather than 1/260th ought to be deducted from an employee's annual pay where that employee had partially performed by going on strike.

[78] See M. Freedland, *The Personal Employment Contract* (Oxford, OUP, 2003) 201–4.

[79] See the discussion in H. Collins, 'Progress towards the Right to Work in the United Kingdom' in V. Mantouvalou (ed.), *The Right to Work: Legal and Philosophical Perspectives* (Oxford, Hart Publishing, 2015) 236 and 239–42.

[80] *Cuckson v Stones* (1858) 1 E & E 248; *Miles v Wakefield* [1987] AC 539, 561A–B and 564G–565B per Lord Templeman; *Miller v Hamworthy Engineering Ltd* [1986] IRLR 461; *BT v Ticehurst* [1992] ICR 383; and *Beveridge v KLM (UK) Ltd* [2000] IRLR 765, 766 per Johnston J.

[81] *Sunrise Brokers LLP v Rodgers* [2015] ICR 272.

[82] [1906] 2 KB 728, 743–4 per Farwell J.

■ M. Freedland, *The Personal Employment Contract* (Oxford, OUP, 2003) 215

> . . . many of [the] inherent uncertainties can be traced back to the varieties in the structure of personal work or employment contracts which we identified in Chapter 2, and in particular to the broad contrast between diffuse relational structures and tight exchange-based structures. The contrast between performance as 'actual work' and performance as 'readiness and willingness to work' can be and frequently has been used to capture and express that structural contrast. In tight exchange-based structures, remuneration is seen as conditional upon 'actual work', while, in looser relational structures, remuneration is regarded as conditional upon 'readiness and willingness to work'. This equation is not absolutely precise, nor are any of the elements which make it up; but it is nevertheless highly persuasive and influential.

This binary divide between remuneration payable for actual work performed and alternatively for 'readiness and willingness to work' correlates approximately with the historical social distinction between manual labourers paid by wages and salaried workers.[83] However, the relevance of that social distinction has now broken down and the current approach is to treat the consideration for remuneration as the employee's readiness and willingness to work in all cases of employment.

It should be stressed that the various statutory protections of earnings cast a long shadow over the implied term impressing a duty to pay wages on the employer. For example, Part II of the ERA precludes employers from making unauthorized deductions from the wages of their employees.[84] Likewise, the National Minimum Wage Act 1998 confers in favour of workers a right to a minimum wage[85] and the terms of Chapter 3 of Part 5 of the Equality Act 2010 provide for equal pay for equal work between the sexes.[86] Furthermore, sections 151 and 155 of the Social Security Contributions and Benefits Act 1992 enjoin an employer to pay statutory sick pay[87] to the employee for the first 28 weeks of incapacity at the current rate of £92.05 per week.[88] Finally, Part III of the ERA furnishes a more powerful degree of constraint on the employer's power of lay-off than that afforded by the common law in *Devonald v Rosser*. It does so by prescribing guarantee payments[89] in respect of any whole day in which an employee, who has been continuously employed for at least one month, is not provided with work because of a diminution in the requirements of the employer's business or other occurrence affecting its normal working.

6.2.3 Duty of an employer to exercise reasonable care for the physical and psychiatric well-being of the employee

The implied term which imposes a duty on the employer to exercise reasonable care for the physical and psychiatric well-being of its employees is the central conduit through which the common law fosters and promotes the policy objectives of care and

---

[83] See Lord Denning, '*Quantum Meruit*: The Case of *Craven-Ellis v. Canons Ltd*' (1939) 55 *Law Quarterly Review* 54, 63–4; M. Freedland, *The Personal Employment Contract* (Oxford, OUP, 2003) 217–18.

[84] See Chapter 8, section 8.2.2.   [85] See Chapter 8, section 8.2.1.   [86] See Chapter 14.

[87] An employer may recover an amount paid out as statutory sick pay if, and only to the extent that, it exceeds a percentage of his liability to pay National Insurance contributions in the income tax month in question: section 159A of the Social Security Contributions and Benefits Act 1992 ('SSCBA'). Sick pay is not payable for the first three days of a period of incapacity by virtue of section 155(1) of the SSCBA. Statutory sick pay is paid at a prescribed weekly rate related to normal weekly earnings.

[88] See article 9 of the Social Security Benefits Up-rating Order (SI 2018/281).

[89] See Chapter 8, section 8.2.2.

co-operation between the parties. It is undoubtedly one of the most important implied terms and has been responsible for some of the most radical developments in the content and performance of contracts of employment over the past 80 years. In its orientation, the policy objective of promoting care in the employment relationship is cross-cut by the other policy goal of mutuality/reciprocity. Support for this proposition is furnished by the fact that employees are also subject to an implied term imposing a duty to exercise reasonable care in the performance of their roles.[90]

In contrast to the implied terms imposing duties on the employer to supply the employee with work and to pay wages, the employer's implied duty to exercise reasonable care is comparatively youthful. This is attributable to the fact that the implied term was not established until the decision of the House of Lords in *Wilsons & Clyde Coal Co. Ltd v English*.[91] Prior to that date, the common law propounded the 'doctrine of common employment', which was a vestige of the old 'master and servant' law. Under that doctrine, an employer would not be liable to an employee where it had delegated its duty to take care of the safety of its employees to competent subordinates and the employee was injured as a result of the negligent actions of the subordinate. This doctrine was discarded by the House of Lords in *Wilsons & Clyde Coal*:

■ *Wilsons & Clyde Coal Co. Ltd v English* [1938] AC 57, 70

Lord Thankerton:

The workman, under his contract of employment, is not to be held impliedly to have taken the risk of want of due care in the provision of a reasonably safe system of working, and the master cannot transfer the duty on to the shoulders of a subordinate. If he appoints a servant to attend to the discharge of such duty, such servant, in this respect, is merely the agent or hand of the master, and the maxim *qui facit per alium facit* per se renders the master liable for such servant's negligence as being, in the view of the law, the master's own negligence.

By ruling that the employer was under a duty to exercise reasonable care for the safety of those in its employment irrespective of any downwards delegation, the House of Lords swept aside the doctrine of common employment. However, it was not wholly clear from the speeches of the Law Lords whether that duty arose in the law of tort, the law of contract, or both. The subsequent decisions in *Lister v Romford Ice & Cold Storage Co.*[92] and *Matthews v Kuwait Bechtel Corp.*[93] put the matter beyond doubt by ruling that this duty could be conceived of as concurrently contractual and tortious. Indeed, the latter has exerted a major degree of influence over the former to the extent that the former is permeated by a highly tort-based mode of reasoning, notwithstanding that the parallel duties remain conceptually and doctrinally distinct. For example, the standard of scrutiny of managerial conduct for the purposes of evaluating whether there has been a breach of the employer's tortious or implied contractual duty is objective.[94] Such an objective standard of review directs an employment judge towards an enquiry of what a reasonable person would have done in the factual circumstances, taking into account in particular the foreseeability of harm, the magnitude of the risk of that harm occurring, the gravity of the potential harm, the cost and practicability of preventing it, and the justifications for running the risk. If the employment judge rules that the reasonable person

---

[90] See the discussion in section 6.3.2.   [91] [1938] AC 57.   [92] [1957] AC 555.
[93] [1959] 2 QB 57.
[94] *Nettleship v Weston* [1971] 2 QB 691, 702 per Denning MR; *Stokes v Guest, Keen and Nettlefold (Bolts and Nuts) Ltd* [1968] 1 WLR 1776, 1783D–E per Swanwick J; *Barber v Somerset County Council* [2004] 1 WLR 1089, 1110 per Lord Walker; and *Sutherland v Hatton* [2002] IRLR 263, 270 per Hale LJ.

on an objective assessment would have acted in a manner, or taken steps, which the employer failed to take, the employer will be deemed to be in breach of duty. Furthermore, as well as the law of tort, the law of constructive dismissal in the statutory regime of unfair dismissal[95] has been another significant driver in the evolution of the content and scope of the implied term.[96] Much of the case law on the implied duty has been generated within the rubric of constructive dismissal claims raised by employees under Part X of the ERA[97] in the employment tribunals and EAT.[98]

In *Wilsons v Clyde Coal Co. Ltd v English*,[99] Lord Wright divided the implied term into three components or sub-duties:

■ *Wilsons & Clyde Coal Co. Ltd v English* [1938] AC 57, 78

Lord Wright:

The same principle, in my opinion, applies to those fundamental obligations of a contract of employment which lie outside the doctrine of common employment, and for the performance of which employers are absolutely responsible. When I use the word absolutely, I do not mean that employers warrant the adequacy of plant, or the competence of fellow-employees, or the propriety of the system of work. The obligation is fulfilled by the exercise of due care and skill. But it is not fulfilled by entrusting its fulfilment to employees, even though selected with due care and skill. The obligation is threefold—'the provision of a competent staff of men, adequate material, and a proper system and effective supervision'; . . .

This tripartite division of the employer's obligations into the provision of competent staff, adequate material and a proper system of work, and effective supervision is supplemented by the employer's statutory obligations under the Health and Safety at Work etc. Act 1974 ('HSWA'), the Management of Health and Safety at Work Regulations 1999 ('MHSW'),[100] and sundry other pieces of health and safety legislation. Although there is some evidence that the statutory obligations have had an impact on the expectations to which an employer will be held in terms of the reasonable care implied term,[101] consistent with the pervasive disintegrated relationship which pertains between the implied terms of the contract of employment and the statutory regulation of the employment relationship,[102] the cross-fertilization of norms between the common law and statutory sources

---

[95] See section 95(1)(c) of the ERA and Chapter 16, section 16.2.2.3.

[96] The catalyst was the approach of the Court of Appeal in the ground-breaking case of *Western Excavating (ECC) Ltd v Sharp* [1978] QB 761.   [97] Or its statutory predecessors.

[98] Some notable examples are *Pagano v HGS* [1976] IRLR 9 (failure of employer to provide employee with safe roadworthy vehicles to drive); *British Aircraft Corp. Ltd v Austin* [1978] IRLR 332 (failure to investigate the employee's complaint about the provision of protective eyewear); *Graham Oxley Tool Steels Ltd v Firth* [1980] IRLR 135 (employer kept the employee waiting outside the workplace for 25 minutes in freezing weather); *Bracebridge Engineering Ltd v Darby* [1990] IRLR 3 (failure of employer to treat an employee's allegation of sexual harassment and assault seriously); and *Waltons & Morse v Dorrington* [1997] IRLR 488 (failure to provide a smoke-free environment reasonably suitable for the performance of the employee's contractual duties).

[99] [1938] AC 57.   [100] SI 1999/3242.

[101] See *Lane v Shire Roofing Co. (Oxford) Ltd* [1995] IRLR 493; *Waltons & Morse v Dorrington* [1997] IRLR 488, 490 per Morison P. However, a breach of the employer's obligation in section 2 of the HSWA to ensure, so far as is reasonably practicable, the health, safety, and welfare at work of all its employees does not give rise to a civil claim for breach of statutory duty: section 47 of the HSWA. See also regulation 22 of the MHSW.

[102] See M. Freedland, *The Personal Employment Contract* (Oxford, OUP, 2003) 142; M. Freedland and N. Kountouris, *The Legal Construction of Personal Work Relations* (Oxford, OUP, 2011) 193; and A.C.L. Davies, 'The Relationship Between Common Law and Statute' in M. Freedland et al. (eds), *The Contract of Employment* (Oxford, OUP, 2016) 73.

has not been as widespread as one might have expected.[103] To that extent, in line with the theme advanced in Chapter 2, the interaction between the two sources can be characterized as something akin to 'oil and water' to the extent that the jurisprudence of both branches has developed largely in isolation.[104]

One area where the implied term has recently expanded is in relation to psychiatric injury caused by work-related stress. The decisions in *Walker v Northumberland County Council*[105] and *Cross v Highland and Islands Enterprise*[106] established that an employer could be liable in contract or tort/delict for work-related stress in English and Scottish law respectively. The subsequent decision of the Court of Appeal in *Sutherland v Hatton*[107] built on that jurisprudence by setting out the parameters of the employer's liability for work-related psychiatric injuries:

■ *Sutherland v Hatton* [2002] EWCA Civ 76, [2002] ICR 613, 631C–632F

Lady Justice Hale: Summary

From the above discussion, the following practical propositions emerge.

(1) There are no special control mechanisms applying to claims for psychiatric (or physical) illness or injury arising from the stress of doing the work the employee is required to do . . . The ordinary principles of employer's liability apply . . .

(2) The threshold question is whether this kind of harm to this particular employee was reasonably foreseeable . . .: this has two components (a) an injury to health (as distinct from occupational stress) which (b) is attributable to stress at work (as distinct from other factors) . . .

(3) Foreseeability depends upon what the employer knows (or ought reasonably to know) about the individual employee. Because of the nature of mental disorder, it is harder to foresee than physical injury, but may be easier to foresee in a known individual than in the population at large . . . An employer is usually entitled to assume that the employee can withstand the normal pressures of the job unless he knows of some particular problem or vulnerability . . .

(4) The test is the same whatever the employment: there are no occupations which should be regarded as intrinsically dangerous to mental health . . .

(5) Factors likely to be relevant in answering the threshold question include: (a) The nature and extent of the work done by the employee . . . Is the workload much more than is normal for the particular job? Is the work particularly intellectually or emotionally demanding for this employee? Are demands being made of this employee unreasonable when compared with the demands made of others in the same or comparable jobs? Or are there signs that others doing this job are suffering harmful levels of stress? Is there an abnormal level of sickness or absenteeism in the same job or the same department? (b) Signs from the employee of impending harm to health . . . Has he a particular problem or vulnerability? Has he already suffered from illness attributable to stress at work? Have there recently been frequent or prolonged absences which are uncharacteristic of him? Is there reason to think that these are attributable to stress at work, for example because of complaints or warnings from him or others?

---

[103] Contrast this with *Gilchrist v Asda Stores Ltd* [2015] CSOH 77 at paras 14 and 15 where Lady Stacey suggested that the breach of health and safety regulations will give rise to breach of duty of care in tort irrespective of section 47 of the HSWA, as the fact that the regulation exists means the harm ought to have been reasonably foreseeable to the employer.

[104] See Chapter 2, section 2.1.1.   [105] [1995] 1 All ER 737.
[106] 2001 SLT 1060.   [107] [2002] EWCA Civ 76, [2002] 2 All ER 1.

(6)   The employer is generally entitled to take what he is told by his employee at face value, unless he has good reason to think to the contrary . . .

(7)   To trigger a duty to take steps, the indications of impending harm to health arising from stress at work must be plain enough for any reasonable employer to realise that he should do something about it . . .

(8)   The employer is only in breach of duty if he has failed to take the steps which are reasonable in the circumstances, bearing in mind the magnitude of the risk of harm occurring, the gravity of the harm which may occur, the costs and practicability of preventing it, and the justifications for running the risk . . .

(9)   The size and scope of the employer's operation, its resources and the demands it faces are relevant in deciding what is reasonable; these include the interests of other employees and the need to treat them fairly, for example, in any redistribution of duties . . .

(10) An employer can only reasonably be expected to take steps which are likely to do some good: the court is likely to need expert evidence on this . . .

(11) An employer who offers a confidential advice service, with referral to appropriate counselling or treatment services, is unlikely to be found in breach of duty . . .[108]

(12) If the only reasonable and effective step would have been to dismiss or demote the employee, the employer will not be in breach of duty in allowing a willing employee to continue in the job . . .

(13) In all cases, therefore, it is necessary to identify the steps which the employer both could and should have taken before finding him in breach of his duty of care . . .

(14) The [employee] must show that that breach of duty has caused or materially contributed to the harm suffered. It is not enough to show that occupational stress has caused the harm . . .

(15) Where the harm suffered has more than one cause, the employer should only pay for that proportion of the harm suffered which is attributable to his wrongdoing, unless the harm is truly indivisible. It is for the [employer] to raise the question of apportionment . . .

(16) The assessment of damages will take account of any pre-existing disorder or vulnerability and of the chance that the [employee] would have succumbed to a stress-related disorder in any event . . .

Lord Walker in *Barber v Somerset County Council*[109] cautioned against treating this passage as possessing 'anything like statutory force'[110] and preferred the statement of general principle about the nature of an employer's liability by Swanwick J in *Stokes v Guest, Keen and Nettlefold (Bolts & Nuts) Ltd*[111] However, he also confirmed that it amounted to useful practical guidance and 'a valuable contribution to the development of the law'.[112] To that extent, this passage has become extremely influential in delimiting the content and scope of the employer's reasonable care obligations in the context of a work-related stress claim.[113] In *Barber*, it was held that the employer had breached the implied term where it failed to take the reasonable steps necessary to prevent the work-related psychiatric

---

[108] On the conclusiveness of this factor, see *Hartman v South Essex Mental Health and Community Care NHS Trust* [2005] IRLR 293; *Daw v Intel Corp. UK Ltd* [2007] EWCA Civ 70, [2007] 2 All ER 126; and *Dickins v O2 plc* [2008] EWCA Civ 1144, [2009] IRLR 58.

[109] [2004] UKHL 13, [2004] 1 WLR 1089.   [110] *ibid.*, 1109H.

[111] [1968] 1 WLR 1776, 1783.

[112] [2004] UKHL 13, [2004] 1 WLR 1089, 1109B, see also Lord Scott at 1092C.

[113] For example, see *Hartman v South Essex Mental Health and Community Care NHS Trust* [2005] IRLR 293; *Harding v Pub Estate Co. Ltd* [2005] EWCA Civ 553; *Hone v Six Continentals Retail Ltd* [2005] EWCA Civ 922, [2006] IRLR 49; *Pakenham-Walsh v Connell Residential* [2006] EWCA Civ 90; *Daw v Intel Corp. UK Ltd* [2007] EWCA Civ 70, [2007] 2 All ER 126; *Dickins v O2 plc* [2008] EWCA Civ 1144, [2009] IRLR 58; and *McCarthy v Highland Council* 2012 SLT 95.

illness of an employee teacher. The employee had a heavy workload of up to 70 hours a week and had been signed off work with a medical certificate stating that he was suffering from stress and depression. In such a case, it was held that the medical certificate ought to have alerted the employer to the fact that the employee had a heightened risk of injury to his mental well-being and that it ought to have taken the reasonable steps.

In practice, many claims of breach of the contractual duty will be defeated on one of the following grounds:

(1) that the harm was not reasonably foreseeable;

(2) that the breach of duty was not causative of the harm; or

(3) that the loss suffered was too remote from the breach of duty.

For example, *Easton v B&Q plc*[114] is a decision in which a store manager's claim for breach of the duty of care failed for an absence of reasonable foreseeability. Here, the manager suffered from depression and was off work for five months. A few days after beginning a phased return to work, his employer recertified him as unfit for work owing to depression. The employee alleged that the depression returned because he felt under pressure from his employer to accept an offer of a temporary position at another branch. The High Court held that there had been no breach of duty because of an absence of reasonable foreseeability and that the employer had been entitled to act on the basis that the employee would be able to assess whether he wished to take up a particular post; likewise in *Boylin v The Christie NHS Foundation*,[115] where it was held that one serious incident was insufficient to establish a breach of the duty of care as this failed on the reasonable foreseeability limb. As for the lack of causation, in *Olulana v Southwark LBC*,[116] an employee was unable to establish a breach of duty in light of evidence to the effect that the development of her schizophrenic condition whilst working for a local authority had been caused as a result of an insidious and inevitable neurobiological deterioration, rather than workplace stress. Further, where the psychiatric harm suffered can be attributed to a loss of status in the workplace caused by the employee's own harmful conduct, namely the abuse of cocaine whilst working undercover, causation will be absent.[117] Turning to the limiting factor of remoteness, in *Yapp v Foreign and Commonwealth Office*,[118] the High Commissioner in Belize was temporarily withdrawn from his post—effectively suspended—in response to various allegations of sexual harassment and bullying that were made against him. The Court of Appeal arrived at the conclusion that the suspension was in breach of duty, but no damages were awarded on the reasoning that the losses suffered were far too remote.[119]

Around about the same time as the parameters of the employer's implied duty of care in relation to an employee's psychiatric well-being were being worked out, an even wider version of the implied term appeared to be emerging, which operated to impress obligations on the employer to exercise reasonable care to protect the employee from *financial* harm. This was in direct contrast with the orthodox position exemplified in a slew of decisions such as *Deyong v Shenburn*[120] and *Reid v Rush & Tompkins Group plc*.[121] Here, the proposition that the contractual duty to exercise reasonable care could be extended to protect an employee from economic losses had been expressly rejected.

[114] [2015] EWHC 880 (QB).   [115] [2014] EWHC 3363 (QB).   [116] [2014] EWHC 2707 (QB).

[117] *AB v Chief Constable of X Constabulary* [2015] IRLR 284.

[118] [2015] IRLR 112. See D. Brodie, 'Risk Allocation and Psychiatric Harm: *Yapp v Foreign and Commonwealth Office*' (2015) 44 *Industrial Law Journal* 270; and D. Cabrelli, 'Liability and Remedies for a Breach of the Contract of Employment at Common Law: Some Recent Developments' (2016) 45 *Industrial Law Journal* 207.

[119] *Monk v Cann Hall Primary School* [2013] IRLR 732 is another case in which the manner of a suspension was such that it ought to be held in breach of the implied term.

[120] [1946] 1 All ER 226.   [121] [1989] 3 All ER 228, [1990] ICR 61.

Notwithstanding this orthodoxy, in *Spring v Guardian Assurance*,[122] the House of Lords held that an employer who gave a reference in respect of a former employee owed that employee a duty to take reasonable care in its preparation and would be liable to him in negligence if he were to fail to do so and the employee thereby suffer economic damage. This was quite a remarkable decision. It recognized that the implied term was operative to exercise constraints over the conduct of the employer notwithstanding that the employment relationship had come to an end. Likewise, in *Scally v Southern Health and Social Services Board*,[123] the House of Lords reached the conclusion that where a contract of employment negotiated between an employer and a representative body contained a particular term conferring on the employee a valuable right contingent upon his acting as required to obtain the benefit, there was an implied obligation on the employer to take reasonable steps to inform the employee of that term if he could not be expected to be aware of it unless it was brought to his attention. It was thought that these decisions could be conceived as subjecting the employer to a duty to exercise reasonable care for the economic welfare of the employee, particularly in light of the following statement:

■ *Spring v Guardian Assurance* [1995] 2 AC 296, 353G–H

Lord Woolf:

As I understand *Scally*, it recognises that, just as in the earlier authorities the courts were prepared to imply by necessary implication a term imposing a duty on an employer to exercise due care for the physical wellbeing of his employees, so in the appropriate circumstances would the court imply a like duty as to his economic wellbeing, the duty as to his economic wellbeing giving rise to an action for damages if it is breached.

In many ways, such a development could be perceived as being wholly natural, given the traditional emphasis in the common law of treating the contract of employment in nothing more than purely economic or financial terms.[124]

However, when we reflect on the subsequent approach of the courts, it is clear that *Spring* and *Scally* represented the high-water mark of the notion of a duty to exercise reasonable care for an employee's economic well-being. The trajectory of the post-*Spring* case law is one of consistent judicial retrenchment,[125] culminating in the decision of the Court of Appeal in *Crossley v Faithful & Gould Holdings Ltd*.[126] Here, a senior employee who had resigned contended that his employer had breached a 'portmanteau' implied term in law enjoining it to exercise reasonable care for his economic well-being by failing to warn him of the adverse financial effects of his resignation on disability scheme benefits for which he had applied. Lord Justice Dyson in *Crossley* rejected the contention that an

---

[122] [1995] 2 AC 296. See also *Kidd v AXA Equity & Law Life Assurance Society plc* [2000] IRLR 301 (employer not liable and duty did not extend to the provision of a reference that was full, fair and comprehensive); *McKie v Swindon College* [2011] IRLR 575 (former employer liable in tort, rather than under the implied term, for allegations set out in an email); *Jackson v Liverpool City Council* [2011] IRLR 1009 (former employer not liable since opinions expressed in reference were fair even though matters had emerged after the employment of the employee had terminated); *AB v A Chief Constable* [2014] IRLR 700 (no liability for breach of duty) and *Abdel-Khalek v Ali* [2016] IRLR 358.

[123] [1992] 1 AC 294 (HL).

[124] The paradigm is the law of wrongful dismissal and the law of damages for a breach of the contract of employment where the social and personal (as opposed to economic and financial) implications of dismissal and/or breach for the employee are treated as irrelevant: see P. Elias, 'The Structure of the Employment Contract' (1982) 35 *Current Legal Problems* 95, 96, 99, and Chapter 15, section 15.3.2.

[125] *University of Nottingham v Eyett* [1999] ICR 721; *Outram v Academy Plastic* [2001] ICR 367; and *Hagen v ICI Chemicals & Polymers Ltd* [2002] IRLR 31.

[126] [2004] IRLR 377. See C. Wynn-Evans, 'Of Portmanteaux and Bridgeheads' (2004) 33 *Industrial Law Journal* 355.

open-textured implied term for the economic welfare of employees had been established by *Scally*. Instead, he confined *Scally* to the proposition that it imposed an implied duty on an employer to draw an employee's attention to a contractual term where it could not reasonably be expected that the employee would be aware of valuable rights conferred by that term. Since the former employee in *Crossley* was a senior employee and director, it was held that the implied duty was not engaged since he possessed the know-how and resources to have taken his own financial advice.[127] Despite the clarity of the decision in *Crossley*, it is not wholly obvious that the reluctance of the courts to recognize a broader implied contractual duty—enjoining an employer to provide a minimum amount of information and advice for the economic benefit of its employees—is sustainable in the long run.[128] In light of the far-reaching nature of the implied term of mutual trust and confidence, a persuasive argument has been advanced by Van Bever[129] that it is inevitable that the former will evolve to impose such a duty where it is 'necessary or reasonable given the legitimate expectations of the [parties]'.[130] Moreover, there is scope for liability for economic loss to be imposed in the law of tort. For example, in *Lennon v Commissioner of Police of the Metropolis*,[131] it was held that an employer may be liable in tort for economic loss for negligently failing to advise an employee of valuable contractual benefits where the employer had voluntarily assumed responsibility for doing so. In light of that jurisprudence, would the Employee in the following Hypothetical A be able to avail herself of the implied term?

Hypothetical A

Cynthia Wordsworth is an employee ('the Employee') who has worked for Danny's Demolishers Ltd ('the Employer') in the latter's Salisbury office for a period of 25 years. She is the overall manager of the Salisbury office and is responsible for all of the 33 employees working at the premises. She reports to the board of directors of the Employer at its head office. The Employee is nearing retirement and has paid contributions into a company occupational pension scheme operated by the Employer for over 20 years. She is completely unaware of the terms and benefits of such a scheme and usually relies on her independent financial adviser to keep her abreast of the benefits available. After she attends a general information seminar run by the Employer at its head office for new entrants into the Employer's pension scheme and learns about the generous lump sums payable to employees on retirement under the scheme, she decides to take early retirement. However, after her retirement, she is horrified to learn that only employees who entered the Employer's pension scheme after 2010 are eligible to receive the lump sum retirement payments and that she is not entitled to such a payment. She sues the Employer on the basis that it breached the implied term of reasonable care by failing to advise her of the terms of the pension scheme relating to the payment of lump sums on retirement. In your view, would the Employee's claim be successful?[132]

[127] Furthermore, the view was taken that a more open-ended implied term imposing a duty on the employer to advise employees of financial benefits would create an unreasonable burden on employers where financial advice was readily available. See also *Coventry University v Mian* [2014] EWCA Civ 1275 where the Court of Appeal held that there was no breach of duty of care where the employer initiated disciplinary proceedings without undertaking due enquiry and the employee developed a psychiatric illness.

[128] However, see the latest example of resistance on the part of the Court of Appeal in *Greenway v Johnson Mathey plc* [2016] IRLR 526.

[129] A. Van Bever, 'An Employer's Duty to Provide Information and Advice on Economic Risks?' (2013) 42 *Industrial Law Journal* 1.

[130] *ibid.*, 33.   [131] [2004] IRLR 385.

[132] The answer is no: (1) she is a senior manager who relies on an independent financial adviser to advise her; and (2) the information session was a general session and the employer would not be liable for any information imparted during it.

We now depart from the notion of 'care' and turn our attention to the concept of 'co-operation'. This is a notion we identified earlier as one of the policy goals pursued by the implied terms. It is fair to say that limited progress has been made in formulating an implied duty on the employer to co-operate. It had once been thought that the obligations of the employer to exercise reasonable care would eventually be systematized and treated as simply one manifestation of a wider reciprocal implied term of co-operation. For example, at the time of the Court of Appeal's decision in *Secretary of State for Employment v ASLEF (No. 2)*[133]—which held that an employee should not act in a way that frustrates the commercial objective of the contract of employment—it was generally regarded as an authority for a much broader co-operation implied term.[134] However, despite certain isolated judicial pronouncements,[135] the general weight of the authorities is opposed to the recognition of such an implied term or duty.[136] It is particularly revealing that cases where the employer's implied duty could have been articulated in terms of co-operation were instead couched as imposing obligations to provide support and training.[137] At a more profound level, many of the developments which an implied duty of co-operation arguably could have generated were instead advanced under the umbrella of the nascent implied term of mutual trust and confidence, to which our consideration now turns.

6.2.4 Implied term of mutual trust and confidence

The failure of an implied duty of co-operation to take root can be understood in light of the inexorable rise in fortunes of the implied term of mutual trust and confidence. Whilst this implied term clearly promotes the policy consideration of trust and confidence, it also advances the cause of co-operation amongst the parties. Although the common law is the source of the implied term of mutual trust and confidence, as explained by Lord Nicholls in *Eastwood v Magnox Electric plc*,[138] it was the statutory concept of 'constructive dismissal' in the unfair dismissal regime which acted as the catalyst for its emergence.[139] By 1979, it had been held that a breach of the implied term would automatically amount to a constructive dismissal under the statutory regime.[140] Throughout the 1980s and early 1990s, a slew of cases decided in the EAT and Court of Appeal acknowledged the existence of the implied term. Finally, in 1997, when employees raised a common law action against their employers for damages on the basis that the latter had breached the

---

[133] [1972] 2 WLR 1370. See also *Isle of Wight Tourist Board v Coombes* [1976] IRLR 413.

[134] See J. F. Burrows, 'Contractual Co-operation and the Implied Term' (1968) 31 *Modern Law Review* 390; B. Napier, 'Working to Rule: A Breach of the Contract of Employment?' (1972) 1 *Industrial Law Journal* 125, 132; and B. Napier, 'Judicial Attitudes towards the Employment Relationship: Some Recent Developments' (1977) 6 *Industrial Law Journal* 1, 7–9.

[135] To the effect that the implied term of co-operation enjoins the employer to co-operate with the employee to enable the latter to fulfil certain conditions necessary to secure certain financial benefits: *Takacs v Barclays Services Jersey Ltd* [2006] IRLR 877, 885 per Master Fontaine.

[136] See M. Freedland, *The Personal Employment Contract* (Oxford, OUP, 2003) 146–51.

[137] *Wigan Borough Council v Davies* [1979] ICR 411 (failure to take reasonable steps to provide the employee with support by preventing harassment from fellow employees); *Cresswell v Board of Inland Revenue* [1984] ICR 508 (employer under a duty to provide support and training to clerical employees in adapting their working methods from the use of paper manual files to computerized records).

[138] [2005] 1 AC 503, 521–2.

[139] For an explanation, see B. Hepple, *Rights at Work: Global, European and British Perspectives* (London, Thomson/Sweet & Maxwell, 2005) 51–2; *Western Excavating (ECC) Ltd v Sharp* [1978] QB 761; M. Freedland, *The Personal Employment Contract* (Oxford, OUP, 2003) 155–6; L. Barmes, 'Common Law Implied Terms and Behavioural Standards at Work' (2007) 36 *Industrial Law Journal* 35, 37–8 and Chapter 16, section 16.2.2.3.

[140] See *Courtaulds Northern Textiles Ltd v Andrew* [1979] IRLR 84, 86 per Arnold J; *Woods v W. M. Car Services* [1981] ICR 666, 672 per Browne-Wilkinson J.

implied term by running a corrupt and dishonest business, the House of Lords took the opportunity to explicitly recognize the implied term:

■ *Malik v BCCI* [1998] AC 20, 45C–46H

Lord Steyn: The implied term of mutual trust and confidence

The [employees] . . . rely on a standardised term implied by law, that is, on a term which is said to be an incident of all contracts of employment . . . Such implied terms operate as default rules. The parties are free to exclude or modify them. But it is common ground that in the present case the particular terms of the contracts of employment of the two [employees] could not affect an implied obligation of mutual trust and confidence. The employer's primary case is based on a formulation of the implied term that . . . imposes reciprocal duties on the employer and employee. Given that this case is concerned with alleged obligations of an employer I will concentrate on its effect on the position of employers. For convenience I will set out the term again. It is expressed to impose an obligation that the employer shall not: 'without reasonable and proper cause, conduct itself in a manner calculated and[141] likely to destroy or seriously damage the relationship of confidence and trust between employer and employee:' see *Woods v. W. M. Car Services (Peterborough) Ltd* [1981] I.C.R. 666, 670 (Browne-Wilkinson J.), approved in *Lewis v. Motorworld Garages Ltd* [1986] I.C.R. 157 and *Imperial Group Pension Trust Ltd v. Imperial Tobacco Ltd* [1991] 1 W.L.R. 589 . . . The evolution of the term is a comparatively recent development. The obligation probably has its origin in the general duty of co-operation between contracting parties: Hepple & O'Higgins, *Employment Law*, 4th ed. (1981), pp. 134–135, paras. 291–292. The reason for this development is part of the history of the development of employment law in this century. The notion of a 'master and servant' relationship became obsolete. Lord Slynn of Hadley recently noted 'the changes which have taken place in the employer–employee relationship, with far greater duties imposed on the employer than in the past, whether by statute or by judicial decision, to care for the physical, financial and even psychological welfare of the employee:' *Spring v. Guardian Assurance [Plc.]* [1995] 2 A.C. 296, 335B. A striking illustration of this change is *Scally's* case [1992] 1 A.C. 294 . . . where the House of Lords implied a term that all employees in a certain category had to be notified by an employer of their entitlement to certain benefits. It was the change in legal culture which made possible the evolution of the implied term of trust and confidence . . . The major importance of the implied duty of trust and confidence lies in its impact on the obligations of the employer: Douglas Brodie, 'Recent cases, Commentary, The Heart of the Matter: Mutual Trust and Confidence' (1996) 25 I.L.J. 121. And the implied obligation as formulated is apt to cover the great diversity of situations in which a balance has to be struck between an employer's interest in managing his business as he sees fit and the employee's interest in not being unfairly and improperly exploited. The evolution of the implied term of trust and confidence is a fact. It has not yet been endorsed by your Lordships' House. It has proved a workable principle in practice. It has not been the subject of adverse criticism in any decided cases and it has been welcomed in academic writings. I regard the emergence of the implied obligation of mutual trust and confidence as a sound development.

The implied term has generated a flood of judicial and academic comment, having been described as (a) an 'overarching obligation implied by law as an incident of the contract of employment',[142] (b) assuming a 'central position in the law of the contract of employment',[143]

---

[141] It has been held that this should be read as 'or' rather than 'and', i.e. disjunctively rather than conjunctively: *Baldwin v Brighton & Hove City Council* [2007] IRLR 232.

[142] *Johnson v Unisys Ltd* [2003] 1 AC 518, 536A per Lord Steyn.

[143] D. Brodie, 'Mutual Trust and the Values of the Employment Contract' (2001) 30 *Industrial Law Journal* 84, 86.

(c) being 'undoubtedly the most powerful engine of movement in the modern law of employment contracts',[144] and (d) forming the 'cornerstone of the legal construction of the contract of employment'.[145] Much of the recent academic literature on this topic has focused on the juridical nature, content, scope of application, and possible future trajectory of the duty of trust and confidence.[146] With regard to the nature of the implied term, academics have argued that it may be rationalized in dignitarian terms.[147] This suggests that it is a term which seeks to respect and promote the human dignity of the worker and to recognize the relational character of the employment relationship. To the extent that it is accepted that the employment relationship is relational[148] in character in the sense that it goes beyond the simple exchange of work for wages[149] and instead provides an employee with a level of self-esteem, personal and social fulfilment, and encompasses a long-term continuous relationship, there is some purchase in the notion that implicit within the implied term lies a recognition that the workplace is a community. Brodie has addressed this idea of the workplace as a community. Essentially, it is a vision of 'the employment relationship . . . involving elements of common interest and partnership, rather than . . . conflict and subordination':[150]

■ **D. Brodie, 'Mutual Trust and the Values of the Employment Contract' (2001) 30 *Industrial Law Journal* 84, 88–9**

It would seem to be worth considering what prompted the emergence of mutual trust and confidence. A number of answers might be given (and not necessarily mutually exclusive ones) and it may be that contemporary interest in communitarian values had a role to play. Selznick has suggested that 'wherever continuity and concerted effort are prized, the (modern) contract model loses force and relevance. As we move to association, and from association to community, mutuality reaches beyond exchange to create more enduring bonds of interdependence, caring and commitment'. Certainly mutual trust, being a positive version of the general duty of cooperation, can be regarded as promoting 'interdependence, caring and commitment'. The implied obligation constitutes judicial recognition of the fact that the employment contract is not just about economic exchange but also social or personal relations. Invoking communitarian values seems more apt given the significance of the community constituted by the workplace.

Chiming with the communitarian underpinnings of the implied term, it has also been described by the judiciary as a managerial obligation to 'act responsibly and in good

---

[144] M. Freedland, *The Personal Employment Contract* (Oxford, OUP, 2003) 166.

[145] H. Collins, *Employment Law*, 2nd edition (Oxford, OUP, 2010) 106.

[146] See the literature cited in the additional reading list with the Online Resources.

[147] See A. Bogg, 'Good Faith in the Contract of Employment: A Case of the English Reserve?' (2011) 32 *Comparative Labor Law & Policy Journal* 729, 759; D. Brodie, 'Mutual Trust and the Values of the Employment Contract' (2001) 30 *Industrial Law Journal* 84, 99; and H. Collins and V. Mantouvalou, 'Human Rights and the Contract of Employment' in M. Freedland et al. (eds), *The Contract of Employment* (Oxford, OUP, 2016) 205–6.

[148] See Chapter 5, section 5.1.1, *Johnson v Unisys Ltd* [2003] 1 AC 518, 532F per Lord Steyn and D. Brodie, 'Relational Contracts' in M. Freedland et al. (eds), *The Contract of Employment* (Oxford, OUP, 2016) 145. Contrast this with D. Brodie, 'How Relational is the Employment Contract?' (2011) 40 *Industrial Law Journal* 232.

[149] D. Brodie, 'Beyond Exchange: The New Contract of Employment' (1998) 27 *Industrial Law Journal* 79; D. Brodie, 'Legal Coherence and the Employment Revolution' (2001) 117 *Law Quarterly Review* 604.

[150] *State of South Australia v McDonald* [2009] SASC 219 at para 231 per Doyle CJ. See also D. Brodie, 'How Relational is the Employment Contract?' (2011) 40 *Industrial Law Journal* 232, 240; B. Napier, 'Judicial Attitudes towards the Employment Relationship: Some Recent Developments' (1977) 6 *Industrial Law Journal* 1, 7, 9, and 17.

faith'[151] and one of 'good faith and fair dealing'.[152] As for what that means, it has been said that the obligation enjoins 'each party [to] have regard to the interests of the other, but not that either must subjugate his interests to those of the other'.[153]

However, in practice, these pronouncements as to the nature of the implied term are expressed at a general level of abstraction and fail to provide content as to the precise manner in which it operates in routine cases. In practical terms, the contribution made by the implied term of mutual trust and confidence to workplace relations is twofold:

(1) it prevents the disappointment of the employee's legitimate or reasonable expectations and instead enables them to be given legal effect;[154] and

(2) it subjects the power and discretion of management to a measure of meaningful control.

Turning first to the notion of 'legitimate expectations', Bogg has identified four ways in which the courts and tribunals have pursued this objective, each of which overlap[155] to some degree:

■ **A. Bogg, 'Good Faith in the Contract of Employment: A Case of the English Reserve?' (2011) 32 *Comparative Labor Law & Policy Journal* 729, 759–60**

> Trust and confidence makes its specific contribution by preventing the disappointment of the employee's reasonable expectations. It does this in four main ways: the requirement of notice in respect of certain discretionary decisions, the requirement of consistency of treatment between employees, the protection of legitimate expectations[,] and the employer's positive obligation to provide information to employees in particular contexts.

We consider each of these four factors in turn.

(1) With regard to the first factor cited by Bogg, the cases of *Commerzbank AG v Keen*,[156] *United Bank v Akhtar*,[157] and *Société Générale (London Branch) v Geys*[158] support the contention that the implied term enjoins the employer to give notice in respect of managerial decision-making.[159] For example, in *Commerzbank*, it was held that an employee was entitled to be supplied with an explanation of the reasons for the exercise of a discretion in respect of additional pay.[160] Likewise, in *United Bank*, an ostensibly unrestricted express contractual power in a mobility clause enabling the employer to move the employee's place of work to Birmingham from Leeds was held to be subject to the implied term, duly imposing an obligation on the employer to give the employee reasonable notice of the exercise of the discretion. As for *Geys*,

---

[151] *Eastwood v Magnox Electric plc* [2005] 1 AC 503, 523G per Lord Nicholls; *Imperial Group Pension Trust Ltd v Imperial Tobacco Ltd* [1991] ICR 524, 533 per Sir Browne-Wilkinson VC.

[152] *Johnson v Unisys Ltd* [2003] 1 AC 518, 536D per Lord Steyn.

[153] *Nottingham University v Fishel* [2000] ICR 1462, 1493C per Elias J.

[154] See Lord Steyn, 'Contract Law: Fulfilling the Reasonable Expectations of Honest Men' (1997) 113 *Law Quarterly Review* 433, 442; D. Brodie, 'Beyond Exchange: The New Contract of Employment' (1998) 27 *Industrial Law Journal* 79, 96–7; and D. Brodie, 'Mutual Trust and the Values of the Employment Contract' (2001) 30 *Industrial Law Journal* 84, 94–6.

[155] A point noted by D. Brodie, 'Mutual Trust and the Values of the Employment Contract' (2001) 30 *Industrial Law Journal* 84, 94–6.   [156] [2007] IRLR 132.

[157] [1989] IRLR 507.

[158] [2012] UKSC 63, [2013] 1 AC 523. For discussion, see the literature cited in the additional reading list with the Online Resources.

[159] See also *Yapp v FCO* [2015] IRLR 112 regarding fair notice of allegations of sexual misconduct.

[160] [2007] IRLR 132, 135 per Mummery LJ. In this case, the complaint was that the employer had failed to give reasons for the non-payment of a discretionary bonus.

Lady Hale ruled that where the employer terminates the employment contract summarily with or without payment in lieu of notice, the implied term of mutual trust and confidence imposes a common law duty on the employer to provide notice of that fact to the employee.[161] The concern for the conferral of prior notice by the employer betrays a judicial predisposition to notions of natural justice.[162]

(2) Meanwhile, the manner in which the implied term requires the employer to treat employees consistently can be seen in the case of *Transco v O'Brien*.[163] Here, all permanent employees were given new contractual terms affording an enhanced redundancy package. When the employer's honest, but erroneous, belief that Mr O'Brien was not a permanent employee resulted in a failure to offer him the same deal, it was held that this inconsistency of treatment was a breach of the implied term.

(3) As for the part played by the implied term in protecting the employee from having his legitimate expectations defeated, the case of *French v Barclays Bank plc*[164] is instructive. Here, the employer had asked the employee to relocate and an interest-free bridging loan had been approved by the employer. When the employer subsequently decided to charge the employee interest on the loan, this was ruled to be a breach of the implied term.

(4) Finally, Bogg cites the role of the implied term in compelling the employer to furnish information to the employee. One example is the case of *Visa International v Paul*,[165] where the employer breached the implied term by failing to inform the employee of the emergence of a new vacancy for which she considered herself suitable.

Turning to the implied term's second principal function in imposing constraints on the exercise of the managerial prerogative, the powers of management are limited by the implied term irrespective of their source, e.g. whether they are conferred by an express term[166] or inherent within the employment relationship as a consequence of the authority/power relation.[167] The implied term intervenes here where there has been an arbitrary, capricious, or abusive exercise of the managerial prerogative to such an extent that trust and confidence have been destroyed or severely undermined.[168] By the same token, the fact that the employer has failed to exercise a power or discretion does not preclude the operation of the implied term's controls. Thus, it can be deployed to call the omissions, as well as the actions, of an employer or employee to account,[169] imposing positive obligations upon an employer or employee. All of this underscores the breadth of the circumstances subject to the scrutiny of the implied term of mutual trust and confidence and

---

[161] [2012] UKSC 63, [2013] 1 AC 523, 548A–H at paras 57–60.

[162] D. Brodie, 'Fair Dealing and the World of Work' (2014) 43 *Industrial Law Journal* 29, 33.

[163] [2002] ICR 721.   [164] [1998] IRLR 646.   [165] [2004] IRLR 42.

[166] For example, a mobility clause (*United Bank v Akhtar* [1989] IRLR 507), suspension clause (*Gogay v Hertfordshire County Council* [2000] IRLR 703; *Milne v Link Asset & Security Co. Ltd* [2005] All ER (D) 143 (September)), garden leave clause (*TFS Derivatives Ltd v Morgan* [2005] IRLR 246), or a flexibility clause (*Land Securities Trillium Ltd v Thornley* [2005] IRLR 765; *Norman v Audit Office* (UKEAT/0276/14/BA, 15 December 2014)).   [167] See Chapter 5, section 5.1.1.

[168] *Gogay v Hertfordshire County Council* [2000] IRLR 703; *Imperial Group Pension Trust Ltd v Imperial Tobacco Ltd* [1991] ICR 524; *Hagen v ICI Chemicals and Polymers Ltd* [2002] IRLR 31; and *Transco v O'Brien* [2002] ICR 721.

[169] See *Croft v Consignia plc* [2002] IRLR 851, 859 per Lindsay P; *Blackburn v Aldi Stores Ltd* [2013] IRLR 846 (failure to hold a proper appeal in respect of a grievance, even where there was no issue as to the original grievance hearing); *Reed v Stedman* [1999] IRLR 299 (failure of the employer to investigate complaints of sexual harassment); *IBM UK Holdings Ltd v Dalgleish* [2015] EWHC 1241 (Ch) (failure to conduct prior consultation with staff about pension changes); *Gebremarian v Ethiopian Airlines* [2014] IRLR 354 (failure to undertake prior consultation, any semblance of a selection process, or a fair redundancy exercise more generally, before deciding to dismiss an employee for redundancy); and *BG plc v O'Brien* [2001] IRLR 496. This can be contrasted with the views of Hart J in *University of Nottingham v Eyett* [1999] ICR 721, 727–8.

the fact that it serves to elaborate general standards of behaviour which the law expects employers and employees to observe in generic situations.

Some general points may be made about the operation of mutual trust and confidence.

(1) By definition, the term is mutual and thus subjects the employee to certain obligations as much as the employer. However, given the long-standing nature of the employee's duty of loyalty, fidelity, and confidence, it is the employer who has been the object of the lion's share of the cases in which a breach has been alleged.[170]

(2) Since its inception in the 1970s until the decision of the House of Lords in *Johnson v Unisys Ltd*,[171] the content of the implied term underwent a steady unprecedented growth, with Lord Hoffmann referring to this process as 'the courts . . . advancing across open country'.[172] However, not unlike the approach which has been adopted by the common law courts in many other areas of the law, a breakthrough development in the law such as that in *Malik v BCCI* was soon followed by a process of judicial retrenchment. For example, in *Johnson*, for three reasons,[173] it was held that the employer's ultimate managerial sanction of dismissal was not subject to control or regulation by the implied term of mutual trust and confidence at common law:

■ *Johnson v Unisys Ltd* [2003] 1 AC 518, 541F

> *Lord Hoffmann:*
>
> In the way it has always been formulated, it is concerned with preserving the continuing relationship which should subsist between employer and employee. So it does not seem altogether appropriate for use in connection with the way that relationship is terminated.

Indeed, this represents the most significant limitation on the power of the term to control managerial behaviour, bearing in mind that it is the employer's power of dismissal which is the most effective disciplinary tool in its armoury and the most potentially devastating exercise of the managerial prerogative for the employee.

(3) The implied term is not concerned with the reasonableness or otherwise of the actions of an employer or employee;[174] instead, the question is whether the actions of the employer or employee destroy or seriously undermine trust and confidence in the relationship between the parties, without reasonable or proper cause. An example of trust-destroying conduct is where the employer treats the employee with a lack

---

[170] See *Malik v BCCI* [1998] AC 20, 46C per Lord Steyn.   [171] [2003] 1 AC 518.

[172] [2003] 1 AC 518, 540A.

[173] First, that the implied term could not cut down the employer's power of dismissal conferred by an express term; second, to recognize the applicability of the implied term in such circumstances would enable the employee to circumvent the statutory regime of unfair dismissal; third, the roadblock presented by *Addis v Gramophone Co. Ltd* [1909] AC 488, on which, see Chapter 15, section 15.3.1.

[174] See *Post Office v Roberts* [1980] IRLR 347; *Marshall Specialist Vehicles Ltd v Osborne* [2003] IRLR 672, 678, and 682 at paras 59 and 83 per Burton P; *BG plc v O'Brien* [2001] IRLR 496 at para 27; *Imperial Group Pension Trust Ltd v Imperial Tobacco Ltd* [1991] ICR 524; and D. Cabrelli, 'Re-establishing Orthodoxy in the Law of Constructive Dismissal: *Claridge v Daler Rowney Ltd* [2008] IRLR 672 and *Bournemouth University Higher Education Corp. v Buckland* [2009] IRLR 606' (2009) 38 *Industrial Law Journal* 403, 409. Reasonableness only has a part to play in the context of the adjudicator's assessment of the employer's cause for the trust-destroying conduct, rather than the conduct itself, but contrast this view with the perceptive arguments in A. Bogg, '*Bournemouth University Higher Education Corp. v Buckland*: Re-establishing Orthodoxy at the Expense of Coherence?' (2010) 39 *Industrial Law Journal* 408.

of respect or basic decency,[175] or subjects the employee to unlawful sex or disability discrimination in contravention of statute.[176]

(4) In line with contractual orthodoxy, whether the duty of trust and confidence has been breached is to be determined objectively,[177] i.e. 'whether . . . from the perspective of a reasonable person in the position of the innocent party, the contract breaker has shown an intention to abandon and altogether refuse to perform the contract'.[178] As such, if the employee subjectively believes there was a breach, this will be irrelevant, since whether there has been a breach is a question of objective fact.[179]

(5) Single acts of negligence will not usually amount to a breach of the implied duty of trust and confidence.[180]

(6) The implied term is also available to strike down a course of conduct or omissions even though the final act or omission itself is not unreasonable or objectionable in law: the so-called 'last straw' doctrine.[181] Further, as expressed by Lord Nicholls in *Eastwood*, the implied term is available to subject conduct or omissions to objective scrutiny at most points in the employment relationship, i.e. the entire managerial decision-making process,[182] including any litigation conducted by the employer against third parties,[183] or even litigation against the employee whilst the latter remains in post.[184] Therefore, the actions or omissions of the employer prior[185] and in relation to the performance,[186] recruitment, suspension,[187] and opportunities for promotion[188] of an employee may be reviewed, as can the events leading up to a dismissal (including the disciplinary procedure),[189] the application or variation of

---

[175] *Courtaulds Northern Textiles Ltd v Andrew* [1979] IRLR 84; *Horkulak v Cantor Fitzgerald International* [2003] IRLR 756; *Private Medicine Intermediaries Ltd v Hodkinson* (UKEAT/0134/15/LA, 15 January 2016).

[176] *Shaw v CCL Ltd* [2008] IRLR 284; *Greenhof v Barnsley Metropolitan Council* [2006] IRLR 98. However, it is not always the case that an act of discriminatory conduct will constitute a breach of the implied term: *Shaw v CCL Ltd* [2008] IRLR 284; *Amnesty International v Ahmed* [2009] IRLR 884; and *Clements v Lloyds Banking plc* [2014] ICR D22.

[177] *Malik v BCCI* [1998] AC 20, 47G per Lord Steyn; *Buckland v Bournemouth University Higher Education Corp.* [2010] EWCA Civ 121, [2011] QB 323, 333C per Sedley LJ.

[178] *Tullett Prebon plc v BGC Brokers LP* [2011] IRLR 420, 423 per Lord Justice Kay; *Watson v University of Strathclyde* [2011] IRLR 458, 461 per Lady Smith.

[179] *Leeds Dental Team Ltd v Rose* [2014] IRLR 8; *Rawson v Robert Norman Associates Ltd* (UKEAT/0199/13/RN, 28 January 2014); and *Eminence Property Developments Ltd v Heaney* [2010] EWCA Civ 1168, [2011] 2 All ER (Comm) 223, 242d–e per Etherton LJ.

[180] *Hagen v ICI Chemicals and Polymers Ltd* [2002] IRLR 31, 39 per Elias J.

[181] *London Borough of Walham Forest v Omilaju* [2005] IRLR 35; *Kearns v Glencore UK Ltd* [2013] EWHC 3697 (QB); *Cook v MSHK Ltd and Ministry of Sound Recordings Ltd* [2009] IRLR 838, 846–7 per Rimer LJ.

[182] *Eastwood v Magnox Electric plc* [2005] 1 AC 503, 523G per Lord Nicholls.

[183] *James-Bowen v Commissioner of Police for the Metropolis* [2016] EWCA Civ 1217.

[184] *Singh v Reading Borough Council* [2013] 1 WLR 3052.

[185] *Tullett Prebon plc v BGC Brokers LP* [2011] IRLR 420.

[186] *Frith Accountants v Law* [2014] IRLR 510 (causing loss of meaningful status by discussing with the employee's son, without her knowledge, her performance and competence to do her job).

[187] *McClory v Post Office* [1993] 1 All ER 457; *Gogay v Hertfordshire County Council* [2000] IRLR 703.

[188] *Visa International Service Association v Paul* [2004] IRLR 42.

[189] *Eastwood v Magnox Electric plc* [2005] 1 AC 503; *Stevens v University of Birmingham* [2015] EWHC 2300 (QB). In *Stevens*, it was held that strict literal adherence to the express terms of the employer's contractual disciplinary procedure amounted to a breach of the implied term of mutual trust and confidence. Here, the breach consisted of the employer's refusal to allow an employee to have a companion of his choice present at an investigatory meeting into the employee's alleged misconduct. *Stevens* can be contrasted with *Chhabra v West London Mental Health NHS Trust* [2013] UKSC 80, [2014] ICR 194 and *Edwards v Chesterfield Royal Hospital NHS Foundation Trust* [2011] UKSC 58, [2012] 2 AC 22, where the failure to adhere to, or serious irregularities in the conduct of, a disciplinary procedure were held to constitute a breach of the implied term of mutual trust and confidence.

■ *Clark v Nomura International plc* [2000] IRLR 766, 774–5

Mr Justice Burton:

My conclusion is that the right test is one of irrationality or perversity (of which caprice or capriciousness would be a good example) ie that no reasonable employer would have exercised his discretion in this way . . . Such test of perversity or irrationality is not only one which is simple, or at any rate simpler, to understand and apply, but it is a familiar one, being that regularly applied in the . . . Administrative Court. In reaching its conclusion, what the court does is thus not to substitute its own view, but to ask the question whether any reasonable employer could have come to such a conclusion. Of course, if and when the court concludes that the employer was in breach of contract, then it will be necessary to reach a conclusion, on the balance of probabilities, as to what would have occurred had the employer complied with its contractual obligations, or, as Timothy Walker J put it in *Clark v BET plc* [1997] IRLR 348, assess, without unrealistic assumptions, what position the employee would have been in had the employer performed its obligation. That will involve the court in assessing the employee's bonus, on the basis of the evidence before it, and thus to that extent putting itself in the position of the employer; but it will only do it if it is first satisfied, on the higher test, not that the employer acted unreasonably, but that no reasonable employer would have reached the conclusion it did acting in accordance with its contractual obligations, and the assessment of the bonus then of course is by way of an award of damages.

Although the small print of the implied term was altered slightly in *Horkulak v Cantor Fitzgerald International*[199] to the effect that standards of arbitrariness were included alongside irrationality, perversity, and good faith, the decision of Lord Justice Mummery in *Keen v Commerzbank AG* illustrates how the standard of scrutiny of managerial conduct is pitched at a particularly forgiving threshold:

■ *Keen v Commerzbank AG* [2007] ICR 623, 632C–H

Lord Justice Mummery:

As Potter LJ said [in *Horkulak v Cantor Fitzgerald International*], the employee was entitled 'to a bona fide and rational exercise [by the employers] of their discretion as to whether or not to pay him a bonus and in what sum'. He made it clear that, although the contract did not contain any particular formula or point of reference for the calculation of the bonus, the obligation was to consider the question of bonus as a rational and bona fide exercise when taking into account the criteria adopted for the purpose of arriving at a decision. He also observed . . . that to do otherwise would be to 'fly in the face of the principles of trust and confidence which have been held to underpin the employment relationship'. In my judgment, the claim that the bonus pool decisions for 2003 and 2004 were irrational or perverse faces difficulties which [the employee] is unable to surmount. First and foremost, the bank has a very wide contractual discretion. [The employee] has to show that the discretion has been exercised irrationally. It cannot be said that the decisions of the bank on bonuses for 2003 and 2004 are irrational on their face. The burden of establishing that no rational bank in the City would have paid him a bonus of less than his line manager recommended is a very high one. It would require an overwhelming case to persuade the court to find that the level of a discretionary bonus payment was irrational or perverse in an area where so much must depend on the discretionary judgment of the bank in fluctuating market and labour conditions. Secondly, there is no independent evidence, expert or otherwise, lending any support to his claim of irrationality in the size of the bonus pools for the two years.

---

[199] [2004] EWCA Civ 1287, [2005] ICR 402.

The end result is that it is a formidable hurdle[200] for an employee to deploy the discretionary benefits term as a means of challenging an employer's exercise of discretion in relation to the non-payment of bonuses or other contractual benefits.[201] To that extent, the term amounts to no more than a modest constraint on the employer's discretion. Indeed, in certain circumstances, it may prove more fruitful for the employee to argue that the contractual term confers an *absolute entitlement to a bonus*, rather than one which is discretionary in nature.[202]

Having been initially confined to the control of decisions relating to express discretionary benefits, a kind of feedback loop between employment and commercial contract law[203] would have appeared to have spawned a much broader role for this implied term. Matters have now developed to such an extent that *any express contractual discretion* conferred in favour of an employer would seem to be regulated by an implied term heavily infused with public law principles.[204] In *Braganza v BP Shipping Ltd*,[205] the issue for the employer to decide was whether one of its employees had committed suicide when he mysteriously disappeared one night on board a vessel, which was his place of work. This was important, since his employment contract would pay out a death-in-service benefit if he had died because he had been lost overboard and drowned owing to an accident. However, if it was decided that he had committed suicide, then the death-in-service benefit would not pay out. In deciding that the employer had erred when it decided that the cause of death was suicide, the Supreme Court explained how an employer should approach the task of exercising an express contractual discretionary power or engaging in an express contractual decision-making process:

■ *Braganza v BP Shipping Ltd* [2015] UKSC 17, [2015] 1 WLR 1661, 1669C–74G

Lady Hale:

Contractual terms in which one party to the contract is given the power to exercise a discretion, or to form an opinion as to relevant facts, are extremely common. It is not for the courts to rewrite the parties' bargain for them, still less to substitute themselves for the contractually agreed decision-maker. Nevertheless, the party who is charged with making decisions which affect the rights of both parties to the contract has a clear conflict of interest. That conflict is heightened where there

---

[200] For example, see *Ridgway v JP Morgan Chase Bank National Association* [2007] EWHC 1325 (QB), [2007] All ER (D) 54 (June); *Humphreys v Norilsk Nickel International (UK) Ltd* [2010] IRLR 976. Breach of a 'reasonable expectation' of an employee will not necessarily constitute an example of irrationality: *IBM United Kingdom Holdings Ltd v Dalgleish* [2018] IRLR 4.

[201] See also *Mallone v BPB Industries Ltd* [2002] IRLR 452; *Khatri v Cooperative Centrale Raiffeisen-Boerenleenbank BA* [2010] EWCA Civ 397, [2010] IRLR 715. For a discussion of the possible policy reasons as to why such a low standard has been adopted, see D. Cabrelli, 'The Hierarchy of Differing Behavioural Standards of Review in Labour Law' (2011) 40 *Industrial Law Journal* 146, 153–4. See also C. Wynn-Evans, 'Discretionary Bonus Awards, UCTA and the Duty to Give Reasons' (2007) 36 *Industrial Law Journal* 207; D. Cabrelli, 'Discretion, Power and the Rationalisation of Implied Terms' (2007) 36 *Industrial Law Journal* 194, 201–3.

[202] For example, see *Small v Boots Co. plc* [2009] IRLR 328; *Dresdner Kleinwort Ltd v Attrill* [2013] IRLR 548. Cf. *Brogden v Investec Bank plc* [2017] IRLR 90, where the opposite situation was the case, i.e. the employee argued that the bonus was discretionary and subject to a rationality review, but this was rejected by the Court of Appeal.

[203] See *Socimer International Bank Ltd v Standard Bank London Ltd* [2008] EWCA Civ 116, and the discussion of the convergence between commercial contract and employment law in D. Brodie, 'Fair Dealing and the World of Work' (2014) 43 *Industrial Law Journal* 29, 40–3. See also Lady Justice Arden, 'Coming to Terms with Good Faith' (2013) 30 *Journal of Contract Law* 199.

[204] See the discussion in M. Freedland and N. Kountouris, 'Common Law and Voice' in A. Bogg and T. Novitz (eds), *Voices at Work* (Oxford, OUP, 2014) 352, 362 and *Paturel v DH Services (UK) Ltd* [2016] IRLR 286, 293 per Mr Justice Singh.   [205] [2015] UKSC 17, [2015] 1 WLR 1661.

is a significant imbalance of power between the contracting parties as there often will be in an employment contract. The courts have therefore sought to ensure that such contractual powers are not abused. They have done so by implying a term as to the manner in which such powers may be exercised, a term which may vary according to the terms of the contract and the context in which the decision-making power is given.

There is an obvious parallel between cases where a contract assigns a decision-making function to one of the parties and cases where a statute (or the royal prerogative) assigns a decision-making function to a public authority. In neither case is the court the primary decision-maker. The primary decision-maker is the contracting party or the public authority. It is right, therefore, that the standard of review generally adopted by the courts to the decisions of a contracting party should be no more demanding than the standard of review adopted in the judicial review of administrative action. The question is whether it should be any less demanding.

The decided cases reveal an understandable reluctance to adopt the fully developed rigour of the principles of judicial review of administrative action in a contractual context. But at the same time they have struggled to articulate precisely what the difference might be . . .

[The relevant authorities were] helpfully summarised by Rix LJ in *Socimer International Bank Ltd v Standard Bank London Ltd* [2008] Bus LR 1304. In his conclusion, at para 66, he substitutes the more modern term 'irrationality' for unreasonableness:

'It is plain from these authorities that a decision-maker's discretion will be limited, as a matter of necessary implication, by concepts of honesty, good faith, and genuineness, and the need for the absence of arbitrariness, capriciousness, perversity and irrationality. The concern is that the discretion should not be abused. Reasonableness and unreasonableness are also concepts deployed in this context, but only in a sense analogous to *Wednesbury* unreasonableness, not in the sense in which that expression is used when speaking of the duty to take reasonable care, or when otherwise deploying entirely objective criteria: as for instance when there might be an implication of a term requiring the fixing of a reasonable price, or a reasonable time. In the latter class of case, the concept of reasonableness is intended to be entirely mutual and thus guided by objective criteria . . . Laws LJ in the course of argument put the matter accurately, if I may respectfully agree, when he said that pursuant to the *Wednesbury* rationality test, the decision remains that of the decision-maker, whereas on entirely objective criteria of reasonableness the decision-maker becomes the court itself.'

The same point was made (albeit in a completely different context, and so *obiter*) by Lord Sumption JSC in *Hayes v Willoughby* [2013] 1 WLR 935, para 14:

'Rationality is not the same as reasonableness. Reasonableness is an external, objective standard applied to the *outcome* of a person's thoughts or intentions . . . A test of rationality, by comparison, applies a minimum objective standard to the relevant person's *mental processes*. It imports a requirement of good faith, a requirement that there should be some logical connection between the evidence and the ostensible reasons for the decision, and (which will usually amount to the same thing) an absence of arbitrariness, of capriciousness or of reasoning so outrageous in its defiance of logic as to be perverse.' (emphasis added)

. . . the test of the reasonableness of an administrative decision which was adopted by Lord Greene MR in *Associated Provincial Picture Houses Ltd v Wednesbury Corpn* [1948] 1 KB 223, 233–234 . . . has two limbs . . .

The first limb focuses on the decision-making process—whether the right matters have been taken into account in reaching the decision. The second focuses on its outcome—whether, even though the right things have been taken into account, the result is so outrageous that no reasonable decision-maker could have reached it. The latter is often used as a shorthand for the *Wednesbury* principle, but without necessarily excluding the former.

There are signs, therefore, that the contractual implied term is drawing closer and closer to the principles applicable in judicial review . . . If it is part of a rational decision-making process to exclude extraneous considerations, it is in my view also part of a rational decision-making process to take into account those considerations which are obviously relevant to the decision in question. It is of the essence of 'Wednesbury reasonableness' (or 'GCHQ rationality') review to consider the rationality of the decision-making process rather than to concentrate on the outcome. Concentrating on the outcome runs the risk that the court will substitute its own decision for that of the primary decision-maker.

It is clear, however, that unless the court can imply a term that the outcome be objectively reasonable—for example, a reasonable price or a reasonable term—the court will only imply a term that the decision-making process be lawful and rational in the public law sense, that the decision is made rationally (as well as in good faith) and consistently with its contractual purpose. For my part, I would include both limbs of the Wednesbury formulation in the rationality test. Indeed, I understand Lord Neuberger PSC (at para 103 of his judgment ... and I to be agreed as to the nature of the test.

But whatever term may be implied will depend on the terms and the context of the particular contract involved . . . it is unnecessary to reach a final conclusion on the precise extent to which an implied contractual term may differ from the principles applicable to judicial review of administrative action. Given that the question may arise in so many different contractual contexts, it may well be that no precise answer can be given. The particular context of this case is an employment contract, which, as Lord Hodge JSC explains, is of a different character from an ordinary commercial contract. Any decision-making function entrusted to the employer has to be exercised in accordance with the implied obligation of trust and confidence. This must be borne in mind in considering how the contractual decision-maker should approach the question of whether a person has committed suicide [in this particular case] . . . Employers can reasonably be expected to inform themselves of the principles which are relevant to the decisions which they have to make. Employment law is complicated and demanding in many legal systems, but employers are expected to know it. They can also reasonably be expected to know how they should approach making the important decisions which they are required or empowered to make under the terms of the employment contract. In my view, a decision that an employee has committed suicide is not a rational or reasonable decision, in the terms discussed above, unless the employer has had it clearly in mind that suicide is such an improbability that cogent evidence is required to form the positive opinion that it has taken place.

This extract from *Braganza* yields the proposition that the rationality test will apply to the employer's decision-making process *and* the product of that process, i.e. the decision itself. The onus will fall on the employer to demonstrate that both the process and outcome were rational. As such, if the employer is unable to lead evidence regarding how it reached its decision, that will generate problems, since the court will be unable to ascertain the basis on which the decision was made.[206] A finding of irrationality will likely follow.

What is somewhat unclear post-*Braganza* is whether there is an overlap between the implied term in play here and the implied term of mutual trust and confidence. In fact, in the extract above, at one point, Lady Hale makes the point that discretions conferred by an express term of the employment contract must be exercised in accordance with the implied term of mutual trust and confidence. Lord Hodge went even further and seemed to treat the implied term of mutual trust and confidence as the only regulatory device performing any role at all here.[207] This can be contrasted with Lord Neuberger's dissenting opinion where he questioned whether the implied term of mutual trust and confidence had any role to play at all in this context. His Lordship said: 'Once it is accepted that [the employer] had to carry out the investigation [into the employee's death] with 'honesty,

---

[206] *Hills v Niksun Inc* [2016] IRLR 715.   [207] [2015] UKSC 17, [2015] 1 WLR 1661, 1679C–H.

good faith and genuineness' and had to avoid 'arbitrariness, capriciousness, perversity and irrationality', I do not see what trust and confidence add[s].'[208] As such, whether the implied term embraced by the Supreme Court in *Braganza* is indeed the implied term of mutual trust and confidence or a much broader application of the discretionary benefits implied term remains unresolved.[209] An additional issue is whether both the *Braganza* implied term and the implied term of mutual trust and confidence are simply facets of a much broader implied term conferring a right to fair treatment.[210] Another possibility is that they will be replaced in time by an abstract common law 'implied term requiring respect for the dignity and autonomy of employees as people'.[211] At this stage, it is simply too early to tell.

Turning now to the anti-avoidance implied term, this is designed to protect the employee from a premature dismissal motivated by an intention on the part of the employer to avoid the payment of certain or contingent contractual benefits conferred by the employment contract. For example, in *Aspden v Webbs Poultry & Meat Group (Holdings) Ltd*,[212] it was held that the anti-avoidance implied term precluded the employer from dismissing (other than summarily dismissing for breach) the employee whilst he was incapacitated for work in order to defeat his contractual entitlement to income replacement benefits under the employers' permanent health insurance scheme, which was dependent upon the continuance of the employment relationship. Likewise, in *Hill v General Accident Fire & Life Assurance Corp. plc (No. 1)*,[213] the employee was made redundant four months short of qualifying for a long-term sickness benefit in terms of his contract of employment. It was held that this breached the anti-avoidance implied term since it was clear that the employee's redundancy was attributable to the employer's desire to avoid the operation of the benefits.[214] *ICTS (UK) Ltd v Visram*[215] is a similar case, in which the EAT ruled that the anti-avoidance implied term prevented the employer from dismissing an employee contractually entitled to long-term disability benefits for the reason of ill-health/capability.

There is a powerful argument that the anti-avoidance implied term should be extended so that it applies beyond the isolated example of dismissal. In such circumstances, the implied term would restrain the employer from exercising an express or implicit managerial power/prerogative in order to avoid an express contractual term conferring the making of certain or conditional payments to the employee.[216] However, such a development would result in overlap with the implied term of mutual trust and confidence, which is also concerned with regulating and controlling the arbitrary and capricious exercise of managerial power. In light of that point, it has been argued that the anti-avoidance term and the discretionary benefit term ought to be reconceptualized as manifestations of the wider implied term of mutual trust and confidence. Given the affinities between the three

---

[208] *Braganza v BP Shipping Ltd* [2015] UKSC 17, [2015] 1 WLR 1661, 1688G. See the discussion in W. Courtney, 'Reasonableness in Contractual Decision-Making' (2015) 131 *Law Quarterly Review* 552, 554.

[209] For example, in holding that the employer had not acted with rationality in fixing an employee's commission, this issue was not considered by the Court of Appeal in *Hills v Niksun Inc* [2016] IRLR 715. Neither was it addressed by Mr Justice Singh in *Paturel v DH Services (UK) Ltd* [2016] IRLR 286, where both the implied term of mutual trust and confidence and the rationality term were pleaded by the employee.

[210] See A. Sanders, 'Fairness in the Contract of Employment' (2017) 46 *Industrial Law Journal* 508.

[211] H. Collins and V. Mantouvalou, 'Human Rights and the Contract of Employment' in M. Freedland et al. (eds), *The Contract of Employment* (Oxford, OUP, 2016) 206.

[212] [1996] IRLR 521.   [213] 1999 SLT 1157, [1998] IRLR 641.

[214] See also *Jenvey v Australian Broadcasting Corp.* [2002] IRLR 520; *Takacs v Barclays Services Jersey Ltd* [2006] IRLR 877. Contrast these successful cases with *Lloyd v BCQ Ltd* [2013] 1 CMLR 41.

[215] (UKEAT/0344/15/LA, 26 July 2016).

[216] See *Takacs v Barclays Services Jersey Ltd* [2006] IRLR 877, 886 per Master Fontaine. Some cases are not always presented in terms of the anti-avoidance implied term, e.g. see *Locke v Candy and Candy Ltd* [2011] IRLR 163.

implied terms, there is much logic from a doctrinal and policy perspective in engineering a recalibration so that a single implied obligation emerges.[217]

Reflection points

1. In light of the source of the implied terms, do you believe that the list of employers' duties is closed?

2. Explore the relationship between the common law implied terms and statutory employment protection rights.

3. Which of the implied terms imposing duties on employers are the most significant in the common law of the contract of employment? Give reasons for your answer.

4. Do you agree that the anti-avoidance implied term and the discretionary benefits implied term can, and ought to, be reformulated as two expressions of the implied term of mutual trust and confidence? Give reasons for your answer.

 For additional reading on the duties of employers, visit the Online Resources for this book at www.oup.com/uk/cabrelli3e/

6.3 DUTIES OF EMPLOYEES

Our attention now turns to the common law implied terms that impress obligations on the employee. In much the same way as the employer's implied duties, the employee's implied duties pursue the policy objectives of mutuality/reciprocity, care and co-operation, and trust and confidence in the employment relationship. However, there is some departure from the employer's implied duties insofar as the central implied duty of fidelity, loyalty, and confidence to which employees are subject is concerned with the promotion of an additional policy goal, namely loyalty and freedom of economic activity/trade. See Figure 6.2 for a summary of the implied terms imposing duties on employees.

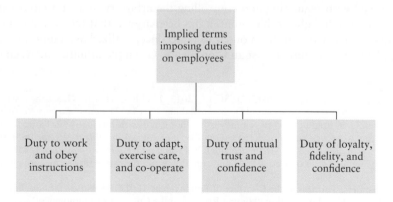

Figure 6.2 *Implied terms imposing duties on employees*

---

[217] For a wider discussion of this point, see D. Brodie, *The Employment Contract: Legal Principles, Drafting, and Interpretation* (Oxford, OUP, 2005) 188 at para 11.13; D. Cabrelli, 'Discretion, Power and the Rationalisation of Implied Terms' (2007) 36 *Industrial Law Journal* 194, 201–3; and M. Freedland, *The Personal Employment Contract* (Oxford, OUP, 2003) 119–27.

6.3.1 Implied term imposing duty on employee to work and obey instructions and orders

As the employer is under a duty to pay wages for work performed, the employee must perform the work in order to attract those wages: this is the mutuality/reciprocity policy goal manifested through the wage–work bargain. The employee owes the employer a duty of obedience.[218] For example, in *Pepper v Webb*,[219] a gardener steadfastly refused to comply with the reasonable instructions of his employer, made derogatory remarks, and walked away from his place of work. When the employee was dismissed without payment in lieu of notice, he claimed that he had been summarily dismissed in breach of contract, but the Court of Appeal ruled that his refusal to obey lawful and reasonable instructions amounted to a repudiatory breach of contract. *Pepper* can be contrasted with the similar case of *Wilson v Racher*,[220] which also concerned a gardener employee who had used obscene and insolent language to his employer. Here, it was held that the employee had not breached the duty of obedience since his employer had been provocative and made unjust accusations against him.

The point ought to be made that the instructions of the employer must be lawful and reasonable. Therefore, it was held that an employee was not in breach of duty where an employer was discourteous, ordered him to fly an aircraft contrary to regulations, and failed to keep the aircraft in a safe condition.[221] This can be contrasted with *Buckoke v Greater London Council*,[222] where firemen refused to follow their employer's order to drive fire engines through red lights in an emergency situation after taking necessary precautions. Notwithstanding the argument that the order would involve the employees in the commission of a statutory offence, the Court of Appeal held that their failure to follow such instructions constituted a breach of the duty of obedience. The Court of Appeal pointed to the proviso that the employees must take necessary precautions before crossing the red lights as the justification for its finding.

At this juncture, it is salutary to make a distinction between the implied term requiring the employee to obey a managerial order and the order itself:

P. Elias, B. Napier, and P. Wallington, *Labour Law: Cases and Materials* (London, Butterworths, 1980) 442–3

. . . there is an analytical point to be made at the outset; while the employer's power to command is derived from contract, it does not follow that his every order is itself a term of the contract. As Lord Denning said in the famous [*Secretary of State for Employment v ASLEF (No. 2)* [1972] 2 QB 455] case (concerning the legality of a work-to-rule on the railways), the contents of British Rail's Rule Book 'are only instructions to a man as to how he is to do his work'. Other imperatives—e.g. an oral direction to an employee to begin a particular piece of work—can be similarly understood. It is quite possible that the general power of command given to the employer by the implied term requiring obedience to his lawful and reasonable orders may be supplemented by other terms

---

[218] This duty pre-dates the contractual backcloth of the employment relationship and can be traced back to the nineteenth-century master and servant laws: *Turner v Mason* (1845) 14 M & W 112. See also S. Deakin and F. Wilkinson, *The Law of the Labour Market: Industrialization, Employment, and Legal Evolution* (Oxford, OUP, 2005) 61–2 and 103; M. Freedland and N. Kountouris, *The Legal Construction of Personal Work Relations* (Oxford, OUP, 2011) 188.

[219] [1969] 2 All ER 216, [1969] 1 WLR 514.   [220] [1974] ICR 428.

[221] *Donovan v Invicta Airlines* [1970] 1 Lloyd's Rep 486; cf. *Bouzourou v Ottoman Bank* [1930] AC 271 (PC) and *Ottoman Bank v Chakarion* [1930] AC 277.   [222] [1971] 2 All ER 254.

dealing with particular matters. Commonly, for example, a contract of employment will contain a mobility clause permitting an employer to direct the employee to work in a different location (e.g. *United Kingdom Atomic Energy Authority v Claydon* [1974] ICR 128) . . . [223]

Mobility clauses have been the subject of an abundance of case law.[224] Such clauses are express terms conferring a power on the employer to transfer the employee to another place of work. Whilst the employee is subject to the implied term demanding obedience to the employer's direction to relocate in accordance with such an express term, the implied term of mutual trust and confidence has been harnessed to confer a measure of protection to the employee. This delicate interplay between these two competing implied terms is channelled through the rule that a discretionary power conferred on an employer by a mobility clause must be exercised in a way that provides reasonable notice of transfer to the employee, that the employer has taken steps to reduce the effect of the move on the employees and offer relocation or other financial allowances.[225] A failure to do so will amount to a breach of the implied term of mutual trust and confidence by the employer. Finally, statutory employment rights in the context of 'whistleblowing', where the employee makes a protected disclosure, will impact on the extent to which an employee is bound to follow the employer's instructions.[226]

6.3.2 Implied term imposing duty on employee to adapt, exercise care, and co-operate

The policy objective of care and co-operation is reciprocal in orientation, and the judicial pursuit of that goal is instantiated by the imposition of duties of care on the employer and duties to adapt, co-operate, and exercise care on the employee. In this section, we are concerned with the latter. Turning first to the duty to adapt, the classic exposition of this duty is found in *Cresswell v Board of Inland Revenue*.[227] Here, clerical assistants and tax officers involved in the administration of the PAYE system resisted a changeover from the traditional manual method of operation to computerization. The Court of Appeal ruled that the alterations to the employees' tasks were insufficiently material to no longer constitute work that the employee had agreed to perform[228] and that they were subject to an implied term requiring them to adapt to new working patterns and methods introduced in the course of employment.[229]

Not only is there a duty to adapt, but the employee is also subject to a duty to exercise reasonable care and skill in the discharge of his/her duties. Therefore, where an employee lorry driver took his co-worker father as a mate and injured him whilst backing up the vehicle, it was held that the employee had breached the duty of care and was liable in damages to his employer in respect of sums the employer had paid out to the father in

---

[223] See also P. Elias, B. Napier, and P. Wallington, *Labour Law: Cases and Materials* (London, Butterworths, 1980) 449.

[224] *O'Brien v Associated Fire Alarms* [1969] 1 All ER 93; *Rank Xerox Ltd v Churchill* [1988] IRLR 280; and *White v Reflecting Roadstuds Ltd* [1991] IRLR 331.

[225] *United Bank v Akhtar* [1989] IRLR 507 and *Kellogg-Brown & Root (UK) Ltd v Fitton* (UKEAT/0205/16/BA, 21 November 2016).

[226] See sections 43A–K of the ERA.   [227] [1984] ICR 508, [1984] IRLR 190.

[228] Contrast this with *Bull v Nottinghamshire and City of Nottingham Fire and Rescue Authority* [2007] ICR 1631, where it was held that the changes required of the employees did not constitute work that the employees had agreed to perform. Here, firefighter employees were required to respond to emergency calls from members of the public reporting potentially life-threatening medical conditions in situations in which the firefighters were in a position to respond more promptly than an ambulance crew.

[229] [1984] ICR 508, 518H–519D per Walton J.

consequence of the employee's negligent driving.[230] Although a narrow interpretation of the employee's duty of care was drawn in a subsequent case,[231] the decision in *Lister* left open the possibility that employers or their insurers would sue their employees where the latter's negligence had resulted in third-party harm/losses for which the employer had been held vicariously liable. However, the insurance industry entered into a gentleman's agreement whereby it would not pursue its rights against negligent employees in such circumstances and the law was changed so that the employer was bound to take out compulsory insurance to cover such claims.[232] This accord is still in place. The employee's implied duty of care not only encompasses an obligation not to be negligent, but also includes an obligation to exercise reasonable care and skill in the completion of a pre-medical questionnaire.[233] Therefore, where the employer suffers loss as a result of careless statements made in such a questionnaire, the employee will be liable in damages.

Closely related to the duty to exercise reasonable care is the duty to co-operate. The leading authority for the duty to co-operate is *Secretary of State for Employment v ASLEF (No. 2)*.[234] Here, the Court of Appeal ruled that employees were in breach of duty when they engaged in a particular form of industrial action referred to as 'work-to-rule'. This entailed strict compliance with the rulebook of their employers with the objective of disrupting the employer's business. It was held that the unreasonable way in which the employees had performed their contractual obligations as a result of the work-to-rule programme constituted a breach of the contract of employment. If the Court had reached the opposite result, the persistence of such 'behaviour [would have] render[ed] the contract of employment dysfunctional'.[235] Subsequently, the decision in *ASLEF* was rationalized as establishing a proposition of law that an employee was under a duty to co-operate with the employer and that the motive of the employee in following orders should not be to unduly frustrate the employer's commercial objectives.

6.3.3 Implied term of mutual trust and confidence

The mutuality of the trust and confidence implied term is underscored by cases such as *Briscoe v Lubrizol Ltd*[236] and *RDF Media Group v Clements*.[237] These two[238] decisions remind us that employees are also bound by the obligations imposed by such a term. In *RDF Media Group*, a senior employee disclosed confidential information to the executives of a competing company about projects on which he was working for the employer. The employee also reached an informal understanding with the competitor that he would attempt to take some of those projects over if he were to take up employment with it. The employee also agreed to co-operate with the competitor in briefing the media so that the public perception of the dispute between the employee and the employer operated to press the employer into negotiating an early release for the employee from certain restrictive covenants in his service agreement and ancillary contractual documentation. The High Court ruled that these informal understandings and agreements between the employee and the competitor amounted to disloyalty on the part of the employee, constituting a

---

[230] *Lister v Romford Ice and Cold Storage Co. Ltd* [1957] AC 555. See also *Harmer v Cornelius* (1858) 5 CB (NS) 236; *Matthews v Kuwait Bechtel Corp.* [1959] 2 QB 57; and *Janata Bank v Ahmed* [1981] ICR 791.   [231] *Harvey v RG O'Dell Ltd* [1958] 1 All ER 657.

[232] See G. Gardiner, '*Lister v The Romford Ice and Cold Storage Company, Ltd*' (1959) 22 *Modern Law Review* 652, 653–5.

[233] *Cheltenham Borough Council v Laird* [2009] IRLR 621, 646 per Mr Justice Hamblen.

[234] [1972] 2 QB 455.

[235] H. Collins, 'The Contract of Employment in 3D' in D. Campbell, L. Mulcahy, and S. Wheeler (eds), *Changing Concepts of Contract* (Basingstoke, Palgrave MacMillan, 2013) 65, 82.

[236] [2002] IRLR 607.   [237] [2008] IRLR 207.

[238] See also *Tubbenden Primary School v Sylvester* [2012] ICR D29; *Thomson Ecology Ltd v APEM Ltd* [2014] IRLR 184.

breach of the implied term of mutual trust and confidence and/or the implied duty of loyalty and fidelity owed to the employer.

RDF Media Group was also an authority for the proposition that an employee was not entitled to claim damages or statutory constructive dismissal on the basis of the employer's repudiatory breach of the implied term of mutual trust and confidence if the employee him/herself was guilty of an anterior repudiatory breach of the implied term of mutual trust and confidence. Whilst this position may seem equitable, it was doubtful whether it was doctrinally sound or desirable from a policy perspective.[239] It would appear to suggest that an employer is given *carte blanche* to mistreat an employee once the employee has committed a repudiatory act of misconduct, free from the risk that the employee leaves and successfully claims damages at common law or as an unfair constructive dismissal in violation of Part X of the ERA:

■ *SG & R Valuation Service Co. v Boudrais and others* [2008] EWHC 1340 (QB) at para 28

> *Cranston J:*
>
> I would be concerned about situations where, if the employee was in repudiatory breach, the employer could take whatever repudiatory breach it wished and the employe[e] could not accept the employe[r]'s repudiation as bringing the employment relationship to an end. That could lead to some very undesirable scenarios in the employment relationship.[240]

In fact, in the decision of the Inner House of the Court of Session in *McNeill v Aberdeen City Council (No. 2)*,[241] the approach in *RDF Media Group* was rejected. It was held that Scots law does not accept the rule that a prior repudiatory breach of the implied term of mutual trust and confidence by the employee will prevent him/her from claiming damages or constructive dismissal where the employer has subsequently breached the same implied term. The position in English law would now appear to be identical to Scots law as a result of the decision of the EAT in *Atkinson v Community Gateway Association*.[242] In *Atkinson*, it was held that an employee was entitled to accept the employer's repudiatory breach and terminate the employment contract even though the employee himself was in anterior repudiatory breach. As such, this element of the decision in *RDF Media Group* must now be suspect.

Finally, we consider the content and operation of the implied term of mutual trust and confidence prior to the formation, and in the dying stages, of the employment relationship. First, it has been held that an employee may be subject to obligations of trust and confidence prior to the actual commencement of employment. For example, in *Tullett Prebon plc v BGC Brokers LP*,[243] whilst employed by one set of brokers, the employees signed 'forward contracts' with a competing firm of brokers. These contracts enjoined the employees to take up employment with the competing firm in the future. It was held

---

[239] See H. Collins, 'Constructive Dismissal and the West Lothian Question: *Aberdeen City Council v McNeill*' (2011) 40 *Industrial Law Journal* 439, who doubted the approach adopted in *RDF Media Group*.

[240] Sourced from BAILII available at http://www.bailii.org/cgi-bin/markup.cgi?doc=/ew/cases/EWHC/QB/2008/1340.html&query=boudrais&method=boolean (last visited 14 November 2017). For similar sentiments, see also *Wilfe Gilbert (Staffs) Ltd v Bunn* (UKEAT/0547/07/ZT, 17 June 2008) at paras 39–40 per HHJ Burke QC; *Tullett Prebon plc v BGC Brokers LP* [2010] IRLR 648, 676 per Jack J; and *Brandeaux Advisers (UK) Ltd and others v Chadwick* [2011] IRLR 224, 231 per Jack J.

[241] [2015] ICR 27. See D. Brodie, 'Common Law Remedies and Relational Contracting: *McNeil v Aberdeen CC (No. 2)* [2013] CSIH 102' (2014) 43 *Industrial Law Journal* 170.

[242] [2015] ICR 1.   [243] [2011] IRLR 420.

that the employees were subject to obligations of trust and confidence to the competing firm in terms of these forward agreements, despite the fact that they were not employment contracts and that the employees continued to owe a duty of trust and confidence to their current employer.[244] The Court of Appeal held that there was no reason why concurrent trust and confidence obligations could not arise and that this analysis could proceed on the basis that the existence of one attenuated the content and scope of the other. Likewise, it has been held that, during a period of garden leave, the operation of the implied terms of trust and confidence and fidelity *may*[245] similarly be attenuated.[246] This suggests that the implied terms must co-exist with each other in harmony with their content carved by reference to one another. However, exactly where the carving knife is applied to establish the boundaries of the content of each of the implied terms is not clear from the judicial pronouncements in *Tullett Prebon*.

6.3.4 Implied term of loyalty, fidelity, and confidence

Although overshadowed, overtaken, and to some extent usurped by the recent growth in importance of the implied term of mutual trust and confidence,[247] it is no exaggeration to say that the employee's duty of loyalty, fidelity, and confidence[248] remains central to the judicial construction of the contract of employment.[249] It represents the primary means by which the policy goals of loyalty and freedom of economic activity are pursued. Of course, the underlying policy objective that employees exhibit loyalty to their employers is in direct conflict with the employer's requirement to respect the right of their employees to engage freely in competitive conduct.[250] Therefore, the content of the duty of loyalty and fidelity as elaborated through the case law amounts to the judicial articulation of how these two opposing policies ought to be reconciled. As will become clear, that process does not result in a uniform degree of content which is applicable to all classes of employees; rather, the duty is self-modulating, to the extent that a more heightened level of obligation attaches to employees in more senior, professional, or managerial roles.

[244] If one treats the 'forward contract' in *Tullett Prebon* as a species of commercial contract, it is not wholly easy to reconcile this decision with the decisions in *Bedfordshire County Council v Fitzpatrick Contractors Ltd* (1998) 62 ConLR 64 and *Jani-King (GB) Ltd v Pula Enterprises Ltd* [2007] EWHC 2433 (QB), [2008] 1 All ER (Comm) 451 that the implied term of mutual trust and confidence does not arise in the context of a commercial contract. However, Lord Justice Kay in *Tullett Prebon* dismissed the contention that the forward contract was a commercial contract as a 'sterile argument' and held that the forward contract was 'more akin to a contract of employment than to a purely commercial agreement': [2011] IRLR 420, 425–6.

[245] *Imam-Siddique v BlueBay Asset Management (Services) Ltd* [2013] IRLR 344.

[246] *Balston v Headline Filters Ltd* [1987] FSR 330; *RDF Media Group v Clements* [2008] IRLR 207, 218 per Bernard Livesey QC; and *Tullett Prebon plc v BGC Brokers LP* [2011] IRLR 420, 425 per Lord Justice Kay. Further, where an employee is not in breach of contract and is contractually obliged to act in the best interests of his/her employer, the employee's duty of trust and confidence cannot be stretched so far as to impose an obligation to waive bonus payments to which the employee is contractually entitled: *Fish v Dresdner Kleinwort Ltd* [2009] IRLR 1035.

[247] For example, rather than classifying the conduct of the employee as a repudiatory breach of the duty of loyalty and fidelity in *RDF Media Group v Clements* [2008] IRLR 207, the High Court couched matters in terms of a repudiatory breach of the implied term of mutual trust and confidence. See also D. Brodie, *The Employment Contract: Legal Principles, Drafting, and Interpretation* (Oxford, OUP, 2005) 117–18.

[248] The actual terminology is often ill-defined, with terms such as 'fidelity', 'loyalty', 'good faith', 'confidence', and 'faithfulness' being used interchangeably: M. Freedland, *The Personal Employment Contract* (Oxford, OUP, 2003) 173.

[249] Like the employee's duty of obedience, it is a duty with a venerable pedigree, pre-dating the obligations of care, co-operation and mutual trust, and confidence: M. Freedland and N. Kountouris, *The Legal Construction of Personal Work Relations* (Oxford, OUP, 2011) 191.

[250] M. Freedland, *The Personal Employment Contract* (Oxford, OUP, 2003) 171.

Figure 6.3 *Content of the implied duty of loyalty, fidelity, and confidence*

Stripped to its core, the duty encompasses an obligation to provide faithful service. For example, in the classic exposition of the employee's obligation in *Robb v Green*,[251] the Court of Appeal held that an employee was in breach of the duty 'to serve his master with good faith and fidelity'[252] when he surreptitiously copied customer lists from his employer's order book with the intention of using them in his own business. This primary obligation is channelled through a number of conduits, which can be categorized as sub-duties in the terms set out in Figure 6.3.

The employee's duty to account and not to make a secret profit out of his/her trust can be dealt with relatively briefly. In *Reading v Attorney-General*,[253] a sergeant in the British Army facilitated the smuggling of illicit spirits by accompanying civilian lorries whilst on duty, for which services he earned £20,000. When found in possession of such sums of money, he was court-martialled, convicted of conduct prejudicial to military discipline, and imprisoned. On release from prison, he sought to recover the money, but the House of Lords held that he was not entitled to recover it on the ground that he had a duty to account for secret profits made at the expense of his employer.

As for the employee's obligation not to compete with the employer, *Hivac v Park Royal Scientific Instruments*[254] demonstrates the breadth of this duty. The case concerned five highly skilled employees who assembled valves for incorporation into hearing aids. They worked for a company in direct competition with their employer on their day off on Sundays, without the knowledge or consent of their employer. No confidential information of the employer was disclosed, applied, or exploited as part of that process. It had been recognized prior to *Hivac* that an employee's duty of loyalty and fidelity included an obligation not to work for competitors whilst the employee was contractually engaged to perform work for the employer.[255] In *Hivac*, the question was whether that obligation was sufficiently broad to preclude employees from working for competitors in their own spare time. One might take the view that what the employees did in their own spare time was of no concern to their employer, provided that the employees discharged their contractual duties as required. However, the Court of Appeal decided that the employees were in breach of duty since what they were doing had the capacity to inflict great harm on the commercial interests of the employer. The requirement that the employee's spare time activities must contribute substantially to the detriment of the employer's

[251] (1895) 2 QB 315.   [252] *ibid.*, 320 per Lord Justice Smith.
[253] [1951] AC 507. See also *Attorney General v Blake* [1998] 2 WLR 805, 814 per Lord Woolf MR.
[254] [1946] Ch 169.   [255] *Wessex Dairies Ltd v Smith* [1935] 2 KB 80.

commercial interests is crucial. Thus, in *Nova Plastics Ltd v Froggett*,[256] an employee was held not to be in breach of duty when he worked as an 'odd job man' in his spare time for a rival company.

It should be stressed that the employee's obligation not to compete will apply to enable the employer to hold the employee (who is seeking to leave to work for a third-party competitor) to a lengthy notice period. In *Elsevier Ltd v Munro*,[257] an employee was seeking to move to a competing employer for the outstanding portion of his 12-month notice period. Since the employer could prove that the employee's breach of contract would cause immeasurable damage to its commercial interests, the High Court was prepared to grant a final injunction as a remedy.

In *Hivac* and *Nova Plastics*, the employees concerned were actually employed by the respective employers. However, once they become former employees, such competition does not constitute a breach of duty, since those employees are free to engage in competitive activities. A substantial number of the cases relating to the employee's obligation not to compete have arisen in the context of employees who are on the verge of leaving the employment of the employer to (a) take up a position with a competing employer or (b) set up their own business which will compete with the employer. This is a particularly fraught area, since in recognition of the public interest present in an employee's freedom to trade the law is anxious to safeguard the employee's legitimate ability to take the knowledge, information, and skill he/she has developed and acquired during the course of his/her employment and apply it for his/her own benefit once he/she has left. The employee is also free to compete with his/her former employer once the employment relationship has terminated. On the other hand, the employer has a legitimate expectation that the law will intervene to protect its commercial interests where the employee engages in wrongful conduct prior to leaving employment. Generally speaking, the law strikes a balance between pre-termination conduct on the part of the employee which can be described as:

- preparatory to future competition; or
- competitive activity itself.

In the latter case, the employee will be in breach of duty, whereas in the former situation, the employee will *generally* be deemed not to be in breach. For example, in *Laughton & Hawley v Bapp Industrial Supplies Ltd*,[258] it was held that employees merely had an intention to compete and were not in breach of duty when, prior to termination, they wrote to ten of their employer's suppliers requesting details of their products and informing them that they intended to start up in business on their own subsequent to the termination of their employment. This can be contrasted with *Lancashire Fire Ltd v SA Lyons Co. Ltd*,[259] where an employee was ruled to be in breach[260] where he set up a business, acquired items and equipment, and rented premises for that business prior to leaving employment, the business being the manufacture of components for would-be clients of his employer. Likewise, in *Gamatronic (UK) Ltd v Hamilton*,[261] where the employees had shown an irrevocable intention to set up a competing business by engaging

---

[256] [1982] IRLR 146.   [257] [2014] IRLR 766.   [258] [1986] ICR 634.

[259] [1997] IRLR 113. See *Tither Barn v Hubbard* (EAT/532/89, Wood J, unreported, 7 November 1991) where it was held that an employee did not breach the duty not to compete where he informed another employee of his plans to do so and offered him a potential job in a competitor firm in the future. Cf. *Thomson Ecology Ltd v APEM Ltd* [2014] IRLR 184.

[260] See also *Reuse Collections Ltd v Sendall* [2015] IRLR 2015 where an employee did not actually engage in competitive activity until his employment contract had terminated. However, in the High Court it was held that he was nonetheless in breach of the implied term, since pre-termination he had incorporated a competing company and attempted to solicit customers and suppliers of his employer. Likewise, see *Energy Renewals Ltd v Borg* [2014] IRLR 713.   [261] [2016] EWHC 2225 (QB).

in the following pre-termination activities: involving themselves in operational matters for the new competing company, acquiring shares in nominee companies, approaching potential customers of the business, and holding themselves out as directors of the company. Ultimately, as decided by the Court of Appeal in *Helmet Integrated Systems Ltd v Tunnard*,[262] the touchstone for what, on the one hand, is permissible preparatory activity and what, on the other hand, is impermissible conduct, is wholly dependent on the nature of the employee's obligations and his/her responsibilities and job. Therefore, everything turns on the facts of each particular case. Having said that, there have recently been some indications that the judiciary have tightened up this area of law to narrow the circumstances in which the employee will be merely engaged in preparatory activity and not in breach of duty. In *QBE Management Services (UK) Ltd v Dymoke*,[263] Haddon-Cove J ruled that directors and senior employees ought to disclose any action taken by others that would lead to competitive activity, and any action of their own, as soon as the irrevocable intention to compete is formed, unless they resign immediately. The extent to which this heralds a new approach on the part of the judiciary remains open to question and we will need to await guidance at an appellate level.

We now turn to the question of whether a sub-duty exists imposing an obligation on the employee to disclose his/her own wrongdoing and that of his/her fellow employees. The starting point for the discussion is the decision of the House of Lords in *Bell v Lever Brothers*[264] and the Court of Appeal in *Sybron Corp. v Rochem Ltd*.[265] Both of these cases expounded a general rule precluding a general duty to report one's own misconduct or that of a fellow employee. However, in *Sybron Corp.*, relying on the authority of *Swain v West (Butchers) Ltd*,[266] Lord Justice Stephenson specifically recognized that a duty to disclose the wrongdoing of fellow employees could arise in a particular case depending on the contract of employment of the particular employee and the whole circumstances of the case. In *Sybron*, the employee was in a senior position in the hierarchy of the employer with an obligation to produce monthly reports pertaining to a geographical sector placed under his supervision. It was ruled that this was relevant to subject him to a duty to report the wrongdoing of his fellow employees superior or subordinate to him in the chain of command. This was despite the fact that it would inevitably reveal the employee's own misconduct. *Sybron* can be contrasted with the approach in *Lonmar Global Risks v West*,[267] where Hickinbottom J held that there is no implied duty compelling an employee to disclose to his/her employer the fact that fellow employees are being recruited by a competitor. However, Hickinbottom J did say that where the facts and circumstances of the case were such that the status of the employee concerned was of a fiduciary nature, a fiduciary obligation would arise duly impressing such a duty on the employee to report.[268] A similar approach was adopted by Lord Justice Lewison in the decision of the Court of Appeal in *Ranson v Customer Systems plc*.[269] We can see that it is somewhat difficult to reconcile *Sybron* with *Lonmar* and *Ranson* given that *Sybron* suggests that even non-fiduciary employees are subject to an obligation to disclose the wrongdoing of colleagues.

Turning now to the issue of confessing to one's own misconduct, notwithstanding the ostensibly unequivocal language employed by Lord Atkin in *Bell*[270] against the

---

[262] [2007] IRLR 126. For a similar decision, see *Imam-Siddique v BlueBay Asset Management (Services) Ltd* [2013] IRLR 344.

[263] [2012] IRLR 458. Cf. *MPT Group Ltd v Peel* [2017] EWHC 1222 (Ch).

[264] [1932] AC 161.

[265] [1983] ICR 801. See M. Freedland, 'High Trust, Pensions, and the Contract of Employment' (1984) 13 *Industrial Law Journal* 25.   [266] [1936] 3 All ER 261.

[267] [2011] IRLR 138, 156.

[268] *Lonmar Global Risks v West* [2011] IRLR 138, 156–7 per Hickinbottom J; *Kynixa Ltd v Hynes* [2008] EWHC 1495.

[269] [2012] IRLR 769.   [270] [1932] AC 161.

proposition that a duty to report one's own misconduct could ever be implied in the case of an employee, in *Item Software (UK) Ltd v Fassihi*[271] Lady Justice Arden in the Court of Appeal adopted the view that Lord Atkin had indeed considered that the existence of a duty of disclosure would depend to some extent on the circumstances.[272] Lady Justice Arden suggested that a director or senior employee below the level of the board of directors may, in appropriate circumstances, be bound by a duty to disclose his/her wrongdoing.[273] This formulation chimes with that of Lord Justice Lewison in the decision of the Court of Appeal in *Ranson v Customer Systems plc*,[274] who opined that an employee may be subject to a duty to disclose his/her own wrongdoing and that whether such a duty is implied is dependent on the terms of his/her employment contract.[275] However, what was left unresolved by Lady Justice Arden's judgment in *Item Software* was the precise set of circumstances that give rise to such a duty of disclosure. Lord Justice Lewison in *Ranson v Customer Systems plc* provided some guidance on this point:

■ *Ranson v Customer Systems plc* [2012] EWCA Civ 841, paras 55–56

Lewison LJ:

That is not to say that an employee can never have an obligation to disclose his own wrongdoing; but any such obligation must arise out of the terms of his contract of employment . . . In *Swain v West (Butchers) Ltd* [1936] 3 All ER 261 the employee manager had a contractual obligation 'to promote, develop and extend the interests of the company.' This contractual obligation required him to disclose misconduct by the managing director. In *QBE Management Services (UK) Ltd v Dymoke* . . . [2012] IRLR 458 Mr Dymoke's contract contained obligations to use his best endeavours to promote and protect the interests of his employer, and a further obligation that he would 'fully and properly disclose to the Board . . . all of the affairs of the Group of which he is aware.' These obligations meant that Mr Dymoke had a duty to disclose his own activities in soliciting fellow employees to defect *en masse*, his misuse of confidential material and solicitation of his employer's customers while he was still employed . . . On the other hand in *Helmet Integrated Systems Ltd v Tunnard*, where Mr Tunnard's contract contained an obligation 'to advise on competitor activity and pricing structures', Mr Tunnard was not in breach by developing his own product (in his own time) which was intended to be a direct competitor of his employer's product, and in not disclosing his activities to his employers . . .[276]

---

[271] [2005] ICR 450.

[272] *ibid.*, 465G–466B. On whether that approach is convincing, see A. Berg, 'Fiduciary Duties: A Director's Duty to Disclose His Own Misconduct' (2005) 121 *Law Quarterly Review* 213; L. Ho and P. Lee, 'A Director's Duty to Confess: A Matter of Good Faith?' (2007) 66 *Cambridge Law Journal* 348, 352–3.

[273] However, doubt has been cast on whether this proposition forms part of Scots law: *Commonwealth Oil & Gas Ltd v Baxter* 2009 SC 156, 162 at para 14 per Lord President Hamilton and 180 at para 82 per Lord Nimmo Smith. [274] [2012] IRLR 769.

[275] Contrast this extract with the unequivocal statement by the Honourable Mr Justice Mitting sitting in the EAT in *The Basildon Academies v Amadi* (UKEAT/0342/14/RN, 27 February 2015) at paras 20–1, to the following effect: '[I]n no case of which I am aware . . . has the proposition ever been advanced, let alone held to be good law, that an employee must disclose to his employer, in the absence of an express contractual term requiring him to do so, an allegation however ill-founded of impropriety against him . . . In my judgment it is clearly not the law that an employee is under such an implied obligation.' However, *Ranson* was not cited before the EAT in *Amadi*, so it is arguable that the decision was decided *per incuriam*.

[276] Sourced from BAILII available at http://www.bailii.org/cgi-bin/markup.cgi?doc=/ew/cases/EWCA/Civ/2012/841.html&query=Customer+and+Systems+and+Plc+and+v+and+Ranson&method=boolean (last visited 13 November 2017).

What is clear from the judgments in *Item Software* and *Ranson* is that employees, generally, will not be treated as fiduciaries:

■ *Nottingham University v Fishel* [2000] ICR 1462, 1491A–1493H

Elias J: Employees as fiduciaries . . .

[An employee's] fiduciary obligations are limited and arise out of the particular circumstances, namely that he is put in a position where he is obliged to account to me for the change he has received. In that case the obligation arises out of the employment relationship but it is not inherent in the nature of the relationship itself . . . the essence of the employment relationship is not typically fiduciary at all. Its purpose is not to place the employee in a position where he is obliged to pursue his employer's interests at the expense of his own. The relationship is a contractual one and the powers imposed on the employee are conferred by the employer himself. The employee's freedom of action is regulated by the contract, the scope of his powers is determined by the terms (express or implied) of the contract, and as a consequence the employer can exercise (or at least he can place himself in a position where he has the opportunity to exercise) considerable control over the employee's decision making powers. This is not to say that fiduciary duties cannot arise out of the employment relationship itself. But they arise not as a result of the mere fact that there is an employment relationship. Rather they result from the fact that within a particular contractual relationship there are specific contractual obligations which the employee has undertaken which have placed him in a situation where equity imposes these rigorous duties in addition to the contractual obligations. Where this occurs, the scope of the fiduciary obligations both arises out of, and is circumscribed by, the contractual terms; it is circumscribed because equity cannot alter the terms of the contract validly undertaken . . . The problem of identifying the scope of any fiduciary duties arising out of the relationship is particularly acute in the case of employees. This is because of the use of potentially ambiguous terminology in describing an employee's obligations, which use may prove a trap for the unwary. There are many cases which have recognised the existence of the employee's duty of good faith, or loyalty, or the mutual duty of trust and confidence—concepts which tend to shade into one another . . . Accordingly, in analysing the employment cases in this field, care must be taken not automatically to equate the duties of good faith and loyalty, or trust and confidence, with fiduciary obligations.[277] Very often in such cases the court has simply been concerned with the question whether the employee's conduct has been such as to justify summary dismissal, and there has been no need to decide whether the duties infringed, properly analysed, are contractual or fiduciary obligations. As a consequence, the two are sometimes wrongly treated as identical: see *Neary v. Dean of Westminster* [1999] I.R.L.R. 288, 290 where the mutual duty of trust and confidence was described as constituting a 'fiduciary relationship.' Accordingly, in determining whether a fiduciary relationship arises in the context of an employment relationship, it is necessary to identify with care the particular duties undertaken by the employee, and to ask whether in all the circumstances he has placed himself in a position where he must act solely in the interests of his employer. It is only once those duties have been identified that it is possible to determine whether any fiduciary duty has been breached . . . It follows that fiduciary duties may be engaged in respect of only part of the employment relationship, as was recognised by Lord Wilberforce, giving judgment for the Privy Council in *New Zealand Netherlands Society 'Oranje' Inc. v. Kuys* [1973] 1 W.L.R. 1126, 1130c . . .

---

[277] On this point, consider the debate between Flannigan and Frazer in R. Flannigan, 'The Fiduciary Duty of Fidelity' (2008) 124 *Law Quarterly Review* 274; R. Flannigan, 'The Fiduciary Duty of Departing Employees' (2008) 14 *Canadian Labour & Employment Law Journal* 357; and A. Fraser, 'The Employee's Contractual Duty of Fidelity' (2015) 131 *Law Quarterly Review* 53.

The exposition of the law in the *Nottingham* extract has been referred to as 'illuminating',[278] 'authoritative',[279] 'masterly',[280] and the 'leading authority'.[281] The fundamental point that an employee is not generally to be treated as a fiduciary qua employee[282] cannot be stressed highly enough—for if it were otherwise and the employment relationship fell within the class of relationships automatically considered to be fiduciary in character, this would have dramatic implications for the position of employees. Leaving aside whether it would be possible for the employee and employer to 'contract out' of such fiduciary obligations,[283] it is suggested that the implications would be four-fold.

(1) Like all other fiduciary offices, the employee would be under a 'no-conflict' duty, which would require him/her to subordinate his/her own personal or commercial interests to those of the employer.

(2) Although the employee's fiduciary obligations would be carved by reference to his/her implied and express contractual obligations, unlike some of the latter duties, the former duties would survive the termination of the contract of employment.

(3) The policy goal that the employee should enjoy freedom of activity, which we considered earlier, would be radically undermined. By requiring the employee to resist the temptation to pursue certain interests or opportunities where these conflict with the interests of the employer, the scope of the employee's freedom to trade would be circumscribed.

(4) Finally, and most importantly, any breach of the employee's fiduciary obligations would give rise to a wider range of remedies, including restitutionary relief. As such, the employer would not be required to prove it suffered loss flowing from the breach of fiduciary duty; instead, it would be entitled to proprietary and personal gain-based damages, an accounting of profits,[284] and restitution generally.

As noted in the *Nottingham* extract, the touchstone of whether an employee is a fiduciary thus depends on 'the particular duties undertaken by the employee, and [whether] he has placed himself in a position where he must act solely in the interests of his employer'. If the employee is in such a position, equity will operate to impose the more rigorous fiduciary obligations upon the employee in addition to his/her implied contractual obligations.

---

[278] *PMC Holdings Ltd v Smith* [2002] All ER (D) 186 (April) at para 5 per Burton J.

[279] *Helmet Integrated Systems Ltd v Tunnard* [2007] IRLR 126, 130 per Moses LJ; see also *Caterpillar Logistics Services (UK) Ltd v de Crean* [2012] EWCA Civ 156 at paras 58–59 per Stanley Burnton LJ. For discussion, see L. Clarke, 'Mutual Trust and Confidence, Fiduciary Relationships and Duty of Disclosure' (1999) 30 *Industrial Law Journal* 348; V Simms, 'Is Employment a Fiduciary Relationship' (2001) 30 *Industrial Law Journal* 101; and D. Brodie, 'The Employment Relationship and Fiduciary Obligations' (2013) 16 *Edinburgh Law Review* 198.

[280] *Ranson v Customer Systems plc* [2012] IRLR 769.

[281] *Samsung Semiconductor Europe Ltd v Docherty* 2012 SLT 806, 811–12 per Lord Glennie; see also *Fish v Dresdner Kleinwort Ltd* [2009] IRLR 1035, 1039–40 per Mr Justice Jack.

[282] For a discussion examining whether there is scope *for the employer to be treated as a fiduciary of the employee*, see J. Murray, 'Conceptualising the Employer as Fiduciary: Mission Impossible?' in A. Bogg, C. Costello, A.C.L. Davies, and J. Prassl (eds), *The Autonomy of Labour Law* (Oxford, Hart Publishing, 2015) 337.

[283] The authorities are divided on the ability of the parties to oust or modify fiduciary obligations in contract. For example, cf. *Kelly v Cooper* [1993] AC 205, 213H–214B per Lord Browne-Wilkinson; *New Zealand Netherlands Society 'Oranje' Incorporated v Kuys* [1973] 1 WLR 1126, 1131–2 per Lord Wilberforce; and *Henderson v Merrett Syndicates Ltd* [1995] 2 AC 145, 206B–D per Lord Browne-Wilkinson with *Re Goldcorp Exchange* [1995] 1 AC 74, 98E per Lord Mustill; and J. Getzler, 'Excluding Fiduciary Duties: The Problems of Investment Banks' (2008) 125 *Law Quarterly Review* 15.

[284] See *One Step (Support) Ltd v Morris-Garner* [2016] IRLR 435. However, this will not cover the recovery of the wrongdoing employee's salary or wages, since this constitutes remuneration for work done, rather than profit: *Milanese v Leyton Orient FC Ltd* [2016] IRLR 601.

For example, amongst other obligations, the Court of Appeal has ruled that the common law will impose a fiduciary duty on the employee not to orchestrate a team move to a competitor of the employer, which the courts will police by a 'springboard' injunction.[285] In most of the cases in which an employee has been treated as a fiduciary, that individual has been in a senior or managerial position or has had a special skill, role, status, expertise, or set of qualities.[286] More often than not, the employer has reposed trust, confidence, and reliance in the employee who has used his/her position as an employee to further his/her own interests, obtained an advantage by virtue of his/her position as an employee, or retained a profit or otherwise kept money, in circumstances which put the employee in breach of his/her contract of employment.[287] In such cases, it has been felt appropriate to impose fiduciary responsibility on the employee. In fact, Brodie has addressed whether senior staff who are not treated by the common law as fiduciaries should nonetheless be subject to a heightened set of implied contractual obligations. Consider the following extract:

■ D. Brodie, 'Fair Dealing and the World of Work' (2014) 43 *Industrial Law Journal* 29, 32

> . . . whilst it would be over simplistic to say that the more senior an employee, the greater the degree of loyalty and diligence required of him, the scope of the duty imposed on someone at high managerial level in a multimillion pound business will involve a heavy burden not to do anything which might result in damage to the interests of that business . . . a senior manager who became aware of a competitive threat to an aspect of the business for which he is responsible would normally come under such a duty, whereas a junior employee without such responsibility would not. The fact that good faith has been placed at the core of the employment relationship has led to the obligations assumed by senior employees moving closer to those owed by fiduciaries.

Finally, we turn to the component of the implied duty of fidelity and loyalty which obliges the employee not to use or disclose the confidential information of the employer. In this context, the balance between the policy goals of loyalty and freedom of economic activity is struck by the common law in such a way that the employer is entitled to be protected from the unwarranted exploitation of its trade secrets and confidential information whilst recognizing that an ex-employee should not be prevented from using the skills and expertise earned over the period of his/her employment, or confidential information or materials he/she can recall from his/her time as an employee. Ultimately, the law achieves this by preventing the employee from using, disclosing, or exploiting the employer's confidential information and trade secrets prior, and subsequent to, the termination of the employment contract. However, the content and scope of the duty is wider during the former period than the latter:

---

[285] *Willis Ltd v Jardine Lloyd Thomson Group plc* [2015] IRLR 844 and *Dorma UK Ltd v Bateman* [2016] IRLR 616.

[286] For example, see *Shepherds Investments Ltd v Walters* [2007] IRLR 110; *Crowson Fabrics Ltd v Rider* [2008] IRLR 288; *Samsung Semiconductor Europe Ltd v Docherty* 2012 SLT 806; *AAH Pharmaceuticals Ltd v Birdi* [2011] EWHC 1625 (QB), [2011] All ER (D) 205 (June); and *Keown v Nahoor* [2015] EWHC 3418 (Ch) (in-house accountant). However, see *Threlfall v ECD Insight Ltd* [2013] IRLR 185 where the employee was a member of the senior management of the employer, but was held not to be a fiduciary.

[287] *Threlfall v ECD Insight Ltd* [2013] IRLR 185.

■ *Faccenda Chicken Ltd v Fowler* [1987] Ch 117, 135G–138H

Neill LJ:

It is sufficient to set out what we understand to be the relevant principles of law. Having considered the cases to which we were referred, we would venture to state these principles:[. . .]

(3)   While the employee remains in the employment of the employer the obligations are included in the implied term which imposes a duty of good faith or fidelity on the employee . . . [I]t may be noted: (a) that the extent of the duty of good faith will vary according to the nature of the contract . . . (b) that the duty of good faith will be broken if an employee makes or copies a list of the customers of the employer for use after his employment ends[288] or deliberately memorises such a list, even though, except in special circumstances, there is no general restriction on an ex-employee canvassing or doing business with customers of his former employer . . .

(4)   The implied term which imposes an obligation on the employee as to his conduct after the determination of the employment is more restricted in its scope than that which imposes a general duty of good faith. It is clear that the obligation not to use or disclose information may cover secret processes of manufacture such as chemical formulae . . . or designs or special methods of construction . . . and other information which is of a sufficiently high degree of confidentiality as to amount to a trade secret. The obligation does not extend, however, to cover all information which is given to or acquired by the employee while in his employment, and in particular may not cover information which is only 'confidential' in the sense that an unauthorised disclosure of such information to a third party while the employment subsisted would be a clear breach of the duty of good faith . . .

(5)   In order to determine whether any particular item of information falls within the implied term so as to prevent its use or disclosure by an employee after his employment has ceased, it is necessary to consider all the circumstances of the case. We are satisfied that the following matters are among those to which attention must be paid:

(a)   The nature of the employment. Thus employment in a capacity where 'confidential' material is habitually handled may impose a high obligation of confidentiality because the employee can be expected to realise its sensitive nature to a greater extent than if he were employed in a capacity where such material reaches him only occasionally or incidentally.

(b)   The nature of the information itself. In our judgment the information will only be protected if it can properly be classed as a trade secret or as material which, while not properly to be described as a trade secret, is in all the circumstances of such a highly confidential nature as to require the same protection as a trade secret eo nomine . . . It is clearly impossible to provide a list of matters which will qualify as trade secrets or their equivalent. Secret processes of manufacture provide obvious examples, but innumerable other pieces of information are *capable* of being trade secrets, though the secrecy of some information may be only short-lived. In addition, the fact that the circulation of certain information is restricted to a limited number of individuals may throw light on the status of the information and its degree of confidentiality.

(c)   Whether the employer impressed on the employee the confidentiality of the information. Thus, though an employer cannot prevent the use or disclosure *merely* by telling the employee

[288] For example, where an employee copies or removes personal and business contacts stored on a database in his employer's computer system, even though some of these contacts pre-dated the commencement of his employment (*PennWell Publishing (UK) Ltd v Isles* [2007] IRLR 700), or where she sends emails from her work account to her personal account containing a significant number of documents concerning the employer's affairs (*Brandeaux Advisers (UK) Ltd and others v Chadwick* [2011] IRLR 224), or where an employee copies the employer's customer and supplier contact details in order to create a rival firm (*Crowson Fabrics Ltd v Rider* [2008] IRLR 288). However, this does not mean that the employer 'owns' the contents of sent emails as property: *Capita plc v Darch* [2017] IRLR 718. Where client contact lists are downloaded without authorization, an employee may also be prosecuted for theft of personal data under section 55 of the Data Protection Act 1998.

that certain information is confidential, the attitude of the employer towards the information provides evidence which may assist in determining whether or not the information can properly be regarded as a trade secret . . .

(d)   Whether the relevant information can be easily isolated from other information which the employee is free to use or disclose . . . For our part we would not regard the separability of the information in question as being conclusive, but the fact that the alleged 'confidential' information is part of a package and that the remainder of the package is not confidential is likely to throw light on whether the information in question is really a trade secret . . .

The passage yields the proposition that, subsequent to the termination of the employment relationship, an employee will be precluded from using, disclosing, or exploiting the trade secrets of the employer or confidential information which is equivalent to such trade secrets. General information of a confidential nature will not attract the same level of legal protection. Meanwhile, the employee's duty during the course of his/her employment is broader, extending to all types of confidential information and trade secrets. As for what constitutes a 'trade secret', plans for the development of new products, and for the discontinuance of existing products, were held to be trade secrets in *Lansing Linde Ltd v Kerr*.[289] Furthermore, in *Lansing Linde*, it was held that a trade secret is information used in a trade or business which, if disclosed to a competitor, would be liable to cause real or significant damage to the owner of the secret. In addition, the owner must limit its dissemination or at least not encourage or permit widespread publication. Trade secrets can thus include not only secret formulae and technical processes for the manufacture of products, but also the names of customers and the goods they buy, and has to be interpreted in the wider context of highly confidential information of a non-technical or non-scientific nature, which may come within the ambit of information the employer is entitled to have protected, albeit for a limited period.

Of course, whilst the judgment of Neill LJ in *Faccenda Chicken* provides some helpful guidance, it acknowledges that making the necessary classifications of information will be a highly factual exercise. In *Faccenda Chicken*, it was held that customer lists, pricing policies, details of prices charged to customers, and other sales data were not trade secrets[290] or confidential information equivalent to a trade secret; likewise in *Crowson Fabrics Ltd v Rider*,[291] where an employer's customer and supplier contact details were not even categorized as confidential information. This can be contrasted with *Sectrack NV v Satamatics Ltd*,[292] where the High Court extended an interim injunction on the basis that there was a serious issue to be tried that a list of customer names and contact details did amount to trade secrets. Meanwhile, *Warm Zones v Thurley*[293] concerned a comprehensive database containing unique information about householders that belonged to a not-for-profit employer who addressed fuel poverty in domestic homes by delivering energy-efficient measures and welfare benefit and energy advice. It was held in the High Court that the database amounted to commercial and proprietary information of a sufficiently confidential nature to justify the grant of a mandatory injunction restraining the employees concerned from copying or disclosing details of the database to a competitor company. All of these decisions underscore the fundamental point that no comprehensive list can be crafted as to what is, and is not, a protectable trade secret or confidential

---

[289] [1991] 1 WLR 251.

[290] There is a definition of 'trade secrets' in the EU's Trade Secrets Directive 2016/943 (OJ 2016 L517/1), on which see Article 2(1). It is open to argument whether this definition may eventually serve to narrow down the definition of confidential information and trade secrets under the common law.

[291] [2008] IRLR 288.

[292] [2007] EWHC 3003 (Comm). See also *Arthur J Gallagher Services UK Ltd v Skriptchenkov* [2016] EWHC 603 (QB).   [293] [2014] IRLR 791.

information equivalent to a trade secret. Much will depend on the factors identified at (a)–(d) in the extract from *Faccenda Chicken*, i.e. the nature of the employment, the nature and quality of the information, whether the employer clarified the nature of the information, and the industry, trade sector, or area in which the employer is concerned.[294] Further, it is crucial that the employee knew that the information was a trade secret and was aware that it was being misused (either by him/herself or a third party).[295]

Turning to the remedies available in the case of a breach of this duty, an injunction, rather than damages is the primary remedy.[296] A springboard injunction is also possible. In certain circumstances, the employer will seek to recover damages, but where it has sustained no financial loss as a result of the breach of duty, the court will only award nominal damages. For example, in *Marathon Asset Management LLP v Seddon*,[297] the employer recovered the paltry sum of £2 in nominal damages.

On the basis of this guidance, in your opinion, does the information which the employee carried away in Hypotheticals B, C, D, and E constitute a trade secret or the equivalent thereof?

Hypothetical B

Danny's Demolishers Ltd ('the Employer') is the leading demolition company in the UK, with numerous subsidiary companies operating throughout the country. It has numerous rival firms, but what makes it stand out from the crowd is its customer care service, after-sales service, competitive prices, and pricing structures. John Thompson ('the Employee') has five years' continuous service with the Employer, but decides to 'jump ship' to a rival firm for higher pay. Shortly after the termination of the Employee's contract of employment, his line manager happens to encounter the Employee on the train and finds him in possession of a copy of a document belonging to the Employer which contains the names and contact details of the Employer's customers and suppliers. The line manager is also aware of it being a document which is jealously guarded under lock and key in the Employer's head office. Is the Employee in breach of the implied term of fidelity, loyalty, and confidence?[298]

Hypothetical C

The facts are the same as in Hypothetical B, subject to the following variations: the line manager finds the Employee in possession of a document containing details of a highly efficient technique adopted by the Employer in the demolition process which enables it to complete demolition projects much faster on average than its rivals. Is the Employee in breach of the implied term of fidelity, loyalty, and confidence?[299]

---

[294] Having said that, it appears reasonably clear that high-level and strategic business plans and information of a technical nature concerning manufacturing processes will always be treated as trade secrets.

[295] *Vestergaard Frandsen A/S v Bestnet Europe Ltd* [2013] IRLR 654.

[296] *D v P* [2016] IRLR 355.   [297] [2017] IRLR 503.

[298] This is a difficult question: it is possibly a breach, if the customer and supplier list is relevant to the discharge of the customer care or after-sales service, but unlikely. This case is somewhat similar to *Churchill Retirement Living Ltd v Luard, Maddams and McCarthy & Stone Retirement Lifestyles Ltd* [2012] EWHC 1479 (Ch).

[299] Yes. This is a commercially sensitive document which enables the Employer to distinguish itself from its competitors.

Hypothetical D

The facts are the same as in Hypothetical C, but assume that the technical process concerned has been patented. Is the Employee in breach of the implied term of fidelity, loyalty, and confidence?[300]

Hypothetical E

The facts are the same as in Hypothetical B, subject to the following variations: the line manager finds the Employee in possession of a copy of a document belonging to the Employer containing details of its pricing policy in respect of Dorset County Council ('DCC') which is clearly marked 'Highly Confidential' on each page. The Employer has not undertaken any demolition projects for DCC for over five years. Is the Employee in breach of the implied term of fidelity, loyalty, and confidence?[301]

If the employer wishes to exert greater control over the post-termination conduct of an employee, the counsel of perfection is for the employer to insert a restrictive covenant/clause in restraint of trade into the employee's contract of employment at the outset of the employment relationship. By doing so, the employer will have greater protection in the law of contract than that provided under the implied term of loyalty, fidelity, and confidence. The law recognizes that clauses in restraint of trade are anti-competitive insofar as they inexorably curtail the freedom of activity of an individual to ply his/her trade. For that reason, they are strictly controlled by the common law. The general rule is that such clauses must be no more than is reasonably necessary to protect the legitimate commercial interests of the employer or the public interest generally. Such clauses are assessed for reasonableness from the perspective of the point in time that they are entered into, i.e. not the later period when the clause is challenged in court.[302] Restrictive covenants come in many shapes and sizes, but the following are the most common encountered in legal practice.

(1) *A non-compete covenant* This is a clause prohibiting or restraining an employee from competing with the employer subsequent to the date of termination of the contract of employment by working for a competitor of the employer or setting up in business in competition with the employer. Such a provision must be no greater than is reasonably necessary for the purposes of *protecting the trade secrets or the customer base of the employer*.[303]

---

[300] No. Since the technical process is patented, it is in the public domain, so is not protected by confidentiality.

[301] Possibly, but the pricing policy might now be outdated.

[302] *Patsystems v Neilly* [2012] IRLR 979 and *Bartholomews Agri Foods Ltd v Thornton* [2016] IRLR 432. However, cf. statements of the High Court in *Egon Zehnder v Tillman* [2017] IRLR 828: this case was subsequently heard by the Court of Appeal ([2017] IRLR 906) who overturned the High Court's decision, but the Court of Appeal did not cover this point.

[303] *Herbert Morris Ltd v Saxelby* [1916] 1 AC 688, 701–2 per Lord Atkinson. In comparison with post-termination covenants restricting the solicitation of, or dealing with, customers, the common law has adopted a stricter approach with respect to the enforcement of non-compete covenants, on which, see *Scottish Farmers' Dairy Co. (Glasgow) Ltd v McGhee* 1933 SC 148 and *Bridge v Deacons* [1984] AC 705, 713 per Lord Bridge.

(2) *A non-solicitation*[304] *of customers or non-dealing*[305] *with customers covenant* This provision prohibits or restricts an employee from soliciting, poaching, canvassing, interfering,[306] or dealing with the customers of the employer subsequent to the date of termination of the employment contract. The protection afforded to the employer by such a clause must be no greater than is reasonably necessary for the purposes of *protecting its goodwill, business/trade connections, and customer base.*[307]

(3) *A non-solicitation of employees covenant* This clause prohibits or restricts an employee from soliciting, poaching, canvassing, or employing the employees of the employer subsequent to the date of termination of the employment contract. Restrictions on the poaching or solicitation of employees must afford protection which is no greater than is reasonably necessary for the purposes of the employer *maintaining a suitable and well-trained workforce.*

It is incumbent upon the court to determine whether the covenant is no more than reasonably necessary to secure and protect the identified legitimate business interest of the employer emphasized in the above. This will involve a balancing exercise, with the consequences of enforcement weighed up against non-enforcement. As such, it is an exercise in proportionality review.[308]

The following are some of the issues which are taken into account to decide whether these covenants are unenforceable.

- *Non-compete clause*
  - The extent of the temporal restriction included in the clause is relevant, e.g. a period of six months may be valid,[309] but a 12-month prohibition or restriction will often[310] be held to be a restraint of trade and unenforceable.[311] Much will depend on the seniority of the employee and whether colleagues of the employee are subject to the same periods of restraint.[312]

---

[304] In *Towry EJ Ltd v Barry Bennett* [2012] EWHC 224 (QB), the word 'solicit' was held to mean 'directly or indirectly request[s], persuade[s] or encourage[s] clients of their former employer to transfer their business to their new employer'.

[305] In *Towry EJ Ltd v Barry Bennett* [2012] EWHC 224 (QB), the point was made that a 'non-dealing' clause will provide stronger protection for an employer than a 'non-solicitation' clause.

[306] See *Bell & Scott LLP v Kaye* [2009] CSOH 111, 2009 GWD 27–434, where the words 'interfere with' were said to involve contemplation of some deliberate action on the part of the former employee to disrupt an existing relationship between the former employer and one of its clients, or to obstruct or impede the development of future business relationships.

[307] *Stenhouse Australia Ltd v Phillips* [1974] AC 391, 400 per Lord Wilberforce; *AGMA Chemicals v Hart* 1984 SLT 246, 248 per Lord Hunter.

[308] M. Freedland, *The Personal Employment Contract* (Oxford, OUP, 2003) 182.

[309] See *Threlfall v ECD Insight Ltd* [2013] IRLR 185 where a six-month non-compete covenant was found to be valid. Likewise, in *Tradition Financial Services Ltd v Gamberoni* [2017] IRLR 698, where the High Court stated that the six-month covenant would have been upheld even if it had run after an initial three-month period of garden leave, i.e. an aggregate nine-month restriction. But contrast these decisions with *Egon Zehnder v Tillman* [2017] IRLR 906; *Bartholomews Agri Foods Ltd v Thornton* [2016] IRLR 432; *Ashcourt Rowan Financial Planning Ltd v Hall* [2013] IRLR 637; *CEF Holdings Ltd v Mundey* [2012] IRLR 912; and *Phoenix Partners Group LLP v Asoyag* [2010] IRLR 594, where the opposite conclusion was drawn.

[310] *Thomas v Farr plc* [2007] ICR 932 and *Merlin Financial Consultations Ltd v Cooper* [2014] IRLR 610 are two rare decisions in which a 12-month non-compete covenant was upheld. Essentially, the employee concerned must be very senior and the employer must have no other protection available, e.g. where the contract contains no non-solicitation of customers or non-dealing with customers clause. However, where the sector involved is financial services, the courts are more ready to uphold 12-month periods on the basis that they are 'industry standard'.

[311] See *Energy Renewals Ltd v Borg* [2014] IRLR 713 and *Prophet plc v Huggett* [2014] IRLR 797 in which 12-month non-compete covenants were held to be unenforceable.

[312] See *Associated Foreign Exchange Ltd v International Foreign Exchange (UK) Ltd* [2010] IRLR 964; *CEF Holdings Ltd v Mundey* [2012] IRLR 912.

- The extent of the geographical restriction included in the non-compete covenant must be restricted. If there is no restricted geographical location for the operation of the covenant, this will often prove fatal to its validity.[313] It is difficult to furnish concrete guidance on an acceptable level of geographical restriction, since much will depend on the nature of the employer's business.[314]

- The scope of the market or business of the employer should be specified clearly and accurately. If the clause seeks to prohibit or restrict the employee from entering into business in competition with the employer and the specific business of the employer is defined too broadly in the clause, it will not be upheld on the basis that it goes beyond what is reasonably necessary to protect the legitimate interests of the employer.[315] A particularly difficult issue arises where the employee develops a new line of business for the employer. When the employee's employment comes to an end and he/she enters into competition with the employer, he/she will not be in breach of the non-compete covenant if the employer ceases to carry out that commercial line of business.[316]

- The competitive activities that the employee is prevented or restricted from carrying out post-termination must be clearly defined, i.e. the nature of activities in the employer's business.[317]

- *Non-solicitation of customers clause*
  - In terms of the extent of the temporal restriction included in the clause, the general rule is that this should be no more than the period of time it would reasonably take the employer to build up a trade connection between the clients looked after by the former employee and his/her replacement. A period of six months will usually be treated as enforceable on the ground that it is 'short',[318] 12 months may be reasonable,[319] but more than two years will require rigorous justification. A rule of thumb often adopted in practice is that the temporal restriction should be closely tied to the employee's notice period; if it exceeds that period, it is likely that it will be excessive.

  - The extent of the geographical restriction will be considered.

  - The non-solicitation of customers clause will commonly provide that the employee is prohibited from soliciting, canvassing, poaching, interfering, or dealing with[320] persons who had been clients or customers of the employer in a particular period immediately prior to the date of termination of the employee's employment contract. In evaluating the reasonableness of the clause, the courts and tribunals will consider the length of that period.

---

[313] See *Axiom Business Computers Ltd v Kenny* 2003 GWD 37–1021; *Ashcourt Rowan Financial Planning Ltd v Hall* [2013] IRLR 637.

[314] For example, in *Office Angels Ltd v Rainer-Thomas and O'Connor* [1991] IRLR 214, a fairly limited radius of 1.2 miles was held to be excessive since the restricted market was as an employment agency office and there was a plethora of such agencies within the relevant 1.2 miles radius of the City of London. The employer could not show any proper functional correspondence between the area circumscribed by the restriction and the area particularly associated with the employees' former place of work. The clause amounted to a valuable protection against general competition, which was wholly unreasonable. See also *Merlin Financial Consultants Ltd v Cooper* [2014] IRLR 610.

[315] See *Scully UK Ltd v Lee* [1998] IRLR 259.

[316] *Threlfall v ECD Insight Ltd* [2013] IRLR 185; *Phoenix Partners Group LLP v Asoyag* [2010] IRLR 594.   [317] *CEF Holdings Ltd v Mundey* [2012] IRLR 912.

[318] *Coppage v Freedom Security Ltd* [2013] IRLR 970. See also *East England Schools CIC (t/a 4my-schools) v Palmer* [2014] IRLR 191.

[319] See *Croesus Financial Services v Bradshaw* [2013] EWHC 3685 (QB); *Romero Insurance Brokers Ltd v Templeton* [2013] EWHC 1198 (QB) and *Pickwell v Pro Cam CP Ltd* [2016] IRLR 761; cf. *Associated Foreign Exchange Ltd v International Foreign Exchange (UK) Ltd* [2010] IRLR 964.

[320] See *Le Puy Ltd v Potter* [2015] IRLR 554.

- In the context of an employment relationship, if a clause attempts to restrict an employee after the date of the termination of the employment contract from soliciting the clients or customers of the employer with whom the employee had had dealings during the period of the employment relationship, is this enforceable? The short answer to this question is 'yes', provided that there is a reasonable period in terms of the range of customers, i.e. that the employee is prohibited from soliciting, canvassing, poaching, or dealing with persons who had been clients or customers of the employer in a particular period immediately prior to the date of termination of the employee's employment contract, e.g. six, nine, or 12 months: *Office Angels Ltd v Rainer-Thomas and O'Connor*;[321] *Stenhouse Australia Ltd v Phillips*;[322] *Cantor Fitzgerald International v Bird*;[323] *Wincanton Ltd v Cranny*;[324] *Croesus Financial Services v Bradshaw*;[325] and *East England Schools CIC (t/a 4myschools) v Palmer*.[326] In covenants of this type, the more significant issue is whether the latter temporal restriction is longer than is reasonably necessary.[327]

- Another issue is whether a non-solicitation of customers or non-dealing with customers clause may be deemed enforceable where it prohibits or restricts an employee after the date of the termination of the employment contract from soliciting persons who had been customers of the employer prior to the commencement of the employment relationship. There is authority which provides that such clauses may be upheld.[328]

- Is a clause valid if it attempts to restrict an employee from soliciting customers of the employer after the date of the termination of the employment contract with whom the employee had had no contact or dealings prior to the date of termination? In the decisions in *Axiom Business Computers Ltd v Kenny*,[329] *Dentmaster (UK) Ltd v Kent*,[330] and *International Consulting Services (UK) Ltd v Hart*,[331] the clauses in the employment contracts were broad enough to restrain the employees from approaching clients of the employer with whom they had made no contact. Nonetheless, they were held to be valid. In *Dentmaster*, the clause incorporated certain self-limiting factors, one of which was the six-month restriction on the class of persons who had been customers. Meanwhile, in *Coppage v Safetynet Security Ltd*,[332] the temporal period of the restriction was limited to six months. However, the positive outcome for the employers in these cases was not replicated in *Bartholomews Agri Foods Ltd v Thornton*,[333] where the covenant was held void. Here, the employee had only dealt with customers responsible for the generation of 12 per cent of the turnover of the former employer.[334]

- Can an employee be prohibited from canvassing or soliciting prospective customers of the employer after the date of termination of the employment contract with whom the employee made initial contact and/or commenced negotiations prior to

---

[321] [1991] IRLR 214, 220 per Sir Christopher Slade.
[322] [1974] AC 391, 401E–F per Lord Wilberforce.   [323] [2002] IRLR 867.
[324] [2000] IRLR 716.   [325] [2013] EWHC 3685 (QB).   [326] [2014] IRLR 191.
[327] See, e.g., *Stenhouse Australia Ltd v Phillips* [1974] AC 391.
[328] In *Axiom Business Computers Ltd v Kenny* 2003 GWD 37–1021, the non-solicitation of customers clause extended to persons who had been customers of the employer prior to the employee commencing employment with the employer. Nevertheless, Lord Bracadale held that the clause was not unreasonably wide. Despite this decision, some caution should be exercised since it is difficult to reconcile with the Court of Appeal decisions in *Gilford Motor Co. Ltd v Horne* [1933] Ch 935 and *Plowman & Son Ltd v Ash* [1964] 2 All ER 10, 12 per Harman LJ, and in the Scottish context, the Outer House decision in *Hinton & Higgs (UK) Ltd v Murphy* [1989] SLT 450, 453D per Lord Dervaird.
[329] 2003 GWD 37–1021.   [330] [1997] IRLR 636.   [331] [2000] IRLR 227.
[332] [2013] IRLR 970.   [333] [2016] IRLR 432.
[334] See also *Capita plc v Darch* [2017] IRLR 718.

the date of termination of the contract of employment? One might assume that such a clause would be enforceable, given that in *Gilford Motor Co. Ltd v Horne*[335] and *Plowman & Son Ltd v Ash*[336] it was held that non-solicitation clauses can be upheld even though they prohibit dealings with customers with whom the employee had never had any contact at all. However, somewhat bizarrely, the law on this point is unclear. For example, in the case of *Gledhow Autoparts Ltd v Delaney*,[337] one of the grounds on which the covenant was held to be too wide was that it covered potential customers with whom the employee had made some sort of initial contact or relationship which might be expected to subsequently develop.

- If a non-solicitation of customers clause attempts to prohibit or restrict an employee from soliciting, poaching, or dealing with persons who become clients or customers of the employer after the date of termination of the employment contract, it is very likely that a clause of this type will be struck down.[338] The reasoning is that such a form of non-solicitation clause extends beyond what is reasonably necessary to secure and protect the identified legitimate business interests of the contracting party seeking such protection.

- *Non-solicitation/poaching of employees clause*

  - The extent of the temporal restriction included in the clause will be relevant. In *TSC Europe (UK) Ltd v Massey*,[339] the period of one year was not commented on adversely by the court. This decision can be contrasted with *CEF Holdings Ltd v Mundey*[340] where a six-month period was held to be unenforceable.

  - The class of employees protected is crucial. In *TSC Europe (UK) Ltd v Massey*, *Dawnay, Day & Co. Ltd v D'Alphen*,[341] *CEF Holdings Ltd v Mundey*,[342] and *NIIT Technologies Ltd v Chaturvedi*,[343] it was held that the clause was invalid because it extended to the solicitation of employees of the employer of all kinds, even the most junior, and employees who may be taken on by the employer during the temporal restriction, i.e. post-termination. Further, in *CEF Holdings Ltd v Mundey*,[344] the clause was not upheld because it covered employees with whom the restricted employee had had no contact in his/her employment.[345] In other words, it is likely that a non-poaching covenant which fails to identify a certain class of employees according to skill, seniority, expertise, or time will be held to be too wide.

Having identified the various rules applicable in the case of such covenants, it should be stressed that the UK Government issued a 'Call for Evidence' exploring the legitimacy of non-compete clauses in May 2016.[346] The Call for Evidence sought the views of consultees on the proposition that non-compete clauses ought to be prohibited on the ground that they stifle 'British entrepreneurship by preventing workers from starting up their own business after leaving a job', and that they might 'unfairly hinder workers from moving freely between employers, and from developing innovative ideas, translating those ideas into a start-up, and growing their business'.[347] In recent years, the academic literature has attributed some of the economic success of 'Silicon Valley' to

---

[335] [1933] Ch 935.   [336] [1964] 2 All ER 10, 12 per Harman LJ.   [337] (1965) 1 WLR 1366.

[338] *Aramark plc v Sommerville* [1995] SLT 749.   [339] [1999] IRLR 22.

[340] [2012] IRLR 912.   [341] [1998] ICR 1068.   [342] [2012] IRLR 912.

[343] [2016] (High Court (QBD), 10 March 2017).   [344] [2012] IRLR 912.

[345] See also *Capita plc v Darch* [2017] IRLR 718.

[346] See 'Non-compete clauses—Call for Evidence' (June 2016), available at https://www.gov.uk/government/consultations/non-compete-clauses-call-for-evidence (last visited 12 November 2017).

[347] 'Non-compete clauses—Call for Evidence' (June 2016), available at https://www.gov.uk/government/uploads/system/uploads/attachment_data/file/525293/bis-16–270-non-compete-clause-call-for-evidence.pdf at page 3 (last visited 11 February 2018). See also pages 4–5.

the technological innovation spurred on by the ban on non-compete clauses in the US State of California.[348] Since the restraint of trade doctrine can be applied to enforce non-compete covenants, the concerns on the part of the UK Government can also be viewed as a thinly veiled criticism of the effectiveness of this common law rule. In essence, the notion here is that by enabling non-compete covenants to be enforced the common law is acting as a barrier to technological innovation. As such, it may be that the UK Government is looking to emulate the success of Silicon Valley by introducing legislation to ban non-compete covenants, but much will depend on the progress of its policy formulation on this issue, which at the moment, is largely unclear. It is yet to respond to the views of consultees and chart a way forward.

Reflection points

1. Rather than drawing a proposition of law that all pre-termination activity preparatory to post-termination competition is unlawful, in *Helmet Integrated Systems Ltd v Tunnard* the Court of Appeal decided that the nature of the employee's job was the principal relevant factor in determining whether the preparatory pre-termination activities breached the implied duty not to compete with his employer. Do you believe that this is a satisfactory rule?

2. Critically evaluate the relationship between the implied term of fidelity, loyalty, and confidence and the implied term of mutual trust and confidence. To what extent do these terms overlap?

3. Explore the relationship between the common law implied term of fidelity, loyalty, and confidence and the fiduciary obligations of an employee treated as a fiduciary. Why is the distinction relevant and is it justifiable?

4. Which of the implied terms imposing duties on employees are the most significant in the common law of the contract of employment? Give reasons for your answer.

5. Do you agree with the flexibility adopted by the common law in drawing up no precise definition of 'trade secrets' and confidential information which is the equivalent of the same?

 For additional reading on the duties of employees, visit the Online Resources for this book at www.oup.com/uk/cabrelli3e/

---

[348] Some of the US literature is as follows: R. J. Gilson, 'The Legal Infrastructure of High Technology Industrial Districts: Silicon Valley, Route 128, and Covenants Not to Compete' (1999) 74 *New York University Law Review* 575; J. J. Prescott, N. D. Bishara, and E. Starr, 'Understanding Non-Competition Agreements: The 2014 Non-Compete Survey Project' (2016) *Michigan State Law Review* 369; N. D. Bishara and E. Starr, 'The Incomplete Non-Compete Picture' (2016) 20 *Lewis & Clark Law Review* 497; and US White House Report, 'Non-Compete Agreements: Analysis of the Usage, Potential Issues, and State Responses' (May 2016), available at https://obamawhitehouse.archives.gov/sites/default/files/non-competes_report_final2.pdf (last visited 11 February 2018).

CHAPTER SEVEN

THE VARIATION, SUSPENSION, AND FUTURE OF THE PERSONAL EMPLOYMENT CONTRACT

7.1 INTRODUCTION

In this chapter, we explore a disparate range of topics, all of which are linked by their connection to the contract of employment. First, we examine the common law rules regulating the variation of the terms of the contract of employment. Although a variation of the contract may be agreed bilaterally by the employer and employee, this chapter will concentrate on the situation where the employer seeks to unilaterally modify the terms of the employment contract. We then move on to address the ability of the employer to suspend the contract of employment. Both the topics of variation and suspension of contract are of cardinal importance for employers, employees, and the wider economy and, as noted elsewhere, share the feature that they are often a 'prelude to its termination'.[1] For instance, the rules concerning variation of contract have been particularly prescient in the context of the economic recession which took place between 2008 and 2013, often as an alternative, or precursor, to the application of the laws governing its termination. In order to avoid redundancies, many employees agreed to variations proposed by their employers to their pay-related contractual terms consisting of pay reductions

---

[1] N. Countouris and A. Sanders, 'Variation and Suspension of the Contract of Employment and its Terms' in M. Freedland et al. (eds), *The Contract of Employment* (Oxford, OUP, 2016) 492.

and freezes.[2] As for suspension, this is a pivotal issue where allegations of improper behaviour or misconduct are made against employees. Finally, the chapter conjectures on the potential future trajectory of the content of the contract of employment.

7.2 VARIATION OF THE PERSONAL CONTRACT OF EMPLOYMENT

Before we embark on an in-depth assessment of the rules on the variation of the contract of employment, it is useful to identify the setting within which variations take place. Although both management and labour may seek modifications to workplace practices, it is with variations advanced by the former[3] that this section is primarily concerned.

7.2.1 Variation: some context

Variation of contract is a central topic, particularly in light of modern pressures on management to demand greater labour flexibility in order to adapt to changing market conditions. For instance, alongside the indefinite and incomplete nature of the contract of employment,[4] the dynamic and evolutionary character of the employment relationship generates internal pressures for regular modifications of job descriptions, the pattern of job tasks and assignments, working arrangements and conditions, and pay-related terms. These factors are complemented by a series of external pressures which also compel employers to apply the managerial prerogative to modify working practices. For example, the requirement for employers to renegotiate the status quo is engendered by labour market and product market pressures as well as 'unexpected production problems'.[5] Further, the managerial requirement for labour flexibility in order to remain a player in the competitive marketplace gives rise to constant monitoring of the way in which work is to be done:

■ W. Brown and D. Rea, 'The Changing Nature of the Employment Contract' (1995) 42 *Scottish Journal of Political Economy* 363, 366

> Because the contract is incomplete, the way it is implemented is profoundly influenced by the power relationship between employer and employee, whether or not this is organised. This relationship is altered by changing labour market and product market pressures, to an extent that is partially moderated through the intervening institutions. In short, the reality of the employment contract is highly changeable, and it does not help our understanding to abstract it from the processes by which it is continually being changed.

■ D. Marsden, *A Theory of Employment Systems* (Oxford, OUP, 1999) 80–1

> A feature of incomplete contracts like the employment relationship is that they have to allow for periodic renegotiation. The transaction rules enable firms to manage task assignments without the

---

[2] See 'Zero Hour is at Hand as Inflation Plunges to Historic 50-Year low' (*The Times*, 24 March 2009); W. Brown and D. Marsden, 'Individualization and Growing Diversity of Employment Relationships' in D. Marsden (ed.), *Employment in the Lean Years: Policy and Prospects for the Next Decade* (Oxford, OUP, 2011) 73, 73–4.

[3] See *Hershaw v Sheffield City Council* [2014] ICR 1120 for a discussion as to whether an internal human resources consultant had the authority to bind the employer in proposing a unilateral variation of the employment contract by letter.   [4] See Chapter 5, section 5.1.1.

[5] D. Marsden, *A Theory of Employment Systems* (Oxford, OUP, 1999) 51.

need for continuous negotiation, but the way they are applied, and sometimes the rules themselves, need to be adapted. Technology and organizational methods change, and job classifications become out of date. Jobs are frequently of long duration, commonly lasting fifteen years and
more even in the US, so some procedure for revision is necessary. For procedural rules especially,
such updating is not straightforward. Commons identified a fundamental consequence of the idea
that employment is always subject to its continuing acceptability to the parties involved: that it is
not a contract as such, but rather a 'continuing implied renewal of contracts at every minute and
hour' (Commons, 1924, ch. 8 § 1). Both parties remain free to terminate the relationship with due
notice, even in western Europe, so there is an ever-present element of negotiation.

Indeed, the change in the underlying structure of the UK economy from a manufacturing to a service-based economy has resulted in a greater need for employers to modify
workplace practices. That is to say that the change from a mass manufacturing relation
of production to a flexible relation of production in a service-based 'knowledge' economy
has generated ever more rapid adaptations of working patterns:

■ H. Collins, 'Regulating the Employment Relation for Competitiveness' (2001) 30 *Industrial Law Journal* 17, 20

What kinds of relations of production are required for successful exploitation of these [new] forces
of production? The answer is certain, though opaque: flexible relations of production . . . The concept of flexibility introduces an implicit contrast with the organisation of production relations that
successfully harnessed the potential of mass production. In the organisation of mass production,
work was divided into numerous discrete tasks or job packages, which were allocated to particular
workers, who performed the same job indefinitely, having mastered the task-specific skill by on-
the-job training. In flexible relations of production the opposite applies. The job has uncertain or
discretionary content. Tasks can be performed by many different workers, often working together
in teams. The work required mutates rapidly, thereby causing the distinct possibility that the function or job will disappear altogether. All of which developments require training for workers in
both firm-specific and general transferable skills.[6]

If one approaches the variation of workplace practices from the perspective of the contractual backcloth of the employment relationship, three challenges present themselves.

(1) First, the lack of congruence between the static contractual framework and the inherently dynamic character of the employment relationship produces a number of
tensions. Employment lawyers cling to the idea that the contract of employment and
its terms are concluded at a definitive point in time, but this is at odds with the fluid
reality of the situation:

■ M. Freedland, *The Personal Employment Contract* (Oxford, OUP, 2003) 237

This, as the present writer and Paul Davies argued in 1984, involve[s] the imposition of an essentially
static contractual model upon an essentially dynamic or evolutionary personal work relationship.
The complex normative fabric of the employment relationship is systematically reduced to an initial treaty which remains in force until its termination unless it is modified by another equally decisive and definitive agreement. As a narrative of the history of the generality of personal work rela-

---

[6] Writer's annotations appear in square brackets throughout this chapter.

tionships, this has much the same artificiality as the theoretical insistence that they are entered into as contracts negotiated between individuals, and that those individuals are freely exercising equal bargaining power. In fact, the two theoretical positions—the individual bargain model and the static contract model—complement and reinforce each other. They combine to produce a composite position which is even more artificial than its constituent parts. It is the static contract model which makes the individual bargain model a particularly contrived or counter-factual one. Most employment relationships are formed on the basis of standardized terms, which have been set by the employing enterprise, whether as the result of collective bargaining or, more commonly, simply as the result of unilateral norm-formation by the enterprise itself. Most of the formal revisions of the terms of employment will be equally standardized, either by employing entities' norm-making or by collective bargaining. Within that formal framework, there may occur much more fragmented or individualized formation of obligations, expectations, or perceived entitlements; but this normally takes place in the course of the employment relationship. Often, the detailed norm-making which really defines the employment relationship does not take place at its inception, nor does it fall neatly into subsequent identifiable episodes or transactions. Much of the real norm-making therefore disappears from view when the employment relationship is viewed through the filter of the static contract model. This deprives the individual bargain model of the slight factual accuracy which it might otherwise possess when applied to the generality of employment relationships.[7]

(2) Another difficulty is that a practice imposed by the employer may simply be a new approach to working or the performance of tasks which has no impact on the existing contractual terms. This possibility is accentuated by the prevailing tendency for job descriptions, responsibilities, and tasks to be specified in writing in a very broad-brush and diffuse manner in order to preserve for the employer a measure of functional flexibility.[8] For example, in *Wetherill v Birmingham City Council*,[9] provisions in a collective agreement which had been expressly incorporated into an employment contract were interpreted in a broad manner to confer a power in favour of the employer to vary unilaterally the terms of a car allowance scheme from a rate appropriate to the engine capacity of the car actually used to a rate appropriate to the duties which were to be performed. Here, the change in working practice introduced by the employer did not entail a variation of the terms of the contract of employment, since the provision regulating car allowances possessed its own inbuilt elasticity which was sufficient to impose the change in practice. Thus, there is an important distinction to be drawn between the unilateral alteration of:

(a) contractual terms which carefully prescribe the employee's job description, duties, and tasks; and

(b) the working conditions, processes, and means of performing the prescribed job description, duties, and tasks.

In the former case, this will amount to a unilateral variation of contract,[10] whereas the latter will not and the employee will be expected to adapt in line with the implied terms

---

[7] See also P. Davies and M. Freedland, *Labour Law: Text and Materials*, 2nd edition (London, Weidenfeld and Nicholson, 1984) 289–90.

[8] D. Marsden, *A Theory of Employment Systems* (Oxford, OUP, 1999) 64–5; H. Collins, 'Regulating the Employment Relation for Competitiveness' (2001) 30 *Industrial Law Journal* 17, 27.

[9] [2007] EWCA Civ 599, [2007] IRLR 781.

[10] For example, *Bull v Nottinghamshire and City of Nottingham Fire and Rescue Authority* [2007] EWCA Civ 240, [2007] ICR 1631, where it was held that the changes required of the employees did not constitute work that the employees had agreed to perform. Here, firefighter employees were required to 'co-respond' to emergency calls from members of the public reporting potentially life-threatening medical conditions in circumstances where the firefighters were in a position to respond more promptly than an ambulance crew.

of the contract of employment.[11] Admittedly, it is not a straightforward task to draw a line between (a) and (b). Matters are further complicated by the fact that employers have the ability to effect changes to working practices without employee consent by simply amending a staff handbook, works rulebook, policy, or procedure which has not been specifically incorporated into the contract of employment. Here, there is no variation of the contract of employment, since the documents on which the original conduct of the employer was based were never ever contractual in the first place.

There is an increasing tendency on the part of employers to include unilateral variation clauses, flexibility clauses, and mobility clauses in the contract of employment. The following are examples of these clauses:

Example of a 'unilateral variation' clause in a contract of employment

The Employer reserves the right to vary the terms and conditions described in this contract of employment and the terms and conditions of your employment generally. Such changes can only be made by a member of the Human Resource Department and must be communicated to you in writing.

Example of a 'flexibility' clause in a contract of employment

You will be required to undertake the type of work outlined in the schedule of principal responsibilities annexed hereto (which schedule is indicative only) and any additional or other necessary work required by the employer in association with your appointment as may be necessary to meet the needs of the employer's business or that of any associated company or body.

Example of a 'mobility' clause in a contract of employment

The Employer may from time to time require you to be transferred temporarily or permanently to any place of business which the Employer may have in the United Kingdom for which a relocation allowance or other allowances may be payable at the discretion of the Employer. The salary and allowances so transferred may be adjusted at the discretion of the Employer.

Such is the degree of elasticity built into such clauses that, if upheld by a court, they allow the employer to modify the express terms of the contract or the duties, job/work, or place of work of the employee without first attaining the consent of the employee. For example, in the case of *Bateman v Asda Stores Ltd*,[12] a unilateral variation clause in a staff handbook, which was incorporated into the employee's contract of employment, provided that the employer 'reserved the right to review, revise, amend or replace the contents of this handbook, and introduce new policies from time to time reflecting the changing needs of the business'. It also purported to give the employer the power to vary terms and conditions without the consent of the employees. When the employer relied on the unilateral variation clause to impose changes in working conditions and pay structures, the EAT upheld the employer's position on the basis that the wording of the variation clause in the handbook was sufficiently wide and clear;[13] likewise in *Sparks v Department for Transport*,[14] where

---

[11] See Chapter 6, section 6.3.2.   [12] [2010] IRLR 370.
[13] For a critique of this decision, see F. Reynold and J. Hendy, 'Reserving the Right to Change Terms and Conditions: How Far Can the Employer Go?' (2012) 41 *Industrial Law Journal* 79.
[14] [2016] IRLR 519.

a provision contained in a contractually incorporated staff handbook prescribed that the employees' contracts of employment 'c[ould] not be changed detrimentally without [thei]r agreement'.[15] A similar point was made in *Wandsworth London Borough Council v D'silva*:

■ *Wandsworth London Borough Council v D'silva* [1998] IRLR 193, 197

Lord Woolf MR:

The general position is that contracts of employment can only be varied by agreement. However, in the employment field an employer or for that matter an employee can reserve the ability to change a particular aspect of the contract unilaterally by notifying the other party as part of the contract that this is the situation. However, clear language is required to reserve to one party an unusual power of this sort. In addition, the court is unlikely to favour an interpretation which does more than enable a party to vary contractual provisions with which that party is required to comply.

The point made in the extract above that 'clear language is required to reserve . . . an unusual power of this sort' is exemplified by the decisions of the EAT in *Hart v St Mary's School (Colchester) Ltd*[16] and *Norman v National Audit Office*.[17] In both of these decisions, two clauses which stipulated that provisions of the contract of employment were 'subject to variation' and 'subject to amendment' were held not to be sufficiently clear or unambiguous to enable the employer to unilaterally vary. The EAT took the view that they failed to clarify which of the parties could amend, and how.

Flexibility clauses and mobility clauses share many affinities with unilateral variation clauses, but differ in that their scope of application is more precise than the latter, with the employer reserving the right to modify (a) the job description and duties of the employee in the case of the flexibility clause and (b) the place of work in the context of the mobility clause.[18] Like unilateral variation clauses, they may be upheld by the judiciary to enable the employer to modify the duties or workplace location without a formal amendment of the contractual terms.[19] However, the employer must ensure that the power to vary conferred by the clause is exercised in a manner which is compliant with the implied term of mutual trust and confidence and/or not indirectly discriminatory on the grounds of age;[20] otherwise, the employer will be in breach of contract.[21]

(3) The final difficulty presented by the contractual framework is that it is not always easy to determine whether there has been a variation of the content of the contract or a termination with the re-engagement of the employee. For example, if an employee refuses to agree to a proposed alteration, rather than unilaterally vary

---

[15] However, in *Sparks*, the employer was ultimately unsuccessful in its attempt to impose variations to its absence management policy on the employees since they were held to be 'detrimental' to the employees concerned.   [16] (UKEAT/0305/14, 8 January 2015).

[17] [2015] IRLR 634.   [18] H. Collins, *Employment Law*, 2nd edition (Oxford, OUP, 2010) 108.

[19] See, e.g., *Home Office v Evans* [2008] IRLR 59.

[20] For example, see the unsuccessful attempt to claim that a variation amounted to indirect age discrimination in *Edie v HCL Insurance BPO Services Ltd* [2015] ICR 713.

[21] See, e.g., *United Bank Ltd v Akhtar* [1989] IRLR 507 (mobility clause); *Land Securities Trillium Ltd v Thornley* [2005] IRLR 765 (flexibility clause); and *Bateman v Asda Stores Ltd* [2010] IRLR 370 (unilateral variation clause). See also *Dresdner Kleinwort Ltd and Commerzbank AG v Attrill* [2013] EWCA Civ 394, [2013] IRLR 548.

the terms of the contract of employment it is open to an employer to terminate the contract with the appropriate period of notice and then re-engage the employee on a fresh contract of employment incorporating the changes proposed. To all intents and purposes, the practical effect is the same as a variation of the contractual terms, but the legal characterization of the process is wholly different. In a similar vein, where the employer modifies the workplace duties of the employee, these may be so substantial that they do not constitute a variation to contractual terms at all, but instead involve the termination of the contract with a subsequent re-engagement on the new terms. The case of *Burdett-Coutts v Hertfordshire County Council*[22] exemplifies how difficult it can be to distinguish between a variation and a termination on notice with re-engagement. In *Burdett-Coutts*, an employer sent a letter to dinner lady employees amending their working arrangements in respect of the provision of school meals, which effectively constituted a pay reduction. The employees had the right to at least 12 weeks' prior notice of the termination of their employment contracts. The letter stipulated that the proposed changes would take effect 12 weeks after the date it was sent and went on to say that it amounted to 'formal notice of . . . changes in your contract of service'. The employer argued that the letter operated to give the employees 12 weeks' prior notice of termination of their employment with an offer to re-employ them on the new terms set out in the letter. However, Mr Justice Kenneth Jones rejected that argument and ruled that the letter could not be interpreted as giving notice to the employees to terminate their employment. The letter informed the addressee that the existing terms and conditions would be amended by the employer and was expressed to be 'formal notice of . . . changes in your contract of service'. Those words were apt, and apt only, to describe an attempt by the employer to vary unilaterally the terms of the contract of employment.

7.2.2 Variation: the law

We now turn to an evaluation of the legal characterization of changes to working practices. Here, it is useful to think of variation as coming in three potential forms:

■ M. Freedland and N. Kountouris, *The Legal Construction of Personal Work Relations* (Oxford, OUP, 2011) 207

Firstly, there might be regulation of the freedom of the employing enterprise to confer upon itself, from the outset of the contractual relation, the power to vary the terms and conditions of employment. Secondly, there may be controls upon subsequent bilateral variation of terms and conditions of employment; and finally there may be controls, which one might expect to be the strictest of the three types of regulation, upon the power of the employing enterprise unilaterally to impose subsequent variation of terms and conditions of employment. We could think of any of these types of control as the regulation of variation either for flexibility if it is permissive in character or for stability if it imposes strict controls. In English law, we find that the common law of the contract of employment tends towards a permissive regime in all these three respects, and that this regime is the subject of a dis-integrated approach, so that it is rather strongly distinguished and separated from other kinds or sources of control of variation. This permissiveness is, in large measure, an expression of that historical combination of liberal contractualism and deference to managerial prerogative which we have remarked upon . . . earlier.

22 [1984] IRLR 91.

Although we will consider the regulation of the first kind of variation mentioned in the extract—namely a written clause in the employment contract conferring the power on the employer to unilaterally vary contractual terms—this will be fairly brief. Instead, the lion's share of our discussion will concentrate on the third example in the passage which concerns the extent to which the common law permits employers unilaterally to impose subsequent variation of terms and conditions of employment. As noted by Freedland and Kountouris, the judiciary in the UK are generally receptive to managerially initiated variations in comparison with other European jurisdictions. The law is characterized by its 'underlyingly libertarian approach to variation of the terms and conditions of the contract of employment'[23] and its tendency to enable the employer to manipulate the rules governing contractual variation to 'compress . . . the claims to job security and stability advanced by workers'.[24] This is particularly the case where there is a pressing business reason for the employer to introduce the changes and have them accepted by the employee. The wholly relaxed attitude of the judiciary to the power of the employer to terminate the contract of employment on providing reasonable notice to the employee is also partially responsible for the general willingness of the courts to empower employers to unilaterally vary contractual terms.[25] However, there is an underlying tension which pervades this area of the law: the permissive approach of the courts and tribunals is puzzling in light of the fact that an employer will be in repudiatory breach of the contract of employment if it unilaterally imposes a variation on the employee. In such circumstances, in accordance with the 'elective' theory of the termination of the contract of employment,[26] the employee will have a claim for damages together with the right to (a) accept the employer's breach and terminate the contract of employment or (b) affirm the contract so that it continues in existence notwithstanding the employer's repudiatory breach.[27] Given the degree of prominence afforded to the consensual nature of the employment contract by the 'elective' approach, the question arises as to how it can be that the judiciary have formulated such a management-friendly approach.

The answer to this question lies partly in an analysis of the various means by which the employment contract may be varied and partly in an examination of the options available to the employee when faced by the proposed imposition of changes to their contractual terms. With regard to the former, the contract may be varied in writing or orally.[28] By far the most difficult kind of case dealt with by the tribunals and courts is where it is alleged that the terms of the contract of employment have been altered by the conduct of the parties. For example, it may be argued that the employee's actions are inconsistent with a refusal to work in accordance with new practices introduced by the employer. Matters here are also complicated by the fact that an employee has a number of options where the change in practice proposed or adopted by the employer amounts to an attempt to modify the terms and conditions of the employee's contract to their detriment.[29] Consider the following Hypothetical A.

---

[23] M. Freedland and N. Kountouris, *The Legal Construction of Personal Work Relations* (Oxford, OUP, 2011) 212.

[24] N. Countouris and A. Sanders, 'Variation and Suspension of the Contract of Employment and its Terms' in M. Freedland et al. (eds), *The Contract of Employment* (Oxford, OUP, 2016) 514.

[25] See M. Freedland, *The Personal Employment Contract* (Oxford, OUP, 2003) 250–2; M. Freedland and N. Kountouris, *The Legal Construction of Personal Work Relations* (Oxford, OUP, 2011) 212; and *Solectron Scotland Ltd v Roper* [2004] IRLR 4.   [26] See Chapter 15, section 15.2.4.2.

[27] *Rigby v Ferodo Ltd* [1988] ICR 29; *Geys v Société Générale (London Branch)* [2012] UKSC 63, [2013] 1 AC 523.

[28] However, the courts will be reluctant to accept that contractual terms have been modified orally by the employer, particularly where the employer has failed to record the alleged variation in contemporaneous written documentation: *Prometric Ltd v Cunliffe* [2016] IRLR 776.

[29] Where the proposed variation is beneficial to the employee and the employee continues to work without protest, it will be presumed that the parties have agreed to the varied term, without the need for any formal acceptance on the part of the employee: *Hershaw v Sheffield City Council* [2014] ICR 1120.

Hypothetical A

Owing to the reduction of orders from clients, Danny's Demolishers Ltd ('the Employer') has decided to impose a 4 per cent reduction in the pay of all of its employees working at its Taunton plant. James Underhill is one of the employees at the Taunton plant ('the Employee') and receives a letter on 3 May from the Employer which states that his pay will be reduced by 4 per cent with effect from 3 September. His written contract of employment provides that he is entitled to 12 weeks' prior notice of termination. The Employee is unhappy about the proposed diminution in his salary and has heard from fellow workers at the plant that employees may respond by choosing one of five available options. He is unsure as to what those five options are and so he seeks advice. His legal adviser lists the five choices as follows:

(1) agree to the variation;

(2) resign and claim constructive dismissal;

(3) do nothing and continue to work without protest;

(4) affirm the contract by working under the new terms under protest and then bring a claim in court for damages for breach of contract or complain to a tribunal of an unlawful deduction from wages under Part II of the Employment Rights Act 1996 ('ERA'); or

(5) refuse to work under the new terms, whereupon the employer has to make a decision to dismiss the Employee or allow the Employee to continue working under the old terms.

See Figure 7.1 for a diagram setting out the five options which are open to the employee.

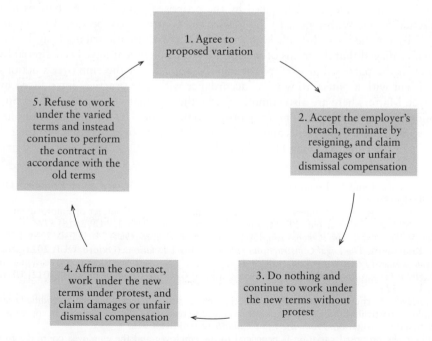

Figure 7.1 *Five options available to an employee where employer proposes a contractual variation*

(1) From Figure 7.1, we can see that the first option is for the employee to (1) expressly agree to the proposed or adopted variation, in which case the contractual terms are formally altered.

(2) Secondly, the employee has the choice to accept the employer's repudiatory breach of the contract of employment, terminate the contract by resigning, and then claim common law damages for a constructive wrongful dismissal or compensation on the basis that he/she has been statutorily constructively unfairly dismissed in terms of Part X of the ERA. Where the employee walks away from the contract, he/she may claim common law damages on the basis of the law of constructive wrongful dismissal, i.e. that the employer has committed a unilateral repudiatory breach of contract by failing to secure his/her agreement to the variation in working practice. This can be compared with the situation where the employee presents a complaint to an employment tribunal that the imposed variation amounted to an unfair constructive dismissal under Part X of the ERA. Although the tribunals and courts are likely to agree with the assertion that the employee has been constructively dismissed, they have been less receptive to the notion that the dismissal was unfair for the purposes of Part X of the ERA. The case of *Catamaran Cruisers Ltd v Williams*[30] is the prime example here. In the context of an employee's failure to accept contractual variations, the EAT in *Catamaran* held that there is no hard-and-fast rule that the employer must demonstrate that the changes imposed were for business reasons so pressing that it was absolutely vital for the survival of the employer's business that the terms be accepted. Instead, the threshold is lower for the employer to satisfy and the tribunal must enquire into the employer's motives for the variations, satisfy itself that they were not sought for arbitrary reasons, and take into account the benefit to the employer in imposing the changes. As such, the judiciary take a holistic approach to the question of statutory fairness, rather than simply analysing the impact of the variation on the employee, which will invariably be prejudicial.

(3) If the employee fails to accept the proposed variation, resign, and claim damages for common law constructive dismissal or compensation for statutory unfair constructive dismissal, the third option available is to do nothing and continue to work under the new imposed terms without protest. This option is one of the most problematic since the question arises as to whether the employee's actions are consistent with him/her having given his/her implied consent to the variation. Ultimately, the question is how the judiciary infer the intentions of the parties from their conduct. In the following extract from *Solectron Ltd v Roper*,[31] we find that the judiciary are wary of rushing to judgment that the employee's continuation of work is tantamount to the provision of implied consent to the variation:

■ *Solectron Scotland Ltd v Roper* [2004] IRLR 4 at paras 30–34

Mr Justice Elias:

The fundamental question is this: is the employee's conduct, by continuing to work, only referable to his having accepted the new terms imposed by the employer? That may sometimes be the case. For example, if an employer varies the contractual terms by, for example, changing the wage or perhaps altering job duties and the employees go along with that without protest, then in those circumstances it may be possible to infer that they have by their conduct after a period of time accepted the change in terms and conditions. If they reject the change they must either

---

[30] [1994] IRLR 386.
[31] [2004] IRLR 4. *Solectron* was approved as the appropriate test by Lord Justice Jacob in the Court of Appeal in *Khatri v Cooperative Centrale Raiffeisen-Boerenleenbank BA* [2010] IRLR 715, 720–1.

refuse to implement it or make it plain that, by acceding to it, they are doing so without prejudice to their contractual rights. But sometimes the alleged variation does not require any response from the employee at all. In such a case if the employee does nothing, his conduct is entirely consistent with the original contract continuing; it is not only referable to his having accepted the new terms. Accordingly, he cannot be taken to have accepted the variation by conduct. So, where the employer purports unilaterally to change terms of the contract which do not immediately impinge on the employee at all—and changes in redundancy terms will be an example because they do not impinge until an employee is in fact made redundant—then the fact that the employee continues to work, knowing that the employer is asserting that that is the term for compensation on redundancies, does not mean that the employee can be taken to have accepted that variation in the contract. The point was put by Browne-Wilkinson J in . . . *Jones v Associated Tunnelling Co Ltd* [1981] IRLR 477 . . . [32] [This] was a case where the employers were asserting in the statutory statement of terms that the terms of the contract contained a wider mobility clause than that which the employee considered to be the case. One of the arguments was that the employee had continued to work with knowledge that this was the term being asserted by the employer and therefore he must have been taken to have accepted it. This tribunal said this:

'22. In our view, to imply an agreement to vary or to raise an estoppel against the employee on the grounds that he has not objected to a false record by the employers of the terms actually agreed is a course which should be adopted with great caution. If the variation relates to a matter which has immediate practical application (eg the rate of pay) and the employee continues to work without objection after effect had been given to the variation (eg his pay packet has been reduced) then obviously he may well be taken to have impliedly agreed. But where, as in the present case, the variation has no immediate practical effect, the position is not the same. It is . . . asking too much of the ordinary employee to require him either to object to an erroneous statement of his terms of employment having no immediate practical impact on him or be taken to have assented to the variation. So to hold would involve an unrealistic view of the inclination and ability of the ordinary employee to read and fully understand such statements. 23. Even if he does read the statements and can understand it, it would be unrealistic of the law to require him to risk a confrontation with his employer on a matter which has no immediate practical impact on the employee . . .'

That case related to an assertion of a new term by the employer in a statutory statement of terms of employment, but the same principle applies, it seems to us, here. In our view, there is no basis at all for . . . contending that in the circumstances of this case the employees could be taken to have accepted that there was a new term replacing the [original] term as a result of their continuing to work in the organisation with knowledge that the employers were offering these different terms in redundancy packages.[33]

This extract enjoins the tribunals and courts to make a distinction between managerially imposed variations which (a) immediately impinge on the employee and (b) those which do not. In the former case, where the employee continues to work for a period of time subsequent to the variation without making an objection—as in the random drug-testing policy introduced by the employer in *O'Flynn v Airlinks The Airport Coach Co. Ltd*,[34] or the changes to the employee's working hours in *Daley v Strathclyde*[35]—the judiciary will be more receptive to the argument that the employee has implicitly consented to the variation of contractual terms. This can be contrasted

---

[32] *Jones* was followed in *Re Leyland DAF Ltd* [1994] 4 All ER 300 and *Aparau v Iceland Frozen Foods* [1996] IRLR 119.

[33] Sourced from BAILII, available at http://www.bailii.org/cgi-bin/markup.cgi?doc=/uk/cases/UKE-AT/2003/0305_03_3107.html&query=solectron+and+limited+and+v+and+roper&method=boolean (last visited 10 October 2017).

[34] [2002] Emp LR 1217.   [35] [1977] IRLR 414.

with (b), as in the case of the changes to the redundancy terms in *Solectron*, where the courts will be more circumspect in attributing to the employee an implied acceptance by conduct;[36] likewise in *Wess v Science Museum Group*,[37] which concerned a variation to the notice period in a contract of employment. Other relevant factors which will be taken into account in assessing whether the employee has impliedly accepted the variations include whether the employee continues to do the same work for the same pay (since that will provide evidence that the varied term is of no immediate practical effect) and whether the employee adopted the method of acceptance of the new terms specifically called for by the employer in order to show assent to the proposed variations (e.g. a signature). It is also relevant whether the employer did not require the employee to sign to evince consent or even query with him/her why he/she had not signed.[38] Furthermore, where the employee is taken to have implicitly accepted the variation, this will arise by virtue of the passage of a period of time. There is no set period prescribed in the case law, although in *O'Flynn v Airlinks The Airport Coach Co. Ltd*,[39] it was held that four months was a sufficient period of time to establish implied consent. Meanwhile, in *Cartwright v Tetrad Ltd*,[40] a unilateral pay cut was taken to have been accepted by the workforce where they had failed to object to it for five months and continued to work without protest. A pay cut can be contrasted with a pay freeze: where the relevant trade union unequivocally declares that it does not accept this change, its continuing silence (and that of the employees) over the subsequent five years does not constitute assent.[41]

(4) If the employee decides to continue to work for the employer, he/she may do so on the basis of the fourth option. In terms of that option, the employee affirms the contract in response to the employer's unilateral repudiatory breach, works in accordance with the new terms expressly under protest, and then brings a claim in court for damages for breach of contract or presents a complaint to an employment tribunal of unauthorized deduction from wages in terms of Part II of the ERA.[42] By working within the varied contract under protest, the employee is providing a clear signal that he/she does not accept the new terms and is treating the changes as a breach of contract.[43] The leading case on working under protest is *Rigby v Ferodo*:

■ *Rigby v Ferodo* [1988] ICR 29, 35C–G

[The headnote to the case sets forth the facts as follows:] The employee was a lathe operator and had been first employed by the employer in 1964. He was a member of a union and in 1982 was entitled to 12 weeks' notice of termination of his contract. In that year the employer encountered serious financial difficulties. In consequence, the employer proposed a 5 per cent reduction in

---

[36] It is not impossible for implied consent to arise in such circumstances: see D. Brodie, *The Employment Contract: Legal Principles, Drafting, and Interpretation* (Oxford, OUP, 2005) 221–3.

[37] (UKEAT/0120/14/DM, 6 October 2014). In *Wess*, the employee was taken to have assented to the variation, having raised no objection to the amended notice period within a nine-year period.

[38] *Khatri v Cooperative Centrale Raiffeisen-Boerenleenbank BA* [2010] IRLR 715, 720 per Lord Justice Jacob; cf. *FW Farnsworth Ltd v Lacy* [2013] IRLR 198.

[39] [2002] Emp LR 1217. In *Watson v Jacobson*, Outer House, 12 January 1995, one month was insufficient. See also *Robinson v GAP Personnel Franchises Ltd* (UKEAT/0342/07, 16 October 2007).

[40] (UKEAT/0262/14/JOJ, 15 January 2015).

[41] *Abrahall v Nottingham City Council* (UKEAT/0010/16/JOJ, 5 May 2016).

[42] See Chapter 8, section 8.2.2.

[43] It should be stressed that affirmation does not preclude the employee from claiming damages in respect of the employer's repudiatory breach since it does not amount to an implicit variation of the employment contract: *MacMullan v Cooke* (Court of Appeal, 14 December 2000).

wages to the union, and warned that, if this were not agreed, it would have to be imposed. In September, the union suggested two alternative proposals, the alternatives being dependent upon whether or not the union members took industrial action. The employer warned that there was no alternative to reductions in wages and, on 18 September, set out in writing the reduced rates which it applied from that date. The union held meetings of its members at which the only votes taken were in relation to the possibility of taking industrial action; no vote was taken on whether or not to accept the wage reductions. The union itself did not agree to accept the reductions, although it indicated to the employer that no industrial action would be taken. The employee instituted proceedings for damages for breach of contract in 1984.

Lord Oliver:

My Lords, the one thing that is clear in this case is that the [employer] had no intention whatever of terminating the contracts of employment with its workforce except by compelling the acceptance of new contractual terms which [the employee] and his fellow [trade union] members were, as they made it quite clear, unwilling to accept and which they never did accept. Faced with that situation the [employer] could have chosen to terminate their contracts on proper notice. It chose not to do so. It could have dismissed them out of hand and faced the consequences. It chose not to do so. It continued to employ them, week by week, under contracts which entitled them to a certain level of wages but withheld from them a part of that entitlement. I can, in those circumstances, see no answer at all to [the employee]'s claim and the trial judge and the Court of Appeal were, in my judgment, plainly right in the conclusions at which they arrived. It has been submitted that there was some sort of implied acceptance on the part of [the employee] of the [employer]'s repudiation by working on. At the trial this was put on the basis of estoppel, waiver and acquiescence. All three were rejected by the trial judge and, in my judgment, he was, on the facts which he found, quite plainly right to reject them. I can, for my part, see no other basis upon which it can be argued that the continued working by [the employee] and his acceptance for the time being and under protest of the wage that the [employer], with full knowledge of his lack of agreement, chose to pay him is to be construed as an acceptance by him either of the repudiation by the [employer] of the original continuing contract or of the new terms which the [employer] was seeking to impose.

The *Rigby* extract clarifies that if the employee affirms the contract and continues to work on the basis of the new terms under protest, he/she is entitled to (a) claim damages in respect of any financial differential between the new terms and the old terms, i.e. to 'stand and sue', or (b) if the variation amounts to a repudiatory breach, ultimately to resign and claim damages for a common law constructive wrongful dismissal or compensation for an unfair statutory constructive dismissal. More importantly, as noted in the extract, the 'ball' is firmly in the court of the employer to decide how to take matters forward if the employee does not resign and claim damages on an ongoing basis. The employer effectively is compelled to abandon its attempt to change the contractual terms or effect the variation indirectly by dismissing the employee and then subsequently re-engaging him/her on a new contract incorporating the varied terms. However, it is crucial that the employee works in compliance with the new terms when he/she protests the variation. As the case of *Robinson v Tescom Corp.*[44] demonstrates, it is not open to the employee to object to the employer's changes and then insist on working under the old terms. If the employee does so and the employer responds by dismissing the employee on the basis that the employee failed to comply with his/her implied

---

[44] [2008] IRLR 408.

duty to follow reasonable instructions,[45] this will not amount to a common law wrongful dismissal[46] or an unfair dismissal for the purposes of the statutory regime in Part X of the ERA.[47]

(5) The final option available to the employee is simply to refuse to work under the varied terms and instead to continue to perform the contract in accordance with the old terms. Once again, the employment contract continues in this case. As the case of *Adamas Ltd v Cheung*[48] clarifies, where the employee refuses to work under the new terms, there is nothing requiring him/her to treat the employment contract as terminated in order to avoid a finding that he/she has signalled his/her agreement to the varied terms. Instead, the onus lies on the employer to take a view as to how it will respond to the employee's position:

■ **Adamas Ltd v Cheung [2011] UKPC 32 at para 25**

Lord Mance:

On one view, the words 'stay in his employment under changed terms' used in *Periag* [*v International Beverages Ltd* 1983 MR 108 (Maur CA)] and later cases might be read as suggesting that any employee, who continues in employment after any breach by his or her employer consisting of a requirement to do work outside the scope of the original employment contract, thereby accepts the new conditions. But this would not represent a rational legal position. If the change demanded was, although outside the scope of the original contract, so minor as not to be repudiatory, the employee would have no right to treat him or herself as constructively dismissed. It could not be right in such circumstances to treat an employee as having waived any claim for damages for the breach. The board understood [counsel for the employer] to accept that whether conduct is sufficiently serious to justify termination of a contract always depends on an analysis of the particular circumstances. It may be open to question whether the change proposed in this case was repudiatory, when Mrs Cheung could simply refuse to undertake deliveries if and when asked. But, even if one assumes that most if not all unilateral changes of job or terms by an employer including the present would be repudiatory if outside the scope of the original contract, the board sees no reason why an employee, faced with an employer's demand for what the employee regards as unjustified changes, should then be obliged to treat the contract of employment as terminated on pain of being held, otherwise, to have accepted such changes. Where, as here, the original contractual job continues to exist and to be capable of performance by the employee, the employee can continue to perform; it is the employer who in such circumstances has to decide what stance to take.[49]

Where the fifth option is adopted by the employee, the *Adamas* extract directs that the burden lies on the employer to decide whether the employee should be allowed to continue to perform the contract under the old terms, or to respond by dismissing the employee and re-engaging him/her on the basis of a new contract of employment, which includes the varied terms. Of course, if the employer elects to terminate the employment contract and re-engage, it must take the risk that the judiciary characterize the termination as a common law wrongful dismissal or as an unfair dismissal under the statutory regime.

---

[45] See Chapter 6, section 6.3.1.   [46] See Chapter 15, section 15.2.4.
[47] See Chapter 16, section 16.3.   [48] [2011] IRLR 1014.
[49] Sourced from BAILII, available at http://www.bailii.org/cgi-bin/markup.cgi?doc=/uk/cases/UKPC/2011/32.html&query=adamas+and+limited+and+v+and+cheung&method=Boolean (last visited 10 October 2017).

Damages for wrongful dismissal will usually be avoided if the employer terminates by giving the employee the requisite period of notice. However, avoiding a finding of unfair dismissal is more fraught, since the employer will need to follow a fair and proper pre-dismissal procedure and show that it has a valid business reason for the variations which chimes with one of the five potentially fair reasons for dismissal delineated in section 98(1), (2), and (3) of the ERA.[50]

A final point to make is that where the employer varies the terms of the employment contract, the process must be conducted in a manner which complies with the implied term of mutual trust and confidence. In other words, trust and confidence must not be destroyed or severely undermined. This is a particularly germane issue where the employer seeks to effect the variation via the auspices of a unilateral variation, flexibility, or mobility clause in the contract of employment.[51] Other areas of employment law may also assume relevance in the context of a variation process. First, if the purported variation of working practices does not actually formally entail a change in contractual terms, the employer will be able to rely on the employee's implied term enjoining him/her to adapt to changes in working methods. Thus a failure by the employee to modify his/her behaviour to align him/herself with the changes introduced by the employer will constitute a breach of contract. At the other extreme is the situation where the variation to the duties of the employee is so radical that it results in the termination of the contract of employment with a subsequent re-engagement on the new terms. In such circumstances, the employer will have to be mindful of the fact that the employee may be treated as redundant for the purposes of the statutory unfair dismissal regime in terms of section 139(1) of the ERA, which ultimately could lead to a finding of unfair dismissal in terms of section 98(4) of the ERA. Finally, there is also scope for the employee to secure injunctive relief to restrain the employer from effecting a proposed unilateral contractual variation. *Hughes v London Borough of Southwark*[52] is one example in which social worker employees were successful in preventing employers from causing their place of work to be moved against their will.[53]

Reflection points

1. Consider the circumstances in which a change of working practices will amount to (a) a variation of contractual terms, (b) a termination of the employment contract with re-engagement on a new contract, (c) a redundancy, and (d) none of (a)–(c).

2. Now list the responses available to the employee faced by an employer imposing contractual variations. Which of the five options do you prefer and why?

3. Describe the general attitude of the judiciary to variations to contractual terms initiated by management. How would you explain this phenomenon in light of the fact that an unaccepted variation is a breach of contract?

 For additional reading on the variation of the contract of employment, visit the Online Resources for this book at www.oup.com/uk/cabrelli3e/

---

[50] See *Slade v TNT (UK) Ltd* (UKEAT/0113/11/DA, 13 September 2011) where the employer was held not to have unfairly dismissed the employee; cf. *Darby & Stilly v Law Society* (UKEAT/0447/07/Zt, 14 August 2008).
[51] See section 7.2.1.   [52] [1988] IRLR 55.
[53] See K. D. Ewing, 'Remedies for Breach of the Contract of Employment' (1993) 52 *Cambridge Law Journal* 405, 418.

7.3 SUSPENSION OF THE PERSONAL CONTRACT OF EMPLOYMENT

In this section, we examine the issue of suspension of the employment contract.

7.3.1 Suspension: some context

Unlike the variation or termination of the contract of employment, suspension has no long-standing effect on contractual terms and merely operates to freeze them in limbo for a period of time pending resumption of the contract on the occurrence or satisfaction of certain matters. By enabling an employee to continue to work and return to his/her old job at the expiration of the period of suspension, from the perspective of the employee, suspension is a wholly preferable option to the alternative of dismissal. Suspension may be sought in a variety of situations:

■ **M. Freedland and N. Kountouris, *The Legal Construction of Personal Work Relations* (Oxford, OUP, 2011) 214**

> [W]e might wish to say that there had been a 'suspension of employment' in situations where the employee is laid off temporarily because of a fluctuation in demand for the product of the employing enterprise, or a temporary interruption in production; or where the employee is in a state of sickness or incapacity not regarded as permanent; or where she is on maternity leave; or where he or she is on strike; or performing military service obligations; or where he or she has been placed on suspension by the employing enterprise for disciplinary or investigatory purposes, or placed on 'garden leave' on a precautionary basis pending the termination of employment.

Either the employer or the employee may seek to suspend the employment contract. The identity of the party calling for suspension will depend on the context. Where the employer suffers a downturn in demand for its products or services, it may purport to suspend the contract of employment; this temporary cessation is often referred to as a 'lay-off'. Suspension is an attractive option to the employer as it enables it to avoid the wage claims of its employees.[54] Indeed, the potentially devastating effects on the wage claims of employees is one of the reasons why the common law fashioned a general rule against the employer having an unrestricted implied power of suspension without pay.[55] An employer may also elect to suspend the employment contract in order to investigate allegations of misconduct against employees for disciplinary purposes or to protect its interests by placing the employee on garden leave during the employee's notice period. Meanwhile, an employee may be keen for the employment contract to be suspended with or without pay where he/she is temporarily absent, e.g. owing to industrial action, maternity leave, paternity leave, incapacity, or illness.

When the contract is suspended, the obligations of the employer and employee require to be determined. This causes us to examine the legal effect of suspension, which is inextricably bound up with the resolution of the question 'suspension of what?' For instance, the word 'suspension' may be a reference to (1) the performance of the work, (2) the employment contract itself, (3) the rights and obligations of the parties, (4) the employee's employment generally, or (5) the employee. The predominant view is that the cases point towards (2), the corollary of which is that (1) and (3) are also suspended:

---

[54] H. Collins, *Employment Law*, 2nd edition (Oxford, OUP, 2010) 114.

[55] See *Hanley v Pease & Partners* [1915] 1 KB 698. Thus, suspension is only possible if an express term gives the employer the power to do so, e.g. *Bird v British Celanese* [1945] KB 336.

■ *Bird v British Celanese* [1945] KB 336, 341

> *Lord Justice Scott:*
>
> The clause operates in accordance with its terms; the whole contract is suspended, in the sense that the operation of the mutual obligations of both parties is suspended; the workman ceases to be under any present duty to work, and the employer ceases to be under any consequential duty to pay. That is the natural meaning of the word 'suspend' when applied to a contract of employment, and I think it is also its legal meaning.

The *Bird* extract sets out the common law position. However, as we noted in section 6.2.2 of Chapter 6, the UK Parliament has intervened to subject the wage–work bargain to statutory regulation, by imposing certain obligations on employers in the context of suspension.

(1) Where an employee has been continuously employed for at least one month, Part III of the ERA obliges the employer to make guarantee payments in respect of any whole day in which the employee has not been provided with work owing to lay-off. This modifies the common law position insofar as *Browning v Crumlin Valley Collieries Ltd*[56] continues to be authoritative.

(2) Where suspension of the employment contract has been the result of sickness or incapacity, the employer must pay statutory sick pay to the employee for the first 28 weeks of such sickness or incapacity at a rate of £92.05 per week[57] in terms of sections 151 and 157 of the Social Security Contributions and Benefits Act 1992.

What is particularly interesting is the extent to which these isolated instances of statutory regulation of suspension have been kept at arm's length from the common law. Indeed, there has been a telling failure to develop the common law of the suspension of the employment contract by analogy with the statutory rights of employees to guarantee payments and sick pay, which provides further evidence of the 'oil and water' relationship between the two sources described in Chapter 2, section 2.1.

7.3.2 Suspension: the law

In Chapter 6, we encountered the common law implied term imposing a duty on the employer to pay wages to the employee where the latter is ready and willing to work.[58] The operation of this rule essentially eliminates the extent to which an employer can lawfully suspend the employment contract for economic rationales.[59] Thus, we find that the common law from a very early point rejected the notion that the employer has an unrestricted implied power of suspension:

■ *Hanley v Pease & Partners Ltd* [1915] 1 KB 698, 705–7

> [The headnote to the case sets forth the facts as follows:] A workman absented himself from his work for one day without leave from his employers. The employers did not dismiss him,

---

[56] [1926] 1 KB 522. See Chapter 6, section 6.2.2.
[57] See Article 9 of the Social Security Benefits Up-rating Order 2018 (SI 2018/281).
[58] See Chapter 6, section 6.2.2, and Chapter 8, section 8.2.2.
[59] *Devonald v Rosser* (1906) 2 KB 728.

but suspended him from working on the following day, whereby the workman was prevented from earning the wages he would have earned on that day had he been allowed to work, namely, 6s. 2d . . .

Lush J:

. . . in the present case after declining to dismiss the workman—after electing to treat the contract as a continuing one—the employers took upon themselves to suspend him for one day; in other words to deprive the workman of his wages for one day, thereby assessing their own damages for the servant's misconduct at the sum which would be represented by one day's wages. They have no possible right to do that. Having elected to treat the contract as continuing it was continuing. They might have had a right to claim damages against the servant, but they could not justify their act in suspending the workman for the one day and refusing to let him work and earn wages . . .

Rowlatt J:

As regards the point of substance it is obvious that the employer has no implied power to punish the workman by suspending him for a certain period of his employment, the contract subsisting all the time. He has power if the occasion arises—but there is no finding in the present case that the occasion had arisen—to dismiss a workman and propose a new employment to begin on the next day which the workman may or may not accept. The facts, however, do not support that view of the case . . .

One of the justifications for denying the employer a broad implied power of suspension is laid bare in this passage. In other words, if the employer is suffering an economic downturn and is unable to pay wages or offer an employee work, it has the option of dismissing that employee. Since the employer enjoys a largely unfettered implied power of dismissal at common law, the judiciary reasoned that this was sufficient justification not to develop a rule permitting the employer to suspend the employment contract.[60] One should also keep in mind that the employer has the additional option of varying the terms of the employment contract in order to make cost savings in the teeth of an economic downturn. The earlier discussion in this chapter showed that the judiciary are generally receptive to managerially initiated variations of contractual terms.

The implication of *Hanley v Pease & Partners* is that the suspension of the employment contract can only proceed on the basis of an express term conferring such a power in favour of the employer.[61] A related issue is whether it is competent for an employer to withhold payment in the context of an express power to suspend. In the case of *Batty v BSB Holdings (Cudworth) Ltd*,[62] the Court of Appeal held that, provided that there is an express term to the effect that remuneration may be withheld, there is no requirement for an employer to pay an employee whilst he/she is off work due to suspension and he/she is not ready and willing to work. To the extent that *Batty* concerned an employee who was not ready and willing to work, the decision of the Court of Appeal appears unremarkable. Therefore, what requires to be examined is whether it is competent for an employer to oust the entitlement of a suspended employee to full pay who is willing to work by deploying an express term to that effect. In this context, the key cases are *Bird v British Celanese*[63] and *McLory v Post Office*.[64] In *British*

---

[60] See also *McArdle v Scotbeef Ltd* 1974 SLT (Notes) 78.
[61] *Bird v British Celanese* [1945] KB 336.   [62] [2002] EWCA Civ 648 at para 33 per Ward LJ.
[63] [1945] KB 336.   [64] [1993] 1 All ER 457.

Celanese, Lord Justices Scott and Lawrence expressed the view that, during the period of suspension, the obligations and rights of the employee and employer are mutually frozen. Therefore, if the express terms of the contract of employment provide that the employee's right to payment is also suspended, this is perfectly valid.[65] In *McLory*, Neuberger QC, sitting as a High Court judge, provided tacit approval of a provision which stated that an employer could suspend an employee without full pay.[66] Thus, the position is particularly clear: the employer's implied duty to remunerate its employees where the latter are ready and willing to work indeed may be disapplied in the context of a suspension.

It should be stressed that the employer's express power of suspension is always subject to the regulatory control of implied terms of the contract of employment, in particular the mutual trust and confidence implied term. Where the power of suspension is exercised in a way which is incompatible with the preservation of trust and confidence, the employer will be in repudiatory breach of contract. In order to illustrate the point in sharper focus, let us consider the following Hypothetical B.

Hypothetical B

In response to an allegation of sexual harassment made by one its employees, Anita Ogston, Danny's Demolishers Ltd ('the Employer') decides to suspend its employee, Michael Darling ('the Employee') on full pay pending the completion of the disciplinary process. The Employer also reports the matter to the police authorities who initiate their own enquiry. Anita Ogston has made seven previous unsubstantiated allegations of sexual harassment against the Employer's employees, each of which were held by the Employer's investigation and police enquiries to have been completely fabricated. Once again, the Employer's investigation and the police enquiry reveal that the allegation was wholly baseless and the Employer agrees to reinstate the Employee. However, the Employee has developed a psychological illness owing to the manner of his suspension. In such circumstances, the Employee is entitled to damages on the basis that the Employer's conduct was in breach of the implied term of mutual trust and confidence.

The factual content of Hypothetical B is similar to that encountered in the cases of *Gogay v Hertfordshire County Council*,[67] *Milne v Link Asset & Security Co. Ltd*,[68] *Yapp v FCO*,[69] *Agoreyo v London Borough of Lambeth*,[70] and *Crawford v Suffolk Mental Health Partnership NHS Trust*.[71] In each of these cases, the courts seem to be concerned about the fair treatment of the employees in advance of any managerial decision to suspend.[72] Indeed, in *Crawford*, Lord Justice Elias provided the following advice to employers:

---

[65] [1945] KB 336, 341 and 342 per Scott LJ and Lawrence LJ. In Kahn-Freund's view, it was not the case that the suspension of the employer's implied duty to pay wages operated only where an express term of the contract of employment evidenced the agreement of the parties, but rather that 'if . . . suspension [of the employer's obligation to pay] occurs, it results neither from a unilateral declaration of either side nor from agreement, but from the event [of the suspension of work] itself *ipso iure*': O. Kahn-Freund, 'Suspension of the Contract of Employment in English Law', Offprint from the *International and Comparative Labour Law Review*, 1970 10(1), Padova (sourced from Otto Kahn-Freund Collection at the Bodleian Law Library on 26 July 2006) 6.

[66] [1993] 1 All ER 457, 464–5 per Neuberger QC.   [67] [2000] IRLR 703.

[68] [2005] All ER (D) 143 (September).   [69] [2015] IRLR 112.

[70] [2017] EWHC 2019 (QB).   [71] [2012] EWCA Civ 138.

[72] See D. Brodie, 'Risk Allocation and Psychiatric Harm: *Yapp v Foreign and Commonwealth Office*' (2015) 44 *Industrial Law Journal* 270, 271–2.

■ *Crawford v Suffolk Mental Health Partnership NHS Trust* [2012] EWCA Civ 138, paras 71–73

Lord Justice Elias:

This case raises a matter which causes me some concern. It appears to be the almost automatic response of many employers to allegations of this kind to suspend the employees concerned, and to forbid them from contacting anyone, as soon as a complaint is made, and quite irre-spective of the likelihood of the complaint being established . . . [Indeed] even where there is evidence supporting an investigation, that does not mean that suspension is automatically justified. It should not be a knee jerk reaction, and it will be a breach of the duty of trust and confidence towards the employee if it is. I appreciate that suspension is often said to be in the employee's best interests; but many employees would question that, and in my view they would often be right to do so. They will frequently feel belittled and demoralised by the total exclu-sion from work and the enforced removal from their work colleagues, many of whom will be friends. This can be psychologically very damaging. Even if they are subsequently cleared of the charges, the suspicions are likely to linger, not least I suspect because the suspension appears to add credence to them. It would be an interesting piece of social research to discover to what extent those conducting disciplinary hearings subconsciously start from the assumption that the employee suspended in this way is guilty and look for evidence to confirm it. It was partly to correct that danger that the courts have imposed an obligation on the employers to ensure that they focus as much on evidence which exculpates the employee as on that which inculpates him . . . [Employers] owe duties to their long serving staff, and defensive management responses which focus solely on their own interests do them little credit. Being under the cloud of possible criminal proceedings is a very heavy burden for an employee to face. Employers should not subject employees to that burden without the most careful consideration and a genuine and reasonable belief that the case, if established, might justify the epithet 'criminal' being applied to the employee's conduct.[73]

 For additional reading on the suspension of the contract of employment, visit the Online Resources for this book at www.oup.com/uk/cabrelli3e/

7.4 THE FUTURE TRAJECTORY OF THE COMMON LAW CONTENT OF THE PERSONAL CONTRACT OF EMPLOYMENT

From the discussion in this chapter, and Chapters 5 and 6, it is self-evident that the implied terms represent the most powerful catalyst in the common law evolution of the rights and obligations of the parties. Therefore, our attention returns to these implied terms in order to predict what the future might hold for the content of the employment contract. Throughout Chapter 6, we commented from time to time on the internal coherence of the law and whether the implied terms might develop in particular direc-tions. In this brief section, we stop to reflect upon the half-life of the implied terms in more detail. In particular, we identify four potential avenues which the common law *might* take.

---

[73] Sourced from BAILII, available at http://www.bailii.org/cgi-bin/markup.cgi?doc=/ew/cases/EWCA/Civ/2012/138.html&query=Crawford+and+v+and+Suffolk+and+Mental+and+Health+and+Partnership +and+NHS+and+Trust&method=boolean (last visited 10 October 2017).

7.4.1 From *ius dispositivum* to *ius cogens* implied terms

In *Malik v BCCI*,[74] Lord Steyn referred to the derogable (i.e. *ius dispositivum*) nature of the implied terms when he remarked that they are 'default rules [and t]he parties are free to exclude or modify them'.[75] Hence, the implied terms are not entrenched (i.e. *ius cogens*) and instead may be ousted by express terms in the sense that the latter will always supplant the former. This formula chimes with general principles of contract law. However, whether—and if so, how—a rule of law ought to emerge whereby implied terms are treated by the common law as mandatory and so impervious to disapplication is a hot topic. Indeed, this issue has generated a great deal of debate in academic circles. As for the potential juridical bases for the emergence of such mandatory implied terms, the common law doctrine of public policy is one possibility. Indeed, both Rudden[76] and Freedland[77] have recognized that concepts of 'over-riding public policy' are useful instruments of analysis in determining the line at which 'the distinction between derogable and inderogable law is . . . drawn'.[78] Nevertheless, there would appear to be little appetite on the part of the judiciary to engage in such a line of movement. Meanwhile, another option is statutory intervention, whereby implied terms are entrenched as mandatory norms by parliamentary diktat. However, once again, this is unlikely, given the lack of enthusiasm amongst parliamentarians for such a reform, which would strike at freedom of contract:

■ **D. Brodie, 'The Employment Contract and Unfair Contracts Legislation'** **(2007) 27 *Legal Studies* 95, 103–5**

[A]ny decision to render the term [obliging employers to take reasonable care for their employees' health and safety] mandatory at common law could be seen as being legitimised by s 2 [of the Unfair Contract Terms Act 1977 ('UCTA')].[79] It is also the case that a failure to take reasonable care for an employee's health and safety will involve a criminal offence under the Health and Safety at Work Act 1974. Nevertheless, where entrenchment is at stake, such conservatism continues to prevail. In *Johnson v Unisys*, for example, none of the Law Lords were willing to hold that mutual trust and confidence was a mandatory term on grounds of public policy. At root, the ideology of the common law dictates that implied terms in law remain 'default rules'. In the absence of legislative fiat the autonomy of the parties is allowed to prevail. In *Johnstone*, the matter was viewed as 'more appropriate for negotiation between the professional bodies . . . or for Parliament, than for resolution by the courts'. This is to be regretted. Implication follows from an assessment that certain obligations are inherent in a particular type of relationship. The framework of the relationship is diminished in their absence. In contracts where there is greater

---

[74] [1998] AC 20. See also *Reda v Flag Ltd* [2002] UKPC 38, [2002] IRLR 747, 753 per Lord Millett.

[75] *Malik v BCCI* [1998] AC 20, 45D–E per Lord Steyn. See also *Johnson v Unisys Ltd* [2003] 1 AC 518, 539F, and 536A–B per Lord Hoffmann and Lord Steyn.

[76] See D. Brodie, 'Beyond Exchange: The New Contract of Employment' (1998) 27 *Industrial Law Journal* 79, 83–6; and D. Brodie, 'The Employment Contract and Unfair Contracts Legislation' (2007) 27 *Legal Studies* 95, 103 for arguments that certain public policy criteria can be used to justify the existence of the implied term of mutual trust and confidence.

[77] See B. Rudden, 'Ius Cogens, Ius Dispositivum' (1980) 11 *Cambrian Law Review* 87, 89–90.

[78] M. Freedland, 'Ius Cogens, Ius Dispositivum, and the Law of Personal Work Contracts' in P. Birks and A. Pretto (eds), *Themes in Comparative Law*, (Oxford, OUP, 2002) 165, 170–1.

[79] UCTA will also apply to entrench the reasonable care duty of the employer in tort. However, it has been held that section 3 of UCTA cannot be deployed to challenge any disapplication of implied contractual duties on the ground that an employee will not be dealing as a 'consumer' or on the employer's 'written standard terms of business': *Commerzbank AG v Keen* [2007] IRLR 132, 138 per Mummery LJ. The position in Scots law diverges: *Chapman v Aberdeen Construction Group plc* 1993 SLT 1205.

equality of bargaining power between the parties, it is appropriate that implied terms operate merely as default rules. In contracts of employment, on the other hand, core rights within employment relations may be dependent on judicial implication. To allow an employment contract to be formed without the benefit of the implied terms in law, or at least some of them, may significantly diminish the social protection afforded to employees by the law. Given the failure of the common law to facilitate entrenchment, I would submit both that statute should provide protection and that s 2 of UCTA offers an appropriate model. There should be no question of an employer being allowed to argue that exclusion is reasonable . . . One must then ask which terms should be protected in this way. The obligation of reasonable care is already protected by [UCTA]. This makes perfect sense. The employer's enterprise should not be run at the risk of damage to the employee's health; at least where that risk could be avoided by the taking of reasonable care. I would further suggest that, to accord with contemporary standards, other implied obligations would now be regarded as fundamental. In particular, mutual trust and confidence would seem to merit protection given that the term aims to protect '. . . the employee's interest in not being unfairly and improperly exploited'. Moreover, it prevents employers mistreating employees by 'harsh and oppressive behaviour or by any other form of conduct which is unacceptable today as falling below the standards set by the implied trust and confidence term'. The foregoing notwithstanding, I would argue that it is also the case that some implied terms are more fundamental—and therefore more apt for entrenchment—than others. In some instances, it is imperative that a term be inalienable. In other cases, modification of the term by the parties may be perfectly acceptable. What of a highly paid executive whose contract provides for 3 months' notice? If no express term existed the application of the standard implied term in law might offer a longer notice period. Nevertheless, the package of terms and conditions, taken as a whole, may be more than reasonable and it could hardly be said that exploitation has taken place. In a yet further group of cases, statutory intervention may not be required even though the term may be regarded as fundamental. For instance, the obligation of fidelity functions entirely for the employer's benefit. Given the employer's superior bargaining power, it is reasonable to conclude that any decision to waive or restrict the term would be genuinely voluntary and, therefore, statutory intervention is not required.

The extract from Brodie adopts a selective approach to the entrenchment of implied terms. In terms of such a scheme, only fundamental implied terms would be treated as inderogable, e.g. the implied term of mutual trust and confidence[80] and the implied term enjoining the employer to exercise reasonable care for the physical and psychiatric well-being of the employee. Meanwhile, the implied term of loyalty, fidelity, and confidence would be subject to disapplication or modification in recognition of the fact that the employer wields the superior bargaining power. The underlying justification for such an exercise in entrenchment is that the contract of employment would be modestly rebalanced to align more closely with the factual reality that the employee is in the weaker bargaining position.

However, Collins is wholly sceptical about the desirability or necessity for the common law implied terms to be treated as inalienable.[81] Instead, he is of the view that the implied terms should be restricted to their current role, an important component of which is to subject express terms conferring discretionary powers upon management to a measure of regulatory control. For Collins, the notion of inderogable implied terms is a 'legal heresy', since it would lead to doctrinal incoherence and ultimately be ineffective and

---

[80] For discussion of the entrenchment of implied terms, see H. Collins, 'Implied Terms in the Contract of Employment' in M. Freedland et al. (eds), *The Contract of Employment* (Oxford, OUP, 2016) 483–90.

[81] H. Collins, 'Legal Responses to the Standard Form Contract of Employment' (2007) 36 *Industrial Law Journal* 2, 9–10.

fruitless.[82] In light of Collins' scepticism, we now move on to address the extent to which the implied terms may evolve in a similar, yet distinct, direction, namely to constrain the operation of express terms in the contract of employment.

7.4.2 From control to disapplication of express terms

A closely related issue is whether the implied terms will harden to such a degree that they may function to override the express terms of the contract of employment. Contractual orthodoxy dictates that this is not possible and this essentially sums up the current legal position.[83] Nevertheless, the regulatory nature of the implied terms has evolved to such a point that they may be harnessed as a means of subjecting the exercise of a managerial power or discretion conferred pursuant to an express term to a measure of constraint. The prime example is the implied term of mutual trust and confidence. This does so by holding that the exercise of an express power or discretion will constitute a breach of the implied term where the employer engages in abusive or arbitrary conduct. Whilst this comes close to an implied term overruling an express term, it is not quite the same thing, since it is not the express term which is being 'trumped', *but rather the way in which the express term is being exercised*. This is conceptualized as the implied term carving the content of the express term. The existing practice whereby the implied and express terms must co-exist in harmony so that they can be read together is attributable to the judgment of Sir Nicolas Browne-Wilkinson V-C in *Johnstone v Bloomsbury Health Authority*:[84]

■ *Johnstone v Bloomsbury Health Authority* [1992] QB 333, 350C–F

Sir Nicolas Browne-Wilkinson V-C:

. . . where there is a contractual relationship between the parties their respective rights and duties have to be analysed wholly in contractual terms and not as a mixture of duties in tort and contract. It necessarily follows that the scope of the duties owed by one party to the other will be defined by the terms of the contract between them. Therefore, if there is a term of the contract which is in general terms (e.g. a duty to take reasonable care not to injure the employee's health) and another term which is precise and detailed (e.g. an obligation to work on particular tasks notwithstanding that they involve an obvious health risk expressly referred to in the contract) the ambit of the employer's duty of care for the employee's health will be narrower than it would be were there no such express term. In the absence of such express term, an employer would be in breach of the normal obligation not knowingly to put the employee's health at risk. But the express term postulated would demonstrate that, in that particular contract, the duty was restricted to taking such care of the employee's health as was consistent with the employee working on the specified high-risk tasks. The express and the implied terms of the contract have to be capable of co-existence without conflict.

Nevertheless, for the same reasons advanced in favour of the entrenchment of implied terms, one might suggest that a more far-reaching approach ought to be adopted whereby

---

[82] However, Collins seems to have since softened his position: H. Collins, 'Implied Terms in the Contract of Employment' in M. Freedland et al. (eds), *The Contract of Employment* (Oxford, OUP, 2016) 489–90.

[83] *Johnson v Unisys Ltd* [2003] 1 AC 518, 539F at para 37 per Lord Hoffmann; *Reda v Flag Ltd* [2002] UKPC 38, [2002] IRLR 747, 753 per Lord Millett.

[84] [1992] QB 333. This judgment was expressly endorsed by the House of Lords in *Johnson v Unisys Ltd* [2003] 1 AC 518, 539 at para 37 per Lord Hoffmann and para 24 per Lord Steyn, and in *Barber v Somerset County Council* [2004] 2 All ER 385, 397e–g per Lord Rodger.

certain implied terms should have the ability to oust express terms. Indeed, in *GMB v Brown*, Elias J expressed the following opinion:

■ *GMB Trade Union v Brown* **(UKEAT/0621/06/ZT, 16 October 2007) at para 40**

> *The Honourable Mr Justice Elias (President):*
>
> We see no reason in principle why it should not be a breach of the duty of trust and confidence to insist upon compliance with the express terms of the contract, albeit only in exceptional circumstances.[85]

A stark example of Mr Justice Elias's approach is supplied by *Stevens v University of Birmingham*.[86] Here, the High Court decided that the employer's strict literal adherence to the express terms of its contractual disciplinary procedure amounted to a breach of the implied term of mutual trust and confidence.[87]

However, the feasibility of such a development is open to doubt. There is an anxiety that the adoption of such an approach would result in the implied terms overreaching themselves, raising questions about their legitimacy. It would also take the common law of the contract of employment down a path involving a serious rupture with general principles of contract law. It would effectively consign the liberal philosophies of freedom of contract and party autonomy espoused by the common law to oblivion. As such, it would be a movement antithetical to the common law approach and for that reason is unlikely to materialize.

7.4.3 From the personal contract of employment to the statutory 'worker' contract

As we noted in Chapter 4, section 4.2.1, there is a class of individual providing personal services who is also entitled to certain statutory employment rights, i.e. the 'worker'.[88] One of the mysteries of employment law concerns the nature and breadth of content of the statutory 'worker' contract: does it, and ought it to, include the implied terms of the contract of employment or some suitably modified version of them?

On the one hand, there is some force in the contention that the common law of the contract of employment has no business implying terms into what is essentially a statutorily recognized contract. On the other hand, although the 'worker' contract is undoubtedly a creature of statute and the application of the common law tests for the establishment of an employment relationship would result in the individual 'worker' being treated as an independent contractor (despite the fact that he/she is not running a business), one might contend that such an individual should not be limited to looking to the common law implied terms of the *contract for services* to discover the content and scope of his/her

---

[85] Sourced from BAILII, available at http://www.bailii.org/cgi-bin/markup.cgi?doc=/uk/cases/UKE-AT/2007/0621_06_1610.html&query=GMB+and+Trade+and+Union+and+v+and+Brown&method=boolean (last visited 10 October 2017).   [86] [2015] EWHC 2300 (QB).

[87] Contrast *Stevens* with the opposite scenario in *Chhabra v West London Mental Health NHS Trust* [2013] UKSC 80, [2014] ICR 194. In *Chhabra, the failure to adhere to, or serious irregularities in the conduct of, a disciplinary procedure* were held to constitute a breach of the implied term of mutual trust and confidence.

[88] These are rights not to suffer unauthorized deductions from wages and whistle-blowing rights under Part II and sections 47B and 48 of the ERA, the Working Time Regulations 1998 (SI 1998/1833), the National Minimum Wage Act 1998, the Part-Time Workers (Prevention of Less Favourable Treatment) Regulations 2000 (SI 2000/1551), and the right to be accompanied at a disciplinary hearing under section 10 of the Employment Relations Act 1999.

obligations and rights vis-à-vis the employing entity.[89] Indeed, if it is accepted that the basis for common law intervention in the contract of employment is the existence of unequal bargaining strength,[90] it is difficult to understand why those terms should not also be operative in the case of the statutory 'worker' who is clearly in a position of subordination and dependency.[91] For that reason, one might argue that the implied terms of the contract of employment ought to be replicated and applied (with any necessary modifications) to impose obligations and confer rights on the 'worker' and the employing entity.

It is in this context that one contemplates the possibility that the implied terms of the contract of employment have leap-frogged, and may continue to leap-frog, over from the common law of the contract of employment to shape the content of the statutory 'worker' contract. To some extent, there is evidence of this process having already begun. Cases such as *Spring v Guardian Assurance*,[92] *Kidd v AXA Equity & Law Life Assurance Society plc*,[93] and *Harmer v Cornelius*[94] are consistent with the stance that some strands of the implied term to exercise reasonable care bind the semi-dependent 'worker' and the employing entity (and vice versa). On the other hand, some cases point in the opposite direction and seem to restrict the operation of this implied term to the contract of employment.[95] Meanwhile, in the cases of *Bedfordshire County Council v Fitzpatrick Contractors Ltd*[96] and *Jani-King (GB) Ltd v Pula Enterprises Ltd*,[97] it was held that the implied term of mutual trust and confidence is of no application to commercial and franchise contracts. In so implying, the courts left open the possibility that contracts analogous to employment could be made subject to such a term. This point was picked up by Lord Justice Kay in the Court of Appeal in *Tullett Prebon plc v BGC Brokers LP*,[98] who held that a 'forward contract' entered into between a prospective employee and a prospective employer, whereby the latter undertook to enter into an employment contract with the former in the future, was sufficiently close in character to an employment contract (e.g. on a classificatory spectrum ranging from commercial contracts at one end to employment contracts at the other) for the term of mutual trust and confidence to be implied. If one applies that reasoning to the statutory 'worker' contract, there is a strong argument that the implied term should be extended from the contract of employment to the 'worker' contract. However, a note of caution should be struck. Other than the reasoning that a forward contract was analogous to employment in line with the authorities of *Bedfordshire County Council* and *Jani-King*, Lord Justice Kay offered no precise or theoretical explanation as to why the far-reaching term of trust and confidence should be implied. For example, the 'necessary incident[s]',[99] 'wider considerations',[100] or 'general considerations' test for implying terms in law into a particular class of contract[101] were

[89] Indeed, if the individual did look to such implied terms of the contract for services, he/she would find a dearth of principles and rules: M. Freedland, 'From the Contract of Employment to the Personal Work Nexus' (2006) 35 *Industrial Law Journal* 1, 5–6.

[90] See Chapter 1, section 1.2.1; *Malik v BCCI* [1998] AC 20, 37H per Lord Nicholls; *Autoclenz v Belcher* [2011] ICR 1157, 1168G–H per Lord Clarke; *Gisda Cyf v Barratt* [2010] UKSC 41, [2010] 4 All ER 851, 862E–F per Lord Kerr; and P. Davies and M. Freedland (eds), *Kahn-Freund's Labour and the Law* (London, Stevens & Sons, 1983) 17–20 and 29–37.

[91] See D. Brodie, 'The Employment Contract and Unfair Contracts Legislation' (2007) 27 *Legal Studies* 95, 109; M. Freedland, *The Personal Employment Contract* (Oxford, OUP, 2003) 151–4 and 168–70.

[92] [1995] 2 AC 296.   [93] [2000] IRLR 301.   [94] (1858) 5 CB (NS) 236.

[95] *Lister v Romford Ice and Cold Storage Co. Ltd* [1957] AC 555; *Janata Bank v Ahmed* [1981] IRLR 457.

[96] (1998) 62 ConLR 64.   [97] [2007] EWHC 2433 (QB), [2008] 1 All ER (Comm) 451.

[98] [2011] IRLR 420, 426. See also *Brandeaux Advisers (UK) Ltd and others v Chadwick* [2011] IRLR 224, 231 per Jack J.

[99] *Lister v Romford Ice and Cold Storage Co. Ltd* [1957] AC 555, 576 per Viscount Simonds; *Liverpool City Council v Irwin* [1977] AC 239, 254F–255C per Lord Wilberforce; and *Scally v Southern Health and Social Services Board* [1992] 1 AC 294, 306G–307F at para 12 per Lord Bridge.

[100] *Scally v Southern Health and Social Services Board* [1992] 1 AC 294, 306G–307F at para 12 per Lord Bridge.   [101] See Chapter 5, section 5.2.4, and Chapter 6, section 6.1.1.

not considered in *Tullet Prebon*. It is suggested that there is every possibility that the absence of such an account is something the traditionally conservative judiciary may refer to in a future case to stymie the extension of the implied terms of the contract of employment to the statutory 'worker' contract.

7.4.4 Recalibration of implied terms under an overarching principle

As the content of the implied terms evolves and expands, greater scope for overlap, duplication, and fragmentation of approach is generated. It also creates the opportunity for the implied terms to be reconstituted under an overarching all-embracing principle. In terms of such a scheme, the recalibrated implied terms would come to be viewed as mere expressions or manifestations of that wider abstract principle. Further, the principle itself could be invoked as a means of expanding or reducing the scope of the individual implied terms and, when taken in aggregate, the content and scope of the implied terms would be greater than the sum of their parts. The disparate variety of circumstances held to be subject to the implied term of mutual trust and confidence reinforces the point that it is undoubtedly the most significant driver in the evolution of the implied obligations of the employer and employee. For that reason, it is the most oft cited candidate for an overarching principle under which each of the other implied terms may come to rest.[102]

However, before we reach the conclusion that the trust and confidence term is the most apt implied term for reconstitution as a super-principle, we must first satisfy ourselves that it would cover the kinds of factual circumstances which have been held to give rise to a breach of the other implied terms. Furthermore, we must be clear that its scope of application is indeed broader than that of the other implied terms. To that end, it is useful to consider judicial pronouncements on the topic, particularly against the other implied term which is widely understood to be broad in its operation, namely the implied term of loyalty, fidelity, and confidence. Indeed, when the implied term of mutual trust and confidence was first recognized by the House of Lords in *Malik v BCCI*,[103] Lord Steyn remarked that, '[i]t is true that the implied term adds little to the employee's implied obligations to serve his employer loyally and not to act contrary to his employer's interests'.[104] As such, here was the suggestion that there was some correlation or match between the scope of the duty of trust and confidence and the duty of loyalty.[105] However, recent case law has downplayed the notion that the content and scope of the duties of trust and confidence and loyalty and fidelity can be conflated. For example, in *Wright v Weed Control*,[106] the approach was taken that the duty of trust and confidence was necessarily distinct from the more specific obligation of confidence and loyalty and that it would not necessarily be inappropriate to treat the latter as falling within the scope of the former. However, the converse was not true, i.e. there would be many breaches of the duty of trust and confidence which would not fall within the scope of what was generally understood to be the province of the obligation of loyalty and confidence. Essentially, it

---

[102] *Johnson v Unisys Ltd* [2003] 1 AC 518, 536A at para 24 per Lord Steyn; D. Brodie, 'The Heart of the Matter: Mutual Trust and Confidence' (1996) 25 *Industrial Law Journal* 121, 123–5; D. Brodie, 'Mutual Trust and the Values of the Employment Contract' (2001) 30 *Industrial Law Journal* 84, 85; M. Freedland, *The Personal Employment Contract* (Oxford, OUP, 2003) 159; and D. Brodie, 'Book Review of "The Personal Employment Contract" by M. R. Freedland' (2004) 33 *Industrial Law Journal* 87, 89.

[103] [1998] AC 20.

[104] *ibid.*, 46C. See M. Freedland and N. Kountouris, *The Legal Construction of Personal Work Relations* (Oxford, OUP, 2011) 188–9.

[105] M. Freedland, *The Personal Employment Contract* (Oxford, OUP, 2003) 175; D. Brodie, *The Employment Contract: Legal Principles, Drafting, and Interpretation* (Oxford, OUP, 2005) 117–18.

[106] [2008] All ER (D) 235 (February) at para 19 per Elias J. Support for the notion of the distinctiveness of these implied terms is also furnished in the judgment of Livesey QC in *RDF Media Group plc v Clements* [2008] IRLR 207, 218 at para 108.

was acknowledged that the two duties would overlap,[107] but that the duty of loyalty was clearly narrower than the duty of trust and confidence.

Insofar as such judicial dicta suggest that its content and scope is much more expansive than the other implied terms, there is clearly a great deal of promise afforded by the trust and confidence term as a candidate for a future overarching principle. However, in light of the reining in of the implied term in the context of dismissal and certain doctrinal studies based on the implied term of reasonable care and the trust and confidence term, an element of caution, and indeed scepticism, has been struck in some quarters about the viability of such a development:

■ M. Freedland and N. Kountouris, *The Legal Construction of Personal Work Relations* (Oxford, OUP, 2011) 199

It remains to be seen whether and if so how far the implied obligation of mutual trust and confidence has retained, in the context of the regulation of the content and performance of contracts of employment, the capacity to operate as a general constraint upon the abuse of law, of rights, and of power on the part of employing enterprises. It may be that its exclusion from the regulation of dismissal has crucially undermined its ability to operate in that way even beyond the sphere of dismissal. Another possibility is that the mutual obligation of trust and confidence will enjoy a vigorous half-life in the limited sphere to which it has been consigned.

■ D. Cabrelli, 'The Implied Duty of Mutual Trust and Confidence: An Emerging Overarching Principle?' (2005) 34 *Industrial Law Journal* 284, 305–7

The previous section of this article sought to demonstrate a lack of functional equivalence between the implied duty to exercise reasonable care and the duty of trust and confidence . . . It is submitted that the evidence cited above demonstrates that the two implied duties aim to achieve different things. Some of the employer's implied duties are fashioned by statute, some by public policy and some by other areas of the law. Each implied duty has a varied scope with different influences bearing upon it. The implied duty to exercise reasonable care emerged in the first half of the twentieth century as a means of securing the abolition of the doctrine of common employment. It then evolved incrementally in the absence of health and safety legislation and in parallel with the tortious duty of care in negligence. In contrast, the implied duty of trust and confidence emerged from those cases which dealt with constructive unfair dismissals in terms of the Industrial Relations Act 1971. Perhaps the definition and nomenclature of the implied duty of trust and confidence itself initially suggested a wider role. However, what we are now witnessing is an inclination by the courts to rein in the doctrine, as exemplified by *Johnson, Eastwood* and the recent case of *Kerry Foods Ltd v Lynch*. The principal point being made here is that the employer's implied duties are distinct stand-alone duties existing at different levels of generality which are at different stages of development with different juridical sources and natures, and each not necessarily operating in tandem with one another. Indeed, some of the implied duties are more advanced than others which are partly for historical reasons and the means by which they interact with statute law. Moreover, it also may explain (i) why the implied duties appear to be pulling in opposite directions from each other at times and (ii) why the state of development of both of them fluctuates between retrenchment and expansion within the space of a few years, if not months . . . After detailed analysis, this article makes the fundamental point that all of the implied duties are

---

[107] See also *Nottingham University v Fishel* [2000] ICR 1462, 1492C per Elias J.

inherently distinct and that, on balance, there is no evidence for the emergence of the implied duty of mutual trust and confidence as an umbrella principle. The trends in the recent case law have emphasised the distinctiveness of the duties to exercise reasonable care and mutual trust and confidence. The article demonstrates that both duties are separate, free-standing duties (sitting on an equal plane in terms of importance) and to rationalise one and/or all of the implied duties, as one of the means by which the super-principle of trust and confidence is, or may be expressed, is to a large extent 'aspirational'.

Indeed, rather than the implied term of mutual trust and confidence, Freedland has opined that the concept of 'fair management and performance' is a more fitting contender for an all-embracing principle.[108] In fact, there is now evidence in the case law to support the emergence of an implied term providing an employee with a right to fair treatment,[109] which could eventually assume the role of an organizing super-principle;[110] although the judiciary are generally more than content to continue to analyse cases in accordance with the traditional language of the implied terms, it is a truism that the category of implied terms is not closed. But striking a note of caution, it is perhaps enough of a major step for the courts to recognize the existence of an implied term, let alone a higher-order norm under which each of those implied terms may assemble.

Reflection points

1. In light of the earlier extracts from Brodie and Collins, do you believe that it is desirable for the implied terms to become entrenched so that they are not susceptible to displacement by express terms? Give reasons for your answer.

2. Consider whether the implied terms ought to be able to displace express terms. What are the impediments confronting such a development?

3. Are you of the view that it is desirable for the implied terms to regulate the content of the statutory 'worker' contract? Give reasons for your answer.

4. What are the advantages and disadvantages of conceptualizing the implied terms of the contract of employment in terms of an abstract organizing principle?

 For additional reading on the future trajectory of the personal contract of employment, visit the Online Resources for this book at www.oup.com/uk/cabrelli3e/

---

[108] M. Freedland, *The Personal Employment Contract* (Oxford, OUP, 2003) 187–8.

[109] *Yapp v FCO* [2015] IRLR 112, 118 per Underhill LJ; *Chhabra v West London Mental Health NHS Trust* [2013] UKSC 80; [2014] IRLR 227, 233 at para 37 per Lord Hodge; *Al-Mishlab v Milton Keynes Hospital NHS Foundation Trust* [2015] EWHC 3096 (QB) at para 17 per Mr Justice Green.

[110] For the definitive case in favour of an implied duty of fair treatment assuming this role, see A. Sanders, 'Fairness in the Contract of Employment' (2017) 46 *Industrial Law Journal* 508.

PART IV
STATUTORY EMPLOYMENT RIGHTS

CHAPTER EIGHT

PAY AND WORKING TIME

8.1 AN EXAMINATION OF THE STATUTORY REGULATION OF PAY AND WORKING TIME

In this chapter, we turn our attention to statutory employment rights for the first time in this book. In particular, we focus on the statutory regulation of (1) the wage–work bargain and (2) the working conditions of 'employees' and 'workers',[1] i.e. the legal protections that incorporate a measure of 'fair exchange' into the contract of employment.[2] The chapter will cover the rights conferred on employees and workers under the National Minimum Wage Act 1998 ('NMWA') and the Working Time Regulations 1998 ('WTR').[3] Both these pieces of legislation possess the capacity to override the mutually agreed contractual arrangements struck by the parties. The provisions of the Employment Rights Act 1996 ('ERA') relating to wages, e.g. the statutory right (a) not to suffer unauthorized deductions from wages and (b) to a guarantee payment, will also be addressed.[4]

---

[1] For the statutory definitions of these terms, see the discussions in Chapter 3, section 3.2.1, and Chapter 4, section 4.2.1.

[2] M. Freedland, 'The Exchange Principle and the Wage-Work Bargain' in M. Freedland et al. (eds), *The Contract of Employment* (Oxford, OUP, 2016) 68.   [3] SI 1998/1833.

[4] The other miscellaneous rights contained in the ERA, such as the various protections for employees from the suffering of detriments, the rights for employees to take time off work for various prescribed reasons, the right for employees to request flexible working, and the protections for employees on the insolvency of their employer, are considered in Chapter 9 and Chapter A of the Online Resources.

8.1.1 Historical and contextual analysis of, and justifications for, the statutory regulation of pay and working time

For an employer's workforce, their pay and conditions of remuneration will be the most important element of the wage–work bargain. For that reason alone, it is a central feature of the employment relationship attracting statutory and common law regulation and demands our attention. We also focus on working conditions in this chapter: the state of the worker's surroundings will often dictate the quality of their performance and the level of their output.

Common law controls on pay and working conditions have tended to be rather limited, e.g. rules on circumstances in which the employer may make deductions from pay. Instead, the traditional forum for the regulation of the wage–work bargain, working time, annual leave/holiday pay, overtime, rest breaks, and night-shift work was the collective agreement struck through voluntary collective bargaining. This system was representative of the collective laissez-faire model of industrial relations which dominated much of the twentieth century, whereby national minimum wage and working time regimes prescribed by legislation were eschewed by successive British Governments.[5] With the exception of the control of hours worked by women and children[6] and other isolated pockets,[7] historically there was no statutory working time regulation in the UK. A few years before the introduction of the WTR, Deakin articulated the following view:

■ S. Deakin, 'Equality under a Market Order: The Employment Act 1989' (1990) 19 *Industrial Law Journal* 1, 2

Britain is currently unique in Western Europe in not providing general legislative standards governing the working hours of adult men. There is no legislation laying down maximum daily, weekly and annual hours for the whole workforce. There has, however, been legislation governing the hours of women and children in industrial employment since the last century.

The terms of the collective agreements struck by the trade unions and employers' associations were superimposed upon the bedrock of a legally enforceable set of minimum terms and conditions and industrially prescribed minimum remuneration laid down by bodies known as 'trade boards' and latterly 'wages councils'.[8] These wages councils, which comprised representatives of employees and employers and were given statutory underpinning by the Wages Councils Act 1945, 1969, and 1979,[9] prescribed minimum wages *for particular sectors of the economy or industries only.* Therefore, there was no such thing as national minimum wage legislation applicable to all employees and workers in the UK. Wages councils were the statutory successors of the trade boards which had been created by the Trade Boards Act 1909[10] to address the hardships suffered by workers employed

[5] See O. Kahn-Freund, 'Minimum Wage Legislation in Great Britain' (1948) 97 *University of Pennsylvania Law Review* 778.

[6] See the Factories Act 1961. The protective regulation of working hours in respect of women and children was dismantled by the Sex Discrimination Act 1986 and the Employment Act 1989.

[7] See the Coal Mines Regulation Act 1908 and the Railway Servants (Hours of Labour) Act 1893.

[8] See also the Holidays with Pay Act 1938, which regulated holiday pay.

[9] See the discussion in P. Davies and M. Freedland, *Labour Law: Text and Materials*, 2nd edition (London, Weidenfeld and Nicholson, 1984) 143–54; P. Davies and M. Freedland, *Labour Legislation and Public Policy* (Oxford, Clarendon Press/OUP, 1993) 29–32 and 541–5; and Lord Wedderburn, *The Worker and the Law: Text and Materials*, 3rd edition (London, Penguin Books, 1986) 350–4.

[10] See S. Deakin and F. Green, 'One Hundred Years of British Minimum Wage Legislation' (2009) 47 *British Journal of Industrial Relations* 205.

in the 'sweated trades',[11] whom it was felt were entities subsidized by the public purse, the system of poor relief, and charities.[12] One of the distinguishing features of the wages councils' regime was its lack of universality in that it only regulated pay in specific industries, leaving large pockets of workers scourged by low pay, wholly untouched. It was also devised as a floor of protection, which it was anticipated would stimulate the emergence of widespread collective bargaining arrangements.

When the Donovan Commission[13] reported in the late 1960s, it recommended the progressive abolition and merger of the wages councils. This was based on their failure to foster growth in voluntary collective bargaining or to raise the level of pay in the industries covered by wages councils at the same rate as the industries covered by voluntary collective bargaining but not subject to wages councils. As such, they had not met the objective of raising the wages of the less well-off. Accordingly, throughout the 1970s and 1980s, a great number of wages councils were wound up or consolidated. Finally, the Conservative Government abolished the wages councils in 1993[14] on the ideological basis that they were a barrier to growth in employment.[15] By the time the New Labour Government secured power in 1997, the number of employees in the UK covered by collective bargaining processes had plummeted from the heights reached in the 1970s.[16] The model devised by the NMWA was based on the idea of 'universality' whereby the minimum wage, unlike the wages councils,[17] would be an entitlement afforded to all employees, irrespective of where or how they worked. This had the advantage of boosting earnings—predominantly for 'young workers, older workers, [women,] ethnic minorities, migrant workers, disabled people, and those with no qualifications'[18]—employed in low-paid industries and occupations, namely 'retail; hospitality; social care; employment agencies; food processing; leisure, travel and sport; cleaning; agriculture; security; childcare; textiles and clothing; and hairdressing'[19] to the level of the newly established minimum wage.

The impact of national legislation prescribing a minimum wage at a single identifiable rate across all industries and sectors of the economy is a hotly debated topic amongst economists. For mainstream economists adopting the orthodox neoclassical model, regimes such as that prescribed by the NMWA are thought to be a bad idea on the ground

---

[11] See S. Keevash, 'Wages Councils: An Examination of Trade Union and Conservative Government Misconceptions about the Effect of Statutory Wage Fixing' (1985) 14 *Industrial Law Journal* 217.

[12] See speech by Winston Churchill MP, Hansard HC, vol. 155, col. 1888, 24 April 1906.

[13] *Report of the Royal Commission on Trade Unions and Employers' Associations 1965–1968* (London, HMSO, Cmnd 3623) para 234.

[14] The Trade Union Reform and Employment Rights Act 1993.

[15] However, the agricultural wages boards established by the Agricultural Wages Act 1948 and Agricultural Wages (Scotland) Act 1949 were maintained. The Agricultural Board for England and Wales was finally wound up in October 2013.

[16] See Chapter 1, section 1.2.1; W. Brown, 'The Contraction of Collective Bargaining in Britain' (1993) 31 *British Journal of Industrial Relations* 189; and W. Brown and D. Rea, 'The Changing Nature of the Employment Contract' (1995) 42 *Scottish Journal of Political Economy* 363, 366–8.

[17] See P. Davies and M. Freedland, *Towards a Flexible Labour Market: Labour Legislation and Regulation since the 1990s* (Oxford, OUP, 2007) 183–5 for an explanation why the New Labour Government decided not to resurrect the wages councils regime when the National Minimum Wage Act 1998 came into force in April 1999.

[18] See *National Minimum Wage: Low Pay Commission Report 2013* (Cm 8565, 2013), available at http://www.lowpay.gov.uk/lowpay/report/pdf/9305-BIS-Low_Pay-Accessible6.pdf page 24 at para 2.15 (last visited 27 November 2017).

[19] See *National Minimum Wage: Low Pay Commission Report 2012* (Cm 8302, 2012), available at https://www.gov.uk/government/publications/national-minimum-wage-low-pay-commission-report-2012 pages 23–4 at paras 2.8–2.11 (last visited 20 November 2017). See also *National Minimum Wage: Low Pay Commission Report 2015* (Cm 9017, 2015), available at https://www.gov.uk/government/publications/national-minimum-wage-low-pay-commission-report-2015 page 37 at para 2.17 (last visited 20 November 2017).

that they impose unnecessary costs and burdens on business. They are generally uniform in their hostility to such minimum wage policies, one scholar retorting that it 'is striking that the labor force effects of minimum wages are predominantly negative'.[20] There are three principal negative impacts cited by neoclassical economists/scholars.

(1) *Increased redundancies*, particularly amongst younger workers,[21] are said to lead to higher youth and adult unemployment:

■ **G. J. Stigler, 'The Economics of Minimum Wage Legislation' (1946) 36** *American Economic Review* **358, 358–61**

Each worker receives the value of his marginal product under competition. If a minimum wage is effective, it must therefore have one of two effects: first, workers whose services are worth less than the minimum wage are discharged (and thus forced into unregulated fields of employment, or into unemployment or retirement from the labor force) . . . The former result, discharge of less efficient workers, will be larger the more the value of their services falls short of the legal minimum, the more elastic the demand for the product, and the greater the possibility of substituting other productive services (including efficient labor) for the inefficient workers' services. The discharged workers will, at best, move to unregulated jobs where they will secure lower returns. Unless inefficient workers' productivity rises, therefore, the minimum wage reduces aggregate output, perhaps raises the earnings of those previously a trifle below the minimum, and reduces the earnings of those substantially below the minimum. These are undoubtedly the main allocational effects of a minimum wage in a competitive industry . . . Although no precise estimate of the effects of a minimum wage upon aggregate employment is possible, we may nevertheless form some notion of the direction of these effects. The higher the minimum wage, the greater will be the number of covered workers who are discharged . . . Whatever the number . . . the direct unemployment is substantial and certain; and it fairly establishes the presumption that the net effects of the minimum wage on aggregate employment are adverse.

---

(2) Stigler argues that the workers discharged as a result of the operation of the minimum wage will be allocated to less well-paid jobs or will be unable to find alternative employment freezing them into a state of long-term unemployment. Accordingly, the second negative effect of a statutory wage floor is the *reduction in aggregate output and productivity* it generates, owing to the stimulus of an inefficient allocation of labour.

(3) The third argument rests on the negative employment effects of minimum wages, namely that they *depress the demand for labour*. The result is fewer jobs in the labour market since fewer workers will be employed by employers owing to the increased costs.[22]

By setting a mandatory wage rate, the effect of the NMWA is to uproot the mutually agreed allocation of risks and reward struck by the contracting parties. The NMWA represents an interference with freedom of contract and accordingly, particularly cogent justifications must be formulated for its introduction or retention.

---

[20] J. Mincer, 'Unemployment Effects of Minimum Wages' (1976) 84 *Journal of Political Economy* S87, S104.

[21] See C. Brown, C. Gilroy, and A. Kohen, 'The Effect of the Minimum Wage on Employment and Unemployment' (1982) 20 *Journal of Economic Literature* 487, 524.

[22] G. Davidov, 'A Purposive Interpretation of the National Minimum Wage Act' (2009) 72 *Modern Law Review* 581, 587–8.

The neoclassical assault on minimum wage legislation has been challenged by new institutional economists. One of the oft-versed arguments presented in favour of a statutorily prescribed minimum wage is that it fosters a 'shock' effect, jolting employers—who are now subject to the requirement to pay the minimum wage above the market rate—into devising techniques and means of increasing their productivity. In the extract from Stigler—who is by no means an advocate of the 'shock' theory—the processes involved therein are described:

■ **G. J. Stigler, 'The Economics of Minimum Wage Legislation' (1946) 36** *American Economic Review* **358, 359**

> Each worker receives the value of his marginal product under competition. If a minimum wage is effective, it must therefore have one of two effects . . . second, the productivity of low-efficiency workers is increased . . . The second and offsetting result, the increase of labor productivity, might come about in one of two ways: the laborers may work harder; or the entrepreneurs may use different production techniques. The threat of unemployment may force the inefficient laborers to work harder . . . The introduction of new techniques by the entrepreneurs is the more common source of increased labor productivity. Here again there are two possibilities. First, techniques which were previously unprofitable are now rendered profitable by the increased cost of labor. Costs of production rise because of the minimum wage, but they rise by less than they would if other resources could not be substituted for the labor . . . Second, entrepreneurs may be shocked out of lethargy to adopt techniques which were previously profitable or to discover new techniques.

A second justification in favour of a statutory wage floor is that it precludes the State subsidization of firms and industries which have been kept afloat by low wages:

■ **S. Deakin and F. Wilkinson, 'Minimum Wage Legislation' in K. Dau-Schmidt, S. D. Harris, and O. Lobel (eds),** *Labor and Employment Law and Economics* **(Cheltenham, Edward Elgar, 2009) 150, 157–8**

> A more radical departure from the orthodox account [of the effects of minimum wage legislation] is provided by theories informed by an institutionalist [economics] view of the labour market . . . This perspective leads to a different view of minimum wage legislation. Rather than being an 'artificial' interference in the free market, it becomes just one form of regulation which, together with other conventions, norms and customer practices, governs the way in which labour is contracted. The case for legislation is that, as a consequence of differences in industrial structure, certain groups in the labour market will not have access to voluntary means of labour organisation, such as collective bargaining or the protection of professional rules governing entry and access to jobs. Hence the industries in which low pay is endemic are those in which there are structural factors, such as ease of entry by both firms . . . and workers . . . which impede the effective organisation of labour and hence the application of common terms and conditions . . . The persistence of these conditions means that low pay is in effect a subsidy enabling otherwise uncompetitive firms and industries to survive. Minimum wage regulation is therefore necessary in order to help create an environment in which firms compete not on the basis of low pay but instead through high labour quality and product and process innovation . . . Equally, placing a floor under wages can augment the purchasing power of workers and thereby underpin effective demand . . . These efficiency-orientated and macroeconomic effects have indeed been prominent among the justifications offered for the introduction of minimum wage regulation in most of the systems adopting it.[23]

---

[23] Writer's annotations appear in square brackets throughout this chapter. See also S. Deakin and F. Wilkinson, 'The Law and Economics of the Minimum Wage' (1992) 19 *Journal of Law and Society* 379, 385–6.

An additional argument in favour of national minimum wage legislation centres on its potential contribution towards an increase in overall productive efficiency in the economy. One of the assumptions underpinning the neoclassical economic account of the effects of minimum wages is that each worker is equally as productive as the next. However, what is referred to as the 'efficiency wage' theory[24] deviates from the neoclassical model insofar as it posits that the output of all workers is not necessarily always equal. In short, some workers shirk and are lazy, particularly when their pay is very low: if you pay peanuts, you get monkeys. By paying more than the market rate, the less productive workers will feel more valued in their jobs and become more loyal and motivated to increase their output.[25] Accordingly, paying an efficiency wage will increase the employer's output and deter workers from being less productive. To that extent, the 'efficiency wage' theory suggests that raising wages above the market rate will have a positive effect on overall productivity rather than reduce output because of increased costs.

Another benefit associated with a minimum wage is sometimes referred to as the 'spillover effect'. This describes a phenomenon which is often seen when minimum wage regimes are introduced. In short, the minimum wage would appear to exert upward pressures on the wage packages of workers situated higher up in the wage distribution chain. In other words, there is research to suggest that the wages of a significant number of workers earning in excess of the minimum wage increase when the minimum wage comes into effect.[26] When the 'spillover effect' is combined with the 'efficiency wage' theory, the overall effect is increased productivity, which benefits everyone in society. Finally, it is often argued that a minimum wage operates to preclude the emergence of a 'race to the bottom' in wages by employers. As such, the national minimum wage prevents the emergence of 'unfair competition', whereby 'reputable firms [are] undercut by competitors solely on the basis of depressed wages'.[27]

The impact of the national minimum wage in the UK casts some doubt on the neoclassical economic position as there is evidence to suggest that it has had a wholly benign effect on the labour market since it was introduced:

■ M. B. Stewart, 'The National Minimum Wage after a Decade' in D. Marsden (ed.), *Employment in the Lean Years: Policy and Prospects for the Next Decade* (Oxford, OUP, 2011) 130–2

... most of the empirical evidence on the impact of the NMW on employment points to an absence of significant negative effects of either the introduction of the NMW or its subsequent upratings. This is particularly true when data on individual employees is used. The only convincing exception to this is the research analysing the residential care homes sector ... Outside this very particular sector, the bulk of the evidence indicates that the NMW has had little or no adverse impact on employment ... It is sometimes suggested that evidence of no negative employment effects, and even possible positive effects, because they are counter to economic theory, must be the result of defective empirical methodology. It is important to remember that this is not the

---

[24] See G. A. Akerlof, 'Labor Contracts as Partial Gift Exchange' (1982) 97 *Quarterly Journal of Economics* 543; G. A. Akerlof, 'Behavioral Macroeconomics and Macroeconomic Behavior' (2002) 92 *American Economic Review* 411.

[25] See C. Shapiro and J. E. Stiglitz, 'Equilibrium Unemployment as a Worker Discipline Device' (1984) 74 *American Economic Review* 433.

[26] See L. F. Katz and A. B. Krueger, 'The Effect of the Minimum Wage on the Fast-Food Industry' (1992) 46 *Industrial and Labor Relations Review* 6; D. Card and A. Krueger, *Myth and Measurement: The New Economics of the Minimum Wage* (Princeton, NJ, Princeton University Press, 1995).

[27] See *The National Minimum Wage: First Report by the Low Pay Commission* (Cm 3796, 1998), available at http://webarchive.nationalarchives.gov.uk/20090609003228/http://www.berr.gov.uk/files/file37987.pdf at page 17 (last visited 21 November 2017).

case. While the simplest economic model predicts that an increase in the minimum wage will reduce employment, more sophisticated and realistic models do not. In the simplest neoclassical model of a competitive labour market, all workers are paid their marginal product. The introduction of a minimum wage above the market clearing wage will induce firms to lay off workers and reduce employment. There is a clear prediction that employment will fall . . . [However, t]here may be 'efficiency wage' effects where firms by paying employees more raise their productivity, for example, by raising employee morale or motivation, or increasing the cost of job loss to the employee, or reducing the quit rate. As a result of these and other potential influences of this type, the effect of an increase in the minimum wage on employment cannot be predicted unambiguously in more complex situations. Firms may have used other routes to adjust to the introduction of, or an increase in, the NMW . . . Some firms may be able to adapt by reorganizing their operations so as to increase the productivity of the affected workers in line with their increase in wages. Some firms may adjust at the hours margin rather than the number of workers. Some firms may be able to pass on the increase in wage costs by raising prices, depending on the degree of competitiveness of the product market in which they operate and the wage structures of their competitors. Some firms may be able to absorb the extra wage costs as a reduction in profits without threatening their survival, depending on the economic rents in the sector and how profitable they were before the change.[28]

Ultimately, the principal lesson to be learnt from the British experience is that the effect the minimum wage will have on a country's economy will depend largely on where the rate is set. In the UK, the rate was fixed at such a level that there was no adverse impact on the employment rate, productivity levels, unemployment, or inflation;[29] neither have the subsequent upratings of the minimum wage had any negative consequences.[30] Nevertheless, there is general agreement amongst economists of all persuasions that if it is set at too high a level, this may have disadvantageous consequences for the economy.[31]

The NMWA, however, was motivated by more than economic goals; it also pursued a number of non-economic objectives:

■ G. Davidov, 'A Purposive Interpretation of the National Minimum Wage Act' (2009) 72 *Modern Law Review* 581, 586–94

Minimum wage laws redistribute resources in favour of low-wage workers. As a positive matter, this has been a major goal of minimum wage laws around the world. In the UK, Mark Freedland and his colleagues have recently argued that one of the goals of the NMW . . . has been 'to make

---

[28] See also M. Fahn, 'Minimum Wages and Relational Contracts' (2017) 33 *Journal of Economics, Law and Organization* 301. For a commentary on the impact of the national minimum wage on earnings, pay, the labour market, productivity, unemployment, and competitiveness, see also D. Metcalf, 'Why Has the British National Minimum Wage Had Little or No Impact on Employment?' (2008) 50 *Journal of Industrial Relations* 489, and *National Minimum Wage: Low Pay Commission Report 2015* (Cm 9017, 2015), available at https://www.gov.uk/government/publications/national-minimum-wage-low-pay-commission-report-2015 pages 49–117 at paras 2.39–2.243 (last visited 8 February 2016).

[29] This was a compromise reached in order to strike a balance between the benefits associated with the arguments of the new institutional economists, whilst also addressing the fears voiced by orthodox neoclassical economists, on which, see W. Brown, 'The Process of Fixing the British National Minimum Wage, 1997–2007' (2009) 47 *British Journal of Industrial Relations* 429.

[30] See M. de Linde Leonard, T. D. Stanley, and H. Doucouliagos, 'Does the UK Minimum Wage Reduce Employment? A Meta-Regression Analysis' (2014) 52 *British Journal of Industrial Relations* 499.

[31] See G. Davidov, 'A Purposive Interpretation of the National Minimum Wage Act' (2009) 72 *Modern Law Review* 581, 589–92.

work pay'—to replace (to some extent) in-work benefits and shift some of their costs to employers. This in effect shows that the NMW . . . has a redistributive goal . . . The basic assumption behind the redistributive goal is that since employers are forced to raise the wages of the lowest-paid, these workers are better off. Empirical evidence supports this assumption and shows that the minimum wage has the effect of compressing the distribution of earnings . . . Respect for the dignity of the worker as a human being dictates that human labour should not be sold for less than a certain minimum. The idea that 'labour should not be regarded merely as a commodity or article of commerce' represents a long-standing understanding that labour power cannot be separated from the self. Since human beings are not things and cannot be bought and sold as such, neither can their labour power. This does not mean that we cannot or should not sell our labour power for a price, but it does mean that some limitations are necessary, and labour and employment regulations accordingly try to protect our health and our rights at work. Some of these regulations are designed to ensure respect for our dignity as human beings . . . The minimum wage can be seen in a similar light . . . By working a full day for the benefit of another, the worker relinquished her freedom to do what she pleases. Our ability to do what we choose with our time is valuable. It is part of our human dignity which everyone else and society at large must honour . . . the minimum wage is more appropriately understood as an attempt to ensure respect for human dignity—including taking into account the indirect costs of employment—than a much too crude attempt to correct market failures . . . minimum wage legislation is based on the belief that people, who are not commodities, should not be required to work for wages below a certain minimum that represents respect for their human dignity.

Accordingly, the Davidov extract contends that the NMWA can be justified in social and moral, rather than purely economic, terms, i.e. a concern for distributive justice and respect for the dignity of the worker. Rogers has made the same point.[32]

The statutory wage floor laid down in the NMWA shares an affinity with the controls placed on working hours and annual leave in the WTR. Both represent a measure of statutory interference in the working conditions of workers and the wage–work bargain. Rather than being motivated by a concern for (1) distributive justice or (2) respect for the dignity of the worker in the same way as the NMWA, or alternatively justified as (3) a response to the demise in collective bargaining, (4) a means of guaranteeing workplace equality, or (5) reconciling the right to work and family life, it is abundantly clear from the Preamble to the Working Time Directive ('WTD'),[33] that the regulation of working time and annual leave is predicated on health and safety policy concerns.[34] The WTD, which has direct effect in terms of EU law,[35] is to be interpreted in light of principles contained in the instruments of the International Labour Organization ('ILO'),[36] such as the ILO Convention on the Hours of Work Industry Convention of 1919[37]

---

[32] B. Rogers, 'Justice at Work: Minimum Wage Laws and Social Equality' (2015) 92 *Texas Law Review* 1543.

[33] Directive 2003/88/EC (OJ 2003 L299/9). The WTR are based on the WTD.

[34] Indeed, in *UK v Council* [1996] ECR I-5755, the European Court of Justice ('ECJ' or 'CJEU') rejected the UK's challenge to the health and safety basis for the WTD. The ECJ has stressed the importance of the WTD towards the enhancement of the working and living conditions of workers, including their physical and mental well-being in the workplace, on which, see *Wippel v Peek & Cloppenburg GmbH & Co.* [2005] IRLR 211, 217 and *Landsshauptstadt Kiel v Jaeger* [2003] IRLR 804, 812.

[35] *Pfeiffer v Deutches Rotes Kreuz* [2005] IRLR 137. The WTD was adopted on the legal basis of then Article 118a of the Treaty of Rome—now enshrined in Article 153(1)(a) of the Treaty on the Functioning of the European Union ('TFEU')   [36] See WTD, Preamble, para 6.

[37] See http://www.ilo.org/dyn/normlex/en/f?p=1000:12100:0::NO::P12100_ILO_CODE:C001 (last visited 27 November 2017).

and ILO Convention 132 of 24 June 1970 concerning Annual Holidays with Pay (Revised):[38]

> **Article 153**
>
> 1. With a view to achieving the objectives of Article 151, the Union shall support and complement the activities of the Member States in the following fields:
>
>   (a) improvement in particular of the working environment to protect workers' health and safety . . .

The language employed here should not be taken to suggest that the WTR is not motivated by a desire to enhance the rights of workers. Instead, as noted by Barnard, the law regulating working time 'is situated in the grey area between traditional health and safety measures and the rights of employed persons'.[39] In other words, the exhausted and overworked worker who is prone to accidents is hardly one whose interests and rights are being protected. In fact, Article 13 of the WTD, which embraces the notion of the 'humanization'[40] of the workplace, is particularly far-reaching insofar as it subverts the traditional convention of subordination experienced by the worker in the power dynamics of the employment relationship. Instead, it is designed to ensure that the organization and pattern of work is adjusted and adapted in line with the needs, availability, and requirements of the worker:

> **Article 13 Pattern of Work**
>
> Member States shall take the measures necessary to ensure that an employer who intends to organise work according to a certain pattern takes account of the general principle of adapting work to the worker, with a view, in particular, to alleviating monotonous work and work at a predetermined workrate, depending on the type of activity, and of safety and health requirements, especially as regards breaks during working time.

Some commentators argue that the WTR is a prime example of misguided paternalistic legislation, since not only is it instrumental in depriving employers of much needed flexibility in their organizational capacity, but it also denies workers the freedom of choice to exercise a preference to work overtime and earn extra pay. Orthodox economic theory posits that statutorily prescribed maximum weekly working hours limits

---

[38] See http://www.ilo.org/dyn/normlex/en/f?p=1000:12100:0::NO::P12100_INSTRUMENT_ID: 312277 (last visited 27 November 2017). This Convention was used as an interpretive tool by the ECJ/CJEU in the cases of *Schultz-Hoff* [2009] IRLR 214, 239 and *KHS AG v Schulte* [2012] IRLR 156, 168, and 170. Domestically, the EAT had recourse to this ILO Convention as an interpretive aid in *Plumb v Duncan Print Group Ltd* [2015] IRLR 711. See also Article 32(2) of the EU Charter of Fundamental Rights of 2000 which provides that '[e]very worker has the right to limitation of maximum working hours, to daily and weekly rest periods and to an annual period of paid leave', available at http://www.europarl.europa.eu/charter/pdf/ text_en.pdf (last visited 27 November 2017).

[39] C. Barnard, *EU Employment Law*, 4th edition (Oxford, OUP, 2012) 533.

[40] See S. Hardy, 'Harmonising European Working Time in an Enlarged EU: A Case of Failed "Humanisation"?' (2006) 22 *International Journal of Comparative Labour Law and Industrial Relations* 543; A. Bogg, 'Of Holidays, Work and Humanisation: A Missed Opportunity?' (2009) 34 *European Law Review* 738.

are misconceived on the ground that the forces of competition will drive employers to tailor working hours to the demands of individual workers:[41]

■ **N. Adnett and S. Hardy, 'Reviewing the Working Time Directive: Rationale, Implementation and Case Law' (2001) 32** *Industrial Relations Journal* **114, 114–15**

Employers who find it hard to match [the preferences of their individual workers in respect of the allocation of working hours] . . . will, in order to recruit and retain workers, have to provide compensation in the form of higher wages. Thus the theory of compensating wage differentials predicts that most individuals will be working their utility maximising number of hours conditional on their wage. Imposing working time restrictions must therefore lower workers' utility and raise employers' unit labour costs, thereby reducing the competitiveness of EU producers.

By tightly controlling working hours with maximum limits, neoclassical economists argue that overall productivity will inevitably fall. However, from a new institutional economics perspective, the relationship between working hours and productivity is more subtle than the simple formula of 'more hours = more economic output'. Instead, the contention is that working longer hours may diminish a worker's output per hour and that, by arranging working practices to prioritize shorter hours and more flexible working arrangements tailored around workers' needs, higher productivity rates will be achieved. Hypothetical A illustrates the point.

Hypothetical A

Kerr Daniels ('KD') is a specialist manufacturer of spare parts for various pieces of machinery involved in the demolition and construction industry. He works 50 hours per week for Danny's Demolishers Ltd ('DD'). His average output is 50 spare parts every week, which equates to one spare part every hour. DD notes that, by reducing KD's hours to 40 hours a week, his output becomes 45 spare parts every week. This is equivalent to 1.125 spare parts per hour, resulting in a higher productivity rate.

There is evidence which reveals that such a dynamic may play out in practice:

■ **ILO,** *The Effects of Working Time on Productivity and Firm Performance: A Research Synthesis Paper* **(Conditions of Work and Employment Series No. 33, 2011) iv–6**

This paper provides a comprehensive synthesis of previous research examining the link between different aspects of working time and outcomes in terms of productivity and firm performance. These aspects include both how the length of working hours affects unit productivity and also how various types of 'flexible' or innovative working time arrangements (i.e., flexi-time, compressed workweeks, hours averaging, working time accounts/time banking, etc.) affect enterprise performance. First, in terms of the volume (quantity) of working hours, the paper finds

---

[41] J. T. Addison, C. Barrett, and W. Siebert, 'The Economics of Labour Market Regulation' in J. T. Addison and W. S. Siebert (eds), *Labour Markets in Europe: Issues of Harmonization and Regulation* (London, Dryden Press, 1997).

that manufacturing productivity does not necessarily increase when hours are lengthened, and that in many industries, it appears that shorter hours are associated with higher output rates per hour . . . Lengthening the duration of hours per employee is likely to add to the level of production per worker, but does it actually improve the productivity rate of labour? In the US, longer hours may be associated with greater output, in a given industry, but they are also associated with diminished output per hour, at least for the period 2000–2005 . . . Shepard and Clifton . . . established that manufacturing productivity does not necessarily improve when hours are lengthened. Their empirical study . . . suggests that the use of overtime hours actually lowers average productivity, measured as output per worker hour, for almost all of the industries in the sample, even when the data are controlled or corrected. More precisely, a 10-per cent increase in overtime resulted, on average, in a 2.4-per cent decrease in productivity measured by hourly output. Indeed, it appears that in many, if not most, industries in the United States, shorter hours are actually associated with higher rates of output per hour . . . The potential theoretical and practical impact of a reduction in hours on productivity was assessed by the [ILO] over twenty years ago (White, 1987). Improvements in the efficiency of labour utilization were evident from a century's worth of research that found some productivity improvement following a reduction in hours, depending, of course, on the accompanying conditions and responses, in the medium if not the short term. Four types of reductions were distinguished, all of which remain relevant to today's conditions. Each creates its own potential for productivity improvements that would offset much, if not all, of the initial costs associated with shorter working hours. The four types are: reductions in excessive hours, gradual reductions in standard hours, accelerated reductions in standard hours, and individualized options for reducing working hours. When implementing the flexible scheduling implied by the last type, White reported, many plants in the United Kingdom and on the European continent included shorter weekly hours or part-time options. He found that the circumstances most likely to produce gains in labour productivity were those involving a cyclical or variable workload. When the workload tapered off, such flexibility allowed workers to match their attendance more closely to their preferred allocation of time.

From an economic standpoint, the same reasoning can be applied in relation to legislation which prescribes a minimum amount of annual leave, namely that workers are more productive if they are afforded the opportunity to take time off to recuperate and refresh themselves. This also benefits employers with greater staff loyalty. Moreover, the ability of employers to retain workers is enhanced by the provision of annual leave, as well as assisting employers in the recruitment of labour. As such, the employer's staff turnover rate is reduced, as are the costs of training and retraining, leading to enhanced efficiency and output. Of course, the neoclassical economist would counter these arguments by pointing to the double costs borne by employers where staff are afforded rights to take annual leave: first, there is the expense of recruiting a replacement worker to cover an employee while he/she is off on annual leave, including the training and salary costs of the former; and secondly, by providing an employee with annual leave, the employer is essentially paying a salary in return for no output for the duration of the period of annual leave. As such, in crude terms, it is paying something for nothing.

Reflection points

1. Which account of the effects of national minimum wage laws, maximum weekly limits on working hours, and annual leave do you prefer, i.e. the neoclassical or new institutional economics analysis? Give reasons for your answer.

2. Now that a National Living Wage has been introduced, do you agree that it has been beneficial to (a) the UK economy and (b) to workers and employees? How does it differ from the 'Living Wage'? See https://www.theguardian.com/society/2017/nov/06/uk-living-wage-rises-to-875-per-hour. Give reasons for your answer.

3. The earlier extract from Davidov's article argues that the national minimum wage is an employment policy designed to redistribute a modest amount of resources and wealth away from employers and their shareholders to workers and the State (via the benefits saved), i.e. distributive justice. In your opinion, is it justifiable for employment policy and laws to be utilized as a means of effecting distributive justice? Or is redistribution a goal which should only be pursued via State fiscal/tax policy?

4. In 2011, the average full-time worker in the UK worked 32.3 hours per week, which is higher than many EU countries.[42] This is demonstrative of the so-called UK 'long hours culture'. Are you convinced that the WTD and WTR should prevent British workers from working as many hours as they like?

 For additional reading on the historical and contextual analysis of, and justifications for, the statutory regulation of pay and working time, visit the Online Resources for this book at www.oup.com/uk/cabrelli3e/

8.2 STATUTORY WAGE REGULATION

In this section, we will address the statutory inroads made into the wage–work bargain. More specifically, section 8.2.1 will focus on the regulation of the minimum wage in the NMWA and the National Minimum Wage Regulations 2015 ('NMWR').[43] Meanwhile, the wage protection legislation found in Parts II and III of the ERA will be the focus of the discussion in section 8.2.2.

8.2.1 National minimum wage legislation

It is a truism that the express or implied terms of the contract of employment are very unlikely to confer any right to an automatic pay increase or pay progression, e.g. an annual uplift based on the rate of inflation.[44] This can be contrasted with statute, which does confer an uplift and progression at the lower end of the scale, i.e. the national minimum wage. The terms of section 1 of the NMWA are deceptively simple inasmuch as they confer an entitlement in favour of workers to the payment of the national minimum wage:

---

[42] See OECD, 'Hours Worked', available at https://data.oecd.org/emp/hours-worked.htm (last visited 27 November 2017); and 'Which Nationalities Work the Longest Hours?' (*The Telegraph*, 24 February 2017), available at http://www.telegraph.co.uk/travel/maps-and-graphics/nationalities-that-work-the-longest-hours/ (last visited 27 November 2017).

[43] SI 2015/621, which repealed the National Minimum Wage Regulations 1999 (SI 1999/584).

[44] See *Thorne v House of Commons Commission* [2014] IRLR 260; *Cabinet Office v Beavan* [2014] IRLR 434; and *EHRC v Earle* [2014] IRLR 845.

Section 1 Workers to be paid at least the minimum wage

(1) A person who qualifies for the national minimum wage shall be remunerated by his employer in respect of his work in any pay reference period at a rate which is not less than the national minimum wage . . .

(3) The national minimum wage shall be such single hourly rate as the Secretary of State may from time to time prescribe.

Section 12 of the NMWA also provides that workers have the right to be given a written statement with each payment containing such information as would enable them to determine whether they have been paid the minimum wage. The national minimum wage was initially set at £3.60 per hour and the current rates are illustrated in Figure 8.1. In April 2016, the national minimum wage was relabelled the 'national living wage' in the case of persons who are 25 years of age or over[45]—not to be confused with the 'living wage', which is a non-legal prescribed rate of hourly pay, set at £8.75 at the time of writing.[46] There is a commitment from the Government to increase the level of the national living wage to £9 per hour by 2020.

The national minimum wage and national living wage do not provide for a compulsory increase in the minimum wage every year in line with earnings or inflation. However, in the February of each year, the Low Pay Commission ('LPC')[47] submits a report to the Government setting out recommendations on the future rate of the minimum wage. As Table 8.1 demonstrates, the minimum wage has been subject to uprating every year since its inception.

The median earnings of employees aged 25 and above in the UK in 2017 were £13.03 per hour.[48] At that time, the minimum wage was £7.50 per hour. Accordingly, the minimum wage equated to 57.55 per cent of the median wage in 2017.

In order to negotiate the architecture of the national minimum wage legislation, it is beneficial to divide the discussion into (1) the relational scope of application of the

Current rates

These rates are for the National Living Wage and the National Minimum Wage. The rates change every April.

Year	25 and over	21 to 24	18 to 20	Under 18	Apprentice
April 2018	£7.83	£7.38	£5.90	£4.20	£3.70

Figure 8.1 *Current rates of national living wage and national minimum wage*
Source: https://www.gov.uk/national-minimum-wage-rates (last visited 27 November 2017).

---

[45] See regulation 4 of the NMWR.

[46] See http://www.livingwage.org.uk/home (last visited 27 November 2017).

[47] The Low Pay Commission was set up under the NMWA to provide advice to the Government about the national minimum wage. It is an independent statutory non-departmental public body, i.e. a 'quango' comprising three trade unionists, three representatives of employers, specialists engaged in industrial relations, and two economists from academia.

[48] See *National Minimum Wage: Low Pay Commission Report 2017* (Cm 9536, 2017), available at https://www.gov.uk/government/uploads/system/uploads/attachment_data/file/661195/Low_Pay_Commission_2017_report.pdf page 62 at para 2.79 (last visited 27 November 2017).

Table 8.1 *The national minimum wage rates since 1999*

From	Adult rate (for workers aged 21+)		Development rate (for workers aged 18–20)	16–17-year-old rate	Apprentice rate
1 Apr 2018	£7.83	£7.38	£5.90	£4.20	£3.70
1 Apr 2017	£7.50	£7.05	£5.60	£4.05	£3.50
1 Oct 2016	£7.20	£6.95	£5.55	£4.00	£3.40
1 Apr 2016	£7.20	£6.70	£5.30	£3.87	£3.30
1 Oct 2015	£6.70		£5.30	£3.87	£3.30
1 Oct 2014	£6.50		£5.13	£3.79	£2.73
1 Oct 2013	£6.31		£5.03	£3.72	£2.68
1 Oct 2012	£6.19		£4.98	£3.68	£2.65
1 Oct 2011	£6.08		£4.98	£3.68	£2.60
1 Oct 2010	£5.93		£4.92	£3.64	£2.50

From	Adult rate (for workers aged 22+)	Development rate (for workers aged 18-21)	16–17-year-old Rate	Apprentice rate
1 Oct 2009	£5.80	£4.83	£3.57	–
1 Oct 2008	£5.73	£4.77	£3.53	–
1 Oct 2007	£5.52	£4.60	£3.53	–
1 Oct 2006	£5.35	£4.45	£3.40	–
1 Oct 2005	£5.05	£4.25	£3.30	–
1 Oct 2004	£4.85	£4.10	£3.00	–
1 Oct 2003	£4.50	£3.80	£3.00	–
1 Oct 2002	£4.20	£3.50	–	–
1 Oct 2001	£4.10	£3.50	–	–
1 Oct 2000	£3.70	£3.20	–	–
1 Apr 1999	£3.60	£3.00	–	–

NMWA and NMWR, i.e. which workers are entitled to claim, and disentitled from claiming, the minimum wage; (2) the definition of working time for the purposes of calculating the minimum wage; (3) which payments received by the worker count towards the worker's wage/remuneration; and (4) the enforcement mechanisms.

8.2.1.1 Relational scope of application

The relational scope of the NMWA is laid down in section 1(2):

Section 1 Workers to be paid at least the minimum wage . . .

(2) A person qualifies for the national minimum wage if he is an individual who—

  (a) is a worker,

  (b) is working, or ordinarily works, in the [UK] under his contract, and

  (c) has ceased to be of compulsory school age . . .

We can see that section 1(2) directs that a 'worker' ordinarily working in the UK under his/her contract who is no longer of compulsory school age is entitled to be paid the minimum wage. Section 54(3) of the NMWA defines 'worker' in the standard statutory manner.[49] Sections 34 and 35 also include agency workers and home workers within the coverage of the NMWA, as are House of Commons and House of Lords staff and individuals in Crown employment specifically covered.[50] Further, section 41 empowers the Secretary of State to include a category of individual 'of a prescribed description who would not otherwise be a worker' within the compass of the word 'worker'.

On the other hand, there are several categories of individual excluded from the NMWA and the NMWR.[51] The following are excluded: the armed forces;[52] share fishermen;[53] unpaid volunteers working for a charity, voluntary organization, associated fund-raising body, or statutory body;[54] residential members of a religious community (except a provider of further or higher education or independent school);[55] prisoners;[56] and workers involved in certain prescribed government training schemes or work experience at a further or higher education institution, e.g. a 'sandwich-type course'.[57] With regard to volunteers, or interns,[58] the requisite mutuality of obligation necessary to establish a 'worker' contract is absent, since there is no obligation impressed on the enterprise to provide work *and pay for it*: the intern[59] and volunteer generally will have no expectation of being paid. Alternatively, it is common for no legally binding contract to be put in place between the enterprise and the volunteer/intern,[60] in which case the definition of 'worker' in section 54(3) cannot be engaged,[61] unless it can be argued that the volunteer/intern's obligation personally to do work for an organization produces some economic value and the intern is paid.[62] As for unpaid pupil barristers, the Court of Appeal held in *Edmonds v Lawson*[63] that they were not workers on the basis that they benefit from work experience, training, and development rather than financial remuneration. Other categories of excluded worker laid down in regulation 57 of the NMWR include au pairs and family household workers, i.e. workers engaged in work relating to the employer's family household activities where the worker is not a family member, but is treated as such, and resides in the family home and participates in the sharing of family chores and activities.[64] Likewise, regulation 58 of the NMWR prescribes that family members living in the family home who are engaged in work

---

[49] See Chapter 4, section 4.2.1   [50] Sections 36, 38, and 39 of the NMWA.

[51] The Secretary of State has broad regulation-making powers under sections 3 and 4 of the NMWA.

[52] Section 37 of the NMWA.   [53] Section 43 of the NMWA.   [54] Section 44 of the NMWA.

[55] Section 44A of the NMWA.   [56] Section 45 of the NMWA.

[57] Regulation 53 of the NMWR. For the position of qualifying trainees, see regulation 54 of the NMWR.

[58] See D. Morris, 'Volunteering and Employment Status' (1999) 28 *Industrial Law Journal* 249, 253–4; B. Simpson, 'The Employment Act 2008's Amendments to the National Minimum Wage Legislation' (2009) 38 *Industrial Law Journal* 57, 59–60; and S. Malik, 'Unpaid Website Intern Celebrates Court Victory' (*The Guardian*, 23 May 2011).

[59] For an analysis of the position of interns, see D. Boffey, 'Revealed: Class Divide at the Heart of Unpaid Internships—Survey Shows How Employers Are Able to Exploit Graduates' Desperation to Find Work' (*The Observer*, 2 December 2012), available at http://www.guardian.co.uk/money/2012/dec/01/interns-rebel-against-unpaid-placements at page 16 (last visited 27 November 2017); https://www.gov.uk/national-minimum-wage-work-experience-and-internships (last visited 27 November 2017). It is possible that training required for actual interning or volunteering can convert the relationship to a 'worker' relationship and also be equated to remuneration, thus demanding the payment of the minimum wage.

[60] For example, see *X v Mid Sussex Citizens Advice Bureau* [2012] UKSC 59, [2013] 1 All ER 1038.

[61] For the effect of illegality on the 'worker' contract, see the analysis in S. Fraser and A. Sher, 'The National Minimum Wage: Under Threat from an Unlikely Source' (2006) 35 *Industrial Law Journal* 289.

[62] See https://www.gov.uk/national-minimum-wage-work-experience-and-internships (last visited 27 November 2017).   [63] [2000] ICR 567.

[64] See *Julio v Jose* [2012] ICR 487 and *Nambalat v Taher* [2012] IRLR 1004. But cf. *Ajai v Abu* [2017] IRLR 1113.

activities in respect of the family's business are not entitled to be paid the national minimum wage in respect of such work.

8.2.1.2 Working time

Once it has been established that an individual is a worker falling within the purview of the operation of the NMWA, the next stage is to consider whether the work that he/she performs is work for which the national minimum wage will be paid. This is to be undertaken on the basis of the express (written or oral) and implied terms of the worker's contract, including the subsequent conduct of the parties.[65] It is a major challenge to formulate the basis on which the minimum wage will be paid, given the diverse range of contractual arrangements for the supply of labour, working time, and remuneration that conceivably may be entered into between workers and enterprises. For example, some workers are paid weekly, some by annual salary, and some based on their productivity, e.g. the 'piece' worker paid 4p per unit he/she manufactures. As such, the regime established by the NMWA and NMWR must be sufficiently robust to be inclusive of all workers, regardless of how they are paid or work. We find that regulation 17 and Chapters 2–5 of Part 5 of the NMWR divide working time into four mutually exclusive categories as follows.

- *Time work* This is work for which the worker is paid by a set period of time, e.g. by the hour.[66] Where the worker is contracted to be at the employer's disposal for a set number of hours in return for which he/she is entitled to remuneration, such a conventional time-based payment system presents no particular difficulty. However, matters become particularly fraught when the working arrangements concerned do not fit the normal pattern, e.g. when 'time work' includes shift work where a worker spends most of the time not performing any work tasks, 'on-call' work, and circumstances where the worker is entitled to sleep whilst working.[67] Matters here are further complicated by the fact that 'sleep-in, on-call' work, i.e. where a time worker is *on call, available, but sleeping and waiting to work*, rather than in fact working, is specifically covered by regulation 32(1) and (2) of the NMWR, in which case on-call work is not accounted for in calculating the minimum wage in two circumstances:

> **Regulation 32 Time work where worker is available at or near a place of work**
>
> (1) Time work includes hours when a worker is available, and required to be available, at or near a place of work for the purposes of working unless the worker is at home.
>
> (2) In paragraph (1), hours when a worker is 'available' only includes hours when the worker is awake for the purposes of working, even if a worker by arrangement sleeps at or near a place of work and the employer provides suitable facilities for sleeping.

Regulation 32 prescribes two exceptions where an on-call worker will be unable to count his/her working time towards the hours worked for the purposes of earning the minimum wage: first, where the on-call worker's home is at or near the workplace *and the time is time at which the worker is at, or entitled to spend at, home*; and secondly, where the worker is afforded the right to sleep at or near the workplace and is provided with sleeping facilities, *it is only time during which he/she is permitted to*

---

[65] *Governing Body of Binfield Church of England Primary School v Roll* [2016] IRLR 670, 671–2 per Judge Hand QC.   [66] Regulation 30 of the NMWR.
[67] See the discussion in L. Rodgers, 'The Notion of Working Time' (2009) 38 *Industrial Law Journal* 80, 83–6.

use those facilities and is awake for the purposes of working that will be treated as payable at the minimum wage rate.

In a slew of conflicting decisions,[68] the Employment Appeal Tribunal ('EAT') and Court of Appeal reached different conclusions as to whether 'sleep-in' and 'on-call' workers who were security guards or working in residential care units for the elderly could count their on-call and sleep-in working time for the purposes of calculating the minimum wage. The main point that could be extracted from these decisions was that 'sleep-in' 'on-call' workers could count time working as 'time work' simply by being present at the workplace. The difficulty for employers was that workers in the care sector were often paid a fixed allowance in respect of such sleep-in periods on the premises, rather than the minimum wage. The workers sought to challenge this practice.[69] The EAT in *Focus Care Agency Ltd v Roberts*[70] recognized that it is difficult to decide whether sleep-in time counts as 'time work' or not (on the basis that regulation 32 applies). The EAT was reluctant to follow the approach adopted in the previous decisions where a 'sleep-in' 'on-call' worker would be held to be working on the basis of 'time work' simply by being present at the workplace. Instead, it counselled tribunals to apply a variety of criteria to ascertain whether a worker is working simply by being present:

■ *Focus Care Agency Ltd v Roberts* [2017] ICR 1186, 1201H–1202D

Simler J (President):

The authorities identify a number of potentially relevant factors. No single factor is determinative and the weight each factor carries (if any) will vary according to the facts of the particular case. The following are potentially relevant factors in determining whether a person is working by being present. (i) The employer's particular purpose in engaging the worker may be relevant to the extent that it informs what the worker might be expected or required to do: for example, if the employer is subject to a regulatory or contractual requirement to have someone present during the particular period the worker is engaged to be present, that might indicate whether and the extent to which the worker is working by simply being present. (ii) The extent to which the worker's activities are restricted by the requirement to be present and at the disposal of the employer may be relevant. This may include considering the extent to which the worker is required to remain on the premises throughout the shift on pain of discipline if he or she slips away to do something else. (iii) The degree of responsibility undertaken by the worker may be relevant . . . [it is possible to distinguish] between the limited degree of responsibility in sleeping in at the premises to call out the emergency services in case of a break-in or a fire on the one hand, and a night sleeper in a home for the disabled where a heavier personal responsibility is placed on the worker in relation to duties that might have to be performed during the night. (iv) The immediacy of the requirement to provide services if something untoward occurs or an emergency arises may also be relevant. In this regard,

---

[68] See *British Nursing Association v IRC* [2003] ICR 19; *Walton v Independent Living Organisation Ltd* [2003] ICR 688 (see the discussion in B. Simpson, 'The National Minimum Wage Five Years on: Reflections on Some General Issues' (2004) 33 *Industrial Law Journal* 22, 29–32); *Scottbridge Construction Ltd v Wright* [2003] IRLR 21; *McCartney v Oversley House Management* [2006] ICR 510; *Burrow Down Support Services Ltd v Rossiter* [2008] ICR 1172; *South Manchester Abbeyfield Society Ltd v Hopkins* [2011] ICR 254; *Whittlestone v BJP Home Support Ltd* [2014] ICR 275; *Esparon (t/a Middle West Residential Care Home) v Slavikovska* [2014] IRLR 598; and *Shannon v Clifton House Residential* [2015] IRLR 982. For commentary, see L. Hayes, 'Care and Control: Are the National Minimum Wage Entitlements of Homecare Workers at Risk under the Care Act 2014?' (2015) 44 *Industrial Law Journal* 492.

[69] The HMRC have specifically targeted employers in the social care sector for investigation as to whether they are paying the minimum wage: see http://www.independent.co.uk/news/health/social-care-sector-sleep-in-carers-back-pay-bill-hmrc-charity-2019-deadline-a8033816.html (last visited 27 November 2017).

[70] [2017] ICR 1186.

it may be relevant to determine whether the worker is the person who decides whether to intervene and then intervenes when necessary, or whether the worker is woken as and when needed by another worker with immediate responsibility for intervening. Regulation 32 is only relevant and to be considered if the tribunal decides, having considered the terms of the relevant contract and the nature of the engagement against the factual matrix, that the worker is not working by being present during the period for which he claims. Each case is likely to turn on the consideration of its own particular facts. There will be cases where the line is a difficult one to draw and the current cases are good examples of difficult factual situations in which these regulations must be applied.

Adopting this multifactorial approach, the EAT ruled that the minimum wage was to be paid for the whole shift as the worker had to be present in the workplace to properly discharge her contractual duties. This could be distinguished from 'on-call' work where the workers could go as they please, provided they could be contacted and respond effectively to such calls: in the latter case, regulation 32 will apply to deny the worker the minimum wage in respect of that period.

Salaried work A worker is a salaried hours worker where he/she is paid solely an annual salary or annual salary and bonus on the basis of a definitive number of hours per year and has a contractual entitlement to be paid in equal weekly or monthly instalments of wages in respect of those hours.[71] Where a salaried hours worker is absent from work, e.g. in respect of holidays or sickness, he/she continues to be entitled to draw his/her salary. Akin to the 'time work' category, a similar regime applies in respect of 'on-call' salaried hours workers, i.e. that where a salaried hours worker is on call, available at or near a place of work, and waiting to work, rather than in fact working, he/she will have a right to be paid in respect of such hours, subject to the same two exceptions adumbrated earlier.[72]

Output work This caters for the 'piece' worker who is paid by reference to the number of pieces made, tasks completed, number or value of sales made or transactions completed by the worker, or as a result of his/her work.[73] As noted by Simpson, '[i]t was always likely that provision for translating a [national minimum wage] expressed as an hourly rate into an acceptable "minimum wage" for workers paid by reference to some measure of the quality of work produced would give rise to difficulties'.[74] Indeed, since the inception of the national minimum wage, the formula has already been changed once. The current position furnishes a pair of options for the calculation of the working hours of output workers. First, the worker may be paid the minimum wage for every hour actually worked.[75] However, if the contract fails to specify any normal, minimum, or maximum set of hours, the minimum wage must be determined on the basis of the mean hourly output rate, sometimes referred to as the 'fair rate'. The following extract from the UK Government website illustrates the calculation:

■ **UK Government website**

Work out the fair rate

1. Find out the average rate of work per hour (tasks or pieces completed).

2. Divide it by 1.2 (this means new workers won't be disadvantaged if they're not as fast as the others yet).

---

[71] See regulation 21 of the NMWR.   [72] See regulation 27(1)(b) and (2) of the NMWR.
[73] See regulation 36 of the NMWR.
[74] B. Simpson, 'The National Minimum Wage Five Years on: Reflections on Some General Issues' (2004) 33 *Industrial Law Journal* 22, 32.   [75] See regulations 37, 42, and 43 of the NMWR.

3. Divide the hourly minimum wage rate by that number to work out the fair rate for each piece of work completed.

Work out the average rate of work per hour

To work out the rate to pay workers, employers must carry out a fair test to see what the average rate of work is.

1. Test some or all of the workers. The group you test must be typical of the whole workforce—not just the most efficient or fastest ones.

2. Work out how many pieces of work have been completed in a normal, average working hour.

3. Divide this by the number of workers to work out the average rate.

4. If the work changes significantly, do another test to work out the new average rate. It's not necessary to do another test if the same work is being done in a different environment, eg work previously done in a factory being done at home.

Example

Workers are paid for each shirt they make. They can produce on average 12 shirts per hour. This number is divided by 1.2 to make 10.

Andy is 25 and is eligible for the national living wage rate of £7.83.

This means he must be paid at least 78.3p per shirt he makes (£7.83 divided by 10).

Source: Available at https://www.gov.uk/minimum-wage-different-types-work/paid-per-task-or-piece-of-work-done (last visited 27 November 2017).

- *Unmeasured work* An individual is an unmeasured worker where his/her work does not constitute any of the time worker, salaried hours worker, or output work categories. The hours of work actually worked by the worker may be counted for the purposes of determining his/her minimum wage,[76] which will include hours spent undergoing training or travelling as part of work.[77] Alternatively, an agreement in writing between the worker and the employer may specify the average daily number of hours the worker is likely to spend in carrying out the duties required of him/her under his/her contract to do unmeasured work.[78]

8.2.1.3 Payments which count towards the calculation of the national minimum wage

Once the nature of a worker's working time has been ascertained, it is then necessary to identify his/her pay reference period. Regulation 6 of the NMWR directs that the pay reference period will be one month. Where the worker is paid by reference to a shorter period, the pay reference period will be one day for the worker who is paid daily and one week in the case of the worker paid on a weekly basis. Regulations 8 and 9 of the NMWR clarify the pay received by the worker that is treated as allocated to the pay reference period. It provides that all sums paid to the worker in the pay reference period are allocated to that period, as are sums earned in the pay reference period whose payment is deferred to the following pay reference period. Consider the following illustration.

---

[76] Regulation 45(a) of the NMWR.

[77] Regulations 46 and 47 of the NMWR. However, time spent involved in industrial action will not be treated as unmeasured work: regulation 49 of the NMWR.

[78] Regulations 49 and 50 of the NMWR. See also *Walton v Independent Living Organisation Ltd* [2003] ICR 688.

Hypothetical B

Eleanor Seagrove is 23 years old, works for Danny's Demolishers Ltd ('the Employer'), and is paid on a weekly basis. She receives £280 gross on Monday 28 January in respect of 40 hours' work she completed from Monday 21 to Sunday 27 January. She does an additional six hours' night-time overtime on Saturday 26 January for which she will receive £90 gross on Monday 4 February. For the purposes of calculating how much is attributed to the one-week pay reference period from 21 to 27 January, both the money paid and earned will be taken into account, namely £280 + £90 = £370 gross for 46 hours' work, which is equivalent to an average hourly rate of £8.04 per hour, i.e. the aggregate remuneration received and allocated to the pay reference period—£370—divided by the total number of hours worked in the pay reference period—46.[79] Therefore, we can see that Eleanor is paid above the national minimum wage rate of £7.38 per hour.

The NMWR provides that some of the remuneration received and earned by the worker in the pay reference period will not be taken into account for the purposes of calculating the national minimum wage.[80] Moreover, it is prescribed that certain payments received by the worker will reduce the amount of his/her total pay taken into account for the purposes of calculating the minimum wage.[81] In addition, certain deductions from pay received will be applied to limit the total pay of the worker for the purposes of the calculation of the minimum wage.[82] We now consider each of these in turn.

Sums paid that are to be taken into account include basic salary, bonus payments, commission, piecework payments, and other payments that incentivize a worker in respect of his/her performance. Moreover, regulations 9(1)(e) and 14–16 provide for an accommodation allowance to be taken into account, which is the only non-cash benefit received by the worker that will be accounted for. The idea behind the allowance is that it acts as a worker protective measure, encouraging employers to provide accommodation to their workers and disincentivizing them from subjecting their workers to excessive accommodation charges. It is provided that the value of the worker's accommodation is equivalent to the number of days it was supplied to the worker during his/her pay reference period multiplied by the daily accommodation allowance of £7.00.[83] That figure is then added to the worker's pay in determining the national minimum wage.

Hypothetical C

By way of example, if Eleanor in Hypothetical B had been provided with accommodation for seven days during her one-week pay reference period, the relevant sum for the purposes of the minimum wage would be £7.00 × 7 = £49.00 + £370 = £419.00. This figure would then be divided by 46 hours to calculate the average hourly rate of £414.80 ÷ 46 = £9.11, which is higher than the national minimum wage rate of £7.38 per hour.

However, if the worker pays a rent for the living accommodation so that it is not a benefit in kind, the value of that rent up to the accommodation allowance is not taken into account, subject to any excess which is applied to reduce the worker's total remuneration

---

[79] See regulation 14 of the NMWR. [80] Regulation 10 of the NMWR.
[81] Regulation 11 of the NMWR. [82] Regulations 12–16 of the NMWR.
[83] See regulation 16(1) of the NMWR.

for the purposes of ascertaining the minimum wage.[84] As for gas and electricity and other service costs associated with the accommodation supplied by the employer, it has been held that these are not included within the accommodation allowance.[85]

We now move on to consider the pay and benefits received by the worker that are disregarded in calculating the national minimum wage. These tend to be payments or allowances that are intended to supplement the worker's wage, rather than form part of it. As noted earlier, benefits in kind are not included, irrespective of whether they have a monetary value or not.[86] Likewise, the following are ignored: employer loans to workers;[87] wage advances;[88] pension, allowance, or gratuity payments in respect of retirement;[89] compensation for loss of office;[90] lump sum retirement payments;[91] redundancy payments;[92] tribunal or court settlement payments;[93] payments made to reward workers under a workplace suggestion scheme;[94] allowances in respect of workplace absences or engagement in industrial action;[95] allowances that are not referable to the worker's performance, such as on-call payments or a London weighting payment;[96] expenses payments or allowances;[97] and travelling expenses allowed as deductions from earnings under section 338 of the Income Tax (Earnings and Pensions) Act 2003.[98] The most significant of the payments ignored in calculating the minimum wage is addressed in regulation 10(m) of the NMWR, namely gratuities, tips, cover charges, and service charges paid by the employer to the worker which represent amounts paid by customers.[99] This provision was introduced in October 2009 and is designed to ensure that employers are prevented from using tips and gratuities to cover their minimum wage obligations. Consider the following Hypothetical D.

Hypothetical D

Erica Osborne is aged 22 and works 20 hours a week in Danny's Demolishers ('DD') head office restaurant in London as a waitress. Erica is paid £160 gross per week, £40 of which comprises tips paid to her by DD in respect of sums received from restaurant

---

[84] See regulation 14 of the NMWR.

[85] In *Leisure Employment Services Ltd v Commissioners for HM Revenue & Customs* [2007] ICR 1056, the Court of Appeal adopted the position that an employer was disentitled from charging its workers £6 per fortnight for gas and electricity where the employer was paying the workers the minimum wage when their wages and the accommodation allowance were added together. Therefore, if the charges applied for gas and electricity were taken into account, the effect was that the workers were being paid less than the minimum wage. That was the case notwithstanding that the gas and electricity charge levied was less expensive than that which the workers would have been obliged to pay to the utility suppliers direct. Davidov has justified the decision arrived at by the Court of Appeal on the basis that it protects workers from abusive managerial practices: G. Davidov, 'A Purposive Interpretation of the National Minimum Wage Act' (2009) 72 *Modern Law Review* 581, 605–6.

[86] See regulation 10(f) of the NMWR. Of course, the accommodation allowance is the only exception.

[87] See regulation 10(a) of the NMWR.   [88] See *ibid*.

[89] See regulation 10(b) of the NMWR.   [90] See *ibid*.   [91] See *ibid*.

[92] See regulation 10(d) of the NMWR.   [93] See regulation 10(c) of the NMWR.

[94] See regulation 10(e) of the NMWR.   [95] See regulation 10(h) of the NMWR.

[96] See regulation 10(k) of the NMWR. See also *Smith v Oxfordshire Learning Disability NHS Trust* [2009] ICR 1395, 1402D–1403B per Underhill J (P) on the status of a sleep-in payment allowance.

[97] See regulation 10(l) of the NMWR.   [98] See regulation 10(n) of the NMWR.

[99] For a fascinating discussion of the difficulties caused by the worker–employer–customer relationship, see E. Albin, 'A Worker–Employer–Customer Triangle: The Case of Tips' (2011) 40 *Industrial Law Journal* 181. See also G. Davidov, 'A Purposive Interpretation of the National Minimum Wage Act' (2009) 72 *Modern Law Review* 581, 603–4; E. Albin, 'Labour Law in a Service World' (2010) 72 *Modern Law Review* 959, 970–2.

customers. Since the £40 in tips represents sums paid by customers in respect of tips, gratuities, cover charge, or service charge, it is ignored for the purposes of calculating Erica's minimum wage by virtue of regulation 10(m) of the NMWR. It is irrelevant whether the £40 is paid through DD's payroll or not. Since the £40 is disregarded, it is clear that DD is in breach of the NMWA: it is paying Erica £120 ÷ 20 hours = £6 per hour, which is less than the national minimum wage rate of £7.38 per hour.

Prior to 1 October 2009, only tips, gratuities, etc. paid directly to the worker by customers or sums paid to a troncmaster (such as a head bar steward or head waiter) and subsequently distributed to the worker[100] would be ignored in the context of the calculation of the worker's minimum wage. If the tips were paid to the worker by the employer through payroll, the employer could include them in ascertaining whether the worker's pay conformed to the minimum wage legislation. However, the government decided to repeal this provision[101] and it is now the case that any payment made by the employer to the worker which amounts to a tip, gratuity, etc. is disregarded. In the following extract, Albin explores the rationale for the change in the law:

■ E. Albin, 'A Worker–Employer–Customer Triangle: The Case of Tips' (2011) 40 *Industrial Law Journal* 181, 184–5

Tip provision has two aspects. It is an act of generosity on the part of the customer, but at the same time it constitutes a distribution of employing functions to the customer. The clearest employing function is the payment for the work performed, but tip provision impacts work relations in more subtle ways. As soon as customers contribute to the worker's earnings, they become involved in the management of the employment relationship. Workers adopt specific behaviours to please customers and fulfil their wishes, not only for the benefit of the establishment owner but also in the hope that, by responding to customer wishes, their earnings will rise, a good word will be said to the employer, etc. Once a worker is more dependent on a third party for earnings, she becomes less loyal to her employer and more biased towards the paying customer. As a consequence, her relationship with her employer might weaken, or in legal terms become more casual, making her employment more precarious. Such precariousness is especially troubling due to the fact that tip receivers are usually located at the lower end of the labour market. Hence, any enhancement of their precarious situation, which may result from the legal approach towards tips, should be considered.

Therefore, at the heart of this change of policy is a recognition that workers generally in receipt of tips are vulnerable and usually found in the hospitality and catering sectors at the lower end of the pay scale. However, whilst persuasive, there is an alternative narrative. This is the claim that rather than workers becoming less loyal when they are dependent on customers to 'top up' their low wages, on the contrary, a stronger relationship may be created between management and workers due to staff performing better in

[100] *Revenue & Customs Commissioners v Annabel's (Berkeley Square) Ltd* [2009] 4 All ER 55.

[101] See Department for Business, Enterprise and Regulatory Reform, *The National Minimum Wage: Governmental Response to Consultation on Service Charges, Tips, Gratuities and Cover Charges* (May 2009), available at https://www.gov.uk/government/publications/national-minimum-wage-code-of-best-practice-on-service-charges-tips-gratuities-and-cover-charges (last visited 28 November 2017); Department for Business, Innovation and Skills, *Code of Best Practice on Service Charges, Tips, Gratuities and Cover Charges* (October 2009), available at https://www.gov.uk/government/publications/national-minimum-wage-code-of-best-practice-on-service-charges-tips-gratuities-and-cover-charges (last visited 28 November 2017).

order to gain better tips. The argument runs that this strengthens the employer-worker relationship. In addition, can it be claimed with any conviction that the receipt of tips make workers more precarious, and if so, then how so?

The Government is currently looking into tipping practices and whether the existing legal regime ought to be reformed. A call for evidence was issued in September 2015[102] and the Government has since issued a consultation paper on tipping in response.[103] The consultation contained a series of policy options including whether to ban or restrict the levying of table sales charges on staff (which is a fee paid by waiting staff based on their sales during a shift) and how the prevalence of well managed tronc systems could be incentivized and increased. However, at the time of writing, the Government had not finalized its policy position and the impetus for reform seems to have hit the buffers owing to more pressing issues such as Brexit.

Finally, we address deductions that must be made from the worker's gross pay in order to calculate his/her pay for the purposes of the national minimum wage. These are deductions in respect of the worker's expenditure in connection with his/her employment, including the following:

- the cost of purchase of tools or equipment or uniform cleaning;[104]

- any deduction made by the employer for its own use and benefit (e.g. a deduction in respect of meals);[105]

- payments to any person (other than the employer) on account of the worker's expenditure in connection with his/her employment unless the expenditure is met, or designed to be met, by a payment paid to the worker by the employer;[106] and

- any payment or deduction made in respect of living accommodation provided by the employer to the extent that it exceeds the maximum accommodation allowance of £49.00 per week;[107]

These sums can be contrasted with the deductions and payments that are not taken into account to reduce the pay of the worker for the purposes of calculating the minimum wage, as follows:

- deductions in respect of the worker's conduct or any other event[108] in respect of which he/she is contractually liable;[109]

- deductions made by the employer in respect of a loan or wage advance;[110]

- deductions attributable to an accidental overpayment of wages;[111]

- deductions in respect of the purchase by the worker of any shares, other securities or share option, or of any share in a partnership;[112]

- any payment by the worker in respect of the purchase of goods or services from the employer, unless the purchase is made in order to comply with a requirement of the worker's contract or otherwise required by the employer in connection with his/her employment;[113]

---

[102] See https://www.gov.uk/government/consultations/tips-gratuities-cover-and-service-charges-call-for-evidence (last visited 28 November 2017).

[103] See https://www.gov.uk/government/uploads/system/uploads/attachment_data/file/521946/bis-16–172-tipping-consultation.pdf (last visited 28 November 2017).

[104] See regulation 13(a) of the NMWR.   [105] See regulation 12(1) of the NMWR.

[106] See regulation 13(b) of the NMWR.   [107] See regulations 14–16 of the NMWR.

[108] This will include a voluntary resignation: *Commissioners for Revenue and Customs v Lorne Stewart plc* [2015] IRLR 187.   [109] See regulation 12(2)(a) of the NMWR.

[110] See regulation 12(2)(b) of the NMWR.   [111] See regulation 12(2)(c) of the NMWR.

[112] See regulation 12(2)(d) of the NMWR.

[113] See regulation 12(2)(e) of the NMWR. In *Leisure Employment Services Ltd v Commissioners for HM Revenue & Customs* [2007] ICR 1056, it was held that deductions for gas and electricity in the case of live-in workers fell under this rule.

- any deduction levied by a higher education institution, further education institution, 16–19 academy, local housing authority, or registered social landlord for accommodation in terms of regulation 14(2) of the NMWR; and
- deductions for tax and National Insurance contributions.[114]

8.2.1.4 Enforcement

The national minimum wage and national living wage are enforced via a combination of private and public means. There are two mechanisms made available for individual private enforcement. First, if the employer fails to pay the minimum wage, section 17 of the NMWA entitles the worker to raise a breach of contract claim in the domestic courts or the employment tribunal. In the case of the domestic courts, the worker has six years from the date of the contractual breach to raise civil proceedings in England and five years in Scotland. Arrears of pay can be claimed for the periods of six or five years, depending on whether the proceedings are raised in England or Scotland. Meanwhile, the worker is only permitted to present a complaint to an employment tribunal for breach of contract if his/her employment has terminated, in which case he/she has three months from the date of termination to claim. Since there is a much longer period available to workers to raise a claim in the courts, they are more likely to proceed through this route given the difficulties involved in ascertaining whether they have been underpaid from an investigation of the employer's records.[115] The second mechanism available to a worker to privately enforce a claim—and, 'the most common form of individual enforcement action'[116]—is to raise an unlawful deduction from wages claim under Part II of the ERA.[117] Since the worker's pay is less than the minimum wage, the shortfall is treated as an unauthorized deduction from pay. Such a claim is raised in the employment tribunal and the worker has three months from the date of the underpayment to bring the complaint. There is no restriction on the period for which arrears of pay may be claimed, so long as the arrears are referable to the same series of unauthorized deductions. Furthermore, there is no cap on the amount of wages which can be claimed. As such it is possible for a worker to claim when he/she has never received any financial remuneration, but receives rent-free accommodation, for example a warden in a Sixth Form College. Finally, it is worth mentioning that these rights to enforce an underpayment are supplemented by additional ancillary rights of action which are designed to protect the former right. For example, section 23 of the NMWA stipulates that a worker has a right not to be subjected to any detriment short of dismissal by any act, or any deliberate failure to act, by his/her employer on the ground that (1) the worker took action or proposed to take such action to enforce his/her rights to be paid the

---

[114] See the archived Department for Business, Enterprise and Regulatory Reform (now the Department for Business, Energy and Industrial Strategy) National Minimum Wage Guide (revised September 2008), available at http://webarchive.nationalarchives.gov.uk/+/http://www.berr.gov.uk/files/file47736.pdf at page 37 (last visited 28 November 2017).

[115] A statutory obligation is imposed on employers to keep records sufficient to establish that they are remunerating the worker at a rate at least equal to the national minimum wage in a single document in terms of section 9 of the NMWA and regulation 59 of the NMWR. Workers have a right to inspect and examine such records under section 10 of the NMWA. For a discussion of the shortcomings of the existing process for accessing records, see B. Simpson, 'Implementing the National Minimum Wage: The 1999 Regulations' (1999) 28 *Industrial Law Journal* 171, 181.

[116] B. Simpson, 'A Milestone in the Legal Regulation of Pay: The National Minimum Wage Act 1998' (1999) 28 *Industrial Law Journal* 1, 21.

[117] A matter of no little interest is the fact that the relational coverage of Part II of the ERA is specifically extended by section 18 of the NMWA for the purposes of enforcing a minimum wage claim as an unauthorized deduction from wages in the employment tribunal. In other words, workers with no contract with the employer, agency workers, and home workers are explicitly given rights of enforcement notwithstanding that they may be unable to establish that they are a 'worker' for the purposes of the standard statutory definition of that term in section 230(3)(b) of the ERA.

minimum wage in the courts or the employment tribunal, (2) the employer was prosecuted under section 31 of the NMWA, or (3) the worker qualifies or might qualify for the minimum wage.[118] Meanwhile, section 104A provides parallel protection where the worker has been dismissed in the same set of circumstances, in which case his/her dismissal is treated as automatically unfair for the purposes of Part X of the ERA.[119]

If we now move on to consider public enforcement of the national minimum wage, section 13 of the NMWA provides for HM Revenue and Customs ('HMRC') officers to be assigned to the task. Such officers are empowered to require the employer to produce records kept by it pursuant to its statutory obligation under section 9 of the NMWA and regulation 59 of the NMWR.[120] The HMRC officers may examine these records and copy them and may at all reasonable times enter any relevant premises in order to exercise such powers.[121] If an HMRC officer is of the opinion that the minimum wage laws are being infringed, he/she has the power to serve a notice of underpayment on the employer.[122] The notice will require the employer to pay to the worker the sum due within 28 days, together with all arrears of pay and a financial penalty comprising 50 per cent of the aggregate value of the arrears, subject to a £20,000 cap.[123] If the employer complies with the notice within 14 days of service, the financial penalty levied is halved.[124] Section 19C of the NMWA directs that an employer may appeal such notice to an employment tribunal on various limited grounds. If the employer fails to comply with the terms of the notice, an HMRC officer may raise proceedings on behalf of the relevant worker in the court against the employer to recover the arrears of pay or present a complaint to an employment tribunal to enforce an unauthorized deduction from wages claim under Part II of the ERA.[125] Finally, it is a criminal offence for an employer to fail to keep records in terms of section 9 of the NMWA or to keep false records or to produce or furnish false information of a material nature.[126]

On paper, the range of enforcement mechanisms available is impressive. However, the problems experienced by workers in discovering whether they have or have not been paid the minimum wage by reference to the employer's records, as well as worker concerns about their job security if they raise a claim, both operate to limit the numbers of worker complaints made to HMRC officers. In addition, a lack of manpower on the part of HMRC officers discourages them from indiscriminately deploying the administrative enforcement measures at their disposal.[127] Instead, HMRC officers have no choice but to prioritize their finite resources and use them intelligently. There is evidence that the HMRC has been adopting such a strategy in recent years,[128] but on

---

[118] Section 23(2) of the NMWA provides that whether or not the worker has the right to claim the minimum wage in the court or the employment tribunal or such a right has been infringed is irrelevant if the worker is in good faith.

[119] For more detail on the reasons for dismissal that are treated as automatically unfair, see Chapter 16, section 16.2.4.2.   [120] Section 14(1(a), (b), and (c) of the NMWA.

[121] Section 14(1)(d) of the NMWA.   [122] Section 19(1) of the NMWA.

[123] Sections 19 and 19A(5B) of the NMWA.   [124] Section 19A(10) of the NMWA.

[125] Section 19D of the ERA.   [126] Section 31 of the NMWA.

[127] See B. Simpson, 'The Employment Act 2008's Amendments to the National Minimum Wage Legislation' (2009) 38 *Industrial Law Journal* 57, 62–4.

[128] For example, the Low Pay Commission commended the HMRC on the progress it had made 'in the way enforcement is carried out, for example targeted enforcement, allocating resources to risk, and the introduction of the Pay and Work Rights Helpline (PWRH)': *National Minimum Wage: Low Pay Commission Report 2012* (Cm 8302, 2012), available at https://www.gov.uk/government/publications/national-minimum-wage-low-pay-commission-report-2012 page 124 at para 4.106 (last visited 28 November 2017). Increasing the awareness of the national minimum wage regime amongst the public has been achieved by raising the profile of the work of HMRC, e.g. naming and shaming campaigns in the media, which is a strategy that is beginning to bear fruit: see *Low Pay commission: Non-Compliance and Enforcement of the National Minimum Wage* (September 2017), available at https://www.gov.uk/government/uploads/system/uploads/attachment_data/file/645462/Non-compliance_and_enforcement_with_the_National_Minimum_Wage.pdf at paras 3.31–3.39 (last visited 28 November 2017).

a more positive note the Government has recently increased the HMRC's enforcement budget[129] from £13 million to £20 million,[130] created a new directorate of labour enforcement and exploitation, and added a new team of criminal prosecutors within the HMRC.

8.2.1.5 Reform

The Taylor review[131] has proposed a package of modest reforms that will impact upon the national minimum wage. In particular, the suggested modifications are principally intended to offset some of the insecurity and vulnerability experienced by 'gig economy' and zero-hours contract workers. For example, it has been recommended that the Government should modify minimum wage legislation to entitle gig economy workers to a piece rate. In addition, it is suggested that the Low Pay Commission ought to analyse whether zero-hours workers should receive the national living wage or minimum wage at a higher rate than the standard rate.[132]

8.2.2 Wage protection legislation

We have noted how the worker protections in the NMWA and NMWR may be enforced by presenting a complaint to an employment tribunal that the worker has suffered an unauthorized deduction from wages under section 23(1) of the ERA. The provisions of sections 13 and 23 of the ERA can be traced back to the Truck Acts passed in the nineteenth century, which were designed to impose limitations on the ability of employers to pay their workers in kind, rather than in coin.[133] They are superimposed upon the common law rules on the withholding of, and deductions from, wages which we addressed in Chapter 6, sections 6.2.1 and 6.2.2. At the heart of the provisions in Part II of the ERA is a direction that the employer must pay the worker at the agreed contractual rate without any deductions or set-off, subject to two exceptions:

(1) where the worker gives his/her prior written agreement to the deduction; or

(2) where the employer has the statutory (e.g. income tax and National Insurance contributions) or contractual right to make the deduction.

The mischief behind these provisions is that transparency is crucial before an employer deducts sums from wages and that the worker should not have sums withheld for incompetence in performance or indiscipline without contractual or statutory foundation:

---

[129] See *National Minimum Wage: Low Pay Commission Report 2015* (Cm 9017, 2015), available at https://www.gov.uk/government/publications/national-minimum-wage-low-pay-commission-report-2015 page 201 at para 5.11 (last visited 28 November 2017).

[130] See *Low Pay commission: Non-Compliance and Enforcement of the National Minimum Wage* (September 2017), available at https://www.gov.uk/government/uploads/system/uploads/attachment_data/file/645462/Non-compliance_and_enforcement_with_the_National_Minimum_Wage.pdf at para. 3.3 (last visited 28 November 2017).

[131] See *Good Work: The Taylor Review of Modern Working Practices* (July 2017), available at https://www.gov.uk/government/uploads/system/uploads/attachment_data/file/627671/good-work-taylor-review-modern-working-practices-rg.pdf at pages 37–8 and 42 (last visited 19 November 2017).

[132] *ibid.*, page 44.

[133] For an examination, see O. Kahn-Freund, 'The Tangle of the Truck Acts' (1949) 4 *Industrial Law Review* 2; S. Deakin, 'Logical Deductions? Wage Protection Before and After *Delaney v Staples*' (1992) 55 *Modern Law Review* 848, 848–50.

Section 13   Right not to suffer unauthorized deductions

(1) An employer shall not make a deduction from wages of a worker employed by him unless—

(a) the deduction is required or authorized to be made by virtue of a statutory provision or a relevant provision of the worker's contract, or

(b) the worker has previously signified in writing his agreement or consent to the making of the deduction.[134]

(2) In this section 'relevant provision', in relation to a worker's contract, means a provision of the contract comprised—

(a) in one or more written terms of the contract of which the employer has given the worker a copy on an occasion prior to the employer making the deduction in question, or

(b) in one or more terms of the contract (whether express or implied and, if express,[135] whether oral or in writing) the existence and effect, or combined effect, of which in relation to the worker the employer has notified to the worker in writing on such an occasion . . .

(6) For the purposes of this section an agreement or consent signified by a worker does not operate to authorize the making of a deduction on account of any conduct of the worker, or any other event occurring, before the agreement or consent was signified . . .

Miscellaneous exceptions to the general prohibition are laid down in section 14. For instance, the employer may deduct without restriction in respect of an overpayment of wages or expenses received, or where the worker has participated in a strike or other industrial action,[136] or in respect of payments to third parties the employer has been authorized to deduct by the worker.[137] Section 24(1) of the ERA directs that where a tribunal finds a section 23 complaint to be well founded, it must make a declaration to that effect, order the employer to pay the amount of the deduction made, and award such other amount as it considers appropriate in all the circumstances to compensate the worker for the financial loses sustained. Unlike the NMWA, enforcement is limited to private enforcement by workers and there are no HMRC officers empowered to take administrative action to force managerial compliance with Part II of the ERA.

The expression 'wages' is afforded an extensive definition:

---

[134] For the purposes of the statutory deduction scheme in Part II of the ERA, a contractual repayment clause is subject to the common law rule against penalties, i.e. in order to determine whether the repayment clause is in fact a penalty clause: *Cleeve Link Ltd v Bryla* [2014] ICR 264.

[135] Part of the tribunals' task here is to apply ordinary principles of contract law to interpret the express terms and implied terms if necessary: *Weatherilt v Cathay Pacific Airways Ltd* [2017] IRLR 609, but cf. *Agarwal v Cardiff University* [2017] IRLR 600.

[136] In *Hartley v King Edward VI College* [2017] 1 WLR 2110 and *Amey v Peter Symonds College* [2014] IRLR 206, the Supreme Court and High Court ruled that 1/365th rather than 1/260th ought to be deducted from an employee's annual pay where that employee had gone on strike. However, cf. *Cooper v Isle of Wight College* [2008] IRLR 124 where it was held 1/260th of the employee's wage/salary is deductible in respect of every day he/she is on strike.

[137] See section 14(1), (5), and (4). Additional protection is conferred on workers in retail employment whereby a ceiling of 10 per cent of wages in a pay day is placed on the employer's liability to deduct for stock deficiencies and cash shortages: sections 17–22 of the ERA.

Section 27 Meaning of 'wages' etc.

(1) In this Part 'wages', in relation to a worker, means any sums payable to the worker in connection with his employment, including—

(a) any fee, bonus,[138] commission,[139] holiday pay[140] or other emolument[141] referable to his employment, whether payable under his contract or otherwise,

(b) statutory sick pay . . .

(c) statutory maternity pay . . .

(ca) . . . statutory paternity pay . . .

(cb) statutory adoption pay . . .

(cc) statutory shared parental pay . . .

(d) a guarantee payment . . .

(e) any payment for time off . . . carrying out trade union duties . . .

(f) remuneration on suspension on medical grounds . . . and . . . on suspension on maternity grounds . . .

(fa) remuneration on ending the supply of an agency worker on maternity grounds . . .

(g) any sum payable in pursuance of an order for reinstatement or re-engagement . . .

(h) any sum payable in pursuance of an order for the continuation of a contract of employment . . .

(j) remuneration under a protective award . . .

The breadth of the expressions 'wages' and 'referable to his employment, whether payable under his contract or otherwise' were considered by the House of Lords in *Delaney v Staples*.[142] The case concerned a Miss Delaney who was summarily dismissed for an alleged breach of her obligation of confidentiality. She raised an unauthorized deduction of wages claim in the tribunal and claimed unpaid commission of £18, accrued holiday pay of £37.50, and one week's wages in lieu of notice to the tune of £82. The question arose as to whether a payment in lieu of notice was wages and could be recovered under the statutory predecessor of what is now Part II of the ERA. Lord Browne-Wilkinson in the House of Lords came to the view that a payment in lieu of notice was not wages for work done, but instead was a payment in connection with the termination of Miss Delaney's

---

[138] See *Farrell Matthews and Weir v Hansen* [2005] IRLR 160 and *Tradition Securities and Futures SA v Mouradian* [2009] EWCA Civ 60 where it was held that a discretionary bonus which had been declared could be recovered as it was a quantifiable sum; cf. *Coors Brewers Ltd v Adcock* [2007] IRLR 440 where the bonus was discretionary and undeclared, in which case, the Court of Appeal held civil proceedings in the ordinary courts was the sole means of enforcement. See also *Small v Boots Co. plc* [2009] IRLR 328 as to the location of the dividing line between a discretionary and guaranteed contractual bonus payment.

[139] This includes discretionary commission payments: *Kent Management Services Ltd v Butterfield* [1992] IRLR 394. Post-termination commission payments were held to be wages rather than payments in connection with the termination of the worker's contract in *Robertson v Blackstone Franks Investment Management Ltd* [1998] IRLR 376.

[140] Enforcement of a failure to pay holiday pay under regulation 13 of the WTR can be pursued as an unauthorized deduction from wages claim: *HMRC v Stringer* [2009] IRLR 677.

[141] In *Atchoe v Camden Primary Care Trust* [2007] EWCA Civ 714, (2007) 151 SJLB 672, the Court of Appeal ruled that a payment made to a worker in respect of him being placed on an out-of-hours 'on-call' roster was supplementary to his pay and did not constitute 'wages'.

[142] [1992] 1 AC 687. For commentary on this case, see S. Deakin, 'Logical Deductions? Wage Protection Before and After *Delaney v Staples*' (1992) 55 *Modern Law Review* 848; A. McColgan, 'Payments in Lieu and the Wages Act 1986' (1992) 21 *Industrial Law Journal* 219.

employment. Therefore, a claim for wrongful dismissal is the appropriate channel to re-cover non-payment of notice pay. Moreover, a damages payment for breach of contract will not qualify as wages:

■ *Delaney v Staples* [1992] 1 AC 687, 692A–C

Lord Browne-Wilkinson:

I must say a word about the nature of wages and payments in lieu of notice . . . the essential char-acteristic of wages is that they are consideration for work done or to be done under a contract of employment. If a payment is not referable to an obligation on the employee under a subsisting contract of employment to render his services it does not in my judgment fall within the ordinary meaning of the word 'wages.' It follows that if an employer terminates the employment (whether lawfully or not) any payment in respect of the period after the date of such termination is not a payment of wages (in the ordinary meaning of that word) since the employee is not under obliga-tion to render services during that period.

The extract from *Delaney* clarifies that not all payments received by the worker will constitute wages. For example, section 27(2) excludes advance payments under a loan or advances of wages, payments in respect of expenses[143] incurred by the worker in carrying out his/her duties, pension or gratuity payments or allowances relating to the worker's retirement or as compensation for loss of office, redundancy-based payments, and pay-ments otherwise than in the worker's capacity as a worker.

Finally, we turn to the statutory protection conferred in favour of employees[144] in the event of lay-off,[145] which is prescribed in Part III of the ERA. Provided that an employee has been continuously employed for a period of one month,[146] he/she is entitled to the pay-ment of a modest sum in respect of any whole day in which he/she has not been provided with work owing to lay-off, i.e. where the employer experiences a reduction in the require-ments of its business for work of the kind which the employee is employed to do or any other occurrence affecting the normal working of its business in relation to work of the kind which the employee is employed to do.[147] The sum is referred to as a statutory guar-antee payment and is capped at £27 per day.[148] Moreover, the payment is only available up to a maximum of five days[149] of lay-off in any period of three months.[150] Hence, the most the employee can receive is 5 × £27 = £135. As such, it is a statutory provision of limited value to employees. It is further limited by the operation of section 30(1) which provides that 'no guarantee payment is payable to an employee in whose case there are no normal working hours on the day in question'. However, where an employee agrees a temporary variation to his/her contract to the effect that he/she no longer works on Fridays in each working week, this does not constitute a modification of normal working hours or create a 'new normal'. Therefore, the employee is entitled to receive a guarantee payment.[151]

---

[143] See *Southwark London Borough v O'Brien* [1996] IRLR 420 where it was held that a mileage al-lowance covered expenses and did not constitute 'wages'.

[144] Since it is an entitlement afforded to employees only, casual workers engaged on contracts where there is no mutuality of obligation present will be unable to avail themselves of the statutory right to a guarantee payment.

[145] The employer must have a contractual entitlement to exercise lay-off. Where there is such an express right, a term in law will not be implied that the period of lay-off must be reasonable. As such, where the period exceeds a reasonable period, the employer will not be in repudiatory breach of contract: *Craig v Bob Lindfield & Son Ltd* [2016] ICR 527.   [146] Section 29(1) of the ERA.

[147] See section 28 of the ERA.   [148] Section 31(1) of the ERA.

[149] See *Cartwright v G Clancey Ltd* [1983] IRLR 355.   [150] Section 31(2) and (3) of the ERA.

[151] *Abercrombie v Aga Rangemaster Ltd* [2013] EWCA Civ 1148, [2013] All ER (D) 178 (October).

Reflection points

1. In your opinion, is the exclusion of voluntary workers, interns, and pupil barristers from the protective coverage of the NMWA justified? If so, why? If not, why not?

2. Do you find the way in which the NMWR approaches 'on-call' working time convincing? Give reasons for your answer.

3. Bearing in mind that a payment in lieu of notice is a sum paid in respect of a period (i.e. the notice period) which the employer has prevented the employee from working, do you agree with the decision in *Delaney v Staples*? Give reasons for your answer.

 For additional reading on statutory minimum wage and wage protection legislation, visit the Online Resources for this book at www.oup.com/uk/cabrelli3e/

8.3 WORKING TIME REGULATION

We now consider the level of statutory interference made by the WTR into the working conditions of workers. We also take the opportunity to test the notion that the transposition of the WTD in the WTR is an example of 'relatively light . . . prescriptive regulation'.[152] The provisions of the WTR can best be analysed by dividing them into:

(1) the relational scope of application of the WTR;

(2) the 'working time' that is subject to the protections contained in the WTR;

(3) the protective limits on working time imposed by the WTR;

(4) the entitlements conferred in favour of workers pursuant to the WTR;

(5) the enforcement of the provisions of the WTR; and

(6) the scope for future reform of the WTD and WTR.

8.3.1 Relational scope of application

Regulation 2(1) of the WTR clarifies that the protections are conferred in favour of workers. The definition of 'worker' equates to that found in section 230(3) of the ERA and section 54(3) of the NMWA.[153] The position under the WTR can be contrasted with that under the WTD, since there is no definition of 'worker' in the latter. One might think that this gives rise to an inference that the EU's intention is to defer the definition to the national law of the Member States.[154] However, that would be incorrect, since it was held in *Union Syndicale Solidaires Isère v Premier Ministre*[155] that the term 'worker' had an autonomous meaning specific to EU law for the purposes of the WTD. The word 'worker' must be 'defined in accordance with objective criteria which distinguish the employment relationship by reference to the rights and duties of the persons concerned [and t]he

---

[152] P. Davies and M. Freedland, *Towards a Flexible Labour Market: Labour Legislation and Regulation Since the 1990s* (Oxford, OUP, 2007) 50.

[153] A number of the cases which have addressed this generic definition of worker have indeed been cases brought under the WTR, e.g. *Byrne Bros (Formwork) Ltd v Baird* [2002] ICR 667; *Redrow Homes (Yorkshire) Ltd v Wright* [2004] EWCA Civ 469, [2004] ICR 1126; *Redrow Homes (Yorkshire) Ltd v Buckborough* [2009] IRLR 34; and *Pimlico Plumbers Ltd v Smith* [2017] IRLR 323.

[154] For example, in the same way as Article 2(1) of the Part-Time Work Directive 97/81/EC (OJ 1998 L14/9) and Article 2(1)(d) of the Acquired Rights Directive 2001/23/EC (OJ 2001 L82/16).

[155] [2011] IRLR 84.

essential feature of an employment relationship . . . is that for a certain period of time a person performs services for and under the direction of another person in return for which he receives remuneration'.[156] In the case of *R v Secretary for Trade and Industry, ex parte BECTU*,[157] the ECJ took this further when it ruled that the WTD applied to 'every worker' including workers employed on short-term engagements. Although the point has not been tested specifically in the UK employment tribunals or courts, it is likely that the domestic definition in regulation 2(1) of the WTR is sufficiently broad to meet the autonomous EU definition adumbrated in *Union Syndicale*.

Other categories of individuals are included within the coverage of the WTR, namely doctors in training,[158] Crown employees,[159] members of the armed forces and the police,[160] House of Lords and House of Commons staff,[161] non-employed trainees,[162] and agricultural workers in Scotland and Wales.[163] Meanwhile, others are explicitly excluded from the entitlements and limits in the WTR, including seafarers,[164] fishing vessel workers[165] and inland waterways workers,[166] individuals below school age,[167] and domestic servants in a private household.[168] Article 17 of the WTD also enables the UK to derogate from the provisions of the WTD in certain carefully controlled circumstances, as follows:

(1) Regulation 20(1) of the WTR deprives workers engaged on 'unmeasured working time' of some (but not all) of their rights under the WTR:

Regulation 20 Unmeasured working time

(1) Regulations 4(1) and (2) [maximum weekly working time], 6(1), (2) and (7) [restrictions on length of night work], 10(1) [daily rest], 11(1) and (2) [weekly rest] and 12(1) [rest breaks] do not apply in relation to a worker where, on account of the specific characteristics of the activity in which he is engaged, the duration of his working time is not measured or predetermined or can be determined by the worker himself, as may be the case for—

(a) managing executives or other persons with autonomous decision-taking powers;

(b) family workers;[169] or

(c) workers officiating at religious ceremonies in churches and religious communities . . .

---

[156] *ibid.*   [157] [2001] ECR I-4881.   [158] Regulation 25A of the WTR.

[159] Regulation 37 of the WTR.

[160] Regulations 38 and 41 of the WTR. However, regulation 18(2) of the WTR carves an exception in respect of front-line members of the armed forces and policemen, i.e. 'where characteristics peculiar to certain specific services such as the armed forces or the police . . . inevitably conflict with the provisions of [the WTR]'. This can be contrasted with members of the armed forces or police engaged in desk jobs who do not fall within regulation 18(2) and so will be covered by the WTR, on which, see the discussion in C. Barnard, 'The Working Time Regulations 1998' (1999) 28 *Industrial Law Journal* 61, 63.

[161] Regulations 39 and 40 of the WTR.   [162] Regulation 42 of the WTR.

[163] Regulation 43 of the WTR. For the position of agricultural workers in England, see the Working Time (Amendment) (England) Regulations 2013 (SI 2013/2228).

[164] Regulation 18(1)(a) of the WTR. Seafarers are protected by Council Directive 1999/63/EC of 21 June 1999, as amended (OJ 1999 L167/33).

[165] See regulation 18(1)(b) of the WTR. Specific protection is conferred by the Fishing Vessels (Working Time: Sea-fishermen) Regulations 2004 (SI 2004/1713).

[166] See regulation 18(1)(c) of the WTR. Specific protection is conferred by the Merchant Shipping (Working Time: Inland Waterways) Regulations 2003 (SI 2003/3049).

[167] *Addison v Ashby* [2003] ICR 667.

[168] Regulation 19 of the WTR. However, they are entitled to rest breaks, daily rest, weekly rest, and annual leave under regulations 10–13A of the WTR.

[169] This does not apply to relief parents who act as the representative of foster parents of children in care on the parents' days off, live during this period with the children in a family-like setting and during this time independently attend equally to the children's and family's needs, as parents generally do: *Hälvä v SOS-Lapsikylä ry* [2017] IRLR 942.

(1) There has been little case law to date on the breadth of the exception in regulation 20. The only case which has considered this provision, albeit rather briefly, was *Sayers v Cambridgeshire County Council*.[170] Here, it was held that the worker could not be categorized as an 'unmeasured working time' worker, since her employment contract regulated her working hours, and although she was a Senior Operations Manager she could not be considered a managing executive or someone with autonomous decision-making powers. As such, there was nothing about the activity in which she was engaged that meant her working time was unmeasured.

(2) A second set of derogations permitted by Article 17(2) and (3) of the WTD,[171] specifically relate to restrictions on night work, daily rest periods, weekly rest periods, and rest breaks. These include workers whose place of work is distant from their place of residence, security and surveillance workers, and workers whose activities[172] entail a requirement for continuity of service or production.[173] Also included within the ambit of the derogation are workers engaged in (a) a trade or industry where there is a foreseeable surge of activity, e.g. agricultural workers, workers in the tourism sector, and postal service workers, and (b) activities affected by (i) an occurrence due to unusual and unforeseeable circumstances beyond the control of the employer, or (ii) exceptional events, the implications of which could not be avoided despite the exercise of all due care by the employer, or (iii) an accident or the imminent risk of an accident. Certain railway transport workers are excluded from the rights and limits in the WTR.

(3) Regulation 22 of the WTR prescribes a third set of derogations for shift workers in respect of the entitlements to daily and weekly rest in certain contexts. In return, the shift workers concerned have the right to compensatory rest.

(4) The fourth package of derogations provides that a number of entitlements and limits laid down in the WTR may be modified or disapplied by a collective or workforce agreement.[174] Regulation 23 of the WTR provides that a collective[175] or workforce agreement[176] may be adopted to vary or exclude the worker's right to daily and

---

[170] [2007] IRLR 29.   [171] See regulation 21 of the WTR.

[172] It has been held that these activities concern those of the worker, rather than those of the employer: *Gallagher v Alpha Catering Services Ltd* [2005] IRLR 102. On that basis, workers employed in delivering food and drink to aircraft were not treated as subject to the derogation, since there was no evidence to suggest that their working time could not be organized so as to have rest breaks every six hours.

[173] For example: residential care and health workers (see *M'bye v Stiftelsen Fossumkollektivet* [2016] IRLR 227); dock and airport workers (*Associated British Ports v Bridgeman* [2012] IRLR 639); communications, media, and emergency workers; utility workers; workers engaged in industries in which work cannot be interrupted on technical grounds; research and development workers; agricultural workers; and workers involved in the carriage of passengers on regular urban transport services.

[174] Although the scope of this derogation is particularly broad, research has revealed that the deployment of collective agreements in this sphere is limited: C. Barnard, S. Deakin, and R. Hobbs, 'Opting out of the 48-Hour Week: Employer Necessity or Individual Choice—An Empirical Study of the Operation of Article [22(1)] of the Working Time Directive in the UK' (2003) 32 *Industrial Law Journal* 223, 244–5. Meanwhile, workforce agreements are 'rarely used' as they are considered 'counter-cultural' to the practice of UK industrial relations: *ibid.*, 245.

[175] Regulation 2(1) of the WTR defines a collective agreement in the same fashion as section 178 of the Trade Union and Labour Relations (Consolidation) Act 1992, on which, see Chapter C of the Online Resources.

[176] Regulation 2(1) of the WTR defines a workforce agreement as a written agreement concluded between an employer and workers employed by it or its representatives which has effect for a period not exceeding five years and is applicable to all of the relevant members of the workforce or such members who belong to a particular group, duly signed by the representatives of the workforce or the group to which the agreement applies. An additional requirement is that copies of the text of the agreement, together with guidance that the workers might reasonably require to fully understand the content of the agreement, must have been provided to the affected workers by the employer before the agreement was made available for signature.

weekly rest, a rest break and the limits in relation to night-shift work in regulations 6, 10, 11, and 12 of the WTR respectively.[177] In return, the workers bound by these modifications or exclusions are entitled to a period of compensatory rest or, where that is not possible, 'such protection as may be appropriate in order to safeguard the worker's health and safety'.[178]

(5) Finally, the fifth derogation in the WTR envisages the individual agreement of the worker to the amendment or disapplication of the 48-hour weekly working time limit. This individual opt-out enables workers to waive the 48-hour limit and will be addressed later in the context of the discussion at section 8.3.3.1.

8.3.2 Working time

Central to the WTR is the concept of working time, however much the definition found therein[179] differs from that prescribed in the NMWA and the NMWR.[180] The former is much more general than the latter and does not divide work types into separate categories.[181] Instead, it consists of three distinct elements:

> **Regulation 2 Interpretation**
>
> (1) In these Regulations—
>
> working time', in relation to a worker, means—
>
> (a) any period during which he is working, at his employer's disposal and carrying out his activity or duties,
>
> (b) any period during which he is receiving relevant training, and
>
> (c) any additional period which is to be treated as working time for the purpose of these Regulations under a relevant agreement; . . .

Guidance previously issued by the now defunct Office of Fair Trading[182] suggested that working time would include working lunches,[183] time spent training, time spent travelling during the working day,[184] and time spent working away from home.[185] Moreover, in

---

[177] Regulation 23(a) of the WTR.

[178] Regulation 24(a) and (b) of the WTR. A collective or workforce agreement may also be used to modify the default 17-week reference period which is used for the purposes of calculating whether the worker has exceeded the 48-hour maximum weekly working time limit laid down in regulation 4 of the WTR (see section 8.3.3.1). The collective or workforce agreement may vary this period up to a maximum of 52 weeks for objective or technical reasons or reasons concerning the organization of work (regulation 23(b) of the WTR). If the 17-week default period is varied upwards, once again, it is stipulated that the worker must be afforded a compensatory rest period or alternative adequate protection to safeguard his/her health and safety (regulation 24(a) and (b) of the WTR).   [179] Regulation 2(1) of the WTR.

[180] In *British Nursing Association v IRC* [2003] ICR 19, 24H, Buxton LJ in the Court of Appeal cautioned against the use of decisions made on the basis of the WTR for the purposes of guiding the proper approach to the notion of working time under the NMWA and NMWR, and vice versa. This sentiment was based on the 'different objectives of the different pieces of legislation'.

[181] As discussed earlier, work types under the NMWA and NMWR are divided into time work, salaried work, output work, and unmeasured work.

[182] See 'Guidance on the Working Time Regulations', available at http://webarchive.nationalarchives.gov.uk/20081112132843/http://www.berr.gov.uk/whatwedo/employment/employment-legislation/employment-guidance/page28978.html (last visited 19 November 2017).

[183] However, lunches taken at the leisure of the worker are not included.

[184] However, time spent travelling to and from the place of work is not counted.

[185] See the discussion in C. Barnard, 'The Working Time Regulations 1998' (1999) 28 *Industrial Law Journal* 61, 70.

Federación de Servicios Privados del Sindicato Comisiones Oberas v Tyco Integrated Security SL,[186] the CJEU arrived at the conclusion that time spent travelling from home to customers' premises in the case of mobile or peripatetic workers was also to be regarded as 'working time' for the purposes of the WTD. Such travel time met the tripartite criteria in regulation 2(1)(a) of the WTR.[187] Likewise, in *Edwards v Encirc Ltd*,[188] the EAT ruled that time spent at a meeting in a trade union capacity qualified as 'working time' for the purposes of the WTR. As such, the judicial interpretation of the definition of 'working time' has been rather broad. This trend is particularly appreciable in the context of the treatment of inactive on-call working time and whether a distinction should be drawn on the basis of the intensity of the worker's working time in such a context. For example, in *Sindicato de Médicos de Asistencia Pública (SIMAP) v Conselleria de Sanidad y Consumo de La Generalidad Valenciana*,[189] the question was whether the entirety of the time spent by doctors on call at their employer's health centre amounted to working time. The ECJ ruled that active and inactive on-call time was included within the definition of working time in such circumstances, irrespective of whether the doctors were in fact called out or not and that the words in regulation 2(1)(a) should be construed cumulatively. However, the ECJ indicated that matters would be different where the worker is engaged in inactive on-call working time but is not required to be present at his/her employer's premises:

■ *SIMAP* [2001] ICR 1116, 1147E–F

Judgment of the Court:

It is clear . . . that to exclude duty on call from working time if physical presence is required would seriously undermine th[e] objective [of protecting the health and safety of workers]. [However], the situation is different where doctors in primary care teams are on call by being contactable at all times without having to be at the health centre. Even if they are at the disposal of their employer, in that it must be possible to contact them, in that situation doctors may manage their time with fewer constraints and pursue their own interests. In those circumstances, only time linked to the actual provision of primary care services must be regarded as working time within the meaning of [Article 2(1) of the WTD].

The subsequent case of *Landsshauptstadt Kiel v Jaeger*[190] concerned circumstances which were similar to the facts of *SIMAP*. The principal difference was that the workers were provided with sleeping facilities and were permitted to sleep at their employer's premises during periods of inactive on-call working time. Nonetheless, the ECJ once again ruled that, since the workers were bound to remain at a location determined by their employer and be at the latter's disposal, the whole of the on-call working time would be counted:

[186] [2015] IRLR 935. However, the fact that such travelling time is 'working time' does not confer any right to payment in favour of the worker for that period: *East v Valentine* [2017] IRLR 878, since the WTR does not deal with the regulation of pay.

[187] See D. McCann, 'Travel Time as Working Time: *Tyco*, the Unitary Model and the Route to Casualisation' (2016) 45 *Industrial Law Journal* 244, 245–7.   [188] [2015] IRLR 528.

[189] [2001] ICR 1116. See J. Fairhurst, '*SIMAP*: Interpreting the Working Time Directive' (2001) 30 *Industrial Law Journal* 236; J. Kenner, 'Re-evaluating the Concept of Working Time: An Analysis of Recent Case Law' (2004) 35 *Industrial Relations Journal* 588, 593–9; T. Nowak, 'The Working Time Directive and the European Court of Justice' (2008) 15 *Maastricht Journal of European and Comparative Law* 447; and L. Rodgers, 'The Notion of Working Time' (2009) 38 *Industrial Law Journal* 80.

[190] [2004] ICR 1528. Similar issues were raised before the ECJ in *Abdelkader Dellas v Premier Ministre* [2006] IRLR 225 and *Vorel v Nemocnice Český Krumlo* (Case C-437/05) [2007] ECR I-331. See the discussion in L. Rodgers, 'The Notion of Working Time' (2009) 38 *Industrial Law Journal* 80, 81–3.

■ *Landsshauptstadt Kiel v Jaeger* [2004] ICR 1528, 1156H–1557B

Judgment of the Court:

[O]n-call duty . . . performed by a doctor where he is required to be physically present in the hospital must be regarded as constituting in its totality working time for the purposes of [the WTD] even where the person concerned is permitted to rest at his place of work during the periods when his services are not required, with the result that [the WTD] precludes legislation of a member state which classifies as rest periods an employee's periods of inactivity in the context of such on-call duty.[191]

The approach in *Jaeger* can be contrasted with that under the NMWA and the NMWR, where it is possible for on-call time spent sleeping not to count as working time.[192] The respective divergences in the notion of working time under the WTR/WTD and the NMWA/NMWR have been noted in the academic literature:

■ L. Rodgers, 'The Notion of Working Time' (2009) 38 *Industrial Law Journal* 80, 88

The particular problem which emerges from a consideration of the WTR and NMWR together is that once it has been determined that on-call time (for instance) must be counted as working time to protect the health and safety of an employee, it is then a difficult conclusion to come to that this work should be remunerated at a different level to other work.[193]

8.3.3 Limits

The limits provided for in the WTR can be divided into two categories:

(1) the maximum ceiling of 48 hours on weekly working time; and

(2) the night-shift restrictions.

We now consider each of these limits in turn.

8.3.3.1 Maximum weekly working time

The primary protective limit found in the WTR is as follows:

Regulation 4 Maximum weekly working time

(1) Unless his employer has first obtained the worker's agreement in writing to perform such work, a worker's working time, including overtime, in any reference period which is applicable in his case shall not exceed an average of 48 hours for each seven days.

---

[191] Of course, if the worker's place of work is his/her home, then inactive on-call time spent sleeping will constitute working time, on which, see *Hughes v Mr Graham and Mrs Lynne Jones (t/a Graylyns Residential Home)* (UKEAT/0159/08/MAA, 14 August 2008). See also *McCartney v Oversley House Management* [2006] ICR 510; cf. *Lynch v Bromley Arts Council* (UKEAT/0390/06/DA, 17 February 2007, HHJ Serota QC, 2007 WL 504776) on the basis that, in *Lynch*, on-call time periods which were not expressly required by an employer and which an employee was not obliged to work in addition to his 40-hour week were not treated as working time.

[192] *Focus Care Agency Ltd v Roberts* [2017] ICR 1186, 1201H–1202D per Simler J (P).

[193] See also the critique in A. C. L. Davies, 'Getting More Than You Bargained For? Rethinking the Meaning of "Work" in Employment Law' (2017) 46 *Industrial Law Journal* 477, 499–500.

> (2) An employer shall take all reasonable steps, in keeping with the need to protect the health and safety of workers, to ensure that the limit specified in paragraph (1) is complied with in the case of each worker employed by him in relation to whom it applies and shall keep up-to-date records of all workers who carry out work to which it does not apply by reason of the fact that the employer has obtained the worker's agreement as mentioned in paragraph (1).

In order to determine whether a worker has exceeded the 48-hour weekly working time limit, the hours he/she has worked are averaged out over a 17-week period. As such, a worker may work more than 48 hours in a particular week, provided that the 17-week average is less than the prescribed maximum.[194] The case of *Barber v RJB Mining (UK) Ltd*[195] was one of the first appellate decisions to address regulation 4(1) of the WTR. Here, it was ruled that regulation 4(1) was a mandatory provision which was applicable to all contracts of employment and conferred a free-standing legal right under the worker's employment contract, breach of which may be enforced by raising a legal action in the domestic civil courts.[196] The ability to enforce regulation 4(1) in the domestic civil courts has the added benefit for workers of enabling them to seek an injunction to prevent a threatened breach of the 48-hour limit. Alternatively, the worker will be entitled to seek a declaration of his/her rights.[197]

The enforcement process in respect of regulation 4(1) can be contrasted with that regarding regulation 4(2) of the WTR. Breach of the latter subjects an employer to criminal sanctions in terms of regulations 28(1) and 29(1) of the WTR. This was a point reinforced by the High Court in its decision in *Sayers v Cambridgeshire County Council*.[198] *Sayers* also established that there is no justification for the establishment of a cause of action for a breach of statutory duty in respect of regulation 4(2) of the WTR.[199] Therefore, an individual has no right to enforce a breach of regulation 4(2) by raising a claim in the courts or presenting a complaint to an employment tribunal, and any enforcement of this provision is limited to criminal proceedings.

Returning to the fine print of regulation 4(1) of the WTR, it is impossible to overestimate the significance of the words 'unless his employer has first obtained the worker's agreement in writing to perform such work'. They give expression to the worker's entitlement to signify his/her individual agreement to opt out of the 48-hour maximum weekly working time limit, which is expressly permitted by Article 22(1) of the WTD. The principal reason why the UK took advantage of the individual derogation option in Article

---

[194] See regulation 4(3), (6), and (7) of the WTR.

[195] [1999] ICR 679. For a critique of the reasoning adopted in this decision, see A. Edwards, '*Barber v RJB Mining* in the Wider Context of Health and Safety Legislation' (2000) 29 *Industrial Law Journal* 280.

[196] The principal rationale adopted for the decision in *Barber* is that if it were held that regulation 4(1) had to be read together with regulation 4(2), 'namely to take reasonable steps to ensure that the specified limit was adhered to, this would leave the maximum number of hours uncertain and to some extent at the whim of the employer[, which] would deprive paragraph (1) of its full effect': *Barber v RJB Mining (UK) Ltd* [1999] ICR 679, 688E per Gage J.

[197] For example, in *Barber*, the workers obtained a declaration from the court to the effect that they had the right to continue working until their average working hours came within the 48-hour limit. As for the remedies available to public sector employees where there has been a breach of the 48-hour limit prescribed in regulation 4(1), this was an issue that was specifically addressed in *Fuß v Stadt Halle (No. 2)* [2011] 2 CMLR 13. *Fuß (No. 2)* decided that such public sector workers also have a right to bring an employment tribunal claim in order to secure reparation for the breach. The extent to which private sector workers will remain barred from this additional remedy conferred in favour of public sector workers is an open question, particularly since it does seem rather specious that its availability is dependent on the sector of the economy in which the worker is situated.   [198] [2007] IRLR 29.

[199] *Sayers v Cambridgeshire County Council* [2007] IRLR 29, 54.

22(1) of the WTD lies in its ability to secure labour market flexibility and managerial adaptability:[200]

■ **C. Barnard, S. Deakin, and R. Hobbs, 'Opting out of the 48-Hour Week: Employer Necessity or Individual Choice—An Empirical Study of the Operation of Article [22(1)] of the Working Time Directive in the UK' (2003) 32** *Industrial Law Journal* **223, 248–9**

The clear implication is that the derogations contained in the [WTD] are an important element in ensuring that the British labour market remains more 'flexible' than its continental European counterparts. More generally, the British model of labour market regulation is one which the government commends to its EU partners: 'flexibility at a UK level should be matched by flexibility in Europe.' . . . [T]he term 'flexibility' appears to be a synonym for 'freedom from external constraint', the constraint, that is, of legal regulation . . . Working time legislation is therefore perceived to represent, in microcosm, the difference between the lightly regulated UK labour market, and the apparently more intensive regulation of the continental systems. Our case studies show that this is a perspective shared not just by some employers but also by some workers and their representatives. Employers see the individual opt-out as necessary if they are to meet customer demands or client requirements which presuppose long working hours. Employees, likewise, accept a long-hours culture which is bound up with access to higher earnings and, in some cases, a feeling of individual autonomy and control over working arrangements.

Although the above study was completed in 2002, it is unlikely that the evidence they unearthed of 'extensive but varied use of [the] individual opt-out'[201] is purely historical. If anything, it is likely that the use of the opt-out will have increased over recent years, given the fears workers harbour about their job security.

Barnard, Deakin, and Hobbs' study reveals that employers will generally have workers sign an individual opt-out by presenting it to them 'for signature at the time of their induction, when they were completing other administrative documentation [or] . . . as a standard contract term which [they] would have to take positive steps to avoid', e.g. by individual negotiation and removal.[202] As such, employers routinely place direct or indirect pressure on their workers to sign the opt-out at the earliest stage possible in the working relationship. In recent years, the ECJ has sought to reduce the potential for employers to exert such pressures by interpreting the terms of Article 22(1) of the WTD in a purposive manner. For example, in order to profit from the flexibility afforded by Article 22(1), in *Fuß v Stadt Halle*[203] the ECJ clarified that strict observance with each of the stringent requirements of that Article is required on the part of the Member State before it can introduce national legislation sanctioning the power of employers to use the individual opt-out. Further, exacting and precise constraints on an employer's ability to exercise the individual opt-out were laid down in *Pfeiffer v Deutsches Rotes Kreuz Kreisverband Waldshut eV*:[204]

---

[200] See P. Davies and M. Freedland, *Towards a Flexible Labour Market: Labour Legislation and Regulation since the 1990s* (Oxford, OUP, 2007) 17–24 on the hallmarks of managerial adaptability.

[201] C. Barnard, S. Deakin, and R. Hobbs, 'Opting out of the 48-Hour Week: Employer Necessity or Individual Choice—An Empirical Study of the Operation of Article [22(1)] of the Working Time Directive in the UK' (2003) 32 *Industrial Law Journal* 223, 237. The reasons why employers and workers use the opt-out are explored in *ibid.*, 237–48.   [202] *ibid.*, 245–6.

[203] [2010] IRLR 1080, 1084.

[204] [2005] ICR 1307. See S. Prechal, 'Case Note on *Pfeiffer v Deutsches Rotes Kreuz Kreisverband Waldshut eV* (Joined Cases C-397/01 to C-403/01) [2004] ECR I-000' (2005) 42 *Common Market Law Review* 1445.

■ *Pfeiffer v Deutsches Rotes Kreuz Kreisverband Waldshut eV* [2005] ICR 1307, 1355C–G

Judgment of the Court:

[The WTD] seeks to guarantee the effective protection of the safety and health of workers by ensuring that they actually have the benefit of, inter alia, an upper limit on weekly working time . . . Any derogation from those minimum requirements must therefore be accompanied by all the safeguards necessary to ensure that, if the worker concerned is encouraged to relinquish a social right which has been directly conferred on him by the [WTD], he must do so freely and with full knowledge of all the facts. Those requirements are all the more important given that the worker must be regarded as the weaker party to the employment contract and it is therefore necessary to prevent the employer being in a position to disregard the intentions of the other party to the contract or to impose on that party a restriction of his rights without him having expressly given his consent in that regard . . . It follows that, for a derogation from the maximum period of weekly working time laid down in article 6 of [the WTD] (48 hours) to be valid, the worker's consent must be given not only individually but also expressly and freely. Those conditions are not met where the worker's employment contract merely refers to a collective agreement authorising an extension of maximum weekly working time. It is by no means certain that, when he entered into such a contract, the worker concerned knew of the restriction of the rights conferred on him by [the WTD] . . . therefore . . . article [22(1) of the WTD must] . . . be construed as requiring consent to be expressly and freely given by each worker individually if the 48-hour maximum period of weekly working time, as laid down in article 6 of the [WTD], is to be validly extended. In that connection, it is not sufficient that the relevant worker's employment contract refers to a collective agreement which permits such an extension.

Pfeiffer ensures that worker autonomy is respected in order for the employer to avail itself of the opt-out. If the worker is subject to a detriment, this will amount to a breach of Article 22 of the WTD. Dismissal of the worker for a failure to consent via an opt-out to working hours in excess of the 48-hour limit will typically constitute a detriment, except where the termination of the worker's contract is 'for reasons which are fully independent of [the worker's] refusal to agree to perform such additional work'.[205] An illustration of this exception is where a worker is dismissed because the employer requires him/her to work additional hours because of urgent operational requirements and this can be justified by the financial situation of the employer.

Notwithstanding the purposive approach adopted in *Pfeiffer*, the terms of Article 22(1) of the WTD and the first 15 words of regulation 4(1) of the WTR serve to weaken materially the effectiveness of the 48-hour weekly working time limit. As such, the opt-out is highly controversial. Repeated attempts by the European Commission have been made to remove it, but have failed on every occasion.[206] Ultimately, Member States which tend to prize labour market flexibility over worker protection are likely to continue to resist any future attempts to withdraw the opt-out. And once the UK has exited the EU and the European Union Withdrawal Bill is brought into force, it is unlikely that the opportunity will be taken to remove the opt-out. The end result is that the central protection afforded by regulation 4(1) will continue to be something of a chimera for the majority of workers:

---

[205] *M'bye v Stiftelsen Fossumkollektivet* [2016] IRLR 227.

[206] Negotiations of the main cross-sectoral social partners at EU level on reform of the WTD began in November 2011, but by mid-December 2012 these attempts to update the WTD had failed once again owing to a lack of consensus among the social partners involved.

■ **C. Barnard, S. Deakin, and R. Hobbs, 'Opting out of the 48-Hour Week: Employer Necessity or Individual Choice—An Empirical Study of the Operation of Article [22(1)] of the Working Time Directive in the UK' (2003) 32** *Industrial Law Journal* **223, 251-2**

> So one conclusion to draw from our study is that as long as the individual opt-out continues in place, a much needed stimulus for the modernisation of working time, which could have come from the [WTD], will fail to materialise . . . The individual opt-out is the principal means by which the potential impact of the [WTD] has been diluted. The opt-out provides employers with a low-cost mechanism to avoid the 48-hour limit, and the ease with which it can be deployed is one of the reasons for the limited use by employers of the collective derogations [in the WTD and the WTR].[207]

The extract from Barnard, Deakin, and Hobbs refers in passing to the ability of the parties to enter into a collective or workforce agreement derogating from the WTR. It is possible to do so by varying the default 17-week reference period prescribed in regulation 4(3). This may be done for a period up to 52 weeks for objective or technical reasons or reasons concerning the organization of work.[208] However, the UK does not have a culture of effective 'employee representation which allows . . . continental systems to achieve flexibility in the application of working time standards'.[209] The number of workers covered by collective agreements in the UK is low and workforce agreements in non-unionized workplaces are very uncommon. For these reasons, the individual opt-out is the preferred choice for employers seeking to derogate from regulation 4 of the WTR.

8.3.3.2 Night-shift work

The second limit found in the WTR concerns night-shift workers.[210] Regulation 2(1) of the WTR stipulates that a night worker is one who:

(1) on the majority of days on which he/she works,[211] works at least three hours of his/her daily working time during (a) 11pm and 6am or (b) a seven-hour period, part of which falls within the period between midnight and 5am, as determined by a relevant agreement; or

(2) is likely, during (a) 11pm and 6am or (b) a seven-hour period, part of which falls within the period between midnight and 5am, as determined by a relevant agreement, to work at least such proportion of his/her annual working time as has been agreed between employer and workers in a collective agreement or workforce agreement.

Regulation 6 directs that a 'night worker's normal hours of work in any reference period . . . shall not exceed an average of eight hours for each 24 hours'. However, there is an

---

[207] Of course, if the individual opt-out were removed, as noted in C. Barnard, S. Deakin, and R. Hobbs, 'Opting out of the 48-Hour Week: Employer Necessity or Individual Choice—An Empirical Study of the Operation of Article [22(1)] of the Working Time Directive in the UK' (2003) 32 *Industrial Law Journal* 223, 251–2, it is highly likely that employers would adjust their practices so that they could rely on the 'unmeasured working time' derogation in regulation 20(1) of the WTD.

[208] Regulation 23(b) of the WTR.

[209] C. Barnard, S. Deakin, and R. Hobbs, 'Opting out of the 48-Hour Week: Employer Necessity or Individual Choice—An Empirical Study of the Operation of Article [22(1)] of the Working Time Directive in the UK' (2003) 32 *Industrial Law Journal* 223, 251.

[210] See C. Barnard, 'The Working Time Regulations 1998' (1999) 28 *Industrial Law Journal* 61, 72–4.

[211] In *R v Attorney-General for Northern Ireland, ex parte Burns* [1999] IRLR 315, it was held that a worker was a night-shift worker where she worked on the basis of a rotating shift cycle during night-time on a regular (from 9pm to 7am one week in three), albeit not exclusive, or predominant, basis. Here, 'regular' was to be distinguished from an 'infrequent or ad hoc basis'.

exception for young workers between the ages of 15 and 17 who are prohibited from working night-shift work between the hours of 10pm and 6am.[212] In the same vein as regulation 4(2), regulation 6(2) imposes an obligation on an employer to take all reasonable steps, in keeping with the need to protect the health and safety of workers, to ensure compliance with the eight-hour limit. Akin to the 48-hour maximum weekly working time limit in regulation 4, the reference period is 17 weeks in the case of night-shift workers. However, where a night-shift worker's work entails special hazards or heavy physical or mental strain, the eight-hour limit is an absolute restriction, rather than one that can be averaged out over the 17-week period.[213]

8.3.4 Entitlements

Akin to the limits in the WTR, the various entitlements can be separated out into rights which relate to (a) working hours, namely a daily rest period, a weekly rest period, an in-work rest break, and compensatory rest, and (b) paid annual leave.

8.3.4.1 Daily rest period

In terms of regulation 10(1), a worker has the right to a rest period of not less than 11 consecutive hours in each 24-hour period during which he/she works for his/her employer. In the case of a young worker, this is increased to 12 consecutive hours in each 24-hour period. In *Commission v UK*,[214] the ECJ held that employers are under a duty to ensure that their workers actually take their daily rest periods rather than simply to give them the opportunity to take them. This was taken further by the ECJ in *Union Syndicale Solidaires Isère v Premier Ministre*.[215] Here, it was stated that the objective of the entitlement to daily rest is 'to enable . . . workers to relax and dispel the fatigue caused by the performance of their duties'.[216] As such, legislation enabling an employer to obviate the daily rest entitlement by reducing the overall number of days worked by a worker in a year was held to be inadequate.

8.3.4.2 Weekly rest period

In a similar vein to regulation 10(1) of the WTR, regulation 11(1) prescribes that a worker is entitled to an uninterrupted break of not less than 24 hours in each seven-day period during which he/she works for his/her employer. The CJEU has ruled that the 24-hour break may be granted on any day within that seven-day period, and there is no requirement for the rest day to be the seventh day following six consecutive working days.[217] An alternative option is specified in regulation 11(2) whereby a worker is afforded the right to either (a) two uninterrupted rest periods of not less than 24 hours in each 14-day period or (b) one uninterrupted rest period of not less than 48 hours in each such 14-day period. Meanwhile, a young worker has the right to a rest period of not less than 48 hours in each seven-day period during which he/she works for his/her employer.

---

[212] Regulation 6A of the WTR.

[213] See regulation 6(7) and (8) of the WTR. Regulation 7 of the WTR goes on to provide night-shift workers with an entitlement to a free and confidential health assessment prior to taking up night work and at regular intervals thereafter. Regulation 7(6) of the WTR provides health protection for night-shift workers by enjoining employers to transfer a night-shift worker to daily shift work to which he/she is suited if a registered medical practitioner advises the employer that the worker is suffering from health problems which are connected to the fact that the worker performs night work.

[214] [2006] IRLR 888.   [215] [2011] IRLR 84.   [216] *ibid.*, 90.

[217] *Maio Marquez da Rosa v Varzim Sol-Turismo Jogo e Animação SA* (Case C-306/16, 9 November 2017).

8.3.4.3   Rest break

In terms of regulation 12(1) and (3) of the WTR, where a worker's working time is in excess of six hours, he/she has the right to an uninterrupted rest break of not less than 20 minutes, which may be spent away from his/her workstation if he/she has one.[218] This is increased to 30 minutes in the case of a young worker. In a series of decisions, the point has been made that it is not enough for an employer to provide rest breaks to workers who have specifically asked for them; instead, employers must take active steps to schedule rest breaks into the working hours of the workers in advance,[219] and rest breaks must be provided even where the worker has never expressly asked for a rest break or is taken to have 'acquiesced' to working without a rest break.[220] As such, where the employer fails to put in place arrangements to facilitate rest breaks, this will be treated as a refusal to permit the worker to take a rest break. Moreover, the employer is not permitted to trawl over the past working hours of workers and re-classify periods where the worker was inactive as his/her rest break;[221] instead, a worker must know in advance that an uninterrupted period of inactivity is to be treated as a rest break, which period is actually uninterrupted in fact. Therefore, a rest break is a period which is neither working time nor a daily or weekly rest period in respect of which the worker may do as he/she pleases. As for the position of a worker who is 'on-call' during his/her rest break where there is a constant risk of interruption, the decision of the Northern Ireland Court of Appeal in *Martin v Southern Health and Social Care Trust*[222] is particularly instructive. Here, it was held that the time spent 'on-call' could not be equated to a rest break since this would undermine the purpose of the WTD in 'ensuring that shifts in excess of six hours could be worked without placing the health and safety of the staff . . . in jeopardy'.[223]

Where the tribunal or court makes a finding that the employer has breached regulation 12 of the WTR, the worker will be entitled to a remedy. However, the worker is precluded from claiming compensation for injury to feelings as part of that remedy, since the wording of regulation 30(4)(a) of the WTR cannot be stretched to permit this.[224] But this may not prevent a claim for compensation for damage to health.

8.3.4.4   Compensatory rest

Regulations 21 and 22 of the WTR enable an employer to derogate from the rest period and rest break requirements in specific circumstances. Where the employer does so and requires the worker to work during a period which would otherwise be a rest period or rest break, regulation 24(a) directs that the employer must, wherever possible, allow the worker to take an equivalent period of compensatory rest. In *Hughes v Corps of Commissionaires Management Ltd (No. 2)*,[225] the Court of Appeal ruled that an equivalent period of compensatory rest in lieu of a rest break must have the characteristics of a rest in the sense of a break from work and must, so far as possible, ensure that the period which is free from work is at least 20 minutes.[226] However, in exceptional cases in which it is not possible to confer an equivalent period of compensatory rest for objective reasons, regulation 24(b) provides that the employer must afford such protection as may be appropriate in order to

---

[218] This provision is subject to the terms of any collective agreement or workforce agreement which has been concluded and applies to the worker, on which, see regulation 12(3) of the WTR.

[219] *Commission v UK* [2006] IRLR 888.   [220] *Grange v Abellio London Ltd* [2017] IRLR 108.

[221] *Gallagher v Alpha Catering Services Ltd* [2005] ICR 673, 684B–C per Gibson LJ.

[222] [2010] IRLR 1048.

[223] *Martin v Southern Health and Social Care Trust* [2010] IRLR 1048, 1052–3.

[224] *Santos Gomes v Higher Level Care Ltd* [2016] IRLR 678.

[225] [2011] IRLR 915. See B. Barrett, 'When is a Work Break Not a Statutory Break?' (2012) 41 *Industrial Law Journal* 363.

[226] [2011] IRLR 915, 921 per Elias LJ. If a break does not possess those characteristics, then it will not meet the criteria of equivalence and compensation.

safeguard the worker's health and safety. The reference to exceptional circumstances here confirms the fact that this derogation is narrow and should be applied restrictively.

8.3.4.5 Paid annual leave

The centrepiece entitlement contained in the WTR is the worker's right to a prescribed period of paid annual leave. The purpose of paid annual leave is set out in the following extract from *Stringer*:

■ *Stringer v Revenue and Customs Commissioners* [2009] ICR 932, 979B

Judgment of the Court:

It is common ground that the purpose of the entitlement to paid annual leave is to enable the worker to rest and to enjoy a period of relaxation and leisure.

The basic right to annual leave and additional annual leave is enshrined in regulations 13(1) and 13A(1) of the WTR which transpose the UK's obligation in Article 7 of the WTD to provide a minimum of four weeks' leave. In the UK, annual leave amounts to 5.6 weeks, i.e. 28 days' paid annual leave in any one leave year, which is higher than the minimum requirement under EU law. The leave year runs from 1 October each year and annual leave may be taken in instalments.[227] Except where the working relationship is terminated, it is provided by regulations 13(9)(b) and 13A(6) of the WTR that an employer is prohibited from making a payment in lieu of annual leave, i.e. a lump sum payment.[228] It has been held that a worker's entitlement to annual leave is not affected by his/her death, so that it carries over and a payment in lieu must be made to the worker's estate, i.e. his/her executors or personal representatives.[229]

One is struck by the straightforwardness and modesty of the set of provisions laid down in regulations 13–16. This throws into sharp relief the plethora of case law and jurisprudence that they have generated over the past ten years. The fact that the House of Lords, Supreme Court, and ECJ/CJEU have been called upon time and again to interpret the annual leave and holiday pay provisions is testament to that fact. In those decisions, referring to Article 31(2) of the EU Charter of Fundamental Rights, the courts have consistently confirmed that the right to paid annual leave is a fundamental social right from which derogations or exceptions should not be brooked:[230]

■ *Zentralbetriebsrat der Landeskrankenhaüser Tirols v Land Tirol* [2010] 3 CMLR 30

Judgment of the Court:

. . . it is important to note first that, according to settled case-law, the right of every worker to paid annual leave must be regarded as a particularly important principle of European Union social law from which there can be no derogations and whose implementation by the competent national authorities must be confined within the limits expressly laid down by [the WTD]. Second, it should be noted that that particularly important principle of European Union social law cannot be interpreted restrictively . . .

---

[227] See regulations 13(3) and (9) and 13A(4) and (6) of the WTR.
[228] See also *FNV v Staat der Nederlanden* [2006] IRLR 561.
[229] *Bollacke v K + K Klaas & Kock BV* [2014] ICR 828.
[230] See *British Airways plc v Williams* [2012] ICR 847, 878A–B; M. Bell, 'Sickness Absence and the Court of Justice: Examining the Role of Fundamental Rights in EU Employment Law' (2015) 21 *European Law Journal* 641, 643–50.

Land Tirol also addressed the effect of transitions in working patterns on a worker's entitlement to annual leave. For example, where the worker moves from a full-time to part-time position, the CJEU decided that there was no basis for the employer to adjust the worker's accrued entitlement to date in order to reflect the reduction in his/her working time. As for the opposite work transition from part-time to full-time, in *Greenfield v The Care Bureau Ltd*,[231] the CJEU held that if a part-time worker increases his/her hours, the employer is not obliged to recalculate the worker's entitlement to annual leave retrospectively, even taking into account the annual leave already accrued and taken. Instead, the holiday entitlement should be recalculated on a forward-looking basis only, i.e. from the point in time at which the working pattern changes.

As a means of countering the potential for abuse, preconditions or prerequisites placed in front of the entitlement are restricted. For example, in *R v Secretary of State for Trade & Industry, ex parte BECTU*,[232] the ECJ held that a 13-week continuous service qualifying period in national legislation was proscribed. Likewise, in *Dominguez v Centre Informatique du Centre Ouest Atlantique*,[233] the ECJ rejected the validity of provisions or practices of national law that made entitlement to paid annual leave conditional on a minimum period of ten days' or one month's actual work during the reference period.

Whilst making the very existence of the right to paid annual leave subject to preconditions is prohibited, it is perfectly acceptable for a Member State to set out conditions for taking paid annual leave. In fact, this is what we find in regulation 15 of the WTR:

Regulation 15 Dates on which leave is taken

(1) A worker may take leave to which he is entitled under regulation 13 and regulation 13A on such days as he may elect by giving notice to his employer in accordance with paragraph (3), subject to any requirement imposed on him by his employer under paragraph (2).

If the worker complies with the notice requirement in regulation 15(1), the employer may respond by serving a counter-notice on the worker under regulation 15(2) of the WTR requiring the worker to take his/her annual leave on particular days or not to take such leave on particular days. In essence, this enables the employer to control the timing of the leave by directing the employee to take leave on particular days which are more suitable to its commercial requirements, rather than when the worker wishes to take the leave, provided that the leave constitutes a genuine break from working time.[234] For example, in *Russell v Transocean International Resources Ltd*,[235] the issue was whether individuals working on offshore installations in the oil and gas industry on the basis of a repeating shift pattern of two or three weeks' work offshore, followed by two or three weeks' onshore leave, were entitled to insist that they take their annual leave on the offshore installation, i.e. out of the time when they were at their employer's disposal. The Supreme Court rejected the workers' argument that they ought to be afforded annual leave whilst offshore. Their justification was that it was sufficient for the employer to require the workers to take their annual leave whilst onshore, since it was irrelevant where the worker was at the time the leave was taken, as was what he/she was doing at that

---

[231] [2016] IRLR 62.   [232] [2001] IRLR 559.

[233] [2012] IRLR 321. Contrast this with *Heimann v Kaiser GmbH* [2013] IRLR 48 where the ECJ accepted that fixing the paid annual leave of short-time workers on the basis of the rule *pro rata temporis* was permitted, thus enabling employers to preclude zero-hours contract workers on temporary short-term working from any entitlement to annual leave.

[234] See *Sumsion v BBC* [2007] IRLR 678, 681 per Lady Smith; *Lyons v Mitie Security Ltd* [2010] ICR 628.

[235] [2012] ICR 185.

time, so long as it was a period when he/she was not working. However, if taken to its logical conclusion, the notion that the power to direct where and when the leave is taken is vested in the employer rather than the employee may lead to absurd consequences, e.g. the proposition that the employer may compel its workers to take the entirety of their 5.6 weeks' annual leave in blocks of less than one week. The most extreme example would be the employer who applies regulation 15(2) of the WTR to instruct a worker to take his/ her leave in periods of one day every other week, e.g. every Monday fortnight, through-out the leave year. For that reason, Lord Hope in *Russell* doubted whether it was viable for the employer to be afforded the right to insist that the worker take his/her leave on the basis of such a staggered period:

■ *Russell v Transocean International Resources Ltd* [2012] ICR 185, 199G–200A

Lord Hope:

The question is not whether a worker can be required to take annual leave during a period when he would not otherwise have been working but whether the worker can be forced to take his en-titlement to annual leave in periods which are shorter than one week. But it is not a problem that has to be answered in this case. There seems to me to be much to be said for the view that, when article 7 of the [WTD] is read together with the purposes identified in the preamble and in the light of what the Court of Justice said in [*Merino Gómez v Continental Industrias del Caucho SA*] [2005] ICR 1040, para 30, the entitlement is to periods of annual leave measured in weeks, not days. The worker can opt to take all or part of it in days, if he chooses to do so. But the employer cannot force him to do so. But I do not need to reach a concluded view on this point, and I have not done so.

During the period of annual leave, regulation 16(1) of the WTR stipulates that a worker has the right to be paid during his/her annual leave at the rate of a week's pay in respect of each week of leave.[236] A week's pay is based on a worker's 'normal working hours'.[237] A particular issue which has generated a great deal of litigation and controversy is what counts as 'pay' and 'normal working hours' for the purposes of regulation 16. The first judicial proclamation on the issue was given in *Bamsey v Albon Engineering Ltd*.[238] Here, the Court of Appeal addressed how a worker should be paid whilst on annual leave where he regularly worked substantial amounts of overtime. The worker argued that his holiday pay should equate to his average earnings inclusive of overtime. The worker's contract directed that he was bound to work overtime, which was discretionary and not guaranteed. The Court of Appeal ruled that only the overtime which the worker's contract absolutely required the employer to provide and the worker to perform will be taken into account in calculating the worker's weekly pay. Therefore, payments made in respect of discretionary overtime were not fixed and did not constitute part of the worker's normal working hours.[239]

However, the analysis of the Court of Appeal in *Bamsey* based on the meaning of a 'week's pay' and 'normal working hours' in sections 221–222 of the ERA does not sur-vive the decision of the ECJ in *British Airways plc v Williams*.[240] *Williams* concerned the remuneration of pilots which comprised a fixed annual salary and flight supplement pay-ments, which varied according to the time the pilots spent flying. When the pilots were on annual leave, their pay was calculated on the basis of their fixed annual salary only, i.e. excluding the supplementary payments. In arriving at the conclusion that this practice

---

[236] A week's pay is determined in accordance with the provisions of sections 221–224 of the ERA.
[237] See sections 221 and 222 of the ERA.   [238] [2004] ICR 1083.
[239] See also *British Airways plc v Noble* [2006] ICR 1227, which considered the appropriate treatment of consolidated shift pay.   [240] [2012] ICR 847.

was unlawful under the WTD on the basis that workers were entitled to be paid their 'normal remuneration' during annual leave, the ECJ made the following observations:

■ *British Airways plc v Williams* [2012] ICR 847, 878C–879H

Judgment of the Court:

The purpose of the requirement of payment for that leave is to put the worker, during such leave, in a position which is, as regards remuneration, comparable to periods of work . . . it follows from the foregoing that remuneration paid in respect of annual leave must, in principle, be determined in such a way as to correspond to the normal remuneration received by the worker . . . [W]here the remuneration received by the worker is composed of several components, the determination of that normal remuneration and, consequently, of the amount to which that worker is entitled during his annual leave requires a specific analysis. Such is the case with regard to the remuneration of an airline pilot as a member of the flight crew of an airline, that remuneration being composed of a fixed annual sum and of variable supplementary payments which are linked to the time spent flying and to the time spent away from base. In that regard, although the structure of the ordinary remuneration of a worker is determined, as such, by the provisions and practice governed by the law of the member states, that structure cannot affect the worker's right . . . to enjoy, during his period of rest and relaxation, economic conditions which are comparable to those relating to the exercise of his employment. Accordingly, *any inconvenient aspect which is linked intrinsically to the performance of the tasks which the worker is required to carry out under his contract of employment and in respect of which a monetary amount is provided which is included in the calculation of the worker's total remuneration,* such as, in the case of airline pilots, the time spent flying, *must necessarily be taken into account for the purposes of the amount to which the worker is entitled during his annual leave.* By contrast, the components of the worker's total remuneration which are intended exclusively to cover occasional or ancillary costs arising at the time of performance of the tasks which the worker is required to carry out under his contract of employment, such as costs connected with the time that pilots have to spend away from base, need not be taken into account in the calculation of the payment to be made during annual leave . . . [A]rticle 7 of [the WTD] . . . must be interpreted as meaning that an airline pilot is entitled, during his annual leave, not only to the maintenance of his basic salary, but also, first, to all the components intrinsically linked to the performance of the tasks which he is required to carry out under his contract of employment and in respect of which a monetary amount, included in the calculation of his total remuneration, is provided and, second, to all the elements relating to his personal and professional status as an airline pilot. It is for the national court to assess whether the various components comprising that worker's total remuneration meet those criteria.[241]

At the very beginning of the *British Airways* extract, the ECJ makes the point that the remuneration of the worker during his/her annual leave must be comparable to that paid during his/her periods of work: the worker must receive his/her normal remuneration for that period of rest in order to enable him/her to take the leave to which he/she is entitled. The CJEU adopted the same 'intrinsically linked' test in *Lock v British Gas Trading Ltd*[242] and held that the worker should be paid their 'normal remuneration'. The liberal approach of the CJEU is rooted in the idea that no barriers should be placed in front of annual leave, as this may deter the worker from actually taking up that entitlement. For example, a worker should not be disincentivized from taking annual leave by reason that if he were on annual leave he would receive less remuneration than if he were at work.

---

[241] Italics added by writer for the purposes of drawing emphasis to the relevant text.
[242] [2014] ICR 813.

On the basis of the CJEU's 'intrinsically linked' test expounded in *British Airways* and *Lock*, the EAT in *Bear Scotland Ltd v Fulton*[243] held that holiday pay should include normal compulsory non-guaranteed overtime. This applies to the 20 days' annual leave entitlement under regulation 13 of the WTR, but does not stretch to the additional 1.6 weeks conferred under regulation 13A, as the latter is a domestic entitlement as opposed to one provided under the WTD. The ruling in *Bear Scotland* has been extended to voluntary overtime that the worker normally works, i.e. voluntary overtime extending over a sufficient period of time on a regular and/or recurring basis as opposed to purely ad hoc or irregular overtime (which does not have to be included).[244] The same position was taken by the Northern Ireland Court of Appeal in *Patterson v Castlereagh Borough Council*[245] on the ground that non-guaranteed overtime should be included in the worker's holiday pay package where it constitutes an appropriately permanent feature of his/her remuneration package. The EAT in *Bear Scotland* also ruled that travel time payments should be included when calculating holiday pay if they are linked intrinsically to the performance of the tasks which the worker is required to carry out under his/her contract of employment. However, allowances designed to cover ancillary or occasional costs borne by the worker ought not to be included in holiday pay where they arise in the ordinary course of the worker's employment. Meanwhile, in *British Gas Trading Ltd v Lock (No. 2)*,[246] the Court of Appeal applied the same CJEU 'intrinsically linked' test to hold that the holiday pay package should include elements of the worker's average results-based commission that is normally earned over an appropriate reference period.[247] What all these cases underline is that it is essential to identify what constitutes the worker's 'normal pay', i.e. what is normally received, which is a purely evidential issue.

Turning to the decision of the ECJ in *Robinson-Steele v RD Retail Services Ltd*,[248] this concerned the status of rolled-up holiday pay,[249] i.e. the situation where the employer does not pay the worker when he/she is on annual leave, but instead pays the worker in respect of his/her annual leave in the form of part-payments staggered across the entire leave year in addition to the worker's normal remuneration for work done. The ECJ ruled that this practice was unlawful since holiday pay and annual leave must be contemporaneous and workers cannot derogate from this by contractual provision. To find otherwise, the ECJ feared, would undermine the worker's right to take paid annual leave and perhaps disincentivize him/her from taking it.[250]

What are the implications for annual leave where the worker is already on leave, e.g. garden, parental, maternity, or sick leave? Should a *subtractive* or an *additive* approach be adopted?[251] A subtractive analysis dictates that a period of garden, maternity, or sick leave should operate to reduce the worker's entitlement to paid annual leave. Here, the notion is that the worker is already on leave from work and so released from his/her

---

[243] [2015] IRLR 15.   [244] *Dudley Metropolitan Borough Council v Willetts* [2017] IRLR 870.
[245] [2015] IRLR 721.   [246] [2016] IRLR 946.
[247] Tribunal claims raised by workers for unpaid holiday pay (e.g. claims for unpaid non-guaranteed overtime, unpaid commission, unpaid travel time payments, or flight supplement payments, etc.) as a statutory unauthorized deductions claim after 1 July 2015 are limited to two years' back pay of such holidays: section 23(4A) and (4B) of the ERA. It is not possible for a worker to raise an arrears of holiday pay claim to recover unpaid holiday pay as a breach of contract action in the court or tribunal: regulation 16(4) of the WTR.   [248] [2006] ICR 932.
[249] Prior to the decision in *Robinson-Steele*, this technique was particularly prevalent in the case of seasonal workers.
[250] However, some commentators have branded the ECJ's approach a form of misguided paternalism which renders the regime unduly inflexible, overlooking the primary role for collective bargaining envisaged by the WTD: A. Bogg, 'The Right to Paid Annual Leave in the Court of Justice: The Eclipse of Functionalism' (2006) 31 *European Law Review* 892.
[251] See the discussion in A. Bogg, 'Paid Annual Leave and the Long-Term Sick: Third Time Lucky for the United Kingdom?' (2007) 36 *Industrial Law Journal* 341, 348–50.

contractual obligations. As such, the subtractive approach posits that it is not possible for the worker to be released from his/her obligations by the taking of paid annual leave whilst he/she is on maternity or sick leave.[252] An illustration is the CJEU's decision in *Maschek v Magistratsdirection der Stadt Wien*[253] where it was held that workers put on garden leave have no right under EU law to pay in lieu of unused holidays they could have taken during the period of garden leave. Therefore, during garden leave, annual leave does not accrue and the employer can count unused but accrued holiday as taken during garden leave. This can be contrasted with an additive analysis that treats each leave period as a distinct entitlement which does not diminish the other. Therefore, where a worker is on maternity or sick leave, his/her entitlement to paid annual leave continues to accrue, which renders it possible for the worker to take paid annual leave whilst absent from work on maternity or sick leave.

In short, although the position has ebbed and flowed over the past decade,[254] the additive approach has clearly won through. In *Zentralbetriebsrat der Landeskrankenhaüser Tirols v Land Tirol*,[255] the ECJ decided that the worker's right to paid annual leave is not lost as a result of the worker having taken a period of parental leave. With regard to maternity leave, in *Merino Gómez v Continental Industrias del Caucho SA*,[256] the ECJ ruled that while a worker is on maternity leave, she cannot lose her entitlement to paid annual leave.[257] Both periods of leave are distinct and cannot be taken contemporaneously. As for sick leave, in *Stringer v HM Revenue and Customs Comrs*,[258] the ECJ held that paid annual leave must continue to accrue during the leave year whilst the worker is absent through sick leave.[259] The ECJ arrived at the conclusion that annual leave and sick leave were mutually exclusive, the former being designed to allow the worker to relax and take some leisure time for general health and safety purposes, whilst the objective of the latter is to enable the worker to recover from illness. Taking annual leave is a particularly attractive route for a worker on long-term sick leave, since paid annual leave is paid at the rate of his/her ordinary contractual remuneration, which will often be higher than statutory sick pay—set at £92.05 per week at the time of writing—which the worker's contract will specify as the applicable rate during sick leave. The ECJ in *Stringer* went on to say that paid annual leave may be taken by the worker whilst he/she is on sick leave, but if a Member State precludes a worker from doing so, then the law of that Member State must enable the worker to take the accrued, but untaken, annual leave during another leave year.[260] The consequence of that finding is to preclude national laws which (1) extinguish the worker's right to take unexercised/unused paid

---

[252] This was the reasoning adopted by the Court of Appeal in the context of sick leave in *Inland Revenue Commissioners v Ainsworth* [2005] ICR 1149. See also A. Bogg, 'Of Holidays, Work and Humanisation: A Missed Opportunity?' (2009) 34 *European Law Review* 738, 741–2.   [253] [2016] IRLR 801.

[254] For example, the exception for garden leave in *Maschek v Magistratsdirection der Stadt Wien* [2016] IRLR 801.   [255] [2010] 3 CMLR 30.

[256] [2005] ICR 1040.

[257] See also regulation 9 of the Maternity and Parental Leave etc. Regulations 1999 and section 71(5) of the ERA which direct that an employee taking ordinary or additional maternity leave is entitled, during the period of that leave, to the benefit of all of the terms and conditions of employment, whether or not they arise under her contract of employment, which would have applied if she had not been absent from work.

[258] [2009] ICR 932. For a critique of this decision, see A. Bogg, 'Of Holidays, Work and Humanisation: A Missed Opportunity?' (2009) 34 *European Law Review* 738. For comment, see M. Bell, 'Sickness Absence and the Court of Justice: Examining the Role of Fundamental Rights in EU Employment Law' (2015) 21 *European Law Journal* 641, 646–50.

[259] The employer's failure to pay holiday pay during the period of paid annual leave can only be recovered via an unauthorized deductions from wages claim under Part II of the ERA: see *HM Revenue and Customs Comrs v Stringer* [2009] ICR 985 and regulation 16(4) of the WTR.

[260] *Stringer v HM Revenue and Customs Comrs* [2009] ICR 932, 979G–980A. See also *Sobczyszyn v Szkola Podstawowa w Rzeplinie* [2016] IRLR 725.

annual leave at the end of the leave year or (2) prevent a carry-over period[261] for unexercised/unused annual leave into the following leave year, where the worker has been on sick leave for the whole or part of the leave year and his/her incapacity to work has persisted until the end of the working relationship, which was the reason why the worker could not exercise his/her right to paid annual leave.[262] This served to cast doubt on the legality of regulation 13(9)(a) of the WTR which articulates the principle of 'use it or lose it' in the following terms:

> **Regulation 13 Entitlement to annual leave**
>
> (9) Leave to which a worker is entitled under this regulation may be taken in instalments, but—
>
> (a) it may only be taken in the leave year in respect of which it is due . . .[263]

In fact, in the subsequent decision of the Court of Appeal in *NHS Leeds v Larner*,[264] it was held that the terms of regulation 13(9) would require to be interpolated with additional wording. Therefore, it should read '[l]eave to which a worker is entitled under this regulation [13(9)] may be taken in instalments but—(a) it may only be taken in the leave year in respect of which it is due, save where the worker was unable or unwilling to take it because he was on sick leave and as a consequence did not exercise his right to annual leave'. Effectively, this elides the notice requirements of regulation 15(1) of the WTR insofar as it obviates any need for the worker on sick leave to give notice, or to make a specific request, to carry over unused paid annual leave prior to the end of the leave year. *NHS Leeds v Larner* also decided that if a worker is on sick leave and his/her employment is terminated before he/she has exercised all of his/her accrued paid annual leave, regulation 14 of the WTR should be modified to provide that the employer must make the worker a payment in lieu equal to the sum due to him/her under regulation 16 of the WTR for the period of untaken leave.

In its decision in *The Sash Window Workshop Ltd v King*,[265] the CJEU expanded upon the foundational jurisprudence of the Court of Appeal in *NHS Leeds v Larner*. To recap, in *NHS Leeds v Larner*, words were added to regulation 13(9) of the WTR to permit the carrying over of annual leave in the case of a worker *on sick leave*.[266] This created an exception to the general rule that carry-over is not allowed, but as will become clear, there is a time limit to this period of carry-over. This exception was further developed by the CJEU in *Sash Window* in circumstances where the worker was prevented from exercising paid annual leave for reasons other than sick leave. Here, the CJEU concluded that where an employer does not allow or enable a worker to exercise his entitlement to paid leave, e.g. where the employer did not put the worker in a position to do so, then the full period of untaken annual leave will carry over indefinitely.[267] The effect of the CJEU's ruling is that where the worker was unable to exercise paid leave for a reason other than

---

[261] In *FNV v Staat der Nederlanden* [2006] IRLR 561, 566, the ECJ had suggested that carry-over of unexercised paid annual leave into the following leave year would be inevitable, since it decided that Article 7(2) of the WTD, which proscribes the payment in lieu of unexercised paid annual leave, should be treated as an inflexible principle.

[262] *Stringer v HM Revenue and Customs Comrs* [2009] ICR 932, 982C–D.

[263] Regulation 13A(6) of the WTR adopts the same principle in relation to the additional paid annual leave of 1.6 weeks.   [264] [2012] ICR 1389.

[265] [2018] IRLR 142.

[266] There is no additional requirement imposed on the worker who wishes to carry over annual leave for the reason of sickness to demonstrate that he/she was unable, by reason of his/her medical condition, to take annual leave: *Plumb v Duncan Print Group Ltd* [2015] IRLR 711.

[267] [2018] IRLR 142, 158.

sickness—for example, because the employer wrongly classified the individual as a non-'worker'—the right to paid leave carries over until the worker is given the chance to exercise it. And, if the worker is never afforded the right to exercise the untaken leave, then on termination of employment, the worker has the right to payment in lieu in respect of the period of annual leave that remains outstanding. Unlike the position in the case of non-exercise of paid annual leave owing to sickness leave, there is no time limit to the period of carry forward. Hence, the worker's claim for untaken leave can go back many years.

The decision of the CJEU in *Sash Window* was preceded by that of the EAT in *Shannon v Clifton House Residential*,[268] which arguably no longer survives the CJEU's approach in *Sash Window*. *Shannon* concerned an on-call night worker who lived free of charge in a studio flat at his place of work (a care home). The care worker had not taken his annual leave for many years and sought to carry forward his paid annual leave entitlement. In the view of the EAT, the worker in *Shannon* could not carry forward the untaken annual leave entitlement, nor was he entitled to pay in lieu of untaken annual leave, since he had chosen not to request his paid annual leave entitlement from his employer despite the fact that he could have done so, nor was there any evidence that he had been unwilling or unable to take annual leave owing to reasons beyond his control. In essence, the EAT ruled that the general rule laid down in regulations 13(9)(a) and 13A(6) of the WTR applied so that the brocard of 'use it or lose it' held good. However, the outcome in *Shannon* must now be suspect, since in *Sash Window*, the CJEU expressly stated that it was irrelevant that the worker had failed to ask the employer to take paid annual leave. As such, post-*Sash Window*, where the worker has not exercised paid annual leave and the reason for the non-exercise is either sickness, or because he/she was unable to do so, or was prevented by the employer from doing so, the general rule of 'use it or lose it' will be inapplicable.

What has not been definitively resolved by the CJEU, however, is the period of time for which workers *on sick leave* are permitted to roll over unused paid annual leave into the following leave years. In *Neidel v Stadt Frankfurt am Main*,[269] the ECJ ruled that a rollover period of nine months was insufficient. Additional guidance was provided by the ECJ's decision in *KHS AG v Schulte*.[270] Here, the ECJ stipulated that it is not permissible for national legislation to prohibit a worker from carrying over accrued, but untaken, paid annual leave indefinitely into subsequent leave years. A period of 15 months of carry-over was ruled to be satisfactory in the context of the facts of *KHS* which provided for a leave year of 12 months.[271] Therefore, the impact of *Neidel*[272] and *KHS*[273] is that European jurisprudence suggests that a rollover period of between 12 and 15 months will be appropriate where a worker is on sick leave and is unable to take all of his/her paid annual leave and the leave year period equates to 12 months. This can be contrasted with the domestic jurisprudence in *Plumb v Duncan Print Group Ltd*,[274] where the EAT held that the carry-over period in the case of a worker unable to take annual leave owing to sickness should be slightly higher. Here, it was held that the carry-over period should be limited to 18 months following the end of the leave year in which the entitlement had accrued. The EAT arrived at this 18-month period on the basis that it was suggested by the ILO in Annual Holiday Convention No. 132,[275] whose jurisprudence the WTD explicitly states ought to be considered.[276]

---

[268] [2015] IRLR 982.   [269] [2012] ICR 1201.

[270] [2012] IRLR 156. See M. Bell, 'Sickness Absence and the Court of Justice: Examining the Role of Fundamental Rights in EU Employment Law' (2015) 21 *European Law Journal* 641, 646–50.

[271] *KHS AG v Schulte* [2012] IRLR 156, 170.   [272] [2012] ICR 1201.   [273] [2012] IRLR 156.

[274] [2015] IRLR 711.

[275] ILO Convention 132 of 24 June 1970 concerning Annual Holidays with Pay (Revised), available at http://www.ilo.org/dyn/normlex/en/f?p=1000:12100:0::NO::P12100_INSTRUMENT_ID:312277 (last visited 20 November 2017).   [276] See para 5 of the Preamble to the WTD.

A separate issue is whether the ECJ's jurisprudence on carrying over accrued but untaken paid annual leave is restricted to the minimum period of four weeks' paid annual leave conferred in favour of workers under EU law by Article 7(1) of the WTD. In the UK, paid annual leave extends to 28 days—which is permitted under EU law[277]—and so is higher than the minimum EU requirement of four weeks. In *Neidel*, the ECJ suggested that it was open to a Member State to provide that the excess period may not be carried over into subsequent leave years.[278] In May 2011, the UK Government published a Consultation Paper on *Modern Workplaces*.[279] Here, it proposed that the WTR be amended to enable employers to limit the carry-over of paid annual leave in sickness cases to the minimum period of four weeks' paid annual leave prescribed in Article 7 of the WTD and regulation 13(1) of the WTR. As such, employers would have the power to prevent the carry-over of the remaining eight days' paid annual leave conferred by regulation 13A(1) of the WTR.[280] However, the Government never published its response to the consultation and it is unclear whether it intends to consider future reform in relation to this matter.

The ECJ has also had the opportunity to pronounce on the situation where the worker becomes sick immediately before or during a scheduled period of paid annual leave. In effect, this situation is the opposite of *Stringer* where the worker wished to take paid annual leave whilst she was off ill on sickness leave. It has given rise to the worker's ancillary 'right to reschedule'. For example, in *Pereda v Madrid Movilidad SA*,[281] the ECJ accepted that where a worker becomes sick immediately before he/she takes a period of planned paid annual leave, Article 7 of the WTD will confer a right to reschedule that planned period of paid annual leave to a future date when he/she is well. The ECJ went on to say that if the worker is unable to reschedule or take the paid annual leave within the same leave year, he/she must be afforded an entitlement to carry over that period into the subsequent leave year. In its subsequent decision in *ANGED v FASGA*,[282] the ECJ took this principle a stage further and held that a worker who became ill during a period of paid annual leave should be permitted to treat that putative period of annual leave as sick leave instead and then reschedule[283] the planned period of annual leave to a later date when he/she is fit for work.[284] As such, it is irrelevant whether the worker's leave was scheduled or booked and workers have the right to enjoy their annual leave at a later date if they become sick.[285] Although consistent with the notion that the worker's right to annual leave enshrined in Article 7 of the WTD is concerned with ensuring a worker takes sufficient rest, relaxation, and leisure, which must be respected without exception, it is not entirely clear how an employer ought to respond where the worker is unable to provide adequate evidence to the effect that he/she actually did indeed become ill during his/her holidays. For example, are employers entitled to place conditions on the worker's right to convert the period of paid annual leave into sick leave, e.g. receipt of a medical certificate? Alternatively, is this precluded by the principle in *BECTU*[286] and *Dominguez*[287] that restrictions on the worker's right to take paid annual leave are prohibited?

---

[277] See *Dominguez v Centre Informatique du Centre Ouest Atlantique* [2012] IRLR 321, 346 at para 50.

[278] *Neidel v Stadt Frankfurt am Main* [2012] ICR 1201, 1208.

[279] See https://www.gov.uk/government/uploads/system/uploads/attachment_data/file/31549/11–699-consultation-modern-workplaces.pdf at pages 48–9 (last visited 20 November 2017).

[280] This would accord with the decision of the EAT in *Sood Enterprises v Healy* [2013] IRLR 865.

[281] [2009] IRLR 959.   [282] [2012] IRLR 779.

[283] In its Consultation Paper on *Modern Workplaces*, the Government proposed to confine this right to reschedule to the minimum period of four weeks' paid annual leave conferred in favour of workers under EU law by Article 7(1) of the WTD: see https://www.gov.uk/government/uploads/system/uploads/attachment_data/file/31549/11–699-consultation-modern-workplaces.pdf at pages 48–9 (last visited 20 November 2017).   [284] *ANGED v FASGA* [2012] IRLR 779, 780–1.

[285] *Sobczyszyn v Szkola Podstawowa w Rzeplinie* [2016] IRLR 725.   [286] [2001] IRLR 559.

[287] [2012] IRLR 321. Contrast this with *Heimann v Kaiser GmbH* [2013] IRLR 48, where the ECJ accepted that fixing the paid annual leave of short-time workers on the basis of the rule *pro rata temporis* was permitted, thus enabling employers to preclude zero-hours contract workers on temporary short-term working from any entitlement to annual leave.

8.3.5 Enforcement, remedies, and additional protection

Regulations 28–34 of the WTR lay down criminal and civil proceedings which can be used to enforce the various provisions of the WTR. The division of labour between these criminal and civil means of enforcement is explained by Barnard as follows:

■ C. Barnard, 'The Working Time Regulations 1998' (1999) 28 *Industrial Law Journal* 61, 64–5

> The distinction between limits and entitlements [in the WTR] is reflected in the way in which the provisions [of the WTR] are enforced. In essence limits are enforced through criminal sanctions against the employer, entitlements through civil action in an Employment Tribunal.

The limits prescribed in the WTR are enforceable by criminal prosecutions and the Health and Safety Executive, and local authorities are also given an enforcement role in this context.[288] Although the means of enforcement of the limits in the WTR are primarily based on the criminal law, it should not be forgotten that workers have the right to enforce an infringement of the 48-hour maximum weekly working time limit in regulation 4(1) of the WTR as a breach of contract in the civil courts.[289] Public sector workers[290] also have an entitlement to rely on Article 6(b) of the WTD to enforce a breach of the 48-hour maximum weekly working time limit against their employer in the domestic courts. Therefore, the law has evolved to enable a measure of civil enforcement of the limits. Meanwhile, the entitlements in the WTR are subject to individual enforcement action by workers presenting a complaint to an employment tribunal.[291] The employment tribunal has the power to award compensation in respect of the worker's loss as a result of the breach of the entitlement on a just and equitable basis. Regulation 30(4) of the WTR stipulates that what is 'just and equitable' will be influenced by the nature of the employer's default in refusing to permit the worker to exercise an entitlement conferred under the WTR and any loss which he/she has sustained. In *Miles v Linkage Community Trust Ltd*,[292] the EAT provided some guidance on the point in time at which the employer will be treated as having committed the requisite 'default'. It was held that two steps must have been fulfilled: first, the worker must seek to exercise his/her entitlement under the WTR; and secondly, the employer must have responded by refusing the worker the permission to do so. Only when the employer has refused permission will it be in 'default'.[293]

8.3.6 Future reform

A pertinent question is whether the provisions of the WTR and WTD are in need of reform, in light of the fact that these instruments have had little impact on the long-hours working culture in the UK. Article 24(3) of the WTD imposes an obligation on the European Commission to monitor and review the operation of the WTD and report on the same on a quinquennial basis to the European Parliament, the Council of Ministers, and the European Economic and Social Committee. The latest attempt by the European Commission in 2004–09 to revise the WTD entailed a legislative proposal that

---

[288] See regulations 28 and 29 of the WTR. [289] *Barber v RJB Mining (UK) Ltd* [1999] ICR 679.

[290] *Fuß v Stadt Halle* [2010] IRLR 1080. [291] See regulation 30 of the WTR.

[292] [2008] IRLR 602.

[293] As for the factors relevant to take into account in relation to the culpability of the employer's default, see *Miles v Linkage Community Trust Ltd* [2008] IRLR 602, 606. Workers are also protected from the suffering of any detriment and from dismissal in respect of action they take to invoke their rights under the WTR, on which, see sections 48(1ZA), 49(1) and (2), and 101A of the ERA.

sought to codify the *SIMAP* and *Jaeger* judgments in relation to inactive 'on-call' time and remove the controversial individual opt-out in Article 22(1) of the WTD. However, the Council of Ministers and the European Parliament were unable to reach agreement and the proposal hit the buffers. The establishment of consensus across the 28 Member States on the future of the 'opt-out' remains the most formidable obstacle to the future reform of the WTD. In effect, it is the existence of the opt-out which provides substantial force for the view that the working time regime in the WTD and WTR is a 'relatively light . . . [form of] prescriptive regulation'.[294] In an effort to gain a better understanding of how the WTD has been implemented in the Member States—including the use of the opt-out—and its consequent social and economic effects, the European Commission commissioned Deloitte Consulting to produce a report in 2010.[295] Deloitte's attitude to the continued retention of the opt-out was far from hostile. Instead, it saw no evidence of systematic abuse of the opt-out on the part of public sector employers and noted that it offered the 'flexibility [required by employers] for dealing with staff and skills shortages, the particular difficulties [faced by employers] in some rural areas, [the need for employers to secure] continuous service provision both in relation to hours and workarounds in relation to the use of on-call time, and the use of volunteers in fire services'.[296] At the time of writing, the prospects for the removal of the opt-out would appear to be bleak, with the European Commission averse to the 're-open[ing of the] debate on its abolition in which no consensus appears possible between the social partners or between the co-legislators'.[297] Instead, the scope of reform has been limited to the tightening up of the requirements for record-keeping and the monitoring of the opt-out. The latest initiative by the European Commission was to consult on a review of the WTD, which consultation process closed in March 2015.[298] Since that period, there has been little movement as regards reform.

Of course, at the domestic level, matters have been complicated by Brexit. Although the European Union Withdrawal Bill incorporates legislation such as the WTR that is derived from European law, there is no longer any obstacle in the way of Parliament repealing or removing all or some of the rights conferred. The courts would also be entitled to overlook future decisions of the CJEU when interpreting the provisions of the WTR and also overrule pre-Brexit CJEU decisions. For instance, Parliament would be entitled to remove the recent case law of the CJEU that provides that workers are entitled to be paid their 'normal remuneration' when they are off on annual leave. An additional issue worthy of consideration at the domestic level is the modest level of reform recommended by the Taylor Review. In particular, Taylor has proposed that reforms be introduced to increase the current pay reference period of 12 weeks to 52 weeks,[299] and to enable workers to receive rolled-up holiday pay—which of course, is currently in breach of EU Law.[300] The latter point underscores how some elements of the Taylor review are inextricably bound up with the freedom of manoeuvre opened up for Parliament by Brexit.

[294] P. Davies and M. Freedland, *Towards a Flexible Labour Market: Labour Legislation and Regulation Since the 1990s* (Oxford, OUP, 2007) 50.
[295] See European Commission, *Study to Support an Impact Assessment on Further Action at European Level Regarding Directive 2003/88/EC and the Evolution of Working Time Organisation* (COM(2010) 801 final, 21 December 2010), available at http://ec.europa.eu/social/main.jsp?catId=706&langId=en&intPageId=205 at pages 143–4 (last visited 20 November 2017).
[296] See *ibid.*, pages 143–4.   [297] See *ibid.*, page 14.
[298] See http://ec.europa.eu/social/main.jsp?catId=333&consultId=14&visib=0&furtherConsult=yes&langId=en (last visited 20 November 2017).
[299] See *Good Work: The Taylor Review of Modern Working Practices* (July 2017), available at https://www.gov.uk/government/uploads/system/uploads/attachment_data/file/627671/good-work-taylor-review-modern-working-practices-rg.pdf at page 47 (last visited 19 November 2017).
[300] *Robinson-Steele v RD Retail Services Ltd* [2006] ICR 932.

Reflection points

1. Do you believe that it is tenable for the scope of 'working time' to diverge for the purposes of the NMWA and the WTR? Give reasons for your answer.

2. In your opinion, should the individual opt-out be retained? If so, why? If not, why not?

3. The flexibility associated with the individual opt-out to the 48-hour limit on weekly working time is not replicated in the context of the worker's right to paid annual leave/holiday pay. To what extent can this rigidity in the case of the latter be justified?

4. Do you agree with the decision in *Grange v Abellio London Ltd* that even where workers have agreed not to have a daily break, they can still claim under the WTR?

 For additional reading on working time regulation, visit the Online Resources for this book at *www.oup.com/uk/cabrelli3e/*

CHAPTER NINE

WORK-LIFE BALANCE

9.1 CONTEXTUAL ANALYSIS OF WORK-LIFE BALANCE

In this chapter, we analyse the statutory employment rights contained in the Employment Rights Act 1996 ('ERA') and subordinate legislation which has a bearing on the work–life balance of employees, workers, and other individuals providing personal services. Coverage will include the protection of pregnant workers, and the statutory arrangements for maternity leave and maternity pay. We will then move on to explore family-friendly measures which seek to achieve a more equal division of family responsibilities between couples, such as the statutory right to shared parental leave and statutory shared parental pay, paternity leave, adoption leave, and parental leave, as well as the right to request flexible working and the right to take time off work to deal with dependants.[1]

---

[1] Owing to constraints of space, the following statutory measures will not be considered in this work, namely (1) the right not to suffer a detriment short of dismissal on various protected grounds unrelated to work–life balance in sections 43M–49 of the ERA, (2) the statutory 'whistle-blowing protection rights' in sections 43A–43L of the ERA, (3) the rights conferred in favour of betting shop workers and in respect of Sunday working in sections 36–43 of the ERA, and (4) the right to time off work for the reasons laid down in sections 50–54 and 58–63K of the ERA.

9.1.1 Family-friendly policies and the reconciliation of work and family life

Human beings encounter a number of demands on their time throughout their lives. It is incumbent on them to divide their time in a manner which balances these conflicting commitments. Leaving aside time needed to sleep, rest, and relax, or time spent pursuing leisure activities or hobbies, the most common demands that people face are those which are imposed on them by their job. Family responsibilities are another major pressure on people's time, such as childcare or caring for elderly parents or relatives. How a rational worker decides to strike an appropriate balance between domestic and working commitments is a central social issue on which basic economics can shed some light. It is also a key topic for employment law and in social policy circles:

■ H. Collins, *Employment Law*, 2nd edition (Oxford, OUP 2010) 79–80

How can a person perform a good job that is well remunerated and also find time to fulfil caring responsibilities, share the household chores fairly, as well as have time for leisure and community activities? The attempt to find practical answers to these questions has been, and will continue to be, one of the central tasks for employment law. A simple economic model can assist our analysis of how employment law tackles this problem. Paid work in the workplace provides an employee with a stream of income. By increasing the time spent in the workplace, an employee can usually obtain greater rewards, either through extra payments for overtime or through promotion for hard work. But the increase in income must be set against the lack of time to perform unpaid domestic work and to enjoy leisure activities. Each employee has to make a trade-off between paid work and unpaid activities. In making this decision, a crucial variable is the amount of additional income obtained from longer working hours. If a job is well paid, the additional income can be spent on buying services or employing others to perform domestic work . . . If work is badly paid, however, a worker may decide that it is more efficient to work few hours, if at all, and to spend time on domestic work, though as a consequence the family may be forced to live in relative poverty. This model assumes that work opportunities will be available for any number of hours that the worker chooses. This assumption usually proves false, however, for employers offer jobs in standard packages, often requiring at least forty hours a week, and they not infrequently expect longer working hours. This barrier to flexible hours of work can effectively exclude workers from many jobs, or more commonly from the better paid jobs. Workers who find that, owing to poor pay and inflexible hours, they have to forego employment opportunities for the sake of domestic responsibilities and other obligations, often become socially excluded.

In the traditional husband and wife family unit, the orthodox method of managing the demands imposed by working and domestic responsibilities was to divide them along gendered lines in accordance with the 'male breadwinner/female carer' model.[2] The male would assume the obligation of going out to work full-time and earn a living for the family. Meanwhile, the female would relinquish her career, work, or occupation, and instead allocate all or the majority of her time to the fulfilment of domestic, child-rearing, and caring duties. As such, prevailing social mores and conventions exclusively allocated the role of caring/nurturing to women. The ability of women to fully participate in the labour market was limited as a result of this traditional child-rearing and caring role in society:

---

[2] See R. Crompton, *Employment and the Family* (Cambridge, CUP, 2006) 1–3 and 35–41; K. Cunningham-Parmeter, '(Un)equal Protection: Why Gender Equality Depends on Discrimination' (2015) 109 *Northwestern University Law Review* 1, 27–30.

■ N. Busby, *A Right to Care* (Oxford, OUP, 2011) 6

Woman's association with care arises from her biological difference and the traditional assumption that nature has better equipped the female sex for unpaid work within the family. In Greek philosophy, on which many of our contemporary conceptions of gender are based, Plato's conviction that the 'female bears and the male begets' encapsulates the belief that the different natures of men and women result in a fundamental predisposition for their respective roles within the family. Aristotle, whose formula that 'likes should be treated alike' is the premise on which current anti-discrimination law is based, was of the view that the male was 'more fitted to rule than the female' placing women within the private confines of the home. As outdated as the dichotomization expounded by the Greek School may appear in current analyses of gender relations, the ideological doctrine intended to explain the relative social positions of women and men is endemic in the philosophy underpinning contemporary social arrangements and supporting institutions. The welfare systems of most industrialized countries are stubbornly predicated on the assumption that the division of labour within families will place men in the position of main earner or 'breadwinner' and women in that of primary carer and 'homemaker', at least during the childbearing and rearing years. That such ideology continues to inform policy-making is not necessarily intentional: there are very few who would claim that men are better suited to participation in paid work than women as well-established sex discrimination legislation demonstrates. However, such beliefs are so entrenched in our psyches that they inform our individual and collective actions and enable our unquestioning acceptance of rules and institutions founded on discriminatory criteria which exist at all levels of society. Furthermore, the relationship between certain social groups and the development of legal systems has led to the furtherance of particular interests through the medium of the law. Male dominance in the 'public sphere', particularly within political institutions, has led to the furtherance of male interests and a corresponding adherence to the *status quo* in unpaid care arrangements despite overwhelming evidence that family formation and labour market participation have irrevocably changed.

By the early twentieth century, the male breadwinner/female carer idea had become so embedded that it could be quite comfortably characterized as one of *the* primary social institutions:

■ R. Crompton, *Employment and the Family*
(Cambridge, CUP, 2006) 2–3

During the course of the twentieth century, the consolidation of the male breadwinner model was accompanied by institutional developments and arrangements that reflected its basic assumptions, from school hours to pensions and the delivery of health and welfare services . . . Men in full-time employment received a 'family wage' and related benefits, women gained benefits, often indirectly, as wives and mothers. This gender/welfare arrangement has been described by Crouch as part of the 'mid [twentieth] century social compromise' . . . This was in a broad sense a class 'compromise'. Governments of left and right supported social protections and increasing welfare, and left parties and their representatives did not seek to radically destabilise existing social arrangements. These arrangements may be described as characteristic of 'Fordism', a term that has been widely employed to describe the industrial and social order that emerged in many advanced capitalist societies after the Second World War. 'Fordism' was characterised by mass production, full employment (at least as far as men were concerned), the development of state welfare and rising standards of consumption.

In a contemporary context, the edges of the traditional male breadwinner/female carer paradigm have begun to fray. This can be ascribed to changes in the composition of family units and attitudes over the past 50 years, e.g.:

(1) the increase in single-parent and same-sex families;

(2) the reduction of 'traditional' family units;

(3) the rise in divorce rates;

(4) the decline of marriage unions between heterosexual couples;[3] and

(5) the realization that the pursuit of an equal opportunities or substantive equality agenda leaves little room in principle for the operation of an assumption that only males can perform full-time work.

Therefore, 'Fordism [has] beg[u]n to unravel'.[4] The prevailing policy emphasis in recent times has been to adopt measures that seek to reconcile the occupational commitments of female and male workers alongside the demands imposed on them by family life. This entails a transition from the traditional 'male breadwinner/female carer' model to a 'dual breadwinner/carer' dynamic, i.e. equal parenting. It is also reflective of a policy preference for the division of domestic and caring roles between males and females by increasing the amount of (1) paid work undertaken by the latter and (2) unpaid care undertaken by the former.[5] This policy prescription seeks to eviscerate the inflexible stereotypical assumption that only females can take care of children and other dependants; rather, it envisages a movement away from a gender-segmented labour market towards the realization of a more equitable distribution of work and care amongst the sexes. The UK Government aims to achieve this through a commitment to 'becom[ing] the most family friendly Government in the world'.[6] Consider the following Hypothetical A.

Hypothetical A

Amelia Pendleton ('AP') works 15 hours a week as a secretary in the Preston office of Danny's Demolishers Ltd ('DD'). She earns £640 per month gross and spends the remainder of her time looking after her 2-year-old twin children. Her husband Nigel also works for DD in Preston as a technician. However, Nigel works full-time (40 hours per week) and is paid £23,000 gross per annum. Therefore, the gross annual earnings of the family unit is £30,680, i.e. £640 × 12 = £7,680 + £23,000 = £30,680. After lengthy discussions, Amelia and Nigel agree that Nigel will reduce his working hours by ten hours a week and that Amelia will increase her working hours in a week by the same amount of time. The time freed up in Nigel's schedule will be spent caring for the twins. The end result is that Amelia's earnings increase to £12,800 per annum and Nigel's reduce to £17,240 per annum, resulting in composite earnings of £30,040, equating to a minor diminution.

---

[3] See E. Reid and E. Caracciolo Di Torella, 'The Changing Shape of the "European Family" and Fundamental Rights' (2002) 27 *European Law Review* 80, 83–4; R. Crompton, *Employment and the Family* (Cambridge, CUP, 2006) 6–7.

[4] R. Crompton, *Employment and the Family* (Cambridge, CUP, 2006) 3.

[5] See S. Fredman, 'Women at Work: The Broken Promise of Flexicurity' (2004) 33 *Industrial Law Journal* 299, 300.

[6] HM Government, *Consultation on Modern Workplaces: Modern Workplaces—Government Response on Flexible Parental Leave* (November 2012), available at http://www.bis.gov.uk/assets/BISCore/employment-matters/docs/M/12–1267-modern-workplaces-response-flexible-parental-leave.pdf at page 2 (last visited 28 November 2017).

Although variations in social mores and conceptions regarding the appropriate division of family responsibilities may be cited as an explanation for family-friendly policies, there are also normative justifications which can be advanced in their favour. The orthodox account of these justifications ranges from factors couched in moral terms to those which highlight their social/structural and economic benefits. Consider the following extract from Jacobsen which identifies three categories/rationalizations for legislative intervention:

■ J. P. Jacobsen, 'Accommodating Families' in K. Dau-Schmidt, S. D. Harris, and O. Lobel (eds), *Labor and Employment Law and Economics* (Cheltenham, Edward Elgar, 2009) 320, 320–2

One category is that of *social justice*, where one might argue that people with families should be treated either the same as people without families, or differently from people without families . . . Whilst most societies appear to have subscribed to an *ex ante* approach in which all persons are considered equally likely to find themselves in a situation where they need accommodation for family-related obligations, *ex post* some individuals may not ever need such accommodation, and may resent having to 'pick up the slack' at the workplace for other employees with families, or end up literally receiving fewer benefits due to not having a family structure that would entitle them to receive them. This latter concern could be mitigated by having cafeteria-style benefit plans—plans where employees can choose from a menu of benefits and/or receive pecuniary compensation if they do not utilize fully the nonpecuniary benefits offered. Another category is that of *maintaining social and cultural structures*, including transmission of values to the younger generations . . . Assuming both women and men continue to work outside the home, the issue arises of ensuring that sufficient adult attention is paid to children to make sure that they are raised well. This may require substitution of other adult time for the mother's time . . . and also substitution of formerly home-produced goods and services by commercial services . . . Given that there are positive externalities to society of having well-educated productive citizens, there is justification for society's subsidizing or requiring certain actions (such as providing compulsory public schooling) so as to encourage development of this human capital, as it is unlikely that the optimal level would arise without intervention. This previous category relates also to simple demographic concerns, which is that countries with high rates of women's employment participation also appear to have low fertility rates, with rates well below replacement levels in many of the more prosperous European countries in particular . . . [A]ssuming that women in particular continue to work in the formal sector, family-friendly policies may be needed in order to encourage families to continue to have sufficient children to maintain stable population sizes . . . Finally, *economic concerns* would relate to the maximisation of societal output, whether measured as only the formal sector economic output or as total societal output, and maintaining good growth of economic measures (though a broader view would be to maximize total societal utility or wellbeing, a controversial concept regarding its measurement). In particular, if society invests in educating women, particularly in skills that are only of significant use in the formal workforce (that is, tertiary education and professional/vocational training), then in order to increase returns on this human capital investment, it is important to keep women in the workforce for more years and in a more continuous fashion (in part so as to maintain one's skills and learn new skills). Again, it is unrealistic to expect any particular employer to bear this burden voluntarily, particularly if the skills involved are general rather than firm-specific, so this opens the door to suggesting legislation that will compel firms to act in particular ways so as to preserve human capital and provide incentives for potential employees to invest in human capital in the first place.[7]

---

[7] Writer's annotations appear in square brackets throughout this chapter. Annotations shown in italics in this extract are the writer's.

In the Jacobsen extract, economic rationales are cited in favour of family-friendly policies. One can also highlight the enhanced performance which will be wrought if workers are contented in the workplace because their requests for flexible working are approved, e.g. more loyal staff, lower staff turnover, decreased absenteeism, and better staff health.[8] Other empirical studies have focused on the impact of work–life policies on wage growth and productivity. The research evidence is summarized in the following extract from Jacobsen:

■ J. P. Jacobsen, 'Accommodating Families' in K. Dau-Schmidt, S. D. Harris, and O. Lobel (eds), *Labor and Employment Law and Economics* (Cheltenham, Edward Elgar, 2009) 320, 333

One early study using US data . . . concludes that [the implementation of family-friendly benefits has productivity-enhancing effects by allowing employees to operate more efficiently and/or making it possible for firms to attract more productive workers and as such wages stay the same or even increase.] However, another study using more recent UK data . . . finds a compensating wage differential of around 20 percent, mainly associated with flexible working schedules, so [there is a clear trade-off between family-friendly benefits and wages], and another more recent US study . . . finds that employers using family-friendly benefits can benefit both from reduced turnover and from being able to pay lower entry-level wages . . . Another UK study that focused on low-income parents also found that there was a perceived trade-off between family-friendly working conditions and income and career prospects . . . Meanwhile, Bloom et al . . . compared manufacturing firms in the US, France, Germany and the UK and found that 'it depends': for some firms, use of work–life balance policies improved productivity, while for others, it didn't . . . Another US study . . . takes a different tack in looking for productivity effects by looking to see if share prices rise after announcements that various Fortune 500 firms were adopting family-friendly policies, and indeed finds positive effects on share prices. Overall the evidence is clearly mixed but promising in arguing that there need not be any negative effect on either firms or workers or instituting such policies.

In contrast, the neoclassical economic account of family-friendly measures, akin to those elaborated in Chapter 8 on working time,[9] emphasizes their depressive effect on productive output. The orthodox economic argument is that State-sanctioned forms of flexible working and family-friendly policies impose red tape and burdens on business which are negative for the economy and general social well-being. In fact, it is argued that they are discriminatory since they 'load disproportionate costs onto those employers with larger than average proportions of employees with caring responsibilities'.[10] Moreover, it is suggested that they are incompatible with the 'long-hours' culture and burgeoning workplace pressures imposed on workers by employers who feel they need to lay down demanding individual performance targets in order to remain afloat in an increasingly globalized competitive marketplace.[11] Further, the contention that it is a rational choice for employers to implement such measures as a means of increasing the loyalty and contentedness of their staff ignores the empirical evidence. A number

---

[8] See C. Wheatley, 'I'm in a Meeting with My Children: Family-Friendly Policies Keep Staff Happy and Can Boost Productivity, Says Catherine Wheatley' (*The Sunday Times*, Business Section, 24 February 2013); A. Asthana, 'These Maternity-Leave Myths are Costing Us Dear' (*The Times*, 1 June 2012) 30; and J. L. Glass and S. B. Estes, 'The Family Responsive Workplace' (1997) 23 *Annual Review of Sociology* 289, 306.   [9] See Chapter 8, section 8.1.1.
[10] R. Crompton, *Employment and the Family* (Cambridge, CUP, 2006) 213.   [11] *ibid.*, 87.

of studies[12] suggest that employers will only harness work–life policies in order to assist employees in discharging their caring responsibilities where those employees are sufficiently senior and valued enough to warrant meeting the attendant costs. Since the majority of an employer's workers may be employed in low-end or atypical jobs, there is little incentive for such employers to voluntarily set in motion family-friendly initiatives. If such measures are statutorily prescribed, the potential outcome is that the costs to the employer may well overshadow the benefits.

As the law currently stands, there is no general employment right to flexible working. Instead, a statutory procedure is laid down which confers a general entitlement in favour of all employees to request a change to their hours and pattern of working.[13] The comparatively recent (2014) extension of the statutory right to request flexible working to all employees is a material development that has not been popular amongst employers, who prefer an approach characterized by voluntarism as opposed to compulsion.[14]

Family-friendly and work–life measures have been introduced in the UK in a somewhat piecemeal and ad hoc fashion. They can be grouped into two categories, which by and large reflect their historical evolution. First, there is the older strand which can be charted back to the Employment Protection Act 1975 that was modernized when the Pregnant Workers' Directive[15] was transposed into UK law,[16] namely the protection of women in birth, pregnancy, and maternity, provision for statutory maternity pay, and the prohibition of workplace discrimination related to pregnancy or maternity. The second group of statutory provisions concerns the right of employees to paternity, parental, and adoption leave and 'family-friendly' provisions which seek to reconcile work and life, such as the rights to request flexible working and to take time off to care for dependants. These provisions were introduced by the Employment Relations Act 1999 (in order to transpose the Parental Leave Directive[17]) and the Employment Act 2002 as part of the review of the law relating to working parents.[18] We consider each of these categories in greater detail in sections 9.2 and 9.3. The most recent generation of family-friendly laws finds its expression in the shared parental leave regime introduced in April 2015.[19] This enables mothers, fathers, mothers' partners, and adopters to share the mother's 50 weeks' maternity leave between them in order to look after their children. In this way, both the baby's parents (or the husband or partner of the mother) can take leave simultaneously in a one-week period or multiple periods of a week. In 2015, the Government announced its

---

[12] S. Dex and C. Smith, *The Nature and Patterns of Family-Friendly Employment Policies in Britain* (York, York Publishing Services, 2002); J. L. Glass and S. B. Estes, 'The Family-Responsive Workplace' (1997) 23 *Annual Review of Sociology* 289, 299–300; and R. Crompton, *Employment and the Family* (Cambridge, CUP, 2006) 213.

[13] Please note that this is not the equivalent of a statutory employment right to flexible working.

[14] See C. Wheatley, 'I'm in a Meeting with My Children: Family-Friendly Policies Keep Staff Happy and Can Boost Productivity, Says Catherine Wheatley' (*The Sunday Times*, Business Section, 24 February 2013). Cf. the criticisms from the perspective of working mothers in G. James, 'Family-friendly Employment Laws (Re)assessed: The Potential of Care Ethics' (2016) 45 *Industrial Law Journal* 477, 486.

[15] Directive 92/85/EC on Pregnant Workers (OJ 1992 L348/1), on which, see E. Ellis, 'Protection of Pregnancy and Maternity' (1993) 22 *Industrial Law Journal* 63; R. Wintemute, 'When is Pregnancy Discrimination Indirect Discrimination?' (1998) 27 *Industrial Law Journal* 23; and S. Honeyball, 'Pregnancy and Sex Discrimination' (2000) 29 *Industrial Law Journal* 43.

[16] By the Trade Union Reform and Employment Rights Act 1993 (now repealed).

[17] Parental Leave Directive 96/34/EC (OJ 1996 L145/4), as amended by Directive 97/75/EC (OJ 1998 L10/24). These Directives are now repealed and parental leave is governed by the EU Parental Leave Directive 2010/18/EU (OJ 2010 L68/13).

[18] Department of Trade and Industry, *Work and Parents: Competitiveness and Choice* (December 2000), available at http://webarchive.nationalarchives.gov.uk/+/http://www.dti.gov.uk/er/g_paper/index.htm (last visited 28 November 2017).

[19] See the Maternity and Adoption Leave (Curtailment of Statutory Rights to Leave) Regulations 2014 (SI 2014/3052), Statutory Shared Parental Pay (General) Regulations 2014 (SI 2014/3051), and the Shared Parental Leave Regulations (SI 2014/3050).

intention to extend shared parental leave and shared parental pay to working grandparents, on the ground that they play a crucial role in providing childcare and in supporting families who are working.[20] However, since the original announcement, little progress has been made on actually implementing that policy.

Reflection points

1. In its Consultation on *Modern Workplaces* in May 2011, available at https://www.
   gov.uk/government/uploads/system/uploads/attachment_data/file/31549/11-699-con-
   sultation-modern-workplaces.pdf (last visited 28 November 2017), the Government
   declared the following at page 2:

   > We want to create a society where work and family life complement one another. One where
   > employers have the flexibility and certainty to recruit and retain the skilled labour they need to
   > develop their business. And one where employees no longer have to choose between a rewarding
   > career and a fulfilling home life.

   In your opinion, to what extent is it feasible for these twin objectives to be reconciled?

2. Consider the arguments in favour of and against the introduction of family-friendly
   laws, including laws which entitle all workers to demand that they work flexibly. In
   your opinion, which of these arguments is/are the most convincing?

 For additional reading on family-friendly policies and the reconciliation of work and family life, visit the Online Resources for this book at www.oup.com/uk/cabrelli3e/

9.2 PROTECTION OF BIRTH, PREGNANCY, AND MATERNITY

In this section, our attention turns to the statutory provisions regulating the interaction between pregnancy and maternity, on the one hand, and work, on the other. This takes us into the territory of statutory maternity leave, maternity pay, and the various protections from dismissal, detriment, discrimination, and redundancy which apply in the case of pregnancy and maternity. An important point is that each of these rights is conferred in favour of employees who are mothers of children,[21] rather than workers or employees generally. For example, in *CD v ST*,[22] the CJEU decided that an employee who was the commissioning non-birth mother in a surrogacy arrangement had no entitlement to maternity leave under the Pregnant Workers' Directive,[23] irrespective of the fact that she had started to breastfeed and mother the child within one hour of its birth. Finally, we examine the entitlement to shared parental leave and pay, which enables mothers, fathers, and adopters to share their parental leave between them.

[20] See https://www.gov.uk/government/news/chancellor-announces-major-new-extension-of-shared-parental-leave-and-pay-to-working-grandparents (last visited 28 November 2017).

[21] Further, it is lawful under EU law for a Member State to exclude an employed father of a child from entitlement to maternity leave, where the mother of the child is not an employee: *Montull v INSS* Case C-5/12 [2013] IRLR 976. It is debatable whether *Montull* can be reconciled with the decision of the CJEU in *Roca Álvarez v Sesa Start España* [2011] 1 CMLR 28.

[22] *CD v ST* [2014] 3 CMLR 15. For commentary on, and criticism of, this decision, see G. De Baere, 'Shall I Be Mother? The Prohibition on Sex Discrimination, the UN Disability Convention, and the Right to Surrogacy Leave under EU Law' (2015) 74 *Cambridge Law Journal* 44; E. Caracciolo di Torella, 'Surrogacy, Pregnancy and Maternity Rights: A Missed Opportunity for a More Coherent Regime of Parental Rights in the EU' (2015) 40 *European Law Review* 52.

[23] Directive 92/85/EC (OJ 1992 L348/1).

9.2.1 **Statutory maternity leave**

An unambiguous exposition of the aims of maternity leave was furnished by the European Court of Justice ('ECJ' or 'CJEU') in *Commission v Luxembourg*:

■ *Commission v Luxembourg* [2005] CMLR 1, 20

> Maternity leave . . . is intended to protect a woman's biological condition and the special relationship between a woman and her child over the period which follows pregnancy and childbirth, by preventing that relationship from being disturbed by the multiple burdens which would result from the simultaneous pursuit of employment.

In light of such a categorical statement, one would be forgiven for thinking that statutory maternity leave has always been a universal and unconditional entitlement. However, prior to the coming into force of the Work and Families Act 2006, there was no general right to statutory maternity leave, the chief precondition being that the employee satisfy a qualifying period of six months' prior continuous employment. Moreover, the period of maternity leave was much shorter than the current provision for 52 weeks, initially being set at 14 weeks by the Trade Union Reform and Employment Rights Act 1993,[24] and then subsequently uprated to 18 weeks,[25] 26 weeks,[26] with a final consolidation of ordinary maternity leave and additional maternity leave into a 52-week period by the Work and Families Act 2006. Another significant point is that there is no such thing as an EU maternity leave Directive;[27] instead, maternity leave is only touched upon briefly by Article 15 of the Recast Equality Directive 2006.[28]

The current statutory provisions on maternity leave find their expression in sections 71–75 of the ERA and regulations 4–12A of the Maternity and Parental Leave etc. Regulations 1999 ('MPLR').[29] These divide maternity leave into 26 weeks of ordinary maternity leave ('OML') and 26 weeks of additional maternity leave ('AML').[30] Unlike the position prior to October 2008,[31] however, there is no substantive difference between the rights enjoyed by employees during bouts of OML and AML, which now amount to a unified block of 52 weeks' leave. During that period,[32] an employee is entitled to the benefit of all of her terms and conditions of employment as would apply if she had not been absent on leave.[33] The employee's 'terms and conditions' include matters connected with her employment whether or not they arise under her contract of employment,[34]

---

[24] Transposing the requirements of the Pregnant Workers' Directive 92/85/EC (OJ 1992 L348/1).

[25] Employment Relations Act 1999.

[26] Regulation 8 of the Maternity and Parental Leave (Amendment) Regulations 2002 (SI 2002/2789).

[27] The EU Commission had proposed a separate Maternity Leave Directive, but this was shelved in July 2015.

[28] Directive 2006/54/EC (OJ 2006 L204/23).   [29] SI 1999/3312.

[30] See sections 71 and 73 of the ERA; regulations 4(1), 7(1), and (4) of the MPLR.

[31] See regulations 4 and 5 of the Maternity and Parental Leave etc. and the Paternity and Adoption Leave (Amendment) Regulations 2008 (SI 2008/1966).

[32] If an employer hires a temporary replacement to cover the employee on OML/AML, the employer is afforded a measure of protection from unfair dismissal proceedings when it dismisses the temp on the return of the employee from OML/AML: see section 106 of the ERA.

[33] See sections 71(4)(a) and 73(4)(a) of the ERA; regulation 9(1)(a) of the MPLR. By the same token, she is subject to all of the obligations arising under those terms and conditions, except insofar as their performance is inconsistent with her statutory right to maternity leave: sections 71(4)(b) and 73(4)(b) of the ERA; regulation 9(1)(b) of the MPLR.

[34] The fact that the terms and conditions need not be contractual is exemplified by the decision of the ECJ in *Thibault v CNAVTS* [1999] ICR 160.

but do not include contractual terms about remuneration, i.e. terms which only concern sums payable to an employee by way of wages or salary.[35] The policy behind the exclusion of terms concerning remuneration is that when the employee is absent on maternity leave, she will be in receipt of statutory maternity pay[36] or maternity payments under an enhanced contractual scheme and, accordingly, will have no need for continued payment of remuneration. The breadth of the word 'remuneration' was considered in *Hoyland v Asda Stores Ltd*.[37] *Hoyland* concerned an annual bonus which the employer paid to its employees based on the sales achieved by the workforce as a whole. Since it was paid in recognition of work undertaken by the employee, the EAT took the view that it was paid as part of the employees' 'wages or salary' and therefore was excluded. Likewise, in *Department for Work and Pensions v Sutcliffe*,[38] it was held that the word 'remuneration' included statutory sick pay. Childcare vouchers paid through salary sacrifice schemes may also be discontinued by the employer.[39] Therefore, unless expressly stated to the contrary in the contract of employment, sick pay will not be payable when an employee is absent on OML or AML.[40]

Subject to the limitations imposed by regulation 6 of the MPLR, section 71(3) of the ERA directs that the employee has the right to choose the date of commencement of OML. The conditions prescribed in regulation 6 stipulate that the employee's period of OML will begin on the earlier of:

(1) the date which she notifies to her employer as the date on which she intends her OML to start; or

(2) the day following the first day after the beginning of the fourth week before the expected week of childbirth ('EWC') that she is absent from work wholly or partly because of pregnancy.[41]

However, it should be stressed that the employee's ability to choose the date of commencement is subject to the condition that she cannot select a date for the commencement of her OML that is earlier than the beginning of the eleventh week before the EWC.[42] Section 72 of the ERA and regulation 8 of the MPLR prohibit an employee from working during the two-week period commencing with the date of childbirth. This is referred to as compulsory maternity leave.

Whilst the earlier statement that there are no prerequisites imposed in respect of the general entitlement to OML is undoubtedly true,[43] certain notification requirements are prescribed by regulation 4 of the MPLR. The employee must notify her employer of her pregnancy, the EWC, the date on which she intends OML to start, and, if required by the employer, she must produce a certificate from a registered medical practitioner or midwife which sets out the EWC.[44] This notice must be embodied in writing if the employer

---

[35] See sections 71(5) and 73(5)(b) of the ERA; regulation 9(2) and (3) of the MPLR.

[36] See section 9.2.2 and the Statutory Maternity Pay (General) Regulations 1986 (SI 1986/1960), and sections 164–167 of the Social Security Contributions and Benefits Act 1992.

[37] [2005] ICR 1235.   [38] (UK/EAT/0319/07/ZT, 1 October 2007, HHJ Peter Clark).

[39] *Peninsula Business Services Ltd v Donaldson* [2016] ICR 565.

[40] The ECJ has held that taking maternity leave cannot affect the employee's right to take any other period of leave guaranteed by EU law such as annual leave under the Working Time Directive 2003/88/EC (OJ 2003 L299/9): *Merino Gómez v Continental Industrias del Caucho SA* [2005] ICR 1040, 1056A–B. Cf. *Boyle v EOC* [1999] ICR 360.

[41] Regulation 6(1)(a) and (b) of the MPLR.

[42] Regulation 4(2)(b) of the MPLR. Provision, however, is made for premature childbirth, in which case regulation 6(2) of the MPLR stipulates that OML begins on the date of birth.

[43] This is also true as regards EU law, e.g. *Terveys-ja sosiaalialan neuvottelujarjesto TSN ry v Terveyspalvelualan Liitto re* [2014] ICR D15, where it was held that there is no minimum period of time that must elapse before an employee is entitled to a second period of maternity leave.

[44] Regulation 4(1) of the MPLR.

requests and must be given to the employer no later than the end of the fifteenth week before her EWC, or otherwise as soon as is reasonably practicable.[45] Regulation 4(1A) of the MPLR recognizes that the employee may amend the intended start date of OML subject to certain restrictions. If childbirth takes place before the employee has given such notification or before the EWC which she notified to the employer, then the employee must simply notify the employer that she has given birth as well as the date of the birth, whereupon OML will start from that date.[46] Once the employer has received the employee's notice, it must serve a counter-notice on the employee within 28 days of (a) receipt of that notice or (b) the date of commencement of OML, as the case may be, notifying the employee of the date on which her period of AML will end,[47] failing which, the employee will be protected from any detriment or dismissal if she does not return to work on the date notified.

Owing to the fact that sections 71(4)(a) and 73(4)(a) of the ERA and regulation 9(1)(a) of the MPLR provide that the employee's terms and conditions continue to subsist during the period of OML and AML, it is self-evident that the employee has a contractual right to return to the workplace once the 52-week composite period of maternity leave has expired. As such, no statutory preconditions to that entitlement can be imposed and the employee enjoys an automatic right to return once the 52 weeks are up.[48] Nonetheless, although arguably superfluous, sections 71(4)(c) and 73(4)(c) of the ERA and regulation 18 of the MPLR explicitly acknowledge that the employee has an entitlement to return to work once the periods of OML and AML have ended. An assumption operates to the effect that the employee's date of return is the date which the employer notified to her in its counter-notice under regulation 7(6) of the MPLR. However, if she decides to return earlier, regulation 11 of the MPLR obliges her to provide no less than eight weeks' notice of the date on which she intends to return, failing which, the employer will have the right to postpone her return to a date such as will ensure that the employer has eight weeks' notice of her return. This is subject to an exception, namely that that date must not post-date the composite 52-week maternity leave period. Regulation 18(1) and (2) of the MPLR prescribes that, where the employee returns after the period of OML or AML, the right to return relates to the job in which she was employed before her absence. However, in the case of a return to work after AML, it is recognized that it may not be reasonably practicable for her to return to her job, in which case she has the right to another job which is both suitable for her and appropriate for her to do in the circumstances.

Statutory guidance on the job in respect of which the right to return operates is governed by regulation 18(3) of the MPLR, which provides that the relevant job is one in which she was employed immediately before the period of her OML or AML began. Moreover, the word 'job' is defined in regulation 2(1) of the MPLR as 'the nature of the work which she is employed to do in accordance with her contract and the capacity and place in which she is so employed'. The scope of these provisions was considered in *Blundell v Governing Body of St Andrews Catholic Primary School*.[49] In *Blundell*, a school teacher complained that, when she returned from maternity leave, she was given a different class to teach and that this constituted a breach of regulation 18 of the MPLR insofar as it was not the 'job in which she was employed before her absence'. The EAT took into account the fact that the MPLR is designed to ensure an element of continuity on the employee's return from maternity leave so that she comes back to a work situation as near as possible to that which she left and any sense of dislocation felt is minimized. This is achieved by the degree of specificity provided in relation to the three factors relating to the employee's pre-leave work narrated in regulation 2(1) of the MPLR, namely

---

[45] Regulation 4(1) and (2)(a) of the MPLR.   [46] Regulation 4(4) of the MPLR.
[47] Regulation 7(6) and (7) of the MPLR.
[48] This complies with the terms of Article 15 of the Recast Equality Directive 2006/54/EC (OJ 2006 L204/23).   [49] [2007] ICR 1451.

its nature and the capacity and place in which it was undertaken. On the basis of these elements of nature, capacity, and place of the work, Langstaff J decided that the employer had not breached the employee's statutory right to return:

■ *Blundell v Governing Body of St Andrews Catholic Primary School* [2007] ICR 1451, 1467E–H

Langstaff J:

[The] claimant could be required to teach any class as asked by her head, and . . . this was a real, not simply a theoretical requirement deriving from the contract alone. The nature of her work, according to her contract, was as a teacher. Her capacity (as a matter of fact) was viewed more realistically as a class teacher than as teacher of reception yellow, since she would in any event have been asked to move after each two-year period, and anyway the identity of the pupils in the reception class would change from year to year simply through age. The place of work could not be said to be the reception classroom, but the school. The claimant complains that the precise position she occupied was as reception teacher. The tribunal held that being a teacher of reception class as such was temporary: it seems plain to us that, where a precise position is variable, a tribunal is not obliged to freeze time at the precise moment its occupant takes maternity leave, but may have regard to the normal range within which variation has previously occurred. The post to which the claimant here was returned was the same post, if the level of specificity was properly to be regarded as 'teacher'. If it was temporarily more specific, because the precise post varied, the question is whether the job on return fell outside the boundary of what was permissible. Was it outside the normal range of variability which the claimant could reasonably have expected? It is clear the tribunal found it was not . . . [and] we see no error in the tribunal decision on this point.

The decision in *Blundell* can be contrasted with *Kelly v Secretary of State for Justice*[50] where it was held that it was not suitable and appropriate to return a 'prison mental health lead' whose contract of employment described her as a 'prison officer' to the role of an ordinary prison officer.

A no less significant point is that regulation 18A(1) of the MPLR provides for certain ancillary rights attaching to the right to return. For example, the employee has the right to return with her seniority, pension rights, and similar rights intact as they would have been if she had not been absent, and on terms and conditions no less favourable than those which would have applied if she had not been absent. For example, the practice in Hypothetical B would be unlawful.

Hypothetical B

Janice Freeman ('JF') works as a salesperson in the Wolverhampton office of Danny's Demolishers Ltd ('DD'). She has a contractual entitlement to a bonus payable at the end of each month and the rate is based on the amount of sales she generates per month. JF takes OML and AML. When she returns from maternity leave, DD informs her that the provision regarding the bonus entitlement has been removed from her contract of employment.

[50] (UKEAT/0227/13/JOJ, 25 November 2013).

A key question is whether the European and domestic protections in Article 15 of the Recast Equality Directive and sections 71(4)(c) and 73(4)(c) of the ERA and regulations 18 and 18A of the MPLR cater sufficiently for the needs of returning mothers. Of particular note is the fact that these provisions confer an entitlement to return to work on the same terms and conditions of employment as those in place before the commencement of the periods of OML and AML. However, what they explicitly do not do is provide any right to return on different contractual terms. Bearing in mind that many returning mothers will wish to switch from full-time to part-time work or to reduce their working hours, it is clear that these statutory provisions fail to establish any means of enabling that preference to be met. In fact, as will become apparent from the examination of the rules regulating part-time work in Chapter 13,[51] other than the law of indirect sex discrimination, which may hold some promise,[52] employment law offers scant comfort to the full-time employee seeking a post-maternity leave work transition to the more flexible part-time work type.

Where the employee is off on maternity leave, regulation 12A of the MPLR recognizes that the employee may work for her employer for a limited number of days without bringing that leave to a premature termination. These days are referred to as 'keeping in touch' ('KIT') days and regulation 12A(1) directs that an employee may carry out up to ten KIT days during maternity leave without bringing such leave to an end. Moreover, an employer is afforded no right to compel the employee to undertake any KIT days and no corresponding right is conferred on the employee to work during maternity leave.[53] This provision enables the employee to preserve some connection with the workplace whilst she is absent on maternity leave. Therefore, it is designed to maintain the parent–workplace relationship and facilitate a smooth transition from childbirth back to the workplace. However, as a policy measure, it has been subjected to a trenchant critique:

■ G. James, 'Enjoy Your Leave But "Keep in Touch": Help to Maintain Parent–Workplace Relationships' (2007) 36 *Industrial Law Journal* 315, 316–17

. . . KIT days might, if handled unsympathetically, be perceived as a requirement rather than an option (either by employers or employees) and may add to the stresses and strains of women's daily lives during what is already an intense period of re-adjustment. Indeed, there are a number of potential flaws with KIT days which suggest a misunderstanding (or lack of research)[54] regarding what is desirable or feasible during the leave period. Firstly, employers are advised to arrange these KIT days *prior to* leave . . . Yet, prior to the birth or adoption of a child employees may have false expectations about what they will feel, or what might be practical, following the birth/adoption and may agree to KIT days which later prove difficult to comply with, due, for example, to lack of sleep, ill health or childcare problems. Second, what an employee is to be paid for working KIT days is not as clear or as fair as one might expect. The Government suggests that pay ought to be agreed in advance but by failing to stipulate that all employees ought to be paid at their contractual rate for any work (or training) they undertake, the Government have provided unscrupulous employers with an opportunity to exploit new parents . . . Third, although legally protected against detrimental treatment and dismissal if she refuses to work during leave, how many women will, in

---

[51] See Chapter 13, section 13.2.1.
[52] See sections 18 and 19 of the Equality Act 2010 and Chapter 10, section 10.2.4.
[53] Regulation 12A(6) of the MPLR.
[54] For a detailed research paper which highlights the high take-up of KIT days, see the joint BIS and EHRC report, 'Pregnancy and Maternity-Related Discrimination and Disadvantage' (BIS Research Paper No. 325), available at http://www.equalityhumanrights.com/sites/default/files/publication_pdf/BIS-15–447-pregnancy-and-maternity-related-discrimination-and-disadvantage.pdf at pages 85–91 (last visited 8 February 2016).

practice, bring a claim if they feel that they have been poorly treated? Research shows a limited invocation of relevant legal avenues by pregnant women and new mothers who experience detrimental treatment . . . KIT days might therefore prove to be unpopular. They may also prove to be unnecessary: They are premised upon the idea that they will (a) help new mothers and adoptive parents stay in touch with workplace developments and ease their return to work, and (b) help employers accommodate leave with minimum disruption to productivity, yet employers are entitled to make 'reasonable contact' during leave. Surely this latter provision is wide enough to ensure employees are kept 'in the loop' regarding developments at work and provides both parties with ample opportunity to make contact during leave should they wish to do so.

9.2.2 Statutory maternity pay

The right to statutory maternity pay ('SMP') was one of the flagship reforms introduced by Michael Foot, Employment Minister in the minority Labour Government of 1974–79. As part of the 'Social Contract' agreed between the Trade Unions Congress and the Government,[55] provision for SMP was included within the Employment Protection Act 1975. Since its introduction, the right to SMP has undergone a series of major reforms. Some of the more radical changes have been spurred by European developments. For example, domestic law had to be modified in 1994 in order to comply with the requirements of the Pregnant Workers' Directive[56] concerning the 'maintenance of a payment to, and/or entitlement to an adequate allowance for, workers [on maternity leave]'.[57] Furthermore, in *Gillespie v Northern Health Board*,[58] although the ECJ dismissed the argument that European equality law required women to be paid full contractual pay whilst on maternity leave, it was decided that maternity pay must not be set by a Member State at so low a rate that it functioned to disincentivize employees from taking up the right to maternity leave. Otherwise, such a practice would undermine the purpose of the latter, namely 'the protection of women before and after giving birth'.[59]

The domestic regulation of SMP is currently found in sections 164–167 of the Social Security Contributions and Benefits Act 1992 ('SSCBA') and the Statutory Maternity Pay (General) Regulations 1986[60] ('SMP Regs'). Although the regime regulating SMP has progressively moved in a worker-friendly direction in response to the European developments outlined earlier, it remains the case that the entitlement is far from universal. For example, SMP (1) does not entail the continuation of full contractual pay throughout the duration of the employee's period of statutory maternity leave and (2) stops short of conferring an allowance for the full 52-week period of OML and AML. Instead, the maternity pay period runs contemporaneously with the 26-week period of OML and the first 13 weeks of AML, resulting in payment for the first 39 weeks of maternity leave only.[61] The pregnant employee will receive 90 per cent of her normal weekly contractual earnings[62] during the first six weeks of OML ('the earnings-related element of SMP'), but the remaining 33 weeks of SMP are paid at the lower of £140.98[63] per week and the

---

[55] See P. Davies and M. Freedland, *Labour Legislation and Public Policy* (Oxford, Clarendon Press/OUP, 1993) ch. 8.   [56] Directive 92/85/EEC (OJ 1992 L348/1).
[57] Article 11(2)(b) of the Pregnant Workers' Directive 92/85/EEC (OJ 1992 L348/1).
[58] [1996] ICR 498.
[59] [1996] ICR 498, 513G. The ECJ also ruled that women on maternity leave should benefit from pay rises awarded before or during that period. See also *Alabaster v Woolwich plc* [2005] ICR 695.
[60] SI 1986/1960.
[61] See regulation 2(2) of the SMP Regs; sections 164–165 of the SSCBA.
[62] This is averaged out over the eight-week period immediately prior to the fourteenth week before the EWC: section 166(1) and (2) of the SSCBA.
[63] This figure is usually increased on an annual basis.

earnings-related element of SMP.[64] Once paid out to the employee, the employer is entitled to recover the majority of the SMP from the State, which is achieved by deducting it from National Insurance contributions and PAYE.[65] The end result is the absence of any link between SMP and the real earnings of pregnant employees, which operates to indirectly motivate workers to return to work prior to the exhaustion of the entire 52-week period of maternity leave.[66] It also suggests the existence of an underlying 'assumption [in policy circles] that [the employee] has a partner who is supporting her financially during [the] period [of maternity leave]'.[67]

Not only is the entitlement limited, but a number of preconditions are imposed on receipt:

Section 164 [SMP]—entitlement and liability to pay . . .

(2) The conditions [on the receipt of SMP] are—

   (a) that [the employee] has been in employed earner's employment with an employer for a continuous period of at least 26 weeks ending with the week immediately preceding the 14th week before the [EWC] . . . but has ceased to work for him . . .;

   (b) that her normal weekly earnings for the period of 8 weeks ending with the week immediately preceding the 14th week before the [EWC] . . . are not less than the lower earnings limit in force [in respect of National Insurance contributions] . . . immediately before the commencement of the 14th week before the [EWC]; and

   (c) that she has become pregnant and has reached, or been confined before reaching, the commencement of the 11th week before the [EWC] . . .

(4) A woman shall be entitled to payments of [SMP] only if—

   (a) she gives the person who will be liable to pay it notice of the date from which she expects his liability to pay her [SMP] to begin; and

   (b) the notice is given at least 28 days before that date or, if that is not reasonably practicable, as soon as is reasonably practicable.

(5) The notice shall be in writing if the person who is liable to pay the woman [SMP] so requests.

Where the employee is ineligible to receive SMP on the basis that she is unable to satisfy these conditions, she may be entitled to claim State maternity allowance, which is a benefit made available by the Department for Work and Pensions.[68]

Section 165 of the SSCBA and regulation 2 of the SMP Regs govern the date of commencement of SMP. The default rule that the period of SMP begins with the eleventh week before the EWC finds its expression in section 165(2) of the SSCBA.[69] Given that some employees on maternity leave will experience pregnancy-related illnesses, an important issue is whether an employee can claim SMP and statutory sick pay concurrently.

---

[64] See regulation 6 of the SMP Regs; section 166(2) of the SSCBA.

[65] Sections 164–167 of the SSCBA. Where there is a contractual maternity scheme in place, e.g. one which provides for full pay to the employee when she is on maternity leave, SMP must be set off against that contractual entitlement.

[66] See G. James, 'The Work and Families Act 2006: Legislation to Improve Choice and Flexibility?' (2006) 35 *Industrial Law Journal* 272, 273–4.

[67] S. Fredman, *Women and the Law* (Oxford, OUP, 1997) 200.

[68] See https://www.gov.uk/maternity-allowance/overview (last visited 29 November 2017).

[69] This is subject to the exception in regulation 2(1) of the SMP Regs which gives a woman an entitlement to choose the date of commencement of her period of SMP. This exception was considered in *Wade v North Yorkshire Police Authority* [2007] IRLR 393.

In *Department for Work and Pensions v Sutcliffe*,[70] HHJ Peter Clark concluded that the payment of sick pay during OML and AML was precluded by section 71(5)(b) of the ERA and regulation 9(3) of the MPLR. These statutory provisions stipulate that the inactive terms and conditions of the employee on maternity leave concern those relating to remuneration, i.e. sums payable by way of wages or salary. Since sick pay is a form of remuneration, the latter clearly includes sick pay, in which case SMP and sick pay cannot be paid contemporaneously.

9.2.3 Right to time off for ante-natal care

Sections 55 and 56 of the ERA provide pregnant employees[71] with an entitlement to paid time off work to attend ante-natal appointments in accordance with the UK's obligations under Article 9 of the Pregnant Workers' Directive.[72] This time off must be paid at the employee's normal rate of pay, calculated at the appropriate hourly rate[73] in respect of the period of absence. Therefore, it is unlawful for the employer to insist that the employee 'make the time up', failing which her pay will be reduced. With the exception of the first ante-natal appointment,[74] certain preconditions are attached to this right, namely that the employee must, if requested to do so, show the employer:

(1) a certificate from a registered medical practitioner, registered midwife, or registered nurse which states that she is pregnant; and

(2) an appointment card or some other document which narrates that an appointment has been made.[75]

Rather surprisingly, the ERA furnishes no definition of an 'ante-natal' appointment or care, although the Statutory Code of Practice on Employment promulgated by the Equality and Human Rights Commission ('EHRC') provides that it 'can include medical examinations, relaxation and parenting classes'.[76] Other examples include appointments with the employee's midwife and ante-natal classes.

Section 57(1)(a) and (b) of the ERA provides that if the employer unreasonably refuses to allow the employee to take time off for ante-natal care or fails to pay any amount to which she is entitled under section 56 of the ERA, the employee may enforce that statutory breach by presenting a complaint to an employment tribunal. In light of the fact that section 55 of the ERA would appear to confer on an employee an absolute right to time off for ante-natal care if the two preconditions in section 55(2) of the ERA are met, the language of section 57(1) is unusual insofar as it limits the employee's ability to enforce an infringement of that statutory right to those circumstances where the employer has unreasonably refused the employee's request. As such, the right is absolute, but the scope for enforcement is restricted. As for what might constitute a reasonable refusal, the ERA is silent, albeit that one might be able to imagine a case where the tribunal concludes

---

[70] (UK/EAT/0319/07/ZT, 1 October 2007, HHJ Peter Clark).

[71] Similar protections are afforded to agency workers, fathers of the expected child, and husbands or partners of pregnant employees under sections 57ZA, 57ZB, 57ZC, 57ZD, and 57ZE of the ERA. Agency workers have the right to be remunerated in respect of such time off, whereas fathers, husbands and partners of the pregnant employee do not. Moreover, in the case of fathers, and such husbands and partners, a maximum of two ante-natal appointments is prescribed in section 57ZE(2) and the maximum period of time that may be taken off in respect of each ante-natal appointment is six-and-a-half hours (section 57ZE(3)).   [72] Directive 92/85/EEC (OJ 1992 L348/1).

[73] Section 56(2) of the ERA defines this as the amount of one week's pay divided by the number of normal working hours in a week for that employee when employed under the contract of employment in force on the day when the time off is taken.

[74] Section 55(3) of the ERA.   [75] Section 55(2)(a) and (b) of the ERA.

[76] See https://www.equalityhumanrights.com/sites/default/files/employercode.pdf at para 17.26 (last visited 29 November 2017).

that the employee ought to have arranged the ante-natal appointment in her own free time. The employee must present her complaint to the employment tribunal within three months of the date of the ante-natal appointment (rather than the employer's unreasonable refusal) or such further period as the tribunal considers reasonable.[77] If the tribunal upholds the employee's complaint, it may make a declaration to that effect.[78] If the complaint that the employer unreasonably refused to permit the employee to take time off is held to be well-founded, the tribunal must order the employer to pay to the employee an amount equivalent to the remuneration to which she would have been entitled under section 56 of the ERA if the employer had not refused.

9.2.4 Protections from dismissal, detriment, discrimination, and redundancy which apply in the case of pregnancy and maternity

The UK Parliament has recognized that much of the aforementioned rights to maternity leave, SMP, and time off for ante-natal care would be rendered ineffective in the absence of corresponding statutory provisions protecting pregnant employees and employees on maternity leave from being subjected to detriments, dismissal, redundancy, or discrimination.

If we turn first to the circumstances in which a pregnant employee suffers a detriment, this is governed by section 47C of the ERA and regulation 19 of the MPLR. The word 'detriment' is not defined in either of the ERA or the MPLR, but it is usually taken to mean some form of action or omission on the part of the employer which is short of dismissal and disadvantageous to the employee.[79] It is provided that an employee must not be subjected to any detriment by any act, or any deliberate failure to act, by her employer which is perpetrated for a 'prescribed reason'. Regulation 19(2) of the MPLR lists the 'prescribed reasons' as the fact that the employee:

(1) is pregnant;[80]

(2) has given birth to a child;

(3) is suspended from work because she is pregnant, has recently given birth, or is breastfeeding;

(4) took, sought to take, or availed herself of the benefits of OML or AML;

(5) failed to return after a period of OML or AML where the employer did not notify her of the date of return and she reasonably believed that the period of OML or AML had not ended, or the employer gave her less than 28 days' notice of the date on which the period of OML or AML would end, and it was not reasonably practicable for her to return on that date; and/or

(6) undertook, considered undertaking, or refused to undertake any KIT days in accordance with regulation 12A of the MPLR.

The employee alleging a breach of any of these rights may complain to an employment tribunal.[81] The tribunal will consider the claim provided that it is presented within three months[82] of

---

[77] Section 57(2) of the ERA.   [78] Section 57(3) of the ERA.

[79] In fact, regulation 19(4) of the MPLR carves a dismissal out of the scope of the word 'detriment' and, accordingly, where the 'detriment' is the dismissal of the employee, the provisions of section 47C and regulation 19 of the MPLR do not apply; instead, section 99 of the ERA and regulation 20 of the MPLR will apply, on which, see later.

[80] In *Ramdoolar v Bycity Ltd* [2005] ICR 368, the EAT held that the tribunal must be satisfied that the employer knew of, or believed in, the existence of the employee's pregnancy. Otherwise, this prescribed reason will not be met.   [81] Section 48(1) of the ERA.

[82] Section 48(3)(a) of the ERA. However, the tribunal may extend the three-month period if it considers it was reasonable in a case where it is satisfied that it was not reasonably practicable for the complaint to be presented before the end of that standard period: section 48(3)(b) of the ERA.

the date of the detriment[83] and, if successful, it must make a declaration that the complaint was well-founded and award compensation.[84] Compensation is fixed on a 'just and equitable' basis, i.e. taking account of all the circumstances having regard to the infringement and the loss suffered by the employee, including any expenses reasonably incurred by the employee in consequence of the employer's actions or inactions and any loss of any benefit which she might reasonably be expected to have had but for that act or failure to act.[85]

Secondly, as we noted, a 'detriment' will not cover a 'dismissal' of an employee for a pregnancy or maternity-related reason. Where an employer dismisses[86] a pregnant employee or an employee off on maternity leave, section 99 of the ERA and regulation 20 of the MPLR direct that, where the reason or principal reason for her dismissal is (a) of a 'prescribed kind' or (b) redundancy and the employer failed to offer her a suitable vacancy in accordance with the statutory right under regulation 10 of the MPLR,[87] she will be treated as automatically unfairly dismissed[88] if the dismissal operates to terminate her period of OML or AML.[89] Regulation 20(2) of the MPLR also provides that if the reason for an employee's dismissal is redundancy and it is demonstrated that the employee was chosen for redundancy because of one of the prescribed reasons in preference to other employees in comparable circumstances, then she will be treated as automatically unfairly dismissed. The employee will need to show that the circumstances constituting the redundancy applied equally to one or more employees in the same undertaking as the employee who held positions similar to that held by her but who had not been dismissed.[90] Reasons of the 'prescribed kind' are laid down in regulation 20(3) of the MPLR and mirror the reasons (1)–(6) in relation to an employee detriment.

There is one major exception to the rule that the employee will be regarded as automatically unfairly dismissed in such circumstances. This is set out in regulation 20(7) of the MPLR:

> **Regulation 20 Unfair dismissal . . .**
>
> (7) Paragraph (1) does not apply in relation to an employee if—
>
>   (a) it is not reasonably practicable for a reason other than redundancy for the employer (who may be the same employer or a successor of his) to permit her to return to a job which is both suitable for her and appropriate for her to do in the circumstances;
>
>   (b) an associated employer offers her a job of that kind, and
>
>   (c) she accepts or unreasonably refuses that offer.

---

[83] Where the detriment consists of a series of acts or omissions and some of those acts or omissions occur outside the three-month limitation period, the Court of Appeal has held that the latter events can be taken into account if there is some link between them and the other events which makes it just and reasonable for them to be treated in time and for the employee to be able to rely on them: *Arthur v London Eastern Railway Ltd* [2007] IRLR 58.   [84] Section 49(1) of the ERA.

[85] Section 49(2) and (3) of the ERA. The employee is under an obligation to mitigate her loss: section 49(4) of the ERA.

[86] Protection from dismissal is prescribed by Article 10 of the Pregnant Workers' Directive 92/85/EEC (OJ 1992 L348/1) and applies from the outset of the pregnancy to the end of maternity leave. Article 10 is directly effective and applies to fixed-term contracts of employment: *Jiménez Melgar v Ayuntamiento de los Barrios* (C-438/99) [2001] ECR I-6915, [2001] IRLR 848.

[87] See Chapter 18, section 18.3.4, for more detail on regulation 10 of the MPLR in the context of a redundancy.

[88] Where a dismissal is automatically unfair, there is no need for the employee to show that she was dismissed in terms of section 95(1) of the ERA and that her dismissal was unreasonable in accordance with section 98(4) of the ERA, on which, see Chapter 16, section 16.2.4.2.

[89] Regulation 7(5) of the MPLR directs that, in such a case, the period of OML or AML ends at the date of dismissal, on which, see *St Alphonsus RC Primary School v Blenkinsop* (UKEAT0082/09/DA18 May 2009, HHJ McMullen QC).

[90] *SG Petch Ltd v English-Stewart* (UKEAT/0213/12/JOJ, 31 October 2012, Honourable Mr Justice Burton).

The question of whether the employee has unreasonably refused an offer of suitable alternative employment is well-trodden ground under the general law of redundancy.[91] As such, although there is no case law construing regulation 20(7), it is likely that the tribunals and courts would adopt the same approach. The fact that regulation 20(8) of the MPLR directs that the onus is on the employer to show that the employee unreasonably refused an offer of alternative employment provides a measure of employment protection for the dismissed worker in such a context.

Although these provisions for automatic unfair dismissal are extremely useful for employees dismissed for the pregnancy-related and maternity-related reasons set out earlier, experience shows that dismissed employees will prefer to label and advance their employment claim as one of direct sex discrimination under section 13 of the Equality Act 2010 ('EA') or pregnancy or maternity discrimination under section 18 of the EA. The principal motivation for this practice is that compensation awards for successful discrimination claims are unlimited, unlike unfair dismissal claims.[92] There is a wealth of European jurisprudence on the kind of conduct which is proscribed under anti-discrimination laws in the context of pregnant employees. For example, in *Dekker v Stichting*[93] and *Webb v EMO Air Cargo (UK) Ltd*,[94] the ECJ ruled that the dismissal of a pregnant worker automatically constitutes direct sex discrimination.[95] Meanwhile, in *Tele Danmark*,[96] the dismissal of a fixed-term pregnant employee was held to amount to direct sex discrimination, notwithstanding that the employee knew that she was pregnant when she was recruited but failed to inform the employer of that fact.[97] Other decisions of the ECJ afford pregnant workers a degree of protection in other contexts.[98]

Finally, we mention briefly regulation 3 of the Management of Health and Safety at Work Regulations 1999 ('MHSW')[99] which imposes an obligation on employers to undertake a risk assessment in respect of all of their employees. Pregnant employees are singled out for specific attention by the MHSW. For example, regulation 17 explicitly provides that an employer must suspend a new or expectant employee who works at night from work for as long as necessary for health and safety grounds if a registered medical practitioner or midwife deems it necessary for the employee's health or safety that she

---

[91] See Chapter 18, section 18.3.4, for more detail.

[92] These are capped at £83,682 or the employee's annual pay, whichever is the lower: see Chapter 17, section 17.3.3.2.

[93] [1992] ICR 325. In *Brown v Rentokil* [1999] ICR 790, a woman was dismissed for absences from work in excess of 26 weeks owing to a pregnancy-related illness and this was held to amount to direct sex discrimination. Contrast *Rentokil* with *Lyons v DWP JobCentre Plus* [2014] ICR 668 where it was held that dismissal for absences relating to post-natal depression arising after maternity leave did not amount to sex, pregnancy, or maternity discrimination.

[94] [1995] ICR 1021. See also *Paquay v Société d'architectes Hoet + Minne SPRL* [2008] 1 CMLR 263.

[95] See also *Handels-og Kontorfuntionaerernes Forbund I Danmark (Union of Clerical and Commercial Employees) (for Hertz) v Dansk Arbejdsgiverforening* [1992] ICR 332. Article 2(2)(c) of the Recast Equality Directive now provides that any less favourable treatment of a woman related to pregnancy or maternity is direct sex discrimination.   [96] [2004] ICR 610.

[97] The thinking here is that the employer is not entitled to take this into account in deciding who to recruit.

[98] For example, in *Jiménez Melgar v Ayuntamiento de los Barrios* (C-438/99) [2001] ECR I-6915, [2001] IRLR 848, where an employer's decision not to renew a fixed-term contract was grounded on the employee's pregnancy, the ECJ took the view that this was also direct sex discrimination. Meanwhile, *Mayr v Bäckerei und Konditorei Gerhard Flöckner Ohg* [2008] 2 CMLR 27 demonstrates how zealous the ECJ can be in upholding the interests of female employees. Here, it was ruled that where an employer dismisses an employee undergoing IVF treatment because of her IVF-related absences from work, the employer's conduct will be regarded as direct sex discrimination because the employee is likely to become pregnant. See also *Metropolitan Police v Keohane* [2014] ICR 1073 where the removal of a dog from a pregnant police dog-handler because she was no longer operational amounted to pregnancy-related discrimination on the basis that it had an impact on her career progression and would result in her losing overtime when she returned to work.   [99] SI 1999/3242.

should not be at work for a particular period of time.[100] An employer's consistent failure to undertake such a risk assessment will also constitute a breach of the implied term of mutual trust and confidence, enabling an employee to claim constructive dismissal at common law or under section 95(1)(c) of the ERA for the purposes of the statutory unfair dismissal regime.[101] Finally, an employee who is subjected to a detriment for having been suspended on maternity grounds is protected under section 47C of the ERA and regulation 19(2)(c) of the MPLR. Likewise a dismissal on such grounds will constitute an automatically unfair dismissal under regulation 20(1) and (3)(c) of the MPLR.

9.3 WORK-LIFE BALANCE PROTECTIONS

At their heart, the statutory provisions regulating shared parental leave ('SPL'), paternity, and parental leave represent an attempt by the UK Parliament to promote the increased participation of fathers in the raising of their children. Ultimately, they cause us to question what a father's role should be and whether it ought to be limited to the 'breadwinner' function. The shared parental leave provisions found in the Shared Parental Leave Regulations 2014 ('SPLR'),[102] the Statutory Shared Parental Pay (General) Regulations 2014 ('SSPPR'),[103] and the Maternity and Adoption Leave (Curtailment of Statutory Rights to Leave) Regulations 2014 ('MAL(C)R'),[104] the parental leave elements of the MPLR, and the paternity leave provisions of the Paternity and Adoption Leave Regulations 2002 ('PALR')[105] are all intended to modify the behaviour of fathers. In particular, they are designed to strike a more equitable division between the sexes for family and care responsibilities. Nonetheless, it has been argued that the current incarnation of work–life protections in domestic law are ineffective in rupturing the gender-segmented labour market by encouraging fathers to reallocate some of their working hours to childcare duties:

■ E. Caracciolo Di Torella, 'New Labour, New Dads: The Impact of Family-Friendly Legislation on Fathers' (2007) 36 *Industrial Law Journal* 318, 328

> . . . family-friendly policies de facto continue to promote the idea of the mother as main carer: they are not geared towards promoting equal parenting or gender equality but simply at 'valuing' mothers' work . . . As a result they reinforce the existing gendered division of unpaid work which is the precondition of inequality in the workplace and more generally in society. This makes the current arrangements 'the most unequal parenting in Europe' . . .

Empirical research has revealed that fathers do not reduce their hours of work in order to increase the amount of time they spend on their parental responsibilities.[106] In fact, many fathers consider themselves to be good parents notwithstanding that they do not spend as much time caring for their children as mothers. This suggests that fathers' perception of their parenting role fails to match that of mothers.[107] The extent to which SPL has

---

[100] Regulations 18 and 18A of the MHSW specify when the employer's duty to carry out a risk assessment is triggered and regulation 16 divides the obligations incumbent on the employer into a series of steps.

[101] *Bunning v GT Bunning & Sons Ltd (No. 2)* [2005] EWCA Civ 104.

[102] SI 2014/3050.   [103] SI 2014/3051.   [104] SI 2014/3052.   [105] SI 2002/2788.

[106] E. Dermott, 'What's Parenthood Got to Do with It? Men's Hours of Paid Work' (2006) *British Journal of Sociology* 619.

[107] E. Dermott, 'Time and Labour: Fathers' Perceptions of Employment and Childcare' (2005) *Sociological Review* 91.

changed this trend is doubtful,[108] particularly since the Achilles heel of this reform is the paltry level at which statutory shared parental pay ('SSPP') is set, namely £140.98 or 90 per cent of the employee's average weekly earnings, per week of leave taken, whichever figure is the lower.[109] In fact, research has revealed that SPL has been far from a roaring success to date. The charity 'Working Families' estimates a mere 0.5–2 per cent take-up rate amongst fathers.[110] The reasons given range from an inter-generational divide on the merits of male parenting, to the stigma associated with taking leave in the workplace, and the complexity[111] of the regulations. In the following extract, James probes further:

■ G. James, 'Family-friendly Employment Laws (Re)assessed: The Potential of Care Ethics' (2016) 45 *Industrial Law Journal* 477, 497–8

There have been various legal changes in the UK that have purportedly sought to en-courage men's role as caregivers, including the paternity [provisions] . . . and more re-cently, the right to claim SPL. All these attempts, while commendable at a superficial level, have been flawed in many ways . . . For example, SPL offers some superficial recognition that parenting is, or should be, a gender neutral undertaking. However, the practical complexity of the provision, the poor payment available, and the fact that it has been developed alongside a long standing, more simplistic 'fall back' of re-lying solely on the traditional, 'tried and tested', maternity leave option, undermines its potential to promote more male caregiving during the first year of the child's life. A policy does not have to be overtly gendered to have normative cores that *are* implic-itly gendered and perpetuate the notion that care-work is, predominantly, a female undertaking. SPL *appears* to promote a more gender neutral approach to care that will challenge traditional ideologies of motherhood and fatherhood but in practice favours, and is likely to perpetuate, the current status quo whereby mothers predom-inantly undertake the majority of childcare responsibilities. The SPL provision has not been adequately funded or promoted and it remains difficult for working parents to, drawing on Williams' useful terminology, 'un-bend' gendered constructions of childcare/workplace relations, and those that attempt to do so will have to overcome more hurdles and might be disadvantaged economically as a result.

With these criticisms fresh in our mind, we now turn to consider SPL in greater detail.

9.3.1 **Shared parental leave**

SPL is a form of 'leave transfer' from the mother to the father/partner.[112] The statutory framework behind the employee's entitlement to SPL and SSPP contained in the SPLR, SSPPR, and MAL(C)R is infinitely labyrinthine and would make the Minotaur's maze look like child's play in comparison. For that reason, only the bare bones of the scheme are set out in this book.

---

[108] See discussion of this criticism in G. Mitchell, 'Encouraging Fathers to Care: The Children and Fam-ilies Act 2014 and Shared Parental Leave' (2015) 44 *Industrial Law Journal* 123, 130–1.

[109] Regulation 40(1) of the SSPPR.

[110] See https://www.workingfamilies.org.uk/workflex-blog/shared-parental-leave-in-the-uk-is-it-working-lessons-from-other-countries/ (last visited 29 November 2017) and the UK Department for Business, En-ergy and Industrial Strategy publicity drive at https://www.gov.uk/government/news/new-share-the-joy-campaign-promotes-shared-parental-leave-rights-for-parents (last visited 13 February 2018).

[111] See G. James, 'Family-friendly Employment Laws (Re)assessed: The Potential of Care Ethics' (2016) 45 *Industrial Law Journal* 477, 484–5.

[112] It replaced the former statutory incarnation of this concept known as 'additional paternity leave'.

Essentially, the SPL regime enables eligible employees—rather than mothers or adopting parents—to share up to 52 weeks' leave as SPL and 39 weeks' SSPP on the birth or adoption of a child. The default position is that mothers will continue to be entitled to ML and SMP, but that mothers with partners[113] who both meet certain qualifying conditions will be permitted to end the mother's ML and SMP and convert it into SPL and SSPP. Accordingly, the untaken balance of ML and SMP will then be available to both the mother and partner as SPL and SSPP and can be taken in blocks of one week. The untaken balance of ML and SMP may be shared in a manner which enables both parents to be on leave concurrently. However, the first two weeks after the child's birth are reserved to the mother as leave and cannot be shared pursuant to SPL.

At the time of writing, SSPP was set at the lower of £140.98 or 90 per cent of the employee's average weekly earnings, per week of leave taken.[114] Of course, it is possible for the employer to give employees a contractual right to receive enhanced shared parental pay, but there is no compulsion to do so.[115] This is one of the main weaknesses in the SPL and SSPP regime, along with the statutory requirement that a mother must consent to the sharing of her period of ML and SMP with the father, husband, civil partner, or partner. Mitchell has classified this legal provision as one which does nothing to uproot the traditional 'male breadwinner/female carer' model:

■ G. Mitchell, 'Encouraging Fathers to Care: The Children and Families Act 2014 and Shared Parental Leave' (2015) 44 *Industrial Law Journal* 123, 131

> . . . the legislation has reinforced mothers' primary caring role, as mothers must declare that they 'consent to the amount of leave which P[arent] intends to take' . . . The whole period of leave is the mother's to use if she wishes; fathers will only be able to access [SPL] if the mother allows them. Therefore, mothers remain the 'gatekeepers of fathers' participation in care,' dictating the role fathers can play . . . This again demonstrates how mothers' caring role has been prioritised by the legislation . . .

Since the introduction of SPL and SSPP in 2015, the Government has announced its intention to extend the regime to cover working grandparents.[116] This is designed as one of the policy responses to the latest 'eldercare–workplace conundrum',[117] i.e. the need to look after and support families and working grandparents involved in the provision of childcare, which is a growing phenomenon. However, at the time of writing, no meaningful progress had been reached with this policy measure and it may be that it has been put on the back-burner for the time being.

---

[113] In other words, the biological father of the child or the mother's husband, civil partner, or partner, whether opposite or same sex.

[114] Regulation 40(1) of the SSPPR. See the Shared Parental Leave Calculator provided by the UK Government, available at https://www.gov.uk/pay-leave-for-parents (last visited 29 November 2017).

[115] Where the employer provides a contractually enhanced maternity pay scheme to its employees who are mothers, but it has a policy of denying an equivalent benefit to its employees who are fathers, this will not amount to direct sex discrimination: *Capita Customer Management Ltd v Ali* (UKEAT/0161/17/ BA, 11 April 2018), but cf. *Hextall v Chief Constable of Leicestershire Police*, available at https://www. serjeantsinn.com/wp-content/uploads/2016/10/2601223–15-Hextall-v-LeicestershirePolice-FH-Aug16- JR.pdf (last visited 29 November 2017).

[116] See https://www.gov.uk/government/news/chancellor-announces-major-new-extension-of-shared-parental-leave-and-pay-to-working-grandparents (last visited 29 November 2017).

[117] G. James and E. Spruce, 'Workers with Elderly Dependants: Employment Law's Response to the Latest Care-Giving Conundrum' (2015) 35 *Legal Studies* 463.

9.3.2 Paternity leave

The provisions for paternity leave ('PL') on birth and adoption[118] are set out in sections 80A–80E of the ERA, and regulations 4–14 of the PALR. An important point worth stressing is that the label 'paternity' leave is something of a misnomer since the leave is made available to partners of mothers of children, rather than fathers as such.[119]

Hypothetical C

Simone Doncaster works as a technician in the Didcot office of Danny's Demolishers Ltd. She has been in a civil partnership with Moira for five years. If Moira gives birth to a child, Simone will meet the definition of 'partner' in regulation 2(1) of the PALR.

An employee will have the right to PL for the purposes of caring for a child[120] or supporting the child's mother if he/she:

(1) has satisfied certain notice, evidential, and declaratory preconditions;[121] and

(2) (a) has been continuously employed for a period of not less than 26 weeks ending with the week immediately preceding the fourteenth week before the expected week of the child's birth and has remained in continuous employment with that employer until the week before the first week of his/her APL;

(b) is either the father of the child, or married to or the partner or civil partner of the child's mother, but not the child's father; and

(c) has, or expects to have:

(i) responsibility for the upbringing of the child if he/she is the child's father; or

(ii) the main responsibility (apart from the child's mother's responsibility) for the upbringing of the child, if he/she is the mother's husband or the partner or civil partner of the mother;[122] and

(d) has not taken any SPL in respect of the child.[123]

Therefore, the primary condition imposed is that the employee must have at least 26 weeks' service in order to be eligible for ordinary paternity leave or additional paternity leave. Consider the disapproval of this requirement in the following extract from James:

■ **G. James, 'The Work and Families Act 2006: Legislation to Improve Choice and Flexibility?' (2006) 35 *Industrial Law Journal* 272, 275**

. . . offering leave only to men who have the stipulated length of service required . . . introduces a divide between fathers who can take leave and those who cannot, based upon length of service which is unfair in practical terms. It also has damaging ideological ramifications because

---

[118] Owing to constraints of space, the rules regulating statutory paternity leave on adoption are not addressed here.

[119] See the definition of 'partner' in regulation 2(1) and (2) of the PALR.

[120] Where the mother gives birth to more than one child, the right to paternity leave is not extended or available more than once: regulation 4(6) of the PALR. Compare this with the argument of the employee in *Zoi Chatzi v Ipourgos Oikonomikon* [2010] ECR I-8489 in the context of parental leave.

[121] Regulation 4(1) of the PALR.   [122] Regulation 4(2) of the PALR.

[123] Regulation 4(1A) of the PALR.

it reinforces the notion that the mother has (and *should* have) the main responsibility for child-care (as her eligibility is not dependent upon length of service), suggesting that the father's role is secondary. This is at best a missed opportunity for fathers who are increasingly interested in caring for their children . . . Indeed, even the two-week ordinary paternity leave entitlement (for which again only SPP is paid) is subject to a length of service qualification. Why is this acceptable for fathers when moves have been made to eliminate this in relation to mothers? Is his role in ensuring children have 'the best start' any less important? The fact that the purpose of [PL] is still promoted as facilitating a need to 'care for the child *and support the mother*' (my emphasis) is also disappointing, as it does little to promote equal parenting in an era when both parents often have responsibilities to employers.

The TUC have recently estimated that the requirement for 26 weeks' service prevented 44,000 fathers from taking PL in 2016.[124] This equates to approximately 10 per cent of all new fathers qualifying as employees in that year.

The notice, evidential, and declaratory preconditions imposed on a father's, partner's/civil partner's entitlement to PL consist of the service of two notices on the employer. The first is a notice of his/her intention to take PL in respect of a child by specifying the expected week of the child's birth, whether the employee has chosen to take one week's PL or two consecutive weeks' PL, and the date on which the employee has chosen that period of PL to begin.[125] The employee must serve this notice on the employer in or before the fifteenth week before the expected week of the child's birth or as soon as is reasonably practicable where that is not possible.[126] Meanwhile, the second notice is one which the employee must give to his/her employer intimating the date on which the child was born, as soon as reasonably practicable subsequent to the child's birth.[127] Both of these notices must be provided in writing if the employer so requests.[128] Furthermore, if the employer so requests, the employee is bound to provide his/her employer with a signed declaration to the effect that the purpose of his/her absence from work is to care for a child or support the child's mother and that he/she satisfies the conditions for the entitlement.[129]

Paternity leave must be taken in a block of one week or two consecutive weeks' leave[130] and begin on the date of the child's birth or on any date thereafter, provided that PL ends within 56 days of the date of birth.[131] Statutory paternity pay ('SPP') is paid at the rate of the lesser of £140.98[132] per week or 90 per cent of the employee's average weekly earnings[133] for a period of two weeks.[134] In the same vein as statutory maternity leave, the employee on PL in receipt of SPP is entitled to the benefit of all of the terms and conditions of his/her employment which would have applied if he/she had not been absent, with the exception of any terms regarding remuneration, i.e. sums payable to him/her

---

[124] See https://www.tuc.org.uk/news/quarter-new-dads-are-missing-out-paternity-leave-and-pay-says-tuc (last visited 29 November 2017).   [125] Regulation 6(1) of the PALR.

[126] Regulation 6(2) of the PALR.   [127] Regulation 6(7) of the PALR.

[128] Regulation 6(8) of the PALR.   [129] Regulation 6(3) of the PALR.

[130] Regulation 5(1) of the PALR.   [131] Regulation 5(2) of the PALR.

[132] This figure is usually increased on an annual basis.

[133] Sections 171ZA and 171ZE of the SSCBA; regulation 2(a) and (b) of the Statutory Paternity Pay and Statutory Adoption Pay (Weekly Rates) Regulations 2002 (SI 2002/2818). Unlike statutory maternity pay, there is no earnings-related element. For a critique of this omission, see G. James, 'The Work and Families Act 2006: Legislation to Improve Choice and Flexibility?' (2006) 35 *Industrial Law Journal* 272, 275.

[134] Section 171ZE(2) of the SSCBA. Section 123(3) of the Children and Families Act 2014 amends section 171ZE(2) of the SSCBA to enable the Secretary of State to make regulations to extend the period of two weeks' SPP. However, at the time of writing, there is no evidence that regulation 8 of the Statutory Paternity Pay and Statutory Adoption Pay (General) Regulations 2002 (SI 2002/2822) has been amended to that effect.

by way of wages or salary.[135] Moreover, regulations 13 and 14 of the PALR provide that the employee has a right to return to work after the expiry of a period of PL with his/her seniority, pension rights, and similar rights left intact, and on no less favourable terms and conditions than those which would have applied if he/she had not been absent. There is also statutory protection from a detriment or dismissal for the reason of paternity leave.[136]

The question is whether PL has promoted the sea-change in the division of responsibilities between the sexes for 'breadwinning' and 'caring' which is so desired by some of the commentators whose work we discussed earlier in this chapter. At a superficial level, the most obvious deficiency in the PL regime is the absence of any link between SPP and the father/partner's weekly earnings. Further, the lack of paternity leave protection in EU labour law does nothing to assist the development of the 'dual carer' model at domestic level. Statistical evidence also shows that very few men take PL. Other commentators have adopted a more principled critique of paternity leave, depicting it as an entitlement labouring under the shadow of maternity leave:

■ E. Caracciolo Di Torella, 'New Labour, New Dads: The Impact of Family-Friendly Legislation on Fathers' (2007) 36 *Industrial Law Journal* 318, 322–4

... a closer look reveals that there are too many shortcomings which make it unlikely that the right will underpin and further promote a change of attitude in parenthood models. The main problem is that the legislation is drafted in such a way to reinforce the idea that mothers rather than fathers are the primary carers. Indeed fathers do not have—unlike mothers—an automatic entitlement to take the leave. They must satisfy certain conditions such as the length of employment and they are not entitled to the same (salary related) level of pay ... Furthermore, the legislation rather obscurely states that fathers can use the leave 'to care for the child' and to 'support the mother'. It has been convincingly argued that this does little to promote the idea of equal parenting, rather it reinforces the message that mothers need to be 'supported' ... Seen in this light, paternity rights are nothing short of a token and as such they are unlikely to promote a cultural change ... This article maintains that, instead of providing more choice, essentially [the existence of PL] complicates even more the position of fathers by making it clear that they only have a 'secondary' right. Indeed their right is not only subordinate to the position of the mother in the workplace but also to her wishes . . ..

9.3.3 Parental leave

Parental leave was introduced by the Employment Relations Act 1999 in order to transpose the terms of the EU Parental Leave Directive,[137] which implemented the framework agreement entered into between the European Social Partners as part of the European Social Dialogue.[138] A helpful explanation of the purpose of parental leave was given by the ECJ in *Commission v Luxembourg*:

■ *Commission v Luxembourg* [2005] CMLR 1, 20

... parental leave is distinct from maternity leave. Parental leave is granted to parents to enable them to take care of their child. This leave may be taken until the child has reached a given age ...[139]

---

[135] Section 80C of the ERA; regulation 12 of the PALR.
[136] Sections 47C(2)(ca) and 99(3)(ca) of the ERA; regulations 28 and 29 of the PALR.
[137] Directive 96/34/EC (OJ 1996 L145/4). This has now been repealed and replaced by the Parental Leave Directive 2010/18/EU (OJ 2010 L68/13).
[138] See C. Barnard, *EU Employment Law* (Oxford, OUP, 2012) 420.

Further, parental leave is a measure designed to foster equal opportunities between men and women and the participation of women in the labour market. It is a form of leave which is available to both parents, albeit one which is non-transferable.[140] Member States must exercise caution in respect of the preconditions they impose on the right to parental leave. For example, if a Member State's law makes a father's entitlement conditional on the mother of the child being in employment or engaged in the exercise of a profession, this will constitute a breach of EU law.[141]

The Government's online guidance suggests that parental leave can be used to allow parents to spend more time with their children, to look at new schools, to settle children into new childcare arrangements, and to spend time with their grandparents.[142] Notwithstanding these lofty intentions, an examination of the statutory detail reveals that parental leave is a particularly modest kind of leave. In many respects, the parental leave framework closely follows the grain of that established for paternity leave. The main difference is that parental leave is an unpaid entitlement. Section 76(1) of the ERA and regulation 13 of the MPLR direct that an employee with continuous service of one year or more who has, or expects to have, responsibility for a child is entitled to be absent from work on parental leave for the purposes of caring for that child.[143] The leave endures for 18 weeks[144] which must be exercised before the child's 18th birthday.[145]

Regulation 16 of the MPLR lays down a default regime which is a kind of model scheme that will apply if the employee's contract of employment or a collective agreement or workforce agreement does not include a provision conferring an entitlement to absence from work for the purpose of caring for a child. The default regime is set out in Schedule 2 to the MPLR and provides for certain preconditions to the entitlement concerning the service of notice[146] which are drawn in similar terms to those pertaining to paternity leave. Of more significance, however, is the statutory direction that an annual limit of four weeks of parental leave is imposed, subject to the employer's agreement to the contrary.[147] Furthermore, parental leave can only be taken in blocks of one week, unless the child is disabled, which underscores the relative inflexibility of the entitlement.[148]

In the same vein as maternity and paternity leave, the employee is entitled to the benefit of all of his/her terms and conditions of employment during the leave period.[149] This includes matters connected with his/her employment whether or not they arise under a contract of employment, but excludes terms concerning remuneration.[150] Regulation 17 directs that the employee is entitled to the benefit of his/her employer's implied obligation of trust and confidence during the period of parental leave, including terms relating to notice of termination of the employment contract, compensation in the event of redundancy, or disciplinary or grievance procedures.[151] Conversely, the employee continues to be subject to the implied obligation of good faith owed to his/her employer, including terms and conditions relating to notice of termination of employment, the disclosure of confidential information, the acceptance of gifts or other benefits, and the employee's participation in any other business.[152]

---

[139] See also Article 33(2) of the Charter of Fundamental Rights of the European Union.

[140] Clause 2(2) of the framework agreement annexed to Directive 96/34/EC (OJ 1996 L145/4).

[141] *Maistrellis v Ypourgos* [2015] IRLR 944.

[142] See https://www.gov.uk/parental-leave/overview (last visited 29 November 2017).

[143] Regulation 13(1) of the MPLR. Where twins are born, a parent will not be entitled to two periods of parental leave: *Zoi Chatzi v Ipourgos Oikonomikon* [2010] ECR I-8489. However, Member States must establish a parental leave regime which ensures that the parents of twins receive treatment taking due account of their particular needs.

[144] Regulation 14(1) of the MPLR.   [145] Regulation 15(1) of the MPLR.

[146] The employee must provide 21 days' prior notice of the intended start date: para 3 of Schedule 2 to the MPLR.   [147] Paragraph 8 of Schedule 2 to the MPLR.

[148] See *Rodway v South Central Trains Ltd* [2005] ICR 1162; E. Caracciolo Di Torella, 'New Labour, New Dads: The Impact of Family-Friendly Legislation on Fathers' (2007) 36 *Industrial Law Journal* 318, 325–6.

[149] Section 77(1) of the ERA; regulation 17(a) of the MPLR.   [150] Section 77(2) of the ERA.

[151] Regulation 17(a) of the MPLR.   [152] Section 77(1)(b) of the ERA; regulation 17(b) of the MPLR.

Section 77(1)(c) and (4) of the ERA and regulations 18(1) and 18A(1) of the MPLR provide the employee on parental leave with a right to return to work after the expiry of leave with seniority, pension rights, and similar rights left intact, and on no less favourable terms and conditions than those which would have applied if he/she had not been absent. Regulation 18(1) and (2) of the MPLR direct that where the employee returns after the period of parental leave, the right to return relates to the job in which he/she was employed before his/her absence. Regulation 18(3) of the MPLR goes on to state that the relevant job is one in which the employee was employed immediately before the period of his/her parental leave began. The word 'job' is defined in regulation 2(1) of the MPLR as 'the nature of the work which she is employed to do in accordance with his/her contract and the capacity and place in which he/she is so employed'. However, if the employee takes in excess of four weeks' parental leave, the right to return applies in respect of the job in which the employee was employed before his/her absence or, if it is not reasonably practicable for the employer to permit him/her to return to that job, to another job which is both suitable and appropriate for him/her to do in the circumstances.[153] In *Riezniece v Zemkopibas ministrija*,[154] the ECJ held that an employer will infringe the Parental Leave Directive when it transfers an employee returning from parental leave to an equivalent role in a different department which it knows is due to be eliminated in the near future. Therefore, it is not always necessary to return the employee to his/her original post, where this is impracticable, provided that the post is not earmarked for abolition.[155]

The principal chink in the armour of the parental leave regime is the absence of payment, which clearly discourages fathers from taking it up:

■ A. McColgan, 'Family-Friendly Frolics? The Maternity and Parental Leave etc. Regulations 1999' (2000) 29 *Industrial Law Journal* 125, 139–42

The House of Commons Select Committee on Social Security, in its report on the social security implications of parental leave . . . remarked on the consensus to the effect that 'the payment of leave in some form would increase the take-up of the new entitlement'; 'the experience of other countries—and the conclusions of successive reviews of the subject—suggest that there is a strong case for parental leave being paid, if it is to be widely used and provide parents with a genuine choice'; 'if unpaid, leave is unlikely to be taken up in sufficient quantities to make a real difference to people's lives and is highly unlikely to be taken up by single parents, the low-paid or fathers'; . . . The firm evidence is that uptake of leave turns on whether it is paid or not . . . All the evidence is, however, that failing to pay parental leave will have the effect that it will be taken almost exclusively by women. This, in turn, will increase the incentives for prospective employers to discriminate against women of child-bearing age and against the mothers of young children . . . the low take-up of parental leave by fathers which is widely anticipated is a matter for concern. The detachment of working fathers from the domestic scene has implications not only for women's aspirations to equality, but also for the relationships which develop between fathers and children. These are vitally important, most especially given that early bonding promotes continued contact between fathers and children in the (ever-more likely) event of family breakdown.[156]

---

[153] Regulation 18(2) of the MPLR.   [154] [2013] IRLR 828.

[155] Akin to maternity leave, an employee has the right not to be subjected to any detriment or dismissal for having taken or sought to take parental leave: sections 47C(2)(c) and 99(3)(c) of the ERA; regulations 19(2)(e)(ii) and 20(3)(e)(ii) of the MPLR. See *Meerts v Proust NV* Case C-116/08 [2009] ECR I-10063 and *Lyreco Belgium NV v Rogiers* [2014] IRLR 656, which address the level of compensation payable to the automatically unfairly dismissed employee.

[156] See also E. Caracciolo Di Torella, 'New Labour, New Dads: The Impact of Family-Friendly Legislation on Fathers' (2007) 36 *Industrial Law Journal* 318, 326–7.

As such, the key criticism to be drawn from this extract is that the existing parental leave framework gives 'parents little of substance to help them balance their
paid work and caring commitments'.[157] This is partly why SPL was introduced in
April 2015.

9.3.4 Adoption leave

An employee is entitled to ordinary adoption leave ('OAL') if he/she (1) satisfies certain prescribed notice and evidential requirements[158] and (2) is the child's[159] adopter,
and has notified the adoption agency that he/she agrees that the child should be
placed with him/her for adoption on the date of placement.[160] Since April 2015, there
has been no length of continuous service condition.[161] If the employee has taken
OAL, provided that he/she has not been (1) notified by the adoption agency that the
placement will not be made or (2) dismissed, he/she will also be eligible for additional adoption leave ('AAL').[162] An employee will be the child's 'adopter' if he/she is
a person matched with a child for adoption or where two people have been matched
jointly, whichever of them has elected to be the child's adopter.[163] Therefore, a couple
must choose who is to take up the right to statutory adoption leave. Bearing in mind
the additional needs of adopted children, the embargo on both adoptive parents
being simultaneously absent from work on adoption leave is arguably one of the
flaws in the statutory regime.[164]

In order to be eligible for OAL, the employee must serve notice[165] on the employer
no more than seven days after the date on which he/she is notified of having been
matched with the child for adoption or, otherwise, as soon as is reasonably practicable.[166] The notice must set out the date on which the child is expected to be placed
with the employee for adoption and the date on which he/she has chosen that his/her
period of OAL should begin.[167] If the employer so requests, the employee must furnish
the employer with documentary evidence issued by the adoption agency that specifies
the name and address of the agency, the date on which the employee was notified that
he/she had been matched with the child, and the date on which the agency expects to
place the child with the employee.[168] The period of OAL will commence on the date
on which the child is placed with the employee for adoption or up to 14 days prior to
the expected date of placement.[169] The period of OAL is 26 weeks,[170] as is the period
of AAL;[171] therefore, the employee may be absent from work on adoption leave for up
to 52 weeks.

---

[157] G. Mitchell, 'Encouraging Fathers to Care: The Children and Families Act 2014 and Shared Parental
Leave' (2015) 44 *Industrial Law Journal* 123, 125.   [158] Regulation 15(1)(b) of the PALR.
[159] Regulation 2(1) of the PALR defines a child as a person who is, or when placed for adoption was,
under 18 years of age.   [160] Regulation 15(1)(a) and (2) of the PALR.
[161] There was a 26 weeks' length of service condition, but this has now been removed.
[162] Regulation 20(1) of the PALR.   [163] Regulation 2(1) of the PALR.
[164] See G. James, 'The Work and Families Act 2006: Legislation to Improve Choice and Flexibility?'
(2006) 35 *Industrial Law Journal* 272, 274. However, both working couples are permitted to share
the 52 weeks of adoption leave between them, so that one takes up part of the 52 weeks as a period of
adoption leave and the other person takes up the remaining period of leave as SPL: regulations 20–27
of the SPLR.
[165] Such notice must be in written form if the employer so requests: regulation 17(6) of the PALR.
[166] Regulation 17(2) of the PALR.   [167] Regulation 17(1) of the PALR.
[168] Regulation 17(3) of the PALR.   [169] Regulation 16(1) of the PALR.
[170] Regulation 18(1) of the PALR.
[171] Regulation 20(2) of the PALR. This is the case unless the child is returned to the adoption agency
or dies, or OAL is disrupted because the child is returned to the adoption agency or dies, or the employee
is dismissed.

The employee on adoption leave is entitled to the benefit of all terms and conditions of employment during the period of OAL and AAL,[172] except terms relating to remuneration, i.e. sums payable by way of wages or salary.[173] The employee also continues to be burdened by the obligations arising under those terms and conditions.[174] The employee has the right to return from OAL to the job in which he/she was employed before his/her absence without serving prior notice on his/her employer.[175] However, where the employee wishes to return early from adoption leave, there is a requirement to provide the employer with at least eight weeks' prior notice of his/her intended date of return.[176] Identical rules apply in the case of AAL, but if it is not reasonably practicable for the employer to permit the employee to return to his/her job, he/she has the right to return to another job which is both suitable for him/her and appropriate for him/her to do in the circumstances.[177] As with maternity leave, the employee on OAL or AAL may carry out work for his/her employer for a period up to ten KIT days without bringing that leave to a premature end.[178]

9.3.5 Right to request flexible working

Employees[179] falling within certain prescribed grounds are entitled by domestic law to ask their employer to rearrange their working hours. This is achieved by modifying the employee's contractual terms and is governed by the Flexible Working Regulations 2014 ('FWR')[180] and sections 80F–I of the ERA:

Section 80F Statutory right to request contract variation

(1) A qualifying employee may apply to his employer for a change in his terms and conditions of employment if—

　(a) the change relates to—

　　(i) the hours he is required to work,

　　(ii) the times when he is required to work,

　　(iii) where, as between his home and a place of business of his employer, he is required to work, or

　　(iv) such other aspect of his terms and conditions of employment as the Secretary of State may specify by regulations . . .

The entitlement is conferred in favour of *any employee* or agency worker[181] who has been continuously employed for a period of at least 26 weeks.[182] The statutory provisions stipulate mandatory requirements regarding the content and form of the employee's application for flexible working. For example, the application must be in writing and

---

[172] Regulation 19(1) of the PALR.

[173] Regulation 19(2) and (3) of the PALR. The provisions for statutory adoption pay also mirror those in force in the context of SMP, including the earnings-related element of statutory adoption pay for the first six weeks.

[174] Sections 75A(3)(b) and 75B(4)(b) of the ERA.　　[175] Regulation 26(1) of the PALR.

[176] Regulation 25(1) of the PALR.　　[177] Regulation 26(2) of the PALR.

[178] Regulation 21A(1) of the PALR. An employee has the right not to be subjected to any detriment or dismissal for having taken or sought to take OAL or AAL: sections 47C(2)(ba) and 99(3)(ba) of the ERA; regulations 28(1)(a) and (b) and 29(3)(a) and (b) of the PALR.

[179] Certain agency workers are specifically included for these purposes: section 80F(8)(b) of the ERA.

[180] SI 2014/1398.

[181] Section 80F(8)(b) of the ERA. An 'agency worker' is defined here as a worker 'supplied by a person ("the agent") to do work for another ("the principal") under a contract or other arrangement made between the agent and the principal'.　　[182] Regulation 3 of the FWR.

dated,[183] and must state whether the employee has made a previous application and if so, when.[184] Once the employee has made an application to rearrange his/her working hours, he/she must not make a further application within 12 months.[185]

When an employer receives such an application, it must deal with the application in a 'reasonable manner' and notify the employee of its decision on the application within a period of three calendar months or such other longer period as may be agreed between it and the employee.[186] However, if it refuses, it must invoke one of the following reasons and there must be a factual basis for that ground:

Section 80G Statutory right to request contract variation

(1) An employer to whom an application under section 80F is made . . .

   (b) shall only refuse the application because he considers that one or more of the following grounds applies—

      (i)   the burden of additional costs,

      (ii)   detrimental effect on ability to meet customer demand,

      (iii)   inability to re-organise work among existing staff,

      (iv)   inability to recruit additional staff,

      (v)   detrimental impact on quality,

      (vi)   detrimental impact on performance,

      (vii)   insufficiency of work during the periods the employee proposes to work,

      (viii) planned structural changes, and

      (ix)   such other grounds as the Secretary of State may specify by regulations.

Although the statutory regime enjoins employers to apply their mind to an employee's request for flexible working, there is no need for them to accede to such requests. Provided that the employer can demonstrate a factual basis for one of the reasons laid down in section 80G(1)(b), it is within its rights to refuse the application. Therefore, the implicit rejection of any notion of a right to *obtain* flexible working clearly functions to dilute the wider social impact of the legislation. However, the reasonableness criterion in section 80G(1)(a) does enable the employee to challenge the employer's refusal. The decision of the EAT in *Commotion Ltd v Rutty*[187] is likely to prove instructive in determining how the tribunal will evaluate the reasonableness of the employer's decision to refuse. Here, it was held that a tribunal was entitled to examine the evidence on which the employer made its decision in order to discover whether the ground in section 80G(1)(b) invoked by the employer as the reason for the refusal was based on incorrect facts. This would entail an investigation of the circumstances surrounding the employee's request, the effect of granting it, any potential disruption, and the attitude of other staff.[188] As such, the requirement to establish correct facts is a measure that empowers a tribunal to consider whether the employer's assertion and conduct generally were reasonable. The pointers provided by *Rutty* are likely to be supplemented by the guidance laid down by ACAS in its June 2014 Code of Practice 5 on 'handling in a reasonable manner requests to

---

[183] Regulation 4(a) and (c) of the FWR.   [184] Regulation 4(c) of the FWR.

[185] Section 80F(4) of the ERA. Like maternity leave, an employee has the right not to be subjected to any detriment or dismissal for having requested, or sought to request, flexible working: sections 47E and 104C of the ERA.

[186] Section 80G(1)(a) and (aa), and (1B) of the ERA.   [187] [2006] ICR 290.

[188] [2006] ICR 290, 302C per Judge Burke QC.

work flexibly'.[189] An additional legal avenue for an employee to challenge an employer's refusal of a request to work flexibly is the law of direct sex discrimination. In *Shaw v CCL Ltd*,[190] an employer was found to have both directly and indirectly discriminated on grounds of sex in turning down the employee's request to be allowed to work flexibly on her return from maternity leave.[191]

Commentators have identified a further crucial deficiency[192] in the effectiveness of the right to request flexible working:

■ **E. Caracciolo Di Torella, 'New Labour, New Dads: The Impact of Family-Friendly Legislation on Fathers' (2007) 36 *Industrial Law Journal* 318, 321**

. . . The right has . . . [a] pitfall . . . it appears that employers continue to assume that mothers, rather than fathers, have a better case for requesting an alteration of their working hours. For example, in the cases of *Robert Jones v Gan Insurance* (2000) which was settled before going to the ET and *Walkingshaw v The John Martin Group* (ET, November 2001) the employers were reluctant to allow fathers to rearrange their working hours, although the same possibility was contemplated for mothers . . . It is therefore little surprise that more women rather than men are taking advantage of this right . . .

At the time of writing, the evidence would appear to suggest that the statutory right to request flexible working is particularly successful in meeting its objectives. For example, in a joint Department for Business, Innovation and Skills and Equality and Human Rights Commission research paper,[193] it is reported that 84 per cent of all employers granted all the requests they had received. However, as noted by Rose, when we scratch below the surface of the apparent success of the right to request flexible working, certain problems emerge:

■ **E. Rose, 'Workplace Temporalities: A Time-Based Critique of the Flexible Working Provisions' (2017) 46 *Industrial Law Journal* 245, 246-7**

. . . the flexible working provisions appears to be highly successful. Evaluations of its operation reveal high levels of positive responses from employers to employee requests for flexibility. But if we consider the spread of flexibility among a broad range of occupations and in a variety of workplaces, a different picture emerges. Certain employees, including managers and professionals, are less likely than others to report having access to flexible working or making requests for working flexibl[y]. Moreover, employees in certain workplaces, including male-dominated, private sector and small workplaces, are less likely to request temporal adjustments to their work. There are hints that the workplace 'culture' may be the problem in some cases, but these observations remain little explored.

---

[189] See http://www.acas.org.uk/media/pdf/f/e/Code-of-Practice-on-handling-in-a-reasonable-manner-requests-to-work-flexibly.pdf (last visited 29 November 2017).

[190] [2008] IRLR 284.

[191] However, this should not be taken to suggest that every refusal of a request to work flexibly will amount to direct sex discrimination. The issue will be whether the employer is able to objectively justify its refusal.

[192] For further critical reflections, see G. James, 'The Work and Families Act 2006: Legislation to Improve Choice and Flexibility?' (2006) 35 *Industrial Law Journal* 272, 275–7; G. Mitchell, 'Encouraging Fathers to Care: The Children and Families Act 2014 and Shared Parental Leave' (2015) 44 *Industrial Law Journal* 123, 128.

[193] See the joint BIS and EHRC report, 'Pregnancy and Maternity-Related Discrimination and Disadvantage', BIS Research Paper No. 235, available at http://www.equalityhumanrights.com/sites/default/files/publication_pdf/BIS-15–447-pregnancy-and-maternity-related-discrimination-and-disadvantage.pdf at pages 13, 90, and 94 (last visited 29 November 2017).

9.3.6 Right to time off for dependants

Clause 3 of the framework agreement annexed to the EU Parental Leave Directive[194] imposed an obligation on Member States to afford employees a right to take time off to care for dependants in emergencies. This provision is motivated by a desire to enable employees to take a reasonable amount of leave 'in the event of domestic crises',[195] unexpected emergencies, and to make any necessary longer term arrangements, e.g. where planned caring arrangements for children are unexpectedly disturbed,[196] children become sick, or there is an accident involving a child. By affording employees such a statutory right, the aspiration was that the number of sick days taken off work by employees would be reduced.

The provision was transposed into UK law by the Employment Relations Act 1999 and is now found in sections 57A and 57B of the ERA. Particularly noteworthy is the absence of any requirement for an employee to have a minimum period of continuous service in order to be eligible for the statutory right in section 57A. What is also conspicuous is the failure to identify what constitutes a 'reasonable amount of [leave] . . . to take action which is necessary'. The guidance in *Qua* furnished by the EAT suggests that only a short period of time will be appropriate:

■ *Qua v John Ford Morrison* [2003] ICR 482, 490A–492A

Mrs Recorder Cox QC:

In determining whether action was necessary, factors to be taken into account will include, for example, the nature of the incident which has occurred, the closeness of the relationship between the employee and the particular dependant and the extent to which anyone else was available to help out . . . in determining what is a reasonable amount of time off work, an employer should always take account of the individual circumstances of the employee seeking to exercise the right. It may be that, in the vast majority of cases, no more than a few hours or, at most, one or possibly two days would be regarded as reasonable to deal with the particular problem which has arisen. Parliament chose not to limit the entitlement to a certain amount of time per year and/or per case . . . It is not possible to specify maximum periods of time which are reasonable in any particular circumstances. This will depend on the individual circumstances in each case and it will always be a question of fact for a tribunal as to what was reasonable in every situation. Where an employee has exercised the right on one or more previous occasions and has been permitted to take time off, for example, to deal with a dependant child's recurring illness, an employer can in our view take into account the number and length of previous absences, as well as the dates when they occurred, in order to determine whether the time taken off or sought to be taken off on a subsequent occasion is reasonable and necessary . . . Further, in determining what is a reasonable amount of time off work, we consider that the disruption or inconvenience caused to an employer's business by the employee's absence are irrelevant factors, which should not be taken into account . . . The operational needs of the employer cannot be relevant to a consideration of the amount of time an employee reasonably needs to deal with emergency circumstances of the kind specified. A dependant child could suddenly fall ill and necessitate action, which requires an employee's absence from work, at a time which the employer could show caused acute or even insurmountable operational problems. Taking into account the employer's needs as relevant to the overall reasonableness of the amount

---

[194] Directive 96/34/EC (OJ 1996 L145/4), as amended by Directive 97/75/EC (OJ 1998 L10/24). These Directives have now been replaced by the Parental Leave Directive 2010/18/EU (OJ 2010 L68/13). The entitlement is now contained in clause 7 of the Framework Agreement annexed to the Parental Leave Directive 2010/18/EU (OJ 2010 L68/13).

[195] A. McColgan, 'Family-Friendly Frolics? The Maternity and Parental Leave etc. Regulations 1999' (2000) 29 *Industrial Law Journal* 125, 135.

[196] See *Royal Bank of Scotland plc v Harrison* [2009] ICR 116.

of time taken off would, in our view, frustrate the clear purpose of the legislation, which is to ensure that employees are permitted time off to deal with such an event, whenever it occurs, without fear of reprisals, so long as they comply with the [statutory] requirements.

As for the maximum period that might constitute a reasonable period of time, the EAT in *Cortest Ltd v O'Toole* made the following points:

■ **Cortest Ltd v O'Toole (UKEAT/0470/07/LA, 7 November 2007) at paras 22–23**

Mr Justice Nelson:

These cases are all fact sensitive but a period as long as one month or even longer for care by a parent would rarely, almost never, fall within s.57A . . . If longer leave is required then a short period of unpaid parental leave is available but that was not so here because it is not available for emergency situations and a request has to be put in writing. We are satisfied that one month especially where there is no evidence that any other arrangements were sought, for example, neighbours or other relatives or any other kind cannot be reasonable on the facts . . . [W]e are also clear that s.57A does not permit a parent to become the child minder for a period as long as occurred here, just short of one month, when the maximum period thought to be possible was two months . . .[197]

Further, there is no need for a situation to arise suddenly or to amount to an emergency for the right to time off to be engaged. For example, in *Royal Bank of Scotland plc v Harrison*,[198] an employee knew two weeks in advance that her childminder would be unavailable to care for her children on a particular date. Nonetheless, the EAT ruled that the need for her to make alternative caring arrangements was 'unexpected' in terms of section 57A(1)(d) of the ERA. A separate issue arose in *Forster v Cartwright Black*[199] concerning the construction of section 57A(1)(c) and whether it could be used in order to enable an employee to take time off for compassionate/bereavement leave. In January 2003, the employee's father died and she was given 12 days' bereavement leave. In May 2003, when her mother died, the employee took five days' bereavement leave and she was signed off work for a further four weeks by her doctor for the reason of a 'bereavement reaction'. The relevant point was whether section 57A(1)(c) of the ERA—which enabled employees to take time off to take action which is necessary in consequence of the death of a dependant—was sufficient to introduce a right to bereavement leave. The EAT decided that it did not; rather, section 57A(1)(c) extended only to enable employees to take time off to make funeral arrangements, attend the funeral, register the death, and, if there is a will, apply for probate and be interviewed by the probate office. Since the decision in *Forster*, ACAS has produced a useful good practice note with the title *Managing Bereavement in the Workplace*.[200] This offers various pointers to employers on how to address the demands and needs of employees who are experiencing a bereavement in the family. A Parental Bereavement Bill is also currently making its way through the Parliamentary process, which if passed, would amend the ERA and SSCBA to entitle mothers and fathers to bereavement leave and statutory bereavement leave pay where their children have died.

---

[197] Sourced from BAILII, available at http://www.bailii.org/cgi-bin/markup.cgi?doc=/uk/cases/UKE-AT/2007/0470_07_0711.html&query=cortest&method=boolean (last visited 29 November 2017).

[198] [2009] ICR 116.   [199] [2004] ICR 1728.

[200] See http://m.acas.org.uk/media/pdf/7/a/Managing-bereavement-in-the-workplace-a-good-practice-guide.pdf (last visited 29 November 2017).

Section 57B(1) and (2) of the ERA directs that an employee may present a complaint to an employment tribunal on the ground that the employer unreasonably refused to permit him/her to take a reasonable amount of time off in terms of section 57A within three months of the refusal or some further period as the tribunal considers reasonable. The tribunal may make a declaration that the complaint was well-founded or award compensation.[201] Compensation is fixed on a 'just and equitable' basis, i.e. taking account of all the circumstances having regard to the employer's default in refusing to permit time off to be taken by the employee and the loss suffered by the employee.[202] The EAT has held that the following factors will be relevant in evaluating the reasonableness of the employer's refusal: how often the emergency had happened before; whether or not there was another way of solving the problem; and the business needs of the employer.[203]

Reflection points

1. Do you agree with the argument that the rate of SMP discourages female employees from taking up their full entitlement to 52 weeks' maternity leave? If so, why? If not, why not?

2. Do you believe that the shared parental leave regime has been successful and, in your opinion, is it desirable? Give reasons for your answer.

3. Consider the statutory measures in relation to paternity pay, parental leave, adoption leave, the right to request flexible working, and the right to time off for dependants as a whole. To what extent do these provisions promote a more equal division of family responsibilities between the sexes? Give reasons for your answer.

4. Consider the following quote in light of the existing statutory provisions for maternity, paternity, parental, and adoption leave and the right to request flexible working and the right to time off for dependants:

   . . . the provision of good quality childcare which is fully or partially publicly funded should be a central tenet of the programme of any government whole-heartedly committed to equal opportunities for men and women.[204]

5. Busby recommends the introduction of a novel legal model, which imposes a duty on employers to take reasonable steps to accommodate requests for flexible working from employees with care-giving responsibilities: N. Busby, *A Right to Care* (Oxford, OUP, 2011) 182–90. Consider the advantages and disadvantages of such an approach in light of the existing statutory regime, including the feasibility of its introduction.

 For additional reading on work–life balance protections, visit the Online Resources for this book at www.oup.com/uk/cabrelli3e/

---

[201] Section 57B(3) of the ERA.   [202] Section 57B(4) of the ERA.

[203] *Truelove v Safeway Stores plc* [2005] ICR 589, 595C per Judge McMullen QC.

[204] S. Fredman, *Women and the Law* (Oxford, OUP, 1997) 214. See also L. Dickens, 'Equality and Work–Life Balance: What's Happening at the Workplace' (2006) 35 *Industrial Law Journal* 445, 447, for an examination of the levels of (a) childcare facilities at the workplace and (b) financial help with childcare, made available voluntarily by employers. Another possible family-friendly measure would be a statutory right to a career break.

PART V
EQUALITY LAW

CHAPTER TEN

INTRODUCTION TO EMPLOYMENT EQUALITY LAW

10.1 CONTEXTUAL ANALYSIS OF EMPLOYMENT EQUALITY LAW

Employment equality laws represent the most far-reaching example of statutory interference in the common law of the contract of employment. Having broken new ground when first introduced in the 1960s, by 2004, the employment equality laws had become scattered across a range of primary and secondary legislation. The Equality Act 2010 ('EA') consolidated and reformed the law. At the heart of the EA is an approach which seeks to combat discrimination in the workplace where it has been perpetrated by an employer against an employee on the ground that the employee possesses one or more of a carefully prescribed set of 'protected characteristics',[1] namely sex, race, disability, religion or belief, sexual orientation, age, pregnancy and maternity, gender reassignment, and marriage and civil partnership. Whilst it is inevitable that an employer must engage in some form of discrimination in order to hire, promote, suspend, or dismiss individuals, the EA seeks to ensure that such decision-making is pursued on wholly meritocratic grounds. As such, the EA incentivizes management to take decisions based on the skills, competence, qualifications, aptitude, and experience of such individuals, rather than suspect grounds such as sex, race, disability, etc. However, this does not mean that the employment equality laws impose an obligation on employers to select the most able candidate available for a vacant position or a promotion, or that they preclude an employer from selecting on the basis of wholly illogical or capricious motives. Provided that the protected characteristics of sex, race, etc. are not the ground for the selection, the employer will escape liability, since an individual's personhood itself is not a protected ground.[2]

---

[1] See section 4 of the EA.
[2] G. Mead, 'Proof of Direct Discrimination' (1992) 21 *Industrial Law Journal* 217; T. Khaitan, *A Theory of Discrimination Law* (Oxford, OUP, 2015) 30.

The normative justifications for anti-discrimination/equality laws are as diverse as they are legion, spanning the recognition and promotion of individualism, personal autonomy, dignity, State neutrality, democratic participation, redistribution, social inclusion, restitution, and procedural justice. Against that backdrop, this chapter will explore the pros and cons of interfering in the labour market via the promulgation of anti-discrimination laws. We will move on to evaluate the basic theoretical constructs which are relevant to a proper understanding of anti-discrimination law in the UK and the EU, including the possible policy responses, e.g. the distinction between formal equality and substantive equality. Having briefly assessed the historical development of anti-discrimination laws in the workplace, the chapter will then analyse key statutory concepts such as direct discrimination, indirect discrimination, harassment, sexual harassment, and victimization.

10.1.1 Contextual introduction to employment equality law

At a superficial level, the ideology underpinning statutory employment laws tackling workplace discrimination is deceptively simple. It is encapsulated in the concept of equality: the basic premise that all persons in the workplace should be treated the same and should not suffer discrimination on the basis of particular grounds. Equality in this sense is proscriptive in that it functions to impose negative obligations on employers,[3] i.e. not to treat a protected class of worker differently from other workers or not to apply criteria or adopt practices which have a negative impact on persons falling within that protected group. The protected classes will be examined in greater detail in Chapter 11, but they tend to be groups who have suffered from societal barriers in the past. Anti-discrimination laws aim to protect those groups by imposing such proscriptive obligations to interfere in the employer's freedom of contract:

■ *Taiwo v Olaigbe* [2016] 1 WLR 2653, 2660H–2661B

> ***Baroness Hale:***
>
> Generally speaking, the suppliers of employment, accommodation, goods and services are allowed to choose with whom they will do business. There is freedom to contract, or to refuse to contract, with whomever one pleases. The [EA] limits that freedom of contract (and also the freedom of suppliers of public services). It does so in order to protect specified groups who have historically been discriminated against by those suppliers, shut out of access to the employment, accommodation, goods and services they supply, for irrelevant reasons which they can do nothing about.

Two points can be made at this juncture about the notion of equality as a basic justification for the anti-discrimination laws we find in UK employment law.

(1) First, if we accept that 'equality' should act as the foundation for such laws, our intuitive response is to say that this means consistency of, or equal, treatment. This will preclude the law from treating a class of worker identified as deserving of protection differently from other workers not belonging to that class, i.e. basic 'consistency of treatment' or 'treat like groups alike'. This may seem entirely logical and appropriate,

---

[3] Contrast this with duties to make reasonable adjustments, or to reasonably accommodate employees falling within a protected class, which are prescriptive rather than proscriptive, on which, see T. Khaitan, *A Theory of Discrimination Law* (Oxford, OUP, 2015) 28, 76–80, 86–7; G. Rutherglen, 'Concrete or Abstract Conceptions of Discrimination' in D. Hellman and S. Moreau (eds), *Philosophical Foundations of Discrimination Law* (Oxford, OUP, 2013) 120–2.

but breaks down when we recognize that that particular class of worker may have suffered from structural discrimination over a sustained period of time to the extent that they are under-represented or inherently disadvantaged in the workplace, e.g. where we find labour segmentation of particular jobs or groups of jobs along gender or racial lines. In such a case, we may decide that such a group ought to be treated differently in the sense of being treated *more favourably* than the mainstream. However, our instinctive sense of equality has an in-built tendency to discourage us from affording more favourable and asymmetrical treatment to that group. This leads us to question whether it can usefully be employed as the all-embracing theoretical bedrock for the entire body of statutory anti-discrimination laws in the UK. Ultimately, what we can take from this discussion is that the basis for UK anti-discrimination laws does not uniformly find its expression in the conception of equality identified with equal treatment of workplace groups;[4] instead, the position is more complex, which causes us to reconsider whether our intuitive understanding of equality as 'consistency of treatment' is perhaps too simplistic—a point we will revisit later in section 10.1.2.

(2) Secondly, one of the paradoxes of the concept of equality is its insistence on treating all persons in the workplace as if they were identical when in fact there is nothing further from the truth. After all, individual employees possess a range of diverse characteristics, e.g. some are men, others women, some black, others white, etc.

■ F. A. Hayek, *The Constitution of Liberty* (London and New York, Routledge Classics, 2006) 756

Equality [before the] law and [of the rules of moral and social] conduct, however, is the only kind of equality conducive to liberty and the only equality which we can secure without destroying liberty. Not only has liberty nothing to do with any other sort of equality, but it is even bound to produce inequality in many respects. This is the necessary result and part of the justification of individual liberty: if the result of individual liberty did not demonstrate that some manners of living are more successful than others, much of the case for it would vanish. It is neither because it assumes that people are in fact equal nor because it attempts to make them equal that the argument for liberty demands that government treat them equally. This argument not only recognizes that individuals are very different but in a great measure rests on that assumption. It insists that these individual differences provide no justification for government to treat them differently. And it objects to the differences in treatment by the state that would be necessary if persons who are in fact very different were to be assured equal positions in life. Modern advocates of a more far-reaching material equality usually deny that their demands are based on any assumption of the factual equality of all men. It is nevertheless still widely believed that this is the main justification for such demands. Nothing, however, is more damaging to the demand for equal treatment than to base it on so obviously untrue an assumption as that of the factual equality of all men. To rest the case for equal treatment of national or racial minorities on the assertion that they do not differ from other men is implicitly to admit that factual inequality would justify unequal treatment; and the proof that some differences do, in fact, exist would not be long in forthcoming. It is of the essence of the demand for equality before the law that people should be treated alike in spite of the fact that they are different.

---

[4] This is reflective of the distinction drawn between anti-discrimination laws and equality laws in M. Bell, *Anti-Discrimination Law and the European Union* (Oxford, OUP, 2002) 147–8 and S. Honeyball, *Great Debates in Employment Law* (Basingstoke, Palgrave Macmillan, 2011) 104–5.

In distinguishing between the concepts of equality and liberty,[5] Hayek notes that a call to factual equality as a justification for measures based on the principle of equality is absurd, since all people possess inherent differences. In fact, it is these very differences which motivate the calls for equality. Hayek makes the additional point that the pursuit of liberty may be wholly detrimental to the achievement of equality.[6] The liberal philosophy underpinning the common law which seeks to protect the individual from undue coercion or interference from the State is strongly associated with the concept of liberty. The idea of liberty in the common law is instantiated through the totemic freedoms lying at the heart of private law, namely the doctrines of individual freedom of contract and the individual's freedom to trade and compete.[7] These individual freedoms may conflict with the pursuit of equality, and the traditional policy of the common law has been to assert the superiority of the former over the latter:

■ *Allen v Flood* [1898] AC 1, 172–3

> *Lord Davey:*
>
> An employer may discharge a workman (with whom he has no contract), or may refuse to employ one from [*sic*] the most mistaken, capricious, malicious or morally reprehensible motives that can be conceived, but the workman has no right of action against him . . . A man has no right to be employed by any particular employer, and has no right to any particular employment if it depends on the will of another.[8]

Therefore, if a law-maker decides to shift the traditional emphasis by promoting equality, this will be achieved at the expense of liberty to some degree, albeit not necessarily inconsistently with democratic principles.[9]

Anti-discrimination laws clearly impinge upon the proper functioning of the labour market. Such State interference in the common law preference for the promotion of individual freedom must command some fairly persuasive arguments in its favour. The justifications for the introduction of anti-discrimination laws are grounded in a diverse range of moral principles and policies, as well as their positive commercial impact.[10] Ultimately, however, they entail the curtailment of the liberty of employers to choose with whom they can or ought to contract in the labour market and on what terms they may do so:

---

[5] For a distinction between liberty-based conceptions of discrimination law and equality-based accounts of discrimination law, see S. Moreau, 'In Defense of a Liberty-Based Account of Discrimination' in D. Hellman and S. Moreau (eds), *Philosophical Foundations of Discrimination Law* (Oxford, OUP, 2013) 71.

[6] However, not all commentators agree, e.g. Sen in A. Sen, *Inequality Re-examined* (Oxford, OUP/ Clarendon Press, 1992) 22–3.

[7] *Allen v Flood* [1898] AC 1, 166 per Lord Shand.

[8] See also C. Barnard, S. Deakin, and C. Kilpatrick, 'Equality, Non-discrimination and the Labour Market in the UK' (2002) 18 *International Journal of Comparative Labour Law and Industrial Relations* 129, 130.

[9] See *Ladele v London Borough of Islington* [2009] EWCA Civ 1357, [2010] 1 WLR 955, 974G per Lord Neuberger MR.

[10] For the business case in favour of anti-discrimination laws, see Department for Business, Innovation and Skills Occasional Paper No. 4, 'The Business Case for Equality and Diversity: A Survey of the Academic Literature' (January 2013), available at https://www.gov.uk/government/uploads/system/uploads/attachment_data/file/49638/the_business_case_for_equality_and_diversity.pdf (last visited 5 December 2017); R. Riley, H. Metcalf, and J. Forth, 'The Business Case for Equal Opportunities' (2013) 44 *Industrial Relations Journal* 216.

■ **R. A. Epstein, *Forbidden Grounds: The Case against Employment Discrimination Laws* (Cambridge MA, Harvard UP, 1992) 3–4**

An antidiscrimination law is the antithesis of freedom of contract, a principle that allows all persons to do business with whomever they please for good reason, bad reason, or no reason at all. . . . The anti-discrimination principle operates as a powerful brake against this view of freedom of contract and the concomitant but limited role of the state. By its nature the antidiscrimination principle is interventionist for reasons that have nothing to do with the prevention of force and fraud. Rather, the principle rests on the collective social judgment . . . that some grounds for private decision are so improper that it is both immoral and illegal for the government to allow employers to use them in deciding whether to hire, retain, or promote workers. The list of forbidden grounds includes race, sex, age, national origin, religious belief, handicap, and in some cases sexual orientation. Decisions made 'on the merits' are allowed, but, subject to a broad and controversial exception of affirmative action, any private reliance on these socially extraneous criteria is prohibited. The defenders of the antidiscrimination principle often treat that principle as though it were a self-evident truth that certain grounds for decision should be banned for moral reasons. On other occasions they treat the principle not as a good in itself but as a means to other ends: to creating an open and equal society with full participation, or to increasing the overall wealth of society by ensuring that all productive labor may be put to its highest use.

Economists such as Epstein argue that statutory intervention intended to secure equality is wholly misguided. Some of the justifications for non-interference are grounded in the ability of the free market to combat discrimination in the absence of State-sanctioned regulation; others, meanwhile, are based on the anti-competitive nature of anti-discrimination legislation. Four principal rationales are advanced in favour of that argument, as follows.

(1) There is the economic argument that if a labour market is functioning efficiently, there will be no need to proscribe employers from engaging in discriminatory practices. The contention is that employers harbouring a 'taste for discrimination'[11] will be forced out of the marketplace. There are two reasons why discriminatory practices will be self-defeating economically in the long run: first, the discriminating employer will become uncompetitive, since competing non-discriminating firms will be able to undercut it by hiring the best people for jobs. The claim here is that market outcomes are inherently egalitarian:

■ **C. Sunstein, *Free Markets and Social Justice* (Oxford, OUP, 1997) 151**

Markets, it is sometimes said, are hard on discrimination. An employer who finds himself refusing to hire qualified blacks and women will, in the long run, lose out to those who are willing to draw from a broader labor pool. Employer discrimination amounts to a self-destructive 'taste'—self-destructive because employers who indulge that taste add to the cost of doing business. Added costs can only hurt. To put it simply, bigots are weak competitors. The market will drive them out.[12]

Secondly, the reputational damage inflicted on employers who engage in discriminatory conduct will be so acute that they will be driven out of the marketplace:

---

[11] A phrase coined by Becker in his seminal work, G. S. Becker, *The Economics of Discrimination*, 2nd edition (Chicago, University of Chicago Press, 1971) 39–52.

[12] Posner makes the same point in R. Posner, *Economic Analysis of Law*, 9th edition (New York, Aspen Publishers, 2014) 939–41, as does Plant in R. Plant, *The Neo-liberal State* (Oxford, OUP, 2010) 117.

■ R. A. Epstein, *Equal Opportunity or More Opportunity?* (London, Civitas, 2002) 38

Nor is there any reason to intervene because most forms of bad employer behaviour are self-limiting. An employer does not want to get a bad reputation for discrimination. Reputation is thought to be a weak regulator but its effects can be huge. A company with a bad reputation will not last. Losses will be suffered by shareholders and there will be a reluctance by consumers to buy its products. What if McDonalds announced that it would have no women in its senior management? How long would it be before it was unable to attract able men to work for it? Market pressures tend to encourage non-discrimination.

However, the claims of economists that discriminatory employers will be eliminated by the spontaneous order of the market is not reflected in the empirical evidence. There are a variety of reasons grounded in economic theory which explain why the outcomes produced by the market are inherently unequal. In effect, employers with a tendency to discriminate can continue to thrive in an efficient and competitive market:

■ S. J. Schwab, 'Employment Discrimination' in K. G. Dau-Schmidt, S. D. Harris, and O. Lobel (eds), *Labor and Employment Law and Economics* (Cheltenham, Edward Elgar, 2009) 301–3

... employers willing to pay for their taste in discrimination with lower profits can remain competitive indefinitely. Two scenarios are imaginable here, the closely held firm and the joint-stock company. An entrepreneur who works alongside his employees may dislike working with blacks, and thus prefer an 8 per cent monetary return with an all-white workforce to a 10 per cent monetary return with an integrated or all-black workforce. He will stay in business if he is willing to reject offers from non-discriminatory entrepreneurs willing to pay the full monetary value (10 per cent return) for the firm. If only a few entrepreneurs with his discriminatory tastes exist, these few firms will be segregated with no market discrimination. If enough discriminatory entrepreneurs exist, discrimination against blacks as well as segregation will occur. The capital market will pressure discriminatory entrepreneurs to sell out, thereby capturing the high monetary return, and retire or go into another business that does not require association with blacks to make high profits. But this repeats the point that if entrepreneurs are willing to pay for their taste in discrimination, the market allows them to do so. The alternate scenario involves dispersed shareholders who do not physically associate with the firm. Some investors might willingly accept lower monetary returns in order to indulge in their taste for investing in discriminatory firms, increasing their overall return as they see it. This is the flip side to the South Africa divestiture movement of the 1980s where investors willingly accepted lower returns by refusing to invest in firms involved in South Africa apartheid. If only a small number of investors act this way, segregation may occur without discrimination. If enough discriminatory investors are willing to accept lower monetary returns, they can permanently lower black wages. Perhaps a more important explanation for long-run discrimination is that profit-maximising employers in competitive markets will cater to the discriminatory tastes of employees or customers. If some customers will pay less for a product or service from a black employee, or some employees demand higher wages to work with blacks, black employees become less valuable. As Strauss ably recounted, the result could be segregation or discrimination ... workers with no taste for discrimination will not undercut workers willing to pay for their taste for discrimination. Other scholars point to clear market imperfections to explain the persistence of discrimination ... Becker pointed to monopolies as a market imperfection. He emphasized that one of the fruits of a product monopoly is the ability to indulge in a taste for discrimination in the labor market without suffering competitive harm. The firm will earn lower profits than if it hired the cheapest possible labor of a given quality, but can still earn above-average profits. Still, if the monopoly is transferable, a discriminating monopolist has pressure to sell out to those without a taste for discrimination, In other words, competitive capital markets as well as competitive product markets put pressure on employers. In a somewhat different vein, Akerlof shows that discrimination can persist in competitive markets with transaction costs. Suppose some traders have a taste for discrimination against blacks while others do not and that it takes time or money to distinguish from others. Firms with black employees will miss out on some trades and be under a perpetual cost disadvantage.

This extract suggests that the market will not necessarily function to eliminate discrimination. Schwab and Donohue III have gone one step further to argue that discrimination laws can be efficient even though they interfere with the market and impede the liberties of employers.[13] As such, State-enforced employment equality laws are justified if managerial practices of a discriminatory nature are to be wiped out.

(2) A second argument against *sex* discrimination laws in particular is advanced by Becker. Becker contends that what might appear to be sex discrimination may in fact amount to no such thing; instead, the wage and occupational differentials between the sexes may simply be a manifestation of the weaker levels of participation and investment made by women in their human capital in the labour market (e.g. the aggregate time out of the labour market to bear and mother children). They may also be attributable to the lifestyle of, or personal choices (more time and effort spent on housework and childcare) made by, females, which inherently affect their productivity and wage-earning capacity:[14]

■ **G. Becker, 'Human Capital, Efforts, and the Sexual Division of Labor' (1985) 3** *Journal of Labor Economics* **S33**

... since child care and housework are more effort intensive than leisure and other household activities, married women spend less effort on each hour of market work than married men working the same number of hours. Hence, married women have lower hourly earnings than married men with the same market human capital, and they economize on the effort expended on market work by seeking less demanding jobs. The responsibility of married women for child care and housework has major implications for earnings and occupational differences between men and women . . . This paper argues that responsibility for child care, food preparation, and other household activities also prevents the earnings of women from rising more rapidly. Child care and other housework are tiring and limit access to jobs requiring travel or odd hours. These effects of housework are captured by a model developed in this paper of the allocation of energy among different activities. If child care and other housework demand relatively large quantities of 'energy' compared to leisure and other nonmarket uses of time by men, women with responsibilities for housework would have less energy available for the market than men would. This would reduce the hourly earnings of married women, affect their jobs and occupations, and even lower their investment in market human capital when they worked the same number of market hours as married men.

---

[13] See the discussion in S. J. Schwab, 'Is Statistical Discrimination Efficient?' (1986) 76 *American Economic Review* 228; J. J. Donohue III, 'Is Title VII Efficient?' (1986) 134 *University of Pennsylvania Law Review* 1411, 1430–1; and S. J. Schwab, 'Law-and-Economics Approaches to Labour and Employment Law' (2017) 33 *International Journal of Comparative Labour Law and Industrial Relations* 115, 120.

[14] R. Posner, *Economic Analysis of Law*, 9th edition (New York, Aspen Publishers, 2014) 450–1.

Consequently, the housework responsibilities of married women may be the source of much of the difference in earnings and in job segregation between men and women ... Moreover, their lower hourly earnings reduce their investment in market capital even when they work the same number of hours as married men.[15]

The counter-argument is that the concentration of childcare and household labour in the female population imposes overall costs on society as it translates into (a) an under-appreciation of female participation in the labour market and (b) an unjustifiable assumption that such responsibilities invariably rest with women. Economists refer to these societal costs as 'externalities' or 'spillovers' from the failure of the market to operate efficiently. In other words, if those females expending energy and labour outside of the labour market were instead included within it, they could well be more efficient than the males filling the roles within the labour market. The argument runs that the ingrained institutional dynamic which assumes that only females can undertake childcare and household chores is by no means predetermined since males can just as effectively perform these roles. As such, anti-discrimination laws are justified along the same lines discussed in Chapter 9 in the case of family-friendly policies, insofar as they:

(a) promote a more even distribution of responsibility for childcare and household labour between men and women, which in turn gives rise to greater scope for men to perform such chores whilst their female partners remain in the labour market; and

(b) chisel away at the institutional perception that female labour is somehow inferior to male labour.

(3) Posner also argues that anti-discrimination laws are unwarranted because they are self-defeating, in the sense that they harm the very constituencies that they are designed to protect. Not only do the costs imposed by anti-discrimination laws outweigh any benefits generated,[16] but the perceived benefits are entirely illusory. The self-defeating nature of these laws is attributable to the incentives they afford to employers to refuse to hire individuals falling within the groups the legal system has earmarked for protection:[17]

■ R. Posner, *Economic Analysis of Law*, 9th edition (New York, Aspen Publishers, 2014) 451–2

... antidiscrimination laws can boomerang against the protected class as employers take rational measures to minimize the laws' impact. For example, the [US] Equal Pay Act requires employers to pay the same wage to men and women doing the same work. If women workers have a lower marginal product, employers will have an incentive to substitute capital for labor inputs in those job classifications in which they employ many women. In addition, having to pay female employees more than their market worth may make employers reluctant to hire women; and though this reluctance may expose the employer to a suit for hiring discrimination, such suits are rare because damages obtaining in such a suit usually are small. The reason is that a job applicant is unlikely

---

[15] See also G. S. Becker, 'Investment in Human Capital: A Theoretical Analysis' (1962) 70 *Journal of Political Economy* 9.

[16] For a critique of this argument, see I. Ayres, 'Alternative Grounds: Epstein's Discrimination Analysis in Other Market Settings' (1994) 31 *San Diego Law Review* 67; J. J. Donohue III, 'Advocacy versus Analysis in Assessing Employment Discrimination Law' (1992) 44 *Stanford Law Review* 1583.

[17] See also R. A. Epstein, *Equal Opportunity or More Opportunity?* (London, Civitas, 2002) 39.

to land a job that pays a great deal more than she could get elsewhere, yet her damages if her application is wrongfully denied will be limited to the difference between what her wage would have been in that job and what it is in her existing job, or if she's not employed then in her best alternative employment. There is a double whammy here. While the expected liability costs of a discriminatory refusal to hire are low, the expected liability costs of a discriminatory firing (call these 'firing costs') are high, since a worker's wage in his current job is likely, because he has firm-specific human capital, to exceed, often by a considerable margin, the wage in the best alternative job that he could land. These costs are avoided by not hiring a member of a class protected by the employment discrimination law. Even if the Equal Pay Act is fully enforced, women may not benefit. Having to pay them a higher wage will increase the employer's costs and may therefore cause him to reduce the wages of all his employees, male and female, or raise those wages more slowly than he otherwise would, or lay off workers. The larger the fraction of the workforce that is female, the less of the employer's added labor costs will be shifted in these ways to the male workers and so the less the women will benefit from the Act. Moreover, some of the costs that antidiscrimination laws impose on employers will be passed on to consumers in the form of higher prices, and female consumers will be hurt along with male. The heterogeneity of women's interests, combined with the financial and altruistic interdependence between men and women, creates further uncertainty as to whether women will be net beneficiaries of antidiscrimination laws. Increased labor costs that are due to payment of pregnancy disability benefits are borne in part by all workers, but while pregnant employees obtain an offset from the benefits themselves, women who are either not employed or not fertile are clear losers.[18]

The charge that anti-discrimination laws will backfire assumes that all employers operate in a perfectly competitive free labour market and that they will respond rationally to all situations they encounter in that market.[19] However, we do not live in a perfect world;[20] rather, the responses of management are entirely unpredictable, particularly in light of the patent imperfections in the operation of the labour market, such as monopoly power, oligarchies, transaction costs, and the imbalances in the level of information possessed by employers and employees, etc. Bearing that in mind, the introduction of anti-discrimination laws as a mechanism for the redistribution of resources away from the over-represented towards the under-represented in the workplace may be justified, safe in the knowledge that they will not necessarily backfire on the group they are intended to benefit.

(4) Finally, there is the view that regulatory interference is an unjustified exercise of State power which compels employers to change their practices involuntarily. This is a perspective strongly associated with neoliberal philosophy and economics.[21] State neutrality beyond the corrective justice[22] achieved by the common law institutions of contract, property, and tort law is to be strongly discouraged, since the extension

---

[18] Writer's annotations appear in square brackets throughout this chapter.

[19] H. Collins, 'Justifications and Techniques of Legal Regulation of the Employment Relation' in H. Collins, P. Davies, and R. Rideout (eds), *Legal Regulation of the Employment Relation* (London, Kluwer, 2000) 13–14.

[20] See R. H. Thaler and C. R. Sunstein, *Nudge: Improving Decisions About Health, Wealth and Happiness* (London, Penguin, 2009) 7.

[21] See, e.g., F. A. Hayek, *The Constitution of Liberty* (London and New York, Routledge Classics, 2006); R. A. Epstein, *Equal Opportunity or More Opportunity?* (London, Civitas, 2002) 15–16; R. A. Epstein, *Forbidden Grounds: The Case against Employment Discrimination Laws* (Cambridge, MA, Harvard UP, 1992); and R. Plant, *The Neo-liberal State* (Oxford, OUP, 2010) 117.

[22] Corrective justice is a form of justice requiring one party to make good, i.e. to 'correct', the loss or harm suffered by another party as a result of a wrong inflicted by the former on the latter, on which, see E. J. Weinrib, *The Idea of Private Law* (Cambridge, MA, Harvard UP, 1995) 62–3; W. Lucy, *The Philosophy of Private Law* (Oxford, OUP, 2007) 268–326; and E. J. Weinrib, *Corrective Justice* (Oxford, OUP, 2012).

of State action via the field of anti-discrimination laws is ultimately redistributive in nature. Redistribution outside of the social security and taxation regimes is misconceived, owing to the fact that (a) it goes against the grain of the neoliberal philosophy that true liberty is freedom from State coercion and (b) no meaningful consensus can ever be reached as to the basis upon which a redistributive strategy is to be pursued, since this is necessarily a matter for moral and political debate upon which most rational people will disagree.

However, the State neutrality argument against anti-discrimination laws overlooks the social costs imposed on society by failures in the operation of the labour market such as social security benefit payments. Such pervasive labour market failures operate as justification for State interference in order to promote transparency and remove limitations on access experienced by excluded constituencies. However, even where the claims in favour of anti-discrimination laws are accepted, experience has shown that Governments of a neoliberal bent can nonetheless quite easily deploy policies designed to constrain the impact, and frustrate the operation, of the equality regime introduced into law.[23]

10.1.2 Designing an employment equality law framework: exploring the theoretical justifications and potential policy objectives

Once a legal system has decided to intervene to regulate the labour market and institute an anti-discrimination law framework, one of a number of policy aims may be pursued in order to achieve that end. These policy preferences are essentially shaped by the philosophical bases on which the framework is to be grounded. Anti-discrimination laws may be justified by calls to abstract theoretical principles such as dignity, identity, personal autonomy, State neutrality, democratic participation, redistribution, social inclusion, restitution, or procedural justice.[24] For example, sections 9 and 10 of the Bill of Rights in the South African Constitution closely link equality with the dignity and identity of the individual employee, e.g. that individual's values, sense of self-worth as an individual human being, and his/her identity.[25] The dignitarian foundation of equality rejects the notion that stereotypical assumptions about the capabilities of individuals can be made on the basis of their race, sex, disability, age, etc. Instead, dignity is grounded in identitarian conceptions of the good, and demands that the individual's identity be respected and that they be judged on their merit.

Behind these various theoretical justifications we find the competing policy objectives of formal/procedural equality and substantive equality.[26] For example, the philosophical

---

[23] See B. Burton, 'Neoliberalism and the Equality Act 2010: A Missed Opportunity for Gender Justice?' (2014) 43 *Industrial Law Journal* 112.

[24] See S. Fredman, 'Equality: A New Generation?' (2001) 30 *Industrial Law Journal* 145; H. Collins, 'Discrimination, Equality and Social Inclusion' (2003) 66 *Modern Law Review* 16; and B. Hepple, 'The Aims of Equality Law' (2008) 61 *Current Legal Problems* 1.

[25] S. Fredman, *Discrimination Law*, 2nd edition (Oxford, OUP, 2011) 19–25; B. Hepple, *Equality: The New Legal Framework*, 2nd edition (Oxford, Hart Publishing, 2014) 20–2; and H. Collins, 'Theories of Rights as Justifications' in G. Davidov and B. Langille (eds), *The Idea of Labour Law* (Oxford, OUP, 2011) 151–3. See also section 3(c) of the Equality Act 2006. See also *National Coalition for Gay and Lesbian Equality v Minister of Justice* [1998] ZACC 15, 1999 (1) SA 6, 1998 (12) BCLR 1517, at paras 120–125 per Sachs J.

[26] See J. Croon-Gestefeld, *Reconceptualising European Equality Law. A Comparative Institutional Analysis* (Oxford, Hart Publishing, 2017) 30–40 and the following works by Collins and Barnard on other policy objectives for employment equality legislation, namely 'social inclusion' and 'solidarity': H. Collins, 'Discrimination, Equality and Social Inclusion' (2003) 66 *Modern Law Review* 16; C. Barnard, 'The Future of Equality Law: Equality and Beyond' in C. Barnard, S. Deakin, and G. S. Morris (eds), *Future of Labour Law. Liber Amicorum Sir Bob Hepple* (Oxford, Hart Publishing, 2004) 227.

precepts of personal autonomy, State neutrality, and procedural justice are associated with the policy prescription of formal/procedural equality. Formal/procedural equality is a conception of equality which is concerned with consistent treatment, whereby likes are treated alike. It is not overly concerned with equality of outcomes or results. Meanwhile, normative justifications for anti-discrimination laws based on dignity, democratic participation, redistribution, and restitution underpin the policy objective of substantive equality. Statutory constructs grounded on substantive equality are redistributive in nature, i.e. concerned with distributive justice, equality of opportunity, equality of results/outcomes, or more favourable treatment of a protected class of worker. Contrary to the conception of formal equality, the substantive equality policy objective acknowledges that certain groups may require to be treated differently from the 'mainstream' in order to enable them to overcome embedded structural disadvantages:

■ **S. Fredman, *Discrimination Law*, 2nd edition (Oxford, OUP, 2011) 2**

How do we explain then how equal treatment can in effect lead to inequality, while unequal treatment might be necessary in order to achieve equality? The apparent paradox can be understood if we accept that equality can be formulated in different ways, depending on which underlying conception is chosen. Equality of treatment is predicated on the principle that justice inheres in consistency; hence likes should be treated alike. But this in turn is based on a purely abstract [conception] of justice, which does not take into account existing distributions of wealth and power. Consistency in treatment of two individuals who appear alike but in fact differ in terms of access to power, opportunities, or material benefits, results in unequal outcomes. An alternative conception of equality, therefore is based on a more substantive view of justice, which concentrates on correcting maldistribution. Such a principle would lead to a focus on equality of results, requiring unequal treatment if necessary to achieve an equal impact. Alternatively, the focus could be on facilitating personal self-fulfilment, by equalizing opportunities.

A distinction is drawn in the passage between equal treatment associated with the policy objective of formal equality, on the one hand, and the conception of substantive equality which is concerned with achieving equality of results/outcomes, on the other hand. This dichotomy between an equal treatment/formal equality[27] and equality of results/outcome/substantive equality[28] model of anti-discrimination law is illustrated in the following Hypotheticals A and B.

Hypothetical A

Olivia Armitage has been employed by Danny's Demolishers Ltd ('DD') for over five years in its Cambridge office. She is aghast to learn from Jeff Wilkinson, one of her male colleagues, that DD has given all of the male members of staff in the Cambridge office a client entertainment budget of £5,000 per annum. This budget is not available to the female members of staff.

Hypothetical A is a clear example of disparate treatment in the sense that female members of DD's staff have not been afforded a client entertainment budget in contrast to their male counterparts. Olivia has been treated less favourably than her male colleagues

---

[27] This is the same as 'direct discrimination'.
[28] In other words, a 'disparate impact' or 'indirect discrimination' model.

since they are entitled to a benefit which she is denied. Here, Olivia has not been treated consistently with Jeff and so 'like' has not been treated the same as 'like'. Accordingly, DD would be held legally liable under a regime predicated solely on the conception of formal equality. In this case, the discrimination meted out to Olivia is overt in nature.[29]

This rudimentary example of a formal equality model in Hypothetical A can be contrasted with the situation where a benign measure is adopted by an employer which has a disparate impact on an employee falling within a protected group. In this case, the affected employee will have been treated wholly consistently with a colleague who cannot be identified as a member of the protected class; nevertheless, a disproportionately adverse impact is experienced by the employee concerned. Consider the following hypothetical.

Hypothetical B

Danny's Demolishers Ltd ('DD') has employed Malik Singh ('MS') as an operations adviser in its Bedford office. MS was born and lived in India until he was 25 years old. He has lived in the UK for the past five years. All of MS's education was conducted in India. DD advertises internally for an operations manager and one of the criteria for the vacancy is that the applicant must have at least three A-level qualifications at a minimum B grade. A white male British colleague of MS who is also an operations adviser is appointed and MS is extremely disappointed that he was unsuccessful. MS is more experienced than the successful colleague but was unable to satisfy the qualifications criterion.

In this illustration, both MS and his colleague have been treated identically: both must satisfy exactly the same qualifications criterion in order to be eligible for the vacancy. However, the effect of insisting on that criterion is much more burdensome on MS than his colleague, owing to the fact that he is of a different racial and national origin and undertook his education and training in a country other than the UK. For that reason, what looks like a neutral qualifications criterion in fact has a disproportionate impact on persons falling within a protected group, namely persons not of British national origin. By proscribing DD from adopting such a job criterion, the concept of indirect discrimination affords a greater equality of results, compelling DD to alter its practices. Such an equality of results model is one instantiation of the broader policy objective of substantive equality.[30]

As will become apparent when we subject the legal concepts of direct discrimination, indirect discrimination, pregnancy discrimination, harassment, victimization, etc. to close scrutiny, UK anti-discrimination laws are not confined to the achievement of only one of the competing notions of formal and substantive equality; instead, both of these conceptions, which manifest themselves through different statutory constructs, are pursued.[31] For example, the statutory notion of direct discrimination is generally understood to represent the formal equality model, whereas indirect discrimination is designed to achieve the equality of results incarnation of the substantive equality model.[32] Meanwhile, pregnant workers or workers on maternity leave[33] are afforded more favourable treatment

---

[29] However, this statement should not be taken as to suggest that direct discrimination can never be covert in nature, on which, see section 10.2.3.

[30] See *R (E) v Governing Body of JFS and another (United Synagogue and others intervening)* [2009] UKSC 15, [2010] 2 AC 728, 757B per Baroness Hale.

[31] H. Collins, 'Discrimination, Equality and Social Inclusion' (2003) 66 *Modern Law Review* 16, 16–17.

[32] See *R (E) v Governing Body of JFS and another (United Synagogue and others intervening)* [2009] UKSC 15, [2010] 2 AC 728, 757B per Baroness Hale.

[33] See section 18 of the EA and regulation 10 of the Maternity and Parental Leave Regulations 1999 (SI 1999/3312), on which, see Chapter 18, section 18.3.4.

in the workplace than ordinary workers who are not on maternity leave, which is an alternative instantiation of substantive equality.[34] Ultimately, Parliament in the UK has sought to tailor the protections afforded to particular groups in accordance with differing conceptions of equality, which are dependent on the level of structural disadvantage, under-representation, or limitations on access to employment that its collective social judgment believes those groups to have experienced. This direct correlation between policy prescriptions and the legal measures that have been adopted enables the latter to be benchmarked in accordance with their effectiveness in achieving the former.[35]

Each of the competing policy objectives, however, has its Achilles' heel. If we take formal equality, the primary objection is that it necessarily requires an external value judgment to be made about what groups are 'alike'. As such, it has been argued that it is 'empty' and devoid of any content:

■ P. Westen, 'The Empty Idea of Equality' (1982) 95 *Harvard Law Review* 537, 546–7

. . . a more natural view of 'like treatment' is suggested by the way 'people who are alike' was interpreted. Just as no categories of 'like' people exist in nature, neither do categories of 'like' treatment exist; treatments can be alike only in reference to some moral rule. Thus, to say that people who are morally alike in a certain respect 'should be treated alike' means that they should be treated in accord with the moral rule by which they are determined to be alike. Hence 'likes should be treated alike' means that people for whom a certain treatment is prescribed by a standard should all be given the treatment prescribed by the standard. Or, more simply, people who by a rule should be treated alike should by the rule be treated alike. So there it is: equality is entirely '[c]ircular.' It tells us to treat like people alike; but when we ask who 'like people' are, we are told they are 'people who should be treated alike.' Equality is an empty vessel with no substantive moral content of its own. Without moral standards, equality remains meaningless, a formula that can have nothing to say about how we should act. With such standards, equality becomes superfluous, a formula that can do nothing but repeat what we already know. As Bernard Williams observed, 'when the statement of equality ceases to claim more than is warranted, it rather rapidly reaches the point where it claims less than is interesting.'[36]

Westen makes the point that the insistence of formal equality on symmetrical treatment begs the question: 'Equal treatment with whom?' The common response is that an exercise in comparison is required whereby the claimant falling within the protected group is compared against a 'comparator' and must be able to show disparate treatment in order for his/her claim to be successful.[37] Our intuitive conception of this elusive 'comparator' is that he ought to be a white, able-bodied, straight male. Hence, the 'mainstream' is implicitly predetermined to be male, which in many ways is disrespectful to the constituencies striving for equality in the workplace inasmuch as it suggests that they are somehow inferior to this male norm.[38] Some commentators have suggested that a

---

[34] See *Thibault v CNAVTS* [1999] ICR 160, 176E.

[35] However, Hepple has warned against such an instrumental approach and called on commentators to see the legal measures applied as simply one of the means to be pursued in order to effect wider legal and attitudinal change: B. Hepple, 'The Aims of Equality Law' (2008) 61 *Current Legal Problems* 1, 21.

[36] In addition, see J. R. Lucas, 'Against Equality' (1965) 40 *Philosophy* 296, 296–7. For commentary on Westen's views, see J. Croon-Gestefeld, *Reconceptualising European Equality Law. A Comparative Institutional Analysis* (Oxford, Hart Publishing, 2017) 27–9.

[37] For example, see the forceful argument in R. Wintemute, 'When is Pregnancy Discrimination Indirect Discrimination?' (1998) 27 *Industrial Law Journal* 23, 25.

[38] S. Fredman, *Discrimination Law*, 2nd edition (Oxford, OUP, 2011) 10–11.

third-party comparison exercise is not required and should be abandoned in favour of self-comparison or no comparison at all:

S. Honeyball, *Great Debates: Employment Law* (Basingstoke, Palgrave Macmillan, 2011) 118

With regard to showing adverse treatment of the claimant because of a protected characteristic, it would appear that the way to establish that would be to keep as many of the features of the scenario as intact as possible between the two sides of the comparison and remove merely the discriminatory feature to establish if there is, or would have been, a difference. In other words, in a case of race discrimination for example, what would need to be involved is the removal of the racial features, but all other variables would remain. This takes out the possibility that it is one of the other, non-racial, features that is the reason for the discrimination. If that is accepted, it would appear to be desirable, and even necessary, that a comparator is not involved, because that comparator would bring with them a host of other features that could form the reason for the discrimination. If only racial features in my example were to be removed that would entail that the comparison would need to be between the claimant with her racial characteristic and the claimant again without her racial characteristic. So, although a comparison would still be required, it would be self-comparison, not comparison with a comparator. The purity, if it can be called that, of the comparison process requires this methodology.

■ T. Macklem, *Beyond Comparison: Sex and Discrimination* (Cambridge, CUP, 2003) 18

Sex discrimination is wrongful, and its wrongfulness is not comparative, but depends, as I have said, on the impact of discrimination, and the misconception it embodies, on the success of some person's life, in this case the life of a woman. In other words, if wrongfulness is noncomparative, then sex discrimination must also be noncomparative, for it is the wrongfulness of sex discrimination that concerns us.

Despite these persuasive arguments, it is undoubtedly the case that the courts and tribunals cling to the practice of applying comparators.[39] Indeed, this is explicitly required by UK equality legislation.[40]

A further objection to the conception of formal equality is that it is inherently individualistic in two senses: first, it elides the group-based characteristics attributable to individuals; and second, it relies on an individual litigation-driven model to achieve equality. The statutory model concentrates on negative anti-discrimination laws which are intensely individualistic, requiring claimants to personally vindicate their legal rights in a tribunal or court. Another limitation of formal equality is the relativity of the treatment afforded to the claimant and the comparator. So long as the claimant is treated the same as the comparator, the employer will avoid liability. Therefore, it is entirely legal for an employer to treat the claimant and comparator equally badly, leading to a 'levelling down', rather than 'levelling up', of protection.[41]

---

[39] *Gillespie v Northern Health and Social Services Board* (Case C-342/93) [1996] 2 CMLR 969, 987.
[40] Section 23 of the EA.
[41] The decision of the European Court of Justice ('ECJ' or 'CJEU') in *Smith v Avdel Systems Ltd* [1994] IRLR 602 is the paradigm, on which, see S. Deakin, 'Levelling down Employee Benefits' (1995) 54 *Cambridge Law Journal* 35; T. Khaitan, *A Theory of Discrimination Law* (Oxford, OUP, 2015) 133 and 153–4.

The major alternative conception of equality is substantive equality, which itself has a variety of incarnations.[42] This policy prescription may be articulated in terms of:

(1) 'equality of opportunity';

(2) 'equality of results/outcomes'; or

(3) positive discrimination, i.e. the direct accommodation or *more favourable treatment* of a particular protected class of worker on the basis of broad values, such as dignity, individual self-worth, and autonomy.

Turning first to the meaning of 'equality of opportunity', this presupposes that members of a protected group are participating in a metaphorical race towards a social good situated at a starting point lying somewhere behind the mainstream: the more entrenched the disadvantage, barriers, or under-representation suffered, the further behind the mainstream the individual will start the race. In terms of such manifestation of the substantive equality conception, the goal of anti-discrimination laws should be fair competition on a 'level playing field':

■ **S. Fredman, 'Reversing Discrimination' (1997) 113** *Law Quarterly Review* **575, 579**

> The approach based on [the] 'equal opportunities'... model rejects a purely formal view of justice, recognising that certain distributive factors need to be considered. Its central tenet, therefore, is that true equality cannot be achieved if individuals begin the race from different starting points. This model also departs from the narrow individualism of the symmetrical approach, acknowledging the extent to which an individual's life chances are distorted by structural discrimination based on group membership. An 'equal opportunities' approach therefore permits sex- or race-based policies if tailored to the purpose of equalising the starting point. It is, however, at this point that the traditional notions of neutrality, symmetry and the primacy of the individual reassert themselves. Once individuals enjoy equality of opportunity, it is argued, the problem of institutional discrimination has been overcome, and fairness demands that they be treated on the basis of their individual qualities, without regard to sex or race. This model therefore specifically rejects policies which aim to correct imbalances in the workforce by quotas or targets whose aim is one of equality of outcome.

A perfunctory glance at the content of UK anti-discrimination legislation reveals that its stated aim is the achievement of equality of opportunity. For example, section 3(d) of the Equality Act 2006 enjoins the Equality and Human Rights Commission ('EHRC') to take steps to encourage and support the development of a society in which each individual has an equal opportunity to participate in society. In addition, the Discrimination Law Review pronounced that '[e]veryone should have an equal chance to make the most of [his/her] natural ability'.[43] Further, section 149(1) of the EA[44] obliges public authorities to have due regard to the need to advance equality of opportunity in the workplace between

---

[42] See C. Barnard and B. Hepple, 'Substantive Equality' (2000) 59 *Cambridge Law Journal* 562, 564–7.

[43] Department for Communities and Local Government, *Discrimination Law Review: A Framework for Fairness—Proposals for a Single Equality Bill for Great Britain* (June 2007), available at http://webarchive.nationalarchives.gov.uk/20120919132719/www.communities.gov.uk/documents/corporate/pdf/325332.pdf page 8 (last visited 5 December 2017) ('the Discrimination Law Review').

[44] Further guidance is furnished by section 149(3) of the EA.

persons falling within one of the protected constituencies and persons not falling therein as part of their decision-making processes.[45]

However, some philosophers and political economists argue that equality of opportunity is not a very desirable goal or form of equality at all. For example, in 2002, Cavanagh wrote a book with the provocative title, *Against Equality of Opportunity*.[46] The following extract provides a flavour of Cavanagh's principal arguments:

■ M. Cavanagh, *Against Equality of Opportunity* (Oxford, OUP, 2002) 132

It should by now be clear why I am opposed to equality—and therefore to equality of opportunity, to the extent that it has anything to do with equality, in any substantial sense. First and most importantly, because it is not clear that equality is something we should be striving for in this area. We just don't conceive of our relations with one another in the right way: we don't think of ourselves as partners in some common enterprise, at least not in the economic sphere. But second, even if we did conceive of our relations with one another in the right way, that would bring us to the next problem. Jobs cannot be shared, so we would have to argue for a different kind of equality: everyone having an equal chance. The problem here is that this kind of equality—everyone having an equal chance to *become unequal*—seems a poor way of expressing the fact that we are all equal partners in some economic enterprise.[47]

If we accept that equality of opportunity suffers from the conceptual shortcomings identified by Cavanagh—that a person's right to liberty must entail a right to inequality—the notion of equality of results/outcomes might seem to harbour more promise. Indeed, in Hypothetical B, we noted that the key statutory concept of indirect discrimination is predicated on such an incarnation of the conception of substantive equality. Anti-discrimination laws devised with the aim of achieving equality of results will seek to ensure that the application of an apparently neutral criterion by an employer does not disproportionately adversely impact on an individual falling within a protected group and the group itself. However, we must acknowledge that indirect discrimination/equality of results also suffers from certain drawbacks. First, it is always necessary for the individual to show that the effect of the application of a criterion leads to individual and group disparity when compared with a comparator falling within the advantaged group. Secondly, the employer is afforded the opportunity to justify the disparate impact by showing that it had a legitimate business requirement and that it had a real need to apply the criterion or practice to achieve that end. Moreover, the focus of indirect discrimination on results does not always lead to the wholesale revision of structures which propagate discrimination.[48]

Against the backdrop of these deficiencies in the equality of results/outcome method, we come to the final possible approach towards substantive equality: positive discrimination, i.e. *more favourable treatment* of a protected constituency. The underlying

---

[45] See also *Equality for Women* (London, HMSO, Cmnd 5724, 1974) at para 17 (this is the White Paper which preceded the Sex Discrimination Act 1975); Department for Communities and Local Government, *Fairness and Freedom: The Final Report of the Equalities Review* (February 2007), available at http://webarchive.nationalarchives.gov.uk/20100807034701/http:/archive.cabinetoffice.gov.uk/equalitiesreview/upload/assets/www.theequalitiesreview.org.uk/equality_review.pdf pages 15–16 (last visited 5 December 2017) ('the Equalities Review'); and the Discrimination Law Review, pages 60–1.

[46] M. Cavanagh, *Against Equality of Opportunity* (Oxford, OUP, 2002).

[47] See also 'Equal Wrongs: John Crace Meets the Philosopher Who Believes that Striving for Equal Opportunities is a Waste of Time' (*The Guardian*, Education Pages, 26 March 2002).

[48] S. Fredman, *Discrimination Law*, 2nd edition (Oxford, OUP, 2011) 10–17.

assumption here is that a particular group is sufficiently different that its members ought to be treated differently from those not belonging to the group. This will involve preferential treatment[49] based on the recognition of an individual's identity[50] and is wholly redistributive in nature. Thus, it runs wholly counter to the orthodox equal treatment approach associated with the formal equality model. It is often justified on the basis that the dignity, identity, autonomy, and self-worth of individuals belonging to a disadvantaged or under-represented group ought to be respected. However, by its very nature it involves formal inequality and (reverse) direct discrimination, i.e. discriminating in favour of a constituency classified as deserving of protection at the expense of the mainstream, which is somewhat paradoxical given that it is a manifestation of an equality policy. Another powerful criticism of positive discrimination is that it is a thinly concealed attempt at social engineering and justice. As such, it is a form of social egalitarianism that attempts to ensure that 'all groups [are] represented in the institutions and occupations of society roughly in proportion to their representation in the population',[51] entailing the imposition of a pattern of distribution of jobs in accordance with a predetermined end. For this reason, any widespread recognition of its legitimacy as the conceptual underpinning of UK anti-discrimination laws, save in isolated pockets,[52] has been resisted by the judiciary. Nonetheless, there are some good reasons why it should not be discounted as one of the means available to tackle embedded inequality in certain carefully identified instances:

■ H. Collins, *Employment Law*, 2nd edition (Oxford, OUP, 2010) 68

Governments and courts seem reluctant to breach the principle of equal treatment contained in the law of direct discrimination. The rejection of quotas and the insistence on the preservation of the principle of allocating jobs on the basis of merit hamper efforts to tackle patterns of disadvantage in the labour market. This reluctance to approve more robust measures of affirmative action seems particularly unsatisfactory in certain kinds of public sector employment, such as the police force, where the representativeness of the officers to the population that they serve may prove a vital ingredient in ensuring the success of the service. In such cases where legitimacy may depend upon diversity of representation, a more systematic recruitment policy of favouring under-represented minorities who are sufficiently qualified to perform the job satisfactorily may be justifiable.

Reflection points

1. Consider the arguments in favour of and against the introduction of anti-discrimination laws. In your opinion, which of these arguments is/are the most convincing?

2. In what circumstances do you believe it is warranted to move beyond the formal equality model to introduce laws whose purpose is grounded in the pursuit of substantive equality? Give reasons for your answer.

---

[49] See C. McCrudden, 'Rethinking Positive Action' (1986) 15 *Industrial Law Journal* 219; L. Barmes, 'Equality and Experimentation: The Positive Action Challenge' (2009) 68 *Cambridge Law Journal* 623; and C. McCrudden, 'A Comparative Taxonomy of "Positive Action" and "Affirmative Action" Policies' in R. Schulze (ed.), *Non-discrimination in European Private Law* (Mohr Siebeck, 2011) 157 for the various forms such favourable treatment might take.

[50] The equal treatment/formal equality model entails overlooking the identity and idiosyncracies of the individual.

[51] M. B. Abram, 'Affirmative Action: Fair Shakers and Social Engineers' (1986) 99 *Harvard Law Review* 1312, 1313.

[52] For example, the duty of the employer to make reasonable adjustments in respect of disabled people, on which, see *Archibald v Fife Council* [2004] ICR 954, 966D–F per Baroness Hale.

3. Is it ever justifiable to statutorily intervene to enable employers to positively discriminate in favour of certain classes of employee, i.e. to treat them more favourably than the mainstream?

 For additional reading on employment equality law, visit the Online Resources for this book at www.oup.com/uk/cabrelli3e/

10.2 AN EVALUATION OF PROHIBITED CONDUCT

In this section, we review the central statutory concepts in the EA such as direct discrimination, indirect discrimination, harassment, sexual harassment, and victimization. First, however, we focus on the historical development of the law.

10.2.1 Historical introduction

The struggle for gender and racial equality can be traced back to the late nineteenth century and is inextricably bound up in the struggle for universal suffrage and the emancipation of women and racial minorities from subordination. The first piece of 'equality' legislation to be passed by Parliament was the Sex Disqualification (Removal) Act 1919, which brought to an end the barriers to entry to certain professions and the civil service faced by women. This statute followed on from a Government report[53] and partly reflected the growing trend for universities in the UK to admit women to study, as well as recognizing the working contribution women had made in the war effort. However, it was not until the 1960s that the first and second generations of modern statutory equality/anti-discrimination laws[54] were introduced in response to the large influx of immigrants from the former British Empire.[55] The Race Relations Acts of 1965 and 1968 brought into effect an equal treatment/formal equality model based on an applicant's or employee's race. Such anti-discrimination laws grew up and came of age within the discipline of employment law, since it was only possible for such laws to be enforced in the context of workplace disputes, i.e. between employee and employer. It was generally accepted that the legislation was generally toothless since there was a convoluted enforcement procedure which vested (i) an obligation in an organization called the Race Relations Board to facilitate conciliation between a complainer and an employer and, ultimately, (ii) the power to raise civil proceedings in the Race Relations Board on behalf of the claimant. Any damages awarded would be remitted to the complainer but could not include an award for injury to feelings.

The deficiencies of the 1965 and 1968 Acts became apparent as the jurisprudence on the other side of the Atlantic became more sophisticated. The US Supreme Court pronounced on the unlawfulness of managerial policies having a disparate impact on disadvantaged groups in 1971[56] and gave free rein to the operation of the equality of results/outcomes incarnation of the substantive equality model. Meanwhile, it was clear there

---

[53] *Report on the War Cabinet Committee on Women in Industry* (London, HMSO, Cmd 135, 1918).

[54] See B. Hepple, *Equality: The New Legal Framework*, 2nd edition (Oxford, Hart Publishing, 2014) 7–12 for a synopsis of the five generations of equality laws.

[55] See A. Lester and G. Bindman, *Race and the Law* (Harmondsworth, Penguin, 1972) for a comprehensive overview of the struggle for racial anti-discrimination laws.

[56] *Griggs v Duke Power* 401 US 424, (1971) 3 Fed 75.

was no equivalent legal concept in the UK which could do the same work. Furthermore, there was a palpable gap in the scope of anti-discrimination laws as women were not earmarked for protection. All of this would be remedied by the emergence of the third generation of equality laws in the Equal Pay Act 1970, the Sex Discrimination Act 1975 ('SDA'), and the Race Relations Act 1976 ('RRA') which imported the 'disparate impact' concept from US law.[57] First, these Acts of Parliament proscribed indirect discrimination without objective justification, i.e. in the absence of an objective justification, an employer was prohibited from adopting apparently neutral measures which had a disparate impact on a protected constituency. Further, protection was extended to women insofar as they were provided with the right not to suffer direct or indirect discrimination in gaining access to employment and in the workplace more generally. Women were also guaranteed equal pay for equal work or work rated as equivalent pursuant to a job evaluation scheme voluntarily formulated by an employer. The third-generation legislation also conferred a free-standing right in favour of individuals to raise proceedings on their own behalf in an employment tribunal and sanctioned awards for injury to feelings. Finally, certain bodies were established such as the Equal Opportunities Commission ('EOC') and the Commission for Racial Equality ('CRE') which were entrusted with the obligation to financially support litigation and provide advice. In 1995, Parliament passed the Disability Discrimination Act 1995 ('DDA') and added disability as one of the protected strands of anti-discrimination law. Concepts such as the employer's duty to make reasonable adjustments to accommodate disabled employees were introduced into UK law. A body known as the Disability Rights Commission ('DRC') was also established to monitor the efficacy of the new laws in the same manner as the EOC and the CRE.

The fourth generation of equality laws can only be understood properly in light of the significant influence exerted by EU law over this area of employment law.[58] When the UK joined the European Economic Community in the 1970s, there was a requirement to comply with Article 119 of the Treaty of Rome[59] and the Equal Pay Directive.[60] These provisions enjoined Member States to adopt and maintain the principle of equal pay for equal work. The Equal Pay Act 1970 came into force in the UK in 1975 and gave effect to these European instruments, although the exact model found in Article 119 was rejected by the then Government. Moreover, the UK also had a responsibility to transpose the requirements of the Equal Treatment Directive,[61] but the Government of the day introduced the SDA without considering the terms of that Directive on the basis that it did not appear to have 'any relevance' to its work.[62] By the time the Race Directive[63] and the Framework Directive[64] were introduced in 2000, the far-reaching implications of EU equality law had been fully exposed in numerous cases. For example, in *Defrenne v SABENA (No. 2)*,[65] the ECJ ruled that Article 119 had direct effect. This meant that it could be invoked by claimants in the national courts of Member States and supplant

---

[57] See L. Dickens, 'The Road is Long: Thirty Years of Equality Legislation in Britain' (2007) 45 *British Journal of Industrial Relations* 463, 464–71 for a summary of the historical development of equality legislation and the internal and external influences shaping the content of the law as it evolved.

[58] See C. O'Cinneide, 'Completing the Picture: The Complex Relationship between EU Anti-Discrimination Law and "Social Europe"' in N. Countouris and M. Freedland (eds), *Resocialising Europe in a Time of Crisis* (Cambridge, CUP, 2013) 118.

[59] Later renumbered to Article 141 of the Treaty of Rome and now Article 157 of the Treaty on the Functioning of the European Union ('TFEU') (OJ 2010 C83/47).

[60] Directive 75/117/EEC (OJ 1975 L45/19).

[61] Directive 76/207/EEC (OJ 1976 L39/40). This has since been repealed and replaced with effect from 15 August 2009 by the Consolidated/Recast Equality Directive 2006/54/EC (OJ 2006 L204/23).

[62] Lord Lester, 'Discrimination: What Can Lawyers Learn from History?' (1994) *Public Law* 224, 227. This attitude is attributable to the general lack of awareness of the potential impact of European legislation on UK law in the early to mid-1970s.   [63] Directive 2000/43/EC (OJ 2000 L180/22).

[64] Directive 2000/78/EC (OJ 2000 L303/16).   [65] [1976] ECR 455.

any inconsistent national legislation. Furthermore, *Defrenne v SABENA (No. 3)*[66] and *Mangold v Helm*[67] emphasized the principle of equality as a fundamental value and constitutional principle of European law. This elevated the equality principle to the status of 'a unique entrenched right, against which even statute cannot stand'.[68] The legal basis for the promulgation of the Race and Framework Directives was the new Article 13 of the Treaty of Rome,[69] which empowered the European Council to take appropriate action to combat discrimination based on sex, racial or ethnic origin, religion or belief, disability, age, and sexual orientation. The Race and Framework Directives targeted the proscription of discrimination in the workplace grounded on race, disability, age, sexual orientation, and religion or belief. The UK transposed these Directives into law via the fourth generation of equality laws, namely the Employment Equality (Religion or Belief) Regulations 2003 ('EE(RB)'),[70] the Employment Equality (Sexual Orientation) Regulations 2003 ('EE(SO)'),[71] and the Employment Equality (Age) Regulations 2006 ('EE(A)').[72]

The coming into force of the Equality Act 2006 and the EA was the final piece of the jigsaw and has been referred to as the fifth generation of equality laws.[73] First, the Equality Act 2006 disbanded the EOC, CRE, and DRC, and replaced them with the EHRC, which was given the statutory remit of promoting and monitoring human rights and protecting, enforcing, and promoting equality across the then six 'protected' grounds. Meanwhile, the EA consolidated, simplified, and reformed employment equality laws, and was the culmination of a long process of deliberation and consultation. In 2007, the Discrimination Law Review and the Equalities Review reported to the Government, which responded with *Framework for a Fairer Future: The Equality Bill*[74] and *The Equality Bill: Government Response to the Consultation*.[75] Ultimately the SDA, RRA, DDA, EE(RB), EE(SO), and EE(A) were repealed and consolidated in the EA. New concepts such as associative discrimination, third-party harassment,[76] and positive action were brought into force. Hepple has argued that this fifth generation of equality laws is concerned with transformative equality:

---

[66] [1978] ECR 1365, 1378.

[67] Case C-144/04 [2006] IRLR 143. See D. Schiek, 'The ECJ Decision in *Mangold*: A Further Twist on Effects of Directives and Constitutional Relevance of Community Equality Legislation' (2006) 35 *Industrial Law Journal* 329; C. Kilpatrick, 'The ECJ and Labour Law: A 2008 Retrospective' (2009) 38 *Industrial Law Journal* 180.

[68] C. Docksey, 'The Principle of Equality between Women and Men as a Fundamental Right under Community Law' (1991) 20 *Industrial Law Journal* 258. Since these decisions, in *Seda Kücükdeveci v Swedex GmbH & Co. KG* [2010] ECR I-365, [2010] IRLR 346 the Grand Chamber of the CJEU has relied on the protections against discrimination on the grounds of sex, race, colour, ethnic or social origin, genetic features, language, religion or belief, political or any other opinion, membership of a national minority, property, birth, disability, age, or sexual orientation in Article 21(1) of the Charter of Fundamental Rights of the European Union (pronounced on 7 December 2000 in Nice (OJ 2000 C364/1) and a second time in Strasbourg on 12 December 2007 (OJ 2007 C303/1) and also published in OJ 2010 C83/389) to hold that national legislation infringed age discrimination law and ought to be disapplied.

[69] Now Article 19 TFEU.

[70] SI 2003/1660. See L. Vickers, 'The Employment Equality (Religion or Belief) Regulations 2003' (2003) 32 *Industrial Law Journal* 188.

[71] SI 2003/1661.

[72] SI 2006/1031. See DTI Consultation Paper, *Equality and Diversity: Coming of Age*, available at http://webarchive.nationalarchives.gov.uk/+/http://www.dti.gov.uk/files/file16397.pdf (last visited 5 December 2017); M. Sargeant, 'The Employment Equality (Age) Regulations 2006: A Legitimisation of Age Discrimination in Employment' (2006) 35 *Industrial Law Journal* 209; and J. Swift, 'Justifying Age Discrimination' (2006) 35 *Industrial Law Journal* 228.

[73] B. Hepple, *Equality: The New Legal Framework*, 2nd edition (Oxford, Hart Publishing, 2014) ch. 1.

[74] (Cm 7431, June 2008), available at http://www.cpa.org.uk/cpa/The_equality_bill_2008.pdf (last visited 5 December 2017).

[75] (Cm 7454, July 2008), available at http://www.official-documents.gov.uk/document/cm74/7454/7454.pdf (last visited 5 December 2017).

[76] This concept has since been repealed, on which, see section 10.2.5.

■ **B. Hepple, *Equality: The New Legal Framework*, 2nd edition (Oxford, Hart Publishing, 2014) 15**

> The fifth generation . . . represented by the Equality Act [2010 is] . . . the start of a period of *transformative equality*, examples of which are gender mainstreaming and positive measures against institutional racism and reasonable accommodation for disabled persons. These policies are not intended to replace traditional anti-discrimination laws but go further, requiring, for example, equality impact assessments and active labour market policies.[77]

Having been raised up into maturity within the bosom of employment law, there is an argument that anti-discrimination law has now broken free of these moorings to become an independent and self-contained branch of the law. For example, the extent to which anti-discrimination laws can better be regarded as a facet of human rights law or constitutional law, rather than labour law, has been debated by scholars:

■ **S. Fredman, 'Equality Law: Labour Law or an Autonomous Field?' in A. Bogg, C. Costello, A. C. L. Davies, and J. Prassl (eds), *The Autonomy of Labour Law* (Oxford, Hart Publishing 2015) 273**

> While the right not to be discriminated against in a work situation remains embedded in labour law, the scope of anti-discrimination law has always extended beyond work to include [access to] education and goods, facilities and services. With the arrival of domesticated human rights law the right to equality can be asserted in an even wider range of cases, often in parallel to labour law, and with different scopes and standards of review. This has made the focus on the employment relationship particularly discordant with the underlying aims of equality, which do not cohere well with the principle that protection should be aligned with subordinate status. Discrimination constitutes an exercise of power which can take place in many sets of relationships, well beyond that of employment.

10.2.2 Eligibility to claim

In Chapter 4, we considered the relational scope of anti-discrimination laws in the UK.[78] We noted that the protections afforded in the context of employment apply not only to employees,[79] but also extend to individuals engaged on the basis of a 'contract personally to do work' in terms of section 83(2)(a) of the EA. Further, in *Jivraj v Hashwani*,[80] the Supreme Court ruled that the individual presenting a complaint of discrimination *must be in a relationship of subordination* vis-à-vis the recipient of his/her services in order to come within the ambit of the 'contract personally to do work'. It stands to reason that this formulation restricts the relational scope of the protections in Part 5 of the EA so that not all individuals engaged in the provision of a personal service will be covered by equality laws. To the extent that the decision of the EAT in *EAD Solicitors LLP v Abrams*[81] might be read as suggesting that a company can present a complaint of direct discrimination under section 13 of the EA against a limited liability partnership where

---

[77] See also S. Fredman, *Discrimination Law*, 2nd edition (Oxford, OUP, 2011) 30–1.
[78] See Chapter 4, section 4.2.3.
[79] However, voluntary workers fall outside the protective coverage of anti-discrimination laws: *X v Mid Sussex Citizens Advice Bureau* [2012] UKSC 59, [2013] 1 All ER 1038.
[80] [2011] UCSC 40, [2011] 1 WLR 1872.   [81] [2015] IRLR 978.

the company is a member of the LLP and, as such, be covered by section 45 of the EA, that would appear to be as far as the *ratio decidendi* of this case goes. Owing to the fact that a company cannot provide a personal service and it would be stretching logic to assert that a company was in a subordinate position vis-à-vis a third-party recipient of its services, it is argued that it would be impermissible for a company to claim that it was an employee *of an employer*, or engaged in work for *an employer* on the basis of a contract personally to do work in terms of section 83(2)(a).

Section 41 of the EA also directs that a 'contract worker' has the right not to suffer discrimination, harassment, or victimization at the hands of a hirer of his/her services where he/she is supplied to work for the latter by a third party such as an employment agency and the contract worker is employed by such agency. Since it is a major challenge for agency workers to establish a contract of employment with the agency, section 41 is unlikely to be particularly useful to agency workers, who are afforded greater protection by regulation 5 of the Agency Workers Regulations 2010,[82] which provision entitles them to parity of pay with a permanent employee or worker of the hirer.[83] Furthermore, police officers,[84] partners in a partnership,[85] members of a limited liability partnership,[86] barristers,[87] advocates,[88] parliamentary staff,[89] members of the armed forces,[90] persons appointed to personal offices[91] or public offices,[92] members of local authorities,[93] and members of trade associations and organizations, including trade unions,[94] inter alia, are covered by the protections within the EA. However, there are a number of exceptions where the EA will not apply, e.g. in relation to acts done for the purposes of safeguarding national security.[95] The other major exemption from the application of the EA finds its expression in the concept of the 'occupational requirement', which we will analyse in more detail in Chapter 11.[96]

The EA is silent on its territorial extent. The Explanatory Notes to the EA clarify that 'following the precedent of the Employment Rights Act 1996 ['ERA'], the [EA] leaves it to tribunals to determine whether the law applies, depending for example on the connection between the employment relationship and Great Britain'.[97] This statement suggests that the parliamentary intention is to adopt a uniform approach across the broad range of statutory employment rights contained in the ERA and the EA.[98] In fact, in *R (on the application of Hottak) v Secretary of State for Foreign and Commonwealth Affairs*,[99] the Court of Appeal held that the territoriality of unfair dismissal and equality law claims under the ERA and EA are identical. As such, the relevant test is that set out in *Ravat v Halliburton Manufacturing and Services Ltd*.[100]

---

[82] SI 2010/93.   [83] See Chapter 4, section 4.3.2.   [84] Section 42 of the EA.

[85] Section 44 of the EA.

[86] Section 45 of the EA. See *EAD Solicitors LLP v Abrams* [2015] IRLR 978.

[87] Section 47 of the EA.   [88] Section 48 of the EA.

[89] Section 83(2)(b), (c), and (d) of the EA.   [90] Section 83(3) of the EA.

[91] Section 49 of the EA.   [92] Section 50 of the EA.   [93] Section 58 of the EA.

[94] Section 57 of the EA.   [95] Sections 191–197 of, and Schedule 22 to, the EA.

[96] See Chapter 11, section 11.4.

[97] Paragraph 15, available at http://www.legislation.gov.uk/ukpga/2010/15/notes/division/2/3/1 (last visited 5 December 2017).

[98] Therefore, where there is an international element to an anti-discrimination claim, the decisions of the House of Lords and the Supreme Court in *Lawson v Serco Ltd* [2006] IRLR 289; *Duncombe v Secretary of State for Children, Schools and Families; Fletcher v Secretary of State for Children, Schools and Families* [2011] UKSC 14, [2011] 2 All ER 417; and *Ravat v Halliburton Manufacturing and Services Ltd* [2012] UKSC 1, [2012] 2 All ER 905 will require to be consulted. See Chapter 16, section 16.2.1.1.

[99] [2016] 3 All ER 935. See L. Merrett, 'The Contract of Employment in Its International and European Law Setting' in M. Freedland et al. (eds), *The Contract of Employment* (Oxford, OUP, 2016) 621, L. Merrett, 'The Extra-Territorial Reach of Employment Legislation' (2010) 39 *Industrial Law Journal* 355, 375–7; and U. Grusic, 'The Territorial Scope of Employment Legislation and Choice of Law' (2012) 75 *Modern Law Review* 722, 725, 735–7.

[100] [2012] ICR 389. See Chapter 16, section 16.2.1.2.

The EA applies across the whole chronology of the employment relationship, from hiring and firing decisions, decisions regarding whether an individual should be trained, promoted, or transferred, including how the terms of the individual's contract should be drawn, to how he/she ought to be treated generally in the workplace. Equality laws applying to the workplace are set out in Part 5 of the EA. Furthermore, the compass of the protections in the EA also extends to discrimination, harassment, or victimization perpetrated *subsequent to the termination of the employment contract or employment relationship*:

Section 39 Employees and applicants

(1) An employer (A) must not discriminate against a person (B)—

   (a) in the arrangements A makes for deciding to whom to offer employment;

   (b) as to the terms on which A offers B employment;

   (c) by not offering B employment.

(2) An employer (A) must not discriminate against an employee of A's (B)—

   (a) as to B's terms of employment;

   (b) in the way A affords B access, or by not affording B access, to opportunities for promotion, transfer or training or for receiving any other benefit, facility or service;

   (c) by dismissing B;

   (d) by subjecting B to any other detriment.

(3) An employer (A) must not victimise a person (B)—

   (a) in the arrangements A makes for deciding to whom to offer employment;

   (b) as to the terms on which A offers B employment;

   (c) by not offering B employment.

(4) An employer (A) must not victimise an employee of A's (B)—

   (a) as to B's terms of employment;

   (b) in the way A affords B access, or by not affording B access, to opportunities for promotion, transfer or training or for any other benefit, facility or service;

   (c) by dismissing B;

   (d) by subjecting B to any other detriment . . .

(7) In subsections (2)(c) and (4)(c), the reference to dismissing B includes a reference to the termination of B's employment—

   (a) by the expiry of a period (including a period expiring by reference to an event or circumstance);

   (b) by an act of B's (including giving notice) in circumstances such that B is entitled, because of A's conduct, to terminate the employment without notice.

Section 40 Employees and applicants: harassment

(1) An employer (A) must not, in relation to employment by A, harass a person (B)—

   (a) who is an employee of A's;

   (b) who has applied to A for employment . . .

> ### Section 108 Relationships that have ended
>
> (1) A person (A) must not discriminate against another (B) if—
>
>   (a) the discrimination arises out of and is closely connected to a relationship which used to exist between them, and
>
>   (b) conduct of a description constituting the discrimination would, if it occurred during the relationship, contravene this Act.
>
> (2) A person (A) must not harass another (B) if—
>
>   (a) the harassment arises out of and is closely connected to a relationship which used to exist between them, and
>
>   (b) conduct of a description constituting the harassment would, if it occurred during the relationship, contravene this Act . . .
>
> (7) But conduct is not a contravention of this section in so far as it also amounts to victimisation of B by A.[101]

Section 39(7) clarifies that a dismissal is inclusive of a constructive dismissal[102] and the situation where an employee's fixed-term contract comes to an end and is not renewed.[103] Therefore, a dismissal which amounts to direct or indirect discrimination will be covered.[104] As for the concept of 'detriment' in section 39(2)(d) and (4)(d), the leading case is *Shamoon v RUC*. Here, the House of Lords stressed that whether the conduct meets the requisite threshold will depend on whether the reasonable worker, objectively construed, would take the view that the employee had been disadvantaged in the circumstances:

■ *Shamoon v RUC* [2003] ICR 337, 349G–373B

> #### Lord Hope:
>
> [What constitutes a detriment entails the application of] a test of materiality. Is the treatment of such a kind that a reasonable worker would or might take the view that in all the circumstances it was to his detriment? An unjustified sense of grievance cannot amount to 'detriment': *Barclays Bank plc v Kapur (No 2)* [1995] IRLR 87. But, contrary to the view that was expressed in *Lord Chancellor v Coker* [2001] ICR 507 on which the Court of Appeal relied, it is not necessary to demonstrate some physical or economic consequence . . .
>
> #### Lord Scott:
>
> [I] am in general agreement with the views expressed by Lord Hope . . . My only reservation is that the test of detriment as expressed by Brightman LJ in *Ministry of Defence v Jeremiah* [1980]

---

[101] It has been held by the Court of Appeal in *Jessemey v Rowstock Ltd* [2014] 1 WLR 3615 that claims for post-employment victimization are not precluded.

[102] Although it is not possible for an employer to 'cure' a repudiatory breach of contract amounting to a constructive dismissal (*Buckland v Bournemouth University Higher Education Corp.* [2010] EWCA Civ 121, [2010] IRLR 445), for the purposes of the EA the employer can indeed 'cure' its perpetration of discrimination by exhausting an internal disciplinary procedure and reinstating the employee to his/her job after an appeal. In such a case, the employee will have no entitlement to claim discrimination: *Little v Richmond Pharmacology* [2014] ICR 85.

[103] Section 39(8) of the EA.

[104] See Chapter 16, section 16.2.1.1. The upshot is that a claimant will have a claim under the EA as well as a claim for unfair dismissal under Part X of the ERA, albeit that pursuing the former claim may prove more attractive owing to the availability of uncapped compensation and the fact that there is no requirement that the claimant establish that he/she has been continuously employed for at least two years.

ICR 13, 31, cited by Lord Hoffmann in *Chief Constable of the West Yorkshire Police v Khan* [2001] ICR 1065, 1077–1078, para 53 . . . namely, that 'a detriment exists if a reasonable worker would or might take the view that the [treatment] was in all the circumstances to his detriment', must be applied by considering the issue from the point of view of the victim. If the victim's opinion that the treatment was to his or her detriment is a reasonable one to hold, that ought, in my opinion, to suffice. In *Khan's* case the complainant, desiring to apply for a new job, wanted a reference to be given by his employers. His employers refused to give one. It was clear that if they had given one it would have been an unfavourable one. It might be said that a reasonable worker would not want an unfavourable reference. But the complainant wanted to be treated like all other employees and to be given a reference. The House concluded that this was a reasonable attitude for him to adopt and that the refusal to give him a reference constituted 'detriment'. He was being deprived of something that he reasonably wanted to have. And, while an unjustified sense of grievance about an allegedly discriminatory decision cannot constitute 'detriment', a justified and reasonable sense of grievance about the decision may well do so.

Shamoon demonstrates that the word 'detriment' will be given a broad construction by the courts and tribunals. Although Lord Scott's formulation involves a subjective evaluation of the reasonable worker's viewpoint from the perspective of the victim/claimant, any difference between this and Lord Hope's approach may be more apparent than real: both recognize that the test includes the application of an objective check on the reasonableness of the worker's belief that the employer's conduct or omissions amounted to a detriment. This is illustrated in the case of *Grant v HM Land Registry*.[105] Here, the Court of Appeal held that a gay employee who disclosed his sexual orientation when he was employed at his employer's Lytham office was not subjected to a detriment when he moved to Coventry and a new manager revealed his sexual orientation to work colleagues there against his wishes, in circumstances in which it was clear that the manager concerned did not have a harassive or discriminatory purpose. This finding was based on the assertion that the claimant was unable to establish a justified sense of grievance: although the claimant may genuinely have considered himself aggrieved, there were no reasonable grounds for so thinking on an objective assessment of the facts and hence no 'detriment', since there was no ill intent or malice in the actions of the new manager. Likewise, in *Singh v Cordant Security Ltd*,[106] it was held that no detriment had been suffered by a claimant where the employer had failed to investigate a grievance that the employer had adopted racially abusive language, because it was clearly fabricated and unmeritorious. Meanwhile, examples of 'detriment' have included transferring an employee to a less desirable post for reporting incidents of racial discrimination,[107] removing a dog from a pregnant police dog-handler because she was no longer operational,[108] and the situation where a hospital's practice included a requirement that male nurses be chaperoned when carrying out an electro-cardiogram on female patients and no comparable arrangements were in place for female nurses conducting the same procedure on male patients.[109]

10.2.3 Direct discrimination

We will address direct discrimination as the starting point for our discussion of the key statutory concepts intended to tackle discrimination, which the EA refers to as 'prohibited conduct'. The other examples of 'prohibited conduct' are indirect discrimination,

---

[105] [2011] ICR 1390.   [106] [2016] IRLR 4.
[107] *Kirby v Manpower Services Commission* [1980] IRLR 229.
[108] *Metropolitan Police v Keohane* [2014] ICR 1073.
[109] *Moyhing v Barts and London NHS Trust* [2006] IRLR 860.

harassment/sexual harassment, and victimization, each of which can be thought of as a type of statutory tort, conferring a remedy of compensation if a claimant's complaint to an employment tribunal is substantiated.[110] Direct discrimination is the embodiment of the formal equality conception of equality, namely that 'likes should be treated alike'. The claimant employee will have been directly discriminated against if he/she is treated less favourably than another for the reason of a 'protected characteristic', namely sex, race, disability, religion or belief, sexual orientation, age, pregnancy/maternity, gender reassignment, or marriage/civil partnership. Hence, less favourable treatment is crucial and simply treating all employees in the same manner will not engage the concept of direct discrimination.[111] Historically, the concept was designed to combat overt instances of discriminatory conduct, which continued to be a feature of the labour market well into the 1970s. An important point is that, save in the case of age discrimination, it is never possible for the employer to justify direct discrimination:

Section 13 Direct discrimination

(1) A person (A) discriminates against another (B) if, because of a protected characteristic, A treats B less favourably than A treats or would treat others.

(2) If the protected characteristic is age, A does not discriminate against B if A can show A's treatment of B to be a proportionate means of achieving a legitimate aim.

(3) If the protected characteristic is disability, and B is not a disabled person, A does not discriminate against B only because A treats or would treat disabled persons more favourably than A treats B.

(4) If the protected characteristic is marriage and civil partnership, this section applies to a contravention of Part 5 (work) only if the treatment is because it is B who is married or a civil partner.

(5) If the protected characteristic is race, less favourable treatment includes segregating B from others.

(6) If the protected characteristic is sex . . .

(b) in a case where B is a man, no account is to be taken of special treatment afforded to a woman in connection with pregnancy or childbirth.

The stages which make up the test of direct discrimination are illustrated in Figure 10.1.[112]

Figure 10.1 *The stages involved in a direct discrimination claim*

---

[110] Sections 120 and 124(2) of the EA.

[111] For example, see *Ladele v London Borough of Islington* [2009] EWCA Civ 1357, [2010] 1 WLR 955, 964C–H per Lord Neuberger MR.

[112] See Article 2(1) and (2)(a) of the Race Directive; Article 2(1) and (2)(a) of the Framework Directive; and Article 2(1)(a) of the Recast Equality Directive for the European provisions, which are very similar to section 13 of the EA.

The starting point for the discussion is that section 13 demands a clear link between the employer's grounds for the less favourable treatment and one of the nine protected characteristics recognized by the law. For that reason, in *Taiwo v Olaigbe*,[113] the Supreme Court rejected the argument that two female claimants suffered direct race discrimination when they were treated less favourably because they were vulnerable migrant workers. Since the particular ground for the employer's treatment—the vulnerable migrant worker status of the claimants—did not completely correspond to one of the protected characteristics, namely race, the claimants were unsuccessful in their argument that their treatment had been unlawful. Of course, a counter-argument to the position of the Supreme Court is that vulnerable migrant worker status and race are so inextricably bound up with each other that it is illogical to treat them as two separate factors.

The words 'because of' in section 13(1) of the EA replaced the words 'on the grounds of', which feature in the Race, Framework and Recast Equality Directives, and featured in the now-repealed SDA, RRA, EE(RB), EE(SO), and EE(A). In the cases in which the courts were called upon to construe the words 'on the grounds of' in the SDA, RRA, EE(RB), EE(SO), and EE(A), they consistently held that they required the claimant to compare his/her treatment with another like person, known as the 'comparator'. The Government speeches in the House of Commons[114] and the Explanatory Notes to the EA[115] demonstrate an absence of any intention on the part of Parliament to change this meaning. Therefore, it is insisted that a claimant will continue to be required to demonstrate less favourable treatment in comparison with a suitable comparator not falling within the protected group.[116] Since the coming into force of the EA in 2010, the courts have stuck to their practice of applying comparators in order to establish direct discrimination, just as the Government asserted that they would.[117]

The fact that section 13 of the EA enjoins B to show less favourable treatment than 'others' begs the question as to what the features of these 'others' might be. It is well established that this formula necessitates a comparison exercise and it is insufficient for the claimant simply to show that he/she has an honest, subjective believe that he/she has been treated less favourably than a third party.[118] Therefore, consistent with the formal equality model, B the claimant, must compare him/herself with an actual individual in the workplace who does not possess the same protected characteristic as the claimant or fall within that protected group. This person is referred to as the 'comparator' and B the claimant must show that his/her treatment was less favourable when compared with that comparator.

More significantly, by virtue of the inclusion of the words, 'would treat' in section 13(1) of the EA and 'would be treated' in the Race, Framework and Recast Equality

---

[113] [2016] 1 WLR 2653.

[114] Hansard, HC Public Bill Committee, Eighth Sitting, col. 242, 16 June 2009 (Solicitor General Vera Baird).

[115] Paragraph 61, available at http://www.legislation.gov.uk/ukpga/2010/15/notes/division/3/2/2/1 (last visited 5 December 2017).

[116] However, this modification in the definition of direct discrimination has been controversial: see the submissions of the Discrimination Law Association, the EHRC, the Equality and Diversity Forum, the TUC, the National Union of Teachers, the University and College Union, the Equality and Diversity Forum, and the Equality Commission for Northern Ireland to the House of Commons Public Equality Bill Committee, available at http://www.publications.parliament.uk/pa/cm200809/cmpublic/cmpbequality.htm (last visited 5 December 2017). See also the reservations of Underhill J (P) in the EAT in *J v DLA Piper UK LLP* [2010] ICR 1052, 1080.

[117] For example, see *CP Regents Park Two Ltd v Ilyas* (UKEAT/0366/14/MC, 16 June 2015) where different comparators were adopted in respect of different points raised in the case; see also the debate about the proper choice of comparator in *Vernon v Azure Support Services* (UKEAT/0192/13/SM, 7 November 2014).

[118] *Burrett v West Birmingham Health Authority* [1994] IRLR 7.

Directives, a claimant may invoke a *hypothetical* comparator, i.e. a fictional employee not falling within the same protected group as the claimant.[119] This clearly broadens the scope of direct discrimination as a regulatory device, since it does not preclude a claimant from raising a claim where there is no suitable individual available in the workplace who can act as a comparator;[120] otherwise, the concept of direct discrimination would be ineffectual as a means of conferring protection in the context of occupations segmented along gender, racial lines, etc. For example, imagine the situation where a woman is engaged as a secretary in a workplace where all of her colleagues are also female. If the employer issues an instruction that requires all employees to wear short skirts at all times in the office, the fact that there are no male employee comparators would not preclude the female claimant from establishing a less favourable treatment claim on the basis that the instruction is a gender-based criterion. As for the attributes of the actual or hypothetical comparator, he/she need not be a 'clone' of the claimant:[121]

Section 23 Comparison by reference to circumstances

(1) On a comparison of cases for the purposes of section 13, 14, or 19 there must be no material difference between the circumstances relating to each case.

(2) The circumstances relating to a case include a person's abilities if—

    (a) on a comparison for the purposes of section 13, the protected characteristic is disability;

    (b) on a comparison for the purposes of section 14, one of the protected characteristics in the combination is disability.[122]

(3) If the protected characteristic is sexual orientation, the fact that one person (whether or not the person referred to as B) is a civil partner while another is married is not a material difference between the circumstances relating to each case.

Hence, the actual or hypothetical comparator must be someone whose situation is broadly similar, albeit not identical, to that of the claimant, but who does not share the same protected characteristic[123] as the claimant or fall within the relevant protected group. This is the effect of the instruction in section 23 that there may be differences between the comparator and the claimant, provided that they are not material.

Another issue of some consequence is the fact that section 13 does not require the claimant him/herself to possess one of the protected characteristics or to fall within the protected group, i.e. section 13(1) does not state 'because of B having a protected characteristic', but instead stipulates 'because of a protected characteristic'. The import of this wording is that the protected characteristic is divorced from the claimant and so associative discrimination and discrimination by perception are covered. The former can be illustrated by the facts of the case of *Coleman v Attridge Law*.[124] Mrs Coleman alleged that

---

[119] For example, see *Chief Constable of West Yorkshire v Vento* [2001] IRLR 124.

[120] When the comparator is hypothetical and the courts must decide how the employer would have acted in relation to that comparator, it was suggested in *Balamoody v United Kingdom Central Council for Nursing, Midwifery and Health Visiting* [2002] ICR 646 that the court should ask how the employer acted in cases which, while not identical, were also not entirely dissimilar. This is reflected in section 23 of the EA.

[121] *Madden v Preferred Technical Group Cha Ltd* [2005] IRLR 46.

[122] See also *Macdonald v Advocate General for Scotland* [2003] UKHL 34, [2004] 1 All ER 339.

[123] For example, see *Smith v Department for Business and Skills* (UKEAT/0308/12/RN, 23 January 2014).

[124] [2008] ECR I-5603, [2008] IRLR 722. See also *Saini v All Saints Haque Centre* [2009] IRLR 74 for a case of associative discrimination in the context of the protected characteristic of religion, and *EAD Solicitors LLP v Abrams* [2015] IRLR 978 where the associative claim was one of age and the claimant was a company.

she had suffered less favourable treatment owing to the fact that she had taken time off to care for her disabled son. The ECJ ruled that the Framework Directive conferred protection from discrimination in the context of the protected characteristic of disability where the claimant did not possess that characteristic. The manner in which section 13 has been drafted suggests that this judgment has been codified and, indeed, the Explanatory Notes to the EA expressly provide that discrimination by association is covered.[125] In fact, taking matters one step further, it has been held in *EAD Solicitors LLP v Abrams*[126] that a company providing services to a third party can raise a direct discrimination claim against that third party under section 13 where the company alleges the third party treated it less favourably because of the age of an individual with whom it is associated.[127] Going even further, it has been held by the Court of Appeal[128] in Northern Ireland—in a case famously dubbed the 'gay cake row'—that where a Christian-owned bakery[129] refused to supply a homosexual activist with a cake bearing a message in support of gay marriage, the bakery had directly discriminated on grounds of sexual orientation. This decision seems to stretch the scope of associative discrimination to include a claimant's general relationship to the LGBT+ community at large in the context of the protected characteristic of sexual orientation.

As for discrimination based on perception, an individual will be subjected to direct perceptual discrimination where an employer erroneously believes that he/she possesses a protected characteristic and treats him/her less favourably than someone who does not have that characteristic. A good example is provided by the case of *English v Thomas Sanderson*.[130] Here, an employee was taunted by his work colleagues for being gay, when they knew full well that he was not gay. Although Mr English was not gay, it was held that he had suffered less favourable treatment on the basis of the protected ground of sexual orientation. As such, the EAT accepted that his claim of direct discrimination had been substantiated.

The first two leading cases on the test to be adopted in the case of a direct discrimination claim were decided by the House of Lords. In *Birmingham City Council v Equal Opportunities Commission*,[131] all of the Law Lords were in agreement that the employer had engaged in direct discrimination, but in *James v Eastleigh Borough Council*,[132] there was a 3:2 majority of the Law Lords in favour of finding the employer guilty of direct discrimination:

---

[125] Paragraph 59, available at http://www.legislation.gov.uk/ukpga/2010/15/notes/division/3/2/2/1 (last visited 5 December 2017). However, section 13(4) provides for one exception where the alleged victim must fall within the protected group and that is where the protected characteristic is marriage or civil partnership. Interestingly, since the decision of the ECJ in *Centrum voor Gelijkheid van Kansen en voor Racismebestrijding v NV Firma Ferijn* [2008] IRLR 732, European jurisprudence does not necessarily require a direct victim of direct discrimination and so a claim can be taken by the EHRC to launch a challenge to an employer's practices.

[126] [2015] IRLR 978.

[127] The nature or closeness of the association which is required between the claimant and the party possessing the protected characteristic is at present unclear. However, it is not entirely clear how the decision in *Abrams* can realistically be applied to the world of work, since it is doubtful whether a company claimant can qualify as an employee or an entity engaged on the basis of a contract personally to do work as defined in section 83(2) of the EA.

[128] *Lee v McArthur* [2017] IRLR 69.

[129] 'Public sides with bakery in gay cake row', available at https://yougov.co.uk/news/2014/11/08/public-sides-bakery-gay-cake-row/ (last visited 5 December 2017).

[130] [2009] IRLR 206. See also *Chief Constable of Norfolk v Coffey* ([2017] UKEAT 0260_16_1912, 19 December 2017).

[131] [1989] AC 1155.   [132] [1990] 2 AC 751.

■ *Birmingham City Council v Equal Opportunities Commission* [1989] AC 1155, 1194A–D

[The headnote to the case sets forth the facts as follows:] The council, the local education authority for Birmingham, had a statutory duty to provide secondary education in their area. In carrying out those duties, it provided selective secondary education in independent, single-sex grammar schools for some five per cent, of the children at the age of 11. Selection for those schools was based on examination results. Because, however, there were more grammar schools for boys than for girls in the area, more places were available for boy pupils, and, as a result, a girl pupil required higher marks in the entrance examination to gain a grammar school place than did a boy. In proceedings for judicial review, the Equal Opportunities Commission alleged that the council in carrying out its statutory duty was discriminating against girls within the meaning of [section 13 of the EA. The House of Lords held that the claim of direct discrimination had been established.]

Lord Goff:

There is discrimination under the statute if there is less favourable treatment on the ground of sex, in other words if the relevant girl or girls would have received the same treatment as the boys but for their sex. The intention or motive of the defendant to discriminate, though it may be relevant so far as remedies are concerned . . . is not a necessary condition of liability; it is perfectly possible to envisage cases where the defendant had no such motive, and yet did in fact discriminate on the ground of sex. Indeed, as Mr Lester pointed out in the course of his argument, if the council's submission were correct it would be a good defence for an employer to show that he discriminated against women not because he intended to do so but (for example) because of customer preference, or to save money, or even to avoid controversy. In the present case, whatever may have been the intention or motive of the council, nevertheless it is because of their sex that the girls in question receive less favourable treatment than the boys, and so are the subject of discrimination under the [EA].

■ *James v Eastleigh Borough Council* [1990] 2 AC 751, 772C–774

[The headnote to the case sets forth the facts as follows:] The plaintiff, who had retired, and his wife, both of whom were 61 years of age, went to a leisure centre run by the . . . council. The wife was admitted free of charge but the plaintiff had to pay an admission fee as the council only provided free admittance, inter alia, to people who had reached state pension age, which in the case of a man was 65 and in that of a woman 60. The plaintiff . . . alleged unlawful sex discrimination [and the House of Lords by a majority 3–2 (Lord Griffiths and Lord Lowry dissenting) held that he had suffered direct discrimination.]

Lord Goff:

. . . I do not read the words 'on the ground of sex' as necessarily referring only to the reason why the [employer] acted as he did, but as embracing cases in which a gender-based criterion is the basis upon which the [employee claimant] has been selected for the relevant treatment. Of course, there may be cases where the [employer's] reason for his action may bring the case within the subsection, as when the [employer] is motivated by an animus against persons of the [employee claimant's] sex, or otherwise selects the [employee claimant] for the relevant treatment because of his or her sex. But it does not follow that the words 'on the ground of sex' refer only to cases where the [employer's] reason for his action is the sex of the [employee claimant]; and, in my opinion, the application by the [employer] to the [employee claimant] of a gender-based criterion which favours the opposite sex is just as much a case of unfavourable treatment on the ground of sex. Such a conclusion seems to me to be consistent with the policy of the Act, which is the active pro-

> motion of equal treatment of men and women . . . Whether or not the treatment is less favourable in the relevant sense, i.e. on the ground of sex, may derive either from the application of a gender-based criterion to the [employee claimant], or from selection by the [employer] of the [employee claimant] because of his or her sex; but, in either event, it is not saved from constituting unlawful discrimination by the fact that the [employer] acted from a benign motive. However, in the majority of cases, I doubt if it is necessary to focus upon the intention or motive of the [employer] in this way. This is because, as I see it, cases of direct discrimination under section [13] can be considered by asking the simple question: would the [employee claimant] have received the same treatment from the [employer] but for his or her sex? This simple test possesses the double virtue that, on the one hand, it embraces both the case where the treatment derives from the application of a gender-based criterion, and the case where it derives from the selection of the [employee claimant] because of his or her sex; and on the other hand it avoids, in most cases at least, complicated questions relating to concepts such as intention, motive, reason or purpose, and the danger of confusion arising from the misuse of those elusive terms.

Two points emerge from these two decisions of the House of Lords.

(1) The House firmly scotched the idea that the employer's subjective motive or purpose in treating the employee in the way that it did was a relevant consideration. In promulgating such a rule, the courts were anxious to ensure that employers do not escape liability where they are guilty of covert, unintentional discrimination or unconscious racism, sexism, etc.[133] In an earlier case, Lord Justice Shaw in the Court of Appeal had held that direct discrimination entailed a measure of hostility on the part of the alleged discriminator towards persons having a particular protected characteristic.[134] However, the approach of the House of Lords in *Birmingham* and *James* effectively rendered such a requirement irrelevant.[135] Interestingly, the House of Lords' rejection of the notion that discrimination had to be conscious or intentional by and large coincided with the publication of a seminal article[136] which furnished strong psychological evidence for the proposition that the source of racism or sexism 'lay principally in unconsciously racist acts'.[137] The upshot of Lord Goff's formulation in *Birmingham* and *James* is that, where the employer's motive or purpose is entirely untainted by discrimination, it may nonetheless be held to have meted out direct discrimination to the claimant. This is the implication of the application of the 'but for' test, which is a particularly lax test for a claimant to satisfy.

(2) The House of Lords ruled that a 'but for' test ought to be applied in order to establish the necessary causal link between the less favourable treatment meted out to the claimant and the relevant protected characteristic. As noted by Lord Justice O'Neill in *King v The Great Britain-China Centre*,[138] the effect of the application of this test is that (a) a difference in the sex, race, etc. of the claimant and the comparator and (b) a difference in the treatment of the claimant and the comparator will be sufficient to

---

[133] See *Nagarajan v London Regional Transport* [2000] 1 AC 501, 511H–512E per Lord Nicholls; G. Mead, 'The Role of Intention in Direct Discrimination' (1990) 19 *Industrial Law Journal* 251.

[134] *Peake v Automotive Products Ltd* [1978] 1 QB 233, 240D; noting the formidable nature of such a requirement, see P. Wallington, 'Ladies First: How Mr Peake was Piqued' (1978) 37 *Cambridge Law Journal* 37.

[135] See M. Gelowitz, 'The Mental State for Direct Discrimination' (1989) 20 *Industrial Law Journal* 247, 248–9 for a useful taxonomy of intention and motive.

[136] See C. R. Lawrence III, 'The Id, the Ego, and Equal Protection: Reckoning with Unconscious Racism' (1987) 39 *Stanford Law Review* 317.

[137] R. A. Lenhardt, 'Understanding the Mark: Race, Stigma, and Equality in Context' (2004) 79 *New York University Law Review* 803, 808.   [138] [1992] ICR 516, 528H–529A.

found direct discrimination.[139] Although possessing the attraction of simplicity, there are compelling concerns associated with this somewhat mechanical approach. First, as noted by Lord Woolf in *Khan v Chief Constable of West Yorkshire*,[140] the application of the 'but for' test will often lead to the treatment of 'a person as [having] act[ed] unlawfully when he ha[s] not been motivated either consciously or unconsciously by any discriminatory motive[, which] is hardly likely to assist the objective of promoting harmonious racial relations'.[141] Secondly, the mechanics of the 'but for' approach call into question the purpose of the words 'because of' in section 13 of the EA which suggest that some account ought to be taken of the reason for the treatment. Accordingly, if the 'but for' test is applied, the words 'because of' seem to be simply otiose. The anxiety that the 'but for' test overstepped the mark in rendering the alleged discriminator's thought processes wholly insignificant is patent in Lord Griffiths' and Lord Lowry's dissenting opinions in *James*.[142] Indeed, in the subsequent cases of *Nagarajan v London Regional Transport*[143] and *Shamoon v RUC*,[144] Lord Nicholls adopted a more refined approach, enjoining a court or tribunal to avoid the 'but for' test and instead, with the 'reason why' test, enquire about why the employer acted in the way that it did:

■ *Nagarajan v London Regional Transport* [2000] 1 AC 501, 510H–511D

Lord Nicholls:

. . . in every case it is necessary to inquire why the [employee claimant] received less favourable treatment. This is the crucial question. Was it on grounds of race? Or was it for some other reason, for instance, because the [employee claimant] was not so well qualified for the job? Save in obvious cases, answering the crucial question will call for some consideration of the mental processes of the [employer]. Treatment, favourable or unfavourable, is a consequence which follows from a decision. Direct evidence of a decision to discriminate on racial grounds will seldom be forthcoming. Usually the grounds of the decision will have to be deduced, or inferred, from the surrounding circumstances. The crucial question just mentioned is to be distinguished sharply from a second and different question: if the [employer] treated the [employee claimant] less favourably on racial grounds, why did he do so? The latter question is strictly beside the point when deciding whether an act of racial discrimination occurred . . . Racial discrimination is not negatived by the [employer]'s motive or intention or reason or purpose (the words are interchangeable in this context) in treating another person less favourably on racial grounds. In particular, if the reason why the [employer] rejected the [employee claimant]'s job application was racial, it matters not that his intention may have been benign. For instance, he may have believed that the applicant would not fit in, or that other employees might make the applicant's life a misery. If racial grounds were the reason for the less favourable treatment, direct discrimination . . . is established.

■ *Shamoon v RUC* [2003] ICR 337, 341B–342C

Lord Nicholls:

When the claim is based on direct discrimination . . . in practice tribunals in their decisions normally consider, first, whether the [employee] claimant received less favourable treatment than the

---

[139] See G. Mead, 'Proof of Direct Discrimination' (1992) 21 *Industrial Law Journal* 217, 218 and the extremely useful illustration of the distinction between the 'but for' and 'reason why' tests in B. Watt, 'Goodbye "But-for", Hello "But-Why"?' (1998) 27 *Industrial Law Journal* 121.
[140] [2000] ICR 1169.
[141] *Khan v Chief Constable of West Yorkshire* [2000] ICR 1169, 1174C per Lord Woolf MR.
[142] *James v Eastleigh Borough Council* [1990] 2 AC 751, 768.
[143] [2000] 1 AC 501.   [144] [2003] ICR 337.

appropriate comparator (the 'less favourable treatment' issue) and then, secondly, whether the less favourable treatment was on the relevant proscribed ground (the 'reason why' issue). Tribunals proceed to consider the reason why issue only if the less favourable treatment issue is resolved in favour of the [employee] claimant. Thus the less favourable treatment issue is treated as a threshold which the [employee] claimant must cross before the tribunal is called upon to decide why the [employee] claimant was afforded the treatment of which she is complaining. No doubt there are cases where it is convenient and helpful to adopt this two step approach to what is essentially a single question: did the [employee] claimant, on the proscribed ground, receive less favourable treatment than others? But, especially where the identity of the relevant comparator is a matter of dispute, this sequential analysis may give rise to needless problems. Sometimes the less favourable treatment issue cannot be resolved without, at the same time, deciding the reason why issue. The two issues are intertwined . . . the less favourable treatment issue is incapable of being decided without deciding the reason why issue. And the decision on the reason why issue will also provide the answer to the less favourable treatment issue. This analysis seems to me to point to the conclusion that employment tribunals may sometimes be able to avoid arid and confusing disputes about the identification of the appropriate comparator by concentrating primarily on why the [employee] claimant was treated as she was. Was it on the proscribed ground which is the foundation of the application? That will call for an examination of all the facts of the case. Or was it for some other reason? If the latter, the application fails. If the former, there will be usually be [*sic*] no difficulty in deciding whether the treatment, afforded to the [employee] claimant on the proscribed ground, was less favourable than was or would have been afforded to others.

Lord Nicholls' 'reason why' test forges a division between (1) the reason or ground for the treatment and (2) the employer's motive for the treatment.[145] The latter is drenched in subjectivity, and although it may be wholly benign, it is always an irrelevant consideration. However, the former—which may be tainted by discrimination when assessed by the tribunal in light of all of the evidence—is always relevant. In this way, the concept of direct discrimination continues to be effectual in addressing covert, unconscious, or unintentional discrimination and stereotypical assumptions about the working potential of individuals falling within one of the protected groups,[146] whilst at the same time not suffering from the accusation that the words 'because of' in section 13 of the EA are rendered obsolete.

However, subsequent to *Nagarajan* and *Shamoon*, two uncertainties abounded. First, Lord Nicholls had not expressly cast doubt on the 'but for' test or *Birmingham* and *James* in *Nagarajan* or *Shamoon*, so the status and continuing relevance of the 'but for' test was examined by scholars[147] who debated whether or not Lord Nicholls' approach amounted to a judicial restatement of the approach to causation in direct discrimination. Secondly, it was not entirely clear how to draw the distinction between (1) the reason or ground for the treatment and (2) the employer's motive for the treatment. If it was indeed clear that evidence of improper motive or intention was not required, what was not entirely clear was what *was* required for these purposes over and above the simple equation of (1) a difference in sex, race, etc. and (2) a difference in treatment. In *R (E) v Governing Body of JFS*,[148] in a 5:4 majority judgment, the Supreme Court adopted the

---

[145] See *Reynolds v CLFIS UK Ltd* [2015] ICR 1010.

[146] Precluding employers from adopting stereotypical assumptions is one of the policies underpinning the concept of direct discrimination: *R (on the application of European Roma Rights Centre) v Immigration Officer at Prague Airport* [2005] IRLR 115; *Aylott v Stockton on Tees Borough Council* [2010] IRLR 994.

[147] See B. Watt, 'Goodbye 'But-for', Hello 'But-Why'?' (1998) 27 *Industrial Law Journal* 121; L. Barmes, 'Promoting Diversity and the Definition of Direct Discrimination' (2003) 32 *Industrial Law Journal* 200, 204–8.

[148] See also the approach of Underhill J in *Amnesty International v Ahmed* [2009] ICR 1450.

partition between the reason for the treatment and the employer's subjective motive or purpose and ruled that the former could be identified on the basis of an *objective* evaluation of all of the facts of the case:

■ *R (E) v Governing Body of JFS* [2009] UKSC 15, [2010] 2 AC 728, 745H–789G

[The headnote to the case sets forth the facts as follows:] The claimant, who was Jewish by birth, wished to send his son to an oversubscribed voluntary aided Jewish school. Under its oversubscription policy, the school gave priority to children who were recognised as Jewish according to the Office of the Chief Rabbi ('the OCR'), such recognition being based on matrilineal descent or conversion in accordance with the tenets of Orthodox Judaism. The school did not make any requirement of practice of the Jewish faith. The child's mother had been converted according to non-Orthodox Judaism, whose conversions were not recognised by the OCR. Applying the oversubscription policy, the school's governing body refused the child a place. The claimant sought judicial review of the decision of the school's governing body and the decision of the school's appeal panel upholding it, claiming, inter alia, that, since the definition of who was a Jew, whether by descent or conversion, was a question of ethnicity, the refusal to admit his son because his mother was not Jewish according to the OCR was unlawful in that it constituted . . . direct discrimination on racial grounds, contrary to section [13 of the EA] . . . [In a 5–4 majority judgment (Lords Hope, Rodger, Walker and Brown delivering minority judgments), the Supreme Court held that the school had treated the child in a directly discriminatory manner.]

Lord Phillips:

In the phrase 'grounds for discrimination', the word 'ground' is ambiguous. It can mean the motive for taking the decision or the factual criteria applied by the [employer] in reaching his decision. In the context of [section 13 of the EA] 'grounds' has the latter meaning. In deciding what were the grounds for discrimination it is necessary to address simply the question of the factual criteria that determined the decision made by the [employer]. This approach has been well established by high authority . . . The difference between the motive for discrimination and the factual criteria applied by the [employer] as the test for discrimination lay at the heart of the division between the majority and the minority of the House of Lords in *James v Eastleigh Borough Council* [1990] 2 AC 751 . . . Th[e] 'but for' test [in *James*] was another way of identifying the factual criterion that was applied by the council as the basis for their discrimination, but it is not one that I find helpful. It is better simply to ask what were the facts that the [employer] considered to be determinative when making the relevant decision . . . Whether there has been discrimination on the ground of sex or race depends upon whether sex or race was the criterion applied as the basis for discrimination. The motive for discriminating according to that criterion is not relevant . . . The observations of Lord Nicholls of Birkenhead in *Nagarajan v London Regional Transport* [2000] 1 AC 501 and *Chief Constable of West Yorkshire Police v Khan* [2001] 1 WLR 1947 . . . throw no doubt on these principles. Those observations address the situation where the factual criteria which influenced the [employer] to act as he did are not plain. In those circumstances it is necessary to explore the mental processes of the [employer] in order to discover what facts led him to discriminate. This can be illustrated by a simple example. A fat black man goes into a shop to make a purchase. The shopkeeper says 'I do not serve people like you'. To appraise his conduct it is necessary to know what was the fact that determined his refusal. Was it the fact that the man was fat or the fact that he was black? In the former case the ground of his refusal was not racial; in the latter it was. The reason why the particular fact triggered his reaction is not relevant to the question of the ground upon which he discriminated. In the *Nagarajan* case [2000] 1 AC 501, Lord Nicholls approved the reasoning in both the *Birmingham* case [1989] AC 1155 and the *James* case [1990] 2 AC 751. At p 511, he identified two separate questions. The first was the question of the factual basis of the discrimination. Was it because of race or was it because of lack of qualification? He then pointed out that there was a second and different question. If the [employer] discriminated on the ground of race, what was his motive for so doing? That question was irrelevant. When, at para 29 in the *Khan* case [2001] 1 WLR 1947, Lord Nicholls spoke of a 'subjective test' he was speaking of the exercise of determining the facts that operated on the mind of the [employer], not his motive for discriminating. The subjective test, described by Lord Nicholls, is only necessary as a seminal step where there is doubt as to the factual criteria that have caused the [employer] to discriminate. There is no need for that step in this case, for the factual criteria that governed the refusal to admit to JFS are clear . . .

Baroness Hale:

[In *Nagarajan*,] Lord Nicholls . . . pointed out that there are in truth two different sorts of 'why' question, one relevant and one irrelevant. The irrelevant one is the [employer]'s motive, intention, reason or purpose. The relevant one is what caused him to act as he did. In some cases, this is absolutely plain . . . The distinction between the two types of 'why' question is plain enough: one is what caused the treatment in question and one is its motive or purpose. The former is important and the latter is not. There are obvious cases, where there is no dispute at all about why the [employee claimant] received the less favourable treatment. The criterion applied was not in doubt. If it was based on a prohibited ground, that is the end of the matter. There are other cases in which the ostensible criterion is something else—usually, in job applications, that elusive quality known as 'merit'. But nevertheless the [employer] may consciously or unconsciously be making his selections on the basis of race or sex. He may not realise that he is doing so, but that is what he is in fact doing . . . There is absolutely no doubt about why the school acted as it did. We do not have to ask whether they were consciously or unconsciously treating some people who saw themselves as Jewish less favourably than others. Everything was totally conscious and totally transparent. M was rejected because he was not considered to be Jewish according to the criteria adopted by the [OCR]. We do not need to look into the mind of the [OCR] to know why he acted as he did. If the criterion he adopted was, as in the *Birmingham* case [1989] AC 1155 or the *James* case [1990] 2 AC 751, in reality ethnicity based, it matters not whether he was adopting it because of a sincerely held religious belief. No one doubts that he is honestly and sincerely trying to do what he believes that his religion demands of him. But that is his motive for applying the criterion which he applies and that is irrelevant. The question is whether his criterion is ethnically based . . .

Lord Mance:

Direct discrimination can arise in one of two ways: because a decision or action was taken on a ground which was, however worthy or benign the motive, inherently racial within the meaning of section [13 of the EA], or because it was taken or undertaken for a reason which was subjectively racial . . . The allegation in the present case is that a decision or action was taken on inherently ethnic grounds within section [13 of the EA], although the school's subjective motivation was its purely religious convictions. I appreciate that even the first part of this allegation involves what may be described as a subjective element—a 'question of fact' in Lord Nicholls's words in *Chief Constable of West Yorkshire Police v Khan* [2001] 1 WLR 1947, para 29—in so far as it requires an answer to the question: why in fact was [the child] refused a place? But there is here no room for doubt about the answer. He was refused a place by reason of the application of the admissions policy . . . With that answer, the next, relevant question is simply whether that policy, religiously motivated as it was, involved grounds for admission or refusal of admission which were in their nature inherently ethnic . . . the Court of Appeal in my view reached the correct conclusion, when it held that as a matter of law the admissions policy followed by JFS was inherently discriminatory, contrary to [the legislation], although the policy was adopted by the school for the most benign, religious motives . . .

Lord Clarke:

I agree with Lord Mance JSC that there are two ways in which direct discrimination can be established. The first is where, whatever the motive and whatever the state of mind of the [employer], the decision or action was taken on a ground that was inherently racial and the second is where the decision or action was taken on a ground that was subjectively racial. Until now this distinction has not perhaps been as clearly identified in the authorities as it should be . . . If, viewed objectively, the [employer] discriminated against the [employee] claimant on racial grounds the reason why he did so is irrelevant. Thus in the *Birmingham* and *James* cases the sex discrimination was objectively plain from the criteria adopted. Once that was established, the state of mind of the [employer] was, as Lord Nicholls put it, strictly beside the point. That, as I see it, is this case. This is a plain or obvious case of the kind Lord Nicholls had in mind because the position is clear from the OCR's criteria. When he said in the first of the italicised passages that, save in obvious cases, answering the crucial question will call for some consideration of the mental processes of the [employer], he had in mind, not this kind of case, which he would have regarded as obvious, but the kind of case he had just mentioned—namely where the [employee] claimant was discriminated against but it was not clear whether that was because of unlawful discrimination on the ground of, say, race or sex, or for some other reason, for instance, because the [employee claimant] was not so well qualified for the job. This is not such a case . . . [As such,] at the initial stage, when the question is whether or not the discrimination was on racial grounds, the [employer]'s motivation may not only be relevant but also necessary, in order to reach an informed decision as to whether or not this was a case of racial discrimination. However, I emphasize the word *may* because, for the reasons I have already given, the [employer]'s motivation or subjective reasoning is not in my opinion relevant in every case. The authorities . . . show that it is not relevant where the criteria adopted or (in Lord Ackner's words) the formula used are or is inherently discriminatory on ethnic grounds. Lord Nicholls has however shown that it is relevant in other cases where, without investigating the state of mind of the [employer], it is not possible to say whether the discrimination was on ethnic grounds or not.

The case extracts in this section stipulate that where an employer adopts, for example, a gender or race-based, criterion, rather than a gender or race-neutral criterion, then, in the words of Lords Mance and Clarke, the employer's decision or action will be *inherently discriminatory*. Alternatively, as Lord Phillips states, the factual criterion or criteria which influenced the employer to act in the way that it did will be inherently discriminatory in such a case. As noted by Lord Clarke, this is an example of a '*plain or obvious case*'[149] of direct discrimination and has since been referred to as a 'criterion' case.[150] Another example of such a 'criterion' case is provided by the facts of the case of *Bull v Hall*,[151] where an hotelier applied a criterion whereby couples would only be admitted to a double room if they were married. Lady Hale in the Supreme Court held that this criterion was inherently based on, or linked to, an individual's sexual orientation and so two homosexuals were held to have been directly discriminated against when they were refused a double room. *Bull* can be contrasted with the situation where the treatment is predicated on a gender-neutral, race-neutral, disability-neutral, etc. criterion, e.g. where it is ostensibly merit-based. In such circumstances, it is *incumbent on the tribunal or court to identify the factual criterion or criteria applied by the employer in arriving at its decision on an objective basis*: this is referred to as a 'reason why' case.[152] This may reveal that the reason for the treatment was based on gender, race, disability, etc., or it may show the opposite, as the case may be. If it demonstrates the former, direct discrimination will be established. Ultimately, the Supreme Court's approach continues to prevent the employer from leading a defence based on a benign motive.

---

[149] *R (E) v Governing Body of JFS* [2009] UKSC 15, [2010] 2 AC 728, 788H per Lord Clarke.
[150] See *Interserve FM Ltd v Tuleikyte* [2017] IRLR 615, 617–18 per Simler J.
[151] [2013] UKSC 73, [2013] 1 WLR 3741.
[152] See *Interserve FM Ltd v Tuleikyte* [2017] IRLR 615, 618 per Simler J.

Post-*JFS*, there are two issues which deserve our attention, as follows:

(1) There may be a mixture of reasons or grounds for the treatment. In such a case, the question is how the tribunals and courts should approach the 'reason why' test. In *Nagarajan*, Lord Nicholls took the view that the relevant approach here was to ask whether a protected characteristic had had a 'significant influence on the outcome'.[153] This has been refined since by Gibson LJ in *Igen Ltd v Wong*, where he stated that the employer will only avoid liability if 'the treatment was in no sense whatsoever' on the protected ground.[154]

(2) As for the status of the 'but for' test post-*JFS*, the position is somewhat confused. Lord Phillips' judgment in *JFS* was plain to the effect that no assistance was to be derived from it. This can be contrasted with Baroness Hale and Lord Clarke who both referred to the 'but for' test, falling short of expressly endorsing its continued application. Connolly has argued that the 'but for' test ought to be abandoned in light of *JFS* on the basis that the 'failure [of the Supreme Court] to show when it should be used did little to recommend it as the template for tribunals'.[155] Indeed, rather than adopt the shorthand of the 'but for' approach, it may well be that tribunals would be best advised to focus on the dichotomy between 'inherently discriminatory' and 'less plain or obvious' cases where the factual criteria which led the employer to treat the employee in the way that it did are unclear.

The reason it is crucial to identify whether the treatment of the employee is based on a protected characteristic or not is that there is a major fault-line between the concepts of direct and indirect discrimination: the former can never be justified,[156] but the employer can objectively justify the latter by convincing a tribunal that it required to apply an indirectly discriminatory provision, criterion, or practice in order to achieve a legitimate aim. The effect of the Supreme Court's decision in *JFS* that the school's admissions policy was directly discriminatory meant that there was no scope for the school to lodge a justificatory defence. The absence of a justification defence intrinsic to the statutory concept of direct discrimination has been a matter of some debate, with commentators such as Bowers, Moran, and Honeyball[157] arguing that its introduction would avoid much of the difficulty experienced by the higher courts in forging a suitable model for the operation of the direct discrimination concept. If an employer could mount a defence to both direct and indirect discrimination claims, the distinguishing criteria between the two statutory constructs would be less important. However, Gill and Monaghan[158] are less convinced. Their principal concern is that, with a justification defence, employers would be able to escape liability by leading defences for discriminatory treatment based on cost and the

---

[153] *Nagarajan v London Regional Transport* [2000] 1 AC 501, 513B per Lord Nicholls.

[154] *Igen Ltd and others v Wong* [2005] ICR 931, 956, para 11 of the Annex.

[155] M. Connolly, 'Racial Groups, Sub-Groups, the Demise of the *But for* Test and the Death of the Benign Motive Defence: *R (on the application of E) v Governing Body of JFS*' (2010) 39 *Industrial Law Journal* 183, 190; for a critique of the decision in *JFS*, see J. M. Finnis, 'Directly Discriminatory Decisions: A Missed Opportunity' (2010) 126 *Law Quarterly Review* 491.

[156] See *Moyhing v Barts and London NHS Trust* [2006] IRLR 860. Where the employer is a natural person, it is no defence for the employer to show that he/she has the same protected characteristic as the claimant: section 24 of the EA. Of course, once direct discrimination has been proven, it is possible for the employer to mount a defence on the ground that it had a genuine occupational requirement for someone to fill a particular role or for treating the claimant less favourably in terms of section 83 of, and Schedule 9 to, the EA. This is a statutorily prescribed exception to the principle of equality.

[157] See J. Bowers and A. Moran, 'Justification in Direct Sex Discrimination Law: Breaking the Taboo' (2002) 31 *Industrial Law Journal* 307; J. Bowers, A. Moran, and S. Honeyball, 'Justification in Direct Sex Discrimination Law: A Reply' (2003) 32 *Industrial Law Journal* 185.

[158] T. Gill and K. Monaghan, 'Justification in Direct Sex Discrimination Law: Taboo Upheld' (2003) 32 *Industrial Law Journal* 115.

protection of their financial interests. Moreover, it is likely that the courts would be less reluctant to uphold an employer's justification where there is clearly no conscious or intentional basis for its actions, thus opening up the scope for stereotypical assumptions about persons possessing the protected characteristics to be left unchallenged. Nevertheless, whatever the merits and demerits of this debate, there is the inescapable truth that the Race, Framework, and Recast Equality Directives preclude the UK from amending section 13 of the EA to enable employers to justify direct discrimination. Therefore, unless Brexit is grasped as an opportunity to adopt an altogether fresh approach and break with EU law in this regard, the domestic tribunals, courts, employers, and employees will have to continue to reject any attempts to justify direct discrimination claims.

10.2.4 **Indirect discrimination**

Earlier, in section 10.1.2, we noted how indirect discrimination is a regulatory device designed to achieve a form of substantive equality known as 'equality of results'. In many ways, it is treated as an inferior concept to direct discrimination insofar as it can be justified but the latter cannot.[159] Rather than assess whether the treatment of the claimant was inconsistent with the treatment of a person not falling within the same protected group as the claimant, indirect discrimination seeks to achieve another objective. It is designed to address circumstances where the treatment of the claimant and the comparator is the same and ostensibly neutral (e.g. merit-based), or the criteria or practice adopted is the same for everyone and neutral, but the outcome of the treatment or the application of the criteria or practice is that a disproportionately adverse impact is suffered by the claimant and the protected group to which he/she belongs.[160] Thus, the target of the concept of indirect discrimination is *group and individual discrimination*. This distinction between direct and indirect discrimination is captured by Baroness Hale in the following judicial statement:

■ *R (E) v Governing Body of JFS* [2009] UKSC 15, [2010] 2 AC 728, 757B–C

Baroness Hale:

The basic difference between direct and indirect discrimination is plain ... The rule against direct discrimination aims to achieve formal equality of treatment: there must be no less favourable treatment between otherwise similarly situated people on grounds of colour, race, nationality or ethnic or national origins. Indirect discrimination looks beyond formal equality towards a more substantive equality of results: criteria which appear neutral on their face may have a disproportionately adverse impact upon people of a particular colour, race, nationality or ethnic or national origins.

There are two major, interlinked consequences of the ruling in *JFS* that the motive, intention, and purpose of the employer are irrelevant. The first is that both direct and indirect discrimination function to address covert, as well as overt, discrimination and the second is that the criteria distinguishing between those concepts is somewhat obscure for a number of reasons.[161] With regard to the latter point in particular, the charge is that the real issue in *James* concerned the application of a *criterion*, namely 'pensionable age', rather

---

[159] See the discussion in O. Doyle, 'Direct Discrimination, Indirect Discrimination and Autonomy' (2007) 27 *Oxford Journal of Legal Studies* 537.

[160] *Mcfarlane v Relate Avon Ltd* [2010] IRLR 872, 876 per Laws LJ.

[161] See section 10.2.4.5 and S. Forshaw and M. Pilgerstorfer, 'Direct and Indirect Discrimination: Is There Something in Between?' (2008) 37 *Industrial Law Journal* 347; N. Cunningham, 'Indirect Discrimination: Between the Wheat and the Chaff' (2009) 38 *Industrial Law Journal* 209.

than the *treatment* of the claimant, and so it ought to have been properly characterized as a case of indirect discrimination.[162] The same point applies in the context of the *JFS* case, where the school's admissions policy entailed the application of the OCR's criteria for the identification of Orthodox Judaism.[163] Nonetheless, despite the argument that the words 'treatment', 'criterion', and 'grounds' have been conflated by the judgments in *James* and *JFS*, it is clear that if 'pensionable age' in *James* and the OCR's criteria for orthodox Judaism in *JFS* are applied by an employer, these will be deemed to be inherently gender-based and ethnicity-based, rather than gender-neutral or ethnicity-neutral criteria. For that reason, they will be addressed by the concept of direct discrimination on the basis that their application amounts to less favourable *treatment*. Meanwhile, where the criteria invoked by the employer are merit-based and wholly gender-neutral, race-neutral, etc., whether the employer is liable or not will be addressed by the regulatory construct of indirect discrimination. The fundamental point to take from this discussion is that, despite their similarities and effects, the concepts are 'mutually exclusive [and y]ou cannot have both at once'.[164]

The statutory formula for indirect discrimination involves four elements, each of which can be thought of as a separate stage (as illustrated in Figure 10.2):

Section 19 Indirect discrimination

(1) A person (A) discriminates against another (B) if A applies to B a provision, criterion or practice which is discriminatory in relation to a relevant protected characteristic of B's.

(2) For the purposes of subsection (1), a provision, criterion or practice is discriminatory in relation to a relevant protected characteristic of B's if—

    (a) A applies, or would apply, it to persons with whom B does not share the characteristic,

    (b) it puts, or would put, persons with whom B shares the characteristic at a particular disadvantage when compared with persons with whom B does not share it,

    (c) it puts, or would put, B at that disadvantage, and

    (d) A cannot show it to be a proportionate means of achieving a legitimate aim.

(3) The relevant protected characteristics are—

    age;

    disability;

    gender reassignment;

    marriage and civil partnership;

    race;

    religion or belief;

    sex;

    sexual orientation.[165]

---

[162] See the arguments of counsel for Eastleigh in *James v Eastleigh Borough Council* [1990] 2 AC 751, 759D.

[163] See *ibid.*, 768 per Lord Lowry; J. Finnis, 'Directly Discriminatory Decisions: A Missed Opportunity' (2010) 126 *Law Quarterly Review* 491.

[164] *R (E) v Governing Body of JFS* [2009] UKSC 15, [2010] 2 AC 728, 757C per Baroness Hale. See G. Mead, 'The Role of Intention in Direct Discrimination' (1990) 19 *Industrial Law Journal* 251. For discussion, see section 10.2.4.5.

[165] See Article 2(1) and (2)(b) of the Race Directive; Article 2(1) and (2)(b)(i) of the Framework Directive; and Article 2(1)(b) of the Recast Equality Directive for the European provisions which are very similar to section 19 of the EA.

We now turn to a consideration of each of these four factors.

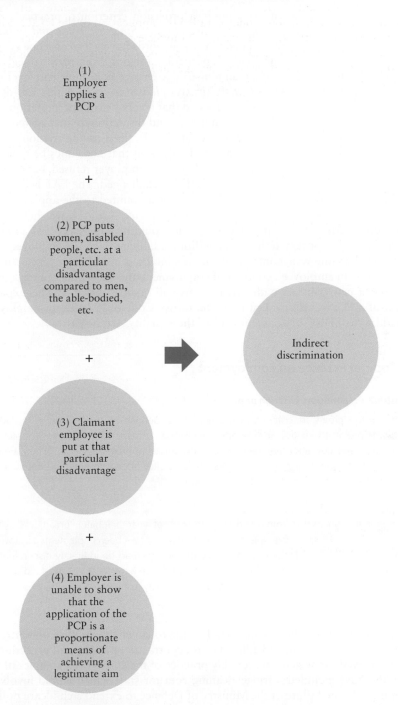

Figure 10.2 *The stages involved in an indirect discrimination claim*

10.2.4.1 Provision, criterion, or practice: section 19(1) and (2)(a) of the EA

The first element to consider is what is meant by a 'provision, criterion, or practice' ('PCP'), for this must be applied by the employer. In *Secretary of State for Trade and Industry v Rutherford (No. 2)*,[166] Lord Walker stated that these words have a 'broad scope . . . [that] may be formal and general or informal and particular, ranging from national legislation applicable to all employment . . . to an administrative change in a single employer's shift system'. The decision of the EAT in *British Airways plc v Starmer*,[167] which was decided prior to the introduction of the EA, also suggested that a very broad interpretation would be applied. In *Starmer*, it was held that a unilateral and discretionary management decision which was *applied to the claimant only* could be classified as a 'provision'. Here, a female pilot returning from maternity leave had requested that her duties be reduced to 50 per cent of her pre-maternity full-time workload. The employer refused, but offered to reduce her hours by 75 per cent, which the employee challenged. The EAT held that the managerial decision to limit the hours to 75 per cent amounted to the application of a 'provision'. Likewise, in *Edie v HCL Insurance BPO Services Ltd*,[168] it was held that the varied contractual terms of an employment contract could be a PCP, as could a managerial requirement to accept new terms and conditions, failing which the employee would be dismissed. In the same vein, contractual changes imposed by an employer pursuant to the termination of an employee's contract of employment and subsequent re-engagement on the basis of a new contract with varied terms will qualify as a PCP. This expansive construction of a PCP is also evident in the Statutory Code of Practice on Employment promulgated by the EHRC under section 14 of the Equality Act 2006:[169]

■ EHRC Code of Practice on Employment

What constitutes a provision, criterion or practice?

4.5 . . . The phrase 'provision, criterion or practice' is not defined by the [EA] but it should be construed widely so as to include, for example, any formal or informal policies, rules, practices, arrangements, criteria, conditions, prerequisites, qualifications or provisions. A [PCP] may also include decisions to do something in the future—such as a policy or criterion that has not yet been applied—as well as a 'one-off' or discretionary decision.

Example:

A factory owner announces that from next month staff cannot wear their hair in dreadlocks, even if the locks are tied back. This is an example of a policy that has not yet been implemented but which still amounts to a [PCP]. The decision to introduce the policy could be indirectly discriminatory because of religion or belief, as it puts the employer's Rastafarian workers at a particular disadvantage. The employer must show that the [PCP] can be objectively justified.

This conceptualization of a PCP is sufficiently wide to cover the exercise of contractual powers and the application of, and adherence to, contractual policies and procedures by the employer, as well as the general everyday practice of the employer. Examples of PCPs in the case law have included a fridge-cleaning rota for staff which would involve the handling of meat,[170] the failure of the Ministry of Defence to extend a childcare policy to

---

[166] [2006] UKHL 19, [2006] ICR 785, 798B.   [167] [2005] IRLR 862.
[168] [2015] ICR 713.
[169] See https://www.equalityhumanrights.com/sites/default/files/employercode.pdf (last visited 5 December 2017).
[170] *Chatwal v Wandsworth Borough Council* [2011] Eq LR 924.

members of the armed forces from outside the UK,[171] and a school's uniform policy that restricted the amount of jewellery schoolchildren could wear.[172]

10.2.4.2 Group disadvantage: section 19(2)(b) of the EA

Lord Justice Sedley asserted in *Eweida v British Airways plc*[173] that the purpose of the concept of indirect discrimination 'is to deal with the discriminatory impact [upon a group] of facially neutral requirements'.[174] It is intrinsic to the concept that the protected group of which the claimant forms part must be able to point to a particular disadvantage which that group has suffered or would suffer as a result of the application or proposed application of a facially neutral PCP in comparison with a group of workers without the protected characteristic. However, there is one situation where there is no requirement for the claimant to establish group disadvantage. This exception applies in the case of the protected characteristic of religion or belief. The effect of the decision of the European Court of Human Rights ('ECtHR') in *Eweida v UK*[175] is that the terms of section 19(2)(b) enjoining the claimant to show group disadvantage require to be read down in a manner which is compatible with the ECtHR's approach to Article 9 of the European Convention on Human Rights ('ECHR'). So long as the claimant's manifestation of his/her religious belief is 'intimately linked'[176] to the religion in question, it is not incumbent on him/her to establish that that particular manifestation is a 'duty mandated by the religion in question'.[177] As such, in *Eweida*, the claimant came within the protection of Article 9 of the ECHR notwithstanding that her insistence on wearing a cross visibly over her uniform was not a doctrinal requirement or central component of the Christian religion, i.e. despite the fact that she was unable to point to an identifiable section of Christian members with the same religious belief that a crucifix should be worn visibly.[178] The upshot of *Eweida* is that if a claimant alleging indirect discrimination on the basis of his/her religious belief satisfies the terms of section 19(1) and (2)(c) of the EA (i.e. the application of a PCP and that he/she has been personally disadvantaged as a result of manifesting his/her religious belief), the onus will immediately shift to the employer to objectively justify its conduct under section 19(2)(d) of the EA.

The decision of the Court of Appeal in *Mba v Mayor and Burgesses of the London Borough of Merton*[179] furnishes an example of the approach sanctioned by *Eweida*. Here, the Court of Appeal held that the claimant's religious belief that Sunday should be a day of rest was 'not a core component of the Christian religion'. Hence, the claimant did not need to show that there was an identifiable group of Christians who believed that this particular belief was a central tenet of the Christian religion and that no group comparison was required in order to show a particular disadvantage suffered by the group. Of course, this would appear to conflict with the wording of section 19(2)(b) which does

---

[171] *Ministry of Defence v DeBique* [2010] IRLR 471.

[172] *R (on the application of Watkins-Singh) v Aberdare Girls' High School Governors* [2008] EWHC 1865 (Admin).   [173] [2010] ICR 890.

[174] *ibid.*, 895D per Sedley LJ.   [175] [2013] IRLR 231.   [176] *ibid.*, 245.

[177] *ibid.*, 245.

[178] The effect of this decision is that an employee claimant will be relieved of the duty to show group disadvantage under section 19(2)(b) of the EA where a practice he/she adopts is a personal religious choice not dictated by official religious dogma or a widespread practice amongst followers of a particular faith, i.e. he/she is a 'solitary believer'. This protects employees who follow a particular religion where (1) no authoritative central authority exists for the articulation of the official beliefs of the faith (such as the Vatican in the case of the Catholic Church) and (2) there is no intra-faith consensus on the nature of the practices imposed by a particular religion, on which, see N. Hatzis, 'Personal Religious Beliefs in the Workplace: How Not to Define Indirect Discrimination' (2011) 74 *Modern Law Review* 287, 292. See also *Mba v Mayor and Burgesses of the London Borough of Merton* [2014] IRLR 145.

[179] [2014] 1 WLR 1501.

demand a group comparison exercise, but this provision was, to all intents and purposes, essentially read down by the Court of Appeal so that it was compatible with the ECtHR's interpretation of Article 9 of the ECHR in *Eweida*.[180]

If we now leave aside this exception to the group comparison exercise which is applicable in the case of the protected characteristic of religion or belief, we turn to consider the validity of an associative indirect discrimination claim. Whilst section 19 of the EA precludes an associative indirect discrimination claim on the basis that its wording clearly requires the claimant to possess the protected characteristic, the decision of the CJEU in *CHEZ Razpredelenie Bulgaria AD v Komisia za zashtita ot diskriminatsias*[181] has arguably set the cat amongst the pigeons. In *CHEZ*, a Bulgarian lady claimed associative indirect discrimination on the basis that a local authority's practice of installing electricity meters at a height of 6 metres in the homes of its residents placed members of the Roma group at a particular disadvantage. Although the claimant was not of Roma origin, she claimed that she had suffered a particular disadvantage as a result of the practice. In a landmark decision, the CJEU held that the claimant was entitled to raise an associative indirect discrimination claim on the grounds of the ethnic origin of the Roma, notwithstanding that she had no connection or association with the Roma group. The decision was based on the wording of the European Race Directive[182] which does not require the claimant to possess the protected characteristic in an indirect race discrimination claim. This decision may mean that the domestic provisions in section 19(2)(b) may need to be read down in a way which is compatible with EU law embodied in *CHEZ*, failing which they are interpreted to be in violation of EU law and will need to be reformed.

Once the claimant has established that he/she forms part of a protected group,[183] the mechanism adopted in order to ascertain whether the protected group has suffered a particular disadvantage in comparison with a comparator group not possessing the protected characteristic is to select a representative pool of workers to whom the PCP was applied. This is known as the 'pool for comparison' and involves a comparison exercise between workers with the protected characteristic and those without it.[184] In deciding who is included within the pool for comparison, section 23 of the EA directs that there must be no material difference between the circumstances relating to each case. For example, in an age discrimination claim, this will mean that a court or tribunal will not be permitted to consider differences between the claimant and a comparator that relate to age.[185] Moreover, employees or persons at large to whom the PCP was not applied should not be included within the pool.[186]

The direction in section 23 of the EA that there should be no material differences between the circumstances relating to the claimant and the comparator can often involve

---

[180] However, Elias LJ was less convinced that it was possible to read down the section 19 test of indirect discrimination so that it was compatible with Article 9 of the ECHR: *Mba v Mayor and Burgesses of the London Borough of Merton* [2014] 1 WLR 1501, 1513G.

[181] [2015] IRLR 746. For discussion, see M. Malone, 'The Concept of Indirect Discrimination by Association: Too Late for the UK?' (2017) 46 *Industrial Law Journal* 144.

[182] Directive 2000/43/EC (OJ 2000 L180/22).

[183] Of course, this statement is subject to what has been discussed in the context of religious indirect discrimination claims in the context of the *Eweida* and *Mba* decisions, and the position in an associative indirect discrimination claim as per *CHEZ*.

[184] See paras 4.21–4.22 of the EHRC's Code of Practice.

[185] For example, the fact that the claimant was younger than the comparator and, as such, was less likely to have a mortgage and family ties, or that she would be likely to recover from a redundancy situation much quicker than the older comparator: *Lockwood v Department of Work and Pensions* [2013] IRLR 941. However, cf. *Smith v Department for Business and Skills* (UKEAT/0308/12/RN, 23 January 2014).

[186] *Briggs v North Eastern Education and Library Board* [1990] IRLR 181.

the making of difficult choices. For example, in *Naeem v Secretary of State for Justice*[187] the claimant complained of indirect religious discrimination attributable to the existence of a greater number of Christian chaplains than Muslim chaplains employed by the Prison Service on higher pay scales owing to the disparate treatment in access to prisoners between the two prior to 2002. Here, there were two potential comparator groups: all Christian prison chaplains irrespective of when they joined the Prison Service; or only those Christian prison chaplains employed since 2002, when parity of treatment of Christian and Muslim chaplains in respect of access to prisoners was initiated. It was held that, since section 23 requires no material difference between the claimant and the comparator, the latter option ought to be preferred. This rendered it more difficult for the claimant to succeed in his case since it arguably factored the circumstances of the claimant and the comparators into the comparison exercise.

The pool will normally comprise the aggregate of the workers advantaged and disadvantaged[188] by the adoption of the PCP.[189] Consider the following hypothetical, which describes how courts and tribunals assess whether there has been a 'group particular disadvantage'.

Hypothetical C

William Crawthorn, Michael Williams, and Henrietta Hogan are disabled secretaries employed by Danny's Demolishers Ltd ('DD') at its Cardiff office. They each use a wheelchair to get around. There are eight persons employed in the Cardiff office in total, five of whom are not disabled. DD has adopted a new practice which requires all of the staff to present a seminar on a different topic to each other every Wednesday in the training room in the basement of the office. There is no disabled access to the basement. As such, the PCP applied by the employer is for employees to present a weekly seminar in the basement training room. Let us imagine that Henrietta raises an indirect discrimination claim. In such a scenario, the ordinary practice would be to select the whole of the group to whom the PCP is applied as the relevant pool, i.e. all of the eight employees. We must then ask what proportion of the employees in the pool who do not share the same protected characteristic as the claimant would be disadvantaged by the application of the PCP. In our case, only five of the eight employees do not share the protected characteristic, and of those five employees, none of them are disadvantaged by the application of the PCP. Therefore, the percentage who are disadvantaged is 0 per cent: let us call that x. Section 19(2)(b) of the EA then enjoins the tribunal to compare x with the proportion of persons in the pool who do share the same protected characteristic[190] as the claimant who is disadvantaged by the application of the PCP. In this example, all of the three disabled employees would be disadvantaged, i.e. 100 per cent: let us call that y. In this example, if x were compared with y, we would find that x would be 0 per cent and y 100 per cent. The next question is whether this difference amounts to a 'particular disadvantage'.

[187] [2014] ICR 472. This decision was appealed to the Supreme Court ([2017] 1 WLR 1343), but the point taken was a separate issue and the matter of the comparator group chosen by the EAT was not addressed by the Supreme Court.

[188] For the difference between adopting an 'advantage-led' and 'disadvantage-led' approach, see *Rutherford v Secretary of State for Trade and Industry (No. 2)* [2006] UKHL 19, [2006] ICR 785 (on which, see C. Barnard, 'The Ageing Model of Indirect Discrimination' (2007) 66 *Cambridge Law Journal* 37) and *Grundy v British Airways plc* [2008] IRLR 74. The authorities would appear to prefer the 'disadvantage-led' test.

[189] *Rutherford v Secretary of State for Trade and Industry (No. 2)* [2006] UKHL 19, [2006] ICR 785, 803A per Lord Walker.

[190] In other words, disability.

It should be stressed that the tribunals are afforded a wide discretion in framing the appropriate pool and, in the case of criteria for a vacant position in a recruitment scenario, the pool may be particularly large given the amount of individuals who may be affected by the PCP, i.e. it may be the entirety of the economically active population.[191] In addition, the burden is imposed on the claimant to select the pool, which may be challenged by the employer and rejected by the tribunal if it is arbitrary or unrealistic. However, the tribunal is not furnished with an entirely broad discretion to reject, since the EAT has held that in 'reaching their decision as to the appropriate pool in a particular case, a tribunal should undoubtedly consider the position in respect of different pools within the range of decisions open to them, but they are entitled to select from that range the pool which they consider will realistically and effectively test the particular allegation before them'.[192]

The onus is placed on the claimant to show the requisite 'particular disadvantage'.[193] The EHRC's Code of Practice directs as follows.

■ EHRC Code of Practice on Employment

> 4.22 . . . Whether a [particular disadvantage exists] will depend on the context, such as the size of the pool and the numbers behind the proportions. It is not necessary to show that the majority of those within the pool who share the protected characteristic are placed at a disadvantage.

Adopting a statistical approach will often be useful,[194] but is not absolutely necessary[195] or necessarily always useful,[196] since the tribunal is afforded sufficient flexibility in determining whether there is a particular disadvantage, taking into account the circumstances of the case and the underlying purpose of the EA. For example, the smaller the pool, or the more 'inadequate or unreliable'[197] the evidence and information available, the less appropriate it will be to adopt a mechanical statistical analysis, since a robust comparison will not necessarily be produced. Where a statistical approach is applied, the courts and tribunals have been reluctant to devise a rule of thumb as to how great the statistical difference between x and y must be; instead, the relevant threshold needed to establish 'particular disadvantage' will vary from case to case. It is difficult to avoid the conclusion that the issue is a largely impressionistic one for the employment tribunal to make, since the EAT and the appellate courts are generally unwilling to overturn the former's finding on the issue. A striking example is the case of *London Underground Ltd v Edwards (No. 2)*,[198] where the employer introduced a new roster for underground train drivers which entailed flexible working. The claimant was a single parent who was unable to comply with the demands imposed by the new practice. All of the 2,000 male employees were able to comply with the new roster, whilst only one of the 21 female workers was unable to comply, i.e. the claimant. Therefore, x was 0 per cent,[199] whereas y was approximately

---

[191] See the discussion in H. Collins, *Employment Law*, 2nd edition (Oxford, OUP, 2010) 61.
[192] *Ministry of Defence v DeBique* [2010] IRLR 471, 482 per Mrs Justice Cox.
[193] *Nelson v Carillion Services Ltd* [2003] ICR 1256; *Redcar and Cleveland Borough Council v Bainbridge* [2009] ICR 133.   [194] See paras 4.12–4.13 of the EHRC's Code of Practice.
[195] See *O'Flynn v Adjudication Officer* [1996] 3 CMLR 103; *Chief Constable of Avon and Somerset Constabulary v Chew* [2001] All ER (D) 101 (September); *Eweida v British Airways plc* [2009] IRLR 78, 84 per Mr Justice Elias (P); *Ministry of Defence v DeBique* [2010] IRLR 471, 482 per Mrs Justice Cox; *Homer v Chief Constable of West Yorkshire Police* [2012] UKSC 15, [2012] ICR 704, 709H per Baroness Hale; and *Games v University of Kent* [2015] IRLR 202, 206–7 per HHJ David Richardson.
[196] S. Fredman, *Discrimination Law*, 2nd edition (Oxford, OUP, 2011) 184.
[197] See para 4.13 of the EHRC's Code of Practice.   [198] [1999] ICR 494.
[199] This was the proportion of men disadvantaged by the application of the PCP.

5 per cent.[200] Despite the fact that the difference was modest, it was held that the fact that 100 per cent of the male train drivers could comply was sufficient to establish the requisite degree of group disadvantage.

Once it has been established that the group with the protected characteristic has suffered a particular disadvantage, the Supreme Court of Appeal in *Essop v Home Office (UK Border Agency)*[201] has held that it is not incumbent on the employer or the claimant to identify the reason why the application of the PCP particularly disadvantages the group sharing the protected characteristic of the claimant. In other words, whether the reason for the particular disadvantage is the protected characteristic or some other factor is entirely irrelevant: this is consistent with the idea that indirect discrimination is about disparate 'impact', rather than 'treatment'. As noted by Baroness Hale, the concept of indirect discrimination only 'requires a causal link between the PCP and the particular disadvantage suffered by the group and the individual'.[202]

A final point which ought to be made is that there is no requirement for the claimant to show that the members of the protected group within the pool were unable to comply with the PCP, so long as a 'particular disadvantage' can be established. Therefore, the members of the protected group within the pool may be able to comply with the PCP, but the manner in which they do so may be such that they suffer a particular disadvantage.[203]

10.2.4.3 Personal disadvantage: section 19(2)(c) of the EA

In the same vein as group disadvantage, in order to demonstrate 'particular disadvantage', there is no requirement for the claimant to show that he/she was unable to comply with the PCP. Therefore, he/she may be able to comply with the PCP, but the manner in which he/she does so is such that she suffers a particular disadvantage.[204] Meanwhile, the words 'would put' in section 19(2)(c) of the EA reveal that the PCP may have been proposed, rather than implemented. Of course, if the claimant does not suffer the particular disadvantage whereas the protected group does, this will be insufficient. For example, in *Little v Richmond Pharmacology*,[205] an employer's decision to reject an employee's request to work part-time was cured when it overturned its earlier decision on a subsequent internal appeal. As such, the employee's complaint of indirect discrimination was unsuccessful on the ground that she had suffered no personal disadvantage.

10.2.4.4 The employer's objective justification/proportionality defence: section 19(2)(d) of the EA

In the words of Fredman, 'the key issue [in indirect discrimination claims is] whether the [PCP] can be justified in the light of the possible alternatives, and if not, how it should be modified or replaced[, which is where] . . . the real focus should lie if indirect discrimination is to get anywhere close to fulfilling its mission of removing unnecessary obstacles to equal opportunity'.[206] This takes us to section 19(2)(d) of the EA. Here, it is stipulated that the employer will be able to avoid liability for indirect discrimination if it satisfies the tribunal that the application of the PCP was a 'proportionate means of achieving a

---

[200] This was the proportion of women disadvantaged by the application of the PCP.

[201] [2017] 1 WLR 1343.

[202] *Essop v Home Office (UK Border Agency)* [2017] 1 WLR 1343, 1353E. For criticism of the decision of the Court of Appeal, see S. Fredman, 'The Reason Why: Unravelling Indirect Discrimination' (2016) 45 *Industrial Law Journal* 231.

[203] *Eweida v British Airways plc* [2009] IRLR 78, 83 per Mr Justice Elias (P).

[204] *ibid.*, 83 per Mr Justice Elias (P).   [205] [2014] ICR 85.

[206] S. Fredman, 'The Reason Why: Unravelling Indirect Discrimination' (2016) 45 *Industrial Law Journal* 231, 243.

legitimate aim'. This wording in section 19(2)(d) must be read in light of the slightly different wording contained in Article 2(2) of the Race Directive, Article 2(2)(b)(i) of the Framework Directive, and Article 2(1)(b) of the Recast Equality Directive.[207] Here, the employer is enjoined to show that the PCP 'is objectively justified by a legitimate aim and the means of achieving that aim are appropriate and necessary'. The interpretation of the European wording applied in *Bilka-Kaufhaus v Weber von Hartz*,[208] *Enderby v Frenchay Health Authority*,[209] and *R v Secretary of State for Employment, ex parte Seymour-Smith and Perez*[210] imposes a requirement on the tribunal or court to adopt a three-stage process. It must ascertain whether the application of the PCP:

(1) corresponds to a real need (i.e. a legitimate aim) on the part of the employer which is unrelated to any discrimination based on any protected characteristic;[211]

(2) is appropriate with a view to achieving that need and capable of doing so; and

(3) is necessary to meet that need and proportionate in light of all the relevant factors, including the possibility of achieving by other means the aims pursued.

This is known as the 'least restrictive means' approach to the employer's objective justification defence. It adopts a slightly different emphasis from the UK 'proportionate means' formulation. Under EU law, if the application of the PCP is not 'appropriate', 'necessary', or 'proportionate' to achieve the real need, the employer's defence is not satisfied. It must be stressed that these three elements are not equally interchangeable, but sequential.[212] It is a high hurdle for an employer to discharge the 'least restrictive means' form of the proportionality standard: if a less restrictive means of achieving the employer's real business need or legitimate aim is found to exist, the employer's objective justification defence will be rejected.[213]

Bamforth, Malik, and O'Cinneide have commented that 'there is concern that the domestic legislation makes use of a weaker formula',[214] imposing a less rigorous standard of review. This is based on the *Hampson v Department of Education and Science*,[215] *Barry v Midland Bank*,[216] and *R (Elias) v Secretary of State for Defence*[217] formulation which is applied domestically. This adopts a standard of review which is variable and, as such, at once forgiving as it may be exacting in its intensity of scrutiny. The domestic formulation entails *balancing* the discriminatory impact or harm suffered by the employee against the employer's need to achieve the legitimate aim. The greater the harm suffered by the employee, the greater must be the employer's need to achieve the legitimate aim:

---

[207] *Homer v Chief Constable of West Yorkshire Police* [2012] UKSC 15, [2012] ICR 704, 711H per Baroness Hale.   [208] [1987] IRLR 317, 320 at para 36.

[209] [1993] IRLR 591.   [210] [1999] 2 AC 554.

[211] In *Hardy & Hansons plc v Lax* [2005] IRLR 726, 731–2 at paras 31–32, Pill LJ held that the proportionality review does not encompass a 'range of proportionate means' standard.

[212] *Homer v Chief Constable of West Yorkshire Police* [2012] UKSC 15, [2012] ICR 704, 711H–712D per Baroness Hale.

[213] See G. Davidov and P. Alon-Shenker, 'Applying the Principle of Proportionality in Employment and Labour Law Contexts' (2013) 59 *McGill Law Journal* 375; G. Davidov, 'The Principle of Proportionality in Labour Law and Its Impact on Precarious Workers' (2012) 34 *Comparative Labor Law & Policy Journal* 63; and S. Fredman, 'Addressing Disparate Impact: Indirect Discrimination and the Public Sector Equality Duty' (2014) 43 *Industrial Law Journal* 349.

[214] N. Bamforth, M. Malik, and C. O'Cinneide (eds), *Discrimination Law: Theory and Context—Text and Materials* (London, Sweet & Maxwell, 2008) 322. See also A. Baker, 'Proportionality and Employment Discrimination in the UK' (2008) 37 *Industrial Law Journal* 305.

[215] [1989] ICR 179.

[216] [1999] 3 All ER 974, 984e–986g per Lord Nicholls.

[217] [2006] 1 WLR 3213. For other examples of the weaker domestic 'balancing' approach, see *Chief Constable of West Midlands Police v Harrod* [2017] ICR 869, 882F–H per Bean LJ; and *Edie v HCL Insurance BPO Services Ltd* [2015] ICR 713.

■ *R (Elias) v Secretary of State for Defence* [2006] 1 WLR 3213, 3246B–3251E

Mummery LJ:

First, the onus is on the [employer] to justify the [PCP] as a matter of law and of objective fact . . . Secondly, one important consequence of the failure of the [employer] to address the indirectly discriminatory effects of the [PCP] is the absence of an evidential basis for justifying the [PCP] or for assessing the comparative discriminatory effects of other possible criteria as a means of [achieving the employer's legitimate aim. Thus the employer must show that it addressed the issue of indirect discrimination when formulating the PCP] . . . A stringent standard of scrutiny of the claimed justification is appropriate [where] the discrimination, though indirect in form, is . . . closely related in substance to the direct form of discrimination . . . The standard of justification in race discrimination is the more exacting E[U] test of proportionality. As held by the [ECJ] in *Bilka-Kaufhaus v Weber von Hartz* . . . the objective of the measure in question must correspond to a real need and the means used must be appropriate with a view to achieving the objective and be necessary to that end. So it is necessary to weigh the need against the seriousness of the detriment to the disadvantaged group. It is not sufficient that the [employer] could reasonably consider the means chosen as suitable for attaining the aim . . . A three-stage test is applicable to determine whether the [PCP is] proportionate to the aim to be achieved . . . First, is the objective sufficiently important to justify limiting a fundamental right? Secondly, is the measure rationally connected to the objective? Thirdly, are the means chosen no more than is necessary[218] to accomplish the objective?

Thus, the domestic formulation which requires a balancing or weighing of the harm suffered by the employee against the reasonable business needs of the employer[219] arguably places a different complexion on the process than the apparently more exacting 'least restrictive means' test.[220] The former approach demands that the greater the harm suffered, the more cogent must be the employer's need to achieve a legitimate objective, whereas the latter simply enquires whether an alternative, less intrusive, measure could have been adopted to secure the legitimate objective. Although similar, there is undoubtedly a measure of space between the two formulations; however, there is some evidence that the domestic courts are now increasingly incorporating the latter exercise as part of the overall proportionality evaluation.[221]

The first part of the process is for the employer to put forward a 'legitimate aim' which justifies the adoption of the PCP. The legitimacy of the employer's objective is evaluated according to an objective standard[222] and is a question of fact for the tribunal.[223] Objectives which the courts and tribunals have been satisfied are legitimate have included: health and safety;[224] rewarding a group of employees for working unsociable hours;[225]

---

[218] This has been interpreted as 'reasonably necessary' rather than the stricter unvarnished 'necessity' test in domestic law: see *Chief Constable of West Midlands Police v Harrod* [2017] ICR 869, 881H–882B per Bean LJ.

[219] *Chief Constable of West Yorkshire Police v Homer* [2012] UKSC 15, [2012] ICR 704, 711E per Baroness Hale; *MacCulloch v Imperial Chemical Industries plc* [2008] ICR 1334; and *HM Land Registry v Benson* [2012] ICR 627.

[220] For example, see the statement in *Cobb v Secretary of State for Employment* [1989] ICR 506, 516H–517B per Wood J.

[221] For example, see *Hardy & Hansons plc v Lax* [2005] ICR 1565; *Azmi v Kirklees Metropolitan Borough Council* [2007] ICR 1154, 1172C–G per Wilkie J; and *Chief Constable of West Yorkshire Police v Homer* [2012] UKSC 15, [2012] ICR 704, 712F–H per Baroness Hale.

[222] *British Airways plc v Starmer* [2005] IRLR 862.

[223] *Ladele v London Borough of Islington* [2010] 1 WLR 955, 968B–E.

[224] See the case of Ms Chaplin in *Eweida v UK* [2013] IRLR 231.

[225] *Blackburn v Chief Constable of West Midlands Police* [2009] IRLR 135.

rewarding loyalty;[226] imposing a coherent pay structure, avoiding privatizations, avoiding job losses and cuts in hours, and preventing members from receiving lower pay;[227] encouraging turnover;[228] maintaining and sustaining a school's religious ethos;[229] promoting equal opportunities;[230] facilitating the recruitment and retention of staff of a suitable calibre;[231] ensuring the future viability of the employer in a market-competitive and non-discriminatory way;[232] and facilitating effective communication between teachers and pupils.[233] Meanwhile, it has been held that applying a PCP with the objective of avoiding statutory protection against discrimination was illegitimate,[234] as was the need to maintain good industrial relations, without more.[235] Indeed, where the employer's aim is itself discriminatory in character, it cannot be legitimate. Nor was there any legitimate aim for a rule preventing schoolchildren from wearing a turban.[236] In addition, the legitimate aim must not be indelibly linked to, or associated with, a prohibited ground of discrimination[237] and it has been held that simple budgetary or cost-related objectives of themselves[238] can never be legitimate:

■ *Woodcock v Cumbria Primary Care Trust* [2012] ICR 1126, 1151D–E

Rimer LJ:

Accepting, as I make clear I do, that the guidance of the [ECJ] is that an employer cannot justify discriminatory treatment 'solely' because the elimination of such treatment would involve increased costs, that guidance cannot mean more than that the saving or avoidance of costs will not, without more, amount to the achieving of a 'legitimate aim'. That is entirely unsurprising. To adopt a simple example given by [Counsel for the Trust], it is hardly open to an employer to claim to be entitled to justify the discriminatory payment to A of less than B simply because it would cost more to pay A the same as B. Such treatment of A could not, without more, be a 'legitimate aim'.[239]

The major exception to the orthodoxy which states that costs alone can never be a sufficient legitimate aim is supplied by the law of disability discrimination, which enjoins an employer to make reasonable adjustments to the workplace to accommodate disabled employees,[240] although the extent to which this exception applies to the statutory wrong of indirect disability discrimination is presently unclear.

---

[226] *MacCulloch v Imperial Chemical Industries plc* [2008] ICR 1334.
[227] *Allen v GMB* [2008] ICR 1407.
[228] *MacCulloch v Imperial Chemical Industries plc* [2008] ICR 1334.
[229] *R (E) v Governing Body of JFS* [2009] UKSC 15, [2010] 2 AC 728; *Board of Governors of St Matthias Church of England School v Crizzle* [1993] ICR 401.
[230] *Ladele v London Borough of Islington* [2010] 1 WLR 955.
[231] *Chief Constable of West Yorskhire v Homer* [2012] ICR 704.
[232] *Edie v HCL Insurance BPO Services Ltd* [2015] ICR 713.
[233] *Azmi v Kirklees Metropolitan Borough Council* [2007] ICR 1154.
[234] *Allonby v Accrington and Rossendale College* [2001] IRLR 364.
[235] *Kenny v Minister for Justice, Equality and Law Reform* [2013] 2 CMLR 50.
[236] *Clymo v Wandsworth London Borough Council* [1989] ICR 250.
[237] *R (Elias) v Secretary of State for Defence* [2006] 1 WLR 3213.
[238] In other words, a 'cost plus' justification will be legitimate, i.e. where the employer is able to identify some other additional justification for its conduct, alongside budgetary considerations, on which, see the discussion in J. Lane, '*Woodcock v Cumbria Primary Care Trust*: The Objective Justification Test for Age Discrimination' (2013) 76 *Modern Law Review* 134.
[239] See also *Ministry of Justice v O'Brien* [2013] 1 WLR 522, 546D–547B per Baroness Hale; *Schmitzer v Bundesministerin für Inneres* [2015] IRLR 331. Cf. *Woodcock* with *HM Land Registry v Benson* [2012] ICR 627 where the EAT held that a 'cheapness' criterion for evaluating applications for voluntary redundancy and early retirement in order to meet the £12 million budget set aside for the early retirement and voluntary redundancy scheme was legitimate.
[240] Sections 20–22 of the EA; *Cordell v Foreign and Commonwealth Office* [2012] ICR 280. See Chapter 12, section 12.3.3.

The second stage is for the tribunal or court to address whether the application of the PCP is capable of achieving, and rationally connected to, the accomplishment of the legitimate objective. Here, the focus is on the degree of contribution which the PCP makes to the achievement of the legitimate aim. For example, in *R (E) v Governing Body of JFS*,[241] four of the majority justices[242] held that the school's admissions policy of restricting entry to children qualifying as Jewish according to the precepts of the OCR (i.e. the PCP) did not accomplish the school's legitimate aim of fostering and promoting the religious ethos of the school. Conversely, in *Homer v Chief Constable of West Yorkshire Police*,[243] the Supreme Court acknowledged that the employer's aim of facilitating the recruitment and retention of staff of an appropriate calibre was legitimate. However, Baroness Hale drew a distinction between recruiting new staff and retaining staff and the aim of retaining recent staff from that of retaining those recruited under a different system. In the case of the latter, Baroness Hale opined that it might not be appropriate to require existing staff to meet the particular PCP applied by the employer, since there may be less exacting non-discriminatory alternatives available, which the employment tribunal had not considered.

The latter point takes us on neatly to the final stage of the proportionality test in section 19(2)(d) of the EA. This enjoins the courts to address whether the application of the PCP is appropriate, (reasonably) necessary,[244] and proportionate to achieve the legitimate aim. The burden here lies on the employer to show that the PCP was proportionate[245] on the basis of a balance of probabilities.[246] In the majority of the cases, the UK courts will approach this requirement by balancing the harm suffered by the claimant, i.e. the discriminatory impact, against the extent to which it is necessary for the employer to adopt the PCP to accomplish the objective. The discriminatory impact must be analysed in terms of the numbers of employees affected, as well as the degree of severity of the harm experienced by the employees falling within the protected group.[247] The greater the impact, the more pressing the employer's need must be to apply the PCP to achieve the legitimate aim. However, an exception is applicable in the case of indirect religious discrimination claims as a result of the Court of Appeal's decision in *Mba*[248] since there is no requirement to assess the disparate impact of the application of the PCP *on the protected group, but only the claimant him/herself*. This elision of the group impact element of the objective justification defence was adopted in *Mba* as a result of the individual-oriented nature of religious protection embodied in Article 9 of the ECHR. As such, the proportionality exercise in an indirect religious discrimination claim entails enquiring whether the application of the PCP was justified in respect of that particular individual employee working for that particular employer in light of its impact on that employee only and the employer's need to achieve the relevant legitimate aim.[249] Where it is only the claimant who is affected by the application of the PCP, this will mean that it ought to be easier for the employer to reasonably accommodate the religious practice of the employee.

An attempt to apply a variation of the range of reasonable responses test in the context of the proportionality defence was rejected by Pill LJ in the case of *Hardy & Hansons plc v Lax*.[250] Pill LJ was of the view that, in undertaking a review based on a proportionality criterion, an adjudicator is invited to form 'its own judgment, upon a fair and detailed

---

[241] [2009] UKSC 15, [2010] 2 AC 728.   [242] Lords Phillips, Mance, Kerr, and Clarke.
[243] [2012] UKSC 15, [2012] ICR 704.
[244] *Chief Constable of West Midlands Police v Harrod* [2015] IRLR 790.
[245] *Rainey v Greater Glasgow Health Board* [1987] ICR 129.
[246] *Singh v Rowntree Mackintosh Ltd* [1979] ICR 554.
[247] *University of Manchester v Jones* [1993] ICR 474.
[248] *Mba v Mayor and Burgesses of the London Borough of Merton* [2014] 1 WLR 1501.
[249] *ibid.*, 1513G–1514C per Elias LJ and 1514E–H per Vos LJ.
[250] [2005] ICR 1565.

analysis of the working practices and business considerations involved, as to whether the proposal is reasonably necessary',[251] i.e. there is no margin of discretion afforded to the employer based on whether the employer's approach came within a range of proportionate responses. An alternative way for the courts to approach the final stage is to adopt the 'least restrictive means' formulation, i.e. the highly stringent European incarnation of the proportionality test. In the UK context, this is not necessarily applicable in every case,[252] but, as recognized by Mummery LJ in *R (Elias) v Secretary of State for Defence*,[253] it will be appropriate to apply it where the discrimination, though indirect in form, is closely related in substance to the direct form of discrimination. This involves the court testing whether there are less intrusive or non-discriminatory means of achieving the legitimate aim.[254] In doing so, it is not appropriate for the court to consider what means could be adopted to achieve different aims, but only to examine the other means of achieving the employer's legitimate aims.[255] Ultimately, the 'least restrictive means' approach enjoins tribunals and courts to subject the managerial prerogative to an acute intensity of scrutiny.[256] This is evident in the analysis of two of the minority justices[257] in *R (E) v Governing Body of JFS*.[258] Lord Hope was of the persuasion that the school had failed to consider whether less discriminatory means could be adopted which would not undermine the achievement of the school's legitimate objective, i.e. the promotion of the religious ethos of the school.[259] For example, this could have included affording consideration:

■ *R (E) v Governing Body of JFS* [2009] UKSC 15, [2010] 2 AC 728, 812B–C

Lord Hope:

. . . to the possibility of admitting children recognised as Jewish by any of the branches of Judaism, including those who were Masorti, Reform or Liberal. Consideration might have been given to the relative balance in composition of the school's intake from time to time between those recognised as Jewish by the OCR who were committed to the Jewish religion and those who were not, and as to whether in the light of it there was room for the admission of a limited number of those committed to the Jewish religion who were recognised as Jewish by one of the other branches.

The objective justification defence will likely prove an inadequate resource where an employer seeks to defend the application of a PCP or the maintenance of a policy if it had no particular justification in mind when it first adopted that PCP or policy. As such, what is referred to as 'retrospective justification', i.e. where the employer subsequently seeks to come up with an *ex post facto* justification for the PCP or policy when the application of the latter is subsequently challenged, is likely to be treated with scepticism by the courts. The reason for this approach is that the courts will treat with more respect a policy or PCP 'which was carefully thought through by reference to the relevant principles at the time when it was adopted . . . [and it will be] difficult for the [employer] to justify the proportionality of the means chosen to carry out their aims if they did not conduct the exercise of examining the alternatives or gather the necessary evidence to inform the choice at that time'.[260]

---

[251] *ibid.*, 1578E–F.   [252] *Hardy & Hansons plc v Lax* [2005] ICR 1565, 1578E per Pill LJ.
[253] [2006] 1 WLR 3213.
[254] *Homer v Chief Constable of West Yorkshire Police* [2012] UKSC 15, [2012] ICR 704, 712F–G per Baroness Hale.   [255] *Blackburn v Chief Constable of West Midlands Police* [2009] IRLR 135.
[256] *Hardy & Hansons plc v Lax* [2005] ICR 1565, 1578F–1579D per Pill LJ; *Azmi v Kirklees Metropolitan Borough Council* [2007] ICR 1154, 1172F per Wilkie J.   [257] Lords Hope and Walker.
[258] [2009] UKSC 15, [2010] 2 AC 728.
[259] *ibid.*, 811F–812D per Lord Hope.
[260] *O'Brien v Ministry of Justice* [2013] 1 WLR 522, 539H–540B per Baroness Hale.

10.2.4.5 Is there a clear dividing line between direct and indirect discrimination?

Earlier, in section 10.2.4, an extract was reproduced from the judgment of Baroness Hale in *R (E) v Governing Body of JFS*,[261] where she remarked that there is a clear dividing line between direct and indirect discrimination and that they are 'mutually exclusive [and y]ou cannot have both at once'.[262] Whilst the judicial rhetoric is to the effect that there is a well-defined chasm between direct and indirect discrimination, this may be difficult to substantiate in conceptual terms, and the courts themselves may sometimes confuse the two concepts.[263] An excellent illustration of this point is provided by the decision of the CJEU in *Achbita v G4S Secure Solutions NV*.[264] In *Achbita*, it was held that where the employer operated a policy establishing a blanket ban on the visible wearing of *any religious, political or philosophical symbols or signs* this conduct did not constitute direct discrimination, but potentially indirect discrimination. The CJEU held that such a rule applied to all staff and treated all workers equally by requiring dress to be neutral. Seen from this perspective, there could be no differential treatment based on religion, i.e. no direct discrimination. The practice was prima facie indirectly discriminatory, however, as it was more likely to impact upon persons from certain religious groups with a requirement to wear a religious emblem/dress. However, the policy was capable of objective justification as the employer's intention to display neutrality in its relations with customers was considered to be a legitimate aim which was not disproportionate. The CJEU also indicated that, in determining whether such discrimination is justifiable, it is necessary to take the following into account, namely the size and conspicuousness of the religious symbol, the nature of the employee's activity, the context in which she has to perform that activity, and the national identity of the Member State concerned. Whilst the policy of the employer in *Achbita* does seem neutral on its face insofar as it applies to everyone in the workplace, an alternative interpretation is to say that by singling out employees of religious faith in its no '*religious, political or philosophical symbols or signs*' policy, it was treating them less favourably than others. But, if that is indeed the proper construction of the circumstances in *Achbita*, then surely that would amount to direct discrimination? It is for that reason that the dividing line between less favourable treatment, i.e. direct discrimination, and the application of an ostensibly neutral policy or practice having a disparate adverse effect on persons with protected characteristics, i.e. indirect discrimination, may in fact be something of a chimera.

10.2.5 Harassment and sexual harassment

Harassment is the third of the statutory torts recognized as 'prohibited conduct' by the EA. This concept dovetails, and to some extent overlaps, with the statutory tort of harassment recognized by the Protection from Harassment Act 1997,[265] the main difference being that there is no requirement for an act or omission to amount to a course of conduct in the context of the EA:

---

[261] [2009] UKSC 15, [2010] 2 AC 728.

[262] *R (E) v Governing Body of JFS* [2009] UKSC 15, [2010] 2 AC 728, 757C per Baroness Hale. See G. Mead, 'The Role of Intention in Direct Discrimination' (1990) 19 *Industrial Law Journal* 251.

[263] See S. Forshaw and M. Pilgerstorfer, 'Direct and Indirect Discrimination: Is There Something in between?' (2008) 37 *Industrial Law Journal* 347; N. Cunningham, 'Indirect Discrimination: Between the Wheat and the Chaff' (2009) 38 *Industrial Law Journal* 209.

[264] [2017] IRLR 466. For a similar case, see *Bougnaoui v Micropole SA* [2017] IRLR 447. For analysis of religious dress codes in the workplace, see K. Alidadi, *Religion, Equality and Employment in Europe—The Case for Reasonable Accommodation* (Oxford, Hart Publishing, 2017) ch. 3.

[265] See *Majrowski v Guy's and St Thomas's NHS Trust* [2007] 1 AC 224.

Section 26 Harassment

(1) A person (A) harasses another (B) if—

    (a) A engages in unwanted conduct related to a relevant protected characteristic, and

    (b) the conduct has the purpose or effect of—

        (i) violating B's dignity, or

        (ii) creating an intimidating, hostile, degrading, humiliating or offensive environment for B.

(2) A also harasses B if—

    (a) A engages in unwanted conduct of a sexual nature, and

    (b) the conduct has the purpose or effect referred to in subsection (1)(b).

(3) A also harasses B if—

    (a) A or another person engages in unwanted conduct of a sexual nature or that is related to gender reassignment or sex,

    (b) the conduct has the purpose or effect referred to in subsection (1)(b), and

    (c) because of B's rejection of or submission to the conduct, A treats B less favourably than A would treat B if B had not rejected or submitted to the conduct.

(4) In deciding whether conduct has the effect referred to in subsection (1)(b), each of the following must be taken into account—

    (a) the perception of B;

    (b) the other circumstances of the case;

    (c) whether it is reasonable for the conduct to have that effect.

(5) The relevant protected characteristics are—

age;

disability;

gender reassignment;

race;

religion or belief;[266]

sex;

sexual orientation . . .

Section 40 Employees and applicants: harassment

(1) An employer (A) must not, in relation to employment by A, harass a person (B)—

    (a) who is an employee of A's;

    (b) who has applied to A for employment . . .[267]

---

[266] See *Saini v All Saints Haque Centre* [2009] IRLR 74.

[267] Section 40(2) of the EA imposed liability on an employer where an employee had been harassed by a third party in the course of the employee's employment. This covered harassment by an employer's customers or suppliers. See *Burton v De Vere Hotels Ltd* [1996] IRLR 596 (cf. *Pearce v Governing Body of Mayfield Secondary School* [2003] IRLR 512). The third-party harassment provisions were repealed in October 2013. This was justified on the basis that the actions of third parties are outside the control of the employer and that section 40(2) of the EA imposed a 'regulatory burden on business to no apparent good purpose': Government Equalities Office, *Equality Act 2010: Employer Liability for Harassment of Employees by Third Parties—A Consultation* (May 2012), available at https://www.gov.uk/government/uploads/system/uploads/attachment_data/file/137748/consultation-document.pdf (last visited 7 December 2017). See J. Hand, 'Employer's Liability for Third-Party Harassment: An "Unworkable" and Superfluous Provision?' (2013) 42 *Industrial Law Journal* 75.

It is particularly conspicuous that the definition of 'relevant protected characteristics' in section 26(5) of the EA excludes harassment relating to pregnancy and maternity and marriage and civil partnership. The Labour Government justified the exclusion of these characteristics on the basis that:

(1) pregnancy and maternity harassment would be addressed by the provisions outlawing direct or indirect sex discrimination;

(2) there was insufficient evidence that harassment on grounds of marriage constituted a sufficiently practical problem; and

(3) civil partnership harassment would be tackled by direct or indirect discrimination on grounds of sexual orientation.[268]

As such, the absence of these protected characteristics from section 26(5) of the EA by no means gives employers a free hand to harass on these grounds with impunity. However, the main difference is that a claimant alleging harassment in these contexts, and invoking the direct or indirect sex or sexual orientation discrimination concepts in order to do so, will be required to show less favourable treatment than a suitable comparator under section 13 of the EA, i.e. a causal link must be established between the treatment and the characteristic.[269] This can be contrasted with harassment claims based on the relevant protected characteristics listed in section 26(5) of the EA. Here, there is no requirement for the claimant to show that he/she was harassed 'because of' one of those relevant protected characteristics—which would entail a comparison exercise; instead, the harassment must be 'related to' one of the relevant protected characteristics, which is much broader than the words 'because of', since it does not impose an obligation on the claimant to show that he/she was treated less favourably than a suitable comparator, i.e. no direct comparison with a comparator is needed.[270] Moreover, the words 'related to' suggest that the claimant employee need not possess the protected characteristic him/herself, although that would not appear to be the case in the context of a disability harassment claim, since in *Peninsula Business Service Ltd v Baker*,[271] the EAT ruled that the claimant must actually prove that he/she is disabled under section 6 of the EA.

Another important point is that section 26(1)(a) of the EA does not say, 'A engages in unwanted conduct related to a relevant protected characteristic which B has or possesses'. Therefore, the clamant need not have or possess the relevant protected characteristic which will enable him/her to raise a harassment claim where the employer:

(1) harasses a colleague of B or a customer on the basis that such colleague or customer has a relevant protected characteristic and thus creates an unpleasant working environment for B;[272] or

(2) perceives B to have the relevant protected characteristic.[273]

The principal point to take from this discussion is that the concepts of harassment and sexual harassment are now free-standing examples of prohibited conduct, which can be

---

[268] See the discussion in B. Hepple, *Equality: The New Legal Framework*, 2nd edition (Oxford, Hart Publishing, 2014) 98–9.

[269] See section 212(1) and (5) of the EA.

[270] See *R (EOC) v Secretary of State for Trade and Industry* [2007] ICR 1234. See also the discussion in L. Barmes, 'Constitutional and Conceptual Complexities in UK Implementation of the EU Harassment Provisions' (2007) 36 *Industrial Law Journal* 446, 452–6; L. Clarke, 'Harassment, Sexual Harassment, and the Employment Equality (Sex Discrimination) Regulations 2005' (2006) 35 *Industrial Law Journal* 161, 167–8.   [271] [2017] ICR 714.

[272] For example, see *Saini v All Saints Haque Centre* [2009] 1 CMLR 38 where H was harassed in connection with the religion of a colleague.

[273] *English v Thomas Sanderson* [2009] IRLR 206.

contrasted with the historical position where it was necessary to 'shoe-horn' such cases within the statutory architecture proscribing direct and indirect discrimination.[274]

Harassment arises where there is unwanted conduct which has the purpose or effect of:

(a) violating B's dignity; *or*

(b) creating an intimidating, hostile, degrading, humiliating, or offensive environment for B.

This disjunction between (a) and (b) is particularly interesting, in light of the definition of harassment in the Race, Framework and Recast Equality Directives which each adopt conjunctive wording.[275] The instruction to the courts and tribunals in section 26(4)(c) of the EA to take into account whether it is reasonable for the conduct to have the effect of (a) or (b) underscores the point that the test of harassment is not subjective. Instead, the evaluative criteria entail the application of a mixture of subjective and objective considerations.[276] Rather than simply ask whether the claimant genuinely believed that the unwanted conduct had the effect set out in (a) or (b), the tribunals must also consider whether the conduct could reasonably be considered to have that effect on an objective evaluation of the circumstances.[277] In adopting this test,[278] it will be relevant for the court or tribunal to consider the intention and motives of the harasser, albeit that there is no requirement that the harasser must have been aware that his/her conduct would be unwelcome.[279] Examples of harassment in the case law have included 'outing' a homosexual or lesbian against his/her will,[280] the regular use of homophobic language such as 'Big Gay Wayne' and 'you are so gay',[281] the employment of language such as 'gollywog' in the presence of the employee claimant who was black and of Afro-Caribbean origin,[282] suspending a disabled support worker at a care home for having her first aid certificate revoked owing to her inability to perform cardio-pulmonary resuscitation and manual handling,[283] and mocking an employee's foreign accent.[284] However, these cases can be contrasted with *Heafield v Times Newspaper Ltd*,[285] where the line manager of a Roman Catholic employee at *The Times* newspaper shouted 'can anyone tell me what's happening to the fu***** Pope?' across the newsroom. The EAT rejected the employee's claim of religious harassment on the ground that it had not been reasonable for him to feel that his dignity had been violated or that an intimidating, hostile, degrading, humiliating, or offensive environment had been created, since in the context, in what was a pressurized environment, it was not intended as an insult to his religion. Likewise, in *Henderson v GMB*,[286] it was held that the use of language

---

[274] For example, see *Porcelli v Strathclyde Regional Council* [1986] IRLR 134; *Pearce v Governing Body of Mayfield School* [2003] IRLR 512.

[275] See Article 2(3) of the Race Directive, Article 2(3) of the Framework Directive, and Article 2(1)(c) of the Recast Equality Directive.

[276] M. Bell, 'A Patchwork of Protection: The New Anti-Discrimination Law Framework' (2004) 67 *Modern Law Review* 465, 471.

[277] For example, see the disability harassment claim in *Betsi Cadwaladr University Health Board v Hughes* (UKEAT/0179/13/JOJ, 28 February 2014).

[278] *Richmond Pharmacology Ltd v Dhaliwal* [2009] IRLR 336.

[279] *Reed and Bull Information Systems Ltd v Stedman* [1999] IRLR 299.

[280] *Grant v HM Land Registry* [2011] ICR 1390, 1405B–C per Elias LJ.

[281] *Smith v Ideal Shopping Direct Ltd* (UKEAT/0590/12/BA, 16 May 2013).

[282] *Lindsay v London School of Economics and Political Science* [2014] IRLR 218. However, the Court of Appeal held that there are not words or terms which are inherently racist and that the context within which the words or expressions were uttered will always have to be taken into account. As such, the 'reason why' the terms were uttered will be relevant.

[283] *Prospects for People with Learning Disabilities v Harris* [2012] Eq LR 781.

[284] *Sheffield City Council v Norouzi* [2011] IRLR 897.

[285] [2013] Eq LR 345. See M. Pearson, 'Offensive Expression and the Workplace' (2014) 43 *Industrial Law Journal* 429.   [286] [2015] IRLR 451.

towards an employee such as 'you are too left-wing' and your actions 'were over the top' were too trivial as to constitute harassment. A similar conclusion was reached in *Quality Solicitors CMHT v Tunstall*,[287] where it was held that there had been no racial harassment when a comment was made by the claimant's colleague to the effect that 'she is Polish, but very nice'. Meanwhile, inaction by an employer will also be covered, e.g. failing to investigate allegations of racial abuse without good cause.[288]

In *Conteh v Parking Partners Ltd*,[289] Langstaff J furnished some useful guidance on the circumstances in which the actions or omissions of an employer 'create' the requisite harassment to engage section 26(1)(b)(ii) of the EA:

■ *Conteh v Parking Partners Ltd* [2011] ICR 341, 348C–349B

Langstaff J:

. . . it must be shown that that conduct has, in this case, the effect—though it may be, in other cases, a purpose—as set out by [section 26(1)(b) of the EA]. That is that inaction has here the effect of creating the proscribed environment. That is a causation question. Here it is worth considering the word which opens [section 26(1)(b)(ii)], 'creating'. Parliament determined to use that word as opposed to an expression such as 'causing'. If a word such as 'causing' had been used, it might be plain that Parliament had intended that the test of causation usually applied in tort claims would apply here too; that is, as is well established at common law, that anyone would be taken to have caused a result if they had caused or materially contributed to it. 'Creating' is a word which, so far as we know, has no such history. It remains unexplored in case law. The use of it suggests to us that the focus is upon what causes the environment to begin to be as it is. However, we are satisfied by the arguments of [counsel for Conteh] that creation does not have to be a matter of an instant. What must be looked at is the environment, and then the question be asked: how was that environment created? Creation may of course take place as a matter of an instant; but it may take place over time. It may be that third party behaviour has created the environment in part, but the actions of an employer, to whom those third parties are not responsible, has made it worse, in which case the environment might be said to have been created by the actions of both. The extent to which the employer had by his actions assisted in that process of creation would be relevant when one came to the question of compensation, but not for the purposes of liability. Since the process of creation envisages a positive change in circumstance, can inaction ever be said to create an environment? An example would be where a failure to act when an employee reasonably required that there be action had itself contributed to the atmosphere in which the employee worked, as for instance where she or he felt unsupported, to the extent that the failure to support him or her actively made the position very much worse, effectively ensuring that there was no light at the end of the tunnel in remedy of the situation with which, as a result of the actions of others, he or she then faced. In exploring that as a matter of theory we do not suggest that such cases will be common. It is perhaps unlikely that they will be readily found and an employment tribunal should only conclude that such has happened if there is cogent evidence to that effect; but we can see it as a possibility which is covered by the wording of the statute. We have greater hesitation in concluding however that 'creating' is apt to include a case where all that can be said against an employer is that he has failed to remedy a situation brought about by the actions of others for whom he is not responsible.

---

[287] [2014] Eq LR 679; cf. *Richmond Pharmacology v Dhaliwal* [2009] ICR 724 where a one-off statement that the employee might be 'married off in India' was held to amount to racial harassment.

[288] *Conteh v Parking Partners Ltd* [2011] ICR 341. However, in *Timothy James Consulting v Wilton* [2015] ICR 764, it was ruled that a constructive dismissal cannot itself constitute an act of harassment for the purposes of section 26 of the Equality Act 2010.   [289] [2011] ICR 341.

Although a single incident can be caught by section 26 and qualify as harassment, it has been held that a one-off incident rather than a course of conduct will generally not be enough to create an intimidating, etc. environment. For example, in *Henderson v GMB*[290] and *Quality Solicitors CMHT v Tunstall*,[291] where some one-off trivial statements are made and a degree of minor upset is caused, the utterance of those words will not be sufficiently material to constitute harassment since they will be treated as an incident rather than such as to create the requisite intimidating, hostile, etc. environment.

A further query is whether claims can be made for harassment occurring at any point during the employment relationship. It is generally accepted that harassment can take place throughout the course of the employment relationship, and in this way, the EA again provides 'day one' protection. However, it was only recently reaffirmed in *Urso v Department for Work and Pensions*[292] that a dismissal could amount to harassment as it could amount to an 'affront to the employee's dignity'. More importantly, harassment is prohibited by sections 40 and 108 of the EA at every stage of employment, and this clearly covers the time before, during, and after employment.

Turning now to section 26(2) of the EA, it is clear that this is designed to combat sexual harassment, i.e. unwanted conduct of a sexual nature which has the purpose or effect of violating the employee's dignity or creating an intimidating, etc. environment for him/her. The EA does not supply any examples of conduct of a sexual nature, but the Explanatory Notes to the EA cited the displaying of 'material of a sexual nature, such as a topless calendar'[293] as sufficient to constitute sexual harassment. Further assistance is supplied by the EHRC's Code of Practice which states that sexual harassment 'can cover verbal, non-verbal or physical conduct including unwelcome sexual advances, touching, forms of sexual assault, sexual jokes, displaying pornographic photographs or drawings or sending emails with material of a sexual nature'.[294] In one case, it was held that an employee's crude comment about the size of a female colleague's breasts amounted to sexual harassment.[295]

In order to establish a harassment claim, it will often be the case that the claimant will be required to establish vicarious liability on the part of the employer, since many instances of harassment and/or sexual harassment are perpetrated by an employee of the employer, i.e. a colleague. Here, section 109 of the EA comes into play insofar as it imposes vicarious liability on the employer C if an employee A commits a discriminatory act against another employee B in the course of A's employment. B may also have a claim against employer C by virtue of the doctrine of vicarious liability where B suffers harassment which cannot be ascribed to any of the relevant protected characteristics. This is by virtue of the decision of the House of Lords in *Majrowski v Guy's and St Thomas' NHS Trust*.[296] Here, it was held that the Protection from Harassment Act 1997 will apply to furnish protection to employee B where there is a course of conduct amounting to

---

[290] [2015] IRLR 451.

[291] [2014] Eq LR 679; cf. *Richmond Pharmacology v Dhaliwal* [2009] ICR 724.

[292] [2017] IRLR 304.

[293] Paragraph 99, available at http://www.legislation.gov.uk/ukpga/2010/15/notes/division/3/2/2/14 (last visited 7 December 2017).

[294] See https://www.equalityhumanrights.com/sites/default/files/employercode.pdf at para 7.13 (last visited 7 December 2017).   [295] *Insitu Cleaning Co. Ltd v Heads* [1995] IRLR 4.

[296] [2006] UKHL 34, [2007] 1 AC 224. See also *Green v DB Green* [2006] IRLR 764; *Cumbria County Council v Carlisle-Morgan* [2007] IRLR 314; *RBS v McAdie* [2008] IRLR 895; *Conn v Sunderland County Council* [2008] IRLR 324; *Gravil v Carroll* [2008] IRLR 829; *Veakins v Kier Islington Ltd* [2010] IRLR 132; *Rayment v Ministry of Defence* [2010] IRLR 768; *Iqbal v Dean Manson* [2011] IRLR 428; *Marinello v City of Edinburgh Council* [2011] IRLR 669; B. Barratt, 'Vicarious Liability for Harassment by an Employee' (2006) 35 *Industrial Law Journal* 431; D. Brodie, 'Deterring Harassment at Common Law' (2007) 36 *Industrial Law Journal* 213; and B. Barratt, 'When Does Harassment Warrant Redress?' (2010) 39 *Industrial Law Journal* 194.

'harassment', which is left undefined. In *Majrowski*, Lord Nicholls distinguished between 'conduct which is oppressive and unacceptable' and 'conduct which is unattractive, even unreasonable'.[297] The former is targeted by the Protection from Harassment Act 1997, whereas the latter is not.

10.2.6 Victimization

Victimization is the final statutory form of prohibited conduct which we consider. This concept is referred to as 'retaliation' in the USA and describes the situation where the employer subjects an employee to a detriment as a result of the employee performing a protected act. There is little purpose in the statutory concepts of direct and indirect discrimination and harassment if the employer can intimidate the employee from bringing or continuing proceedings on one of these bases by subjecting him/her to retaliation:

Section 27 Victimisation

(1) A person (A) victimises another person (B) if A subjects B to a detriment because—

    (a) B does a protected act, or

    (b) A believes that B has done, or may do, a protected act.

(2) Each of the following is a protected act—

    (a) bringing proceedings under this Act;

    (b) giving evidence or information in connection with proceedings under this Act;

    (c) doing any other thing for the purposes of or in connection with this Act;

    (d) making an allegation (whether or not express) that A or another person has contravened this Act.

(3) Giving false evidence or information, or making a false allegation, is not a protected act if the evidence or information is given, or the allegation is made, in bad faith.

(4) This section applies only where the person subjected to a detriment is an individual.

It has been held that the word 'detriment' in section 27(1) of the EA should be given a broad meaning so that it includes less favourable treatment of the claimant in the way certain measures were applied to him/her by the employer, where the explanation for such treatment was the making of a protected act.[298] Further, when read down in light of the Race, Framework, and Recast Equality Directives, section 27 enables a claimant to attain relief where he/she raises an associative victimization claim.[299] In such an associative victimization claim, there is no need for the claimant to establish a particularly close relationship with the person who performed the protected act and all that the claimant is required to demonstrate is factual causation, i.e. that the detriment was suffered as a result of the protected acts. Another point worth stressing is that a claimant will be entitled to raise a post-employment victimization claim.[300] Pre-employment victimization

---

[297] [2006] UKHL 34, [2007] 1 AC 224, 234D–E.
[298] *Deer v University of Oxford* [2015] IRLR 481.
[299] *Thompson v London Central Bus Co.* [2016] IRLR 9.
[300] Section 108(1) of the EA. See also *Jessemey v Rowstock Ltd* [2014] IRLR 368.

claims will also be valid where there is a close connection between the employer and the employee's former employer.[301]

As for the scope of section 27(2)(d) of the EA, the approach of the Court of Appeal in *Woods v Pasab Ltd (t/a Jhoots Pharmacy)* is instructive.[302] Here, it was decided that a protected act will not include the situation where the employee is dismissed for making racist comments about the employer and the employer takes offence at this allegation. As such, the employee's statement that the employer was a 'little Sikh Club that only looks after Sikhs' was not treated as an allegation that the employer had contravened the EA. Meanwhile, although section 26(1) requires a connection between the detriment suffered by the employee and the protected act, it is not necessary for the employee to establish that the employer was motivated by a conscious desire to subject the employee to the detriment because of, or for the reason of, the protected act; rather, it is sufficient if the protected act was a significant cause of, or the significant reason for,[303] the detriment.[304] In determining the significant reason, the real reason why the alleged victimization took place must be identified and a 'but for' test should not be applied.[305] However, there is no requirement for the employee to show less favourable treatment than a suitable comparator as a result of a protected act; instead, all that the claimant need do is show that he/she has been subjected to a detriment. In order to determine whether a detriment has been suffered, the effect on the employee should be considered, rather than the purpose of the employer in treating the employee in the way that it did. Fundamentally, the question is whether a reasonable worker from the perspective of the employee would or might take the view that the treatment was in all circumstances detrimental.[306] Thus, where an employer took appropriate, honest, and reasonable preparatory action by refusing to provide an employee with a reference in order to defend its interests in the context of pending discrimination proceedings brought by that employee, it was held that it had not subjected the employee concerned to a detriment.[307] Likewise, where an employer's real reason for an employee's dismissal was its reasonable belief in the employee's gross misconduct in taking unauthorized holiday leave, rather than the fact that the employee had made a protected act, this did not constitute victimization.[308] This can be contrasted with the situation where an employer publicly announces that the likelihood will be redundancies if a minority of the workforce persist in pursuing their equal pay claims. In such a case, the House of Lords held that this subjected the employees concerned to a detriment.[309]

---

[301] Section 108(1) of the EA and *Butterworth v Police and Crime Commissioner's Office for Greater Manchester* [2016] IRLR 280.

[302] [2013] IRLR 305.   [303] *Burrell v Micheldever Tyre Services Ltd* [2013] Eq LR 695.

[304] *Nagarajan v London Regional Transport* [2000] 1 AC 501, 512H–513B per Lord Nicholls.

[305] *Micheldever Tyre Services Ltd v Burrell* [2014] ICR 935.

[306] *Derbyshire v St Helens Metropolitan Borough Council* [2007] UKHL 16, [2007] 3 All ER 81. Compare and contrast *Woodhouse v West North West Homes Ltd* [2013] IRLR 773 with *Martin v Devonshires Solicitors* [2011] ICR 352. In the latter case, it was held that an employer will be deemed not to have victimized the employee where there are features of the case which suggest that the detriment experienced by the employee can be treated as separable from the protected acts of the employee; in *Woodhouse*, doubt was cast on this approach.

[307] *Chief Constable of West Yorkshire Police v Khan* [2001] 1 WLR 1947.

[308] *Leeds Teaching Hospital NHS Trust v Blake* (UKEAT/0430/14/BA, 15 July 2015).

[309] *Derbyshire v St Helens Metropolitan Borough Council* [2007] UKHL 16, [2007] 3 All ER 81. See the discussion in M. Connolly, 'Discrimination Law: Victimisation' (2000) 29 *Industrial Law Journal* 304; M. Connolly, 'Discrimination Law: Victimisation' (2002) 31 *Industrial Law Journal* 161; M. Connolly, 'Discrimination Law and Victimisation: Reinterpreting *Khan*—Easy Case Makes Bad Law' (2007) 36 *Industrial Law Journal* 364; and M. Connolly, 'Rethinking Victimisation' (2009) 38 *Industrial Law Journal* 149.

Reflection points

1. Do you believe that direct discrimination should cover overt, unconscious, and unintentional discrimination? If not, why not? If so, why?

2. Are you convinced by the distinction drawn between the 'motive' and the 'grounds or reason' for the claimant's treatment adopted by the Supreme Court in *JFS* in relation to direct discrimination claims? Alternatively, do you agree with the view that this distinction is far from clear-cut and that it simply muddies the crucial difference between direct and indirect discrimination?[310]

3. Consider the employer's proportionality defence in the context of the concept of indirect discrimination. Which of the approaches do you think is the most appropriate: (1) the 'least restrictive means' approach; or (2) the 'balancing' approach whereby the harm suffered by the employee is weighed against the employer's need to apply the PCP to achieve the legitimate aim?

 For additional reading on prohibited conduct, visit the Online Resources for this book at www.oup.com/uk/cabrelli3e/

---

[310] On this point, see J. M. Finnis, 'Directly Discriminatory Decisions: A Missed Opportunity' (2010) 126 *Law Quarterly Review* 491, 495.

CHAPTER ELEVEN

THE PROTECTED CHARACTERISTICS

11.1 CONTEXTUAL ANALYSIS OF THE PROTECTED CHARACTERISTICS

Our attention now turns to the grounds recognized as 'protected characteristics' in the Equality Act 2010 ('EA'). The technical analysis of the statutory constructs of direct discrimination, indirect discrimination, harassment, and victimization in Chapter 10 revealed that there is no free-standing right for a claimant to present a complaint on these grounds in the absence of a link to one of the nine protected characteristics. As such, an individual's personhood itself is not protected and it is not competent to raise a discrimination claim based on a factor other than one of the nine fixed protected characteristics. In this chapter, we will probe the rationales for this approach and also question why some characteristics have been earmarked for protection by the law and others have not. This leads us into territory which causes us to theorize about, and contextualize, the protections afforded to certain groups, since the record shows that the recognition of many of the protected characteristics as suspect reasons for discrimination was the product of years of protracted political and social struggle. On another note, the EA treats each of the protected characteristics as distinct, 'exist[ing] and operat[ing] like 'silos' within which each specific form of discrimination [i]s tackled in mutual exclusion [and i]ndividuals [a]re stripped of their plurality so that one [of their] attribute[s i]s magnified clearly before the law'.[1] We will explore why this might be the case, going on to examine each of the protected characteristics in detail, including an analysis of some of the 'boundary disputes' which arise in the case of some of these characteristics. The chapter will then explore the genuine occupational requirements exception, the mechanics of the reversed burden of proof in discrimination cases, and vicarious liability in the discrimination context. Finally, we will analyse the various remedies available to a successful claimant in his/her discrimination complaint before an employment tribunal.

11.1.1 Designing an employment equality law framework: exploring the protected characteristics

In line with the neoliberal philosophy which permeates much of the policy discourse in the current political climate, protection in the EA is concerned with *status* equality, rather than *economic, social, or income* equality. In other words, imbalances in wealth, power, and class are outside the scope of the EA;[2] instead, the EA is designed to address disadvantages associated with an individual's particular status. For example, section 4 of the EA identifies nine characteristics of individuals, which are ranked equally, i.e. there is no hierarchy:

Section 4 The protected characteristics

(1) The following characteristics are protected characteristics—

age;

disability;

gender reassignment;

marriage and civil partnership;

pregnancy and maternity;

race;

religion or belief;

sex;

sexual orientation.[3]

These characteristics are particularly diverse inasmuch as some may affect the ability of employees to perform their job, e.g. age, disability, pregnancy/maternity, and religion or

---

[1] I. Solanke, 'Infusing the Silos in the Equality Act 2010 with Synergy' (2011) 40 *Industrial Law Journal* 336, 337.

[2] Some argue that this is symptomatic of the myopia which blights the political classes, e.g. see R. Wilkinson and K. Pickett, *The Spirit Level: Why Equality is Better for Everyone* (London, Penguin, 2010); J. Stiglitz, *The Price of Inequality* (London, Penguin, 2013).

[3] Section 9(5) of the EA enables a Minister of the Crown to add 'caste' as a protected characteristic: at the time of writing, the Government were consulting on a proposal to introduce 'caste' as a tenth protected characteristic: see https://www.gov.uk/government/consultations/caste-in-great-britain-and-equality-law-a-public-consulation (last visited 6 December 2017). The EAT decided in *Chandhok v Tirkey* [2015] IRLR 195 that 'caste' could form a component of the protected characteristic of 'race', i.e. 'ethnic origins' in section 9(1)(c) of the EA.

belief, whereas others will not, e.g. marriage/civil partnership, race, and sexual orientation. Meanwhile, all but one of them are 'binary' in the sense that one either possesses the characteristic or one does not (e.g. one is either female or male, disabled or able-bodied, etc.). Age is the odd one out, since every employee will have an age:

■ *Seldon v Clarkson, Wright & Jakes* [2012] ICR 716, 720C–E

Baroness Hale:

. . . age is different . . . age is not 'binary' in nature (man or woman, black or white, gay or straight) but a continuum which changes over time. As Lord Walker of Gestingthorpe pointed out in *R (Carson) v Secretary of State for Work and Pensions* [2006] 1 AC 173, para 60: 'Every human being starts life as a tiny infant, and none of us can do anything to stop the passage of the years.' This means that younger people will eventually benefit from a provision which favours older employees, such as an incremental pay scale; but older employees will already have benefited from a provision which favours younger people, such as a mandatory retirement age.

The domestic position can be contrasted with the protection provided under EU law in Article 19 of the Treaty on the Functioning of the European Union ('TFEU')[4] and the Race,[5] Framework,[6] and Recast Equality[7] Directives. Here, the protected characteristics are limited to racial or ethnic origin,[8] religion or belief, disability, age, or sexual orientation,[9] and sex.[10] This can be compared with International Labour Organization ('ILO') Convention 111 of 1958 on Discrimination (Employment and Occupation) which confers protection to race, colour, sex, religion, political opinion, national extraction, or social origin. Meanwhile, the terms of Article 21 of the European Union Charter of Fundamental Rights ('EUCFR')[11] are much broader in remit:

Article 21 Non-discrimination

1. Any discrimination based on any ground such as sex, race, colour, ethnic or social origin, genetic features, language, religion or belief, political or any other opinion, membership of a national minority, property, birth, disability, age or sexual orientation shall be prohibited.

2. . . . any discrimination on grounds of nationality shall be prohibited.

Hepple[12] has produced a useful table contrasting the various positions adopted under the EA, EU law, the European Convention on Human Rights ('ECHR'), and the Universal Declaration of Human Rights ('UDHR'), which is reproduced in Table 11.1.

---

[4] (OJ 2010 C83/47).   [5] Directive 2000/43/EC (OJ 2000 L180/22).
[6] Directive 2000/78/EC (OJ 2000 L303/16).   [7] Directive 2006/54/EC (OJ 2006 L204/23).
[8] Article 1 of the Race Directive.   [9] Article 1 of the Framework Directive.
[10] Article 2(1) of the Recast Equality Directive.
[11] Pronounced on 7 December 2000 in Nice (OJ 2000 C364/1) and a second time in Strasbourg on 12 December 2007 (OJ 2007 C303/1), and also published in OJ 2010 C83/389.
[12] B. Hepple, *Equality: The New Legal Framework*, 2nd edition (Oxford, Hart Publishing, 2014) 36.

Table 11.1 *Table contrasting positions under the EA, EU law, the ECHR, and the UDHR*

	EA	EU	ECHR	UNDHR
Age	✓	✓		
Belief	✓	✓		
Birth			✓	✓
Colour	✓		✓	✓
Disability	✓	✓		
Ethnic origin	✓	✓		
Gender reassignment	✓	✓		
Genetic features		✗		
Irish traveller	✓			
Language			✓	✓
Marriage/civil partnership	✓			
Nationality	✓	✗		
National origin	✓		✓	✓
National minority, association with		✗	✓	
Other status			✓	✓
Political or opinion				✓
Property			✓	✓
Race	✓			✓
Racial origin		✓		
Religion	✓	✓		✓
Sex	✓	✓	✓	✓
Sexual orientation	✓	✓		
Social origin			✓	✓

Source: B. Hepple, *Equality: The New Legal Framework*, 2nd edition (Hart Publishing, 2014) 36.

The striking differences between the models found in the UK, EU law, the EUCFR, the ECHR, and UDHR provoke a number of questions.

(1) On what grounds do UK and EU law justify limiting discrimination protection to a carefully prescribed fixed list of characteristics?

(2) What is it about these particular characteristics that has persuaded the collective judgment of society to accept that they are deserving of anti-discrimination protection under the statutory employment equality regime? Further, what is it about other characteristics that exclude them from the same protective coverage?

These are the two principal questions which will be explored in this section.

If we turn to the first issue, there is a persuasive argument that the application of any form of *arbitrary prejudice* by an employer in deciding how to treat an employee ought to be classified as a civil wrong under the law. Such a wholly unified and open-ended approach to the proscription of discrimination based on the notion of arbitrary prejudice essentially operates to decouple employment equality laws from any protected characteristic at all. It represents a fundamental acceptance of the argument that all forms of unequal treatment predicated on arbitrary prejudice are unjustified. As such, an employee ought to be afforded an anti-discrimination claim where he/she has suffered direct discrimination, indirect discrimination, harassment, or victimization on any ground which is not linked to meritocratic criteria or practices. Pursuant to such a model, if an employee is refused promotion on a ground other than a neutral, meritorious reason such as skills level, competence, experience, qualifications, aptitude, expertise, etc., then the law will intervene to protect the employee. Such an approach presupposes that society has an interest in ensuring that employers apply meritocratic criteria at all times in the process of selection, promotion, dismissal, etc. However, it is not entirely clear that society does have such a right to insist that employers act in such a way. There is the powerful neoliberal argument that although it 'may be rational to give a job to the best person . . . jobs are not at society's disposal and employers have to be allowed to act irrationally'.[13]

Another attraction of an open-ended and unified anti-discrimination regime predicated on the notion of *arbitrary prejudice* is that it eschews the shortcomings prevalent in the existing single-dimension approach to employment equality law whereby a claimant is restricted to claiming discrimination on the basis of a sole protected characteristic.[14] Rather than persisting with a system which lays down a finite set of protected characteristics operating in 'silos' with the inevitable 'boundary issues' which that approach entails, it is possible, under a unified system, for a claimant to raise a claim where non-meritocratic criteria consisting of a combination of suspect categories functioned as the employer's motivation for perpetrating discrimination. For example, the open-ended model would offer redress where an employee suffered direct discrimination—not because he/she is black, homosexual, or an atheist—but because he/she is a black homosexual atheist. This inherent flexibility associated with an open-ended regime therefore enables 'intersectional'/'multiple' discrimination to be tackled, which is something that the UK approach does not currently address:[15]

■ **B. Hepple, *Equality: The New Legal Framework*, 2nd edition (Oxford, Hart Publishing, 2014) 35–6**

There are several advantages to a generalised approach. First, it facilitates proof in cases of multiple discrimination where the precise reason for adverse treatment of a person or group is uncertain; for example, was it because she is a woman, or because she is Black, or because she is pregnant, or a combination of these characteristics? Secondly, an open-ended approach recognises the links between different forms of disadvantage and engenders solidarity between different protected groups. Thirdly, it allows courts and tribunals to develop equality law in response to changing social mores—for example, attitudes to homosexuality and transsexualism changed from the 1970s onwards, but it was not until 1999, when Article 13 of the Treaty of Amsterdam came into force and was implemented in the Framework Employment Directive, that these characteristics were brought within the legal framework. In the future, there is bound to be pressure to add characteristics such as social origin, genetic features and language. [However, i]n the absence of any reference to 'other status' (as in the ECHR), or a general prohibition on any 'unfair' discrimination, the [UK] courts and tribunals will not be in a position to expand the protected characteristics.[16]

---

[13] 'Equal Wrongs: John Crace Meets the Philosopher Who Believes that Striving for Equal Opportunities is a Waste of Time' (*The Guardian*, Education Pages, 26 March 2002).

[14] See the discussion in I. Solanke, *Discrimination as Stigma: A Theory of Anti-Discrimination Law* (Oxford, Hart Publishing, 2017) 47–9.

[15] See *Bahl v Law Society* [2004] EWCA Civ 1070, [2004] IRLR 799; for comment, see I. Solanke, 'Putting Race and Gender Together: A New Approach to Intersectionality' (2009) 72 *Modern Law Review* 723. Section 14 of the EA, which proscribes discrimination on the basis of a combination of two of the protected characteristics, was never brought into force. For the EU law position in relation to intersexuality, see M. Travis, 'Accommodating Intersexuality in European Union Anti-Discrimination Law' (2015) 21 *European Law Journal* 180.

[16] Writer's annotations appear in square brackets throughout this chapter.

However, a powerful counter-argument to the unified model is provided by Advocate-General Sharpston in the case of *Ruiz Zambrano v Office National de l'emploi*.[17] This centres on the legitimacy of such a regime:

■ *Ruiz Zambrano v Office National de l'emploi* [2012] QB 265, 300G–H

Advocate-General Sharpston:

There must be a boundary to every rule granting an entitlement. If there is no such limit, the rule becomes undecipherable and no one can tell with certainty who will, and who will not, enjoy the benefit it confers. That is not in the interests of the member states or the citizen; and it undermines the authority of the court.

Hence, if the touchstone of protection is unequal treatment grounded in arbitrary prejudice on the part of the employer in an open-ended regime, there is a strong contention that the law is deprived of the requisite degree of certainty required to guide employers, employees, courts, and society generally about what constitutes proper behaviour. With flexibility comes uncertainty and an inability to plan, leading to accusations that the law lacks legitimacy. A second argument against the adoption of an open-ended approach is that it often leads to the judicial extrapolation of a hierarchy of protected characteristics. For example, a 'pecking order' of grounds has emerged under the open-ended regime in the ECHR. In this way, some grounds/characteristics are perceived by the judiciary as deserving of a lower level of protection than others, or of the same degree of intensity of scrutiny of managerial conduct.[18] Ultimately, the outcome is a system where some protected characteristics are policed more effectively than others. This may seem invidious, but in many ways is the inevitable product of a unified approach where the values associated with particular protected characteristics vary to such a degree that they may clash in particular cases.[19]

Rather than apply the notion of *arbitrary prejudice* as the justification for an open-ended approach to discrimination law, the criterion of *immutability* has historically functioned as the lynchpin upon which a 'restricted' regime is based. Immutability serves as a useful criterion that guides us towards the identification of a limited set of characteristics for protection from discrimination. This takes us on to the second question we posed earlier, which is essentially a debate about what characteristics should be protected if we reject the open-ended model and instead espouse a restricted regime with a limited set of protected characteristics. Adopting the criterion of *immutability* as the basis for the prescription of protected characteristics is a principled approach. It holds that where certain features of human beings are *unchangeable*, *outside their control*, and *not chosen*, they ought to be protected by law from discrimination. This is on the basis that the protected features ought to be treated by the law as 'normatively irrelevant . . .

---

[17] *Ruiz Zambrano v Office National de l'emploi* [2012] QB 265.

[18] See S. Fredman, *Discrimination Law*, 2nd edition (Oxford, OUP, 2011) 118–30.

[19] For example, where an employer's right to put into practice his/her religious or philosophical belief results in a lesbian employee suffering a detriment at the hands of the employer. Here, we have a clash between the protected characteristics of religious belief and sexual orientation which will entail a degree of prioritization between the two, on which, see A. McColgan, 'Class Wars? Religion and (In)equality in the Workplace' (2009) 38 *Industrial Law Journal* 1; C. O'Cinneide, 'The Uncertain Foundations of Contemporary Anti-Discrimination Law' (2011) 11 *International Journal of Discrimination and the Law* 7.

[in the sense that] possession of these [features or characteristics] should not affect how successful our lives are':[20]

■ **I. Solanke, 'Infusing the Silos in the Equality Act 2010 with Synergy' (2011) 40 *Industrial Law Journal* 336, 349–50**

It has long been the case that [anti-discrimination law ('ADL')] could only be seen as politically legitimate if it served to protect people from mistreatment arising from reasons over which they have little or no control, and are impossible or very difficult to change—in other words, are immutable. Immutability was the reason why protection from discrimination on the grounds of religion was removed from discussions at the UN and in Britain in the 1960s: it was agreed that people should be protected for what they are rather than what they choose. Regional frameworks adopt the same logic: in the case of *TEST-Achat* before the CJEU, Advocate General Kokott described race, ethnic origin and gender as characteristics which are 'inseparably linked' to individuals, 'over which he has no influence' and which is 'not subject to any natural changes'. Immutability is also central in the protection from discrimination in the USA . . . Immutability continues to act as a gatekeeper for ADL—it is argued that weight discrimination is acceptable largely due to the widespread belief that being overweight is a behavioural or voluntary condition. As a result, there is a low level of public sympathy for the overweight and obese. Although 'anti-fat' attitudes are prevalent in society, laws to address this enjoy little political support.

If we accept that *immutability* could be a means of identifying the relevant characteristics which ought to be protected by law from discrimination in a 'restricted' regime, we can ask whether this possesses explanatory force in the context of:

(1) the nine protected characteristics recognized by the EA; and

(2) other attributes of individuals which are often used as a basis for stigmatization in the workplace (and wider society), but are not protected by the EA.

First, if we turn to consider the nine protected characteristics of sex, race, disability, religion or belief, sexual orientation, age, pregnancy/maternity, gender reassignment, and marriage/civil partnership, is it really true to say that these are immutable in nature in the sense that they are unchangeable and unchosen? For example, it has been questioned judicially whether the protected characteristic of religious belief possesses the requisite degree of immutability:

■ *Eweida v British Airways plc* [2010] ICR 890, 901F

Sedley LJ:

One cannot help observing that all of the [protected characteristics in section 4 of the EA] apart from religion or belief are objective characteristics of individuals; religion and belief alone are matters of choice.[21]

---

[20] T. Khaitan, *A Theory of Discrimination Law* (Oxford, OUP, 2015) 56. See the discussion in I. Solanke, *Discrimination as Stigma: A Theory of Anti-Discrimination Law* (Oxford, Hart Publishing, 2017) 49–51 and 54–62.

[21] For a critique, see C. McCrudden, 'Religion, Human Rights, Equality and the Public Sphere' (2011) 13 *Ecclesiastical Law Journal* 26, 32.

Whilst it is true to say that religion is mutable in the sense that the doctrinal tenets of a religion are subject to change over time,[22] the view that religion is a matter of choice is doubtful. This contention assumes that religious and philosophical beliefs are always a matter of choice, and that they ebb and flow in accordance with a person's own free will. This may be accurate for some employees, but a mere moment's reflection leads us to question whether this is necessarily always the case, particularly in light of the dynamic interplay between various social and cultural pressures in the lives of many individuals. Hence, perhaps it is sufficient to conclude that, notwithstanding that religious and philosophical beliefs may be changed in many instances, it is by no means possible to generalize, since in the case of a proportion of the working population such beliefs will necessarily be immutable. Likewise, some commentators have also questioned whether sexual orientation can be categorized as a universal immutable feature over which *all* individuals have absolutely no control:

■ R. Wintemute, *Sexual Orientation and Human Rights* (Oxford, Clarendon Press/OUP, 1997) 174–6

In considering whether sexual orientation is immutable, one should look at the direction of a person's emotional-sexual attraction, because the direction of their conduct is almost certainly chosen. Is the direction of a person's attraction something they cannot change, or is it something they can choose? It is certainly true that many gay men and lesbian women sincerely believe that the direction of their attraction is something they did not choose and cannot change, which makes same-sex emotional-sexual conduct the only viable choice for them. Their own subjective belief in the immutability of their own sexual orientation (as direction of attraction) will often make an immutable status argument seem to them the most appealing response to sexual orientation discrimination. (Indeed, during the first year of my doctoral studies, I was convinced that an immutable status argument was 'the answer', that the connection between attraction and conduct was irrelevant, and that gay men and lesbian women who see their sexual orientation as a choice, as well as bisexual persons, could be 'swept under the carpet'.) A court could merely accept the sincerity of this belief of many gay men and lesbian women, or could find it credible in view of the overwhelming social pressure on them to change. However, there is not yet any way for them to prove the existence and immutability of the direction of their attraction through scientific measurement or observation (e.g. an x-ray, blood test, brain scan or chromosome count), in the way that a person's sex, height, weight or HIV antibody status might be established . . . scientists are still a very long way from conclusively proving that sexual orientation (as direction of attraction) has a 'cause' or combination of 'causes' that precludes individual choice and renders it an 'immutable status'. Nor do all gay men or all lesbian women share this belief. Research does suggest that it is extremely difficult to change the direction of attraction of gay men. But there are gay men who claim that, even though the direction of their attraction may initially have been unchosen, they have succeeded in changing it from same-sex to heterosexual or bisexual . . . The possibility of choice for lesbian and bisexual women has led Didi Herman to question the use of an immutable status argument . . . Thus, it would appear that sexual orientation . . . may be immutable (i.e. impossible to change) for many (perhaps even for most) persons but not for all, and that this immutability cannot be proven conclusively even in those cases where it is said to exist.[23]

[22] See A. McColgan, 'Class Wars? Religion and (In)equality in the Workplace' (2009) 38 *Industrial Law Journal* 1, 23.

[23] See also the article by Matthew Parris, 'Who's Totally Gay? There's No Straight Answer' (*The Times*, 21 April 2012), page 19.

However, is the possibility of change, however rare or difficult, sufficient of itself to deny a characteristic the status of immutability? Gardner argues that it is not:

■ **J. Gardner, 'On the Ground of Her Sex(uality)' (1998) 18 *Oxford Journal of Legal Studies* 167, 172**

> The orientation of our sexual attraction, like our religious faith, might of course change through dramatically life-transforming experiences such as trauma, conversion, or brainwashing. Alienation or *ennui* might also cause us to see the world, including the sexual attractiveness of its occupants, in a different light from before. But the fact that the orientation of one's sexual attraction, or one's religious faith, might change by these means is no consolation to those who are discriminated against on the basis of that orientation or faith. The question for them is not whether their orientation or faith can change, but whether they can now change it by choosing to. Having acquired it, are they stuck with it for the time being? For my money, an affirmative answer to this question makes the status, whether it was originally chosen or not, as immutable as it needs to be to pass the 'immutable status' test.[24]

If we now move on to consider other features harboured by individuals which are often used to subject them to disadvantage in employment and society generally, would the criterion of immutability explain why they are not included in the list of protected characteristics in the EA? For example, if we consider an individual's political opinion or persuasion, this is clearly not a feature which is unchangeable and unchosen, but instead is a behavioural choice. In line with the argument that mutable features ought not to be protected, we find that political views are not one of the nine protected characteristics in section 4 of the EA.[25] The inability to satisfy the criterion of immutability might also explain why we do not proscribe discrimination on the basis of a person's social class, physical appearance or looks,[26] height,[27] or even their weight or size,[28] some or all of which are generally thought (perhaps wrongly) to be subject to change. However, is it

---

[24] See also O. Doyle, 'Direct Discrimination, Indirect Discrimination and Autonomy' (2007) 27 *Oxford Journal of Legal Studies* 537, 544.

[25] See *Redfearn v Serco Ltd* [2006] ICR 1367, 1371F per Mummery LJ, on which, see J. Lewis, 'Discriminating against a Discriminator' (2006) 65 *Cambridge Law Journal* 508. For a more circumspect perspective on the proposition that can be derived from this case, see A. McColgan, 'Class Wars? Religion and (In)equality in the Workplace' (2009) 38 *Industrial Law Journal* 1, 8. However, it must be stressed that political opinion is a protected characteristic in Northern Ireland by virtue of the Fair Employment and Treatment (Northern Ireland) Order 1998 (SI 1998/3162) (on which, see *McConkey v the Simon Community* [2009] IRLR 757). Further, in response to the decision of the ECtHR in *Redfearn v UK* [2013] IRLR 51, the UK Government has introduced a rule whereby any employee who alleges that he/she has been dismissed on the basis of his/her political affiliation is not required to have a minimum of two years' continuous service in order to be eligible to claim unfair dismissal, on which, see section 108(4) of the Employment Rights Act 1996 and Chapter 16, section 16.2.1.1.

[26] The inherent subjectivity of this category may also be another reason.

[27] Taller people seem to be more successful in the workplace: T. Judge and D. Cable, 'The Effect of Physical Height on Workplace Success and Income: Preliminary Test of a Theoretical Model' (2004) 89 *Journal of Applied Psychology* 428.

[28] See T. Hervey and P. Rostant, 'All About That Bass'? Is Non-Ideal-Weight Discrimination Unlawful in the UK?' (2016) 79 *Modern Law Review* 248 and 'Of Course It's OK to Call Another Woman a Hobnob-Guzzling, Lazy Lard-Arse' (*Independent on Sunday*, 18 September 2005), page 24. However, in *Kaltoft v Kommunernes Landsiljforening, acting on behalf of the Municipality of Bullun* [2015] ICR 322 and *Walker v Sita Information Networking Computing Ltd* [2013] Eq LR 476, the European Court of Justice ('ECJ' or 'CJEU') and the EAT held that an obese person could be disabled for the purposes of the European equality law and the EA: see Chapter 12, section 12.1.1.

really true to say that all of the nine protected characteristics in the EA are not matters of choice? *Au contraire*, surely it is true to say that some of the protected characteristics are not immutable at all, but simply manifestations of a fundamental choice exercised by an individual? If so, should this preclude them from protection?

■ S. Fredman, *Discrimination Law*, 2nd edition (Oxford, OUP, 2011) 131–2

Although intuitively appealing, a reliance on immutability does, however, raise a host of further problems. The fact that some aspects of our identity are indeed a matter of personal choice, or can in principle be changed or suppressed, should not be a reason for denying such characteristics the protection of discrimination law. Thus, for many, religion is a matter of personal choice; but does that mean that a person's religion should be a reason for discriminating against her? Pregnancy may or may not be a personal choice. But either way, choice seems irrelevant to the question whether pregnancy should be a protected characteristic. Indeed, even the apparent immutability of sex itself is not unassailable. Many recent cases have concerned discrimination against trans-sexuals: here it is the very mutability of their sex that has triggered the discrimination.

This extract from Fredman impels us to question whether a criterion such as immutability is of itself sufficient to assist us in deciding what characteristics ought to act as the focal point of anti-discrimination laws. Perhaps distinguishing between characteristics on the basis of whether they are a subjective *fundamental choice* or not would be more promising. A fundamental choice is something that every person should have the right to make unconstrained from outside interference. It is distinguishable from a trivial choice by the fact that it is something that is inextricably associated with an individual's pursuit of his/her sense of identity. As such, it is linked to the ideas of personal autonomy, dignity, and identity which we noted in Chapter 10 were particularly forceful ideals in the context of employment equality laws. Although useful up to a point, however, it is not entirely clear how a policy-maker can apply these ideas as a matter of practice to distinguish between fundamental and non-fundamental choices and thus lay down a list of protected characteristics. The following extract provides further clarity:

■ J. Gardner, 'On the Ground of Her Sex(uality)' (1998) 18 *Oxford Journal of Legal Studies* 167, 173–4

... my explanation makes clear that only valuable choices can be fundamental choices, since only valuable choices can contribute to the value of an autonomous life. Whether a choice is valuable depends ... on whether it is a choice between valuable options. This means that not every choice concerning one's own sexuality is made fundamental by the fact that some are. Choosing to have sex with people of one's own sex rather than with people of the opposite sex can be fundamental, because it is a choice between two valuable options, even though choosing to have sex with children or dead bodies rather than living adults would not be, since that is in each case a choice between a valuable option and a base or demeaning one. Thus the test of fundamental choice does not open the door for the morally corrupt or morally deficient to complain of wrongful discrimination when their corruption or deficiency is held against them. The test assists with the protection of gay men and lesbians against discrimination only because ... *there is absolutely nothing wrong with homosexuality*, and the traditional condemnation of it is sheer prejudice or superstition. The implication of this is that the fundamental choice argument ... only yields an improper ground of discrimination when combined with the basic considerations of rationality which it buttresses and extends. It is because those who regard homosexuality as a perversion are mistaken, and hence do not have the reason for their anti-homosexual attitudes and activities that they take themselves to have, that employers and landlords and the occupants of similar roles, even when they do not share in the homophobic mistake themselves, should still not discriminate against homosexual and bisexual people.

The Gardner extract suggests that we can discriminate between choices which are fundamental and those which are not, if the choice is one between (1) two or more competing valuable options and (2) a valuable option and a base or demeaning option: the former is a fundamental choice, but the latter is not.[29] This formula seems simply to swap the word 'valuable' for 'fundamental', which causes an anxiety to take root in our mind that perhaps such a 'fundamental choice' criterion is inadequate as the basis upon which the protected characteristics should be chosen. After all, one person's choice between 'valuable' options is another person's choice between a 'valuable' and a 'demeaning' option.

Perhaps we are looking in the wrong place by focusing on *principles* such as *immutability* and *fundamental choices*. Instead, it may be that more pragmatic criteria grounded in *policy* could act as a more fitting explanation of the state of the protected characteristics in UK and EU law. For example, it may be the fact that an individual's characteristic is subject to widespread arbitrary, inescapable, structural, and punitive *stigmatization*[30] at the hands of the majority in a democratic society that renders it sufficient to earmark that characteristic for protective status. Stigmatization in this context is something more profound than societal disapproval of a particular habit or attribute, such as making smokers light up cigarettes outside buildings. Instead, the notion is rooted in dignitarian concerns about the self-worth of a human individual:

■ R. A. Lenhardt, 'Understanding the Mark: Race, Stigma, and Equality in Context' (2004) 79 *New York University Law Review* 803, 809

... I define ... stigma as a problem of negative social meaning, of 'dishonourable meanings socially inscribed on arbitrary bodily marks [such as skin color], of 'spoiled collective identities.' To be ... stigmatized, under this view, implies more than merely being referred to by a racial[, sexist, ageist, homophobic, etc.] epithet or even the denial of a particular opportunity on the basis of one's race[, sex, disability, religion or belief, sexual orientation, age, pregnancy and maternity, gender reassignment and marriage or civil partnership]. It involves becoming a disfavored or dishonored individual in the eyes of society, a kind of social outcast whose stigmatized attribute stands as a barrier to full acceptance into the wider community. As Loury recently explained, [such] stigmatization 'entails doubting the person's worthiness and consigning him or her to a social netherworld. Indeed, although the language is somewhat hyperbolic, it means being skeptical about whether the person can be assumed to share a common humanity with the observer.'[31]

---

[29] See T. Khaitan, *A Theory of Discrimination Law* (Oxford, OUP, 2015) 60.

[30] See the discussion in I. Solanke, *Discrimination as Stigma: A Theory of Anti-Discrimination Law* (Oxford, Hart Publishing, 2017) ch. 4. For the distinction between stigmatization, subordination, stereotyping, prejudice, and demeaning behaviour, see L. Blum, 'Racial and Other Asymmetries' in D. Hellman and S. Moreau (eds), *Philosophical Foundations of Discrimination Law* (Oxford, OUP, 2013) 187–90.

[31] See also the discussion in I. Solanke, 'Infusing the Silos in the Equality Act 2010 with Synergy' (2011) 40 *Industrial Law Journal* 336, 350–5.

Thus, it is the extent to which society perceives the individual as being detached from the mainstream which categorizes the individual as stigmatized. However, an approach which relies on arbitrary stigmatization as the identifying criterion suffers from the disadvantage that it is hopelessly broad which would bring many characteristics within the scope of protective status. For example, is it truly correct to say that alcoholics and drug addicts do not suffer from arbitrary, structural, and punitive stigmatization in gaining access to the workplace? Rather, is it not the case that they are routinely subjected to a thinly masked degree of opprobrium and segregation? If so, does that of itself make them deserving of special protection from discrimination laws? It would seem that there are differing degrees of stigmatization and it is not wholly clear where the line ought to be drawn between deserving and non-deserving cases.

For that reason, it may be that stigmatization is not necessarily a helpful criterion. In fact, when we examine the historical development of the recognition of the protected characteristics, there is something to be said for the point that 'the decision [to recognize the protected characteristics w]as simply a political one, reflecting the balance of opinion in society at a particular time'.[32] For example, the first ground to be protected was race,[33] which was a political reaction to the large influx of Asian and Afro-Caribbean immigrants into the UK in the 1950s and 1960s from the former imperial colonies.[34] The extent of the discrimination and the size of the group affected were sufficiently weighty to foster the political will to intervene legislatively. Race was followed by sex/gender in the 1970s, which was a response to the economic logic of the European Common Market, which the UK had recently joined. It was deemed contrary to the proper functioning of the Common Market for employers to be permitted to discriminate across the EU in the pay they tendered to their male and female workers: prior to the enactment of the Treaty of Rome in 1957, France had introduced equal pay laws and argued that its corporations could be undercut from competitors situated in other Member States if the principle of equal pay were not established in the Treaty.[35] Thereafter, the characteristics of disability, sexual orientation, religion or belief, and age were recognized by the UK's Disability Discrimination Act 1995 and the Framework Directive in 2000. These legislative interventions were a manifestation of the political will which existed to foster a close sense of citizenship amongst the peoples of the EU[36] and to extend the application of the judicially sanctioned ideal of equality and non-discrimination as a fundamental principle of European law.[37] Other plausible motivations for the recognition of disability and age as protected characteristics might well have been the political and economic desire to promote the increased participation of the elderly and disabled in the labour market, as well as the cross-fertilization of jurisprudence between the CJEU and the European Court of Human Rights ('ECtHR') in construing the ECHR. Of course, widespread public acceptance of the wrongfulness of discrimination based on a person's sexual orientation, disability, age, and religion was a necessary precondition of such political motivation, but by the 1990s it was generally acknowledged that public opinion was sufficiently receptive to the adoption of such a course of action. Changes in public attitudes had been shaped by the increasing acceptance of the ECtHR to interpret the ECHR in a manner which extended protection from discrimination to a broader range of minority groups.

---

[32] S. Fredman, *Discrimination Law*, 2nd edition (Oxford, OUP, 2011) 111.

[33] See the Race Relations Acts of 1965 and 1968.

[34] See H. Goulbourne, *Race Relations in Britain Since 1945* (Basingstoke, Macmillan Press, 1998) ch. 2.

[35] See L. Dickens, 'The Road is Long: Thirty Years of Equality Legislation in Britain' (2007) 45 *British Journal of Industrial Relations* 463, 469.

[36] See M. Bell, 'Equality and Diversity: Anti-Discrimination Law after Amsterdam' in J. Shaw (ed.), *Social Law and Policy in an Evolving European Union* (Oxford, Hart Publishing, 2000) 157; D. Schiek, 'A New Framework on Equal Treatment of Persons in EC Law?' (2002) 8 *European Law Journal* 290, 293–4.   [37] See *Defrenne v SABENA (No. 3)* [1978] ECR 1365, 1378.

Therefore, where does this take our discussion and what kind of conclusion can we draw? Suffice to say that there is no one identifiable 'threshold' criterion which can be applied in order to discern whether a particular characteristic ought to be brought within the protective cloak of anti-discrimination laws. Whilst the criteria of immutability and fundamental choice are indisputably rationales which may be advanced as justifications for the recognition of the nine protected characteristics, they by no means possess full explanatory force when they are placed under the microscope. Instead, an element of political and social recognition that certain stigmatized groups ought to be afforded protection has also held sway over the decision whether to legislate or not. Therefore, we can claim with a measure of confidence that a combination of factors has served to produce the present legal position which we find today.

11.2 AN ASSESSMENT OF THE PROTECTED CHARACTERISTICS

In this section, we place our magnifying glass over the definitions, and judicial interpretation, of eight[38] of the nine protected characteristics in the EA. We will encounter two recurring themes in our discussion of these eight grounds which interlink. These are the themes of (1) 'boundary dispute' and (2) 'spin out', which give rise to new protected characteristics. The interrelationship between these features is shown in Figure 11.1.

In the previous paragraph, we referred to the nine grounds recognized as protected characteristics as a 'fixed' list. The adjective 'fixed' is somewhat misleading, since:

(1) it is by no means the case that the number of protected characteristics will remain static; and

(2) a variety of 'boundary disputes' have arisen in relation to the scope of the nine protected characteristics.

The result of these boundary disputes in some cases has been the expansion of the territory which they occupy, e.g. 'sex' has been interpreted as covering transsexuals. As such, rather than conceive of the protected characteristics as possessing a rigid set of boundaries, it is perhaps beneficial to think of them as malleable with outside walls that oscillate in line with changes in social, political, and cultural attitudes. The first 'boundary disputes' theme is closely related to the second theme, which we may describe in shorthand as 'spin out'. This describes the phenomenon whereby a 'boundary dispute' concerning the extent of the coverage of a protected characteristic x leads to the expansion of that category to include a particular attribute y; thus, x is judicially construed as inclusive of y. After a period of time, social, cultural, and political pressure is brought to bear and policy-makers respond in turn by recognizing y as a protected characteristic in its own right. This dynamic describes how the protected characteristics of gender reassignment, pregnancy, and maternity came to be acknowledged as

Figure 11.1 *Relationship between protected characteristics, 'boundary disputes' and 'spin out'*

[38] Disability is addressed separately in Chapter 12.

separate categories deserving of protection, as they were 'spun out' of the protected characteristic of 'sex'.[39]

11.2.1 Sex, gender reassignment, pregnancy, and maternity discrimination

Sex/gender was the second factor to be recognized as a protected characteristic when the Equal Pay Act 1970 and the Sex Discrimination Act 1975 ('SDA') came into force in the 1970s. The struggle for equality of the sexes before the law was a long political and social struggle. The historical record furnishes ample evidence of the widespread job segregation and wage inequality which were features of the labour market in the nineteenth and twentieth centuries. Women were confined to working roles in the service industries and excluded from certain professions such as law and medicine. Stereotypical societal assumptions about the role of women—as being primarily responsible for childbearing and childcare—were endemic and the prevailing attitude was that the workplace was no place for a woman. Women were perceived to be less productive than men and too emotional to engage in business. Such views were often perpetuated, harnessed, and fostered by the legal system. For example, in the early twentieth century, the judiciary had no hesitation in ruling that an employer was within its rights to dismiss a female teacher for the reason that she had married.[40] Moreover, the following judicial proclamation illustrates how outdated stereotypical attitudes about the ability and suitability of women to perform certain roles continued to persist until well into the 1960s:

■ *Nagle v Fielden* [1966] 2 QB 633, 647D

> *Lord Denning:*
>
> It is not as if the training of horses could be regarded as an unsuitable occupation for a woman, like that of a jockey or speedway-rider.

It is no exaggeration to say that there has been a radical transformation over the past 50 years in societal attitudes to the roles which women can perform: we can now say with a measure of confidence that the opinion expressed in *Nagle v Fielden* is no longer widespread. Women are no longer treated as being unable or unsuitable to work, and can and do act as breadwinners. Highly prized legal protections from workplace discrimination have been pressed into service as a means of chiselling away at outmoded attitudes. Further, the emergence of flexible labour markets has enabled women to structure their working lives around childcare and other commitments. Employees are now entitled to protection from direct and indirect discrimination and harassment on the ground of sex.

With that background in mind, we now move on to consider the terms of the EA.[41] Equality legislation has never given a precise definition of 'sex' and this approach continues into the EA:

---

[39] However, it should be stressed that the recognition of a new protected characteristic does not deprive it from being protected under the auspices of the characteristic from which it was originally derived: in other words, after *y* is statutorily treated as a distinct characteristic, *x* continues to include *y*. This is a matter of some significance where the types of prohibited conduct that *y* is protected from are not comprehensive, which, as we will see, is precisely the case in the context of pregnancy, maternity, marriage, and civil partnership.

[40] *Price v Rhondda Urban District Council* [1923] 2 Ch 372, 391 per Eve J.

[41] For comment on the impact of the EA on gender justice, see B. Burton, 'Neoliberalism and the Equality Act 2010: A Missed Opportunity for Gender Justice?' (2014) 43 *Industrial Law Journal* 112.

Section 11 Sex

(1) In relation to the protected characteristic of sex—

    (a) a reference to a person who has a particular protected characteristic is a reference to a man or to a woman;

    (b) a reference to persons who share a protected characteristic is a reference to persons of the same sex . . .

Section 212 General interpretation

(1) In this Act—

    'man' means a male of any age . . .

    'woman' means a female of any age.[42]

These statutory provisions reveal that UK law essentially adopts a biological, rather than social, construction of gender and the biological differences between the sexes are acknowledged.

One thorny issue is the matter of the segregation of the sexes.[43] Here, in technical terms, both sexes are being treated equally, but are separated from each other. The case of *Chief Inspector of Education, Children's Services and Skills v Interim Executive Board of Al-Hijrah School*[44] concerned the status of OFSTED's policy regarding segregation in mixed schools. This policy stated that there must be good educational reasons for a school to segregate on the basis of sex which must be justified. When a Muslim school was found to engage in sex segregation, this policy was challenged. Mr Justice Jay in the EAT ruled that segregation could not be said to be discrimination as it was not clear whether one sex as a group was being treated 'less favourably' than the other group. He also rejected the idea of 'double discrimination', i.e. both sexes being treated less favourably inasmuch as both lost the opportunity to socialize and learn with the other sex. OFSTED appealed, and when the case was heard by the Court of Appeal it was held that the School's segregation policy caused detriment and less favourable treatment for both male and female pupils alike by reason of their sex and therefore amounted to direct discrimination under the EA. Segregation by gender was a detriment which diminished the quality of a pupil's education, since male and female pupils lost the opportunity to socialize, interact, and learn with, or from, the opposite sex. And perhaps more importantly, section 13 of the EA demands that direct discrimination be approached from the viewpoint of a 'person' rather than a group, i.e. the crucial question is whether segregation results in less favourable treatment for an individual, rather than the group/protected characteristic of which he/she forms part vis-à-vis a comparator group. For that reason, it was an error to assess less favourable treatment from the perspective of groups of females and groups of males.

Circumstances in which the biological condition of a human being is in a mutable state have given rise to the first of the 'boundary disputes' which we referred to earlier. In *P v*

---

[42] Section 13(6) of the EA directs that less favourable treatment of a female employee because she is breastfeeding is to be treated as sex discrimination.

[43] Segregation based on race is automatically treated as direct discrimination: section 13(5) of the EA.

[44] [2017] IRLR 30 (High Court), [2017] EWCA Civ 1426 (Court of Appeal).

S, the issue was whether discrimination against a transsexual qualified as discrimination on the grounds of his/her sex:

■ *P v S and Cornwall County Council* [1996] ICR 795, 813F–814F

> *European Court of Justice:*
>
> [The question here is therefore] whether, having regard to the purpose of the [Recast Equality Directive, Article 14(1)] . . . dismissal of a transsexual for a reason related to his or her gender reassignment . . . [is precluded] . . . the scope of the [Recast Equality] Directive . . . cannot be confined simply to discrimination based on the fact that a person is of one or other sex. In view of its purpose and the nature of the rights which it seeks to safeguard, the scope of the [Recast Equality] Directive is also such as to apply to discrimination arising, as in this case, from the gender reassignment of the person concerned. Such discrimination is based, essentially if not exclusively, on the sex of the person concerned. Where a person is dismissed on the ground that he or she intends to undergo, or has undergone, gender reassignment, he or she is treated unfavourably by comparison with persons of the sex to which he or she was deemed to belong before undergoing gender reassignment. To tolerate such discrimination would be tantamount, as regards such a person, to a failure to respect the dignity and freedom to which he or she is entitled, and which the court has a duty to safeguard. Dismissal of such a person must therefore be regarded as contrary to article [14(1) of the Recast Equality Directive].

If we apply the reasoning in *P v S and Cornwall County Council*, i.e. whether the relevant discrimination 'is based, essentially if not exclusively, on the sex of the person concerned', do you believe that the employees in the following two Hypotheticals A and B would be protected from discrimination on the basis of the protected characteristic of 'sex'?

Hypothetical A

John Hardman ('JH') has been employed by Danny's Demolishers Ltd ('DD') for three weeks in its Cambridge office. JH is a hermaphrodite and is regularly subjected to highly rude and offensive 'jokes' by his manager about his genitalia in the office. The *Oxford English Dictionary* defines a hermaphrodite as a 'person . . . having both male and female sex organs'.

Hypothetical B

Danny's Demolishers Ltd ('DD') employs Charles Campbell ('CC') in its Edinburgh office. CC is a eunuch and is regularly subjected to highly rude and offensive 'jokes' by his manager about his (lack of) genitalia in the office. The *Oxford English Dictionary* defines a eunuch as a 'castrated person of the male sex'.

The recognition of protection for transsexuals within the purview of the ground of 'sex' was subsequently 'spun out' into the separate protected characteristic of 'gender reassignment'[45] in section 7 of the EA, with direct and indirect discrimination and harassment protection explicitly conferred under sections 16, 25, and 26 of the EA. The definition of 'gender reassignment' in section 7 of the EA covers individuals who have embarked on the transition from a man to a woman and vice versa. It is also broader than the pre-EA law, since there is no longer any need for the employee to show that he/she is undergoing medical supervision. The Explanatory Notes to the EA explain that an employee will satisfy the criteria in section 7 notwithstanding that he/she does not consult medical professionals on reassigning his/her gender, but simply starts to live as a member of the opposite sex and 'passes' as a member of the opposite sex without such medical intervention.[46] As for the range of prohibited conduct, the extracts reveal that direct discrimination, indirect discrimination, and harassment on the ground of gender reassignment are covered. Section 16 also protects a transsexual from being treated less favourably than a person who is sick or injured because he/she is proposing to undergo the relevant treatment to change his/her sex. Transsexuals enjoy protection in respect of any period they take off work to undergo gender reassignment 'if they are treated less favourably than they would be treated for absence for reasons other than sickness or injury and it is unreasonable to treat them less favourably'.[47]

A separate 'boundary dispute' arose as to whether discrimination on the basis of an individual's sexual orientation fell within the scope of 'sex' discrimination. In the case of *Grant v Southwest Trains*,[48] the ECJ refused to recognize sexual orientation discrimination as a species of sex discrimination. However, as will become apparent,[49] the struggle for gay, lesbian, and bisexual rights was not defeated. In the Framework Directive,[50] European policy-makers acknowledged that sexual orientation ought to feature as a distinct protected characteristic. However, unlike sexual orientation, in a series of groundbreaking decisions in the 1980s and 1990s, the ECJ was prepared to include pregnancy and maternity within the ambit of 'sex' discrimination.[51] Akin to the gender reassignment category, both pregnancy and maternity were then 'spun out' from 'sex' discrimination and are now protected characteristics by virtue of section 18 of the EA:

Section 13 Direct discrimination . . .

(6) If the protected characteristic is sex—

. . .

(b) in a case where B is a man, no account is to be taken of special treatment afforded to a woman in connection with pregnancy or childbirth . . .

---

[45] See the pre-EA decision of the House of Lords in *A v Chief Constable of West Yorkshire Police* [2004] ICR 806 which effectively recognized gender reassignment as a protected characteristic.

[46] See Explanatory Notes to the EA, available at http://www.legislation.gov.uk/ukpga/2010/15/notes/division/3/2/1/4/3 at para 43 (last visited 6 December 2017).

[47] Explanatory Notes to the EA, available at http://www.legislation.gov.uk/ukpga/2010/15/notes/division/3/2/2/4/1 at para 71 (last visited 6 December 2017).

[48] [1998] ICR 449.

[49] See section 11.2.4.

[50] Directive 2000/78/EC (OJ 2000 L303/16).

[51] *Dekker v Stichting Vormingscentrum Voor Jonge Volwassen (VJV Centrum) Plus* [1990] ECR I-3941; *Hertz* [1990] ECR I-3979; *Webb v EMO Air Cargo (UK) Ltd (No. 1)* [1994] IRLR 482; *Webb v EMO Air Cargo (UK) Ltd (No. 2)* [1995] IRLR 645; and *Tele Danmark A/S v Handels- og Kontorfunctionernes Forbund i Denmark* [2001] IRLR 853.

Section 18 Pregnancy and maternity discrimination: work cases

(1) This section has effect for the purposes of the application of Part 5 (work) to the protected characteristic of pregnancy and maternity.

(2) A person (A) discriminates against a woman if, in the protected period in relation to a pregnancy of hers, A treats her unfavourably—

    (a) because of the pregnancy, or

    (b) because of illness suffered by her as a result of it.

(3) A person (A) discriminates against a woman if A treats her unfavourably because she is on compulsory maternity leave.

(4) A person (A) discriminates against a woman if A treats her unfavourably because she is exercising or seeking to exercise, or has exercised or sought to exercise, the right to ordinary or additional maternity leave . . .

(6) The protected period, in relation to a woman's pregnancy, begins when the pregnancy begins, and ends—

    (a) if she has the right to ordinary and additional maternity leave, at the end of the additional maternity leave period or (if earlier) when she returns to work after the pregnancy;

    (b) if she does not have that right, at the end of the period of 2 weeks beginning with the end of the pregnancy . . .

Employees who are pregnant are entitled to *more favourable treatment* during the protected period calculated in accordance with section 18(6). This can be ascribed to the absence of any requirement for such employees to compare their treatment with that of a suitable comparator.[52] The same point applies in the case of female employees on compulsory, ordinary, or additional maternity leave.[53] This is the effect of:

(1) the requirement in section 18(2) that the pregnant employee or employee on compulsory, ordinary, or maternity leave must show that she was treated 'unfavourably'— rather than 'less favourably' than a comparator;[54] and

(2) Recital (23) of the Preamble to the Recast Equality Directive.

As such, pregnancy discrimination is a form of *positive discrimination* enjoining employers to treat pregnant employees more favourably than the mainstream workforce, which protects the reproductive capacity of women and is a reflection of the biological realities.[55]

---

[52] See also regulation 10 of the Maternity and Parental Leave Regulations 1999 (SI 1999/3312) ('MPLR') which stipulates that, where an employer intends to make an employee on maternity leave redundant as part of an overall redundancy process, such an employee has the right to be offered a suitable available vacancy, i.e. a new contract of employment, in priority to other employees, on which, see Chapter 18, section 18.3.4. However, it should be stressed that an employer's failure to honour the terms of regulation 10 of the MPLR will not of itself constitute direct pregnancy or maternity discrimination: *Sefton Borough Council v Wainwright* [2015] ICR 652.

[53] Arguably, the protection afforded here ought to extend to 'maternity' and not simply compulsory, ordinary, and/or additional maternity leave.

[54] For example, see *Interserve FM Ltd v Tuleikyte* [2017] IRLR 615, 617 per Simler J and *Metropolitan Police v Keohane* [2014] ICR 1073.

[55] See S. Fredman, 'Pregnancy and Parenthood Reassessed' (1994) 110 *Law Quarterly Review* 106. However, this does not mean that the pregnant employee or employee on maternity leave must not show that her 'unfavourable' treatment was 'because' of pregnancy or maternity: *Interserve FM Ltd v Tuleikyte* [2017] IRLR 615, 617 per Simler J. This will entail an evaluation as to whether the case is a 'criterion' or 'reason why' direct discrimination case when the reasons or grounds for the impugned treatment are considered, on which, see Chapter 10, section 10.2.3.

Pregnancy discrimination covers discrimination relating to an employee's pregnancy-related illnesses,[56] but does not extend to unfavourable treatment meted out to an employee who is undergoing IVF treatment where, on the date of the discriminatory act, the employee's ova have been fertilized by her partner's sperm cells, but not yet transferred into her uterus.[57] Examples of direct discrimination 'because of' pregnancy include the failure to renew a pregnant employee's fixed-term contract for the reason of her pregnancy[58] and dismissing a pregnant employee recruited for a fixed period, notwithstanding that she had omitted to inform her employer that she was pregnant when her contract was concluded and she was absent owing to pregnancy for a substantial portion of the period of the fixed-term contract.[59] As for the nature of the causal connection, it has been held that whether the unfavourable treatment is attributable to pregnancy is a question which must be assessed objectively, albeit that there is no requirement that pregnancy be the sole, or even the principal, cause of the treatment.[60] A final matter of some import is that section 18 does not specifically prohibit indirect discrimination or harassment on the grounds of pregnancy or maternity leave,[61] which is a matter of great concern, given that recent evidence has revealed that one in five mothers have reported 'harassment or negative comments related to pregnancy or flexible working from their employer and/or colleagues'.[62]

11.2.2 Race discrimination

Race was the first characteristic to be recognized as a factor deserving of protection. This was partly a UK parliamentary response to the fact that the common law of the contract of employment[63] offered no sanctuary for those employees on the receiving end of racially discriminatory behaviour prior to the coming into force of the Race Relations Acts of 1965 and 1968:

---

[56] *Brown v Rentokil Ltd* [1998] IRLR 445. However, contrast this with *Lyons v DWP JobCentre Plus* [2014] ICR 668 where it was ruled that a dismissal for absences relating to post-natal depression arising after maternity leave did not amount to sex or pregnancy or maternity discrimination under section 13 or 18 of the EA since a man experiencing a similar period of sickness would have been treated identically.

[57] *Mayr v Bäckerei und Konditorei Gerhard Flöckner OHG* [2008] 2 CMLR 27, [2008] IRLR 387; *Brown v Rentokil Ltd* [1998] IRLR 445. However, this is subject to *Sahota v Home Office* [2010] ICR 772, 779, where Underhill J (P) remarked that IVF treatment should be treated as equivalent to pregnancy for the purposes of determining unfavourable treatment in the context of sex discrimination where the treatment has reached the limited stage between the follicular puncture and the immediate transfer of the in vitro fertilized ova into the uterus.

[58] *Jiménez Melgar v Ayuntamiento de Los Barrios* [2001] IRLR 848.

[59] *Tele Danmark A/S v Handels- og Kontorfunctionernes Forbund i Denmark* [2001] IRLR 853.

[60] *O'Neill v Governors of St Thomas More RCVA Upper School* [1996] IRLR 372.

[61] See Chapter 10, section 10.2.5. However, as noted in Chapter 10, section 10.2.5, this does not afford an employer carte blanche to harass employees because they are pregnant or on maternity leave, since pregnant employees and employees on maternity leave may be able to demonstrate that they were indirectly discriminated against or harassed because of their sex. As such, if we refer back to the formulation adumbrated in section 11.2, if 'sex' is x and 'pregnancy' is y, since x has been ruled to include y, the fact that y is only subject to protection from direct discrimination does not prevent an employee with the characteristic y from being successful in a claim that she has been indirectly discriminated against or harassed on the grounds of characteristic x.

[62] See Joint BIS and EHRC report, 'Pregnancy and Maternity-Related Discrimination and Disadvantage' (BIS Research Paper No. 235), 22 March 2016, available at https://www.gov.uk/government/publications/pregnancy-and-maternity-related-discrimination-and-disadvantage-final-reports at page 9 (last visited 6 December 2017).

[63] For a comprehensive and enlightening summary of the attitude of the common law judges to racist behaviour in the workplace and beyond, see A. McColgan, *Discrimination, Equality and the Law* (Oxford, Hart Publishing, 2014) 10–13.

■ *Re Lysaght, Hill v Royal College of Surgeons* [1965] 3 WLR 191, 206C–F

Buckley J:

I accept that racial and religious discrimination is nowadays widely regarded as deplorable in many respects and I am aware that there is a Bill dealing with racial relations at present under consideration by Parliament, but I think that it is going much too far to say that the endowment of a charity, the beneficiaries of which are to be drawn from a particular faith or are to exclude adherents to a particular faith, is contrary to public policy. The testatrix's desire to exclude persons of the Jewish faith or of the Roman Catholic faith from those eligible for the studentship in the present case appears to me to be unamiable, and I would accept . . . that it is undesirable, but it is not, I think, contrary to public policy.

In many ways, the judicial sentiment of Buckley J echoes the pronunciation of Lord Davey in the classic common law case of *Allen v Flood*[64] that 'an employer may discharge a workman . . . or may refuse to employ one from [*sic*] the most mistaken, capricious, malicious or morally reprehensible motives that can be conceived, but the workman has no right of action against him [under the common law]'.[65]

However, the effect of successive waves of parliamentary intervention—the principal example being the Race Relations Act 1976 ('RRA')—is that the common law position is now largely irrelevant. As we noted in Chapter 10,[66] the EA represents the fifth generation of statutory equality laws[67] and race discrimination lies at the very core of the protections conferred. Of course, the racial mix of the population of the UK has changed radically since the 1960s when the first race relations legislation was introduced. Britain is now a much more diverse society. Research has suggested that approximately 13.6 per cent of the UK population belonged to an ethnic minority group in 2016.[68] This is projected to rise to 20 per cent of the overall UK population in 2051.[69] Thus, more of us will belong to an ethnic minority group as the twenty-first century progresses.

Section 9 is the relevant section of the EA which confers protection from discrimination on the basis of 'race'. This is explicitly expressed to include closely related characteristics such as colour, nationality, ethnic origins, and/or national origins. Direct and indirect discrimination and harassment on the ground of race are all proscribed:

Section 9 Race

(1) Race includes—

    (a) colour;

    (b) nationality;

    (c) ethnic or national origins.

---

[64] [1898] AC 1.   [65] *ibid.*, 172–3.   [66] See Chapter 10, section 10.2.1.

[67] See B. Hepple, *Equality: The New Legal Framework*, 2nd edition (Oxford, Hart Publishing, 2014) 11–17 for a synopsis of the five generations of equality laws.

[68] See House of Commons Library Briefing Paper SN01156, 28 June 2017, *Ethnic Minorities in Politics and Public Life*, available at http://researchbriefings.files.parliament.uk/documents/SN01156/SN01156. pdf at page 4 (last visited 6 December 2017).

[69] P. Rees, P. Wohland, P. Norman, and P. Boland, 'Ethnic Population Projections for the UK, 2001– 2051' (2012) 29 *Journal of Population Research* 45.

(2) In relation to the protected characteristic of race—

    (a) a reference to a person who has a particular protected characteristic is a reference to a person of a particular racial group;

    (b) a reference to persons who share a protected characteristic is a reference to persons of the same racial group.

(3) A racial group is a group of persons defined by reference to race; and a reference to a person's racial group is a reference to a racial group into which the person falls.

(4) The fact that a racial group comprises two or more distinct racial groups does not prevent it from constituting a particular racial group.[70]

In one of the first decisions of the House of Lords to consider a claim of race discrimination, Lord Simon recognized that a person's 'race' was not a matter to be determined along scientific or biological lines;[71] instead, in contrast with the characteristic of sex, it is a feature to be evaluated in cultural terms. This line of reasoning was approved by Lord Fraser in the subsequent decision of the House of Lords in *Mandla v Dowell Lee*,[72] in which the relationship between the terms 'race' and 'ethnic origins' in the legislation was addressed:

■ *Mandla v Dowell Lee* [1983] AC 548, 561D–F

Lord Fraser:

My Lords, I recognise that 'ethnic' conveys a flavour of race but it cannot, in my opinion, have been used in the [EA] in a strictly racial or biological sense. For one thing, it would be absurd to suppose that Parliament can have intended that membership of a particular racial group should depend upon scientific proof that a person possessed the relevant distinctive biological characteristics (assuming that such characteristics exist). The practical difficulties of such proof would be prohibitive, and it is clear that Parliament must have used the word in some more popular sense. For another thing, the briefest glance at the evidence in this case is enough to show that, within the human race, there are very few, if any, distinctions which are scientifically recognised as racial.

The House also furnished guidance on how the courts and tribunals should approach the scope of the expression 'ethnic origins' in the legislation. The leading speech on this matter was delivered by Lord Fraser, who adopted a relatively broad formulation:

■ *Mandla v Dowell Lee* [1983] AC 548, 562D–563A

Lord Fraser:

For a group to constitute an ethnic group in the sense of the [EA], it must, in my opinion, regard itself, and be regarded by others, as a distinct community by virtue of certain characteristics. Some of these characteristics are essential; others are not essential but one or more of them will com-

---

[70] Cf. the position in EU law in *Jyske Finans A/S v Ligebehandlingsnaevnet* [2017] IRLR 665.
[71] *Ealing London Borough Council v Commission for Racial Equality* [1972] AC 342, 362D per Lord Simon.   [72] [1983] AC 548.

monly be found and will help to distinguish the group from the surrounding community. The conditions which appear to me to be essential are these: (1) a long shared history, of which the group is conscious as distinguishing it from other groups, and the memory of which it keeps alive; (2) a cultural tradition of its own, including family and social customs and manners, often but not necessarily associated with religious observance. In addition to those two essential characteristics the following characteristics are, in my opinion, relevant; (3) either a common geographical origin, or descent from a small number of common ancestors; (4) a common language, not necessarily peculiar to the group; (5) a common literature peculiar to the group; (6) a common religion different from that of neighbouring groups or from the general community surrounding it; (7) being a minority or being an oppressed or a dominant group within a larger community, for example a conquered people (say, the inhabitants of England shortly after the Norman conquest) and their conquerors might both be ethnic groups. A group defined by reference to enough of these characteristics would be capable of including converts, for example, persons who marry into the group, and of excluding apostates. Provided a person who joins the group feels himself or herself to be a member of it, and is accepted by other members, then he is, for the purposes of the [EA], a member. That appears to be consistent with the words at the end of section [9(3) of the EA]: '[A] reference . . . to a person's racial group [is a reference to a racial group into which the person falls].' In my opinion, it is possible for a person to fall into a particular racial group either by birth or by adherence, and it makes no difference, so far as the [EA] is concerned, by which route he finds his way into the group.

In *R v Governing Body of Jews Free School*,[73] the majority of the Supreme Court went somewhat further than Lord Fraser. They held that the treatment of an employee will be attributable to his/her 'ethnic origin' if he/she is discriminated against on grounds of from whom he/she is descended. Moreover, Lord Clarke expressed the view that the ground for the discrimination was not an 'either/or' question; instead, the ground could be attributable to both an employee's ethnicity *and* religion,[74] with Lord Kerr[75] and Lady Hale[76] both taking a slightly different approach and saying that an individual's origin could be a complex amalgam of ethnicities, e.g. an employee could be discriminated against because he/she was half Italian and half Masorti Jew. The upshot of this approach is that the division between ethnic origins and religion is particularly fine, if not elusive, with Connolly going so far as to claim that they have become 'virtually inseparable' grounds.[77] In addition, it should not be forgotten that section 9(4) provides that sub-groups and separate denominations of racial groups/ethnic origins will be covered, such as Orthodox Jews and Masorti Jews in the *JFS* case.

Lord Fraser's third consideration of 'a common language, not necessarily peculiar to the group' has also been held to be interlinked with the concept of race for the purposes of section 9 of the EA. In *Kelly v Covance Laboratories Ltd*,[78] a Russian laboratory worker claimed she had suffered race discrimination at work after she was instructed not to speak her native tongue, Russian, in the workplace. The lab work involved animal testing and her employer had concerns regarding activists involved in espionage at the lab. The EAT affirmed the tribunal's decision that there was no direct race discrimination because the same instruction would have been given to the 'hypothetical comparator' of

---

[73] *R v Governing Body of Jews Free School* [2009] UKSC 15, [2010] 2 AC 728.
[74] *ibid.*, 784E–G per Lord Clarke.   [75] *ibid.*, 780A–B per Lord Kerr.
[76] *ibid.*, 760G–H per Lady Hale.
[77] M. Connolly, 'Racial Groups, Sub-Groups, the Demise of the *But for* Test and the Death of the Benign Motive Defence: *R (on the application of E) v Governing Body of JFS*' (2010) 39 *Industrial Law Journal* 183, 187.   [78] *Kelly v Covance Laboratories Ltd* [2016] IRLR 338.

any other person who spoke a language other than English. The EAT rejected the argument that this was a case of direct race discrimination, and instead held that the discrimination was indirect instead. This could be objectively justified on the basis that protecting security concerns was a legitimate aim.[79]

Pursuant to the application of Lord Fraser's influential approach in *Mandla v Dowell Lee*, it has been held that gypsies and Irish travellers are distinct ethnic groups,[80] as are Sikhs[81] and Jews.[82] As for the question of caste, it has been decided by the EAT in *Chandhok v Tirkey*[83] that caste falls within section 9 of the EA, notwithstanding that the relevant subordinate legislation specifically recognizing caste as a protected characteristic has not yet been brought into force under section 9(5) of the EA. This can be contrasted with the decision of the Supreme Court in *Taiwo v Olaigbe*,[84] where it was ruled that less favourable treatment of an individual because of his/her 'vulnerable migrant worker status' will not be equated with racial discrimination or discrimination based on ethnic origins.[85] Meanwhile, in *Crown Suppliers (Property Services Agency) v Dawkins*,[86] it was ruled that Rastafarians are not a distinct ethnic group and likewise, in *JH Walker v Hussain*,[87] the EAT took the view that Muslims cannot be characterized as an ethnic group. The fact that Sikhs and Jews are recognized as having separate ethnic origins but Rastafarians and Muslims are not has served to expose the fact that the boundary between race/ethnic origin and religion is particularly fraught. Attempts to slot a religion within the auspices of the 'ethnic origins' category were rendered somewhat[88] superfluous with effect from 2003 when religion was recognized as a separate protected characteristic.[89] Thus, 'religion' effectively has been 'spun out' from race and ethnic origins and now finds itself treated as a separate protected characteristic in section 10 of the EA.

As for 'colour', it is unlikely that an employee would raise a claim based solely on this ground, as it would be more fitting to frame it as a complaint on the ground of race or ethnic origin.[90] However, where a complaint is presented on this basis, the racial group of which the employee forms part may consist of individuals of more than one ethnic origin.[91] Furthermore, in EU law, 'nationality' does not cover acts of discrimination relating to a sub-national group within a State, such as the Scots or Welsh.[92] Nationality is more concerned with citizenship and so the English, Scots, Welsh, and Northern Irish are treated as British and citizens of the UK.[93] However, this does not mean that an employee

---

[79] However, it can be argued that this confuses direct and indirect discrimination. It suggests that employers could, in some contexts, proscribe employees from speaking any language other than English in the workplace on the basis that it is an objectively justifiable form of indirect discrimination, which appears to be a perilous argument which could be open to challenge.

[80] *Commission for Racial Equality v Dutton* [1989] 1 QB 783; *O'Leary v Punch Retail* (Westminster County Court, 29 August 2000, unreported).   [81] *Mandla v Dowell Lee* [1983] AC 548.

[82] *Seide v Gillette Industries Ltd* [1980] IRLR 427; *R v Governing Body of Jews Free School* [2009] UKSC 15, [2010] 2 AC 728.   [83] [2015] ICR 527.

[84] [2016] 1 WLR 2653.

[85] As for the approach of the tribunals and courts to ostensibly racist language, see *Lindsay v London School of Economics and Political Science* [2014] IRLR 218; *Quality Solicitors CMHT v Tunstall* [2014] Eq LR 679.   [86] [1993] ICR 517.

[87] [1996] ICR 291.

[88] This statement is diluted by the word 'somewhat' owing to the accuracy of the point made by Lord Clarke in *R v Governing Body of Jews Free School* [2009] UKSC 15, [2010] 2 AC 728, 784E–G, that an employer's treatment of an individual may be motivated by a mixture of both ethnic and religious grounds.   [89] See section 11.2.3.

[90] *Abbey National v Chagger* [2009] ICR 624, 639F–H per Underhill J. Underhill J's decision in the EAT was overturned by the Court of Appeal ([2010] ICR 397), but his views on 'colour' discrimination cases were not disapproved.

[91] *Lambeth London Borough Council v Commission for Racial Equality* [1990] ICR 768.

[92] *Morsen and Jhanjan* [1983] 2 CMLR 221, 230–3.

[93] *Northern Joint Police Board v Power* [1997] IRLR 610.

is not protected from discrimination on the basis that he/she is Scottish or Welsh, as this would qualify as discrimination on the basis of 'national origins': the latter has been held to include a nation which no longer exists[94] and may be acquired by adoption or adherence,[95] i.e. it is not a simple matter of a person's place of birth.[96]

The point should be made that an employee may suffer discrimination because of the race of a third party, e.g. a customer. For example, in *Showboat Entertainment Centre v Owens*,[97] a white male employee was dismissed for refusing to obey an instruction to exclude all black customers from the premises of his employer. This was deemed to be a dismissal for a refusal to carry out a discriminatory instruction and was unlawful. The employee in *Showboat Entertainment* would now also have an entitlement to raise an associative discrimination claim on the basis of someone else's race if he has suffered 'collateral damage', e.g. been directly or indirectly discriminated against, or victimized because of the race of another.[98]

11.2.3 Religion or belief discrimination

The Framework Directive[99] and the Employment Equality (Religion or Belief) Regulations 2003 ('EE(RB)')[100] provided for religious and philosophical beliefs to be treated as a protected characteristic. Direct and indirect discrimination and harassment[101] on these grounds are now prohibited and the relevant definitions are found in section 10 of the EA:

Section 10 Religion or belief

(1) Religion means any religion and a reference to religion includes a reference to a lack of religion.

(2) Belief means any religious or philosophical belief and a reference to belief includes a reference to a lack of belief.

The statement that religion and religious or philosophical belief include a lack of religion or religious or philosophical belief means that atheists, agnostics, and humanists are equally protected by section 10. Moreover, denominations and sects of a religion, such as Shia and Sunni Muslims, fall within its coverage. However, beyond that, no guidance is furnished by section 10 of the EA as to what constitutes a 'religion'. Much of the difficulty here lies in the fact that no universal definition of 'religion' has been adopted by the courts, which is perhaps unsurprising, given the fluidity of the parameters of the concept:

---

[94] See *Ealing London Borough Council v Commission for Racial Equality* [1972] AC 342, 363H–364E per Lord Simon; *Northern Joint Police Board v Power* [1997] IRLR 610.

[95] *BBC Scotland v Souster* [2001] IRLR 150.

[96] *R (on the application of Elias) v Secretary of State for Defence* [2006] IRLR 934.

[97] [1984] 1 WLR 384.

[98] See *CHEZ Razpredelenie Bulgaria AD v Komisia za zashtita ot diskriminatsias* [2015] IRLR 746; *Thompson v London Central Bus Co.* [2016] IRLR 9. For some discussion of *CHEZ*, see S. Fredman, 'The Reason Why: Unravelling Indirect Discrimination' (2016) 45 *Industrial Law Journal* 231, 235–8.

[99] Directive 2000/78/EC (OJ 2000 L303/16).

[100] SI 2003/1660. See L. Vickers, 'The Employment Equality (Religion or Belief) Regulations 2003' (2003) 32 *Industrial Law Journal* 188.

[101] See *Saini v All Saints Haque Centre* [2009] IRLR 74 for a harassment case.

■ L. Vickers, *Religious Freedom, Religious Discrimination and the Workplace*
(Oxford, Hart Publishing, 2008) 15–16

I What is 'religion'?

Although there are many recognised religions in the world, simple attempts to define the term
'religion' almost immediately run into difficulty. A belief in God, which may unite Judaism, Islam
and Christianity, is clearly insufficient, as some religions such as Hinduism are polytheistic. A
move to 'belief in God or gods' immediately comes up against the fact that Buddhism does not
include belief in a 'god'. And yet these are recognised as major world religions, and they will
have been within the contemplation of those who drafted the various international documents
protecting the right to freedom of religion. The difficulties are compounded once one considers
less well known religions such as various pagan traditions, and the rise in new religions whose
traditions and beliefs may be undocumented and totally unfamiliar to the general population.
And what of the 'religion' adhered to by only a handful or even only one person? Moreover, the
question arises as to whether other belief systems, such as veganism, pacifism or communism,
are protected, and whether their protection is predicated in them being classified in some way
as analogous to religion. What is significant about the court decisions which have dealt with
such questions is the marked reluctance of courts to get involved in creating an all-encompass-
ing definition . . . Tempting as it may be to avoid definition, to do so altogether leaves courts
acting in a vacuum, and without any principles to guide them. It becomes difficult to predict
how a court will make its assessment, and impossible to challenge any individual decision.
Moreover, minority religions are particularly likely to be left unprotected. A working definition
of religion is therefore required, in order to provide a principled basis for deciding cases, and
to help determine when a philosophical belief will qualify for protection. Any definition needs
to be broad enough to be able to respond to new religions, but also clear enough to be applied
to individual cases.

Some assistance on the breadth of the word 'religion' may be derived from the Code of
Practice of the Equality and Human Rights Commission ('EHRC') which specifically
mentions certain religions, namely Buddhism, Christianity, Hinduism, Islam,[102] Jainism,
Judaism, Rastafarianism,[103] Sikhism, Zoroastrianism, and the Baha'i faith.[104] It has also
been held that scientology qualifies as a religion.[105] Provided that there is 'a clear structure and belief system', a religion need not be 'mainstream or well known'.[106] Moreover,
it is by no means necessary that the religion is theistic or concerned with the divine or
supernatural. In a discrimination claim, the appropriate comparator will be persons who
do not share the same religious belief as the claimant and the nature of this belief will
have to be precisely identified.[107]

It should also be stressed that 'religion' is distinguishable from a 'religious belief'. As
noted by Elias J (P) in the EAT in *Eweida v British Airways plc*,[108] 'it is not necessary for
a belief to be shared by others in order for it to be a religious belief, nor need a specific

---

[102] For the relationship between Islam, religiously sanctioned clothing, and employer dress codes, see
Begum v Pedagogy Auras UL Ltd (t/a Barley Lane Montessori Day Nursery) (UKEAT/0309/13/RN, 22
May 2015).

[103] See *Harris v NKL Automotive Ltd* [2007] All ER (D) 68 (November).

[104] See https://www.equalityhumanrights.com/sites/default/files/employercode.pdf at para 2.53 (last
visited 6 December 2017).

[105] *R (on the application of Hodkin) v Registrar General of Births, Deaths and Marriages* [2014] AC
610.

[106] See https://www.equalityhumanrights.com/sites/default/files/employercode.pdf at para 2.54 (last
visited 6 December 2017).

[107] *Lee v McArthur* [2017] IRLR 69, 80 per Lord Chief Justice Morgan.

[108] [2009] ICR 303.

belief be a mandatory requirement of an established religion for it to qualify as a religious belief [and a] person could, for example, be part of the mainstream Christian religion but hold additional beliefs which are not widely shared by other Christians, or indeed shared at all by anyone'.[109] As such, the intensity of scrutiny adopted by the courts is largely subjective and defers to the belief of the employee. Moreover, where an employee's religious belief is wholly personal to the employee, the effect of the decisions of the ECtHR in *Eweida v UK*[110] and of the Court of Appeal in *Mba v Mayor and Burgesses of the London Borough of Merton*[111] is that the employee will be protected from discrimination, provided that that religious belief has attained a 'certain level of cogency, seriousness, cohesion and importance'.[112] As such, the 'solitary believer' will be protected.

Drawing on the jurisprudence of the ECtHR in relation to Article 9 of the ECHR,[113] the courts have also forged a distinction between an employee (a) holding and (b) manifesting a religious belief. An illustration of this distinction is supplied by the EHRC Code:

■ EHRC Code of Practice on Employment

Manifestation of religion or belief

2.60 While people have an absolute right to hold a particular religion or belief under Article 9 of the European Convention on Human Rights, manifestation of that religion or belief is a qualified right which may in certain circumstances be limited. For example, it may need to be balanced against other Convention rights such as the right to respect for private and family life (Article 8) or the right to freedom of expression (Article 10).

2.61 Manifestations of a religion or belief could include treating certain days as days for worship or rest; following a certain dress code; following a particular diet; or carrying out or avoiding certain practices. There is not always a clear line between holding a religion or belief and the manifestation of that religion or belief. Placing limitations on a person's right to manifest their religion or belief may amount to unlawful discrimination; this would usually amount to indirect discrimination.

Example:

An employer has a 'no headwear' policy for its staff. Unless this policy can be objectively justified, this will be indirect discrimination against Sikh men who wear the turban, Muslim women who wear a headscarf and observant Jewish men who wear a skullcap as manifestations of their religion.[114]

The distinction between holding and manifesting a religious belief was touched upon in the decisions[115] of the Court of Appeal in *Ladele v London Borough of Islington*,[116]

---

[109] *ibid.*, 310F–G (this decision was affirmed by the Court of Appeal, but this particular issue was not considered in the appeal). See also *Mba v Mayor and Burgesses of the London Borough of Merton* [2014] 1 WLR 1501, 1507C–1510B per Maurice Kay LJ, 1512D–1513G per Elias LJ, and 1515A–D per Vos LJ.

[110] [2013] IRLR 231.   [111] [2014] 1 WLR 1501.   [112] [2013] IRLR 231, 243.

[113] See *Copsey v WWB Devon Clays Ltd* [2005] IRLR 811, which was a decision relating to the law prior to the recognition of 'religion' and 'religious beliefs' as protected characteristics.

[114] On this illustration, consider the distinction between the facts in *Achbita v G4S Secure Solutions NV* [2017] IRLR 466 and *Bougnaoui v Micropole SA* [2017] IRLR 447, which demonstrate how it can be a fine line between direct and indirect discrimination on the basis of religion or religious belief: see Chapter 10, section 10.2.4.5 for a discussion. For discussion, see Z. Adams and J. O. Adenitire, 'Ideological Neutrality in the Workplace' (2018) *Modern Law Review* 348; A. Humbler, 'Neutrality and Workplace Restrictions on Headscarves and Religious Dresses: Lessons from Achbita and Bougnaoui' (2018) 47 *Industrial Law Journal* 149; and P. Collins, 'Covering Up? Client Embarrassment, Neutral Intolerance and Wearing Headscarves at Work' (2018) 134 *Law Quarterly Review* 31.

[115] The issue was broached by the EAT in *Azmi v Kirklees Metropolitan Borough Council* [2007] ICR 1154, 1172G–1173E per Wilkie J, but it was not deemed relevant to the principal issue to be addressed in the case. *Azmi* was a case about a female Muslim employee employed in a school as a bilingual support worker. Her request to wear a veil covering her head and face (i.e. a niqab) in the classroom was refused by her employer and her claim of religious discrimination was unsuccessful.   [116] [2010] 1 WLR 955.

Eweida v British Airways plc,[117] *MacFarlane v Relate Avon Ltd*,[118] *Mba v Mayor and Burgesses of the London Borough of Merton*,[119] and most recently, *Wasteney v East London NHS Foundation Trust*.[120] In these cases, the employee claimants asserted that a particular practice or belief was a requirement of his/her religion and that the employer's refusal to permit him/her to follow that practice or manifest that belief amounted to religious discrimination. *Ladele* concerned a Christian registrar of births, marriages, and deaths who was disciplined for refusing to conduct civil partnerships between persons of the same sex. *Eweida v British Airways plc* related to a Christian employee who was suspended for wearing a cross over her uniform in non-conformance with her employer's 'no visible jewellery' policy in its staff dress code. As for *MacFarlane*, this concerned a Christian employed as a counsellor who was dismissed for refusing to counsel same-sex couples in cases where issues of psychosexual therapy arose. *Mba* related to a Christian employee who did not wish to work two Sundays in every three in accordance with the employee's rota on the ground that Sundays were a day of rest. In every one of these four cases, the employees were unsuccessful in persuading the Court of Appeal that they had been the victims of indirect discrimination on the grounds of their religious beliefs. Likewise, in the case of *Wasteney* where a junior employee who was a Muslim complained against her boss who was an Evangelical Christian. She claimed that Wasteney was attempting to convert her to Christianity. When the employer took disciplinary action against Wasteney, she brought a claim, alleging that there had been unlawful discrimination and harassment on the basis of religion or belief. The EAT ruled that the disciplinary sanction arose as a result of Wasteney subjecting a subordinate to unwelcome conduct rather than any justifiable manifestation of her religious beliefs. Furthermore, as noted earlier, although Article 9 prescribes a right to 'hold' a particular religion or belief, the right to manifest religion or belief is qualified; it is subject to 'such limitations as are prescribed by law and are necessary in a democratic society in the interests of public safety, for the protection of public order, health or morals, or for the protection of the rights and freedoms of others'.[121] As such, there is no unfettered right to manifest one's religion or belief in the UK, and in addition, the manifestation must not result in unwanted conduct. Cases such as *Wasteney*, where a religious employee has sought to proselytize in the workplace, will inevitably be dealt with on a case-by-case basis, but certainly, where it is clear that manifestations are 'inappropriate' or 'upset members of staff', these will not be tolerated.[122]

When each of the cases of *Eweida*, *Ladele*, and *MacFarlane* were conjoined and heard by the ECtHR in *Eweida v UK*,[123] the ECtHR adopted the distinction between holding and manifesting/acting upon a religious belief.[124] Holding a belief would be protected if it were to reach a 'certain level of cogency, seriousness, cohesion and importance'.[125] Meanwhile, the manifestation of a belief will be subject to the protection of the law where there is a 'sufficiently close and direct nexus between the [employee's] act and the underlying belief'.[126] Further, the manifestation must be 'genuine' in order to be protected. In the case of *Gareddu v London Underground Ltd*,[127] it was held that a Roman Catholic employee's attendance at a religious festival could be a manifestation of his religious belief. However, in this case, the EAT dismissed the claim on the grounds that

---

[117] [2010] ICR 890.   [118] [2010] IRLR 872.   [119] [2014] 1 WLR 1501.

[120] [2016] IRLR 338.   [121] Article 9(1) of the ECHR.

[122] *Grace v Places for Children* (UKEAT/0217/13/GE, 5 November 2013) para 6 per Mr Justice Mitting.

[123] [2013] IRLR 231. See G. Pitt, 'Taking Religion Seriously' (2013) 42 *Industrial Law Journal* 398 for discussion of *Eweida v UK*.   [124] *Eweida v UK* [2013] IRLR 231, 245.

[125] *ibid*.

[126] *ibid*. As such, the sentiment expressed by Lord Rodger in *McConkey v Simon Community Northern Ireland* [2009] ICR 787, 790A–B no longer amounts to good law.   [127] [2017] IRLR 404.

the request was not genuine. As such, simply because there is a manifestation of an employee's religious belief does not mean that there can be no investigation as to whether that manifestation is genuine. Here, it was discovered that the true reason for the employee's request for five consecutive weeks' leave was that he wished to spend time with his family in Sardinia.

Further, there is no need to establish that a group of people with the same religious belief as the claimant are in the habit of acting upon their belief in the same manner as the claimant.[128] For this reason, Ms Eweida's insistence on acting upon her Christian faith by visibly wearing a cross was protected despite the fact that this practice was not a central tenet or requirement of that religion. Since the decision of the Court of Appeal in *Mba*, it is now the law that an employee with a belief not widely shared by practising members of a religion need not show that an actual or hypothetical group of employees sharing the same belief suffered from group disparate impact in an indirect discrimination claim.[129] In such a case, the employer is under no obligation to address the impact on such a group and weigh it against its need to apply the alleged discriminatory provision, criterion, or practice ('PCP') to achieve its legitimate aim; instead, it is only the impact on the employee claimant that is relevant. To that extent, since *Mba*, there is an argument that the legal concept of indirect discrimination as understood in terms of section 19 of the EA—which demands group disadvantage and group disparate impact to be assessed—has essentially given way in the case of religious belief to a particular form of 'reasonable accommodation' law.[130] This is so in the sense that the alleged harm or impact suffered is no longer viewed through a 'group' lens as regards religion, but instead is individualized to the level of the employee claimant and the employer. This is also the case notwithstanding that the ECtHR 'remained silent on [the reasonable accommodation point]'[131] in *Eweida v UK* when it was invoked in that case by the interveners. A number of commentators,[132] including Baroness Hale,[133] have argued that the scope of prohibited conduct in the law should be extended to include the failure of an employer to reasonably accommodate an employee's religious belief, so it is particularly interesting to witness how the courts would appear to be arriving at such a position through an incremental process of natural evolution under the influence of Article 9 of the ECHR.

Sections 10 and 13 of the EA must be construed in line with the approach of the ECtHR in *Eweida v UK*. As such, manifesting a religious belief by adopting a particular practice will be protected under UK law. As noted by Pitt in the following extract, if protection under the EA were limited to *holding* a belief, it would constitute a rather toothless provision:

---

[128] *Eweida v UK* [2013] IRLR 231, 245; *Mba v Mayor and Burgesses of the London Borough of Merton* [2014] 1 WLR 1501, 1507C–1510B per Maurice Kay LJ, 1512D–1513G per Elias LJ, and 1515A–D per Vos LJ.   [129] See Chapter 10, sections 10.2.4.2 and 10.2.4.4.

[130] For the distinction, which it is argued may lie in the difference between negative and positive duties of reasonable accommodation, see G. Pitt, 'Taking Religion Seriously' (2013) 42 *Industrial Law Journal* 398, 404–7. See also R. McCrea, 'Religion in the Workplace: *Eweida and others v UK*' (2014) 77 *Modern Law Review* 277.

[131] T. Lock, 'Religious Freedom and Belief Discrimination in Germany and the United Kingdom: Towards a Common European Standard' (2013) 38 *European Law Review* 655, 676.

[132] K. Alidadi, 'Reasonable Accommodations for Religion and Belief: Adding Value to Art. 9 ECHR and the EU's Anti-Discrimination Approach in Employment?' (2012) 37 *European Law Review* 693; M. Gibson, 'The God "Dilution"? Religion, Discrimination and the Case for Reasonable Accommodation' (2013) 72 *Cambridge Law Journal* 578. For the opposite view, see E. Howard, 'Reasonable Accommodation of Religion and Other Discrimination Grounds in EU Law' (2013) 38 *European Law Review* 360. For a more nuanced approach to the whole issue, see R. Wintemute, 'Accommodating Religious Beliefs: Harm, Clothing or Symbols, and Refusals to Serve Others' (2014) 77 *Modern Law Review* 223.

[133] See https://www.supremecourt.uk/docs/speech-140613.pdf (last visited 6 December 2017).

■ **G. Pitt, 'Keeping the Faith: Trends and Tensions in Religion or Belief Discrimination' (2011) 40 *Industrial Law Journal* 384, 393**

If the E[A], section 10 only protects *holding* a belief as opposed to *acting* on it, then the protection is limited indeed. First of all, discrimination on grounds of merely holding a belief is inherently unlikely, as no one else would necessarily know that the subject held it. A person may hold the most bizarre, misguided, stupid, even pernicious set of beliefs—but provided she keeps them to herself, how would anyone ever know?[134]

In the *Ladele* and *MacFarlane* cases addressed by the ECtHR in *Eweida v UK*, the characteristic of religious belief came into conflict with the protected characteristic of sexual orientation.[135] In both cases, the latter ground was held to 'trump' the former characteristic and the employee's claims of indirect religious discrimination were defeated. How such characteristics can be reconciled where they clash is a particularly fraught matter which we will revisit later at section 11.4 in our evaluation of the genuine occupational requirements exception in employment equality law.

Religious beliefs may also 'clash' with other rights or certainly policy concerns. Some religions, for example, some tenets of Christianity, promulgate a belief in the sanctity of marriage, and that divorce is impermissible in any circumstances, even where one partner has committed a serious crime. *Pendleton v Derbyshire County Council*[136] concerned such a 'test of faith'. A teacher was dismissed after she decided to remain with her husband following his conviction for producing indecent images of children, and also voyeurism. The reason for the school's decision was that her continued relationship with her husband was incompatible with her duty to safeguard pupils. As an Anglican Christian, she believed that her marriage vows were sacred and chose to stay with her husband, convinced by his remorse. She brought a claim for indirect discrimination on grounds of religion or belief. The EAT held that although safeguarding children in a school environment was a legitimate aim, it was necessary to consider whether it was proportionate to dismiss the claimant, or whether another alternative could have been taken. There was no evidence to show that dismissal was a proportionate means of achieving the legitimate aim because the employer had not considered alternatives to dismissal. As such, it was held that Mrs Pendleton had suffered from indirect discrimination on the grounds of religion or belief.

Suffice to say at this stage that the courts are reluctant to treat a claim of religious discrimination as one of direct discrimination which harbours no scope for employer justification. Instead, as shown by *Pendleton*, the judiciary are more comfortable with (re)conceptualizing the case as one of indirect discrimination which allows them to balance the competing interests of the claimant employee, employer, and others pursuant to the proportionality standard of review in section 19(2)(d) of the EA. Such an exercise also enables the court to take into account the interests of those potentially affected by the employee's stance, such as the fundamental rights of others where there is a clear conflict.

As for what constitutes a philosophical belief, in the same vein as a religious belief, a philosophical belief or an employee's manifestation of that belief may be purely personal to him/her.[137] As such, the law does not insist that the employee show that a group of people hold the same philosophical belief, or adopt the same practice, as him/her. The

---

[134] See also N. Hatzis, 'Personal Religious Beliefs in the Workplace: How Not to Define Indirect Discrimination' (2011) 74 *Modern Law Review* 287.

[135] See also C. Fenton-Glynn, 'Replacing One Type of Oppression with Another? Same-Sex Couples and Religious Freedom' (2014) 73 *Cambridge Law Journal* 31.   [136] [2016] IRLR 580.

[137] *Grainger plc v Nicholson* [2010] ICR 360, 371A–B per Burton J.

combined effect of the EHRC Code[138] and *Grainger plc v Nicholson*[139] is that the following criteria must be satisfied:

- the belief need not include faith or worship of a god or gods, but must affect how a person lives his/her life or perceives the world;
- the belief must be genuinely held;[140]
- the belief must be a belief and not an opinion or viewpoint based on the present state of information available;[141]
- the belief must be a belief as to a weighty and substantial aspect of human life and behaviour;
- the belief must attain a certain level of cogency, seriousness, cohesion, and importance;
- it is not a bar to a philosophical belief being protected that it is a one-off belief[142] and not shared by others, a fortiori where it is likely that others do share the belief; and
- the belief must be worthy of respect in a democratic society, not incompatible with human dignity and must not conflict with the fundamental rights of others.

It should be stressed that these seven criteria must be met in order for a belief to fall within the coverage of the term 'philosophical belief', whereas these additional hurdles are irrelevant for the purposes of determining whether a system constitutes a religion or religious belief. One commentator has questioned whether this hierarchy between religious belief and philosophical belief is justifiable, particularly in light of the final criterion:

■ **G. Pitt, 'Keeping the Faith: Trends and Tensions in Religion or Belief Discrimination' (2011) 40 *Industrial Law Journal* 384, 390**

Considering in particular the . . . limitation [that the belief must be worthy of respect in a democratic society, not incompatible with human dignity, and not conflict with the fundamental rights of others], it is the case that much of Christianity, Judaism and Islam institutionalises discrimination against women and regards homosexuality as sinful and a sufficient reason for less favourable treatment. Are such views worthy of respect? Are they compatible with human dignity? Even if one accepted for the sake of argument that they were, it would be impossible, surely, to deny that they conflict with the fundamental rights of others. Yet as long as such views are propounded on the basis of religious beliefs which have been held by millions of people for hundreds of years, they are apparently absolved from scrutiny against these standards.

Perhaps a partial answer to this conundrum lies in the fact that it is inherently illogical to subject a religion or religious doctrine to scrutiny based on reason or standards of cogency, cohesion, and rational coherence. By its very nature, a religion is about faith, rather than reason or logic, and it often 'involves belief in the supernatural [and so] is not always susceptible to lucid exposition or, still less, to rational justification'.[143] As such, to apply such additional criteria to a religious belief may be counter-productive and ultimately wholly unwarranted.

---

[138] See https://www.equalityhumanrights.com/sites/default/files/employercode.pdf at paras 2.55–2.59 (last visited 6 December 2017).   [139] [2010] ICR 360.
[140] It has been recognized that beliefs may change over the lifetime of the person: *Streatfeild v London Philharmonic Orchestra Ltd* [2012] Eq LR 901.
[141] See *McClintock v Department of Constitutional Affairs* [2008] IRLR 29, 45 per Elias J.
[142] For example, veganism and pacifism.
[143] *R v Secretary of State for Education and Employment, ex parte Williamson* [2005] 2 AC 246, 259B–C per Lord Nicholls.

On the basis of these seven criteria, it has been held that the following qualify as a philosophical belief under section 10(2) of the EA: a belief in catastrophic anthropogenic climate change which governed every aspect of the individual's life and work;[144] a belief in public sector broadcasting such as that pursued by the BBC, involving the values of social cohesion, debating of important issues, and cultural interchange;[145] and a belief in the sanctity of life, including the beliefs that hare-coursing and fox-hunting were contrary to such a principle.[146] Pacifism, vegetarianism, and complete abstinence from alcohol may be protected. Moreover, the EHRC Code specifically lists humanism and atheism as qualifying philosophical beliefs,[147] and although a belief in Marxism or communism may be considered political in nature, it has been held that a belief in 'left-wing democratic socialism'[148] is sufficiently philosophical to be characterized as deserving of protection. However, it has been held that a belief that children should not be placed for adoption with civil partners or same-sex couples did not constitute a philosophical belief,[149] nor did a belief in 'the proper and efficient use of public money in the public sector'.[150] Finally, there must be a religious or philosophical viewpoint in which the employee actually believes and it is not enough to have an opinion based on some real or perceived logic or based on information or lack of information available.[151] As for the word 'substantial' in the definition found in *Grainger*, this has been interpreted as meaning 'more than merely trivial,' and the word 'coherence' is to be understood 'in the sense of being intelligible and capable of being understood'.[152] The '*Grainger*' formulation has prompted one commentator to note the irony that 'a stupid, but sincere, belief, based on nothing at all, is within the scope of the protection, but an opinion based on logic and information is not'.[153]

11.2.4 Sexual orientation, marriage, and civil partnership discrimination

In the well-known case of *Grant v Southwest Trains*[154] the ECJ rejected an attempt to characterize discrimination against employees on the basis of their sexual orientation as a form of sex discrimination. This could be contrasted with the position of the ECtHR in the case of *Smith and Grady v UK*,[155] which recognized that Article 8 of the ECHR protected gay and lesbian employees. In a similar vein to the approach adopted by the ECJ, in its decision in *MacDonald v Advocate General for Scotland*,[156] the House of Lords refused to accept that sexual orientation discrimination could be equated with sex discrimination. However, this case was a mere temporary setback to those seeking employment equality for the LGBT community and, in late 2003, the Employment Equality (Sexual Orientation) Regulations 2003 ('EE(SO)')[157] were introduced. The impetus for change was the Framework Directive and the EE(SO) transposed the element of the Directive which provided protection on the grounds of sexual orientation into UK law. The position is now enshrined in section 12 of the EA, which provides that it is unlawful for

---

[144] *Grainger plc v Nicholson* [2010] ICR 360.   [145] *Maistry v BBC* [2014] EWCA Civ 1116.

[146] See *Hashman v Milton Park (Dorset) Ltd (t/a Orchard Park Garden Centre)* (ET/3105555/2009, 4 March 2011).

[147] See https://www.equalityhumanrights.com/sites/default/files/employercode.pdf at para 2.57 (last visited 6 December 2017).   [148] *Henderson v GMB* [2015] IRLR 451.

[149] *McClintock v Department of Constitutional Affairs* [2008] IRLR 29, 34 per Mr Justice Elias (P).

[150] *Harron v Chief Constable of Dorset Police* [2016] IRLR 481.

[151] *McClintock v Department of Constitutional Affairs* [2008] IRLR 29.

[152] *Harron v Chief Constable of Dorset Police* [2016] IRLR 481, 486 per Langstaff J.

[153] G. Pitt, 'Keeping the Faith: Trends and Tensions in Religion or Belief Discrimination' (2011) 40 *Industrial Law Journal* 384, 389.   [154] [1998] ICR 449.

[155] [1999] IRLR 734.   [156] [2003] ICR 937.   [157] SI 2003/1661.

employers to harass employees or directly or indirectly discriminate against them on the grounds of sexual orientation:

Section 12 Sexual orientation

(1) Sexual orientation means a person's sexual orientation towards—

    (a) persons of the same sex,

    (b) persons of the opposite sex, or

    (c) persons of either sex.[158]

A person's sexual orientation will cover the direction of his/her attraction and it is not a qualifying requirement that he/she is sexually active.[159] Like the protected characteristic of religion and religious belief, it has been held that a person's sexual orientation includes the 'manifestation of that orientation in the form of sexual behaviour as it does to sexuality as such',[160] i.e. the expression of a person's sexual attraction, which goes beyond a person's direction of attraction. Furthermore, it is not necessary for the employee to be actually gay, lesbian, or bisexual, i.e. discrimination on the basis of a perception that the employee is gay, bisexual, or a lesbian is also prohibited. For example, in *English v Thomas Sanderson Blinds Ltd*,[161] a male employee was regularly subjected to banter and innuendo of a homophobic nature by his colleagues because they perceived him as having stereotypical characteristics which they associated with a homosexual, in that he had attended a boarding school and lived in Brighton. The employee was not gay and all of his colleagues knew he was not homosexual. Nonetheless, the EAT ruled that the employee had been unlawfully harassed on the basis of the protected characteristic of sexual orientation and it was irrelevant what the employee's sexual orientation, real or imagined, actually was in the circumstances. The policy behind this decision was that no employee should be 'outed' against his/her will pursuant to a sustained campaign of harassment. However, this can be contrasted with *Grant v HM Land Registry*[162] where an employee 'came out' as a homosexual at his employer's Lytham office. However, when he subsequently moved to the Coventry office, he did not reveal he was gay to his new colleagues. Here, it was held that he had not been harassed because of his sexual orientation when his line manager revealed his sexuality to staff, particularly since there was no malicious intent on the part of the line manager.[163]

Of course, in order to succeed in a claim of direct or indirect discrimination on the ground of sexual orientation, an employee will be required to compare him/herself with an appropriate comparator. The nature of the comparator is currently unclear,[164] but

---

[158] See H. Oliver, 'Sexual Orientation Discrimination: Perceptions, Definitions and Genuine Occupational Requirements' (2004) 33 *Industrial Law Journal* 1.

[159] EHRC Code, available at https://www.equalityhumanrights.com/sites/default/files/employercode.pdf at para 2.65 (last visited 6 December 2017). Since there must be a direction of attraction, asexuals fall outside the coverage of section 12 of the EA.

[160] *R (Amicus—MSF Section) v Secretary of State for Trade and Industry* [2007] ICR 1176, 1211B–E per Richards J.

[161] [2009] ICR 543. See M. Connolly, 'Homophobic Harassment Where No One is Gay' (2009) 68 *Cambridge Law Journal* 265.   [162] *Grant v HM Land Registry* [2011] ICR 1390.

[163] Contrast this decision with *Smith v Ideal Shopping Direct Ltd* [2013] Eq LR 943.

[164] For example, see *Grant v HM Land Registry* [2011] ICR 1390, 1404G–H per Lord Justice Elias; *Bull v Hall* [2013] 1 WLR 3741; *Black v Wilkinson* [2013] 1 WLR 2490; *Hay v Credit Agricole* [2014] 2 CMLR 32.

what is readily apparent is that there must be no material difference between the circumstances relating to the case of the employee and the comparator. It is specifically provided in section 23(3) that a civil partner who is treated less favourably than a married person in similar circumstances is entitled to bring a claim for sexual orientation discrimination, i.e. the relevant comparator in such a context will be a married employee.

As the earlier Pitt extract highlights, the tenets of some major religions, such as Islam and Christianity, cast homosexuality as 'sinful' and believe that marriage should only be between one man and one woman. Religious believers may seek to manifest their faiths at work, for example a Christian relationship counsellor may refuse to counsel gay couples,[165] a marriage registrar may refuse to marry a gay couple,[166] or in the infamous 'gay cake row'[167] where the religious owners of a bakery refused to bake a cake with a design advocating gay marriage. In all of these situations, religious employees sought to treat gay persons differently on the basis of their sexual orientation, and as such, sought a 'licence to discriminate'. However, in each of these cases, it was held that the manifestation of their belief was not justifiable or permissible in the work context. These decisions have prompted religious groups to claim that 'asking someone to leave their belief in God at the door of their workplace is akin to asking them to remove their skin colour before coming into the office'[168] and that sexual orientation has 'trumped' religion.

Turning now to protection from discrimination on the basis of an employee's marital status, this is specifically prohibited by virtue of section 8 of the EA. Moreover, an employee must not suffer discrimination for the reason that he/she has entered into a civil partnership.

> ### Section 8 Marriage and civil partnership
>
> (1) A person has the protected characteristic of marriage and civil partnership if the person is married or is a civil partner.

The EHRC Code provides further guidance on the protective coverage of section 8, directing that any formal union of a man and a woman that is legally recognized in the UK will fall within the term 'marriage'.[169] It also goes on to stipulate that a civil partnership is a registered civil partnership in terms of the Civil Partnership Act 2004.[170] As for couples engaged to be married, they are not protected by virtue of the authority of *Bick v Royal West of England Residential School for the Deaf*;[171] likewise in the case of cohabitees, singles, widows, widowers, and divorcees. The tribunals and courts have drawn a distinction between discrimination on the ground of the fact of marriage per se and the ground of being married to a particular person. For example, in *Hawkins v Atex Group Ltd*,[172] the wife and daughter of a manager were hired in direct breach of the employer's policy preventing the recruitment of close relatives of existing employees. When the wife was dismissed, she raised a claim of marital discrimination. The EAT ruled that the wife had not suffered any discrimination because she was married, but instead because she was

---

[165] *Macfarlane v Relate* [2010] IRLR 872.

[166] *Ladele v Islington Borough Council* [2010] 1 WLR 955.

[167] *Lee v McArthur* [2017] IRLR 69.

[168] See the statement from the Archbishop of York in 'Marginalising Christians', available at http://www.christian.org.uk/wp-content/uploads/marginchristians.pdf at page 8 (last visited 6 December 2017).

[169] EHRC Code, available at https://www.equalityhumanrights.com/sites/default/files/employercode.pdf at para 2.32 (last visited 6 December 2017).   [170] *ibid.*, para 2.32.

[171] [1976] IRLR 325. But contrast this with *Turner v Turner* (ET/2401702/04, 11 August 2004).

[172] [2012] IRLR 807.

married to the manager: the former was proscribed by section 8, but the latter was not.[173] Therefore, her claim was rejected. It was also held that an appropriate comparator will be someone in a close relationship which is similar, albeit falling short of marriage, in the context of a direct marital discrimination complaint.[174] It should be pointed out that indirect marital discrimination is also unlawful, whereas harassment related to a person's marital status is not recognized as a specific statutory wrong. In such a case, a married employee would be required to try to reconfigure his/her claim as one of direct or indirect sex discrimination.[175]

11.2.5 Age discrimination

If race is the most venerable of all the protected characteristics, age lies at the opposite end of the spectrum and instead is still in its infancy. For a long time, employees were not protected from age discrimination. Such discrimination is acutely felt by both younger and older workers who are subject to ingrained societal and managerial prejudices. For example, recent research suggests that negative, age-based stereotypes about the competence of workers persist in British society. Younger workers are thought to be less friendly and competent than older workers, with lower moral standards.[176] As for older workers, they are often treated as incompetent and 'past it'.[177] Against the backdrop of demographic change and an ageing population, these are concerning revelations for policy-makers.

Historically, attempts were made by employees to combat age discrimination indirectly by pressing the protected characteristic of sex into service. For example, the case of *Secretary of State for Trade and Industry v Rutherford (No. 2)*[178] concerned a challenge to the (now-repealed) rule disqualifying employees over the age of 65 from presenting a complaint of unfair dismissal to an employment tribunal. An employee dismissed at the age of 67 argued that the upper age limit of 65 was indirectly discriminatory against men on the ground of sex. Ultimately, the House of Lords rejected the indirect discrimination claim, citing the absence of evidence of any disparate impact on men as a group. Nonetheless, this litigation proved to be one of the first forays by elderly workers into the courts and tribunals as a means of upholding their interests.

At the time of the *Rutherford* litigation, the Framework Directive had already come into force. However, it afforded Member States a period of six years to transpose its provisions on age discrimination. The UK Government took advantage of the flexibility and it was not until 2006 that the Employment Equality (Age) Regulations 2006 ('EE(A)')[179] finally came into force. The main driver of the reform was principally economic, rather than philosophical or moral. The economic arguments were twofold. First, policy-makers

---

[173] Contrast this decision with that of the EAT in *Dunn v Institute of Cemetery and Crematorium Management* [2012] ICR 941.

[174] See also *Chief Constable of the Bedfordshire Constabulary v Graham* [2002] IRLR 239.

[175] See Chapter 10, section 10.2.5, for a more in-depth discussion.

[176] See D. Sweiry and M. Willits, *Attitudes to Age in Britain 2010/11* (In-House Research No. 7, Department for Work and Pensions, January 2012), available at http://statistics.dwp.gov.uk/asd/asd5/ih2011–2012/ihr7.pdf at pages 47–9 (last visited 6 December 2017).

[177] See E. Dewhurst, 'Are Older Workers Past Their Sell-by-Date? A View from UK Age Discrimination Law' (2015) 78 *Modern Law Review* 189; see also the facts of *Reynolds v CLFIS UK Ltd* [2015] ICR 1010 where a 73-year-old was dismissed partly for the reason that she was perceived to be incapable of changing the way she worked. [178] [2006] 4 All ER 577.

[179] SI 2006/1031. See Department of Trade and Industry, *Equality and Diversity: Coming of Age*, available at http://webarchive.nationalarchives.gov.uk/+/http://www.berr.gov.uk/files/file26479.pdf (last visited 6 December 2017); M. Sargeant, 'The Employment Equality (Age) Regulations 2006: A Legitimisation of Age Discrimination in Employment' (2006) 35 *Industrial Law Journal* 209; and J. Swift, 'Justifying Age Discrimination' (2006) 35 *Industrial Law Journal* 228.

viewed the extension as a necessity in order to encourage the increased participation of the elderly in the labour market: this was a pragmatic policy choice, reflective of the growth in the average age of the populations of the UK and the EU. Secondly, it was thought that enabling workers to continue in the workplace beyond retirement age was of material benefit to commercial organizations, since more experienced workers would be retained for longer and not lost prematurely:

■ S. Fredman, *Discrimination Law*, 2nd edition (Oxford, OUP, 2011) 102–5

The issue of age discrimination has been pushed to the foreground by several interlocking factors. The first is demographic: the UK is ageing rapidly. Average life expectancy is increasing, and fertility rates have fallen below replacement levels. In the 25 years up to 2008, the population aged 65 and over increased from 15 to 16 per cent; while the population aged 16 and under decreased from 21 to 19 per cent. By 2033, a greater proportion of the population will be old than young. This pattern is repeated throughout the EU: the growth of the working-age population is slowing rapidly; whereas the population over 60 is growing steadily . . . As a result, prolonging labour force participation has become a key labour market objective, both in the UK and the EU more widely. Age discrimination legislation was one of the measures put in place to achieve this end, together with a range of other policy initiatives . . . The new emphasis on combating age discrimination is not, therefore, a result of a sudden appreciation of the need for fairness, but gains its chief impetus from macroeconomic imperatives. Nevertheless, this should not obscure the fact that age discrimination is a source of injustice in its own right, regardless of instrumental justifications . . . The instrumental approach can be contrasted with an intrinsic view of the aims of anti-discrimination law. These emphasize the protection of individual dignity and the expansion of genuine choice for older or younger people.

The recognition of age as a protected characteristic now finds its expression in section 5 of the EA:

Section 5 Age

(1) In relation to the protected characteristic of age—

(a) a reference to a person who has a particular protected characteristic is a reference to a person of a particular age group.

(b) a reference to persons who share a protected characteristic is a reference to persons of the same age group.

(2) A reference to an age group is a reference to a group of persons defined by reference to age, whether by reference to a particular age or to a range of ages.

Age discrimination differs from the standard discrimination law pattern in a variety of ways. Two particular features are singled out for specific consideration here. First, in contrast with the other protected strands, as noted by Baroness Hale in *Seldon v Clarkson, Wright & Jakes*,[180] age is not binary: everyone has an age and it is not an either/or issue.

---

[180] [2012] ICR 716. See section 11.1.1.

Secondly, as Blake J observed in *R (Age UK) v Secretary of State for Business, Innovation and Skills*,[181] age discrimination legislation is approached on a more restrictive basis than other forms of discrimination:

■ *R (Age UK) v Secretary of State for Business, Innovation and Skills* [2010] ICR 260, 297C–E

Blake J:

I accept the submission made on behalf of the [Secretary of State for Business, Innovation and Skills] that use of a specific age as the basis for social policy decisions reflected in the [EA] is somewhat different from use of other criteria such as race, sex, religion or sexual orientation which have either been or have become now regarded as particularly suspect grounds ... This is not to assign age to some diminished worth in a supposed hierarchy of rights. Unlike the immutable characteristics of racial and gender identity all of us grow older each year, and all of us face decisions about retirement. The different nature of discrimination on the grounds of age compared with other grounds is reflected directly in [the Framework Directive] by the fact that article 6 permits justification of direct discrimination on the grounds of age.[182]

It is the latter point that is of paramount importance: as well as indirect age discrimination, direct age discrimination may be objectively justified by the employer invoking the proportionality defence:

Section 13 Direct discrimination

(2) If the protected characteristic is age, A does not discriminate against B if A can show A's treatment of B to be a proportionate means of achieving a legitimate aim.

However, as noted by the Justices in the Supreme Court decision of *Seldon v Clarkson, Wright & Jakes*,[183] although an employer may justify directly discriminatory treatment by demonstrating that the treatment was a proportionate means of achieving a legitimate aim, the objectives that the employer may invoke are more strictly controlled and are not as broad as those available in the case of an indirect age discrimination claim:

■ *Seldon v Clarkson, Wright & Jakes* [2012] ICR 716, 733D

Baroness Hale:

It now seems clear that the approach to justifying direct age discrimination cannot be identical to the approach to justifying indirect discrimination and that ... section 13(2) of the [EA] ... must be read accordingly.

---

[181] [2009] IRLR 1017.

[182] In *Homer v Chief Constable of West Yorkshire Police* [2010] IRLR 619, 623, Mummery LJ agreed that that sentiment might be correct, but did not think it was particularly useful when it came to interpreting a particular statutory provision such as the content of indirect age discrimination, and he was not particularly sympathetic to the notion of a hierarchy of protected characteristics on the basis of the text of the Framework Directive.

[183] [2012] ICR 716.

As for examples of prima facie directly discriminatory treatment because of age, the following have fallen foul of the law: national legislation which stipulated that periods of employment completed before the age of 25 were to be disregarded when calculating the notice period for dismissal;[184] where an offer to take voluntary redundancy was not extended to a bank regional director over the age of 50 on the basis that it would trigger an entitlement to take early retirement, which was an expensive option for the employer;[185] and, in *Prigge v Deutsche Lufthansa*,[186] a collective agreement for Lufthansa pilots which provided for automatic retirement at age 60, which could be contrasted with both international and German legislation enabling commercial pilots to fly between 60 and 65 provided that they did so as part of a crew with at least one pilot under the age of 60.[187] *Prigge* can be contrasted with the decision of the CJEU in *Tyrolean Airways Tiroler Lufthart Gesellschaft v Betriebsrat Bord der Tyrolean Airways*.[188] Here, the CJEU decided that a rule that service with a particular Austrian airline company counted for the purpose of accruing service-related benefits and that comparable service with other airlines in the Austrian airlines group would be completely disregarded was not based on age or an event linked to age, hence did not constitute direct age discrimination. Likewise, in *Reynolds v CLFIS UK Ltd*[189] it was held that there was no direct age discrimination where the employer dismissed a 73-year-old employee after relying upon the reports of colleagues motivated by discrimination. A similar result was reached in *Palmer v RBS*[190] where an employer's failure to allow an employee to change her choice of voluntary redundancy to redeployment, so that she could be taken from age 49 to age 50 whereupon she would qualify for a more favourable option of voluntary retirement, was not an act of direct age discrimination.

However, the paradigm example of direct age discrimination is a managerial policy pursued by the employer—as opposed to the State—which prescribes a mandatory retirement age of 65 years of age, which was precisely the issue for consideration in *Seldon*.[191] The oft-versed justifications an employer will cite in favour of the imposition of a mandatory retirement age have been itemized as follows:

(1) younger workers are more productive than older workers;

(2) wage premiums and monitoring costs would increase if older workers were not compulsorily retired;

(3) older workers need to make room for the young; and

(4) it facilitates workforce planning.

In a study commissioned by the Age and Equality Network,[192] it was found that these rationalizations for a mandatory retirement age[193] could not be substantiated by evidence or social policy needs in general terms. Instead, such justifications would be required to

---

[184] *Kücükdeveci v Swedex GmbH & Co. KG* [2011] 2 CMLR 703.
[185] *Donkor v Royal Bank of Scotland* [2016] IRLR 268.   [186] [2011] IRLR 1052.
[187] *Prigge v Deutsche Lufthansa* [2011] IRLR 1052.   [188] [2012] IRLR 781.
[189] [2015] ICR 1010.   [190] [2014] ICR 1288.
[191] In *Seldon v Clarkson Wright & Jakes (No. 2)* [2014] IRLR 748, Langstaff J in the EAT arrived at the conclusion that the employer's compulsory retirement age of 65 was objectively justified. For commentary, see B. Barrett and M. Sargeant, 'Working in the UK Without a Default Retirement Age: Health, Safety, and the Oldest Workers' (2015) 44 *Industrial Law Journal* 75; for a comparative review, see A. Blackham, 'Managing without Default Retirement in Universities: A Comparative Picture from Australia' (2015) 35 *Legal Studies* 502.
[192] C. Wunsch and J. V. Raman, *Mandatory Retirement in the United Kingdom, Canada and the United States of America* (London, The Age & Employment Network, 2010).
[193] On mandatory retirement ages, see E. Dewhurst, 'The Development of EU Case-Law on Age Discrimination in Employment: 'Will You Still Need Me? Will You Still Feed Me? When I'm Sixty-Four' (2013) 19 *European Law Journal* 517.

be particularized as valid in the context of an employee claimant's case. As we shall see, this formulation is one which has been adopted by the Supreme Court.

In line with Baroness Hale's observation in the extract from *Seldon*, it has been held that it is only possible for an employer to justify a practice that directly discriminates against its employees on the basis of age if it is able to point to a legitimate aim of a *public interest nature* which it is seeking to pursue *which is consistent with the social policy aims of the State*. As such, purely individual reasons that are concerned specifically with the employer's workplace or situation will not suffice as a justification. In *Seldon*, referring to Article 6(1) of the Framework Directive, it was held that employment policy, labour market, or vocational training objectives would qualify as legitimate aims:

Article 6 Justification of differences of treatment on grounds of age

1.... [M]ember states may provide that differences of treatment on grounds of age shall not consti-tute discrimination, if, within the context of national law, they are objectively and reasonably justi-fied by a legitimate aim, including legitimate employment policy, labour market and vocational training objectives, and if the means of achieving that aim are appropriate and necessary. Such differences of treatment may include, among others—(a) the setting of special conditions on access to employment and vocational training, employment and occupation, including dismissal and re-muneration conditions, for young people, older workers and persons with caring responsibilities in order to promote their vocational integration or ensure their protection; (b) the fixing of minimum conditions of age, professional experience or seniority in service for access to employment or to certain advantages linked to employment; (c) the fixing of a maximum age for recruitment which is based on the training requirements of the post in question or the need for a reasonable period of employment before retirement.

Baroness Hale in *Seldon* went on to identify the objectives of inter-generational fair-ness[194] and preserving the dignity of older workers (by avoiding unseemly debates about capacity) as two legitimate aims which possessed the necessary degree of public interest, depending on the circumstances of the employment concerned and provided that the means chosen were appropriate and necessary:

■ *Seldon v Clarkson, Wright & Jakes* [2012] ICR 716, 734C–F

Baroness Hale:

Two different kinds of legitimate objective have been identified by the Luxembourg court. The first kind may be summed up as *inter-generational fairness*. This is comparatively uncontroversial. It can mean a variety of things, depending upon the particular circumstances of the employment con-cerned: for example, it can mean facilitating access to employment by young people; it can mean enabling older people to remain in the workforce; it can mean sharing limited opportunities to work in a particular profession fairly between the generations; it can mean promoting diversity and the interchange of ideas between younger and older workers. The second kind may be summed up as *dignity*. This has been variously put as avoiding the need to dismiss older workers on the grounds of incapacity or underperformance, thus preserving their dignity and avoiding humiliation, and as avoiding the need for costly and divisive disputes about capacity or underperformance. Either way,

---

[194] For a discussion of the appropriateness of this objective, see L. Vickers and S. Manfredi, 'Age Equal-ity and Retirement: Squaring the Circle' (2013) 42 *Industrial Law Journal* 61.

it is much more controversial. As Age UK argue, the philosophy underlying all the anti-discrimination laws is the dignity of each individual, the right to be treated equally irrespective of either
irrational prejudice or stereotypical assumptions which may be true of some but not of others.
The assumptions underlying these objectives look suspiciously like stereotyping. Concerns about
capacity, it is argued, are better dealt with, as they were in *Wolf v Stadt Frankfurt am Main* (Case
C-229/08) [2010] All ER (EC) 939[195] and *Prigge v Deutsche Lufthansa AG* (Case C-447/09) [2011]
IRLR 1052, under article 4(1) [of the Framework Directive], which enables them to be related to the
particular requirements of the job in question.

In *Seldon*, it was ruled that the employer might be required to show that the application
of the directly discriminatory PCP *to the employee claimant in the case at hand* was justified in light of cogent evidence,[196] rather than simply demonstrate that it was justified *in
general*. A large measure of Baroness Hale's approach was inspired by the jurisprudence
of the ECJ/CJEU. This jurisprudence is usefully summarized in the following extract from
Seldon, which also provides a non-exhaustive list of legitimate aims an employer may
justifiably invoke[197] in a direct discrimination claim:

■ *Seldon v Clarkson, Wright & Jakes* [2012] ICR 716, 732C–733B

Baroness Hale:

What messages, then, can we take from the European case law? . . .

(2) If it is sought to justify direct age discrimination under article 6(1) [of the Framework Directive],
the aims of the measure must be social policy objectives, such as those related to employment
policy, the labour market or vocational training. These are of a public interest nature, which is
'distinguishable from purely individual reasons particular to the employer's situation, such as
cost reduction or improving competitiveness' ([*R (on the application of the Incorporated Trustees of the National Council on Ageing (Age Concern England)) v Secretary of State for Business,
Enterprise and Regulatory Reform* [2009] ICR 1080] and *Fuchs* [*v Land Hessen*] [2012] ICR 93).

(3) It would appear from that, as Advocate General Bot pointed out in *Kücükdeveci* [*v Swedex
GmbH & Co. KG*] [2011] 2 CMLR 703, that flexibility for employers is not in itself a legitimate
aim; but a certain degree of flexibility may be permitted to employers in the pursuit of legitimate social policy objectives.

(4) A number of legitimate aims, some of which overlap, have been recognised in the context of
direct age discrimination claims: (i) promoting access to employment for younger people ([*Felix
Palacios de la Villa v Cortefiel Servicios SA* [2007] IRLR 989], *Hütter* [*v Technische Universität Graz*

[2009] ECR I-5325] and *Kücükdeveci* [*v Swedex GmbH & Co. KG* [2011] 2 CMLR 703]); (ii) the efficient planning of the departure and recruitment of staff (*Fuchs* [*v Land Hessen* [2012] ICR 93]); (iii) sharing out employment opportunities fairly between the generations (*Petersen* [*v Berufungsausschuss für Zahnärzte für den Bezirk Westfalen-Lippe* [2010] ECR I-47], *Rosenbladt* [*v Oellerking* [2011] IRLR 51] and *Fuchs* [*v Land Hessen* [2012] ICR 93]); (iv) ensuring a mix of generations of staff so as to promote the exchange of experience and new ideas (*Georgiev* [*v Technicheski Universitet Sofia, Filial Plovdiv* [2011] 2 CMLR 179] and *Fuchs* [*v Land Hessen* [2012] ICR 93]); (v) rewarding experience (*Hütter* [*v Technische Universität Graz* [2009] ECR I-5325] and *Hennigs* [*v Eisenbahn-Bundesamt* [2012] CMLR 484]); (vi) cushioning the blow for long serving employees who may find it hard to find new employment if dismissed (*Ingeniørforeningen i Danmark* [*v Region Syddanmark* [2011] 1 CMLR 1140]); (vii) facilitating the participation of older workers in the workforce (*Fuchs* [*v Land Hessen* [2012] ICR 93]); see also *Mangold v Helm* (Case C-144/04 [2006] All ER (EC) 383); (viii) avoiding the need to dismiss employees on the ground that they are no longer capable of doing the job, which may be humiliating for the employee concerned (*Rosenbladt* [*v Oellerking* [2011] IRLR 51]); or (ix) avoiding disputes about the employee's fitness for work over a certain age (*Fuchs* [*v Land Hessen* [2012] ICR 93]).

(5) However, the measure in question must be both appropriate to achieve its legitimate aim or aims and necessary in order to do so. Measures based on age may not be appropriate to the aims of rewarding experience or protecting long service (*Hütter* [*v Technische Universität Graz* [2009] ECR I-5325], *Kücükdeveci* [*v Swedex GmbH & Co. KG* [2011] 2 CMLR 703] and *Ingeniørforeningen i Danmark* [*v Region Syddanmark* [2011] 1 CMLR 1140]).

(6) The gravity of the effect upon the employees discriminated against has to be weighed against the importance of the legitimate aims in assessing the necessity of the particular measure chosen (*Fuchs* [*v Land Hessen* [2012] ICR 93]).[198]

(7) The scope of the tests for justifying indirect discrimination under article 2(2)(b) [of the Framework Directive] and for justifying any age discrimination under article 6(1) [of the Framework Directive] is not identical. It is for the member states, rather than the individual employer, to establish the legitimacy of the aim pursued ([*R (on the application of the Incorporated Trustees of the National Council on Ageing (Age Concern England)) v Secretary of State for Business, Enterprise and Regulatory Reform* [2009] ICR 1080]).

At a broader conceptual level, we might ask what is so special about direct age discrimination that policy-makers have singled it out as a *justifiable* wrong? The answer lies in the distinction we addressed earlier between the economic rationales for the proscription of age discrimination, on the one hand, and the inherent dignitarian rationales for its prohibition, on the other:

■ S. Fredman, *Discrimination Law*, 2nd edition (Oxford, OUP, 2011) 106

. . . age is set apart from other protected characteristics by permitting direct age discrimination to be justified provided it is an appropriate and necessary means to achieve a legitimate aim. The [Frame-

---

[198] For example, see *Dansk Jurist- og Økonomforbund (on behalf of Toftgaard) v Indenrigs- og Sundhedsministeriet* [2014] IRLR 37 where the harm to civil servants who were 65 or over was disproportionate to the employer's legitimate aim, since those aged 65 or over were essentially forced to draw their pension as they were not entitled to three years' availability pay on dismissal, which was provided to younger civil servants. See also *Schmitzer v Bundesministerin für Inneres* [2015] IRLR 331 where transitional arrangements introduced in respect of public sector payments based on length of service were deemed to be disproportionate.

work] Directive pinpoints a series of aims which are considered legitimate, including employment policy, labour market and vocational training objectives. These span both instrumental and intrinsic objectives. Thus Article 6 [of the Framework Directive] permits differences of treatment to promote the vocational integration or ensure the protection of young people, older workers, and persons with caring responsibilities. These are intrinsic reasons. On the other hand, the right not to be discriminated against on grounds of age can be subordinated to instrumental ends. Thus Article 6 [of the Framework Directive] also potentially permits differences of treatment which fix a minimum condition of age for employment or other benefits; or which fix a minimum of recruitment based on the training requirements of the post or the need for a reasonable period of employment before retirement.

If we now turn to the phenomenon of indirect age discrimination, the most central decision to date has been that of the Supreme Court in *Homer v Chief Constable of West Yorkshire Police*.[199] Here, an employee aged 62 claimed that he had suffered indirect discrimination when his employer altered its policy to require persons performing his job description to have a law degree. Although the case was remitted to the employment tribunal to reconsider the employer's proportionality defence, two things are abundantly clear about the operation of the defence in the case of an indirect discrimination claim: it is not necessary for an employer to invoke a legitimate aim for the application of a PCP which:

(1) has a public interest character in general; and

(2) is consistent with the social policy aims of the State.

Instead, the employer may pinpoint objectives which are wholly particular to its own organization, such as a 'costs plus' objective,[200] the promotion of the recruitment or retention of staff of the requisite talent, capability, and quality, the facilitation of a fair selection process or stable workforce, or the rewarding of loyalty.[201] The proportionality exercise will then entail an enquiry as to whether the employer had no alternative means of achieving the legitimate aim which, if established, will furnish the employer with the requisite objective justification for its conduct.[202]

Similarly, *Chief Constable of West Midlands Police v Harrod*[203] involved claims of indirect age discrimination from claimants who maintained that a provision, criterion, or practice had resulted in a particular disadvantage to them as a result of their age. In *Harrod*, several police offers were compulsorily retired under subordinate legislation on efficiency grounds. However, such forced retirement was subject to a condition that the officers would be entitled to receive a pension equivalent to 2/3rds of average pensionable pay.[204] Officers with more than 30 years' service were prejudiced as a result. However the Court of Appeal held that the employer could objectively justify the restriction of dismissals to officers with more than 20 years' service on the ground that there was no other lawful method of selection available.

---

[199] [2012] ICR 704.

[200] See *Woodcock v Cumbria Primary Care Trust* [2012] IRLR 491, 501–2 per Rimer LJ; Chapter 10, section 10.2.4.4. In *Schmitzer v Bundesministerin für Inneres* [2015] IRLR 331, the CJEU reiterated the point that what will not wash is an argument from an employer that it was too expensive for it not to discriminate.   [201] *Rolls-Royce plc v Unite the Union* [2010] 1 WLR 318.

[202] *Chief Constable of West Yorkshire Police v Homer* [2012] UKSC 15, [2012] ICR 704, 712F–H per Baroness Hale. However, contrast this 'least restrictive means' incarnation of the proportionality test with the more diluted 'balancing' approach adopted by the EAT in *Chief Constable of West Midlands Police v Harrod* [2017] ICR 869, 882F–H per Bean LJ and *Edie v HCL Insurance BPO Services Ltd* [2015] ICR 713 where the contention was rejected that the tribunal has the power to identify or devise a less prejudicial PCP and so the harm suffered by the claimants must be weighed up against the extent of the employer's need to apply the PCP to achieve its legitimate aim.   [203] [2017] ICR 869.

[204] See also *Dansk Industri, acting on behalf of Ajos A/S v Estate of Rasmussen* [2016] IRLR 552.

Two final points ought to be made. First, as decided by the EAT in *EAD Solicitors LLP v Abrams*,[205] a limited company will have the benefit of a direct associative age discrimination claim under section 13 of the EA. Secondly, age discrimination is a fundamental principle of equality in EU law: *Kücükdeveci v Swedex GmbH & Co. KG*.[206] As noted in Chapter 10, section 10.2.1, the upshot of this is that the principle can be engaged as a means of striking down provisions of the common law or UK legislation with which it conflicts.

Reflection points

1. If there is a 'boundary dispute' in respect of one of the protected characteristics *x* which eventually gives rise to a new protected characteristic *y* being 'spun out' therefrom, are you of the view that it is justified for a claimant with protected characteristic *y* to be permitted to continue to raise claims of discrimination based on the protected characteristic *x*? Give reasons for your answer.

2. In your opinion, is the list of protected characteristics fixed? If not, is it feasible for that menu to continue to expand? If not, why not? If so, why?

3. Read the articles by M. Bell and L. Waddington, 'Reflecting on Inequalities in European Equality Law' (2003) 28 *European Law Review* 349; M. Bell, 'A Patchwork of Protection: The New Anti-Discrimination Law Framework' (2004) 67 *Modern Law Review* 465; E. Howard, 'The Case for a Considered Hierarchy of Discrimination Grounds in EU Law' (2006) 13 *Maastricht Journal of European and Comparative Law* 443; and C. O'Cinneide, 'The Uncertain Foundations of Contemporary Anti-Discrimination Law' (2011) 11 *International Journal of Discrimination and the Law* 7. Do you agree with Bell, Waddington, and Howard's argument that current domestic and EU law prescribes a hierarchy of protected characteristics 'with racial or ethnic origin at the top, closely followed by sex, with religion or belief, disability and sexual orientation below this and age at the bottom'? If so, is such a hierarchy justifiable? If so, on what grounds?

 For additional reading on the protected characteristics, visit the Online Resources for this book at www.oup.com/uk/cabrelli3e/

11.3 POSITIVE DISCRIMINATION

The essence of policies promoting the positive discrimination agenda can be expressed in relatively straightforward terms: they are legal measures adopted to realize the substantive equality model by enjoining employers to exercise more favourable treatment of groups or constituencies which have been systematically and/or persistently denied access to labour markets or structurally disadvantaged or under-represented in those labour markets. We now turn to an examination of positive discrimination, including how it can be differentiated from positive action.

11.3.1 Examining positive discrimination and positive action

Advocates of positive discrimination argue that it functions to compensate disadvantaged sections of society from past discrimination. It is contended that it is desirable on

---

[205] [2015] IRLR 978.   [206] [2011] 2 CMLR 703.

the basis that the legal system's traditional dependence on the individual litigation-driven model is overly casuistic, ad hoc, and incapable of addressing deep-seated structural limitations on the capacity of under-represented groups to fully participate in the labour market. Proponents of positive discrimination allege that the legal concepts of direct and indirect discrimination have failed to incentivize employers to alter their behaviour and practices by embedding diversity and equality into their widespread decision-making processes. Positive discrimination is sometimes referred to as 'affirmative action', or 're-verse discrimination' in the literature.[207] Despite the varying nomenclature attached to the concept, what is particularly clear is that it entails discrimination against certain mainstream groups, i.e. less favourable treatment of the mainstream. For example, if disabled employees are identified as deserving of preferential treatment in relation to the terms and conditions attached to their employment and, as such, a positive discrimina-tion policy is implemented, then, all things being equal, non-disabled employees will experience direct discrimination as regards such terms and conditions. This leaves the employer open to direct discrimination proceedings raised by an employee falling within the mainstream constituency and the fact that doctrine dictates that the employer's mo-tives or intentions are irrelevant[208] simply underscores the position.[209] It is for this reason that legislation prescribing various kinds of legal measures associated with positive dis-crimination tends to be carefully drawn to specifically exclude the possibility of claims from the mainstream group.[210]

Measures designed to effect positive discrimination are inherently controversial, pri-marily for the reason that they are unjustifiable or lack legitimacy[211] in the sense that they:

(1) elide the principle of equal treatment;

(2) are capable of instilling resentment in the mainstream group which has been unfavourably treated or patronize the under-represented or disadvantaged group; and

(3) specifically enjoin employers to have regard to the particular identities and character-istics of their existing and prospective employees:

■ **S. Fredman, 'Reversing Discrimination' (1997) 113 *Law Quarterly Review* 575**

Given its deliberate use of race- or gender-conscious criteria, it is not surprising that the legitimacy of affirmative action is highly problematic. Much of the [twentieth] century has been spent con-vincing judges and legislators that race and gender [and age, disability, sexual orientation, religious belief, marital or civil partnership status, pregnancy and maternity, gender re-assignment] are ir-relevant and their use in the allocation of benefits or rights invidious. How then can it be legitimate to permit such use for purportedly remedial purposes?

---

[207] See the discussion in C. McCrudden, 'Rethinking Positive Action' (1986) 15 *Industrial Law Journal* 219, 220–1; see generally C. McCrudden, 'A Comparative Taxonomy of "Positive Action" and "Affirma-tive Action" Policies' in R. Schulze (ed.), *Non-Discrimination in European Private Law* (Tübingen, Ger-many, Mohr Siebeck, 2011) 157.

[208] *Birmingham City Council v Equal Opportunities Commission* [1989] AC 1155; *James v Eastleigh Borough Council* [1990] 2 AC 751.

[209] For example, see *Lambeth London Borough Council v Commission for Racial Equality* [1990] ICR 768; L. Barmes, 'Promoting Diversity and the Definition of Direct Discrimination' (2003) 32 *Industrial Law Journal* 200; and L. Barmes, 'Equality Law and Experimentation: The Positive Action Challenge' (2009) 68 *Cambridge Law Journal* 623, 628.

[210] For example, see sections 13(3), 158, and 159 of the EA.

[211] See the discussion of the various charges and counter-charges in T. Khaitan, *A Theory of Discrimi-nation Law* (Oxford, OUP, 2015) 222–40.

The counter-argument is that positive discrimination ought to be an economically attractive proposition insofar as it enables employers to gain access to a much wider and more diverse pool of talent. Moreover, the symmetrical/equal treatment model grounded in formal justice is not sufficiently attuned to social realities:

■ **S. Fredman, 'Reversing Discrimination' (1997) 113** *Law Quarterly Review* **575, 596**

Formal justice ignores the social fact that discrimination on the grounds of race or sex functions as a continuing and powerful constraint on the circumstances and opportunities of women and black people, a constraint which does not affect those of the privileged race or gender. Equal treatment of individuals who are not socially equal perpetuates the inequalities. This immediately exposes the fallacy of the symmetrical argument: since discrimination on grounds of race or sex has consistently worked to the detriment of black people and women, discrimination in their favour should be viewed quite differently from invidious and detrimental discrimination. A law which genuinely aims to narrow the disparities and eventually achieve equality must tolerate unequal treatment where necessary to achieve more equal results.

The policy objective of positive discrimination may take many forms and, to the extent that it does so, this is precisely how the law in the UK pursues this agenda. The most extreme form of positive discrimination is quotas,[212] which the current law rejects.[213] We find that there are five incarnations of positive discrimination in the UK.

(1) First, it has been judicially recognized that the legal concept in sections 20–22 of the EA which requires employers to make reasonable adjustments in favour of disabled employees entails a measure of positive discrimination in their favour, i.e. more favourable treatment than able-bodied employees:

■ *Archibald v Fife Council* [2004] ICR 954, 958D–969E

Lord Hope:

As the determination of the employment tribunal makes clear, a substantial number of adjustments to the normal procedures were made in [the employee's] case. Some of them involved positive discrimination in her favour, such as her automatic short listing for the available posts. This was within the scope of the duty, as it was necessary for the [employer] to redress the position of disadvantage that she was in due to her disability . . .

Baroness Hale:

The [EA], however, does not regard the differences between disabled people and others as irrelevant. It does not expect each to be treated in the same way. It expects reasonable adjustments to be made to cater for the special needs of disabled people. It necessarily entails an element of more favourable treatment . . . It is common ground that [sections 20–22 of the EA] entail . . . a measure of positive discrimination, in the sense that employers are required to take steps to help disabled people which they are not required to take for others . . .

---

[212] See J. C. Suk, 'Quotas and Consequences' in D. Hellman and S. Moreau (eds), *Philosophical Foundations of Discrimination Law* (Oxford, OUP, 2013) 228.
[213] See section 159(4)(b) of the EA.

The effect of *Archibald* has been explicitly catered for in section 13(3) of the EA which precludes a non-disabled employee from claiming direct discrimination where a disabled employee is treated more favourably than him/her:

> **Section 13 Direct discrimination**
>
> (3) If the protected characteristic is disability, and B is not a disabled person, A does not discriminate against B only because A treats or would treat disabled persons more favourably than A treats B.

We will explore the reasons why it has been considered justifiable to require employers to treat disabled employees more favourably than others in Chapter 12.

(2) A second example afforded by the law relates to pregnant employees and employees on maternity leave, which enjoins such employees to show that they have been treated 'unfavourably'. As we discussed in section 11.2.1, in order to establish a case of discrimination, section 18 of the EA imposes no obligation on a pregnant employee or employee on maternity leave to show that she was treated less favourably than a comparator. The absence of a comparison exercise is consistent with the conception of substantive equality.[214] As such, a degree of positive discrimination is conferred in favour of such employees in order to recognize their biology and to protect their reproductive capacity.[215]

(3) Likewise, a claimant seeking to prove harassment need only show that it 'related to' a protected characteristic, which also negates any need for a comparison exercise.

(4) In each of the three examples of disability, pregnancy/maternity, and harassment, it has been decided by the legislature that there is something so unique or special about these characteristics and concepts that their 'difference' ought to be explicitly recognized; as such, they should be set apart from the standard symmetrical equal treatment model. However, as well as engaging in the pursuit of positive discrimination on such a selective case-by-case basis, policy-makers have recently accepted that an acknowledgement of more general manifestations of positive discrimination also ought to be permitted. For example, following on from the decision of the ECJ in *Marschall v Land Nordrhein Westfalen*,[216] Article 7 of the Framework Directive,[217] Article 5 of the Race Directive,[218] Article 3 of the Recast Equality Directive,[219] and Article 157(4) of the TFEU recognized that Member States should be entitled to introduce laws enabling employers to adopt positive action of a proportionate nature. Such positive action consistent with EU law has been adopted by the UK and finds its expression in sections 158 and 159 of the EA:

> **Section 158 Positive action: general**
>
> (1) This section applies if a person (P) reasonably thinks that—
>
> (a) persons who share a protected characteristic suffer a disadvantage connected to the characteristic,

---

[214] This can be compared to the conception of formal equality which entails treating 'like with like' and so necessarily involves comparison.

[215] See S. Fredman, 'Pregnancy and Parenthood Reassessed' (1994) 110 *Law Quarterly Review* 106.

[216] [1998] IRLR 39; cf. *Kalanke v Freie Hansestadt Bremen* [1995] IRLR 660. For an analysis of the CJEU's jurisprudence, see J. Croon-Gestefeld, *Reconceptualisng European Equality Law* (Oxford, Hart Publishing, 2017) 167–84.   [217] Directive 2000/43/EC (OJ 2000 L180/22).

[218] Directive 2000/78/EC (OJ 2000 L303/16).   [219] Directive 2006/54/EC (OJ 2006 L204/23).

(b) persons who share a protected characteristic have needs that are different from the needs of persons who do not share it, or

(c) participation in an activity by persons who share a protected characteristic is disproportionately low.

(2) This Act does not prohibit P from taking any action which is a proportionate means of achieving the aim of—

(a) enabling or encouraging persons who share the protected characteristic to overcome or minimise that disadvantage,

(b) meeting those needs, or

(c) enabling or encouraging persons who share the protected characteristic to participate in that activity . . .

Section 159 Positive action: recruitment and promotion

(1) This section applies if a person (P) reasonably thinks that—

(a) persons who share a protected characteristic suffer a disadvantage connected to the characteristic, or

(b) participation in an activity by persons who share a protected characteristic is disproportionately low.

(2) Part 5 (work) does not prohibit P from taking action within subsection (3) with the aim of enabling or encouraging persons who share the protected characteristic to—

(a) overcome or minimise that disadvantage, or

(b) participate in that activity.

(3) That action is treating a person (A) more favourably in connection with recruitment or promotion than another person (B) because A has the protected characteristic but B does not.

(4) But subsection (2) applies only if—

(a) A is as qualified as B to be recruited or promoted,

(b) P does not have a policy of treating persons who share the protected characteristic more favourably in connection with recruitment or promotion than persons who do not share it, and

(c) taking the action in question is a proportionate means of achieving the aim referred to in subsection (2).

(5) 'Recruitment' means a process for deciding whether to—

(a) offer employment to a person,

(b) make contract work available to a contract worker . . .

There are two elements to these provisions. First, section 158 enables general positive action measures to be pursued by the employer which are a proportionate means of achieving one of the listed legitimate aims in section 158(2). In terms of this provision, an employer will be permitted to adhere to a policy that seeks to confer a priority on groups which it 'reasonably thinks' are traditionally disadvantaged, possess different and unmet needs which vary from the mainstream, and suffer from a disproportionate lack of participation in workplace activities. The evaluative criterion of reasonableness to be applied to the employer's judgment here is not particularly intense, as shown by the guidance furnished in the EHRC Code:

■ **EHRC Code of Practice on Employment**

What does 'reasonably think' mean?

12.14 . . . some indication or evidence will be required to show that one of the . . . statutory conditions [of disadvantage, different and unmet needs and disproportionate participation] applies. It does not, however, need to be sophisticated statistical data or research. It may simply involve an employer looking at the profiles of their workforce and/or making enquiries of other comparable employers in the area or sector. Additionally, it could involve looking at national data such as labour force surveys for a national or local picture of the work situation for particular groups who share a protected characteristic. A decision could be based on qualitative evidence, such as consultation with workers and trade unions.

Hepple adds some flesh to the bones of this provision to provide examples:

■ **B. Hepple, *Equality: The New Legal Framework*, 2nd edition (Oxford, Hart Publishing, 2014) 159**

Unconditional quotas or reserved places are clearly not lawful [under section 158], but it may be possible to give priority to a particular group provided this is based on objective criteria showing why the group is disadvantaged. So a university in which Black students are under-represented may target particular schools and communities, provide access courses and special support for such students, and deal with practical barriers to their recruitment or academic achievement. But the university cannot have a racial quota or reserve places for particular groups.

This generic provision can be contrasted with section 159 which applies to managerial decision-making regarding recruitment and promotion. Here, employers are afforded the *option* of preferring employees who are members of a group that has been systematically disadvantaged or under-represented in the labour market over employees falling within mainstream groups. However, it is subject to tight control inasmuch as the employer is only entitled to prefer such employees where each of the candidates is equally qualified. Hence the lack of participation, disadvantage, and under-representation acts as a kind of 'tie-breaker' to enable the employer to hire or promote the candidate belonging to the relevant group. Consider the illustration in Hypothetical C.

Hypothetical C

Fifteen employees are employed at the Stirling office of Danny's Demolishers Ltd ('DD'). All of those employees are white males bar one, and only one of the employees is a member of the Asian community. A vacancy for an office junior has arisen and two of the five individuals interviewed for the position have been given an equal scoring of 20 in terms of the objective criteria of skills, experience, suitability, competence, qualifications, and professional attitude.[220] The scores of the other three candidates for the position are below 20.

[220] See the Explanatory Notes to the EA, available at http://www.legislation.gov.uk/ukpga/2010/15/notes/division/3/11/2/2 at para 518 (last visited 6 December 2017).

One of the two candidates is an Asian woman named Aisha Shah. DD decides to offer the position to Aisha Shah because it is keen to increase the number of woman and members of the Asian community working at its Stirling office. Tom Harkness, the unsuccessful candidate, seeks to challenge Aisha's appointment on the ground that he has suffered direct discrimination. Provided that DD is able to show that the selection of Aisha meets the criteria in section 159(2)(3) and (4) of the EA, DD will not be liable in direct discrimination.

(5) Where the employer is a public authority or a private sector entity exercising public functions, it will be subject to the public sector equality duty set out in section 149 of the EA. In exercising such public functions, such employers have a statutory obligation to have regard to the need to (a) eliminate discrimination, harassment, and victimization, (b) advance equality of opportunity between persons sharing a relevant protected characteristic and those who do not share it, and (c) foster good relations between persons sharing a relevant protected characteristic and those who do not share it.[221] Section 149(6) of the EA specifically acknowledges that compliance with this statutory duty may involve treating some persons more favourably than others, i.e. positive discrimination.

11.4 EVALUATING THE GENUINE OCCUPATIONAL REQUIREMENTS EXCEPTION

In this section, we explore a particular statutory construct which, if satisfied, will prevent the operation of the protections set out in the EA: the occupational requirements exception. Seen from this perspective, this concept is remarkable insofar as it permits an employer to lawfully subject an employee to discrimination on the basis of one of the nine recognized protected characteristics.

11.4.1 Exploring the occupational requirements exception

In Chapter 10, section 10.2.2, we noted how sections 191–197 of, and Schedule 22 to, the EA prescribe a number of exceptions where the EA will have no effect, e.g. where an employer's actions are undertaken for the purposes of safeguarding national security. The current domestic framework is based on Article 4(1) of the Framework Directive, Article 4 of the Race Directive, and Article 14(2) of the Recast Equality Directive. Section 83(11) of the EA gives effect to Schedule 9 to the EA, which is the key statutory provision, similarly providing for exceptions, albeit in an indirect manner. The key point is that Schedule 9 to the EA enables an employer to engage in 'prohibited conduct' under the EA on a lawful basis where it is an 'occupational requirement' of the work or job that an employee has a particular protected characteristic and the individual or employee concerned does not meet that requirement, or the employer has reasonable grounds for not being satisfied that such individual or employee meets it:

---

[221] For general discussion of the public sector equality duty, see S. Fredman, 'Breaking the Mould: Equality as a Proactive Duty' in N. Countouris and M. Freedland (eds), *Resocialising Europe in a Time of Crisis* (Cambridge, CUP, 2013) 138; S. Fredman, 'Addressing Disparate Impact: Indirect Discrimination and the Public Sector Equality Duty' (2014) 43 *Industrial Law Journal* 349.

Schedule 9

Work: Exceptions
Part I
Occupational Requirements
1 General

(1)   A person (A) does not contravene a provision mentioned in sub-paragraph (2) by apply-ing in relation to work a requirement to have a particular protected characteristic, if A shows that, having regard to the nature or context of the work—

(a) it is an occupational requirement,

(b) the application of the requirement is a proportionate means of achieving a legitimate aim, and

(c) the person to whom A applies the requirement does not meet it (or A has reasonable grounds for not being satisfied that the person meets it).[222]

The decision of the CJEU in *Bougnaoui v Micropole SA*[223] reminds us that it will only be in very limited circumstances that a characteristic related to one of the protected charac-teristics may constitute a genuine and determining occupational requirement. The EHRC Code furnishes guidance on the breadth of the term 'occupational requirement' and states that the 'requirement must not be a sham or pretext and there must be a link between the requirement and the job'.[224] For example, if the employer is casting actors for a con-ventional theatre performance of Andrew Lloyd Webber's musical *Jesus Christ Superstar*, it could be a genuine occupational requirement that the role of Jesus be filled by an employee who is male and able-bodied, rather than female and disabled. If a female disa-bled worker were to raise a claim of direct discrimination against the employer, the latter would have a defence under paragraph 1 of Schedule 9 to the EA on the ground that she does not meet the occupational requirement that the individual cast as Jesus be male and able-bodied. Another example applies where general tenets of privacy and decency call for persons of a particular protected characteristic to occupy the job. Requiring a person with a specific protected characteristic will not contravene the EA in such circumstances, e.g. that a prison officer in an all-female prison be female, rather than male.

It should be stressed that it is necessary for the employer to show that its requirement for an individual with a particular protected characteristic to fill the job is a proportion-ate means of achieving a legitimate aim. For example, in the earlier example regarding the female prison officer, the employer would be required to demonstrate that it was a proportionate means of achieving the legitimate aim of securing decency and privacy to hire such a female prison officer, rather than a male prison officer. In doing so, the employer would be obliged to satisfy the tribunal or court that a less restrictive alterna-tive to secure the legitimate aim did not exist, e.g. by demonstrating that it would be disproportionate for it to adjust working practices or physical aspects of the workplace to accommodate male prison officers to be hired in the female prison. Subjective consid-erations, such as the employer acceding to a key client's demand that it no longer wishes to have the employer's services provided by a worker wearing an Islamic headscarf will not be a genuine occupational requirement that is proportionate.[225]

---

[222] Paragraph 1(3) of Schedule 9 to the EA provides that, in the context of the protected characteristics of gender reassignment, marriage, and civil partnership, the requirement is not to be a transsexual person, married, or a civil partner.

[223] [2017] IRLR 447.

[224] EHRC Code, available at https://www.equalityhumanrights.com/sites/default/files/employercode. pdf at para 13.7 (last visited 6 December 2017). See also *Bougnaoui v Micropole SA* [2017] IRLR 447, 465.   [225] *Bougnaoui v Micropole SA* [2017] IRLR 447.

Unlike the predecessor statutory regime in the context of sex and race discrimination in section 7 of the SDA and section 5 of the RRA, the framework in Schedule 9 is open-ended and unlimited. Nonetheless, some general guidance can be supplied on the scope of the exception in Schedule 9 to the EA. The most logical way to approach Schedule 9 is to divide it into its parts which are of (a) general application and (b) particular to specific protected characteristics.

11.4.2 Occupational requirements exception: general application

Unlike section 7 of the SDA and section 5 of the RRA, there is a glaring absence of specific examples of genuine occupational requirements in the context of sex, race, etc. in Schedule 9 to the EA. However, the now-repealed provisions of the SDA and RRA are likely to be of some influence and relevance in construing the content of the open-ended framework in paragraph 1(1) of Schedule 9 to the EA. Therefore, the following examples are likely to continue to constitute genuine occupational requirements and defeat an employee's complaint of direct or indirect discrimination.

(1) *Sex* Genuine occupational requirements in the context of sex include that:

(a) the job calls for a person of one sex rather than the other for reasons of physiology (excluding physical strength or stamina) or, in dramatic performances or other entertainment, for reasons of authenticity, so that the essential nature of the job would be materially different if carried out by a person of the other sex;

(b) the job needs to be held by a person of one sex rather than the other to preserve decency or privacy or, where the job is likely to involve working or living in a private home, because objection might reasonably be taken to allowing a person of the other sex the degree of physical or social contact with an inmate of the home or the knowledge of intimate details of his/her life which is likely on account of the nature or circumstances of the job or the home;

(c) it is impracticable for the employee to live elsewhere than in premises provided by the employer which are normally lived in by, and equipped with accommodation for, persons of one sex and it is not reasonable to expect the employer either to equip these premises with accommodation for the other sex or to provide other premises;

(d) the premises within which the work is to be done are part of a hospital, prison, or other establishment for persons requiring special care, supervision, or attention and these persons are all of one sex, and it is reasonable, having regard to the essential character of the establishment, that the job should not be held by a person of the other sex;

(e) the holder of the job provides individuals with personal services, promoting their welfare or education or the like, and these services can most effectively be provided by a person of one sex rather than the other;

(f) the job needs to be held by a person of one sex rather than the other because it is likely to involve the performance of duties outside the UK in a country whose laws or customs are such that the duties could not effectively be performed by a person of the other sex; or

(g) the job is one of two to be held by a married couple.

(2) *Race* Genuine occupational requirements in the context of race include:

(a) that the job calls for a person of one race rather than another for reasons of authenticity in theatrical, dramatic, or artistic works (e.g. plays or modelling), or in a specific setting such as an ethnic restaurant;

    (b) where personal services are provided to members of a racial group and can best be provided by members of that group; or[226]

    (c) Parliament or the Government is entitled to discriminate directly or indirectly against a person on the ground of race by applying to that person a PCP which relates to that person's place of ordinary residence or the length of time that the person has been present or resident in or outside the UK or an area within it.[227]

11.4.3 Occupational requirements exception: specific application

Paragraphs 2–20 of Schedule 9 to the EA cater for particular circumstances in which the EA will be taken not to have been contravened. We now examine the most significant of these provisions in the context of the protected characteristics of religious belief and age.

11.4.3.1 Religion or belief

If we turn first to the exceptions applicable in the case of religious belief, there are two genuine occupational requirement provisions ('GOR exceptions') to consider.[228] These GOR exceptions are the most morally and politically contentious of the GORs since they have the potential to clash with the broader equality agenda. This is evident in the case of the first GOR exception found in paragraph 2 of Schedule 9 to the EA which concerns an occupational requirement of an employer (who may be or may not be a religious organization) that an individual be of a particular sex, not be transsexual, not be married or in a civil partnership, or not be married to, or the civil partner of, a person who has a living former spouse or civil partner.[229] Moreover, such employer may also impose a requirement relating to circumstances in which a marriage or civil partnership came to an end or a requirement relating to sexual orientation.[230]

    Essentially, this first GOR exception permits a qualifying employer to directly or indirectly discriminate against persons because of their sex, current or former marital status, or sexual orientation, and because they are or were in a civil partnership. Hepple notes that this first GOR exception in the context of religious belief 'makes it possible . . . for the Catholic Church to require that its priests be men'[231] and the EHRC Code clarifies that it would enable an 'orthodox synagogue . . . [to] apply a requirement for its rabbi to be a man' or an 'evangelical church . . . [to] require its ministers to be married or heterosexual if this enables the church to avoid a conflict with the strongly held religious convictions of its congregation'.[232] The decision of Mr Justice Richards in the case of *R (on the application of Amicus-MSF Section) v Secretary of State for Trade and Industry*[233] indicates that, since the first GOR exception is a derogation from the principle of equal treatment, it is to be applied sparingly and interpreted strictly. As such, Mr Justice Richards opined that it would be difficult to satisfy each of its individual elements, and that

---

[226] See *London Borough of Lambeth v Commission for Racial Equality* [1990] ICR 768.

[227] Paragraph 1 of Schedule 23 to the EA.

[228] For a discussion, see G. Pitt, 'Keeping the Faith: Trends and Tensions in Religion or Belief Discrimination' (2011) 40 *Industrial Law Journal* 384, 401–3; A. McColgan, 'Class Wars? Religion and (In)Equality in the Workplace' (2009) 38 *Industrial Law Journal* 1, 3–5.

[229] Paragraph 2(4)(a), (b), (c), and (d) of Schedule 9 to the EA.

[230] Paragraph 2(4)(e) and (f) of Schedule 9 to the EA.

[231] B. Hepple, *Equality: The New Legal Framework*, 2nd edition (Oxford, Hart Publishing, 2014) 112. See the Church of England priest in *Pemberton v Inwood* [2017] IRLR 211 who married his long-term male civil partner.

[232] EHRC Code, available at https://www.equalityhumanrights.com/sites/default/files/employercode. pdf at para 13.12 (last visited 6 December 2017).   [233] [2007] ICR 1176.

the scope of application of the derogation was very limited and would be restricted to the recruitment of religious teachers and leaders.[234]

In order for an employer to avail itself of this first GOR exception, it must show that:

(1) the employment concerned is for the purposes of an organized religion;

(2) either one of the 'compliance' or 'no-conflict' principles is engaged; and

(3) the disappointed individual or employee claimant to whom the requirement was applied did not meet it or the employer has reasonable grounds for not being satisfied that he/she meets it.[235]

Rather unhelpfully, there is no definition of 'employment for the purposes of an organized religion',[236] although Mr Justice Richards in the case of *R (on the application of Amicus-MSF Section) v Secretary of State for Trade and Industry*[237] took the view that this was a narrower expression than 'for the purposes of a religious organisation' or the expression 'where an employer has an ethos based on religion or belief',[238] since 'employment as a teacher in a faith school' is likely to be 'for purposes of a religious organisation' but not 'for purposes of an organised religion'.[239] Thus, '... whilst an "organised religion" will also be a "religious organisation", it is not the case that a "religious organisation" is always an "organised religion"'.[240]

As for the compass of the 'compliance' principle, paragraph 2(5) of Schedule 9 to the EA indicates that it will be engaged if the employer's occupational requirement is applied so as to comply with the doctrines of the religion. Mr Justice Richards expressed the following view of the 'compliance' principle:

■ *R (on the application of Amicus-MSF Section) v Secretary of State for Trade and Industry* [2007] ICR 1176, 1210F–G

Mr Justice Richards:

[It is] to be read not as a subjective test concerning the motivation of the employer, but as an objective test whereby it must be shown that employment of a person not meeting the requirement would be incompatible with the doctrines of the religion. That is very narrow in scope.

Turning now to the 'non-conflict' principle, paragraph 2(6) of Schedule 9 to the EA states that this will be applicable 'if because of the nature or context of the employment, the requirement is applied so as to avoid conflicting with the strongly held religious convictions of a significant number of the religion's followers'. Once again, this is a provision which operates to hem in the breadth of coverage of this first GOR exception:

---

[234] *ibid.*, 1210C–E per Mr Justice Richards; cf. *Reaney v Hereford Diocesan Board of Finance* Case no. 1602844/2006, Cardiff Tribunal, 17 July 2006, unreported but available at http://www.secularism.org. uk/uploads/reaney-judgement.pdf (last visited 6 December 2017), which is a case about a Diocesan youth worker.   [235] Paragraph 2(1)(a), (b), and (c) of Schedule 9 to the EA.

[236] The Government had provided a definition when the EA was progressing through Parliament as a Bill. It restricted the meaning of this expression to employment that wholly or mainly involved leading or assisting in the observation of liturgical or ritualistic practices of the religion or promoting or explaining the doctrine of the religion (whether to followers of the religion or otherwise). However, the inclusion of this wording was defeated in the House of Lords at committee stage, on which, see S. Fredman, *Discrimination Law*, 2nd edition (Oxford, OUP, 2011) 85.   [237] [2007] ICR 1176.

[238] *ibid.*, 1210E per Mr Justice Richards.   [239] *ibid.*, 1210E per Mr Justice Richards.

[240] R. Sandberg and N. Doe, 'Religious Exemptions in Discrimination Law' [2007] 66 *Cambridge Law Journal* 302, 308.

■ *R (on the application of Amicus-MSF Section) v Secretary of State for Trade and Industry* [2007] ICR 1176, 1210G–1211B

Mr Justice Richards:

. . . this is in my view an objective, not subjective, test. Further, the conflict to be avoided is with religious convictions, which must be strongly held; and they must be convictions of a significant number of the religion's followers. This is going to be a very far from easy test to satisfy in practice. The fact that reference is made to 'a significant number' rather than to all or the majority of a religion's followers not only restricts the desirability of avoiding detailed statistical analysis . . . but also ensures that proper account is taken of the existence of differing bodies of opinion even within an organised religion. Sexual orientation is a matter on which some followers of a religion may hold stronger religious convictions than others. In my view it is legitimate to allow for the possibility of applying a relevant requirement even if the convictions in question are held only by a significant minority of followers.

Meanwhile, the second GOR exception finds its expression in paragraph 3 of Schedule 9 to the EA. It applies where an employer having a particular ethos based on religion or belief has an occupational requirement that the individual or employee concerned be of a particular religion or belief having regard to the particular ethos and to the nature or context of the work.[241] If the individual or employee claimant fails to meet the requirement, or the employer has reasonable grounds for not being satisfied that the claimant meets it, and adopting the occupational requirement is proportionate, then the employer will defeat the claimant's discrimination claim.[242] This provision is designed to permit qualifying employers to employ, promote, etc. persons who are of a particular religion or belief to posts and thus exclude persons of other religions or none.[243] The Explanatory Notes to the EA provide as follows:

■ Explanatory Notes to the Equality Act

796. . . .

Example

- A religious organisation may wish to restrict applicants for the post of head of its organisation to those people that adhere to that faith. This is because to represent the views of that organisation accurately it is felt that the person in charge of that organisation must have an in-depth understanding of the religion's doctrines. This type of discrimination could be lawful. However, other posts that do not require this kind of in-depth understanding, such as administrative posts, should be open to all people regardless of their religion or belief.[244]

The principal element of this second GOR exception is that the employer must have 'an ethos based on religion or belief'. The EHRC Code provides the following:

---

[241] Paragraph 3 of Schedule 9 to the EA.

[242] Paragraph 3(a), (b), and (c) of Schedule 9 to the EA.

[243] For example, at para 13.18 of the EHRC Code, it is narrated that it could be lawful for a Humanist organization promoting Humanist philosophy to prescribe that its chief executive be a Humanist.

[244] See the Explanatory Notes to the EA, available at http://www.legislation.gov.uk/ukpga/2010/15/notes/division/3/16/26/1/2 at para 796 (last visited 6 December 2017).

■ **EHRC Code of Practice on Employment**

> 13.17 ... the employer must be able to show that their ethos is based on a religion or belief, for example, by referring to their founding constitution. An 'ethos' is the important character or spirit of the religion or belief. It may also be the underlying sentiment, conviction or outlook that informs the behaviours, customs, practices or attitudes of followers of the religion or belief.

Thus, there is no requirement for the employer to be a religious organization itself, provided that it has an ethos based on a religion or belief. To that extent, it is 'simply [an] extension . . . of the normal occupational requirement exemption'[245] in paragraph 1 of Schedule 9 to the EA. The decision of the EAT in *Glasgow City Council v McNab*[246] exemplifies how the requirement that the employer must have 'an ethos based on religion or belief' functions as a major limitation on the coverage of this second GOR exception. *McNab* concerned a Roman Catholic school situated in Scotland which was maintained by a local education authority in accordance with statute. Statute provided that the local education authority was solely responsible for the appointment of teachers, subject to the proviso that appointments to certain posts had to be approved by the Roman Catholic Church, including the post of 'principal or assistant principal teacher of guidance'. Mr McNab, an atheist, applied for a temporary post of acting principal teacher of pastoral care. He was an existing teacher of personal and social education at the school where the vacancy had arisen. The responsibilities undertaken by pastoral care teachers had previously been the responsibility of guidance teachers; hence special approval of the Roman Catholic Church was required. The application he submitted was unsuccessful and he was not even offered an interview. It was established that, had he been a Roman Catholic, an interview would have been forthcoming. The EAT held that the GOR exception was not engaged and that McNab had suffered discrimination, hence it was not an occupational requirement for a principal teacher of pastoral care to be a Roman Catholic. Moreover, Lady Smith in the EAT ruled that McNab's legal employer, i.e. the local authority, did not 'have any business having an ethos'[247] based on religion or belief, notwithstanding that it had a statutory obligation to maintain Roman Catholic schools. Moreover, it was held to be irrelevant that the employer could demonstrate that a part of its organization has a religious ethos.

What is unclear, however, from paragraph 3 of Schedule 9 to the EA is whether it enables an employer to insist on appointing a person to a post (a) who belongs to a particular religion and (b) whose behaviour complies with the doctrinal instructions of that religion. For example, could an organization set up for the propagation of the Islamic faith in England and Wales insist that its chairman be a Muslim and remain celibate, if he is gay? Although the employer would appear to be warranted in requiring him to be a Muslim, it is not wholly apparent that the expression 'a requirement to be of a particular religion or belief' is sufficiently broad to allow the employer to insist that he remain celibate.[248] However, the counter-argument is that the expression 'occupational requirement' in paragraph 3(a) of Schedule 9 to the EA might be broad enough to enable an employer to require the individual to adjust his/her behaviour so that it is also in conformance with the tenets of the religion.

---

[245] R. Sandberg and N. Doe, 'Religious Exemptions in Discrimination Law' [2007] 66 *Cambridge Law Journal* 302, 306.   [246] [2007] IRLR 476.

[247] *ibid.*, 481.

[248] Hepple has argued that this is one area in which para 3 of Schedule 9 to the EA fails to comply with the more broadly defined terms of the Framework Directive: B. Hepple, *Equality: The New Legal Framework*, 2nd edition (Oxford, Hart Publishing, 2014) 112–13.

Ultimately, many of the difficulties generated by the GOR exceptions in paragraphs 2 and 3 of Schedule 9 to the EA can be attributed to the fraught interplay between the protected characteristics of religion or belief, on the one hand, and sex, sexual orientation, marital, and civil partnership status, on the other.[249] This is captured eloquently by Fredman in the following extract:

■ S. Fredman, *Discrimination Law*, 2nd edition (Oxford, OUP, 2011) 73–4

. . . the relationship between religion and other grounds of discrimination is shifting and often conflicting. Religions find their source of authority in faith rather than reason, and in some cases, their allegiance is to God and a transcendental morality, rather than to the democratic legal system. This might make it difficult to find common ground either between one religion and another or between individual religions and a secular human rights regime . . . Perhaps most problematic is the reliance on religious belief to justify other forms of discrimination. Should individuals be permitted to discriminate against others on the grounds that this is required by their religion or belief? . . . More common are attempts to defend sexism or homophobia on the grounds of religion . . . [and] both British and EU law have permitted priority to be given in specific circumstances to religious belief over the protection of others' rights, particularly those of women and homosexuals. These conflicts have led some to argue that protection against religious discrimination has no place within the traditional lexicon of British discrimination law. McColgan argues that 'requiring the accommodation of practices or beliefs categorised as "religious" tends to perpetuate practices and beliefs which are problematic on equality and other grounds'. Further complexities are added by the fact that it is not only religious belief, but also the right not to believe, that is usually protected by discrimination law. Other forms of belief are included too, usually encapsulated in the formula 'religion or belief'. This raises the troublesome question on whether all kinds of belief should be equally protected.

11.4.3.2 Age

We now move on to address the GOR exceptions that are applicable in the context of age discrimination. An employer will be entitled to subject an individual or employee claimant to direct or indirect age discrimination in carefully controlled circumstances. For example, paragraphs 11–12 and 15 of Schedule 9 to the EA permit differences in national minimum wage rates and childcare provision. In addition, paragraph 13 of Schedule 9 to the EA enables an employer to provide enhanced redundancy payments on the basis of seniority. However, the most central exception applies in the context of benefits, facilities, or services offered by the employer based on length of service, e.g. pay increments, holiday entitlement, access to company cars, or financial advice. Here, paragraph 10 of Schedule 9 to the EA directs that the employer is not liable for direct or indirect discrimination where it puts a worker B at a disadvantage in comparison with another worker C in relation to the provision of such a benefit, facility, or service because B has a shorter period of service than C. However, where B's period of service exceeds five years, an employer must negotiate the additional criterion enjoining it to demonstrate

---

[249] For a discussion of the 'clash of equalities', see A. McColgan, *Discrimination, Equality and the Law* (Oxford, Hart Publishing, 2014) 150–74; A. McColgan, 'Class Wars? Religion and (In)Equality in the Workplace' (2009) 38 *Industrial Law Journal* 1; and R. Wintemute, 'Accommodating Religious Beliefs: Harm, Clothing or Symbols, and Refusals to Serve Others' (2014) 77 *Modern Law Review* 22.

that it 'reasonably believes that [providing benefits, facilities or services based on length of service] . . . fulfils a business need'.[250] The EHRC Code explains that a 'business need' could include 'rewarding higher levels of experience, or encouraging loyalty, or increasing or maintaining the motivation of long-serving staff'.[251] Further exploration of this expression is adumbrated as follows:

■ EHRC Code of Practice on Employment

14.24 This test of 'fulfilling a business need' is less onerous than the general test for objective justification for indirect discrimination . . . However, an employer would still need evidence to support a reasonable belief that the length of service rule did fulfil a business need. This could include information the employer might have gathered through monitoring, staff attitude surveys or focus groups. An employer would be expected to take into account the interests of their workers and not be motivated simply by financial self-interest.

In the case of *Rolls-Royce plc v Unite the Union*,[252] the employer had entered into two collective agreements with the recognized trade union. The collective agreements included a series of selection criteria for making redundancies and one of those criteria, designed to act as a 'tie-breaker', was length of service, i.e. the latter was the deciding factor where employee scores were the same in a redundancy selection exercise. Although the length of service criterion was not as crude as a 'last in, first out' matrix,[253] the employer brought proceedings in order to ascertain whether its inclusion amounted to unlawful age discrimination. The Court of Appeal held that the length of service criterion was lawful on the basis that it was a proportionate means of achieving a legitimate aim under the statutory predecessor of section 19(2)(d) of the EA and also under the statutory predecessor of what is now the length of service derogation in paragraph 10(2) of Schedule 9 to the EA. In the circumstances, the employer had established a clear business need for the length of service criterion in accordance with the requirements of paragraph 10(2) of Schedule 9 to the EA. Length of service was but one of a number of criteria in the overall context of the redundancy selection process, was by no means determinative, and had been agreed between the employer and the union. As such, viewed objectively, the length of service provision was justified for the purposes of achieving the legitimate commercial aims of (a) achieving a stable workforce in the context of a fair process of redundancy selection and (b) rewarding loyalty.

 For additional reading on positive discrimination and the genuine occupational requirements exception, visit the Online Resources for this book at www.oup.com/uk/cabrelli3e/

---

[250] Paragraph 10(2) of Schedule 9 to the EA.

[251] EHRC Code, available at https://www.equalityhumanrights.com/sites/default/files/employercode.pdf at para 14.23 (last visited 6 December 2017).

[252] [2010] 1 WLR 318. See also *MacCulloch v Imperial Chemical Industries plc* [2008] ICR 1334; *Loxley v BAE Systems (Munitions & Ordnance) Ltd* [2008] ICR 1348, on which, see C. Wynn-Evans, 'Age Discrimination and Redundancy' (2009) 38 *Industrial Law Journal* 113.

[253] See Chapter 18, section 18.3.2.2, for more commentary on the 'last in, first out' criterion.

11.5 LIABILITY AND ENFORCEMENT

Enforcement of the provisions in the EA is divided between individual employee claimants and the EHRC. Essentially, the EA continues to rely on an individual litigation-driven enforcement model.[254] As such, the EHRC is disentitled from raising class actions for the benefit of a group of claimants.[255]

In this section, we concentrate on some aspects of the machinery for the individual adjudication of employment equality disputes through the employment tribunal system: other works[256] and Chapter 2, section 2.3.3, should be consulted for an in-depth assessment of the responsibilities of the EHRC. These duties extend to undertaking investigations,[257] conducting inquiries,[258] issuing unlawful act notices,[259] seeking court injunctions or interdicts to prevent unlawful acts of discrimination,[260] and using prescribed, but limited, enforcement powers in direct and indirect discrimination cases.[261]

11.5.1 Burden of proof

We turn first to the party upon whom the onus of proving a discrimination claim lies. Employers will often take steps to conceal any evidence that their internal thought processes evinced an intention to deliberately discriminate against an employee on the ground of one of the nine protected characteristics. For that reason, inferences of discrimination will have to be drawn by the court or tribunal, since direct evidence 'will seldom be forthcoming'.[262] The odds are further stacked against employee claimants by the fact that many instances of discriminatory conduct involve a subtle build-up of events over a period of time. As noted in a report by DTI Employment Relations:

■ **Department of Trade and Industry,** *The Experience of Claimants in Race Discrimination Employment Tribunal Cases* (Employment Relations Research Series, No. 55, April 2006) 149–50

> Claimants felt that the requirements of proving within an adversarial legal system that discrimination had occurred placed them at a considerable disadvantage. They also felt that this type of discrimination, often being subtle and incremental, was particularly difficult for them to prove. Claimants' experiences of taking cases had led them to conclude that the 'system' inherently favoured [the employer], and some claimants believed that the employer would almost always win.[263]

---

[254] Having said that, an identifiable claimant is not necessary under EU law, i.e. the Framework Directive, on which, see *Asociatia ACCEPT v Consiliul National pentru Combaterea Discriminarii* [2013] ICR 938.

[255] See Hansard HC, vol. 501, col. 1135, 2 December 2009 (Lynne Featherstone) and Hansard HL, vol. 716, col. 980, 19 January 2010 (Baroness Royall of Blaisdon) for the (rejected) proposal that the EHRC or a recognized trade union be entitled to take such class or representative action.

[256] See B. Hepple, *Equality: The New Legal Framework*, 2nd edition (Oxford, Hart Publishing, 2014) 177–91; B. Hepple, 'Enforcing Equality Law: Two Steps Forward and Two Steps Backwards for Reflexive Regulation' (2011) 40 *Industrial Law Journal* 315.

[257] Section 20 of the Equality Act 2006.   [258] Section 16 of the Equality Act 2006.

[259] Section 21 of the Equality Act 2006.   [260] Section 24 of the Equality Act 2006.

[261] Section 24A of the Equality Act 2006.

[262] *Nagarajan v London Regional Transport* [2000] 1 AC 501, 511B–512B per Lord Nicholls. See also *R v Immigration Officer at Prague Airport and another, ex parte European Roma Rights Centre and others* [2004] UKHL 55, [2005] AC 1, 55F per Baroness Hale.

[263] Available at http://webarchive.nationalarchives.gov.uk/20121212135622/http://www.bis.gov.uk/files/file27818.pdf (last visited 6 December 2017).

Owing to the formidable obstacles placed in front of claimants, the law provides that the burden of proof is reversed. The current law propounds a two-stage test and is found in section 136 of the EA, which transposes Article 8 of the Race Directive,[264] Article 10 of the Framework Directive,[265] and Article 19 of the Recast Equality Directive[266] into domestic law:

Section 136 Burden of proof

(1) This section applies to any proceedings relating to a contravention of this Act.

(2) If there are facts from which the court could decide, in the absence of any other explanation, that a person (A) contravened the provision concerned, the court must hold that the contravention occurred.

(3) But subsection (2) does not apply if A shows that A did not contravene the provision . . .

(6) A reference to the court includes a reference to—

   (a) an employment tribunal; . . .

The first stage involves the court or tribunal adducing facts from which it could decide that the employer has committed a discriminatory act in the absence of an adequate explanation from the employer. In the context of a direct sex discrimination claim,[267] this will place the initial onus of proof on the employee and will involve the court enquiring whether there is a difference in sex between the claimant and the relevant comparator and also whether there is a difference in treatment.[268] At this stage, the court or tribunal must ignore any adequate explanation furnished by the employer. If a difference in sex and a difference in treatment are established at this first stage, this is indicative of the possibility of sex discrimination.[269] The burden will then shift to the employer at the second stage to show that the factual criterion or criteria which influenced it to act in the way that it did were in no way attributable to the claimant's sex, i.e. the 'reason why'. Whether a non-discriminatory reason is established by the employer will be evaluated by the court or tribunal on an objective basis.[270] As for an indirect sex discrimination claim, at the first stage, the claimant will be required to establish that the application of a PCP by the employer placed him/herself and persons of the same sex as him/herself at a particular disadvantage. The burden then moves to the employer at the second stage, who must satisfy the court that the application of the PCP was a proportionate means of achieving a legitimate aim.

More detailed guidance on the mechanics of the two-stage burden of proof was provided by the Court of Appeal in *Igen Ltd v Wong*.[271] This case concerned how employment tribunals ought to apply the pre-EA statutory provisions, but in the decision of the EAT in *Maksymiuk v Bar Roma Partnership*[272] it was accepted that the detailed elaboration of the two-stage test in *Igen* remained good law in the context of the EA:

---

[264] Directive 2000/43/EC (OJ 2000 L180/22).   [265] Directive 2000/78/EC (OJ 2000 L303/16).

[266] Directive 2006/54/EC (OJ 2006 L204/23).

[267] The same process is applicable in the case of the other protected characteristics.

[268] *Ayodele v Citylink Ltd* [2017] EWCA Civ 1913.

[269] *Madarassy v Nomura International plc* [2007] ICR 867, 878H per Mummery LJ.

[270] There is one exception: where the comparator is hypothetical, it has been held by the Court of Appeal in *Brown v Croydon London Borough Council* [2007] ICR 909 that it is not an error of law for the court or tribunal to proceed directly to stage 2 without having first addressed or exhausted stage 1.

[271] [2005] ICR 931. See N. Cunningham, 'Discrimination through the Looking-Glass: Judicial Guidelines on the Burden of Proof' (2006) 35 *Industrial Law Journal* 279.

[272] (UKEATS/0017/12/BI, 19 July 2012).

■ *Igen Ltd v Wong* [2005] ICR 931, 956E–957F

Peter Gibson LJ:

(1) Pursuant to [section 136 of the EA], it is for the claimant who complains of . . . discrimination to prove on the balance of probabilities facts from which the tribunal could conclude, in the absence of an adequate explanation, that the employer has committed an act of discrimination against the claimant which is unlawful by virtue of [the EA]. These are referred to below as 'such facts'.

(2) If the claimant does not prove such facts he or she will fail . . .

(5) It is important to note the word 'could' in section [136 of the EA]. At this stage the tribunal does not have to reach a definitive determination that such facts would lead it to the conclusion that there was an act of unlawful discrimination. At this stage a tribunal is looking at the primary facts before it to see what inferences of secondary fact could be drawn from them.

(6) In considering what inferences or conclusions can be drawn from the primary facts, the tribunal must assume that there is no adequate explanation for those facts.

(7) These inferences can include, in appropriate cases, any inferences that it is just and equitable to draw in accordance with section [138(3) and (4) of the EA] from an evasive or equivocal reply to a questionnaire or any other questions that fall within section [138 of the EA].[273]

(8) Likewise, the tribunal must decide whether any provision of any relevant code of practice is relevant and, if so, take it into account in determining such facts pursuant to section [136 of the EA]. This means that inferences may also be drawn from any failure to comply with any relevant code of practice.

(9) Where the claimant has proved facts from which conclusions could be drawn that the employer has treated the claimant less favourably on the ground of sex, then the burden of proof moves to the employer.

(10) It is then for the employer to prove that he did not commit, or as the case may be, is not to be treated as having committed, that act.

(11) To discharge that burden it is necessary for the employer to prove, on the balance of probabilities, that the treatment was in no sense whatsoever on the grounds of [any of the protected characteristics] . . .

(12) That requires a tribunal to assess not merely whether the employer has proved an explanation for the facts from which such inferences can be drawn, but further that it is adequate to discharge the burden of proof on the balance of probabilities that [one of the protected characteristics] was not a ground for the treatment in question.

(13) Since the facts necessary to prove an explanation would normally be in the possession of the [employer], a tribunal would normally expect cogent evidence to discharge that burden of proof. In particular, the tribunal will need to examine carefully explanations for failure to deal with the questionnaire procedure and/or code of practice.

It has been stressed that slavish adherence to each of these stages is not required. Therefore, no error of law is committed if the tribunal fails to go through each of the stages in

---

[273] It should be noted that the statutory right of an employee to compel the employer to respond to an equality questionnaire in terms of section 138 was repealed on 6 April 2014.

sequential order.[274] An illustration of the operation of the two-stage test in accordance with the guidance in *Igen* is set out in Hypothetical D.

Hypothetical D

Jennifer Marsh ('JM') is employed as an operations manager at the Bedford office of Danny's Demolishers Ltd ('DD'). She is responsible for managing ten staff, all of whom are male. One of the staff, George Hansen ('GH'), is routinely verbally abusive, aggressive, and hostile towards JM at the weekly management meetings they hold on Tuesday mornings. At one meeting, GH questioned JM's integrity and competence. Unsurprisingly, JM was extremely upset about this incident. She contacted her line manager David Wordsworth ('DW') and a meeting was arranged. At the meeting, JM informed DW that she was not prepared to continue working with GH and that she would be considering her position. DW was not particularly sympathetic and told JM that she needed to manage GH more effectively. JM then resigned and claimed sex discrimination and constructive dismissal. JM pointed to the circumstances of the operations manager William Black ('WB'), who had held the position at the Bedford office immediately prior to JM's appointment to the role. Similar incidents and difficulties with GH had been experienced by WB, and when WB had complained to DW about GH, DW had rearranged working duties so that WB was no longer responsible for managing GH and GH was assigned to another manager. When WB left DD and JM had been appointed, GH had been moved back to operations so that JM was now his responsible manager.

In such a case, the court or tribunal would ask whether it could adduce facts to the effect that there was a difference in sex between JM and WB and a difference in DD's treatment of JM and WB. In doing so, it must ignore any adequate explanation that DD might have had for its behaviour. If the court or tribunal is satisfied that this first stage of the two-stage test has been met, it then falls to DD to prove that the factors which influenced it to act in the way that it did in no way were attributable to JM's sex, i.e. that there was a non-discriminatory reason for her treatment, duly evaluated on an objective basis.[275]

11.5.2 Vicarious liability

Not only may an employer be held personally liable for discriminatory acts under the EA, but it may also incur liability:

(1) for the discriminatory conduct of its employees on a vicarious basis;

(2) where it knowingly assists another to breach the EA; or

(3) where it instructs, causes, or induces another to do anything in relation to a third party which amounts to a contravention of the EA.

---

[274] *Laing v Manchester City Council* [2006] ICR 159. Furthermore, in *Igen* and *Madarassy v Nomura International plc* [2007] EWCA Civ 33, [2007] ICR 867, the courts and tribunals were reminded that there is no substitute for the exact statutory language and that this guidance should in no way supplant the wording of section 136 of the EA. The formulation in *Igen* was approved by the Supreme Court in *Hewage v Grampian Health Board* [2012] UKSC 37, [2012] ICR 1054.

[275] Where an individual has a significant degree of influence over an employer, the burden of proof will be on the employer to rebut the presumption of discrimination where the former makes a discriminatory statement, e.g. by making a public announcement putting clear water between itself and the individual's offending comments or establishing that it had an equal opportunities recruitment policy: *Asociatia ACCEPT v Consiliul National pentru Combaterea Discriminarii* [2013] ICR 938.

Moreover, the legislation provides that an employee may be entitled to bring a free-standing claim against another employee without making a claim against the mutual employer in certain circumstances.[276] The relevant provisions are found in sections 109, 110, 111, and 112 of the EA, but we focus here in particular on section 109 which addresses vicarious liability:

Section 109 Liability of employers and principals

(1) Anything done by a person (A) in the course of A's employment must be treated as also done by the employer . . .

(3) It does not matter whether that thing is done with the employer's or principal's knowledge or approval.

(4) In proceedings against A's employer (B) in respect of anything alleged to have been done by A in the course of A's employment it is a defence for B to show that B took all reasonable steps to prevent A—

    (a) from doing that thing, or

    (b) from doing anything of that description.

The touchstone of vicarious liability in the context of direct discrimination, indirect discrimination, and harassment is whether the employee[277] committed the discriminatory act in the course of his/her employment. On its face, this would appear to exculpate the employer if the employee's conduct were so extravagant or extreme that there would be no logical foundation to classify it as having occurred during the employee's employment. However, the courts and tribunals have adopted a broad interpretation of the expression 'course of employment'. The leading authority is *Jones v Tower Boot Co. Ltd.*[278] Here, a 16-year-old employee of mixed ethnic parentage working in a shoe factory was subjected to regular physical and verbal racial abuse of an extreme nature from his co-workers.[279] Relying on the common law tests for vicarious liability,[280] the employer argued that it had a defence on the basis that the actions of the co-workers were unauthorized modes of carrying out the work which they had been authorized by the employer to do. However, the Court of Appeal held that the common law test for the imposition of vicarious liability in the law of tort had no application to statutory employment equality laws. Instead, the Court of Appeal ruled that whether the discriminatory conduct took place in the course of the employee's employment is a question of fact for the tribunals and courts to determine:

---

[276] See section 110 of the EA and the decision in *Barlow v Stone* [2012] IRLR 898.

[277] Of course, by virtue of the relational scope of the legislation prescribed in section 83(2) of the EA, individuals providing services to the employer on the basis of a contract personally to do work are also included.   [278] [1997] ICR 254.

[279] The most extreme examples of such abuse consisted of burning his arm with a hot screwdriver, whipping him on the legs with a piece of welt, throwing metal bolts at his head, attempting to put his arm in a lasting machine, and calling him racially abusive names.

[280] The common law test has changed slightly since 1998, as expounded in the classic decision of the House of Lords in *Lister v Hesley Hall Ltd* [2002] 1 AC 215. Moreover, since the decision in *Jones*, a claim that an employer is vicariously liable for harassment perpetrated by one of its employees is now competent under the Protection from Harassment Act 1997 by virtue of the decision of the House of Lords in *Majrowski v Guy's and St Thomas' NHS Trust* [2006] UKHL 34, [2007] 1 AC 224, on which, see Chapter 10, section 10.2.5.

■ *Jones v Tower Boot Co. Ltd* [1997] ICR 254, 263H–265D

> *Waite LJ:*
>
> [Counsel for the employer submits that] the more heinous the act of discrimination, the less likely it will be that the employer would be liable . . . I would reject that submission entirely. It cuts across the whole legislative scheme and underlying policy of [section 109 of the EA] which is to deter racial and sexual harassment in the workplace through a widening of the net of responsibility beyond the guilty employees themselves, by making all employers additionally liable for such harassment, and then supplying them with the reasonable steps defence under section [109(4) of the EA] which will exonerate the conscientious employer who has used his best endeavours to prevent such harassment, and will encourage all employers who have not yet undertaken such endeavours to take the steps necessary to make the same defence available in their own workplace . . . It would be particularly wrong to allow racial harassment on the scale that was suffered by the employee in this case at the hands of his workmates—treatment that was wounding both emotionally and physically—to slip through the net of employer responsibility by applying to it a common law principle evolved in another area of the law to deal with vicarious responsibility for wrongdoing of a wholly different kind. To do so would seriously undermine the statutory scheme of the [EA] and flout the purposes which [it was] passed to achieve. The tribunals are free, and are indeed bound, to interpret the ordinary, and readily understandable, words 'in the course of his employment' in the sense in which every layman would understand them . . . The application of the phrase will be a question of fact for each industrial tribunal to resolve, in the light of the circumstances presented to it, with a mind unclouded by any parallels sought to be drawn from the law of vicarious liability in tort.

As for the employer's 'reasonable steps' defence in section 109(4), it is not open to the employer who has failed to take reasonable steps to argue that it is not liable because if it had taken such steps, that would have not made any difference or prevented the alleged conduct from occurring.[281] The EHRC Code suggests that the existence of any evidence that an employer has not adopted, adhered to, or provided training to its employees on an equality and diversity policy *prior to the alleged discriminatory conduct or harassment*[282] is more likely than not to cause a tribunal or court to conclude that its reasonable steps defence must fail.[283] Moreover, there is a strong argument that the employer would also be held personally liable in such circumstances for failing to promote a conducive working environment free from harassment and discriminatory conduct on the basis of one of the protected characteristics. Alongside implementing an equality policy, ensuring workers are aware of such a policy, and providing equal opportunities training, the EHRC Code directs that reasonable steps might include reviewing its equality policy as appropriate and dealing effectively with employee complaints.[284] It goes on to stipulate that, in evaluating whether a step is reasonable, 'an employer should consider its likely effect and whether an alternative step could be more effective[, but] a step does not have to be effective to be reasonable'.[285] Ultimately, in assessing the employer's reasonable steps defence, much will come down to the rigour of the employer's equality policy, the extent of the awareness training of its staff in relation to its equality policy, the nature of the supervisory process, the measures it has inculcated to monitor compliance, and the seriousness with which it treats allegations of discrimination committed by its employees.

---

[281] *Canniffe v East Riding of Yorkshire Council* [2000] IRLR 555.

[282] See *Canniffe v East Riding of Yorkshire Council* [2000] IRLR 555; *Mahood v Irish Centre Housing Ltd* [2011] Eq LR 586.

[283] EHRC Code, available at https://www.equalityhumanrights.com/sites/default/files/employercode.pdf at para 10.52 (last visited 6 December 2017).   [284] *ibid.*, para 10.52.

[285] *ibid.*, para 10.51. See also *Croft v Royal Mail Group plc* [2003] ICR 1425, 1446B–D per Pill LJ.

11.5.3 **Remedies**

Once an individual employee's discrimination claim has succeeded,[286] attention will turn to the appropriate remedies. Only the employment tribunal ('ET') has jurisdiction to determine complaints of discrimination in respect of employment.[287] The remedies which are available where a case of discrimination under the EA has been made out are governed by section 124 of the EA, namely a declaration of rights, and compensation:[288]

Section 124 Remedies: general . . .

(2) The [ET] may—

(a) make a declaration as to the rights of the complainant and the respondent in relation to the matters to which the proceedings relate;

(b) order the respondent to pay compensation to the complainant;

(c) make an appropriate recommendation.[289]

(3) An appropriate recommendation is a recommendation that within a specified period the respondent takes specified steps for the purpose of obviating or reducing the adverse effect on the complainant of any matter to which the proceedings relate . . .

(7) If a respondent fails, without reasonable excuse, to comply with an appropriate recommendation, the tribunal may—

(a) if an order was made under subsection (2)(b), increase the amount of compensation to be paid;

(b) if no such order was made, make one.

An employee claimant has a period of three months starting with the date of the act to which the complaint relates to present a complaint of discrimination to an ET.[290] The ET may extend that three-month period if it thinks it just and equitable to do so, and this power to entertain claims out of time has been applied freely by the courts and tribunals.

Compensation is the principal remedy in the case of successful discrimination claims. Compensation is an individual-oriented, rather than group-based, remedy, in that it furnishes an award directly to the claimant rather than the protected group of which the claimant forms part. Unlike the unfair dismissal jurisdiction,[291] there is no upper limit on the amount of compensation which may be awarded,[292] although whether this feature of UK discrimination law survives for long after Brexit is a good question. Since discrimination is a type of statutory

---

[286] Representative and class actions are not permitted, so a separate complaint must be presented by every affected employee where the employer adopts a practice which has a detrimental and discriminatory effect on more than one member of the workforce.   [287] Section 120 of the EA.

[288] The power of the tribunal to make 'wider recommendations' under section 124(3)(b) was removed with effect from 1 October 2015.

[289] The ET has no power to make an order for re-engagement or reinstatement, i.e. to restore the employee to his/her job, or a job with his/her employer, if he/she had been dismissed. However, such orders may be considered where the claimant has been the victim of an unfair discriminatory dismissal, i.e. an order under sections 114 and 115 of the ERA.   [290] Section 123(1) of the EA.

[291] Where compensation falls to be awarded both under the unfair dismissal jurisdiction in Part X of the ERA and the EA, section 126 of the ERA provides that an ET must not award compensation under either of those Acts in respect of any loss or other matter which is or has been taken into account under the other by the tribunal (or another ET) in awarding compensation on the same or another complaint in respect of that act of discrimination.

[292] See *Marshall v Southampton and South West Area Health Authority (No. 2)* [1993] ECR I-4367, [1994] QB 126. The Beecroft Report, available at http://www.bis.gov.uk/assets/biscore/employment-matters/docs/r/12–825-report-on-employment-law-beecroft.pdf at page 8 (last visited 6 December 2017), recommended a cap on the level of compensation, but this was rejected on the ground that it would likely infringe EU law which requires compensation payments in respect of discrimination claims to be 'effective, proportionate and dissuasive', on which, see Article 25 of the Recast Equality Directive, Article 15 of the Race Directive, and Article 17 of the Framework Directive. Of course, after Brexit, there will no longer be any impediment to removing the compensation cap.

tort, the principle to be applied in calculating compensation is identical to that applied in the case of a civil tort claim: rather than adopt the contractual measure of damages, the employee must be placed in the position in which he/she would have been had he/she not been the victim of the discriminatory conduct.[293] The principal elements of the compensation package will consist of the employee's past and future loss of earnings and pension loss. An award may also be made for injury to feelings to compensate for the effect of the discrimination on the employee. Guidance on how tribunals and courts should approach the calculation of injury to feelings awards was set out in *Vento v Chief Constable of West Yorkshire Police*,[294] *Da'Bell v NSPCC*,[295] and *Perera de Souza v Vinci Construction (UK) Ltd*.[296] In those cases, ETs were directed to apply three distinct bands of compensation. The lowest band is between £800 and £8,400 for less serious cases, e.g. where the conduct is an isolated incident, such as a racist remark.[297] The middle band of between £8,400 and £25,200 is reserved for serious cases, and the highest band of between £25,200 and £42,000, for a campaign of discriminatory conduct. Only in exceptional circumstances will an award above £42,000 be competent and awards below £800 are not to be made at all. Recent statistics reveal that the average awards for injury to feelings in 2013 and 2014 were £5,564 and £8,162 respectively, while the median award for the same years was £5,000 and £6,600.[298] The EAT has also decided that an award of aggravated or exemplary damages will be competent where the employer has been shown to be guilty of oppressive, arbitrary, or unconstitutional action and if the award otherwise payable would not suffice by way of punishment and deterrence.[299] Such exemplary damages may be additional to an injury to feelings award. Although some extremely high awards of compensation have been the focus of press reports,[300] the median level of awards depicts an altogether different picture (for example, see Table 11.2).

In terms of section 124 of the EA, ETs also have the power to make recommendations alongside awards of compensation. Such recommendations may enjoin an unsuccessful employer to take measures within a specified period of time to obviate or reduce the adverse effect of its practices vis-à-vis the employee claimant.

Reflection points

1. What are the deficiencies of relying on the individual enforcement of anti-discrimination laws?

2. Are you convinced that it is justifiable in terms of policy for employers to be held vicariously liable for the discriminatory actions of their employees?

3. In your opinion, are the remedies available in the context of successful discrimination claims adequate? Give reasons for your answer.

4. Should it be that one protected characteristic can trump another, for example, considering the conflict between religion and sexual orientation?

For additional reading on liability and enforcement, visit the Online Resources for this book at www.oup.com/uk/cabrelli3e/

---

[293] *Ministry of Defence v Cannock* [1994] ICR 918; *Ministry of Defence v Wheeler* [1998] 1WLR 637.
[294] [2003] IRLR 101.   [295] [2010] IRLR 19.
[296] [2017] IRLR 844. See also the joint Presidential Guidance of the Employment Tribunals, available at https://www.judiciary.gov.uk/wp-content/uploads/2015/03/vento-bands-presidential-guidance-20170905.pdf (last visited 6 December 2017).
[297] *Ministry of Defence v Kemeh* [2014] ICR 625.
[298] 'Compensation Awards 2014: Part 1' (2015) 259 *Equal Opportunities Review* 9, 11: Table 2. The latest updated statistics are unavailable.
[299] *Hackney London Borough Council v Sivanandan* [2011] ICR 1374.
[300] See 'Doctor is Awarded £4.5m Compensation for Workplace Discrimination Claims' (*The Guardian*, 16 December 2011).

Table 11.2 *Compensation Awarded by Tribunals—Mean and Median Amounts, 2007/8 to 2016/17*

	2007/08	2008/09	2009/10	2010/11	2011/12	2012/13	2013/14	2014/15	2015/16	2016/17
Race Discrimination jurisdictions										
Number of claims awarded compensation	65	73	68	72	58	51	56	38	27	22
Median award	£8,120	£5,568	£5,392	£6,277	£5,256	£4,831	£5,513	£8,025	£13,760	£13,141
Average (mean) award	£14,566	£33,026	£18,584	£12,108	£102,259	£8,945	£11,203	£17,040	£14,185	£36,853
Sex Discrimination jurisdictions										
Number of claims awarded compensation	151	176	151	173	166	113	122	77	36	34
Median award	£5,200	£7,000	£6,275	£6,078	£6,746	£5,900	£8,039	£13,500	£13,500	£8,381
Average (mean) award	£11,263	£11,061	£19,499	£13,911	£9,940	£10,552	£14,336	£23,478	£85,622	£19,152
Disability Discrimination jurisdictions										
Number of claims awarded compensation	92	82	73	72	78	82	130	85	72	77
Median award	£8,363	£7,203	£8,553	£6,142	£8,928	£7,536	£7,518	£8,646	£11,309	£10,235
Average (mean) award	£19,523	£26,023	£52,087	£14,137	£22,183	£16,320	£14,502	£17,319	£21,729	£31,988
Religious Discrimination jurisdictions										
Number of claims awarded compensation	2	5	7	10	10	10	5	1	4	7
Median award	£.*	£4,291	£5,000	£6,892	£4,267	£4,759	£3,191	£1,080	£16,174	£12,045
Average (mean) award	£3,203	£33,937	£4,886	£8,515	£16,725	£6,137	£8,131	£1,080	£19,647	£20,344
Sexual Orientation Discrimination jurisdictions										
Number of claims awarded compensation	8	5	15	12	10	6	10	9	1	4
Median award	£2,103	£12,462	£5,000	£5,500	£13,505	£6,319	£6,824	£6,000	£20,192	£6,314
Average (mean) award	£7,579	£21,709	£20,384	£11,671	£14,623	£10,757	£8,701	£17,515	£20,192	£6,026
Age Discrimination jurisdictions										
Number of claims awarded compensation	22	23	28	26	23	24	25	9	4	14
Median award	£1,526	£3,816	£5,868	£12,697	£6,065	£4,499	£6,000	£7,500	£8,417	£15,198
Average (mean) award	£3,334	£8,430	£10,931	£30,289	£19,327	£8,079	£18,801	£11,211	£9,025	£35,663

Source: ET database.

Notes

'Compensation awarded' is that of which the tribunal is aware. Awards validated by the data owners, Performance and Reporting team in HMCTS.

* Not available.

CHAPTER TWELVE

DISABILITY DISCRIMINATION

12.1 CONTEXTUAL ANALYSIS OF DISABILITY DISCRIMINATION LAW

Laws against disability discrimination form an integral component of the employment equality regime laid down in the Equality Act 2010 ('EA'). In this chapter, we focus on disability discrimination as a separate protected characteristic. This is justified on the basis that there is a tendency to treat the concepts deployed in the EA which tackle disability discrimination as a specialized and sui generis set of norms.[1] They are often thought of as an adjunct to mainstream employment equality law since they do not fit neatly within the standard pattern established under the other strands such as sex, race, age, etc.[2] Bearing that point in mind, we begin our examination of disability discrimination by focusing on the historical context and the possible conceptual approaches to the protection of disabled workers. We then move on to address the definition of 'disability' in section 6 of the EA. Thereafter, the employer's duty to make reasonable adjustments and the 'discrimination arising from disability' concepts will be analysed. Finally, some comments and observations will be offered on the current state of disability discrimination law generally, taking into account the recent introduction of the EA and European developments.

---

[1] See D. Wasserman, 'Is Disability Discrimination Different?' in D. Hellman and S. Moreau (eds), *Philosophical Foundations of Discrimination Law* (Oxford, OUP, 2013) 269.

[2] See the judicial sentiments expressed by Mummery LJ in *Clark v Novacold Ltd* [1999] ICR 951, 959A–B and *Stockton on Tees Borough Council v Aylott* [2010] ICR 1278, 1281B.

12.1.1 Contextual and historical examination of disability discrimination laws

Statistical analyses produced by the Office of National Statistics relating to the third quarter of 2016 reveal that the working age disabled account for approximately 7.2 million of the UK population, of whom 3.47 million are adults of working age.[3] As for the proportion of disabled persons in the labour market, this is characterized by exclusion and segregation with a mere 48.3 per cent of disabled persons in employment, which equates to a disability employment gap of 32.2 per cent,[4] i.e. approximately 80.5 per cent of non-disabled persons were in employment during the same period. Meanwhile, of those disabled persons incorporated within the labour market in 2014, one-third were employed full-time, which can be contrasted with the figure of three-fifths in the case of non-disabled persons.[5]

Disabled persons have encountered structural and systematic barriers to admission to the labour market for a considerable period of time. The historic social attitude towards the treatment of disabled persons was to extend welfare and social protection via the auspices of the State. Thus, disabled persons were deemed deserving of State generosity via the welfare and benefits system, combined with individual charitable attention. Such an approach has been labelled 'custodialism' by commentators.[6] Custodialism was inherently paternalistic and had the potential to be oppressive, since it perceived disabled people as deserving of pity and sympathy. The tacit philosophy underpinning this approach was that the inbuilt incapacities of the disabled rendered them inherently incapable of participating in the labour market. In response, disabled persons began to insist on rights rather than charity in the 1960s in an effort to facilitate their full participation in the workplace and wider society. A disability rights movement emerged which employed 'rights' arguments as a means of advancing the claims of disabled persons. Various justifications for change were, and continue to be, put forward. The first rationale is predicated on the philosophical notion of social justice. The precepts of social justice demand that law ought to be harnessed to dismantle employment barriers for disabled persons so that broader opportunities are extended to them. Differing theoretical conceptions of the social justice justification can be found,[7] but at the heart of this approach is an insistence on the intrinsic worth of laws that protect disabled persons from discrimination and remove obstacles to their labour market participation. A separate justification for protecting the disabled in the workplace is grounded in economics. The economic rationale embraces the idea that there is a large section of society that is excluded from employment and that this is an untapped, but rich, resource to which the labour market is being denied access. The argument goes that the skills base of the economy would be broadened by the involvement of disabled persons in employment, which would translate into the recovery of a greater amount of taxation by the State. However, some of the deficiencies of this economic justification are laid bare in the following extract from Alldridge:

[3] See the House of Commons Library Briefing Paper No 7540, 16 December 2016, available at http://researchbriefings.files.parliament.uk/documents/CBP-7540/CBP-7540.pdf at pages 3 and 4 (last visited 6 December 2017).

[4] See *ibid*., pages 3 and 4.

[5] See ODI, Disability Equality Indicators, available at http://odi.dwp.gov.uk/disability-statistics-and-research/disability-equality-indicators.php at B1 (last visited 6 December 2017).

[6] See J. tenBroek and F. W. Matson, 'The Disabled and the Law of Welfare' (1966) 54 *California Law Review* 809, 815–16; M. C. Weber, 'Disability and the Law of Welfare: A Post-Integrationist Examination' (2000) *University of Illinois Law Review* 889, 899–901.

[7] See D. Mabbett, 'Some Are More Equal than Others: Definitions of Disability in Social Policy and Discrimination Law in Europe' (2005) 34 *Journal of Social Policy* 215, 218–21.

■ P. Alldridge, 'Locating Disability Law' (2006) 59 *Current Legal Problems* 289, 311

Of the three justifications for government involvement . . . in the area of the treatment of disabled people the two economic reasons given for trying to improve the lot of disabled people are: net benefits to the economy, widening the skills base and an increase in productivity; and increased tax revenues and lower spending on incapacity benefits. As to the first, it is clear that there will be benefits to the economy from the widening of the skills base and an increase in productivity, but whether or not they are net benefits depends upon how much it costs to bring about that widening. There is no reliable information upon which to make the decision. It is also evident that for every disabled person in employment who would otherwise be receiving benefit, there will be increased tax revenues and reduced expenditure on incapacity benefits, if this could be accomplished at no cost. However, whether it is a net benefit will turn on how much it would cost, and what it will cost depends upon the other effects of securing a job for the disabled person. So the economic arguments are weak compared to the social justice argument.

Indeed, rather than being necessarily economically beneficial, there are particularly fraught economic trade-offs to be made in conferring anti-discrimination protections in favour of disabled persons:

■ *Clark v Novacold Ltd* [1999] ICR 951, 954F–G

Mummery LJ:

The whole subject [of disability discrimination law] presents unique challenges to legislators and to tribunals and courts, as well as to those responsible for the day-to-day operation of the [EA] in the workplace. Anyone who thinks that there is an easy way of achieving a sensible, workable and fair balance between the different interests of disabled persons, of employers and of able-bodied workers, in harmony with the wider public interests in an economically efficient workforce, in access to employment, in equal treatment of workers and in standards of fairness at work, has probably not given much serious thought to the problem.

If we reflect on how the 'rights' model may be advanced in favour of disabled persons, there is force in the contention that this may be done in three particular ways.[8]

(1) The first entails continuity with the body of equality law whereby the notion of equal treatment and the formal conception of equality are adopted. According to this formulation, disabled persons are afforded the right not to be treated less favourably than able-bodied persons in a like-for-like situation. The flaw in this approach, however, is that it fails to reflect the reality that disabled people do not necessarily require the same treatment as the able-bodied norm; instead, the character of their situation may demand different treatment, which may indeed entail an element of preference. Thus, the nature of disability as a protected characteristic is such that its discreteness and difference ought to be reflected in the promotion of the substantive, rather than the formal, model of equality. This is essentially a debate about whether the concept of equality should regulate for 'sameness' or 'difference', and chimes with the second means of promoting the rights of the disabled, namely the 'minority group' approach,

---

[8] This tripartite division draws on the approach of Fredman in S. Fredman, *Discrimination Law*, 2nd edition (Oxford, OUP, 2011) 95–7.

which emphasizes the 'difference', 'discreteness', or 'insularity' associated with disability.[9]

(2) The underlying idea behind the 'minority group' approach is that disabled employees are a kind of homogenous minority group with specific issues which diverge from the mainstream able-bodied constituency in the labour market—in particular, that disabled persons have been subjected to detrimental impacts, restrictions, and limitations based on stereotypical assumptions about their capabilities because of the manner in which the labour market and occupations are generally organized. Indeed, the EA exhibits an element of political recognition that disabled persons and employees are not seeking equal treatment from a comparator situated on the 'opposite side of the same coin', but instead *different treatment*. The demerits of this argument, however, are set out by Fredman in the following extract:

■ S. Fredman, *Discrimination Law*, 2nd edition (Oxford, OUP, 2011) 131–2

The advantage of this analysis is to emphasize the political and social aspect of disability. However, it also has some problematic implications. As a start, it depends on identifying people as 'disabled', which has proved notoriously difficult, both in the field of discrimination law and in that of social security. This, argue opponents of minority group analysis, is not just a technical legal difficulty. It reflects the social reality that disabled people do not form a discrete and insular group at all. Moreover, it is argued, a 'minority group' analysis sets people with disabilities apart as different and distinct. Disability is characterized as fixed and dichotomous: either one has a disability or one does not.

The principal objection here is that the disabled cannot be meaningfully classified as a distinct group with a shared social history and sense of shared solidarity.

(3) These criticisms have given rise to a third model for the advancement of rights for the disabled. This is often referred to as the 'universal' approach whereby the protection of disabled employees is decoupled from anti-discrimination laws.[10] Rather than focusing on disabled persons as an homogeneous group which deserves to be the target of protective laws, disability is conceived of as something that everyone has that can be plotted across a spectrum. Thus, the 'universalist' philosophy involves an acknowledgement of the diverse capacities of the disabled. Of further significance is the fact that rights are conferred on all, rather than disabled persons alone, pursuant to the 'universalist' model. The upshot is that the normality of disability is underscored and the disabled are no longer thought of as belonging to the 'other'. This 'universalist' model 'reconfigures the normal rather than attempting to reconfigure the disabled person',[11] and offers the potential to effect a transformation of existing social practices and structures in the workplace to accommodate the needs of the disabled.[12]

---

[9] Indeed, as we will see, the ideology of 'difference' permeates certain legal concepts which feature in those parts of the EA that proscribe disability discrimination.

[10] E. Albin, 'Universalising the Right to Work of Persons with Disabilities: An Equality and Dignity Based Approach' in V. Mantouvalou (ed.), *The Right to Work: Legal and Philosophical Perspectives* (Oxford, Hart Publishing, 2015) 61.

[11] P. Alldridge, 'Locating Disability Law' (2006) 59 *Current Legal Problems* 289, 305.

[12] See I. K. Zola, 'Towards the Necessary Universalising of a Disability Policy' (1989) 67 (Supp 2, Pt 2) *Millbank Quarterly* 401; J. E. Birkenbach, S. Chatterji, E. M. Badley, and T. B. Ustun, 'Models of Disablement, Universalism and the International Classification of Impairments, Disabilities and Handicaps' (1999) 48 *Journal of Social Science and Medicine* 1172; and M. A. Stein, 'Same Struggle, Different Difference: ADA Accommodations as Antidiscrimination' (2004) 153 *University of Pennsylvania Law Review* 579.

Current UK domestic policy is to adopt a mixture of the 'minority group' and 'universal' approaches, i.e. to treat the disabled as a special group deserving of protection whilst recognizing that certain attributes of the workplace require modification to cater for the requirements of all, rather than the disabled alone. This has been coupled with an emphasis on another key theme lying at the centre of the existing disability discrimination regime prescribed in the EA. This theme operates at a cross-cutting level to the debate on the three ways of advancing disability rights we examined earlier and is the idea that the EA applies the 'medical' model of disability. The 'medical' model presumes that a person's disability is not attributable to external environmental influences, but to the individual's own impairment which functions to marginalize his/her capacity to engage in normal day-to-day activities:

■ P. Bartlett, 'The United Nations Convention on the Rights of Persons with Disabilities and Mental Health Law' (2012) 75 *Modern Law Review* 752, 758

> Under the medical model, the disability is viewed as a medical condition that requires fixing. As such, it is viewed as contained in the body of the person with disability. The person with disability is in turn perceived as a passive recipient of medical care, leading to the marginalisation and objectification of that person.

It is fundamental to the 'medical' model that a definition of disability is drawn. This gives rise to one of the key drawbacks of the model, i.e. that an individual must marshal sufficient clinical evidence to satisfy a tribunal or court that he/she suffers from an impairment affecting his/her ability to undertake normal day-to-day activities as a matter of fact, *albeit one which is not so serious as to render them unemployable, i.e. such that it does not impede his/her ability to engage in professional life.*[13] Alternative justifications for challenging the 'medical' model are set out in the following Wells extract:

■ K. Wells, 'The Impact of the Framework Employment Directive on UK Disability Discrimination Law' (2003) 32 *Industrial Law Journal* 253, 258

> . . . the tendency of tribunals and courts to focus upon medical questions relating to the nature of diagnosis of the condition restricts the number of individuals who may claim protection under the [EA]. The narrow and formal interpretation often given to the [EA] excludes individuals who may be very susceptible to disability discrimination, because they fail to establish the nature of their impairment or its severity. The complexity of the procedure due to its medical, technical nature may also deter applicants from pursuing their claims . . . the medical approach has wider negative implications for disability rights in the workplace. Placing the focus on substantial medical impairment and requiring extensive evidence of the particular nature of the condition may serve to perpetuate the labelling and stigma faced by disabled people trying to access and participate in the labour market. An employer may believe that an individual is less capable of working because he or she is perceived as differing in some way from physical or mental norms and thus the employer may discriminate against that individual. If that individual is to benefit from the [EA], he or she must first spell out the nature of the condition, and then prove that it results in a level of impaired functioning. The emphasis is on what is wrong with the individual, and what the individual

---

[13] As such, there is no equivalence between the effect of an individual's impairment on his/her ability to (1) engage in professional life and (2) carry out normal day-to-day activities, on which, see the decision of the Court of Justice of the European Union ('CJEU' or 'ECJ') in *HK Danmark, acting on behalf of Ring v Dansk almennyttigt Boligselskab* [2013] ICR 851.

consequently cannot do. Making claimants prove these factors is in itself unpalatable. Further, such an approach is unlikely to encourage equal consideration of disabled people and individuals who have no physical or mental impairments: it reinforces the line between 'normal' and 'disabled'.

Lawson has also remarked on the serious impact of the public examination of a person's disabilities which are involved in disability discrimination cases grounded in the 'medical' model:

■ A. Lawson, 'Disability and Employment in the Equality Act 2010: Opportunities Seized, Lost and Generated' (2011) 40 *Industrial Law Journal* 359, 361–2

[This process has] proved so gruelling and personally invasive that it has been likened to the cross-examination of rape victims. Unsurprisingly perhaps, evidence suggests that defendants often deliberately choose to challenge the disabled status of a claimant as a strategy for intimidating and pressurising them into settling or withdrawing the case. An associated difficulty is that the disability definition requirement risks distracting judicial and other attention from the behaviour of the alleged discriminator and focusing it instead on the functional limitations of the victim. The gravity of this risk is demonstrated by the estimate that almost a fifth of all [disability discrimination] tribunal cases fail because of the disability definition.

An alternative conceptual approach towards the design of disability discrimination laws centres on the acknowledgement that social constructions of disability function to disadvantage disabled people and therefore require a degree of reconfiguration. This is known as the 'social' model. This model espouses the idea that the nature, meaning, methods, patterns, and organization of work are social creations and the product of deep-seated historical attitudes to the efficiency of disabled waged labour. For the past 200–300 years, society has been structured in accordance with values that promote commercial activity, and which strive to galvanize the workplace in ways which increase productivity and overall profit. In line with this philosophy, disabled persons have been systematically excluded from labour markets, and may be less happy in their jobs,[14] owing to the perception that the effects of their impairments lead to lower economic output, i.e. that they are inefficient. The 'social' model, however, perceives the limitations experienced by the disabled as not attributable to their physical or mental ailments at all but to the social and economic conditions embedded in cultural and institutional norms. The absence of disabled persons from the labour market has perpetuated the problem by virtue of the fact that the working environment has been consistently aligned along able-bodied needs. At the heart of the 'social' model is the demand that it is society that must adapt to the needs of the disabled:

■ C. Barnes, 'A Working Social Model? Disability, Work and Disability Politics in the 21st Century' (2000) 20 *Critical Social Policy* 441, 441–5

In contrast to the earlier more orthodox views the social model centres on environmental and cultural factors as the primary cause of disabled people's marginalization. Of particular concern for disabled people and their organizations has been the systematic exclusion of people with accredited impairments from the world of work . . .

---

[14] See F. Perales and W. Tomaszewski, 'Happier with the Same: Job Satisfaction of Disadvantaged Workers' (2016) 54 *British Journal of Industrial Relations* 685.

[The fundamental notion is that] the way society is organized [is] to the detriment of people with perceived impairments and their families . . .

From a social model or materialist perspective then, perceptions of impairment and disability are inextricably linked to the 'mode of production' or the social organization of work. Consequently, there are several important points to be made about a social model analysis of work. One, it does not automatically mean that individually based interventions, whether they be medically, rehabilitative, educational or employment based, are of no value or always counter-productive. Two, it signifies a concerted attempt to shift attention away from the real or imagined functional limitations of individuals with perceived impairments and on to the difficulties caused by disabling environments both physical and social. Three, it rejects the notion that unemployment and underemployment among disabled workers can be understood in isolation from other factors such as education, transport, the built environment, access, ideology and culture. Finally, it recognizes that within the present context, policy developments in the employment field can have only a limited impact on the employment problems of disabled people and that, as a consequence, meaningful change is only likely through a radical reformulation of the meaning of and the organization of work.[15]

Many disability rights commentators prefer the 'social' model over the 'medical' model on the ground that it eschews (1) the need for a definition of disability and (2) the insensitive and public scrutiny associated with the latter. In its conception, it is a wholly more palatable approach to the employment protection of disabled persons. Indeed, there are indications that the approach in the EA has moved closer towards the 'social' model since it enables claimants to obtain relief where the employer has treated them less favourably because it has the mistaken belief that the claimant is disabled, i.e. discrimination by perception. Moreover, where a claimant has suffered discrimination because he/she is associated with a disabled person, e.g. he/she is the parent, son, daughter, carer, or friend of a disabled person, he/she will have a right to a remedy, which is referred to as discrimination by association. In both cases, the claimant will not be required to establish that he/she falls within the definition of disability in section 6 of the EA. Moreover, the UK domestic legislation in the EA, and EU law in the Framework Directive,[16] must be interpreted in line with the UN Convention on the Rights of Persons with Disabilities ('CRPD').[17] Since the latter adopts the 'social' model, there is a strong argument that the EA ought to be construed in conformance with the CRPD.[18]

However, one of the principal challenges to the 'social' model is grounded in pragmatism and historical experience. Recent research has revealed a deep-seated propensity on the part of the judiciary to cling to a medicalized conception of disability:

[15] See also M. Oliver and C. Barnes (eds), *Disabled People and Social Policy: From Exclusion to Inclusion* (London, Longman, 1998).

[16] See *HK Danmark, acting on behalf of Ring v Dansk almennyttigt Boligselskab* [2013] ICR 851, 874F–876B.

[17] See section 2(1) of the European Communities Act 1972; European Communities (Definition of Treaties) (United Nations Convention on the Rights of Persons with Disabilities) Order 2009, SI 2009/1181.

[18] See S. F. Butlin, 'The UN Convention on the Rights of Persons with Disabilities: Does the Equality Act 2010 Measure up to UK International Commitments?' (2011) 40 *Industrial Law Journal* 428; P. Bartlett, 'The United Nations Convention on the Rights of Persons with Disabilities and Mental Health Law' (2012) 75 *Modern Law Review* 752. In fact, since the decision of the CJEU in *HK Danmark, acting on behalf of Ring v Dansk almennyttigt Boligselskab* [2013] ICR 851, there is some evidence that the EAT has started to veer towards the application of the social model: see *Sobhi v Commissioner of Police of the Metropolis* [2013] Eq LR 785.

■ V. Perju, 'Impairment, Discrimination, and the Legal Construction of Disability in the European Union and the United States' (2011) 44 *Cornell International Law Journal* 279, 284–8

At the core of the [social] model, one finds both a transformative insight and its central shortcoming. The insight is that the cause of disability is not a medical impairment but society's reaction to that impairment. Over the past four decades, this insight has formed the basis of disability reforms and changed the status of persons with disabilities from passive 'objects of rehabilitation and cure' to rights holders entitled to make demands on social institutions. The shortcoming, as we have seen, is the readiness to gloss over medical impairments altogether, and in this process, to generate distortion effects that courts have been unwilling or unable to rectify . . .

The good news is that, formally speaking, changes in the judicial definition of disability would go a long way to change the current disability law regime. Defining disability without reference to medical impairments would bring courts closer to a discrimination-centered approach to disability. The bad news is that an impairment-free definition is highly unlikely. There is a path dependency in how concepts are defined, and medical impairments have so often been at the center of the meaning of disability that it might be difficult to shift course radically at this stage. However one envisions the future of disability law, it helps to understand the judicial definition of disability as reflecting deep tensions in the arguments and argumentative strategies in support of the social model.

As will become apparent from our analysis of the law later, the UK approach which relies on an explicit legal definition of 'disability' is anchored firmly within the 'medical' model,[19] albeit that there are undoubtedly some elements of the 'social' model at play, e.g. discrimination by perception or association. This can be contrasted with the position in EU law which is now[20] wedded to the 'social' model subsequent to the decisions of the CJEU in *HK Danmark, acting on behalf of Ring v Dansk almennyttigt Boligselskab* ('*Ring*'),[21] *Z v A Government Department*,[22] and *Fag og Arbejde, acting on behalf of Kaltoft v Kommunernes Landsforening, acting on behalf of the Municipality of Bullund*.[23] This approach has emerged under the influence of the social model embedded within Article 27 of the CRPD. Rather than being under an obligation to show that a medical condition or illness substantially affects his/her ability to carry out normal day-to-day activities, it is instead incumbent on the disabled employee to satisfy the court that he/she suffers from a 'limitation which results in particular from physical, mental or psychological impairments which in interaction with various barriers may hinder the full and effective participation of the person concerned in professional life on an equal basis with other workers'.[24] It is the emphasis on the relationship between the 'barriers' in society and the workplace experienced by the disabled worker and the impairment which

[19] See S. Fredman, *Discrimination Law*, 2nd edition (Oxford, OUP, 2011) 97–8 and 171–3 for an analysis of whether the legal concepts of (1) the employer's duty to make reasonable adjustments in sections 20–22 of the EA and (2) 'discrimination arising from disability' in section 15 of the EA are articulations of the 'medical' or 'social' models.

[20] The current position is in stark contrast to the original EU approach, with its uncompromising reliance on the 'medical' model, in *Chacón Navas v Eurest Colectividades SA* [2007] ICR 1. Here, the ECJ firmly scotched the notion that the Framework Directive embraced the 'social' model.

[21] [2013] ICR 851.   [22] [2014] IRLR 563, [2014] 3 CMLR 20.

[23] [2015] IRLR 146. For commentary, see T. Hervey and P. Rostant, '"All About That Bass"? Is Non-Ideal-Weight Discrimination Unlawful in the UK?' (2016) 79 *Modern Law Review* 248.

[24] *HK Danmark* [2013] ICR 851, 874H–875A. See also *Z v A Government Department* [2014] IRLR 563, 574; *Kaltoft v Kommunernes Landsiljforening, acting on behalf of the Municipality of Bullun* [2015] ICR 322, 344E–346A.

suggests the relevance of the 'social' model to EU law.[25] It should be noted that the 'social' model derived from EU law has now been followed domestically in the EAT in *Banaszc-zyk v Booker Ltd* and should be included when interpreting the definition of 'disability'.[26]

At this juncture in our discussion, we move on to consider the nature of the discriminatory conduct which is proscribed in the context of disability. For example, if a disabled worker experiences a barrier of some sort in the workplace, must we jump to the conclusion that he/she has been discriminated against? Bearing in mind that disabled workers have different needs from the mainstream and that they are not necessarily desirous of formal equality and symmetrical treatment, is it truly accurate to depict employers who fail to comply with disability discrimination laws as 'guilty' of discrimination?[27] Although they may be morally innocent, employers will be held liable under the law in such circumstances, since what is now clear is that the EA demands positive discrimination in favour of disabled workers. This was a slow realization on the part of lawyers and the general public, but ultimately was brought fully into the foreground by the landmark decision of the House of Lords in *Archibald v Fife Council*[28] in 2004. Here, the legal requirement for preferential treatment for the disabled pursuant to the legal concept of the duty to make reasonable adjustments was underscored in no uncertain terms: how far the rights of the disabled had come from their humble origins in legislation originally hailing from the tail end of the Second World War. For example, in response to the numbers of former servicemen returning disabled from war, in 1944, Parliament passed the Disabled Persons (Employment) Act 1944 ('DP(E)A'). The DP(E)A enjoined employers with at least 20 employees to ensure that up to 3 per cent of their total workforce comprised individuals who were registered as disabled persons. However, this statutory quota was 'more honoured in the breach than the observance'[29] by employers, and enforcement was negligible. The result was the perpetuation of the occupational segregation and exclusion of the disabled from the labour market. The DP(E)A was finally repealed by the Disability Discrimination Act 1995 ('DDA'), which introduced a modern framework for the proscription of disability discrimination. The DDA was amended in 2005 in order to prohibit disability discrimination by public bodies and to conform to the requirements of the Framework Directive. Finally, the DDA was repealed when the provisions on disability discrimination contained in the EA came into force. Having briefly introduced the key approaches to the protection of disabled workers from discrimination in the EA, we turn to a more detailed analysis of the definition of disability in section 12.2.

Reflection points

1. Which of the 'medical' or 'social' model approaches to the protection of the disabled do you prefer? Give reasons for your answer.

2. Do you agree that the formal equality model (conferring a right to equal treatment) is insufficient in the context of disability? If not, why not? If so, why?

3. Critically evaluate the decisions of the CJEU in *Ring* and *Kaltoft*.

 For additional reading on the context and history of disability discrimination laws, visit the Online Resources for this book at www.oup.com/uk/cabrelli3e/

---

[25] For an opposite view that *HK Danmark* and *Kaltoft* do not embody the social model but are examples of the persistent adoption of the medical model, see D. Hosking, 'Fat Rights Claim Rebuffed: *Kaltoft v Municipality of Billund*' (2015) 44 *Industrial Law Journal* 460.   [26] [2016] IRLR 273.

[27] See the discussion in the column in the *Times* newspaper by Matthew Parris on 16 May 1994.

[28] [2004] UKHL 32, [2004] ICR 954.

[29] B. Doyle, 'Disabled Workers' Rights, the Disability Discrimination Act and the UN Standard Rules' (1996) 25 *Industrial Law Journal* 1, 10.

12.2 THE DEFINITION OF DISABILITY

A variety of sources must be consulted in order to determine whether an individual is disabled as a matter of fact. In *Gallop v Newport City Council*,[30] the Court of Appeal emphasized the point that it is incumbent on the employer to make a factual judgment as to whether or not an employee is disabled and that it should not simply rely on an external opinion from an occupational health professional. Further, the EAT in *Gallop v Newport City Council (No. 2)*[31] explained that the 'knowledge of the employer' related to the 'actual motivation, intention and knowledge of the decision-maker'. The various sources comprise primary and secondary legislation, extra-statutory guidance, and case law, each of which performs a gate-keeping role. The starting place for the discussion is section 6 of, and Schedule 1 to, the EA:

Section 6 Disability

(1) A person (P) has a disability if—

   (a) P has a physical or mental impairment, and

   (b) the impairment has a substantial and long-term adverse effect on P's ability to carry out normal day-to-day activities.

(2) A reference to a disabled person is a reference to a person who has a disability.

(3) In relation to the protected characteristic of disability—

   (a) a reference to a person who has a particular protected characteristic is a reference to a person who has a particular disability;

   (b) a reference to persons who share a protected characteristic is a reference to persons who have the same disability . . .

(6) Schedule 1 (disability: supplementary provision) has effect . . .

Schedule 1 . . .

Paragraph 6 Certain medical conditions

(1) Cancer, HIV infection and multiple sclerosis are each a disability.

(2) HIV infection is infection by a virus capable of causing the Acquired Immune Deficiency Syndrome.

Paragraph 7 Deemed disability

(1) Regulations may provide for persons of prescribed descriptions to be treated as having disabilities.

(2) The regulations may prescribe circumstances in which a person who has a disability is to be treated as no longer having the disability . . .

The regulations promulgated pursuant to Schedule 1 to the EA are the Equality Act 2010 (Disability) Regulations 2010 ('the Regulations'),[32] which specifically exclude certain conditions from the coverage of qualifying impairments for the purposes of section 6(1)

---

[30] [2014] IRLR 211. cf. *Urso v Department for Work and Pensions* [2017] IRLR 304.
[31] *Gallop v Newport City Council (No. 2)* [2016] IRLR 395.
[32] SI 2010/2128.

of the EA, such as exhibitionism,[33] voyeurism,[34] seasonal allergic rhinitis, addictions to alcohol, nicotine or other substances, and a tendency to set fires, steal, or to physically or sexually abuse other persons.[35] Moreover, certain features are also expressly identified as qualifying as a disability, such as blindness, and persons certified as severely sight impaired or partially sighted by a consultant ophthalmologist.[36] The statutory provisions are supplemented by extra-statutory guidance which has been produced pursuant to section 6(5) of, and paragraphs 10 and 11 of Schedule 1 to, the EA ('the Guidance')[37] which, although not possessing the force of law, must be taken into account by the tribunals and courts in adjudicating disputes.[38]

12.2.1 Impairment

Although this may seem obvious, the employee must prove as a preliminary issue that they are actually disabled under section 6 of the EA. If they cannot prove that they are disabled according to this definition, their claim will be bound to fail.[39] What is particularly striking about the definition of 'disability' in section 6 of the EA is that the whole edifice is constructed upon the cornerstone of the expression 'physical or mental impairment';[40] this reflects the underlying 'medical' model prevalent in the disability discrimination provisions of the EA. Somewhat surprisingly, no definition of the key word 'impairment' is given in the EA. However, the courts[41] and the Guidance[42] take the view that it must be afforded its ordinary and natural meaning. The latter sets out a non-exhaustive list of impairments, some of which may not be 'readily identifiable'.[43]

■ The Guidance

A5

A disability can arise from a wide range of impairments which can be:

- sensory impairments, such as those affecting sight or hearing;

- impairments with fluctuating or recurring effects[44] such as rheumatoid arthritis, myalgic encephalitis (ME)/chronic fatigue syndrome (CFS), fibromyalgia, depression[45] and epilepsy;

---

[33] Regulations 3 and 4 of the Regulations.

[34] For example, see *Hickford v Commissioners for HMRC* (UKEAT/0158/13/SM, 5 December 2013) where an employee was dismissed for gross misconduct because he was accessing inappropriate websites on his employer's computer equipment. His claim that he was prone to 'flights of escapism' attributable to depression and so was disabled was rejected by the EAT.

[35] Regulations 3 and 4 of the Regulations.   [36] Regulation 7 of the Regulations.

[37] See *Guidance on the Matters to be Taken into Account in Determining Questions Relating to the Definition of Disability*, available at http://odi.dwp.gov.uk/docs/wor/new/ea-guide.pdf (last visited 6 December 2017).   [38] Paragraph 12 of Schedule 1 to the EA.

[39] *Peninsula Business Services Ltd v Baker* [2017] IRLR 394.

[40] For the approach of the tribunals and courts towards mental impairments and sickness-related absences, see the discussion in M. Bell, 'Sickness Absence and the Court of Justice: Examining the Role of Fundamental Rights in EU Employment Law' (2015) 21 *European Law Journal* 641; M. Bell, 'Mental Health at Work and the Duty to Make Reasonable Adjustments' (2015) 44 *Industrial Law Journal* 194; A. De Paor and C. O'Mahony, 'The Need to Protect Employees with Genetic Predisposition to Mental Illness? The UN Convention on the Rights of Persons with Disabilities and the Case for Regulation' (2016) 45 *Industrial Law Journal* 525.

[41] *McNicol v Balfour Beatty Rail Maintenance Ltd* [2002] ICR 1498, 1503F–G per Mummery LJ.

[42] See the Guidance, para A3.   [43] See the Guidance, para A8.

[44] It has been held that type 2 diabetes is not a disability: *Metroline Travel Ltd v Stoute* [2015] IRLR 465. However, this decision seems to explicitly contradict the Guidance, para B14 and the EHRC Code, available at https://www.equalityhumanrights.com/sites/default/files/employercode.pdf at para 2.614 (last visited 6 December 2017).

[45] It will not be competent for an employment tribunal to do its own internet research in order to decide that a person was not disabled because the dosage of his/her anti-depressant medication was too low: *East of England Ambulance Service NHS Trust v Sanders* [2015] IRLR 277.

- progressive, such as motor neurone disease, muscular dystrophy, forms of dementia;

- auto-immune conditions such as systemic lupus erythematosis (SLE);

- organ specific, including respiratory conditions, such as asthma, and cardiovascular diseases, including thrombosis, stroke and heart disease;

- developmental, such as autistic spectrum disorders (ASD),[46] dyslexia[47] and dyspraxia;

- learning disabilities;

- mental health conditions with symptoms such as anxiety, low mood, panic attacks, phobias, or unshared perceptions; eating disorders; bipolar affective disorders; obsessive compulsive disorders; personality disorders; post traumatic stress disorder, and some self-harming behaviour;

- mental illnesses such as depression and schizophrenia;

- produced by injury to the body, including to the brain.

Of fundamental significance is the point that it is not a prerequisite for the establishment of an impairment that there must be some underlying cause, recognized illness, or medical condition. Moreover, even if the substantial adverse effect of the impairment suffered by the employee is self-inflicted, he/she may nevertheless be treated as disabled, e.g. mobility problems and discomfort when working in some cases of obesity.[48] What is of central importance is *the effect* of the impairment on the individual,[49] irrespective of whether the employee wholly or partially contributed to the substantial adverse effect suffered.[50] Therefore, a claimant will be obliged to show that he/she has an impairment and the effects of that impairment, but it is not necessary for him/her to show *why* he/she has that impairment. In the following extract, Lord Penrose provides compelling justifications for his view that the question of impairment ought to be divorced from the separate issues of cause, illness, and condition:

■ *Millar v Inland Revenue Commissioners* [2006] IRLR 112, 116

Lord Penrose:

[M]any forms of physical impairment result from conditions that cannot be described as 'illness'. Genetic deformity, for example, may not be a manifestation of 'illness' in any sense. A deficit resulting from trauma has its origins in an event that may have required medical intervention. But an amputee, for example, does not have an 'illness'. One would expect it to be sufficient for such a person to point to his or her current physical condition as establishing an impairment before turning to the other requirements of the [EA].

As such, an individual may be covered under the EA notwithstanding that it is impossible for clinicians to attribute his/her impairment to a physical or mental cause, or even where his/her past behaviour or lifestyle choice is the sole cause of the disability.

[46] This will include Aspergers' syndrome: *Islam v Abertawe Bro Morgannwg University Local Health Board* [2015] EWCA Civ 259.

[47] See *Paterson v Commissioner of Police of the Metropolis* [2007] ICR 1522.

[48] *Walker v SITA Information Networking Computing Ltd* [2013] Eq LR 476. See also *Kaltoft* [2015] ICR 322, on which, see D. Hosking, 'Fat Rights Claim Rebuffed: *Kaltoft v Municipality of Billund*' (2015) 44 *Industrial Law Journal* 460.

[49] See *Millar v Inland Revenue Commissioners* [2006] IRLR 112; the Guidance, para A13; *Walker v SITA Information Networking Computing Ltd* [2013] Eq LR 476; and *Foster v Cardiff University* [2013] Eq LR 718.

[50] *J v DLA Piper* [2010] ICR 1052; *Kaltoft* [2015] ICR 322.

12.2.2 The effect of the impairment

Once a claimant has satisfied the tribunal or court that he/she has a physical or mental impairment, consideration will turn at the next stage to an assessment of its 'effect' on the worker, i.e. whether that impairment has:

- had an adverse effect on his/her ability to carry out normal day-to-day activities, which effect is:
  - long-term; and
  - substantial.

In *J v DLA Piper UK LLP*,[51] Underhill J (P) in the EAT provided some input on how tribunals ought to approach the (1) impairment and (2) effect stages involved in evaluating whether an individual has a disability:

■ *J v DLA Piper UK LLP* [2010] ICR 1052, 1070H–1072C

Underhill J (President):

There are indeed sometimes cases where identifying the nature of the impairment from which a claimant may be suffering involves difficult medical questions; and we agree that in many or most such cases it will be easier—and is entirely legitimate—for the tribunal to park that issue and to ask first whether the claimant's ability to carry out normal day-to-day activities has been adversely affected—one might indeed say 'impaired'—on a long-term basis. If it finds that it has been, it will in many or most cases follow as a matter of common sense inference that the claimant is suffering from a condition which has produced that adverse effect—in other words, an 'impairment'. If that inference can be drawn, it will be unnecessary for the tribunal to try to resolve difficult medical issues of the kind to which we have referred. [Thus,] in cases where there may be a dispute about the existence of an impairment it will make sense . . . to start by making findings about whether the claimant's ability to carry out normal day-to-day activities is adversely affected (on a long-term basis), and to consider the question of impairment in the light of those findings.

Accordingly, the separate questions of (1) impairment and (2) effect need not be approached sequentially and the latter may be addressed first.

We now analyse each of the three components associated with the effect of the impairment in turn.

12.2.2.1 Normal day-to-day activities

The first factor to consider is what constitutes 'normal day-to-day activities'. Once again, there is no definition furnished in the EA or the Regulations. Prior to the enactment of the EA, the DDA included eight factors such as speech; physical co-ordination; continence; manual dexterity; eyesight; hearing; memory or ability to concentrate, learn, or understand; awareness of the risk of physical danger; and mobility. These factors were to be considered in evaluating whether the claimant was able to undertake normal day-to-day activities. However, this list was removed from section 6 of, and Schedule 1 to, the EA. Hepple has somewhat tellingly remarked that this 'change should make it easier for people whose impairments do not readily match any of the eight capacities to show that they meet the definition of a disabled person'.[52] In *Goodwin v Patent Office*,[53]

---

[51] [2010] ICR 1052.
[52] B. Hepple, *Equality: The New Legal Framework*, 2nd edition (Oxford, Hart Publishing, 2014) 44.
[53] [1999] ICR 302.

Morison J underscored the somewhat ephemeral nature of this functional requirement in the definition of disability:

■ **Goodwin v Patent Office [1999] ICR 302, 309F–G**

Morison J:

What is a day-to-day activity is best left unspecified: easily recognised, but defined with difficulty. What can be said is that the inquiry is not focused on a particular or special set of circumstances. Thus, it is not directed to the person's own particular circumstances either at work or home.

However, the Guidance does shed some light on the expression, pointing towards the relevance of the frequency of the activity in question, as follows:

■ **The Guidance**

D3

. . .. day-to-day activities are things people do on a regular or daily basis, and examples include shopping, reading and writing, having a conversation or using the telephone, watching television, getting washed and dressed, preparing and eating food, carrying out household tasks, walking and travelling by various forms of transport, and taking part in social activities.[54]

In *Ekpe v Commissioner of the Police for the Metropolis*,[55] the EAT ruled that a day-to-day activity will be 'normal' if it is not abnormal or unusual as a regular activity on an objective evaluation and that anything done by many men or women will constitute a 'normal' day-to-day function, e.g. applying make-up and putting in rollers were 'normal' activities for many women. Moreover, *Ekpe v Commissioner of the Police for the Metropolis* highlighted the need for tribunals and courts to conduct an overall assessment of the activities that the claimant is unable to do, taking into account the evidence as a whole, rather than focusing on each activity in isolation. The courts have also stressed time and again that concentration must be focused on the things that the claimant either cannot do or can only do with difficulty, as opposed to what he/she can do.[56] Furthermore, it is impermissible for a tribunal to balance what the claimant cannot do against what he/she can do as a means of assessing the claimant's condition.[57]

An altogether separate, albeit key, issue is whether the reference to 'normal day-to-day' activities excludes the ability of a tribunal or court to take into account whether the claimant retains the capacity to perform work activities. The Guidance suggests so, as it stipulates that work activities are not to be taken into account in determining the parameters of the expression 'normal day-to-day activities'.[58] However, this appears to fly in the face of the definition of 'disability' in EU law inasmuch as the ECJ in *Chacón Navas v Eurest Colectividades SA* and *Ring* requires the claimant to identify a limitation resulting from a physical, mental, or psychological impairment which hinders the participation of the person concerned in 'professional life'.[59] For example, in *Z v A Government*

---

[54] See also the EHRC Code, available at https://www.equalityhumanrights.com/sites/default/files/employercode.pdf at page 288 (last visited 6 December 2017).   [55] [2001] ICR 1084.

[56] *Goodwin v Patent Office* [1999] ICR 302; *Leonard v Southern Derbyshire Chamber of Commerce* [2001] IRLR 19.

[57] *Ahmed v Metroline Travel Ltd* [2011] Eq LR 464; *Billett v MoD* [2015] EWCA Civ 773.

[58] See Guidance, para D5–D7; *Banaszczyk v Booker Ltd* [2016] IRLR 273.

[59] For a discussion, see D. Hosking, 'A High Bar for EU Disability Rights' (2007) 36 *Industrial Law Journal* 228.

Department,[60] the CJEU reached the conclusion that a fertile female employee with no uterus who had no capacity to become pregnant and have children was not disabled, since her physical impairment did not hinder or prevent her from accessing, taking part, or advancing in her employment and career. Likewise, in *Chief Constable of Dumfries & Galloway Constabulary v Adams*,[61] the EAT ruled that it is relevant to address whether the claimant is limited in an activity which is to be found across a range of employment situations and something that a person does only at work may be categorized as normal if it is not a specialized skill but is common to different types of employment. For example, in *Adams*, the ability to partake in night shift work was deemed to be a normal day-to-day activity for a police officer, and in *Paterson v Commissioner of the Police for the Metropolis*[62] the EAT held that carrying out an examination or assessment is properly to be described as a normal day-to-day activity for a policeman applying for promotion since it is relevant to that individual's participation in professional life. One of the criticisms levelled at the decisions of the CJEU/ECJ in *Ring, Chacón Navas v Eurest Colectividades SA*, and *Z v A Government Department*, and the EAT in *Paterson v Commissioner of the Police for the Metropolis*—that general participation in or access to professional life constitutes a day-to-day activity—is that the status of a person for the purposes of disability discrimination law would be governed by the manner in which the employer reacted to the impairment.[63] *Paterson v Commissioner of the Police for the Metropolis* may also be criticized on the ground that it seems to make the individual's disability status dependent on the nature of his/her job, including the work activities involved in that job. That surely cannot be correct, since the disability status of an individual then hinges on his/her occupation.

12.2.2.2 Long-term effect

Once it has been established that the claimant's impairment has an effect on his/her capacity to undertake normal day-to-day activities, it is incumbent on him/her to show that the impact is 'long-term' and 'substantial'. As for the former, paragraph 2 of Schedule 1 to the EA provides as follows:

Schedule 1

Paragraph 2 Long-term effects

(1) The effect of an impairment is long-term if—

    (a) it has lasted for at least 12 months,

    (b) it is likely to last for at least 12 months, or

    (c) it is likely to last for the rest of the life of the person affected.

(2) If an impairment ceases to have a substantial adverse effect on a person's ability to carry out normal day-to-day activities, it is to be treated as continuing to have that effect if that effect is likely to recur.

(3) For the purposes of sub-paragraph (2), the likelihood of an effect recurring is to be disregarded in such circumstances as may be prescribed.

(4) Regulations may prescribe circumstances in which, despite sub-paragraph (1), an effect is to be treated as being, or as not being, long-term.

---

[60] [2014] IRLR 563.   [61] [2009] ICR 1034.   [62] [2007] ICR 1522.
[63] See *Chief Constable of Lothian and Borders Police v Cumming* [2010] IRLR 109.

Paragraph 2(1)(a) of Schedule 1 to the EA is fairly self-explanatory. Paragraph 2(1)(b) of Schedule 1 to the EA is designed to cater for circumstances in which the effect of the impairment on the claimant has not yet lasted for 12 months when the employer's alleged discriminatory conduct took place, but is likely to continue for at least 12 months subsequent to when it commenced. In the decision of the House of Lords in *SCA Packaging Ltd v Boyle*,[64] it was ruled that the word 'likely' in paragraph 2(1)(b) of Schedule 1 to the EA should be interpreted as meaning 'could well happen', in the sense that there is a significant risk of something happening,[65] rather than 'more probable than not'. This construction considerably lowers the bar for claimants. Meanwhile, paragraph 2(1)(c) of Schedule 1 to the EA covers the situation where the claimant is unlikely to continue to live for the period of 12 months from the date on which his/her impairment started to have an effect on his/her ability to carry out normal day-to-day activities. Meanwhile, if the effect of the impairment has not had a substantial adverse effect on the claimant's ability to undertake normal day-to-day activities for the requisite 12-month period, paragraph 2(2) of Schedule 1 to the EA provides that the individual is disabled if (1) it is likely to recur for (2) at least 12 months, beginning with the date of the initial occurrence of the effect. Hence paragraph 2(2) looks to cover intermittent, as well as constant, effects on the individual's capacities. The Guidance provides the following example of when an individual will satisfy paragraph 2(2):

■ The Guidance

> ### C6
>
> A young man has bipolar affective disorder, a recurring form of depression. The first episode occurred in months one and two of a 13-month period. The second episode took place in month 13. This man will satisfy the requirements of the definition in respect of the meaning of long-term, because the adverse effects have recurred beyond 12 months after the first occurrence and are therefore treated as having continued for the whole period (in this case, a period of 13 months).

Once again, the word 'likely' in the expression 'likely to recur' in paragraph 2(2) of Schedule 1 to the EA will be taken to mean 'could well happen' by virtue of the decision of the House of Lords in *SCA Packaging Ltd v Boyle*.[66] As for the proper approach towards the evaluation of the likelihood of the claimant's impairment recurring, the question is whether events subsequent to the alleged discriminatory conduct, such as actual recurrences of the impairment, can be taken into account by the tribunal or court? That is, should the adjudicator exercise hindsight? In *Richmond Adult Community College v Mc-Dougall*,[67] the Court of Appeal ruled that the assessment as to whether the effect is likely to last for at least 12 months must be judged on the basis of evidence available at the time of the employer's alleged discriminatory conduct, rather than the later time of the tribunal hearing.[68] As such, a tribunal or court has no right to have regard to the later recurrence of the claimant's impairment and must 'close its eyes' to subsequent factual events. As noted by Petts, this approach—which is designed to avoid the peril of 'hindsight bias'—is grounded in fairness to the employer, but may generate certain practical challenges:

---

[64] [2009] UKHL 37, [2009] ICR 1056, 1071E per Baroness Hale.

[65] *ibid.*, 1069C per Lord Rodger.

[66] *ibid.*, 1078D–F per Lord Brown and 1079B per Lord Neuberger.   [67] [2008] ICR 431.

[68] For example, see *Donelien v Liberata UK Ltd* (UKEAT/0297/14/JOJ, 16 December 2014) where the EAT ruled that the employer could not have reasonably known that the employee was disabled. In this case, the employee had a poor sickness record and had exhibited symptoms of a stress-related illness two months prior to her dismissal, which was likely to last for a year or more and which significantly and adversely affected her day-to-day living.

■ J. E. Petts, 'Prognoses for Disability Discrimination Following *McDougall*'
(2008) 37 *Industrial Law Journal* 268, 273–7

The Court of Appeal has therefore adopted a subjective approach in the assessment of likelihood: if a person's decisions are to be criticised, and sanctions applied for getting them wrong, the reasoning goes, they should be assessed on the basis of what was known to the person at the time, and not what became known later. More interestingly, Pill LJ envisages a specific decision about *whether* a person is disabled as a quite separate decision from a decision about how to treat that person, that decision itself being one, so his reasoning goes, which also ought not to be criticised except in so far as it was wrong on the basis of the information before the person making it at the time that it was made. The underlying principle appears to be that it would be wrong in principle if a person could be liable for disability discrimination despite neither knowing nor being in a position where he or she could reasonably be expected to know that the person against whom he or she allegedly discriminated was disabled . . .

If the court or tribunal must decide whether a substantial adverse effect of an impairment was likely to recur, or last for more than twelve months, on the basis only of evidence available to the defendant/respondent at the time of the alleged discrimination, it could be argued that medical reports obtained subsequently for the purposes of bringing the claim must be ignored when determining that question, since those reports could not have formed the basis of the earlier impugned decision, and therefore that such a decision cannot be criticised on the basis of information contained in those reports . . .

Even if tribunals strain the rule in *McDougall* to allow medical reports on the question of likelihood of continuance or recurrence, presumably, those reports would have to be written on the basis of what the employer (etc.) knew at the time of the impugned decision, excluding subsequent information, including, it would follow, diagnostic tests performed for the purposes of the report. This might be very difficult in practice for medical professionals to achieve, especially since the report on every issue other than prognosis will be able to be compiled with all the information before the medical professional in question.[69]

This extract from Petts reflects the decision of the EAT in *Patel v Oldham Metropolitan Borough Council*[70] where it was held that the claimant's period of suffering from mild myelitis (inflammation of the spinal cord) could be aggregated with the subsequent period during which she suffered from a secondary myofascial pain syndrome (painful muscular trigger points) for the purpose of satisfying the long-term threshold criterion. Accordingly, 'fine distinctions between one medical condition and its development into another are to be avoided [and] the effect of an illness or condition likely to develop or which has developed from another illness or condition forms part of the assessment of whether the effect of the original impairment is likely to last or has lasted at least 12 months'.

Perhaps controversially, a lack of evidence as to length of incapacity could also bolster the 'long-term' element of the definition. In *Daouidi v Bootes Plus SL*[71] it was held that the requirement for a disability to be 'long-term' could be evidenced by the fact that, at the time the alleged discrimination took place, the incapacity of the disabled person did not have a clear prognosis as to the length of incapacity.

A final point worth highlighting is the Guidance's insistence that 'it is not necessary for the effect to be the same throughout the period which is being considered in relation to determining whether the "long-term" element of the definition is met [and so a] person may still satisfy the long-term element of the definition even if the effect is not the same throughout the period'.[72]

---

[69] See also F. Reynold QC and A. Palmer, 'What Place for Hindsight in Deciding Whether a Claimant Was Disabled?' [2007] 36 *Industrial Law Journal* 486.   [70] [2010] ICR 603.
[71] [2017] IRLR 151.   [72] [2010] ICR 603, 609G–610A per Slade J.

12.2.2.3 Substantial effect

We now move on to address whether the adverse effect suffered by the claimant as a result of the impairment is 'substantial' in nature. This is important since it means that the existence of a mental or physical impairment such as anxiety or depression will of itself be insufficient for an employee to be treated as disabled;[73] instead, it is a requirement for a direct or indirect causal link to exist between the impairment and the substantial and long-term adverse effect on the ability of the employee to carry out normal day-to-day activities. The EAT in *Goodwin v Patent Office*[74] adopted the view that these words signify that the impairment must be 'more than minor or trivial', rather than 'very large', which is now codified in section 212(1) of the EA. Additional guidance on the relationship between 'trivial/insubstantial' and 'substantial' effects was provided in *Aderemi v London and South Eastern Railway Ltd.*[75] Here, it was ruled that there is no such thing as 'a sliding scale between matters which were clearly of substantial effect and those which were clearly trivial, [and] unless an effect could be classified as trivial or insubstantial it was necessarily substantial'.[76] Meanwhile, in *Abadeh v British Telecommunications plc,*[77] the EAT decided that it was not for a medical expert to dictate to a tribunal whether the impairment was substantial or not as the case may be, but rather that this was a matter for the tribunal to answer based on the medical evidence. In *Goodwin v Patent Office*, the claimant was a patent examiner and was diagnosed with paranoid schizophrenia. He suffered from auditory hallucinations which caused him to believe that others could access his thoughts. Although his condition affected his ability to concentrate for any sustained period of time, he was able to carry out domestic activities without assistance, such as cooking, shopping, and caring for himself at home, all of which were undertaken to a satisfactory standard. Work colleagues complained about his behaviour and the employer responded by dismissing him. The employment tribunal held that the effect of the schizophrenia on his capacities was not substantial owing to the fact that he was able to undertake domestic activities without difficulty. However, the EAT granted an appeal on the basis that the tribunal had failed to appreciate the significance of the fact that the claimant was simply unable to carry on a normal day-to-day conversation with work colleagues, and that his capacity to concentrate and communicate had been adversely affected to a material degree. On balance, this was sufficient to establish a substantial adverse effect.

Further, it has been held that where there is only a small chance of a progressive condition worsening, this can be sufficient to prove that the adverse effect is substantive. It was held in *Taylor v Ladbrokes Betting and Gaming Ltd*[78] that if there is only a small chance of deterioration of the condition, in this case Type 2 Diabetes, this is enough to make it 'likely' to result in the individual having a 'substantive adverse effect'.

The Guidance directs that two factors will be particularly relevant in addressing whether the effect of an individual's impairment is substantial. First, it will be revealing that the time taken by the claimant to carry out a normal day-to-day activity is much longer than that which would be taken if he/she did not have the impairment.[79] Secondly, the way in which the claimant carries out a normal day-to-day activity ought to be compared with the way that he/she might be expected to carry out the activity if he or she did not have the impairment.[80] In *Paterson v Commissioner of the Police for the Metropolis,*[81] Elias J (President) provided the following take on these two factors:

---

[73] *Saad v University Hospital Southampton NHS Trust* (UKEAT/0184/14/DM, 4 December 2014); *Department for Work and Pensions v Conyers* (UKEAT/0375/13/KN, 5 November 2014).
[74] [1999] ICR 302.   [75] [2013] ICR 591.   [76] *ibid.*, 596D–F per Langstaff J (P).
[77] [2001] ICR 156.   [78] [2017] IRLR 253.   [79] Guidance, para B2.
[80] Guidance, para B3.   [81] [2007] ICR 1522.

■ *Paterson v Commissioner of the Police for the Metropolis* [2007] ICR 1522, 1529C–D

Elias J (President):

In order to be substantial the effect must fall outwith the normal range of effects that one might expect from a cross section of the population. However, when assessing the effect, the comparison is not with the population at large. As paragraphs [B]2 and [B]3 make clear, what is required is to compare the difference between the way in which the individual in fact carries out the activity in question and how he would carry it out if not impaired.

The Guidance also ensures that the cumulative effects of an impairment on normal day-to-day activities must be addressed as a whole where there is no substantial effect on a person's ability to carry out a particular activity in isolation.[82] Moreover, the tribunal or court must assess the extent to which the claimant 'can reasonably be expected to modify his or her behaviour . . . to prevent or reduce the effects of an impairment on normal day-to-day activities'.[83]

Notwithstanding the existence of the free-standing concept of 'substantial . . . [adverse]' effect in section 6(1)(b) of the EA, certain statutory provisions operate to deem certain effects to be 'substantial' as a matter of course:

Schedule 1

Paragraph 3 Severe disfigurement

(1) An impairment which consists of a severe disfigurement is to be treated as having a substantial adverse effect on the ability of the person concerned to carry out normal day-to-day activities . . .[84]

Paragraph 5 Effect of medical treatment

(1) An impairment is to be treated as having a substantial adverse effect on the ability of the person concerned to carry out normal day-to-day activities if—

(a) measures are being taken to treat or correct it, and

(b) but for that, it would be likely[85] to have that effect.

(2) 'Measures' includes, in particular, medical treatment[86] and the use of a prosthesis or other aid.[87]

(3) Sub-paragraph (1) does not apply—

(a) in relation to the impairment of a person's sight, to the extent that the impairment is, in the person's case, correctable by spectacles or contact lenses or in such other ways as may be prescribed;

(b) in relation to such other impairments as may be prescribed, in such circumstances as are prescribed . . .

---

[82] Guidance, paras B4–B6.   [83] Guidance, para B7.

[84] Regulation 5 of the Regulations specifically provides that the following will not constitute a 'severe disfigurement': (1) a tattoo and/or (2) a body piercing for decorative or other non-medical purposes, including any object attached through the piercing.

[85] In *SCA Packaging Ltd v Boyle* [2009] UKHL 37, [2009] ICR 1056, the House of Lords held that this means 'could well happen'.

[86] See *Kapadia v London Borough of Lambeth* [2000] IRLR 699 where it was ruled that counselling sessions for an individual with depression constituted medical treatment.

[87] The EAT held in *Carden v Pickerings Europe Ltd* [2005] IRLR 721 that the surgical insertion of a plate and pins in a claimant's ankle could amount to 'other aid'.

Paragraph 8 Progressive conditions

(1) This paragraph applies to a person (P) if—

   (a) P has a progressive condition,

   (b) as a result of that condition P has an impairment which has (or had) an effect on P's ability to carry out normal day-to-day activities, but

   (c) the effect is not (or was not) a substantial adverse effect.

(2) P is to be taken to have an impairment which has a substantial adverse effect if the condition is likely to result in P having such an impairment.

In the Guidance, it is narrated that birthmarks, limb or postural deformation, scars, or diseases of the skin will constitute severe disfigurements, and the location of the disfigurement on the body will be relevant in determining whether it is 'severe', i.e. whether it is on the face or on the back of the individual. In *Cosgrove v Northern Ireland Ambulance Service*,[88] the Northern Ireland Court of Appeal adopted a narrow construction of the words 'consists of a severe disfigurement' in paragraph 3 of Schedule 1 to the EA. The case concerned an individual with severe psoriasis who was rejected for an ambulance post (following a pre-employment medical) for the reasons that his skin condition might (1) place him at an increased risk of infection or (2) increase the risk of infection for patients. The Court ruled that the impairment must relate solely to the cosmetic aspect of the condition, as opposed to the factor which increases the risk of infection: the former was covered, but the latter was not.

As for the rather curious rule in paragraph 5 of Schedule 1 to the EA, it is taken as meaning that the beneficial effects of the continuing measures or medical treatment on the individual are to be completely ignored as if he/she were 'not having the treatment and the impairment was completely unchecked'.[89] However, where a permanent improvement has been secured as a result of the continuing medical treatment, it has been held that the effects of that treatment should be accounted for.[90] Moreover, the impact of the words 'are being taken to treat or correct it' is such that the veil of ignorance must be lifted if the measures have ceased and been concluded.[91] Finally, paragraph 8 of Schedule 1 to the EA directs that an individual with a progressive condition the effect of which is not (or was not) substantial or adverse will nonetheless be deemed to have an effect which is substantial and adverse. The purpose of this provision is to ensure that an individual is treated as disabled before a deteriorative condition has a substantial adverse effect when he/she is diagnosed with that condition and some of the effects of that condition first arise. The Guidance provides the following examples:

■ The Guidance

B20

Examples of progressive conditions to which the special provisions apply include systemic lupus erythematosis (SLE), various types of dementia, and motor neurone disease. This list, however, is not exhaustive.

   A young boy aged 8 has been experiencing muscle cramps and some weakness. The effects are quite minor at present, but he has been diagnosed as having muscular dystrophy. Eventually it is

---

[88] [2007] IRLR 397.
[89] *SCA Packaging Ltd v Boyle* [2009] UKHL 37, [2009] ICR 1056, 1066A per Lord Rodger.
[90] *Abadeh v British Telecommunications plc* [2001] ICR 156. See also Guidance, para C11.
[91] *Abadeh v British Telecommunications plc* [2001] ICR 156.

> expected that the resulting muscle weakness will cause substantial adverse effects on his ability to walk, run and climb stairs. Although there is no substantial adverse effect at present, muscular dystrophy is a progressive condition, and this child will still be entitled to the protection of the [EA] under the special provisions in Sch1, Para 8 of the [EA] if it can be shown that the effects are likely to become substantial.

The decision of the EAT in *Mowat-Brown v University of Surrey* underlines the point that it is insufficient for the claimant to establish merely that he/she has been diagnosed with a progressive illness:

■ **Mowat-Brown v University of Surrey [2002] IRLR 235**

Reid (J):

The question to be asked is whether, on the balance of probabilities, the claimant has established that the condition in his case is likely to have a substantial adverse effect. It is not enough simply to establish that he has a progressive condition and that it has or has had an effect on his ability to carry out normal day-to-day activities. The claimant must go on and show that it is more likely than not that at some stage in the future he will have an impairment which will have a substantial adverse effect on his ability to carry out normal day-to-day activities. How the claimant does this is up to him. In some cases, it may be possible to produce medical evidence of his likely prognosis. In other cases, it may be possible to discharge the onus of proof by statistical evidence.[92]

Paragraph 8 of Schedule 1 to the EA directs that the claimant must demonstrate that he/she has suffered an effect on his/her ability to carry out normal day-to-day activities as a result of the progressive condition. In *Kirton v Tetrosyl Ltd*,[93] the claimant had been diagnosed with prostate cancer and underwent surgery, as a result of which he developed urinary incontinence. Although the latter could not be attributed directly to the prostate cancer, it fell within the definition of disability in terms of paragraph 8 since it was the ordinary consequences of an operation to relieve the disease.

12.2.3 Departure from the 'medical' model in section 6 of the EA

We have noted how the prevalent philosophy which underpins section 6 of, and Schedule 1 to, the EA and the Regulations is that a claimant must show that he/she falls within the medicalized definition of disability. To that extent, a claimant who fails to satisfy this underlying 'medical' model will be unable to avail him/herself of protection from discrimination. However, there are three strands by which the EA exhibits a rupture from this general approach, and in each of these situations the claimant is subject to the protective cloak of disability discrimination laws notwithstanding that he/she is unable to satisfy the definition of disability. First, a person who was disabled in the past and has recovered will be deemed to be disabled by virtue of section 6(4) of, and paragraph 9 of Schedule 1 to, the EA. The Guidance furnishes the following example:

---

[92] Sourced from BAILII, available at http://www.bailii.org/cgi-bin/format.cgi?doc=/uk/cases/UKE-AT/2001/462_00_1012.html&query=(mowat-brown)+AND+(v)+AND+(university) (last visited 7 December 2017).

[93] [2003] ICR 1237.

■ **The Guidance**

> *A16*
>
> Four years ago, a woman experienced a mental illness that had a substantial and long-term adverse effect on her ability to carry out normal day-to-day activities, so it met the [EA]'s definition of disability. She has experienced no recurrence of the condition, but if she is discriminated against because of her past mental illness she is still entitled to the protection afforded by the [EA], as a person with a past disability.

The second and third situations where a claim will be valid despite the fact that the claimant is not disabled arise only in the context of a direct disability discrimination claim under section 13 of the EA.[94] The second example applies where the non-disabled claimant complains of direct discrimination because he/she is associated with someone who is disabled, e.g. where the claimant is a carer of a disabled child, as in the case of *Coleman v Attridge Law*,[95] or where he/she has a disabled spouse. Since a claimant is under no obligation to satisfy a tribunal or court that he/she was treated less favourably than a suitable comparator because he/she was disabled but rather because of disability itself—which may be the disability of a third party—section 13(1) of the EA operates to divorce the protected characteristic of disability from the individual claimant him/herself. Meanwhile, the third example is concerned with perceptual discrimination, i.e. where the employer incorrectly assumes that the non-disabled claimant is actually disabled. In such circumstances, the claimant will be entitled to have his/her case that he/she was treated less favourably than a comparator considered notwithstanding that he/she is not actually disabled. Once again, this arises by virtue of the wording of section 13(1), which merely requires the claimant to demonstrate less favourable treatment because of disability, rather than his/her disability specifically.[96] However, the difficulty with this notion of perceptual discrimination lies in how the tribunal or court is to evaluate whether the employer subjectively laboured under a mistaken belief that the claimant was in fact disabled or simply thought that the claimant, for example, was ill or sick:

---

[94] See also section 24(1) of the EA. Therefore, the claimant must be disabled him/herself in order to be permitted to raise a 'discrimination arising from disability' claim under section 15 of the EA, a 'duty to make reasonable adjustments' claim under sections 20–22 of the EA, and an indirect discrimination claim under section 19 of the EA, on which, see *Hainsworth v Ministry of Defence* [2014] IRLR 728. For a critique of the exclusion of an associative discrimination claim in the context of these concepts, see C. O'Brien, 'Equality's False Summits: New Varieties of Disability Discrimination, "Excessive" Equal Treatment and Economically Constructed Horizons' (2011) 36 *European Law Review* 26, 31–7 and 40–2. However, whether the decision in *Hainsworth* survives the decisions of the CJEU and the EAT in *CHEZ Razpredelenie Bulgaria AD v Komisia za zashtita ot diskriminatsias* [2015] IRLR 746 and *Thompson v London Central Bus Co.* [2016] IRLR 9 is unclear. In *CHEZ* and *Thompson*, it was held it was competent for a claimant to raise an associative indirect discrimination claim and an associative victimization claim, on which, see Chapter 10, sections 10.2.4.2 and 10.2.6. However, in both *CHEZ* and *Thompson*, the associative indirect discrimination and associative victimization claims were not raised on the basis of disability, so the position as regards whether these decisions can be extended to cover the protected characteristic of disability is yet to be resolved.

[95] [2008] ICR 1128; *EBR Attridge Law v Coleman (No. 2)* [2010] ICR 242; *McCorry v McKeith* [2017] IRLR 253. See also M. Pilgerstorfer and S. Forshaw, 'Transferred Discrimination in European Law' (2008) 37 *Industrial Law Journal* 384; P. Roberts, 'Caring for the Disabled? New Boundaries in Disability Discrimination' (2009) 72 *Modern Law Review* 635, 643–7.

[96] For the pre-EA law in relation to the interpretation of direct disability discrimination in section 3A(5) of the DDA, see *Aitken v Commissioner of Police of the Metropolis* [2011] EWCA Civ 582, [2012] ICR 78.

■ **A. Lawson, 'Disability and Employment in the Equality Act 2010: Opportunities Seized, Lost and Generated' (2011) 40** *Industrial Law Journal* **359, 373–4**

[Perceptual discrimination claims are] likely to raise some difficult questions in the disability context. These arise largely from the detail and complexity of the [EA] definition of disability. Scrutinising an employer's mistaken perception of the claimant to ascertain whether it meets all the requirements of that statutory definition is an exercise which would be both difficult and undesirable. It would require examination of whether the employer (who would be keen to deny anything that might attract liability) perceived the claimant to have a physical or mental impairment which had a substantial and long-term effect on their ability to carry out normal day-to-day activities. In the words of Underhill P [in *J v DLA Piper UK LLP* [2010] ICR 1052, 1080A–D]:

What the putative discriminator perceives will not always be clearly identifiable as 'disability'. If the perceived disability is, say, blindness, there may be no problem: a blind person is necessarily disabled. But many physical or mental conditions which may attract adverse treatment do not necessarily amount to disabilities, either because they are not necessarily sufficiently serious or because they are not necessarily long-term. If a manager discriminates against an employee because he believes her to have a broken leg, or because he believes her to be 'depressed', the question whether the effects of the perceived injury, or of the perceived depression, are likely to last more or less than twelve months may never enter his thinking, consciously or unconsciously (nor indeed, in the case of perceived 'depression', may it be clear what he understands by the term). In such a case, on what basis can he be said to be discriminating 'on the ground of' the employee's—perceived—disability?

. . . Claimants (even those who are clearly disabled) will undoubtedly be tempted to base their case on discrimination by perception if there is a chance that a less invasive approach to the disability definition will be adopted in this context. Focusing on the perception of the employer might avoid the intrusive examination of functional abilities which has become routine in disability cases. Discrimination by perception thus has the potential to circumvent, at least in direct discrimination cases, the hazards of the definitional gateway through which claimants have previously had to pass. Ironically, however, the strictness of the direct discrimination comparator requirement is likely to render any such circumvention of use to very few claimants.

The Chief Constable of Norfolk v Coffey[97] is the only appellate decision to date to address such a perceptual disability discrimination claim. In this decision of the EAT, HHJ David Richardson provided some guidance on the proper approach to be adopted in the case of perceptual discrimination claims. First, it is irrelevant that the employer perceives the employee to be disabled as a matter of law. Instead, the issue is whether the employer perceives the employee to have an impairment with the features prescribed in the legislation, i.e. a physical or mental impairment having a substantial and long-term adverse effect on the employee's ability to carry out normal day-to-day activities. Secondly, where the employer is aware of the fact that the employee has an impairment and does not consider it as having a substantial adverse effect at the time it makes its assessment, but perceives in error that the impairment may have such an effect in the future, this will amount to perceptual disability discrimination. If that were not the case, it would create a lacuna in the protection offered by the statute.

 For additional reading on the definition of disability, visit the Online Resources for this book at www.oup.com/uk/cabrelli3e

[97] (UKEAT/0260/16/BA, 19 December 2017, HHJ David Richardson).

12.3 PROHIBITED CONDUCT AND THE DUTY TO MAKE REASONABLE ADJUSTMENTS

At the core of the provisions proscribing disability discrimination in the EA reside four legal concepts. Three of these concepts are labelled by the EA as incarnations of 'prohibited conduct', which are shown at the bottom of Figure 12.1. The final construct is the 'duty to make reasonable adjustments'.

Thus, in contrast with the position in the case of the other eight protected characteristics, the disability discrimination laws in the EA contain an additional two legal concepts which are wholly distinctive, namely:

(1) 'discrimination arising from disability'; and

(2) the 'duty to make reasonable adjustments'.

The former is to be distinguished from direct disability discrimination. Meanwhile, the duty to make reasonable adjustments is undoubtedly the most far-reaching insofar as it harbours the potential to enjoin employers to afford preferential treatment to disabled workers.

12.3.1 Direct disability discrimination

A disabled employee is protected from direct disability discrimination. Unlike the standard anti-discrimination model in the EA which proceeds on the basis of symmetrical treatment pursuant to the formal equality model, section 13(3) of the EA underlines the point that an able-bodied colleague of a disabled worker will be disentitled from complaining of direct discrimination where the latter is treated more favourably, e.g. where an employer complies with its statutory duty to make reasonable adjustments. As such, a direct discrimination claim by able-bodied workers is precluded where a disabled worker enjoys the benefits of positive discrimination. Consider the illustration in Hypothetical A.

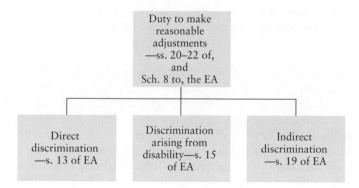

Figure 12.1 *Prohibited conduct*

Hypothetical A

Terry Wilson ('TW'), James French ('JF'), Barry Pryde ('BP'), and Patrick Maher ('PM') are health and safety officers employed by Danny's Demolishers Ltd ('DD'). TW is dyslexic,[98] but JF, BP, and PM have no disability. The post of health and safety director becomes available when their boss retires, and TW, JF, BP, and PM apply for promotion. DD decides to hold a 3-hour professional exam as part of the selection process and gives TW an additional hour on top. When TW's application for promotion to the post of health and safety director succeeds, JF, BP, and PM raise direct discrimination claims under section 13 of the EA. They are extremely unhappy that TW was provided with four hours to complete the exam. The employment tribunal strikes out their claims on the ground that section 13(3) prevents them from being considered.

As for the protective potential of the direct disability discrimination concept, this is minimal inasmuch as the circumstances in which a disabled worker will resort to such a claim are limited. A number of reasons can be cited in favour of this proposition. First, rather than show that he/she was treated less favourably than a comparator because of the impact of his/her disability, the claimant *must establish that the disability itself* was the reason for the less favourable treatment: absent particular cases of mental illness, it is unlikely that an employer will have the claimant's disability in mind as the reason for the detrimental treatment.[99] Therefore, the employer must know about the employee's disability for the direct disability discrimination concept to be engaged.[100] This is compounded by the terms of section 23(1) and (2)(a) which narrowly define the comparator the claimant may invoke, circumscribing the latter to an able-bodied person, (1) in a situation that is not materially different from the disabled claimant, (2) with the same abilities as the disabled claimant, minus, of course, the disability itself.[101] An example is provided in Hypothetical B.

Hypothetical B

Niall Pontefract ('NP') is employed by Danny's Demolishers Ltd ('DD') and is required to drive as part of his employment duties. Unfortunately, NP's driving skills are below the standard to be expected. Colleagues accompanying him in the passenger seats on work journeys regularly complain to DD that NP is unable to drive safely. NP suffers from multiple sclerosis. DD dismisses NP. In such circumstances, NP would need to show that he would have been treated less favourably than a comparator who was also unable to drive safely, but who was not disabled. For obvious reasons, this will be a challenge for NP.

In *JP Morgan Europe Ltd v Chweidan*,[102] the Court of Appeal ruled that it is not incumbent on the claimant to satisfy the tribunal or court that his/her disability was the sole reason for the treatment; rather, it is sufficient if it is 'one which [was] significant in the sense of more than trivial'.[103]

---

[98] Dyslexia was recognized as a disability in *Paterson v Commissioner of the Police for the Metropolis* [2007] ICR 1522.

[99] Of course, in ascertaining the 'reason why' the claimant was treated less favourably than the able-bodied comparator, the tribunal or court will adopt the objective approach fashioned by the Supreme Court in *R (E) v Governing Body of JFS* [2009] UKSC 15, [2010] 2 AC 728, on which, see *Cordell v Foreign and Commonwealth Office* [2012] ICR 280 and Chapter 10, section 10.2.3.

[100] *Patel v Lloyds Pharmacy Ltd* (UKEAT/0418/12/ZT, 6 February 2013, Mitting J).

[101] For example, see *High Quality Lifestyles v Watts* [2006] IRLR 850; *Cordell v Foreign and Commonwealth Office* [2012] ICR 280.   [102] [2012] ICR 268.

[103] *ibid.*, 271F per Elias J.

In the preceding paragraph, the proposition was made that it will generally be improbable that employers will have treated a worker less favourably than a comparator for the reason of his/her disability, rather than the effects of that disability. However, this was made subject to a proviso, namely the case of mental illness. Unfortunately, it is still the case that some employers demote or dismiss workers simply because they suffer from a psychological impairment such as depression, anxiety, bipolar effective disorder, etc. In such contexts, employers will be proceeding on the basis of stereotypical or generalized assumptions about the incapacities generated by such mental disorders. Accordingly, the tribunals and courts will be entitled to exclude particular behavioural traits generated by the claimant's mental disability from the characteristics of the hypothetical comparator.[104] The decision of the Court of Appeal in *Stockton on Tees Borough Council v Aylott* is a classic example of this approach:

■ *Stockton on Tees Borough Council v Aylott* [2010] ICR 1278, 1291A–1292B

[The headnote to the case sets forth the facts as follows:] The claimant, who suffered from bipolar affective disorder and was disabled for the purposes of the [EA], experienced difficulties in his working relationships with colleagues and presented a list of complaints to his employers. His complaints were investigated under the employers' dignity at work procedure while he was on paid leave, but subsequently rejected, and after he returned to work he was placed in a different post with a different working team where he was required to meet deadlines and his work was monitored weekly. The claimant's performance and behaviour continued to be unsatisfactory and he was suspended on full pay pending a disciplinary investigation. As the claimant was then unwell, the suspension was withdrawn and the disciplinary proceedings discontinued. The claimant remained on sick leave for five months until he was dismissed on health grounds. He made a number of claims to an employment tribunal including allegations of unlawful direct disability . . . discrimination . . . The employment tribunal upheld [the] . . . finding that the imposition of deadlines and monitoring, and also his dismissal, were based on the employers' stereotypical view of mental illness; and that, in relation to his claim of direct disability discrimination, an appropriate comparator was someone who had been absent from work for a similar period but did not have the claimant's disability . . . The [EAT] allowed an appeal by the employers, in respect of [the] direct . . . discrimination claim . . . on the ground, inter alia, that the tribunal had used the wrong hypothetical comparators . . .

Mummery LJ:

The hypothetical comparator as a person who did not have the claimant's particular disability, but had a similar sickness absence record, was a comparator choice reasonably open to the employment tribunal . . .The employment tribunal are not, and cannot be, criticised for leaving the claimant's particular disability out of the circumstances of the hypothetical comparator. Section [13(1) of the EA] stipulates that the comparator does not have the disability. In my judgment, there was no error in the employment tribunal also leaving out of those circumstances particular results caused by the claimant's disability: the move to another post and the behavioural and performance difficulties resulting from the particular disability would not be relevant circumstances of a hypothetical comparator who did not have that particular disability. Secondly, I am unable to accept that, in the circumstances of this case, the employment tribunal's reference to the council's 'stereotypical view of mental illness' was too vague to support the finding of direct discrimination. Direct discrimination can occur, for example, when assumptions are made that a claimant, as an

---

[104] Contrast this with *Aitken v Commissioner of Police of the Metropolis* [2012] ICR 78, on which, see A. Lawson, 'Disability and Employment in the Equality Act 2010: Opportunities Seized, Lost and Generated' (2011) 40 *Industrial Law Journal* 359, 372–3.

individual, has characteristics associated with a group to which the claimant belongs, irrespective of whether the claimant or most members of the group have those characteristics: see *R (European Roma Rights Centre) v Immigration Officer at Prague Airport (United Nations High Commissioner for Refugees intervening)* [2005] 2 AC 1 . . .The council's decision to dismiss the claimant was based in part at least on assumptions that it made about his particular mental illness rather than on the basis of up-to-date medical evidence about the effect of his illness on his ability to continue in the employment of the council.

The decision in *Stockton on Tees Borough Council v Aylott* has the effect of lowering the bar for claimants with mental impairments who are intent on raising direct disability discrimination claims. However, this should not obscure the point that few employers will treat disabled persons less favourably than others simply because of their disability. For that reason, the legal concept of 'discrimination arising from disability' in section 15 of the EA is a necessary innovation in order to address those circumstances in which employers subject disabled employees to a disadvantage because of the *effects or outcomes* of their disability, rather than the disability itself.

12.3.2 Discrimination arising from disability

Section 15 of the EA gives expression to the notion of 'discrimination arising from disability':

Section 15 Discrimination arising from disability

(1) A person (A) discriminates against a disabled person (B) if—

(a) A treats B unfavourably because of something arising in consequence of B's disability, and

(b) A cannot show that the treatment is a proportionate means of achieving a legitimate aim.

(2) Subsection (1) does not apply if A shows that A did not know, and could not reasonably have been expected to know, that B had the disability.

The statutory predecessor of this new provision was section 3A(1) of the DDA which proscribed 'disability-related discrimination'. The latter concept entailed a comparison exercise, but was not transposed into the EA; instead, 'discrimination arising from disability' was introduced in response to the restrictive decision of the House of Lords in *Lewisham Borough Council v Malcolm*.[105] This case rendered the 'disability-related discrimination' concept practically useless and weakened the protection available to disabled workers, owing to the narrow way in which the House of Lords approached the comparator.[106] The word 'unfavourably' in section 15(1)(a) is intended to remove any requirement for a comparison exercise. Indeed, the Statutory Code of Practice on Employment promulgated by the Equality and Human Rights Commission ('EHRC') under section 14 of the Equality Act 2006 ('the EHRC Code') directs that 'there is no need to compare a disabled person's treatment with that of another person [and i]t is only necessary to demonstrate that the unfavourable treatment is because of something arising in

---

[105] [2008] UKHL 43, [2008] AC 1399.

[106] See R. Horton, 'The End of Disability-Related Discrimination in Employment?' (2008) 37 *Industrial Law Journal* 376; P. Roberts, 'Caring for the Disabled? New Boundaries in Disability Discrimination' (2009) 72 *Modern Law Review* 635, 637–42; and A. Lawson, 'Disability and Employment in the Equality Act 2010: Opportunities Seized, Lost and Generated' (2011) 40 *Industrial Law Journal* 359, 364–7.

consequence of the disability'.[107] This interpretation has been tested judicially, and the proposition that the use of the word 'unfavourably' in section 15 of the EA avoids the need for any comparison exercise has been approved by the Supreme Court in *Akerman-Livingstone v Aster Communities Ltd*.[108] Another implication of the word 'unfavourably' is that it will be insufficient for the disabled claimant to simply point towards treatment which differs from that accorded to his/her able-bodied colleagues; rather, it denotes an element of disadvantageous treatment. The threshold of disadvantage required, however, is not wholly clear. It is possible to say that the necessary degree of disadvantage for unfavourable treatment will not have been satisfied where the treatment meted out to the employee confers advantages on him/her, but would have conferred greater advantages had his/her disability arisen more suddenly.[109] But precisely when the disadvantage is substantial enough to satisfy the test of unfavourable treatment remains unresolved.

As for the meaning of the phrase, 'something arising in consequence of B's disability', two points can be raised.

(1) This will enjoin the disabled claimant to relate the effect, result, or outcome of his/her disability (rather than the disability itself) to the unfavourable or disadvantageous treatment. As such, proof of a causal link between these two factors is required.[110] However, *Hall v Chief Constable of West Yorkshire*[111] establishes the rule that there is no requirement for a claimant to demonstrate that disability or the effect or impact of the disability is the sole reason for the employer's treatment; instead, proof of the disability or its effect as the effective cause, i.e. one cause out of several causes, is sufficient.

(2) Owing to the fact that the effect, result, or outcome of the disability must concern the claimant's disability, the possibility of perceptual or associative discrimination is excluded.[112]

Meanwhile, as decided in *Akerman-Livingstone v Aster Communities Ltd*,[113] the employer's proportionality defence in section 15(1)(b) of the EA mirrors the same defence in the concept of indirect discrimination in section 19(2), and so recourse to Chapter 10, section 10.2.4, should be made for a wider discussion. However, specifically within this disability context, two points should be stressed. First, it should be noted that if an employer fails to comply with its duty to make reasonable adjustments under sections 20–22, and Schedule 8, it is extremely unlikely that it would succeed in the proportionality defence in section 15(1)(b).[114] Secondly, the decision of the Court of Appeal in *O'Brien v Bolton*

---

[107] EHRC Code, available at https://www.equalityhumanrights.com/sites/default/files/employercode. pdf at para 5.6 (last visited 7 December 2017).

[108] [2015] AC 1399, 1414E per Baroness Hale. However, the Court of Appeal adopted the opposite conclusion and held that a comparator was required in *Williams v Trustees of Swansea University Pension Scheme* [2017] IRLR 882, 888 per Bean LJ.

[109] *Williams v Trustees of Swansea University Pension Scheme* [2017] IRLR 882.

[110] However, there is no requirement to show a causal connection between the disability itself and the negative treatment: *Pnaiser v NHS England* [2016] IRLR 170. The claimant is only required to demonstrate that there was a reason in the employer's mind for the disadvantageous treatment, e.g. the employee's significant absence record which was linked to his disability.

[111] [2015] IRLR 893. However, the employer's subjective reason or motive is not part of the enquiry for the same reason as that explained in the context of direct discrimination claims, on which, see the Supreme Court decision in *R (E) v Governing Body of JFS* [2009] UKSC 15, [2010] 2 AC 728. See also *Pnaiser v NHS England* [2016] IRLR 170.

[112] However, this statement of the law may have to be reconsidered in light of the decisions of the CJEU and the EAT in *CHEZ Razpredelenie Bulgaria AD v Komisia za zashtita ot diskriminatsias* [2015] IRLR 746 and *Thompson v London Central Bus Co.* [2016] IRLR 9 which establish that there is no impediment to a claimant raising an associative indirect discrimination claim and an associative victimization claim.

[113] [2015] AC 1399, 1416C–G per Baroness Hale.

[114] Contrast this with *Monmouthshire County Council v Harris* (UKEAT/0332/14/DA, 23 October 2015).

St Catherine's Academy[115] would appear to dilute the intensity with which the courts and tribunals will scrutinize the conduct of the employer when they apply the proportionality test. In *O'Brien*, Lord Justice Underhill equated the proportionality standard of review with that of the range of reasonable responses standard applicable in the statutory regime of unfair dismissal.[116] This would appear to conflate two radically different standards of review, which somewhat jars against the orthodox understanding of matters,[117] albeit that Lord Justice Underhill's basic point in *O'Brien* that a dismissal that is not a proportionate means of achieving an employer's legitimate aim will inevitably fall outside the range of reasonable responses open to that employer, is a sound one.

Further, simply because it has complied with the reasonable adjustments obligation does not mean that the employer's proportionality defence under section 15(1)(b) will invariably succeed, which may arise where 'the adjustment is unrelated to the particular treatment complained of'.[118] Consider the following hypothetical.

Hypothetical C

Owen Burt ('OB') is employed by Danny's Demolishers Ltd ('DD') at its Liverpool factory. OB suffers from multiple sclerosis and DD makes a reasonable adjustment to his working hours by enabling him to start work at 9:30am instead of 9am. However, after a period of absence comprising three months' sick leave, DD dismisses OB for absenteeism. If OB raises a 'discrimination arising from disability' claim in respect of his dismissal, the prior adjustment of his working hours will be irrelevant in considering the alleged unfavourable treatment, namely OB's dismissal for disability-related sickness absence. As such, notwithstanding that reasonable adjustments were made, there will still be discrimination arising from disability unless the treatment is justified.

However, although the objective justification defence will not function to permit the employer to objectively justify discrimination arising from disability on the basis of previous reasonable adjustments made for the benefit of the employee, the decision of the Court of Appeal in *Williams v Trustees of Swansea University Pension Scheme*[119] demonstrates that the case may not even get to this stage of the enquiry in the first place. In *Williams*, the employer had complied with its duty to make reasonable adjustments by reducing the employee's working hours. The employee subsequently claimed that the reasonable adjustment itself had resulted in discrimination arising from disability since the pension payments to which he was entitled were less than if he had been working full-time. Nevertheless, Lord Justice Bean held that there was no unfavourable treatment suffered by the disabled employee since the relevant reasonable adjustments previously made by the employer could in no way be treated as unfavourable or subjecting the employee to any disadvantage. Since there was no unfavourable treatment, whether the treatment was objectively justifiable or not was irrelevant.

Finally, section 15(2) of the EA addresses the state of the employer's knowledge at the time of the unfavourable treatment. It provides that the employer will not be liable if it did not know, and could not reasonably have been expected to know, that B had the disability. In this context, the statutory embargo in section 60 on pre-employment health and disability questionnaires will be relevant. Whilst the knowledge proviso in section

---

[115] [2017] IRLR 547.   [116] *ibid.*, 555.
[117] See the discussion in Chapter 16, sections 16.3.1 and 16.3.2.
[118] EHRC Code, paras 5.20–5.23.   [119] [2015] ICR 1197.

15 seems to afford an employer an additional defence based on lack of knowledge of disability, this is tempered by the EHRC Code. The EHRC Code interprets the phrase 'could not reasonably have been expected to know' as imposing an obligation on the employer to 'do all they can reasonably be expected to do to find out if a worker has a disability'.[120] This enjoins the employer to take positive steps, rather than 'sit in the sun' and do nothing.

12.3.3 The duty to make reasonable adjustments

If a disabled claimant is placed at a substantial disadvantage in comparison with a non-disabled person by virtue of:

(1) a provision, criterion, or practice ('PCP') adopted by the employer,

(2) a physical feature of the employer's premises, or

(3) the failure to provide an auxiliary aid,

the employer will be obliged to take certain steps to modify the workplace in conformance with its statutory duty to make reasonable adjustments. Such duty is 'central to most, if not all [disability discrimination] claims':[121]

Section 20 Duty to make adjustments

(1) Where this Act imposes a duty to make reasonable adjustments on a person, this section, sections 21 and 22 and the applicable Schedule apply; and for those purposes, a person on whom the duty is imposed is referred to as A.

(2) The duty comprises the following three requirements.

(3) The first requirement is a requirement, where a provision, criterion or practice of A's puts a disabled person at a substantial disadvantage in relation to a relevant matter in comparison with persons who are not disabled, to take such steps as it is reasonable to have to take to avoid the disadvantage.

(4) The second requirement is a requirement, where a physical feature puts a disabled person at a substantial disadvantage in relation to a relevant matter in comparison with persons who are not disabled, to take such steps as it is reasonable to have to take to avoid the disadvantage.

(5) The third requirement is a requirement, where a disabled person would, but for the provision of an auxiliary aid, be put at a substantial disadvantage in relation to a relevant matter in comparison with persons who are not disabled, to take such steps as it is reasonable to have to take to provide the auxiliary aid . . .

Section 21 Failure to comply with duty

(1) A failure to comply with the first, second or third requirement is a failure to comply with a duty to make reasonable adjustments.

(2) A discriminates against a disabled person if A fails to comply with that duty in relation to that person.

In its conception, the duty to make reasonable adjustments is an encapsulation of the 'social' model of disability and also represents the articulation of the substantive model

---

[120] EHRC Code, paras 5.14–5.19.
[121] P. Hughes, 'Disability Discrimination and the Duty to Make Reasonable Adjustments: Recent Developments' (2004) 33 *Industrial Law Journal* 358, 365.

of equality. For example, the duty acknowledges that environmental factors may place obstacles in front of a disabled person's participation within the workplace. Those workplace arrangements may need to be modified and more favourable/asymmetrical treatment afforded to the disabled worker. Meanwhile, the degree of positive discrimination in favour of the disabled person will oscillate in line with (1) the circumstances of each case and (2) what is 'reasonable', rendering the duty sufficiently open-ended, flexible, and, as will become apparent later, far-reaching.

Unlike the concept of indirect discrimination, the duty to make reasonable adjustments is entirely individual, rather than group-based, in nature. Hence the onus is on the claimant to establish that the employer's application of a PCP, a physical feature of the employer's premises, or the absence of an auxiliary aid puts him/her at a *substantial* (rather than *particular*) disadvantage in comparison with persons who are not disabled. Accordingly, it is not incumbent on the claimant to show that disabled persons generally are also placed at the same substantial disadvantage as the claimant. Moreover, in *Hainsworth v MoD*,[122] it was decided that an employee is precluded from raising an associative duty to make a reasonable adjustments claim, i.e. a claim that reasonable adjustments should be made for the benefit of the employee because of his/her association with a disabled person.[123]

There are four steps which ought to be taken by a tribunal or court in deciding whether a reasonable adjustment should be made. First, the nature of the PCP must be identified. Secondly, the relevant physical feature of the premises should be established. The third stage is to determine the nature of the non-disabled comparator (if appropriate), and the final stage is to consider the nature and extent of the substantial disadvantage suffered by the employee.

The first part of the process is to identify the PCP. If we now turn to consideration of the meaning of this expression, the first point to make is that it is apparent that there is no definition in the EA. As such, it can be difficult to pinpoint the correct PCP in a reasonable adjustments claim,[124] particularly where the case concerns the operation of an employer's absence management policy.[125] What is clear is that a PCP will entail a measure of repetitive conduct on the part of the employer. As such, a dismissal will not qualify as a PCP.[126] The concept of PCP has been approached broadly by the tribunals and courts. For instance, it will include not only the employer's selection criteria for a vacant post and the formula or matrix upon which it calculates how much its workers are to be paid, but also the requirements of the disabled worker's job description[127] and common rules applied throughout the workforce,[128] as well as failure to make a reasonable adjustment to avoid a dismissal.[129] The provisions of the EHRC Code also support the view that the notion of PCP should be interpreted broadly:

■ EHRC Code of Practice on Employment

6.10...
[A PCP will include] any formal or informal policies, rules, practices, arrangements or qualifications including one-off decisions and actions . . .

---

[122] [2014] IRLR 728.

[123] Nevertheless, this may be affected by the decisions of the CJEU and the EAT in *CHEZ Razpredelenie Bulgaria AD v Komisia za zashtita ot diskriminatsias* [2015] IRLR 746 and *Thompson v London Central Bus Co.* [2016] IRLR 9 which establish that there is no impediment to a claimant raising an associative indirect discrimination claim and an associative victimization claim.

[124] For example, see *Prospere v Secretary of State for Justice* (UKEAT/0412/14/DA, 30 April 2015).

[125] For such cases, it may be more appropriate for the claim to be raised under section 15 of the EA as opposed to a reasonable adjustments claim under sections 20–22: *General Dynamics Information Technology Ltd v Carranza* [2015] IRLR 43.   [126] *Fox v BA* (UKEAT/0315/14/RN, 22 April 2015).

[127] *Archibald v Fife Council* [2004] UKHL 32, [2004] ICR 954.

[128] *O'Hanlon v Revenue and Customs Commissioners* [2007] ICR 1359.

[129] *Fareham College v Walters* [2009] IRLR 991.

> **Example:**
>
> An employer has a policy that designated car parking spaces are only offered to senior managers. A worker who is not a manager, but has a mobility impairment and needs to park very close to the office, is given a designated car parking space. This is likely to be a reasonable adjustment to the employer's car parking policy.

As for a 'physical feature' of the premises occupied by the employer, further guidance is furnished by section 20(9) and (10) of the EA:

> **Section 20 Duty to make adjustments . . .**
>
> (9) In relation to the second requirement, a reference in this section or an applicable Schedule to avoiding a substantial disadvantage includes a reference to—
>
>   (a) removing the physical feature in question,
>
>   (b) altering it, or
>
>   (c) providing a reasonable means of avoiding it.
>
> (10) A reference in this section, section 21 or 22 or an applicable Schedule . . . to a physical feature is a reference to—
>
>   (a) a feature arising from the design or construction of a building,
>
>   (b) a feature of an approach to, exit from or access to a building,
>
>   (c) a fixture or fitting, or furniture, furnishings, materials, equipment or other chattels, in or on premises, or
>
>   (d) any other physical element or quality . . .

Meanwhile, the EHRC Code suggests that an auxiliary aid 'is something which provides support or assistance to a disabled person [and] can include provision of a specialist piece of equipment such as an adapted keyboard or text to speech software'.[130]

Once the claimant has identified the relevant PCP, physical feature, or auxiliary aid, it must then show a causal link between the application of the PCP, the physical feature, or the absence of the auxiliary aid and the 'substantial disadvantage' which he/she has suffered. Section 212(1) of the EA defines 'substantial' as something more than minor or trivial. Moreover, the decision of the EAT in *Paul v National Probation Service*[131] establishes that it is insufficient for the claimant to simply point towards his/her disability and argue that that itself constitutes the substantial disadvantage. The claimant must also identify the nature and extent of the substantial disadvantage,[132] and it has been held that a disabled worker may be substantially disadvantaged by the adoption of a PCP even though he/she him/herself was not required to comply with it.[133] Likewise, where an employee was subjected to redundancy selection criteria based on length of service, absences, skill set, productivity (including mistake levels), flexibility, and discretionary effort, it was held that the use of selection criteria evaluating productivity and accuracy put the employee at a substantial disadvantage.[134] In *Chawla v Hewlett Packard Ltd*,[135]

---

[130] EHRC Code, para 6.13.   [131] [2004] IRLR 190.

[132] *Environment Agency v Rowan* [2008] ICR 218.

[133] *Roberts v North West Ambulance Service* [2012] ICR D.14.

[134] *Dominique v Toll Global Forwarding Ltd* (UKEAT/0308/13/LA, 7 May 2014).

[135] [2015] IRLR 356.

the email and intranet access of an employee who was off on long-term sick leave was blocked for security reasons and the employee did not receive email communications about share schemes. This was held to be material enough to amount to a substantial disadvantage. These decisions can be contrasted with *Secretary of State for Work and Pensions v Higgins*.[136] Here, it was held that there was no substantial disadvantage when the employer refused to extend or review a phased return to work that it had furnished previously to the employee, since there was no evidence of the substantial disadvantage that the review or extension would prevent.

What is clear is that the expression 'substantial disadvantage' entails the claimant subjecting his/her situation to a comparison exercise. However, unlike direct or indirect disability discrimination, 'there is no requirement to identify a comparator or comparator group whose circumstances are the same or nearly the same as the disabled person's'.[137] In light of the absence of a 'like for like' comparison, the tribunals and courts have adopted a purposive approach to the nature of the appropriate comparator. In *Archibald v Fife Council*,[138] it was held that the comparator is not confined to non-disabled people doing the same job, but rather the non-disabled generally, which means that 'the duty is triggered where an employee becomes so disabled that she can no longer meet the requirements of her job description'.[139] In *Smith v Churchill Stairlifts*,[140] Kay LJ applied a gloss to the approach in *Archibald* to the effect that the proper comparator is readily identified by reference to the disadvantage caused by the relevant PCP:

■ *Smith v Churchill Stairlifts* [2006] ICR 524, 538B–D

[The headnote to the case sets forth the facts as follows:] The applicant suffered from lumbar spondylosis which made walking and lifting objects difficult. He explained his disability when he applied for a position as a salesman with the respondent company, which entailed demonstrating in a client's home a radiator cabinet. The applicant was offered a place on a training course, successful completion of which would lead to employment as a salesman. The company subsequently decided that salesmen would be required to transport a full-sized sample radiator cabinet as a sales aid and that the applicant would be unable to carry one. Accordingly, it withdrew the offer of the training place. When the company refused to consider the applicant's request to work for a trial period on a commission only basis and to use as a sales aid a modified cabinet made by him which was lighter and easier to lift, the applicant brought a complaint of disability discrimination . . . The employment tribunal found that the duty . . . to make reasonable adjustments did not arise, in relation to the requirement to carry the cabinet, as the applicant had not been placed at a substantial disadvantage in comparison with persons who were not disabled, because the majority of the population would have had difficulty carrying the cabinet . . .

Kay LJ:

. . . it is apparent from each of the speeches in *Archibald's* case that the proper comparator is readily identified by reference to the disadvantage caused by the relevant [PCP]. On this basis, the approach of the majority of the employment tribunal is not sustainable. Even if the only relevant [PCP] had been the requirement to carry a full-sized radiator cabinet, the proper comparators

---

[136] [2014] ICR 341.

[137] EHRC Code, para 6.16; section 23 of the EA does not apply in the context of the duty to make reasonable adjustments.

[138] [2004] UKHL 32, [2004] ICR 954.

[139] *Archibald v Fife Council* [2004] UKHL 32, [2004] ICR 954, 972A–D per Baroness Hale. See also *Fareham College v Walters* [2009] IRLR 991, 998 per Cox J, who stated that 'the comparator group is other employees of the [employer] who are not disabled and who are able forthwith to attend work and to carry out the essential tasks required of them in their post'.   [140] [2006] ICR 524.

would still have been the six successful candidates who were subject to the requirement but not disadvantaged thereby because they were not rejected as a result. However, if (as I have held to be so) the relevant PCP included susceptibility to withdrawal of the offer, the proper comparators were the nine people who were admitted to the course. Did the [application of the PCP] as a whole place the applicant at a substantial disadvantage in comparison with persons who were not disabled? In my judgment, there is only one answer to this question and that is in the affirmative.

Hence the manner in which the relevant comparative exercise is structured renders it relatively straightforward for a claimant to establish a disadvantage.[141] The key question to be posed is whether the PCP puts the disabled person at a substantial disadvantage in comparison with a non-disabled person and the fact that they were both treated the same does not remove the disadvantage if the PCP has a harsher impact on the disabled or a category of them, than it did on the able-bodied. Once the comparator is identified, it is not open to the employer to adopt a 'bastard' defence, i.e. to argue that no substantial disadvantage can be established on the basis that the comparator would have been treated just as badly as the claimant.[142]

Once the claimant has established a causal connection between the substantial disadvantage and the PCP, physical feature, or failure to provide an auxiliary aid, the employer's obligation to make reasonable adjustments is triggered. As such, the statutory duty is clearly 'reactive' in character in the employment context: paragraphs 2(2)(c) and 20 of Schedule 8 to the EA only require a substantial disadvantage to be removed if it is suffered by an 'interested disabled person'. As such, there is no obligation on the employer to anticipate working practices, policies, or criteria, or physical features of its estate which might put disabled persons at a disadvantage and then remove them.

We now turn our attention to what might constitute a 'reasonable' adjustment. In the academic literature, Waddington has argued that the UK adopts a dual approach to the notion of 'reasonableness' so that it is taken to 'convey both that the accommodation must be effective and [secondly,] that it must not impose significant inconvenience or cost on the employer'.[143] Nonetheless, certain scholars have subjected the formula of 'reasonable' adjustments to a trenchant critique on the basis that it is a construct which is insufficiently radical, uncertain, and inegalitarian:

■ A. Lawson, *Disability and Equality Law in Britain: The Law of Reasonable Adjustments* (Oxford, Hart Publishing, 2008) 279–84

5.1 Insufficiently Radical . . .

A number of proponents of disability equality have drawn attention to the relatively limited nature of the concept of reasonable adjustments or accommodation. This concept, it is argued, is premised on the acceptance of a non-disabled norm from which some departures will be required in order to accommodate the needs of people with impairments. Because such departures will be required only if they are deemed to be 'reasonable', they will necessarily be modest and limited. A departure from normal practice will not be deemed reasonable, and therefore not required, if it would inflict an undue level of hardship on the duty-bearer . . .

[141] *Griffiths v SSWP* [2017] ICR 160, 176H–177B per Elias LJ.
[142] *Eagle Place Services Ltd v Rudd* [2010] IRLR 486, 496 per Serota J.
[143] L. Waddington, 'When it is Reasonable for Europeans to be Confused: Understanding when a Disability Accommodation is "Reasonable" from a Comparative Perspective' (2008) 29 *Comparative Labor Law & Policy Journal* 317, 339.

5.2 Uncertain . . .

[Employers are] under no obligation to make an adjustment which is unreasonable. The divide between reasonable and unreasonable thus separates cases in which failure to make an adjustment will result in potentially expensive liability for discrimination from those in which it will be regarded as entirely legitimate. The point at which this divide is located, however, may be extremely difficult to predict and is likely to vary from case to case in accordance with the particular factual scenarios in question . . . Predictably, therefore concern has been expressed about the uncertainty inherent in the notion of reasonable adjustment or accommodation . . .

5.3 The Inegalitarian Tendency of Reasonableness . . .

There is a powerful body of literature devoted to the exposure of the inegalitarian impact which the reasonable person . . . has had on the various areas of law in which s/he has operated. The reasonable person is often endowed with qualities of averageness or ordinariness—attributes which are inherently conservative and therefore unlikely to yield results which alter or challenge the status quo . . . The averageness of the reasonable person would thus appear to render him an inappropriate arbiter of delicate equality-related issues. Too often it will endow him with the very prejudices and stereotypical notions which equality law was intended to challenge . . .

However, the anxieties expressed in this extract concerning the aptness of the reasonableness prescription have not been borne out in the case law. Indeed, some of the decisions have required the employer's practices to be adapted to such an extent that they may be labelled as genuinely radical. It has been recognized judicially that the duty may enjoin an employer 'to depart from the usual arrangements in particular circumstances to meet the needs of particular disabled employees',[144] i.e. to deviate from normal working practices specifically for a disabled worker. This can be partly attributed to the consistency with which the judiciary have clung to the notion that the reasonableness of an adjustment must be approached on the basis of an objective test.[145] As such, rather than the employer's perspective, it is 'the view of the employment tribunal of what is reasonable that matters'.[146] This formulation means that if an employee refuses to co-operate with the employer when the adjustments that the latter suggests are reasonable on the basis of an objective evaluation of the circumstances, the employer will have discharged its duty notwithstanding that it is the employee's subjective opinion that they are not reasonable.[147]

One of the most high profile reasonable adjustments cases of late was *First Group Ltd v Paulley*.[148] First Group had a policy that if the disabled bay at the front of the bus was occupied by an able-bodied person e.g. by a mother with a pram, then the bus driver was obliged to ask that person to move but was not required to do any more if they refused. However the Supreme Court held that further reasonable steps ought to be taken by the bus driver, such as persuading the able-bodied passenger to move or not moving the bus until space was made for the disabled person. The lesson borne from this case is that some reasonable adjustments will require able-bodied persons to accept restrictions they might not appreciate or like. This reaffirms that disability may trump other protected characteristics when seen from the perspective of the statutory duty to make reasonable adjustments, i.e. enjoin employers to afford preferential treatment to the disabled. Here disability arguably trumped the characteristic of sex as

---

[144] See *Heathrow Express Operating Co. Ltd v Jenkins* [2007] All ER (D) 144 (February), para 41 per Elias J.

[145] See *Collins v Royal National Theatre Board Ltd* [2004] 2 All ER 851; *Smith v Churchills Stairlifts plc* [2006] ICR 524, 539C–E per Kay LJ.

[146] *Smith v Churchills Stairlifts plc* [2006] ICR 524, 539G per Kay LJ. However, the tribunals and courts have resisted finding that the employer's failure to undertake a risk assessment or to consult the claimant about the adjustment that might be made will necessarily be a breach of duty (*Tarbuck v Sainsbury's Supermarkets Ltd* [2006] IRLR 664), albeit that such failures are likely to result in such a finding (*Project Management Institute v Latif* [2007] IRLR 579), on which, see EHRC Code, para 6.32.

[147] *Makuchova v Guoman Hotel Management (UK) Ltd* (UKEAT/0279/14/DA, 11 December 2014).

[148] [2017] IRLR 258.

mothers with children may have to fold up their buggies and sit elsewhere on the bus. It is easy to see how this might be particularly contentious in the workplace.

A number of factors will be taken into account in establishing whether an adjustment is reasonable. For this purpose, it is absolutely essential that the nature of the step should be identified very clearly[149] and the reasonableness of that potential adaptation will then be evaluated. For obvious reasons, one of the key matters will be the financial cost to the employer of adopting the modification and whether it will impose a disproportionate burden. In *Cordell v Foreign and Commonwealth Office*,[150] the EAT provided some useful guidance on the issues to consider in this context:

■ Cordell v FCO [2012] ICR 280, 291H–292B

Underhill J (President):

... the relevant considerations may include (and we are not intending to be exhaustive): the size of any budget dedicated to reasonable adjustments (though this cannot be conclusive . . .); what the employer has chosen to spend in what might be thought to be comparable situations; what other employers are prepared to spend; and any collective agreement or other indication of what level of expenditure is regarded as appropriate by representative organisations. But such considerations can only help up to a point: even when they have been identified, they can be of no more than suggestive or supportive value . . .Ultimately there remains no objective measure for calibrating the value of one kind of expenditure against another.

In *Cordell*, the total cost of providing the necessary adjustments amounted to an annual cost of over £1 million (which was five times Ms Cordell's salary), would have taken up a large part of the employer's disability budget, and exceeded the next largest adjustment made for an employee by £200,000. On this ground, the EAT upheld the tribunal's rejection of Ms Cordell's claim that the employer had breached its reasonable adjustments duty. Hence what is reasonable will depend on the financial implications for the employer,[151] and if there is a perception that making an adjustment will impose too heavy a burden, the employer will be exonerated.

The EHRC Code stipulates that the other factors to be considered include the following:

■ EHRC Code of Practice on Employment

6.28 . . .

• whether taking any particular steps would be effective in preventing the substantial disadvantage;

• the practicability of the step;[152]

• the . . . extent of any disruption caused;

• the extent of the employer's financial or other resources;

• the availability to the employer of financial or other assistance to help make an adjustment (such as advice through Access to Work); and

• the type and size of the employer.

---

[149] *HM Prison Service v Johnson* [2007] IRLR 951.   [150] [2012] ICR 280.

[151] Where the employer is a school maintained by a local education authority, difficult issues may arise in identifying whether it is the former or latter's financial resources which are relevant, e.g. *Murphy v Slough Borough Council* [2005] ICR 721.

[152] See also *O'Hanlon v Revenue and Customs Commissioners* [2007] ICR 1359, where the financial burden imposed by the adjustment for employers generally was held to be relevant.

Ultimately, in applying these factors, the conclusion reached pursuant to the reasonableness standard is highly context-dependent.[153] Further, the application of the objective reasonableness standard affords a tribunal or court the power to subject the managerial prerogative to a particularly intense measure of scrutiny. This exacting standard of scrutiny complements the notion that the statutory duty may encompass positive discrimination in favour of the disabled worker,[154] a fact which is highlighted by the case law. For example, depending on the facts of a case, a reasonable adjustment may consist of offering a disabled employee the opportunity to fill an existing vacancy in preference to other applicants by waiving its standard requirement for a competitive interview. For example, in *Archibald v Fife Council*,[155] after a routine surgical procedure, a road sweeper employed by the council became virtually unable to walk, with the effect that she could no longer perform the requirements of her post. She applied for a number of sedentary office-based jobs, but was unsuccessful and was eventually dismissed. In the circumstances of the case, the House of Lords arrived at the decision that the employer's statutory obligation entailed transferring the employee into an existing vacancy at the same or a higher grade in preference to other more suitably qualified candidates.

One might argue that *Archibald v Fife Council* stretched the duty too far, as the employer was effectively bound to promote the employee to a position for which she was unsuitable. This concern is reflected in the case law. For example, in *Wade v Sheffield Hallam University*,[156] it was held that it was not reasonable for the employer to move a disabled employee on long-term sick leave to a vacant role without the need for her to undertake a competitive interview, particularly where the employer genuinely believed the individual would be unsuitable for the post. The similarity between the facts of *Wade* and *Archibald* but the divergent results essentially underscore the point that what is reasonable is dependent on the facts and circumstances of each case.

Other reasonable adjustments have included:

(1) allocating a car parking place to a disabled employee;[157]

(2) offering a 'job swap' whereby a non-disabled employee was transferred from post A to post B to enable the disabled employee to fill post A;[158]

(3) 'creating' a vacancy/new job for the disabled worker in substitution for his/her existing post;[159]

(4) paying full contractual sick pay to a disabled worker;[160]

(5) paying for private psychiatric services and counselling for an employee who was suffering from a severe depressive episode triggered by work-related stress;[161]

(6) altering the duties of a manager returning to work subsequent to a bout of depression to enable him/her to cope without stress;[162]

---

[153] *Chief Constable of South Yorkshire Police v Jelic* [2010] IRLR 744.

[154] See D. Cabrelli, 'The Hierarchy of Differing Behavioural Standards of Review in Labour Law' (2011) 40 *Industrial Law Journal* 146, 164, and 167.　　[155] [2004] UKHL 32, [2004] ICR 954.

[156] [2013] Eq LR 951.　　[157] *Environment Agency v Donnelly* [2014] Eq LR 13.

[158] See *Chief Constable of South Yorkshire Police v Jelic* [2010] IRLR 744.

[159] *Southampton City College v Randall* [2006] IRLR 18; *Chief Constable of South Yorkshire Police v Jelic* [2010] IRLR 744; cf. *Tarbuck v Sainsbury's Supermarkets Ltd* [2006] IRLR 664.

[160] *Nottinghamshire County Council v Meikle* [2004] 4 All ER 97. However, as noted in *O'Hanlon v Revenue and Customs Commissioners* [2007] ICR 1359, it will be a rare case where a reasonable adjustment is held to enjoin an employer to continue paying full salary when a disabled worker is off on sick leave. Furthermore, where a contractual or statutory sick pay scheme terminates, it will not often be a reasonable adjustment to extend its operation, on which, see *Royal Bank of Scotland plc v Ashton* [2011] ICR 632.　　[161] *Croft Vets Ltd v Butcher* [2013] Eq LR 1170.

[162] *Greenhof v Barnsley Metropolitan Council* [2006] IRLR 98.

(7) adjusting the rules of an absence management policy where the employee's disability makes them more likely to be absent from work than able-bodied colleagues;[163] and

(8) protecting the higher level of pay of a disabled employee when subsequently allocated to a less well-paid position.[164]

However, there are limits. In *Newcastle upon Tyne Hospitals NHS Foundation Trust v Bagley*,[165] the EAT decided that topping up a disabled employee's part-time earnings during a phased return to work would not amount to a reasonable adjustment. Likewise, assessing the alternatives to dismissal in the case of an employee who had been convicted of theft, dangerous driving, and battery was not a reasonable adjustment in the circumstances.[166] It has also been ruled that exempting an employee from the requirements of the employer's absence management policy did not constitute a reasonable adjustment where the employee had a protracted history of intermittent absences from work, followed by a long-term absence.[167] Meanwhile, in *Salford NHS Primary Care Trust v Smith*,[168] the argument that a career break would constitute a reasonable adjustment was rejected on the ground that it would not afford the claimant a right to return to work. Hence reasonable adjustments are concerned with modifications to working practices that will remove[169] the substantial disadvantage caused by the PCP, physical feature, or absence of the auxiliary aid *and enable a disabled claimant to continue in his/her post*. On the same basis, it has been held that the failure of an employer to facilitate a disabled worker's ill-health retirement application was not a breach of duty.[170]

It should also be stressed that the EHRC Code provides an illustrative list of other adjustments which may potentially be considered reasonable:

■ EHRC Code of Practice on Employment

6.33 . . .

Making adjustments to premises . . .

Providing information in accessible formats . . . Allocating some of the disabled person's duties to another worker . . .

Altering the disabled worker's hours of work or training . . .

Assigning the disabled worker to a different place of work or training or arranging home working[171] . . .

Allowing the disabled worker to be absent during working or training hours for rehabilitation, assessment or treatment . . .

Giving, or arranging for, training or mentoring (whether for the disabled person or any other worker) . . .

Acquiring or modifying equipment . . .

Modifying procedures for testing or assessment . . .

Providing a reader or interpreter . . .

---

[163] *Griffiths v SSWP* [2017] ICR 160.

[164] *G4S Cash Solutions (UK) Ltd v Powell* [2016] IRLR 820.   [165] [2012] Eq LR 634.

[166] *Howorth v North Lancashire Teaching Primary Care NHS Trust* (UKEAT/0294/13/RN, 22 August 2014).

[167] *Jennings v Barts and the London NHS Trust* [2013] Eq LR 326. Contrast this with *Griffiths v SSWP* [2017] ICR 160 and *HMRC Commissioners v Whiteley* (UKEAT/0581/12/MC, 12 May 2013).

[168] [2011] Eq LR 119.

[169] At the very least, there must be a real prospect that the adjustment will remove the substantial disadvantage: *Leeds Teaching Hospital NHS Trust v Foster* [2011] Eq LR 1075.

[170] *Tameside Hospitals NHS Foundation Trust v Mylott* (UKEAT/0352/09/DM, 11 March 2011).

[171] Cf. *Environment Agency v Rowan* [2008] ICR 218.

Providing supervision or other support . . .

Employing a support worker to assist a disabled worker . . .

Modifying disciplinary or grievance procedures for a disabled worker . . .

Adjusting redundancy selection criteria for a disabled worker . . .

Modifying performance-related pay arrangements for a disabled worker . . .

A particularly important issue is whether the employer can mount a defence to a reasonable adjustments claim on the basis that it did not know that the claimant was disabled. Here, a distinction must be drawn between disabled persons who are (1) applicants or potential applicants for a vacancy and (2) existing workers. In the case of the former, paragraph 20(1)(a) of Schedule 8 to the EA directs that the employer will not be liable if it did not know, and could not reasonably be expected to know, that the claimant was disabled.[172] Once again, this underscores the entirely reactive nature of the duty. It is also instructive that section 60 of the EA imposes an embargo (subject to certain exceptions)[173] on the employer making enquiries about the disability and general health of applicants. As noted by Hepple, the 'reason for this provision is that pre-employment questionnaires can be a powerful deterrent for potential applicants who are disabled, often leading them to hide their disability or not to apply'.[174] As for the state of the employer's knowledge in the case of existing workers, paragraph 20(1)(b) of Schedule 8 to the EA provides that the statutory duty is triggered if the employer knew, and could be reasonably expected to know, that the claimant is (1) disabled *and* (2) likely to be placed at a substantial disadvantage by the application of the PCP, physical feature, or the absence of an auxiliary aid. In the case of *Secretary of State for Work and Pensions v Alam*,[175] the EAT supplied further assistance on how this knowledge requirement will operate in practice:

■ *Secretary of State for Work and Pensions v Alam* [2010] ICR 665, 671F–672H

Lady Smith:

. . . it seems to us clear, as a matter of statutory interpretation and giving the language of those provisions their ordinary meaning, that to ascertain whether the exemption from the obligation to make reasonable adjustments provided for by [sections 20 and 21 of the EA] applies, two questions arise. They are: (1) did the employer know both that the employee was disabled and that his disability was liable to affect him in the manner set out in [section 20(3), (4) or (5)]? If the answer to that question is: 'no' then there is a second question; namely (2) ought the employer to have known both that the employee was disabled and that his disability was liable to affect him in the manner set out in [section 20(3), (4) or (5)]? If the answer to that second question is: 'no', then [paragraph 20(1)(b) of Schedule 8 to the EA] does not impose any duty to make reasonable adjustments. Thus, the employer will qualify for the exemption from any duty to make reasonable adjustments if *both* those questions are answered in the negative. That interpretation takes proper account not only of the use, twice, of the word 'and' but also of the comma after 'know' . . .

---

[172] For example, see *Ridout v TC Group* [1998] IRLR 628.
[173] See section 60(6) of the EA.
[174] B. Hepple, *Equality: The New Legal Framework*, 2nd edition (Oxford, Hart Publishing, 2014) 96.
[175] [2010] ICR 665.

12.3.4 Indirect disability discrimination

Prior to the coming into force of the EA, there was no separate statutory tort of indirect disability discrimination. This was thought to be anomalous, particularly in light of the fact that the three modes of tackling disability discrimination were all individual-oriented. For example, if a claimant were successful in his/her claim for (1) direct disability discrimination, (2) discrimination arising from disability, or (3) a breach of the duty to make reasonable adjustments, this would be entirely reactive and could conceivably only operate to the benefit of the individual claimant, rather than the disabled group at large of which he/she formed part. Hence there was a lacuna in the law insofar as there was no statutory machinery enjoining employers to address PCPs, physical features, etc. which might put disabled persons *generally as a group* at some form of disadvantage. Of course, whilst there is some merit in the argument that the concept of indirect discrimination might not be the most fitting means of addressing group disadvantage 'because disabilities are so many and so varied',[176] this can be addressed to some extent by a provision such as section 6(3)(b) of the EA, which requires the 'group' to share the same disability as the claimant. For example, if the claimant suffers from multiple sclerosis (MS), then the group sharing the protected characteristic of disability for the purposes of section 19 will be a group of individuals suffering from MS. Of course, this will result in difficulties and very small pools for comparison where the disability of the claimant is one which is rare indeed. In essence, however, as noted in the following extract, the function of the concept of indirect disability discrimination is to dislodge practices which entrench barriers experienced by a group of disabled workers:

■ A. Lawson, 'Disability and Employment in the Equality Act 2010: Opportunities Seized, Lost and Generated' (2011) 40 *Industrial Law Journal* 359, 376

> Given its group dimension, indirect discrimination is better placed than reactive reasonable adjustment to challenge and break down systemic barriers. In addition, its extension to the arena of disability employment law carries the important symbolic message that disability discrimination is not an entirely individualised affair but one that demands scrutiny of general policies and organisational structures and practices. Attention has been drawn in other jurisdictions to the importance of exploiting the potential of indirect discrimination or disparate impact provisions as well as to the fact that they often appear to be little used.

On this basis, one can perceive the introduction of the concept of indirect discrimination as an additional step in the direction of the 'social' model, since the mischief here is to remove societal and environmental factors which impede the ability of an entire group of disabled workers from participating fully in working life.

Alongside the absence of a group element, the duty to make reasonable adjustments differs from indirect disability discrimination[177] in two other respects, both of which are concerned with the gateway criteria for the operation of these concepts. For example, the concept of indirect disability discrimination will only be engaged where the employer adopts a PCP, whereas the reasonable adjustments duty arises where (1) a PCP that is

---

[176] M. Connolly, *Discrimination Law*, 2nd edition (London, Sweet & Maxwell, 2011) 414. See also *Lewisham Borough Council v Malcolm* [2008] UKHL 43, [2008] 1 AC 1399, 1437H–1438B per Lord Brown.

[177] It should be stressed that the concept of indirect disability discrimination will function in identical terms to the standard indirect discrimination model under section 19 of the EA. Accordingly, reference to Chapter 10, section 10.2.4, should be made here in order to complete the discussion.

adopted, (2) a particular physical feature, or (3) the failure to provide an auxiliary aid gives rise to a form of disadvantage. Moreover, indirect disability discrimination will be established where the claimant and the disabled group of which he/she forms part are subjected to a 'particular' disadvantage. This can be contrasted with the duty to make reasonable adjustments where the threshold criterion is 'substantial' disadvantage.

Reflection points

1. Compare and contrast the legal concepts of direct disability discrimination and 'discrimination arising from disability'. To what extent does the decision of the Court of Appeal in *Stockton on Tees Borough Council v Aylott* conflate the two concepts?

2. Are you of the opinion that the manner in which the judiciary have approached the statutory duty to make reasonable adjustments has overstepped the mark, imposing unwarranted disproportionate burdens on employers? Give reasons for your answer.

3. Compare and contrast the employer's duty to make reasonable adjustments and the concept of indirect disability discrimination.

4. Critically evaluate the employer's duty to make reasonable adjustments.

 For additional reading on prohibited conduct and the duty to make reasonable adjustments, visit the Online Resources for this book at www.oup.com/uk/cabrelli3e/

12.4 FINAL ASSESSMENT OF DISABILITY DISCRIMINATION LAW

One of the main deficiencies in the disability discrimination architecture is its functional reliance on managerial reaction to, rather than anticipation of, disadvantage. The reactive nature of the obligation in the context of employment and the workplace is distinguishable from its anticipatory counterpart in Schedule 4 to the EA, which applies to premises generally. The anticipatory obligation is engaged without the necessity for any intervention on the part of a claimant, thus enjoining an employer to apply its mind to (1) those PCPs or features which environmentally disenfranchise or impose constraints on disabled workers and then (2) removing or modifying them. Lawson has argued that[178] the latter possesses greater transformative potential and provides much greater scope to drive forward systemic change to the benefit of the disabled.[179] Indeed, the promulgation of both a reactive duty, to ensure an effective response to an individual's needs on a case-by-case basis, and an anticipatory one, to target provisions which may affect disabled persons generally, would undoubtedly advance the cause of disabled employees in the workplace. However, as the law stands in relation to employment, it is principally the reactive duty that is currently propounded under the EA, albeit that there is an argument that the concept of indirect disability discrimination harbours some promise insofar as it may function to encourage management to undertake risk assessments and remove structural barriers for the disabled without the need for individuals to engage in prior litigation.

[178] A. Lawson, 'Disability and Employment in the Equality Act 2010: Opportunities Seized, Lost and Generated' (2011) 40 *Industrial Law Journal* 359, 369.

[179] See also S. Fredman, 'Breaking the Mould: Equality as a Proactive Duty' in N. Countouris and M. Freedland (eds), *Resocialising Europe in a Time of Crisis* (Cambridge, CUP, 2013) 138 for an examination of more proactive initiatives in the context of anti-discrimination law more generally.

CHAPTER THIRTEEN

PART-TIME AND FIXED-TERM WORK

13.1 CONTEXTUAL ANALYSIS OF PART-TIME AND FIXED-TERM WORK

This chapter is devoted to an examination of the measures that have been adopted to strike a balance between the twin policy objectives of labour market flexibility and enhanced job quality in the context of part-time work and fixed-term work. This will entail an evaluation of the equal treatment regimes contained in the Part-Time Workers (Prevention of Less Favourable Treatment) Regulations ('PTWR')[1] and the Fixed-Term Employees (Prevention of Less Favourable Treatment) Regulations ('FTER').[2] In doing so, we will address the Framework Agreement and Directive on Part-time Work ('PTWD')[3] and the Agreement on Fixed-term Work and the Fixed-term Work Directive ('FTWD').[4]

13.1.1 Contextual and historical introduction to part-time and fixed-term work

If we consult the statistics compiled by the Office for National Statistics, a picture is presented of the prevalence of part-time and fixed-term work in the UK labour market. An examination of labour market statistics shows that from September 2017 to November 2017, there were 32.21 million people in employment in the UK and 8.55 million persons were working on a part-time basis, equating to approximately 26.59 per cent of the entire workforce.[5] The incidence of part-time work in the UK 'expanded in the postwar era . . . grew steadily [from] the 1940s then increased exponentially from the early 1970s, from 15 per cent of the workforce in 1971'.[6] Meanwhile, EUROSTAT statistics narrate

---

[1] SI 2000/1551.   [2] SI 2002/2034.   [3] Directive 97/81/EC (OJ 1998 L14/9).
[4] Directive 99/70/EC (OJ 1999 L175/43).
[5] See Office of National Statistics, *Labour Market Statistic Bulletin* (January 2018), available at https://www.ons.gov.uk/employmentandlabourmarket/peopleinwork/employmentandemployeetypes/bulletins/uklabourmarket/january2018 at page 1 and Table 3 (last visited 16 February 2018).
[6] D. McCann, *Regulating Flexible Work* (Oxford, OUP, 2008) 56. Writer's annotations are shown in square brackets throughout this chapter.

that approximately 1.545 million individuals were working on a temporary basis in the UK labour market in 2016.[7] These figures for part-time and fixed-term work are astonishingly high and are a testament to the general flexibility of the labour market in the UK. The flexibility which accompanies part-time and fixed-term positions presents certain positive advantages. For example, it enables workers to secure working hours that are tailored around their domestic and social responsibilities.[8] It is also argued that part-time and fixed-term work both serve as a gateway or stepping stone for the unemployed into full-time permanent employment in the labour market.[9] By the same token, part-time and fixed-term working patterns are also attractive to employers insofar as they generate cost efficiencies: employers can deploy part-time and fixed-term workers when needed, in order to react to rises and falls in the demand for their products or services.[10]

In Chapter 4, we noted how both part-time and fixed-term employment are two forms of atypical,[11] flexible working arrangements.[12] On the negative side, non-standard employment such as part-time and fixed-term work also poses certain challenges. Such working patterns tend to be associated with precarious, low-pay,[13] low-status, and low-satisfaction jobs, with less job security, fewer benefits, lower productivity,[14] and more disadvantageous working conditions than full-time permanent roles.[15] Such jobs are predominantly occupied by single women with childcare and household responsibilities, younger people entering the labour market for the first time, and elderly workers making their final excursion into the labour market. For example, the statistical data reveals that approximately 6.291 million of the 8.55 million part-time workers in the UK are female, i.e. approximately 73.57 per cent.[16] Meanwhile, 835,400 of the approximate 1.545 million fixed-term workers are women, which equates to around 54.07 per cent.[17] Indeed, it has historically been the case that the majority of part-time positions have been filled

---

[7] See http://appsso.eurostat.ec.europa.eu/nui/submitViewTableAction.do (last visited 24 September 2017).

[8] See A. Iseke, 'The Part-Time Job Satisfaction Puzzle: Different Types of Job Discrepancies and the Moderating Effect of Family Importance' (2014) 52 *British Journal of Industrial Relations* 445.

[9] See A. Booth, M. Francesconi, and J. Frank, 'Temporary Jobs: Stepping Stones or Dead Ends?' (2002) 112 *Economic Journal* F189–F213; and D. McVicar, M. Wooden, F. Leung, and N. Li, 'Work-Related Training and the Probability of Transitioning from Non-Permanent to Permanent Employment' (2016) 54 *British Journal of Industrial Relations* 623. For a critique of the 'stepping stones' argument, see A. Davies, 'Regulating Atypical Work: Beyond Equality' in N. Countouris and M. Freedland (eds), *Resocialising Europe in a Time of Crisis* (Cambridge, CUP, 2013) 238–42.

[10] DTI, *Success at Work: Protecting Vulnerable Workers, Supporting Good Employers* (London, HMSO, 2006) 16.

[11] They are atypical in the sense that one of the following elements will be absent: (1) a full-time contract (2) with a single employer (3) for an indefinite period of time to (4) perform personal services (5) at the employer's premises (6) irrespective of whether the employer has sufficient work to provide the employee or not.

[12] See A. Ludera-Ruszel, 'Typical or Atypical: Reflections on the Atypical Forms of Employment Illustrated with the Example of a Fixed-Term Employment Contract—A Comparative Study of Selected European Countries' (2016) 37 *Comparative Labor Law & Policy Journal* 407, 409–11.

[13] The literature refers to a 'part-time pay penalty': see S. Connolly and M. Gregory, 'The Part-time Pay Penalty: Earnings Trajectories of British Women' (2009) 61 (Suppl: 1) *Oxford Economic Papers* i76–97; and A. Manning and B. Petrongolo, 'The Part-Time Pay Penalty for Women in Britain' (2008) 118 *Economic Journal* F28–51.

[14] M. Damiani, F. Pompei, and A. Ricci, 'Temporary Employment Protection and Productivity Growth in EU Economies' (2016) 155(4) *International Labour Review* 587.

[15] See S. Connolly and M. Gregory, 'Moving down: Women's Part-Time Work and Occupational Change in Britain 1991–2001' (2008) *Economic Journal* F52, F72; D. McCann, *Regulating Flexible Work* (Oxford, OUP, 2008) 104–5.

[16] See Office for National Statistics, Labour Market Statistics, (January 2018), available at https://www.ons.gov.uk/employmentandlabourmarket/peopleinwork/employmentandemployeetypes/bulletins/uklabourmarket/january2018 at Table 3 (last visited 16 February 2018); M. Bell, 'Achieving the Objectives of the Part-Time Work Directive? Revisiting the Part-Time Workers Regulations' (2011) 40 *Industrial Law Journal* 254, 268–9.

[17] See http://appsso.eurostat.ec.europa.eu/nui/submitViewTableAction.do (last visited 24 September 2017).

by women, who command lower earnings than male workers.[18] There is also some evidence to suggest that there are divergences in the skill levels of part-time and full-time workers.[19]

The correlation between (a) part-time/fixed-term work and (b) female labour participation opens up the possibility that female part-time and fixed-term workers might be able to challenge preconditions to statutory employment protection on the ground that they constitute indirect sex discrimination. For example, in the case of *R v Secretary of State for Employment, ex parte Equal Opportunities Commission*,[20] qualifying thresholds for access to unfair dismissal protection based on higher length of service for part-time workers were challenged in the courts. The thresholds were two years of continuous employment for employees who worked for 16 or more hours per week, and five years of continuous employment for employees who worked between 8 and 16 hours per week. The argument raised by the part-time workers was that considerably more women than men worked part-time and, as such, the thresholds discriminated against women. The House of Lords decided that the Secretary of State had failed to establish that the thresholds were a proportionate means of achieving the social policy objective of increasing the availability of part-time work. As such, it was held that the relevant domestic legal provisions were incompatible with EU sex discrimination law. The Government's response to the decision of the House of Lords was to repeal these provisions.[21] However, the pressing of the law of indirect sex discrimination into service as a means of affording protection to part-time workers could never be treated as some form of absolute panacea. Gender equality laws do not offer a wholesale solution to the problems experienced by part-time and fixed-term workers, since, as a conceptual device, they will inevitably fail to safeguard their interests on a uniform basis. The following extract from Barnard explains the rationale for this in the context of part-timers, but the point made is of equal application to fixed-term workers:

■ C. Barnard, *EU Employment Law*, 4th edition (Oxford, OUP, 2012) 431

> The drawback with the indirect discrimination approach to dealing with less favourable treatment of part-time workers is that it is dependent on the part-timers showing that the rule actually [subjected female part-timers to a particular disadvantage in comparison with] . . . men. Thus, female part-time workers have to show disparate impact; male part-time workers cannot make the claim at all. In this respect, the [PTWD] represented an important step forward in terms of protection for all part-time workers, both male and female.[22]

The steady increase in the numbers of part-time and fixed-term workers in the UK has generated an anxiety that a two-tier labour market is being allowed to open up, with standard full-time permanent employees entitled to the enjoyment of the full suite of employment protection legislation, whilst individuals providing personal services on the basis of non-standard forms of employment such as part-time and fixed-term work are denied the very same rights. The basis for this concern is that a substantial proportion of

---

[18] See S. Horrell, J. Rubery, and B. Burchell, 'Unequal Jobs or Unequal Pay?' (1989) 20 *Industrial Relations Journal* 176, 178.

[19] See *ibid.*, 190.   [20] [1995] 1 AC 1.

[21] See regulation 2 of the Employment Protection (Part-time Employees) Regulations 1995 (SI 1995/31). Cf. *R v Secretary of State for Employment, ex parte Seymour-Smith* [2000] ICR 244 and see the discussion in D. McCann, *Regulating Flexible Work* (Oxford, OUP, 2008) 62–3 which sets out the many examples where part-time and fixed-term workers were able to use the law of direct or indirect sex discrimination to successfully challenge their employer's practices.

[22] See also D. McCann, *Regulating Flexible Work* (Oxford, OUP, 2008) 64–6.

part-time and fixed-term workers work on a casual, ad hoc basis and so will fail to meet the common law tests for the establishment of employment status.[23] Our discussion in Chapter 4 demonstrated that the standard policy response to the potential evolution of a two-tier labour market and the difficulties generated by atypical working types has been to adopt one or more of the following three regulatory techniques:

(1) carefully recalibrating the criteria for the identification of the contract of employment by adjusting them in a worker-friendly direction;

(2) establishing intermediate legal categories lying somewhere between the contract of employment and the personal contract for services; or

(3) abandoning the contractual paradigm altogether and instead recognizing certain personal relationships for the performance of work as deserving of employment protection.[24]

However, such a taxonomy of the techniques available does not fit particularly well with the regulatory arrangements one encounters in the case of certain forms of non-standard employment. Instead, we find that part-time and fixed-term work have been specifically identified as forms of non-standard employment which should be regulated sui generis. This somewhat piecemeal regulatory response has entailed the promulgation of legislation that is designed to capture the competing policy aims of labour market flexibility and enhanced job quality specifically within the context of part-time and fixed-term work. To that extent, the arrangements adopted share some commonalities with that employed in the case of the regulation of agency work[25] in terms of the Agency Workers' Directive.[26]

The tailored regulation of part-time and fixed-term work which we find in domestic law is attributable to policy initiatives pursued at the European level through the auspices of the 'European social dialogue'.[27] Unlike previous European attempts in the early 1980s and early 1990s to regulate 'atypical' part-time and fixed-term work which hit the buffers,[28] the key factor influencing the content of the PTWD and FTWD was the conviction that flexible working arrangements could act as drivers of job creation. The PTWD and FTWD were envisaged by the European Commission and the European Social Partners as the first two pieces of legislation in a 'sequence of measures which between them would comprehensively regulate the relationship between standard and non-standard forms of employment'.[29] As noted earlier, the model adopted was one based on equal treatment and parity of terms, with the FTWD having the additional objective of preventing employers from abusively deploying successive fixed-term employment contracts. Clause 1(a) in each of the framework agreements annexed to the PTWD and FTWD reveals the underlying objectives of these Directives, which can be summarized as follows:

---

[23] For a discussion of these common law tests, see Chapter 3, section 3.2.1.

[24] See Chapter 4, section 4.1.1; M. Freedland and N. Kountouris, 'The Legal Characterization of Personal Work Relations and the Idea of Labour Law' in G. Davidov and B. Langille (eds), *The Idea of Labour Law* (Oxford, OUP, 2011) 202.

[25] See Chapter 4, section 4.3.2. However, the PTWD and the FTWD adopt a model based on the parity of *all* terms and conditions between (a) part-time and full-time workers and (b) fixed-term workers and permanent workers, whereas the Agency Workers' Directive only ensures parity in respect of the *pay-related terms and conditions* of the agency worker and a permanent worker recruited directly by the end-user.

[26] Directive 2008/104/EC (OJ 2008 L327/9).

[27] This process involved the coming together of cross-industry organizations, referred to as the 'European Social Partners', namely the Union of Industrial and Employer's Confederations of Europe ('UNICE') and the European Centre of Enterprises with Public Participation ('CEEP') for employers, on the one hand, and the European Trade Union Confederation ('ETUC') for workers and trade unions, on the other.

[28] See OJ 1982 C62/7 and OJ 1982 C128/2, amended in 1983 and 1984 by OJ 1983 C18/5 and COM(84) 159 final.

[29] P. Davies and M. Freedland, *Towards a Flexible Labour Market: Labour Legislation and Regulation since the 1990s* (Oxford, OUP, 2007) 87.

- to provide for the removal of discrimination against part-time and fixed-term workers and to improve the quality of part-time and fixed-term work;

- to facilitate the development of part-time work on a voluntary basis and to contribute to the flexible organization of working time in a manner which takes into account the needs of employers and workers; and

- to establish a framework to prevent abuses arising from the adoption of successive fixed-term employment contracts or relationships.

Essentially, these policy prescriptions coalesce into the promise of flexibility in labour markets, on the one hand, and enhanced social protection for part-time and fixed-term workers, on the other. Whilst admirable, some commentators writing when the PTWD came into force questioned the compatibility and deliverability of these objectives.[30] As will become apparent from our analysis of the content of the PTWR, the manner in which the PTWD was transposed in the UK furnishes some support for this view.

The PTWD and the FTWD were transposed into UK law by the PTWR and the FTER. On the introduction of the PTWR, then Secretary of State for Trade and Industry Stephen Byers heralded their arrival as a ground-breaking moment in the protection of part-time workers. The terms of the PTWD and the FTWD were such that they afforded EU Member States a number of options in respect of the transposition of some of their provisions. Close inspection of the detail of the PTWR and FTER reveals that the preference of the UK Government was to pursue the policy objective of 'managerial adaptability' at the expense of job security and worker protection in exercising the choices offered by the PTWD and FTWD:

■ P. Davies and M. Freedland, *Towards a Flexible Labour Market: Labour Legislation and Regulation since the 1990s* (Oxford, OUP, 2007) 21–2

The concept of managerial flexibility describes the capacity of, and the propensity for, employing enterprises to engage in job re-structuring and institutional re-structuring. Where employing enterprises assert managerial flexibility, they engage in processes of evolution which amount to the re-contracting of personal work relations. The pursuit or exercise of managerial flexibility may take the form of, or result in, frequent or even continuous re-contracting of those relationships. The processes of re-contracting will take place at the initiative of the controllers and managers of employing enterprises, and will be conducted by their managers. In a state of managerial flexibility, the articulation and introduction of new contractual structures or frameworks will tend to be a unilateral management activity . . . In short, this re-contracting may be partly on a uniform basis across a whole group of workers, but partly individuated; it could be considered as the re-constituting of the internal labour market and the re-locating of it with regard to the external labour market. Managerial flexibility is the capacity to make those adaptations . . . the importance of managerial flexibility . . . consists . . . in the way that [it] became, we suggest, a guiding ideal for public policy during the [period from 1992 to 2007], perhaps for labour legislation in general but certainly for the aspects of legislation and regulation of personal work relations with which we are concerned . . .

The policy desire to harness a sufficient level of managerial flexibility in personal contractual relations is evident in the context of the vexed question of the relational scope of the PTWR and the FTER. For example, both the PTWD and FTWD provide that they apply to part-time workers or fixed-term workers 'who have an employment contract

---

[30] M. Jeffery, 'Not Really Going to Work? Of the Directive on Part-Time Work, "Atypical Work" and Attempts to Regulate It' (1998) 27 *Industrial Law Journal* 193, 212.

or employment relationship as defined in law, collective agreements or practice in each Member State'.[31] These words have no particular meaning in European law[32] and, in *O'Brien v Ministry of Justice*,[33] the Court of Justice of the European Union ('CJEU' or 'ECJ') ruled that the scope of the protective coverage of the implementing regulations is devolved to the EU Member States.[34] Interestingly, the UK Government decided to adopt divergent approaches to the relational scope of the PTWR and FTER. Turning first to the transposition of the FTWD, we find that regulation 1 of the FTER provides that the FTER is of limited application, covering a fixed-term 'employee' only, rather than the broader category of fixed-term 'worker'. This policy choice on the part of the UK Government functioned to exclude a broad range of individuals providing personal services on temporary and fixed-term contracts, owing to the fact that they would be unable to meet the common law tests for the characterization of their contracts as contracts of employment. This can be contrasted with the transposition of the PTWD via the PTWR which adopts a broader approach. The PTWR extended the protection conferred so that it covers a part-time 'worker' as well as a part-time 'employee'. As such, the PTWR will apply to an individual providing personal services to an employing entity on the basis of a part-time 'worker' contract, i.e. an individual working part-time pursuant to a contract of employment or a contract 'whereby the individual undertakes to do or perform personally any work or services for another party to the contract whose status is not by virtue of the contract that of a client or customer of any profession or business undertaking carried on by the individual'.[35] However, the more extensive definition in the PTWR should not be taken to mean that it has had a greater degree of success than the FTER in enhancing the job or employment security of atypical workers; instead, as we will see, both the PTWR and the FTER supply a number of avenues to employers to justify the less favourable treatment of part-time and fixed-term workers vis-à-vis full-time permanent comparators. It is upon those justifications that we will shine the spotlight in sections 13.2 and 13.3.

Reflection points

1. Do you believe that the PTWD and FTWD were essentially designed to further the European employment policy of labour market flexibility at the expense of statutory protection for part-time and fixed-term workers?

2. In your opinion, what are the economic advantages of limiting the operation of the FTER to fixed-term 'employees' rather than 'workers'?

 For additional reading on the contextual and historical introduction to part-time and fixed-term work, visit the Online Resources for this book at www.oup.com/uk/cabrelli3e/

---

[31] See Article 2(1) of the PTWD; Article 2(1) of the FTWD.

[32] *Foreningen af Arbejdsledere I Danmark v Danmols Inventar* [1985] ECR 2639; *O'Brien v Ministry of Justice* [2012] ICR 955, 975.

[33] [2012] ICR 955. This case can be contrasted with the earlier approach of the ECJ and CJEU in interpreting these words in the FTWD in *Angelidaki v Organismos Nomarkhiaki Aftodiikisi Rethimnis* [2009] ECR I-3071, [2009] 3 CMLR 15; and *Del Cerro Alonso v Osakidetza-Servicio Vasco de Salud* [2007] ECR I-7109, [2008] ICR 141, 158C.

[34] However, see the opinion of Advocate-General Kokott in *Wippel v Peek & Cloppenburg GmbH & Co. KG* [2004] ECR I-9483 to the effect that domestic provisions adopted by the Member State should not be drawn so narrowly that the protective purpose of the PTWD is frustrated, on which, see the discussion in M. Freedland and N. Kountouris, *The Legal Construction of Personal Work Relations* (Oxford, OUP, 2011) 392.

[35] See regulation 1(2)(b) of the PTWR. For a detailed examination of the hallmarks of the statutory 'worker' contract, see Chapter 4, section 4.2.1.

13.2 THE REGULATION OF PART-TIME WORK

The primary protection lying at the heart of the PTWR is found in regulation 5(1) and (2):

> **Regulation 5 Less favourable treatment of part-time workers**
>
> (1) A part-time worker has the right not to be treated by his employer less favourably than the employer treats a comparable full-time worker—
>
> (a) as regards the terms of his contract; or
>
> (b) by being subjected to any other detriment by any act, or deliberate failure to act, of his employer.
>
> (2) The right conferred by paragraph (1) applies only if—
>
> (a) the treatment is on the ground that the worker is a part-time worker, and
>
> (b) the treatment is not justified on objective grounds.

Thus, if the part-time worker is treated less favourably than a comparable full-time worker in respect of the terms of his/her contract or by being subjected to a detriment because he/she is a part-time worker, then the employer will be liable unless it can show the treatment was objectively justified. It has been held that, in the case of less favourable treatment in relation to holiday entitlement[36] and access to occupational pensions, the amount of the pension and the amount of the worker's periodic contribution[37] will relate to the 'terms of [the part-time worker's] contract' under regulation 5(1) of the PTWR. Likewise, in *Ministry of Justice v Burton*,[38] the EAT held that there was less favourable treatment where the contractual terms of part-time judges of the Residential Property Tribunal provided that they would be paid for time taken to write up judgments at the discretion of the employer, whereas full-time tax tribunal judges were paid for their writing time as a matter of course. Further, it is likely that a dismissal of a part-time worker will constitute a 'detriment'.

In evaluating whether there has been less favourable treatment in the terms and conditions of the part-timer's contract in comparison with the comparable full-time workers, the pro rata principle is to be applied, unless it is inappropriate.[39] The 'pro rata principle' means that where a comparable full-time worker receives or is entitled to receive pay or any other benefit, a part-time worker is to receive or be entitled to receive not less than the proportion of that pay or other benefit that the number of his/her weekly hours bears to the number of weekly hours of the comparable full-time worker.[40]

There are four principal issues which require to be considered in order to establish whether a part-time worker is entitled to the equal treatment right under the PTWR. The first issue concerns the definition of 'part-time' and the second issue involves a detailed analysis of the comparison exercise relative to a full-time worker. Thirdly, there is the important matter of how one ought to approach the question of causation, i.e. whether the disparity in treatment is attributable to the part-time worker's part-time status. Finally, of no little importance is the employer's objective justification defence where a prima facie case of less favourable treatment is established.

---

[36] *Zentralbetriebsrat der Landeskrankenhaüser Tirols* (Case C-486/08) [2010] IRLR 631.

[37] *INPS v Bruno* [2010] IRLR 890. However, in *Copple v Littlewoods plc* [2012] IRLR 121, the Court of Appeal ruled that the part-timer could be required to establish by evidence that she would have joined the pension scheme during the period she was denied access to it.

[38] [2016] IRLR 100.   [39] Regulation 5(3) of the PTWR.   [40] Regulation 1(2) of the PTWR.

13.2.1 An examination of the PTWR

The expression 'part-time' is defined in regulation 2(2) of the PTWR:

Regulation 2 Meaning of full-time worker, part-time worker and comparable full-time worker . . .

(2) A worker is a part-time worker for the purposes of these Regulations if he is paid wholly or in part by reference to the time he works and, having regard to the custom and practice of the employer in relation to workers employed by the worker's employer under the same type of contract, is not identifiable as a full-time worker.

Thus, the definition of 'part-time' hinges on the definition of 'full-time', which is found in regulation 2(1) of the PTWR:

Regulation 2 Meaning of full-time worker, part-time worker and comparable full-time worker . . .

(1) A worker is a full-time worker for the purposes of these Regulations if he is paid wholly or in part by reference to the time he works and, having regard to the custom and practice of the employer in relation to workers employed by the worker's employer under the same type of contract, is identifiable as a full-time worker.

Unlike the standard employed for the compilation of statistical data by Labour Market Trends,[41] which treated fewer than 30 hours work a week as part-time work, whether a worker is deemed to be part-time or full-time is subject to the custom and practice of the employer's workplace. The only two decisions to date that have examined whether a claimant satisfied the definition of a part-time worker are *Ministry of Justice v O'Brien*[42] and *Hudson v University of Oxford*.[43] In *O'Brien*, the Supreme Court decided that part-time judges referred to as 'recorders' were part-time workers for the purposes of the PTWR, notwithstanding that they were judicial office-holders. As such, they were entitled to gain access to the occupational pension scheme made available to full-time judges.[44] Meanwhile, in a somewhat surprising decision, the Court of Appeal held in *Hudson* that a worker performing a full-time job could be a part-time worker for the purposes of the PTWR, on the basis that his job actually comprised two separate part-time positions.

Once a court or tribunal is satisfied that a worker is a part-time worker, it is incumbent on the claimant to show that he/she has been treated less favourably than a comparable full-time worker.[45] Hence a part-time worker is required to conduct a successful comparison exercise in order to substantiate his/her case. This has led some commentators to suggest that the philosophy of the PTWR is to downplay the inherent worth of part-time work and to stymie the full potential of the regulatory regime:

---

[41] This was a series published by the Office of National Statistics which has now been discontinued.
[42] [2013] 1 WLR 522.   [43] [2007] EWCA Civ 336.
[44] In *O'Brien v Ministry of Justice* [2017] UKSC 46, the question was whether, when calculating the pension entitlement of part-time fee-paid judges, should only their period of service from the date on which the Part-Time Work Directive came into force in 2000 be taken into account, or the period from the date on which the service of the judges actually commenced? The Supreme Court referred this question to the CJEU for resolution.   [45] Regulation 2(4) of the PTWR.

■ M. Bell, 'Achieving the Objectives of the Part-Time Work Directive? Revisiting the Part-Time Workers Regulations' (2011) 40 *Industrial Law Journal* 254, 257

> Insofar as the [PTWR] erect full-time work as the norm against which equal treatment claims must be measured, there is an implicit tendency to reinforce working arrangements that have been historically organised around the working lives of men rather than women. This squashes the possibility to challenge disadvantages encountered by part-time workers where there is no genuine comparison with the experience of full-time workers. Take, for example, the situation of a part-time worker employed as part of a job-share arrangement. Her job-share partner leaves the enterprise and the employer decides that there should be a full-time replacement. The employer is willing for the remaining job-share worker to increase her hours to full-time work, but this is not possible for the worker because of caring responsibilities. As a result, she is dismissed for business reasons. Can this be characterised as less favourable treatment compared to a full-time worker? It is difficult because in reality this is a situation that only affects part-time workers. Reference to the standard of full-time work has the effect of obscuring disadvantages that are specific to part-time work.

Hence the comparison exercise involved prevents part-time workers from obtaining redress where they have suffered a disadvantage but there is no comparable full-time worker with whom a meaningful comparison can be made. For example, in *Advocate General for Scotland v Barton*,[46] the Court of Session decided that a part-time worker's claim was precluded where he sought to compare himself with a former colleague who had worked 70 per cent of a normal five-day week. As for the actual substance of the comparison, the level of detail involved is astonishingly high for what one would think ought to be a somewhat straightforward exercise:

> *Regulation 2 Meaning of full-time worker, part-time worker and comparable full-time worker . . .*
>
> (4) A full-time worker is a comparable full-time worker in relation to a part-time worker if, at the time when the treatment that is alleged to be less favourable to the part-time worker takes place—
>
> (a) both workers are—
>
>   (i) employed by the same employer under the same type of contract, and
>
>   (ii) engaged in the same or broadly similar work having regard, where relevant, to whether they have a similar level of qualification, skills and experience; and
>
> (b) the full-time worker works or is based at the same establishment as the part-time worker or, where there is no full-time worker working or based at that establishment who satisfies the requirements of sub-paragraph (a), works or is based at a different establishment and satisfies those requirements . . .

Regulation 2(4) prescribes four criteria that the part-time worker must negotiate, which can be summarized briefly as:

(1) 'the same employer';

(2) 'the same establishment' or another establishment of the employer if no comparable full-time workers are employed by the employer at the part-time claimant's establishment;

(3) 'the same type of contract'; and

(4) 'the same or broadly similar work'.

---

[46] [2016] IRLR 210.

We take each of these criteria in turn.

(1) The first condition that the part-time worker must meet in the context of the comparison exercise is that he/she is working or employed by the same employer as the comparable full-time worker. This is defined in regulation 1(2) as 'the person by whom the employee or worker is or (except where a provision of [the PTWR] otherwise requires) where the employment has ceased, was employed'. This does not take us much further forward but clearly excludes a comparison with a full-time worker employed by an *associated employer*.[47]

(2) As for the second condition, little guidance is provided on the scope of an 'establishment'. Suffice to say that European Directives in the employment field often adopt such an expression[48] and recourse to the interpretations of the ECJ or CJEU in those other contexts may shed some light on its meaning: in the European context, it is generally taken to denote a physical location.

(3) Turning to the third criterion, this is undoubtedly the most controversial. It enjoins the part-time worker to establish that he/she is working on the basis of the same kind of contract as the comparable full-time worker. This can serve to frustrate the part-timer's claim at the first base in two ways.

   (a) First, the part-timer must find an actual 'living, breathing'[49] comparable full-time comparator and, as such, hypothetical comparators are disallowed: unlike section 13(1) of the Equality Act 2010, which does permit hypothetical comparators in the context of a direct discrimination claim, regulation 5 does not stipulate that 'a part-time worker has the right not to be treated by his employer less favourably than the employer treats *or would treat* a comparable full-time worker'.[50] Hence, subject to two exceptions specifically laid out in regulations 3 and 4,[51] it is not possible for the part-timer to attempt to construct a comparable full-time worker who does not actually exist.

   (b) Secondly, the part-timer's full-time comparator must be engaged on the 'same type of contract' as the part-timer. As such, if the part-timer is engaged on the basis of a 'worker' contract and the comparable full-timer is instead employed on a contract of employment, the former will be prevented from comparing him/herself with the latter. This is fortified by the aforementioned refusal of the PTWR to countenance hypothetical comparators: only an actual comparable full-time worker/employee may be invoked, and if he/she is engaged on a different contract to the part-timer, the latter's claim will be precluded. Further guidance on the kinds of contractual relationships which will be treated as dissimilar is articulated in regulation 2(3) of the PTWR:

---

[47] For the definition of an associated employer in the context of the equal pay regime, see section 79(9)(a) and (b) of the Equality Act 2010 and Chapter 14, section 14.2.1.4.

[48] For example, see the meaning of the word 'establishment' in the Collective Redundancies Directive 98/59/EC (OJ 1998 L225/16), on which, see Chapter 20, section 20.3.1.5.

[49] A. McColgan, 'Missing the Point? The Part-Time Workers (Prevention of Less Favourable Treatment) Regulations 2000' (2000) 29 *Industrial Law Journal* 260, 261.

[50] See *McMenemy v Capita Business Services Ltd* [2006] IRLR 761; *Carl v University of Sheffield* [2009] ICR 1286, 1289C–1291F per Judge Peter Clark.

[51] Where (a) a worker is in transition from full-time to part-time work, or (b) a full-time worker who has been absent from work for a period of less than 12 months subsequently returns to work on a part-time basis, he/she is entitled to retain his/her terms and conditions. In evaluating the terms and conditions, a comparison with a hypothetical full-time comparator is specifically permitted, i.e. the claimant prior to the transition to the part-time position: see *Fidessa plc v Lancaster* (UKEAT/0093/16/LA, 16 January 2017) where a worker returning to work as a part-time worker could compare herself with her own pre-absence full-time position.

Regulation 2 Meaning of full-time worker, part-time worker and comparable full-time worker . . .

(3) For the purposes of paragraphs (1), (2) and (4), the following shall be regarded as being employed under different types of contract—

(a) employees employed under a contract that is not a contract of apprenticeship;

(b) employees employed under a contract of apprenticeship;

(c) workers who are not employees;

(d) any other description of worker that it is reasonable for the employer to treat differently from other workers on the ground that workers of that description have a different type of contract.[52]

On its face, regulation 2(3) enables employers to circumvent the operation of the PTWR by compartmentalizing part-time and full-time labour in a manner which ensures that the former are contracted on a different basis than the latter. Consider the illustration in Hypothetical A.

Hypothetical A

The Edinburgh office of Danny's Demolishers Ltd ('DD') is a Georgian period listed building situated in Edinburgh's new town. DD decides to hire Alfred Wanchope ('AW') as a full-time employee to provide tours of the listed building to the paying public. AW is employed 9am to 5:30pm, Monday to Friday, every week. The first three weeks of tours are extremely positive and it becomes apparent that more tour guides are needed to shepherd visitors around the building. DD hires two Edinburgh law students, Gina Patterson ('GP') and Richard Rockham ('RR') as part-time ad hoc casual workers on the basis of a zero-hours contract. The arrangement between DD and GP and RR is such that DD will offer GP and RR work when there is tour guide work to be had, which work GP and RR may accept or refuse depending on their commitments.

If GP were to raise a claim that she had suffered a disadvantage or detriment, she would be precluded from invoking AW as a comparator. AW is contracted on the basis of a contract of employment with fixed working hours, whereas GP and RR are not: the requisite mutuality of obligation required for the constitution of an employment contract is absent in the case of GP's and RR's contract with DD.

The authority for the proposition that zero-hours, casual, part-time workers are precluded from invoking a full-time employee with prescribed working hours as a comparator is *Wippel v Peek & Cloppenburg GmbH & Co. KG*.[53] This somewhat crude approach, however, is tempered to some extent by the purposive interpretation of regulation 2(3) that was adopted by the House of Lords in *Matthews v Kent & Medway Towns Fire Authority*:

---

[52] This latter category will cover 'home workers', i.e. atypical workers engaged to work at home on an ad hoc basis. In *Matthews v Kent & Medway Towns Fire Authority* [2006] ICR 365, the House of Lords ruled that part-time, retained, i.e. 'on-call', firefighters did not fall within this 'catch-all' category of worker.   [53] [2004] ECR I-9483.

■ *Matthews v Kent & Medway Towns Fire Authority* [2006] ICR 365, 368E–G

Lord Hope:

... the question whether a full-time worker is employed under the same type of contract as a part-time worker is to be approached broadly, having regard to the purpose of the agreement set out in clause 1 [of the framework agreement annexed to the PTWD]. This is to provide for the removal of discrimination against part-time workers and to improve the quality of part-time work, to facilitate the development of part-time work on a voluntary basis and to contribute to the flexible organisation of working time in a manner which takes into account the needs of employers and workers. The use of the word 'type' fits in with this approach. When one thinks of a type of person or a type of car, for example, one looks for a broad characteristic that separates one type from another. One ignores the many variations and differences within each type and looks instead for something that brings them all together within the same category. An over-precise view as to what makes one type of contract different from another would tend to undermine the purpose of the [framework agreement annexed to the PTWD] ...

Notwithstanding the liberal approach adopted by the House of Lords in *Matthews*, the decision does not dislodge the reality that regulation 2(3) of the PTWR ensures that 'those part-time workers whose employment relationship diverges furthest from the full-time norm are unlikely to be working under the same "type" of employment contract'.[54] Indeed, the manner in which the comparison exercise has been constructed in the PTWR has prompted McColgan to remark that the effect of regulation 2 is to undermine its effectiveness:

■ A. McColgan, 'Missing the Point? The Part-Time Workers (Prevention of Less Favourable Treatment) Regulations 2000' (2000) 29 *Industrial Law Journal* 260, 263

It is ... [the comparison exercise] that explains the government's own estimate that, of over six million part-time workers in the UK, only one sixth would be able to provide a comparator. (Of these million workers, the Regulatory Impact Assessment (RIA) estimated that some 400,000 (fewer than 7% of all part-time workers) would benefit directly from the [PTWR].) [Therefore, w]hat is clear is that the requirement for a comparator excludes the vast majority of part-time workers from the benefit of the [PTWR].[55]

The 'dead hand' of the comparison exercise also functions to constrain the ability of the PTWR to chip away at the occupationally segregated nature of part-time employment. The difficulties here are particularly acute in the context of transitions in working patterns, e.g. where a worker wishes to switch from part-time to full-time work or full-time to part-time work. Admittedly, the PTWR provides some assistance to workers where a transition from full-time to part-time work has been approved by the employer, in which case the worker is entitled to retain his/her terms and conditions.[56]

---

[54] M. Bell, 'Achieving the Objectives of the Part-Time Work Directive? Revisiting the Part-Time Workers Regulations' (2011) 40 *Industrial Law Journal* 254, 259.

[55] See also the three criticisms of comparison exercises in D. McCann, *Regulating Flexible Work* (Oxford, OUP, 2008) 81.

[56] See regulations 3 and 4 of the PTWR. Full-time workers who have been absent from work for a period of less than 12 months and subsequently return to work on a part-time basis are also entitled to retain their terms and conditions. The decision of the EAT in *Fidessa plc v Lancaster* (UKEAT/0093/16/LA, 16 January 2017) enables a worker returning to work as a part-time worker under regulation 4 of the PTWR to compare herself with her own pre-absence full-time position. As such, it is one (albeit limited) exception to the general rule that hypothetical comparators are not permitted.

However, where the employer refuses a full-time worker's request to adjust working hours to part-time, there is little purchase in the worker relying on the PTWR to launch a claim:

■ **D. McCann, *Regulating Flexible Work* (Oxford, OUP, 2008) 89**

[The PTWR] stop short, however, of granting a right for workers to transfer to part-time work, a weakness that reflects their parent Directive, which has been criticized for failing to establish such a legal obligation, the relevant provision one that encourages employers, 'as far as possible', to consider requests from workers to transfer between full-time and part-time work. The [PTWD] also, however, stipulates that a worker's refusal to transfer to full-time work, or vice versa, should not in itself constitute a valid reason for termination of employment, a provision that is not contained in the PTW[R], despite calls from the Select Committee on Education and Employment for it to be included.

The absence of protection included in the PTWR in the context of work transitions is patent if we subject the various possibilities to analysis. If we turn first to a part-time employee's request that he/she move to full-time work, the question arises whether it is possible for such a part-timer to establish less favourable treatment than a comparable full-time worker where the employer refuses: after all, '[t]he problem with constructing this as less favourable treatment lies in the comparator test; an identical situation does not arise for full-time workers'.[57] Moreover, where an employer demands that a part-timer transfer to full-time work or risk redundancy but the part-timer refuses—e.g. where the employer engages in a business reorganization eliminating a part-time post—the jurisprudence of the EAT currently conflicts. In *Hendrikson Europe Ltd v Pipe*,[58] the EAT took the view that the part-timer's redundancy for a refusal to transfer constituted less favourable treatment. However, the EAT in *Tyson v Concurrent Systems Inc.*[59] rejected the part-timer's claim on the basis that the part-timer was seeking to apply a hypothetical comparator, i.e. it is impossible for an actual comparable full-time worker to shift to full-time work.[60] Furthermore, in the same scenario, it is unclear whether the dismissal of the part-timer will be protected under the PTWR:

■ **A. McColgan, 'Missing the Point? The Part-Time Workers (Prevention of Less Favourable Treatment) Regulations 2000' (2000) 29 *Industrial Law Journal* 260, 266**

The 'detriment' from which workers are protected under Reg 5(1)(b) presumably covers dismissal. However, a dismissal for refusing to transfer to full-time work will breach the [PTWR] only where it is categorised by a tribunal as (1) a dismissal 'on the ground that the worker is a part-time worker' [by virtue of regulation 5(2)(a)] and (2) less favourable treatment than that accorded to an actual full-time comparator (Presumably one who had refused to transfer to full-time work?).

---

[57] M. Bell, 'Achieving the Objectives of the Part-Time Work Directive? Revisiting the Part-Time Workers Regulations' (2011) 40 *Industrial Law Journal* 254, 275.

[58] (EAT/0272/02, 15 April 2003).   [59] (EAT/0028/03, 9 April 2003).

[60] In such circumstances, it may be preferable for a part-time worker to bring an indirect sex discrimination claim, as there is evidence that the courts and tribunals are more agreeably disposed to such claims, e.g. *London Underground v Edwards (No. 2)* [1999] ICR 494, on which, see the discussion in D. McCann, *Regulating Flexible Work* (Oxford, OUP, 2008) 72–3.

Some support for the suggestion in this extract that a worker would be prevented from harnessing the PTWR or PTWD to challenge an actual or constructive dismissal where a part-time employment contract is unilaterally converted into a full-time one is provided by the CJEU's decision in *Mascellani v Ministero della Giustizia*.[61] In *Mascellani*, an employee's part-time employment contract was terminated by the employer and she was immediately re-engaged on the basis of a full-time contract of employment. This unilateral conversion was undertaken without her consent. In the circumstances, she sought to challenge the process, but the CJEU decided that clause 5.2 of the PTWD—which provides that it is not a valid reason for termination of employment that the employee objects to a transfer from part-time to full-time work or vice versa—does not preclude an employer from terminating a part-time contract and replacing it with a full-time employment contract without the consent of the employee concerned. In addition, the CJEU reached the conclusion that the unilateral conversion of a part-time employment contract to a full-time contract cannot be compared with, or equated to, the conversion of a full-time employment contract into a part-time contract since there is a qualitative difference between enjoining an employee to take on extra hours and enjoining the employee to reduce his/her working hours.

As for a managerial instruction to switch from full-time to part-time work which is resisted by the worker, the same logic adopted by the CJEU in *Mascellani* on the basis of clause 5.2 of the PTWD ought to apply to disentitle an employee from claiming less favourable treatment under regulation 2 of the PTWR. Furthermore, yet again, the required comparison exercise will erect a barrier: a full-time worker has no right to avail him/herself of the PTWR since he/she is not a part-time worker. By the same token, where a female full-time employee seeks to switch to part-time employment on her return from maternity leave and the employer refuses, the mechanics of the comparison exercise will again prevent a claim from being successful. In such a case, there is arguably greater scope for the worker to be successful by relying on the law of indirect sex discrimination where the courts have exhibited a greater willingness in recent times to scrutinize the conduct of employers in refusing requests to reduce working hours.[62] Hence the PTWR offers nothing to assist *prospective* part-time workers, i.e. those seeking access to part-time employment as a transition from full-time work. The same point applies where an individual is looking to use part-time work as an initial path into the labour market, since regulation 2(2) requires the worker to be in a contractual relationship, rather than seeking to be in such a relationship.[63] In such a case, the statutory right to request flexible working under section 80F of the ERA may be more promising, albeit that it is a procedural, rather than substantive, right.[64]

(4) The final criterion the part-timer must satisfy as part of the comparison exercise is that the comparable full-time worker be engaged in the 'same or broadly similar work having regard, where relevant, to whether they have a similar level of qualification, skills and experience'. The scope of this condition was examined by the House of Lords in *Matthews v Kent & Medway Towns Fire Authority*.[65] Matthews concerned a claim by part-time, retained, i.e. 'on-call', firefighters who were seeking to invoke their full-time firefighter counterparts as comparable full-time workers. Unlike the part-timers, the full-timers operated on a regular shift pattern and had additional duties involving community work and home fire risk assessments. The employment tribunal took the view that there were pivotal divergences in qualifications, experience, and skill levels between the part-timers and full-timers and that they were not

---

[61] [2015] 1 CMLR 36.

[62] See the discussion in D. McCann, *Regulating Flexible Work* (Oxford, OUP, 2008) 69–72 and 73–4.

[63] M. Bell, 'Achieving the Objectives of the Part-Time Work Directive? Revisiting the Part-Time Workers Regulations' (2011) 40 *Industrial Law Journal* 254, 270–3.

[64] See Chapter 9, section 9.3.4, for a more detailed discussion.   [65] [2006] ICR 365.

engaged in the same or broadly similar work. However, the House of Lords adopted a different perspective, instructing tribunals and courts to recognize the inevitability of the fact that part-timers will be undertaking fewer and different tasks than full-timers in evaluating whether the overall nature of the work is the same or broadly similar:

■ *Matthews v Kent & Medway Towns Fire Authority* [2006] ICR 365, 371F–380C

Lord Hope:

The question whether [the work of the part-time, retained firefighters] was 'broadly similar' was . . . a question of fact and degree which one would have thought the tribunal having heard the evidence were best placed to answer. I am not confident however that the tribunal gave sufficient weight to the extent to which the work on which both groups of fire fighters were engaged was 'the same' work. The painstaking way in which they addressed themselves to the various differences was a necessary and admirable reaction to the way the evidence was presented and the issues were argued before them. But it led them to concentrate on the differences and not to assess the weight that ought to be given to the similarities. Their conclusion that the job of the whole-time fire fighter was a fuller wider job than that of the retained fire fighter was not, as they appear to have thought, the end of the exercise. They still had to address the question posed by the statute which was whether, notwithstanding the fact that the job of the whole-time fire fighter was a fuller and wider job, the work on which both groups were engaged could nevertheless be described as broadly similar . . . [T]he tribunal held that, putting together the fuller wider role and the higher level of qualification and skills which they found to be the inevitable inference from the evidence before them, the necessary comparability could not be established. The way this sentence is expressed indicates to me that they did not take the final and vital step of addressing their minds, in the light of these findings, to the test laid down by the statute. For these reasons . . . I think that the decision which they reached was defective and must be set aside . . .

Baroness Hale:

. . . while there are similarities between the two types of comparison, they are not the same. The sole question for the tribunal at this stage of the inquiry is whether the work on which the full-time and part-time workers are engaged is 'the same or broadly similar'. I do not accept the . . . argument, put at its highest, that this involves looking at the similarities and ignoring any differences. The work which they do must be looked at as a whole, taking into account both similarities and differences. But the question is not whether it is different but whether it is the same or broadly similar. That question has also to be approached in the context of [the PTWR] which are inviting a comparison between two types of worker whose work will almost inevitably be different to some extent. In making that assessment, the extent to which the work that they do is *exactly the same* must be of great importance. If a large component of their work is exactly the same, the question is whether any differences are of such importance as to prevent their work being regarded overall as 'the same or broadly similar'. It is easy to imagine workplaces where both full- and part-timers do the same work, but the full-timers have extra activities with which to fill their time. This should not prevent their work being regarded as the same or broadly similar overall. Also of great importance in this assessment is the importance of the same work which they do to the work of the enterprise as a whole. It is easy to imagine workplaces where the full-timers do the more important work and the part-timers are brought in to do the more peripheral tasks: the fact that they both do some of the same work would not mean that their work was the same or broadly similar. It is equally easy to imagine workplaces where the full-timers and part-timers spend much of their time on the core activity of the enterprise . . . The fact that the full-timers do some extra tasks would not prevent their work being the same or broadly similar. In other words, in answering that question particular weight should be given to the extent to which their work is in fact the same and to the importance of that work to the enterprise as a whole. Otherwise one runs the risk of giving too much weight to differences which are the almost inevitable result of one worker working full-time and another working less than full-time.

In *Matthews*, the approach to the 'same or broadly similar work' test produced a result that enabled the retained part-time firefighters to succeed in their claim. This can be contrasted with *Moultrie v Ministry of Justice*[66] where the *Matthews* test was adopted and great store was placed on the final section of the extract from Baroness Hale's judgment, where she stressed the centrality of evaluating the importance to be assigned to the differences in the tasks between the work of the part-timers and the full-timers. Around 85 per cent of the work of part-time, fee-paid tribunal members and full-time, salaried tribunal members was identical. However, the EAT ruled that the remaining 15 per cent differed in a way which was of significant importance to the enterprise as a whole. As such, the similarities in the work done were outweighed by the importance attached to the differences, which comprised recruitment, training, and appraisal duties.

Whether it is the case that the progressive interpretation of the expression 'the same or broadly similar work' in *Matthews* has also been reflected in the evaluation of the expression 'the [less favourable] treatment [of the part-time worker] is on the ground that the [part-time] worker is a part-time worker' in regulation 5(2)(a) of the PTWR is presently unclear. The latter takes us to the question of causation, i.e. the establishment of a causal link between the less favourable treatment of the part-time worker and the fact that he/she is a part-timer. Confusingly, the EAT has produced conflicting decisions on whether the part-timer must demonstrate that he/she was treated less favourably solely because he/she works part-time. In the case of *McMenemy v Capita Business Services Ltd*,[67] the EAT decided that the part-time work must be the *sole* cause of the less favourable treatment. As such, if the employer can identify some other reason for the treatment, it would not be liable. However, the decisions of the EAT in *Sharma v Manchester City Council*[68] and *Carl v University of Sheffield*[69] demonstrated the opposite approach to that in *McMenemy*:

■ *Carl v University of Sheffield* [2009] ICR 1286, 1295D–F

Judge Peter Clark:

The expression 'on the ground that' or 'on the grounds of' frequently appears in our domestic legislation. It was considered by the Court of Appeal in *English v Thomas Sanderson Blinds Ltd* [2009] ICR 543 . . . where the majority . . . read the domestic provisions consistently with the Equal Treatment Framework Directive 2000/78/EC (OJ 2000 L303, p 16) . . . we agree with Elias J in *Sharma* that, whereas domestic legislation must provide the protection contained in the [PTWD], it is not limited to such protection. 'On the ground that' in regulation 5(2)(a) [of the PTWR] means what Mummery J said [in *O'Neill v Governors of St Thomas More Roman Catholic Voluntarily Aided Upper School* [1997] ICR 33, 43F] . . . Part-time work must be the effective and predominant cause of the less favourable treatment complained of; it need not be the only cause.

It is argued that Judge Peter Clark's approach in *Carl* is to be preferred to that of the EAT in *McMenemy* for three reasons: first, it accords with that adopted in the context of section 13 of the Equality Act 2010;[70] secondly, it appears to be the most sensible way of furthering the objective of tackling discrimination in the PTWD; and finally, it removes the possibility of the employer justifying the treatment of the part-time worker by reference to its motive and/or intention—for if the employer need only show that the part-time nature of the work was not the sole cause of the less favourable treatment, this indirectly enables it to advance evidence that its reason or motive for its actions were some other factor.

---

[66] [2015] IRLR 264.   [67] [2006] IRLR 761.   [68] [2008] ICR 623.   [69] [2009] ICR 1286.
[70] See *Nagarajan v London Regional Transport* [2000] 1 AC 501, 512H–513B per Lord Nicholls; Chapter 10, section 10.2.3.

We now move on to address the employer's objective justification defence in regulation 5(2)(b) of the PTWR. There has been a dearth of domestic case law addressing the mechanics of this defence. Indeed, one commentator has remarked that it is 'indicative of the many preceding hurdles that British case law has rarely considered in detail how th[is] test is to be interpreted'.[71] The only decision of the EAT to date in *Besong v Connex Bus (UK) Ltd*[72] proposed that the objective justification defence ought to be approached in the same manner as the employer's proportionality defence in the context of an indirect discrimination claim under section 19 of the Equality Act 2010.[73] Hence the employer must show that it has a genuine need or legitimate aim to pursue in adopting differential treatment between its part-time and full-time workers and that it was appropriate and necessary for it to treat the part-timer less favourably than the full-timer in order to achieve that need or legitimate objective. The jurisprudence of the ECJ also provides some guidance on the nature of the objective justification defence. The FTWD has the same wording as that contained in the PTWD in respect of the objective justification defence. In the case of *Del Cerro Alonso v Osakidetza-Servicio Vasco de Salud*[74] and *De Diego Porras v Ministerio de Defensa*[75] the ECJ interpreted the wording in the FTWD. Here, it was held that the standard formulation of the proportionality defence in the context of indirect discrimination law ought to be pursued, i.e. genuine need/legitimate aim, appropriateness and necessity. Therefore, by extrapolation, this would suggest that the defence under the PTWD and the PTWR is identical to that applicable in the case of the FTWD and the FTER and that the EAT in *Besong v Connex Bus (UK) Ltd* applied the correct approach. However, it should be highlighted that the EAT in *Besong* displayed a degree of deference to the employer in determining whether its actions were objectively justified, which underlines the relevance of the following warning sounded by McCann:

■ D. McCann, *Regulating Flexible Work* (Oxford, OUP, 2008) 86

> . . . there is a risk that the defence could curb [the effectiveness of the PTWR] by inviting courts and tribunals to attach substantive results to their views on the role and value of part-time work, the nature and import of labour market flexibility, the role of labour law in harmonizing work and family life, and the appropriate balance between flexibility and fairness to workers.

In fact, a rather restricted approach to objective justification was adopted by the CJEU in *Österreichischer Gewerkschaftsbund v Verband Österreichischer Banken und Bankiers*[76] where it treated the employer's defence as shaped by the *pro rata temporis* principle laid down in regulation 5(3) of the PTWR. Here, a child allowance provided by the employer was reduced proportionately in the case of part-time workers to account for the reduced hours that they worked. A part-time employee challenged the employer's practice in court and the CJEU held that the reduced allowance was objectively justified on the basis of the *pro rata temporis* principle. With respect, it is suggested that this approach was misconceived, as it confuses the role that the pro rata principle plays in the PTWR and PTWD. The pro rata principle is applicable in the *a priori* question as to whether the part-time worker has suffered less favourable treatment in comparison with a comparable full-time worker, rather than as a core component of the *ex post* objective justification defence. Furthermore, if it is to be applied consistently with the approach in indirect sex,

---

[71] M. Bell, 'Achieving the Objectives of the Part-Time Work Directive? Revisiting the Part-Time Workers Regulations' (2011) 40 *Industrial Law Journal* 254, 263.
[72] *Besong v Connex Bus (UK) Ltd* [2005] All ER (D) 261 (May), para 48.
[73] See Chapter 10, section 10.2.4.4, for a detailed discussion.
[74] [2007] ECR I-7109, [2008] ICR 141, 161G–H.
[75] [2016] IRLR 964.   [76] [2015] IRLR 67.

race, etc. discrimination cases, the proportionality element of the objective justification defence ought to entail a more intensive scrutiny of the employer's managerial practices than the mere invocation of the *pro rata temporis* principle.

Finally, we should add that part-time workers have a right to receive a written statement of the employer's reasons for treating them less favourably than a full-timer in terms of regulation 6. Further, it is not possible for the employer and part-timer to expressly disapply the rights conferred on the latter in the PTWR by contractual agreement.[77] The rights afforded to part-timers are enforced by presenting a complaint to an employment tribunal[78] and part-timers are entitled to treat themselves as automatically unfairly dismissed if they are dismissed for presenting such a complaint.[79]

13.3 THE REGULATION OF FIXED-TERM WORK

Before we turn to consider the provisions of the FTER, it is important not to lose sight of the fact that general employment laws have an impact on fixed-term workers. For example, employment law tends to handicap fixed-term workers by requiring them to meet qualifying thresholds to gain access to certain statutory rights. Employees must have two years' continuous service in order to enjoy the right to receive a redundancy payment[80] and unfair dismissal.[81] Further, there is a 26-week qualifying period before the statutory right to paternity leave is triggered.[82] There is also a qualifying period of one year for parental leave.[83] Fixed-term contracts are often interrupted by short breaks, which can also be fatal to the preservation of continuity of employment, disabling the employee from reaching the relevant qualifying period. For example, if an employee has been working for the same employer for a period of 22 months and there is then a break from work of 28 days, if the employee subsequently returns to work for the employer on a six-month contract, the employee would not be entitled to avail him/herself of the right to unfair dismissal. Leaving aside the possibility that the employee might be able to satisfy the criteria set out in section 212 of the Employment Rights Act 1996 ('ERA'), the effect of the 28-day gap is such that the fixed-term contractual periods of 22 months and six months will not be bridged.[84]

Although they fail to (a) tackle the ability of fixed-term employees to meet these statutory qualifying thresholds or (b) link up breaks in continuous employment, a measure of protection, however, is conferred upon fixed-term employees by the FTER. The FTER do so in two particular ways:

(1) Regulation 8 of the FTER prevents an employer from employing a fixed-term employee on a succession of fixed-term contracts for four years or more. Hence if an employee has been continuously employed under

(a) a fixed-term contract that has been continually renewed, or

(b) a succession of different fixed-term contracts (some of which may have been renewed),

for a period of four years or more, the employee concerned is entitled to convert his/her fixed-term contract into a permanent contract of employment.[85]

(2) The parity or equal treatment model in the FTER operates in broadly similar terms to that contained in the PTWR. Thus, if a fixed-term employee is treated less favourably than a comparable permanent employee in respect of the terms of his/her contract or subjected to a detriment because he/she is a fixed-term employee, then the employer will be liable unless it can show the treatment was objectively justified.[86]

---

[77] Regulation 9 of the PTWR.   [78] Regulation 8 of the PTWR.   [79] Regulation 7 of the PTWR.
[80] Section 155 of the ERA.   [81] Section 108(1) of the ERA.
[82] Regulation 4(2)(a) of the Paternity and Adoption Leave Regulations 2002 (SI 2002/2788).
[83] Regulation 13(1) of the Maternity and Parental Leave etc. Regulations 1999 (SI 1999/3312).
[84] See sections 210 and 211 of the ERA; Chapter 3, section 3.2.2.   [85] Regulation 8 of the FTER.

However, the FTER deviate from the PTWR in a variety of ways.

(1) The relational scope of application differs. The FTER only protect an employee who is employed on the basis of a fixed-term contract, whereas the PTWR are broader in their coverage, extending to 'workers'.[87] Moreover, agency workers are excluded from the operation of the FTER.[88]

(2) Unlike the interpretation of the PTWR, the dismissal of a fixed-term employee will not necessarily constitute a detriment. For example, in *Department for Work and Pensions v Webley*,[89] the non-renewal of a fixed-term contract immediately prior to the employee satisfying the qualifying threshold triggering the statutory right to unfair dismissal could not of itself constitute (a) a detriment or (b) less favourable treatment by comparison with that given to a permanent employee, since the contract had simply been terminated by the effluxion of time in accordance with its terms.

(3) Another difference between the PTWR and the FTER lies in the latter's 'overall package' approach. Regulation 4(1) of the FTER directs that where a contractual term of a fixed-term employee is less favourable than the same term in the comparator permanent employee's contract of employment, such treatment will nonetheless be deemed to be justified on objective grounds if the terms of the fixed-term employee's contract of employment, taken as a whole, are at least as favourable as the terms of the comparable permanent employee's contract of employment. Hence, if there is parity in the overall contractual package of the fixed-term employee and the comparable permanent employee or the former's package is actually better than the latter, the employer will not be liable.

However, there are some commonalities between the PTWR and the FTER. Akin to the PTWR, the pro rata principle is to be applied, unless it is inappropriate, when assessing whether there has been less favourable treatment in the terms and conditions of the fixed-term employee's contract in comparison with those applying to the comparable permanent employee.[90] The 'pro rata principle' means that where a comparable permanent employee receives or is entitled to receive pay or any other benefit, a fixed-term employee is to receive or be entitled to such proportion of that pay or other benefit as is reasonable in the circumstances, having regard to the length of his/her contract of employment and to the terms on which the pay or other benefit is offered.[91]

13.3.1 An examination of the FTER

The expressions 'fixed-term', 'fixed-term employee', and 'permanent employee' are defined in regulation 1(2) of the FTER:

> **Regulation 1 Citation, commencement and interpretation . . .**
>
> (2) In these Regulations—
>
> . . . 'fixed-term contract' means a contract of employment that, under its provisions determining how it will terminate in the normal course, will terminate—

---

[86] Regulation 3(1) and (3) of the FTER.

[87] This includes former fixed-term employees, i.e. a fixed-term employee whose status subsequently changes to that of a permanent employee is entitled to bring a complaint of less favourable treatment because of fixed-term employment in respect of the previous periods of service as a fixed-term employee: *Valenza v Autorita Garante della Concorrenza e del Mercato* [2013] ICR 373.

[88] Regulation 19 of the FTER.   [89] [2005] ICR 577.

[90] Regulation 3(4) of the FTER.   [91] Regulation 1(2) of the FTER.

> (a) on the expiry of a specific term,
>
> (b) on the completion of a particular task, or
>
> (c) on the occurrence or non-occurrence of any other specific event other than the attainment by the employee of any normal and bona fide retiring age in the establishment for an employee holding the position held by him,
>
> and any reference to 'fixed-term' shall be construed accordingly . . .
>
> 'fixed-term employee' means an employee who is employed under a fixed-term contract;
>
> 'permanent employee' means an employee who is not employed under a fixed-term contract, and any reference to 'permanent employment' shall be construed accordingly.

The definition of a 'fixed-term contract' in regulation 1(2) of the FTWR is intended to flesh out the basic provision in clause 2(1) of the FTWD and the more extensive direction in clause 3(1) of the FTWD, which both set out the coverage of that Directive. It is stipulated in clause 2(1) that the FTWD applies to 'fixed-term workers who have an employment contract or employment relationship as defined in law, collective agreements or practice in each Member State'. Meanwhile, clause 3(1) states that 'fixed-term worker' means 'a person having an employment contract or relationship entered into directly between an employer and a worker where the end of the employment contract or relationship is determined by objective conditions such as reaching a specific date, completing a specific task, or the occurrence of a specific event'. These provisions in the FTWD were evaluated by the CJEU in *Poclava v Toledano*,[92] which concerned the status of individuals engaged in work on probation for a defined period of time. It was ruled that a probationary period in an employment contract cannot be classified as a fixed-term contract under clause 2(1) of the FTWD since a probationary period is designed to make 'it possible for a worker's aptitude and skills to be checked, whilst a fixed-term employment contract is used if the end of the employment contract or relationship is determined by objective conditions'.[93]

In the same vein as the PTWR, regulation 2 of the FTER requires the fixed-term employee to demonstrate less favourable treatment in comparison with a suitable comparator. As demonstrated by *DJ Hall v Xerox Ltd*,[94] it is essential that the employer is responsible for the less favourable treatment, rather than some other third party. In approaching the less favourable treatment test, the fixed-term employee must invoke a comparable permanent employee employed by the same employer at the same establishment (or, where there is no comparable permanent employee working or based at that establishment, at a different establishment and satisfying the requirements) who is engaged in the same or broadly similar work having regard, where relevant, to whether they have a similar level of qualification and skills.[95] If a permanent employee's contract has been terminated, he/she cannot be adopted as the comparable permanent employee.[96] Further, hypothetical comparators are disallowed. Consider the illustration in Hypothetical B.

---

[92] [2015] IRLR 403.   [93] *Poclava v Toledano* [2015] IRLR 403, 406.

[94] (UKEAT/0061/14/JOJ, 11 July 2014). Here, a term in a PHI policy restricted fixed-term employees from being entitled to benefits in the event that their employment contracts came to an end prior to the end of a 26-week qualifying period and the EAT ruled that it was the behaviour of the PHI insurer that constituted less favourable treatment.

[95] The fixed-termer and the comparator both must be employed on the basis of a contract of employment.

[96] Regulation 2(2) of the FTER.

Hypothetical B

Andrew Paxman ('AP') is an IT manager employed on a five-year fixed-term contract of employment at the Cambridge office of Danny's Demolishers Ltd ('DD'). DD hires Mathew Quinn ('MQ') as an IT consultant at the Cambridge office on the basis of an open-ended 'worker' contract, i.e. MQ is a 'worker' in terms of section 230(3)(b) of the ERA since he is not bound by a continuing contractual obligation to perform work when DD provides work to him and DD is under no continuing contractual commitment to provide MQ work when it is available. MQ's job is broadly similar to that of AP, but AP's salary is £50,000 per annum and the salary commanded by MQ is £90,000 per annum. Unfortunately, AP would be unable to invoke MQ as a comparator as MQ is not a permanent *employee*. Furthermore, since the FTER prevent the deployment of hypothetical comparators, AP would be unable to attempt to recategorize MQ's permanent worker contract as a permanent employment contract.

In contrast to the PTWR, there is no case law on what is meant by (1) 'the same employer' and (2) 'the same establishment'. However, it is likely that the same approach would be adopted as under the PTWR. As for (3) 'the same or broadly similar work', the CJEU in *Valenza v Autorita Garante della Concorrenza e del Mercato*[97] decided that a range of factors would have to be taken into account by a domestic court or tribunal in order to assess whether a permanent employee was in a comparable situation. This includes the training requirements, working conditions involved, and the nature of the work, i.e. whether the duties performed by the fixed-term employee correspond with those of the permanent employee.[98]

Clause 4 of the FTWD and regulation 3(3)(b) of the FTER also provide the employer with an 'objective justification' defence. In *De Diego Porras v Ministerio de Defensa*, the CJEU ruled that the very fact that a worker was part-time could not, of itself, amount to a valid objective ground. Here, Spanish legislation provided that workers engaged on temporary employment contracts would be denied the general statutory right to a severance payment on the termination of their employment. The CJEU remarked that the 'objective grounds' concept in the FTWD demanded that any:

> . . . unequal treatment found to exist [must] be justified by precise, specific factors, characterising the employment condition to which it relates, in the particular context in which it occurs and on the basis of objective, transparent criteria in order to ensure that that unequal treatment in fact meets a genuine need, is appropriate for achieving the objective pursued and is necessary for that purpose [and t]hose factors may result, in particular, from the specific nature of the tasks for the performance of which fixed-term contracts have been concluded and from the inherent characteristics of those tasks or, as the case may be, from pursuit of a legitimate social-policy objective of a Member State.[99]

The main difference between the PTWR and the FTER lies in the latter's specific control of successive abuse of fixed-term contracts. As noted earlier, regulation 8 of the FTER provides that if a fixed-term employee is employed on the basis of (a) a fixed-term contract that has been continually renewed or (b) a series of fixed-term contracts (some of which may have been renewed) for a period in excess of four years, the employee is afforded a right to convert his/her contract into a permanent contract of employment of

[97] [2013] ICR 373.
[98] *ibid.*, 382F; cf. *Matthews v Kent & Medway Towns Fire Authority* [2006] ICR 365.
[99] *De Diego Porras v Ministerio de Defensa* [2016] IRLR 964, 968.

indefinite duration.[100] In the following extract, Baroness Hale explained the purpose of the corresponding provisions in the FTWD:

■ *Duncombe v Secretary of State for Children, Schools and Families* [2011] **ICR 495, 500D–F**

Baroness Hale:

The preamble and general considerations in the [FTWD] . . . recognise that 'fixed-term employment contracts respond, in certain circumstances, to the needs of both employers and workers' and that they 'are a feature of employment in certain sectors, occupations and activities which can suit both employers and workers'. But the substantive provisions of the . . . [FTWD] do not attempt to define the circumstances in which fixed-term employment is acceptable. Instead they concentrate on preventing or limiting the abuse of successive fixed-term contracts, the abuse being to disguise what is effectively an indefinite employment as a series of fixed-term contracts, thus potentially avoiding the benefits and protections available in indefinite employment.

Whilst the prevention of successive use of fixed-term contracts as a form of disguised indefinite employment is an admirable purpose, there are numerous difficulties with this notion of automatic conversion. The first difficulty is insurmountable and is posed by the common law, namely that 'the transformation . . . of the underlying contract of employment from a fixed-term contract into a contract apparently of indeterminate duration may have the ironical effect of rendering the contract terminable by notice of a much shorter duration than that of the fixed term of the original contract'.[101] That conundrum is attributable to the operation of the common law rule empowering an employer to dismiss an employee on providing a reasonable period of notice.[102] The other difficulties arise as a consequence of deficiencies inherent within the model which has been devised by the FTER. These defects are sufficiently weighty to suggest that the objective of preventing the abusive rollover of fixed-term contracts has been frustrated. Two are highlighted in the following extract from McCann:

■ D. McCann, *Regulating Flexible Work* (Oxford, OUP, 2008) 133–4

A [first] limitation of this regulatory model is the absence of any measures tailored towards protecting temporary workers during the four years preceding the contract renewal that triggers the right to a permanent contract. The regulations do not intervene, for example, to assert the value of job security by requiring that permanent jobs be paired with open-ended contracts . . . [Secondly, the FTER] apply the rules on continuity contained in the ERA to the determination of whether an employee has been 'continuously employed' under successive fixed-term contracts during the four years in which these contracts are permitted. As a result, periods of longer than a week in which no employment contract subsists rupture the continuity and prevent the application of the regulations . . . The implications of the use of this model . . . are both predictable and destructive, transplanting to the [FTER] the exclusion of many casual workers and those whose working patterns are subject to 'contract breaks' from the right to an indefinite contract.

---

[100] The fixed-term employee has the right to demand a written statement from the employer confirming that the employee's contract is no longer fixed-term or that he/she is now a permanent employee: regulation 9 of the FTER. Where the contract is converted, the employer is entitled to make certain modifications to the employee's terms and conditions, so long as they are not sufficiently material to render the overall contractual package unfavourable to the employee: *Huet v Université de Bretagne occidentale* [2012] ICR 694.   [101] M. Freedland, *The Personal Employment Contract* (Oxford, OUP, 2003) 317.
[102] See Chapter 15, section 15.1.1.

A further dilution of the protection conferred concerns the four-year period. Regulation 8(5) of the FTER directs that it may be modified by a collective or workforce agreement and there is nothing to prescribe that that period functions as a minimum floor, i.e. it would appear that the threshold four-year period can be increased.[103] Furthermore, the FTER do not absolutely outlaw the use of successive fixed-term contracts beyond the four-year period, since an employer will be perfectly entitled to do so if it can harness the objective justification defence.[104] In accordance with the formulation adopted by the ECJ in *Del Cerro Alonso v Osakidetza-Servicio Vasco de Salud*,[105] it is incumbent on the employer to establish that it had a genuine need and that the less favourable treatment of the fixed-term employee was 'appropriate [to] achiev[e] the objective pursued and . . . necessary for that purpose'.[106] The domestic approach to the objective justification defence has been particularly deferential to management. For example, in *Duncombe v Secretary of State for Children, Schools and Families*,[107] a teacher was seconded on the basis of a series of two-year, three-year, and four-year fixed-term contracts to a school in Europe for children of parents working in the European institutions. A treaty between the European Communities and the Member States prescribed that the school would be governed by an international board. The board laid down a general rule that teachers would be seconded for no more than nine years. When the claimant sought to convert her fixed-term contract into a permanent employment contract, the Supreme Court held that the employer was objectively justified in refusing to do so. This was on the ground that the claimant's complaint was really about the fixed-term nature of the nine-year period itself which had been prescribed by the international board, rather than the use of the successive two-year, three-year, and four-year fixed-term contracts to make up the nine-year period of employment.

This somewhat relaxed construction in the domestic courts can be contrasted with the approach of the ECJ to objective justification in *Adeneler v Ellinikos Organismos Galaktos*.[108] Here, Greek legislation transposing the FTWD stipulated that fixed-term contracts could only be regarded as successive contracts insofar as they were not separated by more than 20 working days. It was held that this was too restrictive and did not achieve the aims of the FTWD. It could be easily circumvented by employers simply allowing a 21-day period to elapse at the end of each fixed-term employment contract before subsequently concluding another fixed-term contract with the same employee. As for the nature of the 'objective reasons' that the employer may advance as justification, the ECJ also ruled that they must 'be understood as referring to precise and concrete circumstances characterizing a given activity, which . . . may result . . . from the specific nature of the tasks for the performance of which such contracts have been concluded and from the inherent characteristics of those tasks or, as the case may be, from pursuit of a legitimate social-policy objective of a member State'.[109] This necessitates the drawing of a link between the commercial activity pursued by the employer and the use of successive fixed-term contracts, i.e. that there is something about the former that demands the latter. Hence, if the employer's requirements for an activity are indefinite, fixed, or permanent, it will be an uphill struggle for the employer to establish that it needed to employ a fixed-term employee.[110] A good example of the link between an activity and fixed-term work is afforded by *Kücük v Land Nordrhein-Westfalen*.[111] Here, the fact that an activity was being covered by a fixed-term

---

[103] See also regulation 18 of the FTER, on which, see *Hudson v Department of Work and Pensions* [2013] IRLR 32.

[104] Regulation 8(2)(b) of the FTER.   [105] [2007] ECR I-7109, [2008] ICR 141.

[106] *ibid.*, 161G–H.   [107] [2011] ICR 495.   [108] [2006] 3 CMLR 30.

[109] *Del Cerro Alonso v Osakidetza-Servicio Vasco de Salud* [2007] ECR I-7109, [2008] ICR 141, 161C–D.

[110] For an example, see *Pérez López v Servicio Madrileno de Salud (Comunidad de Madrid)* [2016] IRLR 970 where the employer's need was not of a temporary, auxiliary, or extraordinary nature, but instead was permanent and fixed. In such a case, the use of a fixed-term worker on a successive basis was unwarranted.   [111] [2012] ICR 682.

worker for permanent staff off on temporary leave was held to establish the requisite link between the economic activity of the employer and the operation of successive fixed-term contracts. The employer was held to be justified in employing a fixed-term employee as replacement cover for temporary absences, notwithstanding that she had been engaged for more than 11 years on a total of 13 fixed-term contracts. The CJEU adopted a similar approach in *Marquez Samohano v Universitat Pompeu Fabra*,[112] which concerned the appointment of fixed-term associate lecturers at a university. Associate lectureships at UPF were filled by professionals employed outside the university in order to impart specialist practical teaching and knowledge to students, in a similar fashion to lectures and seminars delivered as part of the postgraduate Legal Practice Course in England and Wales or the Diploma in Professional Legal Practice in Scotland. The CJEU classified the duties of the associate lecturers as temporary rather than fixed and permanent, since the professional activities of the associate lecturers in the private sector would be resumed at the end of the contract on a full-time basis, and the associate lectureships were not being used by the employer to meet fixed and permanent needs of the universities in terms of the employment of teaching staff. As such, any alleged rollover of the fixed-term associate lectureship contracts could be justified on objective grounds.

As for the practical mechanics of the objective justification defence under regulation 8 of the FTER, the following extract from Barnard is particularly helpful:

■ **C. Barnard, *EU Employment Law*, 4th edition (Oxford, OUP, 2012) 443**

So how might the rules on objective justification apply in practice? Take a rather familiar example of a researcher working in a university being awarded a grant for five years. The researcher is given a five-year fixed-term contract. In the UK, at least, this initial decision does not need to be objectively justified. At the end of that five-year period some more money is found to give the researcher another two years of employment to finish the research. In principle, the renewal would trigger the provision on abuse and so that second contract would become permanent unless an objectively justified case could be made as to why not. Here the justification would relate to the limited pot of money and the completion of the research. The second contract would therefore probably continue to be fixed-term.

There are a number of final issues to mention. First, fixed-term employees are entitled to be informed of permanent vacancies in the employer's establishment[113] and to receive a written statement of the employer's reasons for treating them less favourably than a permanent employee,[114] and the rights conferred on them are enforced by presenting a complaint to an employment tribunal.[115] Fixed-term employees have a right to be treated as automatically unfairly dismissed if they are dismissed for presenting a complaint to a tribunal in terms of regulation 6, and there is a prohibition on the ability of the employer and employee to contract out of the latter's rights under the FTER.[116] As for the success or otherwise of the FTER, recent research findings have shown that there is no evidence for any diminution in the wage gap between female fixed-term workers and female permanent workers.[117] As such, seen from the perspective of the elimination of gender wage disparities,[118] there is clearly more work to do before the FTER's legal intervention into the fixed-term labour market can be characterized as an unmitigated victory for women's rights.

---

[112] [2014] ICR 609.   [113] Regulation 3(6) and (7) of the FTER.
[114] Regulation 5 of the FTER.   [115] Regulation 7 of the FTER.   [116] Regulation 10 of the FTER.
[117] A. Salvatori, 'The Effects of the EU Equal Treatment Directive for Fixed-Term Workers: Evidence from the UK' (2015) 53 *British Journal of Industrial Relations* 278.
[118] See Chapter 14 for more detailed consideration of this issue.

Reflection points

1. Would you agree with Bell's view that the 'shortcomings of the [PTWR] lies in their limited capacity to dig beneath the manifest examples of discrimination . . . [and] that gender equality [laws] remain . . . more effective in tackling barriers in access to part-time working'?[119] If so, why? If not, why not?

2. Are the protections afforded to fixed-term employees by the FTER 'paper thin'? If so, why? If not, why not?

3. Assume that you answered questions 1 and 2 in the affirmative. Do you believe that the PTWR and FTER should be amended to bolster the protection afforded to part-time and fixed-term workers? If so, how? If not, why not?

4. In your opinion, is there any justification for the adoption of an approach to the employer's objective justification defence in the PTWR and the FTER that differs from the employer's defence in an indirect discrimination claim? Give reasons for your answer.

5. To what extent do you believe that the FTER and PTWR are safe from repeal in the post-Brexit era?

 For additional reading on the regulation of part-time and fixed-term work, visit the Online Resources for this book at www.oup.com/uk/cabrelli3e/

---

[119] M. Bell, 'Achieving the Objectives of the Part-Time Work Directive? Revisiting the Part-Time Workers Regulations' (2011) 40 *Industrial Law Journal* 254, 278.

CHAPTER FOURTEEN

EQUAL PAY LAW

14.1 CONTEXTUAL ANALYSIS OF EQUAL PAY LAW

This chapter examines the principle of equal pay for equal work irrespective of a worker's gender, which is enshrined in Chapter 3 of Part 5 of the Equality Act 2010 ('EA'). In the opening section, consideration will be given to the stubbornness of the gender pay gap in the UK and the EU, as well as the justifications for intervention in the labour market via the auspices of equal pay laws. The chapter then goes on to discuss the legal machinery in the EA which confers an entitlement on employees of one sex to the same remuneration as suitable employee comparators of the opposite sex. The focus will then turn to the content of the 'sex equality clause', which is a term imposed into every employee's contract of employment by virtue of section 66 of the EA. The distinction between the three legal criteria of 'like work', 'work rated as equivalent', and 'work of equal value' in section 65 of the EA and the employer's defence to an equal pay claim will then be addressed. The relationship between Chapter 3 of Part 5 of the EA and (1) the general sex discrimination regime in the EA and (2) Article 157 (ex Articles 141 and 119 of the European Treaty) of the Treaty on the Functioning of the European Union ('TFEU')—which secures equal pay for equal work at the level of European law—will also be taken into account throughout the discussion in this chapter. Although it is assumed that Article 157 of the TFEU will no longer be relevant for domestic equal pay law post-Brexit, it is covered in this chapter as it will continue to apply at least until some period in 2019.

14.1.1 Contextual and historical examination of equal pay laws

In the same vein as the statutory inroads made into the 'wage–work' bargain that we explored in Chapter 8,[1] anti-discrimination/equality law has also been harnessed as a means of regulating the pay-related contractual terms and conditions of employees and

---

[1] Namely the National Minimum Wage Act 1998 and Part II of the Employment Rights Act 1996 ('ERA').

workers.[2] The issue of equal pay for equal work is one which has never been far off the public agenda, with one commentator referring to it as 'a constant feature of political and legal debate'.[3] Pay inequality amongst the sexes has been a feature which has been with us for a considerable period of time. However, there have been profound changes in social attitudes since the following statement was made by Lord Atkinson in the House of Lords in the early twentieth century:

■ *Roberts v Hopwood* [1925] AC 578, 594E–F

Lord Atkinson:

The council would, in my view, fail in their duty if, in administering funds which did not belong to their members alone, they put aside all these aids to the ascertainment of what was just and reasonable remuneration to give for the services rendered to them, and allowed themselves to be guided in preference by some eccentric principles of socialistic philanthropy, or by a feminist ambition to secure the equality of the sexes in the matter of wages in the world of labour.

Approximately 40 years after the coming into force of equal pay legislation in the UK, notwithstanding that the gender pay gap in the UK since the 1970s[4] has undergone a 'dramatic and substantially larger [decline] than that experienced in the US',[5] a marked difference in pay between men and women persists to the present day.[6] As the following extract reveals, the level of the pay disparity between the sexes varies depending on whether the median or mean earnings are taken as the relevant barometer:

■ Office for National Statistics, *Annual Survey of Hours and Earnings: 2016 Provisional Results* (October 2016) 8

Gender pay differences

While there is no single measure that adequately deals with the complex issue of the differences between men's and women's pay, we prefer to use median hourly earnings (excluding overtime). Including overtime can skew the results because men work relatively more overtime than women, and using hourly earnings better accounts for the fact that men work on average more hours than women. The median is less affected by a relatively small number of very high earners than the mean, and therefore gives a better indication of typical pay . . .

It should be noted that the figures do not show differences in rates of pay for comparable jobs, as they are affected by factors such as the proportion of men and women in different occupations. For example, a higher proportion of women work in occupations such as administration and caring, which tend to offer lower salaries . . . The gender pay gap is calculated as the difference between average hourly earnings (excluding overtime) of men and women as a proportion of average hourly earnings (excluding overtime) of men's earnings. Given the strong influence of the balance between full-time and part-time employees, the majority of detailed analyses of the gender pay gap in this bulletin are presented for full-time employees alone. Figures for full-time and part-time

---

[2] The expression 'workers' here is used in a generic, rather than legal, sense.

[3] S. Honeyball, *Great Debates in Employment Law* (Basingstoke, Palgrave Macmillan, 2011) 105.

[4] There was a decrease in the gender pay gap from 37% in 1970 to 23% in 1990 based on average hourly earnings for full-time employees: M. Drolet and K. Mumford, 'The Gender Pay Gap for Private-Sector Employees in Canada and Britain' (2012) 50 *British Journal of Industrial Relations* 529, 532.

[5] *ibid.*, 532.

[6] For an analysis of the gender pay gap from the perspective of career advancement, see I. Noback, L. Broersma, and J. van Dijk, 'Career Advancement in Financial Services and the Influence of Flexible Work-Time Arrangements' (2016) 54 *British Journal of Industrial Relations* 114.

employees combined (as well as part-time employees alone) are included in the downloadable spreadsheets accompanying the charts.

In April 2016 the gender pay gap (for median earnings) for full-time employees decreased to 9.4%, from 9.6% in 2015 . . . This is the lowest since the survey began in 1997, although the gender pay gap has changed relatively little in recent years. When part-time employees are included, the gap decreased from 19.3% in 2015 to 18.1% in 2016, the largest year-on-year drop since 2010. This is also the lowest gender pay gap since the survey began in 1997, when the gap for all employees was 27.5%. For part-time employees separately, women are paid more on average, resulting in a 'negative' gender pay gap. Although the part-time gender pay gap has decreased from minus 6.8% in April 2015 from minus 6.0% in April 2016, there is evidence that the part-time gender pay gap has widened in the long-term. [see Figure 14.1].[7]

Although a gender pay gap—currently standing at 18.1 per cent—clearly persists, it should be pointed out that some progress has been made at certain levels of the workplace and in certain age groups (see Figure 14.1). For example, in the case of women in their 20s and early 30s, the gender pay gap has reversed, i.e. women are now earning more than men.[8] In addition, Geiler and Renneboog's research shows that there is little evidence of pay discrimination at the top level of the company boardroom, e.g. in the case of the chief executive officer ('CEO').[9] On the other hand, however, at the 'sub-top' level of the boardroom, e.g. deputy CEO, chief operating officer, and chief financial officer, deep-seated and endemic pay disparities remain.[10]

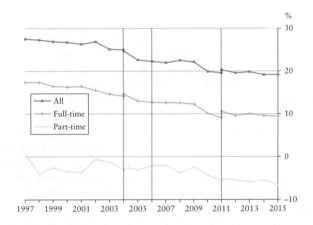

Figure 14.1 *Gender pay gap for median gross hourly earnings (excluding overtime), UK, April 1997 to 2016*

Source: 2016 ONS statistical bulletin (Provisional Results) Annual Survey of Hours and Earnings, available at https://www.ons.gov.uk/employmentandlabourmarket/peopleinwork/earningsand-workinghours/bulletins/annualsurveyofhoursandearnings/2016provisionalresults#gender-pay-diffe rences Figure 6, at page 10 (last visited 8 October 2017).

[7] Available at https://www.ons.gov.uk/employmentandlabourmarket/peopleinwork/earningsandwork-inghours/bulletins/annualsurveyofhoursandearnings/2016provisionalresults#gender-pay-differences (last visited 8 October 2017).

[8] See http://www.telegraph.co.uk/finance/jobs/11240532/The-gender-pay-gap-has-fallen-to-a-record-low.html (last visited 8 October 2017).

[9] P. Geiler and L. Renneboog, 'Are Female Top Managers Really Paid Less?' (2015) 35 *Journal of Corporate Finance* 345.

[10] See also the detailed summary of the gender pay gap in the House of Commons Library Research Briefing Paper No. 07068, available at http://researchbriefings.files.parliament.uk/documents/SN07068/SN07068.pdf (last visited 8 October 2017).

The latest empirical research has revealed that the differentials in the median (and mean) gross hourly earnings between the sexes cannot be attributed alone, or in aggregate, to market forces, differences in human capital, occupation/job characteristics, or workplace segregation. This has led scholars to conclude that these variations in pay between men and women can be imputed to unconscious sex discrimination,[11] which is known in economic terms as the 'discrimination coefficient'.[12] Consider the following extracts:

■ S. Deakin, C. McLaughlin, and D. Chai, 'Gender Inequality and Reflexive Law: The Potential of Different Regulatory Mechanisms' in L. Dickens (ed.), *Making Employment Rights Effective: Issues of Enforcement and Compliance* (Oxford, Hart Publishing, 2012) 116

While the pay gap can be partially explained by wider social structures, including occupational segregation, the undervaluation of women's work and the unequal division of family responsibilities, it is generally accepted in policy circles that discriminatory practices by employers also contribute to the ongoing inequality in pay. The assumption is that while some pay discrimination may be deliberate, it is more likely in practice to be systemic, and as such only identifiable through systematic evaluation of payment systems by employers.

■ A. McColgan, 'Regulating Pay Discrimination' in H. Collins, P. Davies, and R. Rideout (eds), *Legal Regulation of the Employment Relation* (London, Kluwer, 2000) 204–5

In the case of women doing the same jobs and/or working in the same workplaces as men, women's wages are held down by their lower levels of seniority, their exclusion from bonus payment schemes and, in cases where such schemes do apply to their jobs, by discriminatory methods of appraisal. Women are less able to work overtime in respect of which, at least in the manual sector, significant premia apply. This inability is not simply the result of child-care commitments—employers are also less likely to organise female jobs around the expectation of full-time work but are, instead, likely to introduce part-time shift work. And, whereas male shift working is generally paid a premium, female 'twilight shifts' are frequently not so rewarded because they are seen as convenient to working mothers. Finally, part-time workers are generally not entitled to overtime pay until they have exceeded normal full-time hours. To these factors may be added those of occupational and workplace segregation, women frequently working in smaller, less profitable organisations and in occupations in which the availability of cheap, (particularly part-time) female labour keeps wages down . . . traditional economists tend to take the view that discrimination does not persist within the market and that, therefore, women's lower wages must be explicable by their lower levels of human capital and/or their preference for non-monetary compensation. These 'human capital'[13] and 'compensating differentials' approaches do not withstand scrutiny. The factual assumptions upon which they rely (*i.e.*, that women are less educated and less productive, that their jobs are less skilled, that the gender-pay gap can be attributed in large part to differential levels of experience by sex, that 'female' jobs have better terms and conditions than those generally done by men), are incorrect. Further, they are suffused with stereotypical assumptions about women and the nature and value of typically female jobs . . .

[11] See the comprehensive analysis in A. McColgan, *Just Wages for Women* (Oxford, Clarendon Press, 1997) 214–82; K. Mumford and P. N. Smith, 'The Gender Earnings Gap in Britain: Including the Workplace' (2007) 75 *The Manchester School* 653, 670.

[12] G. S. Becker, *The Economics of Discrimination*, 2nd edition (Chicago, University of Chicago Press, 1971).

[13] See G. S. Becker, 'Investment in Human Capital: A Theoretical Analysis' (1962) 70 *Journal of Political Economy* 9; G. S. Becker, 'Human Capital, Effort, and the Sexual Division of Labor' (1985) 3 *Journal of Labor Economics* S33–S58.

In stark contrast to the sentiments articulated in these passages, other commentators are less convinced that the stubbornness of the gender pay gap can be ascribed to managerial practices which are inherently sexually discriminatory. Instead, it is contended that disparities in pay can be attributed to non-discriminatory factors such as the differing roles assumed by men and women in society, with the latter more likely to perform a dual role, i.e. as an economic actor labouring for wages in the workplace whilst also bearing a disproportionate share of family caring responsibilities in their social lives. The argument runs that the time spent on these caring duties which are non-remunerated depresses the female worker's earning potential and productivity in the labour market[14] and that this is one of the consequences of the transition from the traditional 'male breadwinner'/'female carer' model to the 'dual breadwinner'/'dual carer' model:

■ S. Honeyball, *Great Debates: Employment Law* (Basingstoke, Palgrave Macmillan, 2011) 106–8

. . . it is inevitable that women will be paid, on the whole, less than men. This is because there are several reasons why men and women are paid differently that, although related to the sex differences between employees, cannot be attributed to sex discrimination. What are these non-sex reasons? First, it is still the case that women take career breaks far more frequently than men, and it is inevitable that employees who take career breaks are likely to be paid less than those who do not, for several reasons. They may not return to the same job, for example, and therefore start a new career. [Women may] look more for a job that allows shorter hours, of itself resulting in a lower income. And these types of jobs are more likely to be of a lower status than those which are more career-orientated and therefore are lower paid. The counter-argument to this, however, is that it is true that, at least to a degree, the reasons why women take more career breaks than men can be attributed to societal pressure on women to be the primary partner in a mixed-sex couple to look after children, at least in their early years. It may not be something that women desire more than men but they would feel more obligated than men to fulfil. In other words, this is a form of sex discrimination in that women take career breaks for child-rearing because of a stereotypical assumption that society makes about them that is not inevitable. Of course, in the early stages, when there may be breastfeeding, physical recovery and other issues to consider, certain sex-related factors have an inevitable role, but after that time, there is no reason why men should not play an equal part in the child-rearing responsibilities which could involve them in taking career breaks at least as much as their partners. They do not do so, the argument runs, because of societal assumptions and traditions which themselves display a form of sex discrimination in that the result is that women are adversely treated. The difficulty with this argument, for the purposes of legal protection of women against sex discrimination, is that it does not amount to discrimination by an employer but by society at large. It is hardly feasible to construct legislation that gives a claim to women which they can exercise against society at large . . . It also needs to be remembered that women who take career breaks for the purposes of child-rearing may not only lose the time that they have taken off work and the lack of progression in seniority that this entails compared with their previous male counterparts who have continued to climb the tree, but that frequently women will return to a different occupation, or if they remain in the same field of work possibly to a different employer. It is inevitable that such a move will entail lower pay on average. The second reason why women may be paid less on the whole than men that cannot be put down to discrimination, at least by their employer, is that the work that men and women do are quite different when considered generally. Twice as many men as women are self-employed. Of these, a greater proportion of men work full-time and women part-time . . . It does not necessarily follow that the self-employed are paid more than those who are employed, but it might follow that there is a

[14] See also A. McColgan, *Just Wages for Women* (Oxford, Clarendon Press, 1997) 214–82 and 391–7.

greater incentive to work longer hours more profitably if workers do so for themselves rather than for another . . . It is also true that women traditionally have worked in those sectors of the economy that are more fragmented, with a few employees scattered here and there. These types of workers are less likely to belong to a trade union than those who work in labour-intensive situations such as a factory or national firms. Hairdressing, hotels, catering and so on, with a dispersed workforce, have lower density union membership. Trade unions find these types of workers particularly difficult to recruit . . . Such are the arguments in favour of the idea that, perhaps, the figures on the relative pay of men and women reflect a non-discriminatory profile of differences between male and female working. There are certainly differences between the sexes in pay, but these are to be expected given the differences in working patterns between them which are not caused by discrimination (at least by employers) but by individual and couple choices, and by societal attitudes towards the differing roles that men and women play in child-rearing . . .

Whatever one's perspective on these competing positions, to the extent that the gender pay gap persists, this does appear to be symptomatic of the ineffectiveness of 40 years of equal pay legislation in the UK.[15] A number of structural features inherent within the equal pay model in the EA have been identified as barriers to the eradication of the existing pay disparity:

(1) The simplistic notion of formal equality that females doing the same, broadly similar, or equivalent jobs as males should be paid at the same rate as the latter—underpinning the current incarnation of the equal pay regime is insufficiently radical to uproot ingrained gender pay inequalities. Commentators have advocated responses to the phenomenon of pay inequality which are much more innovative than the existing individual litigation-driven model based on symmetrical treatment.[16]

(2) This is compounded by the rigidity of the equal pay regime and its relative inability to (a) address occupational segregation[17] where jobs are structured along gender lines, e.g. the '3Cs' of catering, caring, and cleaning, and (b) confront the adverse effects on labour market participants of flexibilization in the relations of production in the productive economy, which have been charted by scholars such as Fredman and Collins.[18]

   (a) With regard to the phenomenon of job segregation, this is an expression descriptive of the situation where certain occupations or jobs are performed exclusively by women. Where a woman is situated in such an environment and no man is to be found working for her employer in the same trade, job, or profession, the rules in Chapter 3 of Part 5 of the EA are not sufficiently flexible to assist the female claimant in her quest for equal pay. In such circumstances, the rules are restrictive, since the female claimant is disentitled from invoking a hypothetical

---

[15] See T. Bawden and S. Rogers, '40 Years Since the Equal Pay Act, Equality Remains a Dream' (*The Guardian*, 8 March 2011), available at http://www.guardian.co.uk/uk/2011/mar/08/four-decades-on-equal-pay-yet-to-come?INTCMP=SRCH (last visited 8 October 2017).

[16] See S. Fredman, 'Reforming Equal Pay Laws' (2008) 37 *Industrial Law Journal* 193, 215–18; S. Deakin, C. McLaughlin, and D. Chai, 'Gender Inequality and Reflexive Law: The Potential of Different Regulatory Mechanisms' in L. Dickens (ed.), *Making Employment Rights Effective: Issues of Enforcement and Compliance* (Oxford, Hart Publishing, 2012) 116.

[17] For a discussion of occupational segregation, see B. R. Bergmann, *The Economic Emergence of Women* (New York, Basic Books, 1986) chs. 5 and 6; J. Browne, *Sex Segregation and Inequality in the Modern Labour Market* (Bristol, Polity Press, 2006); A. McColgan, *Just Wages for Women* (Oxford, Clarendon Press, 1997) 22–7, 35–40, 45–52, and 57–60; and S. Fredman, *Women and the Law* (Oxford, Clarendon Press, 1997) 111.

[18] See S. Fredman, *Discrimination Law*, 2nd edition (Oxford, OUP, 2011) 156–61; S. Fredman, 'Reforming Equal Pay Laws' (2008) 37 *Industrial Law Journal* 193, 195–201; and H. Collins, 'Regulating the Employment Relation for Competitiveness' (2001) 30 *Industrial Law Journal* 17, 20.

male comparator in her equal pay claim;[19] instead, she must identify an actual comparator working for the same employer (or an associated employer) in the same establishment or an alternative establishment operating on the basis of common terms and conditions.[20] Given the absence of an actual male comparator in segregated workplaces, this will stop the female claimant's equal pay claim in its tracks from the very beginning.

(b) The flexibilization of the relations of production associated with the modern service-based economy (e.g. franchising, outsourcing, joint venture networking, public/private partnering, etc.) have resulted in the fragmentation and rapid adaptation of working patterns away from the traditional bilateral relationship forged between an employer and an employee or worker. As such, there is greater scope for female workers to find that their employment relationship has been reconfigured entailing a change of employer and the emergence of a tripartite or multilateral relationship, e.g. owing to the employee's former employer having engaged in a process of contracting out, contracting in, service provision change, or where an employment agency is inter-positioned between the employee and the former employer. In such circumstances, the potential for current equal pay legislation to apply is minimal to non-existent inasmuch as it insists that a female claimant must select a male comparator working for the same (or an associated) employer at the same establishment or an alternative establishment with common terms and conditions.[21] In short, the claimant may well find that she is 'unable to bring [an] equal pay claim . . . on the basis of a comparison with colleagues with whom [she] work[s] at the same establishment, because [her] employer has been changed [and differs from the employer of those colleagues].'[22]

Of course, at a more technical level, other defects exist in the equal pay regime. For example, it is a real challenge for a potential female claimant to procure information about earnings levels in order to establish a pay disparity.[23] As part of the solution to this problem, the UK Government introduced section 139A of the EA and the Equality Act (Equal Pay Audits) Regulations 2014,[24] which empower a tribunal to order an employer who has been found to have breached equal pay law to conduct an equal pay audit. In addition, the UK Government activated the provisions of section 78 of the EA with effect from April 2017.[25] The 2017 Regulations impose mandatory gender pay gap reporting on private[26] and voluntary sector employers with 250 employees[27] or more, with a

---

[19] However, this is subject to: (a) section 71 of the EA which would enable the female claimant to invoke a hypothetical comparator pursuant to any direct discrimination claim (rather than an equal pay claim under Chapter 3 of Part 5 of the EA) she might raise under section 13 of the EA (see Chapter 10, section 10.2.3) in relation to her payment terms, on which, see section 14.2.1.2; and (b) the female claimant's entitlement to invoke a male worker as a hypothetical comparator where he was a predecessor in her role (see section 64(2) of the EA and *Macarthys Ltd v Smith* [1980] IRLR 210).

[20] See section 79 of the EA. [21] See section 79 of the EA.

[22] S. Fredman, 'Women at Work: The Broken Promise of Flexicurity' (2004) 33 *Industrial Law Journal* 299, 316.

[23] See *South Lanarkshire Council v Scottish Information Commissioner* [2013] 1 WLR 2421, where a local authority unsuccessfully attempted to block a freelance journalist's access to information about the particular points on the pay scales assigned to posts.

[24] SI 2014/2559.

[25] The Equality Act 2010 (Gender Pay Gap Information) Regulations 2017 (SI 2017/172) ('2017 Regulations').

[26] There is a separate duty for public sector employers with 250 employees or more, and this takes effect as a component of a public authorities' 'public sector equality duty': The Equality Act 2010 (Specific Duties and Public Authorities) Regulations 2017 (SI 2017/353).

[27] The explanatory note to the 2017 Regulations provides that the word 'employment' extends to the definition contained in section 83(2) of the EA. As such, it will include employees and individuals working for the employer on the basis of a contract personally to do work, on which, see Chapter 4, section 4.2.2. However, there is no statutory provision in the 2017 Regulations which reflects this assertion in the explanatory note.

phased implementation dependent on the size of the employer and the number of employees. Employers are bound to publish the difference between the average hourly rate of pay paid to male and female employees, the difference between the average bonus paid to male and female employees, the proportions of male and of female employees who receive bonuses, and the relative proportions of male and female employees in each quartile pay band of the workforce. More significantly, however, the UK Government simultaneously took steps to impede a claimant's access to information about earnings when it repealed the statutory 'obtaining information' process set out in section 138 of the EA and regulation 3 of, and Schedule 2 to, the Equality Act 2010 (Obtaining Information) Order 2010[28] in April 2014. Seen from the perspective of enabling claimants to gain access to the relevant information that they need to evaluate the existence of firm-specific gender pay gaps, the UK Government's approach has been somewhat schizophrenic.

There is an additional glaring deficiency in the legislation insofar as a female claimant's successful equal pay claim may result in the 'levelling down' of the male comparator's pay rather than the 'levelling up' of the claimant's pay to that of the male comparator:[29]

■ A. McColgan, *Just Wages for Women* (Oxford, Clarendon Press, 1997) 394

> The primary shortcoming of any legislation directed specifically at the gender-pay gap is that it fails to address *substantive*, as opposed to *relative*, justice. Even if legislation were to be drawn so as to require the adjustment of wages on a proportional basis . . . equal pay legislation will not, as a rule, prevent an employer from paying male and female employees *equally* badly.

The courts and tribunals have stated numerous times that it is not a function of the equal pay legislation to secure 'fair' pay.[30] Furthermore, if the employer does raise the pay of the successful female claimant to that of the comparator, this does no more than modify the claimant's contract and there is nothing in the legislation compelling the employer to alter the overall pay structure for the benefit of the claimant's female colleagues. This underscores the absence of a collective dimension to the equal pay regime and lays bare the shortcomings of the emphasis on the individual litigation-driven model in the legislation. Accordingly, for a more equitable distribution of pay, claimants are left to have recourse to collective bargaining, which in the past has failed female employees to some extent.[31]

An additional defect in the equal pay regime is that it is not designed to pay workers what they are actually worth. As such, the problem of 'justified proportionate inequality' is not addressed in the legislation. Consider Hypothetical A.

Hypothetical A

Charles Le Roux ('CLR') is employed by Danny's Demolishers Ltd ('DD') as a labourer at its Canterbury depot. He is paid £2,300 gross per month. Anita Falcon ('AF') is the deputy head of the Canterbury depot, which is two pay grades higher than CLR. AF is

[28] SI 2010/2194. ACAS has issued a guidance note on asking and responding to questions about equal pay and discrimination in the workplace, available at http://www.acas.org.uk/media/pdf/m/p/Asking-and-responding-to-questions-of-discrimination-in-the-workplace.pdf (last visited 9 October 2017).

[29] See the discussion in S. Fredman, *Discrimination Law*, 2nd edition (Oxford, OUP, 2011) 162.

[30] *Glasgow City Council v Marshall* [2000] 1 WLR 333, 334H–335A per Lord Slynn.

[31] For example, the negotiation of the single status pay agreement, on which, see the discussion in C. McLaughlin, 'Equal Pay, Litigation and Reflexive Regulation: The Case of the UK Local Authority Sector' (2014) 43 *Industrial Law Journal* 1; L. J. Hayes, 'Women's Voice and Equal Pay: Judicial Regard for the Gendering of Collective Bargaining' in A. Bogg and T. Novitz (eds), *Voices at Work* (Oxford, OUP, 2014) 35.

paid £2,500 gross per month. She complains to DD that she ought to be paid considerably more than her current salary on the basis that a pay differential of £200 gross per month between her pay and that of CLR is marginal taking into account the fact that CLR is two pay grades below her on the pay scale. AF presents a claim to an employment tribunal claiming that her pay would have been much higher than her current rate if she had been male and invokes CLR as a comparator. Unfortunately, the EA does not proscribe disproportionate pay differentials. Therefore, the employment tribunal has no option but to strike out AF's claim.[32]

Furthermore, we will also discover how an employer is not liable if it can convince a tribunal or court that the pay disparity is attributable to a material factor which is not tainted by direct sex discrimination or, if indirectly discriminatory, can be objectively justified as a proportionate means of achieving a legitimate aim. As such, there is an explicit defence at the heart of the equal pay model which enables an employer to be excused from equalizing the pay of its male and female staff. As our analysis of the detail of equal pay law will reveal in section 14.2, other defences available involve the employer establishing that the claimant and her comparator are not doing equal work and/or that the comparator selected by the claimant is disallowed.[33] Allied to the fact that the equal pay regime is notorious for being bedevilled by complexity and inordinate delays in its enforcement, there is something to be said for the contention that these factors combine to give rise to a 'denial of justice'.[34]

 For additional reading on the context of equal pay laws, visit the Online Resources for this book at www.oup.com/uk/cabrelli3e/

14.2 EQUAL 'PAY' AND THE SEX EQUALITY CLAUSE

The edifices erected by Chapter 3 of Part 5 of the EA and Article 157 TFEU are constructed around the notion of the regulation of 'terms' and 'pay'. In domestic law, this is achieved by the statutory imposition of a contractual term which is referred to as the 'sex equality clause'. A failure to comply with the sex equality clause will amount to a breach of contract and the claimant will have the option of enforcing her claim by (1) presenting a complaint to an employment tribunal within six months of the date of termination of employment[35] or (2) raising a common law claim for damages for breach of contract

---

[32] See *Evesham v North Hertfordshire Health Authority* [2000] ICR 612, 628F per Roch LJ; *Redcar and Cleveland Borough Council v Bainbridge* [2007] IRLR 984; and I. Steele, 'Beyond Equal Pay' (2008) 37 *Industrial Law Journal* 119. For mechanisms that could be deployed in order to tackle disproportionate pay, see S. Fredman, 'Reforming Equal Pay Laws' (2008) 37 *Industrial Law Journal* 193, 199–200. However, there is an argument that the decision of the European Court of Justice ('ECJ' or 'CJEU') in *Murphy v An Bord Telecom Eireann* [1988] ECR 673 is authority for the proposition that EU law would allow a female claimant a 'justified proportionate inequality' claim in the circumstances adumbrated in Hypothetical A.

[33] See the Statutory Code of Practice on Equal Pay, available at https://www.equalityhumanrights.com/sites/default/files/equalpaycode.pdf at para 74 (last visited 9 October 2017). The Code of Practice is admissible in evidence in criminal, or civil, proceedings, and if an employer fails to adhere to this Code of Practice, this must be taken into account by a court or tribunal in any case in which it appears to the court or tribunal to be relevant: section 15(4) of the Equality Act 2006.

[34] See L. Dickens, 'The Road is Long: Thirty Years of Equality Legislation in Britain' (2007) 45 *British Journal of Industrial Relations* 463, 478.   [35] Section 129 of the EA.

in the courts.[36] There are slight differences in the approaches adopted by European and domestic law towards the regulation of 'terms' and 'pay', which will form the focus of section 14.2.1. The relationship between the equal pay regime and the provisions in the EA which proscribe direct discrimination will also be discussed in section 14.2.1, whereupon we will move on to address the comparison exercise to be pursued in the case of the former regime. Meanwhile, section 14.2.2 will examine the components of the 'sex equality clause', which will necessitate consideration of the three key legal concepts in the equal pay legislation, namely the 'like work', 'work rated as equivalent', and 'work of equal value' criteria in section 65 of the EA.

14.2.1 Equal 'pay', equal 'terms', sex discrimination, and the nature of the comparator

14.2.1.1 Equal pay and equal terms

The equal pay rules are intended to eliminate sex discrimination in 'terms' and 'pay'. Article 157 TFEU provides as follows:

Article 157

(1) Each Member State shall ensure that the principle of equal pay for male and female workers for equal work or work of equal value is applied.

(2) For the purposes of this Article, 'pay' means the ordinary basic or minimum wage or salary and any other consideration, whether in cash or in kind, which the worker receives directly or indirectly, in respect of his employment, from his employer. Equal pay without discrimination based on sex means:

  (a) that pay for the same work at piece rates shall be calculated on the basis of the same unit of measurement;

  (b) that pay for work at time rates shall be the same for the same job . . .

In contrast, the cumulative effect of sections 66 and 80 of the EA is such that it is concerned with the parity of contractual 'terms'[37] rather than 'pay':

Section 66 Sex equality clause

(1) If the terms of A's work do not (by whatever means) include a sex equality clause, they are to be treated as including one.

(2) A sex equality clause is a provision that has the following effect—

  (a) if a term of A's is less favourable to A than a corresponding term of B's is to B, A's term is modified so as not to be less favourable;

  (b) if A does not have a term which corresponds to a term of B's that benefits B, A's terms are modified so as to include such a term . . .

---

[36] Sections 127 and 128 of the EA. Section 128(1) enables a court to strike out an equal pay claim if it is of the view that it could be determined more conveniently by an employment tribunal, on which, see *Abdulla v Birmingham City Council* [2012] UKSC 47, [2012] ICR 1419.

[37] Contrast this with the adoption of the word 'pay' for the purposes of the domestic law on the unauthorized deduction from wages in section 27 of the ERA: see Chapter 8, section 8.2.2.

> *Section 80 Interpretation and exceptions . . .*
>
> (1) The terms of a person's work are—
>
> > (a) if the person is employed, the terms of the person's employment that are in the person's contract of employment, contract of apprenticeship or contract to do work personally . . .

The significance of the difference in wording between European and domestic law is more than cosmetic. At first blush, the word 'terms' in section 80(2)(a) of the EA would appear to be more expansive than the word 'pay' in Article 157 TFEU. However, the ECJ has interpreted the word 'pay' more broadly than one might expect.[38] For example, it has been held to include pay increments based on seniority,[39] contractual or statutory sick pay,[40] payments in respect of time off work for training purposes,[41] statutory unfair dismissal compensation,[42] *ex gratia* Christmas bonuses,[43] occupational pension benefits,[44] pension contributions,[45] overtime payments,[46] piece rates,[47] and contractual or statutory redundancy payments.[48] Meanwhile, the domestic regime has been held to cover fringe contractual benefits such as mortgage interest allowances[49] and removal expenses.[50] Although there is considerable overlap between the domestic and EU regimes, non-contractual benefits and pay will be excluded from consideration under Chapter 3 of Part 5 of the EA[51] whilst falling within the purview of Article 157 TFEU. For example, in *Garland v British Rail Engineering*,[52] it was held that non-contractual concessionary travel facilities granted to retired male employees and their families constituted 'pay' for the purposes of EU law. This is important, since it has been held by the EAT that Article 157 TFEU has direct effect in a claim founded on equal pay for work of equal value, i.e. that a claimant can invoke Article 157 in the domestic courts or tribunals, at the very least until a formal Brexit.[53] On the opposite side of the coin, however, one can conceive of contractual 'terms' which bear no relation to 'pay', in which case, the domestic regime will be more inclusive than Article 157 TFEU.[54]

The emphasis on the word 'term' in section 66 of the EA underscores the point that a claimant must compare his/her contractual term with a 'corresponding' contractual term of a comparator—i.e. a term dealing with the same or similar subject-matter—in order to substantiate his/her claim that he/she has suffered inequality of pay. Hence an employer will be unable to defeat a female claimant's claim if a contractual term of her pay or salary is less advantageous than the same contractual term of a male comparator, but her

---

[38] However, social security payments such as State pension payments and unemployment benefits are not included within the coverage of Article 157 TFEU, but instead fall within the Equal Treatment Directive in relation to State Social Security 79/7/EEC (OJ 1979 L6/24).

[39] *Nimz v Freie und Hansestadt Hamburg* [1991] IRLR 222.

[40] *Rinner-Kühn v FWW Spezial-Gebäudereinigung GmbH & Co. KG* [1989] IRLR 493.

[41] *Arbeiterwohlfahrt der Stadt Berlin eV v Bötel* [1992] IRLR 423.

[42] *R v Secretary of State for Employment, ex parte Seymour-Smith and Perez* [1999] ICR 447.

[43] *Lewen v Lothar Denda* [2000] ICR 648.

[44] *Barber v Guardian Royal Exchange* [1991] 1 QB 344.

[45] *Griesmar v Ministre de l'Economie, des Finances et de l'Industrie* (Case C-366/99) [2003] 3 CMLR 95.

[46] *Arbeiterwohlfahrt der Stadt Berlin eV v Bötel* [1992] IRLR 423.

[47] *Danfoss* [1996] ICR 51.

[48] *Barber v Guardian Royal Exchange* [1991] 1 QB 344.

[49] *Sun Alliance and London Insurance Ltd v Dudman* [1978] ICR 551.

[50] *Durrant v North Yorkshire Health Authority* [1979] IRLR 401.

[51] However, in such a case, a claimant will have the right to rely on the direct sex discrimination provisions in section 13 of the EA.

[52] [1982] 2 All ER 402.

[53] *Asda Stores Ltd v Brierley* (2017) UKEAT/0011/17; [2017] All ER (D) 141 (August).

[54] For example, contractual terms providing for annual leave would not necessarily be categorized as 'pay', but clearly amount to 'terms' under section 80(2)(a) of the EA.

overall remuneration package is no less favourable, or indeed is more generous, than that of the male comparator: In essence, an 'overall remuneration package' approach is rejected in favour of a 'term-by-term' analysis.[55]

By adopting the 'term-by-term' approach,[56] this gives rise to the potential for 'piggyback' claims. A 'piggyback' claim describes the situation in Hypothetical B.

Hypothetical B

Monica Swift ('MS') and Daniel Osborne ('DO') both work for Danny's Demolishers Ltd ('DD') as warehouse operatives and are paid £14 per hour basic salary. The work of William Jenkins ('WJ') as a demolitions labourer is rated as equivalent to that of MS and DO pursuant to a job evaluation study[57] undertaken by DD. WJ is paid £17 per hour. MS presents a complaint to an employment tribunal that she is paid less than WJ. She is successful at an employment tribunal. Accordingly, her pay is increased to £17 per hour. DO then raises an equal pay claim against DD on the basis that he is employed on like work to that of MS, who is now being paid £3 per hour more than him.

In *Hartlepool Borough Council v Llewellyn*,[58] the EAT held that such a piggyback claim is valid. Moreover, it would be competent for DO to present such a complaint on a contingent basis prior to the tribunal's determination of MS's claim and to claim arrears of pay in respect of the period he spent working alongside MS. Of course, such piggyback claims have the scope to generate the ratcheting up of pay across all elements of the contractual remuneration package of workers. Conversely, the alternative is that the employer 'levels down' the pay[59] of WJ in order to scotch the emergence of pay inflation.

14.2.1.2 Interaction between the equal pay and sex discrimination regimes in the EA

The relationship between the equal pay regime in Chapter 3 of Part 5 of the EA and the general prohibition on direct and indirect sex discrimination in the EA can be described as particularly beguiling and complex. The former is limited to the parity of contractual terms, whereas the sex discrimination infrastructure is much broader in scope, encompassing an evaluation of the general treatment of female workers and the application of criteria, provisions, and practices by management to those workers. In order to understand how these two separate strands interact, we must consider the terms of section 70 of the EA:

Section 70 Exclusion of sex discrimination provisions

(1) The relevant sex discrimination provision has no effect in relation to a term of A's that—

   (a) is modified by, or included by virtue of, a sex equality clause or rule, or

   (b) would be so modified or included but for section 69 or Part 2 of Schedule 7.

---

[55] *Hayward v Cammell Laird Shipbuilders Ltd* [1988] AC 894, 907G–908B per Lord Goff.
[56] See also *Brownbill v St Helens and Knowsley Hospitals NHS Trust* [2012] ICR 68 and *Barber v Guardian Royal Exchange* [1991] 1 QB 344, 402D.
[57] See section 14.2.2.2 for an explanation of a job evaluation study.   [58] [2009] ICR 1426.
[59] Since the formal model of equality lies at the centre of the equal pay regime in the EA, there is no impediment to such 'levelling down', on which, see section 14.1.1.

(2) Neither of the following is sex discrimination for the purposes of the relevant sex discrimination provision—

(a) the inclusion in A's terms of a term that is less favourable as referred to in section 66(2)(a);

(b) the failure to include in A's terms a corresponding term as referred to in section 66(2)(b).

The effect of this somewhat opaque provision is to exclude the sex discrimination regime in respect of any term of a female claimant's contract that is subject to the operation of the sex equality clause by virtue of section 66 of the EA. Thus, the equal pay regime is self-contained and partitioned off from the sex discrimination provisions, and only one can apply at the same time.

Where the provisions relating to the sex equality clause in section 66 of the EA do not apply to the female claimant's case, i.e. she is precluded from raising an equal pay claim under Chapter 3 of Part 5 of the EA, section 71 of the EA directs that a female claimant will be able to avail herself of the concept of direct discrimination in section 13 of the EA in the general sex discrimination regime. This situation will arise where a female claimant is unable to identify an *actual* male comparator:

(1) working for the same employer (or an associated employer) at the same establishment or an alternative establishment operating on the basis of common terms and conditions;[60] or

(2) who is engaged in 'like work', 'work rated as equivalent' under a job evaluation scheme, or 'work of equal value'[61] as her own:

Section 71 Sex discrimination in relation to contractual pay

(1) This section applies in relation to a term of a person's work—

(a) that relates to pay, but

(b) in relation to which a sex equality clause or rule has no effect.

(2) The relevant sex discrimination provision (as defined by section 70) has no effect in relation to the term except in so far as treatment of the person amounts to a contravention of the provision by virtue of section 13 . . .

As such, where section 71 of the EA is operative, section 13 of the EA will apply, thus enabling the female claimant to establish that she was treated less favourably than a *hypothetical* male comparator in respect of her contractual payment-related terms because of her sex.[62] To that extent, the equal pay framework is clearly more restrictive than the general sex discrimination regime in relation to the nature of the comparators which may be selected by the claimant. It is to the issue of comparators that we now turn.

14.2.1.3 Comparators: general

The equal pay regime is notably liberal in respect of the nature of the comparator that may be invoked by the claimant. Provided that the claimant conforms with the provisions

---

[60] See sections 14.2.1.4 and 14.2.1.5.

[61] See sections 14.2.2.1, 14.2.2.2, and 14.2.2.3 for a detailed explanation of these concepts.

[62] However, such a claim will be difficult to sustain owing to the fact that the claimant would be required to establish that the factor which influenced the employer to pay her less than the hypothetical male comparator was the fact that she was female, in accordance with the 'reason why' approach to direct discrimination claims expounded in *R (E) v Governing Body of JFS* [2009] UKSC 15, [2010] 2 AC 728, on which, see Chapter 10, section 10.2.3.

of section 79 of the EA, she will have the right to select *any* actual male engaged in 'like work', 'work rated as equivalent', or 'work of equal value' as a comparator pursuant to sections 64 and 65 of the EA:

Section 79 Comparators . . .

(2) If A is employed, B is a comparator if subsection (3) or (4) applies.

(3) This subsection applies if—

(a) B is employed by A's employer or by an associate of A's employer, and

(b) A and B work at the same establishment.

(4) This subsection applies if—

(a) B is employed by A's employer or an associate of A's employer,

(b) B works at an establishment other than the one at which A works, and

(c) common terms apply at the establishments (either generally or as between A and B) . . .

14.2.1.4 Comparators: 'same employment', 'same establishment', and 'cross-establishment' comparisons

Section 79 restricts the comparator to a worker who is of the opposite sex to the claimant, who is working (1) for the same employer or an associate of the claimant's employer (2)(a) at the same establishment as the claimant or (2)(b) at another establishment where terms common to those applicable at the claimant's establishment are applied generally or as regards the claimant and the comparator. As such, the claimant and the comparator do not need to work for the same employer and may be spread across different sites, but the extent to which the employers may differ is circumscribed to 'associated employers'. Section 79(9) of the EA provides that the employers of the claimant and comparator will be associated if they are subsidiary companies of a parent company[63] or one of the employers is a parent company of the other employer.[64] In *Glasgow City Council v Fox Cross Claimants*,[65] the Inner House of the Court of Session held that the words 'company' and 'companies' in section 79(9) of the EA will also include any vehicle comprising an association of persons formed for an economic purpose, e.g. a limited liability partnership ('LLP').

As for the meaning of an 'establishment', there is no explicit definition in the EA. In the case of *City of Edinburgh Council v Wilkinson*,[66] the Inner House of the Court of Session ruled that female claimants employed by the council in schools, hostels, libraries, and social work were disentitled from comparing themselves with manual male workers employed by the council at different locations from the claimants as refuse collectors, road workers, grave diggers, and gardeners, since the word 'establishment' connoted a geographical association with a particular locality:

■ *Edinburgh City Council v Wilkinson* [2011] CSIH 70

Lord Eassie:

In my view the context in which the phrase 'at [the same] establishment' is used in [section 79(2)(b) of the EA]—the preposition deployed is 'at', not 'in'—similarly conveys an association with a locality;

---

[63] Section 79(9)(b) of the EA.   [64] Section 79(9)(a) of the EA.   [65] [2014] IRLR 532.
[66] [2012] IRLR 202.

'establishment' is not, to my mind, being deployed simply in the incorporeal sense of being a body or an undertaking. That is not to say that organisational matters are not relevant to identifying the establishment and its location . . . [Whilst] a distinct geographical separation might not be essential for the constitution of such a 'unit', it respectfully appears to me that a distinct geographical location may, depending on the circumstances, constitute an important definitional element in identifying the establishment. In these circumstances I consider that . . . the term 'establishment' [in section 79(2)(b) of the EA] is largely directed to the place of work. By that I did not understand [this] to mean an individual's particular place of work in the sense that, within any factory complex, or grouping of buildings, an individual may have his own workplace in a particular room or building, but rather the broader notion of a place of work consisting, for example, of a complex or the grouping of buildings as a whole.[67]

As for the circumstances in which a claimant will be entitled to pursue a cross-establishment comparison, i.e. where the claimant and comparator are spread across two different sites, the most obvious situation arises where the employer of the claimant and the comparator is bound to observe a centralized sector-level or national collective agreement.[68] Of course, the statutory injunction that the terms and conditions of the claimant and the comparator at the other establishment must be 'common' imposes no requirement on the claimant to show that both her terms and those of the comparator are exactly the same; otherwise, this portion of the legislation would be absurd, rendering it impossible for a claimant to establish any pay disparity with the comparator based at the different establishment.

Accordingly, where the comparator's job exists at the claimant's establishment, the court will simply ask whether the comparator's terms and conditions at his establishment are 'common' to those which apply to the same job at the establishment of the claimant. Consider the illustration in Hypothetical C.

Hypothetical C

Gareth Jones ('GJ') is employed by Danny's Demolishers Ltd ('DD') as a warehouse operative at DD's Manchester plant at a rate of £18 per hour. Michelle Coleridge ('MC') is employed at DD's Blackburn, Lancashire, plant as a clerical assistant in its office and is paid £14 per hour basic salary. GJ's and MC's jobs have been rated as equivalent pursuant to a job evaluation study undertaken by DD. Although warehouse operatives employed by DD at its Blackburn office are paid £17.50 per hour, DD's agreement with a recognized trade union provided that warehouse operatives employed in Manchester would enjoy a local variation to offset the costs of living in the Manchester area. If MC presented a 'work rated as equivalent' complaint that there was unequal pay when her salary is compared to that of GJ, she would have to establish as a preliminary issue that GJ's terms and conditions were 'common' to those he would have had if he had been employed as a warehouse operative at the Blackburn plant. Since there is only a 50p difference per hour and this is attributable to the local variation provided for in the agreement with the union, it is likely that they would be deemed to be sufficiently common.

[67] Sourced from BAILII available at http://www.bailii.org/scot/cases/ScotCS/2011/2011CSIH70.html (last visited 9 October 2017). The writer's annotations are shown in square brackets throughout this chapter.   [68] *Leverton v Clwyd County Council* [1989] ICR 33.

The principal difficulty arises, however, where the comparator's post does not exist at the claimant's establishment, i.e. if there had been no warehouse operative positions at the Blackburn plant in Hypothetical C. The central authorities here are the decisions of the House of Lords, Inner House of the Court of Session, and the Supreme Court in *British Coal Corp. v Smith*,[69] *Edinburgh City Council v Wilkinson*,[70] and *Dumfries and Galloway Council v North*,[71] who arrived at a position whereby the courts must enquire whether the comparator would have been employed on common terms and conditions if he had been employed doing the same job at the establishment of the claimant. In that case, tribunals and courts are instructed to entertain a 'thought experiment' and hypothesize whether the comparator would have been employed on broadly similar terms and conditions if he had been employed in his same job at the claimant's establishment.[72] In *Dumfries and Galloway Council v North*,[73] the Supreme Court ruled that there is nothing in the legislation enjoining the court or tribunal to consider whether it is feasible that the comparators could be co-located at the claimants' workplace; rather, it is taken as read that the comparators are transferred to do their present jobs in the workplace of the claimant, however unlikely that might be in reality. In following that process, the claimant has no obligation to show that the terms and conditions of the comparator are or would have been common 'in the sense that all the terms are the same, since necessarily his terms must be different in some respect if she is to show a breach of the [sex] equality clause, or in regard to terms other than that said to constitute the discrimination'.[74] Instead, Lord Slynn in *British Coal Corp.* remarked that 'the terms and conditions do not have to be identical, but [it is sufficient that] on a broad basis [they are] substantially comparable'.[75] As such, it is permissible for the tribunals and courts to take into account the similarity between the claimant's and comparator's terms (except those that are the subject of the claim). Moreover, the fact that the origins, genesis, and history of the claimant's and comparator's terms are different does not preclude them from being treated as 'common'.[76] Accordingly, if a collective agreement which applies to both the terms and conditions of the claimant and comparator at the different establishment is modified at a local level specifically for the comparator or generally for workers performing the same work as the comparator at that different establishment, this will not necessarily preclude the claimant from pursuing an equal pay case.[77]

14.2.1.5 Comparators: EU law and the 'single source' test

There is an additional argument that the domestic regime which limits the claimant to a 'same establishment' or cross-establishment comparison contravenes the 'single source'

---

[69] [1996] ICR 515.   [70] [2012] IRLR 202.   [71] [2013] ICR 993.

[72] See *British Coal Corp. v Smith* [1996] ICR 515; *Edinburgh City Council v Wilkinson* [2012] IRLR 202.

[73] [2013] ICR 993.

[74] See *British Coal Corp. v Smith* [1996] ICR 515, 526E per Lord Slynn; *Edinburgh City Council v Wilkinson* [2012] IRLR 202, 209 per Lord Eassie.

[75] [1996] ICR 515, 530D. See also *Asda Stores Ltd v Brierley* [2017] UKEAT/0011/17; [2017] All ER (D) 141 (August).

[76] *Asda Stores Ltd v Brierley* [2017] UKEAT/0011/17; [2017] All ER (D) 141 (August).

[77] However, notwithstanding this high authority, there is an argument that the difference between the wording of section 79(4)(c) of the EA—that the terms and conditions must be common generally or *as regards the claimant and comparator specifically*—and the now-repealed Equal Pay Act 1970 (on which the decisions in *British Coal Corp. v Smith* and *Edinburgh City Council v Wilkinson* were based) alters the complexion of matters. Rather than assessing whether the terms and conditions of the comparator would be common or substantially comparable if he/she were employed at the claimant's workplace, the direction in section 79(4)(c) of the EA that it is appropriate to consider whether the terms and conditions of the claimant and comparator would be common arguably shifts the nature of the enquiry to the commonality of the terms of the claimant and comparator only.

test applicable in EU law.[78] The relationship between the domestic and EU regimes is explored in the Statutory Code of Practice on Equal Pay[79] which directs that, if their application leads to differing results, 'European Union law may be applied to produce a remedy'.[80] This is a point of some significance if one takes into account the fact that Article 157 TFEU has both vertical and horizontal direct effect and, as such, claimants have the power to invoke it in the national courts of the Member States in order to fill gaps in, or supplant, national legislation.[81] Instead of enquiring whether the claimant and comparator are engaged by the same employer, associated employers, at the same establishment, or suitable cross-establishments, the EU approach cuts across this entirely and instead enquires whether a 'body [can be identified] which is responsible for the inequality and which could restore equal treatment'.[82] As such, attention is fixed on the requirement for a single identifiable entity to absorb the burden for the discrimination and to have the power to remedy it, which is an intrinsically fault-based prescription.[83] The fact that Article 157 TFEU bypasses the 'same employer', 'associated employers', and 'establishment' tests in domestic law gives rise to the possibility for the claimant to invoke it as a free-standing basis for her claim where her circumstances fail those domestic criteria.[84]

The 'single source' test differs from the domestic framework to the extent that it is both over-inclusive and under-inclusive of the latter.[85] It is over-inclusive inasmuch as a claimant working for one employer may be entitled to compare her/himself with a comparator working for a wholly unrelated employer if there is evidence to suggest that the contractual terms of both entities are regulated in harmony, e.g. by virtue of legislation, a collective agreement, or evidence of direct control: see *Lawrence v Regent Office Care Ltd*,[86] *Allonby v Accrington and Rossendale College*,[87] and *Glasgow City Council v Fox Cross Claimants*.[88] Accordingly, in certain circumstances, cross-firm and cross-industry comparisons are possible. However, it is also under-inclusive of the domestic regime insofar as a claimant may be unsuccessful in her/his claim where he/she works for

---

[78] Another difference between Article 157 TFEU and Chapter 3 of Part 5 of the EA concerns the relational scope of equal pay laws. The EA applies to persons providing services on the basis of a 'contract personally to do work' in terms of section 83(2) of the EA, but Article 157 applies to the broader concept of 'workers' under EU law and *Allonby v Accrington and Rossendale College* [2004] ICR 1328, which does not hinge on the existence of a contract. Accordingly, there is no need for a contractual relationship or mutuality of obligation and so long as the individual performing services is in a position of subordination to the enterprise, is providing a personal service, and is under the direction of the enterprise and receives remuneration in return for the provision of those services, that individual is protected.

[79] See https://www.equalityhumanrights.com/sites/default/files/equalpaycode.pdf (last visited 8 October 2017).

[80] See *ibid.*, para 57. [81] *Defrenne v SABENA (No. 2)* [1976] ECR 455.

[82] *Lawrence v Regent Office Care Ltd* [2003] ICR 1092, 1108H; *Glasgow City Council v Fox Cross Claimants* [2014] IRLR 532, 543 per Lord Brodie.

[83] I. Steele, 'Tracing the Single Source: Choice of Comparators in Equal Pay Claims' (2005) 34 *Industrial Law Journal* 338, 341.

[84] *Asda Stores Ltd v Brierley* [2017] UKEAT/0011/17; [2017] All ER (D) 141 (August).

[85] If the claimant has satisfied the domestic requirements in section 79(2), (3), and (4) of the EA, there is no need for him/her to go on to satisfy the 'single source' test. The claimant will only be required to negotiate the 'single source' test if he/she brings a claim directly under Article 157 TFEU, in which case the domestic criteria can be bypassed: *North Cumbria Acute Hospitals NHS Trust v Potter* [2009] IRLR 176 and *Asda Stores Ltd v Brierley* [2017] UKEAT/0011/17; [2017] All ER (D) 141 (August).

[86] [2003] ICR 1092.

[87] [2004] ICR 1328. However, as the decisions in *Lawrence* and *Allonby* both demonstrate, a claimant will face an uphill struggle where he/she was a former colleague of the comparator whom he/she invokes but subsequently finds him/herself employed by an agency or an unconnected employer whilst continuing to work alongside the comparator at the premises of the former employer, i.e. in a standard 'contracting out' situation. This has caused Fredman to comment that the single source test is unable to 'see beyond the formal boundaries of the employing enterprise render[ing] equal pay law impotent in the face of employers who deliberately fragment the supervisory and remunerative dimensions of the managerial function': S. Fredman, 'Marginalising Equal Pay Laws' (2004) 33 *Industrial Law Journal* 281. [88] [2014] IRLR 532.

the same employer as the comparator. For example, in *Robertson v DEFRA*,[89] a number of male civil servants working for the Department for the Environment, Food and Rural Affairs sought to compare themselves with female civil servant comparators working for the Department for Transport, Environment and the Regions. Despite the fact that the claimants and the comparators were in common employment with the Crown—an entity employing over half a million employees—the Court of Appeal held that such a comparison was precluded by virtue of the application of the 'single source' test. Indeed, Lord Justice Mummery thought the submission that every civil servant was entitled to compare him/herself with any other civil servant of the opposite sex was 'extravagant'.[90] As noted by Barrett, the approach adopted in this decision 'obviously renders the applicability of [equal pay] law vulnerable in large measure to decisions by large employers to decentralise control over terms of employment'.[91]

14.2.1.6 Comparators: hypothetical comparators, predecessors, and successors

The domestic equal pay framework is notorious for the fact that the claimant is unable to invoke a hypothetical comparator: the identification of an actual comparator is essential.[92] However, this is subject to three exceptions.

(1) A claimant may select a predecessor in her post as a comparator if he/she happens to be a member of the opposite sex.[93] This is justified on the ground that the predecessor is not a hypothetical comparator: '[H]ad the predecessor . . . continued in employment he would have received at least the same pay subsequently when the claimant was employed as he had done before she was employed . . . [which is] a legitimate inference, if only because it would generally be a breach of contract to reduce the wage.'[94] In invoking such a predecessor as a comparator, it is not open to the claimant to argue what would have happened to the comparator's pay if he/she had remained in employment, i.e. to infer likely pay increases which he/she would have enjoyed. As such, the contractual terms of the predecessor at the termination of his/her employment are to be taken for the purposes of the comparison.

As for the sustainability of a claimant engaging in a comparison exercise with a successor to her post, this was an avenue that was categorically blocked off by the EAT in *Walton Centre for Neurology & Neuro Surgery NHS Trust v Bewley*.[95] It was rejected on the basis that it was 'too hypothetical' an exercise which 'reconstructs virtual rather than actual history . . . ask[ing] how events would have progressed had things been otherwise'.[96] Notwithstanding this rejection, there is some force in the contention that domestic law may well now enable a claimant to invoke a successor

[89] [2005] ICR 750. See *Armstrong v Newcastle upon Tyne Hospitals NHS Trust* [2006] IRLR 124 for a similar result.

[90] *Robertson v DEFRA* [2005] ICR 750, 758E. Legal responsibility for pay negotiations had been devolved from the Crown to the individual government departments by virtue of a series of enactments between 1992 and 1996. Accordingly, it was the individual departments, rather than the Crown, that could be identified as the 'single source(s)' liable for rectifying the pay disparities.

[91] G. Barrett, '"Shall I Compare Thee to . . . ?": On Article 141 EC and *Lawrence*' (2006) 35 *Industrial Law Journal* 93, 99. See also S. Fredman, 'Marginalising Equal Pay Laws' (2004) 33 *Industrial Law Journal* 281; I. Steele, 'Tracing the Single Source: Choice of Comparators in Equal Pay Claims' (2005) 34 *Industrial Law Journal* 338.

[92] See *Coloroll Pension Trustees Ltd v Russell* [1997] ICR 179.

[93] *Macarthys Ltd v Smith* [1980] ECR 1275.

[94] *Walton Centre for Neurology and Neuro Surgery NHS Trust v Bewley* [2008] ICR 1047, 1060E per Elias J (P).

[95] [2008] ICR 1047.   [96] *ibid.*, 1060D per Elias J (P).

as a comparator.[97] Section 64(2) of the EA—which had no counterpart in the Equal Pay Act 1970—prescribes that the work of the claimant need not be done contemporaneously with that of the chosen comparator. The breadth of this new statutory provision has yet to be tested in the tribunals and courts, but there is an argument that the inference can be drawn that domestic legislation now permits comparisons with successors as well as predecessors.

(2) As articulated earlier, section 71 of the EA will function to enable a claimant to adopt a hypothetical comparator where he/she is unable to raise an equal pay claim under Chapter 3 of Part 5 of the EA, i.e. where the provisions relating to the sex equality clause in section 66 of the EA do not apply to the female claimant's case because there is no actual comparator engaged in 'like work', 'work rated as equivalent', or 'work of equal value'. In that case, the claimant may rely on the concept of direct sex discrimination pursuant to section 13 of the EA in respect of her pay, which of course, does permit hypothetical comparators.[98]

(3) Finally, where the claimant is seeking to challenge a provision of Chapter 3 of Part 5 of the EA on the basis that it is inconsistent with EU law, it is open to her to select a hypothetical male comparator in order to do so.[99]

14.2.2 Sex equality clause

The stages which a claimant must follow in order to pursue an equal pay claim under Chapter 3 of Part 5 of the EA are illustrated in Figure 14.2.

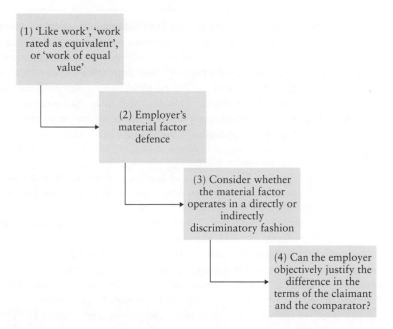

Figure 14.2 *Stages of an equal pay claim*

---

[97] See B. Hepple, *Equality: The New Legal Framework*, 2nd edition (Oxford, Hart Publishing, 2014) 126.

[98] See Article 2(1) and (2)(a) of the Race Directive; Article 2(1) and (2)(a) of the Framework Directive; and Article 2(1)(a) of the Recast Equality Directive for the European provisions, which are very similar to section 13 of the EA.   [99] *Allonby v Accrington and Rossendale College* [2004] ICR 1328.

Section 64 of the EA stipulates that the sex equality clause in section 66 applies where the claimant is employed on work that is equal to the work of the comparator. The notion of 'equal work' gives rise to the three central concepts in Chapter 3 of Part 5 of the EA for the purposes of equal pay claims, namely 'like work', 'work rated as equivalent', or 'work of equal value':

Section 65 Equal work

(1) For the purposes of this Chapter, [the claimant]'s work is equal to that of [the comparator] if it is—

    (a) like [the comparator]'s work,

    (b) rated as equivalent to [the comparator]'s work, or

    (c) of equal value to [the comparator]'s work.

The starting point for our discussion is that section 65(1) prescribes no hierarchy between the notions of 'like work', 'work rated as equivalent', or 'work of equal value', i.e. the second and third concepts are in no way subordinated to the first. This ensures the prevention of the emergence of a 'token man' phenomenon, i.e. the situation where the employer seeks to circumvent a claimant's 'work rated as equivalent' or 'work of equal value' claim by employing a token man to do 'like work', namely the same job, on the same pay and benefits, as the claimant:

■ Pickstone v Freemans plc [1989] AC 66, 111F–112D

[The headnote to the case sets forth the facts as follows:] The employers employed both men and women as warehouse operatives and as checker warehouse operatives. The [claimants], female warehouse operatives, claimed against the employers that they were entitled to equal pay with a male checker warehouse operative on the basis that they were doing work of equal value within the meaning of section [65(1)(c) of the EA] . . . An industrial tribunal dismissed the claim holding that because the [claimants] were employed on like work with other male employees in the same establishment . . . they were not entitled to rely on the equal value provisions contained in section [65(1)(c) of the EA] . . . or upon any rights derived from [Article 157 TFEU] . . .

Lord Keith of Kinkel:

The question is whether [section 65(1)(c) of the EA is only] . . . intended to have effect whenever the employers are able to point to some man who is employed by them on like work with the woman claimant within the meaning of [section 65(1)(a) of the EA] or work rated as equivalent with hers within the meaning of [section 65(1)(b) of the EA], or whether they are intended to have effect only where the particular man with whom she seeks comparison is employed on such work. In my opinion the latter is the correct answer. The opposite result would leave a large gap in the equal work provision, enabling an employer to evade it by employing one token man on the same work as a group of potential women claimants who were deliberately paid less than a group of men employed on work of equal value with that of the women. This would mean that the United Kingdom had failed yet again fully to implement its obligations under [Article 157 TFEU] and the [Recast Equality] Directive . . . It is sufficient to say that the words must be construed purposively in order to give effect to the manifest broad intention of . . . Parliament.

Pickstone v Freemans plc[100] is now codified in section 65(6) of the EA which prescribes that there will be a 'work of equal value' claim if the work of the claimant is neither 'like' (i.e. the same or broadly similar) nor 'rated as equivalent' to that of the comparator, i.e.

[100] [1989] AC 66.

where the 'like work' and 'work rated as equivalent' categories have been 'held . . . not to apply in respect of the work of the [claimant] and the work of the [comparator] with whom she seeks parity of pay'.[101]

We now subject each of the 'like work', 'work rated as equivalent', and 'work of equal value' categories to closer scrutiny.

14.2.2.1 Sex equality clause: 'like work'

Section 65(2) and (3) of the EA furnishes additional guidance on the content of the 'like work' category:

Section 65 Equal work

(2) A's work is like B's work if—

  (a) A's work and B's work are the same or broadly similar, and

  (b) such differences as there are between their work are not of practical importance in relation to the terms of their work.

(3) So on a comparison of one person's work with another's for the purposes of subsection (2), it is necessary to have regard to—

  (a) the frequency with which differences between their work occur in practice, and

  (b) the nature and extent of the differences.

Hence the key element is that the work of the claimant and the comparator must be the same or broadly similar. The direction that any differences in the nature of the work of the claimant and the comparator should not be of practical importance, taking into account their frequency, nature, and extent, was explored by the EAT in *Capper Pass Ltd v Lawton*:

■ *Capper Pass Ltd v Lawton* [1977] ICR 83, 87D–88C

Phillips J:

In such cases where the work is of a broadly similar nature (and not of the same nature) there will necessarily be differences between the work done by the woman and the work done by the man. It seems clear to us that the definition requires the industrial tribunal to bring to the solution of the question, whether work is of a broadly similar nature, a broad judgment. Because, in such cases, there will be such differences of one sort or another it would be possible in almost every case, by too pedantic an approach, to say that the work was not of a like nature despite the similarity of what was done and the similar kinds of skill and knowledge required to do it. That would be wrong. The intention, we think, is clearly that the industrial tribunal should not be required to undertake too minute an examination, or be constrained to find that work is not like work merely because of insubstantial differences. It seems to us that in most cases the inquiry will fall into two stages. *First*, is the work of the same, or, if not, 'of a broadly similar' nature? This question can be answered by a general consideration of the type of work involved, and of the skill and knowledge required to do it. It seems to us to be implicit in the words of [section 65(2) and (3) of the EA] that it can be answered without a minute examination of the detail of the differences between the work done by the man and the work done by the woman. But, *secondly*, if on such an examination the answer is that the work is of a broadly similar nature, it is then necessary to go on to consider

---

[101] *ibid.*, 123A per Lord Templeman.

the detail and to inquire whether the differences between the work being compared are of 'practical importance in relation to [the] terms [of their work].' . . . it seems to us, trivial differences, or differences not likely in the real world to be reflected in the terms and conditions of employment, ought to be disregarded. In other words, once it is determined that work is of a broadly similar nature it should be regarded as being like work unless the differences are plainly of a kind which the industrial tribunal in its experience would expect to find reflected in the terms and conditions of employment . . . The only differences which will prevent work which is of a broadly similar nature from being 'like work' are differences which in practice will be reflected in the terms and conditions of employment.

In the decision of the Court of Appeal in *Shields v E. Coomes (Holdings) Ltd*,[102] the point was emphasized that the references to 'differences' in section 65(2)(b) and (3)(a) and (b) of the EA necessitate a comparison between the things that each of the claimant and comparator actually does and the frequency with which they are actually done, rather than between their respective contractual obligations. Therefore, if the claimant and comparator are employed in the same job and the comparator (but not the claimant) is under a contractual obligation to undertake additional duties, but this flexibility has never been utilized in practice by the employer, this will not be a difference of practical importance.[103]

Three relevant considerations to take into account are the level of responsibility or control assumed by the claimant and comparator, i.e. whether any element of supervision is involved in their duties, along with the skills involved in their respective jobs: these will be deemed to be differences of genuine practical importance.[104] An example of the significance of differing degrees of responsibility is afforded by *Eaton Ltd v Nutall*.[105] Here, it was held that the following differences were of sufficient importance not to engage the 'like work' concept on the basis that if the male comparator were to make a mistake, there would be more serious consequences for him than for the claimant: the female claimant was a production scheduler with responsibility for ordering supplies of 2,400 items up to a value of £2.50 each, whereas the comparator male production scheduler had responsibility for 1,200 items between the values of £5 and £1,000 each. This can be contrasted with the time at which the claimant and comparator perform their work, which can often be disregarded as a factor, e.g. whether the claimant undertakes a particular task at night and the comparator does so in the late morning will generally be irrelevant.[106]

14.2.2.2 Sex equality clause: 'work rated as equivalent'

Owing to the fact that '[f]ew cases arise nowadays under [the 'like work'] category, which is largely of historical interest',[107] the 'work rated as equivalent' and 'work of equal value' concepts are of greater importance. We turn first to the 'work rated as equivalent' construct, which finds its expression in section 65(4) of the EA:

---

[102] [1978] 1 WLR 1408.   [103] *Electrolux Ltd v Hutchinson and others* [1976] IRLR 410.

[104] See *Waddington v Leicester Council for Voluntary Services* [1977] 1 WLR 544; *Morgan v Middlesbrough Borough Council* [2005] EWCA Civ 1432.

[105] [1977] 1 WLR 549.

[106] *Dugdale v Kraft Foods Ltd* [1977] ICR 48; *National Coal Board v Sherwin* [1978] ICR 700. However, where a comparator works night shift, alone and without supervision, the additional responsibility that entails may indeed constitute a difference of practical importance to preclude the claimant from mounting a 'like work' comparison: *Thomas v National Coal Board* [1987] ICR 757.

[107] See B. Hepple, *Equality: The New Legal Framework*, 2nd edition (Oxford, Hart Publishing, 2014) 126.

> **Section 65 Equal work . . .**
>
> (4) A's work is rated as equivalent to B's work if a job evaluation study—
>
> (a) gives an equal value to A's job and B's job in terms of the demands made on a worker, or
>
> (b) would give an equal value to A's job and B's job in those terms were the evaluation not made on a sex-specific system.
>
> (5) A system is sex-specific if, for the purposes of one or more of the demands made on a worker, it sets values for men different from those it sets for women.

It should be stressed that the inclusion of the word 'if' in section 65(4) demonstrates that it is not a mandatory requirement for the employer to produce such a job evaluation study, i.e. it is purely a voluntary exercise. Moreover, a job evaluation study must have been accepted or adopted by the employers and employees as a valid study regulating their relationship in order to be treated as complete and valid.[108] It is also clear from the terms of section 65(4) that the demands made on the workers will be crucial in the context of the compilation of a job evaluation study, which is further elaborated upon in section 80(5) of the EA:

> **Section 80 Interpretation and exceptions . . .**
>
> (5) A job evaluation study is a study undertaken with a view to evaluating, in terms of the demands made on a person by reference to factors such as effort, skill and decision-making, the jobs to be done—
>
> (a) by some or all of the workers in an undertaking or group of undertakings . . .

Thus, a job evaluation functions as a means of systematically assessing the relative value of different jobs and enables a claimant to compare his/her job with the job of a comparator—which is completely different—but has been graded and ranked as equivalent.[109]

Pursuant to such an exercise, a broad range of differing jobs are graded on an analytical basis in terms of the levels of effort, skill, and decision-making which they entail. Other relevant factors include the degree of responsibility and level of training associated with the various jobs. Once graded, the jobs are given scores and then ranked accordingly. In producing such a job study, only factors associated with the requirements of each job ought to be considered, duly divorced from the person actually doing the job, i.e. 'how well someone is doing the job is not relevant'.[110] Alongside this evaluation, the employer must engage in the fixing of grade boundaries.[111] The jobs are then slotted into the grade boundaries in accordance with the scores reached. Further guidance on the process to be adopted is furnished on the website of the Equality and Human Rights Commission,[112] and in the decisions of the Court of Appeal and EAT in *Bromley v H & J Quick Ltd*[113] and *Eaton Ltd v Nutall*,[114] respectively. Both these decisions highlighted the importance of grading each component of the jobs concerned (e.g. according to the degree of effort, skill, decision-making, responsibility, etc.)—instead of the whole job itself—in a broad-brush manner:

---

[108] *Arnold v Beecham Group Ltd* [1982] ICR 744.

[109] See https://www.equalityhumanrights.com/sites/default/files/equalpaycode.pdf at para 39 (last visited 9 October 2017).

[110] See *ibid.*, para 41.

[111] *Bainbridge v Redcar and Cleveland Borough Council (No. 2)* [2007] IRLR 494, 498 per Elias J (P).

[112] See https://www.equalityhumanrights.com/en/advice-and-guidance/job-evaluation-schemes (last visited 9 October 2017).

[113] [1988] ICR 623.   [114] [1977] 1 WLR 549.

■ *Bromley v H & J Quick Ltd* [1988] ICR 623, 633C–E

> **Dillon LJ:**
>
> In my judgment, the [requirement for an analytical study] is not a gloss [on the statute], but indicates conveniently the general nature of what is required by the section, viz. that the jobs of each worker covered by the study must have been valued in terms of the demand made on the worker under various headings . . . It is not enough, in my judgment, that . . . bench-mark jobs [have been evaluated] . . . on [a] . . . factor demand basis [as] . . . required by [the equal pay legislation] . . . if the jobs of the [claim]ants and their comparators were not.

■ *Eaton Ltd v Nutall* [1977] 1 WLR 549, 555C–E

> **Phillips J:**
>
> [The equal pay legislation] can only apply to what may be called a valid evaluation study. By that, we mean a study satisfying the test of being thorough in analysis and capable of impartial application. . . . It will be in order to take into account such matters as merit or seniority, etc., but any matters concerning the work (e.g. responsibility) one would expect to find taken care of in the evaluation study. One which does not satisfy that test, and requires the management to make a subjective judgment concerning the nature of the work before the employee can be fitted into the appropriate place in the appropriate salary grade, would seem to us not to be a valid study for the purpose of [the equal pay legislation].

As such, the key issue is that the analytical process is sufficiently objective[115] so that sex-specific elements are isolated and excised. If the job evaluation fails to adequately measure the demands (in terms of effort, skill, level of responsibility and decision-making) imposed by each of the tasks comprised within the employee's job, then it will be open to challenge.[116]

If the job evaluation study grades the claimant's job higher than that of the comparator, but she is paid less, she can nonetheless pursue a 'work rated as equivalent' equal pay claim.[117] A final point to make concerning job evaluation studies is that they are not a precise science. This is borne out in the judgment of Elias J (P) in *Bainbridge v Redcar and Cleveland Borough Council (No. 2)*:

■ *Bainbridge v Redcar and Cleveland Borough Council (No. 2)* [2007] IRLR 494, 498

> **Elias J (P):**
>
> In effect there are two elements to a job evaluation study. First, there is the evaluation of the jobs; then there is the fixing of grade boundaries. These may be more or less complex. It is not uncommon for jobs to be fitted into grades where there may be real distinctions in the value of the jobs[, since i]t may be simpler for an employer to introduce pay scales which embrace a relatively wide class of jobs even although the value of the jobs at the higher end of a particular grade may be

---

[115] However, it has been recognized judicially that some degree of subjectivity may be inevitable, whereupon care must be exercised to ensure 'that discrimination is not, inadvertently, let in': *Bromley v H & J Quick Ltd* [1988] ICR 623, 632F per Dillon LJ.

[116] *Russell v South Lanarkshire Council* [2012] Eq LR 723.

[117] *Redcar and Cleveland Borough Council v Bainbridge* [2008] ICR 238.

significantly higher than those lower down. That may be a pragmatic and sensible approach enabling the employer to select relatively simplified pay scales, even though it does not closely relate pay to value.

14.2.2.3 Sex equality clause: 'work of equal value'

The principal deficiency with the 'work rated as equivalent' category is that it fails to bite as a concept where the employer refuses to produce a job evaluation study. In the absence of a job evaluation study, there will be no comparator for the claimant to invoke in a 'work rated as equivalent' equal pay claim. Prior to 1983, this resulted in a dead end for a claimant where there was no comparator undertaking 'like work', thus negating the potential of the equal pay legislation to undertake cross-job comparisons: at that time, the Equal Pay Act 1970 only contained the 'like work' and the 'work rated as equivalent' concepts. A challenge was launched by the European Commission to the legal position in the UK[118] on the basis that it was contrary to the Equal Pay Directive.[119] These proceedings before the ECJ were successful, culminating in the introduction of the 'work of equal value' concept by virtue of the Equal Pay (Amendment) Regulations 1983.[120] It is now laid down in section 65(6) of the EA:

Section 65 Equal work . . .

(6) A's work is of equal value to B's work if it is—

  (a) neither like B's work nor rated as equivalent to B's work, but

  (b) nevertheless equal to B's work in terms of the demands made on A by reference to factors such as effort, skill and decision-making.

The exceptionality of the work of equal value category is that it harbours the greatest potential of each of the three statutory categories to achieve a modest measure of 'fair pay', since it permits cross-comparisons across a diverse variety and range of work types:

■ **S. Fredman, 'Reforming Equal Pay Laws' (2008) 37** *Industrial Law Journal* **193, 207–8**

In one important respect, [equal pay legislation] holds out the promise of radical change. This takes the form of the principle of equal value. By penetrating job labels to examine the characteristics of women's work, the notion of equal value opens up dramatic possibilities for transcending evaluations of women's work which depend on deeply held stereotypes and entrenched inequalities in women's bargaining power. Properly handled, the concept of equal value reveals the extent to which women's work shares characteristics usually attributed only to men's work, such as heavy work and responsibility. It also requires recognition of chronically undervalued elements of women's work, such as manual dexterity and caring. As a result, a cook has been compared to a carpenter; a home help to a refuse collector and learning support assistants to painters, drivers and street cleaners.

---

[118] *EC Commission v UK* [1982] ICR 578.

[119] Directive 75/117/EEC (OJ 1975 L45/19), subsequently repealed by the Recast Equality Directive 2006/54/EC (OJ 2006 L204/23).

[120] Regulation 2(1) of SI 1983/1794.

However, independent research has revealed that such are the highly technical and complex processes involved in adjudicating 'work of equal value' claims that they often become bogged down in protracted delays[121] generated by preliminary issues.[122] For example, the procedure prescribed in Schedule 3 to the Employment Tribunals (Constitution and Rules of Procedure) Regulations 2013[123] entails an employment tribunal engaging in three stages of hearings. At the first-stage hearing, an employment judge must consider whether the equal value claim ought to be struck out or referred to an independent expert, designated as such by ACAS,[124] to produce a report. Such a claim must be struck out where a pre-existing job evaluation scheme voluntarily undertaken by the employer does not rate the work of the claimant and comparator as equivalent.[125] However, this is subject to the decision of the Court of Appeal in *Hovell v Ashford & St Peter's Hospital NHS Trust*[126] and section 131(6) and (7), which both prescribe exceptions to that rule. First, in *Hovell*, Lord Justice Elias recognized that it is open to a tribunal to be persuaded that it ought not to strike out or refer an equal value claim to an independent expert where there are small differences in the scoring of the jobs of the claimant and comparator.[127] Secondly, section 131(6) and (7) stipulates that where the tribunal has reasonable grounds to suspect that the employer's job evaluation study was tainted by sex discrimination[128] or is otherwise unreliable, it may refuse to strike out the claimant's 'work of equal value' claim.

If the tribunal makes a reference to an independent expert at the first-stage hearing, the judge must order:

(1) the parties to (a) copy to the independent expert all information which they are required by an order to disclose or agree between each other and (b) produce a joint agreed statement of job descriptions and facts;

(2) the independent expert to prepare a report;

(3) the claimant to (a) disclose in writing to the employer the name of any comparator or, if the claimant is unable to so, to instead disclose such information enabling the employer to identify the comparator and (b) identify to the employer in writing the period in relation to which he/she considers that his/her work and that of the comparator are to be compared; and

(4) fix a date for the second-stage equal value hearing.

Paragraph 6 of Schedule 3 to the 2013 Regulations prescribes that the tribunal must make a determination of facts on which the parties are unable to agree which relate to the dispute at the second-stage hearing and also enjoin the independent expert to prepare his/her report on the basis of facts jointly agreed between the parties or determined by the tribunal. A date is also set for the independent expert to produce the report. Once the independent expert has produced the report—which, it should be stressed, will be similar to a job evaluation study voluntarily prepared by an employer under sections 65(4) and

---

[121] See the indicative time periods set out in Schedule 3 to the Employment Tribunals (Constitution and Rules of Procedure) Regulations 2013 (SI 2013/1237).

[122] K. Godwin, 'Equal Value: Justice Denied?' (2009) 186 *Equal Opportunities Review* 16.

[123] SI 2013/1237.

[124] See section 131(8) of the EA.

[125] On the other hand, if the employer's job evaluation scheme ranks the jobs of the claimant and comparator as equivalent from a particular date, this does not give rise to any presumption that they were of equal value prior to the implementation of the scheme, even where the jobs have not changed to any material extent: *Hovell v Ashford & St Peter's Hospital NHS Trust* [2009] ICR 1545.

[126] *ibid.*   [127] *ibid.*, 1553D–E per Elias LJ.

[128] It will be tainted by sex discrimination if the difference (or coincidence) between values that the scheme sets on different demands is not justifiable regardless of the sex of the person of whom the demands are made: section 131(7) of the EA.

80(5) for the purposes of a 'work rated as equivalent' claim—a third-stage hearing will take place before the tribunal, at which the independent expert's report will be admissible unless it rules that the report is not based on the facts relating to the question in the dispute. The tribunal may then decide the 'work of equal value' claim or order another independent expert to produce a different report.

Of course, if the expert's report places the claimant and the comparator in the same grading with the same score or value attributed to each of their jobs, then the tribunal will be entitled to determine that the claimant's 'work of equal value' claim should succeed. If not, however, then the claim must fail.

14.3 THE 'MATERIAL FACTOR' DEFENCE

Once a claimant has established that his/her work is equal to that of his/her chosen comparator and his/her contract contains a term that is less favourable than a corresponding term in the comparator's contract, the sex equality clause will take effect to equalize the claimant's contractual term with that of the latter by virtue of section 66(2)(a) of the EA. Alternatively, if the claimant's contract does not include the same contractual term as the comparator, then the former contract is modified so as to contain such a term by virtue of section 66(2)(b) of the EA. As such, pay parity is secured. However, the employer has a defence. If the employer is able to discharge the burden of establishing that the pay variation is attributable to a material factor which does not itself discriminate against the claimant either directly or indirectly because of his/her sex, this defence will operate to relieve the employer of any liability:

> **Section 69 Defence of material factor**
>
> (1) The sex equality clause in A's terms has no effect in relation to a difference between A's terms and B's terms if the [employer] shows that the difference is because of a material factor reliance on which—
>
> (a) does not involve treating A less favourably because of A's sex than the [employer] treats B, and
>
> (b) if the factor is within subsection (2), is a proportionate means of achieving a legitimate aim.
>
> (2) A factor is within this subsection if A shows that, as a result of the factor, A and persons of the same sex doing work equal to A's are put at a particular disadvantage when compared with persons of the opposite sex doing work equal to A's.

Section 69 can be explored by dividing it into two elements, namely the available material factors and the impact of the law of direct and indirect sex discrimination on the former.

14.3.1 The material factors

The first element of the employer's defence set up by section 69 is that the employer must satisfy the tribunal or court that the disparity in the pay of the claimant and the comparator is attributable to a 'material factor'. Some general guidance on the meaning of the word 'material' was furnished in the decision of the House of Lords in *Rainey v Greater Glasgow Health Board*,[129] where the point was made that the differences between the

---

[129] [1987] 1 AC 224.

cases of the claimant and comparator must be proven to be 'significant and relevant'.[130] Moreover, Lord Keith of Kinkel went on to say that what is 'material' may well involve the court going beyond consideration of the 'personal qualities by way of skill, experience or training which the [claimant] brings to the job . . . [to include] difference[s] which . . . [are] connected with economic factors affecting the efficient carrying on of the employer's business',[131] i.e. external matters such as market forces[132] *may*[133] qualify as a material factor if the pay differentials they generate are genuinely gender-neutral in the sense of not being tainted by sex discrimination. For example, where the NHS needed to recruit 20 prosthetists from the private sector to plug a labour market shortage, it was held to be justifiable to offer private sector pay rates to attract such staff, even though such rates were higher than those paid to female prosthetists working for the NHS. Additional assistance can be derived from the speech of Lord Nicholls in the House of Lords in *Glasgow City Council v Marshall*:

■ *Glasgow City Council v Marshall* [2000] 1 WLR 333, 339C–F

Lord Nicholls:

In order to discharge th[e] burden [that the difference between the claimant's pay and the comparator's is not tainted by sex,] the employer must satisfy the tribunal on several matters. First, that the proffered explanation, or reason, is genuine, and not a sham or pretence. Second, that the less favourable treatment is due to this reason. The factor relied upon must be the cause of the disparity. In this regard, and in this sense, the factor must be a 'material' factor, that is, a significant and relevant factor. Third, that the reason is not 'the difference of sex.' This phrase is apt to embrace any form of sex discrimination, whether direct or indirect. Fourth, that the factor relied upon is or . . . may be a 'material' difference, that is, a significant and relevant difference, between the woman's case and the man's case.

As for the specific criteria which have been held to qualify as material factors, it is perhaps best to approach them as:

(1) establishing a rebuttable presumption of gender-neutrality (i.e. the claimant may dispel the presumption by showing that the material factor is indeed tainted by sex discrimination); and

(2) to divide them into (a) factors reflecting personal differences in the attributes of the comparator vis-à-vis the claimant which are wholly unrelated to sex and (b) external factors.

Turning first to (2)(a), i.e. the personal qualities of a comparator that may be presumed to be untainted by sex discrimination, it has been held that this will include:

• seniority/longer service;[134]

• regional differentiations in pay reflecting the geographical location at which the comparator works, e.g. a 'London weighting';[135]

---

[130] *ibid.*, 235D per Lord Keith of Kinkel.   [131] *ibid.*, 235E per Lord Keith of Kinkel.

[132] See also *Enderby v Frenchay Health Authority* [1994] ICR 112.

[133] Market forces will not always qualify as a material factor defence, e.g. where the work is segregated according to gender lines, as in *Ratcliffe v North Yorkshire County Council* [1995] 3 All ER 597.

[134] This is on the ground that seniority or length of service criteria in managerial pay structures operate to reward the loyalty and firm-specific experience of workers, which is a legitimate commercial aim: *Cadman v Health and Safety Executive* [2006] ICR 1623, 1647B–D. Another potential legitimate aim of a length of service criterion would include the retention of labour.

[135] *Navy, Army and Air Force Institutes v Varley* [1977] 1 WLR 149.

- night-shift working;[136]

- bonuses to reward higher levels of productivity;[137] or

- superior experience, training, or qualifications,[138] i.e. merit-based factors.[139]

Of course, the claimant may lead evidence to convince a tribunal or court that the material factor is indeed tainted by sex discrimination. For example, with regard to the 'length of service' material factor, the presumption that it is gender-neutral will be dislodged where the employee casts 'serious doubts as to whether recourse to the criterion of length of service is, in the circumstances, appropriate to attain the . . . objective [of rewarding the loyalty and experience of its workers]'.[140] As such, if the claimant can establish that women are generally disadvantaged by the length of service criterion in the pay scheme on the basis that a material number of female employees of the employer have in fact taken career breaks for child-rearing and caring purposes, the burden will fall on the employer to objectively justify its pay practice as a proportionate means of achieving the legitimate aim of rewarding the loyalty and experience of its workers; likewise where the material factor advanced by the employer for the disparity in the pay of the claimant and the comparator is 'productivity': if there is statistical evidence showing that the productivity bonuses are paid to workers in jobs that are composed exclusively or mainly of males, but not to workers in jobs consisting exclusively or predominantly of females,[141] this will set up an inference of sex discrimination and impose a burden on the employer to objectively justify the productivity bonus, i.e. to show that the bonus was a proportionate means of achieving a legitimate commercial aim pursuant to the proportionality standard of review applied in indirect discrimination cases.[142]

We now move on to consider (2)(b), i.e. external factors which are not related to the personal qualities of the comparator that may be classified as sufficiently material factors for pay disparities. Provided that they are shown to be free from any sex bias, these may include:

- market forces;[143]

- the effects of separate collective bargaining arrangements and collective agreements;[144]

- where the operation of regulation 4(2) of the Transfer of Undertakings (Protection of Employment) Regulations 2006[145] caused the pay disparity;[146]

- mistake;[147] or

---

[136] *Blackburn v Chief Constable of West Midlands Police* [2009] IRLR 135.

[137] *Cumbria County Council v Dow (No. 1)* [2008] IRLR 91; cf. *Council of the City of Sunderland v Brennan* [2012] ICR 1216.

[138] *Kenny v Minister for Justice, Equality and Law Reform* [2013] IRLR 463.

[139] *Secretary of State for Justice v Bowling* [2012] IRLR 382.

[140] *Cadman v Health and Safety Executive* [2006] ICR 1623, 1647E.

[141] Or the former group are routinely in receipt of payments that are higher than those of the latter group.

[142] The process here is the same as the employer's defence in the context of an indirect discrimination claim, i.e. section 19(2)(d) of the EA, on which, see Chapter 10, section 10.2.4.4.

[143] *Rainey v Greater Glasgow Health Board* [1987] 1 AC 224.

[144] That is, the claimant and comparator were traditionally represented by different trade unions resulting in different collective bargaining arrangements and disparities in pay associated with two different collective agreements where the claimant's work was exclusively or mainly composed of females and the comparator's jobs wholly or predominantly filled by males, on which, see *Enderby v Frenchay Health Authority* [1994] ICR 112; *Redcar and Cleveland Borough Council v Bainbridge; Middlesbrough Borough Council v Surtees* [2008] IRLR 776; and *Grundy v British Airways plc* [2008] IRLR 815.

[145] SI 2006/246.   [146] *Skills Development Scotland Co. Ltd v Buchanan* [2011] Eq LR 955.

[147] *Yorkshire Blood Transfusion Service v Plaskitt* [1994] ICR 74; *Strathclyde Regional Council v Wallace* [1998] ICR 205; and *Parliamentary Commissioner for Administration v Fernandez* [2004] ICR 123. See C. Kilpatrick, 'Deciding when Jobs of Equal Value can be Paid Unequally: An Examination of s 1(3) of the Equal Pay Act 1970' (1994) 23 *Industrial Law Journal* 311, 324–5.

- red-circling[148] and pay protection schemes.[149]

These can be contrasted with cost/budgetary constraints,[150] 'the interests of good industrial relations',[151] and 'supervening cause'[152] which, taken in isolation, will not be categorized as material factors.

However, once again, if the material factor advanced by the employer for the pay disparity is one of the aforementioned external features, i.e. 'market forces', or that the claimant and the comparator's work type were historically covered by separate collective bargaining processes and agreements, etc., and the claimant is able to show that these justifications are tainted by indirect sex discrimination, it will then be incumbent on the employer to comply with section 69(1)(b) or (2) in order to avoid liability. We now subject this section to a greater degree of scrutiny.

14.3.2 Direct and indirect discrimination

Section 69(1)(a) of the EA directs that any material factor advanced by the employer as a defence must be rejected by the tribunal or court if it is directly discriminatory, e.g. where the variation in the pay of the claimant and the comparator is attributable to a material factor which involves treating the claimant less favourably than the comparator because of the claimant's sex. An obvious, albeit rather crude,[153] example would be where an employer specifically decides to pay pregnant employees less than non-pregnant employees and invokes 'pregnancy' as a material factor defence. In such a case, the employer is afforded no means of justifying the directly discriminatory pay practice.

Much trickier to address are those cases in which the employer's material factor defence is tainted by indirect sex discrimination. This forms the target of section 69(1)(b) and (2) of the EA. The current orthodoxy in the case law is to acknowledge that there are two distinct kinds of indirect discrimination[154] which may arise in the context of equal pay.

(1) Where the contractual terms of the claimant and comparator engaged in 'like work', 'work rated as equivalent', or 'work of equal value' are identical, i.e. there is no variation in pay, but the employer applies a provision, criterion, or practice ('PCP') which puts or would put the claimant and women generally at a particular disadvantage

---

[148] This describes the situation where a male comparator's work (which is rated as equivalent or of equal value to that of the female claimant's work) attracts a higher rate of pay than that of the claimant's job for some reason attributable to a past event, e.g. where it is 'necessary to protect the wages of an employee, or a group of employees, moved from a better paid type of work to a worse paid type of work, perhaps because the first is no longer being undertaken': *Snoxell v Vauxhall Motors Ltd* [1978] 1 QB 11, 22B–C per Phillips J.

[149] *Haq v Audit Commission* [2012] EWCA Civ 1621, [2013] IRLR 206; *Redcar and Cleveland Borough Council v Bainbridge; Surtees v Middlesbrough Borough Council* [2008] IRLR 776; and *Middlesbrough Borough Council v Surtees* [2007] IRLR 869. However, it will be a challenge to objectively justify a pay protection scheme, e.g. see *Glasgow City Council v Unison claimants* [2017] IRLR 739.

[150] *Jorgensen v Foreningen* [2000] IRLR 726.

[151] *Kenny v Minister for Justice, Equality and Law Reform* [2013] IRLR 463.

[152] *Coventry City Council v Nicholls* [2009] IRLR 345. Here, the employers attributed the pay disparity to the alleged intransigence of the trade unions in forging an agreement on single status pay structures. The EAT held that trade union hostility to changing pay arrangements did not establish a supervening cause neutralizing the historical pay variations and as such could not be a material factor.

[153] See also the example provided in the Statutory Code of Practice on Equal Pay, available at https://www.equalityhumanrights.com/sites/default/files/equalpaycode.pdf at para 82 (last visited 9 October 2017): 'Male maintenance workers in a bank were paid more than female administrators because the bank had always regarded and rewarded men as family breadwinners. This is directly discriminatory and cannot be justified.'

[154] See *Bury Metropolitan Borough Council v Hamilton* [2011] IRLR 358, EAT. The decision of the EAT was upheld on appeal to the Court of Appeal in *Council of the City of Sunderland v Brennan* [2012] ICR 1216.

when compared with men. The classic example of this 'PCP form of indirect discrimination' in equal pay cases arises where the employer offers its employees a form of contingent benefit which fewer women are able to satisfy than men, e.g. a contractual term that enables employees to participate in a non-contributory occupational pension scheme if they work full-time. In such a case, section 66(2)(a) and (b) offers no redress to the claimant, since she is not seeking equalization of her contractual terms with that of the comparator—they are already identical—but instead a modification of her terms stripped of the indirectly discriminatory component.

(2) Where there are statistics showing that the claimant's work exclusively or predominantly comprises females who are paid less than an exclusively or mainly male group, which includes the comparator doing 'like work', 'work rated as equivalent', or 'work of equal value' to the claimant. Alternatively, it is sufficient if the statistics establish that there is a substantial disparity in the gender composition of the two groups.

Section 69(1)(b) and (2) of the EA is primarily directed at the situation in (2). This is often referred to in shorthand as '*Enderby*-type indirect discrimination', named after the decision of the ECJ in *Enderby v Frenchay Health Authority*.[155] In such a case, there is no requirement for the claimant to identify a PCP; instead, the statistical discrepancy in the gender make-up of the two groups is generally treated as enough to set up a presumption of prima facie indirect discrimination.[156] However, what is not wholly clear from section 69(2) of the EA is whether the employer is entitled to dislodge the presumption of indirect discrimination by showing that the differential in pay did not arise as a consequence of a factor placing the claimant and 'persons of the same sex doing work equal to' the claimant at a particular disadvantage: in other words, that the statistical disparity is attributable to a material factor wholly unrelated to sex.[157] This will be a particularly germane issue in the situation described by Smith LJ in *Gibson*:

■ *Gibson v Sheffield City Council* [2010] ICR 708, 730A–E

Smith LJ:

In *Middlesbrough Borough Council v Surtees* [2007] ICR 1644 in the [EAT] Elias J (President) sought for examples of the kind of case in which it might be possible for an employer to explain how a statistical gender imbalance had arisen without there being any sex taint. It appears to me that he found it hard to think of any such circumstances and gave only one example, at para 54 of his judgment. He postulated two groups of workers (A and B), both, in the past, comprising only or mainly men but where group A workers were always paid more than group B. Over the course of time, the composition of group B changed so as to become predominantly female but group A remained predominantly male. If the work of the two groups was rated as equivalent and if the women in group B complained of unequal pay, the statistics would show an adverse impact on them. Elias J said that a tribunal would readily be persuaded that the difference in pay was not sex-tainted notwithstanding the statistical analysis showing an adverse impact on the women in group B. The employer would then establish the [material factor] defence without the need to justify. I agree

---

[155] [1994] ICR 112.

[156] In such circumstances, 'it will be difficult for the employer to prove an absence of sex discrimination': Statutory Code of Practice on Equal Pay, available at https://www.equalityhumanrights.com/sites/default/files/equalpaycode.pdf at para 86 (last visited 9 October 2017). See also *Gibson v Sheffield City Council* [2010] ICR 708, 730A per Smith LJ.

[157] See *Armstrong v Newcastle upon Tyne NHS Hospital Trust* [2006] IRLR 124; *Gibson v Sheffield City Council* [2010] ICR 708; and *Newcastle upon Tyne Hospitals NHS Foundation Trust v Armstrong* [2010] ICR 674, which decided that the employer was entitled to do so, albeit that this would appear to be contrary to EU law as set out in *Enderby v Frenchay Health Authority* [1994] ICR 112.

with him that that is an example of a situation in which the employer could show the absence of sex taint and would avoid justification even though there was disparate impact. I am not saying, of course, that the circumstances envisaged by Elias J are the only ones in which it will be possible for the employer to demonstrate that the adverse impact was not sex tainted. There will be others although I cannot think of any.

Hepple is of the opinion that the employer is barred from advancing a defence that the statistical disparity between groups A and B is attributable to a material factor entirely unrelated to sex.[158] Hepple's position is supported by the fact that there was no reference in the Explanatory Notes to the EA to such a defence. However, there is an argument that the statutory language 'as a result of the factor' in section 69(2) does indeed enable the employer to dislodge the presumption set up by the statutory disparity. At present, the position is unresolved, albeit that it is certain that the courts will be called upon to pronounce on the issue at some point in the near future.[159]

Where the employer advances a material factor and the claimant dislodges the presumption of an absence of a sex taint associated with that material factor with statistics showing that the claimant's work exclusively or predominantly comprises females who are paid less than an exclusively or mainly male group which includes the comparator doing 'like work', 'work rated as equivalent', or 'work of equal value'—leaving aside the earlier question as to whether the employer has the right to establish that the statistical disparity is attributable to a material factor wholly unrelated to sex—section 69(2) provides that the employer must objectively justify the pay differential by showing that it is a proportionate means of achieving a legitimate aim. Accordingly, the employer has a defence which is assessed by the tribunal in accordance with the proportionality standard of review.[160] As for what will constitute legitimate aims, from our earlier discussion in section 14.3.1 it is clear that rewarding loyalty and experience and the retention of labour have been recognized as such in the context of the 'length of service/seniority' material factors.[161] Meanwhile, section 69(3) of the EA directs that the long-term objective of reducing inequality between men's and women's terms of work is always to be regarded as a legitimate aim. For more substantive guidance on the operation of the employer's objective justification/proportionality defence in the equal pay context, the EHRC Statutory Code of Practice on equal pay provides very useful illustrations and guidance.[162]

Reflection points

1. In light of the discussion in section 14.1.1, do you agree that the UK and EU gender pay gaps are attributable to unconscious sex discrimination on the part of employers? Give reasons for your answer.

2. Would you support a legislative proposal to liberalize the equal pay regime by removing the restrictions on comparisons in section 79(2), (3), and (4) of the EA specifically

[158] B. Hepple, *Equality: The New Legal Framework*, 2nd edition (Oxford, Hart Publishing, 2014) 128–9. Fredman would also appear to concur: S. Fredman, *Discrimination Law*, 2nd edition (Oxford, OUP, 2011) 165.

[159] See I. Steele, 'Sex Discrimination and the Material Factor Defence under the Equal Pay Act 1970 and the Equality Act 2010' (2010) 39 *Industrial Law Journal* 264, 274.

[160] For a full discussion of the proportionality defence, see Chapter 10, section 10.2.4.4.

[161] *Cadman v Health and Safety Executive* [2006] ICR 1623.

[162] See https://www.equalityhumanrights.com/sites/default/files/equalpaycode.pdf at paras 87–89 (last visited 9 October 2017).

to enable claimants to make cross-firm, cross-site, and cross-sector comparisons without restriction? Give reasons for your answer.

3. In your opinion, is the prohibition of hypothetical comparators justified? If so, why? If not, suggest how a tribunal or court might draw up the features and earning capacity of the hypothetical comparator.

4. Throughout this chapter, a number of references have been made to differences which arise between the domestic equal pay regime and the EU regime under Article 157 TFEU. Can you identify each of these disparities?

 For additional reading on the sex equality clause and the material factor defence, visit the Online Resources for this book at www.oup.com/uk/cabrelli3e/

PART VI
COMMON LAW AND STATUTORY REGULATION OF DISMISSALS

CHAPTER FIFTEEN

WRONGFUL DISMISSAL

15.1 INTRODUCTION TO THE TERMINATION OF THE CONTRACT OF EMPLOYMENT AND WRONGFUL DISMISSAL

In this chapter, we turn our attention to the legal consequences where *an employer* lawfully or unlawfully terminates the contract of employment. Since the default position prescribed by law is that the contract of employment is open-ended/indefinite in duration,[1] the common law imposes a number of constraints on the employer's power of dismissal. As such, the unilateral termination of the employment contract by the employer may be *lawful* or *wrongful* at common law. Of course, this presupposes that there are sufficient policy grounds to justify the judiciary pressing the common law of the contract of employment into service as a means of curbing the exercise of the managerial power of dismissal, which is an issue we will consider. The chapter will also include an examination of the competing elective theory of termination and automatic theory of termination, together with the statutory intervention in the guise of the minimum periods of notice in section 86 of the Employment Rights Act 1996 ('ERA'). Finally, the remedies available to employees in the case of a wrongful dismissal are addressed.

---

[1] See Chapter 5, section 5.1.1.

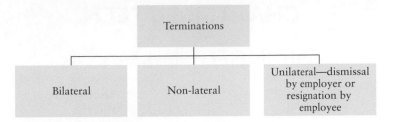

Figure 15.1 *Taxonomy of contractual terminations*

15.1.1 Dismissal and the termination of the contract of employment: a contextual and comparative analysis

A basic starting point for our discussion is to stress the importance of the application of proper terminology in this field of law. For example, one must understand that the dismissal of an employee and the termination of the contract of employment are not necessarily descriptive of the same phenomenon. When an employee is dismissed, the employer may well have brought the contract of employment to an end,[2] but the termination of the contract does not necessarily imply a dismissal. Hence a distinction ought to be drawn between the two. Once that has been clarified, we can classify the kinds of terminations one encounters, in Figure 15.1. A useful taxonomy of terminations is furnished by Freedland, who forges a distinction between:

(1) bilateral terminations;

(2) non-lateral terminations; and

(3) unilateral terminations.[3]

Bilateral termination is a reference to the employer and employee terminating the contract by mutual agreement.[4] This can be contrasted with non-lateral termination, which is descriptive of a termination by operation of law independent of the volition of the parties, e.g. frustration or the death[5] or insolvency[6] of the employer. Finally, unilateral termination may be effected by the employer, i.e. a lawful or unlawful/wrongful dismissal, or by the employee, which is referred to as a 'resignation' in common parlance. In this chapter, it must be stressed that we are principally concerned with the employer's unilateral termination of the contract of employment, i.e. a dismissal, whether lawful or unlawful/wrongful. Therefore, we will not be addressing unilateral termination by the employee, or bilateral or non-lateral termination.

Meanwhile, the law relating to dismissals can be properly understood by dividing the analysis into the following categories, namely:

(1) lawful and unlawful/wrongful dismissals; and

(2) outright/summary and constructive dismissals.

There is an element of overlap here, since an outright/summary and constructive dismissal may be lawful or unlawful/wrongful. See Figure 15.2, which distinguishes dismissals according to their legality and their nature.

---

[2] See the discussion in section 15.2.4.2 regarding when the employment contract is terminated in the context of a dismissal.

[3] M. Freedland, *The Personal Employment Contract* (Oxford, OUP, 2003) 408–9.

[4] For example, *Birch v University of Liverpool* [1985] ICR 470.

[5] The death of the employee (*Stubbs v The Holywell Railway Co.* (1867) LR 2 Exch 311) or employer (*Farrow v Wilson* (1869) LR 4 CP 744, 766 (Willes J)).

[6] See B. G. Graham, 'The Effect of Liquidation on Contracts of Service' (1952) 15 *Modern Law Review* 48.

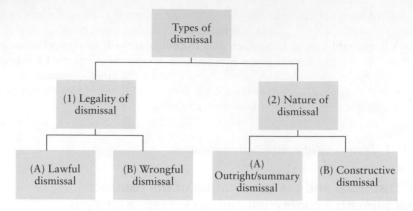

Figure 15.2 *Taxonomy of dismissals*

We focus our attention on the distinction between lawful and wrongful dismissals by the employer. In the case of a contract of employment of an indefinite duration, the common law will treat an employer as having terminated the contract of employment unlawfully/wrongfully where it fails to provide the employee with reasonable notice of dismissal. Therefore, the employer will be in breach where a reasonable period of notice of the termination of an employee's employment contract is not given to the employee nor a payment made to the employee in lieu of notice. This will afford an employee a 'wrongful dismissal' claim for damages in respect of his/her net wages or salary and other contractual benefits during the notice period. By the same token, if the employer provides the employee with a reasonable period of notice of termination, it stands to reason that the employer will have unilaterally terminated the employment contract on a lawful basis.[7]

What amounts to a 'reasonable' period of notice under the common law is not a precise art[8] and is contingent on three factors, namely the custom of the employee's trade, the standing of the individual's job (i.e. professional or otherwise),[9] and the frequency of the payment of the wage or salary (e.g. one week's notice where payment is weekly or one month's notice in the case of a monthly salary). This common law rule is restricted to contracts of employment of an indefinite period:

■ *Reda v Flag Ltd* [2002] UKPC 38, 38

Lord Millett:

The true rule, which is not confined to contracts of employment but applies to contracts generally, is that a contract *which contains no express provision for its determination* is generally (though not invariably) subject to an implied term that it is determinable by reasonable notice . . . The implication is made as a matter of law as a necessary incident of a class of contract which would otherwise be incapable of being determined at all. Most contracts of employment are of indefinite duration and are accordingly terminable by reasonable notice in the absence of express provision to the contrary.[10]

---

[7] *Baxter v Nurse* (1844) 6 Man & G 935; *Robson v Overend* (1878) 6 R 213; and *McClelland v Northern Ireland General Health Services Board* [1957] 1 WLR 594, 599 per Lord Oaksey.

[8] *Wilson v Anthony* 1958 SLT (Sh Ct) 13. For the case in favour of the reasonable notice rule, see R. Arnow-Richman, 'Mainstreaming Employment Contract Law: The Common Law Case for Reasonable Notice of Termination' (2014) 66 *Florida Law Review* 1513.

[9] See *Hill v CA Parsons & Co. Ltd* [1972] Ch 305, 313D, and 316F per Lord Denning MR and Sachs LJ; *Wray v The University of the West Indies* [2007] UKPC 14.

[10] Sourced from BAILII available at http://www.bailii.org/cgi-bin/markup.cgi?doc=/uk/cases/UKPC/2002/38.html&query=Reda+and+v+and+Flag+and+Ltd&method=boolean (last visited 5 October 2017).

In the modern workplace, it will only be on rare occasions that there is no express term as to notice in an employee's contract.[11] This express period may be higher than the common law's 'reasonable' period, in which case the employer will be compelled to provide notice in compliance with the former. Furthermore, section 86(1) of the ERA prescribes certain statutory minimum periods of notice with which the employer must comply. The general position under section 86 of the ERA is that an employee is entitled to one week's notice where he/she has been continuously employed for a period between one month and two years, which increases by a week for each year of continuous employment beyond two years, subject to a maximum of 12 weeks' notice. Once again, where the period calculated under this statutory provision improves upon the period of reasonable notice or the express period set out in the employee's employment contract, the employer must honour the higher statutory period.

The inherent common law power of the employer to unilaterally terminate the employment contract on a lawful basis is known in shorthand as the employer's 'unrestricted notice power'. Similarly, the common law rule which sanctions the employer's prerogative of dismissal can be referred to as the 'unrestricted reasonable notice rule'. Commentators have argued that it furnishes the employer with an unfettered discretion.[12] The effect of that discretion is that the employee is afforded a very limited degree of economic security in respect of his/her employment, bearing in mind that the notice period may be as low as one week in the case of a wage-earner paid on a weekly basis. The unrestricted reasonable notice rule, however, is by no means the only 'default' position upon which a jurisdiction's legal system may settle. It is not inconceivable that a jurisdiction could decide to develop the law of the contract of employment to craft a 'just cause' regime that bars an employer from dismissing an employee in the absence of a just cause.[13] For example, French private law is sufficiently malleable to harness a doctrine known as *abus de droit*, which enables an employee to successfully challenge an employer's power to terminate on reasonable notice. Indeed, even within the common law tradition the unrestricted reasonable notice rule is something of a peculiarly British phenomenon which can be contrasted with the policy choice adopted by the American strand of the common law. In the USA, the employment-at-will doctrine developed, which provided for lawful termination on summary, rather than reasonable, notice. The American vision of the employment relationship amounts to a particularly flexible approach to hiring and firing, and it is often argued that it is one of the contributing factors towards the comparative suppleness of the US labour market:

■ H. Collins, *Employment Law*, 2nd edition (Oxford, OUP, 2010) 163–5

For the disciplinary sanction of dismissal, an interesting divergence arose in the common law. In the United States, the courts developed the default rule that contracts of employment could be terminated 'at will', for any reason at any time. It remains normal practice for American employers to dismiss employees peremptorily and to tell them to leave with their personal belongings im-

---

[11] This is attributable to the statutory direction in section 1(4)(e) of the ERA that the employer must give the employee written particulars of any notice period within two months of the commencement of the employee's employment, on which, see Chapter 5, section 5.2.1.

[12] M. Ford, 'Re-thinking the Notice Rule' (1998) 27 *Industrial Law Journal* 220.

[13] For the possible options and permutations, see G. Davidov and E. Eshet, 'Intermediate Approaches to Unfair Dismissal Protection' (2015) 44 *Industrial Law Journal* 167; G. Davidov, 'In Defence of (Efficiently Administered) "Just Cause" Dismissal Laws' (2007) 23 *International Journal of Comparative Labour Law and Industrial Relations* 117; and J. Howe, 'Poles Apart? The Contestation between the Ideas of No Fault Dismissal and Unfair Dismissal for Protecting Job Security' (2013) 42 *Industrial Law Journal* 122.

mediately. Although English courts agreed that employers could terminate employment for any reason at any time, they also applied the normal rule for contracts of indefinite duration that such contracts contain an implied term that only permits unilateral termination on giving reasonable notice. The period of reasonable notice was usually assumed to be the period between payments, so that if the worker was paid by the day, the contract could be terminated lawfully by giving a day's notice. The remedy open to the employee for breach of the implied term of reasonable notice was confined to a claim (known as 'wrongful dismissal') for the net wages during the notice period. This amounts to a sum equivalent to wages during the notice period, minus the normal deductions such as taxation, and also subject to the employee's duty to mitigate loss. The implied term of reasonable notice thus places scant constraint upon an employer's power to terminate the contract at will.

As for the motivations of the judiciary in harnessing the common law as a means of developing the unrestricted notice rule, three suggestions have been made.

(1) By affording the employer a generous power of dismissal, the unrestricted reasonable notice rule also protected the freedom of the worker to strike.[14]

(2) When the modern common law of the contract of employment was evolving in the nineteenth and early twentieth centuries, 'it was thought preferable to preserve some of the elements of pre-[industrial-] nineteenth-century master and servant law in the . . . exposition of the contract of employment so that it would operate as a framework of discipline for employees'.[15] The line of argument here is that the unrestricted reasonable notice rule enables employers to maintain discipline in the workplace. The employee's understanding that he/she can be fired lawfully with a comparatively limited amount of prior notice operates to focus his/her mind and incentivizes him/her to be conscientious.

(3) It has been suggested that the role played by the unrestricted reasonable notice rule can be conceived of in something more than instrumental terms, and that it represents the judicial articulation of a philosophical approach towards the common law of the contract of employment:

■ M. Freedland, *The Personal Employment Contract* (Oxford, OUP, 2003) 330–1

The notion of the unrestricted notice power was part and parcel of the common law view of the very structure of the contract of employment at the outset of the present era of employment law (that is to say in the early 1960s) and has largely remained so. It was structurally integral to the core conception of the contract of employment in the following sense . . . The key feature of th[e] archetypal [employment] contract, the characteristic which defined its duration, was its terminability by notice. Inherent to that understanding of the 'notice rule' is the idea that the power of termination by notice which it confers upon the employ[er] (and for that matter upon the employee, but that is a somewhat secondary feature) is an unrestricted one. There are various ways in which we can explain the treatment of the unrestricted notice rule, at the outset of the period we are discussing, as a self-evident or unquestioned proposition. It might be seen as the product simply

---

[14] For example, if the contract of employment stipulates that the employee is to be paid daily, the presumption would be that reasonable notice of termination on the part of the employer would be one day, thereby conferring a fairly liberal right to dismiss in favour of the employer. By the same token, by giving one day's prior (reasonable) notice to the employer, the employee would also be entitled to terminate/resign, thus protecting his/her freedom to strike without committing a breach of contract.

[15] P. Davies and M. Freedland, *Labour Legislation and Public Policy* (Oxford, Clarendon Press/OUP, 1993) 430.

of general thinking about freedom of contract, or as a product of the 'collective laissez-faire' approach to industrial relations whereby *de facto* joint regulation by collective bargaining was not closely integrated into the legal norms. Perhaps the best explanation lies in the fact that this vision of the archetypal contract of employment simply did not seem to be a matter of controversy in the common law courts; it hardly ever came into question before the higher or appellate courts. The courts could and did accept a received orthodoxy which treated the unrestricted notice rule as an axiomatic feature of the legal contract of employment even if that orthodoxy was sometimes out of accord with the social and economic reality of employment relationships by the early 1960s . . .

The dissonance referred to in this Freedland extract between the social and political demands for greater protection from dismissal and the prevailing common law philosophy channelled through the unrestricted reasonable notice rule had generated a great deal of tension by the mid-to-late 1960s. By then, a spotlight had been shone on the uncompromising nature of the common law by the House of Lords in *Ridge v Baldwin*[16] and *Malloch v Aberdeen Corp.*[17] Ultimately, this incongruity was a major contributing factor towards the introduction of the statutory unfair dismissal regime, which was intended to confer a higher degree of security of tenure in favour of employees than that afforded by the common law.

Reflection points

1. Consider the attractions of a legal regime that enables an employer to terminate an employee's contract of employment by providing the employee with (a) reasonable notice or (b) summary notice.

2. Now list the disadvantages of such legal regimes. Which of the two options do you prefer and why?

3. What is your view of a 'just cause' regime, i.e. an approach that prohibits the employer from dismissing an employee if it does not have one of a limited class of prescribed reasons for dismissal?

 For additional reading on dismissal and the termination of the contract of employment, visit the Online Resources for this book at www.oup.com/uk/cabrelli3e/

15.2 DISMISSAL AND BREACH OF THE CONTRACT OF EMPLOYMENT AT COMMON LAW

We will first concentrate on the circumstances in which an employer will be taken to have lawfully dismissed an employee. This will entail differentiating between the dismissal of the employee by reasonable notice, for cause (summary dismissal), and dismissal by non-renewal of a fixed-term contract. We will then go on to consider the law of wrongful dismissal and when the termination of the contract of employment in such circumstances takes effect. The latter will involve an exposition of the competing merits of the automatic and elective theories of termination.

---

[16] [1964] AC 40. See C Mummé, 'From Control through Command to the Control of Discretion: Labour Time, Labour Property and the Tools of Managerial Control in Early Twentieth Century Ontario' (2016) 45 *Industrial Law Journal* 176 for a discussion of the historical development of wrongful dismissal as a legal concept.　　　　　　　　　　　　　　　　　　　　　　[17] [1971] 1 WLR 1578.

15.2.1 The employer's unrestricted power of dismissal by reasonable notice

The *obiter* statements of Lord Reid in the cases of *Ridge v Baldwin*[18] and *Malloch v Aberdeen Corp.*[19] demonstrate the imbalance of power inherent within the employment relationship. They clarify that the common law does not require an employer to have any reason or a good reason to dismiss an employee[20]—or even to hear the employee prior to dismissal or give reasons for dismissal. The only requirement imposed is to give the employee:

(1) reasonable notice of termination,[21]

(2) the notice period prescribed in the employee's written contract of employment, or

(3) the statutory minimum period prescribed in section 86 of the ERA,

whichever period is the higher, failing which the employee will have a claim for damages in wrongful dismissal:[22]

■ *Ridge v Baldwin* [1964] AC 40 (HL), 65

Lord Reid (with whom the majority of Law Lords agreed, Lord Evershed dissenting):

The law regarding master and servant is not in doubt. There cannot be specific performance of a contract of service, and the master can terminate the contract with his servant at any time and for any reason or for none. But if he does so in a manner not warranted by the contract he must pay damages for breach of contract. So the question in a pure case of master and servant does not at all depend on whether the master has heard the servant in his own defence: it depends on whether the facts emerging at the trial prove breach of contract.

■ *Malloch v Aberdeen Corp.* [1971] 1 WLR 1578 (HL), 1581F–G

Lord Reid (with whom the majority of Law Lords agreed, Lords Guest and Morris of Borth-y-Gest dissenting):

At common law a master is not bound to hear his servant before he dismisses him. He can act unreasonably or capriciously if he so chooses but the dismissal is valid. The servant has no remedy unless the dismissal is in breach of contract and then the servant's only remedy is damages for breach of contract.

Lord Reid's *obiter dicta* exposed the lack of job security available to employees and the lack of protection against arbitrary termination of their contracts of employment.[23]

---

[18] [1964] AC 40.   [19] [1971] 1 WLR 1578.

[20] See *Alexander v Standard Telephones & Cables (No. 2)* [1991] IRLR 286, 296 at para 53 per Hobhouse J (as he then was).

[21] Once served, notice may not be retracted: *Willoughby v CF Capital plc* [2012] ICR 1038.

[22] In M. Ford, 'Re-thinking the Notice Rule' (1998) 27 *Industrial Law Journal* 219, Ford has argued that 'the [unrestricted reasonable notice] rule is taken to be so obvious that it is usually repeated [by the judiciary] without authorities or analysis to support it'. However, in English law and Scots law there are clear authorities to that effect, e.g. *Baxter v Nurse* (1844) 6 Man & G 935; *Reda v Flag Ltd* [2002] UKPC 38, [2002] IRLR 747, 754 per Lord Millett; *Morrison v Abernethy School Board* (1876) 3 R 945; *Robson v Overend* (1878) 6 R 213; and *Cooper v Henderson* (1825) 3 S 619. See also M. Freedland, *The Personal Employment Contract* (Oxford, OUP, 2003) 329–32.

[23] *Allen v Flood* [1898] AC 1, 173 per Lord Davey. Moreover, in these excerpts, Lord Reid seems to engage in the assimilation of a complex set of ideas about the employer's valid and invalid exercise of the power of dismissal and the consequences of such an exercise, i.e. the notions of lawful termination, unlawful termination, and the issue of remedies are all interwoven together, on which, see M. Freedland, *The Personal Employment Contract* (Oxford, OUP, 2003) 352–3.

Where the employer gives notice of termination of the employee's employment contract, the notice period will not commence until the notice is actually received by the employee having taken delivery of it personally, rather than when the notice was sent or when it arrived at the home of the employee.[24] This will impact on the effective date of termination of the contract of employment at common law.

Despite its harshness, the unrestricted reasonable notice rule has proven to be remarkably impervious to assaults launched against its pre-eminence. These challenges have come from two directions.

(1) Attempts to press public law principles into service as a means of controlling the exercise of the employer's unrestricted notice ultimately proved to be fruitless despite promising beginnings.[25]

(2) Furthermore, in the cases of *Johnson v Unisys Ltd*,[26] *Reda v Flag Ltd*,[27] and *Eastwood v Magnox Electric plc*,[28] the House of Lords and Privy Council ruled that the common law of the contract of employment could not be adapted in order to mount a challenge. Here, the idea that the implied term of mutual trust and confidence could be applied to place constraints on the unrestricted reasonable notice rule was rejected.

However, as stressed by Lord Millett in *Reda v Flag Ltd*,[29] the unrestricted reasonable notice rule is merely an implied default term; as such, it may be displaced. For example, a contractual job security clause which limits the employer to dismiss for good cause only, amounts to a specific carve-out from the implied term that a general hiring is indefinite and can be terminated lawfully by reasonable notice.

Hypothetical A

Danny's Demolishers Ltd ('the Employer') appoints Mark Underwood ('MU') as a sales director who will sit on its board of directors. MU's service agreement provides that he can only be dismissed for 'gross misconduct' or 'long-term ill-health'. Two years into MU's appointment, the Employer dismisses him for the reason of redundancy on six months' prior notice. MU challenges his dismissal as a breach of contract.

In the situation described in Hypothetical A, MU has the benefit of a form of contractual job security, since the express terms of his employment contract restrict the termination of his contract to 'gross misconduct' and 'long-term ill-health' only, i.e. these are the two 'good causes'. If neither of these two 'good cause' criteria are met, the Employer will be in breach by terminating MU's contract of employment on what may or may not be reasonable notice, since such a power is not implied.[30] Accordingly, the effect of the express

---

[24] *Newcastle upon Tyne NHS Foundation Trust v Haywood* [2018] UKSC 22. Cf. *Gisda Cyf v Barratt* [2010] UKSC 41, [2010] ICR 1475.

[25] See *R v East Berkshire Health Authority, ex parte Walsh* [1984] ICR 743 (CA) and the discussion in M. Freedland, *The Personal Employment Contract* (Oxford, OUP, 2003) 332–7.

[26] [2001] UKHL 13, [2003] 1 AC 518, 541F–H per Lord Hoffmann.

[27] [2002] UKPC 38, [2002] IRLR 747, 753 per Lord Millett.

[28] [2005] 1 AC 503.   [29] [2002] UKPC 38, [2002] IRLR 747, 754.

[30] See *McClelland v Northern Ireland General Health Services Board* [1957] 1 WLR 594; G. Pitt, 'Dismissal at Common Law: The Relevance in Britain of American Developments' (1989) 52 *Modern Law Review* 22, 24–5.

term is that MU will be entitled to be compensated in respect of the consequences of losing his job.[31]

15.2.2 The employer's power of summary dismissal for cause without notice

Where an employee commits a repudiatory breach of an express or implied term of the contract of employment, this will entitle the 'innocent' party, i.e. the employer, to summarily terminate the contract by unilaterally accepting the breach. In such a case, the employer will not be required to serve reasonable notice or make a payment in lieu of notice. As for the kind of conduct on the part of the employee that will amount to a repudiatory breach of contract to justify summary dismissal, suffice to say that it must be such that it 'makes the continuance of the contract of service impossible'.[32] Where the employee's conduct so undermines the trust and confidence which is inherent in the employment relationship that the employer should no longer be required to retain the employee in its employment, that will be sufficient.[33] However, whether there has been such a repudiatory breach is a classic 'jury question' for the trial judge to determine and an appellate court will be slow to interfere.[34] In *Williams v Leeds United Football Club*,[35] Mr Justice Lewis remarked that it would be appropriate to consider 'all the relevant circumstances including the nature of the contract and the relationship it creates, the nature of the contractual term that has been breached, the nature and degree of the breach and the consequences of the breach [including] . . . the nature of the business and the position held by the employee'.[36]

---

[31] However, the extent to which an express term can circumscribe the power of dismissal has been cast into doubt somewhat by a passage in the speech of Lord Hoffmann in *Johnson v Unisys Ltd* [2001] UKHL 13, [2003] 1 AC 518, 546 at para 66, and the treatment of that passage by Lords Dyson and Mance in the Supreme Court decision of *Edwards v Chesterfield Royal Hospital NHS Foundation Trust* [2011] UKSC 58, [2012] 2 AC 22. In *Edwards*, an express term of an employee's employment contract specifically incorporated a disciplinary procedure. When that procedure was not followed properly prior to the dismissal of the employee, the employee claimed damages. Lord Mance implicitly endorsed the speech of Lord Hoffmann in *Johnson* when he stated that the incorporation of a 'contractual disciplinary procedure cannot "have been intended to qualify the employer's common law power to dismiss without cause on giving such [i.e. due contractual] notice"': *Edwards v Chesterfield Royal Hospital NHS Foundation Trust* [2011] UKSC 58, [2012] 2 AC 22 at para 108; *Johnson v Unisys Ltd* [2001] UKHL 13, [2003] 1 AC 518, 546 at para 66. At best, the upshot of the approach of Lords Hoffmann, Dyson, and Mance is that clear and unequivocal language is required to satisfy a court or tribunal that an express term is designed to dislodge the unrestricted reasonable notice rule. In the absence of such clarity, there is scope for the unrestricted reasonable notice rule to remain firmly in position.

[32] *Wilson v Racher* [1974] ICR 428, 432 per Edmund Davies LJ.

[33] *Sinclair v Neighbour* [1967] 2 QB 279 (CA); *Pepper v Webb* [1969] 1 WLR 514 (CA); *Laws v London Chronicle (Indicator Newspapers) Ltd* [1959] 1 WLR 698 (CA); *Denco Ltd v Joinson* [1991] IRLR 63; *Neary v Dean of Westminster* [1999] IRLR 288; *Dunn v AAH Ltd* [2010] IRLR 709; *Jervis v Skinner* [2011] UKPC 2; *Milanese v Leyton Orient Football Club* [2016] IRLR 601; and *Adesokan v Sainsbury's Supermarkets Ltd* [2017] IRLR 346. Such conduct may amount to gross misconduct, which is a matter to which we will return in detail in Chapters 16 and 17, sections 16.2.4.3.2 and 17.2.2.1. See *R (Shoesmith) v OFSTED* [2011] IRLR 679 where it was held that the employer had no power to summarily dismiss an employee on the basis of a breakdown in trust and confidence where the concern about the employee related to her competence or capability.

[34] *Clouston & Co. Ltd v Corry* [1906] AC 122; *McCormack v Hamilton Academical Football Club Ltd* [2011] CSIH 68, 2011 GWD 39–801; and *Richards v I P Solutions Group Ltd* [2017] IRLR 133.

[35] [2015] IRLR 383.

[36] *ibid.*, 389. In *Williams*, it was held that using the employer's internal email to send obscene images to friends and work colleagues constituted a repudiatory breach, even though these incidents had occurred many years before. The employer was entitled to accept these repudiatory breaches by summarily dismissing the employee because it had been previously unaware of them having taken place. cf. *Farnan v Sunderland Association Football Club* [2016] IRLR 198 and *A v B Local Authority* [2016] IRLR 779.

Once it has been established that the employee has committed a repudiatory breach of the contract of employment, the question is how the 'innocent' employer ought to manifest its acceptance of the employee's repudiation. Rigidity is rejected, so no particular form is required as long as the conduct or communication clearly and unequivocally conveys to the repudiating employee that the aggrieved employer is treating the contract as at an end.[37] The employer's failure to give the employee work to do will not necessarily satisfy the requirement for the employer to communicate an unequivocal intention to terminate the employee's contract.[38] Although section 86 of the ERA recognizes the right of an employer to summarily dismiss an employee without providing the statutory minimum period of notice, it is no exaggeration to say that the statutory regulation of dismissals via the unfair dismissal scheme in Part X of the ERA has functioned to constrain the ability of an employer to dismiss for cause without notice. For example, paragraphs 22–23 of the ACAS Code of Practice 1 on Disciplinary and Grievance Procedures[39]—which prescribe when a pre-dismissal procedure will be deemed 'fair'—place restrictions on the power of the employer to dismiss summarily for gross misconduct.[40] As such, many employers will seek to adhere to a disciplinary process rooted in the basic building blocks of the ACAS Code, rather than summarily dismiss an employee who it is alleged has been culpable of gross misconduct. One of the fundamental elements is the employee's right to appeal the decision of a disciplinary hearing to dismiss him/her. Where the employee's appeal is successful and the disciplinary procedure was contractual, it has been held that the old contract of employment is revived, notwithstanding that the employer may not have communicated the success of the appeal to the employee.[41]

Finally, the point should be made that if an employer summarily dismisses an employee without cause or prior notice of termination, this will be lawful and not in breach of contract if the employer dismisses by making a payment in lieu of notice ('PILON') to the employee where there is a PILON clause in the contract of employment: an employee has no legal right to 'keep the contract alive against his employer's will by refusing to accept wages in lieu of notice'.[42] The term 'payment in lieu of notice' can describe a number of situations,[43] but in this context it is a reference to an express term affording the employer the right to summarily dismiss the employee[44] in exchange for a lump sum payment in lieu of wages and other contractual benefits payable *as a debt, rather than damages*, to the employee and corresponding to the employee's notice period.[45] Where there is no express PILON clause in the employee's employment contract empowering the employer to terminate by PILON, the effect of the common law is that there is little scope for an

---

[37] *Potter v RJ Temple plc (in liquidation)* (UKEAT/0478/03/LA, 18 December 2003).

[38] *Sandle v Adecco UK Ltd* [2016] IRLR 941.

[39] See http://www.acas.org.uk/?articleid=2174 for the March 2015 version (last visited 6 October 2017) and the Online Resources for this book for the full version of the ACAS Code.

[40] This is reflective of the fact that the tribunals and courts will often be reluctant to make a finding that a dismissal has not been unfair under Part X of the ERA where the employer has failed to follow a fair and proper pre-dismissal process, on which, see Chapter 17.

[41] *Salmon v Castlebeck Care (Teesdale) Ltd* [2015] ICR 735.

[42] B. Hepple, 'The Right to Work at One's Job' (1974) 37 *Modern Law Review* 681, 685.

[43] See the four categories of payment in lieu of notice analysed in *Delaney v Staples* [1992] 1 AC 687, 692C–H per Lord Browne-Wilkinson.

[44] Conversely, the express term may confer a right in favour of the employee to be summarily dismissed by the employer making a payment in lieu of notice.

[45] *Abrahams v Performing Rights Society Ltd* [1995] IRLR 486. However, where a payment in lieu of notice is made in the absence of such an express term, such payment will be on account of damages payable to the employee in respect of the employer's breach of contract: *Delaney v Staples* [1992] 1 AC 687, 692C–H per Lord Browne-Wilkinson. Cf. the position in Scots law, on which, see V. Craig, 'Pay in Lieu of Notice: Damages or Debt?' (2005) 9 *Edinburgh Law Review* 139; *Morrish v NTL Group Ltd* 2007 SC 805, 2007 SLT 1074.

implied power to arise to enable it do so.[46] As such, the immediate termination of the contract by PILON will constitute a breach of contract in such circumstances.[47] In such a case, if the employer fails to pay wages and other contractual benefits in respect of the entirety of the notice period, then this will amount to a wrongful dismissal[48] giving rise to damages,[49] unless the employer was justified in summarily dismissing without notice[50] or paying the employee a sum less than the full economic value of the notice period.

15.2.3 Dismissal by non-renewal of a fixed-term contract

An employer may lawfully dismiss an employee by failing to renew a fixed-term contract at the end of its duration, since the common law dictates that the contract is determined automatically at the end of the period prescribed.[51] Unlike an employment contract of indefinite duration, there is no implied term that an employer may determine a fixed-term contract by reasonable notice.[52] The common law jurisprudence has been supplemented by case law interpreting certain statutory provisions specifically enacted in order to confer protections in favour of employees with fixed-term contracts. For example, the definitions of 'fixed-term contract' in regulation 1(2) of the Fixed-term Employees (Prevention of Less Favourable Treatment) Regulations 2002[53] and a 'limited-term contract' in section 235(2A) and (2B) of the ERA[54] are sufficiently broad to include 'task' and 'purpose' contracts, i.e. contracts terminable on the completion of performance of a particular task or the occurrence or non-occurrence of a specific event. Moreover, a fixed-term contract that is determinable by notice before its term qualifies as a fixed-term contract.[55]

15.2.4 Wrongful dismissal

Stripped to its basic core, a common law action for wrongful dismissal is an action by an employee that *the employer has dismissed him/her in repudiatory breach of contract*. Hence it is essentially an action for damages in respect of a breach of contract. The various stages involved are shown in Figure 15.3.

15.2.4.1 Introduction

A dismissal will be in repudiatory breach where it involves the breach of an implied[56] or express[57] term which goes to the root of the contract of employment. Since it is an implied term that the employer may terminate the employment contract by giving the employee prior reasonable notice, a failure on the part of the employer to do so will

---

[46] *Delaney v Staples* [1992] 1 AC 687 (HL), 692 per Lord Browne-Wilkinson; *Morrish v NTL Group Ltd* [2007] CSIH 56, 2007 SC 805 at para 13 per Lord Nimmo-Smith.

[47] See *Rabess v London Fire and Emergency Planning Authority* [2014] All ER (D) 188 (EAT) (September).

[48] *Pepper v Webb* [1969] 1 WLR 514 (CA).   [49] See section 15.3.1.

[50] For example, *Pepper v Webb* [1969] 1 WLR 514 (CA).

[51] *R v Secretary of State for Social Services, ex parte Khan* [1973] 2 All ER 104.

[52] *Reda v Flag Ltd* [2002] UKPC 38, [2002] IRLR 747, 754 at para 57 per Lord Millett.

[53] SI 2002/2034. See Chapter 13, section 13.3.1.

[54] Part X of the ERA directs that the termination of a 'limited-term contract' is a dismissal for the purposes of the statutory unfair dismissal regime. The Fixed-Term Employees (Prevention of Less Favourable Treatment) Regulations 2002 (SI 2002/2034) ensure parity of contractual terms for those individuals employed on the basis of a 'fixed-term contract'.   [55] *Dixon v BBC* [1979] ICR 281.

[56] However, where the employer dismisses the employee by serving lawful notice of termination and then immediately re-engages him/her with the same level of continuous employment on different terms, it was held that this did not amount to a repudiatory breach of contract: *Kerry Foods Ltd v Lynch* [2005] IRLR 680.

[57] For example, where an employer dismisses in breach of an express term as to notice, or by making a PILON, or the dismissal amounts to a failure to comply with an express term, e.g. a job security clause such as that in *McClelland v Northern Ireland General Health Services Board* [1957] 1 WLR 594.

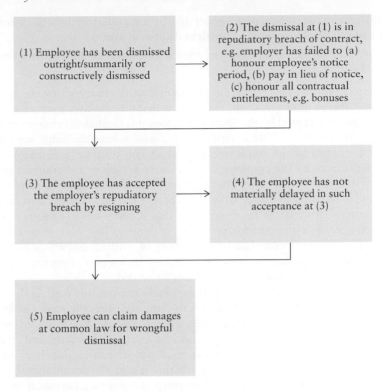

Figure 15.3 *Stages involved in a wrongful dismissal claim*

inextricably lead to a finding of wrongful dismissal. Indeed, the failure of the employer to provide the employee with the requisite period of notice of termination or to make a payment in lieu of notice on a summary dismissal is the paradigm example of a wrongful dismissal. Ordinary contractual principles are applied in order to ascertain whether there has been a repudiatory breach. Therefore, the conduct of the employer is evaluated in accordance with an objective test[58] and must be such that it 'evince[s] an intention no longer to be bound by the contract'.[59] An example is provided by the decision of the High Court in *Smith v Trafford Housing Trust*.[60] Here, an employee's purported demotion for posting a comment against gay marriage on his personal Facebook account was held to amount to a wrongful dismissal.

15.2.4.2 'Elective' versus 'automatic' theory of termination

Our conception of wrongful dismissal is broad enough to include the constructive wrongful dismissal of the employee, i.e. a repudiatory breach of contract on the part of the employer short of outright dismissal which is sufficiently serious to warrant the employee in treating him/herself as having been dismissed.[61] Indeed, for the purpose of ascertaining the precise legal effect of the employer's repudiation, there is a large degree of purchase in making a distinction between:

---

[58] *Forslind v Bechely-Crundall* 1922 SC (HL) 173, 179 per Viscount Haldane; *Pedersen v Camden London Borough Council* [1981] ICR 674.

[59] *General Billposting Co. Ltd v Atkinson* [1909] AC 118, 122 per Lord Collins.

[60] [2013] IRLR 86.

[61] For a comprehensive account of constructive dismissal, see Chapter 16, section 16.2.2.3.

(1) a *constructive* wrongful dismissal generated by a repudiatory breach of contract on the part of the employer short of outright dismissal; and

(2) an *outright/actual* wrongful dismissal by the employer giving rise to a repudiatory breach of contract.

With regard to the former, i.e. (1), there are many authorities that endorse the applicability of the 'elective' theory of termination. This directs that an employer's repudiatory breach of contract must be accepted by the employee before it is treated as effective to terminate the employment contract.[62] This is especially the case where the employer's unilateral variation of the terms of the employment contract constitutes a repudiatory breach.[63] Therefore, confronted by the employer's repudiatory breach of the contract of employment short of dismissal, the 'elective' theory of termination furnishes the employee with a choice. He/she is required to decide whether to accept the breach and claim constructive wrongful dismissal or to affirm the contract so that it continues in existence. This 'elective' approach accords with orthodox principles of contract law.[64] It is generally accepted as preferable over the competing 'automatic' theory of termination, which posits that the employer's unilateral repudiatory breach of contract, howsoever constituted, operates to automatically bring the contract of employment to an end.

However, in its conception, the 'elective' theory lacks explanatory force in the context of an outright wrongful dismissal, i.e. (2), where the employer fires the employee in repudiatory breach of contract. In such circumstances, what meaningful role is played by 'election' on the part of the employee?[65] For example, once an employer has dismissed an employee (whether lawfully or wrongfully), surely the employment relationship is at an end? As such, one would be forgiven for questioning whether it is at all relevant that the employee has elected to accept the repudiatory breach or affirm the contract. Further, if the employee chooses to affirm the contract, how can it be possible that he/she can compel the employer to continue to furnish him/her with employment against its will, particularly where all trust and confidence has broken down?[66] This is compounded by the fact that English law is generally unwilling to grant equitable remedies such as orders for specific performance or injunction to enforce the employee's rights pursuant to the employment contract.[67] In fact, in light of these criticisms, a number of authorities suggested that the employer's unilateral act of dismissal did indeed operate to automatically bring the contract of employment to an end.[68] Furthermore, although the Court of Appeal in *Gunton v Richmond upon Thames*[69] adopted the elective theory of termination in the context of an outright wrongful

---

[62] *Thomas Marshall (Exports) Ltd v Guinlé* [1978] ICR 905; *Gunton v Richmond upon Thames London Borough Council* [1981] 1 Ch 448; *Photo Production Ltd v Securicor Transport Ltd* [1980] AC 827; *London Transport Executive v Clarke* [1981] IRLR 166; *Rigby v Ferodo Ltd* [1987] IRLR 516; *Dietman v Brent London Borough Council* [1987] IRLR 259; *Boyo v London Borough of Lambeth* [1994] ICR 727; and *Soares v Beazer Investments Ltd* [2004] EWCA Civ 482 at para 17 per Kay LJ.

[63] For example, *Rigby v Ferodo Ltd* [1987] IRLR 516.

[64] *White and Carter (Councils) Ltd v McGregor* [1962] AC 413.

[65] P. Elias, B. Napier, and P. Wallington, *Labour Law: Cases and Materials* (London, Butterworths, 1980) 492–3; M. Freedland, *The Personal Employment Contract* (Oxford, OUP, 2003) 368–96.

[66] For a comprehensive account of the competing arguments in favour of the elective and automatic theories in the context of an outright wrongful dismissal, see M. Freedland, *The Personal Employment Contract* (Oxford, OUP, 2003) 368–96 and the articles cited in the reading list on the Online Resources for this book.

[67] *De Francesco v Barnum* (1890) 45 Ch D 430, 438 per Fry LJ; *Ridge v Baldwin* [1964] AC 40, 65 per Lord Reid; and *Wilson v St Helen's Borough Council* [1999] 2 AC 52, 84A–B per Lord Slynn of Hadley.

[68] *Francis v Municipal Councillors of Kuala Lumpur* [1962] 1 WLR 1411, 1417 per Lord Morris of Borth-Y-Gest; *Denmark Productions Ltd v Boscobel Productions Ltd* [1969] 1 QB 699, 737E–F per Harman LJ; *Decro-Wall International SA v Practitioners in Marketing Ltd* [1971] 1 WLR 361, 381 per Buckley LJ; *Vine v National Dock Labour Board* [1957] AC 488, 500 per Viscount Kilmuir LC; and *Sanders v Ernest A Neale Ltd* [1974] 3 All ER 327, 333 per Sir John Donaldson P.

[69] [1981] 1 Ch 448.

(d) If, as was held by the House of Lords in *Rigby v Ferodo Ltd* [1988] ICR 29, a fundamental breach *other* than by way of purported dismissal (namely in that case, the employer's unilateral reduction in wages below the contractual level) does not in any event attract application of the automatic theory, what would be the rationale for treating other fundamental breaches (namely purported dismissals and resignations) differently? Why should wrongful actions more clearly designed to strike at the continuation of the contract be crowned with that significant degree of legal success? As Cabrelli and Zahn suggest in their article entitled 'The Elective and Automatic Theories of Termination at Common Law: Resolving the Conundrum' (2012) 41 ILJ 346, 354, any such difference would be counter-intuitive.

(e) Is the *Rigby* case not inconsistent with the implied suggestion of Lord Sumption JSC in para 129 below that the automatic theory should extend to constructive dismissals? Inherent in the notion of a constructive dismissal is resignation in response to fundamental breach: *Western Excavating (ECC) Ltd v Sharp* [1978] QB 761, 769, 770 (Lord Denning MR). So is there not inherent in it the need for acceptance which the *Rigby* case establishes?

(f) Would the automatic theory extend to wrongful repudiations of contracts of services as well as of contracts of employment? The provision of numerous services pursuant to contract—take, by way of easy examples, those of an accountant, a dentist and a builder—depends upon the co-operation of the other party. If the rationale behind the automatic theory is both the unavailability of specific performance and the inability to claim the contractual remuneration rather than damages, why should it not extend to contracts of services to which the law attaches those same two consequences? [Counsel for *Société Générale*] was wise to decline to answer this question.

In proposing that the court should endorse the automatic theory, [*Société Générale*] invites it to cause the law of England and Wales in relation to contracts of employment to set sail, unaccompanied, upon a journey for which I can discern no just purpose and can identify no final destination. I consider, however, that we should keep the contract of employment firmly within the harbour which the common law has solidly constructed for the entire fleet of contracts in order to protect the innocent party, as far as practicable, from the consequences of the other's breach.

However, what remains unclear is whether the Supreme Court has adopted a genuine form of the elective theory, as advocated by Ewing,[78] whereby an 'employee dismissed in breach of a substantive or procedural term of his or her contract or, in the absence of such a provision, without notice, c[an] elect either to accept the repudiation and sue for damages (however they may be calculated where there is no power to dismiss) or to keep the contract alive by seeking some form of equitable relief, most likely an injunction'.[79] As Blackham has rightly noted, 'there is no indication that the decision in [*Geys*] will make it any easier [for an employee who has affirmed the contract of employment] to obtain an equitable remedy (such as an injunction) to keep a repudiated employment contract on foot'.[80] Therefore, the vexed issue of the hostility of the courts to orders of specific performance and injunctive relief in favour of employees has been deferred to another day. This is a matter which will have to be resolved one way or another, since post-*Geys* it is not entirely clear what happens next when an employee decides to affirm the contract in response to the employer's repudiatory outright dismissal. There is an argument that injunctive relief should be available to an employee in the case of a threatened wrongful

---

[78] K. Ewing, 'Remedies for Breach of the Contract of Employment' (1993) 52 *Cambridge Law Journal* 405.

[79] *ibid.*, 415. Ewing cites the Australian case of *Turner v Australasian Coal and Shale Employees' Federation* (1984) 55 ALR 635 (Federal Court of Australia, Full Court) as an example of this approach.

[80] A. Blackham, 'Uncertain Junctures between Employment and Contract Law' (2013) 72 *Cambridge Law Journal* 269, 272.

breach of contract or termination by the employer as a result of the Supreme Court's decisions in *Geys* and *Edwards*. An additional consequence of *Geys* is that the employee who has affirmed the employment contract should be entitled to recover unpaid wages from the employer as a debt rather than damages where the employer fails to pay him/her, provided that he/she is ready and willing to work, albeit not actually working.[81] As for the position where it is the employee who commits a repudiatory breach, the decision of the Court of Appeal in *Sunrise Brokers LLP v Rodgers*[82] is particularly instructive. It was held that where the employee's repudiatory breach comprises a failure to give the proper amount of notice coupled with a refusal to return to work, the employer will nonetheless be entitled to affirm the contract and keep it alive.[83]

Reflection points

1. Consider the unrestricted reasonable notice rule. Do you believe its adoption in the case of the common law of the contract of employment to be appropriate and desirable? If so, why? If not, why not?

2. Consider the pros and cons of the automatic and elective theories of termination. On balance, which one do you prefer and why?

3. Why is the automatic versus elective debate of any practical relevance?

4. Post-*Geys*, if the employee affirms the employment contract subsequent to the employer's outright wrongful dismissal, what legal remedies does he/she have?

 For additional reading on the termination of the contract of employment and wrongful dismissal, visit the Online Resources for this book at www.oup.com/uk/cabrelli3e/

15.3 REMEDIES

A close analysis of the employee's remedies for wrongful dismissal reveals that they are largely devoid of any potency, being restricted to a relatively moderate amount of damages. Damages awards are invariably low, which is perhaps to be expected, given that the general rule is that the sum payable to the employee will be confined to the payment of his/her net wages/salary and other contractual benefits for the notice period. As for non-monetary remedies, despite the common law's acceptance of the elective theory of termination, the scope for the enforcement of the contract of employment through an order for specific performance or an injunction remains unclear. Although the courts have shown themselves willing to grant extended damages awards and equitable relief on occasion, as we will see, the circumstances in which such remedies will be made is particularly narrow. All of this points towards the fact that the common law of remedies for wrongful dismissal has failed to keep in step with the recent expansion of common law individual employment rights—via the medium of the implied terms of the contract of employment.[84] In this section, we will address damages, before going on to briefly examine specific remedies.

---

[81] See *Sunrise Brokers LLP v Rodgers* [2015] ICR 272, 292B per Longmore LJ; and D. Cabrelli, 'The Mutuality and Enforceability of the Employment Contract: *Sunrise Brokers LLP v Rodgers*' (2015) 19 *Edinburgh Law Review* 280.   [82] [2015] ICR 272.

[83] In certain circumstances, the employer will not be required to pay the employee during the period of the employee's refusal to return to work and will also have the right to restrain the employee from working for a rival firm: *Sunrise Brokers LLP v Rodgers* [2015] ICR 272.

[84] See Chapter 6, section 6.2.

15.3.1 **Damages**

A damages claim is the principal remedy available where an employee's wrongful dismissal action is successful. Unlike a claim in debt for unpaid wages, damages are subject to the ordinary rules of contract law on causation, remoteness of damage, mitigation of loss, and contributory fault. To that extent, damages are not a particularly attractive remedy. A damages claim for wrongful dismissal is a common law claim, and so it must be raised and pursued in the courts.[85] As for the heads of loss which can and cannot be recovered in damages, our understanding is assisted by employing the illustration in Hypothetical B.

Hypothetical B

Danny's Demolishers Ltd has expanded exponentially owing to a large uptake in orders. It decides to convert the business to a public limited company. As such, Danny's Demolishers plc is born. It is a large multinational company operating throughout the UK. One of its subsidiary companies, namely Demolishers (Cardiff) Limited ('the Employer') has a ten-year contract with Cardiff City Council ('the Council') which gives it the exclusive rights to demolish any properties owned by the Council. Margaret Copperfield ('the Employee') is appointed as the Employer's finance director which entitles her to a seat on the Employer's board of directors. Her service agreement provides that she is entitled to nine months' prior written notice of the termination of her contract and it also provides that she is entitled to free private medical insurance and the use of a company car whilst she is an employee. The contract also stipulates that the Employee is entitled to be paid a bonus at the end of each calendar year, which is subject to the absolute discretion of the Employer. Moreover, the Employer's disciplinary procedure is incorporated into the Employee's service contract. It includes a number of pre-dismissal procedural safeguards for the Employee.

Precisely one year and 48 weeks into her appointment, in November 2017, the Employee is suspended by the Employer on full pay without explanation. One week later, she is summarily dismissed without warning or any payment in lieu of notice. The meeting at which she is dismissed is particularly nasty, as the chief executive and chairman of the Employer verbally insult her a number of times, and make disparaging comments about her abilities and professionalism, and she is unceremoniously bundled out of the Employer's premises by three extremely burly security guards without being afforded the opportunity to bid farewell to her erstwhile colleagues. The manner of her dismissal causes the Employee to be very distressed, which ultimately develops into a career-ending, long-term psychiatric illness. One month after the Employee is dismissed, a public scandal reveals that the chief executive and chairman of the Employer had been engaged in the widespread bribery of Council officials.

The scenario described in Hypothetical B gives rise to a potential number of heads of loss which we will now address in turn. The starting point for our discussion is to clarify the basic measure of damages for wrongful dismissal. This can be put quite briefly: damages are restricted to financial loss only, and this will be the employee's net wages/salary and

---

[85] However, there is an exception: by virtue of article 10 of the Employment Tribunals Extension of Jurisdiction (England and Wales) Order 1994 (SI 1994/1623) and sections 3 and 44 of the Employment Tribunals Act 1996, the employment tribunals have jurisdiction to award damages for wrongful dismissal or a breach of the contract of employment up to a maximum of £25,000.

other contractual benefits during the notice period.[86] On one view, this stands to reason, since a wrongful dismissal is a dismissal in repudiatory breach of contract and an employer will be in breach by failing to give reasonable notice. It also accords with the general measure of damages in contract law, whereby the employee ought to be 'placed in the position in which he would have been had his contract been properly performed, and any consequential loss within the contemplation of the parties, but no more'.[87] However, on another view, this approach is unduly narrow and does not properly reflect the measure of damages in contract law, since 'it is arguable that the loss which flows naturally from the breach [of the contract of employment] can only be determined by asking how long the employment would otherwise have been likely to endure'.[88] Furthermore, it is out of step with the 'judicial recognition that the employee's interest in employment relations is not purely financial (*William Hill v Tucker* [1998] IRLR provides one such example)'.[89]

The leading authority for the proposition that damages are confined to wages/salary and other contractual benefits during the notice period is the much-criticized decision of the House of Lords in *Addis v Gramophone Co. Ltd*.[90] *Addis* is generally taken as an authority for three limbs:[91]

(1) injury to the employee's feelings, anxiety, and mental distress arising as a result of the breach will not be compensated;

(2) by extension, such damages are unavailable in respect of the manner of the employee's dismissal; and

(3) any losses the employee might suffer as a result of being unable to secure alternative employment will not be compensated. Thus, the employee has no right to be compensated for the longer-term consequences of the loss of a job.

Applying this reasoning to Hypothetical B, the Employee would have the right to be paid a sum equivalent to nine months' net salary and the costs of private medical insurance premiums for the period of nine months, as well as the notional value of the use of the company car for the same period. However, no damages would arise in respect of the mental distress attributable to the manner of her dismissal.

Addis is a decision reached in 'the heyday of a judicial philosophy of market individualism in respect of what was then called the law of master and servant[, where] in the eyes of the law the position of a servant was a subordinate one [which] seemed natural and inevitable'.[92] Unsurprisingly, it has been subjected to a great deal of judicial[93] and academic[94] criticism. Indeed, over the past 20 years, the general rule that an employee has no claim for compensation in a wrongful dismissal action in respect of harm of a non-financial nature has been subject to attack from two directions:[95]

---

[86] *Gunton v Richmond upon Thames London Borough Council* [1981] 1 Ch 448, 469C per Buckley LJ (CA); *Edwards v Chesterfield Royal Hospital NHS Foundation Trust* [2011] UKSC 58, [2012] 2 AC 22, 54C per Lord Mance.

[87] *Edwards v Chesterfield Royal Hospital NHS Foundation Trust* [2011] UKSC 58, [2012] 2 AC 22, 59D per Baroness Hale.

[88] D. Brodie, *The Contract of Employment* (Edinburgh, Thomson/W Green/Scottish Universities Law Institute, 2008) 226.

[89] D. Brodie, 'Protecting Dignity in the Workplace: The Vitality of Mutual Trust and Confidence' (2004) 33 *Industrial Law Journal* 349, 352. [90] [1909] AC 488.

[91] For example, see C. Barnard, 'Cherries: One Bite or Two?' (2006) *Cambridge Law Journal* 27.

[92] *Johnson v Unisys Ltd* [2003] 1 AC 518, 531 per Lord Steyn.

[93] *ibid.*, 526–7, and 530–3 per Lord Steyn; *Johnson v Gore Wood & Co.* [2002] 2 AC 1, 50B–E per Lord Cooke; and *Eastwood v Magnox Electric plc* [2005] 1 AC 503, 535–6 per Lord Steyn.

[94] D. Brodie, 'Protecting Dignity in the Workplace: The Vitality of Mutual Trust and Confidence' (2004) 33 *Industrial Law Journal* 349, 351; J. Fudge, 'The Spectre of *Addis* in Contracts of Employment in Canada and the UK' (2007) 36 *Industrial Law Journal* 51; and D. Brodie, 'The Beginning of the End for *Addis v The Gramophone Company*?' (2009) 38 *Industrial Law Journal* 228.

[95] An earlier attempt to challenge the hegemony of *Addis* was unsuccessful in *Bliss v South East Thames Regional Health Authority* [1987] ICR 700 (CA).

(1) in the case of *Malik v BCCI*,[96] the House of Lords was asked to reconsider the limb of *Addis* which disentitled an employee from recovering compensation for a loss of earning capacity or reputation as a result of being unable to attain fresh employment in breach of contract; and

(2) in *Johnson v Unisys Ltd*,[97] the question raised was whether the implied term of mutual trust and confidence could circumscribe the operation of the employer's untrammelled prerogative of dismissal, thus enabling an employee to claim compensation for the manner of his/her dismissal.

The results of these two assaults have been mixed. For example, in *Malik*, the challenge was successful. This was achieved by crafting an exception which is confined within particularly limited bounds, rather than the dismantling of the general rule. It was held that, on a breach of the employment contract, an employee would be entitled to 'stigma' damages where the employer had run a dishonest and corrupt business and it was reasonably foreseeable that the employee's future employment opportunities would be compromised as a result. In such circumstances, the employee can recover the financial losses sustained in respect of the damage to his/her reputation. Of course, this represents an exception to the third limb of *Addis*. However, in practical terms, it is extremely challenging for an employee to succeed in a claim for such a head of loss. As noted by Lord Steyn in *Malik v BCCI*,[98] loss of reputation is intrinsically difficult to establish and the usual contractual techniques of causation, remoteness of damages, mitigation of loss, and contributory fault 'present formidable obstacles to such claims succeeding'.[99] Translated to Hypothetical B, if the Employee is able to demonstrate that she suffered a loss of reputation as a result of the public scandal engulfing the Employer which adversely affected her employment prospects, she will be entitled to 'stigma damages'. However, taking into account the fact that she suffered a career-ending psychiatric illness as a result of the manner of her dismissal, it is clear that she is not in a position to work post-termination, thus suggesting that a 'stigma' damages claim would be precluded.

In contrast to the employee's limited success in *Malik*, the employee's challenge to *Addis* in *Johnson v Unisys Ltd*[100] came to nought. *Johnson* concerned an employee who suffered a psychological breakdown as a result of the manner of his dismissal. His claim for unfair dismissal under Part X of the ERA was successful in the employment tribunal. He subsequently commenced court proceedings against the employer for damages for wrongful dismissal. The employee sought to press the burgeoning implied term of mutual trust and confidence into service as a means of constraining the employer's power to dismiss employees on reasonable notice, i.e. that the employer was under an obligation not to dismiss in a manner calculated and likely to destroy or severely damage the relationship of trust and confidence without proper and reasonable cause. Of course, had the House of Lords held that the implied term had no application to dismissal, then there would be no breach of contract and he would be denied damages for the psychological harm suffered:

■ *Johnson v Unisys Ltd* [2003] 1 AC 518, 539–50

Lord Hoffmann:

My Lords, the first question is whether the implied term of trust and confidence . . . applies to a dismissal . . . The problem lies in extending or adapting any of these implied terms to dismissal. There are two reasons why dismissal presents special problems. The first is that any terms which the courts imply into a contract must be consistent with the express terms. Implied terms may supplement the express terms of the contract but cannot contradict them. Only Parliament may

---

[96] [1998] AC 20.   [97] *Johnson v Unisys Ltd* [2003] 1 AC 518 (HL).
[98] [1998] AC 20.   [99] *ibid.*, 53D.   [100] *Johnson v Unisys Ltd* [2003] 1 AC 518 (HL).

actually override what the parties have agreed. The second reason is that judges, in developing the law, must have regard to the policies expressed by Parliament in legislation. Employment law requires a balancing of the interests of employers and employees, with proper regard not only to the individual dignity and worth of the employees but also to the general economic interest. Subject to observance of fundamental human rights, the point at which this balance should be struck is a matter for democratic decision. The development of the common law by the judges plays a subsidiary role. Their traditional function is to adapt and modernise the common law. But such developments must be consistent with legislative policy as expressed in statutes. The courts may proceed in harmony with Parliament but there should be no discord . . . In the way [the implied term of mutual trust and confidence] has always been formulated, it is concerned with preserving the continuing relationship which should subsist between employer and employee. So it does not seem altogether appropriate for use in connection with the way that relationship is terminated . . . although in my opinion it would be jurisprudentially possible to imply a term which gave a remedy in this case, I do not think that even if the courts were free of legislative constraint (a point to which I shall return in a moment) it would necessarily be wise to do so. It is not simply an incremental step from the duty of trust and confidence implied in *Mahmud v Bank of Credit and Commerce International SA* [1998] AC 20. The close association between the acts alleged to be in breach of the implied term and the irremovable and lawful fact of dismissal give rise to special problems . . . Some of the potential problems can be illustrated by the facts of this case, in which Mr Johnson claims some £400,000 damages for the financial consequences of psychiatric damage. This form of damage notoriously gives rise at the best of times to extremely difficult questions of causation. But the difficulties are made greater when the expert witnesses are required to perform the task of distinguishing between the psychiatric consequences of the fact of dismissal (for which no damages are recoverable) and the unfair circumstances in which the dismissal took place, which constituted a breach of the implied term . . . It follows, my Lords, that if there was no relevant legislation in this area, I would regard the question of whether judges should develop the law by implying a suitable term into the contract of employment as finely balanced. But now I must consider the statutory background against which your Lordships are invited to create such a cause of action . . . My Lords, [a] statutory system for dealing with unfair dismissals was set up by Parliament to deal with the recognised deficiencies of the law as it stood at the time of *Malloch v Aberdeen Corpn* [1971] 1 WLR 1581. The remedy adopted by Parliament was not to build upon the common law by creating a statutory implied term that the power of dismissal should be exercised fairly or in good faith, leaving the courts to give a remedy on general principles of contractual damages. Instead, it set up an entirely new system outside the ordinary courts, with tribunals staffed by a majority of lay members, applying new statutory concepts and offering statutory remedies. Many of the new rules, such as the exclusion of certain classes of employees and the limit on the amount of the compensatory award, were not based upon any principle which it would have been open to the courts to apply. They were based upon policy and represented an attempt to balance fairness to employees against the general economic interests of the community . . . So Parliament adopted the practical solution of giving the tribunals a very broad jurisdiction to award what they considered just and equitable but subject to a limit on the amount. In my opinion, all the matters of which Mr Johnson complains in these proceedings were within the jurisdiction of the industrial tribunal . . . The question is whether the courts should develop the common law to give a parallel remedy which is not subject to any such limit. My Lords, I do not think that it is a proper exercise of the judicial function of the House to take such a step. Judge Ansell, to whose unreserved judgment I would pay respectful tribute, went in my opinion to the heart of the matter when he said:

['T]here is not one hint in the authorities that the . . . tens of thousands of people that appear before the tribunals can have, as it were, a possible second bite in common law and I ask myself, if this is the situation, why on earth do we have this special statutory framework? What is the point of it if it can be circumvented in this way? . . . it would mean that effectively the statutory limit on compensation for unfair dismissal would disappear. [']

I can see no answer to these questions. For the judiciary to construct a general common law remedy for unfair circumstances attending dismissal would be to go contrary to the evident intention of Parliament that there should be such a remedy but that it should be limited in application and extent . . . [101]

Lord Millett:

[The implied term of mutual trust and confidence] is an inherent feature of the relationship of employer and employee which does not survive the ending of the relationship. The implied obligation cannot sensibly be used to extend the relationship beyond its agreed duration. Moreover, manipulating it for such a purpose would be unrealistic . . . the creation of the statutory right [not to be unfairly dismissed] has made any such development of the common law both unnecessary and undesirable. In the great majority of cases the new common law right would merely replicate the statutory right; and it is obviously unnecessary to imply a term into a contract to give one of the contracting parties a remedy which he already has without it. In other cases, where the common law would be giving a remedy in excess of the statutory limits or to excluded categories of employees, it would be inconsistent with the declared policy of Parliament. In all cases it would allow claims to be entertained by the ordinary courts when it was the policy of Parliament that they should be heard by specialist tribunals with members drawn from both sides of industry. And, even more importantly, the coexistence of two systems, overlapping but varying in matters of detail and heard by different tribunals, would be a recipe for chaos. All coherence in our employment laws would be lost. For these reasons it is a step which, for one, I am not prepared to take.

The principal reason[102] Lord Hoffmann gave in *Johnson* for rejecting the argument that the employer's power of dismissal was constrained by the implied term of mutual trust and confidence was that it would be unconstitutional. Parliament had introduced a carefully crafted scheme for the regulation of dismissals now found in Part X of the ERA. That statutory code offered compensation for unfair dismissals and so it was undesirable and unwarranted for the common law to evolve in order to confer damages at large for the manner of a dismissal; otherwise, there was the danger that the common law would outflank the statutory regime. This reasoning is controversial.[103] Indeed, it is symptomatic of a chronic inability on the part of the judiciary to conceptualize the unfair dismissal regime as giving rise to a floor of rights upon which the common law can build.

---

[101]   See also *Reda v Flag Ltd* [2002] UKPC 38, [2002] IRLR 747.

[102]   The remaining reasons were that implied terms should not be able to qualify or cut down the employer's express power of dismissal and that the implied term of mutual trust and confidence could only be deployed whilst the employment relationship was subsisting, rather than in relation to its termination. For a similar result in the context of a distribution contract and consultancy contract, see *Ilkerler Otomotiv v Perkins Engines Co. Ltd* [2017] EWCA Civ 183, [2017] 4 WLR 144; and *Monde Petroleum SA v Westernzagros Ltd* [2016] EWHC 1472 (Comm), [2017] 1 All ER (Comm) 1009, on which, see L. Richardson, 'Exercising a Contractual Right to Terminate: What's Good Faith Got to do with it?' (2017) 21 *Edinburgh Law Review* 88.

[103]   For a critique, see L. Barmes, 'The Continuing Conceptual Crisis in the Common Law of the Contract of Employment' (2004) *Modern Law Review* 435, 450. The reception to the decision in *Johnson* in academic circles has been generally unenthusiastic or outright hostile, on which, see H. Collins and M. Freedland, 'Claim for Unfair Dismissal' (2001) 30 *Industrial Law Journal* 305; B. Hepple and G. Morris, 'The Employment Act 2002 and the Crisis of Individual Employment Rights' (2002) 31 *Industrial Law Journal* 245, 253–5; B. Hepple, *Rights at Work: Global, European and British Perspectives* (London, Thomson/Sweet & Maxwell, 2005); and M. Freedland, *The Personal Employment Contract* (Oxford, OUP, 2003) 342–3. For a more positive view, see A. Bogg and H. Collins, 'Lord Hoffmann and the Law of Employment: The Notorious Episode of *Johnson v Unisys Ltd*' in P. S. Davies and J. Pila (eds.), *The Jurisprudence of Lord Hoffmann* (Oxford, OUP, 2014) 185; and A. Bogg and M. Freedland, 'The Wrongful Termination of the Contract of Employment' in M. Freedland et al. (eds.), *The Contract of Employment* (Oxford, OUP, 2016) 549–56.

Instead, parliamentary intervention in the guise of the unfair dismissal regime is treated as sufficient justification to exercise a break on the evolution of common law principles, a point noted by Baroness Hale in her dissenting judgment in *Edwards v Chesterfield Royal Hospital NHS Foundation Trust*:

■ *Edwards v Chesterfield Royal Hospital NHS Foundation Trust* [2011] UKSC 58, [2012] 2 AC 22, 58F–H

> *Baroness Hale:*
>
> There is no reason at all to suppose that, in [introducing the statutory unfair dismissal regime], Parliament intended to cut down upon or reduce the remedies available to employees whose employers acted in breach of their contracts of employment. Quite the reverse. Parliament intended to create a new statutory remedy for unfair dismissal which would supplement whatever rights the employee already had under his contract of employment. Parliament did that because most employees had very few rights under their contracts of employment.

Returning to Hypothetical B, since the Employee's psychiatric illness brought her career to a premature end, the financial losses suffered could be sizeable. However, on the application of *Johnson*, the Employee would be barred from claiming damages in respect of the psychiatric illness she suffered. The rationale for this conclusion is that the illness arose as a result of the distressing manner of her dismissal and so falls within the '*Johnson* exclusion area';[104] only the unfair dismissal regime can offer her relief. Rather bizarrely, if we modify the scenario in Hypothetical B slightly, so that the Employee's psychiatric illness was occasioned as a consequence of the suspension, the legal position would differ as a result of *Gogay v Hertfordshire County Council*.[105] Since a suspension of the contract of employment must invariably occur during the course of the employment relationship—rather than at the point of termination as in the case of dismissal itself—and no statutory code exists to regulate suspensions, the decision in *Gogay* does not conflict with *Johnson*, or *Addis*.[106] The end result is a paradox: it is preferable for the employer to dismiss an employee rather than to suspend him/her, since common law damages may be awarded in respect of the manner of a suspension in breach of the implied term, whereas a claim for damages in the context of the manner of a dismissal would be dismissed.[107] Thus, had the Employee's suspension in Hypothetical B caused or contributed to the development of her illness, damages would have been available.

Now let us imagine that the Employee's psychiatric illness in Hypothetical B was attributable to the manner in which a disciplinary hearing (to put the Employer's allegations and hear the Employee's case) was conducted three days prior to her dismissal. Is the hearing sufficiently proximate to the dismissal to fall within the '*Johnson* exclusion

---

[104] See *Eastwood v Magnox Electric plc* [2005] 1 AC 503, 528 per Lord Nicholls; *Edwards v Chesterfield Royal Hospital NHS Foundation Trust* [2011] UKSC 58, [2012] 2 AC 22, 30E at para 2 per Lord Dyson. [105] [2000] IRLR 703 (CA).

[106] As such, it will be possible for an employee to recover damages for a suspension amounting to a repudiatory breach of contract, e.g. *Agoreyo v London Borough of Lambeth* [2017] EWHC 2019 (QB) and *Yapp v Foreign and Commonwealth Office* [2015] IRLR 112, although as this decision shows, the remoteness of damages rule will present a formidable obstacle for the employee to surmount, i.e. that the harm suffered is not too remote from the breach of the implied contractual duty. See D. Brodie, 'Risk Allocation and Psychiatric Harm: *Yapp v Foreign and Commonwealth Office*' (2015) 44 *Industrial Law Journal* 270 for a discussion; and D. Cabrelli, 'Liability and Remedies for Breach of the Contract of Employment at Common Law: Some Recent Developments' (2016) 45 *Industrial Law Journal* 207.

[107] *Gogay v Hertfordshire County Council* [2000] IRLR 703 (CA), 711 per Lady Hale; *Eastwood v Magnox Electric plc* [2005] 1 AC 503, 529C per Lord Nicholls.

area' or can it be said to exist independently of the dismissal, thus giving rise to common law damages? This raises the issue of the location of the boundary line between the operation of common law actions for damages and the statutory unfair dismissal scheme, which was addressed by the House of Lords in *Eastwood v Magnox Electric plc*.[108] Lord Nicholls gave the leading speech and held that, where a distinct cause of action arises prior to the employee's dismissal, the path is clear for common law damages to be awarded in respect of that action.[109] Thus, the implied term of mutual trust and confidence applies to restrain the conduct of the employer during the 'dying stages'[110] of the employment relationship, i.e. events leading up to the dismissal such as the manner of a suspension, the conduct of the employer's investigation into the allegations against the employee, the conduct of the disciplinary hearing,[111] and the conduct of the employer during the employee's notice period.[112] In *Eastwood*, an employee suffered a psychiatric disorder as a result of a failure on the part of the employer to investigate properly the allegations made against the employee or to conduct the disciplinary hearing on a proper basis. The illness generated financial losses and the House of Lords held that the employee was entitled to an award of damages. In the circumstances, the implied term had been breached which brought about a cause of action to compensate losses attributable to an event which occurred prior to, and was independent of, the dismissal.

This finding may appear to be employee-friendly, but we must not lose sight of the fact that the employee's financial losses must be wholly separate from the dismissal itself in order to be compensated. This places a considerable hurdle in front of an employee, since, as Lord Nicholls recognized,[113] it is unusual for such losses to crystallize unless the employee is dismissed. As such, in the lion's share of cases, the reason for the materialization of such losses will be the dismissal itself. It will only be in exceptional circumstances that unfair treatment preceding a dismissal gives rise to financial loss which is in no way connected to the dismissal. Another implication of the boundary line is that:

■ *Eastwood v Magnox Electric plc; McCabe v Cornwall County Council* [2005] 1 AC 503, 528G–H

> **Lord Nicholls:**
>
> . . . [the employer's] conduct, typically a disciplinary process followed by dismissal, may have to be chopped artificially into separate pieces. In cases of constructive dismissal, a distinction will have to be drawn between loss flowing from antecedent breaches of the trust and confidence term and loss flowing from the employee's acceptance of these breaches as a repudiation of the contract.[114] The loss flowing from the impugned conduct taking place before actual or constructive dismissal lies outside the *Johnson* exclusion area, the loss flowing from the dismissal itself is within that area.

(See Figure 15.4 as to the location of the '*Johnson* exclusion area'.)

This somewhat bizarre exercise in division lays bare the extent to which the co-existence of the common law and statutory systems is particularly fraught,[115] leading to the

---

[108] [2005] 1 AC 503.

[109] *ibid.*, 528C. This would not be a wrongful dismissal action, but an action for damages arising as a result of a repudiatory breach of contract.

[110] C. Barnard, 'Cherries: One Bite or Two?' (2006) *Cambridge Law Journal* 27, 29.

[111] See *Stevens v University of Birmingham* [2015] IRLR 899; *Hendy v MOJ* [2014] IRLR 856; cf. *Coventry University v Mian* [2014] EWCA Civ 2014.

[112] This will include an employee being excluded from her workplace in a public manner: *Monk v Cann Hall Primary School* [2013] IRLR 732.   [113] [2005] 1 AC 503, 528D.

[114] This is a particularly fraught endeavour, e.g. see *GAB Robins (UK) Ltd v Triggs* [2008] IRLR 317; *Gebremariam v Ethiopian Airlines Enterprise* [2014] IRLR 354.

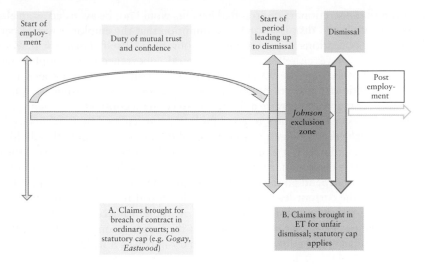

Figure 15.4 *The effect of the decisions in Johnson and Eastwood*

Source: C. Barnard and L. Merrett, 'Winners and Losers: Edwards and the Unfair Law of Dismissal' (2013) 72 *Cambridge Law Journal* 313, 323.

duplication of proceedings in the court and tribunals. The Law Lords recognized the fact that the position was unsatisfactory—which they attributed to the statutory cap on compensation for unfair dismissal under Part X of the ERA—and urged Parliament to intervene urgently to address the situation. However, their call would appear to have fallen on deaf ears.

Returning to Hypothetical B, we can see that the Employee was dismissed one year and 48 weeks into her appointment. An employee is precluded from presenting a complaint of unfair dismissal to an employment tribunal unless he/she has been 'continuously employed for a period of not less than two years ending with the effective date of termination'.[116] Hence, on the face of matters, the employment tribunal has no jurisdiction to hear the Employee's claim. However, we should consider whether the Employee might be able to argue that the Employer's failure to give her the requisite nine months' notice deprived her of the right to claim unfair dismissal, giving rise to a common law damages claim for the loss of the opportunity to present such a complaint. One could argue that the application of orthodox contractual principles would entitle the Employee to such damages, bearing in mind that they are designed to put the Employee in the position in which she would have been had the employment contract been performed. However, the Court of Appeal rejected that argument in *Harper v Virgin Net Ltd*.[117] It held that *Johnson* prevented a claim for damages for the loss of the opportunity to claim unfair dismissal, since such damages arose out of the fact and manner of the dismissal itself.[118]

Hypothetical B also provides that the Employer has a discretion whether to award a bonus payment to the Employee at the end of each calendar year. We can take for granted that the Employee did not receive such bonus prior to her dismissal and so we must query whether she may claim a sum in damages in respect of that failure. It was formerly the

---

[115] See the broader discussion in Chapter 2, section 2.1.1.   [116] Section 108(1) of the ERA.

[117] [2004] EWCA Civ 271, [2005] ICR 921, [2004] IRLR 390. This decision overturned *Raspin v United News Shops Ltd* [1999] IRLR 9.

[118] Another reason for its decision was that section 97(2)(b) of the ERA postpones the effective date of termination until the end of the statutory minimum period of notice prescribed in section 86 of the ERA. However, such statutory postponement did not extend to the end of the contractual period of notice, which was an intentional policy choice on the part of Parliament.

legal position that discretionary contractual benefits would not be awarded as an element of damages for wrongful dismissal on the assumption that the employer would perform its discretionary obligations in a way most favourable to itself: *Lavarack v Woods of Colchester Ltd*.[119] However, reflective of the central importance of the implied term of mutual trust and confidence, the common law has now been adapted to impose fetters on the express discretionary powers of the employer. It does so by imposing a requirement that the employer must not exercise a discretion to confer a contractual benefit or power irrationally, perversely, or contrary to good faith.[120] As articulated by Lord Justice Mummery in *Commerzbank AG v Keen*,[121] this 'rationality' test is a very high threshold for an employee to meet. Ordinarily, it would take 'an overwhelming case to persuade the court . . . that the level of a discretionary bonus payment was irrational or perverse in an area where so much must depend on the discretionary judgment of the [employer]'.[122] For that reason, although the current legal position has developed in a pro-employee direction, it does not really take us much further forward than the prior common law orthodoxy in *Lavarack*. The upshot is that it is unlikely that the Employee in Hypothetical B would enjoy success in claiming the loss of a discretionary bonus as a head of loss in the damages claim.

The final point meriting our attention in Hypothetical B concerns the Employee's options in relation to the Employer's failure to comply with the contractual disciplinary procedure.[123] Here, we must ask if there is scope for the Employee to attain damages at large on the ground that she would not have been dismissed if the Employer had properly followed the contractually binding disciplinary procedure.[124] If the effect of the dismissal is that the employee is prevented from securing further employment in the same line of work, e.g. because he/she suffers a career-ending psychiatric injury, damages for such a head of loss could be quite substantial. The Supreme Court had cause to examine this matter in *Edwards v Chesterfield Royal Hospital NHS Foundation Trust*.[125] Lord Justice Dyson gave the leading judgment[126] and held that damages at large were excluded. The principal obstacle to the availability of damages was said to be the decision in *Johnson*. First, it was held that the damages claim was connected to the manner of the dismissal, since the issue involved speculation as to the impact that proper compliance with the contractual disciplinary procedure might have had on the employer's decision to

---

[119] *Lavarack v Woods of Colchester Ltd* [1967] QB 278.

[120] See Chapter 6, section 6.2.5; *Clark v BET plc* [1997] IRLR 348; *Clark v Nomura International plc* [2000] IRLR 766; *Mallone v BPB Industries Ltd* [2002] ICR 1045; *Horkulak v Cantor Fitzgerald International* [2004] IRLR 942; and *Commerzbank AG v Keen* [2007] ICR 623.

[121] [2007] ICR 623.

[122] *ibid.*, 632G–H. For example, see *Humphreys v Norilsk Nickel International (UK) Ltd* [2010] IRLR 976.

[123] The central problem is identical where the Employer does indeed adhere to the contractual disciplinary procedure, but there is a defect in its execution, e.g. if the Employer failed to abide by the provisions of the policy on the composition of the disciplinary panel or did not enable the Employee to present her case properly in breach of the policy's terms, e.g. by not permitting her to lead or cross-examine witnesses.

[124] See J. McMullen, 'Enforcing Contracts of Employment: "Going Back to Basics" in the Resolution of Employment Rights Disputes' (1995) 24 *Industrial Law Journal* 353, 360–1; J. McMullen, 'Wrongful Dismissal' (1988) 17 *Industrial Law Journal* 182, 187; and F. Reynold QC, 'Non-compliance with a Prescribed Disciplinary Procedure: Do Ordinary Contractual Principles Apply?' (2010) 39 *Industrial Law Journal* 420.

[125] [2011] UKSC 58, [2012] 2 AC 22. For extensive commentary, see L. Barmes, 'Judicial Influence and *Edwards v Chesterfield Royal Hospital NHS Trust & Botham v Ministry of Defence*' (2013) 42 *Industrial Law Journal* 192; C. Barnard and L. Merrett, 'Winners and Losers: *Edwards* and the Unfair Law of Dismissal' (2013) 72 *Cambridge Law Journal* 313; K. Costello, '*Edwards v Chesterfield Royal Hospital*: Parliamentary Intention and Damages Caused by Maladministration of a Contractual Dismissal Procedure' (2013) 76 *Modern Law Review* 134; and A. Bogg, 'Express Disciplinary Procedures in the Contract of Employment: Parliamentary Intention and the Supreme Court' (2015) 131 *Law Quarterly Review* 15.

[126] Lords Mance and Walker agreed with Lord Dyson. Lord Phillips also agreed, but for other reasons, whilst Baroness Hale and Lord Kerr gave dissenting judgments, Lord Wilson agreeing with Lord Kerr.

dismiss. Secondly, since Parliament had prescribed the statutory unfair dismissal regime as the exclusive mechanism for affording relief to dismissed employees, a common law action for damages for the chance that the employee might not have been dismissed was excluded.[127] Once again, the judiciary were reluctant to expand the scope of the common law for fear that it would marginalize the effectiveness of the statutory code on dismissal adumbrated by Parliament. These two factors were treated as justification for the conclusions that 'provisions about disciplinary procedure[s] . . . incorporated as express terms into an employment contract . . . are not ordinary contractual terms[128] agreed by parties to a contract in the usual way',[129] and '[it cannot have been] intend[ed by the parties] that a failure to comply with contractually binding disciplinary procedures will give rise to a common law claim for damages'.[130] Whilst perhaps a seductive proposition constitutionally and from a policy perspective, the notion that the express terms of a contract are somehow not 'ordinary contractual terms' has been described by Barmes as coming at 'an exceptionally high cost in terms of legal confusion and incoherence'.[131] This 'curious result'[132] is somewhat tendentious doctrinally and philosophically on a number of fronts, as follows.

(1) It is impossible to reconcile with general principles of contract law, the freedom of contract doctrine, and the notion of party autonomy and consent.

(2) Further, the fact that this approach treats contractual terms 'as discretionary and susceptible to abandonment at will'[133] is also perplexing.

(3) Finally, *Edwards* is particularly odd in that the employee would be unable to secure damages for breach of contract but would not be excluded from seeking an injunction: the fact that an injunction may be an adequate remedy, whereas damages will not, ultimately turns contractual orthodoxy on the law of remedies on its head. As rightly noted by Bogg, *Edwards* 'has isolated a contractual term whose remedial status is surely unique in the English common law'.[134]

An additional question thrown up post-*Edwards* is whether it continues to be permissible for an employee to claim damages for the reasonable period of time (over and above the notice period) that it would have taken the employer to conduct the disciplinary procedure if it had been conducted and completed by the employer with reasonable expedition. Reverting back to Hypothetical B, let us imagine that two months would be a reasonable period for the Employer to take to exhaust the disciplinary process. In

---

[127] For a critique of this aspect of the majority's reasoning, see K. Costello, '*Edwards v Chesterfield Royal Hospital*: Parliamentary Intention and Damages Caused by Maladministration of a Contractual Dismissal Procedure' (2013) 76 *Modern Law Review* 134, 135–7; C. Barnard and L. Merrett, 'Winners and Losers: *Edwards* and the Unfair Law of Dismissal' (2013) 72 *Cambridge Law Journal* 313, 325–300.

[128] Having said that, Lord Dyson recognized that a breach of a contractually binding disciplinary procedure will indeed give rise to a common law claim for damages if the parties to an employment contract so 'expressly agree': *Edwards v Chesterfield Royal Hospital NHS Foundation Trust* [2011] UKSC 58, [2012] 2 AC 22, 41C at para 39 per Lord Dyson. See also *ibid.*, 54G–H at para 94 per Lord Mance.

[129] *ibid.*, 40H at para 38 per Lord Dyson.

[130] *ibid.*, 41C at para 39 per Lord Dyson and 54G–H at para 94 per Lord Mance.

[131] L. Barmes, 'Judicial Influence and *Edwards v Chesterfield Royal Hospital NHS Foundation Trust & Botham v Ministry of Defence*' (2013) 42 *Industrial Law Journal* 192, 197.

[132] [2011] UKSC 58, [2012] 2 AC 22, 71A at para 154 per Lord Kerr. For comment, see M. Freedland and N. Kountouris, 'Common Law and Voice' in A. Bogg and T. Novitz (eds.), *Voices at Work* (Oxford, OUP, 2014) 352, 355–6.

[133] B. Hepple and G. Morris, 'The Employment Act 2002 and the Crisis of Individual Employment Rights' (2002) 31 *Industrial Law Journal* 245, 255.

[134] A. Bogg, 'Express Disciplinary Procedures in the Contract of Employment: Parliamentary Intention and the Supreme Court' (2015) 131 *Law Quarterly Review* 15, 16.

essence, the issue here is whether the Employee would be entitled to net wages/salary and other contractual benefits for that period. Such damages over and above the damages for the notice period are referred to as 'Gunton damages' or the 'Gunton extension' after the decision of the Court of Appeal in *Gunton v Richmond upon Thames London Borough Council*.[135] In the following excerpt, Collins considers the position of such 'Gunton damages' post-*Edwards*:

■ H. Collins, 'Compensation for Dismissal: In Search of Principle' (2012) 41 *Industrial Law Journal* 208, 219

An employer's failure to follow a contractual disciplinary procedure was held by the Court of Appeal in *Gunton v Richmond-upon-Thames* to justify an additional award of damages. Logically, that award of damages should have reflected the underlying claim for stigma damages, but, no doubt bearing in mind *Addis v Gramophone Co.*, the Court of Appeal preferred to treat the award as simply as [sic] an extension of the notice period to take into account the time that the disciplinary procedure would have taken. Is the *Gunton* extension still possible, or does it fall within the *Johnson* exclusion zone? Strictly speaking, the issue did not arise in *Edwards* because the employer had not appealed the decision of Nicol J in the High Court to award damages in accordance with the *Gunton* extension . . . however, it seems to follow that a *Gunton* extension is still possible. There is an enforceable breach of contract, and the claim is not for stigma damages. Nevertheless, it must be noted that the application of the *Johnson* exclusion zone to a contractual disciplinary procedure in a case of wrongful dismissal was approved by a majority in *Edwards*, and it is hard to see a claim for a *Gunton* extension as falling outside the sphere of dismissals that Parliament has been said to have pre-empted by the law of unfair dismissal. It should be noted, as well, that *Gunton* itself may have been based on the point that [the employee] was entitled to be suspended on full pay pending the outcome of the disciplinary procedure, so that in other cases, where there is no right to pay during the disciplinary process, the extension may not be available.

15.3.2 Non-monetary remedies

The common law approach has been to assume that damages will be an adequate remedy in a wrongful dismissal claim.[136] The recognition that the contract of employment is personal in nature led to the courts rejecting claims for it to be enforced through equitable remedies such as specific performance and injunction. The judicial concern over the practicalities of supervising any order for specific performance or injunction also contributed towards this stance.[137] Injunctions granted in the context of the employment relationship were generally confined[138] to negative post-termination constraints on the activities *of an employee* ruled not to be in restraint of trade. As for injunctions granted in favour of employees, they were conspicuous by their rarity. On one view, this may be justified by the statutory bar on a court granting an order for

---

[135] [1981] Ch 448. For example, *Dietman v London Borough of Brent* [1988] IRLR 299 is one case in which 'Gunton damages' were allowed.

[136] *De Francesco v Barnum* (1890) 45 Ch D 430, 438 per Fry LJ; *Ridge v Baldwin* [1964] AC 40, 65 per Lord Reid; *Wilson v St Helen's Borough Council* [1999] 2 AC 52, 84A–B per Lord Slynn of Hadley; and *Ashworth v Royal National Theatre* [2014] 4 All ER 238.

[137] *CH Giles & Co. Ltd v Morris* [1972] 1 All ER 960.

[138] However, injunctions will be granted in exceptional circumstances where the court is convinced that the injunctive relief (prohibiting the employee from working for anyone other than the employer) will not compel the employee to continue to work for the employer or face idleness or starvation: *Warren v Mendy* [1989] 1 WLR 853; *Sunrise Brokers LLP v Rodgers* [2015] ICR 272.

specific performance or an injunction which would have the effect of compelling an employee to work.[139]

Since the decision of the Court of Appeal in *Hill v CA Parsons & Co. Ltd*[140] and the recognition that the 'elective' theory of termination applies, this once hard-line approach has been relaxed, leading to significant developments in the sphere of remedies for breach of contract. Equitable relief is now possible in the context of procedural and substantive constraints on dismissal in the contract of employment. Thus, on a breach of contract by the employer, an injunction may be granted by the court to restrain a summary dismissal if damages are not an adequate remedy,[141] trust and confidence between the parties has not broken down, and the employer has failed to follow or misapplied the terms of a disciplinary process.[142] An injunction may also be granted to prevent a unilateral variation of the contract of employment[143] or, more controversially, to prevent a dismissal from taking effect. For example, with regard to the latter, Lord Prosser granted a decree for interim interdict restraining a dismissal in breach of a 'last in, first out' redundancy selection procedure in *Anderson v Pringle*[144] and Lord Penrose granted interdict in *Peace v City of Edinburgh Council*[145] to prevent an employee from being disciplined in accordance with a disciplinary process which was contrary to that required by his contract of employment. Although the courts held in *Alexander v Standard Telephones*[146] that an injunction will be refused if trust and confidence between the parties has been destroyed, in *Wadcock v London Borough of Brent*[147] an injunction was granted since a workable solution between the parties could be found. There is a forceful argument that *Wadcock* ought to be preferred, particularly if one considers that the employer would be able to avoid the scope for an injunction to be granted by unilaterally withdrawing trust and confidence.[148]

A final point to make is that the decision of the Supreme Court in *Edwards v Chesterfield* would appear to have generated a surge in applications from employees for an injunction where a binding disciplinary procedure has been breached. In *West London Mental Health NHS Trust v Chhabra*,[149] the Supreme Court granted an injunction in favour of an employee, duly restraining the employer from proceeding with a disciplinary procedure in breach of the employee's contract of employment. It is particularly telling that one of the reasons cited in support of the injunction was that damages were not available to the employee as a result of the decision in *Edwards v Chesterfield*.[150] The court will be prepared to intervene in a disciplinary process if the employee is able to demonstrate that the proceedings are being conducted on a basis which makes their conduct a breach of contract. The irregularity in the procedure must amount to a breach of contract, and the breach itself must reach a certain threshold of seriousness or severity. In *Chhabra*, it was decided that it will be sufficient if the procedural errors or irregularities make the continued pursuit of the disciplinary proceedings unfair in a way which cannot be remedied with or by the proceedings themselves. As for orders

---

[139] Section 236 of the Trade Union and Labour Relations (Consolidation) Act 1992.

[140] [1972] Ch 305.

[141] This may be attributable to the fact that it will be a challenge to quantify non-compliance with a procedure in monetary terms.

[142] *Irani v Southampton and South-West Hampshire Health Authority* [1985] ICR 590; *Jones v Lee & Guilding* [1980] IRLR 67; and *Robb v London Borough of Hammersmith* [1991] ICR 514.

[143] *Powell v London Borough of Brent* [1988] 1 Ch 176.

[144] [1998] IRLR 64.   [145] 1999 SLT 712.   [146] [1990] ICR 291.   [147] [1990] IRLR 223.

[148] P. Elias, 'The Structure of the Employment Contract' (1982) 35 *Current Legal Problems* 95, 101.

[149] [2013] UKSC 80.

[150] *ibid.*, para 39 per Lord Hodge. *McMillan v Airedale NHS Foundation Trust* [2014] EWCA Civ 1031, [2015] ICR 747 is another example of a successful application for injunctive relief. Contrast this with the unsuccessful applications in *Hendy v Ministry of Justice* [2014] IRLR 856 and *Al-Mishlab v Milton Keynes Hospital NHS Foundation Trust* [2015] EWHC 3096 (QB).

for specific performance, the decision in *Geys* may also herald an increase in applications from employees who have been wrongfully dismissed. Further, if the employee can keep the contract on foot and compel the employer to perform in such a case, as noted by Lord Justice Longmore in *Sunrise Brokers LLP v Rodgers*,[151] it is open to question why the employee should not be permitted to recover any unpaid salary or wages as a debt.[152]

 For additional reading on remedies, visit the Online Resources for this book at www. oup.com/uk/cabrelli3e/

---

[151] [2015] ICR 272.

[152] *ibid.*, 292B. For discussion, see D. Cabrelli, 'The Effect of Termination on Post-Employment Obligations' in M. Freedland et al. (eds), *The Contract of Employment* (Oxford, OUP, 2016) 573–5.

CHAPTER SIXTEEN

INTRODUCTION TO UNFAIR DISMISSAL AND SUBSTANTIVE FAIRNESS

16.1 CONTEXTUAL AND HISTORICAL INTRODUCTION TO UNFAIR DISMISSAL LAW

The purpose of this chapter is to explore the range of measures which legislation may adopt, and has adopted, in order to regulate arrangements pursued by employers that result in the dismissal of their employees. In the introductory section, we highlight the features encountered by legislators and policy-makers in deciding whether to promulgate unfair dismissal or redundancy laws which place restrictions on the employer's power to dismiss on economic or other grounds. For example, it is by no means a *fait accompli* that a State will introduce unfair dismissal laws: some economists argue that, by interfering in contractual exchanges between employers and employees, normative controls on dismissal impede the efficient operation of labour markets and should be avoided. In other words, there is a negative correlation between the efficiency of markets and the strength of employment protection legislation. However, if, despite such arguments, a jurisdiction elects to introduce a statutory unfair dismissal regime, the nature, content, and shape of that scheme is a separate issue which needs to be addressed. As such, the policy responses available to the State are also examined in this section. For example, should that regime confer a measure of job property in favour of the employee? Alternatively, should the law be designed to limit job security, focus on employment security, and afford employers a measure of flexibility, thus realizing the amalgam which is referred to as 'flexicurity'? Finally, the chapter moves on to a comprehensive exposition of the substantive law within a contextual, as well as historical, framework.

16.1.1 The efficiency of unfair dismissal laws

There is undoubtedly an interconnection between laws which impose limitations on the ability of employers to offload excess labour, on the one hand, and the efficiency, flexibility, and dynamism of external labour markets, on the other. In Chapter 1,[1] we were introduced to the research of Botero et al.,[2] which examined the link between a jurisdiction's legal origin and the extent of its regulatory intervention in the field of labour law. Botero et al.'s work suggests that there is a direct correlation between the legal origin of a jurisdiction (e.g. whether it belongs to the common law or civil law tradition) and the strength of its labour regulations and laws.[3] In the following extract, Botero et al. explain that the traditional justification for unjust dismissal laws is that they are efficient and have a positive effect on the external labour market of a country's economy. They go on to explore the claims of some commentators that although laws which protect employees from unfair dismissal interfere in labour markets, they have a salutary effect, since they correct or limit the scope for market failures, e.g. decisions by employers to discharge employees for arbitrary, absurd, or discriminatory reasons. They explain that some commentators assert that legal intervention is warranted on the basis that dismissals generate adverse social costs for employees, governments, and taxpayers through the social security and pension systems:

■ **J. C. Botero, S. Djankov, R. La Porta, F. Lopez-De-Silanes, and A. Shleifer, 'The Regulation of Labor' (2004) 119** *The Quarterly Journal of Economics* **1339, 1342**

Why do governments intervene in the labor market? The theory underlying most interventions is that free labor markets are imperfect, that as a consequence there are rents in the employment relationship, and that employers abuse workers to extract these rents, leading to both unfairness and inefficiency. For example, employers discriminate against disadvantaged groups, underpay workers who are immobile or invest in firm-specific capital, fire workers who then need to be supported by the state, force employees to work more than they wish under the threat of dismissal, fail to insure workers against the risk of death, illness or disability, and so on. In response to the perceived unfairness and inefficiency of the free market employment relationship, nearly every state intervenes in this relationship to protect the workers.

Regulation of labor markets aiming to protect workers from employers takes [a number of] forms . . . [G]overnments regulate employment relationships by, for example, restricting the range of feasible contracts and raising the costs of both laying off workers and increasing hours of work . . . [4]

Botero et al. go on to reject the contention that unfair dismissal laws are efficient; instead, they argue, their research reveals that 'heavier regulation of labor is associated with lower

---

[1] See Chapter 1, section 1.2.1.

[2] J. C. Botero, S. Djankov, R. La Porta, F. Lopez-De-Silanes, and A. Shleifer, 'The Regulation of Labor' (2004) 119 *Quarterly Journal of Economics* 1339.

[3] Further quantitative studies appear to have corroborated these findings: J. Armour, S. Deakin, P. Lele, and M. Siems, 'How Do Legal Rules Evolve? Evidence from a Cross-Country Comparison of Shareholder, Creditor and Worker Protection' (2009) 57 *American Journal of Comparative Law* 579, 616; S. Deakin, P. Lele, and M. Siems, 'The Evolution of Labour Law: Calibrating and Comparing Regulatory Regimes' (2007) 146 *International Labour Review* 133, 154; Z. Adams and S. Deakin, 'Quantitative Labour Law' in A. Ludlow and A. Blackham (eds), *New Frontiers in Empirical Labour Law Research* (Oxford, Hart Publishing, 2015) 31, 42–50; and Z. Adams, P. Bastani, L. Bishop, and S. Deakin, 'The CBR-LRI Dataset: Methods, Properties and Potential of Leximetric Coding of Labour Laws' (2017) 33 *International Journal of Comparative Labour Law and Industrial Relations* 59, 76–89.

[4] Writer's annotations appear in square brackets throughout this chapter.

labor force participation and higher unemployment'.[5] If this hypothesis is accurate, and protective labour laws which impose normative controls on unjust or arbitrary dismissals can only be achieved at the expense of a dynamic and flexible labour market, then the implications are twofold:

(1) a jurisdiction must pause before deciding to adopt such a system and consider whether it should abandon the idea; and

(2) if it does opt to forge ahead, it ought to select a regulatory model very carefully when engaged in the process of designing and planning for its introduction.

The policy choice pursued by various States in the USA is particularly instructive in this context. In Chapter 15,[6] we noted that the employment-at-will model is the predominant form the employment relationship takes in the USA.[7] The 'at-will' doctrine, which has formed the cornerstone of US employment law for over 100 years,[8] posits that the employer and employee are both entitled to terminate their relationship at any time, for a good or bad cause, or no cause at all—and without providing prior reasonable notice to the other.[9] Since the default position under US employment law enables the parties to terminate the employment relationship at will, the doctrine is paradigmatic of a legal institution which operates in the absence of a carefully crafted statutory system of fetters on dismissal. It provides an indication of how the labour market functions in a world without protective dismissal legislation. Mirroring the arguments of Botero et al., proponents of the 'at-will' doctrine have invoked the advantages of economic efficiency,[10] increased job creation/employment rates, higher productivity,[11] and pragmatic notions of legal and commercial certainty to defend it against any attacks, and in favour of its setting as a 'default rule' around which employers and employees may contract:

■ R. A. Epstein, 'In Defence of Contract at Will' (1984) 51 *University of Chicago Law Review* 947, 951–2 and 982

[T]he parties should be permitted as of right to adopt this form of contract [i.e. employment-at-will] if they so desire. The principle behind this conclusion is that freedom of contract tends both to advance individual autonomy and to promote the efficient operation of labor markets. Second, the contract at will should be respected as a rule of construction in response to the perennial question

---

[5] J. C. Botero, S. Djankov, R. La Porta, F. Lopez-De-Silanes, and A. Shleifer, 'The Regulation of Labor' (2004) 119 *Quarterly Journal of Economics* 1339, 1379.   [6] See Chapter 15, section 15.1.1.

[7] For an examination of the 'employment-at-will' approach in the USA in a comparative light, see S. Estreicher and J. M. Hirsch, 'Comparative Wrongful Dismissal Law: Reassessing American Exceptionalism' (2014) 92 *North Carolina Law Review* 343; J. M. Hirsch, 'A Comparative Perspective on Unjust Dismissal Laws', available from SSRN at http://papers.ssrn.com/sol3/papers.cfm?abstract_id=2095336 (last visited 26 October 2017).

[8] The first case to judicially endorse the 'at-will' rule was *Payne v Western & Atlantic Railroad* Co. 81 Tenn. 507 (1884) and the judicial imprimatur of the US Supreme Court was provided in *Adair v United States*, 208 US 161, 28 S. Ct. 277, 52 L. Ed. 436 (1908), 27.

[9] Various exceptions to the at-will doctrine have been crafted by the common law courts and legislatures in the USA, namely the 'public policy', 'implied-in-fact', and 'implied covenant of good faith and fair dealing' exceptions. However, as noted by C. W. Summers, 'Employment At-Will in the United States: The Divine Right of Employers' (2002) 3 *University of Pennsylvania Journal of Labour & Employment Law* 65, 77, the efficacy of these exceptions is marginal.

[10] J. P. Frantz, 'Market Ordering versus Statutory Control of Termination Decisions: A Case for the Inefficiency of Just Cause Dismissal Requirements' (1996–97) 20 *Harvard Journal of Law & Public Policy* 555; A. P. Morriss, 'Bad Data, Bad Economics, and Bad Policy: Time to Fire Wrongful Discharge Law' (1996) 74 *Texas Law Review* 1901.

[11] See F. Baumann, 'On Unobserved Worker Heterogeneity and Employment Protection' (2010) 29 *European Journal of Law and Economics* 155, 171.

of gaps in contract language: what term should be implied in the absence of explicit agreement on the question of duration or grounds for termination? . . . When the law introduces a just-cause requirement, it flies in the face of ordinary understandings and thus rests upon an assumption that just-cause arrangements are in the broad run of cases either more frequent or desirable than the contract at will, though neither is the case . . . The critics of the contract at will all point out imperfections in the current institutional arrangements, but they do not take into account the nonlegal means of preserving long-term employment relationships, and they ignore the greater imperfections that are created under alternative legal rules. Contracts at will are consistent with public policy and should be welcomed by it, not because they are perfect, but because in many contexts they respond to the manifold perils of employment contracts better than any rivals that courts or legislatures can devise . . . The recent trend toward expanding the legal remedies for wrongful discharge has been greeted with wide approval in judicial, academic, and popular circles, [but] the modern trend rests in large measure upon a misunderstanding of the contractual processes and the ends served by the contract at will. No system of regulation can hope to match the benefits that the contract at will affords in employment relations. The flexibility afforded by the contract at will permits the ceaseless marginal adjustments that are necessary in any ongoing productive activity conducted, as all activities are, in conditions of technological and business change. The strength of the contract at will should not be judged by the occasional cases in which it is said to produce unfortunate results, but rather by the vast run of cases where it provides a sensible private response to the many and varied problems in labor contracting . . . The doctrine of wrongful discharge is the problem and not the solution. This is one of the many situations in which courts and legislatures should leave well enough alone.

Epstein's analysis of unfair dismissal laws[12] is a classic example of the application of neo-classical economics. Statistical evidence suggests that there may be some force in the contention that unfair dismissal laws impact upon the efficiency and dynamism of labour markets. This can be demonstrated through a comparison of US, EU, and UK labour market statistics. On the basis of a study conducted by Block, Berg, and Roberts, a lower level of labour protection may be ascribed to the USA in comparison with the EU.[13] These research findings demonstrated that labour standards at the EU level are much higher in the areas of redundancy and employee dismissal rights on the change of ownership of the employer. The divergence in the degree of labour protection links in with statistics released by the US Bureau of Labor Statistics and the Office of National Statistics in the UK. The US Bureau of Labor Statistics notes the rate of dismissals in the USA, where approximately 13–15 per cent of the US working population are involuntarily dismissed or made redundant by their employers each year.[14] This can be contrasted with approximately 263,000 workers per quarter[15] out of an aggregate 32.1 million workers in the UK,[16] equating to approximately 0.9 per cent of the working population each quarter

[12] Epstein refers to them as 'wrongful discharge' laws.

[13] See R. Block, P. Berg, and K. Roberts, 'Comparing and Quantifying Labour Standards in the United States and the European Union' (2003) 19 *International Journal of Comparative Labour Law and Industrial Relations* 441, 443–8.

[14] This is based on the assumption that a steady 1.2% of the working population in the USA are involuntarily discharged or made redundant each month, see, e.g., US Bureau of Labor Statistics, 'Job Openings and Labor Turnover, August 2017', 11 October 2017 (USDL 17–1366), available at https://www.bls.gov/news.release/jolts.nr0.htm Table 5 at page 3 (last visited 26 October 2017).

[15] See Office for National Statistics, *Labour Market Economic Commentary* (October 2017), available at https://www.ons.gov.uk/employmentandlabourmarket/peopleinwork/employmentandemployeetypes/articles/labourmarketeconomiccommentary/latest Table 2 at page 10 (last visited 26 October 2017).

[16] See Office for National Statistics, *Labour Market Statistics*, October 2017, available at https://www.ons.gov.uk/employmentandlabourmarket/peopleinwork/employmentandemployeetypes/bulletins/uklabourmarket/october2017 (last visited 26 October 2017).

and 3.3 per cent each year in the UK. This represents a difference of anything between 10 per cent and 11 per cent between the UK and USA, which is a remarkable statistic. The comparative ease with which a US employer can discharge an employee, coupled with the limited exposure to legal risk, undoubtedly makes a material contribution to the divergence we witness in this context. It may also explain the difference between the US statistics and those of the UK, where exposure to legal risk (and therefore compensatory damages) is higher.[17]

The attitude of neo-classical economics to statutory unfair dismissal protection can be contrasted with the alternative perspective advanced by new institutional economists. The latter do not approach calls for social legislation protecting employees from unjust or arbitrary dismissals or redundancies with scepticism; instead, they are unconvinced of the arguments of neo-classical economists, which suggest that markets will always achieve efficient outcomes. Here, there is recognition that unfair dismissal intervention may indeed be efficient and have a beneficial effect on employment markets.[18] An Australian study examining the interconnection between the costs associated with unfair dismissal laws and labour market participation appears to lend support to the arguments of new institutional economists. Freyens and Oslington's research[19] compared the differences between dismissal costs before and after a change in Australian unfair dismissal laws that relaxed the scope of application of the latter so that small businesses employing fewer than 100 employees would be exempt.[20] What is particularly interesting is that the impact of the modification of the unfair dismissal laws was found to be benign. As such, there was little change in the dismissal costs employers were required to bear, nor any significant effects on the functioning of labour markets.[21]

Nonetheless, there is undoubtedly room for argument on the economic merits of unfair dismissal laws and, at best, the literature is not entirely conclusive.[22] This is compounded by the fact that perception plays a significant role, since amongst commercial operators there is a strong feeling that unfair dismissal laws impose costs and 'red tape' on business. The salience of this perception is reflected in the degree of significance which the UK Government[23] and key international institutions such as the Organisation for Economic Co-operation and Development ('OECD') afford to labour laws. For example, the OECD publishes statistics which chart the strength of protective collective dismissal

---

[17] See Collins' exposition of this analysis in H. Collins, *Justice in Dismissal* (Oxford, Clarendon Press, 1992) 252–4.

[18] See the summary of the academic literature in J. Howe, 'Poles Apart? The Contestation between the Ideas of No Fault Dismissal and Unfair Dismissal for Protecting Job Security' (2013) 42 *Industrial Law Journal* 122, 146–8. See also B. Freyens, 'Measuring Firing Costs: The Case for Direct Methods' (2010) 149 *International Labour Review* 287; S. Deakin and F. Wilkinson, 'Labour Law and Economic Theory: A Reappraisal' in H. Collins, P. Davies, and R. Rideout (eds), *Legal Regulation of the Employment Relation* (Kluwer, London, 2000) 29, 55–6; S. Deakin and P. Sarkar, 'Assessing the Long-Run Economic Impact of Labour Law Systems: A Theoretical Reappraisal and Analysis of New Time Series Data' (2008) 39 *Industrial Relations Journal* 453; and S. Deakin, 'The Contribution of Labour Law to Economic and Human Development' in G. Davidov and B. Langille (eds), *The Idea of Labour Law* (Oxford, OUP, 2011) 156.

[19] B. Freyens and P. Oslington, 'Dismissal Costs and Their Impact on Employment: Evidence from Australian Small and Medium Enterprises' (2007) 83 *The Economic Record* 1.

[20] Section 170CE(5E) of the Workplace Relations Act 1996, inserted by paragraph 113 of Schedule 1 to the Workplace Relations Amendment (Work Choices) Act 2005. This legislation has since been repealed by the Fair Work Act 2009.

[21] B. Freyens and P. Oslington, 'Dismissal Costs and Their Impact on Employment: Evidence from Australian Small and Medium Enterprises' (2007) 83 *The Economic Record* 1, 1 and 13.

[22] See J. Howe, 'Poles Apart? The Contestation between the Ideas of No Fault Dismissal and Unfair Dismissal for Protecting Job Security' (2013) 42 *Industrial Law Journal* 122, 146–8.

[23] See the Employment Red Tape Challenge, available at http://www.redtapechallenge.cabinetoffice. gov.uk/themehome/employment-related-law/ (last visited 26 October 2017).

laws.[24] Such statistics on the relative rigidity of unjust dismissal and redundancy laws are undoubtedly consulted by multinational companies in forming a judgment as to whether they ought to invest in a particular country. The argument runs that such corporates will prefer to invest in countries with lower unfair dismissal costs. This serves to incentivize jurisdictions not to promulgate overly inflexible laws that deter inward investment.

16.1.2 The structure, nature, content, and shape of unfair dismissal laws

Where a jurisdiction makes a conscious policy decision to intervene in the labour market and introduce unfair dismissal laws, a second major issue which it must address is the design and form those laws will take. This is a question of regulatory strategy and is conditioned by multifarious factors, e.g. economic policy, social policy, fiscal policy, legal culture, and the political persuasions of the legislature, policy-makers, and judiciary. For example, should that jurisdiction adopt a regulatory regime which deploys a strong model of protection to espouse a notion of job security (i.e. the idea that an employee has property or ownership in his/her work/job with the employer), thus supplementing the baseline of protection offered by the common law wrongful dismissal regulation of the employment relationship in countries such as the UK? Alternatively, should the law seek to achieve a more modest degree of protection by striking an even balance between the demands of employers and employees? Such a balanced approach could afford employers the capacity to engage in a measure of flexibility by focusing energy on drawing up a system which stresses the employment security and enhanced employability of their employees rather than job security and job property.

The expressions 'job security' and 'employment security' are sometimes confused, so it is crucial to distinguish between the two. First, there are a number of ways of conceptualizing the notion of job security. In crude terms, job security can be expressed in a 'strong' or 'positive' form whereby the law accepts that employees have a fundamental human right not to be deprived of their job, i.e. a right to a 'job for life'. This is associated with the notion that an employee has invested as much time, energy, and resources into his/her job as the employer and that the employee's right of property in the job should be vindicated. Thus, if the employer purports to deprive an employee of his/her job and terminate the contract of employment, the State should treat that ostensible dismissal as null and void via the medium of its legal system. This can be contrasted with the alternative 'weak' form of job security. Here, the State recognizes the right of employers to dismiss workers, but harnesses mechanisms which undertake to procure that the employer makes available adequate monetary compensation to the employee for his/her future loss of earnings.[25] These 'strong' and 'weak' conceptions of 'job security' can be set apart from the separate concepts of 'employment security' and 'employability'. Regulations which seek to champion job security traditionally function to entrench the position of an employee in a job as effectively as possible or to offer sufficient monetary compensation in return for the recognition of the employer's power to dismiss, whereas inherent within the latter concept of employment security is a concession that, during their working lives, employees will be expected to adapt to changing methods of work, to reskill, and even to lose their jobs:

---

[24] See http://www.oecd.org/els/emp/oecdindicatorsofemploymentprotection.htm (last visited 26 October 2017).

[25] See W. Njoya, *Property in Work: The Employment Relationship in the Anglo-American Firm* (Aldershot, Ashgate, 2007) 6–7; C. Mummé, 'Property in Labor and the Limits of Contracting' in U. Mattei and J. D. Haskell (eds), *Research Handbook on Political Economy and Law* (Cheltenham, Edward Elgar, 2015) 413–15; and also K. D. Ewing, 'Job Security and the Contract of Employment' (1989) 18 *Industrial Law Journal* 217.

■ H. Collins, 'Regulating the Employment Relation for Competitiveness' (2001)
30 *Industrial Law Journal* 17, 29

> The increasing pace of innovation is likely to destroy job packages more quickly. Thus employees can have no expectation of job security. The best that can be offered by employers to employees is either employment security by the firm or enhanced employability. Employment security means that the employment relation will continue indefinitely, but the employee will have to perform different kinds of work, for which training will be required. Employability due to high levels of skills means that the redundant worker has a much better than average chance of obtaining a good job with another employer.[26]

In the teeth of the accelerating pace of innovation and technological change, Collins notes that States must prioritize employment security and enhanced employability over policies designed to promote job security and property in order to ensure that their respective economies remain competitive. Pursuant to an employment security policy, States invest in active labour market policies that attempt to minimize the period during which dismissed employees are out of work. They do so by offering support to enable employees to secure suitable alternative employment.

As far as the position in UK law is concerned, historically, in the 1960s and 1970s, there was a perception that the job security/property model was the preference of the UK Government. Proponents of this theory could point to the Contracts of Employment Act 1963, which introduced requirements for employers to provide employees with minimum periods of notice prior to dismissal. Furthermore, it was also possible to refer to the provisions of the Redundancy Payments Act 1965[27] and the original incarnation of the unfair dismissal regime in the Industrial Relations Act 1971, which afforded rights of reinstatement and re-engagement to unfairly dismissed employees:

■ P. Davies and M. Freedland, *Labour Law: Text and Materials*, 2nd edition
(London, Weidenfeld and Nicholson, 1984) 431–2

> . . . the unfair dismissal legislation, however much eviscerated in its application and construction, has demonstrated four very important propositions about job property. The first is that the protection of job security and hence job property is very powerfully served by a process which requires *reasons* for dismissal to be substantiated, for such a process exposes the merits of those reasons to scrutiny. The second is that job property is likewise vindicated by a process which exposes the *procedure* of dismissal to scrutiny, for such scrutiny tends to establish control over the substantive decisions. The third proposition is that adequate control over duration of employment requires control over the content of employment as well; for otherwise job property can be undermined by adverse action by employers falling short of dismissal. In other words, there has to be the capacity to control constructive dismissal as well as outright dismissal. The fourth proposition is that the protection of job property depends crucially upon the availability of remedies which place the employer under some real pressure to reinstate the worker whose job security it is sought to vindicate.

In terms of the fourth proposition highlighted by Davies and Freedland, as Ewing has argued, the traditional hostility of the courts towards the 'strong' or 'positive'

---

[26] See also H. Collins, 'Flexibility and Stability of Expectations in the Contract of Employment' (2006) 4 *Socio-Economic Review* 139, 143–6.

[27] See the discussion in the *Report of the Royal Commission on Trade Unions and Employers' Associations 1965–1968* (London, HMSO, Cmnd 3623) 141, at para 523.

conception of job property appeared to wane during the 1970s and 1980s when they became more open to the possibility of offering a more effective range of remedies for wrongful or unfair dismissal.[28] However, despite the strength of such arguments, three factors strongly suggest that the current UK position exhibits a preference for the conceptions of employment security and enhanced employability over job property or security, as follows.

(1) The influence of EU social policy should not be underestimated. EU policy has focused on the desire to achieve 'flexicurity'.[29] Flexicurity is a leitmotif for laws which promote flexibility in employment contract arrangements and employment security over job security.[30] It perceives the employment engagement in a transitional sense whereby it represents an employee's opportunity to acquire greater skills before moving on to subsequent engagements with other employers. This is coupled with State support through the provision of comprehensive lifelong learning, active labour market policies, and modern, generous social security systems. The flexicurity approach also empowers employers to engage in 'numerical' and 'functional' flexibility. Numerical flexibility entails the offloading of labour where there is a diminution in an employer's demand for particular tasks carried out by a section of its workforce, which can be distinguished from functional flexibility which enjoins employees to re-skill themselves to adapt to new technological innovations and methods and patterns of work.[31]

(2) Particularized to the law of unfair dismissal in the UK, as the range of reasonable responses test became entrenched in the early 1980s,[32] the courts sent a signal that the standard of review they would apply to the application of the managerial prerogative to dismiss would be drawn at a particularly lax level. As the courts continued to marshal the range of reasonable responses test as a means of interfering sparingly in the judgment of the employer to dismiss, it became clear that the primary focus of the unfair dismissal legislation had shifted from the *substantive fairness* to the *procedural fairness* of an employee's dismissal. There is a forceful argument that the evisceration of a concern for the substantive fairness of the dismissal is consistent with a judicial abandonment of the notion of job security.

(3) The disinclination of the tribunals and courts to order the reinstatement or re-engagement[33] of unfairly dismissed employees in terms of the power conferred upon them by sections 113–115 of the Employment Rights Act 1996 ('ERA') provides further evidence of the preference for employment security and enhanced employability

---

[28] See K. D. Ewing, 'Job Security and the Contract of Employment' (1989) 18 *Industrial Law Journal* 217; K. D. Ewing, 'Remedies for Breach of the Contract of Employment' (1993) 52 *Cambridge Law Journal* 405, 435–6.

[29] See EC Green Paper, *Modernising Labour Law to Meet the Challenges of the 21st Century* (COM(2006) 708 final, 22 November 2006); Communication from the Commission to the Council, the European Parliament, and others, *Outcome of the Public Consultation on the Commission's Green Paper 'Modernising Labour Law to Meet the Challenges of the 21st Century'* (COM(2007) 627 final, 22 November 2006); and J. Rojot, 'Security of Employment and Employability' in R. Blanpain (ed.), *Comparative Labour Law and Industrial Relations in Industrialised Market Economies*, 8th edition (The Hague, Kluwer, 2004) 375–94.

[30] See G. Davidov and E. Eshet, 'Intermediate Approaches to Unfair Dismissal Protection' (2015) 44 *Industrial Law Journal* 167, 176–8.

[31] For an examination of functional and numerical flexibility, see H. Collins, 'Regulating the Employment Relationship for Competitiveness' (2001) 30 *Industrial Law Journal* 17, 26–9.

[32] In the seminal case of *Iceland Frozen Foods Ltd v Jones* [1983] ICR 17 (EAT), on which, see section 16.3.2.

[33] Reinstatement involves the reversal of the dismissal so that the employee gets his/her old job back. Re-engagement is slightly different and describes the situation where an employee is re-employed by his/her employer but works in a different job.

over job security and property. For example, it is particularly telling that, during the period from April 2016 to April 2017, employment tribunal statistics[34] reveal that the employment tribunals ordered reinstatement or re-engagement in a mere three cases out of a total of 2,139 unfair dismissal claims which proceeded to an employment tribunal hearing.[35]

16.1.3 The rationale for the introduction of the unfair dismissal laws in the UK

A number of factors coalesced in the 1960s and early 1970s to provide the impetus for the promulgation of the law of unfair dismissal in the Industrial Relations Act 1971. In the 1960s, Parliament had introduced a modest measure of statutory protection in the context of dismissal, e.g. the Contracts of Employment Act 1963 enjoined employers to provide employees with minimum periods of notice prior to dismissal, whilst the Redundancy Payments Act 1965 conferred rights on employees to be notified prior to an economic dismissal and a right to a statutory redundancy payment. However, beyond these measures, the common law of wrongful dismissal in the 1960s and 1970s had stressed the comparatively weak position of the employee where he/she had been dismissed. Cases such as *Ridge v Baldwin*[36] and *Malloch v Aberdeen Corp.*,[37] which were considered in Chapter 15,[38] underscored the imbalance of power associated with the common law 'unrestricted reasonable notice rule'. The general common law rule is that an employer is not required to have any reason or a good reason to dismiss an employee[39]—or even to hear the employee prior to dismissal or to give reasons for dismissal.[40] The only requirement imposed on an employer is to give the employee reasonable notice of termination or the statutory minimum period prescribed in section 86 of the ERA, whichever period is the longer, failing which the employee will have a claim for damages in wrongful dismissal.[41]

In the 1960s and 1970s, the lack of employment protection against arbitrary termination looked particularly anomalous given that the UK had adopted Article 2 of the International Labour Organization's ('ILO') Recommendation 119 of 1963 on the termination of employment. This provision recommended a restriction of the employer's power of dismissal by requiring it to have valid reasons for dismissals. Article 4 of the ILO's Convention 158 of 1982 on Termination of Employment which superseded Recommendation 119 of 1963 now provides as follows:

---

[34] See Ministry of Justice, *Employment Tribunal and Employment Appeal Tribunal Tables 2016 to 2017*, available at https://www.gov.uk/government/statistics/tribunals-and-gender-recognition-certificate-statistics-quarterly-april-to-june-2017-and-2016-to-2017 Table E2 (last visited 26 October 2017).

[35] For a discussion of these statistics, see J. Howe, 'Why Do So Few Employees Return to Their Jobs? In Pursuit of a Right to Work Following Unfair Dismissal' in V. Mantouvalou (ed.), *The Right to Work* (Oxford, Hart Publishing, 2015) 255.   [36] [1964] AC 40.

[37] [1971] 1 WLR 1578.

[38] See Chapter 15, section 15.2.1.

[39] See *Alexander v Standard Telephones & Cables (No. 2)* [1991] IRLR 286, 296 at para 53 per Hobhouse J (as he then was).

[40] Ironically, these general propositions of law were articulated in *Ridge v Baldwin* and *Malloch v Aberdeen Corp.* against the backdrop of factual circumstances which triggered particular rules conferring special protection against dismissal upon the employees concerned.

[41] '[T]he rule is taken to be so obvious that it is usually repeated [by the judiciary] without authorities or analysis to support it': M. Ford, 'Re-thinking the Notice Rule' (1998) 27 *Industrial Law Journal* 220, 220. However, in Scots law there are clear authorities to that effect, e.g. *Morrison v Abernethy School Board* (1876) 3 R 945; *Robson v Overend* (1878) 6 R 213; and *Cooper v Henderson* (1825) 3 S 619. See also M. Freedland, *The Personal Employment Contract* (Oxford, OUP, 2003) 329–32.

> *Article 4*
>
> The employment of a worker shall not be terminated unless there is a valid reason for such termination connected with the capacity or conduct of the worker or based on the operational requirements of the undertaking, establishment or service.

The Labour Government, voted into power in the UK in 1964, set up a Royal Commission in 1965 to 'consider relations between managements and employees and the role of trade unions and employers' associations in promoting the interests of their members and in accelerating the social and economic advance of the nation, with particular reference to the law'.[42] At the same time, the Labour Government referred the question of the desirability of the promulgation of unfair dismissal laws to a sub-committee of an organization called the National Joint Advisory Council ('NJAC'). The recommendations of the sub-committee of the NJAC in its report entitled *Dismissal Procedures*[43] preferred an approach which would reform the existing traditional, voluntarist method of regulating dismissals in the absence of law—which was consistent with the then prevailing attitude of avoiding a system that served to 'juridify' the regulation of industrial relations through the medium of legislation. However, the Donovan Commission also considered the potential for the reform of the law of dismissal in the UK and, in its final report, it concluded that it was 'urgently necessary for workers to be given better protection against unfair dismissal'.[44] It recommended that a statutory, rather than voluntary, regime was the preferable means of achieving the desired objectives. The reforms suggested by the Donovan Commission were enacted by sections 22–32 of the Industrial Relations Act 1971.

In its conception, the purpose of the Industrial Relations Act 1971 was to confer upon employees a floor of rights in the context of dismissal. Therefore, employers were entitled to build upon the regime contained therein by incorporating more generous provisions via the express terms of the contract of employment. Moreover, the statutory unfair dismissal regime operated as a superstructure duly resting upon the basic, yet separate, contractual rights of employees, standards set by collective agreements, and the common law of wrongful dismissal. The following judicial pronouncement is reflective of the prevailing sentiment at the time:

■ *Tomlinson v Dick Evans 'U' Drive Ltd* [1978] ICR 639, 642

> *Bristow J:*
>
> It is true that the rights with which we are concerned are creatures of statute, superimposed upon the contractual rights of employees and employers which they enjoy under the common law. But the prerequisite to the existence of these rights is that the person who seeks to enforce them has been employed under a contract. The rights, though creatures of statute, in our judgment depend on, or arise from the contract just as do the common law rights which arise from the contract itself . . .

---

[42] The Royal Commission, which was chaired by Lord Donovan ('the Donovan Commission') was concerned with the perceived post-war inflationary wage demands of the trade unions and the future role and shape of industrial democracy in the UK.

[43] Ministry of Labour, *Dismissal Procedures: Report of a Committee of the National Joint Advisory Council* (1967) para 180.

[44] *Report of the Royal Commission on Trade Unions and Employers' Associations 1965–1968* (London, HMSO, Cmnd 3623) 141, 143, and 146 at paras 523, 529, and 544.

Although the common law and statutory regimes were and are clearly distinct, any notion that the latter had been designed to inhibit the development of the former or vice versa does not appear to have been given any serious thought at the time.[45] Of course, since the decision of the House of Lords in *Johnson v Unisys*[46]—which we discussed in Chapter 15[47]—where Lord Hoffmann took the view that the intention of the UK Parliament was for the unfair dismissal regime to check the expansion of the common law of wrongful dismissal, we now know that the House of Lords' perception of matters was somewhat different. What can be asserted with a great deal of confidence is that the inter-relationship between the contractual rights of employees, the common law of the contract of employment, and the statutory regime has been a vexed one. Throughout this chapter, we will be reminded of the relevance of the issues we addressed in Chapter 2,[48] i.e. the 'oil and water' interaction between the common law and employment protection legislation. Indeed, we will note that the statutory unfair dismissal laws have somewhat paradoxically resorted to the apparatus of the common law of the contract of employment[49] in order to forge a distinctive system regulating the termination of the contract of employment. This might seem counter-intuitive, but as we progress through this chapter the pervasiveness of the influence of the common law on the statutory system will be exposed.[50]

Reflection points

1. Read the following article: G. Davidov and E. Eshet, 'Intermediate Approaches to Unfair Dismissal Protection' (2015) 44 *Industrial Law Journal* 167. In light of the arguments in this piece, would you devise a legal system which included a law protecting employees and workers against dismissals for arbitrary or unjust reasons?

2. Do you believe that the European concept of 'flexicurity' is achievable?

3. What does it mean to say that in the way the judiciary have approached the unfair dismissal legislation, the 'primary focus ha[s] shifted from the *substantive fairness* to the *procedural fairness* of an employee's dismissal'? Why do you think that the judiciary are more comfortable with reviewing the procedural fairness of a dismissal, rather than its substantive fairness?

4. What is your reaction to the statistics revealing that very few orders of reinstatement or re-engagement are made by an employment tribunal? Can you explain such reluctance on the part of the tribunals?

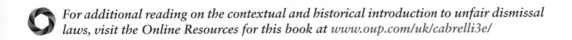 *For additional reading on the contextual and historical introduction to unfair dismissal laws, visit the Online Resources for this book at www.oup.com/uk/cabrelli3e/*

---

[45] See H. Collins and M. Freedland, 'Claim for Unfair Dismissal' (2001) 30 *Industrial Law Journal* 305, 306–7.   [46] [2001] IRLR 279.

[47] See Chapter 15, section 15.3.1.   [48] See Chapter 2, section 2.1.1.

[49] For example, *Western Excavating (ECC) Ltd v Sharp* [1978] QB 761, [1978] IRLR 27; *Buckland v Bournemouth University Higher Education Corp.* [2010] EWCA Civ 121, [2010] IRLR 445.

[50] In other situations, the judiciary have rejected the contention that any assistance can be derived from the common law of the contract of employment, e.g. see *Gisda Cyf v Barratt* [2010] UKSC 41.

16.2 EXAMINING THE ARCHITECTURE OF PART X OF THE ERA

The statutory unfair dismissal regime is now contained in Part X of the ERA and can be divided into a series of basic steps. The flow chart in Figure 16.1 is particularly useful.

The first step in the process involves the employee satisfying an employment tribunal that he/she is eligible to present a complaint of unfair dismissal. Certain essential criteria must be negotiated and the employee must not fall within an excluded category.

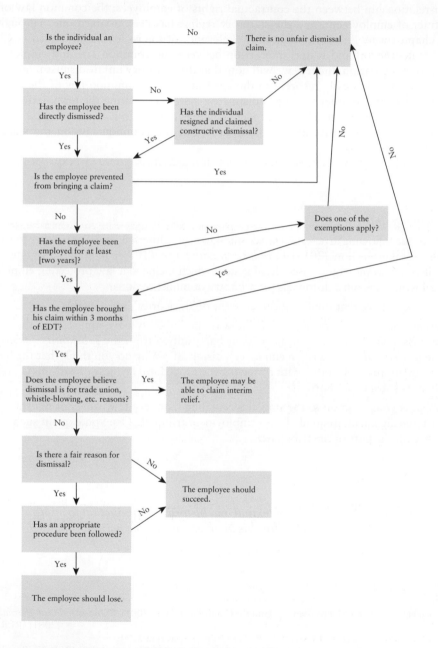

Figure 16.1 *Steps involved in a statutory unfair dismissal claim*

Source: A. Korn, D. Brown, J. Bowers, and S. Forshaw (eds), *Blackstone's Employment Law Practice*, 5th edition (Oxford, OUP, 2010) 445. By permission of Oxford University Press.

Secondly, the employee must also establish that he/she has been dismissed in terms of the definition set out in section 95(1) of the ERA. If the employee discharges that burden, the onus of proof passes to the employer to demonstrate that it had a valid reason for the dismissal of the employee in terms of section 98(1), (2), and (3) of the ERA. Alternatively, the employee may seek to prove that the reason for his/her dismissal was one of the many automatically unfair dismissals recognized by employment protection legislation. Finally, the 'reasonableness' of the dismissal is examined in light of the language of section 98(4) and the case law which interprets that subsection.

The absolute protection of an employee from unfair dismissal finds its expression in section 94 of the ERA. Interestingly, the protection is articulated as a right in favour of the employee in positive terms, rather than expressed as an obligation on the employer in negative terms:

Section 94 The right

(1) An employee has the right not to be unfairly dismissed by his employer.

Section 111 of the ERA prescribes how the unfair dismissal right is enforced:

Section 111 Complaints to employment tribunal

(1) A complaint may be presented to an employment tribunal against an employer by any person that he was unfairly dismissed by the employer.

Curiously, section 111 does not provide that a complaint 'must' be presented to an employment tribunal, but rather states that it 'may' be. This might suggest that some other body—such as the common law courts—also has jurisdiction to hear unfair dismissal claims. However, the obstacle confronting such an argument is that a common law court would insist that sufficient evidence be presented to satisfy it that a breach of the statutory right not to be unfairly dismissed also amounted to a breach of the common law of the contract of employment—and the general rule is that such an assertion is misconceived.[51] The implication is that an employee is not entitled to raise an action of unfair dismissal in the courts: the UK Parliament intended for unfair dismissal claims to be dealt with by specialist employment tribunals which are staffed by personnel experienced in the resolution of such disputes. These personnel act as an 'industrial jury'.[52]

16.2.1 Eligibility to claim

In order to be entitled to present a claim under section 111 of the ERA, an individual must satisfy certain basic criteria. The issue of eligibility to present a complaint of unfair dismissal can be analysed by dividing the discussion into (1) essential criteria which must be fulfilled and (2) excluded categories of individuals.

---

[51] *Doherty v British Midland Airways Ltd* [2006] IRLR 90, 94–5 at paras 25–27 per McMullen QC J, although it is not impossible, e.g. see *Greenhof v Barnsley Metropolitan Borough Council* [2006] IRLR 98.

[52] The notion of the 'industrial jury' goes back to the 1970s when the statutory unfair dismissal regime was first introduced. It encouraged the employment tribunal to apply its own understanding of the fairness and reasonableness of an employer's decision to dismiss an employee, e.g. *Priddle v Dibble* [1978] ICR 149, 152 per Bristow J. However, the salience of the 'industrial jury' concept has waned over the years, in terms of explaining how the law is, and ought to be, applied: see H. Collins and M. Freedland, 'Finding the Right Direction for the "Industrial Jury": *Hadden v Van den Bergh Foods Ltd/Midland Bank plc v Madden*' (2000) 29 *Industrial Law Journal* 288, 289–91.

16.2.1.1 Essential criteria

Certain factors must be satisfied before an individual providing personal services to an employing entity will be entitled to enforce his/her unfair dismissal rights against the employing entity. For example, section 94(1) of the ERA makes it clear that the individual must be an 'employee'. Therefore, the discussion of the binary divide between employees and self-employed independent contractors and the distinguishing common law criteria which we encountered in Chapter 3 assumes central importance here.[53] In addition, section 108(1) of the ERA directs that an employee must have been 'continuously employed for a period of not less than two years[54] ending with the effective date of termination'.[55] However, there is an exception from the two-year requirement: section 108(4) of the ERA directs that any employee who alleges that he/she has been dismissed on the basis of his/her political affiliation is not required to have a minimum of two years' continuous service in order to be eligible to claim unfair dismissal.[56]

The concept of 'continuous employment' is governed by sections 210–218 of the ERA and was analysed in detail in Chapter 3.[57] The definition of 'effective date of termination' is found in section 97 of the ERA.[58] Furthermore, in terms of section 111(2) of the ERA, the complaint must be presented before the end of the period of three months beginning with the effective date of termination of the employee, or some longer period which the tribunal considers reasonable where it is satisfied that it was not reasonably practicable for the complaint to be presented before the end of the three-month period.

16.2.1.2 Excluded categories

There are a number of categories of individual who are prevented from presenting a complaint of unfair dismissal to an employment tribunal in terms of statute. For example, section 10 of the Employment Tribunals Act 1996 stipulates that an employee who was dismissed for reasons of national security is excluded from unfair dismissal protection. Furthermore, employees who are governed by a dismissal procedures agreement entered into between an independent trade union and the employer which is designated by order of the Secretary of State as satisfying certain criteria will be excluded.[59] In terms of sections 199 and 200 of the ERA, the right not to be unfairly dismissed does not apply to share fishermen and police officers.[60] Finally, certain classes of employee are excluded from the right to make a complaint of unfair dismissal based on the geographical location where the work is being undertaken. Section 196 of the ERA, which provided as follows, was repealed by the UK Government in 1999:

> **Section 196 Employment outside Great Britain**
>
> (2) [The right to unfair dismissal protection] do[es] not apply to employment where under the employee's contract of employment he ordinarily works outside Great Britain.

---

[53] See Chapter 3, section 3.2.1. This classificatory exercise is but one example of the grip which the common law of the contract of employment has exerted over the statutory system.

[54] Prior to 6 April 2012, the period was one year.

[55] For trenchant criticism of this qualifying threshold, see K. Ewing and J. Hendy, 'Unfair Dismissal Law Changes: Unfair?' (2012) 41 *Industrial Law Journal* 115; H. Collins and V. Mantouvalou, '*Redfearn v UK*: Political Association and Dismissal' (2013) 76 *Modern Law Review* 909, 914–15.

[56] Section 108(4) of the ERA was introduced by the UK Government in response to the decision of the European Court of Human Rights in *Redfearn v UK* [2013] IRLR 51, on which, see H. Collins and V. Mantouvalou, '*Redfearn v UK*: Political Association and Dismissal' (2013) 76 *Modern Law Review* 909.

[57] See Chapter 3, section 3.2.2.   [58] See Chapter 16, section 16.2.3.

[59] Section 110 of the ERA. Such agreements are very rare.

[60] The latter is fairly self-explanatory, but the concept of 'share fisherman' requires further elucidation. A 'share fisherman' is essentially an employee crew member of a fishing vessel who is remunerated only by a share in the profits or gross earnings of the vessel.

The effect of the repeal of this statutory provision was to leave a gap in the legislation[61] and to dispense with a sophisticated body of case law which had been built up around it.[62] It was unclear whether the employee with some foreign element to his/her employment ought to demonstrate that he/she was employed in Great Britain at the point of his/her dismissal or whether some other criterion should be adopted.

The position was clarified by the leading decisions of the House of Lords and Supreme Court in the cases of *Lawson v Serco Ltd*,[63] *Duncombe v Secretary of State for Children, Schools and Families*,[64] and *Ravat v Halliburton Manufacturing & Services Ltd*.[65] In *Serco*, Lord Hoffman in the House of Lords divided employees generally into four separate camps. He held that unfair dismissal protection would apply to employees falling within the following four categories as a matter of statutory construction:

(1) The first category, which Lord Hoffmann referred to as 'the standard case: working in Great Britain' applied to workers ordinarily working in Great Britain who worked abroad from time to time as part of their employment duties. In such a situation, if the employee is working in Great Britain at the date of dismissal, he/she falls under the protective coverage of the statutory unfair dismissal regime.

(2) The second category concerned 'peripatetic employees', e.g. airline pilots, international salesmen, seafarers,[66] or international consultants.[67] Lord Hoffman stressed the importance of treating the base of a peripatetic employee at the date of dismissal as his/her place of employment, rather than where he/she actually was at the date of dismissal.

(3) The third grouping were referred to as 'expatriate employees', which covered employees posted abroad by a British employer for the purposes of a business carried on in Great Britain or operating within an extra-territorial British enclave in a foreign country. The former would include foreign correspondents working overseas for a British broadcaster or newspaper, or a UK citizen recruited in the UK to work for the British Council overseas.[68] Meanwhile, an employee working in a military base or the British embassy would fall within the latter 'enclave' category. It should be stressed, however, that the employee does not necessarily need to be posted abroad to be treated as an expatriate employee, since it will suffice if the employee is working abroad remotely for a British employer whose other staff work in Britain.[69] It will also be relevant that the peripatetic employee has structured his residential and tax affairs in a way that ensures he is not subject to the British tax regime.[70] Alternatively, it will be of no little import that the employee has notional UK income tax deducted from his salary, or has an entitlement to a UK civil service pension.[71]

---

[61] For the reasons behind the repeal, see U. Grusic, 'The Territorial Scope of Employment Legislation and Choice of Law' (2012) 75 *Modern Law Review* 722, 725; and L. Merrett, 'The Contract of Employment in its International and European Law Setting' in M. Freedland et al. (eds), *The Contract of Employment* (Oxford, OUP, 2016) 624–7.

[62] *Wilson v Maynard Shipping Consultant* [1977] IRLR 491; *Janata Bank v Ahmed* [1981] IRLR 457; and *Carver v Saudi Arabian Airlines* [1999] IRLR 370.   [63] [2006] IRLR 289.

[64] [2011] UKSC 36, [2011] ICR 1312.

[65] [2012] UKSC 1, [2012] ICR 389. For detailed commentary, see L. Merrett, 'New Approaches to Territoriality in Employment Law' (2015) 44 *Industrial Law Journal* 53.

[66] *Windstar Management Services Ltd v Harris* [2016] ICR 847.

[67] For a peripatetic seaman, see *Diggins v Condor Marine Crewing Services Ltd* [2010] IRLR 119; for a peripatetic flight attendant, see *Hunt v United Airlines Inc.* [2008] ICR 934.

[68] *Jeffery v British Council* [2016] IRLR 935.

[69] *Lodge v Dignity & Choice in Dying* [2015] IRLR 184.

[70] *Olsen v Gearbulk Services Ltd* [2015] IRLR 818.

[71] *Jeffery v British Council* [2016] IRLR 935.

(4) The fourth category was the exceptional case of other expatriate employees with 'equally strong connections with Great Britain and British employment law'. In *Duncombe*, the Supreme Court was of the view that expatriate teachers employed by the Secretary of State for Children, Schools and Families to work in European schools educating the children of EU officials and employees fell within this residual fourth category. However, Afghan interpreters engaged by the British Government to work exclusively in Afghanistan did not.[72] Where an employee seeks to persuade a tribunal or court that it has jurisdiction to hear a claim on the basis that he/she is an expatriate employee, it will not be open to him/her to justify this on the ground that a comparison of the local law with British unfair dismissal law tends to show that the former is weaker than the latter.[73]

The end result of the *Lawson* case is that it is insufficient for an employee simply to point to his/her British nationality or the fact that he/she works for a company or other organization registered or headquartered in Great Britain.

However, what was left unresolved by *Lawson* was whether Lord Hoffmann intended these four categories to be exhaustive. For example, in *YKK Europe Ltd v Heneghan*,[74] the EAT was of the view that Lord Hoffmann had established a closed classificatory list. However, this approach was rejected in *Ravat*[75] and in doing so the Supreme Court marginalized the prescriptive approach adopted by Lord Hoffmann. Lord Hope clarified that 'the starting point . . . is that the employment relationship must have a stronger connection with Great Britain than with the foreign country where the employee works . . . [and i]t will always be a question of fact and degree as to whether the connection is sufficiently strong to overcome the general rule that the place of employment is decisive'.[76] Lord Hope's formulation of the correct test is clearly much more open-textured and reduces Lord Hoffmann's four categories to factors which provide useful guidance. Although Lord Hope's 'stronger connection' test is broad and not always wholly straightforward to apply in practice, on the positive side it has the advantage of making it difficult for unscrupulous employers to arrange their affairs in a manner designed to circumvent the operation of the statutory unfair dismissal laws. One of the deficiencies of Lord Hoffmann's more detailed and precise test was that it could lead to deliberate evasion of statutory unfair dismissal laws by employers.

Another significant point was made in *Duncombe* and *Ravat*. Here, it was ruled that a clause in an employment contract which provides that English law governs any contractual disputes between the parties will be a relevant consideration in determining the territorial jurisdiction of the employment tribunal in the case of an unfair dismissal complaint.[77]

 For additional reading on eligibility to claim, visit the Online Resources for this book at www.oup.com/uk/cabrelli3e/

---

[72] *R (on the application of Hottak) v Secretary of State for Foreign and Commonwealth Affairs* [2015] IRLR 827.   [73] *Creditsights Ltd v Dhunna* [2014] IRLR 953.

[74] [2010] IRLR 563.   [75] *Ravat v Halliburton Manufacturing & Services Ltd* [2012] ICR 389.

[76] *ibid.*, 399E–400E per Lord Hope. Where an employee is dismissed and subjected to detriments because he made a public interest disclosure, i.e. he blew the whistle on his employer, the same sufficiently close connection test will apply: *Smania v Standard Chartered Bank* [2015] IRLR 271. The application of the sufficiently close connection test is a question of fact: *Olsen v Gearbulk Services Ltd* [2015] IRLR 818.

[77] For example, see *Jeffery v British Council* [2016] IRLR 935; and *Green v Sig Trading Ltd* (UKEAT/0282/16/DA, 24 May 2017).

16.2.2 **Definition of dismissal**

If an employee establishes that he/she is eligible to present a complaint of unfair dismissal to an employment tribunal under section 111 of the ERA, the focus of enquiry shifts to the concept of 'dismissal' under section 95 of the ERA. The burden lies on the employee to satisfy an employment tribunal that he/she has been dismissed and 'dismissal' is given a specific statutory definition for this purpose. At this stage in the process, the employer's reason or reasons for the dismissal are irrelevant, as is the question of the fairness or reasonableness of the employer in dismissing the employee.

Section 95 of the ERA provides as follows:

Section 95 Circumstances in which an employee is dismissed

(1) An employee is dismissed by his employer if (and, subject to subsection (2), only if)—

   (a) the contract under which he is employed is terminated by the employer (whether with or without notice),

   (b) he is employed under a limited-term contract and that contract terminates by virtue of the limiting event without being renewed under the same contract, or

   (c) the employee terminates the contract under which he is employed (with or without notice) in circumstances in which he is entitled to terminate it without notice by reason of the employer's conduct.

The first two limbs of section 95(1), i.e. 95(1)(a) and 95(1)(b), involve an outright act of termination by the employer, namely the situation where the employer takes the decision to 'sack' or 'fire' the employee. However, in contrast, the third limb, i.e. section 95(1)(c), refers to a particular type of resignation by an employee. The approaches adopted by the judiciary to the three forms of dismissal will be analysed against the backdrop of the various ways in which the contract of employment of an employee may be terminated. This will reveal the degree to which the concept of dismissal can be both under-inclusive and over-inclusive.

16.2.2.1 Termination of the contract of employment by the employer

Section 95(1)(a) of the ERA covers the situation where a contract of employment of indefinite duration is terminated by the employer. This will also include a summary dismissal where the employer responds to an employee's repudiatory breach of the contract of employment by terminating it immediately without notice by reason of the employee's gross misconduct.[78]

The law does not demand the observance of any specific formalities for the purposes of the termination of a contract of employment and so the means of communication are not crucial; instead, the focus is placed on the intention of the employer and how a reasonable employee would have treated or understood the employer's communication, i.e. was there an intention to terminate the contract and would a reasonable employee have appreciated that this was the employer's intention from the latter's writings, words, or conduct?[79] The dismissal must also be communicated, e.g. in writing, orally, or by conduct and the employee has to be aware of the communication and actions of the employer.[80]

---

[78] See section 140 of the ERA. A contrast can be drawn between summary dismissal and instant dismissal by the fact that, in the latter case, it is incumbent on the employer to make a payment to the employee in lieu of notice.   [79] *Tanner v DT Kean Ltd* [1978] IRLR 110, 111 per Phillips J.
[80] *Sandle v Adecco UK Ltd* [2016] IRLR 941.

This is a question of fact for the employment tribunal to adduce from the evidence, rather than a question of (a) law or (b) mixed fact and law.[81] Occasionally, it may be difficult for an employment tribunal to ascertain what an employer intended by certain remarks and whether they were of sufficient quality to amount to a 'dismissal' under section 95(1) (a) of the ERA. For example, if an employer says something vague to an employee such as 'your performance is not conducive to the future well-being of this company', it is not wholly obvious how an employment tribunal should interpret that statement.[82] Conversely, where the conduct of, or the words written or spoken by, the employer unambiguously communicate that an employee's contract has been terminated, is it always the case that the law will treat this as conclusive? Alternatively, does the law provide that an employment tribunal should nevertheless exercise a degree of caution? In *Chesham Shipping Ltd v Rowe*,[83] Phillips J stressed how critical it would be for an employment tribunal to assess the evidence with the question of the intention of the employer at the forefront of its mind.[84] There will be certain cases in which the words written or uttered bear no other meaning than one of dismissal when examined in light of the context. However, on occasion, notwithstanding that the writing or words expressed may seem to evince an unequivocal intention to dismiss, on closer inspection or analysis of the factual context and matrix it may become apparent that there was in fact no serious intention on the part of the employer to terminate the contract of employment, e.g. because the words were uttered in haste, jest, or anger. Here, the onus is on the employment tribunal to apply its objective powers of observation in order to ascertain the true position.

The courts have also held that a finding of dismissal under section 95(1)(a) of the ERA may be made where the employer alters the terms of the employee's contract of employment and the employee continues to work in accordance with the modifications imposed: this is the so-called 'rule in *Hogg v Dover College*',[85] which has been followed in a number of subsequent cases.[86] A degree of guidance was given by the EAT in the case of *Alcan Extrusions Ltd v Yates*[87] as to the extent to which the contract must have been modified to amount to a 'dismissal' for the purposes of section 95(1)(a) of the ERA:

■ *Alcan Extrusions v Yates* [1996] IRLR 327

Judge C Smith QC:

We entirely agree . . . that it is only where, on an objective construction of the relevant letters or other conduct on the part of an employer, it is plain that an employer must be taken to be saying, 'Your former contract has, from this moment, gone' or 'Your former contract is being wholly withdrawn from you' that there can be a dismissal under [section 95(1)(a) of the ERA] other than, of course, in simple cases of direct termination of the contract of employment by such words as 'You are sacked'. Otherwise, we agree [that] the case must stand or fall within [section 95(1)(c) of the ERA]. However, in our judgment, it does not follow from that that very substantial departures by an employer from the terms of an existing contract can only qualify as a potential dismissal under [section 95(1)(c) of the ERA]. In our judgment, the departure may, in a given case, be so substantial as to amount to the withdrawal of the whole contract. In our judgment . . . the learned judge in

---

[81] *Martin v Glynwed Distribution Ltd (t/a MBS Fastenings)* [1983] ICR 511, 521D per Sir Denys Buckley.

[82] A similar issue is whether an employee's words evince an intention to resign. For example, see *Secretary of State for Justice v Hibbert* (UKEAT/0289/13/GE, 30 July 2013); and *Ogilvie Construction Ltd v Brown* (UKEATS/0003/16/JW, 10 August 2016).   [83] [1977] IRLR 391.

[84] *ibid.*, 392.   [85] [1990] ICR 39.

[86] *Alcan Extrusions Ltd v Yates* [1996] IRLR 327; *Hardy v Tourism South East* [2005] IRLR 242.

[87] [1996] IRLR 327.

Hogg was quite correct in saying that whether a letter or letters or other conduct of an employer has such an effect is a matter of degree and, we would hold accordingly, a question of fact for the industrial tribunal to decide. We fully accept that in many cases to construe letters or other conduct on the part of an employer which puts forward no more than variations in a contract of employment as amounting to a termination or withdrawal of such a contract would be quite inappropriate and wrong. But in our judgment, counsel for the appellants was driven to the untenable position, as we believe it to be, that even very substantial departures from an original contract of employment could never amount, on an objective construction, to the termination of the original contract and its replacement by the offer of a different and inferior contract of employment but must always be characterised as breaches of the original contract. In our judgment, counsel for the respondents, Mr Bowers, was correct in submitting that whether or not the action of an employer in imposing radically different terms has the effect of withdrawing and thus terminating the original contract must ultimately be a matter of fact and degree for the industrial tribunal to decide, provided always they ask themselves the correct question, namely, was the old contract being withdrawn or removed from the employee? In our judgment, [the industrial tribunal] was entitled to conclude that the new terms were so radically different from the old as to pass beyond mere repudiatory variation of the old contract, so that they could properly be characterised as the removal of the old contract and the offer, by way of substitution, of a new and substantially inferior contract. In our judgment, that amounted to a finding of fact, which was correctly arrived at by the industrial tribunal on a correct application of the principle in *Hogg*. In our judgment, it is neither practicable nor appropriate to lay down any hard and fast rule as to when such conduct on the part of an employer will have such an effect and when it will not, provided that the principle is understood, namely that the conduct must amount to the withdrawal or removal of the old contract . . .'[88]

Alcan Extrusion forges a distinction between the situation where an employer makes a 'substantial departure' from the terms of an employee's existing contract and a variation of an existing contract of employment.[89] The former situation is treated as a termination of the employee's original contract and a re-engagement of the employee on the basis of a new contract of employment; it is not a variation of the original contract. Since section 95(1)(a) of the ERA proffers a definition of dismissal in terms of the termination of the contract of employment, rather than the employment relationship, this means that the employee is entitled to remain in position[90] whilst he/she makes a claim against the employer for unfair dismissal on the basis that he/she has been dismissed under section 95(1)(a) of the ERA.

In practice, the difficulty for an employment tribunal is how it ought to distinguish between a modification amounting to a variation of the original contract and one which is so radically different that the old contract is brought to an end with the employment relationship continuing on the basis of a new contractual engagement. For example, in the case of *Robinson v Tescom Corp.*,[91] the EAT ruled that an employer's decision to double the territorial sales remit of a sales manager was not sufficiently serious to amount to a withdrawal and termination of the contract of employment, but was rather a variation of the contract. The best that can be said is that this is a matter of fact and degree.

---

[88] Sourced from BAILII available at http://www.bailii.org/cgi-bin/markup.cgi?doc=/uk/cases/UKE-AT/1996/980_95_0502.html&query=alcan+and+extrusions&method=boolean (last visited 31 October 2017).

[89] See Chapter 7, section 7.2.2, for a discussion of the law of variation of the contract of employment.

[90] Of course, if the employee resigns in response to the employer's repudiatory breach of contract, this will amount to a constructive dismissal governed by section 95(1)(c) of the ERA.

[91] [2008] IRLR 408.

Reflection points

1. Do you think that it is right or fair that in circumstances such as those in *Hogg* and *Alcan Extrusion* an employee may be treated as having been dismissed even though he/she remains in the employment of his/her employer?

2. In the following extract, Lord Justice Elias puts the case in favour of the current law when he discusses the decision of the Court of Appeal in *Marriott v Oxford and District Co-operative Society (No. 2)* [1970] 1 QB 186 which was decided before *Hogg*[92] and *Alcan Extrusions*. Do you agree with Elias's argument or do you believe that it is stretching matters for the law to classify matters as a termination, rather than a variation of the original contract of employment, unjustifiably enabling the employee to 'have his cake and eat it'?

■ P. Elias, 'Unravelling the Concept of Dismissal—I' (1978) *Industrial Law Journal* 16, 20–1

> The logic of . . . [*Marriott v Oxford and District Co-operative Society (No. 2)* [1970] 1 QB 186] is that where an employer repudiates the contract, an employee can claim for unfair dismissal or redundancy even though he accepts the fresh terms of employment. As has been mentioned, this possibility stems from the fact that dismissal is defined in terms of the employment contract rather than the employment relationship. In principle, there is nothing unsatisfactory about this. After all, in circumstances such as arose in Marriott's case, the employee is entitled to redundancy compensation if he leaves and rejects the new terms offered, and a new employee will replace him on those terms. Should the redundant employee be precluded from receiving the compensation merely because he happens to be the person who accepts these new terms? There would appear to be no logical or, indeed, moral reason why he should . . .

We now turn to a separate issue. In Chapter 15, we examined the distinction between the 'automatic' and 'elective' theories of the termination of the contract of employment. We noted[93] that the elective theory applies, i.e. the general rule under the common law of the contract of employment is that a repudiated contract is not terminated unless and until the repudiation is accepted by the innocent party. The question is whether it is also appropriate to resort to this theory for the purposes of section 95(1)(a) of the ERA since it also refers to a termination of the contract of employment by the employer. If the 'elective' theory is applicable, it could lead to bizarre results where an employee commits a repudiatory breach of contract. Consider Hypothetical A.

Hypothetical A

Danny's Demolishers plc ('the Employer') has employed Steven Finch as an employee at one of its sales branches in Carlisle. Steven's wife is Iranian and the couple have agreed to travel to Iran for six weeks so that they can look after his mother-in-law. Steven ap-

---

[92] In *Hogg*, the EAT referred to *Marriott*, but the judgments of Lord Denning MR, Winn LJ, and Cross LJ in the Court of Appeal in the latter case do not appear to have been construed by the EAT to be in any way inconsistent with the view it subsequently reached. For an argument that *Hogg* and *Alcan Extrusions* are contrary to the decision in *Marriott* and other authorities, see R. White, 'Repudiatory Breach and the Definition of Dismissal' (1997) 26 *Industrial Law Journal* 252.   [93] See Chapter 15, section 15.2.4.

proaches the Employer for permission to request six weeks' unpaid leave. However, the Employer rejects this request. Nevertheless, Steven decides to go to Iran, where he stays for six weeks. While he is away, the Employer writes a letter to him and sends it to his residential address. The letter requests an explanation for Steven's absence and stipulates that a failure to respond within three weeks will be treated as a repudiatory breach of contract. The Employer receives no response from him within the three-week period and sends a letter to Steven intimating that it accepts his repudiatory breach of contract and that it is holding the contract of employment to be terminated. When Steven returns from Iran and reviews the correspondence, he claims that he has been dismissed under section 95(1)(a) of the ERA by the employer's second letter. He alleges that his dismissal was unfair.

On a straight application of the 'elective theory' of the termination of the contract of employment, the employer's second letter would be sufficient to terminate the contract of employment. Therefore, the employee would be dismissed by the employer under section 95(1)(a) of the ERA. However, there is an alternative analysis: that the employee's repudiatory breach of contract in travelling without the employer's permission is completely inconsistent with the continued existence of the contract of employment and that he effectively 'sacked himself', i.e. that his repudiatory conduct was such that he should be treated as having been 'self-dismissed'. The significance of this line of analysis is that section 95(1)(a) would not apply, thus shutting the employee off from access to the protection of the unfair dismissal regime. At one time, this appeared to be good law. For example, in *Gannon v J C Firth Ltd*[94] and *Kallinos v London Electric Wire*,[95] it was held that the employee's repudiatory breach was sufficient to automatically bring the contract to an end without the need for any subsequent acceptance by the employer. However, this line of reasoning was rejected by the Court of Appeal in *London Transport Executive v Clarke*.[96] The end result is that the notion of 'self-dismissal' has been rejected by the courts; instead, in a case such as Hypothetical A, there will be a dismissal by the second letter in terms of section 95(1)(a) of the ERA.

Let us now move on to consider another set of circumstances falling within section 95(1)(a) of the ERA. This is the idea of a 'forced resignation'. It is a form of resignation by the employee. As such, one would be forgiven for assuming that there had been no dismissal under section 95(1)(a) of the ERA on the ground that there had been no termination of the employment contract by the employer. However, where the evidence reveals that the employee's resignation has been obtained by undue pressure, deception, or pursuant to a threat or ultimatum, the courts and tribunals have shown themselves willing to stretch the compass of section 95(1)(a) of the ERA and apply a purposive interpretation to cover such a factual situation. Therefore, the judiciary will look to the reality of the situation and identify the chief orchestrator of the termination of the contract. If it was the employer, the employee will be taken to have been dismissed on the basis of a 'forced resignation', whereas the opposite conclusion will be reached if it was the employee:

■ *Martin v Glynwed Distribution Ltd (t/a MBS Fastenings)* [1983] ICR 511, 511–520A

[The headnote to the case sets forth the facts as follows:] The employee, a warehouse manager, was told by his employers that there would be an inquiry into an incident in which the employee had severely damaged the employers' mini-bus by driving it into three stationary cars. He was also told

---

[94] [1976] IRLR 415.   [95] [1980] IRLR 11.
[96] [1981] ICR 355. See also *Zulhayir v JJ Food Services Ltd* (UKEAT/0593/10/SM, 26 July 2011).

that the inquiry would probably result in his dismissal and that it would be in his best interests to resign. The employee did resign and, on his complaint of unfair dismissal, he alleged that he had been dismissed since the employers had given him no option but to resign. The industrial tribunal held that the employee had voluntarily terminated his employment and dismissed his complaint. On appeal, the appeal tribunal by a majority held that the industrial tribunal had erred in law in finding that the employee had not been dismissed.

Sir John Donaldson MR:

Whatever the respective actions of the employer and employee at the time when the contract of employment is terminated, at the end of the day the question always remains the same, 'Who *really* terminated the contract of employment?' If the answer is the employer, there was a dismissal within [section 95(1)(a) of the ERA]. If the answer is the employee, a further question may then arise, namely, 'Did he do so in circumstances such that he was entitled to do so without notice by reason of the employer's conduct?' If the answer is 'Yes', then the employer is nevertheless to be treated as if he had dismissed the employee, notwithstanding that it was the employee who terminated the contract.

The extract from *Martin* underscores the point that whether there has been a dismissal or resignation is a matter of fact and degree to be weighed up on the basis of the evidence.[97] For example, if we slightly amend the facts in *Martin* to those in *Haseltine Lake & Co. v Dowler*,[98] the outcome would be somewhat different. In *Haseltine Lake & Co.*, an employee with ten years' service was informed by his employer that he ought to look for another job and that his failure to do so would result in his eventual dismissal. No specific date for his dismissal was specified. The employee continued to work for his employer and, every now and again, the employer offered reminders that its expectation was that the employee would leave within a few months' time. The employee was offered another job with another company and approached the employer to ask if his failure to accept that job would result in his immediate dismissal. The employer responded by saying that he would not be instantly dismissed in such a situation, but that this did not mean that he would not be asked to leave in the near future. With that in mind, the employee gave notice of termination of his contract of employment and accepted the job offer which had been made to him. The relevant issue here was whether the threat of future dismissal was enough to convert what appeared to be an employee resignation into a dismissal by the employer under section 95(1)(a) of the ERA. Waterhouse J in the EAT reached the conclusion that the employer's actions were insufficient to demonstrate a breach or termination of the contract of employment. Instead, the contract of employment had been brought to an end by the employee in accordance with its terms and there were no grounds on which it could be said that the employer had committed a constructive termination through the medium of an anticipatory breach of the contract of employment. By simply expressing a desire or intention to terminate the contract in the future, the employer had not 'constructively' terminated it and so there was no 'dismissal' in terms of section 95(1)(a) of the ERA. Waterhouse J articulated the point in the following manner:[99]

---

[97] See also *Jones v Mid-Glamorgan County Council* [1997] IRLR 685, 687 at para 6 per Waite LJ; *Sandhu v Jan de Rijk Transport Ltd* [2007] IRLR 519, 524 at paras 44–5 per Wall LJ.

[98] [1981] ICR 222. *International Computers Ltd v Kennedy* [1981] IRLR 28 is a similar case.

[99] The EAT also ruled that the facts in *Haseltine Lake & Co.* would not give rise to a constructive dismissal under section 95(1)(c) of the ERA since the employer's conduct did not amount to a repudiatory breach of contract.

■ *Haseltine Lake & Co. v Dowler* [1981] ICR 222, 228–9

> In our judgment, there was no question here of an inevitable breach of contract on the basis of what the employers said and did. A contract of employment is not an agreement for perpetual servitude from which neither master nor servant can escape without committing a breach, and termination in accordance with the agreed terms does not itself constitute such a breach.

Now let us assume that the facts in *Haseltine Lake & Co.* were slightly different. What do you think that the legal position would be in the case of Hypothetical B?

Hypothetical B

Danny's Demolishers plc ('the Employer') is gradually losing patience with Amy Hunt, a junior employee working as a secretary in one of its offices located in Plymouth. One day in July, Ms Hunt leaves the office at 3:30pm, having failed to type a letter for her line manager, Dorothy, which had been clearly marked 'Urgent—Please Type and Pass to me for Approval by 5pm Today'. Dorothy is furious and consults the Employer's board of directors. They all agree that Amy 'will have to go'. The next morning, Dorothy summons Amy to a meeting at which she explains that the Employer has no option but to ask Amy to look for another job. Dorothy then hands Amy a letter serving written notice of the Employer's intention to terminate Amy's employment within one week of the date of the meeting. One day later, Amy serves a letter on the Employer which provides that Amy wishes to terminate the contract of employment with immediate effect. At the same time, she leaves her employment and, a few days later, she presents a complaint of unfair dismissal to an employment tribunal claiming that she has been dismissed in terms of section 95(1)(a) of the ERA.

In the situation in Hypothetical B, one might come to a number of views as to how the law might classify these events. First, one might conclude that the employer and the employee have terminated the contract of employment by mutual consent: in such a case, section 95(1)(a) does not apply.[100] Alternatively, one might posit that the employee's counter-notice was tantamount to a resignation. On the basis of both of these positions, the employer would not be treated as having terminated the contract of employment under section 95(1)(a) of the ERA, i.e. the employee would not be regarded as dismissed. However, whilst the common law of the termination of the contract of employment recognizes the proposition that a contract may be determined by the mutual agreement of the parties,[101] over a period of time it has evolved so that a palpable degree of scepticism has emerged regarding the utility of this notion where the employer has already served written notice of termination upon the employee. This cynicism is primarily attributable to a judicial recognition that the employee is vulnerable and would not usually volunteer, or willingly agree with the employer, to relinquish his/her valuable rights.[102] Moreover,

---

[100] *Khan v HGS Global Ltd* (UKEAT/0176/15/DM, 16 November 2015).

[101] *Marriott v Oxford and District Co-operative Society (No. 2)* [1970] 1 QB 186; *S W Strange Ltd v Mann* [1965] 1 All ER 1069.

[102] *McAlwane v Boughton Estates* [1973] 2 All ER 299; *Lees v Arthur Greaves Ltd* [1974] 2 All ER 393; and *Optare Group Ltd v TGWU* [2007] IRLR 931. However, cases such as *Lipton Ltd v Marlborough* [1979] IRLR 179; *Birch v University of Liverpool* [1985] IRLR 165; and *Scott v Coalite Fuels & Chemicals Ltd* [1988] IRLR 131 do not close the book on the potential for termination by mutual consent to arise.

this may also be one example of the common law evolving by analogy with the growth in statutory protection conferred upon employees,[103] since the reluctance of the common law courts to readily infer that an employee and employer have mutually brought the contract of employment to an end coincided with the introduction of what is now set out in section 95(2) in the early 1970s.[104]

Section 95 Circumstances in which an employee is dismissed

(2) An employee shall be taken to be dismissed by his employer for the purposes of this Part if—

    (a) the employer gives notice to the employee to terminate his contract of employment, and

    (b) at a time within the period of that notice the employee gives notice to the employer to terminate the contract of employment on a date earlier than the date on which the employer's notice is due to expire; and the reason for the dismissal is to be taken to be the reason for which the employer's notice is given.

Thus, section 95(2) of the ERA provides that an employee will have been dismissed by his/her employer where the employer serves notice of termination and the employee responds by serving a counter-notice for 'early termination' prior to the expiry of the period of notice stipulated in the employer's initial notice. Two points can be made in relation to section 95(2):

(1) for the purposes of the unfair dismissal regime, there is no requirement for the employee's counter-notice to be tendered in writing;[105] and

(2) the employee's counter-notice does not need to be of any particular length,[106] provided that it is tendered after the service of the employer's notice, but before the expiry of the prescribed period.

Nevertheless, one should note that if the length of notice served by the employee is less than the period stipulated in the contract of employment or the statutory minimum prescribed by section 86(2) of the ERA, whichever is the longer, he/she will be in breach of contract and liable to the employer in damages.

Reflection points

1. Do you think it is right that there is no minimum duration specified in section 95(2) for the employee's counter-notice? What are the implications of the absence of such a provision?

2. Why do you think the terms of sections 95(2) and 136(3) differ? Does the divergence make any logical sense?

---

[103] See Chapter 2, section 2.1.1.

[104] Section 23(3) of the Industrial Relations Act 1971. This provision directed that the employee was required to serve a counter-notice 'in writing'.

[105] This can be contrasted with section 136(3) of the ERA which does impose an obligation on the employee to serve the counter-notice in writing in order to establish a dismissal for the reason of redundancy in terms of section 139 of the ERA. This is necessary where the employee wishes to claim a statutory redundancy payment under section 135 of the ERA: see Chapter 18, section 18.2.3.

[106] *Ready Case Ltd v Jackson* [1981] IRLR 312.

16.2.2.2 Termination of a limited-term contract of employment by the employer

An employee will be dismissed pursuant to section 95(1)(b) of the ERA if 'he is employed under a limited-term contract and that contract terminates by virtue of the limiting event without being renewed under the same contract'. Now let us consider Hypothetical C in light of section 235 of the ERA.

Hypothetical C(1)

Danny's Demolishers plc ('the Employer') obtains a research and development grant from the Department for Business, Energy and Industrial Strategy ('BEIS') to fund a health and safety researcher's salary for two years. James Small is employed by the Employer on the basis of a two-year fixed-term contract to fill the post. Nine months into the job, James' contract of employment is terminated by the Employer. James claims that he has been dismissed under section 95(1)(b) of the ERA.

Hypothetical C(2)

The facts are the same as in Hypothetical C(1), subject to the following variations: first, the grant funds a health and safety researcher's salary on an open-ended basis; second, one of the conditions attached to the grant provides that it is the intention of BEIS that the grant will be terminated at some point in the future; and third, James Small is employed on the basis of a contract which states that it will come to an end once the health and safety research funded by BEIS is completed in full.

Hypothetical C(3)

The facts are the same as in Hypothetical C(2), subject to the following variation: James Small is employed on the basis of a contract which states that it will come to an end once BEIS decides to terminate the research grant.

Section 235 Other definitions

(2A) For the purposes of this Act a contract of employment is a 'limited-term contract' if—

  (a) the employment under the contract is not intended to be permanent, and

  (b) provision is accordingly made in the contract for it to terminate by virtue of a limiting event.

(2B) In this Act, 'limiting event', in relation to a contract of employment means—

  (a) in the case of a contract for a fixed-term, the expiry of the term,

  (b) in the case of a contract made in contemplation of the performance of a specific task, the performance of the task, and

  (c) in the case of a contract which provides for its termination on the occurrence of an event (or the failure of an event to occur), the occurrence of the event (or the failure of the event to occur).

It is submitted that the fixed-term contract in Hypothetical C(1), the 'purpose'/'task' contract in Hypothetical C(2),[107] and the contract which terminates on the determination of the research grant in Hypothetical C(3) each constitute a 'limited-term contract' under section 95(1)(b) since there is a 'limiting event' in all three cases under section 235(2B) (a), (b), and (c). Since those 'limited-term contracts' have been brought to an end by the employer in Hypothetical C(1), (2), and (3), the employee is dismissed for the purposes of section 95(1)(b) of the ERA. However, what do you think the legal position would be where a contract of employment directs that it is to endure for a specific period of time, but is terminable early by notice? Is this a fixed-term contract or limited-term contract notwithstanding the fact that either party may terminate early by notice? In the case of *BBC v Ioannou*,[108] Lord Denning MR in the Court of Appeal took the view that a contract which purports to be fixed-term or limited-term cannot be 'unfixed' by either party providing for early termination by notice; instead, to truly amount to a fixed-term or limited-term contract, the parties would have to be tied to the period set out in the agreement. This decision was controversial since it deprived employees of their statutory protection on the basis of what appeared to amount to a technicality. In *Dixon v BBC*,[109] the Court of Appeal reversed this aspect of its earlier decision in *BBC v Ioannou*. In *Dixon*, Lord Denning realized that his earlier opinion in *Ioannou* could lead to absurdity. Hence he held that the words 'a fixed term' or 'limited-term' must include fixed-term or limited-term contracts that are nonetheless determinable by notice within their terms. Therefore, the effect of this authority is that an employee in such circumstances would be able to establish that he/she had been 'dismissed' under section 95(1)(b).

Reflection points

1. If a contract of employment states that it will terminate on the occurrence of some event, is that a 'limited-term contract' under section 235 of the ERA, notwithstanding that the stipulated event never actually happens?

2. Imagine that a contract of employment provides that it is to endure for three years and either party has an option to terminate early after 18 months. Is the employment contract a 'limited-term contract' for the purposes of section 235 of the ERA? Does it make a difference that neither of the parties exercised the option to terminate early?

16.2.2.3 Termination of a contract of employment by the employee

Section 95(1)(c) of the ERA provides that an employee will have been dismissed for the purposes of the statutory unfair dismissal regime if 'the employee terminates the contract under which he is employed (with or without notice) in circumstances in which he is entitled to terminate it without notice by reason of the employer's conduct'. A 'dismissal' under section 95(1)(c) of the ERA is referred to as a 'constructive dismissal', since the employer has not actively terminated the employee's contract; instead, the employee treats the conduct of the employer as being so serious that it confers an entitlement to walk away from the contract of employment. As such, the actions of the employee resemble an express resignation of his/her post or a resignation by conduct (i.e. walking away from the job, never to return). Constructive dismissal can be usefully broken down into separate components and analysed in terms of the flow chart in Figure 16.2.

---

[107] Under the common law, where the 'task' is performed or the 'purpose' is fulfilled under a 'task contract' or 'purpose contract', those contracts are treated as having been discharged by performance, rather than terminated, e.g. see *Wiltshire County Council v NATFHE* [1980] ICR 455.

[108] [1975] IRLR 184.   [109] [1979] IRLR 114.

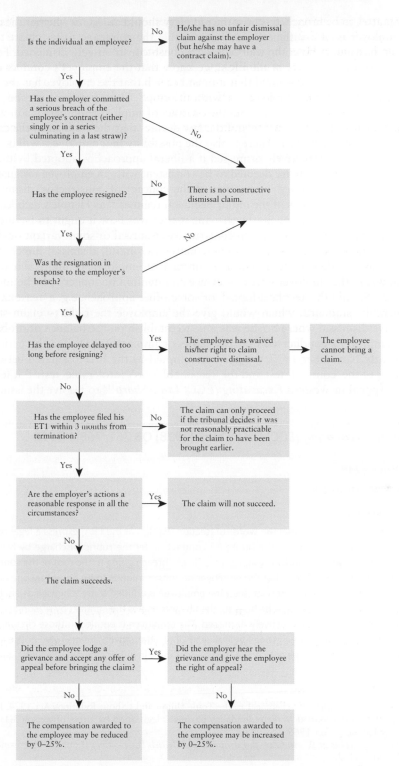

Figure 16.2 *Steps involved in a statutory constructive dismissal claim*

Source: **A. Korn, D. Brown, J. Bowers, and S. Forshaw (eds),** *Blackstone's Employment Law Practice,* **5th edition (Oxford, OUP, 2010) 439. By permission of Oxford University Press.**

The key matter to be broached is how the judiciary should ascertain whether the conduct of the employer is of a sufficient quality to enable the employee to terminate the contract of employment and claim that he/she has been constructively dismissed. From the wording of section 95(1)(c) of the ERA, we know that the employer's conduct must be serious, since it is explicitly stated that it must be such that the employee has the right to terminate the contract of employment 'without notice'. However, since section 95(1)(c) envisages that the employee terminates the contract of employment, there is a danger that he/she will be taken to have resigned if the law decides that the conduct of the employer must be of an extreme nature. There is also the possibility that employees will be deemed not to have been constructively dismissed if a liberal approach is adopted by the courts towards the factors which are deemed to be consistent with an employee resignation.

When the initial statutory incarnation of the concept of constructive dismissal was introduced for the purposes of the unfair dismissal regime,[110] as Hepple's recollections of the mid-1970s reveal, a particularly germane matter was how it ought to be interpreted and whether the common law test of constructive dismissal or some variant ought to be adopted.[111] The common law test of constructive (wrongful) dismissal directs that the employee has the right to terminate the contract of employment and claim wrongful dismissal where the employer's actions 'evince an intention no longer to be bound by the contract'.[112] Should this test be adopted, or some other approach, e.g. a 'reasonableness' or 'intolerable' standard, which would give the employee the right to claim statutory constructive dismissal where he/she was able to establish on the balance of probabilities that the employer's conduct was unreasonable or intolerable? During the period from 1974 to early November 1977, the position adopted by the EAT oscillated between the application of the 'contract' test and the 'reasonableness'/'intolerable' test.[113] It fell to the Court of Appeal in *Western Excavating (ECC) Ltd v Sharp*[114] to resolve the issue:

■ *Western Excavating (ECC) Ltd v Sharp* [1978] QB 761, 768H–772D

Lord Denning MR:

The rival tests are as follows.

The contract test

On the one hand, it is said that the words of [section 95(1)(c) of the ERA] express a legal concept which is already well settled in the books on contract under the rubric 'discharge by breach.' If the employer is guilty of conduct which is a significant breach going to the root of the contract of employment, or which shows that the employer no longer intends to be bound by one or more of the essential terms of the contract, then the employee is entitled to treat himself as discharged from any further performance. If he does so, then he terminates the contract by reason of the employer's conduct. He is constructively dismissed. The employee is entitled in those circumstances to leave at the instant without giving any notice at all or, alternatively, he may give notice and say he is leaving at the end of the notice. But the conduct must in either case be sufficiently serious to

---

[110] See paragraph 5(2)(c) of Schedule 1 to the Trade Union and Labour Relations Act 1974. It had existed since 1965 in the context of the redundancy payments legislation by virtue of section 3(1)(c) of the Redundancy Payments Act 1965.

[111] B. Hepple, *Rights at Work: Global, European and British Perspectives* (London, Thomson/Sweet & Maxwell, 2005) 51–2.

[112] *General Billposting Co. Ltd v Atkinson* [1909] AC 118, 122 per Lord Collins. This is a form of a common law wrongful dismissal.

[113] *Scott v Aveling Barford Ltd* [1978] 1 WLR 208; *Turner v London Transport Executive* [1977] ICR 952, 964 per Megaw LJ; and *Gilbert v Goldstone Ltd* [1977] ICR 36.

[114] [1978] QB 761, [1978] IRLR 27.

entitle him to leave at once. Moreover, he must make up his mind soon after the conduct of which he complains: for, if he continues for any length of time without leaving, he will lose his right to treat himself as discharged. He will be regarded as having elected to affirm the contract.

The unreasonableness test

On the other hand, it is said that the words of [section 95(1)(c) of the ERA] do not express any settled legal concept. They introduce a new concept into contracts of employment. It is that the employer must act reasonably in his treatment of his employees. If he conducts himself or his affairs so unreasonably that the employee cannot fairly be expected to put up with it any longer, the employee is justified in leaving. He can go, with or without giving notice, and claim compensation for unfair dismissal . . .

The result

In my opinion, the contract test is the right test. My reasons are as follows. (i) The statute itself draws a distinction between 'dismissal' in [section 95(1)(c) of the ERA] and 'unfairness' in [section 98(4) of the ERA]. If Parliament intended that same test to apply, it would have said so. (ii) 'Dismissal' in [section 95(1) of the ERA] goes back to 'dismissal' in the Redundancy Payments Act 1965. Its interpretation should not be influenced by [section 98(4) of the ERA] which was introduced first in 1971 in the Industrial Relations Act 1971. (iii) [Section 95(1)(c) of the ERA] uses words which have a legal connotation, especially the words 'entitled' and 'without notice.' If a non-legal connotation were intended, it would have added 'justified in leaving at once' or some such non-legal phrase. (iv) [Section 95(1)(a) and (c) of the ERA] deal with different situations. [Section 95(1)(a) of the ERA] deals with cases where the employer himself terminates the contract by dismissing the man with or without notice. That is, when the employer says to the man: 'You must go.' [Section 95(1)(c) of the ERA] deals with the cases where the employee himself terminates the contract by saying: 'I can't stand it any longer. I want my cards.' (v) The new test of 'unreasonable conduct' of the employer is too indefinite by far. It has led to acute difference of opinion between the members of tribunals. Often there are majority opinions. It has led to findings of 'constructive dismissal' on the most whimsical grounds. The Employment Appeal Tribunal tells us so. It is better to have the contract test of the common law. It is more certain: as it can well be understood by intelligent laymen under the direction of a legal chairman. (vi) I would adopt the reasoning of the considered judgment of the Employment Appeal Tribunal in *Wetherall (Bond St. W1) Ltd v. Lynn* [1978] I.C.R. 205, 211:

[']Parliament might well have said, in relation to whether the employer's conduct had been reasonable having regard to equity and the substantial merits of the case, but it neither laid down that special statutory criterion or any other. So, in our judgment, the answer can only be, entitled according to law, and it is to the law of contract that you have to look.[']

(vii) The test of unreasonableness gives no effect to the words 'without notice.' They impose a legal test which no test of 'unreasonableness' can do . . .

In this extract from *Western Excavating (ECC) Ltd*, the Court of Appeal harnessed the common law of the contract of employment in order to flesh out the concept of statutory constructive dismissal. Borrowing from the common law of constructive dismissal, the tribunals and courts subsequently adopted the approach that a fundamental breach of an express term, or a common law implied term, of the contract of employment by the employer would be considered sufficiently serious to constitute a constructive dismissal.[115] As such, it is not enough for an employee to point to a breach of an express term or common law implied term; rather, the employee must satisfy a court or tribunal

---

[115] M. Freedland, *The Personal Employment Contract* (Oxford, OUP, 2003) 155–6; L. Barmes, 'Common Law Implied Terms and Behavioural Standards at Work' (2007) 36 *Industrial Law Journal* 35, 37–8.

that the breach is serious enough to amount to a *repudiatory* breach of an express or implied term.[116]

Since a constructive dismissal will be established where there has been a repudiatory breach of contract on the part of the employer, as noted by Lord Justice Sedley in *Buckland v Bournemouth University Higher Education Corp.*,[117] orthodox contractual doctrines duly apply more generally. For example, employment tribunals must enquire whether there has been a repudiatory breach of contract on the part of the employer in accordance with an *objective*, as opposed to a *subjective*, test.[118] This compels the court to apply a standard of review that enables it to subrogate itself to an employer and freely apply its mind as to whether the employer's actions, conduct, or omissions were repudiatory in nature or not and to examine objectively the extent of the impact of that conduct on the employee.[119] Thus, it is evident that an objective measure of scrutiny enables a court and tribunal to substitute its own judgment for that of the employer, thus harnessing a more intensive appraisal of the employer's conduct.[120]

Another example of contractual orthodoxy being imported into the statutory notion of constructive dismissal was the adoption in *Buckland v Bournemouth University Higher Education Corp.*[121] of the rule that it is not possible for an employer in repudiatory breach of the contract of employment to cure or rectify that breach by his/her unilateral conduct.[122] Therefore, if the employer's conduct constitutes a repudiatory breach of contract, this is incapable of being expunged at the behest of the employer alone; instead, the elective approach applies. Hence the employee has an option to:

(1) accept the repudiation, walk away, and claim constructive dismissal under section 95(1)(c) of the ERA; or

(2) affirm the contract, whereupon the contract of employment continues.

Reflection point

Reconsider the cases of *Hogg v Dover College* [1990] ICR 39 and *Alcan Extrusions v Yates* [1996] IRLR 327, which we discussed earlier. Where an employer commits a repudiatory breach of contract and offers to re-engage the employee on different terms

---

[116] A breach of the implied term of the contract of employment which enjoins the employer to exercise reasonable care for the well-being of its employees will not necessarily be repudiatory: *Marshall Specialist Vehicles Ltd v Osborne* [2003] IRLR 672, 674 at para 9 per Burton J. However, this can be contrasted with a breach of the implied term of the contract of employment which enjoins an employer to pay an employee's wages where he/she is ready and willing to work. Such a breach will always amount to a repudiatory breach of contract where it is persistent, deliberate, or unexplained or where the employer unilaterally reduces the employee's salary or wage package: see *Cantor Fitzgerald International v Callaghan* [1999] ICR 639, 649E–G per Judge LJ and the *obiter* comment by Sedley LJ in *Buckland v Bournemouth University Higher Education Corp.* [2010] EWCA Civ 121, [2010] IRLR 445, 448 at para 28. Moreover, the tribunals and courts have ruled a number of times that a breach of the implied term of trust and confidence automatically amounts to a repudiatory breach which goes to the root of the contract—*Courtaulds Northern Textiles Ltd v Andrew* [1979] IRLR 84, 86 per Arnold J; *Woods v W. M. Car Services* [1981] ICR 666, 672 per Browne-Wilkinson J; and *Morrow v Safeway Stores* [2002] IRLR 9—forming one particular basis upon which an employee's claim that he/she had been statutorily constructively dismissed could succeed.   [117] [2010] EWCA Civ 121, [2010] IRLR 445.
[118] *ibid.*, 448 at paras 23–27. This was a point decided earlier in *Post Office v Roberts* [1980] IRLR 347. See also *The Leeds Dental Team Ltd v Rose* [2014] ICR 94.
[119] *Hilton v Shiner Ltd* [2001] IRLR 727.
[120] A particularly emphatic version of this formulation was articulated by Rix LJ in *Socimer International Bank Ltd (in liquidation) v Standard Bank London Ltd* [2008] 1 Lloyd's Rep 558, 577 at para 66, where he stated that, on the application of an objective standard, 'the decision maker becomes the court itself'.   [121] [2010] EWCA Civ 121, [2010] IRLR 445.
[122] *ibid.*, 449 at para 44. But contrast this decision with *Assamoi v Spirit Pub Co. (Services) Ltd* (UKEAT/0050/11/LA, 30 July 2012).

and conditions, do you think that it is satisfactory that an employee is entitled to pursue a complaint of unfair dismissal by claiming that he/she has been (a) dismissed under section 95(1)(a) of the ERA even though he/she remains in the employment of his/her employer albeit on the basis of a new contract of employment or (b) constructively dismissed under section 95(1)(c) of the ERA where he/she has resigned from his/her post with or without notice, having rejected the offer of the fresh contract? Alternatively, are you of the opinion that the employee should be deprived of such a choice, and if so, why?

Now let us consider the following Hypothetical D.

Hypothetical D

Archie Jones has worked for Danny's Demolishers plc ('the Employer') as a sales manager for three years. An expensive piece of drilling equipment goes missing from the Employer's Plymouth factory where Archie is based on a day-to-day basis. Without any investigation, the Employer accuses Archie's colleague and friend Mike Aldershot of stealing the equipment and Mike is interviewed by the police when the Employer calls them in. Archie is disillusioned with the Employer as a result of Mike's experience and approaches his line manager saying: 'The situation with Mike has made me sick with you lot—I've had enough of this place.' Archie walks out there and then and does not return to work. He does not hand in any written notice of resignation to the Employer or inform the Employer that he is quitting. He subsequently presents a complaint of unfair dismissal to an employment tribunal. He claims that he has been constructively dismissed under section 95(1)(c) of the ERA. The Employer's defence is that Archie has resigned.

Hypothetical D has been designed to highlight how the judiciary assess whether a contract of employment has been terminated by virtue of an employee resignation, rather than a constructive dismissal. It is not altogether clear that the conduct of the employer in Hypothetical D can be classified in any way as coming close to a repudiatory breach of the contract of employment. Applying the test set forth in *Western Excavating (ECC) Ltd v Sharp*,[123] it is submitted that an argument that the employer no longer intends to be bound by one or more of the essential terms of Archie's employment contract would be unsustainable. Therefore, the analysis would turn to whether Archie has resigned. On this point, perhaps surprisingly, the case law does not forge a presumption in favour of resignation. Although one encounters decisions such as *Sothern v Franks Charlesly & Co.*,[124] where it was held that the declaration 'I am resigning', 'I resign', or 'I am resigning now' by an employee were deemed unambiguously to evince a present intention to resign, one equally finds cases in the mould of *Sovereign House Security Services Ltd v Savage*,[125] where the Court of Appeal ruled that a pronouncement by an employee that he was 'jacking the job in' was sufficiently equivocal and effusive not to amount to a resignation.[126] The Court of Appeal in both *Sothern v Franks Charlesly & Co.* and

---

[123] [1978] QB 761.   [124] [1981] IRLR 278.   [125] [1989] IRLR 115.

[126] See also *Secretary of State for Justice v Hibbert* (UKEAT/0289/13/GE, 30 July 2013) and *Ogilvie Construction Ltd v Brown* (UKEATS/0003/16/JW, 10 August 2016). It is also possible for a resignation to be conditional, in which case a letter of conditional resignation will not bring the contract to an end: see *Heaven v Whitbread Group plc* (UKEAT/0084/10/JOJ, 8 April 2010).

Sovereign House Security Services Ltd v Savage cautioned tribunals against taking utterances by an employee at face value, particularly in situations where the statement was made in the heat of the moment, the employee displayed a degree of immaturity, or the employer had coerced the employee into making a particular statement. Therefore, the court will adopt a cautious approach towards finding that an employee has resigned.[127] However, this is not as surprising as one might think, since a liberal approach to resignation could easily lead to the undesirable result that employees would be unjustifiably deprived of unfair dismissal rights in marginal cases for the want of a 'dismissal'. Indeed, where it was alleged in *Sandhu v Jan de Rijk Transport Ltd*[128] that an employee had resigned in the same factual setting as his dismissal was discussed with his employer, it was held that there was in fact no resignation. The basis of the decision in *Sandhu* was that an employee's offer to resign will usually be a considered decision not taken lightly, often tendered after the employee has had the opportunity to take independent advice.

In *Western Excavating (ECC) Ltd v Sharp*, Lawton LJ made the following remark:

■ **Western Excavating (ECC) Ltd v Sharp [1978] QB 761, 768H–772D**

Lawton LJ:

I do not find it either necessary or advisable to express any opinion as to what principles of law operate to bring a contract of employment to an end by reason of an employer's conduct. Sensible persons have no difficulty in recognising such conduct when they hear about it . . . what is required for the application of this provision is a large measure of common sense.[129]

The key issue is whether there has been a repudiatory breach of an express or implied term or the employer has evinced an intention to no longer be bound by the contract's essential terms. It is irrelevant whether the employer intended to dismiss: what is important is whether the employer has by its conduct, objectively judged, repudiated the contract.[130] For a repudiatory breach to be established, it is sufficient that the employer's conduct played a part in the employee's resignation, i.e. it does not need to be the principal reason.[131] Examples in the case law of sufficiently serious conduct constitutive of constructive dismissal include:

- an employer's failure to investigate complaints of sexual assault[132] or harassment;[133]
- a failure on the part of the employer to deal adequately with an employee's complaints about exposure to cigarette smoke in the workplace,[134] or to provide and implement an independent/impartial procedure to (a) deal with an employee's grievances[135] or (b) allow an appeal from a grievance decision;[136]

---

[127] Furthermore, in ascertaining whether the employee has indeed resigned, the courts have stressed time and again that the facts of prior authorities will be of little value in deciding a case before them, e.g. *Jones v Mid-Glamorgan County Council* [1997] IRLR 685 and *Sandhu v Jan de Rijk Transport Ltd* [2007] IRLR 519.

[128] *Sandhu v Jan de Rijk Transport Ltd* [2007] IRLR 519, 523 at para 37 per Wall LJ.

[129] [1978] QB 761, 772D–773A.

[130] *Grewals (Mauritius) Ltd v Koo Seen Lin* [2016] IRLR 638. However, that is not to say that evidence of intention will not inform the objective assessment.

[131] *Nottinghamshire County Council v Meikle* [2005] ICR 1; *Wright v North Ayrshire Council* [2014] ICR 77.   [132] *Bracebridge Engineering v Darby* [1990] IRLR 3.

[133] *Reed v Stedman* [1999] IRLR 299.   [134] *Waltons & Morse v Dorrington* [1997] IRLR 488.

[135] *W A Goold (Pearmak) Ltd v McConnell* [1995] IRLR 516 and *Nicholson v Hazel House Nursing Home Ltd* (UKEAT/0241/15/LA, 12 May 2016).   [136] *Blackburn v Aldi Stores Ltd* [2013] IRLR 846.

- subjecting an employee to an unsubstantiated allegation of theft;[137]
- failing to provide an employee with suitable special eye protectors to perform his/her work;[138]
- an employer maintaining vehicles in an unroadworthy state in spite of numerous complaints by the employee,[139] or subjecting the employee to gross and abusive language[140] or unduly harsh and frozen working conditions;[141]
- an employer meting out a disproportionate sanction in response to an employee's behaviour;[142]
- an employer removing a key component of an employee's role[143] or job satisfaction,[144] suspending an employee,[145] or reducing an employee's salary,[146] status,[147] or benefits;[148]
- a breach of the employer's statutory duty to make reasonable adjustments for its disabled employees, which can amount to repudiatory conduct,[149] as can an employer's refusal of an employee's statutory request under section 80F of the ERA to return from maternity leave on a flexible and part-time working basis,[150] but not every failure of an employer to observe a statutory employment right will necessarily amount to a repudiatory breach;[151]
- where an employer gives an employee lawful notice of termination of the employment contract, i.e. asserts a contractual right or power, the general rule is that this will not constitute a repudiatory breach of contract,[152] but where the employer exercises that contractual right or power contrary to good faith or the implied term of mutual trust and confidence, there is ample authority to suggest that it will have committed a repudiatory breach;[153]
- where an isolated event or incident is not itself sufficiently serious to amount to a repudiatory breach of contract on the part of the employer, there may nevertheless be prior events or incidents which when taken cumulatively establish a course of conduct. A constructive dismissal may be held to arise as a result of the course of conduct, even though the final act or omission itself is not unreasonable or objectionable in law:[154]

---

[137] *Robinson v Crompton Parkinson* [1978] ICR 401; *Fyfe and McGrouther Ltd v Byrne* [1977] IRLR 29.

[138] *British Aircraft Corp. Ltd v Austin* [1978] IRLR 332.   [139] *Pagano v HGS* [1976] IRLR 9.

[140] *Isle of Wight Tourist Board v Coombes* [1976] IRLR 413; *Palmanor Ltd v Cedron* [1978] IRLR 303; *Ogilvie v Neyfor-Weir Ltd* [2003] All ER (D) 201 (October); and *Cantor Fitzgerald v Horkulak* [2003] IRLR 756.   [141] *Graham Oxley Tool Steels Ltd v Firth* [1980] IRLR 135.

[142] *Stanley Cole (Wainfleet) Ltd v Sheridan* [2003] IRLR 52.

[143] *Land Securities Trillium Ltd v Thornley* [2005] IRLR 765; *Brown v Merchant Ferries Ltd* [1998] IRLR 682; and *McBride v Falkirk Football & Athletic Club* [2012] IRLR 22. But cf. the demotion case of *Wells v Countrywide Estate Agents t/a Hetheringtons* (UKEAT/0201/15/BA, 11 February 2016).

[144] *Hilton v Shiner Ltd* [2001] IRLR 727.

[145] *Agoreyo v London Borough of Lambeth* [2017] EWHC 2019 (QB); *Yapp v Foreign and Commonwealth Office* [2015] IRLR 112.

[146] *Industrial Rubber Products v Gillon* [1977] IRLR 389; *Gillies v Richard Daniels & Co.* [1979] IRLR 457.

[147] For example, a demotion, on which see *Lewis v Motorworld Garages Ltd* [1985] IRLR 465.

[148] *French v Barclays Bank plc* [1998] IRLR 646.

[149] *Greenhof v Barnsley Metropolitan Borough Council* [2006] IRLR 98; *Ishaq v Royal Mail Group Ltd* [2017] IRLR 208.   [150] *Shaw v CCL Ltd* [2008] IRLR 284.

[151] *Doherty v British Midland Airways Ltd* [2006] IRLR 90; *Shaw v CCL Ltd* [2008] IRLR 284. Neither will a breach of 'discrimination law' on the part of the employer necessarily be determinative of the different question of whether the employer has committed a repudiatory breach of contract: *Amnesty International v Ahmed* [2009] IRLR 884.

[152] *Kerry Foods Ltd v Lynch* [2005] IRLR 680.

[153] *United Bank v Akhtar* [1989] IRLR 507; *Land Securities Trillium Ltd v Thornley* [2005] IRLR 765.

[154] *London Borough of Waltham Forest v Omilaju* [2005] IRLR 35; *Lewis v Motorworld Garages Ltd* [1985] IRLR 465.

the so-called 'last straw' doctrine. The 'final straw' does not itself need to amount to a breach of contract, but it must be an act in a series of earlier acts which cumulatively amount to a repudiatory breach. Moreover, the 'last straw' does not have to be of the same character as the earlier acts.

Once it is has been established that the employer has committed a repudiatory breach of contract, one must ask whether there is a requirement for the employee to do anything further, i.e. must he/she acknowledge the employer's breach in some way or does the contract of employment terminate automatically? In English law, as noted in Chapter 15,[155] the legal position is that the elective theory of termination applies for the purposes of a wrongful constructive dismissal at common law.[156] But what is the position in the context of the statutory notion of constructive dismissal under section 95(1)(c) of the ERA? Here, the common law of the contract of employment appears to have fed back into the statutory concept of constructive dismissal, since the elective theory of termination is also applicable. Therefore, there is a requirement that the repudiatory breach of contract is *accepted* by the employee. In addition, once the employee has accepted the repudiatory breach, he/she must walk away by terminating the contract:[157]

■ *WE Cox Toner (International) Ltd v Crook* [1981] ICR 823, 828E–829H

Browne-Wilkinson J:

[T]he general principles applicable to a repudiation of contract are as follows. If one party ('the guilty party') commits a repudiatory breach of the contract, the other party ('the innocent party') can choose one of two courses: he can affirm the contract and insist on its further performance or he can accept the repudiation, in which case the contract is at an end. The innocent party must at some stage elect between these two possible courses: if he once affirms the contract, his right to accept the repudiation is at an end. But he is not bound to elect within a reasonable or any other time. Mere delay by itself (unaccompanied by any express or implied affirmation of the contract) does not constitute affirmation of the contract; but if it is prolonged it may be evidence of an implied affirmation: *Allen v Robles* [1969] 1 WLR 1193. Affirmation of the contract can be implied. Thus, if the innocent party calls on the guilty party for further performance of the contract, he will normally be taken to have affirmed the contract since his conduct is only consistent with the continued existence of the contractual obligation. Moreover, if the innocent party himself does acts which are only consistent with the continued existence of the contract, such acts will normally show affirmation of the contract. However, if the innocent party further performs the contract to a limited extent but at the same time makes it clear that he is reserving his rights to accept the repudiation or is only continuing so as to allow the guilty party to remedy the breach, such further performance does not prejudice his right subsequently to accept the repudiation: *Farnworth Finance Facilities Ltd v Attryde* (1970) 1 WLR 1053 . . . An employee faced with a repudiation by his employer is in a very difficult position. If he goes to work the next day, he will himself be doing an act which, in one sense, is only consistent with the continued existence of the contract, he might be said to be affirming the contract. Certainly, when he accepts his next pay packet (ie, further performance of the contract by the guilty party) the risk of being held to affirm the contract is very great: see *Saunders v Paladin Coachworks Ltd* (1968) 3 ITR 51. Therefore, if the ordinary principles of contract law were to apply to a contract of employment, delay might be very serious, not in its own right but because any delay normally involves further performance of the contract by both parties. It is not the delay which may be fatal but what happens during the period of the delay: see

---

Bashir v Brillo Manufacturing Company [1979] IRLR 295 . . . to our mind . . . provided the employee makes clear his objection to what is being done, he is not to be taken to have affirmed the contract by continuing to work and draw pay for a limited period of time, even if his purpose is merely to enable him to find another job . . . It seems to us that the question whether or not the conduct of the innocent party amounts to an affirmation of the contract is a mixed question of fact and law . . .

This extract from *WE Cox Toner (International) Ltd v Crook* highlights some of the difficulties which arise in determining whether an employee has accepted a managerial repudiation of the contract of employment or affirmed the contract. In fact, the questions of acceptance and affirmation are interlocked: if the employee has accepted the repudiation, he/she has not affirmed the contract; if he/she has affirmed the contract, he/she has not accepted the repudiation—which suggests a dividing line or point in time where one gives way to the other. Nevertheless, an employment tribunal is not invariably required to ascertain the real point in time at which an employee has affirmed the contract or accepted a repudiation.[158] This is particularly relevant where the employee's delay is cited in support of the proposition that there has been an affirmation. In the case of *Simms v Sainsburys Supermarkets*, where the employer failed to make payments due to the employee, it was held that affirmation will be implied if there has been a sufficient delay on the part of the employee to formally repudiate after the employer has made its final decision to refuse to pay wages sufficiently clear.[159] However, the courts are wary of rushing to judgment that an employee's delay in accepting a repudiatory breach is evidence of affirmation, since the key issue is whether his/her conduct demonstrates an intention to continue with the employment contract.[160] For instance, where the employee is ill, draws sick pay, and delays in accepting the employer's repudiation, this will not invariably mean that he/she has affirmed the contract,[161] particularly if the employee is a long-serving employee,[162] or where he/she draws the sick pay for a restricted period of time whilst protesting the situation.[163] However, where the employee serves a period of notice of termination which is longer than the period prescribed by the employment contract, it has been held that this will constitute affirmation.[164]

The case of *Cook v MSHK Ltd*[165] serves to underscore the point that a decision to affirm the contract of employment is irrevocable.[166] If an employer is in repudiatory breach, but the employee continues to work and benefit from payment of wages or salary, this might entitle the employee to claim that he/she has been 'dismissed' for the purposes of section 95(1)(a).[167] However, it is not a constructive dismissal under section 95(1)(c). Where the employee is working under protest and makes this clear to the employer, this is tantamount to the employer reserving a right to accept the repudiation at a future point in time.[168] Nevertheless, the employee must make his/her choice whether to accept or affirm within a reasonable period and cannot work under protest indefinitely.

---

[158] *Simms v Sainsburys Supermarkets* [2005] All ER (D) 144 (March).

[159] See also *Hadji v St Luke's Plymouth* (UKEAT/0095/12/BA, 2 July 2013).

[160] *Chindove v Morrisons Supermarkets* (UKEAT/0201/13/BA, 26 March 2014). It will be uncommon for the employee to be in a position where he/she is held to have contributed to his/her constructive dismissal, since in such a case there will be no reasonable and proper cause for the employer's conduct: *Frith Accountants Ltd v Law* [2014] ICR 805.

[161] *El-Hoshi v Pizza Express Restaurants Ltd* [2004] All ER (D) 295 (June); *Bashir v Brillo Manufacturing Co. Ltd* [1979] IRLR 295.

[162] *Adjei-Frempong v Howard Frank Ltd* (UKEAT/0044/15/DM, 25 May 2015).

[163] *Colomar Mari v Reuters Ltd* (UKEAT/0539/13/MC, 30 January 2015).

[164] *Cockram v Air Products plc* [2014] ICR 1065.

[165] [2009] IRLR 838.   [166] *Cook v MSHK Ltd* [2009] IRLR 838, 847 at para 65 per Rimer LJ.

[167] See *Hogg v Dover College* [1970] 1 QB 186 and *Alcan Extrusions v Yates* [1996] IRLR 327, i.e. the employee would have to show that he/she was working on the basis of a fresh contract of employment.

[168] *Colomar Mari v Reuters Ltd* (UKEAT/0539/13/MC, 30 January 2015).

Another important issue is whether it is an absolute requirement for the employee to communicate the fact that he/she is walking away from the contract of employment in response to the employer's repudiatory breach. In the case of *Weathersfield Ltd v Sargent*,[169] it was held that there is no principle of law which behoves an employee to inform the employer at the time of termination of his reason for leaving employment; instead, the test is simply one of factual causation, i.e. was the employee's departure caused by the employer's conduct? Nevertheless, where the employee communicates no reason for leaving at the time of departure, the tribunal may more readily conclude that the repudiatory conduct was not the real reason for the employee leaving. This rule does not relieve the employee of the obligation to communicate in writing, verbally, or by conduct that he/she is terminating the contract of employment.[170] This is attributable to the wording of section 95(1)(c) of the ERA which enjoins the employee to terminate the contract with or without notice. Further, where the employee fails to communicate that he/she is resigning and there is more than one possible reason for that resignation, it is sufficient for the employee to establish that the employer's repudiatory breach played a part in his/her decision to resign: there is no requirement for him/her to show that the repudiatory breach was the principal reason.[171]

Finally, it is crucial to understand that a constructive dismissal is not automatically unfair under section 98(4) of the ERA. Consider the decision in *Savoia v Chiltern Herb Farms Ltd*,[172] where the employer modified the employee's job, which was clearly demonstrative of a repudiatory breach of contract on an objective assessment of the facts.[173] The evidence was that the employee had accepted the employer's repudiatory conduct in good time and so there was no suggestion of affirmation. Therefore, it was clear that the employee had been constructively dismissed in terms of section 95(1)(c) of the ERA. Nevertheless, there were reasonable grounds to assume that the employer had good reason for its repudiatory conduct and, therefore, there was the possibility that the employee's constructive dismissal might be held to be fair under section 98(4) of the ERA, e.g. by virtue of the employee's failure to co-operate:

■ *Savoia v Chiltern Herb Farms Ltd* [1982] IRLR 166, 167–8

Waller LJ:

If the statute had intended to exclude from consideration in s. [98(4) of the ERA] cases of constructive dismissal arising under s. [95(1)(c) of the ERA] it would have said so. Although it will be more difficult for an employer to say that a constructive dismissal was fair, nevertheless in my view there may well be circumstances where it is perfectly possible to do so. We were referred to a number of authorities of Employment Appeal Tribunals—two in Scotland and some five in England. I list them simply for the sake of completeness: *The Gaelic Oil Co Ltd v M C Hamilton* [1977] IRLR 27, *Logabax Ltd v R H Titherley* [1977] IRLR 97; *Industrial Rubber Products v C Gillon* [1977] IRLR 389 . . . In every single one of those cases, with the exception of the very first one which I mentioned, namely the *Gaelic Oil Co Ltd* [1977] IRLR 27 in which Lord McDonald thought afterwards that it had gone too far, the Employment Appeal Tribunal came to the same conclusion as that which I have already indicated, namely, that a constructive dismissal although more likely than not to be an unfair dismissal, may nevertheless, in certain circumstances, be a fair dismissal. In my judgment in this case the Industrial Tribunal were entitled to consider whether or not a constructive dismissal was unfair or not.

---

[169] [1999] IRLR 94.   [170] *Edwards v Surrey Police* [1999] IRLR 456.
[171] *Logan v Celyn House Ltd* (UKEAT/0069/12/JOJ, 19 July 2012).   [172] [1982] IRLR 166.
[173] *Buckland v Bournemouth University Higher Education Corp.* [2010] EWCA Civ 121, [2010] IRLR 445, 448 at para 28 per Sedley LJ.

Of course, as Waller LJ recognized, it will be a formidable challenge for an employer to convince a court or tribunal that its conduct in constructively dismissing an employee fell within the range of reasonable responses open to a reasonable employer and was fair under section 98(4).[174] This is particularly true in a case where the employer's primary argument (which it has lost) is that there was no constructive dismissal in terms of section 95(1)(c) of the ERA at all.[175] However, that is not to say that it is impossible, as exemplified by case law such as *Savoia, Industrial Rubber Products v Gillon*,[176] and *Logabax v R H Titherley*.[177] These are three cases in which the contention that a constructive dismissal would inevitably be automatically unfair under the then identical equivalent of section 98(4) of the ERA was expressly rejected.

 For additional reading on the definition of 'dismissal', visit the Online Resources for this book at www.oup.com/uk/cabrelli3e/

16.2.3 The effective date of termination

Once it has been established that section 95(1) of the ERA has been engaged and an employee has been dismissed, the focus of enquiry shifts to the date of termination, i.e. at what point in time will the statutory unfair dismissal regime treat the contract of employment as having come to an end? Here, section 97 of the ERA introduces the statutory construct known as the effective date of termination ('EDT').[178] Ascertaining when the effective date of termination has crystallized is important for two principal reasons:

(1) the employee must have been continuously employed for at least two years at the EDT in order to be eligible to raise an unfair dismissal claim;[179] and

(2) section 111(2) of the ERA directs that a complaint of unfair dismissal must be presented before the end of the period of three months beginning with the employee's EDT, so it is possible that it will be held that a complaint has been presented out of time, depending on the EDT.[180]

Section 97 Effective date of termination

(1) Subject to the following provisions of this section, in this Part 'the effective date of termination'—

(a) in relation to an employee whose contract of employment is terminated by notice, whether given by his employer or by the employee, means the date on which the notice expires,

---

[174] *Buckland v Bournemouth University Higher Education Corp.* [2010] IRLR 445, 450 at para 47 per Sedley LJ; *Burton, McEvoy & Webb v Curry* (UKEAT/0174/09/SM, 21 April 2010) at paras 14 and 18; and *Nationwide Building Society v Niblett* (UKEAT/0524/08/ZT EAT, 2 July 2009) at para 43.

[175] *Derby City Council v Marshall* [1979] IRLR 261, 263 at para 16 per Mr T. P. Rogers; P. Elias, B. Napier, and P. Wallington, *Labour Law: Cases and Materials* (London, Butterworths, 1980) 564.

[176] [1977] IRLR 389. *Industrial Rubber* disapproved of the decision in *Gaelic Oil Co. v Hamilton* [1977] IRLR 27 which had held that a constructive dismissal would invariably be automatically unfair under the then equivalent of section 98(4) of the ERA.   [177] [1977] IRLR 97.

[178] However, for the purposes of a statutory redundancy payment, the concept is known as the 'relevant date' in terms of section 145 of the ERA. To all intents and purposes, the criteria are the same.

[179] See section 108(1) of the ERA. Whether there was a sufficient period of continuous employment to claim unfair dismissal was the issue in *Stapp v Shaftesbury Society* [1982] IRLR 326, *Robert Cort & Son Ltd v Charman* [1981] ICR 816, and *M-Choice UK Ltd v Alders* (UKEAT/0227/11/DA, 10 August 2011).

[180] This was the issue in *Gisda Cyf v Barratt* [2010] UKSC 41; *Fitzgerald v University of Kent at Canterbury* [2004] ICR 737; *Palfrey v Transco plc* [2004] IRLR 916; and *Thompson v GEC Avionics Ltd* [1991] IRLR 488.

(b) in relation to an employee whose contract of employment is terminated without notice, means the date on which the termination takes effect, and

(c) in relation to an employee who is employed under a limited-term contract which terminates by virtue of the limiting event without being renewed under the same contract, means the date on which the termination takes effect.

Section 97(1)(a) does not cause too much difficulty, since where a letter or other communication dismisses an employee subject to a period of notice the EDT will arise when the stipulated period of notice has expired.[181] However, a point of some importance is how the courts should approach the situation where the employer serves a letter of dismissal without notice in terms of section 97(1)(b) of the ERA.[182] In this context, what is meant by 'the date on which the termination takes effect'? Is it the date on which:

- the employer does everything necessary to send the communication to the employee;

- the employee reads a letter sent or other communication despatched by the employer which intimates his/her summary dismissal without notice; or

- the employee had, or ought to have had, a reasonable opportunity of reading such letter or communication, i.e. when the communication could be expected in the normal course of things to have come to the employee's attention?

The common law of wrongful dismissal applies the general law of contract. As such, it treats the date of termination of the contract as the point in time at which the employer had done everything that could reasonably be required of it to communicate its decision to terminate the contract of employment.[183] However, in *Gisda Cyf v Barratt*,[184] the Supreme Court rejected the contractual approach for the purposes of section 97(1)(b). Lord Kerr in the Supreme Court ruled that the date of termination occurs once the employee has been informed and knows, or at least has had a reasonable chance of finding out, that he/she has been dismissed.[185] In *Gisda Cyf*, the Supreme Court forged a clear line of demarcation between principles relating to (1) the common law of the contract of employment and (2) statutorily prescribed employment rights.[186] The point was made that the latter represented a separate system for protecting employee interests and that a more employee-friendly interpretation towards section 97(1) of the ERA should be taken. As such, the EDT is at a later date/time than when the employer has done everything necessary to send the communication to the employee.

In light of *Gisda Cyf*, a question which arises is whether it ought to be possible for the parties to fix the EDT amongst themselves. In the case of *Fitzgerald v University of Kent at Canterbury*,[187] the Court of Appeal ruled that contractual autonomy did not extend to

---

[181] It has been held that where an employee is dismissed verbally or in writing by notice on day one, the notice will start to run the following day, i.e. day two, rather than day one, when it is sent, or when it is read: *Wang v University of Keele* [2011] ICR 1251. If the period of notice articulated in the notice is insufficient, i.e. it is less than (a) that expressly stipulated by the contract of employment, (b) the period which emerges from the application of the common law 'reasonable notice' rule, or (c) the minimum statutory period of notice set out in section 86 of the ERA, the EDT nevertheless will be fixed at the date when the insufficient notice expired, rather than when it ought to have expired under (a), (b), or (c).

[182] For an interesting decision in which section 97(1)(b) of the ERA was held to be applicable, see *Hawes & Curtis Ltd v Arfan* [2012] ICR 1244.

[183] *The Brimnes, Tenax Steamship Co. Ltd v Brimnes (owners)* [1975] QB 929.

[184] [2010] UKSC 41, [2010] ICR 1475.   [185] *ibid.*, 1487A–F.

[186] See the discussion in Chapter 2, section 2.1.1. However, cf. the common law position subsequent to the decision of the Court of Appeal in *Newcastle upon Tyne NHS Foundation Trust v Haywood* [2018] UKSC 22, on which, see Chapter 15, section 15.2.1.   [187] [2004] ICR 737.

permitting the parties to agree the EDT. Like Lord Kerr in *Gisda Cyf*, Sedley LJ was keen to underscore the distinctive nature of the statutory unfair dismissal regime. Therefore, contracting out of the statutory EDT is impermissible and will be treated as a violation of section 203(1) of the ERA.[188] As noted by Pugsey HHJ in the EAT in *Heaven v Whitbread Group plc*,[189] all 'depends on what has happened between the parties and not on what they may agree to treat as having happened'.[190]

However, what is the position if the employee and the employer vary the notice of termination on which the EDT is based? In the case of *Palfrey v Transco plc*,[191] the EAT ruled that the notice that determines the EDT can be varied. Hence a distinction must be drawn between the EDT and the notice on which the EDT is based. In *Palfrey*, an employee who was under notice of dismissal requested that the date of termination ought to be brought forward and the employer acceded to this request. This was held to represent a withdrawal of the original notice of dismissal and the substitution, by way of a fresh notice, of a shorter period. Therefore, there was a direct impact on the EDT, which was also brought forward, as was the point in time at which the three-month time limit for presenting an unfair dismissal complaint began to run.

Turning to the EDT in the case of a constructive dismissal under section 95(1)(c) of the ERA, section 97 is strangely silent. However, *BMK Ltd v Logue*[192] is authority for the proposition that a constructive dismissal comes within the coverage of section 97(1)(b) of the ERA. It also held that there was no universally applicable rule that the EDT in a constructive dismissal case will be the date on which the employee's acceptance of the employer's repudiatory conduct took effect, i.e. the date on which the employee walks away from the contract of employment.[193]

Finally, where an internal appeal overturns a decision to summarily dismiss an employee for the reason of gross misconduct, but the employee is dismissed anyway on the basis of a payment in lieu of notice, this will have no effect on the EDT, which will remain the same.[194] It will be classified as a section 97(1)(b), rather than a section 97(1)(a) case, in such circumstances.

16.2.4 The reason for the dismissal

Once the EDT has been identified, the onus lies on the employer to identify its reason or reasons for the dismissal of the employee. The employer's reason must be one of the five potentially valid reasons that are recognized by section 98 of the ERA.[195] The ERA and other employment protection legislation sets out a number of reasons for dismissal which are treated as automatically unfair. These three issues will now be considered in turn, i.e. how the courts approach the task of determining:

(1) the real reason for the employer's dismissal;

(2) whether the reason of the employer is one of the automatically unfair reasons for dismissal delimited in employment protection legislation; and

---

[188] Section 203(1) of the ERA directs that any provision in an agreement (whether a contract of employment or not) is void insofar as it purports to exclude or limit the operation of any provision of the ERA or to preclude a person from bringing any proceedings under the ERA before an employment tribunal. See Chapter 2, section 2.1.1, for a broader discussion.

[189] (UKEAT/0084/10/JOJ, 8 April 2010).   [190] *ibid.*, para 8.

[191] [2004] IRLR 916. Contrast this decision with *Wedgewood v Minstergate Hull Ltd* (UKEAT/0137/10/DA, 13 July 2010).   [192] [1993] ICR 601.

[193] For example, see the decision in *G. W. Stephens & Son v Fish* [1989] ICR 324 where it was held that the EDT was the employee's acceptance of the employer's repudiation where that acceptance was in fact three months after the date of the employer's repudiation.

[194] *Rabess v London Fire and Emergency Planning Authority* [2017] IRLR 147.

[195] Section 98(1) of the ERA; *Maund v Penwith District Council* [1984] IRLR 24.

(3) whether the employer's reason is one of the five potentially fair reasons for dismissal set out in section 98 of the ERA.

16.2.4.1 Ascertaining the employer's reason

Section 98(1)(a) of the ERA provides that the employer must have at least one reason for the dismissal of an employee.[196] An initial question is how one should approach the task of identifying the reason or principal reason (if more than one) for the dismissal of an employee, i.e. is it a question of fact or law?

■ *Wilson v Post Office* **[2000] EWCA Civ 3036, paras 21 and 30**

> *Buxton LJ:*
>
> . . . In the light of what was said in *Abernethy* [*v Mott, Hay & Anderson* [1974] ICR 323], it is in my judgment a question of legal analysis to determine under which part of s[ection] 98 [of the ERA] the reason in fact given by the employer falls. Here the tribunal erred in assuming, simply on the basis of one sentence in the notice of appearance, that this was a case of capability . . . the error in this case was an error of law. It was an error of characterisation, an error of thinking that because the word 'capability' had been used in the proceedings, the case had to be characterised under s[ection] 98(2)(a) [of the ERA]: when in fact, as the Employment Appeal Tribunal rightly found, as a matter of legal identity it fell under s[ection] 98(1)(b) [of the ERA].[197]

Although it is clear from this extract that the identification of the reason for the dismissal is a matter of legal analysis for the employment tribunal[198] and that a mis-characterization of the reason is an error of law, the question arises as to what standard of review the court or tribunal should apply to the employer's state of mind. The ERA does not directly address the point, but the authorities are clear that the tribunal and the court must look to discover what it was that *subjectively* motivated the employer; it is irrelevant that the subjective belief of the employer was in fact incorrect.[199] This results in a somewhat lax approach since it is straightforward for an employer to satisfy the standard of review. This is significant as it may be that an employer has labelled the dismissal as a redundancy, i.e. for economic reasons owing to a downturn in business, when in fact the dismissal was motivated by a desire to discharge a particularly difficult or incompetent employee. In such a case, the question arises as to whether the employer should be penalized for officially attributing a wrong reason for the dismissal. Interestingly, the Court of Appeal has held that the employer's defective categorization of the reason for the dismissal will not necessarily be fatal[200] to the employer:

---

[196] See also section 107 of the ERA which provides that, in ascertaining an employer's reason or principal reason for an employee's dismissal, no account must be taken of any pressure placed on the employer to dismiss the employee where the employee has been engaged in industrial action.

[197] Sourced from BAILII available at http://www.bailii.org/cgi-bin/markup.cgi?doc=/ew/cases/EWCA/Civ/2000/3036.html&query=Wilson+and+v+and+Post+and+Office&method=boolean (last visited 29 October 2017).

[198] In its judgment, the employment tribunal not only must set out the facts that it finds to have been proved in relation to the identification of the reason for the dismissal but must also give an explanation as to why it concludes that a potentially fair reason has or has not been established: *Elliott v University Computing Co.* [1977] ICR 148, 152 per Phillips J.

[199] *Ford v Libra Fair Trades Ltd* [2008] All ER (D) 106.

[200] See also *Hannan v TNT-IPEC (UK) Ltd* [1986] IRLR 165; *Screene v Seatwave Ltd* (UKEAT/0020/11/RN, 26 May 2011).

■ *Abernethy v Mott, Hay & Anderson* [1974] ICR 323, 323–331C

[The headnote to the case sets forth the facts as follows:] From 1950 the [employee], a well qualified civil engineer, was employed by the [employer] on large scale projects and from 1964 worked from their head office. At the end of 1971 the employer suggested that the [employee] be seconded to the Greater London Council on a project which involved working and living on the site. He declined the offer, saying that he preferred to work from head office. On February 25, 1972, the employer gave him notice to terminate his employment on March 31 on the ground of 'redundancy.' They offered him [a] redundancy payment of £850 and a further ex gratia payment of £750. He declined those payments and began proceedings for compensation for unfair dismissal under the Industrial Relations Act 1971 . . . [The Court of Appeal ruled that though the employer had erred in law in telling the employee that his dismissal was by reason of redundancy, the wrong legal label did not matter so long as there was a set of facts which the tribunal could find was the principal reason for the dismissal.]

Cairns LJ:

A reason for the dismissal of an employee is a set of facts known to the employer, or it may be of beliefs held by him, which cause him to dismiss the employee. If at the time of his dismissal the employer gives a reason for it, that is no doubt evidence, at any rate as against him, as to the real reason, but it does not necessarily constitute the real reason. He may knowingly give a reason different from the real reason out of kindness or because he might have difficulty in proving the facts that actually led him to dismiss; or he may describe his reasons wrongly through some mistake of language or of law. In particular in these days, when the word 'redundancy' has a specific statutory meaning, it is very easy for an employer to think that the facts which have led him to dismiss constitute a redundancy situation whereas in law they do not; and in my opinion the industrial tribunal was entitled to take the view that that was what happened here: the employers honestly thought that the facts constituted redundancy, but in law they did not. So the reason for the dismissal was not redundancy but something else. The tribunal found that the principal reason for the dismissal related to the capability of the applicant for work of the kind which he was employed to do . . . Now, the only work which the [employee] at the material time was willing to do was work at head office. That was work of one of the kinds which the [employee] was employed to do; and the reason why he was not given such work was because of the limitation of his capabilities. Those circumstances, according to the finding of the tribunal, constituted the principal reason for his dismissal, and in my opinion it is impossible to say that that reason did not relate to his capability for work of the kind which he was employed to do.

Therefore, in *Abernethy*, it was emphasized that a reason for dismissal is a set of facts known to the employer, or a set of beliefs which it holds, which cause it to dismiss the employee. As such, it is a subjective test.[201] The reasoning of the Court of Appeal in *Abernethy* is consistent with the approach of the House of Lords in *W Devis & Sons Ltd v Atkins*.[202] In *Atkins*, the House of Lords ruled that it was not competent for an employer to rely on reasons for dismissal of which it had no knowledge at the date of dismissal;[203] instead, the date of dismissal is the point in time on which the focus of enquiry should be locked.

---

[201] However, the subjective test, which operates effectively in general, is tested where the matter at issue is whether the employer's reason for the dismissal is one of the automatically unfair reasons for dismissal, on which see *Beatt v Croydon Health Services NHS Trust* [2017] IRLR 748 and section 16.2.4.2.
[202] [1977] AC 931.
[203] This is in stark contrast to the common law position: *Boston Deep Sea Fishing & Ice Co. v Ansell* (1888) 39 Ch D 399.

16.2.4.2 Reasons for dismissal which lead to a finding of automatic unfairness

Since the coming into force of the statutory unfair dismissal regime, the legislature has prescribed a series of instances in which an employee will be taken to have been automatically unfairly dismissed. If an employee is able to establish that the reason or principal reason for his/her dismissal was attributable to one in a carefully prescribed series of factors, there is no requirement for the employee to proceed to establish that the dismissal was fair/unfair or reasonable/unreasonable in terms of section 98(4) of the ERA. To that extent, these categories of protection in Table 16.1 have been formulated by the UK Parliament in a manner which deliberately sets themselves apart from the standard statutory unfair dismissal regime.

Table 16.1 *Non-exhaustive list of automatically unfair reasons for dismissal*

(1)   The employee is dismissed for a reason connected with pregnancy, childbirth, or maternity,[1] antenatal leave, paternity leave, adoption leave, and for taking time off to care for dependents under section 57A of the ERA—section 99 of the ERA and regulation 20 of the Maternity and Parental Leave Regulations 1999[2]

(2)   The employee is dismissed on the basis that he/she was a member of a trade union or was not a member of a trade union, or for the reason that he/she was engaged in participating in trade union activities—section 152 of the Trade Union and Labour Relations (Consolidation) Act 1992 ('TULRCA')[3]

(3)   The employee is dismissed for failing to forgo a right under the Working Time Regulations 1998,[4] or for failing to comply with a requirement which the employer imposed (or proposed to impose) in contravention of the employee's rights under the Working Time Regulations 1998, e.g. a breach of the 48-hour working week—section 101A of the ERA[5]

(4)   The employee is dismissed for performing any function or functions as a trustee of a relevant occupational pension scheme relating to his employment—section 102 of the ERA

(5)   The reason for the employee's dismissal is that he/she was a shop worker or betting worker who had been continuously employed since 1995 and had refused to work on Sundays—section 101 of the ERA

(6)   The employee is dismissed for the sole or principal reason of a transfer of an undertaking in terms of the Transfer of Undertakings (Protection of Employment) Regulations 2006[6] ('TUPE') and the transfer is not an economic, technical, or organisational reason entailing a change in the transferor's or transferee's workforce—regulation 7 of TUPE

(7)   The reason for the dismissal was that the employee participated in protected industrial action in terms of section 219 of TULRCA either during the first 12 weeks of that action or, if the employee has stopped taking part in industrial action, after this period—section 238A of TULRCA

(8)   The employee is dismissed for one of a prescribed series of health and safety-related reasons in terms of section 100 of the ERA

(9)   The employee is dismissed for having been involved or refusing to get involved in an application for the recognition of a trade union—paragraph 161 of Schedule A1 to TULRCA

(10)   The employee is dismissed for having exercised his/her rights to request flexible working under sections 80F or 80H of the ERA—section 104C of the ERA

(11)   The dismissal of the employee is related to the fact that he/she features on a blacklist in terms of regulation 3 of the Employment Relations Act 1999 (Blacklists) Regulations 2010 ('ERB') and either the employer has contravened regulation 3 of the ERB in relation to that prohibited list, or the employer relies on information supplied by a person who contravenes that regulation

in relation to that list, and knows or ought reasonably to know that the information relied on is supplied in contravention of that regulation—section 104F of the ERA

(12) The employee is dismissed for having exercised his/her rights in relation to study or training leave from work under sections 63D, 63F or 63I of the ERA—section 104E of the ERA

(13) The employee is dismissed for the reason that he/she was performing his/her role as an employee representative for the purposes of the information and consultation requirements in the context of collective redundancies or transfers of an undertaking under Chapter II of Part IV of TULRCA or regulations 9, 13 and 15 of TUPE, or where the employee was dismissed for seeking election as an employee representative—section 103 of the ERA

(14) The employee is dismissed for making a protected disclosure in terms of the Public Interest Disclosure Act 1998, i.e. he/she has acted as a 'whistleblower'—section 103A of the ERA[7]

(15) The employee is dismissed for taking action to enforce his/her right or the rights of others to be paid the national minimum wage in terms of the National Minimum Wage Act 1998, irrespective of whether the employee had that right or whether it was infringed—section 104A of the ERA

(16) The dismissal of the employee was attributable to the fact that he/she accompanied a colleague at a disciplinary or grievance hearing or was accompanied by a colleague at such a hearing—section 12 of the Employment Relations Act 1999

(17) The employee was dismissed for taking action to enforce his/her right or the right of others to receive tax credits in terms of the Tax Credits Act 2002, irrespective of whether the employee had that right or whether it was infringed—section 104B of the ERA

(18) The employee's dismissal was attributable to his/her participation in activities relating to the European works councils under the Transnational Information and Consultation of Employees Regulations 1999[8] ('TICE') or information and consultation bodies under the Information and Consultation of Employees Regulations 2004[9] ('I&C Regs')—regulation 28 of TICE and regulation 30 of the I&C Regs

(19) The reason for the dismissal was that the employee sought to enforce his/her rights under the Part-Time Workers (Prevention of Less Favourable Treatment) Regulations 2000[10] ('PTWR') or the Fixed-term Employees (Prevention of Less Favourable Treatment) Regulations 2002[11] ('FTER')—regulation 7 of the PTWR and regulation 6 of the FTER

(20) The employee is dismissed for (a) bringing proceedings against the employer to enforce one of the following statutory rights or (b) alleging that the employer had infringed one of the following statutory rights:

(a) any right conferred by the ERA for which the remedy for its infringement is by way of the presentation of a complaint or reference to an employment tribunal;

(b) the right to receive a statutory minimum period of notice in terms of section 86 of the ERA;

(c) various rights in sections 68, 86, 145A, 145B, 146, 168, 168A, 169 and 170 of TULRCA which relate to deductions from pay, trade union activities and time off;

(d) the rights conferred on employees by the Working Time Regulations and related provisions;

(e) the rights conferred on the employee by virtue of TUPE[12]

(21) The employee is dismissed for the reason that he/she has been convicted of a criminal offence, but that conviction is spent under the Rehabilitation of Offenders Act 1974—section 4(3)(b) of the Rehabilitation of Offenders Act 1974

(22) The employee is dismissed for having been summoned to undertake jury service, or because he/she was absent from work on that ground—section 98B of the ERA

(23) The employee is dismissed for having refused to accept an offer by the employer for the employee to become an employee shareholder within the meaning of section 205A of the ERA—section 104G of the ERA

Notes
1. See *SG Petch Ltd v English-Stewart* (UKEAT/0213/12/JOJ, 31 October 2012).
2. SI 1999/3312.
3. See *Metrolink Ratpdev Ltd v Morris* (UKEAT/0113/16/RN, 15 December 2016).
4. SI 1998/1833.
5. Where an employee was dismissed for falling asleep on the job, this was not automatically unfair on the basis that the dismissal contravened his rights under the Working Time Regulations 1998: *Ajayi v Aitch Care Homes (London) Ltd* [2012] ICR D22.
6. SI 2006/246.
7. See *Beatt v Croydon Health Services NHS Trust* [2017] IRLR 748; *Eiger Securities LLP v Korshunova* [2017] IRLR 115; *Chesterton Global Ltd v Nurmohamed* [2017] IRLR 837; and *Royal Mail Group Ltd v Jhuti* [2018] IRLR 251.
8. SI 1999/3323.
9. SI 2004/3426.
10. SI 2000/1551.
11. SI 2002/2034.
12. Section 104 of the ERA.

Importantly, where a complaint is presented by an employee to an employment tribunal that there has been an automatically unfair dismissal, the qualifying period of two years' continuous employment of the employee in terms of section 108(1) of the ERA will be inapplicable.[204] Furthermore, in the case of an employee who has been dismissed for health and safety related reasons or for making a protected disclosure, section 124(1A) of the ERA stipulates that the cap on compensation for a finding of unfair dismissal which is applicable under section 124 of the ERA does not apply.

16.2.4.3 The five potentially fair reasons for dismissal

Assuming that the court or employment tribunal is satisfied that the reason or principal reason for the employee's dismissal does not fall within one of the 'automatically unfair' categories, its attention will turn to the five potentially fair reasons for dismissal delineated in section 98(1), (2), and (3) of the ERA. The onus lies on the employer to prove that the reason which motivated it to dismiss was one of those five valid reasons, failing which the dismissal will be held to be unfair. However, if the employer is able to discharge this burden, it does not lead to the proposition that the dismissal was fair; instead, it is simply the case that a prima facie case has been made that the dismissal was fair and the focus of enquiry then turns to the reasonableness criterion under section 98(4) of the ERA. In that respect, the five reasons enumerated in section 98 of the ERA simply act as 'gateways'[205] to the evaluative scrutiny of the employer's claim that it was reasonable for it to treat one of those reasons as sufficient to dismiss the employee in terms of section 98(4) of the ERA.[206] In the case of *Mercia Rubber Mouldings Ltd v Lingwood*,[207] Sir John Donaldson stated that a reason in section 98(1), (2), and (3) of the ERA is one 'which *can* justify the dismissal, not which *does* justify the dismissal'.[208] To that extent, in its conception, the statutory unfair dismissal regime clearly divorces the reason for the dismissal from the question of the reasonableness of the dismissal itself.

---

[204] Section 108(3) of the ERA.
[205] J. Bowers and A. Clarke, 'Unfair Dismissal and Managerial Prerogative: A Study of "Other Substantial Reason"' (1981) 10 *Industrial Law Journal* 34.
[206] *Priddle v Dibble* [1978] ICR 149, 152 per Bristow J; *Cobley v Forward Technology Industries plc* [2003] IRLR 706, 708 at para 22 per Mummery LJ.   [207] [1974] IRLR 82.
[208] *ibid.*, 83.

It should be stressed that the greater the number of potentially fair reasons, the greater the scope for the employer to establish that the dismissal of an employee was fair. Moreover, the manner in which those five reasons are interpreted will determine whether the employer is afforded a substantial degree of manoeuvre:

■ **P. Davies and M. Freedland, *Labour Law: Text and Materials*, 2nd edition (London, Weidenfeld and Nicholson, 1984) 469–71**

> . . . so far as reasons are concerned, the notable point is how widely, openly and inclusively the category of reasons capable of constituting fair reasons is defined . . . the basic trend of the legislation is to define fairness by reference to a category of positively acceptable reasons for dismissal. That category is, however, such a wide one that most dismissals which are rationally motivated and not merely arbitrary will fall within it. As a result, [section 98(1), (2), and (3) of the ERA] operates primarily as a procedural rather than a substantive requirement—a procedural requirement that it is the employer who must establish the grounds for dismissal rather than a substantive requirement that he justify the dismissal in any exacting sense.[209]

From a cursory glance at section 98 of the ERA, one is struck by the degree of overlap between the statutorily prescribed categories:

Section 98 General

(1) In determining . . . whether the dismissal of an employee is fair or unfair, it is for the employer to show—

    (a) the reason (or, if more than one, the principal reason) for the dismissal, and

    (b) that it is either a reason falling within subsection (2) or some other substantial reason of a kind such as to justify the dismissal of an employee holding the position which the employee held.

(2) A reason falls within this subsection if it—

    (a) relates to the capability or qualifications of the employee for performing work of the kind which he was employed by the employer to do,

    (b) relates to the conduct of the employee,

    (c) is that the employee was redundant, or

    (d) is that the employee could not continue to work in the position which he held without contravention (either on his part or on that of his employer) of a duty or restriction imposed by or under an enactment.

(3) In subsection (2)(a)—

    (a) 'capability', in relation to an employee, means his capability assessed by reference to skill, aptitude, health or any other physical or mental quality, and

    (b) 'qualifications', in relation to an employee, means any degree, diploma or other academic, technical or professional qualification relevant to the position which he held.

Arguably, the reason identified in section 98(1)(b), i.e. 'some other substantial reason' ('SOSR'), is the most beguiling of the lot. As will become apparent, SOSR has been construed as something of a 'catch-all' provision. The wide construction of SOSR by the

---

[209] See also P. Elias, 'Fairness in Unfair Dismissal: Trends and Tensions' (1981) 10 *Industrial Law Journal* 201, 201.

courts lends support to the sentiment advanced by Davies and Freedland that section 98(1), (2), and (3) of the ERA functions as a procedural, rather than meaningful, constraint on the employer's power of dismissal.

16.2.4.3.1 Capability/qualifications

The definition of a 'capability' reason for an employee's dismissal in section 98(2)(a) of the ERA is sufficiently widely drawn to justify the employer invoking it as the reason for the dismissals in each of the examples in Hypothetical E.

Hypothetical E(1)

Over the past six months, Danny's Demolishers plc ('the Employer') has been disappointed with the poor productivity rate of Owen Arbuthnott, one of its employees in the plant hire and sales department. During the past six months, the employee has only hired out two Hitachi EX800 80 ton excavators fitted with demolition pulverisers and breakers ('plant') to clients. The average number of plant hired out by his colleagues numbered ten over the same six-month period. Moreover, one year before, the employee arranged 20 hires of plant in a six-month period and the current lack of performance is not attributable to any recessionary pressures: the plant hire and sale market is booming due to huge tax breaks offered by the UK Government for property demolitions. Moreover, in the past, the employee's application, presentation, client-handling skills, communication skills, and general attitude were consistently graded as excellent. The Employer dismisses the employee for the reason of (lack of) capability under section 98(2)(a) of the ERA. The employee presents a complaint to the employment tribunal that he has been unfairly dismissed on the basis that the Employer has failed to discharge the burden of showing that the reason for the employee's dismissal related to his capability to perform his role.

Hypothetical E(2)

The facts are the same as in Hypothetical E(1), subject to the following variation: the employee's attitude, application, presentation, client handling, and communication skills have rapidly deteriorated over the past six months, with a number of reports of aggressive behaviour and physical violence towards colleagues and clients. The Employer dismisses the employee for the reason of (lack of) capability under section 98(2)(a) of the ERA.

Hypothetical E(3)

David Smith is employed in the plant hire and sales department of Danny's Demolishers plc ('the Employer'). David has been off work for a considerable period of time due to a long-standing kidney infection. After a period of absence of 72 weeks, the Employer decides to dismiss David on the basis of an independent medical report which concludes that it was unclear whether David will ever be fit to return to his duties at work. The Employer attributes the (lack of) capability of David as the reason for the dismissal in terms of section 98(2)(a) of the ERA. David presents a complaint to the employment tribunal that he has been unfairly dismissed on the ground that the Employer has failed to discharge the burden of showing that the reason for his dismissal related to his capability to perform his role.

Hypothetical E(4)

Robert Makalene is employed as an in-house solicitor by Danny's Demolishers plc ('the Employer'). On his appointment as an employee, when specifically asked, Robert informed the Employer that he had passed the Legal Practice Course ('LPC') subsequent to the completion of his undergraduate LLB degree. However, this was untrue. When the Employer discovers that Robert did not possess the LPC, which it is necessary to have in order to practise as a solicitor, it was extremely unhappy and took the decision to dismiss him. The Employer attributed Robert's (lack of) qualifications as the reason for the dismissal in terms of section 98(2)(a) of the ERA. Robert presents a complaint to the employment tribunal that he has been unfairly dismissed on the basis that the Employer has failed to discharge the burden of showing that the reason for his dismissal related to his qualifications to perform his role.

In Hypothetical E(1), the employee's poor performance is attributable to an innate inability on his part to harness the full range of talent which he possesses, rather than incompetence or carelessness. The opposite is true in Hypothetical E(2), where a mixture of ineptitude and a poor attitude has led to the employee's dismissal. Meanwhile, the case of Hypothetical E(3) is an example of a sustained period of absence attributable to illness, i.e. that the employee lacks the capability to work. In the case of *Sutton & Gates (Luton) Ltd v Boxall*,[210] the EAT adopted a particularly restricted construction towards the compass of the capability reason. The EAT enjoined courts and tribunals to 'distinguish in their own minds how far [the reason for dismissal] is a question of sheer incapability due to an inherent incapacity to function, compared with a failure [of the employee] to exercise to the full such talent as is possessed'.[211] Therefore, in circumstances such as Hypothetical E(2) where the employee 'has not come up to standard through his own carelessness, negligence or maybe idleness[, such cases] are much more appropriately dealt with as cases of conduct or misconduct rather than of capability'.[212] This point is significant for the purposes of ascertaining the procedural fairness of the dismissal of an employee in such circumstances, i.e. that misconduct-related pre-dismissal procedures should be applied by employers. Meanwhile, on the basis of what was expressed in *Boxall* and *Abernethy v Mott, Hay & Anderson*,[213] Hypotheticals E(1) and E(3) are undoubtedly both cases where the employee has exhibited a 'sheer incapability due to an inherent incapacity to function', i.e. lack of capability due to (a) inflexibility and lack of adaptability in the case of Hypothetical E(1) and (b) illness in the context of E(3).[214]

With regard to Hypothetical E(4), there would appear to be a lack of a relevant 'qualification' in terms of the employee's failure to complete the LPC. Section 98(3)(b) directs that a qualification means 'any degree, diploma or other academic, technical or professional qualification relevant to the position which [the employee] held'. In the case of *Blue Star Ship Management Ltd v Williams*,[215] Phillips J in the EAT held that it is incumbent on the employer to satisfy the tribunal or court that the qualification he lacked was

---

[210] [1978] IRLR 486.   [211] *ibid.*, 488 per Kilner Brown J.   [212] *ibid.*, 488 per Kilner Brown J.
[213] [1974] ICR 323.
[214] In *Shook v London Borough of Ealing* [1986] IRLR 46, it was held that, in cases of dismissal for a lack of capability, the employer's reason for dismissal must relate to the capability for performing work of the kind the employee was employed to do. Therefore, this is a broad-brush formulation and it is misconceived for an employee to assert that there is a requirement for an employer to satisfy the court or tribunal that the employee lacked the capacity to perform *every single task* which the employer was entitled by law to call upon that employee to discharge.   [215] [1978] ICR 770.

one which was 'substantially concerned with the aptitude or ability of the person to do the job'.[216] Applying that reasoning to Hypothetical E(4), it is suggested that the issue is not clear-cut, since although the lack of a practical legal training qualification will impede the employee's ability to perform his work as a practising solicitor, he will undoubtedly have had the benefit of at least two years of a traineeship which could compensate. Indeed, much will depend on the nature of the legal work which the employee was employed to do and the extent to which he had prior exposure to that kind of work as a trainee.

16.2.4.3.2 Conduct

The 'conduct' reason in section 98(2)(b) of the ERA covers a multitude of sins. For example, criminal convictions will fall within its remit,[217] as will incompetence, poor performance, and breaches of the employment contract or indiscipline[218] and wilful disobedience of a managerial order.[219] Where an employer suspects that an employee has committed a crime within the workplace and this is the motivation for a dismissal, it must demonstrate that it believed that the employee was guilty of the relevant misconduct at the time it took the decision to dismiss.[220] A genuine, even if mistaken, belief on the part of the employer as to the conduct of the employee relied upon will be sufficient to discharge the burden of establishing misconduct as a reason for dismissal,[221] but it will not invariably amount to a fair dismissal, especially if there were no reasonable grounds for that belief or no reasonable investigation was undertaken.[222]

It is unclear how carelessness or general bad behaviour ought to be classified and whether this is included within the compass of 'conduct' in section 98(2)(b) of the ERA. Consider the case of *Thomson v Alloa Motor Co. Ltd*, in which a petrol pump attendant was dismissed for misconduct by her employer after she drove a car into a petrol pump at her workplace:

■ *Thomson v Alloa Motor Co. Ltd* [1983] IRLR 403, 404

Lord McDonald:

In our opinion conduct within the meaning of the subsection means actings of such a nature whether done in the course of the employment or outwith it that reflect in some way upon the employer–employee relationship. Applying that test to the facts of the present case we are of opinion that the majority of the Tribunal have erred in concluding that the reason for the dismissal was shown to be conduct in this sense. The fact that [the employee] had caused this damage did not in any way affect her capacity to perform her duties as a petrol pump attendant. Accordingly if the incident is capable of being described as due to conduct in the widest sense it was not conduct that reflected in any way upon the [employee]'s capacity to perform her duties nor did it expose the [employer] to any risk of similar damage being caused in the future. There is a specific finding in fact by the Tribunal that in consequence of the incident the [employee] decided to give up her intention to learn to drive and there was little likelihood of a recurrence of the incident. Accordingly no valid statutory reason has been established for the dismissal in terms of [section 98(2)(b) of the ERA] and in that situation the further question of reasonableness does not arise.

---

[216] *ibid.*, 774–5.   [217] *Murphy v Trust House Forte Hotels Ltd* [1977] IRLR 186.
[218] For example, physical violence or fighting on the job.
[219] *Redbridge London Borough Council v Fishman* [1978] ICR 569.
[220] *British Home Stores Ltd v Burchell* [1978] IRLR 379. However, if the motivation for dismissal was a criminal conviction which has been spent under the Rehabilitation of Offenders Act 1974, this will amount to an automatically unfair dismissal in terms of section 4(3)(b) of the Rehabilitation of Offenders Act 1974.
[221] *Trust House Forte Leisure Ltd v Aquilar* [1976] IRLR 251; *Maintenance Co. Ltd v Dormer* [1982] IRLR 491.   [222] *British Home Stores Ltd v Burchell* [1978] IRLR 379.

The premise to be drawn from this passage is that the conduct of the employee which the employer treats as sufficient justification for dismissal must have some connection to the rights and duties of the parties in terms of the employment relationship. If an incident or series of incidents are unrelated or divorced from the employee's job, it is unlikely that they will constitute 'conduct' as a reason for dismissal. For example, in *CJD v Royal Bank of Scotland plc*,[223] an employee who was involved in a relationship with a female colleague and living with her pushed her onto a sofa in self-defence after she scratched him in the face. The employee was charged with assault, but his plea of not guilty was accepted by the Crown. In the circumstances, the Inner House of the Court of Session held that such conduct of the employee in a domestic context in no way reflected upon the employee–employer relationship and as such could not be characterized as misconduct caught by section 98(2)(b) of the ERA. Of course, there is a fine line to be drawn here, since criminal convictions arising from incidents occurring wholly outside the workplace may nevertheless afford sufficient reason for an employer to dismiss on the basis of misconduct.[224] For example, the case of *X v Y*[225] concerned an employee who worked for a charity which promoted personal development among young people. His post involved liaising with the local probation service and working with young offenders and those at risk of offending in the 16–25 age group. The employee was dismissed when he was arrested for gross indecency, having pulled into a lay-by when he was off duty and gone to the toilet, where he engaged in consensual sexual activity with a man he had never met before. The employment tribunal, EAT, and the Court of Appeal held that the reason for dismissal was the employee's misconduct, despite the fact that the activities had taken place outside the workplace. *X v Y* can be contrasted with the case of *Pay v Lancashire Probation Service*.[226] Here, a probation officer who worked predominantly with sex offenders was dismissed after his employers discovered photographs of him involved in acts of bondage, domination, and sado-masochism on the internet, and learned that he was involved in the merchandising of products relating to such activities and that he performed shows in hedonist and fetish clubs. It was held by the employment tribunal and the EAT that the reason for the dismissal of the probation officer was 'some other substantial reason' under section 98(1)(b) of the ERA rather than for misconduct.

A case such as *Thomson v Alloa Motor Co. Ltd* also begs the question as to the circumstances in which the employer will have the right to summarily dismiss an employee for the reason of gross misconduct. Consider the case of *Neary v Dean of Westminster*:

■ *Neary v Dean of Westminster* [1999] IRLR 288, 290–1

Lord Jauncey:

The character of the institutional employer, the role played by the employee in that institution and the degree of trust required of the employee vis-à-vis the employer must all be considered in determining the extent of the duty and the seriousness of any breach . . . Whether misconduct justifies summary dismissal of a servant is a question of fact . . . What degree of misconduct justifies summary dismissal? . . . [The case law] demonstrate[s] clearly that conduct amounting to gross misconduct justifying dismissal must so undermine the trust and confidence which is inherent in the particular contract of employment that the master should no longer be required to retain the servant in his employment.[227]

---

[223] [2014] IRLR 25.   [224] For example, crimes of theft or dishonesty.   [225] [2004] IRLR 625.
[226] [2004] IRLR 129.
[227] See also *Jervis v Skinner* [2011] UKPC 2 and *Adeshina v St George's University Hospital* [2017] EWCA Civ 257. In *Dunn v AAH Ltd* [2010] IRLR 709, Rix LJ in the Court of Appeal held that there is no distinction to be crafted between gross misconduct and repudiatory conduct evincing an intention no longer to be bound by the contract of employment.

Building on the jurisprudence of Lord Jauncey in *Neary*, in *West London Mental Health Trust v Chhabra*[228] Lord Hodge distinguished between serious misconduct and gross misconduct, reaching the conclusion that it would be a rare occurrence where the latter would cover conduct which did not entail the wilful or deliberate breach of a rule.

Although this guidance as to when an employer will have the right to summarily dismiss an employee is useful, as noted by Clark J in the case of *Farrant v The Woodroffe School*,[229] it is common for examples of gross misconduct to be delimited in the employer's disciplinary procedure, staff handbook, or a collective agreement negotiated and agreed with a recognized trade union. For example, see the guidance as to what is best practice in the ACAS Code:[230]

■ ACAS Code of Practice 1: Disciplinary and Grievance Procedures, paras 23–24

Some acts, termed gross misconduct, are so serious in themselves or have such serious consequences that they may call for dismissal without notice for a first offence. But a fair disciplinary process should always be followed, before dismissing for gross misconduct. Disciplinary rules should give examples of acts which the employer regards as acts of gross misconduct. These may vary according to the nature of the organisation and what it does, but might include things such as theft or fraud, physical violence, gross negligence or serious insubordination.

16.2.4.3.3 Redundancy

Section 98(2)(c) of the ERA directs that redundancy is a potentially fair reason for dismissal. There is a statutory definition of redundancy which is set out in section 139(1) of the ERA. It is examined in greater detail in Chapter 18.[231]

16.2.4.3.4 Breach or contravention of a duty or statute

Where an employer terminates the contract of employment of an employee for the reason that the employee has breached a duty or statutory provision, this is a potentially fair reason for dismissal by virtue of section 98(2)(d) of the ERA. Where an employer has a genuine, but mistaken, belief that an employee has contravened a legal enactment and that the continuation of the contract of employment would be unlawful, the case of *Bouchaala v Trusthouse Forte Hotels Ltd*[232] is authority for the proposition that this will not be a section 98(2)(d) reason for the dismissal of that employee. On a related note, if the reason for the dismissal is that the employee could not continue to work in the position which he/she held without contravention of a duty or restriction imposed by statute, will it always be reasonable for an employer to dismiss the employee? The case of *Kelly v University of Southampton*[233] answered this question in the negative. Instead, it is for the tribunal to decide whether it was unreasonable or not for an employer to dismiss in terms of section 98(4) of the ERA and the fact that to continue to employ someone could be a breach of legislation is not of itself conclusive.

16.2.4.3.5 SOSR

Finally, we come to the fifth potentially fair reason for dismissal, namely 'some other substantial reason' ('SOSR') under section 98(1)(b) of the ERA. SOSR is particularly enigmatic phraseology. Unfortunately, not a great deal of assistance on the meaning of

---

[228] [2014] ICR 194.   [229] [1998] IRLR 176, 179.
[230] Available at http://www.acas.org.uk/?articleid=2174 (last visited 29 October 2017).
[231] See Chapter 18, section 18.2.2.   [232] [1980] IRLR 382.   [233] [2008] ICR 357.

SOSR can be derived from the case law. In *Hollister v NFU*, Lord Justice Eveleigh gave some indication of the width of the concept when he stated: 'I do not think it is right to lay down as a general rule what is and what is not some other substantial reason within the meaning of [section 98(1)(b) of the ERA].'[234] Likewise, in *SW Global Resourcing Ltd v Docherty*,[235] Lady Smith in the EAT remarked that the 'hurdle imposed by s.98(1)(b) is a modest one', and in *Garside and Laycock Ltd v Booth*[236] Mr Justice Langstaff recognized that SOSR under section 98(1)(b) of the ERA 'is a broad category of case'. Some further pointers can be gleaned indirectly from the case law.

(1) Since the reason must be 'substantial', it is clear that it must not be whimsical or trivial in nature.[237]

(2) The dismissal will be for SOSR where the employer dismisses an employee in order to protect its legitimate business interests and the employer is able to establish a sound business reason for dismissal.[238] For example, where the employer engages in a reorganization which reallocates patterns of work amongst the workforce, if an employee is dismissed, this will be deemed to be SOSR if the employer's motivation for the process was not to make employees redundant in the sense that its requirements for the number of employees in the workforce had reduced. Indeed, an appreciable number of the cases have decided that SOSR represents the reason for reorganizations[239] which can be distinguished from redundancy situations. This has served to limit the concept of 'redundancy' as defined in section 139 of the ERA.[240]

Beyond reorganizations, other examples of SOSR include the rejection of a unilateral reduction in pay,[241] circumstances in which the employer experiences a substantial breakdown of trust and confidence in the employee,[242] where the employer had a genuine and reasonable belief that an employee was not permitted to work in the UK,[243] and the dismissal of an employee who was found to have a difficult personality or unfortunate manner.[244] On a related note, the dismissal of an employee due to personality clashes with colleagues was found to be SOSR.[245] Moreover, where an employer dismissed an employee at the behest of its key client, this was held to be for SOSR.[246] The dismissal of a chief executive by the shareholders of his employer subsequent to its takeover was also ruled to be SOSR in *Cobley v Forward Technology Industries plc*.[247] As such, the case law has imported some content and meaning into the concept in a manner which highlights the degree to which it sometimes operates to eviscerate the scope of the other four potentially fair reasons for dismissal. In fact, it is particularly seductive to regard the expansion of SOSR as inversely proportional to the contraction of the category of 'redundancy'.[248]

---

[234] [1979] ICR 542, 553.

[235] [2012] IRLR 727, 732 and *Ssekisonge v Barts Health NHS Trust* (UKEAT/0133/16/LA, 2 March 2017).   [236] [2011] IRLR 735, 738–9.

[237] *Harper v National Coal Board* [1980] IRLR 260, 261 per Lord McDonald.

[238] *Robinson v British Island Airways Ltd* [1978] ICR 304; *Hollister v NFU* [1979] ICR 542.

[239] *Bowater Containers Ltd v McCormack* [1980] IRLR 50. See also J. Bowers and A. Clarke, 'Unfair Dismissal and Managerial Prerogative: A Study of "Other Substantial Reason"' (1981) 10 *Industrial Law Journal* 34, 36–9.   [240] See Chapter 18, section 18.2.2.

[241] *Garside and Laycock Ltd v Booth* [2011] IRLR 735.

[242] *Leach v Office of Communications* [2012] ICR 1269; *Ezsias v North Glamorgan NHS Trust* [2011] IRLR 550; and *Tubbenden Primary School v Sylvester* [2012] ICR D29.

[243] *Nayak v Royal Mail Group* (UKEATS/0011/15/SM, 15 February 2016).

[244] *Perkin v St George's Healthcare NHS Trust* [2005] IRLR 934.

[245] *C A Treganowan v Robert Knee & Co. Ltd* [1975] IRLR 247.

[246] *Scott Packing and Warehousing Co. Ltd v Paterson* [1978] IRLR 166; *Henderson v Connect (South Tyneside) Ltd* [2010] IRLR 466. Contrast these decisions with *Handshake Ltd v Summers* (UKEAT/0216/12/KN, 22 October 2012).   [247] [2003] IRLR 706.

[248] See Chapter 18, section 18.2.2.

For additional reading on the effective date of termination and the 'reasons for dis-
missal', visit the Online Resources for this book at www.oup.com/uk/cabrelli3e/

16.3 THE SUBSTANTIVE FAIRNESS OF THE DISMISSAL

There are a number of discrete areas of private law in which the UK Parliament has intervened to subject decisions of a legal person to scrutiny under a 'fairness' or 'reasonableness' standard.[249] In each of these instances, the legislature is essentially enjoining a court
or tribunal to undertake a value judgment as to the lawfulness of those decisions in accordance with such criteria. Taken in isolation, the criteria of 'fairness' or 'reasonableness'
are sufficiently open-textured to attract a number of interpretations and there is the danger that the construction adopted will prove to be somewhat chimerical. On occasion, Parliament specifically imports a range of pointers which serve to instantiate the notions of
'fairness' or 'reasonableness' in particular fact-specific situations. For example, in section
62 of the Consumer Rights Act 2015—which is a piece of legislation designed to protect
consumers from unfair terms in consumer contracts—it is stipulated that a contract term
will be 'unfair' if, 'contrary to the requirement of good faith, it causes a significant imbalance in the parties' rights and obligations arising under the contract, to the detriment of
the consumer'. This can be contrasted with legislative provisions that afford little guidance
as to how the courts or tribunals should apply the 'fairness' or 'reasonableness' standards.

When the standard of review which an adjudicator is enjoined to apply is articulated
at a high level of generality such as 'fairness' or 'reasonableness', in the absence of additional statutory guidance, the judiciary must step in to fix the intensity of scrutiny. By far
the most common intensities of scrutiny which one encounters in the field of employment
law (in order of the highest to the lowest measure of scrutiny) are as follows.

(1) *An 'objective' fairness or reasonableness standard* This empowers an adjudicator to
    subrogate itself to a legal person and freely apply its mind as to whether that person's
    decision, actions, conduct, or omissions were lawful or not. This measure enables an
    adjudicator to substitute its own judgment for that of the legal person in light of all
    of the facts and circumstances, thus harnessing a particularly intensive appraisal of
    that person's conduct. A particularly emphatic version of this formulation was articu-
    lated by Rix LJ in *Socimer International Bank Ltd (in liquidation) v Standard Bank
    London Ltd*, where he stated that, on the application of an objective standard, 'the
    decision maker becomes the court itself'.[250]

(2) *A 'range of reasonable responses' standard* We will discuss the nature of this in more
    detail shortly.

(3) *A 'subjective' fairness or reasonableness standard* This standard disentitles an adjudi-
    cator from second-guessing the decisions, actions, omissions, or conduct of the legal
    person; rather, the adjudicator is merely directed to ensure that the decision-maker
    itself had a genuine belief that (a) its decisions, actions, omissions, or conduct were
    reasonable or fair, or (b) the reason for its decisions, actions, omissions, or conduct
    were reasonable or fair.

In light of these three possibilities, let us now turn to the statutory unfair dismissal
regime. Here, a measure of statutory assistance is provided as to the means by which
the judiciary should mould the appropriate intensity of scrutiny of managerial action:

---

[249] For example, sections 2, 3, 16, and 17 of the Unfair Contract Terms Act 1977.
[250] [2008] 1 Lloyd's Rep 558, 577 at para 66; approved by the Supreme Court in *Braganza v BP Shipping Ltd* [2015] UKSC 17, [2015] 1 WLR 1661.

Section 98 General

(4) In any other case where the employer has fulfilled the requirements of subsection (1), the determination of the question whether the dismissal is fair or unfair (having regard to the reason shown by the employer)—

    (a) depends on whether in the circumstances (including the size and administrative resources of the employer's undertaking) the employer acted reasonably or unreasonably in treating it as a sufficient reason for dismissing the employee, and

    (b) shall be determined in accordance with equity and the substantial merits of the case.

As such, the 'reasonableness' criterion is conditioned and influenced by the following three factors:

- the size and administrative resources of the employer's undertaking—which is clearly a subjective criterion;
- equity and the substantial merits of the case—what this entails requires judicial resolution; and
- whether it was reasonable or unreasonable for the employer to treat the reason for the dismissal as a sufficient reason for that dismissal—which appears to involve an objective evaluation.

We should keep each of these three factors in mind and reconsider each in light of the 'range of reasonable responses' test, which we will address shortly.

16.3.1 Substantive fairness: basic concepts

There are two aspects of the dismissal of an employee which the judiciary have assessed by reference to the reasonableness test set out in section 98(4).

(1) The legislative terminology has been marshalled to pose a broadly evaluative question as to the reasonableness of the *substance* of the employer's decision to dismiss, i.e. whether it was *substantively fair* for the employer to treat the reason identified in terms of section 98(1), (2), and (3) of the ERA as sufficient to dismiss the employee. This *substantive fairness* evaluative function engages the courts and tribunals in a process of adjudication which may or may not interfere quite liberally in the managerial prerogative, depending on how the content of the applicable standard of review is drawn by the courts. It is with substantive fairness that we are concerned in this Chapter 16.

(2) Section 98(4) also functions to subject the *procedural* mechanisms applied by the employer in advance of the decision to dismiss to a degree of scrutiny. This aspect of the evaluative endeavour is referred to as the *procedural fairness* of the dismissal and will be considered in detail in Chapter 17.

The relationship between substantive fairness and procedural fairness is particularly crucial: if the dismissal is held to be substantively fair, this does not necessarily mean that an employee's dismissal will be found to be fair overall, since the process leading up to the dismissal may be deemed to have been procedurally unfair; however, if a tribunal or court rules that the substance of the dismissal was unfair, it is inevitable that it will be deemed to be unfair overall, notwithstanding the fact that the pre-dismissal procedure adopted was flawless.

Initially, the concept of the 'industrial jury' was employed in the case law towards the question of the substantive fairness of the dismissal. This connoted a purely objective measure of scrutiny of the managerial prerogative. It was thought that such a notion empowered an employment tribunal to act in a way similar to a jury in a criminal trial. For example, the employment tribunal, staffed with two laypersons experienced in industrial relations and a legally qualified employment judge, would draw on their own expertise of workplace relations and decide whether it was fair that a particular employee was dismissed in the case before it on the basis that this was a question of fact.[251] This interpretation of the approach to substantive fairness rejects the importation of technical legal norms or conventions and the suggestion that the tribunal or court has no power to second-guess the decision of the employer to dismiss. Writing in 1981, whilst exploring the relationship between the employment tribunal and appellate courts, Elias described and criticized the industrial jury notion in the following terms:

■ P. Elias, 'Fairness in Unfair Dismissal: Trends and Tensions' (1981) 10
Industrial Law Journal 201, 209–10

[A]n analogy which is frequently employed when this emphasis is given in fairness cases is to treat the industrial tribunal as a special jury whose decision should not be reviewed. Donaldson J. the first president of the National Industrial Relations Court, occasionally used this analogy, [*Earl v Slater & Wheeler (Airlyne) Ltd* [1973] 1 All ER 1 and *James v Waltham Holy Cross UDC* [1973] ICR 398] and it has since been followed by other judges. Such a strong assertion of tribunal autonomy does not altogether sit happily with the view that the tribunal must not substitute its own view for that of the employer. Yet the Court of Appeal has continued to adopt this perspective. In so doing it is reflecting the view, which it frequently espouses, that Parliament intended industrial tribunals to resolve dismissal disputes in a quick, cheap and informal manner, without resort to legal refinements, and that this policy will be undermined if tribunal decisions are too closely scrutinised . . . it was always naive to assume that vague formulae used in a statute can be interpreted according to the dictates of some innate industrial common sense and without resort to traditional legal reasoning, but the Court of Appeal continues to cling to the myth that they can. This is in contrast with the E.A.T. which has not adopted such a non-interventionist stance. Perhaps the presence of industrial relations experts in the latter body gives it a greater confidence in its ability to pass judgment on tribunals. This emphasis on tribunal autonomy is reinforced in three ways. First, there is a tendency to emphasise that decisions on reasonableness are, like all jury questions, matters of fact and not subject to appeal. This is misleading for, as has been mentioned, they are questions of mixed law and fact. Secondly, the Court of Appeal has warned the E.A.T. not to scrutinise the decisions of industrial tribunals with a fine toothcomb 'to see if some error can be found here or there—to see if one can find a little cryptic sentence,' and in this connection it has advised tribunals that detailed reasons are not necessary and that it is sufficient merely 'to tell the parties in broad terms why they lose or, as the case may be, win.' Finally, in *Bailey v. BP Oil (Kent Refinery) Ltd* [[1980] IRLR 287], the Court of Appeal even advised the E.A.T. that its attempts to provide guidance to industrial tribunals was misdirected. Lawton LJ., delivering the judgment of the court, commented: 'In our judgment it is unwise for this court or the Employment Appeal Tribunal to set out guidelines and wrong to make rules and establish presumptions for industrial tribunals to follow or take into account.' This seeks to deny the model building role which the E.A.T. has seen as its principal function in this area. But this advice is surely misplaced; it is the function of appellate courts to ensure some consistency between the large number of industrial tribunals and setting guidelines can assist in this process, provided it is made clear that they should not be treated as binding rules of law. The alternative . . . is that each tribunal will be a law unto itself.

---

[251] *Priddle v Dibble* [1978] ICR 149, 152 per Bristow J.

The purchase in the idea that tribunal autonomy is and ought to be mediated through the industrial jury concept has waned significantly over the years. In fact, the suggestion that the substantive fairness of an employee's dismissal could ever be approached in terms of a formulation which was devoid of legal tests and niceties was always doubtful, as noted by Freedland in the following extract:

■ **M. Freedland, 'Finding the Right Direction for the "Industrial Jury":** *Haddon v Van den Bergh Foods Ltd/Midland Bank plc v Madden'* (2000) 29 *Industrial Law Journal* 288, 289

> The notion of the industrial jury is a misleading one because it makes, what is to my mind, a false analogy with the role of a jury in a criminal trial . . . in order to answer the question, 'was this dismissal unfair?', at least in the particular way that question is posed by section 98, the employment tribunal has to engage in an adjudication which is much less like deciding whether 'the wrong of unfair dismissal has been committed', than like engaging in judicial review of the employer's action and decision-making judged to amount to dismissal. What does it imply to assert that unfair dismissal adjudication is more like judicial review than like arriving at jury verdicts in criminal trials? I think the point is that judicial review is quite highly interactive with the administrative action and decision-making which is the subject of the review. The criminal trial model encourages, perhaps even demands, that those arriving at the verdict place themselves at a distance from the accused and ask themselves, in quite a remote way, whether they find the accused guilty as charged. Those engaged in judicial review, because it is a broadly more evaluative function, become more implicated in the administrative action and decision-making which they are reviewing. This in two senses; firstly, in that they cannot escape the awareness of the influence of their review upon subsequent administrative action; and secondly, in that they invariably, and I think inevitably, end up considering, in some shape manner or form, whether they would have approached the administrative action or decision-making in the way in which it was approached, or in some different way. For in the end, if we are called upon to engage in a broad scrutiny of other people's administrative action or decision-making, that is how we do it. I think I can probably decide whether you have stolen a car without standing in your shoes, but I do not think I can decide whether you have 'acted fairly' without to some extent placing myself in your shoes . . . It will have emerged that I think that the statute law of unfair dismissal, and especially the formulation embodied in what is now section 98, created a very judicial-review-like function for employment tribunals exercising their jurisdiction. The framers of the legislation may not have intended this; they may well have thought that they were giving the tribunals a simpler more directly defined task. But in the event, they were placing the tribunals, and the courts of appeal from the tribunals, squarely into the dilemma, or under the tension, which is at the heart of the judicial review function as I have identified it above.

The major insight to be drawn from this passage is that the fairness of a dismissal is not a factual question for a jury-like body to decide; instead, the language of 'fairness' and 'reasonableness', in section 98(4) of the ERA, indicates the presence of a standard against which the employer's behaviour must be evaluated. Thus, it is more a question of judgment rather than fact, and the role of the tribunal and court has more affinity with the process adopted by the judiciary in a negligence action in tort law or under judicial review in administrative law than a jury in a criminal trial. But what do we mean by a 'standard'? Essentially, a standard is a legal command which signposts expectations about the behaviour of a legal person in an open-textured manner. Standards represent a less peremptory or compelling form of normativity than a legal rule and entail a value judgment to be exercised by an adjudicator about the behaviour of a legal person's decision, action, or conduct in terms of a legal formulation.[252] Words and phrases such as 'reasonable', 'fair', 'fairness', 'proportionate', 'rational', 'due care', 'equitable', 'adequate', and 'appropriate' are classic examples of standard-like language.[253]

Of course, for a dismissal to be found to be unfair, section 98(4) of the ERA directs that the standard of 'reasonableness' is to be used. In construing whether a dismissal is fair or unfair under section 98(4) of the ERA, the courts and tribunals have adopted a legal formulation which entails the application of a standard of review known as the 'range of reasonable responses' test:

■ *Iceland Frozen Foods Ltd v Jones* [1982] ICR 17, 24F–25A

Browne-Wilkinson J:

. . . in law the correct approach . . . to adopt in answering the question posed by [section 98(4) of the ERA] is as follows.

(1) the starting point should always be the words of [section 98(4) of the ERA] themselves;

(2) in applying the section an Industrial Tribunal must consider the reasonableness of the employer's conduct, not simply whether they (the members of the Industrial Tribunal) consider the dismissal to be fair;

(3) in judging the reasonableness of the employer's conduct an Industrial Tribunal must not substitute its decision as to what was the right course to adopt for that of the employer;

(4) in many (though not all) cases there is a band of reasonable responses to the employee's conduct within which one employer might reasonably take one view, another quite reasonably take another;

(5) the function of the Industrial Tribunal, as an industrial jury, is to determine whether in the particular circumstances of each case the decision to dismiss the employee fell within the band of reasonable responses which a reasonable employer might have adopted. If the dismissal falls within the band the dismissal is fair: if the dismissal falls outside the band it is unfair.

As such, instead of the tribunal or court enquiring whether the employer's decision to dismiss was reasonable or unreasonable on a purely objective basis, and thus substituting its own judgment for that of the employer, the tribunal must ask whether dismissal was one of the reasonable responses which an employer might take to the employee's conduct. The effect of the range of reasonable responses standard of review is that the employer's decision to dismiss the employee is evaluated in accordance with a particularly deferential intensity of scrutiny. Consider the following Hypothetical F.

Hypothetical F

Terry Grantchester is employed by Danny's Demolishers plc ('the Employer') as a security guard in one of its factories in Edinburgh. Terry's mother suffers from multiple sclerosis. On a routine inspection of his work locker, the Employer discovers 2 kg of

---

[252] C. S. Diver, 'The Optimal Precision of Administrative Rules' (1983) 93 *Yale Law Journal* 65, 67; L. Kaplow, 'Rules versus Standards: An Economic Analysis' (1992–93) 42 *Duke Law Journal* 557, 561.

[253] D. Kennedy, 'Form and Substance in Private Law Adjudication' (1975–76) 89 *Harvard Law Review* 1685, 1688.

cannabis. Terry admits that the cannabis belongs to him, but explains that he had bought it from a dealer before he came into work that day and that it is for his ailing mother. Terry explains that his mother uses cannabis to relieve the pain of her multiple sclerosis. The Employer decides to dismiss Terry with immediate effect for the reason of gross misconduct. Terry claims that he has been unfairly dismissed.

When approaching the enquiry, an adjudicator should put its own perspective as to how it would have dealt with the issue to one side. In contrast, it should ask how different reasonable employers might respond to the employee's conduct in the same set of circumstances. For example, reverting to Hypothetical F, a tribunal might find that one reasonable employer would decide to take no action and apply no sanction. Another reasonable employer might take the view that a verbal warning would suffice. It may also be the case that a third reasonable employer would react more strongly by serving a final written warning on the employee. Finally, a fourth reasonable employer might perhaps take the decision that dismissal was the appropriate sanction. Therefore, the employment tribunal's task is to construct a list of sanctions which reasonable employers might adopt. If dismissal features on that list, the decision to dismiss falls within the range of reasonable responses and so a prima facie case arises that the dismissal was substantively fair. If dismissal is not on that list of sanctions, then the decision to dismiss would be ruled to be unfair. Since it is more likely than not that dismissal would feature as one of the options available to a reasonable employer in the case of Hypothetical F, the Employer's decision to dismiss Terry Grantchester will be held to have been fair.

However, as some commentators have argued, the difficulty with the 'range' test is that the same result could often be attained by simply enquiring whether 'no reasonable employer would have taken the decision to dismiss', which the employer in the case at hand had actually taken.[254] The latter approach is known as a 'perversity' test, which is notoriously narrow in latitude:

■ H. Collins, 'Finding the Right Direction for the "Industrial Jury": *Haddon v Van den Bergh Foods Ltd/Midland Bank plc v Madden*' (2000) 29 *Industrial Law Journal* 288, 294

> The most frequent criticism of the 'range or band of reasonable responses' test has been that it fails to create a standard that secures a stable middle position. In practice, it often degenerates into a test of perversity. It upholds the justice of dismissals that are 'harsh but fair'.[255]

This was one of the grounds on which the 'range of reasonable responses' standard was held by the EAT not to be good law in the 1990s in the case of *Haddon v Van Den Burgh Foods Ltd*.[256] In other words, the enquiry would often find its expression in asking whether no reasonable employer would have taken the decision to dismiss in the same circumstances as the defendant employer, rather than whether the hypothetical range of reasonable employers would have responded by dismissing the claimant employee for the

---

[254] See *Scottish Prison Service v Laing* [2013] IRLR 859, 864 per Lady Stacey.
[255] See also H. Collins, *Employment Law* (Oxford, OUP, 2003) 173–4.
[256] [1999] IRLR 672, 675 at para 26. See also H. Collins, *Justice in Dismissal* (Oxford, Clarendon Press, 1992) 8 and 38–9; A. Freer, 'The Range of Reasonable Responses Test: From Guidelines to Statute' (1998) 27 *Industrial Law Journal* 335.

reason of his/her conduct, lack of capability, retirement, redundancy, etc. However, one could argue that this critique is misplaced and that a distinction can be drawn between a perversity test and the range of reasonable responses standard, albeit a subtle one.[257] By emphasizing what is 'reasonable' rather than what is 'unreasonable' or 'perverse', the focus of the 'range' test is different from that of a perversity test, which leads towards the point of demarcation between what is reasonable and unreasonable being fixed at a different spot than if the question were posed in terms of unreasonableness or perversity. In other words, the content of the question influences the nature of the answer. Since the outcome of the application of the two standards is that the line between what is reasonable and unreasonable is drawn at different places, it makes no sense to argue that the two concepts are conflated. If the standards were the same and simply expressions of the same approach, there would be no difference in the demarcation point.[258] In addition, it has been recognized judicially that although the range test provides a large measure of latitude in decision-making to the employer, 'the band is not infinitely wide'[259] and has inherent limits.

In the case of *Post Office v Foley*, the Court of Appeal restored the primacy of the range of reasonable responses standard. It also rejected the criticism of the range of reasonable responses test in *Haddon* that the rule against the tribunal substituting its own judgment for that of the employer placed an unacceptable 'judicial gloss' on the terms of section 98(4) of the ERA and was an interpretation which was not warranted by its wording:

■ *Post Office v Foley; HSBC Bank plc v Madden* [2000] ICR 1283, 1287C–1293C

Mummery LJ:

Since employment tribunals throughout Great Britain decide thousands of unfair dismissal cases every month, it is crucial that uncertainty about the law to be applied by them should be dispelled as soon as possible. In my judgment, the employment tribunals should continue to apply the law enacted in s.98(1), (2) and (4) of the [ERA], giving to those provisions the same interpretation as was placed for many years by this court and the Employment Appeal Tribunal on the equivalent provisions in s.57(1), (2) and (3) of the Employment Protection (Consolidation) Act 1978 ('the 1978 Act'). This means that for all practical purposes: (1) 'The band or range of reasonable responses' approach to the issue of the reasonableness or unreasonableness of a dismissal, as expounded by Browne-Wilkinson J in *Iceland Frozen Foods Ltd v Jones* [1982] IRLR 439 at 442–443 and as approved and applied by this court . . . remains binding on this court, as well as on the employment tribunals and the Employment Appeal Tribunal. The disapproval of that approach in *Haddon* [1999] IRLR 672 (see p.676, 25–26) on the basis that (a) the expression was a 'mantra' which led employment tribunals into applying what amounts to a perversity test of reasonableness, instead of the statutory test of reasonableness as it stands, and that (b) it prevented members of employment tribunals from approaching the issue of reasonableness by reference to their own judgment of what they would have done had they been the employers, is an unwarranted departure from binding authority . . . Unless and until the statutory provisions are differently interpreted by the House of Lords or are amended by an Act of Parliament, that is the law which should continue to be applied to claims for unfair dismissal. In so holding I am aware that there is a body of informed opinion which is critical of this interpretation of the 1996 Act . . . the interpretation placed by the tribunals and courts, including this court, on the provisions of the 1978 Act in the cases of *Iceland Foods* [1982] IRLR

---

[257] See the analysis in P. Elias, 'Fairness in Unfair Dismissal: Trends and Tensions' (1981) 10 *Industrial Law Journal* 201, 205–6.
[258] So the writer would disagree with Freer that there is no difference between the two standards.
[259] *Newbound v Thames Water Utilities Ltd* [2015] IRLR 734.

439 and *Burchell* [1978] IRLR 379 has not led Parliament to amend the relevant provisions, even though Parliament has from time to time made other amendments to the law of unfair dismissal, since those authoritative rulings on interpretation were first made. So those rulings, which have been followed almost every day in almost every employment tribunal and on appeals for nearly 20 years, remain binding . . .

Perversity point

It was made clear in *Iceland Foods* [1982] IRLR 439 at pp.442–443, 25 that the provisions of s.57(3) of the 1978 Act (which were re-enacted in s.98(4) of the [ERA]) did not require 'such a high degree of unreasonableness to be shown that nothing short of a perverse decision to dismiss can be held to be unfair within the section'. The tribunals were advised to follow the formulation of the band of reasonable responses approach instead. If an employment tribunal in any particular case mis-interprets or misapplies that approach, so as to amount to a requirement of a perverse decision to dismiss, that would be an error of law with which an appellate body could interfere. The range of reasonable responses approach does not, however, become one of perversity nor is it rendered 'unhelpful' by the fact that there may be extremes and that (as observed in *Haddon* [1999] IRLR 672 at p.676, 26) 'dismissal is the ultimate sanction'. Further, that approach is not in practice required in every case. There will be cases in which there is no band or range to consider. If, for example, an employee, without good cause, deliberately sets fire to his employer's factory and it is burnt to the ground, dismissal is the only reasonable response. If an employee is dismissed for politely say-ing 'Good morning' to his line manager, that would be an unreasonable response. But in between those extreme cases there will be cases where there is room for reasonable disagreement among reasonable employers as to whether dismissal for the particular misconduct is a reasonable or an unreasonable response. In those cases it is helpful for the tribunal to consider 'the range of reason-able responses'.

Substitution point

It was also made clear in *Iceland Foods* [1982] IRLR 439 at p.442, 24–25 that the members of the tribunal must not simply consider whether they personally think that the dismissal is fair and they must not substitute their decision as to what was the right course to adopt for that of the employer. Their proper function is to determine whether the decision to dismiss the employee fell within the band of reasonable responses 'which a reasonable employer might have adopted'. In one sense it is true that, if the application of that approach leads the members of the tribunal to conclude that the dismissal was unfair, they are in effect substituting their judgment for that of the employer. But that process must always be conducted by reference to the objective standards of the hypothetical reasonable employer which are imported by the statutory references to 'reasonably or unreason-ably' and not by reference to their own subjective views of what they would in fact have done as an employer in the same circumstances. In other words, although the members of the tribunal can substitute their *decision* for that of the employer, that decision must not be reached by a process of substituting *themselves* for the employer and forming an opinion of what they would have done had they been the employer, which they were not.

The effect of *Post Office v Foley* was to restore orthodoxy to the law of unfair dismissal. The Court of Appeal asserted that the range of reasonable responses standard was not a formulation which the judiciary had arrived at by modifying the terms of section 98(4). There is an insistence by Mummery LJ that the judiciary are simply interpreting the lan-guage of section 98(4) of the ERA. However, this is not wholly convincing and there is an argument that, by arriving at the range of reasonable responses test, the judiciary have been involved in something more profound than an interpretative process. This point can perhaps be clarified by querying how intensive the degree of scrutiny associated with the range test actually is. For example, whilst the range of reasonable responses standard is not a subjective test from the perspective of the employer, it undoubtedly represents a much less searching intensity of scrutiny of the managerial prerogative than that associated with an objective test of reasonableness which would permit the tribunal/court to conduct a wider enquiry and substitute its judgment for the employer more freely:

■ **D. Cabrelli, 'Rules and Standards in the Workplace: A Perspective from the Field of Labour Law' (2011) 31 *Legal Studies* 21, 30–1**

[T]he judiciary have consistently stated that section 98(4) ERA requires an adjudicator to apply the 'range of reasonable responses' test.[260] This formula represents a self-generated modification of the standard of review by an adjudicator. It channels the adjudicator towards a consideration of the band of responses which a reasonable employer might take in the face of the particular actions or omissions of the employee. Importantly, the 'range' test deprives the court or tribunal [of] a free hand to substitute its own judgment for that of the employer or to articulate what ought to have been done by the employer by reference to the standards or mores of society at large. Instead, it entails the application of a mixture of objective and subjective considerations: objective to the extent that the tribunal or court must identify how different reasonable employers might react to the employee's actions or omissions; yet, subjective[261] in (i) a 'weak' form in the sense that section 98(4) ERA enjoins the tribunal or court to take into account subjective criteria, such as the size and administrative resources of the employer, thus enjoining the adjudicator to afford 'some allowance not only for external facts, but also for personal characteristics of the actor himself'[262] and (ii) in a 'strong' sense to the extent that, by adopting internal practices and formal, written procedures and policies which underscore the particular economic interests of the organisation, there is clearly scope for the employer to channel the parameters of an adjudicator's evaluation of the employer's decision-making and conduct towards a more lenient subjective assessment.[263]

What have been the motives or rationales for the emergence of the 'range of reasonable standard'? As remarked by Collins, the reasons for the adoption of such a test have not been clearly articulated by the judiciary.[264] Three particular explanations may be identified, which can be expressed in utilitarian or instrumental terms.

(1) The first explanation invokes the judicial reluctance towards the second-guessing of managerial decisions. Elias has echoed this point by reformulating it in terms to the effect that the judiciary are less comfortable with engaging in a review of the substance of managerial decisions than they are with scrutinizing the procedural fairness of the process applied by the employer in reaching such decisions.[265]

(2) Secondly, the application of the standard can be perceived as a means of avoiding an over-intrusive approach to adjudication which might otherwise dissipate valuable, limited resources. As such, the standard represents a compromise between managerial efficiency/autonomy and the protection of employees.

---

[260] *Post Office v Foley* [2000] IRLR 827, 829 at para 9 per Mummery LJ.

[261] From the viewpoint of the employer, not the adjudicator.

[262] J. Fleming, *The Law of Torts*, 9th edition (Sydney, Law Book Co., 1998) 119. See also W. Seavey, 'Negligence: Subjective or Objective' (1927) 41 *Harvard Law Review* 1, 27–8.

[263] See H. Collins, *Justice in Dismissal* (Oxford, OUP, 1992) 97–8 and 100. To that extent, the argument that the range test excludes subjective considerations is rejected, on which, see A. Freer, 'The Range of Reasonable Responses Test: From Guidelines to Statute' (1998) 27 *Industrial Law Journal* 335, 342–3.

[264] H. Collins and M. Freedland, 'Finding the Right Direction for the "Industrial Jury": *Haddon v Van den Bergh Foods Ltd/Midland Bank plc v Madden*' (2000) 29 *Industrial Law Journal* 288, 289–95.

[265] P. Elias, 'Fairness in Unfair Dismissal: Trends and Tensions' (1981) 10 *Industrial Law Journal* 201, 211.

(3) Another explanation is that the judiciary are anxious to avoid a negative view of the legitimacy of their role. This is reflective of a judicial response to the 'flood-gates' argument[266] and *a conception of justice in dismissal articulated in terms of the restriction of judicial intervention to circumstances where the conduct of the employee in question has not resulted in harm to the employer's legitimate commercial interests.*[267] In Collins' view, the 'range test' does not actually *set* standards, but instead *reflects* managerial standards based on existing boundaries, i.e. the standard is variable, rather than fixed.[268] Indeed, other than in exceptional cases, the focus of the 'range test' is on the conduct of the employer in deciding to dismiss, rather than on the effect of the decision to dismiss on the employee or any injustice caused to the employee.[269] Collins argues that a more fitting conception of justice in dismissal would be captured by a test expressed in terms of a proportionality standard:

■ **H. Collins, 'Finding the Right Direction for the "Industrial Jury":** *Haddon v Van den Bergh Foods Ltd/Midland Bank plc v Madden*' (2000) 29 *Industrial Law Journal* 288, 295–6

My own suggestion for a route to avoid the pitfalls of the range of reasonable responses test of fairness in unfair dismissal is to imitate the move in administrative law towards a test of proportionality. This test has been developed precisely to strengthen judicial review of administrative decisions in a context where tests of perversity appeared too weak to provide a satisfactory balancing mechanism between the rights of individuals and the legitimate policy objectives of government. A test of proportionality investigates whether the decision-maker is pursuing a legitimate objective, and then asks whether the means that were adopted were necessary and appropriate to achieve that objective. Under this test the court scrutinises the means chosen closely in order to ensure that they did not unnecessarily or disproportionately interfere with the rights of an individual. In the context of employment, the test of proportionality would assume that the employer needs to exercise a disciplinary power over the workforce for the legitimate aim of efficient production, but would subject dismissal decisions both to the question whether the employer was in fact pursuing such a goal of efficiency, and to the question whether dismissal was a necessary and proportionate means for achieving that goal in the circumstances. The right that would normally serve as the balancing mechanism in this enquiry would be the right to claim unfair dismissal, but in some cases other rights, especially those contained in the Human Rights Act 1999,[270] would also inform the judgment about proportionality.[271]

---

[266] H. Collins and M. Freedland, 'Finding the Right Direction for the "Industrial Jury": *Haddon v Van den Bergh Foods Ltd/Midland Bank plc v Madden*' (2000) 29 *Industrial Law Journal* 288, 289–95.

[267] H. Collins, *Justice in Dismissal* (Oxford, Clarendon Press, 1992) 93–102.

[268] *ibid.*, 38 and 98–100; H. Collins, 'Capitalist Discipline and Corporatist Law' (1982) 11 *Industrial Law Journal* 78, 92–3. This point is also made by A. Freer, 'The Range of Reasonable Responses Test: From Guidelines to Statute' (1998) 27 *Industrial Law Journal* 335, 342.

[269] *W Devis & Sons Ltd v Atkins* [1977] AC 931, 952G per Viscount Dilhorne; *Henderson v Connect (South Tyneside) Ltd* [2010] IRLR 466. However, contrast this approach with the trend established in decisions such as *A v B* [2003] IRLR 405; *Salford Royal NHS Trust v Roldan* [2010] IRLR 721; and *Turner v East Midlands Trains Ltd* [2013] ICR 525.

[270] For examples of the way in which the European Convention on Human Rights can be applied to overturn a dismissal which is a disproportionate interference with a Convention right, see *Rubins v Latvia* [2015] IRLR 319 and *Matuz v Hungary* [2015] IRLR 74.

[271] See also H. Collins, *Employment Law* (Oxford, OUP, 2003) 174; H. Collins, *Justice in Dismissal* (Oxford, OUP, 1992) 97–8.

Reflection points

1. If Collins is correct that the range test should be replaced by a proportionality test, what would the effect be on employers? Would this result in an unwarranted intrusion into the decision-making prerogative of the employer?

2. Do you agree with the opinion of Morison J in *Haddon v Van Den Burgh Foods Ltd* [1999] IRLR 672 that the range test was an unjustifiable judicial gloss on the statutory language in section 98(4) of the ERA?

With these insights in mind, let us now turn to the methodology of the substantive fairness enquiry.

16.3.2 The 'substantive fairness' criterion in action

The starting point for our discussion is an analysis of the burden of proving 'reasonableness' under section 98(4) of the ERA. In *Boys and Girls Welfare Society v McDonald*,[272] it was held that the burden of proof is neutral, rather than weighted against the employer. The fairness of the employer's decision to dismiss must be reviewed at the EDT, rather than the point in time at which the notice of termination was proffered or the employer's decision to dismiss was exercised.[273] Another point to make is that the nature of the *reason* for the dismissal in terms of section 98(1), (2), and (3) of the ERA will have a bearing on whether the substance of the employer's decision fell within or outside the range of reasonable responses. For example, in the case of *British Home Stores Ltd v Burchell*, it was held that where the reason for the dismissal of an employee was based on his/her misconduct in terms of section 98(2)(b) of the ERA, the employer will have failed to fulfil the range of reasonable responses test if one of three criteria has not been met:

■ *British Home Stores Ltd v Burchell* [1980] ICR 303, 304B–F

Mr Justice Arnold:

What the Tribunal have to decide every time is, broadly expressed, whether the employer who discharged the employee on the ground of the misconduct in question (usually, though not necessarily, dishonest conduct) entertained a reasonable suspicion amounting to a belief in the guilt of the employee of that misconduct at that time. That is really stating shortly and compendiously what is in fact more than one element. First of all, there must be established by the employer the fact of that belief; that the employer did believe it. Secondly, that the employer had in his mind reasonable grounds upon which to sustain that belief. And thirdly, we think, that the employer, at the stage at which he formed that belief on those grounds, at any rate at the final stage at which he formed that belief on those grounds, had carried out as much investigation into the matter as was reasonable in all the circumstances of the case. It is the employer who manages to discharge the onus of demonstrating those three matters, we think, who must not be examined further. It is not relevant, as we think, that the Tribunal would itself have shared that view in those circumstances. It is not relevant, as we think, for the Tribunal to examine the quality of the material which the employer had before him, for instance to see whether it was the sort of material, objectively

---

[272] [1996] IRLR 129.
[273] *Stacey v Babcock Power Ltd* [1986] IRLR 3; *Parkinson v March Consulting Ltd* [1997] IRLR 308; and *White v South London Transport Ltd* [1998] ICR 293.

> considered, which would lead to a certain conclusion on the balance of probabilities, or whether it was the sort of material which would lead to the same conclusion only upon the basis of being 'sure' as it is now said more normally in a criminal context, or, to use the more old-fashioned term, such as to put the matter 'beyond reasonable doubt'. The test, and the test all the way through, is reasonableness; and certainly, as it seems to us, a conclusion on the balance of probabilities will in any surmisable circumstance be a reasonable conclusion.

What is clear from the tripartite test in *Burchell* is that it is not for a tribunal to check whether the employer established beyond all reasonable doubt that the employee was guilty of the alleged misconduct. Neither is there any requirement for the tribunal to be satisfied that the employer has shown that the employee was 'culpable' in some way at the point the employer decided to dismiss the employee for the reason of misconduct.[274]

If the tribunal's findings of fact do not support the conclusion that the employee had engaged in misconduct and/or it disagrees with what the employer did in the circumstances, that is beside the point. This is not a ground which will entitle the tribunal to find that the dismissal was substantively unfair since that would involve it in substituting its own judgment for that of the employer. A good example is the case of *London Ambulance v Small*.[275] A complaint was lodged by a woman against a paramedic (Mr Small) who had attended the home of her elderly mother, who subsequently died of heart disease. The grounds for the complaint were that Mr Small had not arranged for the patient to be carried down a set of stairs and instead had had her walk down them herself, that he had not done enough for the deceased in light of her high blood pressure and diabetic condition, and that he had made inappropriate remarks about the deceased's incontinence and criticized her daughter for failing to administer paracetamol to relieve her pain. The employment tribunal held that Mr Small's dismissal was unfair and made findings of fact that there was no evidence that Mr Small had failed to carry out a risk assessment before asking the patient to walk down the stairs, nor had the daughter told him that her mother was hypertensive and diabetic. In the Court of Appeal, Lord Justice Mummery held that the tribunal had erred in law:

■ *London Ambulance v Small* [2009] EWCA Civ 220, paras 40–43

Mummery LJ:
B. Substitution and misapplication

The main criticism of the [employment tribunal ('ET')]'s decision is that it fell into the very trap that, as it warned itself several times, it should avoid: 'We are conscious that we must not substitute our own view for that of the respondent.' (paragraph 6.3) Mr Reynold submitted that the ET failed to observe this warning. It did not apply the legal principles correctly stated by it. I agree. On the liability issue the ET ought to have confined its consideration to facts relating to the trust's handling of Mr Small's dismissal: the genuineness of the trust's belief and the reasonableness of the grounds of its belief about the conduct of Mr Small at the time of the dismissal. Instead, the ET introduced its own findings of fact about the conduct of Mr Small, including aspects of it that had been disputed at the disciplinary hearing. For example, the ET found that the daughter, who did not give evidence to the ET, had not told Mr Small that her mother was hypertensive and diabetic. Further, on the point whether Mr Small had done a risk assessment before asking the patient to walk, the ET held that there was no evidence that he had failed to carry out a risk assessment, but Mr Suter gave evidence to the ET that the crucial issue before the disciplinary panel was that Mr Small had

---

[274] *JP Morgan Securities plc v Ktorza* (UKEAT/0311/16/JOJ, 11 May 2017).
[275] [2009] IRLR 563.

not carried out a proper patient assessment before the decision was made. The ET used its findings of fact to support its conclusion that, at the time of dismissal, the trust had no reasonable grounds for its belief about Mr Small's conduct and therefore no genuine belief about it. By this process of reasoning the ET found that the dismissal was unfair. In my judgment, this amounted to the ET substituting itself and its findings for the trust's decision-maker in relation to Mr Small's dismissal. It is all too easy, even for an experienced ET, to slip into the substitution mindset. In conduct cases the claimant often comes to the ET with more evidence and with an understandable determination to clear his name and to prove to the ET that he is innocent of the charges made against him by his employer. He has lost his job in circumstances that may make it difficult for him to get another job. He may well gain the sympathy of the ET so that it is carried along the acquittal route and away from the real question—whether the employer acted fairly and reasonably in all the circumstances at the time of the dismissal.[276]

This extract from *London Ambulance v Small* confirms that the tribunal must confine itself to ascertaining whether the employer believed in the employee's misconduct and had reasonable grounds upon which to sustain that belief at the date of the dismissal: this is a subjective test.[277] If it is satisfied that these criteria are present, it must then go on to consider whether there is evidence to show that the employer undertook as much investigation into the allegations of misconduct as was reasonable in all the circumstances of the case.[278] Where the employer has a reasonable belief that an employee is guilty of gross misconduct and has undertaken the requisite degree of investigation, subject to any mitigating factors,[279] dismissal will almost always fall within the range of reasonable responses.[280] However, ultimately, the tribunal must not substitute its own judgment for that of the employer: a tribunal must only intervene sparingly.

The same point can be said for the EAT, i.e. that it should not readily interfere with the decision of the employment tribunal by substituting its own judgment for that of the tribunal. This point has been reiterated recently by the Court of Appeal and Inner House of the Court of Session in *Fuller v London Borough of Brent*,[281] *North West London Hospitals NHS Trust v Bowater*,[282] *Salford Royal NHS Trust v Roldan*,[283] *Crawford v*

---

[276] Sourced from BAILII available at http://www.bailii.org/cgi-bin/markup.cgi?doc=/ew/cases/EWCA/Civ/2009/220.html&query=London+and+Ambulance+and+Service+and+NHS+and+Trust+and+v+and+Small&method=boolean (last visited 31 October 2017). See also *Tayeh v Barchester Healthcare Ltd* [2013] IRLR 387 and *Secretary of State for Justice v Lown* [2016] IRLR 22 at paras 57–58 per Judge Eady QC, which are both illustrations of the Court of Appeal and EAT ruling that the employment tribunal had substituted their own perspective of the evidence to illegitimately find that a dismissal was unfair. In both cases, the tribunal's finding of unfairness was overturned.

[277] For example, see *Orr v Milton Keynes Council* [2011] EWCA Civ 62, [2011] ICR 704. The tribunal must not consider matters which the employer had not taken into account at the decision to dismiss: *Nejjary v Aramark* (UKEAT/0054/12, 31 May 2012).

[278] See *Sainsbury's Supermarkets Ltd v Hitt* [2003] ICR 111.

[279] For example, where the employee admits his misconduct at the outset of the process, this should be factored into the question whether the dismissal fell within the range of reasonable responses: *Cro Ports London Ltd v Wiltshire* (UKEAT/0344/14/DM, 23 January 2015). See also *Brito-Babapulle v Ealing Hospital NHS Trust* (UKEAT/0358/12/BA, 14 June 2013). Likewise, the employee's previous unblemished work record ought to be taken into account: *A v B (Local Authority)* [2016] IRLR 779. Where two employees were found culpable of the same acts of gross misconduct in respect of the same incident, it has been held that this disparity of treatment will not necessarily be relevant to the reasonableness assessment, as the circumstances of both cases must be 'on all fours' or parallel for disparate treatment to be necessarily unreasonable: *MBNA Ltd v Jones* (UKEAT/0120/15/MC, 1 September 2015).

[280] See *Shresha v Genesis Housing Association Ltd* [2015] IRLR 399 for an analysis of how the range test impacts on the extent and nature of the employer's investigation.

[281] [2011] EWCA Civ 267, [2011] ICR 806.   [282] [2011] EWCA Civ 63, [2011] IRLR 331.

[283] [2010] IRLR 721, 728 at para 51 per Lord Justice Elias.

Suffolk Mental Health Partnership NHS Trust,[284] *Stuart v London City Airport Ltd*,[285] *Newbound v Thames Water Utilities Ltd*,[286] and *Docherty v SW Global Resourcing Ltd*.[287] In each of these decisions, the Court of Appeal and Inner House had cause to reflect upon the interplay between the roles of the employer, the employment tribunal, and the EAT in a dismissal case:

■ *London Borough of Brent v Fuller* [2011] ICR 806, 810A–813C

Lord Justice Mummery:

A summary of the allocation of powers and responsibilities in unfair dismissal disputes bears repetition: it is for the employer to take the decision whether or not to dismiss an employee; for the tribunal to find the facts and decide whether, on an objective basis, the dismissal was fair or unfair; and for the [EAT] (and the ordinary courts hearing employment appeals) to decide whether a question of law arises from the proceedings in the tribunal. As appellate tribunals and courts are confined to questions of law they must not, in the absence of an error of law (including perversity), take over the tribunal's role as an 'industrial jury' with a fund of relevant and diverse specialist expertise . . . Unfair dismissal appeals to this court on the ground that the tribunal has not correctly applied section 98(4) can be quite unpredictable. The application of the objective test to the dismissal reduces the scope for divergent views, but does not eliminate the possibility of differing outcomes at different levels of decision. Sometimes there are even divergent views amongst appeal tribunal members and the members in the constitutions of this court. The appellate body, whether the EAT or this court, must be on its guard against making the very same legal error as the tribunal stands accused of making. An error will occur if the appellate body substitutes its own subjective response to the employee's conduct. The appellate body will slip into a similar sort of error if it substitutes its own view of the reasonable employer's response for the view formed by the tribunal without committing an error of law or reaching a perverse decision on that point. Other danger zones are present in most appeals against tribunal decisions. As an appeal lies only on a question of law, the difference between legal questions and findings of fact and inferences is crucial. Appellate bodies learn more from experience than from precept or instruction how to spot the difference between a real question of law and a challenge to primary findings of fact dressed up as law. Another teaching of experience is that, as with other tribunals and courts, there are occasions when a correct self-direction of law is stated by the tribunal, but then overlooked or misapplied at the point of decision. The tribunal judgment must be read carefully to see if it has in fact correctly applied the law which it said was applicable. The reading of an employment tribunal decision must not, however, be so fussy that it produces pernickety critiques. Over-analysis of the reasoning process; being hypercritical of the way in which the decision is written; focusing too much on particular passages or turns of phrase to the neglect of the decision read in the round: those are all appellate weaknesses to avoid.

■ *Bowater v North West London Hospitals NHS Trust* [2011] EWCA Civ 63, paras 18–19

Lord Justice Longmore:

. . . dismissal of the [employee] for her lewd comment was outside the range of reasonable responses open to a reasonable employer in the circumstances of the case. The EAT decided that the ET had substituted its own judgment for that of the judgment to which the employer had come.

---

[284] [2012] IRLR 402.   [285] [2013] EWCA Civ 973.   [286] [2015] IRLR 734.
[287] [2013] IRLR 874.

> But the employer cannot be the final arbiter of its own conduct in dismissing an employee. It is for the ET to make its judgment always bearing in mind that the test is whether dismissal is within the range of reasonable options open to a reasonable employer. The ET made it more than plain that that was the test which they were applying . . . The EAT apparently did not believe that the ET were being true to their word, but there is just no evidence of that. It is important that, in cases of this kind, the EAT pays proper respect to the decision of the ET. It is the ET to whom Parliament has entrusted the responsibility of making what are, no doubt sometimes, difficult and borderline decisions in relation to the fairness of dismissal. An appeal to the EAT only lies on a point of law and it goes without saying that the EAT must not, under the guise of a charge of perversity, substitute its own judgment for that of the ET.[288]

There is a persuasive argument that the insistence on appellate restraint in these decisions amounts to an attempt to soften the harsh impact of the application of the range of reasonable responses test in the Court of Appeal's earlier decisions in *Post Office v Foley*[289] and *London Ambulance v Small*.[290] In *Fuller*, *Crawford*, and *Bowater*, the Court of Appeal stressed that appellate bodies should be slow to chastise employment tribunals for slipping into the 'substitution mindset'.[291] By doing so, these cases would appear to suggest a modest departure from the unvarnished range test adumbrated in *Post Office v Foley*:[292] *Foley* had looked to appellate bodies to pay close attention to the reasoning of the tribunal for signs that it had substituted its judgment for that of the employer.

The Court of Appeal has arguably adopted another route to dilute an element of the harshness associated with the range test. As noted earlier, the 'range test' looks to the conduct of the employer in deciding to dismiss, rather than on the effect of the decision to dismiss on the employee or any injustice caused to the employee.[293] This approach underscores the one-dimensional nature of the range of reasonable responses standard. This can be contrasted with the two-dimensional nature of the proportionality standard of review adopted in the human rights context. Proportionality enjoins an adjudicator to focus on:

(1) the decision-maker's conduct in reaching its decision and whether that decision was consistent with a legitimate aim; as well as

(2) the effect of that decision on the rights of the employee, e.g. the extent of the injustice caused to him/her.[294]

An adjudicator is compelled to balance factors (1) and (2) against each other. Perhaps aware of the fact that the emphasis in the range of reasonable responses and the proportionality standards differ slightly,[295] the EAT and the Court of Appeal in *A v B*,[296] *Salford Royal NHS Trust v Roldan*,[297] and *Turner v East Midlands Trains Ltd*[298] have drawn

---

[288] Sourced from BAILII available at http://www.bailii.org/cgi-bin/markup.cgi?doc=/ew/cases/EWCA/Civ/2011/63.html&query=bowater&method=boolean (last visited 31 October 2017).

[289] [2000] ICR 1283.   [290] [2009] IRLR 563.

[291] See also *JJ Food Service Ltd v Kefil* [2013] IRLR 850.   [292] [2000] ICR 1283.

[293] *W Devis & Sons Ltd v Atkins* [1977] AC 931, 952G per Viscount Dilhorne; *Henderson v Connect (South Tyneside) Ltd* [2010] IRLR 466.

[294] For an extensive discussion of the operation of the proportionality standard in the labour law and dismissal context, see G. Davidov, *A Purposive Approach to Labour Law* (Oxford, OUP, 2016) 165–6 and 180–96.

[295] However, see the insistence in *Turner v East Midlands Trains Ltd* [2013] ICR 525, 540F–543B per Elias LJ that the range of reasonable responses test is equivalent to the proportionality standard of review. For a contrary view, see H. Collins and V. Mantouvalou, '*Redfearn v UK*: Political Association and Dismissal' (2013) 76 *Modern Law Review* 909, 920–1.   [296] [2003] IRLR 405.

[297] [2010] ICR 1457.   [298] [2013] ICR 525.

out some of the sting associated with the range test. They have done so by holding that the more serious the consequences of a dismissal for the employee, the more rigorous the investigation that is required from the employer.[299] As such, the range of reasonable responses test is self-modulating and sufficiently flexible to 'allow . . . for a heightened standard to be adopted where th[e] consequences [for the employee] are particularly grave'.[300]

A final point to stress is that there is an element of overlap between the *substantive fairness* and *procedural fairness* evaluative stages of a dismissal in the unfair dismissal regime. Although these two aspects of the fairness enquiry in section 98(4) are conceptually distinct, there is undoubtedly some interplay between them. However, if one of the three criteria highlighted in *Burchell* has not been satisfied by the employer, this does not mean that the employer will have invariably unfairly dismissed the employee. In *Boys and Girls Welfare Society v McDonald*,[301] Judge Peter Clark stressed that the primary focus should be on the range of reasonable responses test, i.e. whether the employer's actions fell within the range. Further, it is by no means the case that an employee's dismissal will be held to be unfair where the employee's conduct does not amount to a repudiatory breach of contract entitling the employer to summarily dismiss under common law.[302] The common law test for a finding of wrongful dismissal is to be sharply distinguished from the test for the establishment of an unfair dismissal.

For additional reading on the 'substantive fairness of the dismissal', visit the Online Resources for this book at www.oup.com/uk/cabrelli3e/

---

[299] Where the employee is a long-serving employee, this would also appear to be a relevant factor: *Newbound v Thames Water Utilities Ltd* [2015] IRLR 734.

[300] *Turner v East Midlands Trains Ltd* [2013] ICR 525, 541D per Elias LJ.

[301] [1996] IRLR 129.

[302] *Redbridge London Borough v Fishman* [1978] ICR 569, 574 per Phillips J; *Farrant v Woodroffe School* [1998] ICR 184, 195B–C per Judge Peter Clark; *Ford v Libra Fair Trades Ltd* [2008] All ER (D) 106; and *Weston Recovery Services v Fisher* (UKEAT/0062/10/ZT, 7 October 2010).

CHAPTER SEVENTEEN
PROCEDURAL FAIRNESS AND REMEDIES

17.1 INTRODUCTION TO THE PROCEDURAL FAIRNESS OF A DISMISSAL

This chapter will begin by examining the various potential conceptions of procedural fairness. These conceptions operate as abstract moral justifications for a regulatory regime which places emphasis on procedure. The chapter then underscores the diversity and adaptability of the standards of procedural fairness. Here, the statutory approach and judicial attitude has ebbed and flowed over the years, and the chapter will draw out the extent to which procedural safeguards have been weakened by the Employment Act 2008. Thereafter, the approach of the tribunals and courts to the standards of procedural fairness will be charted in light of the basic building blocks of a fair and proper procedure laid down in the ACAS[1] Code of Practice 1 on Disciplinary and Grievance Procedures ('ACAS Code').[2] The scrutiny of the stages of a procedurally fair process in this chapter will demonstrate the somewhat paradoxical nature of the applicable standards: they are expressed to be entrenched and immutable, but at once diverse and adaptable.

17.1.1 Conceptions of procedural fairness

The evaluation of the employer's pre-dismissal procedure is a central element of the tribunal's or court's overall assessment of the reasonableness of a dismissal under section 98(4) of the Employment Rights Act 1996 ('ERA'). An employer may be found to have

---

[1] The Advisory, Conciliation and Arbitration Service.
[2] See http://www.acas.org.uk/?articleid=2174 (last visited 7 November 2017) and the Online Resources for this book.

breached its statutory obligation not to unfairly dismiss an employee notwithstanding the fact that the decision to dismiss was substantively fair, having satisfied the 'range of reasonable responses' test in *Post Office v Foley*.[3] This will be the case where the procedure adopted by the employer was irregular and failed to meet the requisite standards prescribed by law. In fact, in most cases where an employee has been held to have been unfairly dismissed, it has been attributable to a lack of procedural fairness on the part of the employer rather than any want of substantive fairness.[4] This emphasis on proceduralism may seem surprising given the absence of any express reference to any requirement to adopt and apply fair and proper procedures in Part X of the ERA.[5] However, the prominence placed by the tribunals and courts on the employer's obligation to engage in a fair pre-dismissal procedure has cemented the crucial role of the standards of procedural fairness in the statutory unfair dismissal enquiry.

Since the inception of the statutory unfair dismissal regime in the Industrial Relations Act 1971, the tribunals and courts have attached great weight to procedural fairness in considering the reasonableness of a dismissal. Inherent within this judicial position lies the central notion that employment disputes about dismissals are best resolved at an early stage outside the tribunal system. One might think of two reasons for this. First, the avoidance of tribunal litigation entails a saving to the public purse. Secondly, and more importantly, if employees believe that they have had some opportunity to influence the outcome of a disciplinary process via certain procedural safeguards afforded to them by law, they are more likely to accept the employer's decision to dismiss and less likely to resort to litigation. One can argue that the notions of influence, control, participation, and consultation are embedded within the DNA coding of the procedural process which is prescribed by the law. As such, the argument runs that the standards of procedural fairness are not designed to impede the managerial prerogative to dismiss or to act as a deterrent to dismissals; instead, they function as a means of ensuring that employees are engaged, participate, and feel as if they have a degree of ownership in the pre-dismissal process.

Having decided that standards of procedural fairness assist in determining 'reasonableness' for the purposes of the unfair dismissal regime, one must then identify the ingredients of a fair and proper procedure. When constructing the various elements of a fair pre-dismissal process from a clean slate, it is useful to have regard to the abstract conceptions which might serve as justifications for such a procedure. Collins identifies three differing justifications for the emphasis on proceduralism, which he argues account for the inherent diversity and adaptability of those standards:

■ H. Collins, *Justice in Dismissal* (Oxford, OUP, 1992) 106–12

Respect for Dignity

. . . [T]he State should observe the rules of natural justice or due process before any deprivation of liberty or property, or any denial of some important legitimate expection [*sic*], for the sake of demonstrating respect for the individual affected by the decision. The rules of natural justice focus

---

[3] [2000] IRLR 827.

[4] This resonates with the idea that we developed in Chapter 16, namely that the judiciary are more inclined to scrutinize the reasonableness of the process applied by the employer leading up to the decision to dismiss than they are with the substance of the decision to dismiss itself, on which, see P. Elias, 'Fairness in Unfair Dismissal: Trends and Tensions' (1981) 10 *Industrial Law Journal* 201, 211. However, tribunals and courts are enjoined to assess the substantive and procedural fairness of a dismissal together, rather than separately, which form part of the same question: *Taylor v OCS Group Ltd* [2006] ICR 1602, 1615G–1616C per Lady Justice Smith.

[5] See H. Collins, 'Capitalist Doctrine and Corporatist Law—Part I' (1982) 11 *Industrial Law Journal* 78, 87–8.

on the right to an impartial hearing, because decision-makers have a duty to show that they are considering and taking into account the interests of the individual. Important elements of the right to an impartial hearing include an unbiased tribunal, the right to know the charges or allegations, and the opportunity to rebut them . . . These strict standards of natural justice could be applied without substantial modification to disciplinary dismissals. An employer could be required before making a dismissal for misconduct or incompetence to inform the employee of the reasons for the dismissal, to carry out a thorough investigation of the facts, and to give the employee the opportunity at a hearing before an independent person or committee to rebut the charges or explain mitigating circumstances. Any breach of these procedural requirements would then render the dismissal unfair . . .

Democratic Participation . . .

The focus here is . . . on the maximization of democratic participation in decisions affecting people's lives to the extent consistent with effective government. Participation contributes to open decision-making, which in turn is conducive to results which are generally morally acceptable. At the same time participation requires those involved to develop and refine their own moral viewpoints . . . In the context of dismissals, this model suggests that the workforce and the individuals concerned should be consulted prior to dismissals . . . This justification for procedural fairness therefore regards an impartial hearing as insufficient, for it demands an opportunity for workers to be consulted and to participate in decisions at every stage of the procedures leading to dismissals . . .

Efficiency

A third model of procedural fairness recognizes that careful decisions are often the best ones. It therefore demands that the employer's procedure prior to dismissals should be designed to ensure so far as possible that the decision is based on the best information available at reasonable cost concerning the facts and the likely consequences. In addition, efficiency considerations require, within reasonable bounds of administrative cost, careful consideration of the facts ascertained in order to ensure that all relevant factors are considered and irrelevant ones ignored. This model combines the aim of achieving the best results from the point of view of the aims of the decision-maker, whilst at the same time it is recognized that considerations of costs must place limits upon the scope of any investigation and hearing prior to a decision being reached. In applying this efficiency model of procedural fairness to dismissals, the key idea is that thorough procedures avoid costs to employers arising from erroneous dismissals. By dismissing only those workers who are either disruptive to production, seriously incompetent, or genuinely no longer needed, and no others, the employer achieves the most efficient use of his labour force. Erroneous dismissals of satisfactory employees may incur unnecessary costs with respect to search, hiring, and training for firm-specific skills, as well as the possible deleterious effects of the replacement workers being less efficient and a general sense of grievance arising among the workforce which would undermine the authority of management. But against these advantages of ensuring that only efficient dismissals are made should be weighed the administrative burden of a sophisticated disciplinary and selection process which generates the best information available and acts on it carefully. These efficiency considerations can account well for both the diversity and flexibility of procedural standards . . . we should not be surprised to discover a paternalist and managerialist orientation in the conception of procedural fairness in the law of unfair dismissal. The underlying moral principle, here supporting procedures required by efficiency, is one of maximizing general welfare. The general welfare standard is interpreted primarily as requiring support for the profitability and efficiency of business, though benefits to welfare are increased also by the satisfaction of employees' desire for fair procedures.[6]

---

[6] Writer's annotations appear in square brackets throughout this chapter.

The 'respect for dignity' and 'democratic participation' conceptions of procedural fairness would appear to link quite neatly to the notions of influence, control, participation, and consultation that we identified earlier as those inherent within the legal standards of procedural fairness. However, if we ask which of Collins' three justifications for procedural fairness best represents the current state of the law, it soon transpires that that would be too simplistic a conclusion to draw. For example, the 'respect for dignity' model entails the routine application of the strict standards of natural justice prior to the dismissal of an employee. Nevertheless, in a number of decisions, the tribunals and courts have shown that they do not accord the principles of natural justice the fullest of priority in the context of the regulation of dismissals in the workplace.[7] For example, in *Slater v Leicestershire Health Authority*,[8] it was held that a failure to follow the rules of natural justice does not of itself form an independent ground upon which a decision to dismiss may be attacked.[9] Moreover, in *Ayanlowo v IRC*,[10] it was held that an employee has no absolute entitlement to an oral hearing to make representations where he/she is afforded the right to make written representations.[11] Justifications for the marginal endorsement of the principles of natural justice in pre-dismissal procedure include the costs of compliance to the employer and the perceived need to reflect the fact that it is unrealistic to expect small employers to fully comply with the requirements of natural justice.[12]

Turning to the 'democratic participation' rationale, this envisages a central role for consultation and participation in the context of both disciplinary and economic dismissals. Although we will discover that consultation plays an important role in the requirements for a fair and proper process where the reason for the dismissal is redundancy, reorganization, or the capability/ill-health of the employee, it is not so easily transplantable to disciplinary dismissals for the reason of misconduct or incompetence/inadequate performance. For example, in disciplinary dismissals concerning allegations of misconduct, pre-dismissal consultations with employees are not the norm. Meanwhile, the notion of democratic participation would entail some involvement of the employee in the employer's decision to dismiss. However, examination of the basic requirements of the ACAS Code reveals that the prior participation of employees in the managerial decision to dismiss is even less of a hallmark of the standards of procedural fairness than consultation. This is perhaps understandable in light of the parliamentary and judicial reluctance to interfere in the managerial prerogative. Therefore, we are left with the 'efficiency' model of procedural fairness and the extent to which this is the best fit with the existing interpretation of proceduralism applied by the tribunals and courts:

■ H. Collins, *Justice in Dismissal* (Oxford, OUP, 1992) 120–4

3. An Interpretation of Procedural Fairness

To which of the three models of procedural justice described above does the current practice of the courts and tribunals most closely conform? . . . The third model of procedural justice based upon

---

[7] For a wider discussion of the relationship between natural justice and procedural fairness in the context of unfair dismissal, see S. Fredman and S. Lee, 'Natural Justice for Employees: The Unacceptable Faith of Proceduralism' (1986) 15 *Industrial Law Journal* 15.   [8] [1989] IRLR 16.

[9] See also the dismissal of the argument that the *audi alteram partem* rule applies in the context of the unfair dismissal legislation in *Earl v Slater and Wheeler (Airlyne) Ltd* [1972] ICR 508.

[10] [1975] IRLR 253.

[11] In *Ulsterbus Ltd v Henderson* [1989] IRLR 251; *Voluntary Hostels Group v Horn* [2003] All ER (D) 22 (January); *Santamera v Express Cargo Forwarding (t/a IEC Ltd)* [2003] IRLR 273; and *Rhondda Cynon Taf County Borough Council v Close* [2008] IRLR 868, it was held that it is not generally a breach of the principle of fairness to refuse an employee a right to cross-examine witnesses at his/her disciplinary hearing.

[12] This accords with the direction in section 98(4) that a tribunal or court must take into account the size and administrative resources of the employer in deciding whether the dismissal of the employee was reasonable or not. But cf. *Henderson v Granville Tours Ltd* [1982] IRLR 494.

efficient managerial decisions accords much more closely with the practice of the tribunals. Under this model the aim is to require procedures which will produce efficient decisions for management. The required procedures will often involve investigations and hearings. The degree of investigation must be such that it amounts to reasonable inquiries appropriate to the circumstances . . . Where the facts are clear . . . or the offence so serious that mitigating factors could not change the decision, then it would be a waste of expenditure to conduct an investigation or a hearing: so the law does not require one. In addition, the nature of the required procedure must reflect the cost consideration pertaining to personnel management, so that cumbersome and expensive procedures which comply with principles of natural justice need not be adopted . . . In short, the reasonable employer is the efficient employer, the one who adopts procedures conducive to cost effective manpower management. It is this subtle combination of the costs and benefits of dismissal procedures which best accounts for the diversity and flexibility of the courts' and tribunals' standards of procedural fairness.

This passage clarifies that the efficiency model, which operates as the foundation for the standards of procedural fairness, ensures that the employer engages in proper reflection on its decision to dismiss an employee. It functions to question the employer's initial reason or reasons for dismissal by affording it particular devices to re-evaluate the prudence of that decision in light of the aims and needs of its business. This questioning and reflection process is primarily channelled through the requirement in the ACAS Code for the employer to conduct pre-dismissal investigations and hearings.[13] The end result is that better managerial decision-making is secured from the perspective of what is in the best interests of the employer's business.

In many ways, the efficiency model of procedural fairness shares a number of similarities with the conception of substantive fairness which we examined in Chapter 16. Both conceptions[14] have as their focus the interests and conduct of the employer, rather than that of the employee. For example, in the case of *E C Cook v Thomas Linnell & Sons Ltd*,[15] it was held that the procedural requirement of a formal hearing in the context of an employee's inability to satisfy the demands of a job owing to poor performance could be forgone on the basis that it would otherwise impede the employer unreasonably in the efficient management of its business. This might seem somewhat counter-intuitive to the extent that the statutory unfair dismissal regime would appear to have the employee as its primary focus, i.e. the statutory command in section 94 of the ERA that *an employee* has the right not to be unfairly dismissed. This has been tempered to an extent by the requirement for employers to take into account the interests of an employee where the consequences of a finding of dismissal are likely to be serious.[16] However, in a number of cases, the courts have stressed time and again that tribunals assessing whether there

---

[13] *ILEA v Gravett* [1988] IRLR 497 (EAT); *A v B* [2003] IRLR 405 (EAT); and *Salford Royal NHS Foundation Trust v Roldan* [2010] ICR 1457.

[14] We noted that the 'range of reasonable responses' test in the law of unfair dismissal represents the expression of a conception of justice in dismissal which restricts judicial interference with the managerial prerogative to circumstances where the actions of an employee have not resulted in harm to the employer's legitimate commercial interests, on which, see H. Collins, *Justice in Dismissal* (Oxford, OUP, 1992) 93–102. The notion that the managerial decision to dismiss will only be second-guessed where it is commercially damaging to the employer resonates with the efficiency model of procedural fairness.

[15] [1977] IRLR 132. The employer had brought its opinion of his poor performance forcibly to the attention of the employee over a long period of time and, in these circumstances, the usual requirement for a disciplinary hearing prior to dismissal was set aside.

[16] See *Turner v East Midlands Trains Ltd* [2013] ICR 525; *Salford Royal NHS Foundation Trust v Roldan* [2010] IRLR 721 (CA); and *A v B* [2003] IRLR 405.

has been an unfair dismissal must concentrate their attention on the employer and its conduct, rather than on whether there has been any injustice caused to the employee.[17] As such, the mainstream view is that the injustice of the dismissal from the viewpoint of the employee is irrelevant.[18] Instead, as will become clear in our discussion of the employee's remedies for unfair dismissal later in this chapter, the question of injustice to the employee is a relevant consideration in assessing the compensation to be awarded to an employee, rather than the issue of liability.

The attitude of the legislature and the judiciary to the weight to be attached to the standards of procedural fairness has varied over the life of the unfair dismissal regime.[19] At the moment it is accorded a large degree of significance by virtue of the fact that the full force of the decision of the House of Lords in *Polkey v A E Dayton Services Ltd*[20] has been resurrected since the coming into force of the Employment Act 2008 on 6 April 2009. Therefore, as the law currently stands, although it is not compulsory for an employer to observe the procedural standards in the ACAS Code prior to dismissal, any failure to follow one of the stages of a proper procedure as set down in the ACAS Code could well result in a finding of unfair dismissal. The House of Lords in *Polkey* rejected the so-called 'no-difference' rule, which had been established by the decision of the Employment Appeal Tribunal ('EAT') in *British Labour Pump Co. Ltd v Byrne*.[21] This rule stipulated that if an employer's decision to dismiss an employee fell within the range of reasonable responses, the overall fairness of the dismissal would not be impugned notwithstanding the fact that the employer had not taken any or sufficient procedural steps prior to dismissal. As such, an employer could argue successfully that a dismissal ought to be held to be fair and its failure to follow proper pre-dismissal procedures should be excused since its conduct fell within the band of reasonable responses and the observance of procedural standards would have made no difference to its decision to dismiss. In contrast with the 'no-difference' rule adopted in *British Labour Pump*, the House of Lords in *Polkey* held that the evaluation of the reasonableness of a dismissal under section 98(4) should depend on the facts which were known to the employer at the time of the dismissal and what it had done, rather than what the position would have been if the employer had acted differently.[22] Therefore, the effect of *Polkey* is to accord a large degree of prominence to the application of procedural standards such as a reasonable investigation of the employee's case and affording the employee a disciplinary and appeal hearing. If the employer fails to comply with such standards, this will result in a finding of unfair dismissal.

However, the line of reasoning in *Polkey* does not mean that employers are expected to adhere slavishly to procedural standards in every case; instead, the House of Lords provided for an exception. In circumstances where a range of reasonable employers would conclude that compliance with procedural standards would be 'utterly useless'[23] or 'futile',[24] the employer's failure will be excused and the dismissal will nevertheless be held to be fair. One obvious situation covered by that exception is where an employee is caught red-handed in the commission of an act of gross misconduct.[25]

---

[17] *W Devis & Sons Ltd v Atkins* [1977] IRLR 314 (HL), 319 at paras 39–42 per Viscount Dilhorne; *Polkey v A E Dayton Services Ltd* [1988] AC 344, 355B–C per Lord Mackay of Clashfern. It is a matter of debate whether this construction is justified, given the stipulation in section 98(4) of the ERA that the reasonableness of the employee's dismissal must be considered in light of 'equity and the substantial merits of the case'.

[18] See the discussion in S. Anderman, 'Termination of Employment: Whose Property Rights?' in C. Barnard, S. Deakin, and G. S. Morris (eds), *The Future of Labour Law: Liber Amicorum Bob Hepple QC* (Oxford, Hart Publishing, 2004) 118–22.

[19] For a comprehensive account of the various swings of the pendulum, see H. Collins, *Justice in Dismissal* (Oxford, Clarendon Press, 1992) 112–20.   [20] [1988] AC 344.

[21] [1979] ICR 347.   [22] [1988] AC 344, 355A–B per Lord Mackay of Clashfern.

[23] *ibid.*, 355C per Lord Mackay of Clashfern.   [24] *ibid.*, 364G per Lord Bridge of Harwich.

[25] See also *Duffy v Yeomans and Partner Ltd* [1995] ICR 1.

Over the past 20 years, the prevailing efficiency conception of procedural fairness has been buttressed by an aspiration on the part of successive Governments to encourage:

(1) employers to adopt and apply disciplinary and grievance procedures as a matter of practice or as part of the contracts of employment of their employees; and

(2) employees and employers to settle their disputes about dismissals outside the tribunal system.

The pursuit of (1) and (2) has been motivated by a desire to reduce the volume of the caseload of the tribunals. The means adopted by successive British Governments to achieve these desired outcomes have varied quite considerably since 1994. In 2001, the Labour Government published a Consultation Paper entitled *Routes to Resolution: Improving Dispute Resolution in Britain*,[26] which articulated a concern about the lack of incidence of workplace disciplinary and grievance procedures and the attendant growth in employment disputes flowing through the tribunal system. Not long thereafter, the Employment Act 2002 and the Employment Act 2002 (Dispute Resolution) Regulations 2004[27] introduced the short-lived statutory disciplinary and dismissals procedures ('SDDP' and 'SDDPs') with effect from September 2004. In terms of this legislation, the rule in *Polkey* was partially reversed and an employer was bound to comply with the SDDPs prior to dismissing an employee, failing which the employee would be treated as automatically unfairly dismissed under the now-repealed section 98A(1) of the ERA. The subsequent review of the SDDPs by Gibbons[28] reported that the SDDPs had formalized, exacerbated, and accelerated unfair dismissal disputes and increased the numbers of employment tribunal applications. Ultimately, Gibbons recommended their repeal. The Government was in broad agreement with Gibbons' findings and the Employment Act 2008 abolished the SDDPs, albeit that Northern Ireland still adheres to statutory dismissal procedures.[29] Rather than rendering compliance with statutorily prescribed procedures a compulsory requirement, the Employment Act 2008 places greater prominence on the role of the ACAS Code. The principle in *Polkey* was reasserted. However, one should not draw the conclusion from this change of policy that the standards of procedural fairness imposed on employers can now be considered sufficiently robust from the perspective of employee protection:

■ **A. Sanders, 'Part One of the Employment Act 2008: "Better Dispute Resolution?"' (2009) 38 *Industrial Law Journal* 30, 47–8**

Problems arise because the . . . ACAS Code . . . is noticeably weaker than predecessor ACAS Codes . . . The difficulty is that the new Code replicates to a large extent the SDDPs even though it is widely recognised (including by tribunals) that the SDDPs were the bare minimum. The situation previously was that dismissals in breach of the SDDPs were 'automatically' unfair however tribunals could go on to find the dismissal 'ordinarily' unfair by s 98(4) ERA under the stricter standards of earlier ACAS Codes. It means there will be a deeper imprint of the statutory procedures on the law of unfair dismissal long after their repeal . . . Employees could be deprived of important protections under previous ACAS Codes such as the requirement that the employer's disciplinary action

---

[26] Available at http://webarchive.nationalarchives.gov.uk/+/http://www.dti.gov.uk/er/individual/resolution.pdf (last visited 7 November 2018).   [27] SI 2004/752.

[28] M. Gibbons, *Better Dispute Resolution: A Review of Employment Dispute Resolution in Great Britain* (DTI, 2007). The Gibbons Review was accompanied by a DTI Consultation Paper entitled *Success at Work: Resolving Disputes in the Workplace* (DTI, March 2007).

[29] Disciplinary and Grievance Procedures (April 2011), available at https://www.lra.org.uk/images/publications/44301_final_low_res_web_-4_and_intro.pdf (last visited 7 November 2018).

must be proportionate to the circumstances. This is a significant decline indeed when employees' protection against dismissal is nearly exclusively procedural, given tribunals' reluctance to examine the substantive fairness of dismissals.[30]

The Employment Act 2008 is unlikely to be the final instalment in the saga of government intervention in the area of procedural standards. On the contrary, the previous Coalition Government introduced legislation that places greater importance on the role of ACAS and alternative dispute resolution machinery in advance of tribunal litigation: the Enterprise and Regulatory Reform Act 2013 ('ERRA') and the Employment Tribunals (Early Conciliation: Exemptions and Rules of Procedure) Regulations 2014.[31] By introducing sections 18A and 18B of the Employment Tribunals Act 1996, the ERRA imposed an obligation on ACAS to provide conciliation services in individual workplace disputes. Before a prospective employee claimant lodges an employment claim with the tribunal, he/she is obliged to notify ACAS of his/her intention to do so.[32] This process builds on the pre-claim conciliation service that has been offered by ACAS since 2009, which, although voluntary, appeared to have enjoyed a measure of success.[33] Once again, the main driver for this recent reform was the desire to lighten the caseload of the employment tribunals. In conjunction with the introduction of employment tribunal and EAT issue and hearing fees in July 2013, the evidence from statistics published by ACAS revealed that the pre-claim conciliation provisions have served to further depress the number of cases pursued in the tribunals and courts. For example, in the period between April and September 2015, 16 per cent of cases were successfully settled by ACAS, an additional 66 per cent of employee claimants decided not to take their claim further, and only 18 per cent progressed to an employment tribunal claim.[34] Furthermore, the number of multiple claims taken to tribunals decreased from 5,847 before the implementation of the fees system, to just 1,740 in the year afterwards (2014–15), a reduction of 70 per cent.[35] Of course, in July 2017, the Supreme Court held that the imposition of tribunal fees represented a significant barrier to 'access to justice' and abolished the fees regime.[36] The Government was ordered to repay up to £27 million in fees.[37] Furthermore, it was held that the fees system resulted in indirect discrimination against women, who were much more likely to (a) suffer from maternity and sex discrimination, but were (b) much less likely to be able to afford the fees and so elect not to bring claims.

 For additional reading on the conceptions of procedural fairness, visit the Online Resources for this book at www.oup.com/uk/cabrelli3e/

[30] Cf. Sanders' analysis of the weakness of standards of procedural fairness given the dilution of the protection in the ACAS Code with Anderman's remark that the judiciary are willing 'to maintain relatively high procedural standards': S. Anderman, 'Termination of Employment: Whose Property Rights?' in C. Barnard, S. Deakin, and G. S. Morris (eds), *The Future of Labour Law: Liber Amicorum Bob Hepple QC* (Oxford, Hart Publishing, 2004) 128.   [31] SI 2014/254.

[32] See Chapter 2, section 2.3.4.

[33] See ACAS Annual Report 2010/11, available at http://www.acas.org.uk/media/pdf/p/0/Acas_Annual_Report_Accounts_2010–11_colour.pdf at pages 6, 7, and 14–15 (last visited 7 November 2017); A. Denvir, S. O'Regan, M. Williams, A. Cox, D. Pearmain, and H. Hooker, *Pre-Claim Conciliation Pilot: Evaluation Summary Report*, Research Paper 02/29, available at http://www.acas.org.uk/media/pdf/0/t/0209_PCC_pilot_summary_v2_010709.pdf (last visited 7 November 2017).

[34] See ACAS's early conciliation statistics, available at http://www.acas.org.uk/ECupdate at Table 2 (last visited 7 November 2017).

[35] 'Unions blame 70% fall in employment tribunal cases on fees', available at https://www.theguardian.com/money/2017/jan/31/employment-tribunal-cases-down-70-since-fees-introduced (last visited 7 November 2017).   [36] *R (on the application of UNISON) v Lord Chancellor* [2017] 3 WLR 409.

[37] 'Ministers vow to end employment tribunal fees after court defeat', available at https://www.theguardian.com/money/2017/jul/26/union-supreme-court-fees-unfair-dismissal-claims (last visited 7 November 2017).

17.1.2 Diversity and flexibility in procedural fairness

One of the paradoxes of the standards of procedural fairness is that they are rigid and immutable but at once diverse and adaptable:

■ *McLaren v National Coal Board* [1988] ICR 370, 377E–G

> *Sir John Donaldson MR:*
>
> What industrial warfare may do is to create a situation in which conduct which would not normally justify dismissal becomes conduct which does justify dismissal . . . You have the position that acceptable reasons for dismissing may change in a varying industrial situation, but the standards of fairness never change. They are immutable but are applied in a different situation. What the industrial tribunal was here saying is that the standards are not immutable. They are saying that standards of fairness do change, and that I cannot accept.

In order to fully understand how it can be that the various standards of procedural fairness vary according to the circumstances of the employee's case, it is useful to analyse matters in terms of standards found in the ACAS Code.

These are fleshed out in the case law and ACAS's non-statutory guide on the ACAS Code, namely *Discipline and Grievances at Work*[38] ('ACAS Non-Statutory Guide'). These basic elements may be thought of as comprising:

(a) a letter informing the employee of the allegations against the employee or the problem;

(b) suspension with pay, if necessary;

(c) a reasonable investigation;

(d) discussion and consultation with the employee;

(e) a disciplinary hearing;

(f) a managerial decision to impose a disciplinary sanction; and

(g) an appeal hearing.

The question as to whether the employer is bound to undertake all or some of the procedural standards (a)–(g) is largely dependent on the employer's reason for the dismissal of the employee, e.g. whether it is misconduct, redundancy or capability, breach of statute/duty, or some other substantial reason ('SOSR').[39] The nature of the reason for dismissal dictates the extent to which the employer is bound to comply with the standards of procedural fairness which we identified as (a)–(g). The speech of Lord Bridge of Harwich in *Polkey* provides support for this contention:

■ *Polkey v A. E. Dayton Services Ltd* [1988] AC 344, 364B–E

> *Lord Bridge of Harwich:*
>
> Employers contesting a claim of unfair dismissal will commonly advance as their reason for dismissal one of the reasons specifically recognised as valid by section [98(1), (2), or (3) of the ERA] . . . But an employer having prima facie grounds to dismiss for one of these reasons will in the great majority of

[38] See http://www.acas.org.uk/media/pdf/9/g/Discipline-and-grievances-Acas-guide.pdf (last visited 7 November 2017).   [39] Section 98(1)—(3) of the ERA.

cases not act reasonably in treating the reason as a sufficient reason for dismissal unless and until he has taken the steps, conveniently classified in most of the authorities as 'procedural,' which are necessary in the circumstances of the case to justify that course of action. Thus, in the case of incapacity, the employer will normally not act reasonably unless he gives the employee fair warning and an opportunity to mend his ways and show that he can do the job; in the case of misconduct, the employer will normally not act reasonably unless he investigates the complaint of misconduct fully and fairly and hears whatever the employee wishes to say in his defence or in explanation or mitigation; in the case of redundancy, the employer will normally not act reasonably unless he warns and consults any employees affected or their representative, adopts a fair basis on which to select for redundancy and takes such steps as may be reasonable to avoid or minimise redundancy by redeployment within his own organisation.

Having appreciated that the standards of procedural justice are diverse and adaptable in nature, and adjusted in tandem with the employer's reason for dismissal, we now move on to consider their content in some detail.

17.2 THE APPLICABLE STANDARDS OF PROCEDURAL FAIRNESS

In this section, we provide a framework for the analysis of a fair and proper disciplinary procedure, which an employer must adopt in advance of dismissing an employee.

17.2.1 Plotting the basic framework

The basic ingredients of a fair and proper procedure are found in the ACAS Code. The intensity of the employer's procedural obligations will be sculpted in light of the reason for the dismissal. The elements of a procedurally fair process which we listed as features (a)–(g) in section 17.1.2 are relevant irrespective of the reason for the dismissal and deserve special attention. Therefore, we turn to consideration of these first. However, it should be noted that we will not consider feature (d) here, namely discussion and consultation, since it is covered in our treatment of redundancy dismissals in Chapter 18[40] and in section 17.2.2.2 in relation to capability dismissals in the context of employee incompetence/poor performance.

17.2.1.1 The ACAS Code

Section 207 of the Trade Union and Labour Relations (Consolidation) Act 1992 ('TUL-RCA') enjoins a tribunal to take into account the provisions of the ACAS Code[41] in determining the fairness of a dismissal.[42] Turning to the scope of the ACAS Code, paragraph 1

---

[40] See Chapter 18, section 18.3.3.

[41] For the full version of the ACAS Code, please see the Online Resources for this book or http://www.acas.org.uk/?articleid=2174 (last visited 7 November 2017). For an evaluation of the success of the ACAS Code, see N. Rahim, A. Brown, and J. Graham, 'Evaluation of the Acas Code of Practice on Disciplinary and Grievance Procedures', Research Paper 06/11, available at http://www.acas.org.uk/media/pdf/4/r/Evaluation-of-the-Acas-Code-of-Practice-on-Disciplinary-and-Grievance-procedures-accessible-version-.pdf at page 55 (last visited 7 November 2017).

[42] See also *Lock v Cardiff Railway Co. Ltd* [1998] IRLR 358, where it was held that a failure on the part of the employment tribunal to examine whether the ACAS Code has been complied with will amount to an error of law.

specifically provides that it is of no relevance to dismissals for the reason of redundancy or a dismissal pursuant to the non-renewal of a fixed-term contract of employment on its expiry. It has also been held that it does not apply to dismissals for SOSR or capability/ill-health.[43] Therefore, in our ensuing discussion of the ACAS Code, we will not be addressing redundancy, SOSR or capability/ill-health dismissals and reference should be made to sections 17.2.2.1 and 17.2.2.2 and Chapter 18, section 18.3, for a comprehensive examination of standards of procedural fairness in such contexts.

The provisions of the ACAS Code prescribe a series of basic incremental steps, which, taken cumulatively, combine to form the procedural expectations the law has of an employer prior to a dismissal. These are not exhaustive. Hence it is not the case that an employer's pre-dismissal procedure will be treated as automatically procedurally fair for the purposes of section 98(4) of the ERA if the employer complies with the basic requirements of the ACAS Code.[44] That may or may not be the case depending on the nature of the employer and the circumstances of the employee's case, which is reflective of the command in section 98(4) of the ERA that the tribunal should take into account the 'size and administrative resources of the employer's undertaking' and 'equity and the substantial merits of the case' in its overall evaluation of the fairness of the dismissal. In certain contexts, the law will require the employer to go over and above the standard of procedural fairness set by the ACAS Code and thus confer additional employment protection and safeguards. Much will depend on the circumstances of each case as to whether bare compliance with the ACAS Code is sufficient. The Code is best thought of as a foundation upon which the tribunal builds the requisite standards of procedural fairness.

A useful flow chart identifying the basic incremental steps comprised in a procedurally fair dismissal is provided by ACAS in the ACAS Non-Statutory Guide.[45] This is replicated in Figure 17.1.

The way the ACAS Code is drawn demonstrates that it is designed to strike an appropriate balance between the objectives of certainty and flexibility. With that point in mind, we now turn to consider the incremental steps and other essential factors which are highlighted by the ACAS Code.

17.2.1.2 Suspension of an employee

Paragraph 8 of the ACAS Code provides that an employer may suspend an employee where this is 'considered necessary' in the circumstances of the case. Where the contract of employment is suspended, the employee will be required to remain away from the place of employment. The recommendation is made that any period of suspension should be paid,[46] kept as brief as possible and under regular review, and that it should be clarified that it is not being treated as a disciplinary sanction. In particular, it will be appropriate where the employer is investigating alleged 'breach of duty or statute' or 'misconduct' on the part of the employee in terms of the reasons in section 98(2)(d) or (b) of the ERA, e.g. where an allegation of dishonesty or inappropriate behaviour is made.[47] It may also be necessary for an employer to suspend where the reason for a potential future dismissal

---

[43] *Phoenix House Ltd v Stockman* [2016] IRLR 848; *Holmes v Qinetiq Ltd* [2016] IRLR 664.

[44] Conversely, if the employer fails to conform to the provisions of the ACAS Code, this will not necessarily result in a finding of unfair dismissal: *Buzolli v Food Partners Ltd* [2013] All ER (D) 340 (February). See also Chapter 2, section 2.2.3.

[45] See http://www.acas.org.uk/media/pdf/9/g/Discipline-and-grievances-Acas-guide.pdf (last visited 7 November 2017).

[46] It should be noted that it is technically incorrect to say that the contract of employment may be suspended with pay, since, as noted by Scott LJ in *Bird v British Celanese Ltd* [1945] KB 336, 341, the natural and legal meaning of 'suspension' is that the employee ceases to be under an obligation to work and the employer is relieved of the corresponding obligation to pay, on which, see Chapter 7, section 7.3.

[47] *Clark v Civil Aviation Authority* [1991] IRLR 412, 415 per Mr Justice Wood.

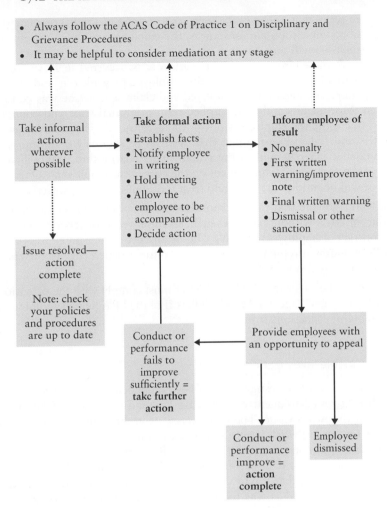

Figure 17.1 *Basic elements of a procedurally fair dismissal*

Source: *The Non-Statutory Guide on the ACAS Code Entitled Discipline and Grievances at Work*, at http://www.acas.org.uk/media/pdf/9/g/Discipline-and-grievances-Acas-guide.pdf at page 5 (last visited 7 November 2017).

is 'capability' under section 98(2)(a) and (3) of the ERA, e.g. where the capability issue is the incompetence or poor performance of the employee and an investigation is required.

However, before exercising the power to suspend, employers should be mindful of certain important restrictions and other legal issues, as follows:

(1) The courts have cautioned employers against being too hasty to suspend employees. For example, in *Crawford v Suffolk Mental Health Partnership NHS Trust*,[48] Elias LJ warned employers that they ought not to 'subject employees to [suspension] without the most careful consideration and a genuine and reasonable belief that the case, if established, might justify the epithet "criminal" being applied to the employee's conduct'.[49]

---

[48] [2012] IRLR 402. See Chapter 7, section 7.3.2 and the high threshold for suspension set in *Agoreyo v London Borough of Lambeth* [2017] EWHC 2019 (QB). [49] [2012] IRLR 402, 410.

(2) The implied terms that police every contract of employment also regulate the power of suspension.[50] In certain circumstances, the employee will have a right to work[51] and so suspension will amount to a breach of the terms of the contract of employment.[52] Where those circumstances are satisfied, as occurred in *Bosworth v Angus Jowett & Co. Ltd*,[53] this will enable the employee to walk out and resign before the disciplinary investigation is completed and claim that he/she was constructively dismissed. More significantly, the implied term of mutual trust and confidence will function to control the employer's power of suspension.[54] Therefore, where the suspension is undertaken in a manner that destroys or seriously undermines the trust and confidence inherent within the employment relationship, this will result in a breach of the contract of employment on the part of the employer.[55] Once again, the employee will be entitled to resign and treat the employer in constructive dismissal.[56]

(3) One should also note that the common law admits of no managerial power to suspend the employee without pay.[57] As such, an employer must rely on an express term of the contract of employment to do so. In the absence of such an express entitlement, this will amount to a repudiatory breach of contract which entitles the employee to claim constructive dismissal.[58]

(4) During a period of suspension, the employer must comply with the provisions of the National Minimum Wage Act 1998 and Part II of the ERA, which prohibits the making of unlawful deductions from wages.

17.2.1.3 Reasonable investigation

The fact that a reasonable investigation is a key component of a fair pre-dismissal procedure has been stressed frequently in the case law and is a requirement enshrined in paragraph 4 of the ACAS Code. The *locus classicus* in the context of an allegation of misconduct is set out in *British Home Stores Ltd v Burchell*.[59] Here, in the context of a misconduct[60] case under section 98(2)(b) of the ERA, Arnold J stated that an employer must be able to show that it had reasonable grounds for its genuine belief in the misconduct of the employee and that it had undertaken as much investigation into the allegations of the employee's case as was reasonable in all the circumstances, at the stage at which it formed that belief on those grounds and, at any rate, at the final stage at which

---

[50] See Chapter 6, section 6.2.   [51] See Chapter 6, section 6.2.1.

[52] For example, where the employee is a 'piece-worker' (*Devonald v Rosser & Sons* [1906] 2 KB 728) or requires to work in order to avoid a loss of reputation or publicity (e.g. actors, as in *Clayton & Waller Ltd v Oliver* [1930] AC 209), or to maintain or develop key skill levels or keep up to date with developments in the industry, sector, or trade within which he/she works (e.g. the spread-better in *William Hill Organisation Ltd v Tucker* [1998] 1 IRLR 313 and the sales director in *Bosworth v Angus Jowett & Co. Ltd* [1977] IRLR 374).   [53] [1977] IRLR 374.

[54] *Gogay v Hertfordshire County Council* [2000] IRLR 703 (CA); see also Chapter 6, section 6.2.4.

[55] For example, see *Yapp v FCO* [2015] IRLR 112; D. Brodie, 'Risk Allocation and Psychiatric Harm: *Yapp v Foreign and Commonwealth Office*' (2015) 44 *Industrial Law Journal* 270.

[56] For example, see *Milne v Link Asset & Security Co. Ltd* [2005] All ER (D) 143 (September).

[57] *Hanley v Pease & Partners Ltd* [1915] 1 KB 698; *Bird v British Celanese Ltd* [1945] KB 336.

[58] *Morrison v Amalgamated Transport and General Workers Union* [1989] IRLR 361.

[59] [1980] ICR 303. Approved by the Court of Appeal in *W Weddel & Co. Ltd v Tepper* [1980] ICR 286.

[60] The guidelines in *British Home Stores Ltd v Burchell* on the requirements for the employer to have a reasonable belief in the employee's misconduct and to undertake a reasonable investigation have been held to be of equal application where the employee's reason for dismissal is 'some other substantial reason' under section 98(1)(b) of the ERA: *Perkin v St George's Healthcare NHS Trust* [2005] IRLR 934. Meanwhile, where the employer's reason for dismissal is the 'capability' of the employee in terms of section 98(2)(a) of the ERA, the nature of what constitutes a reasonable investigation will differ from that applicable in a conduct case, which is a matter to which we will return in section 17.2.2.2.

it formed that belief on those grounds.[61] Therefore, the rigour, nature, and extent of the investigation will be conditioned by the circumstances of the case. Factors such as the size and resources of the employer, the severity of the allegations against the employee,[62] the consequences for the employee if the allegations are substantiated,[63] whether the employer undertook to investigate allegations by a third party, but then failed to do so,[64] and the fact that the employee may have admitted his/her misconduct will flavour the degree of investigation required. As such, the standard of the investigation will vary according to the context.[65]The tribunal must apply a range of reasonable responses test in evaluating whether the employer has conducted sufficient investigation in all of the circumstances of the case:

■ *Sainsbury's Supermarkets Ltd v Hitt* [2002] EWCA Civ 1588, [2003] ICR 111, 119–20

Lord Justice Mummery:
Conclusion . . .

[T]he majority [of the employment tribunal] considered that the investigation was not reasonable. They arrived at that conclusion by substituting their own opinion as to what was a reasonable and adequate investigation, instead of applying . . . the objective standard of the reasonable employer as to what was a reasonable investigation. The employment tribunal were understandably faced with a confusing state of the law as between, on the one hand, the long established approach laid down by Arnold J in the [EAT] in *British Home Stores Ltd v Burchell (Note)* [1980] ICR 303 and, on the other hand, the more recent decisions of the [EAT] in *Haddon v Van den Bergh Foods Ltd* [1999] ICR 1150 and *Midland Bank plc v Madden* [2000] 2 All ER 741. I had hoped that that confusion would have been removed by the subsequent decision of the Court of Appeal on the appeal in *Foley v Post Office* and *HSBC Bank plc (formerly Midland Bank plc) v Madden* [2000] ICR 1283, and that it had been made clear in the judgments that it was necessary to apply the objective standards of the reasonable employer to *all* aspects of the question whether the employee had been fairly and reasonably dismissed. Unfortunately, it appears that the law has not been made as clear as it should have been, since experienced members of the [EAT] have in this case interpreted what was said in *Madden's* case, in relation to the objective standards of reasonableness and the range of reasonable responses test, as not applying to the question whether an investigation into the alleged or suspected misconduct was reasonable in the circumstances of the case . . . The range of reasonable responses test (or, to put it another way, the need to apply the objective standards of the reasonable employer) applies as much to the question whether the investigation into the suspected misconduct was reasonable in all the circumstances as it does to the reasonableness of the decision to dismiss for the conduct reason.

This passage reiterates that recourse to the range of reasonable responses test is not only relevant for the purposes of determining the substantive fairness of the employer's decision to dismiss, but also must be applied in the evaluation of this critical element

---

[61] [1980] ICR 303, 304D. See also *Sneddon v Carr-Gomm Scotland Ltd* [2012] IRLR 820; *Stuart v London City Airport Ltd* [2013] EWCA Civ 973.

[62] *Tykocki v Royal Bournemouth & Christchurch Hospitals NHS Foundation Trust* (UKEAT/081/16/JOJ, 17 October 2016).

[63] *A v B* [2003] IRLR 405. The greater the injustice a dismissal causes an employee, the more exacting the investigation must be: *Turner v East Midlands Trains Ltd* [2013] ICR 525; *Salford Royal NHS Foundation Trust v Roldan* [2010] IRLR 721 (CA). The EAT has observed that this principle is not restricted to circumstances in which the dismissal may result in the employee being disqualified from their profession and as such, applies in all cases: *Moncrieffe v London Underground Ltd* (UKEAT/0235/16/DA, 20 January 2017).

[64] *Scott v EC Maritime PCC Ltd* (UKEAT/0032/16/LA, 10 October 2016).

[65] *ILEA v Gravett* [1988] IRLR 497, 499 per Mr Justice Wood.

of the procedural fairness of the dismissal. For example, in *Shrestha v Genesis Housing Association Ltd*,[66] the Court of Appeal rejected the employee's argument that where the employee provides several explanations to the allegations made against him/her and raises other lines of defence, then it is incumbent on the employer to investigate each of these factors unless they are clearly false or unarguable. Rather, the Court of Appeal ruled that there is no requirement for the employer to undertake a forensic investigation into each explanation advanced by the employee in respect of the allegations made, since the duty of the employer is to conduct a reasonable investigation only. Likewise, in *NHS24 v Pillar*.[67] Here the employee alleged that the employer had undertaken too much investigation by inserting references to two past incidents of similar misconduct which had not been subjected to disciplinary action at the time. This was rejected by the EAT on the grounds that the inclusion of such references was relevant, material, and reasonable in the circumstances.

Another significant matter is whether an employer will have satisfied the standards of procedural fairness where the individual identified as having sufficient skill and experience to conduct the employer's investigation also carries out the disciplinary hearing. Paragraph 6 of the ACAS Code directs that 'where practicable, different people should carry out the investigation and disciplinary hearing'.[68] However, the words 'where practicable' are of paramount importance. In certain contexts, it will not be reasonable to expect the employer to divide the responsibility for the investigation and the hearing between two different individuals. An example is provided by the case of *Slater v Leicestershire Health Authority*.[69] Here, the Court of Appeal held that an employee's dismissal was not rendered unfair by the fact that the manager who had carried out a preliminary investigation also conducted the disciplinary hearing and took the decision to dismiss. Acting in a dual capacity did not preclude the individual from conducting a fair inquiry. The key factor is impartiality.

Of course, an investigation will not always be necessary in a case of gross misconduct, i.e. where an employee is dismissed without notice or payment in lieu of notice. However, paragraph 23 of the ACAS Code reminds us that 'a fair disciplinary process should always be followed, before dismissing for gross misconduct'. This may entail a disciplinary hearing at which the employee is afforded the opportunity to present his/her case, but may not involve an investigation. Once again, much will depend on the facts and circumstances of each case. For example, in the case of *Spence v Department of Agriculture and Rural Development*,[70] it was held that a fair procedure will normally require an employer to consider disclosing anything in its possession which may be of assistance to an employee who is contesting the disciplinary charge or wishes to make submissions in relation to the disciplinary penalty.

When an investigation is organized by the employer, the ACAS Non-Statutory Guide recommends that an investigating officer be appointed to conduct the investigation.[71] The employer must exercise caution where its human resources ('HR') department offers advice to the investigating officer to ensure that the input of the latter is limited to legal advice and advice about procedure, rather than straying into the merits of the allegations made against the employee. For example, where the investigating officer changed the disciplinary sanction from a final warning to dismissal following the strong advice of the HR department, it was held that this was a procedural irregularity

---

[66] [2015] IRLR 399.   [67] (UKEATS/0005/16/JW, 21 April 2017).

[68] Paragraph 27 of the ACAS Code also recommends that the identity of the personnel involved in the disciplinary hearing and the appeal hearing should differ. However, the case of *Rowe v Radio Rentals Ltd* [1982] IRLR 177 indicates the circumstances in which this may be impracticable.

[69] [1989] IRLR 16.   [70] [2011] IRLR 806.

[71] See http://www.acas.org.uk/media/pdf/9/g/Discipline-and-grievances-Acas-guide.pdf at page 17 (last visited 7 November 2017).

and that the employee's dismissal was unfair.[72] In particular, this could trap employers where the investigating officer is inexperienced in such matters and extensively relies on HR advice.

An additional issue which has cropped up in recent years in the context of disciplinary investigations concerns the employee's rights under Article 8 of the European Convention on Human Rights ('ECHR'). In particular, a number of cases have addressed whether an employer has infringed the employee's right to privacy under Article 8 ECHR by accessing the employee's emails, materials, photos, documents, etc. stored on their personal devices (such as mobile phones) or the employer's work equipment, as part of the investigation. The decision in *Garamukanwa v Solent NHS Trust*[73] can be contrasted with *Barbulescu v Romania*.[74] In *Garamukanwa*, the EAT ruled that there was no breach of the employee's right to privacy because Article 8 was not engaged where the employer used his private photos and documents as part of its internal disciplinary process where they had been passed to them by the police. However, in *Barbulescu* the opposite conclusion was reached. The Grand Chamber of the European Court of Human Rights held that the employer's monitoring of the employee's emails that had been sent using his work equipment had invaded his privacy rights and infringed Article 8. This is a fast-growing area of law, which has more content and guidance to come from the courts.

17.2.1.4 Hearings

Disciplinary and appeal hearings are two of the key planks of the pre-dismissal procedure contained in the ACAS Code.[75] In this section, we analyse the disciplinary hearing. The disciplinary hearing is the principal forum in which the employee will present his/her case and side of the story.[76] There is no prescribed format for a disciplinary hearing and the ACAS Code is particularly flexible in that regard. In the case of *Clark v Civil Aviation Authority*,[77] the EAT provided guidance additional to that contained in the ACAS Code about the purpose and content of the meeting:

■ *Clark v Civil Aviation Authority* [1991] IRLR 412

Mr Justice Wood (President):

After due investigation and before reaching any final decision, a disciplinary hearing is obviously necessary as are any appeal hearings. The practice at such hearings will follow the rules of natural justice, which are really matters of fairness and common sense . . . [T]he procedure may vary from one situation to another, but the industrial members would suggest a broad approach on the following lines: explain the purpose of the meeting; identify those present; if appropriate, arrange representation; inform the employee of the allegation or allegations being made; indicate the evidence whether in statement form or by the calling of witnesses; allow the employee and representative to ask questions; ask whether the employee wishes any witnesses to be called; allow the employee or the representative to explain and argue the case; listen to argument from both sides upon the allegations and any possible consequence, including any mitigation; ask the employee

---

[72] *Ramphal v Department of Transport* [2015] IRLR 985; *Dronsfield v University of Reading* [2016] ICR 1107. [73] [2016] IRLR 476.

[74] [2017] IRLR 1032.

[75] For example, each of paragraphs 4, 11, 12, 13, 14, 15, 16, 17, 25, and 28 of the ACAS Code have some bearing on the form which those hearings will take.

[76] Where the charge against the employee is not one of gross misconduct and the employer refuses to afford the employee the opportunity to put his/her case, this will be procedurally unfair: *R (Shoesmith) v OFSTED* [2011] IRLR 679. [77] [1991] IRLR 412.

> whether there is any further evidence or enquiry which he considers could help his case. After due deliberation the decision will almost certainly be reduced into writing, whether or not an earlier oral indication has been given.[78]

This excerpt highlights the essential role performed by the hearing in affording the employee the opportunity to hear the case, charge, and/or allegations made against him/her. In *Strouthos v London Underground Ltd*,[79] the exact parameters of the employer's obligations of disclosure at the hearing[80] were clarified. In particular, it was narrated that it will be a breach of procedural justice in most circumstances to permit an employer to lead additional evidence that crops up during the disciplinary process and substantiates the allegations or to include additional charges or allegations against the employee during the course of the disciplinary process. Of particular importance is the requirement for the employer to carefully prescribe the charge against the employee. For example, in *Celebi v Scolarest Compass Group UK & Ireland Ltd*,[81] it was alleged that the employer's money had gone missing. The EAT held that money could go missing for a variety of reasons, including inefficiency, negligence/mistake, the crimes of others, or the theft/dishonesty of the employee subject to disciplinary proceedings. In such a case, the employee should be provided with the rationale for the disciplinary process, e.g. theft/dishonesty or poor performance, since the nature of the rationale would colour his/her attitude and approach to the procedure. Any employee accused of dishonesty should have had that point put to him/her in no uncertain terms.

What is abundantly clear is that employers should be extremely cautious about proceeding with a disciplinary hearing in the employee's absence. This may render a dismissal unfair. In *Nabili v The Norfolk Community Health & Care NHS Trust*,[82] the EAT advised tribunals to focus on two issues: first, whether the presence of the employee would have been futile; and secondly, whether at the time of the dismissal, the employer had acted reasonably in the circumstances in deciding that the employee's attendance would have had no impact on the decision to dismiss. As such, both questions must be posed and it is not enough to ask one only.

Turning to paragraphs 13–17 of the ACAS Code, these provide for representation at the meeting. They are supplemented by the provisions of section 10 of the Employment Relations Act 1999 ('ERelA 1999') which confer a statutory right in favour of a 'worker'[83] to be accompanied by a companion at a disciplinary hearing:

Section 10 Right to be accompanied

(1) This section applies where a worker—

    (a) is required or invited by his employer to attend a disciplinary or grievance hearing, and

    (b) reasonably requests to be accompanied at the hearing . . .

---

[78] Sourced from BAILII available at http://www.bailii.org/cgi-bin/markup.cgi?doc=/uk/cases/UKEAT/1991/362_89_1806.html&query=clark+and+v+and+civil+and+aviation&method=boolean (last visited 7 November 2017).   [79] [2004] EWCA Civ 402, [2004] IRLR 636.

[80] See also *Spence v Department of Agriculture and Rural Development* [2011] IRLR 806, discussed in section 17.2.1.3, where it was ruled that a fair procedure will normally require an employer to consider disclosing anything in its possession which may be of assistance to an employee who is contesting the disciplinary charge, or wishes to make submissions in relation to penalty.

[81] (UKEAT/0032/10/LA, 28 July 2010).   [82] (UKEAT/0039/16/RN, 21 June 2016).

[83] See Chapter 4, section 4.2.

(2A) Where this section applies, the employer must permit the worker to be accompanied at the hearing by one companion who—

    (a) is chosen by the worker; and

    (b) is within subsection (3).

(2B) The employer must permit the worker's companion to—

    (a) address the hearing in order to do any or all of the following—

        (i) put the worker's case;

        (ii) sum up that case;

        (iii) respond on the worker's behalf to any view expressed at the hearing;

    (b) confer with the worker during the hearing.

(2C) Subsection (2B) does not require the employer to permit the worker's companion to—

    (a) answer questions on behalf of the worker;

    (b) address the hearing if the worker indicates at it that he does not wish his companion to do so; or

    (c) use the powers conferred by that subsection in a way that prevents the employer from explaining his case or prevents any other person at the hearing from making his contribution to it.

(3) A person is within this subsection if he is—

    (a) employed by a trade union of which he is an official within the meaning of sections 1 and 119 of the Trade Union and Labour Relations (Consolidation) Act 1992,

    (b) an official of a trade union (within that meaning) whom the union has reasonably certified in writing as having experience of, or as having received training in, acting as a worker's companion at disciplinary or grievance hearings, or

    (c) another of the employer's workers.

It is apparent from the terms of section 10(2A) and (3) above that the class of persons who may lawfully accompany the employee at a hearing is carefully circumscribed: that right is limited to a trade union[84] official or colleague.[85] If the employee's chosen companion meets these criteria, the employer is precluded from challenging the identity of that individual.[86] Nonetheless, damages for an employer's breach of this statutory obligation will be minimal. In *Gnahoua v Abellio London Ltd*,[87] nominal damages of the paltry sum of £2 were awarded to the employee in recognition of the employer's breach of section 10. However, the compensation package may be augmented where the employer refuses to allow the employee to have a companion of his/her choice present at a meeting into his/her alleged misconduct on the ground that to permit the employee to do so would result in the employer breaching the express terms of its contractual disciplinary procedure, since this can amount to a breach of the implied term of mutual trust and confidence.[88]

---

[84] It is worth noting that there is nothing in section 10 of the ERelA 1999 that says the trade union must be recognized by the employer.

[85] A study has indicated that the effectiveness of these statutory provisions—from the perspective of their impact on the disciplinary process and outcome—is marginal at best where the employee is represented by a non-union companion, on which, see R. Saundry, C. Jones, and V. Antcliff, 'Discipline, Representation and Dispute Resolution: Exploring the Role of Trade Unions and Employee Companions in Workplace Discipline' (2011) 42 *Industrial Relations Journal* 195. Moreover, the evidence revealed that the effect of union companions on the outcome of disciplinary procedures was variable, which begs the question as to whether the employee would be better served at disciplinary hearings by legal representation.

[86] *Toal v GB Oils Ltd* [2013] IRLR 696; paragraph 14 of the ACAS Code.

[87] (2303661/2015, 26 February 2017).

[88] *Stevens v University of Birmingham* [2015] IRLR 894.

It should be stressed that the statutory provision does not permit the employee to be accompanied by a legal representative, such as a solicitor or barrister, who would undoubtedly be particularly adroit at utilizing the rights set out in section 10(2B) of the ERelA 1999, thus enhancing the overall effectiveness of the presentation of the worker's case. One could argue that enabling the worker to be legally represented would better align the disciplinary hearing with the principles of natural justice. In that vein, it is particularly noteworthy that in *Kulkarni v Milton Keynes Hospital NHS Trust*[89] and *R (on the application of G) v Governors of X School ('G v X')*,[90] notwithstanding the restricted scope of these statutory provisions, the Court of Appeal ruled that Article 6 of the ECHR—which guarantees an employee the right to a fair trial by an independent and impartial tribunal—operated where disciplinary hearings had been scheduled to consider serious allegations of sexual assault and inappropriate conduct against members of the medical and teaching professions respectively.[91] In both cases, the charges were of considerable gravity and, if proven, would effectively bar the employees from practising their professions as a doctor and teacher respectively. The Court of Appeal implied a right in favour of those employees to be legally represented. However, when *G v X*[92] was appealed to the Supreme Court, the Justices ruled that the teacher in issue was not entitled to legal representation since Article 6 of the ECHR was not engaged. The majority[93] of the Supreme Court took the view that the employer's disciplinary proceedings would not have a substantial influence or effect on the determination by a regulator of the teacher's civil right to practise his profession in a second set of proceedings. Only in cases where the disciplinary proceedings would determine, or have a substantial effect on, subsequent regulatory proceedings, would Article 6 of the ECHR be applicable. The effect of the Supreme Court's decision in *G v X* has been to curtail severely the employee's right to have a legal representative present at the disciplinary hearing[94] and, from the angle of employment protection, one could argue that it was somewhat disappointing.

17.2.1.5 Disciplinary sanctions and warnings

The disciplinary manager[95] will have a range of disciplinary sanctions at his/her disposal. Where dismissal is deemed to be too severe, but some disciplinary response is deemed to be appropriate, a mild form of disciplinary action is to order that the employee be given a written warning.[96] Much autonomy is afforded to the employment tribunal in determining whether a written warning ought to have been given by the employer by the operation of the rule that this is a matter of fact for it to decide in light of the circumstances of the case.[97] For instance, in *Ham v Governing Body of Beardwood Humanities College*,[98]

---

[89] [2009] EWCA Civ 789, [2009] IRLR 829. See also *R (on the application of Kirk) v Middlesbrough Borough Council* [2010] EWHC 1035 (Admin), [2010] IRLR 699; *R (on the application of Puri) v Bradford Teaching Hospitals NHS Foundation Trust* [2011] EWHC 970 (Admin), [2011] IRLR 582.

[90] [2010] EWCA Civ 1, [2010] 2 All ER 555.

[91] For commentary, see A. Sanders, 'A Right to Legal Representation (in the Workplace) during Disciplinary Proceedings?' (2010) 39 *Industrial Law Journal* 166.

[92] *R (on the application of G) v Governors of X School* [2011] UKSC 30, [2011] 3 WLR 237.

[93] Lord Kerr delivered a dissenting opinion.

[94] For example, see *Mattu v University Hospitals of Coventry and Warwickshire NHS Trust* [2012] IRLR 661; *Ministry of Justice v Parry* [2013] ICR 311.

[95] We have already considered who that individual ought to be in our discussion in section 17.2.1.3. Moreover, the person who takes the decision regarding disciplinary action ideally should be the person who conducted the hearing (*Bugden & Co. v Thomas* [1976] ICR 344; *Sartor v P&O European Ferries (Felixstowe) Ltd* [1992] IRLR 271; and *Byrne v BOC Ltd* [1992] IRLR 505), but a failure to divide responsibilities in this way will not inevitably lead to a finding of procedural unfairness (*Rowe v Radio Rentals Ltd* [1982] IRLR 177).   [96] Paragraph 18 of the ACAS Code.

[97] *Grant v Ampex Great Britain Ltd* [1980] IRLR 461.   [98] [2017] EWCA Civ 1629.

the question was whether a number of relatively minor acts of misconduct could be aggregated to justify a fair dismissal without a prior warning. The EAT ruled that a dismissal without first giving a warning fell within the range of reasonable responses open to the employer in this particular case.

However, where the reason for the warning is incapacity/capability, it will be reasonable for the employer to provide the employee with an opportunity to rectify matters if there is scope for improvement. A written warning should be served on the employee personally rather than a trade union official[99] and is useful for evidential purposes in any subsequent proceedings.[100] In particular, where a period for improvement in a warning has expired without any failure on the part of the employee to comply with its requirements, the subsequent invocation and treatment of that expired warning is a matter of some importance.[101]

Where the misconduct or inadequate performance of the employee is sufficiently serious, the employer may decide to take a more robust approach by directing that a final written warning be given to the employee.[102] A final written warning will 'normally' be appropriate where the employee has been served with a written warning and has committed a further act of misconduct or fails to improve his/her performance within the deadline set in the warning.[103] If a tribunal is satisfied that a final written warning was tendered in good faith and is not manifestly inappropriate in the circumstances, that there were prima facie grounds for issuing it, and that there are no indications of some ulterior motive on the part of the employer, it ought not to interfere to overturn the judgment of the employer.[104] As such, where a final warning has been issued in bad faith:

> [It ought not] to be taken into account in deciding whether there is, or was, sufficient reason for dismissing an employee . . . [and a]n employer would not be acting reasonably in taking into account such a warning when deciding whether the employee's conduct was sufficient reason for dismissing him; and it would not be in accordance with equity or the substantial merits of the case to do so . . . [because t]o hold

---

[99] *Brooks & Son v Skinner* [1984] IRLR 379.   [100] *McCall v Castleton Crafts* [1979] IRLR 218.

[101] In this context, the cases of *Diosynth Ltd v Thomson* [2006] IRLR 284 and *Airbus UK Ltd v Webb* [2008] ICR 561 merit attention. In *Diosynth*, an employee had an expired warning of a duration of 12 months on his record for a breach of health and safety procedures. Subsequently, an explosion occurred in the employers' factory resulting in the death of a colleague of the employee. A full investigation revealed that the explosion was attributable to the failure of the employee and other colleagues to observe safety procedures and he was dismissed. The Inner House of the Court of Session ruled that the dismissal was unfair since the employer had treated the existence of the prior expired warning as *the determining factor* in its decision to dismiss. In *Airbus*, however, the Court of Appeal ruled that an employer's dismissal of an employee was not unfair where it had considered the employee's previous misconduct which had been the subject of an expired warning in its decision to dismiss the employee for the reason of misconduct. *Diosynth* was distinguished on the ground that the employer in that case had taken the previous misconduct referred to in the expired warning as the feature which 'tipped "the balance in favour of dismissal" as the other factors taken together would not have' (*Airbus UK Ltd v Webb* [2008] ICR 561, 575 per Mummery LJ) and that this provided justificatory reason for the dismissal. This could be contrasted with the position in *Airbus* where the subsequent misconduct was sufficient in itself to justify the employer in dismissing the employee without recourse to evidence of the unexpired warning of the previous misconduct. See also *Stratford v Auto Trail VR Ltd* (UKEAT/0116/16/JOJ, 31 October 2016); *Bandara v BBC* (UKEAT/0335/15/JOJ, 9 June 2016); *Appiah v Compass Group UK & Ireland Ltd* (UKEAT/0129/16/DM, 8 September 2016); *Trye v UKME (UK Mission Enterprise Ltd)* (UKEAT/0066/16/DA, 12 July 2016); and *John-Charles v NHS Business Services Authority* (UKEAT/0105/15/BA, 12 October 2015).

[102] Paragraph 19 of the ACAS Code.

[103] Paragraph 18 of the ACAS Code. If the employee on a final written warning commits disciplinary misconduct of a different kind, the treatment of the final written warning in deciding whether to dismiss was considered in *Wincanton Group plc v Stone* [2013] IRLR 178.

[104] *Davies v Sandwell Metropolitan Borough Council* [2013] EWCA Civ 135, [2013] IRLR 374; *Stein v Associated Dairies Ltd* [1982] IRLR 447.

otherwise would be inconsistent with the decisions in *Davies [v Sandwell Metropolitan Borough Council]* and *Wincanton Group [v Stone]*.[105]

Paragraph 21 of the ACAS Code provides that a written warning should set out the nature of the misconduct or poor performance, the behaviour necessary to improve the performance within a specified timescale, and the consequences for failure to improve such performance. There is no recommendation as to the length a warning should take. In the case of *Bevan Ashford v Malin*,[106] the EAT held that any ambiguities in the content of a warning will be construed *contra proferentem*. Therefore, it is vital that its terms are set out clearly to enable the employee to be in no doubt as to the requirements and timescales set.

Demotion of the employee is another form of disciplinary sanction. However, the employer must exercise caution. If it fails to adopt the correct approach, the employee could claim that the demotion was a repudiatory breach of contract entitling him/her to claim constructive dismissal. Nevertheless, the case of *Nunn v Royal Mail Group*[107] provides employers with a not inconsiderable degree of manoeuvre. Here, an employee was dismissed after he refused to accept a demotion, which the employer had applied initially as a disciplinary sanction. It was held that unless there was a glaringly obvious reason why the demotion was unfair, a tribunal will not be obliged to examine in detail the precise allegations and the procedure adopted by the employer. Ultimately, if the employee alleges the demotion constituted a repudiatory breach, the employee should resign and claim constructive dismissal.

Finally, the most extreme disciplinary response is for the employer to dismiss the employee. An employee with two years' or more continuous employment[108] with the employer at the effective date of termination[109] will be entitled to written reasons for his dismissal within 14 days of submitting a request for such reasons. Paragraph 22 of the ACAS Code directs that '[t]he employee should be informed as soon as possible of the reasons for the dismissal, the date on which the employment contract will end, the appropriate period of notice and their right of appeal'. It is to the employee's right of appeal that we now turn.

17.2.1.6 Appeals

The speech of Lord Bridge in the decision of the House of Lords in *West Midlands Co-operative Society Ltd v Tipton*[110] cemented the appeal hearing as a crucial feature of a fair and proper pre-dismissal procedure:

■ *West Midlands Co-operative Society Ltd v Tipton* [1986] AC 536, 548D–F

Lord Bridge of Harwich:

. . . a dismissal may be held to be unfair when the employer has refused to entertain an appeal to which the employee was contractually entitled and thereby denied to the employee the opportunity of showing that, in all the circumstances, the employer's real reason for dismissing him could not reasonably be treated as sufficient. There may, of course, be cases where, on the undisputed

---

[105] *Way v Spectrum Property Care Ltd* [2015] IRLR 657, 662 per Lord Justice Christopher Clarke.
[106] [1995] IRLR 360.   [107] [2011] ICR 162.
[108] Section 92(3) of the ERA. This is subject to certain exceptions in section 92(4) and (4A) where such two years' continuous employment is not required.
[109] This is defined in section 97 of the ERA, on which, see Chapter 16, section 16.2.3.
[110] [1986] AC 536.

facts, the dismissal was inevitable, as for example where a trusted employee, before dismissal, was charged with, and pleaded guilty to, a serious offence of dishonesty committed in the course of his employment. In such a case the employer could reasonably refuse to entertain a domestic appeal on the ground that it could not affect the outcome. It has never been suggested, however, that this was such a case.

Paragraph 4 of the ACAS Code underscores the significance of the appeal hearing, providing that 'employers should allow an employee to appeal against any formal decision made'. Paragraph 26 of the ACAS Code prescribes how the employee ought to respond to the employer's offer of an appeal. First, the employee should put the grounds for the appeal in writing, and second, the employer should hold the appeal without unreasonable delay at an agreed time and place. If an employee does not appeal against his/her dismissal, the decision of *Chrystie v Rolls-Royce (1971) Ltd*[111] is an authority for the proposition that this should not be equated to acquiescence in dismissal on the part of the employee. There is one situation where an appeal is not necessary: where the reason for the dismissal is SOSR, the failure to permit the employee a right of appeal will not result in a finding of unfair dismissal. This is justified on the basis that the absence of an appeal will not necessarily be sufficiently material in such a context.[112]

It was once thought that treating the appeal hearing as a rehearing of the employee's case could cure a procedural defect at an earlier stage in the pre-dismissal process which had rendered the employee's dismissal unfair. In other words, if there was a defect in the conduct of the employer's investigation of the case or an irregularity in the execution of the disciplinary hearing, by affording the employee the opportunity to have his/her case completely considered afresh at the appeal hearing the employer could avoid a finding of unfair dismissal on the ground of procedural unfairness at the earlier stage.[113] However, the decision of the Court of Appeal in the case of *Taylor v OCS Group Ltd*[114] placed a different complexion on the requirements which the employer would have to follow in order to be excused a finding of unfair dismissal in such circumstances. The issue was whether the utilization of the appeal hearing as a forum for the mere 'review', as opposed to a 'rehearing', of the original decision to dismiss was (a) a proper analysis of matters and (b) sufficient to 'cure' a procedural defect at an earlier stage of the procedure, which of itself had been of sufficient gravity to have rendered the employee's dismissal unfair:

■ *Taylor v OCS Group Ltd* [2006] ICR 1602, 1602 and 1614–17

Lady Justice Smith:

. . . the distinction between a review and a rehearing is hard to define in the abstract and even harder to apply in practice . . . What matters is not whether the internal appeal was technically a rehearing or a review but whether the disciplinary process as a whole was fair . . . The use of the words 'rehearing' and 'review', albeit only intended by way of illustration, does create a risk that employment tribunals will fall into the trap of deciding whether the dismissal procedure was fair or unfair by reference to their view of whether an appeal hearing was a rehearing or a mere review. This error is avoided if employment tribunals realise that their task is to apply the statutory test. In doing that, they should consider the fairness of the whole of the disciplinary process. If they find

[111] [1976] IRLR 336.
[112] *Hussain v Jurys Inn Group Ltd* (UKEAT/0283/15/JOJ, 3 February 2016).
[113] *Clark v Civil Aviation Authority* [1991] IRLR 412; *Sartor v P&O European Ferries (Felixstowe) Ltd* [1992] IRLR 271.   [114] [2006] ICR 1602.

that an early stage of the process was defective and unfair in some way, they will want to examine any subsequent proceeding with particular care. But their purpose in so doing will not be to determine whether it amounted to a rehearing or a review but to determine whether, due to the fairness or unfairness of the procedures adopted, the thoroughness or lack of it of the process and the open-mindedness (or not) of the decision-maker, the overall process was fair, notwithstanding any deficiencies at the early stage. In saying this, it may appear that we are suggesting that employment tribunals should consider procedural fairness separately from other issues arising. We are not; indeed, it is trite law that section 98(4) of the [ERA] requires the employment tribunal to approach its task broadly as an industrial jury. That means that it should consider the procedural issues together with the reason for the dismissal, as it has found it to be. The two impact upon each other and the employment tribunal's task is to decide whether, in all the circumstances of the case, the employer acted reasonably in treating the reason it has found as a sufficient reason to dismiss.

As such, whether the appeal hearing can of itself function to cure an antecedent procedural irregularity should be assessed in the round without any need to consider whether it constituted a 'review' or 'rehearing'. Indeed, the fundamental point to take from *Taylor* is that a prior procedural defect can be rectified by a fair and proper appeal process. A closely connected issue is whether the appeal panel ought to take into account fresh evidence at the appeal hearing that has come to light since the original disciplinary hearing. In *O'Brien v Bolton St Catherine's Academy*,[115] the Court of Appeal considered the impact of such fresh evidence and ruled that it was disproportionate and unreasonable for the employer to disregard that evidence without at least a further assessment by its own occupational health advisers.

Paragraph 27 of the ACAS Code directs that an appeal should be dealt with by a manager who has not previously been involved in the case, which was considered by the EAT in *Adeshina v St George's University Hospitals NHS Foundation Trust*,[116] and is accompanied by a direction in the ACAS Non-Statutory Guide that '[the appeal should] wherever possible provide for the appeal to be heard by someone senior in authority to the person who took the disciplinary decision'.[117] In *Adeshina*, a member of the appeal panel was a senior member of staff who also happened to be a mentor of one of the victims of the employee's alleged misconduct. The EAT decided that the dismissal was not unfair despite this fact, on the ground that it was unrealistic and unworkable for such relationships to be avoided, particularly in a tight-knit workplace. In addition, although a junior member of staff formed part of the appeal panel, the fact that a more senior member had taken the original decision did not invalidate the appeal process since the panel included two directors and the junior staff member had access to professional advice from senior colleagues at all times.

It has been held that a failure on the part of the employer to explain the reasons for rejection of the appeal in the appeal conclusion letter and the fact that no member of the appeal panel gave witness evidence at the original disciplinary hearing will not make the dismissal unfair.[118] Where the disciplinary procedure incorporating the appeal is clothed with contractual effect, it has been found to be incompetent for an employer to increase the disciplinary sanction on finding that the employee's appeal was unsuccessful.[119] No such implied contractual power will exist. Conversely, where the employee's appeal is successful, it has been ruled that there is no legal requirement for that decision to be communicated to the employee for the latter's contract of employment to revive; instead,

---

[115] [2017] ICR 737.

[116] [2015] IRLR 704. The Court of Appeal dismissed an appeal from the EAT's decision: [2017] EWCA Civ 257.

[117] See http://www.acas.org.uk/index.aspx?articleid=2179 at page 34 (last visited 8 November 2017).

[118] *Elmore v Governors of Darland High School* (UKEAT/0209/16/DM, 4 May 2017).

[119] *McMillan v Airedale NHS Foundation Trust* [2015] ICR 747.

it will be reactivated automatically on the formal resolution of that decision.[120] As such, the original 'dismissal' will vanish and the employee will be prevented from subsequently claiming unfair dismissal.[121] Finally, it is stipulated in paragraph 28 of the ACAS Code that the employee has the right to be accompanied at an appeal hearing. Whilst section 10 of the ERelA 1999 does not explicitly state that the statutory right does apply to an appeal hearing, the interpretation of the term 'disciplinary hearing' in section 13(4) of the ERelA 1999 clarifies that this is the case.

17.2.1.7 Agreed disciplinary and grievance procedures

Paragraph 2 of the ACAS Code strongly encourages employers to promulgate their own written, specific, and clear disciplinary and grievance procedures on the ground that they enhance the 'fairness and transparency' of any pre-dismissal process. The ACAS Code goes on to say that employees and their representatives[122] ought to have some input into the development of such procedures and that reasonable efforts should be made to ensure that employees understand those rules and how they are to be used.[123] The incentive for the employer in having a set of disciplinary procedures agreed with employee representatives lies in its capacity to ensure that management and employees (subject to the threat of dismissal) 'buy into' and accept it as an authoritative set of guidelines. Of course, there is little point in an employer crafting an elaborate set of disciplinary rules and procedures if it fails to apply them. However, one should not presume that compliance with the terms of a disciplinary procedure will inevitably lead to a finding of a fair dismissal; instead, the requisite standards of procedural fairness are said to be 'superimposed' onto the employer's own disciplinary process. Hence any rules in such agreed disciplinary procedures that are complied with, but that are suspect in light of the standards which procedural fairness demands, may result in a dismissal being held to be unfair. This point is demonstrated by the decision of the Inner House of the Court of Session in the case of *Ladbroke Racing Ltd v Arnott*.[124] Here, the disciplinary rules of the employer provided that any employee placing bets with Ladbrokes would be immediately dismissed. When three employees were dismissed for a breach of this rule, the Court of Session held that their dismissals were unfair, since the standards of procedural fairness—which were higher—had not been met:

■ *Ladbroke Racing Ltd v Arnott* **[1981] SC 159, 182 and 184**

Lord Dunpark:

. . . the terms of [section 98(4) of the ERA] require an employer to consider all the circumstances of the case, including equity and the substantial merits, in order to treat the employee fairly. If, therefore, the employer incorporates in a code of practice, known to the employee, a rule prohibiting a specified act or specified acts for which the stated penalty is instant dismissal, he may not have acted reasonably if all that he does is to say to the employee: 'The rule which you have broken specifies the penalty of dismissal for breach. You are therefore dismissed.' The standard of 'acting reasonably,' set by [section 98(4) of the ERA], requires an employer to consider all the facts relevant to the nature and cause of the breach, including the degree of its gravity . . .

---

[120] *Salmon v Cattlebeck Care (Teesdale) Ltd* [2015] IRLR 189.
[121] *Folkestone Nursing Home Ltd v Patel* (UKEAT/0348/15/DM, 1 June 2016).
[122] For example, trade union representatives.
[123] The prevalence of agreed disciplinary procedures was examined in N. Rahim, A. Brown, and J. Graham, 'Evaluation of the Acas Code of Practice on Disciplinary and Grievance Procedures', Research Paper 06/11, available at http://www.acas.org.uk/media/pdf/4/r/Evaluation-of-the-Acas-Code-of-Practice-on-Disciplinary-and-Grievance-procedures-accessible-version-.pdf at page 25 (last visited 8 November 2017).
[124] [1981] SC 159.

There is a flip side to this point. That is the proposition that it is by no means a foregone conclusion that a failure to abide by the terms of the agreed procedure will inevitably lead to a finding of unfair dismissal. Examples of this proposition are furnished by *Bailey v BP Oil (Kent Refinery) Ltd*[125] and *Westminster City Council v Cabaj*:[126]

■ *Bailey v BP Oil (Kent Refinery) Ltd* [1980] ICR 642, 648D–F

> **Lord Justice Lawton:**
>
> The dismissal in such a case would not be any the less fair because the employers did not follow a disciplinary procedure agreement with a number of trade unions containing the kind of provisions which are under consideration in this appeal. In most cases, if not all, a failure to comply with such an agreement would be a factor to be taken into account; but the weight to be given to it would depend on the circumstances. An industrial tribunal should not base its decision on reasoning to the effect that because there has been a failure to comply, the dismissal must have been unfair.

Therefore, whilst tribunals and courts will have regard to agreed disciplinary procedures for evidential purposes, the degree to which reliance can be placed on their provisions will depend on the circumstances of each case.[127]

Disciplinary procedures ought not to be perceived as some kind of monolithic structure; instead, rather than a standardized formulaic approach, one finds a great deal of variety in procedures adopted by employers across a range of economic sectors. For example, a comparison of the University of Edinburgh's[128] disciplinary policy with that of University College London[129]—which both feature on the Online Resources for this book—demonstrates the point. In the same vein, a single employer may legitimately decide to have a range of agreed disciplinary procedures carefully crafted to cover a variety of situations, e.g. one procedure may deal with misconduct cases and another with capability cases. It is fairly common for employers to deal with misconduct under a disciplinary policy, and to deal with capability under a performance management or capability policy, thereby treating a 'lack of will' and a 'lack of skill' under separate policies. Alternatively, as in the case of *Sarkar v West London Mental Health NHS Trust*,[130] the employer may decide to promulgate an informal procedure for minor cases of misconduct and disciplinary sanctions short of dismissal which sits alongside a more formal disciplinary procedure for cases of greater magnitude. In such circumstances, the employer must exercise caution when it decides whether the employee's case should be treated under the informal or formal procedure. For example, where the employer initiated the disciplinary process by applying its minor procedure which did not afford the employer the sanction of dismissal, but then shifted the employee's case onto the formal procedure halfway through the process, the Court of Appeal in the case of *Sarkar v West London Mental Health NHS Trust* ruled that the employee's dismissal fell outside the band of reasonable responses.

An agreed disciplinary procedure may feature in/on, or as, a staff handbook, policy document, and/or staff intranet or even in an employee's employment contract. The employer must decide whether the agreed disciplinary and grievance procedure is to be incorporated into the employee's contract of employment. Such 'contractual' status may be achieved by incorporating the procedure directly into the employee's employment

---

[125] [1980] ICR 642.   [126] [1996] ICR 960.   [127] *Securicor Ltd v Smith* [1989] IRLR 356.

[128] See http://www.docs.csg.ed.ac.uk/HumanResources/Policies/Disciplinary-Policy.pdf (last visited 8 November 2017).

[129] See http://www.ucl.ac.uk/hr/docs/disciplinary_procedure.php (last visited 8 November 2017).

[130] [2010] EWCA Civ 289, [2010] IRLR 508.

contract.[131] However, if the procedure, policy, and rules are to be contractual, care should be taken, since if any of the provisions of the procedure are not observed by the employer, no matter how trivial, the employer will technically be in breach of contract.[132] By the same token, where an employer has justification to dismiss an employee in terms of the provisions of the agreed disciplinary procedure, the dismissal may nonetheless be unfair, i.e. a contractually valid dismissal nevertheless may be unfair under Part X of the ERA.

17.2.1.8 The effect of a procedural defect

So far in this section, we have identified some of the pitfalls which can lead to an error of procedure in the pre-dismissal process. Once it has been established that the employer is guilty of a procedural defect, this begs the question as to whether the tribunal or court has no option but to make a finding of unfair dismissal. The answer to this query is addressed in the case of *Fuller v Lloyds Bank*:

■ *Fuller v Lloyds Bank* [1991] IRLR 336, 338–9

Mr Justice Knox:

The actual [procedural] defect has, however, to be analysed in the context of what has occurred, and it may be that that analysis will produce the conclusion that there was a defect of such seriousness that the procedure was not fair. In that event there will have been necessarily an unfair dismissal, although there may well be a conclusion that the compensation has to be severely limited because of the potential justification for the decision that the employer took albeit in an unfair way. What will not be a relevant subject of enquiry, in our view, is the motivation of the employer in adopting the policy which led to the procedural defect. That has to be judged by its fruits rather than by the reason for its adoption. The other possibility is that the procedural defect does not produce a procedure which is in itself unfair, but it may nevertheless be that the results taken overall are unfair, and there again, the conclusion that the Industrial Tribunal will reach will be that the dismissal cannot in those circumstances be upheld as anything other than unfair.

We can take from this passage that the tribunals and the courts must take a broad-brush approach to the fairness of the overall procedure applied. This suggests that an isolated procedural error will have to be substantial to lead to the classification of a dismissal as unfair.

An altogether different question is whether there is sufficient moral or statutory justification for the range of reasonable responses test to have permeated each of the stages in a procedurally fair process.[133] For instance, the band of reasonable responses test applies

---

[131] In *Hussain v Surrey and Sussex Healthcare NHS Trust* [2011] EWHC 1670 (QB), at para 168 Mr Justice Andrew Smith ruled that five variables ought to be considered in order to assess whether the employer's disciplinary procedure had contractual effect, namely (1) the importance of the provision to the working relationship, (2) the level of detail prescribed by the provision, (3) the certainty of what the provision required, (4) the context of the provision, and (5) whether the provision was workable.

[132] Where the employer fails to adhere to a contractually binding disciplinary procedure, the employee will be entitled to damages for the period it would have taken the employer to complete the procedure if it had complied (*Gunton v Richmond upon Thames* [1981] 1 Ch 448), but it will not be possible for the employee to recover unrestricted damages at large for career-ending dismissal (*Edwards v Chesterfield Royal Hospital NHS Foundation Trust* [2011] UKSC 58, [2012] 2 AC 22): see Chapter 15, section 15.3.1. A threatened breach of a contractual disciplinary procedure may be restrained by injunction: *West London Mental Health NHS Trust v Chhabra* [2014] ICR 194.

[133] See *Union of Construction, Allied Trades and Technicians v Brain* [1981] ICR 542, 550 per Donaldson LJ; *Sillifant v Powell Duffryn Timber Ltd* [1983] IRLR 91, 97 per Browne-Wilkinson J; *Whitbread plc v Hall* [2001] ICR 699, 705E–707B per Lady Justice Hale; *Sainsbury's Supermarkets Ltd v Hitt* [2002] EWCA Civ 1588, [2003] ICR 111, 119–20 per Mummery LJ; *Taylor v OCS Group* [2006] ICR 1602, 1615–16 per Lady Justice Smith; and *Leeds Teaching Hospital NHS Trust v Blake* (UKEAT/0430/14/BA, 15 July 2015) at para 57 per HHJ David Richardson.

to the conduct of the employer's investigation, the fact-finding process, the disciplinary meeting, the appeal hearing, and the disciplinary sanction.[134] As we will discover later, a major consequence of the application of the range test is that the actual (a) culpability of the employee in a misconduct case, or (b) the ability of the employee to undertake the demands of the job in a capability case, is wholly irrelevant. In fact, a number of factors coalesce to render the standards of procedural fairness sufficiently weak. As such, the conclusion can be drawn that they fail to counter-balance the general laxity of the standards of substantive fairness we examined in Chapter 16.

17.2.2 The influence of the reasons for dismissal on the standards of procedural fairness

Having addressed the sequential stages of a procedurally fair pre-dismissal process in the context of the ACAS Code, relevant statutory provisions, and case law, let us now move on to examine the second level at which one might subject the standards of procedural fairness to scrutiny. In other words, we will consider the extent to which the standards of procedural fairness vary in accordance with the employer's statutory reason for dismissal in section 98(1), (2), and (3) of the ERA. In particular, we will divide disciplinary dismissals into dismissals for the reason of:

(1) misconduct, breach of duty or statute, or 'some other substantial reason';[135] and

(2) capability, in the sense of long-term illness or poor performance/incompetence.[136]

17.2.2.1 Misconduct, breach of duty or statute, and some other substantial reason

The starting point for our discussion of misconduct dismissals is that where an employee has allegedly committed an act of misconduct, an employer *'will normally not act reasonably'*[137] if it fails to conduct a reasonable investigation or afford the employee the opportunity to defend him/herself. In *Polkey*, Lord Bridge was careful not to exclude the possibility that an employer may reasonably dismiss without engaging in such procedural steps in the context of a misconduct case. Paragraphs 23–24 of the ACAS Code furnish guidance on the situations where the pursuance of pre-dismissal procedures may be inappropriate in such circumstances. These circumstances are referred to as examples of 'gross misconduct'[138] and were recognized by Lord Mackay of Clashfern in *Polkey* as giving rise to the right to summarily dismiss without the exhaustion of procedure.[139]

---

[134] *Leeds Teaching Hospital NHS Trust v Blake* (UKEAT/0430/14/BA, 15 July 2015) at para 57 per HHJ David Richardson.

[135] The ACAS Code will apply to dismissals for 'some other substantial reason' under section 98(1)(b) of the ERA where the underlying rationale for the dismissal relates to misconduct or poor performance of the employee, e.g. where there has been a breakdown in trust and confidence: *Lund v St Edmund's School, Canterbury* [2013] ICR D26. However, where the nature of the SOSR is not related to the employee's capability or conduct, the ACAS Code will be inapplicable: *Phoenix House Ltd v Stockman* [2016] IRLR 848. This has been justified on the basis that some of the provisions of the ACAS Code will be irrelevant in such non-conduct and non-capability contexts, e.g. an investigation, etc.

[136] A fair and proper procedure to be applied in a redundancy dismissal will be dealt with separately in Chapter 18, on which, see Chapter 18, section 18.3.

[137] *Polkey v A. E. Dayton Services Ltd* [1988] AC 344, 364D–E per Lord Bridge of Harwich. The writer has shown certain words in italic text for the purposes of emphasis.

[138] For the test of what constitutes gross misconduct, see Chapter 16, section 16.2.4.3.2, and *R (Shoesmith) v OFSTED* [2011] IRLR 679.

[139] *Polkey v A. E. Dayton Services Ltd* [1988] AC 344, 358A–B. It will often, but not necessarily always, be the case that a dismissal will be fair where an employee is found to be culpable of gross misconduct: *Arnold Clark Automobiles Ltd v Spoor* [2017] IRLR 500.

Paragraph 24 of the ACAS Code and the ACAS Non-Statutory Guide provide more concrete examples of 'gross misconduct' in the context of procedural standards to include theft[140] or fraud,[141] physical violence, gross negligence,[142] serious insubordination,[143] and more.[144] However, one should not take from this list that the types of conduct treated as 'gross misconduct' are fixed, since each case must be judged in light of its own facts and circumstances.[145] Paragraph 24 of the ACAS Code, which directs that what amounts to gross misconduct 'may vary according to the nature of the organization and what it does', reflects this. Accordingly, the more serious the act and the smaller the organization, the more likely that the employer will be entitled to summarily dismiss. In *West London Mental Health Trust v Chhabra*,[146] Lord Hodge opined that it would be unlikely for gross misconduct to encompass conduct which does not entail the wilful or deliberate breach of a workplace or disciplinary rule.

Paragraph 24 of the ACAS Code also clarifies that employers should provide examples of acts which they will consider to be 'gross misconduct' in their agreed disciplinary rules and procedures. In fact, as Clark J noted in the case of *Farrant v The Woodroffe School*,[147] it is not uncommon for an employer to do so. However, one should not form the impression from this that a failure by the employer to itemize examples of what it will treat as 'gross misconduct' will automatically disentitle it from summarily dismissing an employee for that reason.[148] Furthermore, an employer should reflect on whether a procedure should be followed at all where there are sufficient grounds for the employer to believe that the employee has committed a serious act of misconduct. This is in accordance with the decision in *Polkey* and the efficiency model of procedural justice, i.e. that recourse to proceduralism should be abandoned where it would be utterly futile in the circumstances.

Of course, the majority of conduct cases will not concern gross misconduct. The classic exposition of the procedure which an employer must follow prior to dismissal for the reason of misconduct more generally is set out in *British Home Stores Ltd v Burchell*.[149] As we noted in Chapter 16,[150] the employer must believe that the employee was guilty

---

[140] See *Carr v Alexander Russell Ltd* [1976] IRLR 220; *Scottish Special Housing Association v Linnen* [1979] IRLR 265.

[141] See *Jervis v Skinner* [2011] UKPC 2, where the employer's reason of fraud for summary dismissal was not made out. [142] See *Dietman v Brent London Borough Council* [1988] ICR 842.

[143] See *Orr v Milton Keynes Council* [2011] ICR 704.

[144] For example, physical violence or bullying, deliberate and serious damage to property, serious misuse of an organization's property or name, the deliberate accessing of internet sites containing pornography, offensive, or obscene material, unlawful discrimination or harassment, bringing the organization into serious disrepute, incapability at work attributable to alcohol or drug abuse (*Dairy Produce Packers Ltd v Beverstock* [1981] IRLR 265), a serious breach of health and safety rules, or a serious breach of confidence (the ACAS Non-Statutory Guide at page 32). To that can be added dishonesty (*Brezan v Zimmer Ltd* [2009] All ER (D) 17 (October)), serious computer misuse (*Spence v Department of Agriculture and Rural Development* [2011] IRLR 806), deliberate and persistent failure to follow reasonable instructions (*Dunn v AAH Ltd* [2010] IRLR 709; *Laws v London Chronicle (Indicator Newspapers) Ltd* [1959] 1 WLR 698 (CA)), and the failure, without explanation or excuse, to attend a meeting to discuss the employee's position at the request of the employer and his/her failure thereafter to reply to the employers' requests to contact him/her (*Briscoe v Lubrizol Ltd* [2002] IRLR 607).

[145] *Carr v Alexander Russell Ltd* [1976] IRLR 220, 221 per Lord McDonald; *Scottish Special Housing Association v Linnen* [1979] IRLR 265. [146] [2014] ICR 194.

[147] [1998] IRLR 176, 179.

[148] For example, in *Ulsterbus Ltd v Henderson* [1989] IRLR 251, a bus conductor was summarily dismissed without notice or payment in lieu thereof on the grounds of complaints made by passengers that he had failed to issue tickets in return for fares collected. Notwithstanding the fact that it was not made clear in the employer's disciplinary rules and procedures that an offence of that nature would attract the ultimate sanction of dismissal, the Northern Ireland Court of Appeal ruled that the dismissal was fair on the basis that any employee would consider it obvious that a failure to issue tickets in return for payment was a most serious offence. Cf. *Dairy Produce Packers Ltd v Beverstock* [1981] IRLR 265.

[149] [1980] ICR 303. Approved by the Court of Appeal in *W Weddel & Co. Ltd v Tepper* [1980] ICR 286.

[150] See Chapter 16, section 16.3.2.

of the misconduct charged. Secondly, the employer must have had reasonable grounds to sustain that belief. Finally, the employer must have carried out as much investigation into the allegation as was reasonable in all the circumstances of the case by the time that it had formed that belief or at any rate at the final stage at which it formed that belief on those grounds.[151] One of the consequences of the *Burchell* test is that the actual guilt of an employee is irrelevant; what matters is whether the employer had reasonable grounds for its belief in the misconduct of the employee when it took the decision to dismiss.[152] Hence, if an employee is arrested and charged[153] but is later acquitted by a criminal court, this will not render an employee's dismissal unfair:[154]

■ *Harris (Ipswich) Ltd v Harrison* [1978] ICR 1256, 1258D–1259A

Phillips J:

Where an employee is charged with a criminal offence alleged to have been committed in the course of his employment, and consequently dismissed, it does not follow that because he is later acquitted the dismissal by the employers was unfair. The function of the industrial tribunal is not to determine the employee's guilt or innocence of the crime alleged, but to consider the behaviour of the employers in the terms of [section 98(4) of the ERA]; that is to say, whether they have shown that in the circumstances, having regard to equity and the substantial merits of the case, they acted reasonably in treating the employee's involvement in the alleged offence as a sufficient reason for dismissing him . . .

This is the effect of the approach of the House of Lords in *W Devis & Sons Ltd v Atkins*[155] that the date of dismissal is the point in time at which the tribunal's focus of enquiry should be fixed.

A further matter for consideration is the role of precedent in the evaluation of the employer's conduct. For example, consider an employee who behaves in a particular way and is punished by dismissal. Is it the case that any employee subsequently acting in much the same way must also be dismissed? Disparity of treatment is indeed a valid means of challenging the fairness of dismissal, as demonstrated by the decision of the Court of Appeal in *The Post Office v Fennell*.[156] However, in *Hadjioannou v Coral Casinos Ltd*,[157] the EAT formulated an approach which limited the scope for arguments based on inconsistency of treatment. First, Waterhouse J recommended that tribunals and courts should apply strict parity requirements when it comes to a comparison between the dismissed employee and the relevant comparator invoked.[158] Secondly, Waterhouse J accentuated

---

[151] *British Home Stores Ltd v Burchell* [1980] ICR 303, 304C–F per Arnold J.

[152] Where the evidence of different witnesses results in conflicting versions of events, the Court of Appeal provided guidance in *Salford Royal NHS Foundation Trust v Roldan* [2010] IRLR 721 on how the employer should proceed.

[153] For the argument that the law of unfair dismissal should approach dismissals in the context of convictions of employees for conduct outside the workplace differently from those dismissals relating to workplace behaviour, see A. Sanders, 'The Law of Unfair Dismissal and Behaviour outside Work' (2014) 34 *Legal Studies* 328.

[154] *Harris (Ipswich) Ltd v Harrison* [1978] ICR 1256. However, for the situation where the police are investigating but have not yet charged the employee and the employer dismisses, see *Z v A* [2014] IRLR 244.

[155] [1977] AC 931.   [156] [1981] IRLR 221.

[157] [1981] IRLR 352. See also *Paul v East Surrey District Health Authority* [1995] IRLR 305 (CA); *MBNA Ltd v Jones* (UKEAT/0120/15/MC, 1 September 2015).

[158] For example, in the case of *Honey v City and County of Swansea* (UKEAT/0465/09/JOJ, 16 April 2010), the dismissed employee was a senior legal executive and the comparator was a mobility assistant, having been engaged previously as a manual worker. It was held that the invocation of the comparator was misconceived on the grounds of a lack of comparable seniority and different job descriptions. For a similar result, see *MBNA Ltd v Jones* (UKEAT/0120/15/MC, 1 September 2015).

the importance of maintaining flexibility. This is particularly relevant in relation to the consideration of mitigating and aggravating factors.[159]

17.2.2.2 Capability/qualifications

Dismissal for the reason of capability is broad enough to cover (a) incompetence/inadequate performance and (b) ill-health/sickness.[160] As noted earlier, many employers will deal with such dismissals through specific capability or performance policies, or in the case of ill-health, through an absence management policy.[161] At the heart of both these examples of 'capability' dismissals lies the issue of employee absence. The phenomenon of workplace absence is a matter which generates a great deal of managerial angst and media attention, particularly in the context of discussions concerning its economic implications:

■ P. Taylor, I. Cunningham, K. Newsome, and D. Scholarios, '"Too Scared to Go Sick": Reformulating the Research Agenda on Sickness Absence' (2010) 41 *Industrial Relations Journal* 270, 270–1

> Popular discourse insists that malingering is endemic in 'sick note Britain',[162] with workers 'swinging the lead', or, to use the currently fashionable term, taking 'duvet days' . . . Particular opprobrium is directed at public sector workers, whose absenteeism levels are compared unfavourably with those in the private sector. Driven by austere budgets, public sector organisations have taken concerted action against their allegedly misbehaving workforces. Both short-term absences, a category associated with workers 'throwing a sickie', and long-term sickness, which statistically contributes most to absence rates, are subject to increasing employer intervention.

In 2017, a report from the Centre for Economic and Business Research highlighted that the cost of absences to the UK economy currently stands at £18 billion.[163] Since Taylor et al. reported on 'duvet days' and 'endemic malingering', it can be shown that many companies actually embrace the concept of 'duvet days' in an attempt to discourage malingering.[164] Hand-in-hand with a 'gentler touch' in the adoption of duvet days from some employers, most companies adopt some form of absence management policy as noted earlier. It can be argued that the trend towards increased absence procedures to manage workforce

---

[159] See *Paul v East Surrey District Health Authority* [1995] IRLR 305 (CA); *London Borough of Harrow v Cunningham* [1996] IRLR 256; and *Procter v British Gypsum Ltd* [1992] IRLR 7. An employer is entitled to engage in blanket dismissals under carefully controlled circumstances: *Monie v Coral Racing Ltd* [1981] ICR 109. The Court of Appeal in *Monie* decided that if an employer has reasonable grounds for its belief that misconduct is the work of one of two employees or possibly both, but cannot distinguish between them, it can act reasonably if it dismisses both employees. It is not necessary for an employer to demonstrate that it had an actual belief in the employee's misconduct and it is sufficient for it to have a reasonable suspicion of the employee's dishonesty. Where there is a reasonable suspicion that one of two or possibly both employees must have acted dishonestly, it is not necessary for the employer to believe that either of them acted dishonestly. However, where the number of employees who may have committed the act is greater than two, additional requirements are imposed on the employer: *Parr v Whitbread & Co. plc* [1990] ICR 427. [160] See Chapter 16, section 16.2.4.3.1.

[161] For example, see the University of Edinburgh's policy, available at http://www.docs.csg.ed.ac.uk/HumanResources/Policies/Absence_Management_Policy.pdf.

[162] Dismissal of an employee for 'pulling a sickie' will be for the reason of conduct, rather than 'capability': *Metroline West Ltd v Ajaj* (UKEAT/0185/15/RN, 3 December 2015).

[163] 'Cost of Absence to UK Economy Rises to £18 Billion', available at http://www.personneltoday.com/pr/2017/03/cost-of-absence-to-uk-economy-rises-to-18-billion/ (last visited 9 November 2017).

[164] 'Would you implement a duvet day?', Active Absence, available at http://www.personneltoday.com/pr/2015/03/would-you-implement-a-duvet-day/ (last visited 9 November 2017).

absences is attributable in no small part to the interpretation of the statutory requirements imposed on employers by section 98(4) of the ERA. Indeed, if we turn to pages 71–76 of the ACAS Non-Statutory Guide,[165] even a perfunctory glance reveals how detailed the basic requirements imposed on employers are. Another matter which is striking is the extent of the variation in the processes, depending on the reasons for the employee's absence. Once again, we come back to the idea of diversity and adaptability of standards of procedural fairness, which we considered at the outset of this chapter.

There will undoubtedly be some variation in the standards of procedural fairness applicable in an (a) incompetence/inadequate performance and (b) ill-health/sickness dismissal—which is affirmed by the approach in the ACAS Non-Statutory Guide.[166] Nonetheless, the two themes that are common to both are the importance of 'reasonable grounds for the employer's belief' and 'fair warning'/'consultation'.

(1) The first feature reflects the requirement we discussed in the context of the standards of procedural fairness in misconduct cases, i.e. that the employer must have reasonable grounds for its belief that the employee is no longer competent to perform the demands of the job.[167] As with misconduct cases, it is irrelevant that the employee is indeed able to perform the job, or has undertaken to return to the workplace after a period of absence,[168] so long as the employer has undertaken sufficient investigation to enable it to reach the decision that dismissal is the only option.[169]

(2) Meanwhile, the need for the employer to give the employee 'fair warning and an opportunity to mend his ways and show that he can do the job' stems from the speech of Lord Bridge of Harwich in *Polkey*.[170] The terminology of 'warning', however, is not appropriate in the case of a capability procedure on ill-health grounds.[171] Here, the preferable language is that of 'consultation', since the employee is not being asked to modify or improve his/her conduct.[172] Instead, the process of discussion and consultation is designed to ensure that the true medical position is revealed, that the employer has not overlooked important matters,[173] and that the employee feels that he/she has had an opportunity to put forward his/her point of view.[174] Ultimately, the benefit of consultation is that it enables an employer to weigh up the situation, 'balancing the employer's need for the work to be done on the one hand, against the employee's need for time to recover his health on the other'.[175] The nature and rigour of that consultation exercise will be determined by the known circumstances of each case.[176]

Turning to capability dismissals on the grounds of incompetence or poor performance, as we noted earlier in section 17.1.1, the efficiency model of procedural fairness is reiterated by Mr Justice Phillips in *E C Cook v Thomas Linnell & Sons Ltd*.[177] Here, it was

---

[165] See http://www.acas.org.uk/index.aspx?articleid=2179 (last visited 9 November 2017) and the Online Resources for this book.

[166] See http://www.acas.org.uk/index.aspx?articleid=2179 at pages 71–6 (last visited 9 November 2017).

[167] *Alidair Ltd v Taylor* [1978] ICR 445.

[168] *D B Schenker Rail (UK) Ltd v Doolan* (UKEATS/0053/09/BI, 13 April 2011), per Lady Smith.

[169] In relation to the rigour of the employer's investigation into the true medical situation in a 'capability' dismissal, there are no grounds for the assertion that the standard of enquiry is higher than in a misconduct case: *D B Schenker Rail (UK) Ltd v Doolan* (UKEATS/0053/09/BI, 13 April 2011), at para 33 per Lady Smith; *Dundee City Council v Sharp* (UKEATS/0009/11/BI, 11 October 2011).

[170] *Polkey v A. E. Dayton Services Ltd* [1988] AC 344, 364D–E.

[171] *Spencer v Paragon Wallpapers Ltd* [1976] IRLR 373 (EAT); *Lynock v Cereal Packaging Ltd* [1988] IRLR 510; cf. *A Links & Co. Ltd v Rose* [1991] IRLR 353, 355–6 per Lord McCluskey.

[172] *East Lindsey District Council v Daubney* [1977] IRLR 181 (EAT).   [173] *ibid.*

[174] *Williamson v Alcan (UK) Ltd* [1977] IRLR 303 (EAT).

[175] *Taylorplan Catering (Scotland) Ltd v McInally* [1980] IRLR 53, 55 per Lord McDonald; *Spencer v Paragon Wallpapers Ltd* [1976] IRLR 373 (EAT).

[176] *East Lindsey District Council v Daubney* [1977] IRLR 181 (EAT).   [177] [1977] IRLR 132.

remarked that the requirements of procedural justice should not curtail the employer's ability to manage its commercial operations effectively. Such an approach to the standards of procedural justice in the case of underperformance/incompetence inevitably leads to the imposition of fairly basic requirements on an employer prior to dismissal. The idea that fair warning and time for improvement will not always be necessary was picked up in *James v Waltham Holy Cross UDC*[178] and *Alidair Ltd v Taylor*.[179] In *Alidair*, it was held that these procedural safeguards may be dropped where the professional standards expected of an employee are extremely high and the implications of any departure from those standards are very serious. Some of the examples given in *Alidair* of employees with high professional standards are the passenger-carrying airline pilot or a scientist operating a nuclear reactor.

Complementing the idea of diverse procedural standards, the relevant approach to be applied in cases of long-term ill-health is very different: in fact, the ACAS Code will not apply to such ill-health dismissals.[180] First, as noted in the case of *Spencer v Paragon Wallpapers Ltd*,[181] the basic question that has to be asked is whether, in all the circumstances, the employer can be expected to wait any longer, and if so, for how much longer? This will involve considering whether the employee has received all of the sick pay to which he/she is entitled, whether it was possible for the employer to hire temporary cover, and the size of the organization.[182] There is no standard period of absence beyond which all dismissals will be treated as unfair. For instance, in *Brighton and Sussex University Hospitals NHS Trust v Akinwunmi*,[183] a dismissal in the context of a 20-month period of absence was held to be unfair. As such, all depends on the reasonableness of the employer's decision. Secondly, the question as to when and whether the employer is entitled to dismiss is a managerial decision, rather than a medical one.[184] To enable the employer to determine how long it should wait, it must take into account the nature of the illness, the likely length of the continuing absence, its need to have done the work which the employee was engaged to do, and the circumstances of the case. Whether the employer will need to consult with the employee's general practitioner or commission its own medical enquiries will depend in each case on the relative rigour of the consultation required.[185] In addition, an employer may be required to search for suitable alternative positions for the employee,[186] and the expectations imposed on the employer in this regard will be higher where the ill-health of the employee has been prolonged or exacerbated by the conduct of the employer.[187]

 For additional reading on the standards of procedural fairness, visit the Online Resources for this book at www.oup.com/uk/cabrelli3e/

---

[178] [1973] ICR 398, 404E–G per Sir John Donaldson.   [179] [1976] IRLR 420 (EAT).

[180] *Holmes v Qinetiq Ltd* [2016] IRLR 664.   [181] [1976] IRLR 373 (EAT).

[182] See *BS v Dundee City Council* [2014] IRLR 131 and *Monmouthshire County Council v Harris* (UKEAT/0332/14/DA, 23 October 2015).   [183] (UKEAT/0345/16/BA, 29 June 2017).

[184] *D B Schenker Rail (UK) Ltd v Doolan* (UKEATS/0053/09/BI, 13 April 2011), at para 35 per Lady Smith; *East Lindsey District Council v Daubney* [1977] IRLR 181 (EAT).

[185] *East Lindsey District Council v Daubney* [1977] IRLR 181 (EAT); *Patterson v Messrs Bracketts* [1977] IRLR 137 (EAT).   [186] *Carricks (Caterers) Ltd v Nolan* [1980] IRLR 259 (EAT).

[187] *Royal Bank of Scotland v McAdie* [2007] EWCA Civ 806, [2008] ICR 1087. The fact that the employer's conduct contributed to the onset of the employee's illness does not lead inexorably to a conclusion of unfair dismissal, although it will be relevant in the context of (1) the evaluation of the fairness of the dismissal under section 98(4) of the ERA, (2) any common law claim that the employer has breached the implied term of the contract of employment which enjoins it to exercise reasonable care for the physical and psychiatric well-being of the employee (*London Fire and Civil Defence Authority v Betty* [1994] IRLR 384; *Royal Bank of Scotland v McAdie* [2007] EWCA Civ 806, [2008] ICR 1087), and (3) a claim that the employee has been unfairly constructively dismissed in terms of sections 95(1)(c) and 98(4) of the ERA.

17.3 REMEDIES

Chapter II of Part X of the ERA[188] prescribes three remedies where an employee has established his/her claim for unfair dismissal. Reinstatement is prioritized as the primary remedy. Where a reinstatement order is made, the employee is entitled to return to his/her old job. If the application of certain statutory criteria guides the tribunal away from making a reinstatement order, it has the power to order re-engagement. This is where an employee returns to work for their former employer, albeit in a different position. If the tribunal fails to make a reinstatement or re-engagement order, it must award compensation to the employee which comprises a basic and compensatory award.[189] Before making an award of compensation, the tribunal is duty-bound to consider whether an order of reinstatement or re-engagement would be preferable.[190] Besides the aforementioned three remedies, the tribunal also has the power to make interim relief orders under TULCRA[191] and the ERA[192] if it appears to the tribunal likely that it will find that the employee has been unfairly dismissed for one or more prescribed reasons.[193] The tribunal has an additional power to order an employer to pay a financial penalty of between £10 and £5,000 where it loses a claim and there are aggravated features.[194]

The statistical evidence[195] demonstrates that employment tribunals routinely eschew orders of reinstatement or re-engagement in favour of awarding compensation to employees. This is particularly unfortunate for the employee where the labour market is slow and unemployment is high. It serves to reinforce their status as something of a 'lost remedy',[196] providing support for the contention that the conceptions of 'job property' or 'job security' are in reality bankrupt explanations for the motivations which underpin the current practices adopted by the employment tribunals and the courts. A number of commentators have argued that the judicial preference for compensation was to some extent inevitable, since the inclinations of both employers *and* employees—in many ways for fairly self-explanatory reasons[197]—lead inexorably down that path: employees would appear to prefer to receive compensation rather than reinstatement or re-engagement orders, and the tribunals and ACAS are generally averse to promoting the latter as remedies.[198] With these thoughts in mind, let us now consider the relevant statutory provisions.

---

[188] Sections 111–132 of the ERA.   [189] Section 112(4) of the ERA.

[190] *King v Royal Bank of Canada (Europe) Ltd* [2012] IRLR 280.

[191] Sections 161–166 TULCRA 1992.

[192] Sections 128–132 of the ERA. The employee must present an application for interim relief to the tribunal before the end of the period of seven days immediately following the effective date of termination in terms of section 97 of the ERA. This seeks to ensure that a lengthy period does not elapse between the date of termination and any interim award of reinstatement or re-engagement.

[193] For example, where it is alleged that the dismissal is attributable to the employee's membership or non-membership of a trade union, participation or non-participation in the activities of a trade union at an appropriate time, or the making of a protected disclosure under the Public Interest Disclosure Act 1998, and other reasons which mirror the circumstances in which an employee will be held to have been automatically unfairly dismissed: see Chapter 16, section 16.2.4.2.

[194] Section 12A of the Employment Tribunals Act 1996.   [195] See Chapter 16, section 16.1.2.

[196] See J. Howe, 'Why Do So Few Employees Return to Their Jobs? In Pursuit of a Right to Work Following Unfair Dismissal' in V. Mantouvalou (ed.), *The Right to Work* (Oxford, Hart Publishing, 2015) 255.

[197] For example, as noted by Lord Johnston in *Wood Group Heavy Industrial Turbines Ltd v Crossan* [1998] IRLR 680, where all trust and confidence between the employer and employee has irretrievably broken down, it is difficult to see how reinstatement or re-engagement will ever be possible.

[198] See L. Dickens, M. Hart, M. Jones, and B. Weekes, 'Re-employment of Unfairly Dismissed Workers: The Lost Remedy' (1981) 10 *Industrial Law Journal* 160; P. Lewis, 'An Analysis of Why Legislation Has Failed to Provide Employment Protection for Unfairly Dismissed Employees' (1981) 19 *British Journal of Industrial Relations* 316; L. Dickens, M. Hart, M. Jones, and B. Weekes, 'Why Legislation Has Failed to Provide Employment Protection: A Note' (1982) 20 *British Journal of Industrial Relations* 257; P. Lewis, '"A Note on Applications" Choice of Remedies in Unfair Dismissal Cases' (1983) 21 *British Journal of Industrial Relations* 232; L. Dickens, M. Jones, B. Weekes, and M. Hart, *Dismissed: A Study of Unfair Dismissal and the Industrial Tribunal System* (Oxford, Blackwell, 1985); K. Williams, 'Unfair Dismissal: Myths and Statistics' (1983) 12 *Industrial Law Journal* 157; and P. Davies and M. Freedland, *Labour Law: Text and Materials*, 2nd edition (London, Weidenfeld and Nicholson, 1984) 493–7.

17.3.1 Reinstatement

The starting point for any discussion of the reinstatement remedy is sections 113, 114(1) and (2), and 116(1) and (2) of the ERA. Section 113 sets out the options of reinstatement or re-engagement and sections 114 and 116 provide additional details:

Section 114 Order for Reinstatement

(1) An order for reinstatement is an order that the employer shall treat the [employee] in all respects as if he had not been dismissed.

(2) On making an order for reinstatement the tribunal shall specify—

   (a) any amount payable by the employer in respect of any benefit which the [employee] might reasonably be expected to have had but for the dismissal (including arrears of pay) for the period between the date of termination of employment and the date of reinstatement,

   (b) any rights and privileges (including seniority and pension rights) which must be restored to the employee, and

   (c) the date by which the order must be complied with . . .

Section 116 Choice of Order and its Terms

(1) In exercising its discretion under section 113 the tribunal shall first consider whether to make an order for reinstatement and in so doing shall take into account—

   (a) whether the [employee] wishes to be reinstated,

   (b) whether it is practicable for the employer to comply with an order for reinstatement, and

   (c) where the [employee] caused or contributed to some extent to the dismissal, whether it would be just to order his reinstatement.

Section 114(1) describes the basic nature of a reinstatement order. Essentially, it means that the employee gets his/her old job back with no adverse effect on his/her continuity of employment. As such, if an employment tribunal orders reinstatement of the employee to a post with the employer, but to a different role with slightly different responsibilities, that is an error of law.[199] It will also be an error of law for a tribunal to order reinstatement on terms that modify the contractual provisions of the employee's employment. For example, in *Scottish Police Services Authority v McBride*,[200] the employment tribunal ordered reinstatement of the employee to a position as a fingerprint officer, but changed her responsibilities to the effect that she was prohibited from attending court as an expert. In the view of Lord Hodge, this did not constitute an alteration of the terms of the employee's employment contract, but was simply a practical restriction on the scope of the employee's work that was attributable to circumstances beyond the control of the parties.[201] In fact, for many years the employee had worked without ever having been asked to give evidence as an expert witness in court. As such, the reinstatement order was sound.

---

[199] *McBride v Strathclyde Police Joint Board* [2013] IRLR 297.
[200] [2016] UKSC 27, [2016] ICR 788.   [201] *ibid.*, 797D–780G.

The period beginning with the effective date of termination and ending with the date of reinstatement is counted towards the employee's continuity of employment.[202] Section 114(2) is designed to supplement that right by providing an entitlement to back pay and compensates the employee for sums accrued, but unpaid, which are attributable to the period between the date of termination and reinstatement.

The stumbling block to an order of reinstatement is the practicability of the employer being ordered to give the employee his/her job back.[203] Practicability is not the same thing as 'expediency' and the onus is on the employer to show impracticability.[204] The tribunals have been directed to take a 'broad common sense view' in their evaluation of the practicability of reinstatement[205] and, in exercising their judgment, they are acting as an industrial jury, which makes it next to impossible to successfully challenge a tribunal's decision on the ground of perversity in an appeal.[206] In *Wood Group Heavy Industrial Turbines Ltd v Crossan*,[207] it was held that it would be impracticable for an employee to be reinstated or re-engaged where all trust and confidence between the parties had irretrievably broken down. On a similar note, in the case of a small employer with few staff where the maintenance of close personal working relationships is essential, it is not appropriate to make a reinstatement order if the employer is reluctant to re-hire the employee and there are insufficient grounds to show that the order will be successful.[208] If a reinstatement order will result in significant overstaffing, the test of practicability will not be satisfied, since to make the order in such circumstances 'would be contrary to common sense and justice'.[209] Conversely, the absence of work for the reinstated employee to do has been held to be an important factor.[210] The implications of a reinstatement order are also relevant in evaluating its practicability: in the case of *Coleman and Stephenson v Magnet Joinery Ltd*,[211] a reinstatement or re-engagement order was held to be inappropriate where the return of the employee to the workplace would lead to serious industrial strife. Furthermore, where an employer would have to make an employee redundant in order to comply with the reinstatement order, this was held not to satisfy the practicability test in the case of *Cold Drawn Tubes Ltd v Middleton*.[212] In both *Cold Drawn Tubes* and *Coleman and Stephenson*, the courts were motivated by a desire to avoid the negative employment relations implications of making a reinstatement order.

If an order of reinstatement is made by the tribunal, its effect is to treat the employee as if he/she had not been dismissed. Therefore, the employee is entitled to be re-employed on no more,[213] or no less,[214] favourable terms than he/she was previously employed. Of course, some adjustments must be made for improvements in terms and conditions of employment since the date of dismissal of the employee,[215] but these are restricted to

---

[202] Regulation 3(2) of the Employment Protection (Continuity of Employment) Regulations 1996 (SI 1996/3147).   [203] Section 116(1)(b) of the ERA.

[204] *Qualcast (Wolverhampton) Ltd v Ross* [1979] ICR 386, 394B per Arnold J.

[205] *Meridian Ltd v Gomersall* [1977] ICR 597, 602D per Kilner Brown J; *Cold Drawn Tubes Ltd v Middleton* [1992] ICR 318, 322A per Tucker J.

[206] *Clancy v Cannock Chase Technical College* [2001] IRLR 331.   [207] [1998] IRLR 680 (EAT).

[208] *Enessy Co. SA (t/a The Tulchan Estate) v Minoprio and Minoprio* [1978] IRLR 489, 490 per Lord McDonald.   [209] *Cold Drawn Tubes Ltd v Middleton* [1992] ICR 318, 324B per Tucker J.

[210] *ibid.*, 323D–324A per Tucker J.   [211] [1974] IRLR 343.

[212] [1992] ICR 318, 323B per Tucker J; see also *Freemans plc v Flynn* [1984] ICR 874. Where the employer has engaged an individual as a permanent replacement to the dismissed employee, the provisions of section 116(5) and (6) of the ERA assume importance. Here, it is provided that the tribunal must not take that fact into account unless the employer can show that (a) it was impracticable for it to arrange for the dismissed employee's work to be done without engaging a permanent replacement, or (b) it engaged the replacement after the lapse of a reasonable period of time, without having heard from the dismissed employee that he/she wished to be reinstated or re-engaged, and that when the replacement was engaged it was no longer reasonable for the employer to arrange for the dismissed employee's work to be done except by a permanent replacement.   [213] *Rank Xerox (UK) Ltd v Stryczek* [1995] IRLR 568 (EAT).

[214] *Artisan Press v Strawley and Parker* [1986] IRLR 126 (EAT).   [215] Section 114(3) of the ERA.

improvements in *contractual terms only*.[216] The principal difficulty with a reinstatement order is that it is wholly unenforceable.[217] Therefore, where an employer fails to comply with its terms in whole or in part, the employee's remedy is restricted to that set out in section 117 of the ERA, namely an award of compensation. However, any provisions in the order as to monetary payments do not create a cause of action which may be enforced through the civil courts.

Two somewhat similar situations are addressed by section 117, as follows.

(1) First, as discussed, where a reinstatement order is made by the tribunal and the employee is duly reinstated, but the employer fails to comply fully with its terms, the tribunal must make an award of compensation. The award is calculated in accordance with the terms of section 124 of the ERA, but a key point is that the sum may exceed the statutory cap of £83,682 or 52 weeks' pay, whichever is the lower, which is ordinarily imposed on a compensatory award.[218]

(2) The second situation covered by section 117(3) and (4) is where the employer fails to comply with the reinstatement order by not reinstating the employee. Here, the tribunal must make an award of compensation for unfair dismissal. This will consist of the payment of a basic award and compensatory award in line with the ordinary provisions applicable in the case of an award of compensation.[219] However, the tribunal is also instructed to make an 'additional award' and the amount of that award is specified in section 117(3)(b). The employer will be excused from paying an additional award of compensation where it satisfies the tribunal that it was impracticable for it to comply with the reinstatement order. Hence there are two 'practicability' evaluations incumbent on a tribunal: the first is applicable where the tribunal considers whether the reinstatement order ought to be made at all; and the second applies where the employer fails to comply with the reinstatement order and is seeking to persuade the tribunal that an additional award of compensation should not be made on the grounds that it was not practicable.[220]

17.3.2 Re-engagement

Re-engagement describes the situation where the tribunal is of the view that the employee should not return to his/her old job, but that the employer, a successor of the employer, or an associated employer should be enjoined to employ the employee in suitable and comparable employment.[221] In much the same vein as a reinstatement order, the re-engagement order must specify the terms on which re-engagement is to take place, including the date for compliance with the order. The terms are more extensive than in the case of a reinstatement order and must include confirmation of the identity of the employer, the nature of, and remuneration for, the employment, details of back pay and other sums accrued but unpaid in respect of the period between the dates of termination and re-engagement, and confirmation of any rights and privileges, including seniority and pension rights, which

---

[216] *O'Laoire v Jackel International Ltd (No. 2)* [1991] ICR 718, 728G per Sir Nicholas Browne-Wilkinson, V-C.

[217] *O'Laoire v Jackel International Ltd* [1990] ICR 197, 206EG per Lord Donaldson of Lymington MR.

[218] See section 124(3) of the ERA. The sum in excess of the £83,682 or 52 weeks' pay statutory limit in section 124(1ZA)(a) of the ERA and article 3 of, and the Schedule to, the Employment Rights (Increase of Limits) Order 2017 (SI 2017/175) will reflect the monetary sums the tribunal ordered to be paid under section 114(2) of the ERA, i.e. arrears of back pay, accrued, but unpaid, rights attributable to the period between the termination date and the reinstatement date, pension rights, etc.

[219] See section 17.3.3.

[220] On the distinctiveness of these two 'practicability' assessments, see *Port of London Authority v Payne* [1994] ICR 555, 569B–570H per Neill LJ. [221] Section 115(1) of the ERA.

must be restored.[222] The precision of the terms of the order is of fundamental importance. In *Lincolnshire County Council v Lupton*,[223] one of the largest employers in the area was the subject of a re-engagement order. The employment tribunal's order stated that re-engagement was restricted to term-time only with part-time hours of 18.5 hours per week, within school hours in the Grantham area. The order also provided that the employment must be suitable in light of the employee's experience and background comparable to that from which she was dismissed or other suitable employment. This order was successfully challenged on the ground that expecting the employer to find a generally suitable post for the employee regardless of the existing vacancies was too imprecise.

The issue of 'practicability' also raises its head in the case of a re-engagement order[224] and the factors discussed earlier, in section 17.3.1, apply with equal force. For instance, in *Lupton*, the EAT observed that re-engagement was not to be used to impose a duty on the employer to search for and find a 'generally suitable place within the ranks for a dismissed employee irrespective of actual vacancies. That . . . puts the duty too high. An employer does not necessarily have a duty to create space for a dismissed employee to be re-engaged. The question at the end of the day is one of fact and degree by reference to what is capable of being carried into effect with success'.[225] In this context, 'practicable' means 'more than merely possible' and is a mandatory consideration. The EAT has also ruled that the tribunal must take into account relevant considerations such as whether modifications could be made to full-time job vacancies to render them suitable for part-time working or job-sharing. However, this does not give rise to a statutory presumption that the employer must displace a colleague where the employer asserts that the relationship has irretrievably broken down. Its reliance on this defence must be tested: first, the tribunal must enquire whether the employer's belief that the relationship has broken down is genuine and secondly, whether it was not irrational.[226]

Finally, since section 117 of the ERA applies to both reinstatement and re-engagement orders, an additional award of compensation may be also ordered where the employer fails to comply with its terms and, accordingly, the discussion in section 17.3.1 is also relevant in this context.

The decision of the EAT in *British Airways plc v Valencia*[227] concerned an employee who had been held to have been unfairly dismissed who had contributed 80 per cent to his dismissal. In the circumstances, the tribunal felt that it was inappropriate to order reinstatement and instead ordered re-engagement of the employee to the same job on identical contractual terms. The EAT overturned the decision of the tribunal, ruling that this approach was impermissible, since it amounted to reinstatement by the back door. In the view of the EAT, re-engagement cannot be to the same job, since the terms of section 115 of the ERA demand that the employee can only be re-engaged 'in a different role (albeit comparable or otherwise suitable) and may involve a change in the identity of the employer, the nature of the employment or the terms as to remuneration'.[228] This decision underscores the point that re-engagement must involve the employee being assumed into the employment of the employer in order to discharge a different job.

17.3.3 Compensation

Where a reinstatement or re-engagement order is not made, the tribunal must award compensation,[229] which comprises a basic and compensatory award.[230] Since reinstatement and re-engagement are ordered very rarely, one could argue that the enforcement of

---

[222] Section 115(2) of the ERA.   [223] [2016] IRLR 576.   [224] Section 116(3)(b) of the ERA.
[225] [2016] IRLR 576, 578 per Mrs Justice Simler DBE.
[226] *United Lincolnshire Hospitals NHS Foundation Trust v Farren* [2017] ICR 513.
[227] [2014] IRLR 683.   [228] [2014] IRLR 683, 687 per Mrs Justice Simler DBE.
[229] Section 112(4) of the ERA.   [230] Section 118(1)(a) and (b) of the ERA.

the unfair dismissal right is nothing more than the monetization of an employee's claim. This is especially true if one considers the rule in *Norton Tool Co. Ltd v Tewson*,[231] which restricts the compensatory award to pecuniary/financial losses sustained and precludes compensation for injury to feelings and distress. We now turn to consider this point and others within the headings of the basic award and compensatory award.

17.3.3.1 Basic award

The purpose of the basic award is to compensate the employee in respect of the continuity of employment which he/she has lost as a result of being dismissed.[232] Unlike the compensatory award, it is based on the *gross* weekly pay of the employee. It is calculated in the same way as the statutory redundancy payment under section 162 of the ERA,[233] as follows:

- half a week's pay[234] for each full year of service where the employee's age during the year is under 22, with half a week's pay being capped at £508;

- one week's pay for each full year of service where the employee's age during the year is 22 or over, but under 41, with a week's pay being capped at £508; and

- one-and-a-half weeks' pay for each full year of service where the employee's age during the year is 41 or over, with one-and-a-half weeks' pay being capped at £508.

The maximum amount payable at the time of writing is currently £15,240[235] in 2018–19, i.e. £508 × 30 (which is the highest multiplier) = £15,240, but such maximum limit is increased annually in line with changes in the retail prices index.[236]

The sum payable to the employee may be reduced under the provisions of sections 121 and 122 of the ERA. Section 121 provides that a redundant employee's basic award will be reduced to two weeks' pay where the employment of the employee was renewed or he/she was re-engaged or he/she unreasonably refused or left suitable alternative employment. Meanwhile, subject to certain exceptions,[237] the tribunal may reduce the basic award where it is of the view that any conduct of the employee before the dismissal was such that it would be just and equitable to reduce, or further reduce, the amount of the basic award to any extent.[238] For obvious reasons, this will be particularly relevant in the context of a misconduct dismissal. Unlike the compensatory award, the rules on mitigation of loss do not operate to validate deductions from the basic award.[239] Finally, it is provided that the basic award will be reduced by the amount of any payment made to the employee for the reason of redundancy under statute or otherwise in respect of the same dismissal.[240]

17.3.3.2 Compensatory award

The compensatory award is a sum payable to the employee in terms of sections 123 and 124 of the ERA. Section 123(1) directs that the tribunal must fix the compensatory

---

[231] [1973] 1 WLR 45, [1972] ICR 501.

[232] The basic award finds its expression in sections 119 and 227(1)(a) of the ERA and article 3 of, and the Schedule to, the Employment Rights (Increase of Limits) Order 2018 (SI 2018/194).

[233] See Chapter 18, section 18.2.3.2.   [234] This is calculated according to sections 220–229 of the ERA.

[235] It ought to be highlighted that in circumstances where the employee has been dismissed for the reason of redundancy attributable to trade-union-related reasons or activities in terms of section 152 or 153 of TULRCA, for the reason that he/she was a health and safety representative (in relation to working time matters) or employee representative in terms of sections 100(1), 101A(1)(d), or 103 of the ERA, or for engaging in activities as a pension scheme trustee under section 102 of the ERA, section 120(1) of the ERA prescribes that the minimum payment of the basic award will be not less than £6,203.

[236] Section 34 of the ERelA 1999.   [237] See section 122(3) of the ERA.

[238] See section 122(2) of the ERA.   [239] *Lock v Connell Estate Agents* [1994] ICR 983.

[240] See section 122(4) of the ERA.

award in accordance with what it considers just and equitable in all the circumstances having regard to the loss sustained by the employee in consequence of the dismissal insofar as that loss was attributable to action taken by the employer. The 'just and equitable' loss referred to in section 123(1) is taken[241] to include any expenses reasonably incurred by the employee in consequence of his/her dismissal and any loss of benefit which the employee might reasonably be expected to have had but for the dismissal. It is not the objective of the compensatory award to punish the employer; rather, it is intended to indemnify the employee in respect of any financial losses which he/she has suffered as a result of the dismissal. There is a statutory cap[242] on the compensatory award which currently stands at £83,682 or the employee's annual pay, whichever is the lower.[243] Like the basic award, it is increased annually in line with the retail prices index.[244]

The maximum award has been subjected to a great deal of criticism for being particularly low. Indeed, successive Governments allowed it to be eroded by the operation of inflation during the late 1970s, 1980s, and 1990s. Notwithstanding the fact that the overall limit is fixed at the lower of £83,682 and a full-year salary of the employee, in the vast number of cases the compensatory award will often be much more modest. For example, statistical evidence for 2016–17[245] reveals that the average level of the compensatory award was £16,543 and the median award was £7,521. Particularly noteworthy is the fact that the compensatory award was less than £4,000 in 21 per cent of the cases where an employee was successful in an unfair dismissal claim.

Norton Tool Co. Ltd v Tewson[246] is the key authority on the heads of loss recoverable under the compensatory award. A great number of issues emerge from the judgment of Sir John Donaldson, including the fact that the rules for the calculation of the compensatory award represent a departure from the common law with the potential to offer more extensive compensation.[247] As noted by Collins, in *Norton Tool*, the courts adopted 'the tort measure of compensation, so that, unlike the common law remedy, losses arising from the probable period of unemployment following an unfair dismissal were treated as . . . recoverable':[248]

■ *Norton Tool Co. Ltd v Tewson* [1972] ICR 501, 504D–507E

Sir John Donaldson:

The measure of compensation for that statutory wrong [of unfair dismissal] is itself the creature of statute and is to be found in the [ERA] and nowhere else. But we do not consider that Parliament intended the court or tribunal to dispense compensation arbitrarily. On the other hand, the amount has a discretionary element and is not to be assessed by adopting the approach of a conscientious and skilled cost accountant or actuary. Nevertheless, that discretion is to be exercised judicially and upon

---

[241] Section 123(2) of the ERA.

[242] However, the maximum award does not apply where the dismissal of the employee is attributable to health and safety grounds in conformance with section 100 of the ERA, where the employee has made a protected disclosure under the Public Interest Disclosure Act 1998 in line with the terms of section 103A of the ERA, or where the employee was selected for redundancy for health and safety related reasons or on public interest disclosure grounds in terms of section 105(3) or (6A) of the ERA: section 124(1A) of the ERA.

[243] Section 124(1), (1ZA) of the ERA; article 3 of, and the Schedule to, the Employment Rights (Increase of Limits) Order 2018 (SI 2018/194).   [244] Section 34 of the ERelA 1999.

[245] Ministry of Justice, *Tribunals and Gender Recognition Certificate Statistics Quarterly: ET and EAT Annual Tables*, available at https://www.gov.uk/government/statistics/tribunals-and-gender-recognition-certificate-statistics-quarterly-april-to-june-2017-and-2016-to-2017 at Tables E4 and E5 (last visited 9 November 2017).   [246] [1973] 1 WLR 45, [1972] ICR 501.

[247] See also *Leonard v Strathclyde Buses Ltd* 1999 SC 57.

[248] H. Collins, 'Compensation for Dismissal: In Search of Principle' (2012) 41 *Industrial Law Journal* 208, 209.

the basis of principle. The court or tribunal is enjoined to assess compensation in an amount which is just and equitable in all the circumstances, and there is neither justice nor equity in a failure to act in accordance with principle. The principles to be adopted emerge from [sections 123 and 124] of the [ERA]. First, the object is to compensate, and compensate fully, but not to award a bonus; save possibly in the special case of a refusal by an employer to make an offer of employment in accordance with the recommendation of the court or a tribunal. Secondly, the amount to be awarded is that which is just and equitable in all the circumstances, having regard to the loss sustained by the complainant. 'Loss' in the context of section 116 does not include injury to pride or feelings. In its natural meaning the word is not to be so construed, and that this meaning is intended seems to us to be clear from the elaboration contained in section [123(1) of the ERA]. The discretionary element is introduced by the words 'having regard to the loss.' This does not mean that the court or tribunal can have regard to other matters, but rather that the amount of the compensation is not precisely and arithmetically related to the proved loss . . . it is not sufficient for an appellant to satisfy this court that, within the range of discretion conferred upon the tribunal, it might or even would have reached a different conclusion. If an appellant is to succeed, he must satisfy this court that the tribunal has erred in principle . . .

(a) Immediate loss of wages

[Section 86 of the ERA] entitles a worker with more than ten years' continuous employment to not less than [ten] weeks' notice to terminate his employment. Good industrial practice requires the employer either to give this notice or pay [ten] weeks' wages in lieu . . . In an action for damages for wrongful, as opposed to unfair, dismissal he could have claimed that [ten] weeks' wages, but would have had to give credit for anything which he earned or could have earned during the notice period . . . In the context of compensation for unfair dismissal we think that it is appropriate and in accordance with the intentions of Parliament that we should treat an employee as having suffered a loss in so far as he receives less than he would have received in accordance with good industrial practice. Accordingly, no deduction [should be] . . . made for [the employee's] earnings during the [employee's] notice period . . .

(b) Manner of dismissal

As the employee secured employment within four weeks of his dismissal and we have taken full account of his loss during this period, we need only consider whether the manner and circumstances of his dismissal could give rise to any risk of financial loss at a later stage by, for example, making him less acceptable to potential employers or exceptionally liable to selection for dismissal . . .

(c) Future loss of wages

There is no evidence to suggest that the employee's present employment is any less secure than his former employment, and we have therefore taken no account of possible future losses due to short-time working, lay-off or unemployment, apart from loss of rights in respect of redundancy and unfair dismissal which are considered separately below.

(d) Loss of protection in respect of unfair dismissal or dismissal by reason of redundancy

These losses may be more serious. So long as the employee remained in the employ of the employers he was entitled to protection in respect of unfair dismissal. He will acquire no such rights against his new employers until he has worked for them for two years . . . Accordingly, if he is unfairly dismissed during that period, his remedy will be limited to claiming damages for wrongful dismissal, which are unlikely to exceed [ten] weeks' wages and may be less. Furthermore, upon obtaining further employment he will be faced with starting a fresh two-year period. This process could be repeated indefinitely, so that he was never again protected in respect of unfair dismissal. Whilst it is impossible for us to quantify this loss, which must be much affected by local conditions, we think that we shall do the employee no injustice if we include [a nominal sum].[249]

---

[249] Nowadays, it is common practice for tribunals to award a nominal sum of £350 in respect of the loss of statutory rights: *Fox v British Airways* [2013] ICR 51, 54 per Langstaff J (P); *University of Sunderland v Drossou* [2017] ICR D23.

This extract from *Norton Tool* informs our understanding of the compensatory award insofar as it enjoins tribunals to approach the calculation of awards in terms of four categories, or heads, of loss. To these heads of loss, we can add (e) loss of use of a company car, (f) loss of benefits in kind, and (g) loss of life insurance[250] and pension rights,[251] including the loss of a chance to claim death-in-service benefits payable under the employer's pension scheme following the employee's unfair dismissal,[252] which is reflective of the direction in section 123(2)(a) of the ERA.[253] However, our commentary will be restricted to categories (a), (b), and (c) in *Norton Tool* only, particularly considering that (a) and (c) are the heads of loss which make up the lion's share of the sums in any compensatory award.

(a) Immediate loss of earnings up to the date of the tribunal seeks to compensate the employee in respect of lost pay *net* of taxation from the date of termination up to the date of the hearing. Alternatively, if the employee has secured another job prior to the date of the hearing which pays the same or more than his/her earnings pre-dismissal, the 'immediate loss of earnings' head will compensate him/her up to the date the new employment was secured. The loss attributable to the dismissal cannot be revived if that employment is lost either through the employee's own action or that of the new employer. The original employer cannot rely on the employee's increased earnings to reduce the loss sustained prior to the employee taking up the new employment.[254] The employee must give credit for wages paid in lieu of notice and sums earned in other employments. The fact that the employee is unable to secure alternative employment during the notice period is not relevant.[255] However, in *Langley v Burlo*,[256] it was held that there is no requirement for such credit to be given in respect of sums earned from other employers during the notice period where the employee has been dismissed without full payment in lieu of notice.[257]

(b) Although *Norton Tool* refers to the manner of a dismissal as a head of loss, it is now clear from the decision of the House of Lords in *Dunnachie v Kingston upon Hull City Council*[258] that an employee cannot recover compensation for the loss arising from the manner of his/her dismissal, including humiliation, injury to feelings, and distress. At a broader level of principle, the House of Lords in *Dunnachie* approved the part of the judgment of Sir John Donaldson in *Norton Tool* which stressed that the construction of the word 'loss' in section 123 of the ERA is restricted to financial loss and so non-economic losses are excluded. Therefore, losses in respect of lost job satisfaction cannot be compensated. Likewise, compensation for loss of reputation can only be compensated where there is cogent evidence to show that it will be extremely difficult for the employee to find alternative employment.[259] This demonstrates the

---

[250] *Fox v British Airways* [2013] ICR 1257.

[251] See *ibid.*; *Sibbit v Governors of St Cuthbert's Catholic Primary School* (UKEAT/0070/10/ZT, 20 May 2010); *Griffin v Plymouth Hospital NHS Trust* [2014] IRLR 962; and the guidance provided in a booklet entitled *Employment Tribunals: Principles for Compensating Pension Loss* (4th edn, August 2017), available at https://www.judiciary.gov.uk/wp-content/uploads/2015/03/principles-for-compensating-pension-loss-20170810.pdf (last visited 9 November 2017). This booklet provides useful, albeit not binding, assistance to the tribunal: *Bingham v Hobourn Engineering Ltd* [1992] IRLR 298.

[252] *Fox v British Airways* [2013] ICR 1257.

[253] In other words, the compensatory award should include any expenses reasonably incurred by the employee in consequence of his/her dismissal and any loss of benefit which he/she might reasonably be expected to have had but for the dismissal.

[254] *Whelan (t/a Cheers Off Licence) v Richardson* [1998] ICR 318, [1998] IRLR 114.

[255] *Babcock FATA Ltd v Addison* [1988] QB 280, 293C–E per Ralph Gibson LJ.

[256] [2006] EWCA Civ 1778, [2007] ICR 390.

[257] In the case of *Stuart Peters Ltd v Bell* [2009] IRLR 941, the Court of Appeal ruled that this principle does not apply in the case of a constructive dismissal.   [258] [2005] 1 AC 226.

[259] *Vaughan v Weighpack Ltd* [1974] ICR 261.

close grip that traditional common law reasoning encapsulated by the decisions of the House of Lords in *Addis v Gramophone Co. Ltd*[260] and *Johnson v Unisys Ltd*[261] exerts over this field of law.

(c) Future loss of earnings will be awarded where the employee is unemployed at the date of the hearing or is in employment which is remunerated below what he/she had been paid by the employer. Thus, future loss of earnings is intended to mirror closely the employee's loss of earnings net of taxation, taking into account the period for which he/she might be expected to be unemployed. Of course, the calculation of future loss is far from easy as it involves accounting for what might have happened in the absence of dismissal, as well as what may happen in the future. Therefore, contingencies such as illness or redundancy, the likelihood that the employee would have changed jobs, and the likelihood that the employee would be employed by another employer will all be factored into the computation to reduce the sum. The general rule of thumb is that the employee's financial loss will be assessed up to the point at which he/she would be likely to obtain an equivalent job at the same level of salary (i.e. more than 50 per cent).[262] Particular difficulty is caused by the situation where the dismissal is potentially career-ending: it will be rare for compensation to be awarded over a career lifetime.[263]

Having considered the principal heads of loss, one must recall that the compensatory award may be increased in accordance with section 124A of the ERA and section 207A of TULRCA. As we noted earlier, the tribunals and the courts are entitled to increase the employer's compensatory award by up to 25 per cent if it is just and equitable in the circumstances where the employer has failed to comply with the ACAS Code.[264]

Conversely, the tribunals and courts are also entitled to make five different kinds of deductions to reduce the level of the compensatory award, as follows.

(1) Section 123(1) of the ERA confers a broad degree of discretion in favour of the tribunal to award a sum lower than the full amount of the loss if it is just and equitable to do so. Therefore, the question of injustice to the employee is a relevant consideration in assessing the compensation to be awarded to an employee. By the same token, as noted by Sir John Donaldson in *Norton Tool*, it is equally unjust for the compensatory award to confer a windfall on the employee. For example, it has been held that employees must give credit for *ex gratia* payments paid by the employer.[265] Certain statutory deductions must also be made. Section 123(7) of the ERA directs that enhanced statutory or contractual redundancy payments must be deducted to the extent they exceed the basic award. Moreover, there are statutory recoupment provisions which are applicable in respect of statutory benefits received by the employee, e.g. jobseeker's allowance, universal credit, or income support.[266]

(2) Turning to mitigation of the employee's loss, section 123(4) of the ERA stipulates that '[i]n ascertaining the loss referred to in [section 123(1) of the ERA] the tribunal

---

[260] [1909] AC 488.   [261] [2001] UKHL 13, [2003] 1 AC 518.

[262] *Wardle v Credit Agricole Corporate and Investment Bank* [2011] ICR 1290.

[263] ibid., 1306D–1307D per Elias LJ.

[264] See *Allma Construction Ltd v Laing* (UKEATS/0041/11/BI, 25 January 2012) for guidance on the relevant factors to take into account in fixing the compensatory uplift. But see *Phoenix House Ltd v Stockman* [2016] IRLR 848 and *Holmes v Qinetiq Ltd* [2016] IRLR 664.

[265] *Finnie v Top Hat Frozen Foods Ltd* [1985] ICR 433, 436–7 per Lord McDonald.

[266] However, the tribunal does not deduct these sums from the compensatory award. Instead, part of the award is 'prescribed' and the employer must pay this element to the Department for Business, Energy and Industrial Strategy ('BEIS') which had paid the jobseeker's allowance or income support to the employee: Employment Protection (Recoupment of Benefits) Regulations 1996 (SI 1996/2349). Hence this mechanism enables BEIS to recover the sum paid, although these Regulations do not apply where the dispute is settled before or after the tribunal makes an unfair dismissal finding.

shall apply the same rule concerning the duty of a person to mitigate his loss as applies to damages recoverable under the common law of England and Wales or (as the case may be) Scotland'. This obligation translates into a requirement that the employee must take reasonable steps to obtain alternative employment. However, the expectations of the employee in respect of alternative employment must be realistic. For example, in *Cooper Contracting Ltd v Lindsey*,[267] the EAT provided a synopsis of key principles applicable in the case of the duty to mitigate: first, the burden of proof rests with the employer to demonstrate a failure to mitigate; secondly, the employer must show that the employee acted unreasonably as opposed to not reasonably in failing to mitigate; thirdly, the determination of unreasonableness is a factual question and account must be taken of the employee's opinions and wishes, although this will be subject to an overall objective evaluation; fourth, the tribunal must not put employees on trial in a way that suggests they are at fault; fifth, there is no obligation on the employee to take all reasonable steps to lessen the loss, as if this were the law, the employer could act in a way that served to reduce the employee's compensation by identifying reasonable steps which were not taken; and finally, and perhaps most significantly, the employee's failure to accept better paid jobs does not necessarily satisfy the test. If the employer fails to discharge the obligation to mitigate, the tribunal will have to assess what would have happened if the employee had mitigated the loss. This will often result in the reduction of the compensatory award.

(3) The third kind of deduction which may be made is the *Polkey* deduction. Our discussion in section 17.1.1 highlighted the fact that an employer who has failed to follow fair and proper disciplinary procedures prior to dismissal will be entitled to have the compensatory award reduced to the extent that observance of such procedures would have made no difference to its decision to dismiss. Therefore, the award must be reduced by a percentage to reflect the extent to which it was possible that the employee would have been dismissed if a fair and proper procedure had been followed. In certain cases, a *Polkey* deduction may reduce the compensatory award by 100 per cent, especially where the employee is guilty of misconduct.[268]

(4) The fourth type of deduction is governed by section 123(6) of the ERA. This provision prescribes that the tribunal must reduce the compensatory award to the extent that the employee caused or contributed to his/her dismissal and it is just and equitable to do so having regard to that finding.[269] Contributory fault will be particularly relevant where the employer's reason for the dismissal was misconduct, and in such circumstances it will also be possible for a 100 per cent reduction in the award to be made.[270]

(5) Turning to the fifth possible form of deduction from the compensatory award, in terms of section 124A of the ERA the compensatory award may be reduced by up to 25 per cent if it is just and equitable in the circumstances where the employee has failed to comply with the ACAS Code. This will be relevant where the employee has failed to follow the grievance procedure in the ACAS Code before he/she presents a complaint to an employment tribunal for unfair dismissal.[271]

---

[267] [2016] ICR D3.

[268] For example, in the case of theft: *Fisher v California Cake & Cookie Ltd* [1997] IRLR 212. There are certain circumstances where a '*Polkey*' deduction must be made: *Express Medicals v O'Donnell* (UKE-AT/0263/15/DA, 9 February 2016).

[269] Likewise, where a part of the illness giving rise to the employee's loss is attributable to a divisible cause not connected to the unlawful conduct of the employer in unfairly dismissing the employee, the compensatory award should be apportioned accordingly: *BAE Systems (Operations) Ltd v Konczak* [2014] IRLR 676.

[270] See *W Devis & Sons Ltd v Atkins* [1977] IRLR 314 (HL); *London Ambulance Service NHS Trust v Small* [2009] IRLR 563.

[271] See *Allma Construction Ltd v Laing* (UKEATS/0041/11/BI, 25 January 2012) for guidance on the relevant factors to take into account in reducing the compensatory award.

Reflection points

1. In your opinion, to what extent is the marginalization of the reinstatement and re-engagement remedies an inevitable or desirable development?

2. If such marginalization is not desirable, on what basis would you justify such a response?

3. If you believe that side-stepping these two remedies is sensible, why would you prefer to rely on compensation as an effective mechanism?

 For additional reading on remedies, visit the Online Resources for this book at www. oup.com/uk/cabrelli3e/

17.4 FINAL EVALUATION OF THE UNFAIR DISMISSAL REGIME

In our analysis of the statutory unfair dismissal regime in Chapter 16 and this chapter, we have flagged up a number of issues which serve to highlight the point that a litany of obstacles are placed in front of an employee enforcing his/her statutory right to unfair dismissal.

(1) One can argue that the application of the range of reasonable responses test combined with a conception of proceduralism grounded in managerial efficiency crystallizes into an underlying judicial policy of abstentionism towards the unfair dismissal legislation.[272] We have also witnessed how the range test has become so embedded that it now shapes the standards of procedural fairness. Hence an employer is required simply to satisfy the tribunal or court that its investigation, fact-finding process, consultation, disciplinary hearing, and/or appeal hearing fell within the band of reasonable responses. Such judicial abstentionism has clearly operated to dilute the wider social impact of the legislation. A connection can be drawn here with the theme identified in Chapter 2[273] on the somewhat paradoxical interplay between employment protection legislation, on the one hand, and the common law, on the other. For example, we have seen how common law conceptions are so ingrained within the culture of the courts that they have been reluctant on a number of occasions to conceive of the legislation as an autonomous body of law with its own internal structure, coherence, and logic.[274]

(2) Similar to the theme we considered in Chapter 1, our examination of the unfair dismissal law has revealed a dichotomy between considerations of substantive fairness and procedural fairness. We have seen how the evaluation of the substantive justice of an employee's dismissal is subordinated to that of procedural justice. The judiciary are prepared to focus on the merits of the process leading up to the dismissal, rather than the outcome, i.e. the dismissal itself. This feature is suggestive of a tacit judicial policy of non-interference in the managerial prerogative, which is endemic in their approach to the enforcement of employment protection laws.

---

[272] See H. Collins, 'Capitalist Doctrine and Corporatist Law—Part I' (1982) 11 *Industrial Law Journal* 78; H. Collins, 'Capitalist Doctrine and Corporatist Law—Part II' (1982) 11 *Industrial Law Journal* 170; and H. Collins, 'Compensation for Dismissal: In Search of Principle' (2012) 41 *Industrial Law Journal* 208.

[273] See Chapter 2, section 2.1.1.

[274] For example, the formulation of the law of constructive dismissal under section 95(1)(c) of the ERA, the test of gross misconduct for the purposes of the standards of procedural fairness, and the judicial approach to remedies.

(3) The coverage of the protection offered by the unfair dismissal legislation is particularly restricted. Indeed, the range of barriers to qualification is extensive. For example, an individual must be an 'employee' with two years' continuous service who does not fall within the scope of certain excluded categories. All of this means that the legislation is beyond the reach of a substantial number of employees.

(4) Even if an employee is able to satisfy the relevant criteria and succeeds with an unfair dismissal claim, our examination of the range of remedies available has demonstrated how they offer no more than a modest degree of financial protection to employees. This is demonstrated by the low level of the median and average compensatory awards for unfair dismissal.[275] The effectiveness of the reinstatement and re-engagement remedies has been marginalized through an incremental process of judicial interpretation. Such interpretation can be conceptualized as a clear judicial rejection of the notions of job property or job security. [276] In fact, the position of the courts is symptomatic of an approach which is primarily concerned with the preservation and defence of the *employer's* property and common law rights.

From the perspective of employment protection, the conclusion can be drawn that the unfair dismissal regime is in a state of disrepair. In the following extract, Anderman surveys the potential for law reform and advances a number of suggestions. Such suggestions might more faithfully reflect the original intentions of Parliament in promulgating the unfair dismissal legislation:

■ S. Anderman, 'Termination of Employment: Whose Property Rights?' in C. Barnard, S. Deakin, and G. S. Morris (eds), *The Future of Labour Law: Liber Amicorum Bob Hepple QC* (Oxford, Hart Publishing, 2004) 128

The Law Lords could adjust the pattern of judicial interpretation of section 98(4) by holding that the range of reasonableness test should be kept within narrow limits. Stressing the importance of the need to take into account 'equity and the substantial merits of the case' in tribunal decisions would be one way to achieve this aim . . . If there is no sign of self-imposed judicial change, what will it take to produce a change in the UK pattern of judicial interpretation of section 98(4)? Despite all the arguments for deregulation, the case for adequate legislative protection of individuals against arbitrary dismissals by employers is as strong as ever. The arguments are based on the moral right of individuals to be fairly treated in cases of dismissals. Fair treatment of individual employees by management helps to remove a ground for resentment by the workforce collectively and contributes to a more efficient management. One possibility, even if a remote one, is a legislative amendment of section 98(4) to spell out that it is a 'just cause' test[277] in which tribunals apply a proportionality test to ensure that arbitrary dismissals cannot be found to be fair by employment tribunals. Another possibility, less remote but still not likely to occur in the short term, is that the European influence can one day produce a change in the test of unfair dismissals . . . European social policy may one day produce a Directive on individual dismissals to improve the minimum standards of fairness in dismissals in the United Kingdom.

---

[275] See section 17.3.3.2.

[276] See Chapter 16, section 16.1.2; W. Njoya, *Property in Work: The Employment Relationship in the Anglo-American Firm* (Aldershot, Ashgate, 2007) 6–7; and C. Mummé, 'Property in Labor and the Limits of Contracting' in U. Mattei and J. D. Haskell (eds), *Research Handbook on Political Economy and Law* (Cheltenham, Edward Elgar, 2015) 413–15.

[277] On 'just cause' fetters on dismissal, see B. Hepple, 'The Fall and Rise of Unfair Dismissal' in W. McCarthy (ed.), *Legal Intervention in Industrial Relations: Gains and Losses* (Oxford, Blackwell, 1993) 95; G. Davidov, 'In Defence of (Efficiently Administered) "Just Cause" Dismissal Laws' (2007) 23 *International Journal of Comparative Labour Law and Industrial Relations* 117; and G. Davidov and E. Eshet, 'Intermediate Approaches to Unfair Dismissal Protection' (2015) 44 *Industrial Law Journal* 167, 169–76.

Although there is some evidence of the Supreme Court taking a more purposive interpretation of the legislation in recent times, e.g. *Gisda Cyf v Barratt*,[278] *Duncombe v Secretary of State for Children, Schools and Families*,[279] and *Ravat v Halliburton Manufacturing & Services Ltd*,[280] it is doubtful whether this represents a sea-change in the attitude of the judiciary. Even if one could argue that it does suggest some development in the judicial position, government hostility towards unfair dismissal laws on the grounds that they deter employers from hiring employees and generate higher levels of unemployment, lower employment rates, and sclerotic labour markets[281] means that it is unlikely that the unfair dismissal regime will be enhanced any time soon to inject it with a meaningful set of constraints upon the employer's power to dismiss. Indeed, if anything, the very opposite is much more likely.[282]

---

[278] [2010] UKSC 41.   [279] [2011] UKSC 36, [2011] IRLR 840.

[280] [2012] UKSC 1, [2012] 2 All ER 905.

[281] See the Beecroft report, available at http://www.bis.gov.uk/assets/biscore/employment-matters/docs/r/12–825-report-on-employment-law-beecroft.pdf at pages 4–5 (last visited 9 November 2017).

[282] See K. Ewing and J. Hendy, 'Unfair Dismissal Law Changes: Unfair?' (2012) 41 *Industrial Law Journal* 115; J. Howe, 'Poles Apart? The Contestation between the Ideas of No Fault Dismissal and Unfair Dismissal for Protecting Job Security' (2013) 42 *Industrial Law Journal* 122.

CHAPTER EIGHTEEN
REDUNDANCY

18.1 INTRODUCTION TO STATUTORY REDUNDANCY PROTECTION

According to section 135 of the Employment Rights Act 1996 ('ERA'), an employee is entitled to the payment of a **statutory redundancy payment** if he/she is dismissed by reason of redundancy. An employee also has the right not to be unfairly dismissed for the reason of redundancy in terms of section 98 of the ERA. Despite the use of the word 'redundancy' in everyday language, one must not lose sight of the fact that it was originally, and is still, a legal concept. It was introduced by statute in the 1960s, namely the Redundancy Payments Act 1965 ('the 1965 Act'), and is a type of **economic dismissal**, i.e. a dismissal by the employer for a reason related to a reduction in its need for labour generally or at a particular location. Other economic dismissals may arise as a result of a workplace or corporate **reorganization** or business transfer. However, 'redundancy' is treated as a distinctive form of dismissal for the purposes of the statutory unfair dismissal regime.

In this chapter, we will consider the extent to which a statutory redundancy payment offers sufficient compensation for the loss of the employee's job and the financial and emotional disruption caused by the necessity to search for other employment. Furthermore, we consider what other protections are available to the employee who is about to be, or has been, made redundant. We then go on to assess how the present statutory regime evolved and whether it strikes an appropriate balance between the personal financial costs and adverse social costs shouldered by UK taxpayers and the economy, on the one hand, and the costs to the productive economy and the labour market, on the other.

The alternatives to redundancy, which an employer like Danny's Demolishers plc might consider in the event of spiralling operational costs, are also addressed.

18.1.1 Historical and contextual introduction

Prior to the introduction of the 1965 Act, workers in the UK were afforded no statutory employment rights when they were made redundant. This did not mean that there was absolutely no extra-legal or legal regulation of economic dismissals. For example, collective agreements struck between trade unions and employers or employers' organizations, which covered particular workplaces in the UK, might provide that an employee was entitled to a contractual payment on redundancy. Alternatively, the collective agreement might provide for an elaborate process of consultation with the trade union, prior to the onset of redundancies, in order to minimize their impact or avoid them altogether.[1] At the level of legal regulation, the common law would control redundancies in certain discrete respects, albeit that such protection was clearly limited. For instance, the law of wrongful dismissal[2] would offer the employee the right not to be made redundant in breach of his/her contract of employment. However, in the absence of breach, few, if any, safeguards were furnished to the employee.

There are a range of reasons why an employer may choose to make part of its workforce redundant. The most common can be summarized as follows:

- efficiencies generated as a result of social change, technological developments, or corporate takeovers;
- reduced demand for the employer's goods or services generally, or attributable to a recession or economic slowdown;[3]
- overreaching, i.e. too much, or too swift an, expansion; and
- corporate restructuring, reorganization, and outsourcing of economic or operational functions.[4]

There is a persuasive theory that the nature of the UK economy and shareholder capitalism in the UK has a negative effect on the capacity of employers to avoid redundancy exercises in response to challenging economic conditions and pressing financial circumstances. The UK is categorized as a 'liberal market economy' by the 'varieties of capitalism' literature.[5] Large public corporations in liberal market economies such as the UK (and the USA) are characterized by corporate governance systems which have widely dispersed share ownership and a strong corporate takeover market, with the latter exerting a tight control over the conduct of management. Unlike corporations in 'co-ordinated market economies', such as those of Germany and Japan, where there are structures and institutions in place to co-ordinate the governance of companies between management and labour, the impact of financial pressures on corporations in the UK are more likely to result in adverse consequences for their labour forces. UK companies are liable to 'downsize' their workforces to a greater extent than companies in Germany in order to remain efficient and competitive:

---

[1] However, it should be stressed that such extra-legal protections in collective agreements were historically rare. Trade unions did not wish to be seen to be involved in a process whereby they could be accused of legitimizing in advance the prerogative of management to undertake large-scale lay-offs: P. Elias, B. Napier, and P. Wallington, *Labour Law: Cases and Materials* (London, Butterworths, 1980) 647.

[2] See Chapter 15, section 15.2.

[3] For example, see the facts of *Allwood v William Hill Ltd* [1974] IRLR 258 and *Williams v Compair Maxam Ltd* [1982] ICR 156.   [4] For example, see *Safeway Stores plc v Burrell* [1997] ICR 523.

[5] P. A. Hall and D. Soskice, *Varieties of Capitalism: The Institutional Foundations of Comparative Advantage* (Oxford, OUP, 2001); B. Hancké, M. Rhodes, and M. Thatcher, *Beyond Varieties of Capitalism: Conflict, Contradictions, and Complementarities in the European Economy* (Oxford, OUP, 2007).

■ **A. Pendleton and H. F. Gospel, 'Markets and Relationships: Finance, Governance, and Labour in the United Kingdom' in A. Pendleton and H. F. Gospel (eds),** *Corporate Governance and Labour Management: An International Comparison* **(Oxford, OUP, 2004) 59–60**

It has become widely argued . . . that the UK finance and corporate governance system has adverse consequences for the performance of the firm and its employees. In a best-selling book, Hutton argues that the UK system prioritizes high returns to shareholders and subjugates the interests of firms and their workforces to the dictates of the City. The threat of takeover means that listed companies have to deliver high short-term returns to investors to secure their loyalty. As a result, 'technical innovation and building market share take second place to financial imperatives' (Hutton 1996: 134). Only those investment projects with high rates of return and low risk can be approved. The 'destructive relationship' between the City and industry means that investment, R&D, and workforces have to be sacrificed when firms face adverse economic circumstances.

This stakeholder line of argument has much in common with that found in the 'varieties of capitalism' literature and the corporate governance literature in Financial Economics. All emphasize the role of market forces in the UK capital and ownership system, with signals from stock trading activity as a key instrument causing firms to take particular courses of action. Hall and Soskice view market-based forms of coordination between actors and institutions as the key characteristic of the US and UK economies ('liberal market economies'), contrasting this with relationship-based forms of coordination in the German and Japanese economies ('coordinated market economies'). 'Institutional complementarities' mean that large, active equity markets in Anglo-American countries are accompanied by a greater reliance by firms on external labour markets than elsewhere, along with relatively low levels of statutory labour regulation. As a result, firms typically respond to economic shocks by adjustments to labour management (for instance, lay-offs). By contrast, in coordinated market economies there is a greater likelihood that these shocks will be absorbed by capital.[6]

The relative ease with which an employer may offload excess labour in response to a lowering of economic demand in a liberal market economy such as the UK is supported by statistical evidence. For example, in August 2007, before the onset of the economic recession, statistics produced by the Office for National Statistics ('ONS') revealed that there were approximately 1,667,000 people unemployed in the UK and there had been 134,000 redundancies in the third quarter (June–September) of 2007.[7] At that time, the unemployment rate, which is the percentage of the labour force without jobs, was 5.4 per cent.[8] By July 2009, and in the thick of the financial crisis, the economic circumstances had changed, the unemployment count had increased to 2,470,000, some 246,000 people had been made redundant in the three months to July 2009, and the unemployment rate had increased to 7.9 per cent.[9] However, in the three months to July 2017, when the ONS conducted interviews, labour market statistics demonstrated that the unemployment rate had dropped to 4.3 per cent, the number of unemployed was 1.46 million and 111,000 people had become redundant in the three months before that

---

[6] Subject to two minor caveats, Pendleton and Gospel's research revealed that the theory matched the reality in the UK, on which, see A. Pendleton and H. F. Gospel, 'Markets and Relationships: Finance, Governance, and Labour in the United Kingdom' in A. Pendleton and H. F. Gospel (eds), *Corporate Governance and Labour Management: An International Comparison* (Oxford, OUP, 2004) 80–1; H. F. Gospel and A. Pendleton, 'Finance, Corporate Governance and the Management of Labour: A Conceptual and Comparative Analysis' (2003) 41 *British Journal of Industrial Relations* 557.

[7] Office for National Statistics, *Economic & Labour Market Review* (August 2007) at page 16.

[8] *ibid.*, pages 12–13.

[9] Office for National Statistics, *Labour Market Statistic Bulletin* (September 2009) 4 and 6–7.

period.[10] Meanwhile, in Germany, the unemployment rate was 8.7 per cent in 2007 and had actually reduced to 3.8 per cent by June 2017.[11] These statistics suggest that there may be some correlation between downward trends in productive enterprise and the scale of redundancies in liberal market economies.

If it is accepted that some form of statutory intervention is required,[12] any law which seeks to confer protection on employees who are the subject of redundancies must necessarily involve a trade-off between the interests of industry, which demands the prerogative to engage in such reorganization of work patterns and allocations in order to remain domestically and globally competitive, and the interests of the taxpayer in seeking to minimize the adverse social costs of redundancies and the accompanying increase in unemployment. The taxpayer will demand that the adverse social costs associated with unemployment are kept to a minimum. The public purse will have the responsibility of meeting these costs and the danger is that an unregulated market for the hiring and firing of employees will lead to a kind of moral hazard, where industry knows that it can offload as much labour as it wishes onto the labour market without having to pick up the bill. However, it should be noted that the interests of the taxpayer do not entirely flow in one direction. Whilst taxpayers will have no desire to saddle the public purse with the expectation of having to meet an indeterminate amount of unemployment, retraining, health service, criminal justice, and other costs generated by lay-offs in the economy,[13] neither is it in their own interests or those of the wider economy to force employers to soak up the costs of low productivity. The same point can be made about low labour mobility and overstaffing, each of which could be easily addressed by promulgating laws that enable employers to engage in the rationalization of their workforces within a carefully prescribed environment.

In light of these opposing interests of industry and the taxpayer, and confronted with the social ills and hardships which large-scale redundancies generate, a number of policy options are available to a law-maker, as follows:

(1) It would be open to a law-maker to design a statutory regime which seeks to address the source of the economic insecurity of the worker. This could be achieved by constraining the managerial prerogative and conferring an enforceable right to work in favour of the employee. However, for the principal reason that such an approach is perceived to be extreme and potentially self-defeating—in that it would have adverse economic consequences—it is unrealistic to expect a policy-maker to apply it.

(2) A second policy choice might be to permit employers to effect redundancies, but to impose a legal obligation on them to make a severance payment to outgoing employees. This could be calculated on the basis of the employee's length of service, experience, age, and final salary, and with reference to the period it is likely to take the employee to secure alternative employment at a broadly similar rate of pay. In accordance with such a scheme, little, if any, responsibility for the costs of unemployment, etc. would be shouldered by the public purse; instead, the brunt of the costs of redundancies would be met by employers.

(3) Another policy option is the polar opposite of the first, whereby social security measures would be radically improved through increased earnings-related payments to

---

[10] Office for National Statistics, *Labour Market Statistic Bulletin* (March 2016), available at https://www.ons.gov.uk/employmentandlabourmarket/peopleinwork/employmentandemployeetypes/bulletins/uklabourmarket/september2017#redundancies at pages 25–6 and 34 (last visited 19 September 2017).

[11] See Eurostat website, available at http://ec.europa.eu/eurostat/tgm/table.do?tab=table&init=1&language=en&pcode=tipsun30&plugin=1 (last visited 19 September 2017).

[12] The arguments in favour of, and against, regulatory interference are the same as those discussed in Chapter 16, section 16.1.1.

[13] For a comprehensive treatment of the social costs of redundancy, see H. Collins, *Justice in Dismissal* (Oxford, OUP, 1992) 170–83.

unemployed workers. For example, in Denmark, the 'flexicurity' agenda pursued by the Danish Government involves generous social welfare provision for those who lose their jobs.[14]

(4) The final policy choice combines elements of options (2) and (3). This option reflects the fact that the law-maker has decided that both the taxpayer and industry should share the burden of unemployment. Of course, how far one constituency is benefited at the expense of the other depends on where the law draws the line. This is a point to which we will return later, in section 18.2.3, when we evaluate the section 135 right to a redundancy payment, which is a key plank of the statutory regulation of redundancies in UK law.

The 1965 Act gave expression to the legislature's initial policy preference. It represented a form of compromise between the demands of the taxpayer and the workforce, on the one hand, and that of industry and the wider economy, on the other. Employers were compelled to make severance payments to employees who fell within the definition of 'redundancy' in section 1 of the legislation, i.e. to a limited class of employees who had been dismissed.[15] Since 1965, the amount of the redundancy payment payable to the employee has been increased, unsurprisingly, to take account of inflation. However, at the time of writing, the maximum amount payable was fixed at the modest sum of £15,240.[16] Hence in no way can it be said that the magnitude of the payment operates to produce a 'disincentive effect', in the sense that the receipt of a redundancy payment discourages employees from seeking fresh employment.[17] On the contrary, the level at which the statutory redundancy payment has been fixed furnishes cogent evidence for the proposition that the balance between the managerial prerogative and the taxpayer has been struck in a manner which offers the worker no more than a moderate degree of protection. To that extent, the 1965 Act might be considered a failure, but perhaps its greatest contribution was unanticipated when it came into force. This lies in the crucial groundwork it laid towards the future introduction of the statutory unfair dismissal regime in 1971 and the cementing of the industrial tribunal system as the appropriate forum for the specialist resolution of labour disputes:

■ **P. Davies and M. Freedland, *Labour Law: Text and Materials*, 2nd edition (London, Weidenfeld and Nicholson, 1984) 529–30**

The [1965 Act] probably had the *narrow aim* of rendering redundancy due to technological change acceptable to the workers affected by it and hence to the country at large (rather than the aim of 'protecting job property' in a positive sense) . . . Its *effects* were wider than its aims because for the first time it turned dismissal into a prima facie compensable event rather than a generally non-compensable event. Moreover, since the *raison d'être* of industrial tribunals was in truth the general adjudication upon dismissal issues it was not surprising that the [1965 Act] should be treated by all concerned as the peg upon which to hang a wide jurisdiction over dismissals generally. This

---

[14] This is accompanied by a flexible workforce with high labour mobility and active labour market policies pursued by government agencies which are designed to get people back into employment, on which, see H. Jørgensen and P. K. Madsen, 'Flexicurity and Beyond: Reflections on the Nature and Future of a Political Celebrity' in H. Jørgensen and P. K. Madsen (eds), *Flexicurity and Beyond: Finding a New Agenda for the European Social Model* (DJØF Publishing, 2007) ch. 1.

[15] However, beyond that, its objectives were not particularly clear: P. Davies and M. Freedland, *Labour Law: Text and Materials*, 2nd edition (London, Weidenfeld and Nicholson, 1984) 528–30; P. Elias, B. Napier, and P. Wallington, *Labour Law: Cases and Materials* (London, Butterworths, 1980) 646–7; and Lord Wedderburn, *The Worker and the Law: Text and Materials*, 3rd edition (London, Penguin Books, 1986) 217–18.   [16] Section 119 of the ERA.

[17] R. H. Fryer, 'The Myths of the Redundancy Payments Act' (1973) 2 *Industrial Law Journal* 1, 10–11.

approach was in a sense encouraged and fostered by certain of the *techniques* employed in the legislation, namely the introduction of a statutory seniority system and the establishment of a Redundancy Fund to act as an insurance mechanism for compensation . . . In a sense the [1965 Act] carried the seeds, if not of its own destruction, then at least of its own diminution in importance. The perhaps unintended logic of the [1965 Act] led directly to a truly generalized system for adjudication upon dismissals which was, of course, realized in the unfair dismissal [regime in the Industrial Relations Act 1971]. With the coming of that legislation the [1965 Act] was somewhat relegated to a back seat. The unfair dismissal legislation held out the prospect of far more substantial compensation for dismissal than that afforded under the 1965 Act, especially with the introduction of the dual basis—basic and compensatory—of awards of compensation for unfair dismissal in 1975.[18]

When the unfair dismissal regime was brought into force by the Industrial Relations Act 1971 ('the 1971 Act'), it provided that a dismissal could be unfair for the reason of redundancy. Therefore, unlike the 1965 Act, which merely afforded employees the right to a seniority and earnings-related redundancy payment, the door was left open for the courts and industrial tribunals to engage in an intensive evaluation of the employer's commercial rationales for the redundancies and then to treat those reasons as 'unfair' on the employee. The potential was thus present for the substantive fairness of the employer's decision to dismiss for the reason of redundancy to be overturned. However, that did not happen; instead, as we will see in section 18.2.4, the 'range of reasonable responses' test was held to be the applicable standard of review in all cases alleging unfair dismissal, including economic dismissals for redundancy.[19] As we noted in Chapter 16,[20] this standard entails a particularly lax intensity of scrutiny of the managerial prerogative. For that reason, it is scarcely an exaggeration to say that the contribution made by the inclusion of redundancy within the unfair dismissal machinery introduced by the 1971 Act lies more in the procedural safeguards which it afforded to employees, via the medium of proper selection procedures and advance information and consultation rights, than in any review of the substance of the employer's decision to dismiss. In cases coming before the employment tribunals and courts today, the probability is that any dismissal which is held to be unfair for the reason of redundancy will have been grounded on the procedural unfairness, rather than the substantive unfairness, of the employer's decision to dismiss.

Akin to much of the employment protection legislation introduced by the UK Parliament, the current statutory regime constructs a floor of redundancy rights, above which the employer and employee may contractually agree to derogate upwards by enhancing the level of protection. The statutory regulation of redundancy is currently set out in Parts X and XI of the ERA and Chapter II of Part IV of the Trade Union and Labour Relations (Consolidation) Act 1992 ('TULRCA'). Introduced in order to meet the UK's European obligations pursuant to the Collective Redundancies Directive[21] and representing the final chink in the regulatory armour, the provisions of TULRCA enjoin employers to engage in prior consultation with trade union or employee representatives. Therefore, we now have a three-pronged approach to the statutory regulation of redundancy—namely a regime which entitles employees to:

(1) a statutory redundancy payment;

(2) protection from unfair redundancy; and

(3) the right to advance information and consultation.

---

[18] Writer's annotations appear in square brackets throughout this chapter.
[19] *James W. Cook & Co. (Wivenhoe) Ltd (in liquidation) v Tipper* [1990] ICR 716.
[20] See Chapter 16, section 16.3.1.   [21] Directive 75/129/EEC (OJ 1975 L48/29).

We will consider the first and second of these features in this chapter, but will return to the last feature in Chapter 20 in the context of the narrative on the other protections available to employees on the business reorganization of the employer.

Reflection points

1. If the theory that UK employers are more prone to engage in large-scale redundancies subsequent to corporate takeovers[22] or in the event of difficult economic conditions is accurate, are you convinced that the UK Parliament's regulatory response to the phenomenon of redundancies has been adequate and appropriate?

2. If so, on what basis would you justify such a response?

3. If not, why would you prefer the adoption of a more interventionist stance and what would it look like?

 For additional reading on the historical and contextual introduction, visit the Online Resources for this book at www.oup.com/uk/cabrelli3e/

18.1.2 **Alternatives to redundancy**

So far, in our hypothetical case study of Danny's Demolishers plc's business, we have traced the expansion of the business from a minor undertaking to a large multinational plc. Demand for the construction of new buildings has soared and so Danny's Demolishers has benefited commercially. However, when the economic climate sours dramatically, that demand begins to fall away very quickly and, for the first time in its existence, the business has had to look at ways of minimizing its operational costs.

Danny's Demolishers may respond in a number of ways. Of course, this may entail a round of redundancies across the business or perhaps at a particular location where business is slow. But redundancies will by no means be the only option available to an employer such as Danny's Demolishers. Indeed, there is evidence to suggest that organizations will treat redundancy as a last resort and will first exhaust alternative means of effecting reorganizations of their labour requirements.[23] This is perhaps not surprising, since, when an employer is proposing to make staff redundant, there is a legal obligation to consider whether there are alternative ways of dealing with the issues which have generated the perceived commercial need for such redundancies.[24]

What do such alternatives to redundancy look like? Consider Hypothetical A.

---

[22] For evidence of the negative employment impact of takeovers, see M. Conyon, S. Girma, S. Thompson, and P. Wright, 'Do Hostile Mergers Destroy Jobs?' (2001) 45 *Journal of Economic Behavior and Organization* 427; M. Conyon, S. Girma, S. Thompson, and P. Wright, 'The Impact of Mergers and Acquisitions on Company Employment in the United Kingdom' (2002) 46 *European Economic Review* 31. As for the negative employment effects of private equity-backed acquisitions, see M. Goergen, N. O'Sullivan, and G. Wood, 'The Employment Consequences of Private Equity Acquisitions: The Case of Institutional Buy-outs' (2014) 71 *European Economic Review* 67.

[23] N. Milward, M. Stevens, D. Smart, and W. R. Hawe, *Workplace Industrial Relations in Transition: The ED/ESRC/PSI/ACAS Surveys* (Aldershot, Dartmouth, 1992) ch. 9.

[24] A failure to consider such alternatives in advance of the declaration of redundancies may result in such redundancies being treated by a court as unfair dismissals entitling the redundant employees to compensation: *Allwood v William Hill Ltd* [1974] IRLR 258.

Hypothetical A

Danny's Demolishers plc ('the Employer') has experienced a severe downturn in its fortunes owing to a general economic recession. Danny calls a meeting of the board of directors to consider all the options, including compulsory redundancies. A briefing note on all of the potential ways of saving money is prepared by a firm of management consultants.[25]

One option advanced is to vary the terms and conditions of the employees by reducing their salaries by 5 per cent.[26] A similar idea is to attempt to persuade the employees to take a salary sacrifice or pay 'holiday'. The briefing note refers to the example of Willie Walsh, chairman of British Airways, who suggested in June 2009 that all staff of BA should agree to forgo their wages for one month. The argument was that this would save jobs by staving off the need for compulsory redundancies.[27] The briefing note also refers to another option which would involve exercising the Employer's rights under the mobility clauses in the contracts of employment of the employees. This would enable the Employer to redeploy some workers from location A to location B.

Other options include an outright recruitment freeze or seconding the employees to other organizations, but Danny and the board think that the former option seems to miss the point of the exercise and they cannot think of anywhere to second their employees. The briefing report also refers to the possibility of recommending that employees take sabbaticals from work or that staff levels be reduced over time by natural wastage. The former might seem promising, but Danny has been told that the workers are unlikely to accept this if put to them. Meanwhile, the latter is a non-starter in the board's view, as the savings which are likely to be generated will not come soon enough, reliant as they are on staff voluntarily handing in their resignations. One further possibility which the briefing note mentions is voluntary redundancy. This would involve offering the workers a severance payment in excess of the statutory minimum redundancy payment, in order to incentivize them to accept. However, in Danny's opinion, the figures involved are too high and he cannot see how the Employer could afford them.

Another option mentioned in the briefing note is to simply dismiss all of the agency staff. Since they are not employees of the Employer, they have no unfair dismissal rights and so can be sacked at will. Danny and the board are reluctant to take this step, as they recall the negative press associated with BMW's decision to adopt this strategy in 2009.[28]

Having rejected all of the options, the Employer asks its solicitor to present the legal options at a hastily convened meeting of the board of directors. Nothing is to be ruled out, including compulsory redundancies.

The report of the solicitor refers to three options: lay-off; short-time working; and redundancy.

Lay-off is a form of suspension of the contract of employment and so, when operative, the contract remains in force. When the employee is 'laid off' as defined in section 147(1) of the ERA, the employer and the employee agree that the latter will not work or be paid for a particular period of time. Lay-off is possible in blocks of one week or more. However, there are protections for the employee, where the lay-off has endured for a period in excess of four consecutive weeks or in excess of six weeks within a period of 13 weeks. In such a context, the employee will be entitled to be paid a statutory redundancy payment if he/she gives the requisite contractual or statutory period of notice

---

[25] The options compiled by the management consultants in Hypothetical A are not intended to be exhaustive.   [26] For an example, see *Garside and Laycock v Booth* [2011] IRLR 735.

[27] See http://news.bbc.co.uk/1/hi/magazine/8104924.stm (last visited 12 February 2016).

[28] See http://news.bbc.co.uk/1/hi/business/7892174.stm (last visited 12 February 2016).

(whichever is the longer) to his/her employer terminating his/her contract of employment and indicating his/her intention to claim such statutory redundancy payment on the ground of lay-off.[29]

An employee is engaging in *short-time working* in terms of section 147(2) of the ERA where he/she earns less than half his/her normal week's pay in a week period. Like lay-off, short-time working does not result in the termination of the contract of employment. The process and conditions are identical to those in lay-off.

Danny considers the options of lay-off and short-time working, but dismisses them on the basis that they seem to amount to temporary fixes, which do not address the nub of the Employer's problems, namely the generally poor economic climate. Unfortunately, this compels him to decide in favour of compulsory redundancies and it is to the statutory regulation of redundancy that we now turn.

18.2 DEFINITION OF REDUNDANCY AND STATUTORY RIGHTS

The two principal statutory rights enjoyed by employees on redundancy that we will address in this chapter are the right to be paid a statutory redundancy payment and the right not to be unfairly dismissed for the reason of redundancy. It should be stressed that the triggers for the statutory rights on redundancy are that (1) the employee must have been dismissed, (2) for the reason of redundancy.

18.2.1 Dismissal

As in the case of the unfair dismissal regime, which we analysed in Chapter 16, 'dismissal' in this context has a distinct legal meaning. The definition of dismissal for the purposes of redundancy is set out in section 136 of the ERA and is broadly similar to the definition in relation to unfair dismissal claims in section 95 of the ERA. However, there are some important differences:

Section 136 Circumstances in which an employee is dismissed

(1) Subject to the provisions of this section . . . for the purposes of this Part an employee is dismissed by his employer if (and only if)—

  (a) the contract under which he is employed by the employer is terminated by the employer (whether with or without notice),

  (b) he is employed under a limited-term contract which terminates by virtue of the limiting event without being renewed under the same contract, or

  (c) the employee terminates the contract under which he is employed (with or without notice) in circumstances in which he is entitled to terminate it without notice by reason of the employer's conduct.

(2) Subsection (1)(c) does not apply if the employee terminates the contract without notice in circumstances in which he is entitled to do so by reason of a lock-out by the employer . . .

---

[29] Section 148 of the ERA.

(5) Where in accordance with any enactment or rule of law—

   (a) an act on the part of an employer, or

   (b) an event affecting an employer (including, in the case of an individual, his death), operates to terminate a contract under which an employee is employed by him, the act or event shall be taken for the purposes of this Part to be a termination of the contract by the employer.

Section 136(1)(a) applies where the employee is positively dismissed by the employer for the reason of redundancy. Meanwhile, where a fixed-term contract comes to an end without renewal by reason of redundancy, section 136(1)(b) applies. Finally, section 136(1)(c) describes the situation where an employee is deemed to have been made redundant by virtue of the conduct of the employer, i.e. there has been a constructive dismissal. It is section 136(5) which deviates from the definition of dismissal in section 95, as it covers constructive terminations of the contract of employment as a result of the actions of, or events affecting, the employer. For example, the death or bankruptcy of the employer or the eradication of the employer's business will amount to a dismissal.[30] This protects the employee, since if the employer's death or bankruptcy was not covered by a statutory provision such as section 136(5), it could be argued that the employment contract had been frustrated. Frustration would deprive the employee of the right to claim dismissal for the reason of redundancy and also the right to a statutory redundancy payment.

Subject to certain exceptions,[31] where an employee is summarily dismissed, this will not amount to a dismissal for the purposes of section 136 of the ERA:

Section 140 Summary dismissal

(1) An employee is not entitled to a redundancy payment by reason of dismissal where his employer, being entitled to terminate his contract of employment without notice by reason of the employee's conduct, terminates it either—

   (a) without notice,

   (b) by giving shorter notice than that which, in the absence of conduct entitling the employer to terminate the contract without notice, the employer would be required to give to terminate the contract, or

   (c) by giving notice which includes, or is accompanied by, a statement in writing that the employer would, by reason of the employee's conduct, be entitled to terminate the contract without notice.

18.2.2 Redundancy

Once it has been established that an employee has been dismissed, the next question to consider is whether that person has been made redundant. For the purposes of the redundant employee's right to be paid a statutory redundancy payment, an employee's dismissal is presumed to have been by reason of redundancy in terms of section 163(2) of the ERA. However, it should be stressed that this does not apply where the employer seeks to argue that the reason for the dismissal was redundancy for the purposes of the

---

[30] However, see *Rose v Dodd* [2006] 1 All ER 464.

[31] For example, where an employee is dismissed for misconduct owing to his/her participation in a strike: section 140(2) of the ERA.

unfair dismissal regime. In such circumstances, the burden of proving redundancy will lie with the employer.

The statutory definition of redundancy is laid down in section 139 of the ERA:

Section 139 Redundancy

(1) For the purposes of this Act an employee who is dismissed shall be taken to be dismissed by reason of redundancy if the dismissal is wholly or mainly attributable to—

   (a) the fact that his employer has ceased or intends to cease—

      (i) to carry on the business for the purposes of which the employee was employed by him, or

      (ii) to carry on that business in the place where the employee was so employed, or

   (b) the fact that the requirements of that business—

      (i) for employees to carry out work of a particular kind, or

      (ii) for employees to carry out work of a particular kind in the place where the employee was employed by the employer, have ceased or diminished or are expected to cease or diminish.

(2) For the purposes of subsection (1), the business of the employer together with the business or businesses of his associated employers shall be treated as one (unless either of the conditions specified in paragraphs (a) and (b) of that subsection would be satisfied without so treating them) . . .

(6) In subsection (1) 'cease' and 'diminish' mean cease and diminish either permanently or temporarily and for whatever reason.

Three initial points can be made before detailed consideration of the statutory provisions:

(1) There is no need for the party seeking to establish 'redundancy' to prove that the employer was at fault, i.e. the legislation is non-fault-based.

(2) The effect of the words 'or are expected to cease or diminish' is that it is possible for a dismissed employee to be redundant notwithstanding the fact that the employer's requirements to carry on the business, or for employees, etc. have not yet ceased or diminished. In such a case, this will constitute what might be usefully referred to as an anticipatory redundancy.

(3) Finally, the definition of redundancy in section 139 of the ERA is of relevance in the context of the employee's statutory rights:

   (a) to receive a redundancy payment; and

   (b) not to be unfairly dismissed.

It has no application to the employer's statutory duty to inform and consult trade union or employee representatives on the redundancy of an employee, which is broader, and prescribed in section 195 of TULRCA.[32]

18.2.2.1 General cessation of the employer's business

Section 139(1)(a)(i) of the ERA applies where there is a complete cessation of the employer's business[33] or a proposal to do so, e.g. owing to a voluntary decision to cease

---

[32] See Chapter 20, section 20.3.1 for further details.

[33] Section 235(1) of the ERA directs that the word 'business' includes a trade or profession and includes any activity carried on by a body of persons (whether corporate or unincorporated).

trading or the insolvency of the employer. In the case of *Thomas v Jones*,[34] it was held that it is not necessary to show that the employer was the owner of the business, since the words 'carry on the business' are used in a general sense to describe the person in *control* of the business. The point here is that it will not necessarily be the legal proprietor of the business who will exercise control, e.g. a pub business that is owned by a brewery, but run and administered by a named manager with decision-making power over the pub's employees.[35] Meanwhile, section 139(1)(a)(ii) is engaged where there is a *partial* cessation of the employer's business, e.g. where a particular office, plant, factory, or unit is closed down. The words 'in the place where the employee was so employed' are broadly similar to the wording of section 139(1)(b)(ii) and their scope has exercised the tribunals and courts. We will consider them in section 18.2.2.3 in the context of section 139(1)(b).

18.2.2.2 Cessation or diminution in the business's requirements for work of a particular kind

Experience has shown that the meaning of section 139(1)(b) of the ERA has been the most fraught element of the definition of redundancy. It encompasses both a cessation and diminution in the employer's requirements for work, and it is through the interpretation of this particular provision that the attitude of the courts and tribunals to the statutory objective of employee protection on redundancy has been laid bare. The point being made here can be elaborated best by making a distinction between the *techniques* pursued by the judiciary and the *consequence* of the application of those techniques. Prior to the inclusion of redundancy as a potentially fair reason for dismissal under the statutory unfair dismissal regime, the case law in the late 1960s and early 1970s which construed the 1965 Act[36]—the statutory predecessor of section 139(1)(b)—developed a body of jurisprudence which underlined the courts' general philosophy of deferring to the managerial prerogative and the right of management to direct its labour force as it saw fit.[37] The tribunals and courts did so by adopting two inter-related and overlapping *techniques*, some of which were inherent within the mischief of the 1965 Act itself and persist to this day, permeating the reasoning of the courts. The *consequence* of the application of both of those techniques was the limitation of the scope to which the conduct of the employer would be redressed by the redundancy protection legislation, exposing a deep-seated deference to the managerial prerogative.

   The first technique involved the courts rejecting the notion that the definition of 're-dundancy' could be applied in order to second-guess the commercial motives or rationales for the employer's decision to make the employee redundant, i.e. the reasons for the redundancy and the employer's need to do so. This technique is exemplified by cases such as *James W. Cook & Co. (Wivenhoe) Ltd (in liquidation) v Tipper*[38] and *Moon v Home-worthy Furniture (Northern) Ltd.*[39] A second technique involved the courts specifically adapting themselves to the way in which the establishment of the unfair dismissal regime had influenced the identity of the party who would be seeking to establish a redundancy. Prior to the introduction of the unfair dismissal regime, the judiciary took a broad view of the statutory reference to 'work of a particular kind' now contained in section 139(1)(b) of the ERA, which operated to narrow down the concept of redundancy. For example, when a boatbuilding business changed from wooden to fibreglass construction in *Hindle*

---

[34] [1978] ICR 274, 276F–G per Phillips J.

[35] Contrast this with the more restrictive legal position in respect of the statutory information and consultation obligations on collective redundancies, on which, see Chapter 20, section 20.3.1.6.

[36] Section 1(2)(b) of the 1965 Act.

[37] For example, see P. Elias, B. Napier, and P. Wallington, *Labour Law: Cases and Materials* (London, Butterworths, 1980) 648–9.   [38] [1990] ICR 716.

[39] [1977] ICR 117.

v Percival Boats Ltd,[40] the Court of Appeal held that an employee who was a skilled woodworker had not been dismissed for the reason of redundancy, since the boatbuilding function continued to exist. The reason for his dismissal was that he was unable to adapt to the employer's new working methods and was thus unprofitable. Likewise, in *Lesney Products Co. Ltd v Nolan*,[41] an employer reorganized the arrangements for machine maintenance by changing its employee machine setters' shifts from one long day shift plus overtime to two day shifts. Initially, the employer required the engagement of 36 machine setters; when certain employees objected to the changed shift pattern and were replaced, it was held that their dismissal did not amount to redundancy, since the function of machine maintenance for which they had been employed remained the same.[42] This can be contrasted with cases decided subsequent to the introduction of the unfair dismissal regime,[43] which furnish evidence of a change in the outlook of the tribunals and courts. Rather than taking a narrow view of the statutory concept of redundancy, the judges assumed a more broad-brush approach. This can perhaps be explained as a response to the somewhat bizarre reality that it is now the employer, rather than the employee, who will be the most keen to argue that a dismissed employee is redundant. If the employer can show that the employee was dismissed for redundancy, it is open to the employer to argue that the dismissal was fair and so restrict the employee to the receipt of a statutory redundancy payment, rather than the more substantial compensatory award[44] under the statutory unfair dismissal regime.[45]

Against the backdrop of the application of those two techniques, two schools of thought emerged as to how the courts and tribunals ought to evaluate whether the employer's requirements for 'work of a particular kind' generally or 'in [a] place' had ceased or diminished. These were the narrower 'job package'/'contract' test and the wider 'function' test. Both of the tests treated the question of redundancy as a matter of law, rather than fact:

■ Lord Wedderburn, *The Worker and the Law: Text and Materials,* 3rd edition (London, Penguin Books, 1986) 225–8

> As the present writer suggested in 1966, [section 139(1)(b)] has come to 'provide a lawyers' field day'. Such a definition was bound to leave out many workers who to the ordinary person are dismissed for 'redundancy' . . . [The advent of the unfair dismissal regime] magnified a more difficult issue. The test of redundancy may turn more either upon an interpretation of the contract (styled by Davies and Freedland the 'job package' approach) or upon an investigation of the actual work done (the 'job function' approach). Both appear in the cases and both have their difficulties. The second leaves the court more free to take its own view of the 'kind of work' . . . ; the first entangles the test of redundancy with the manipulated express and implied terms. Both can be trimmed to suit the needs of the day by the [*Hindle v Percival Boats Ltd* [1969] 1 WLR 174] test, giving the employer's subjective reasoning pride of place. [Each] give[s] the judges wide scope.

Thus, the 'job package'/'contract' test considered the work that the employee was, *or could be*, under a duty to perform by virtue of his/her contract of employment. It represents yet another example of the trend we examined in Chapter 2, section 2.1.1, namely

---

[40] [1969] 1 WLR 174. See also *Vaux and Associated Breweries Ltd v Ward* (1968) 3 ITR 385.
[41] [1977] ICR 235.   [42] See M. R. Freedland, 'Redundancy' (1977) 6 *Industrial Law Journal* 237.
[43] *Robinson v British Island Airways Ltd* [1978] ICR 304; *Murphy v Epsom College* [1985] ICR 80; *Murray v Foyle Meats Ltd* [2000] 1 AC 51; and *Packman v Fauchon* [2012] ICR 1362.
[44] See Chapter 17, section 17.3.3.2.
[45] For example, see *Safeway Stores plc v Burrell* [1997] ICR 523; *High Table Ltd v Horst* [1998] ICR 409.

the general inclination of the judiciary to resort to the machinery of the common law of the contract of employment in order to infuse content into statutory provisions, rather than treating them as self-contained concepts with their own internal logic. In terms of the test, the judges would query what the employee could be required to do in terms of his/her contract of employment, irrespective of the fact that this bore no relation to the work which he/she had actually been doing or was ever likely to be asked to do.[46] In terms of this test, where the terms of the contract conferred an option on the employer to require an employee to fulfil additional duties as the employer's requirements dictated, it would be difficult to establish redundancy, since the scope of the work which the employee might be required to do was drawn extremely widely. For example, the inclusion of a 'flexibility' clause in the contract of employment of an employee would limit the scope for an inference to be drawn that the employee was redundant.[47]

The 'job package'/'contract' test could be contrasted with the 'function' test, which instead looked at the work the employer *actually did*, in isolation from the terms of the contract. This was more straightforward a test to satisfy, since if the duties and the functions of the employee were in actual fact modified, the employee would be treated as redundant. A good example is the case of *Lesney Products v Nolan*.[48]

Different cases applied the two different legal tests leading to differing results, but the courts generally leaned towards the application of the 'job package'/'contract' test. However, in *Murray v Foyle Meats Ltd*,[49] the House of Lords criticized both the 'contract' and 'function' tests, and ruled that the question was one of simple factual causation, i.e. a matter of fact, rather than law.

■ *Murray v Foyle Meats Ltd* [2000] 1 AC 51, 55–8

Lord Irvine of Lairg LC:

My Lords, Foyle Meats Ltd ('the company') carry on business as slaughterers in Londonderry. They employed the applicants as 'meat plant operatives.' Both normally worked in the company's slaughter hall, but they could under their contracts of employment be required to work elsewhere and occasionally did so. Employees who worked in other parts of the factory, such as the boning hall or the loading bay, were engaged on similar terms. In 1995 there was a decline in business and the company decided to reduce the number of 'killing lines' in the slaughter hall from two to one. This meant that fewer employees were required in the hall . . . The applicants were selected for redundancy and dismissed on 27 March 1995. Both made a complaint of unfair dismissal to an industrial tribunal . . . My Lords, the language of [section 139(1)(b) of the ERA] is in my view simplicity itself. It asks two questions of fact. The first is whether one or other of various states of economic affairs exists. In this case, the relevant one is whether the requirements of the business for employees to carry out work of a particular kind have diminished. The second question is whether the dismissal is attributable, wholly or mainly, to that state of affairs. This is a question of causation. In the present case, the tribunal found as a fact that the requirements of the business for employees to work in the slaughter hall had diminished. Secondly, they found that that state of affairs had led to the applicants being dismissed. That, in my opinion, is the end of the matter. This conclusion is in accordance with the analysis of the statutory provisions by Judge Peter Clark in *Safeway Stores Plc. v. Burrell* [1997] I.C.R. 523 and I need to say no more than that I entirely agree with his admirably clear reasoning and conclusions . . . [But I should stress that] both the contract test and the function test miss the point. The key word in the statute is 'attributable' and there is no reason in law why

---

[46] See *Nelson v BBC (No. 2)* [1980] ICR 110 and *Haden Ltd v Cowen* [1983] ICR 1, which are examples of the application of this approach.

[47] See Chapter 7, section 7.2.1, for a description and example of a 'flexibility' clause.

[48] [1997] ICR 235.   [49] [2000] 1 AC 51.

the dismissal of an employee should not be attributable to a diminution in the employer's need for employees irrespective of the terms of his contract or the function which he performed. Of course the dismissal of an employee who could perfectly well have been redeployed or who was doing work unaffected by the fall in demand may require some explanation to establish the necessary causal connection. But this is a question of fact, not law.

There is a strong argument that redundancy will be inevitable in many cases owing to the emphasis which the causation test places on the requirement to establish a drop in the employer's need for employees to perform work, rather than in respect of the individual employee claimant's job. The materialization of this causation test is symptomatic of the judiciary's tendency to construe the statutory provisions in a manner which is pro-employer and defers to the employer's managerial prerogative.[50]

The decision in *Murray v Foyle Meats Ltd* is particularly important in the context of the phenomenon of 'bumping'[51] in redundancies. 'Bumping' describes the situation where a particular position disappears and the employee occupying that post is transferred to another position, duly bumping the employee occupying the latter out of a job. A common reason for an employer to adopt such an approach is that it wishes to retain the individual with the most experience, skills, and qualifications. Now, let us consider the following Hypothetical B in light of the outcomes which would be reached pursuant to the application of the 'job package'/'contract', 'function', and causation tests.

Hypothetical B

Danny's Demolishers plc ('the Employer') has identified the potential for efficiencies in its IT department and has decided that it no longer requires an IT director. Rather than lose the skills of the current IT director, James Squire, the Employer decides to terminate the contract of employment of IT assistant Andrew Short. James Squire then moves into Andrew Short's position as an IT assistant. Andrew Short loses his job, so is he redundant?

Under the 'contract' test, Andrew Short is not redundant, since the Employer's requirement for the position of IT assistant, as described and set out in Andrew Short's terms and conditions of employment, continues to exist. Likewise, the application of the 'function' test would lead to the same result, as the actual work of an IT assistant has not ceased and instead has now been taken up by James Squire. However, if the causation test in *Murray v Foyle Meats Ltd* is applied, Andrew Short would indeed be redundant. As delineated in the speech of Lord Irvine of Lairg LC, the causation test entails asking two questions. First, have the requirements of the Employer's business to carry out work of a particular kind diminished? This question can be answered in the affirmative, since the Employer's requirements for an IT director have ceased. Secondly, is Andrew Short's dismissal attributable, wholly or mainly, to that state of affairs? Again, the answer to that question must be 'Yes', since Andrew Short's employment was terminated in response to that state of affairs.[52]

[50] As we noted earlier, the emergence of the unfair dismissal legislation in 1971 switched the incentives in respect of the raising of unfair redundancy claims. As such, it is now more often than not in the interests of the employer, rather than the employee, to establish redundancy. By making it undemanding for an employer to satisfy the test of redundancy, the House of Lords once again refused to interfere in the managerial prerogative, a point noted in the case of *Church v West Lancashire NHS Trust (No. 1)* [1998] ICR 423.   [51] 'Bumping' is also sometimes referred to as 'transferred redundancy'.
[52] See *Church v West Lancashire NHS Trust (No. 1)* [1998] ICR 423 for an example of 'bumping' in the case law.

The House of Lords' decision in *Murray v Foyle Meats Ltd* informs our understanding of the proper approach to be applied to 'bumping' situations and redundancy generally. It tells us that it is misconceived to ask whether the employer's need for the *employee claimant* to perform *his/her particular job or function* has ceased or diminished; instead, the question is whether an employee's dismissal is caused by a reduction in an employer's need for *employees* to perform *work of a generic type*. The result is that 'bumped' employees will more often than not be treated as redundant.[53] In the same vein, where there is less work available for existing employees, e.g. a reduction in the number of hours available for the employer's staff, an employee will be able to establish a redundancy if he/she is dismissed as a result: the most telling example of this point is the decision of the EAT in *Packman v Fauchon*,[54] where it was held that an employee was redundant when there was a material reduction in his working hours because the employer needed less work of the sort done by that employee. As such, staff numbers and functions/jobs might remain the same, but so long as there is evidence of a substantial reduction in the employer's need for work or hours of work, a dismissed employee will be entitled to claim that he/she is redundant. In addition, the 'diminishing requirements' element of the definition has been construed to include circumstances where it is clear that the employer has a labour surplus, i.e. that it requires fewer employees for existing work. Owing to the fact that the emphasis is on the change in the employer's *requirements* for individuals to do work, i.e. whether there is overstaffing,[55] the amount of work available might stay the same, but technical innovation, social change, or a reorganization[56] by the employer might lead to efficiencies which result in a surplus of labour.[57] In such a case, a dismissed employee will be treated as redundant. The word 'requirements' is absolutely key in section 139(1)(b), as it means that a reduction in work or head count is inconclusive, the emphasis being on whether the employer's requirements for work, head count, or working hours has reduced. As such, even where the actual work available and numbers of employees actually increases, e.g. where a single post is replaced by two new posts that were materially different from the former, an employee will be redundant on the basis that the employer's requirements for the work performed by the employee in the old single post had ceased.[58]

To that extent, the courts have severed the employee and the employee's particular job or function from the requisite analysis, effectively eliding the words 'work of a particular kind' in section 139(1)(b)(i) and (ii) of the ERA by, at best, revising them to mean 'work of a *general* kind' and, at worst, simply ignoring them. To what extent this construction is justified or amounts to an unwarranted gloss on the statutory wording, is a wholly separate and controversial issue. This is especially true, since Parliament could have defined redundancy more easily in terms of a requirement to show a diminution in the employer's need for employees if it was its intention to reach the particular outcome in *Murray v Foyle Meats Ltd*.

As noted earlier, what the approach in *Murray v Foyle Meats Ltd* also disturbs is the requirement for some identifiable function to disappear for section 139(1)(b) of the ERA to be engaged. The question then arises as to what evaluative criteria ought to be applied in order to determine what is meant by 'work of a particular kind'. It is by responding to this question that it becomes apparent that the broad interpretation and pro-employer

---

[53] For example, see *Contract Bottling Ltd v Cave* (UKEAT/0525/12/DM, 23 April 2013).

[54] [2012] ICR 1362.

[55] See *Shawkat v Nottingham City Hospital NHS Trust (No. 2)* [2002] ICR 7; *Martland v Co-operative Insurance Society Ltd* [2008] All ER (D) 166 (April).

[56] A reorganization will not necessarily lead to a redundancy, but instead may amount to some other substantial reason for the employee's dismissal in terms of section 98(1)(b) of the ERA, e.g. where an employee refuses to abide by changes to his/her terms and conditions of employment.

[57] *Delanair Ltd v Mead* [1976] ICR 522; *McCrea v Cullen & Davison Ltd* [1988] IRLR 30.

[58] *Hakki v Instinctif Partners Ltd (formerly College Hill Ltd)* (UKEAT/0112/14/RN, 16 July 2014).

nature of the decision in *Murray v Foyle Meats Ltd* has been tempered slightly by the judiciary, i.e. that the judicial conceptualization of what is meant by the statutory reference to 'work of a particular kind' has served to narrow somewhat the concept of redundancy. For instance, the tribunals and courts have generally held that an employee is not redundant where the amount of work remains the same and the number of staff needed to discharge that work is broadly the same or even greater, *but there is a reduction in the employer's need for certain skills or specialisms with an attendant change in the organization of the responsibilities which the employee is required to perform.*[59] Once again, the tribunals and courts have taken a broad view of what is meant by 'work of a particular kind'. The result has been a slight narrowing of the concept of redundancy, since the case law reveals that the extent to which the work must change is considerable before it can constitute work of a different kind.

Reflection points

1. Bearing in mind that it has brought about a widening of the concept of redundancy, do you agree with the decision of the House of Lords in *Murray v Foyle Meats Ltd*? If so, on what basis would you justify it? If not, why not?

2. With regard to the nature of the work which must no longer be required by the employer, in your opinion to what extent ought it to have changed before the court finds that it constitutes work of a different kind? For example, 20 per cent, 50 per cent, 51 per cent, 80 per cent, 100 per cent? What would be the policy implications of your choice?

18.2.2.3 'In the place where the employee was employed by the employer'

Section 139(1)(a)(ii) and (b)(ii) of the ERA assumes significance where an employer's requirements to carry on its business or for certain employed positions ceases or diminishes in a particular place, e.g. the post of clerical assistant is no longer needed at a particular branch, office, or factory. In much the same way as the evaluation of the concept of a cessation or diminution in the employer's requirements for work of a particular kind in section 139(1)(b) generated interpretive challenges, the assessment of the words 'place where the employee was employed by the employer' has oscillated between the adoption of a narrower 'job package'/'contract' test and the wider 'factual' test. If the 'job package'/'contract' test is applied where a mobility clause[60] is present in the contract of employment of an employee, one could argue that the employee is not redundant. If the employee was dismissed and that dismissal was caused by a reduction in the employer's requirements for work at a particular place, the application of the 'job package'/'contract' test would leave it open to a party to claim that he/she was not truly redundant on the basis of the wide scope of the mobility clause, i.e. the place or places under the contract where the employee *could* legally be required to work.[61] Moreover, notwithstanding the absence of a mobility clause, the application of the 'job package'/'contract' test would generate the same result, since the courts were (and are) prepared to imply a term requiring the employee to move from one location to another, provided that the travelling distance from the employee's home was (is) reasonable.[62]

---

[59] However, cf. *Barot v London Borough of Brent* (UKEAT/0539/11/BA, 17 January 2013); *Hakki v Instinctif Partners Ltd (formerly College Hill Ltd)* (UKEAT/0112/14/RN, 16 July 2014).

[60] See Chapter 7, section 7.2.1, for a description and example of a 'mobility' clause.

[61] For example, see *United Kingdom Atomic Energy Authority v Claydon* [1974] ICR 128.

[62] *O'Brien v Associated Fire Alarms Ltd* [1968] 1 WLR 1916.

The ascendancy of the 'job package'/'contract' test was brought to an end in the late 1990s, rejected as 'def[ying] common sense' by Lord Justice Peter Gibson in the decision of the Court of Appeal in *High Table Ltd v Horst*:[63]

■ *High Table Ltd v Horst* [1998] ICR 409, 419–20

Lord Justice Peter Gibson:

The question . . .—where was the employee employed by the employer for the purposes of the business?—is one to be answered primarily by a consideration of the factual circumstances which obtained until the dismissal. If an employee has worked in only one location under his contract of employment for the purposes of the employer's business, it defies common sense to widen the extent of the place where he was so employed, merely because of the existence of a mobility clause. Of course the refusal by the employee to obey a lawful requirement under the contract of employment for the employee to move may constitute a valid reason for dismissal, but the issues of dismissal, redundancy and reasonableness in the actions of an employer should be kept distinct. It would be unfortunate if the law were to encourage the inclusion of mobility clauses in contracts of employment to defeat genuine redundancy claims. Parliament has recognised the importance of the employee's right to a redundancy payment. If the work of the employee for his employer has involved a change of location, as would be the case where the nature of the work required the employee to go from place to place, then the contract of employment may be helpful to determine the extent of the place where the employee was employed. But it cannot be right to let the contract be the sole determinant,[64] regardless of where the employee actually worked for the employer. The question what was the place of employment is one that can safely be left to the good sense of the industrial tribunal.

Therefore, in the same vein as the House of Lords in *Murray v Foyle Meats Ltd*, the Court of Appeal characterized the appropriate test as one of fact, i.e. the relevant issue is where the employee actually worked. However, the Court of Appeal subjected this general rule to the proviso that the terms of the contract will be relevant where a mobility clause has in fact been invoked by the employer in the past. In such a case, *High Table Ltd v Horst* suggests that the employee will not be redundant. However, it does not necessarily follow from this that an employee will be redundant where an employer enforces a mobility clause in an employee's contract of employment where its need for work diminishes at a particular location.[65] Therefore, the crucial factor is that the employer invoked the mobility clause, and the employee in fact moved in response to that invocation, *in the past*.

 For additional reading on the definition of redundancy and statutory rights, visit the Online Resources for this book at www.oup.com/uk/cabrelli3e/

18.2.3 The right to receive a statutory redundancy payment

18.2.3.1 The entitlement and excluded categories

The cumulative effect of sections 135 and 155 of the ERA is that a redundant employee who has been continuously employed for a period of two years or more has the right to receive a statutory redundancy payment. In terms of section 163(2), where an employee

---

[63] [1998] ICR 409, 419F.
[64] On this point, see *EXOL Lubricants v Birch* (UKEAT/0219/14/KN, 13 November 2014).
[65] *Home Office v Evans* [2008] ICR 302; *Kellogg Brown & Root (UK) Ltd v Fitton* (UKEAT/0205/16/BA, 21 November 2016).

makes a complaint to an employment tribunal that he/she has not received his/her statutory redundancy payment, there is a rebuttable presumption that the employee has been dismissed for the reason of redundancy. There are certain exceptions where a dismissed employee's right to receive a statutory redundancy payment will be denied.

(1) As noted in section 18.2.1, if the employee was summarily dismissed by the employer for misconduct, section 140 stipulates that he/she will forfeit his/her right to receive the statutory redundancy payment.

(2) Employees of foreign governments, civil servants, public officials, share fisherman, and certain categories of employees that have been excluded by the Secretary of State (in cases where there is a collective agreement in place which governs redundancy issues) are excluded from the right to receive a statutory redundancy payment.[66]

(3) An employee will lose the right to a redundancy payment on the operation of an elaborate set of statutory provisions concerning the service of notices and counter-notices between the employee and the employer.[67] The employee must first give to the employer notice terminating his/her employment contract on a date earlier than the date on which the employer's notice of termination of the contract is due to expire and the employer must respond by serving a written counter-notice before the expiry of the period of notice in the employee's notice. It is a requirement that the employee fails to comply with the terms of the employer's counter-notice. The employer's written counter-notice must require the employee to withdraw his/her notice terminating the contract of employment and to continue in employment until the date on which the employer's notice terminating the contract expires. It must also state that, unless the employee satisfies that condition, the employer will contest any liability to pay him/her a redundancy payment.

(4) Most importantly, one must consult section 141:

Section 141 Renewal of contract or re-engagement

(1) This section applies where an offer (whether in writing or not) is made to an employee before the end of his employment—

    (a) to renew his contract of employment, or

    (b) to re-engage him under a new contract of employment, with renewal or re-engagement to take effect either immediately on, or after an interval of not more than four weeks after, the end of his employment.

(2) Where subsection (3) is satisfied, the employee is not entitled to a redundancy payment if he unreasonably refuses the offer.

(3) This subsection is satisfied where—

    (a) the provisions of the contract as renewed, or of the new contract, as to—

        (i)   the capacity and place in which the employee would be employed, and

        (ii) the other terms and conditions of his employment, would not differ from the corresponding provisions of the previous contract, or

    (b) those provisions of the contract as renewed, or of the new contract, would differ from the corresponding provisions of the previous contract but the offer constitutes an offer of suitable employment in relation to the employee.

---

[66] Sections 157, 159, 160, and 199(2) of the ERA.   [67] Section 142 of the ERA.

This legislative extract shows that an employee will not be entitled to be paid the statutory redundancy payment if the employer makes an offer of suitable alternative employment and the employee unreasonably refuses that offer. The question of whether the alternative employment offered was suitable and unreasonably refused will be evaluated in accordance with a mixed objective/subjective standard of review, rather than a range of reasonable responses test.[68] The relevant legal authorities were considered and the law helpfully summarized in the following decision of the EAT:

■ *Bird v Stoke-on-Trent Primary Care Trust* (UKEAT/0074/11/DM, 21 July 2011), paras 17–21

The Legal Framework

In the light of ss 141(2) and 141(3)(b) of the [ERA], the questions for the tribunal were whether the offers of either of the two posts constituted offers of suitable employment for Ms Bird, and whether her refusal of either of those offers was reasonable. Apart from occasional cases which have suggested otherwise—of which the decision of the [EAT] in Scotland (Lord McDonald presiding) in *Tocher v General Motors Scotland Ltd* [1981] IRLR 55 at 13 is one—the law has always been that those two questions have to be considered separately . . . But that does not mean that the two questions are completely unrelated. The more suitable the offer, the easier it may be for the employer to show that the employee's refusal of the offer was unreasonable: see . . . *Commission for Healthcare Audit and Inspection v Ward* (UKEAT/0579/07/JOJ) at 18 . . .[69] The issue of suitability is conveniently (and correctly) summarised in *Harvey on Industrial Relations and Employment Law*, Vol 1, Division E, Issue 204, para 1489, which reads:

[']Under "suitability" you must consider the nature of the employment offered. It is for the tribunal to make an objective assessment of the job offered (*Carron Co v Robertson* (1967) 2 ITR 484, Ct of Sess). It is not, however, an entirely objective test, in that the question is not whether the employment is suitable in relation to that *sort* of employee, but whether it is suitable in relation to that *particular* employee. It comes really to asking whether the job matches the person: does it suit his skills, aptitudes and experience? The whole of the job must be considered, not only the tasks to be performed, but the terms of employment, especially wages and hours, and the responsibility and status involved. The location may also be relevant, because "commuting is not generally regarded as a joy" (*Laing v Thistle Hotels plc* [2003] SLT 37, Ct of Sess, *per* Lord Ordinary Eassie). No single factor is decisive; all must be considered as a package. Was it, in all the circumstances, a reasonable offer for that employer to suggest that job to that employee? And the sole criterion by which that is to be judged is "suitability".[']

There has been talk in some of the cases that the new post should be 'substantially' or 'broadly' equivalent to the existing one (see, for example, Lord Parker CJ in *Taylor v Kent County Council* [1969] 2 QB 560 at p 566B . . . and Lord Eassie in *Laing*), but that was doubted—correctly, we think—by Bridge J (as he then was) in *Collier v Smith's Dock Co Ltd* (1969) 4 ITR 338[70] on the basis that it puts an unwarranted gloss on the statutory language. In other words, the fact that the post which is being offered is different from the employee's existing post does not necessarily mean that it is unsuitable for that employee, but by analogy with the approach in *Ward*, the more different the posts are, the more difficult it may be for the employer to show that the post which is being offered is suitable for the employee. The issue of reasonableness is also conveniently (and correctly) summarised in *Harvey, op cit*, para 1552:

---

[68] See *Devon Primary Care Trust v Readman* [2013] IRLR 878; *Hudson v George Harrison Ltd* [2003] All ER (D) 381 (March). The onus of proving an unreasonable refusal of alternative employment falls on the employer: *Jones v Aston Cabinet Co. Ltd* [1973] ICR 292.

[69] See also *Spencer v Gloucestershire County Council* [1985] IRLR 393.

[70] See also *Standard Telephones v Yates* [1981] IRLR 21 on this point.

['']The question is not whether a reasonable employee would have accepted the employer's offer, but whether that particular employee, taking into account his personal circumstances, was being reasonable in refusing the offer: did he have sound and justifiable reasons for turning down the offer?[']

As the [EAT] (Phillips J presiding) said in *Executors of J F Everest v Cox* [1980] ICR 415 at p 418C, the question whether the employee had sound and justifiable reasons for refusing the offer has to be judged from the employee's point of view, on the basis of the facts as they appeared, or ought to have appeared, to the employee at the time the offer was refused.

In *Cambridge and District Co-operative Ltd v Ruse* [1993] IRLR 156, the . . . [EAT] said that loss of status was a factor which could make the employee's refusal of the offer reasonable. It also said at 18 that 'as a matter of law, it is possible for the employee reasonably to refuse an objectively suitable offer on the ground of his personal perception of the employment offered'. Indeed, that could be so even if other people think that 'the personal perception' of the employee might be wholly unreasonable. That was not the case in *Ruse* because the industrial tribunal had merely found it possible that 'he was being a little sensitive'. But an employee's refusal of an otherwise suitable offer can still be said to be reasonable when he personally thinks that the post he is being offered involves a loss of status, even if that view might be groundless in the eyes of others, provided that it is not groundless from his point of view . . . [the decision in] *Denton v Neepsend Ltd* [1976] IRLR 164 . . . supports the view that the employee's reasons for refusing the offer had only to be 'sound and justifiable' *from the employee's point of view*, even if others might not have thought that his reasons were sound and justifiable.[71]

The point being made about the subjective nature of the assessment of the reasonableness of the employee's refusal towards the end of the passage should perhaps not be stretched too far. Some limits will be set by the tribunals and courts. For example, in *Fuller v Stephanie Bowman (Sales) Ltd*,[72] the tribunal was prepared to hold that an employee's refusal was unreasonable on the basis that there was absolutely no foundation for her genuine belief that her motives for refusal were reasonable. Finally, it should be noted that, where the employer makes the employee an offer of alternative employment and the employee is uncertain whether to accept it or not, the employee has a statutory right under section 138 of the ERA to engage in a trial period. That trial period is four weeks or such longer period as may be agreed between the employee and employer.

18.2.3.2 Calculation of the statutory redundancy payment

The statutory redundancy payment is calculated in the same way as the basic award in the case of a successful unfair dismissal claim.[73] The effect of section 162 of the ERA is that the redundancy payment is calculated in the following manner:

- half a week's pay for each full year of service where the employee's age during the year is under 22, with half a week's pay currently being capped at £508;

- one week's pay for each full year of service where the employee's age during the year is 22 or over, but under 41, with a week's pay being capped at £508; and

- one-and-a-half weeks' pay for each full year of service where the employee's age during the year is 41 or over, with one-and-a-half week's pay being capped at £508.

---

[71] Sourced from BAILII available at http://www.bailii.org/cgi-bin/markup.cgi?doc=/uk/cases/UKEAT/2011/0074_11_2107.html&query=bird+and+v+and+stoke&method=boolean (last visited 19 September 2017). See also *Dunne v Colin & Avril Ltd (t/a Card Outlet)* (UKEAT/0293/16/DA, 8 March 2017).

[72] [1977] IRLR 87.   [73] See Chapter 17, section 17.3.3.1.

With effect from 6 April 2018, the maximum amount payable is £15,240,[74] but such maximum limit is increased annually.

18.2.3.3 Enhanced redundancy payments

The tension between the taxpayer, employees, and the employer that we discussed earlier in this chapter[75] was resolved by constructing a floor of statutory redundancy rights. It is then open to the employer and employee to add flesh to the framework erected by the statutory regime by contracting 'upwards', via the medium of enhanced redundancy packages. Indeed, this is a common phenomenon in the public sector[76] and large private sector organizations.[77] The process for the establishment of an enhanced redundancy package may be taken forward by one of two means:

(1) an employer may negotiate and agree a redundancy agreement with a trade union or elected employee representatives; or

(2) alternatively, it may establish a redundancy policy in the absence of consultation, negotiation, or agreement with a trade union or employee representatives.

A redundancy agreement or policy will contain procedures which the employer will observe and comply with when it contemplates the rationalization of its workforce and redundancies. Redundancy agreements and redundancy policies also sometimes include provisions which bind the employer to pay sums to redundant employees in excess of the amounts to which those employees are entitled under the statutory scheme. Thus, such schemes, which pay more than the statutory requirements, are referred to as 'enhanced' schemes and the payments are known as 'enhanced' redundancy payments. On occasion, the enhanced redundancy scheme may form part of an employee's contract of employment, e.g. by express incorporation of its terms. Where that is the case, all of the issues concerning the incorporation and breach of such a contractual scheme/policy addressed in Chapter 5[78] will assume relevance. On the other hand, the enhanced package may be clothed with contractual effect as an implied term of the contract of employment. Whether that is the case will depend on the employer and whether there is sufficient evidence to show that it has evinced an intention to become contractually bound to make available that benefit to its employees as of right.[79]

Provisions for enhanced redundancy payments are often contained within an employer's redundancy policy. A major benefit of adopting and applying a fair redundancy procedure in terms of an agreement or policy[80] is that an employment tribunal will take it into account in any future case where an employee claims unfair redundancy. A booklet issued by ACAS[81] furnishes useful examples of the kinds of provisions which an employer should seek to include in a redundancy agreement or policy. For example, an agreement or policy ought to detail the procedures to be followed by the employer when it intends

---

[74] See the Schedule to the Employment Rights (Increase of Limits) Order 2018 (SI 2018/194).

[75] See section 18.1.1.

[76] For example, see *Lockwood v Department for Work and Pensions* [2013] EWCA Civ 1195, [2013] IRLR 941.

[77] For example, see *Ali v Petroleum Co. of Trinidad and Tobago* [2017] UKPC 2, [2017] IRLR 432.

[78] See Chapter 5, section 5.2.1.

[79] See *Shumba v Park Cakes Ltd* [2013] IRLR 800; *Allen v TRW Systems Ltd* [2013] ICR D13.

[80] A distinction can be made between a redundancy agreement and a redundancy policy. In the case of the former, the employer will have negotiated and agreed it with trade union or employee representatives, whereas in the case of the latter, no such negotiation or agreement will have occurred.

[81] See ACAS, *Handling Large-Scale Redundancies*, available at http://www.acas.org.uk/index. aspx?articleid=4547 at pages 30 and 48–52 (last visited 12 February 2016). The ACAS guidance note is not legally binding, but provides a useful indication of best practice.

to implement redundancies. Such agreement or policy may also clarify how the employer will approach the avoidance of redundancies.

 For additional reading on the right to receive a statutory redundancy payment, visit the Online Resources for this book at www.oup.com/uk/cabrelli3e/

18.2.4   Unfair dismissal for redundancy

Once a dismissal is found to be for the reason of redundancy, the employee will have not only the right to be paid a statutory redundancy payment, but also the right to claim unfair dismissal. Unlike the right to a statutory redundancy payment,[82] the onus lies on the employee to establish a dismissal for the reason of redundancy where the employee's complaint is one of unfair dismissal.[83] In the case of a dismissal for redundancy, there are two[84] ways in which an employee may be treated as unfairly dismissed.

(1) The effect of section 153 of TULRCA and section 105 of the ERA is that a dismissal will be deemed to be unfair where an employee establishes that the circumstances constituting redundancy applied equally to other comparable employees in the same undertaking who were not dismissed and the reason for the employee's dismissal was one of a number of statutorily prescribed reasons. The list of reasons include health- and safety-related grounds, the employee's membership of a trade union, participation in trade union activities or use of trade union services, the making of a protected disclosure in terms of the Public Interest Disclosure Act 1998, discharging duties as an employee representative for certain statutory purposes, etc.[85]

(2) A dismissal for the reason of redundancy may also be generally unfair under the provisions of section 98 of the ERA. In the context of a treatment of the general unfairness of a redundancy, it is opportune to revisit what Lord Justice Peter Gibson had to say in *High Table Ltd v Horst*[86] and underscore the importance of the sequential process to be followed:

■ *High Table Ltd v Horst* [1998] ICR 409, 419F

> **Lord Justice Peter Gibson:**
> . . . the issues of dismissal, redundancy and reasonableness in the actions of an employer should be kept distinct.

As mentioned in Chapter 16,[87] redundancy is one of the employer's five potentially fair reasons for dismissal by virtue of section 98(2)(c) of the ERA. It is open to an employee

---

[82] See section 163(2) of the ERA.

[83] The bizarre implication of this rule is that it is possible for a tribunal or court to find an employee to be redundant and entitled to a statutory redundancy payment, but that it is not satisfied that the employer dismissed him for redundancy for the purposes of the general unfair dismissal regime: *Midland Foot Comfort Centre Ltd v Moppett* [1973] ICR 219, 224A–D per Sir John Donaldson.

[84] Historically, there were three reasons, the third being that an employee was dismissed for redundancy in violation of a redundancy procedure or arrangement collectively agreed with trade unions: section 59(b) of the Employment Protection (Consolidation) Act 1978.

[85] These statutorily prescribed reasons mirror the automatically unfair dismissals, on which, see Chapter 16, section 16.2.4.2.   [86] [1998] ICR 409, 419F.

[87] See Chapter 16, section 16.2.4.3.

to claim that his/her redundancy was unfair under section 98(4), i.e. that the employer acted unreasonably in treating redundancy as a sufficient reason for dismissing the employee. Here, as with the general unfair dismissal regime, we must make a distinction between the substantive and procedural unfairness of a dismissal: substantive fairness is concerned with an assessment of the employer's decision to dismiss and its outcome, whereas procedural fairness looks to evaluate the *process* leading up to the employer's decision. With regard to the substantive fairness of the employer's decision to dismiss for redundancy, rather unsurprisingly, the law dictates that the tribunal or court must apply the range of reasonable responses standard of review as the applicable test.[88] If the employer is able to demonstrate that there were legitimate commercial pressures or grounds which would lead a reasonable employer to form the view that operational changes leading to redundancy were required and furnishes some evidence that there was some requirement for efficiencies, this will be sufficient to discharge the range test.[89] With regard to the requisite cogency of such evidence, it has been held that it is material for the tribunal to know whether the company was making profits or losses.[90] A tribunal or court has no power to second-guess the economic rationales advanced by the employer for the redundancies on the basis of an objective measure of scrutiny or to enquire whether it would have been fairer for the employer to act in some other way.[91] Therefore, it is unlikely that the evaluative technique of subjecting the employer's prerogative to a test of substantive fairness will operate to overturn the commercial judgment of management.[92] Indeed, it is questionable whether it is realistic at all to expect a tribunal, court, or third-party agency to be in a position to assess the substantive fairness of a managerial decision to dismiss for redundancy, bound up as it is with issues of commercial and economic judgment:

■ H. Collins, *Justice in Dismissal* (Oxford, OUP, 1992) 155

Is it possible to devise a form of legal regulation of economic dismissals which permits a neutral third party such as a tribunal or government official to evaluate the grounds of management's decision to make economic dismissals? Apart from the considerable social cost of administering such a system, many doubt whether any agency or court has the expertise and confidence to second-guess business decisions concerning the product and capital markets. Although the difficulties surrounding such an exercise should not be exaggerated, since so much of the decision will depend upon unverifiable business judgment, it is hard to insist that government agencies would make better decisions in even the majority of cases. The French and Dutch experience with such second-guessing of management's decisions does not provide one with much encouragement.

---

[88] For a comprehensive assessment of the 'range of reasonable responses' test, see Chapter 16, section 16.3.1.

[89] *Moon v Homeworthy Furniture (Northern) Ltd* [1977] ICR 117; *Ladbroke Courage Holidays Ltd v Asten* [1981] IRLR 59, 62 per Waterhouse J; *Orr v Vaughan* [1981] IRLR 63, 65 per Slynn J; *James W. Cook & Co. (Wivenhoe) Ltd (in liquidation) v Tipper* [1990] ICR 716, 729G per Neill LJ; and *Green v London Borough of Barking and Dagenham* (UKEAT/0157/16/DM, 10 March 2017).

[90] *Ladbroke Courage Holidays Ltd v Asten* [1981] IRLR 59, 62 per Waterhouse J.

[91] *Williams v Compair Maxam Ltd* [1982] ICR 156, 161 per Browne-Wilkinson J.

[92] *Jackson v Stephenson College* (UKEAT/0045/13/JOJ, 5 July 2013) is one of those rare cases where the range test was applied to find a dismissal substantively unfair. In this case, A was made redundant, despite the fact that B had offered to take voluntary redundancy, which the employer had rejected. Both A and B had similar skill sets. After A had been dismissed, B resigned. It was held that A's dismissal was unfair on the basis of a breach of the range of reasonable responses test, i.e. that dismissal was a decision that no reasonable employer would have taken in the circumstances.

Instead, it is in the evaluation of the procedural fairness of the redundancy that a claim for unfair dismissal on economic grounds stands any chance of being successful, and it is to this issue that we move in section 18.3.

 For additional reading on unfair dismissal for redundancy, visit the Online Resources for this book at www.oup.com/uk/cabrelli3e/

18.3 PROCEDURAL FAIRNESS: POOLS, SELECTION CRITERIA, AND CONSULTATION

It cannot be stressed enough how crucial it is for an employer to follow and apply proper and fair redundancy procedures. This point is amplified when it is understood that an employment tribunal or court may rule that a dismissal for redundancy is substantively fair, yet that it is unfair overall for a want of procedural fairness. In the case of *Polkey v A. E. Dayton Services Ltd*,[93] the House of Lords emphasized the importance of management following procedures prior to taking the decision to dismiss. In much the same way as we identified that the 'efficiency' model of procedural fairness is the most fitting account of the unfair dismissal regime,[94] the procedural requirements imposed on employers in the context of redundancy generally operate to ensure that the managerial decision to make employees redundant is taken with care. They also ensure that it is the wisest available option in the circumstances, that it is the least expensive for the employer to take, and that the alternatives such as redeployments are considered. The purchase of this reflective element of the efficiency model lies in its potential to (1) assist the employer in identifying whether it has downplayed the scope for its employees to accept wage concessions and (2) dispel managerial misconceptions about the negative consequences of failing to engage in downsizing on the productive capabilities of the organization.

The philosophy of reflection inherent within the efficiency model is instantiated through the main components of what is treated as a 'proper and fair' procedure in the context of redundancy. For example, the ACAS booklet, *Handling Large-Scale Redundancies*,[95] stresses the need for the employer to *consult* individual employees about the redundancies and the alternatives, including the importance of applying fair and objective *selection criteria* as a means of deciding the members of staff to be made redundant. The ACAS booklet broadly follows the basic ingredients of a fair redundancy procedure, which were set out in *Polkey v A. E. Dayton Services Ltd*[96] and *Williams v Compair Maxam Ltd*[97] as follows:

■ *Polkey v A. E. Dayton Services Ltd* [1988] AC 344, 364E

Lord Bridge of Harwich:

[A]n employer having prima facie grounds to dismiss for [the reason of redundancy] will in the great majority of cases not act reasonably in treating the reason as a sufficient reason for dismissal unless and until he has taken the steps, conveniently classified in most of the authorities as 'procedural,' which are necessary in the circumstances of the case to justify that course of action. Thus

---

[93] [1988] AC 344.   [94] See Chapter 17, section 17.1.1.
[95] See http://www.acas.org.uk/index.aspx?articleid=4547 at pages 10, 21, 31, 46, and 49–50 (last visited 12 February 2016), where a basic ACAS guide to handling small-scale redundancies, i.e. of fewer than 20 employees, is also available.   [96] [1988] AC 344.
[97] [1982] ICR 156.

... in the case of redundancy, the employer will normally not act reasonably unless he warns and consults any employees affected or their representatives, adopts a fair basis on which to select for redundancy and takes such steps as may be reasonable to avoid or minimise redundancy by redeployment within his own organisation.

■ *Williams v Compair Maxam Ltd* [1982] ICR 156, 162-7

Browne-Wilkinson J:

The two lay members of this appeal tribunal hold the view that it would be impossible to lay down detailed procedures which *all* reasonable employers would follow in *all* circumstances: the fair conduct of dismissals for redundancy must depend on the circumstances of each case. But in their experience, there is a generally accepted view in industrial relations that, in cases where the employees are represented by an independent union recognized by the employer, reasonable employers will seek to act in accordance with the following principles:

1. The employer will seek to give as much warning as possible of impending redundancies so as to enable the union and employees who may be affected to take early steps to inform themselves of the relevant facts, consider possible alternative solutions and, if necessary, find alternative employment in the undertaking or elsewhere.

2. The employer will consult the union as to the best means by which the desired management result can be achieved fairly and with as little hardship to the employees as possible. In particular, the employer will seek to agree with the union the criteria to be applied in selecting the employees to be made redundant. When a selection has been made, the employer will consider, with the union whether the selection has been made in accordance with those criteria.

3. Whether or not an agreement as to the criteria to be adopted has been agreed with the union, the employer will seek to establish criteria for selection which so far as possible do not depend solely upon the opinion of the person making the selection but can be objectively checked against such things as attendance record, efficiency at the job, experience, or length of service.

4. The employer will seek to ensure that the selection is made fairly in accordance with these criteria and will consider any representations the union may make as to such selection.

5. The employer will seek to see whether instead of dismissing an employee he could offer him alternative employment.

The lay members stress that not all these factors are present in every case since circumstances may prevent one or more of them being given effect to. But the lay members would expect these principles to be departed from only where some good reason is shown to justify such departure. The basic approach is that, in the unfortunate circumstances that necessarily attend redundancies, as much as is reasonably possible should be done to mitigate the impact on the work force and to satisfy them that the selection has been made fairly and not on the basis of personal whim. That these are the broad principles currently adopted by reasonable employers is supported both by the practice of the industrial tribunals and to an extent by statute. A very large number of appeals on cases of alleged unfair selection for redundancy come before this appeal tribunal. In the experience of all of us, without exception hitherto the approach of the industrial tribunals has reflected the canons of good industrial relations set out above ... We must add a word of warning. For the purpose of giving our reasons for reaching our exceptional conclusion that the decision of the industrial tribunal in this case was perverse, we have had to state what in our view are the steps which a reasonable and fair employer at the present time would seek to take in dismissing unionised employees on the ground of redundancy. We stress two points. First, these are not immutable principles which will stay unaltered for ever. Practices and attitudes in industry change with time and new norms of acceptable industrial relations behaviour will emerge. Secondly the factors we have stated are *not* principles of law, but standards of behaviour. Therefore in future cases before this appeal tribunal there should be no attempt to say that an industrial tribunal which did not have regard to or give effect to one of these factors has misdirected itself in law.

Despite Browne-Wilkinson J's assertion that the principles enunciated in *Williams v Compair Maxam Ltd* are not points of law, the indications are that they have since more or less been treated as such.[98] It is worth highlighting that the five-point schema set out in this passage also applies where the workforce is not unionized. Therefore, where references are made to trade unions in the extract from Browne-Wilkinson J's judgment, the employer's obligation will be owed to the employees individually in a non-unionized workplace. In light of that clarification, we will now explore the selection of the appropriate pool for redundancy and the nature and content of fair and objective selection criteria and selection procedures.

18.3.1 The pool for redundancy

In making the decision as to the identity of the members of the workforce who will be made redundant, the employer must:

- choose an appropriate pool of employees for redundancy;
- apply transparent, fair, and proper selection criteria to that chosen pool; and
- apply transparent, fair, and proper selection procedures.

The first question which must be addressed is how the employer ought to decide which group of employees should be included in the pool for redundancy. It is against this pool that the employer's selection criteria will be applied as a means of ascertaining who will be earmarked for redundancy. The general rule is that the pool ought to include all employees carrying out work of the particular kind for which the employer's requirements have ceased or diminished, i.e. all employees performing that kind of work ought to feature within the pool. However, the pool may be extended to include other employees whose jobs are similar to, or interchangeable with, the jobs cited in terms of the requisite skills, qualities, and aptitude. Similarity or interchangeability will be assessed in light of the contractual terms and working patterns of the employees alleged to be performing such similar or interchangeable functions. The criterion of similarity and interchangeability will often serve to determine whether it is appropriate for selection to operate across the organization as a whole or on a divisional or departmental basis. In assessing interchangeability and the reasonableness of the pool which the employer has chosen, an employment tribunal or court does not have the right to substitute its own judgment for that of the employer; instead, the task of the tribunal or court is to adopt the 'range of reasonable responses' test when it decides whether the employer has acted reasonably in selecting the pool for redundancy.[99] As such, the tribunal or court can only overturn the employer's decision if the pool selected falls outside the range of pools which reasonable employers would have chosen in the particular circumstances of the employer's case. The tribunal or court should only interfere where the employer's choice of pool generates arbitrary outcomes. The upshot of all this is that if the employer has genuinely applied its

---

[98] For example, see *Langston v Cranfield University* [1998] IRLR 172; *Fairbrother v Hendy Banks City Print Ltd* [2005] All ER (D) 142 (May).

[99] See *Taymech Ltd v Ryan* (UKEAT/663/94, 15 November 1994); *Fairbrother v Hendy Banks City Print Ltd* [2005] All ER (D) 142 (May).

mind to who should feature in the pool, it will be a major challenge for the employee to persuade the tribunal to interfere.[100]

An employer may decide to make one post redundant and limit the pool to one person, i.e. the employee filling the role that the employer is intending to do away with.[101] However, that does not automatically entitle the employer to limit the pool for selection to the individual fulfilling that role;[102] instead, the employer ought to consider the possibility of 'bumping'.[103] The pool ought to include the person in the subordinate role where the two posts and the remuneration packages for both are similar, and the relative length of service and qualifications of the two employees are similar. In such a situation, there should also be consultation with the employees concerned about the pool. However, in accordance with the decision of the House of Lords in *Polkey v A. E. Dayton Services Ltd*,[104] where consultation would be absolutely futile this will not lead inexorably to a finding of unfair dismissal, even in the absence of evidence of a deliberate decision not to consult for that reason on the part of the employer.[105]

18.3.2 **The selection criteria**

18.3.2.1 The choice and nature of the selection criteria

Once the employer has settled on the individuals to be included within the pool for redundancy, advance warning of potential redundancies should be given to the employees within the pool in terms of the first point set out in Browne-Wilkinson J's judgment in *Williams v Compair Maxam Ltd*. This will entail the service of an 'at risk' letter to those affected employees. If there are no pre-existing selection criteria contained within a redundancy agreement, the employer's redundancy policy, or a collective agreement, selection criteria should be chosen which are transparent, fair, and proper. The criteria must be applied properly by the employer, agreed with trade unions or employee representatives, and be objective, neutral, and objectively verifiable against evidence. If the criteria are objective, then, in the absence of bias, bad faith, or an obvious mistake, their application will usually not be procedurally unfair.[106] For example, where employees are graded according to skills, qualifications, experience, performance, aptitude, appraisal ratings, time-keeping, work attendance record, disciplinary record, abilities, and other neutral criteria, these will be deemed to be fair and objective.[107] However, if the criteria are 'forward-looking', such as assessment centre competency tests, although objective, their application may be found to be unfair.[108] If the criteria are subjective, the employer should consult with the employees in the pool about the selection criteria.[109] Indeed, it is advisable for an employer to consult the employees in the chosen pool about the selection criteria generally, i.e. even where they are objective, since a failure to consult with individual employees about the selection process and criteria may well result in a finding of unfair dismissal.[110] Where the

---

[100] See *Capita Hartshead Ltd v Byard* [2012] ICR 1256; *Family Mosaic Housing Association v Badmos* (UKEAT/0042/13/SM, 3 March 2013).

[101] For example, see *Capita Hartshead Ltd v Byard* [2012] ICR 1256.

[102] See *Wrexham Golf Co. Ltd v Ingham* (UKEAT/0190/12/RN, 10 July 2012).

[103] *Leventhal Ltd v North* [2005] All ER (D) 82 (January); *Fulcrum Pharma (Europe) v Bonassera* (UKEAT/0198/10/DM, 22 October 2010).   [104] [1988] AC 344.

[105] *Duffy v Yeomans & Partners Ltd* [1995] ICR 1.

[106] *Dabson v David Cover & Sons Ltd* [2011] All ER (D) 139 (May).

[107] *British Aerospace plc v Green* [1995] ICR 1006; see also ACAS, *Handling Large-Scale Redundancies*, available at http://www.acas.org.uk/index.aspx?articleid=4547 (last visited 12 February 2016).

[108] *Mental Health Care (UK) Ltd v Biluan* (UKEAT/0248/12/SM, 28 February 2013).

[109] *Pinewood Repro Ltd (t/a County Print) v Page* [2011] ICR 508; *Peninsula Business Services Ltd v Rees* (UKEAT/0407/10/RN, 21 April 2011).

[110] *E-zec Medical Transport Service Ltd v Gregory* [2008] All ER (D) 193 (December). Moreover, see ACAS, *Handling Large-Scale Redundancies*, available at http://www.acas.org.uk/index.aspx?articleid=4547 (last visited 12 February 2016).

selection criteria applicable are to be deployed alongside an inherently subjective factor, e.g. the 'overall requirements of the business', this will be procedurally unfair, leading to a finding of unfair dismissal.[111] The end result will be the same where subjective criteria which favour those 'who, in the opinion of the managers concerned, would be able to keep the company viable' are applied by the employer.[112]

18.3.2.2 The scoring process

The usual process followed by the employer is to apply the selection criteria to the employees within the pool, who are then assessed by giving them a numerical scoring.[113] It is standard for the employees with the lowest scores to be selected for redundancy. For example, if the employer has chosen to make ten employees redundant from a pool of 48 clerical staff, then employees in clerical positions with the lowest ten scores according to the selection criteria would be made redundant. Where an employee challenges the fairness of the manner in which the selection criteria were applied in practice and the scoring process, the test is whether the system applied and the scoring process fell within the range of reasonable responses.[114] If the selection criteria are applied in conjunction with evidence such as official employee records, appraisal forms, and personnel files, the scoring process is unlikely to fall outside the band of reasonable responses. However, it is pivotal that the employer retains evidence of the redundancy process adhered to and the material against which the selection criteria were applied to reach the scoring (e.g. personnel files, appraisal forms).[115] Therefore, the general rule is that it is not open to an employee to enjoin a tribunal or court to engage in an overly meticulous examination of the redundancy procedure, selection criteria, the extent of the consultation, and the bases for reaching the scores attributed to the employees. A similar point was made in *Dabson v David Cover & Sons Ltd*,[116] i.e. that it will normally be inappropriate for the tribunal or court to subject the employer's scoring to a forensic assessment, unless there are exceptional circumstances, e.g. bias or an obvious mistake.[117] However, in recent times, the tribunals and courts appear to be adopting a more interventionist, 'hands-on' approach. There is evidence that they are prepared to subject the scoring and points systems to a closer degree of scrutiny. For example, in the case of *Northgate HR Ltd v Mercy*,[118] the Court of Appeal detected a 'glaring inconsistency' in the application of the selection criteria to the pool when the employer scored the complainant employee's 'capabilities in technical skills and project management . . . on the mean side'.[119] Although this 'glaring inconsistency' was made in good faith, the Court of Appeal held that this could sometimes be sufficient to establish a lack of procedural fairness amounting to an unfair dismissal for the reason of redundancy. Moreover, in *Pinewood Repro Ltd (t/a County Print) v Page*,[120] and *Peninsula Business Services Ltd v Rees*,[121] it was held that if the selection criteria are subjective, the employer should consult with the employees in

---

[111] *Watkins v Crouch (t/a Temple Bird Solicitors)* [2011] IRLR 382.
[112] *Williams v Compair Maxam Ltd* [1982] ICR 156, 166 per Browne-Wilkinson J.
[113] For example, see *Eversheds Legal Services Ltd v De Belin* [2011] ICR 1137.
[114] *British Aerospace plc v Green* [1995] ICR 1006.
[115] *E-zec Medical Transport Service Ltd v Gregory* [2008] All ER (D) 193 (December).
[116] [2011] All ER (D) 139 (May).
[117] See *Nicholls v Rockwell Automation Ltd* (UKEAT/0540/11/SM, 25 June 2012). Therefore, where an employee had been transferred to a new employer pursuant to a 'relevant transfer' in terms of the Transfer of Undertakings (Protection of Employment) Regulations 2006 (SI 2006/246), a failure to moderate the scores between the employees in the pool who had been employed by the transferor and the employees who had always been employed by the transferee did not amount to unfair dismissal since the overall process was fair under the range test: *First Scottish Searching Services Ltd v McDine* (UKEAT/S/0051/10/BI, 17 February 2011).   [118] [2008] ICR 410.
[119] *ibid*., 417–18 per Kay LJ.   [120] [2011] ICR 508.   [121] (UKEAT/0407/10/RN, 21 April 2011).

the pool about the scoring process and enable them to challenge their scores and express their views on the matter.

A particularly important matter is whether the employer ought to make available the selection criteria applied and scoring matrices of the claimant employee where the latter requests them. In the case of *Alexander v Brigden Enterprises Ltd*,[122] the EAT ruled that the employer must notify the employee of the selection criteria which have been used, and also the assessment and scoring matrix of the employee. Although this case was decided within the framework of the now-repealed statutory disciplinary procedures in Part 1 of Schedule 2 to the Employment Act 2002 and the Employment Act 2002 (Dispute Resolution) Regulations 2004,[123] it appears to continue to be good practice in part, albeit not necessarily good law.[124] *Alexander v Brigden Enterprises Ltd* and *British Aerospace plc v Green*[125] also make the point that there is no legal obligation imposed on the employer to make available to the selected employee the scores and assessment records of those employees *who were not selected* for redundancy where the tribunal or court is satisfied that the scoring process fell within the range of reasonable responses.[126] Nevertheless, in line with the preparedness of the courts in recent times to intervene and examine the scoring process, it is submitted that it is good practice to do so. For example, in the case of *King v Eaton Ltd (No. 2)*,[127] which was decided subsequent to the decision of the Court of Appeal in *British Aerospace plc v Green*, the Inner House of the Court of Session in Scotland held that a tribunal or court had the power to inquire into the individual scores of the employees in the pool, which would, of course, involve the disclosure of the scores of *all* of the employees.[128]

It is not uncommon for an employer to set aside a particular criterion as a 'tie-breaker' which can be applied as a deciding factor where more than one employee is scored equally.[129] Provided that the process is open and transparent, and applied properly, the benefit of such an approach is that it is based on meritocratic, rather than discriminatory, criteria. However, where a favoured employee attains a lower score than the claimant employee and additional criteria are then applied to ensure that the claimant employee is selected for redundancy, it has been held that the overall scoring process will not fall within the band of reasonable responses.[130]

18.3.2.3 Potentially discriminatory selection criteria

Selecting and applying objective selection criteria and engaging in consultation with employees may be sufficient to evade liability for unfair dismissal on the grounds of procedural fairness, but the potential for liability to arise on other legal grounds remains. In particular, the anti-discrimination provisions in the Equality Act 2010 and the Maternity and Parental Leave etc. Regulations 1999[131] will assume significance when the employer chooses its selection criteria. In the past, objective and ostensibly neutral criteria such as

---

[122] [2006] ICR 1277.   [123] SI 2004/752.

[124] Unlike the previous ACAS guidance note *Handling Redundancies*, there is nothing explicit in the ACAS booklet *Handling Large-Scale Redundancies* on this point, although Appendix 2 does imply that the selection criteria should be agreed and provided to the employees, but says little about the release of the scoring matrices: available at http://www.acas.org.uk/index.aspx?articleid=4547 (last visited 12 February 2016).   [125] [1995] ICR 1006.

[126] *British Aerospace plc v Green* [1995] ICR 1006, 1016–17 per Waite LJ. This provides further cogent evidence of the rejection of a 'natural justice' conception of procedural fairness to which we referred in Chapter 17, section 17.1.1.   [127] [1998] IRLR 686.

[128] Rather interestingly, the ACAS booklet *Handling Large-Scale Redundancies* is silent on this point: available at http://www.acas.org.uk/index.aspx?articleid=4547 (last visited 12 February 2016).

[129] See, e.g., *Rolls-Royce v Unite the Union* [2010] 1 WLR 318.

[130] *Watkins v Crouch (t/a Temple Bird Solicitors)* [2011] IRLR 382.

[131] SI 1999/3312. Transposing provisions of the Pregnant Workers' Directive 92/85/EEC (OJ 1992 L348/1) and the Parental Leave Directive 2010/18/EU (OJ 2010 L68/13).

'last in, first out' ('LIFO'), 'first in, first out' ('FIFO'), length of service, absence record, part-time work and fixed-term work, etc. were often applied as a means of selecting employees for redundancy. However, in recent times, such criteria are usually avoided, or at best applied with caution, on the basis that their application could potentially indirectly or directly discriminate against workers based on:

(1) age and religious belief (LIFO, FIFO, and the length of service criteria);[132]

(2) sex (the part-time work and fixed-term work criteria);[133]

(3) disability (absence record);[134] and

(4) parental leave.[135]

Although employment equality laws permit a degree of positive discrimination in favour of certain employees, e.g. disabled employees[136] and employees on maternity leave, the application of selection criteria during the redundancy scoring process ought not to be conducted in a manner which serves to disadvantage employees within the pool who do not fall within that constituency. For example, in *Eversheds Legal Services Ltd v De Belin*,[137] the weighting of scores in favour of an employee on maternity leave was held to directly discriminate against the other male employee in the pool. On a related note, it will not necessarily be a requirement for an employer to adjust the chosen selection criteria to take account of the presence of a disabled employee within the pool.[138] The point should also be made that, although criteria such as attendance record and time-keeping continue to be adopted by employers, an employer will have to exercise care in order that their application does not fall foul of the disability discrimination provisions in the Equality Act 2010.[139]

However, one ought to stress that it is by no means a foregone conclusion that the application of criteria such as LIFO, FIFO, and length of service, etc. will inevitably fall foul of the anti-discrimination legislation. It is worth recalling that it is possible for an employer to objectively justify *indirect discrimination* and *direct age discrimination* claims successfully on the basis of the 'proportionality' defence. Although LIFO, FIFO, and/or length of service, etc. will indirectly discriminate against certain employees in the pool on the grounds of age, sex, etc., it is open to an employer to objectively justify the use of such criteria by demonstrating that the choice of these selection criteria is a proportionate means of achieving a legitimate commercial aim.[140] On this point, the case

---

[132] For example, see *Osoba v Chief Constable of Hertfordshire* (UKEAT/0055/13/BA, 11 July 2013); *Naeem v Secretary of State for Justice* [2014] ICR 472.

[133] Most workers falling within these categories tend to be female, on which, see *Clarke v Eley (IMI) Kynoch Ltd* [1983] ICR 165. Therefore, such treatment could be in contravention of sections 13 or 19 of the Equality Act 2010.

[134] See *TW Espie v Balfour Beatty Engineering Services Ltd* (UKEAT/0321/12/DM, 30 November 2012).

[135] *Riezniece v Zemkopibas minisrija* [2013] IRLR 828.

[136] For example, in *Dominique v Toll Global Forwarding Ltd* (UKEAT/0308/13/LA, 7 May 2014), where the redundancy selection criteria were based on length of service, absences, skill set, productivity (including mistake levels), flexibility, and discretionary effort, it was held that the deployment of selection criteria evaluating productivity and accuracy put a disabled employee at a substantial disadvantage and constituted a breach of the duty to make reasonable adjustments under sections 20–22 of the Equality Act 2010.   [137] [2011] ICR 1137 (EAT).

[138] In the case of *Lancaster v TBWA Manchester* (UKEAT/0460/10/DA, 14 June 2011), Slade J DBE held that a failure to adjust the chosen selection criteria did not amount to a breach of the employer's statutory duty to make reasonable adjustments for its disabled employees under what are now sections 20–22 of the Equality Act 2010. Contrast this decision with *Dominique v Toll Global Forwarding Ltd* (UKEAT/0308/13/LA, 7 May 2014).

[139] For example, in the context of a disability discrimination claim, see *TW Espie v Balfour Beatty Engineering Services Ltd* (UKEAT/0321/12/DM, 30 November 2012).

[140] The employer may also succeed with an argument that the application of selection criteria which directly discriminate against employees on the basis of their age is proportionate and lawful in terms of section 13(2) of the Equality Act 2010.

of *Rolls-Royce v Unite the Union*[141] is particularly instructive, since the employer's proportionality defence was successful. *Rolls-Royce v Unite the Union* concerned a collective agreement which had been concluded with the employer's trade union and adopted 'length of service' as a 'tie-breaker', i.e. the deciding factor, where employees' scores were the same in a redundancy selection exercise. The employer sought clarification from the courts as to whether the inclusion of the length of service criterion was indirectly discriminatory on the grounds of age. It argued that it had a legitimate commercial objective in applying the selection criteria of 'length of service' as a deciding factor, i.e. that it had adopted it as a means of (1) rewarding staff 'loyalty' and (2) ensuring that it maintained a 'stable workforce'. The Court of Appeal accepted the employer's argument. When the employer's requirements to reward loyalty and achieve a stable workforce were balanced against the harm suffered by the selected employees as a result of the application of the length of service criterion, the Court held that the process was not disproportionate. A further important factor was that the proportionality of the means adopted was amply demonstrated by the fact that the length of service criterion was only one of a substantial number of criteria for measuring employee suitability for redundancy and that it was by no means determinative.

18.3.3 **Consultation**

Another kernel of procedural fairness in the redundancy context is for employees and their representatives (trade union or otherwise) to be consulted individually and in groups.[142] The requirement for the employer to engage in individual and group consultation permeates the entire length of the pre-redundancy procedure, from the assessment of whether redundancies are required, to the selection of the pool for redundancy, to the point at which the selection criteria are chosen and the potential for suitable alternative employment within the employer's organization.[143] The entire consultation process itself must be fair, meaningful, and genuine overall in the sense that the employees consulted must be afforded a fair and proper opportunity to understand fully the matters about which they are being consulted and to express their views on those subjects.[144] Where consultation is perfunctory or insensitive, this is likely to render the redundancy an unfair dismissal.[145] Except in the unusual situation where consultation will be futile, i.e. in an exceptional case,[146] a failure by the employer to individually consult will result in a finding of procedural unfairness. The employer is bound to consider those views properly and genuinely. Written notes of the meetings between the employer and the employees or their representatives (trade union or otherwise) ought to be taken and the employer should revert to those employees, their employee representatives, and trade unions in writing about any proposals they raised at the meetings, e.g. about avoiding redundancies, and the employer's response to those proposals. During the consultation process, an employer ought not to present the redundancies as a *fait accompli* and instead they

---

[141] [2010] ICR 1. See also *MacCulloch v ICI plc* [2008] ICR 1334; *Loxley v BAE Systems (Munitions & Ordnance) Ltd* [2008] ICR 1348.

[142] *British Aerospace plc v Green* [1995] ICR 1006, 1018B per Millett LJ.

[143] Or that of an associated employer. An associated employer is (a) one which is directly or indirectly controlled by the employer or (b) one which is directly and indirectly controlled by a third party who also directly or indirectly controls the employer: section 231 of the ERA.

[144] *Rowell v Hubbard Group Services Ltd* [1995] IRLR 195. Therefore, if there has been adequate consultation at one stage in the redundancy process, it does not follow that the tribunal must find that the consultation overall was adequate: *Air 2000 Ltd v Mallam* [2004] All ER (D) 119 (September).

[145] *Thomas v BNP Paribas Real Estate Advisory and Property Management UK Ltd* (UKEAT/0134/16/ JOJ, 13 October 2016).

[146] For example, *Ashby v JJB Sports plc* (UKEAT/0114/12/JOJ, 18 September 2012) where there were financial pressures on the employer and matters were of a highly sensitive commercial nature.

should be couched in terms of 'proposed redundancies'. Hence persons falling within the pool who are selected for redundancy should be referred to as having been 'provisionally selected' for redundancy. At all times, it should be made clear that the employer will take all reasonable steps to avoid redundancies and search for suitable alternatives insofar as that is practicable in the circumstances.

Of course, where it is proposing to make 20 or more employees redundant at a single establishment, an employer will be under a statutory obligation to inform and consult with trade union or employee representatives under Chapter II of Part IV of TULRCA.[147] Where the statutory duties are engaged, this does not relieve the employer of the responsibility of consulting individually. Therefore, it is crucial that the employer complies with the individual information and consultation requirements in terms of the process set out in *Williams v Compair Maxam Ltd*, as well as the statutory obligations where the latter are applicable. In such a case, the employer will be required to individually consult contemporaneously with the trade union or employee representatives, i.e. double consultation will be required. It is probable, but not a foregone conclusion, that a failure to comply with the statutory obligations will result in a dismissal being held to be unfair.[148] However, where the employer has not engaged in individual consultation, it will not necessarily avoid liability for unfair dismissal where it has informed and consulted trade union representatives in terms of its obligations under TULRCA.[149]

18.3.4 Suitable alternative employment

An integral part of the pre-redundancy process is for the employer to consider whether suitable alternative employment could be offered to the employees provisionally selected for redundancy. A failure to find and offer suitable alternative employment will mean that the procedure was flawed and the redundancy situation will amount to an unfair dismissal.[150] For example, if it is proposed to make a PA redundant, the employer should consider whether a secretarial post might be made available and offered to the PA. Furthermore, the employer should provide the employee with sufficient information about the financial prospects attached to such alternatives to properly equip the employee to make an informed and meaningful decision.[151]

A related question is whether an employer has an obligation to prioritize employees provisionally selected for redundancy for vacancies or alternative employment that it may have. The answer to this question depends on the context and it is worth noting that such an issue often arises where the redundancies have been implemented pursuant to a reorganization. The matter is usually left to the good faith discretion of the employer. However, on occasion, the tribunal or court will decide that a departure from this approach is warranted. For example, in the case of *Ralph Martindale & Co. Ltd v Harris*,[152] the EAT ruled that the requirements of reasonableness in the particular case dictated that two employees who were at risk of redundancy be given priority for existing vacancies.

---

[147] See Chapter 20 for more detail.

[148] *Hough v Leyland DAF Ltd* [1991] ICR 696; cf. *Forman Construction Ltd v Kelly* [1977] IRLR 468.

[149] *Rolls-Royce Motor Cars Ltd v Price* [1993] IRLR 203; cf. *Mugford v Midland Bank plc* [1997] ICR 399.

[150] *Vokes v Bear* [1974] ICR 1; *Langston v Cranfield University* [1998] IRLR 172. However, if the employer seeks to evade that rule by finding suitable alternative employment and asking employees to apply for it, the employer's selection process cannot be used as a means of simply turning the employee down out of bad faith, since some measure of fairness must be satisfied by the employer: *Ralph Harris v Martindale & Co. Ltd* [2007] All ER (D) 347 (December); *Finch v Parfums Givenchy Ltd* [2010] All ER (D) 365 (July). A failure to find suitable alternative employment when a secondment ends may also amount to unlawful direct age discrimination: *London Borough of Tower Hamlets v Wooster* [2009] IRLR 980.

[151] *Fisher v Hoopoe Finance Ltd* [2005] All ER (D) 51 (June).

[152] [2007] All ER (D) 347 (December).

This involved ensuring that (1) objective recruitment criteria were applied for the purposes of ascertaining who should be selected for the vacancies, and (2) the promotion of the vacancy was restricted so that it ought not to be opened up to the employer's workforce by internal advertisement until it had become clear that neither of the two employees at risk of redundancy were suitable for the vacancy.

The recruitment criteria applied to consider who is to receive alternative employment usually ought to be objective and disclosed to all employees provisionally selected for redundancy,[153] although the criteria need not be exactly the same as the selection criteria. For instance, in *Morgan v The Welsh Rugby Union*,[154] the EAT ruled that when the application of the selection criteria results in the provisional selection of particular employees for redundancy, the employer is entitled to take into account subjective criteria when it is deciding which of those employees would be suitable for an available vacancy. Here, the relative performance of the individuals at the interviews for the vacancy was deemed to be a relevant factor in opting for one employee over another. As such, in these circumstances, the courts have recognized that such a process entails the application of commercial judgment.

Where there is no existing vacancy, an employer's failure to consider the possibility of 'bumping' may result in a finding of unfair dismissal.[155] As such, the employer ought to examine whether there is the opportunity to save the jobs of senior employees provisionally selected for redundancy at the expense of more junior staff. Finally, attention should be drawn to regulation 10 of the Maternity and Parental Leave Regulations 1999,[156] which involves a measure of positive treatment in favour of employees on account of maternity.[157] It is provided that where the employer intends to make an employee on maternity leave redundant as part of an overall redundancy process, such an employee has the right to be offered a suitable available vacancy, i.e. a new contract of employment, in priority to other employees. That is the case despite the fact that the employee on maternity leave may not be the best candidate for the available vacancy:[158]

Regulation 10 Redundancy during maternity leave

(1) This regulation applies where, during an employee's ordinary or additional maternity leave period, it is not practicable by reason of redundancy for her employer to continue to employ her under her existing contract of employment.

(2) Where there is a suitable available vacancy, the employee is entitled to be offered (before the end of her employment under her existing contract) alternative employment with her employer or his successor, or an associated employer, under a new contract of employment which complies with paragraph (3) (and takes effect immediately on the ending of her employment under the previous contract).

(3) The new contract of employment must be such that—

   (a) the work to be done under it is of a kind which is both suitable in relation to the employee and appropriate for her to do in the circumstances, and

   (b) its provision as to the capacity and place in which she is to be employed, and as to the other terms and conditions of her employment, are not substantially less favourable to her than if she had continued to be employed under the previous contract.

---

[153] The failure to disclose the recruitment criteria to an employee made redundant and rejected at interview for suitable alternative employment will furnish grounds for unfair dismissal where the employee who was successful at interview for such alternative employment had enjoyed full disclosure: *Somerset County Council v Chaloner* (UKEAT/0600/12/JOJ, 14 October 2013).

[154] [2011] IRLR 376. See also *Green v London Borough of Barking and Dagenham* (UKEAT/0157/16/DM, 10 March 2017).   [155] *North v Lionel Leventhal Ltd* [2005] All ER (D) 82 (January).

[156] SI 1999/3312.   [157] See Chapter 9, section 9.2.4.

[158] For example, see *Sefton Borough Council v Wainwright* [2015] ICR 652.

Sefton Borough Council v Wainwright[159] is arguably the leading case on the scope of regulation 10 so far. The case concerned an employee on maternity leave who was informed that her job was at risk and that she should apply for a newly created single post which would combine her position and that of another employee provisionally earmarked for redundancy. She was unsuccessful at interview and the job was offered to the other employee on the basis that he was the stronger candidate. The EAT ruled that her dismissal was automatically unfair in terms of regulation 10, since the newly created role was suitable alternative employment and ought to have been offered to the employee, even though she was the weaker candidate at interview. However, the EAT questioned whether an employee on maternity leave would have an entitlement to be offered every suitable alternative vacancy where there is more than one available in the circumstances. Moreover, an automatically unfair dismissal is not necessarily unfavourable treatment entailing pregnancy or maternity discrimination under section 18 of the Equality Act 2010.

In the case of *Simpson v Endsleigh Insurance Services Ltd*,[160] the EAT addressed the two requirements in regulation 10(3) and held that they must be read together and satisfied, rather than treated separately. Hence it is not open to the employee to argue that a suitable post ought to have been offered to her if the terms and conditions of the contract were less favourable. *Simpson v Endsleigh Insurance Services Ltd* is also an authority for the proposition that whether or not a vacancy was suitable is an objective decision for the commercial judgment of an employer, taking into account the claimant's personal circumstances and work experience. Therefore, there is no need for the employee to be involved in that decision-making process.

18.3.5 Intimation of selection for redundancy

Once the employer has completed consultation, discharged its obligation to engage in good industrial practice, sought suitable alternative employment, etc., it will finally have to inform the unfortunate employees that they are to be made redundant. A letter intimating notice of dismissal/termination for redundancy should be sent to each of these employees. That letter should explain the background to the redundancies, as well as the fact that the changes envisaged will result in that person's post becoming obsolete. The employee should be paid in lieu of notice of dismissal if it is intended to make the employee redundant immediately, i.e. he/she ought to receive his/her pay and the monetary value of all contractual benefits for the period of notice of termination. Moreover, the employee should be paid the relevant statutory redundancy payment—assuming that all of the criteria for the payment of such sum have been satisfied.[161]

18.3.6 Appeals against selection for redundancy

A key issue for an employer to consider is whether the letter intimating redundancy must offer the employee a right to appeal the employer's decision to dismiss for redundancy. Before 1 April 2009, the statutory dismissal and disciplinary procedures under Part 1 of Schedule 2 to the Employment Act 2002 and the Employment Act 2002 (Dispute Resolution) Regulations 2004[162] applied. Those statutory procedures provided that employers were obliged to offer the relevant employees a right of appeal to an appeal committee. However, since those statutory provisions are now no longer good law, the question remains as to whether there is an absolute obligation on the employer to do so. The guidance issued by ACAS in its publication *Handling Large-Scale Redundancies* suggests that employers should consider offering such a right of appeal;[163] but the ACAS Code of Practice 1 on

[159] [2015] ICR 652.   [160] [2011] ICR 75.   [161] See section 18.2.3.   [162] SI 2004/752.
[163] See page 31, available at http://www.acas.org.uk/index.aspx?articleid=4547 (last visited 12 February 2016).

Disciplinary and Grievance Procedures,[164] which does provide employees with a right of appeal, does not apply to redundancies. Therefore, it would appear that it is not strictly a legal requirement.[165] However, in order to minimize the potential for claims of unfair dismissal for the reason of redundancy, it is opined that offering an appeal amounts to good practice and underlines the employer's concern for consultation. Indeed, there is an added incentive for employers in offering an internal appeal, since in the case of *Peninsula Business Services Ltd v Rees*[166] the EAT held that a fair and independent appeal process can operate to cure any defects in the pre-appeal procedure.

 For additional reading on procedural fairness: pools, selection criteria, and consultation, visit the Online Resources for this book at www.oup.com/uk/cabrelli3e/

---

[164] See page 1 of the March 2015 version, available at http://www.acas.org.uk/?articleid=2174 (last visited 12 February 2016) and the Online Resources for this book.

[165] See the basic ACAS guide to handling small-scale redundancies, i.e. of fewer than 20 employees, which is available at http://www.acas.org.uk/index.aspx?articleid=4555 (last visited 12 February 2016).

[166] (UKEAT/0407/10/RN, 21 April 2011).

PART VII

BUSINESS REORGANIZATIONS, CONSULTATION, AND INSOLVENCY

CHAPTER NINETEEN

TRANSFERS OF UNDERTAKINGS

19.1 AN INTRODUCTION TO THE REGULATION OF TRANSFERS OF UNDERTAKINGS

In this chapter, we engage in a critical examination of the Transfer of Undertakings (Protection of Employment) Regulations 2006 ('TUPE').[1] First, we will assess the legal position prior to the introduction of the Acquired Rights Directive 2001 ('the ARD'),[2] which is the source of TUPE. This will involve placing TUPE and the ARD in their historical context. We will then move on to analyse the principal implications of TUPE and the content of its provisions. This entails an assessment of the circumstances in which TUPE will apply and recognition of the extent to which TUPE has been interpreted progressively to include economic transactions and arrangements which transcend the transfer of an organization's business and assets. Thereafter, the impact of TUPE on the contract of employment will be examined. In particular, we will note how liabilities, obligations, and rights arising from the contract of employment are transferred to the transferee and that employees are protected where they are dismissed for the reason of

---

[1] SI 2006/246.

[2] Council Directive 2001/23/EC of 12 March 2001 on the approximation of the laws of the Member States relating to the safeguarding of employees' rights, in the event of transfers of undertakings, businesses or parts of undertakings, or businesses (OJ 2001 L82/16).

the 'relevant transfer'. Finally, the information and consultation obligations imposed on transferors will be discussed. The analysis throughout the chapter will be conducted within the context of the requirements imposed on the UK by virtue of the ARD. It is strongly recommended that any examination of the legal detail is considered from the standpoint of the wider social and economic aims of the framework articulated in the ARD and TUPE.

19.1.1 Historical and contextual introduction

In Chapters 3 and 5, particular attention was drawn to the personal nature of the contract of employment. This personal foundation translates into the imposition of an obligation of personal service on the employee with corresponding personal obligations impressed on the employer. Therefore, if one of the parties to the contract is unable to perform through incapacity[3] or dies,[4] the contract is terminated. In this context, if the employee is the 'innocent' party, he/she will be entitled to damages for wrongful dismissal.[5] Underpinning such a contract lay the notions of reciprocity/mutuality of intention to be bound and consensus. The implication of the reciprocity doctrine is that 'if the contract of employment be not binding on the employee . . . then it cannot be binding upon the employer'.[6] Closely allied to the idea of reciprocity/mutuality is the concept of 'consent': the common law tradition treats the employment contract as a personal contract and its assignment/transfer without mutual consensus is not permitted. The case of *Nokes v Doncaster Amalgamated Collieries Ltd*[7] is the principal authority to propound the doctrine of the personal non-transferable nature of the contract of employment:[8]

■ *Nokes v Doncaster Amalgamated Collieries Ltd* [1940] AC 1014, 1018–33

Viscount Simon (LC):

It is, of course, indisputable that (apart from statutory provision to the contrary) the benefit of a contract entered into by A to render personal service to X cannot be transferred by X to Y without A's consent, which is the same thing as saying that, in order to produce the desired result, the old contract between A and X would have to be terminated by notice or by mutual consent and a new contract of service entered into by agreement between A and Y. The rule is so strict that if the contract is between individuals on both sides and X dies, the contract of service is immediately dissolved . . .

It will be readily conceded that the result contended for by the [new employer] in this case would be at complete variance with a fundamental principle of our common law—the principle, namely, that a free citizen, in the exercise of his freedom, is entitled to choose the employer whom he promises to serve, so that the right to his services cannot be transferred from one employer to another without his assent . . .

---

[3] *Condor v Barron Knights Ltd* [1966] 1 WLR 87.
[4] *Stubbs v The Holywell Railway Co.* (1867) LR 2 Exch 311; *Farrow v Wilson* (1869) LR 4 CP 744, 746 per Willes J; *Ranger v Brown* [1978] ICR 603, 605G per Phillips J; and see *Hoey v MacEwan and Auld* (1867) 5 M 814 and section 33(1) of the Partnership Act 1890, in the case of the dissolution of a partnership employer caused by the death of a partner.
[5] *Brace v Calder* [1895] 2 QB 253.
[6] *Pitcher v United Oil & Gas Syndicate Inc.* 174 La. 66 (1932), 69.   [7] [1940] AC 1014.
[8] In the USA, the position is similar to the common law rule in *Nokes*: see *Howard Johnson Co. v Detroit Local Joint Executive Board* 417 US 249 (1974); *National Labor Relations Board v Burns International Security Services Inc.* 406 US 272 (1972).

> I do not agree with the view . . . that a right to the service of an employee is the property of the transferor company. Such a right cannot be the subject of gift or bequest; it cannot be bought or sold; it forms no part of the assets of the employer for the purpose of administering his estate . . .
>
> ### Lord Atkin:
>
> . . . I confess it appears to me astonishing that apart from overriding questions of public welfare power should be given to a court or anyone else to transfer a man without his knowledge and possibly against his will from the service of one person to the service of another. I had fancied that ingrained in the personal status of a citizen under our laws was the right to choose for himself whom he would serve: and that this right of choice constituted the main difference between a servant and a serf . . .
>
> My Lords, I should have thought that the principle that a man is not to be compelled to serve a master against his will is just as deep-seated in the common law of this country . . . and that here there is no clear, definite, or positive enactment overturning it.[9]

Here, we have some forceful language emphasizing the great value of *freedom to* contract, *freedom to quit* employment, and the rejection of the notion that the employer has a common law property right to the service of an employee. These passages champion the liberty of employees to choose the party with whom they contract. By invoking the 'freedom' of choice of the employee, one can approach the decision of the House of Lords from the standpoint that it constituted something of a victory for employment protection. After all, the employee won the case and was held to be entitled to walk away from his employment contract and work for someone else. However, whilst *Nokes* decided that an employee is free to choose his/her employer, it is as much an authority for the proposition that the new employer is equally free to choose its employees. Let us illustrate the point with Hypothetical A.

Hypothetical A

Danny's Demolishers plc ('the Employer') is a large multinational company with a subsidiary company called Danny's Demolishers (Essex) Ltd ('Essex Ltd'). Essex Ltd has a workforce of 120 employees operating from a plant in Brentwood. Owing to a recession, the performance of Essex Ltd has not been satisfactory and a buyer called Almsville Ltd steps forward to acquire the entire business and assets of Essex Ltd. Almsville Ltd is of the view that the business can be profitable if its workforce is drastically reduced after the acquisition. An employee of Essex Ltd, namely Walter Brownsword, reports for work at the Brentwood plant as usual one day only to be told by a representative of Almsville Ltd that it has purchased Essex Ltd's business and assets and that his services are no longer required. Walter is incensed as he wishes to continue in employment with Almsville Ltd. However, owing to the decision in *Nokes*, his contract of employment is personal and non-transferable. As such, Almsville Ltd cannot be compelled to employ him.[10]

---

[9] Writer's annotations appear in square brackets throughout this chapter.
[10] See *Gabriel v Peninsula Business Services Ltd* (UKEAT/0190/11/MA, 23 February 2012) for a modern example of the application of the principle in *Nokes*.

Hypothetical A underscores the point that there are a number of hidden dangers for employees where there is a change of employer and they wish to continue in employment. As noted by Sir Wilfred Greene MR in the Court of Appeal in *Nokes*, 'the position of the . . . [employee] would be . . . unfortunate, since by the dissolution of the transferor company their remedy against it, if any, would have disappeared and all that they could do . . . would be to sue the transferee company for breach of the contract by repudiation on the part of the transferor company . . .'.[11] In other words, where the transferor disposes of its business and assets to a transferee, the employees who wish to continue working for the new employer could be left 'high and dry' by the transferee, since their contracts of employment with the transferor would have automatically terminated. Those employees wishing to continue in employment would need to rely on the benevolence of the transferee and pray that it decides to rehire them, as their continuity of employment would have been severed by the transfer.

The ARD and TUPE dispense with the common law's insistence on the personal non-transferable nature of the employment relationship by providing for the automatic transfer of the contract of employment through the process of statutory novation.[12] Therefore, party freedom is over-ridden and the commercial considerations of the transferor or transferee enterprises are subordinated to considerations of employment protection. For example, it has been held that the restriction of free enterprise is 'an inherent part of the purpose of the [ARD] itself which aims, in the interests of the employees, to transfer to the transferee the obligations arising from the contract of employment or employment relationships'.[13] This policy decision to over-ride a contracting party's freedom of choice is quite a drastic step and a number of justifications have been offered for this regulatory interference, as follows:

(1) Commentators have argued that the rule in *Nokes* providing for the automatic severance of the contract of employment on a change in the nominal employer was something of a legal fiction. In particular, it failed to recognize the fact that the human capital of workers is increasingly invested in specific 'enterprise-organizations', which are entities consisting of persons and assets assigned to the performance of an economic activity pursuing a specific objective.[14] Despite the change in nominal owner of that enterprise-organization and any concomitant change in the employer, its commercial objectives would not have been materially altered, which begs the question as to why the worker ought to be dislodged from employment in such circumstances. In the following extract, Hepple was commenting on the original draft of the ARD, but the sentiments expressed apply with equal force to the ARD in its current form:

■ **B. Hepple, 'Workers' Rights in Mergers and Takeovers: The EEC Proposals'**
(1976) 5 *Industrial Law Journal* 197, 210

[The provisions in the ARD] mean the end of the legal fiction of the personal non-transferable nature of the employment relationship and replace this by the principle of automatic transfer, reflecting the reality of modern working in an *enterprise*. It is in the acceptance of this notion of the

---

[11] *Donoghue v Doncaster Amalgamated Collieries Ltd* [1939] 2 KB 578, 584–5.

[12] See *Wilson v St Helens Borough Council* [1999] 2 AC 52, 76D–E per Slynn LJ. For an elaboration of the effect of the provisions in TUPE on the contract of employment, see M. Freedland, *The Personal Employment Contract* (Oxford, OUP, 2003) 409–10 and 491–515.

[13] See *d'Urso v Ercole Marelli Elettromeccanica Generale SpA* (Case C-362/89) [1992] IRLR 136, 138. However, cf. *Alemo-Herron v Parkwood Leisure Ltd* [2013] ICR 1116.

[14] See G. Barrett, 'Light Acquired on Acquired Rights: Examining Developments in Employment Rights on Transfers of Undertakings' (2005) 42 *Common Market Law Review* 1053, 1055.

ongoing life of an enterprise despite changes of ownership of the physical assets and of the share capital that the [ARD] signposts a radical new direction for labour law. The law of the enterprise recognises acquired rights, based on length of service, which transcend the fictions of personal and corporate employment.

(2) The second argument in favour of the regime in the ARD is linked to notions of commercial pragmatism. The automatic transfer of the employment contract through the process of novation limits the scope for businesses to engage in the dubious practice of 'asset stripping'. 'Asset stripping' describes the situation where a transferor disposes of its business and assets to a transferee acquirer, distributes the sale proceeds to its shareholders via dividend payments, and ultimately puts itself into insolvency, thus leaving the employees with legal claims against the insolvent entity.

(3) The third rationale for the imposition of constraints on free enterprise in terms of the ARD and TUPE is concerned with the effects of business transfers on employment. For example, independent research supports the contention that takeovers of businesses can have negative post-acquisition consequences for the workforce that manifest themselves principally through reduced job tenure and security.[15] The new management are more likely to consider firing some of the transferring employees subsequent to the transfer of a business in a wholly unregulated marketplace. Alternatively, the new owners might be tempted to impose downward variations to the contracts of employment of the transferring employees in order to generate efficiencies or harmonize contractual terms with those of their existing workforces. As such, the provisions of the ARD and TUPE are designed to constrain or remove outright the potential adverse social consequences which may be generated as a result of the application of the common law rule in *Nokes*.

Our understanding of the ARD is enhanced if we subject the policy aim behind the original 1977 Acquired Rights Directive ('Original ARD')[16] to closer examination. In particular, European policy-makers recognized that the objective of furthering internal market integration of commercial organizations throughout Europe would inevitably lead to corporate restructurings. As such, the Original ARD was motivated by a desire to introduce measures supportive of social rights in the context of reorganizations necessitated by closer European market integration:

■ P. Davies and M. Freedland, *Labour Legislation and Public Policy* (Oxford, Clarendon Press/OUP, 1993) 577–8

The [Original ARD] was one of the products of the Social Action Programme adopted by the Council of Ministers in 1974. The general aim of the Social Action Programme was to ensure that the development of social policy within the Community kept pace with the economic

---

[15] B. Black, H. Gospel, and A. Pendleton, 'Finance, Corporate Governance and the Employment Relationship' (2007) 46 *Industrial Relations: A Journal of Economy and Society* 643, 644–8; M. Conyon, S. Girma, S. Thompson, and P. Wright, 'Do Hostile Mergers Destroy Jobs?' (2001) 45 *Journal of Economic Behavior and Organization* 427; and M. Conyon, S. Girma, S. Thompson, and P. Wright, 'The Impact of Mergers and Acquisitions on Company Employment in the United Kingdom' (2002) 46 *European Economic Review* 31; M. Goergen, N. O'Sullivan, and G. Wood, 'The Employment Consequences of Private Equity Acquisitions: The Case of Institutional Buy-outs' (2014) 71 *European Economic Review* 67.

[16] Council Directive 77/187/EEC of 14 February 1977 on the approximation of the laws of the Member States relating to the safeguarding of employees' rights in the event of transfers of undertakings, businesses or parts of undertakings or businesses (OJ 1977 L61/26).

integration which the Community was bringing about. One specific product of that general aim was the policy of recognizing the interests of employees in changes of ownership or control of the enterprises employing them, these being changes which the EEC had the aim and effect of facilitating. This is the rationale for the acquired rights approach; a rationale which can sustain either a narrow approach to acquired rights which says that employees should enjoy the same rights against the new owner or controller of the enterprise as they enjoyed against the old one, or a broad approach which goes on to say that they should also be able to influence the decision whether to transfer ownership or control. Both approaches were at best foreign to, at worst antithetical to, the labour law of the UK. The narrow approach challenged a conscious denial in the common law of the contract of employment of the unilateral transferability of contracts between employers—a doctrine evolved in the context of company amalgamations, and expressed in the decision of the House of Lords in 1940 in *Nokes v Doncaster Amalgamated Collieries Ltd.* The broad approach seemed to involve the adoption of different patterns of industrial relations from those current in the UK; it threatened to require processes of consultation with directly elected representatives of the workforce via Works Councils and, in the Draft Directive of 1974, envisaged compulsory arbitration of employment issues arising out of proposed takeovers and mergers, where British unions still strongly preferred a voluntarist approach. The fact that both approaches are evident in the [Original ARD] of 1977 helps to explain its reception in the UK.[17]

Although there is some evidence in the current ARD and TUPE regime of the broad approach referred to in this extract from Davies and Freedland, our analysis of the consultation provisions in section 19.4 will expose the material limitations on the ability of representatives of transferring employees to participate in the commercial decision to change the ownership or control of an enterprise. Instead, we will note in section 19.3 how the narrow approach of guaranteeing the contractual rights of the transferring employees against the new owner or controller of the enterprise is afforded much greater priority.

19.1.2 Illustration of the main implications of the ARD and TUPE

In summary, what the ARD and TUPE do is preserve the continuity of employment of transferring employees where there is a change of employer. This is achieved by the automatic transfer of the contract of employment through a process of statutory 'novation' in terms of regulation 4(1) of TUPE, which is the first major implication of the ARD and TUPE. The other four principal implications of the ARD and TUPE are to some extent linked to the operation of that rule and can be listed as follows:

(1) all rights, powers, duties, and liabilities arising under or in connection with the contracts of employment of the transferring employees are transferred to, and so are inherited by, the transferee;[18]

(2) the dismissal of any employee for the sole or principal reason of the transfer is treated as an automatically unfair dismissal;[19]

(3) the transferor is obliged to inform and consult with the representatives of the transferring employees;[20] and

---

[17] See also S. Hardy, 'The Acquired Rights Directive: A Case of Economic and Social Rights at Work' in H. Collins, P. Davies, and R. Rideout (eds), *Legal Regulation of the Employment Relation* (London, Kluwer, 2000) 479.

[18] ARD, Article 3(1); TUPE, regulation 4(2).

[19] ARD, Article 4(1); TUPE, regulation 7(1). See Chapter 16, section 16.2.4.2, for a list of the automatically unfair dismissals prescribed by statute.

[20] ARD, Article 7(1); TUPE, regulation 13.

(4) an obligation is imposed on the transferor to furnish written information about the transferring employees to the transferee.[21]

Our understanding of the operation of each of (1)–(4) can be assisted with the aid of Hypothetical B.

Hypothetical B

Danny's Demolishers plc ('the Employer') is a large multinational company with a subsidiary company called Danny's Demolishers (Yorkshire) Ltd ('Yorkshire Ltd'). Yorkshire Ltd has a workforce of 324 employees operating from one plant in Leeds. Unfortunately, a recession in the construction sector in Yorkshire has led to severe cash-flow problems for the company and the decision is taken to identify a buyer for the business of Yorkshire Ltd. A company called Partnership Construction plc steps forward to acquire the entire business and assets of Yorkshire Ltd, and a business sale and acquisition agreement is concluded between the parties. The business of Yorkshire Ltd is transferred to Partnership Construction plc on 12 July, which is the date of the transfer.

Wilson Jones is one of the transferring employees. His contract of employment provides that he is entitled to be paid an annual bonus of £3,000. He has recently presented a complaint to an employment tribunal against Yorkshire Ltd seeking compensation of £23,000 in respect of an allegation of disability discrimination. However, as at the date of transfer, the employment tribunal hearing to consider his disability discrimination claim has not yet taken place and is scheduled for November. It is the policy of Partnership Construction plc not to pay bonuses to its staff.

Alf Tweeding is another of the transferring employees. When he turns up for work as usual on 13 July, he is summoned to the office of a new manager called William Swindle, whom he has never met before. William explains that he has been appointed as a manager by Partnership Construction plc, pursuant to the transfer of the business and assets of Yorkshire Ltd on 12 July. He informs Alf of the fact of the transfer and notifies him that he is dismissed with immediate effect. When Alf asks why he has been dismissed, William responds by saying that Partnership Construction plc has decided to dismiss 11 of the existing 324 employees in order to generate efficiencies in the operation of the business and that Alf is only one of that number. Alf is extremely unhappy that (1) he has been dismissed and (2) not a single member of the workforce was given advance warning of the transfer of Yorkshire Ltd's business to Partnership Construction plc.

It soon becomes apparent to William Swindle that the workforce at the Leeds plant is well in excess of the 324 employees of which Yorkshire Ltd had informed them. Instead, William calculates that there must be something like 462 employees. William notifies Grant Sinclair, one of the directors of Partnership Construction plc, who is furious, because the additional 138 employees means that the deal is no longer a good one for Partnership Construction plc.

Advise Wilson, Alf, and William on their rights under the ARD and TUPE.

If we turn first to Wilson Jones' case, the relevant provisions to consider are Article 3(1) of the ARD and regulation 4(2) of TUPE. The latter stipulates that all of the transferor's rights, powers, duties, and liabilities under, or in connection with, the contracts of employment of transferring employees transfer to the transferee. It is abundantly clear that

---

the existing contractual terms and conditions of Wilson Jones, including any accrued rights, are automatically transferred over to Partnership Construction plc. Since Wilson Jones' right to be paid a bonus is contractual, Partnership Construction plc is liable as the transferee to honour this commitment. Meanwhile, any liability of Yorkshire Ltd in respect of the disability discrimination claim will also transfer over to Partnership Construction plc. The transferee will inherit that claim notwithstanding the fact that it is (1) technically a *contingent statutory* (rather than contractual) liability and it has arisen (2) pursuant to an act or omission of the transferor *prior to the date of the transfer* 'in relation to . . . a person assigned to that organised grouping of resources or employees'.[22] Therefore, Partnership Construction plc will find itself a respondent to the case with the responsibility of defending Wilson Jones' disability discrimination claim at the future employment tribunal hearing.

Turning to Alf Tweeding's case, two issues merit our attention:

(1) Article 4(1) of the ARD and regulation 7(1) of TUPE are engaged. Alf has been dismissed and it is clear that the sole or principal reason for his dismissal is the transfer of Yorkshire Ltd's business. The law treats him as having been automatically unfairly dismissed for the purposes of Part X of the Employment Rights Act 1996 ('ERA'),[23] and he is entitled to the usual remedies for unfair dismissal, which we considered in Chapter 17, section 17.3, without having to prove the substantive or procedural unfairness of his dismissal.

(2) The second issue relates to the provisions of Article 7(1) of the ARD and regulation 13 of TUPE, which impose statutory duties on Yorkshire Ltd as the transferor to inform and consult representatives of the transferring employees about the impending transfer of its business to the transferee. Regulation 13(2) of TUPE directs that such consultation should take place '[l]ong enough before a relevant transfer to enable the employer of any affected employees to consult the appropriate representatives of any affected employees'. In Alf Tweeding's case, neither Yorkshire Ltd nor Partnership Construction plc undertook any such pre-transfer consultation. In terms of regulation 15(9) of TUPE, both the transferor and transferee are jointly and severally liable for any compensation ordered under regulation 15(8) of TUPE for a breach of regulation 13 of TUPE.

Finally, William Swindle's case invokes the provisions of regulation 11 of TUPE, whereby Yorkshire Ltd as transferor is obliged to provide Partnership Construction plc with written notification of details about the transferring employees. The failure to comply with regulation 11 will entitle Partnership Construction plc to obtain compensation from Yorkshire Ltd for an amount the employment tribunal considers just and equitable in the circumstances, having regard to the loss it has sustained. The diagram in Figure 19.1 is a useful representation of how the ARD and TUPE function to confer protection on the transferring employees.

The ARD replaced the Original ARD and TUPE replaced the Transfer of Undertakings (Protection of Employment) Regulations 1981 ('TUPE 1981').[24] TUPE was enacted in order to:

(1) account for numerous revisions which had been made to TUPE 1981, the repeal of the Original ARD, and the introduction of the ARD;[25]

---

[22] See *DJM International Ltd v Nicholas* [1996] ICR 214.

[23] See Chapter 16, section 16.2.4.2, for a list of the reasons which lead to a finding of automatic unfair dismissal. [24] SI 1981/1794.

[25] See the discussion in J. McMullen, 'TUPE: Ringing the (Wrong) Changes: The Collective Redundancies and Transfer of Undertakings (Protection of Employment) (Amendment) Regulations 2014' (2014) 43 *Industrial Law Journal* 149, 150–2.

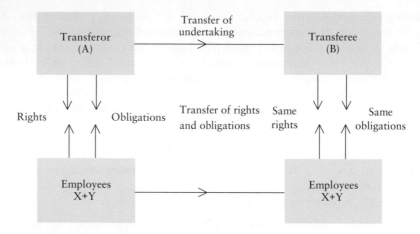

Figure 19.1 *Effect of the ARD and TUPE*
Source: C. Barnard, *EU Employment Law*, 4th edition (Oxford, OUP, 2012) 579.

(2) incorporate into UK law the jurisprudence of the European Court of Justice ('ECJ' or 'CJEU'), which had been developed over the previous 25 years;[26] and

(3) put into effect two governmental policy objectives, namely the desire:

   (a) to incentivize transferors to inform and consult with appropriate representatives of the transferring employees by requiring them to notify transferees of the identities of the transferring employees prior to the transfer; and

   (b) to facilitate the sales of insolvent businesses and thus promote the 'rescue culture' philosophy.

The cross-party political attitude in the UK to the Original ARD was particularly frosty and TUPE 1981 was introduced into domestic law in early 1982. It was brought into force in order to comply with the UK's obligations under the European Treaty by a somewhat hostile Conservative Government with 'a remarkable lack of enthusiasm',[27] which was attributable to the perceived burdens it imposed on businesses. For the first seven years of its existence, its impact was limited, being described as 'almost a dead letter'.[28] However, over the past 30 years, the provisions of TUPE 1981 and TUPE have been afforded a shot in the arm by the courts, particularly insofar as they enthusiastically embraced arguments that its coverage ought to extend to transactions other than the straightforward disposal of a business. Indeed, it can now be said with some confidence that the transfer of undertakings regime is a generally accepted part of the firmament of merger and acquisition deals in the UK and as such, is unlikely to be repealed post-Brexit. Furthermore, to a large extent, it has met the social expectations of workers as regards their rights on the transfer of their employer. With that thought in mind, let us now turn to a consideration of the provisions of TUPE and, in particular, to a preliminary assessment of the definition of a 'relevant transfer', upon which the whole edifice rests.

---

[26] See J. McMullen, 'An Analysis of the Transfer of Undertakings (Protection of Employment) Regulations 2006' (2006) 35 *Industrial Law Journal* 113, 113–14.

[27] Hansard HC, vol. 691, col. 680, 7 December 1981 (Mr David Waddington MP, Under-Secretary of State for Employment). See the discussion in P. Davies and M. Freedland, *Labour Legislation and Public Policy* (Oxford, Clarendon Press/OUP, 1993) 577–9; B. Hepple, 'The Transfer of Undertakings (Protection of Employment) Regulations' (1982) 11 *Industrial Law Journal* 29, 29–30.

[28] H. Collins, 'Transfer of Undertakings and Insolvency' (1989) 18 *Industrial Law Journal* 144, 144.

Reflection points

1. Would you devise a legal regime that seeks to protect employees by preserving their continuity of employment on the transfer of a business?

2. If so, on what basis or bases would you justify the introduction of such a regime and what would it look like?

3. If not, why would you prefer a laissez-faire contractual approach which prioritizes freedom of choice and preserves the ability of the employer and employee to choose with whom they contract?

19.2 EVALUATION OF THE CONCEPT OF A 'RELEVANT TRANSFER'

Article 1(1) of the Original ARD provided as follows:

Article 1

(1) This Directive shall apply to the transfer of an undertaking, business or part of a business to another employer as a result of a legal transfer or merger.

It was reasonably clear that the Original ARD and TUPE 1981 applied where a transferor disposed of the entirety or part of its business to a transferee pursuant to a trade sale or a merger in return for the payment of consideration. In both of these 'typical' examples of a transfer—i.e. sale and merger—the employer of the employees would change and so they would be protected by the safeguards included in the legislation. However, the ECJ soon adopted a much more expansive approach. Employees involved in 'atypical' forms of business restructurings or reorganizations in both the private and public sectors, such as 'contracting out',[29] 'contracting in',[30] and 'outsourcing'[31] situations, were equally included within the coverage of the regime:

■ J. Hunt, 'The Court of Justice as a Policy Actor: The Case of the Acquired Rights Directive' (1998) 18 *Legal Studies* 336, 337

The [ECJ] has reached beyond the 'typical' methods of business transfer, such as sale and merger, and has brought a range of 'new' methods of business reorganisation within the ambit of the directive. Since the 1970s, an increasing number of 'atypical' transactions have emerged which break with the 'typical' form of business reorganisation (involving the 'transfer of a business from one

---

[29] This entails the divestiture of an in-house function undertaken by an organization in the private sector or public sector and its investiture in an external third-party 'service provider' organization. The third party subsequently discharges that function for the former organization pursuant to a contractual agreement, for a defined period of time, and in return for payment. This will often involve the transfer of assets, employees, and clients from the organization to the third-party service provider.

[30] This describes the situation where the third-party 'service provider' ceases to discharge the function and the former organization takes it back in-house. This process of divestiture will also often entail the transfer of assets, employees, and clients from the third-party service provider to the organization.

[31] This is a generic term which is used to convey the idea of a transfer of responsibility for the discharge of certain functions from one organization to another. It will include contracting out and contracting in.

employer (often corporate) to another employer for consideration') which the directive sought to cover. By the mid-1990s, the court had ensured that these new forms of reorganisation, such as 'outsourcing . . . competitive tendering, facilities management, and third party administration may all be caught by the Directive'.

It is the court's application of the directive in the field of the contracting out of services which has proved perhaps most controversial. The practice of contracting out of services previously performed in-house to outside contractors has become increasingly prevalent in both the private and public sectors in many EU states. The primary motivation behind contracting out is 'to enable the client to bring the forces of competition to bear on the provision of the services that it requires'. One route to cost cutting by contractors is undoubtedly through offering employees reduced rates of pay and lower terms and conditions than previously offered by the in-house employer. The ability of contractors to offer services at lower costs in this way has however, been greatly constrained following the decisions of the [ECJ] which indicate that the directive applies in the event of a transfer of (a part of) an undertaking through the mechanism of contracting out. The protection offered by the directive means that the transferred employees retain the same pay and conditions vis-à-vis the new employer as they had in relation to the original, in-house employer. The 'protectionist' line pursued by the [ECJ] in this regard has arguably resulted in removing much of the attraction of contracting out as a cost saving mechanism.[32]

The approach adopted by the ECJ whereby such instances of 'atypical transfers' have been included within the compass of the Original ARD and the ARD has evolved over a period of 30 years since its decision in *Spijkers*[33] and *Süzen*.[34] In short, the test enjoins adjudicators to consider whether there has been a transfer of a stable economic entity which retains its identity post-transfer, and a multi-factorial approach is adopted in order to answer that question.[35] This is something more than a simple (1) contracting out of services, (2) change of contractor, or (3) transfer of a particular economic activity.

The definition of a 'relevant transfer' in regulation 3 of TUPE incorporates the jurisprudence of the ECJ. Nevertheless, it departs from the approach of the ECJ in two ways.

(1) We find that regulation 3(1) divides the definition of a 'relevant transfer' in two. As such, provision is made for:

---

[32] See also J. McMullen, 'Atypical Transfers, Atypical Workers and Atypical Employment Structures: A Case for Greater Transparency in Transfer of Employment Issues' (1996) 25 *Industrial Law Journal* 286.

[33] [1986] 2 CMLR 296. The following are some of the most significant cases: *Redmond (Dr Sophie) Stichting v Bartol* (Case C-29/91) [1992] IRLR 366; *Rask and Christiensen v ISS Kantineservice A/S* (Case C-209/91) [1993] IRLR 133; *Schmidt v Spar und Leihkasse der Früheren Ämter Bordersholm* (Case C-392/92) [1995] ICR 237; *Ayse Süzen v Zehnacker Gebäudereinigung GmbH Krankenhausservice* (Case C-13/95) [1997] ICR 662; *Vidal (Francisco Hernandez) SA v Gomez Peres* (Case C-127/96) [1999] IRLR 132; *Allen v Amalgamated Construction Co. Ltd* (Case C-234/98) [2000] ICR 1316; *Oy Liikenne Ab v Liskojarvi* (Case C-172/99) [2002] ICR 155; *Temco Service Industries SA v Imzilyen* (Case C-51/00) [2002] IRLR 214; *Sánchez Hidalgo v Asociación de Servicios Aser* (Case C-173/96) [2002] ICR 73; *Abler v Sodexho MM Catering Betriebsgesellschaft mbH* (Case C-340/01) [2004] IRLR 168; *CLECE SA v Valor* (Case C-463/09) [2011] ICR 1319; *Alemo-Herron v Parkwood Leisure Ltd* (Case C-426/11) [2013] ICR 1116; *Amatori v Telecom Italia SpA* (Case C-458/12) [2014] IRLR 400; *Ferreira da Silva e Brito v Estado Portugues* (Case C-160/14) [2015] IRLR 1021; *Administrador de Infraestructuras Ferroviarias (ADIF) v Aira Pascual* [2016] IRLR 156; *Osterreichischer Gewerkschaftsbund* [2015] IRLR 67, on which, see E Brameshuber, 'Balancing vs Preservation of rights under the Acquired Rights Directive' (2016) 45 *Industrial Law Journal* 443; and *Federatie Nederlandse Vakvereniging v Smallsteps BV* [2017] IRLR 852.

[34] *Ayse Süzen v Zehnacker Gebäudereinigung GmbH Krankenhausservice* (Case C-13/95) [1997] ICR 662.

[35] *Spijkers v Gebroeders Benedik Abattoir CV* [1986] 2 CMLR 296; *Balfour Beatty Power Networks Ltd v Wilcox* [2006] EWCA Civ 1240, [2007] IRLR 63.

(a) a 'standard' transfer, namely the 'transfer of an undertaking, business or part of an undertaking or business';[36] and

(b) a service provision change.[37]

(2) As the McMullen extract makes clear, this domestic reconceptualization of the meaning of a 'relevant transfer' in TUPE takes it some way beyond the interpretation afforded by the ECJ. As such, additional protection has been conferred domestically on a wider class of transferring employees, sometimes referred to as the 'gold-plating' of EU law.[38] As McMullen explains, the continuing relevance of the case law of the ECJ is confined to the regulation 3(1)(a) 'standard' transfer, i.e. the 'transfer of an undertaking, business or part of an undertaking or business',[39] since it is no longer of import in relation to the 'service provision change' concept in regulation 3(1)(b):

■ **J. McMullen, 'An Analysis of the Transfer of Undertakings (Protection of Employment) Regulations 2006' (2006) 35** *Industrial Law Journal* **113, 115–16**

One significant aspect of the 2006 Regulations is the new definition of a 'relevant transfer', which for most transfers of an undertaking, consolidates European Court case law and its requirement for the transfer of an economic entity which retains its identity. However, for service provision changes there is a special, supplementary, definition which means that, subject to a couple of exceptions, TUPE will apply on the service provision change without resort to the test under European Court case law such as . . . *Süzen* . . . Thus, subject to specified exceptions, it will no longer be necessary, in deciding whether a service provision changeover is covered by TUPE, to apply European Court case law, (ie find the transfer of an economic entity and to take into account whether assets or staff are transferred over the transaction . . .). Unlike the European Court case law position under *Ayse Süzen*, the contract change effects the transfer. (Under *Ayse Süzen*, the mere changeover of a contractor was held not to amount to a transfer of an undertaking without more.) Service provision changeovers then, in the UK, are to be treated differently from most other jurisdictions in the EU and from the [ECJ]'s interpretation of the [ARD]. Employees are better treated, as a result, than is strictly required under [Article 8 of] the [ARD] . . . it is important to stress that all other types of putative transfers of undertakings which do not satisfy the definition of a service provision changeover (and indeed transactions which might otherwise be caught by the service provision changeover but which are specifically excepted (eg where it is intended that the contract is for a single specific event or task of short duration or is one for the supply of goods)) remain covered by the test of a transfer of an economic entity retaining its identity and the European Court case law relevant thereto.

To that extent, it is clear that the new 'service provision change' concept in regulation 3(1)(b) of TUPE can be interpreted from the position of a *tabula rasa* without recourse to the standards set by European case law. Indeed, in the case of *Metropolitan Resources Ltd v Churchill Dulwich Ltd*,[40] it was described in the EAT as a 'wholly new statutory

---

[36] TUPE, regulation 3(1)(a).   [37] TUPE, regulation 3(1)(b).

[38] J. McMullen, 'TUPE: Ringing the (Wrong) Changes: The Collective Redundancies and Transfer of Undertakings (Protection of Employment) (Amendment) Regulations 2014' (2014) 43 *Industrial Law Journal* 149, 150–2; C. Wynn-Evans, 'In Defence of Service Provision Changes?' (2013) 42 *Industrial Law Journal* 152, 167–71.

[39] TUPE, regulation 3(1)(c).   [40] [2009] ICR 1380.

concept'.[41] With these thoughts in mind, we now move on to subject the 'standard transfer' and 'service provision change' concepts to a closer degree of scrutiny.

19.2.1 The definition of a 'relevant transfer' in TUPE

Let us now consider the relevant provisions of regulations 2 and 3 of TUPE:

> **Regulation 2 Interpretation**
>
> (1) In these Regulations . . .
>
> references to 'contractor' in regulation 3 shall include a sub-contractor . . .
>
> references to 'organised grouping of employees' shall include a single employee . . .[42]
>
> 'relevant transfer' means a transfer or a service provision change to which these Regulations apply in accordance with regulation 3 and 'transferor' and 'transferee' shall be construed accordingly and in the case of a service provision change falling within regulation 3(1)(b), 'the transferor' means the person who carried out the activities prior to the service provision change and 'the transferee' means the person who carries out the activities as a result of the service provision change . . .

> **Regulation 3 A relevant transfer**
>
> (1) These Regulations apply to—
>
> (a) a transfer of an undertaking, business or part of an undertaking or business situated immediately before the transfer in the United Kingdom to another person[43] where there is a transfer of an economic entity which retains its identity;
>
> (b) a service provision change, that is a situation in which—
>
>   (i)   activities cease to be carried out by a person ('a client') on his own behalf and are carried out instead by another person on the client's behalf ('a contractor');
>
>   (ii) activities cease to be carried out by a contractor on a client's behalf (whether or not those activities had previously been carried out by the client on his own behalf) and are carried out instead by another person ('a subsequent contractor') on the client's behalf; or
>
>   (iii) activities cease to be carried out by a contractor or a subsequent contractor on a client's behalf (whether or not those activities had previously been carried out by the client on his own behalf) and are carried out instead by the client on his own behalf,
>
> and in which the conditions set out in paragraph (3) are satisfied.
>
> (2) In this regulation 'economic entity' means an organised grouping of resources which has the objective of pursuing an economic activity, whether or not that activity is central or ancillary.
>
> (2A) References in paragraph (1)(b) to activities being carried out instead by another person (including the client) are to activities which are fundamentally the same as the activities carried out by the person who has ceased to carry them out.

---

[41] [2009] ICR 1380, 1383H and 1389F per Burke J. See also the explanation by Elias LJ in *Hunter v McCarrick* [2013] ICR 235, 239E–G.

[42] For an example of a single employee constituting an 'organized grouping', see *Rynda (UK) Ltd v Rhijnsburger* [2015] IRLR 394.

[43] See *Hyde Housing Association Ltd v Layton* [2016] IRLR 107.

(3) The conditions referred to in paragraph (1)(b) are that—

    (a) immediately before the service provision change—

        (i) there is an organised grouping of employees situated in Great Britain which has as its principal purpose the carrying out of the activities concerned on behalf of the client;

        (ii) the client intends that the activities will, following the service provision change, be carried out by the transferee other than in connection with a single specific event or task of short-term[44] duration; and

    (b) the activities concerned do not consist wholly or mainly of the supply of goods for the client's use.[45]

(4) Subject to paragraph (1), these Regulations apply to—

    (a) public and private undertakings engaged in economic activities whether or not they are operating for gain . . .

(5) An administrative reorganisation of public administrative authorities or the transfer of administrative functions between public administrative authorities is not a relevant transfer.

(6) A relevant transfer—

    (a) may be effected by a series of two or more transactions; and

    (b) may take place whether or not any property is transferred to the transferee by the transferor.

The analysis of these provisions is usefully assisted by dividing matters into the two kinds of 'relevant transfer', namely a regulation 3(1)(b) 'service provision change' and a regulation 3(1)(a) 'standard' transfer of 'an undertaking, business or part of an undertaking'.

19.2.1.1 Service provision change

Regulation 3(1)(b) of TUPE divides a 'service provision change' into three categories.

(1) Regulation 3(1)(b)(i) provides for the situation where a private or public person referred to as 'the client' ceases to carry out an economic activity and outsources/contracts out the responsibility for the provision of that activity to a third party. The third party then provides the activity to the client. An example of this scenario is provided by Hypothetical C.

Hypothetical C

Danny's Demolishers plc, ('the Client') is a large multinational company. It is approached by a private company called IT Outsourcing Ltd ('ITL'), which offers to provide all of its information technology ('IT') support requirements at a cost of £350,000 per annum for a period of five years. The Client calculates that it currently costs it £550,000 per annum to perform these IT support services in-house, so it decides to go ahead and outsource its IT support services function to ITL on the terms agreed. All of the assets and staff of the Client relating to the provision of IT support services are transferred to ITL as part of that process.

---

[44] See *Swanbridge Hire & Sales Ltd v Butler* (UKEAT/0056/13/BA, 13 November 2013); *Liddell's Coaches v Cook* [2013] ICR 547; *ICTS UK Ltd v Mahdi* [2016] IRLR 113; and *SNR Denton UK v Kirwan* [2013] ICR 101 for guidance on whether the activities constitute a 'single specific event or task of short-term duration'.

[45] For such an example, see *Pannu v Geo W King Ltd (in liquidation)* [2012] IRLR 193.

The commercial arrangement described in Hypothetical C is also sometimes referred to as 'first-generation contracting out'.

(2) Turning now to the second situation referred to in regulation 3(1)(b)(ii) of TUPE, this can be illustrated by the example in Hypothetical D.

Hypothetical D

After five years, Danny's Demolishers plc, ('the Client') severs its contract with ITL in respect of the provision of IT support services by ITL to the Client. Pursuant to a tender process, the Client selects a private company called Outsourcing of IT Ltd ('OIT') to provide such services for the next five years. All of the assets and staff of ITL relating to the provision of IT support services to the Client are transferred to OIT as part of that process.

Regulation 3(1)(b)(ii) of TUPE is not restricted to a 'second-generation contracting out' situation as narrated in Hypothetical D. It will also cover any subsequent generation contracting out. The central issue is whether there has been a reassignment of the contractor performing the services or activities for the Client and it is essential that the service is provided to the same client or clients[46] throughout, both before and after the change of contractor.[47]

(3) Finally, we turn to regulation 3(1)(b)(iii), which describes the situation where the client decides to sever the outsourcing arrangements and take responsibility for a particular function or service back in-house.

Hypothetical E

After ten years of outsourcing its IT support services function, Danny's Demolishers plc, ('the Client') severs its contract with OIT in respect of the provision of IT support services by OIT to the Client. The Client transfers its IT support services function back in-house from OIT. All of the assets and staff of OIT relating to the provision of IT support services to the Client are transferred to the Client as part of that process.

Each of these three situations will constitute a 'relevant transfer' and invoke the employment protections in TUPE only if the criteria highlighted in regulation 3(3) are also satisfied. As such, once the relevant activity undertaken by the client is identified, it is crucial that it is established that there was an organized grouping of employees situated in the UK before the service provision change, which had as its principal purpose[48] the carrying out of the relevant activities concerned on behalf of the client.[49]

---

[46] In *Ottimo Property Services Ltd v Duncan* [2015] ICR 859, it was decided that the word 'client' could be interpreted as including the plural 'clients' as a result of the terms of the Interpretation Act 1978.

[47] *Hunter v McCarrick* [2013] ICR 235, 246H per Elias LJ; *SNR Denton UK LLP v Kirwan* [2012] IRLR 966; *Taurus Group Ltd v Crofts* (UKEAT/0024/12/CEA, 22 May 2012); *Horizon Security Services Ltd v Ndeze* [2014] IRLR 854; and *CT Plus (Yorkshire) CIC v Stagecoach* (UKEAT/0035/16/DM, 3 August 2016), although cf. *Jinks v London Borough of Havering* (UKEAT/0157/14/MC, 23 February 2015) where there was a change of client on the termination of a sub-contract, yet it was held that the requirements of regulation 3(1)(b) had been satisfied.

[48] See *Tees Esk & Wear Valley NHS Foundation Trust v Harland* [2017] IRLR 486 and *Amaryllis Ltd v McLeod* (UKEAT/0273/15/RN, 9 June 2016).

[49] *Kimberley Group Housing Ltd v Hambley* [2008] ICR 1030, 1038H–1039A per Langstaff J.

The relevant activity in question must not be wholly or mainly concerned with the supply of goods for the client's use and, prior to the service provision change, it must have been the intention of the client that the relevant activity (1) be undertaken by the transferee following the service provision change and (2) not be connected 'with a single specific event or task of short-term duration'.[50] The direction that the activity must neither relate to a single identifiable occurrence nor constitute a task that endures for a limited period of time is particularly crucial. For example, where a company was appointed to undertake security services in respect of a site pending its proposed demolition in eight or nine months, it was held that this qualified as a task of a short-term duration.[51] As such, there was no service provision change and TUPE did not apply. It has been held that whether an activity is a single specific event or a task of short-term duration is a matter of fact and degree, which must be assessed in light of relevant commercial, industrial, or financial practices.[52] Having said that, it is important to note that the words 'single specific event or task of short-term duration' in regulation 3(3)(a)(ii) are circumscribed to some extent by the requirement that the client must 'intend' that the activities are of such a nature. As such, this demands something more concrete than factual evidence of a single specific event or task of short-term duration, which will not be enough if there is no client intention. Events occurring after the prima facie transfer should be taken into account in evaluating the intention of the client and may cast doubt upon whether the activities were in fact intended to be short term.[53] In addition, a mere 'wish' or 'hope' on the part of the client that the engagement of a service provider in the execution of the activities will be short-term in duration is insufficient.[54]

The key difference between a relevant transfer which is classified as a regulation 3(1)(b) 'service provision change' and one falling within a regulation 3(1)(a) 'standard transfer' of an undertaking, business or part of an undertaking or business' lies in the absence of any requirement to establish an economic entity which retains its identity in the case of the former. As such, the focus in a 'service provision change' case is on the *activity* carried on prior, and subsequent, to the putative transfer, rather than the existence of an economic *entity* and whether it retained its identity post-transfer. Whether the contracting out, outsourcing, or contracting in of an activity or the reassignment of a contractor satisfies the 'service provision change' test is a question of law. However, the identification of the activity in question is a matter of fact,[55] and it is sufficient that the activity undertaken before and after is broadly similar, albeit not identical, which represents a departure from the prevalent jurisprudence prior to the introduction of TUPE:

■ *Metropolitan Resources Ltd v Churchill Dulwich Ltd* [2009] ICR 1380, 1390B–1392C

His Honour Judge Burke:

In a case in which regulation 3(1)(b) is relied upon, the employment tribunal should ask itself simply whether, on the facts, one of the three situations set out in regulation 3(1)(b) existed and

---

[50] There has been a measure of disagreement in the EAT regarding whether the words 'a single specific event' and 'task' in regulation 3(3)(a)(ii) are both to be qualified by the words 'of short-term duration' or the words 'a single specific event' ought to be read as standing on their own and the words 'of short-term duration' are to be linked to the word 'task' alone: contrast the opinion of Mr Justice Langstaff in *Liddell's Coaches v Cook* [2013] ICR 547 with that of Lady Smith in *SNR Denton UK v Kirwan* [2013] ICR 101.

[51] *Horizon Security Services Ltd v Ndeze* [2014] IRLR 854.

[52] *Liddell's Coaches v Cook* [2013] ICR 547.   [53] *ICTS UK Ltd v Mahdi* [2016] IRLR 113.

[54] *Sage Ltd (t/a Prestige Nursing Care) v O'Connell* [2014] IRLR 428. Here, the client had a mere wish or hope that a transitional arrangement for the delivery of care to a vulnerable adult would be short-term.

[55] *Ward Hadaway Solicitors v Love* (UKEAT/0471/09/SM, 25 March 2010); *Metropolitan Resources Ltd v Churchill Dulwich Ltd* [2009] ICR 1380, 1389H per Judge Burke QC.

whether the conditions set out in regulation 3(3) are satisfied. The statutory words require the employment tribunal to concentrate upon the relevant activities; and tribunals will inevitably be faced, as in this case, with arguments that the activities carried on by the alleged transferee are not identical to the activities carried on by the alleged transferor because there are detailed differences between what the former does and what the latter did or in the manner in which the former performs and the latter performed the relevant tasks. However, it cannot, in my judgment, have been the intention of the introduction of the new concept of service provision change that that concept should not apply because of some minor difference or differences between the nature of the tasks carried on after what is said to have been a service provision change as compared with before it or in the way in which they are performed as compared with the nature or mode of performance of those tasks in the hands of the alleged transferor. A common sense and pragmatic approach is required to enable a case in which problems of this nature arise to be appropriately decided . . . The tribunal needs to ask itself whether the activities carried on by the alleged transferee are fundamentally or essentially the same as those carried out by the alleged transferor. The answer to that question will be one of fact and degree, to be assessed by the tribunal on the evidence in the individual case before it . . . For the reasons I have set out there is, in my judgment, in a regulation 3(1)(b) case no call for a formal list of factors which the tribunal must consider before it can make a decision as to whether there was or was not a relevant transfer, in contrast to the position in a regulation 3(1)(a) case where the . . . approach [in *Cheesman v R Brewer Contracts Ltd* [2001] IRLR 144] is required. The tribunal did not, in my judgment, err in law in failing to adopt the *Cheesman* approach.

Metropolitan Resources Churchill Ltd v Dulwich Ltd is the leading authority to date on how tribunals and courts should evaluate the nature of the activities[56] conducted by the putative transferor and transferee in order to establish the existence or non-existence of a 'service provision change'. It has been applied by the EAT in many cases[57] and approved by Elias LJ in the Court of Appeal in *Hunter v McCarrick*.[58] Indeed, this passage underscores the central point that tribunals and courts must focus on whether the activities performed after the putative transfer are fundamentally or essentially the same as those carried out pre-transfer.[59] A minor difference, or differences, between the nature of the tasks carried on will be overlooked.[60] In shorthand, this test can be referred to as the

[56] It is possible for there to be two activities: *Arch Initiatives v Greater Manchester West Mental Health NHS Foundation Trust* [2016] IRLR 406.

[57] *Enterprise Managed Services Ltd v Connect-up Ltd* [2012] IRLR 190. See also *Campbell v Johnson Controls* (UKEAT/0041/12/JOJ, 14 February 2012), [2012] All ER (D) 220; *London Borough of Islington v Bannon* (UKEAT/0221/12/KN, 25 September 2012); *Lorne Stewart plc v Hyde* (UKEAT/0408/12/GE, 1 October 2013); *Qlog Ltd v O'Brien* (UKEAT/0301/13/JOJ, 21 March 2014); and *Anglo Beef Processors UK v Longland* (UKEATS/0025/15/JW, 7 December 2016).

[58] [2013] ICR 235.

[59] Its application in the case of *OCS Group UK Ltd v Jones* [2010] All ER (D) 33 (September) resulted in a finding that there was no 'service provision change'. The EAT held that the activity carried out pre-transfer was not merely the provision of food for staff but a full catering service for staff. The degree of changes to the food service implemented post-transfer (kiosks selling snacks and sandwiches) justified the employment tribunal in forming the conclusion that there were substantial differences in he new contract. Meanwhile, the assignation of a lease from one tenant to another is insufficient to trigger the operation of regulation 3(1), since there must be a transfer of an economic activity intrinsically linked to the tenanted property: *LOM Management Ltd v Sweeney* (UKEATS/0058/11/BI, 11 May 2012).

[60] For example, although the incoming contractor's business model was completely different from that of the previous contractor in *Qlog Ltd v O'Brien* (UKEAT/0301/13/JOJ, 21 March 2014) and the incoming contractor sub-contracted out a part of the activities, the activities pre-transfer and post-transfer remained fundamentally the same. The same conclusion was reached in *Salvation Army Trustee Co. v Bahi* [2017] IRLR 410 notwithstanding that changes were made by the transferee to the services provided to the homeless. See also *Anglo Beef Processors UK v Longland* (UKEATS/0025/15/JW, 7 December 2016).

'fundamentally or essentially different' test and was codified in regulation 3(2A) when it came into force in January 2014.

Two issues have cropped up in the cases which have applied *Metropolitan Resources*, having the capacity to abrade the certainty that the introduction of the 'service provision change' concept was intended to create:

(1) First, where there is a change of service provider and the original contractor's contract is 'run off', it would appear that this may preclude the operation of the protections afforded by TUPE. For example, in *Ward Hadaway v Love*,[61] it was held that solicitors processing legal cases for the Nursing and Midwifery Council ('NMC') were not transferred to a new contractor where the NMC terminated the original contractor's contract and awarded an exclusive contract to a new contractor. The EAT ruled that the 'service provision change' concept was not engaged since the new contractor's responsibility was to process new cases only, and the original contractor/ transferor had a 'run-off' period to close out the existing caseload, which meant that there was no need for it to transfer files to the new contractor. As such, where there is a planned incremental transition in service provision with the old and new service provider contemporaneously discharging the services for a period of time, it would appear that the 'service provision change' concept is insufficiently flexible to engage the protections of TUPE.

(2) The extent to which it is possible for the activity concerned to undergo an element of modernization or improvement post-transfer, without engaging the 'fundamentally or essentially different' test, is now particularly uncertain. Indeed, in many of the cases considered, a finding of fragmentation of the activities post-transfer has resulted in the invocation of the 'fundamentally or essentially different' test to negate a 'service provision change'.[62] This would appear to conflict with the Government's intention when it introduced the 'service provision change' concept into UK law. For example, it had been intended that, where an incoming service provider undertakes the activities in a new, efficient, or 'innovative' manner,[63] the 'service provision change' criterion would be nonetheless satisfied, provided that any deviations in practice are not so material that the activity is transformed into something which is 'fundamentally' or 'essentially' different.

A further point of considerable significance is that, prior to the putative service provision change, there must be in existence an organized grouping of employees situated in the UK which has as its principal purpose the carrying out of the activities concerned on behalf of the client.[64] In *Rynda (UK) Ltd v Rhijnsburger*,[65] the Court of Appeal furnished guidance on the proper approach to be taken in determining whether an employee is assigned to an organized grouping of employees dedicated to the provision of the activities:

---

[61] (UKEAT/0471/09/SM, 25 March 2010).

[62] See *Nottinghamshire Healthcare NHS Trust v Hamshaw* (UKEAT/0037/11/JOJ, 19 July 2011) where the residents of a residential care home operated by the NHS trust were rehoused in individual homes. They continued to receive supported living and welfare services from the local authority. The employee care workers, who were formerly employed by the NHS trust, were offered employment by Hamshaw and the other respondents to the case. In the majority of cases, the care workers were required by the contractors, Hamshaw, and others to sleep in at the homes of the former care home residents. The care workers claimed that there had been a 'service provision change' under regulation 3(1)(b) of TUPE, but the EAT rejected that contention. The EAT held that the activities concerned had undergone a sufficient degree of fragmentation post-transfer to warrant the engagement of the 'fundamentally or essentially different' test. *Clearsprings Management Ltd v Ankers* [2009] All ER (D) 261 (February) is a very similar decision.

[63] See the analysis in J. McMullen, 'An Analysis of the Transfer of Undertakings (Protection of Employment) Regulations 2006' (2006) 35 *Industrial Law Journal* 113, 123.

[64] Regulation 3(3)(a)(i) of TUPE.   [65] [2015] IRLR 394.

■ *Rynda (UK) Ltd v Rhijnsburger* [2015] EWCA Civ 75, para 44

Lord Justice Jackson:

I would summarise the principles which emerge from the authorities as follows. If company A takes over from company B the provision of services to a client, it is necessary to consider whether there has been a service provision change within regulation 3 of TUPE. The first stage of this exercise is to identify the service which company B was providing to the client. The next step is to list the activities which the staff of company B performed in order to provide that service. The third step is to identify the employee or employees of company B who ordinarily carried out those activities. The fourth step is to consider whether company B organised that employee or those employees into a 'grouping' for the principal purpose of carrying out the listed activities.[66]

A number of additional issues can be highlighted in the context of the concept of the 'organized grouping', as follows:

(1) A single employee can be an organized grouping of employees.[67]

(2) It is essential that such an organized grouping of employees is dedicated to the provision of the service to the client. This will be particularly problematic where a group of workers is not allocated to the service of a client, but instead to a particular function, involving a number of clients of their employer. In *Eddie Stobart Ltd v Moreman*,[68] the Court of Appeal decided that employees did not transfer under TUPE when they were not structured into a team by reference to the requirements of the client in question. That was despite the fact that the majority of their time was occupied with tasks related to a particular contract, *part of which* involved servicing a particular client. The difference here lies in the distinction between a 'group' of employees and an 'organized grouping' of employees.[69]

(3) Where an employee has been subjected to lay-off, or is on maternity leave or holiday leave prior to a transfer, or there has been a temporary closure or suspension of an undertaking with a resulting absence of staff at the time of the transfer,[70] that does not preclude that employee from being assigned to an organized grouping of employees.[71] However, the opposite conclusion will be reached where the employee is permanently absent from work owing to sickness or illness.[72] Further, where a third party instructs an employer to remove an employee from certain work duties connected with transferring activities, that does not necessarily mean that that employee

---

[66] Sourced from BAILII available at http://www.bailii.org/cgi-bin/markup.cgi?doc=/ew/cases/EWCA/Civ/2015/75.html&query=rynda&method=boolean (last visited 22 October 2017).

[67] *Rynda (UK) Ltd v Rhijnsburger* [2015] IRLR 394, 398 per Jackson LJ; regulation 2(1) of TUPE.

[68] [2012] ICR 919.

[69] See also *Ceva Freight (UK) Ltd v Seawell Ltd* [2013] IRLR 726, 730–2; *Amaryllis Ltd v McLeod* (UKEAT/0273/15/RN, 9 June 2016).

[70] *Inex Home Improvements Ltd v Hodgkins* [2016] ICR 71; *Mustafa v Trek Highways Services Ltd* [2016] IRLR 326. For commentary on *Inex*, see J. McMullen, 'The Developing Case Law on TUPE and Service Provision Change' (2016) 45 *Industrial Law Journal* 220. In certain circumstances there may be cases where a temporary lay-off generated by an absence of work will warrant a finding that the organized grouping of employees has been dissolved and the relevant factors to take into account for that purpose will be the nature, purpose, and length of the cessation of the work.

[71] There have been contrasting judicial opinions regarding the status of an employee suspended prior to a transfer, e.g. contrast *Sage Ltd (t/a Prestige Nursing Care) v O'Connell* [2014] IRLR 428, on the one hand, with *Jakowlew v Nestor Primecare Services Ltd (t/a Saga Care)* [2015] ICR 1100 and *Inex Home Improvements Ltd v Hodgkins* [2016] ICR 71, on the other.

[72] *BT Managed Services Ltd v Edwards* [2015] IRLR 994.

has ceased to be assigned to the organized grouping of employees dedicated to the carrying out of those activities: the basis for this rule is that it should not be possible for an incoming contractor or the client to dictate who is assigned to an organized grouping.[73]

(4) The expression 'organized grouping of employees' connotes a group of employees smaller than the entire workforce of the employer.[74]

(5) Employees who have different employers cannot fall within the expression 'organized grouping of employees'.[75]

(6) The amount of time dedicated by an employee towards the carrying out of the relevant activities is not determinative;[76] instead, the courts and tribunals will focus on the nature of the employee's contractual obligations, rather than the work that they are actually performing, together with the status of that employee within the organizational framework of the contractor that is providing the service.

(7) Finally, if there are certain employees whose role is such that they are not directly involved in the delivery of the service to the client, it is likely that they will not fall within the requisite 'organized grouping of employees'. For example, in *Edinburgh Home-Link Partnership v City of Edinburgh Council*,[77] it was found that directors of a housing charity that provided a service to a single client did not transfer under TUPE because they were not assigned to the organized grouping of the charity's workforce engaged in the service of the client.

19.2.1.2 A 'standard' transfer of an undertaking or business

Unlike the 'service provision change' category, a 'standard' transfer of an undertaking or business under regulation 3(1)(a) of TUPE arises where an economic entity is transferred which retains its identity post-transfer. The first step is to identify the 'economic entity' and the second is to evaluate whether its operation has actually been continued or resumed.[78] An economic entity is something more than an economic activity or a collection of individual employees or workers contracted to perform a particular service.[79] The mere fact that a putative transferee carried on the same activities, or supplied the same services, as the putative transferor is not by itself determinative of a transfer under regulation 3(1)(a) of TUPE, nor does it by itself support a conclusion that an entity retained its identity.[80] This distinction between an 'economic entity' and an 'economic activity' is what differentiates regulation 3(1)(a) of TUPE from the 'service provision change' concept in regulation 3(1)(b) of TUPE. The former approach is reflective of the 'enterprise-organization' conception of an undertaking found in Article 1(1)(b) of the ARD and regulation 3(2) of TUPE, which we considered earlier in section 19.2, i.e. the notion that an economic entity is 'an organized grouping of resources which has the objective of pursuing an economic activity, whether or not that activity is central or ancillary'.[81]

---

[73] *Jakowlew v Nestor Primecare Services Ltd (t/a Saga Care)* [2015] ICR 1100.

[74] *Argyll Coastal Services Ltd v Stirling* (UKEATS/0012/11/BI, 15 February 2012).

[75] *ibid*.

[76] *London Borough of Hillingdon v Gormanley* (UKEAT/0169/14/KN, 19 December 2014); *Costain Ltd v Armitage* (UKEAT/0048/14/DA, 2 July 2014).

[77] (UKEATS/0061/11/BI, 10 July 2012).

[78] *Spijkers v Gebroeders Benedik Abattoir CV* [1986] 2 CMLR 296, 304.

[79] *Wain v Guernsey Ship Management Ltd* [2007] EWCA Civ 294, [2007] ICR 1350.

[80] *RCO Support Services Ltd v Unison* [2002] EWCA Civ 464, [2002] ICR 751.

[81] See G. Barrett, 'Light Acquired on Acquired Rights: Examining Developments in Employment Rights on Transfers of Undertakings' (2005) 42 *Common Market Law Review* 1053, 1055–6.

The reasoning developed in the case law of the ECJ on the scope of the concept of an 'economic entity' is pivotal in the assessment of a 'standard' transfer for the purposes of regulation 3(1)(a) of TUPE. In *Cheesman v R Brewer Contracts Ltd*,[82] Lindsay J (President) reviewed the evaluative criteria applicable for the purposes of regulation 3(1)(a). The following guidance has since been adopted by the domestic courts and tribunals as a definitive summary of the legal position:

■ *Cheesman v R Brewer Contracts Ltd* [2001] IRLR 144, paras 10–12

Mr Justice Lindsay (President):

We shall attempt, although it is not always a clear distinction, to divide considerations between those going to whether there is an undertaking and those, if there is an undertaking, going to whether it has been transferred . . . Thus:

(i)   As to whether there is an undertaking, there needs to be found a stable economic entity whose activity is not limited to performing one specific works contract, an organised grouping of persons and of assets enabling (or facilitating) the exercise of an economic activity which pursues a specific objective . . .

(ii) In order to be such an undertaking it must be sufficiently structured and autonomous but will not necessarily have significant assets, tangible or intangible . . .

(iii) In certain sectors such as cleaning and surveillance the assets are often reduced to their most basic and the activity is essentially based on manpower . . .

(iv) An organised grouping of wage-earners who are specifically and permanently assigned to a common task may in the absence of other factors of production, amount to an economic entity . . .

(v)   An activity of itself is not an entity; the identity of an entity emerges from other factors such as its workforce, management staff, the way in which its work is organised, its operating methods[83] and, where appropriate, the operational resources available to it . . .

As for whether there has been a transfer:—

(i)   As to whether there is any relevant sense a transfer, the decisive criterion for establishing the existence of a transfer is whether the entity in question retains its identity, as indicated, inter alia, by the fact that its operation is actually continued or resumed . . .

(ii) In a labour intensive sector it is to be recognised that an entity is capable of maintaining its identity after it has been transferred where the new employer does not merely pursue the activity in question but also takes over a major part, in terms of their numbers and skills, of the employees specially assigned by his predecessors to that task. That follows from the fact that in certain labour intensive sectors a group of workers engaged in the joint activity on a permanent basis may constitute an economic entity . . .

(iii) In considering whether the conditions for existence of a transfer are met it is necessary to consider all the factors characterising the transaction in question but each is a single factor and none is to be considered in isolation . . . However, whilst no authority so holds, it may, presumably, not be an error of law to consider 'the decisive criterion' in (i) above in isolation; that, surely, is an aspect of its being 'decisive', although, as one sees from the 'inter alia' in (i) above, 'the decisive criterion' is not itself said to depend on a single factor.

---

[82] [2001] IRLR 144. See also *ECM (Vehicle Delivery Service) Ltd v Cox* [1998] ICR 631.

[83] Even where an autonomous organizational structure has been removed, an entity may nonetheless retain its identity post-transfer: *Ferreira da Silva e Brito v Estado Portugues* [2015] All ER (D) 47 (September).

(iv)   Amongst the matters thus falling for consideration are the type of undertaking, whether or not its tangible assets are transferred, the value of its intangible assets at the time of transfer, whether or not the majority of its employees are taken over by the new company, whether or not its customers are transferred, the degree of similarity between the activities carried on before and after the transfer, and the period, if any, in which they are suspended . . .

(v)   In determining whether or not there has been a transfer, account has to be taken, inter alia, of the type of undertaking or business in issue, and the degree of importance to be attached to the several criteria will necessarily vary according to the activity carried on . . .

(vi)   Where an economic entity is able to function without any significant tangible or intangible assets, the maintenance of its identity following the transaction being examined cannot logically depend on the transfer of such assets . . .

(vii) Even where assets are owned and are required to run the undertaking, the fact that they do not pass does not preclude a transfer . . .

(viii) Where maintenance work is carried out by a cleaning firm and then next by the owner of the premises concerned, that mere fact does not justify the conclusion that there has been a transfer . . .

(ix)   More broadly, the mere fact that the service provided by the old and new undertaking providing a contracted-out service or the old and new contract-holder are similar does not justify the conclusion that there has been a transfer of an economic entity between predecessor and successor . . .

(x)   The absence of any contractual link between transferor and transferee may be evidence that there has been no relevant transfer but it is certainly not conclusive as there is no need for any such direct contractual relationship: *Sanchez Hidalgo* paragraphs 22 and 23.[84]

(xi)   When no employees are transferred, the reasons why that is the case can be relevant as to whether or not there was a transfer . . .

(xii) The fact that the work is performed continuously with no interruption or change in the manner or performance is a normal feature of transfers of undertakings but there is no particular importance to be attached to a gap between the end of the work by one sub-contractor and the start by the successor . . .

More generally the cases also show:—

(i)   The necessary factual appraisal is to be made by the National Court . . .

(ii)   The [ARD] applies where, following the transfer, there is a change in the natural person responsible for the carrying on of the business who, by virtue of that fact, incurs the obligation of an employer vis-a-vis the employees of the undertaking, regardless of whether or not ownership of the undertaking is transferred . . .

(iii) The aim of the [ARD] is to ensure continuity of employment relationships within the economic entity irrespective of any change of ownership . . . and our domestic law illustrates how readily the Courts will adopt a purposive construction to counter avoidance . . .[85]

This extract clarifies that it is helpful to classify the undertaking which is the subject of examination as 'asset-reliant' or 'labour-intensive'. Where the undertaking is 'asset-reliant' in the sense that its operation is primarily dependent on the employment of assets,

---

[84] See also *Temco Service Industries SA v Imzilyen* (Case C-51/00) [2002] IRLR 214.
[85] Sourced from BAILII available at http://www.bailii.org/cgi-bin/markup.cgi?doc=/uk/cases/UKE-AT/2000/909_98_3011.html&query=cheesman+and+v+and+r+and+brewer&method=boolean (last visited 22 October 2017).

rather than people, e.g. in the case of a commercial coach transport operator,[86] or the handling of transport units requiring numerous pieces of equipment,[87] it is necessary for a significant amount of tangible assets such as moveable property or buildings to be transferred so that their use is taken over by the transferee. Otherwise, the protections of the ARD are not engaged. On the other hand, where the undertaking can be categorized as 'labour-intensive' in nature and thus the key or essential element of the service offered by the undertaking hinges on manpower rather than assets for its proper functioning, e.g. cleaning or security surveillance services,[88] the protections in the ARD will not apply unless a majority of the workforce engaged in the discharge of the relevant function is transferred to the transferee.

This dichotomy between labour-intensive and asset-reliant undertakings causes difficulties for the reasons expertly captured in the following Davies extract:

■ P. Davies, 'Transfers: The UK Will Have to Make up Its Own Mind' (2001) 30 *Industrial Law Journal* 231, 234

In contracting out of services the impact of the [ARD] has become, if not voluntary, at least highly contingent upon the structuring of the commercial deal by which the contracting out, contracting in or reassignment of the contract is effected. Where assets are an essential part of the business, the application of the [ARD] can be avoided by not transferring the assets; where the business is 'based essentially on manpower', [i.e. 'labour-intensive'] it can be avoided, it seems, by the new employer not offering jobs to the former employer's workforce. It is true that in some cases the new employer may be unable to follow such a course of action, for example, where the former employer's assets or workforce are highly specialised and cannot be easily replaced by going into the market. However, this response simply highlights the arbitrary impact of the [ARD]. It is precisely workers who are not skilled and who might be thought to be most in need of the protection of the law (such as cleaners) whom the new employer is most likely to be able to replace by going into the labour market and thereby avoid the application of the [ARD] (in the case of 'activities based essentially on manpower').

For those reasons, it has been held that the subjective motive of the employer in failing to take over a majority of the workforce in the context of a labour-intensive undertaking will be a relevant matter to be taken into account. For example, where the evidence demonstrates that the decision not to assume the majority of the workforce was reached to avoid the operation of TUPE in the context of a labour-intensive undertaking, this will be part of the factual matrix to be considered by the court or tribunal in its evaluation of the position.[89]

19.2.1.3 Matters of general application

A number of matters are of general application to a 'relevant transfer' irrespective of whether the concept invoked for the engagement of the protective provisions of TUPE

---

[86] *Oy Liikenne Ab v Liskojarvi* (Case C-172/99) [2002] ICR 155.
[87] *Administrador de Infraestructuras Ferroviarias (ADIF) v Aira Pascual* [2016] IRLR 156. See J. McMullen, 'Recent CJEU Case Law on the Transfer of Asset-Reliant Undertakings' (2016) 45 *Industrial Law Journal* 455.
[88] *Vidal (Francisco Hernandez) SA v Gomez Peres* (C-127/96) [1999] IRLR 132; *Sánchez Hidalgo v Asociación de Servicios Aser* (C-173/96) [2002] ICR 73.
[89] See *ECM (Vehicle Delivery) Service Ltd v Cox* [1999] IRLR 559; *ADI (UK) Ltd v Firm Security Group Ltd* [2001] IRLR 542; *RCO Support Services Ltd v Unison* [2002] ICR 751; *Astle v Cheshire County Council* [2005] IRLR 12; and *Mustafa v Trek Highways Services Ltd* [2016] IRLR 326.

is contained within regulation 3(1)(a) or (b). For example, Article 1(1)(a) of the ARD dictates that there must be a change of employer as a result of a legal transfer or merger. Hence, a mere change in ownership of the shares of a corporate employer will not trigger the provisions in TUPE.[90] A similar approach was adopted by the Court of Appeal in *Brookes v Borough Care Services Ltd*,[91] where the 'share membership' of a company limited by guarantee which operated a care home was transferred outright to an industrial and provident society. Here, there was clear evidence that the transaction had been structured in this way in order to avoid the operation of the protective regime in TUPE. Nonetheless, the Court ruled that the motives of the parties in arranging the deal in such a manner were irrelevant. However, an exception to the general rule that a transfer of the shares of a corporate employer will not involve the operation of TUPE was propounded in *Print Factory (London) 1991 Ltd v Millam*.[92] Here, the Court of Appeal ruled that if day-to-day control of a corporate employer is effectively assumed by the transferee of the shares of that company, TUPE will apply, notwithstanding that there has been no change in the employer of the employees. The central issue is whether the 'business' in which the employee was employed had been transferred from one entity to another and the new party had become responsible for carrying on the business, had incurred the obligations of an employer, and had taken over the day-to-day running of the business.[93]

Other provisions of TUPE cast light on its general application. For example, regulation 3(6)(b) explicitly directs that the transfer of property is not necessary for TUPE to be engaged, which is consistent with the jurisprudence of the ECJ. Moreover, the effect of regulation 3(4)(a) is that charitable and not-for-profit organizations can be caught.[94] Meanwhile, regulation 3(5) stipulates that the reorganization of public bodies or the transfer of public functions between public bodies does not constitute a relevant transfer. In such a context, matters are governed by the Cabinet Office Statement of Practice on Staff Transfers in the Public Sector.[95]

With regard to the timing of the transfer, regulation 3(6)(a) of TUPE prescribes that a relevant transfer may be effected by a series of two or more transactions. As such, as recognized by the ECJ in *Celtec Ltd v Astley*,[96] it is possible for a transfer to be undertaken over a period of time. Nevertheless, the ECJ ruled that the ARD required a specific 'date of a transfer'. This would be fixed in line with the actual date on which responsibility as employer for carrying on the business of the economic activity or entity moved from the transferor to the transferee.[97] This means that it is not open to the parties to postpone the date of the transfer to another mutually convenient date. One must also recall that regulation 3(6)(a) of TUPE directs that a TUPE transfer 'may' be implemented by a series of two or more transactions. The significance of the word 'may' is underscored by the

---

[90] *Initial Supplies Ltd v McCall* 1992 SLT 67.   [91] 1998 ICR 1198.

[92] [2007] ICR 1331. See also *Jackson Lloyd v Smith* (UKEAT/0127/13/LA, 4 April 2014) where the business of the target company was incorporated into the business of the share purchaser's holding company.

[93] *ICAP Management Services Ltd v Berry* [2017] IRLR 811.

[94] See *Redmond (Dr Sophie) Stichting v Bartol* [1992] IRLR 366.

[95] See https://www.gov.uk/government/publications/staff-transfers-in-the-public-sector (last visited 22 October 2017) and *Henke v Gemeinde Schierke and Verwaltungsgemeinschaft Brocken* [1997] ICR 746. The so-called 'Henke' exception, which precludes the applicability of TUPE where the nature of the relevant function is derived from the exercise of public authority, was afforded a particularly broad interpretation in the case of *Law Society of England and Wales v Secretary of State for Justice* [2010] IRLR 407. This case related to the transfer of authority for the determination of complaints against solicitors from the Legal Complaints Service of the Law Society ('LCS') to a newly constituted Office for Legal Complaints ('OLC'). It was held that the LCS was a public administrative body which was engaged in the discharge of administrative, public, and regulatory functions, which were to be transferred to the OLC, which would statutorily assume responsibility for those functions. Therefore, regulation 3(5) applied to negate the operation of a TUPE transfer despite the fact that the Law Society is not a public sector body. See also *Scattolon v Ministero dell'Istruzione, dell'Universita' e della Ricerca* [2011] IRLR 1020.

[96] [2005] ICR 1409, 1433H–1434A.

[97] See also *Housing Maintenance Solutions Ltd v McAteer* [2015] ICR 87.

decision of the ECJ in *Temco Service Industries*.[98] Here, the ECJ indicated that it is not strictly necessary for the transfer to be effected pursuant to a contract between the transferor and the transferee; instead, a unilateral act, judicial decision, or a statutory assignment in the absence of any contractual relationship between the transferor and transferee may be sufficient to trigger a 'relevant transfer' covered by the ARD and TUPE.[99]

 For additional reading on a 'relevant transfer', visit the Online Resources for this book at www.oup.com/uk/cabrelli3e/

19.3 LEGAL IMPLICATIONS OF A 'RELEVANT TRANSFER'

It is no exaggeration to say that there are far-reaching legal consequences where it is held that there has been a 'relevant transfer' under regulation 3 of TUPE. These implications are of profound social and economic significance for the employees transferred and the transferee employer. In this section, we will divide our analysis into four separate elements in order to facilitate the discussion, namely:

(1) what and who transfers;

(2) the status of variations to the contract of employment;

(3) the status of dismissals; and

(4) the special case of insolvency.

19.3.1 What and who transfers?

Regulation 4 of TUPE is the starting point for our discussion of the identification of the transferring employees and what the transferee acquires pursuant to a TUPE transfer. In particular, the primary right of a transferring employee to have his/her continuity of employment preserved[100] finds its expression in regulation 4(1):

Regulation 4 Effect of relevant transfer on contracts of employment

(1) Except where objection is made under paragraph (7), a relevant transfer shall not operate so as to terminate the contract of employment of any person employed by the transferor and assigned to the organised grouping of resources or employees that is subject to the relevant transfer, which would otherwise be terminated by the transfer, but any such contract shall have effect after the transfer as if originally made between the person so employed and the transferee.

(2) . . . on the completion of a relevant transfer—

  (a) all the transferor's rights, powers, duties and liabilities under or in connection with any such contract shall be transferred by virtue of this regulation to the transferee; and

  (b) any act or omission before the transfer is completed, of or in relation to the transfer in respect of that contract or a person assigned to that organised grouping of resources or employees, shall be deemed to have been an act or omission of or in relation to the transferee.

---

[98] [2002] IRLR 214. See G. Barrett, 'Light Acquired on Acquired Rights: Examining Developments in Employment Rights on Transfers of Undertakings' (2005) 42 *Common Market Law Review* 1053, 1078–84.

[99] See also *Albron Catering BV v FNV Bondgenoten* [2011] IRLR 76, where there was no contract of employment between the transferring employee and the transferor.

[100] For example, see *Services for Education (S4E) Ltd v White* (UKEAT/0268/13/SM, 10 August 2015).

Regulation 4(1) preserves continuity by deeming the contract of employment not to have been terminated. As such, it is treated as having been entered into between the transferring employee and the transferee. As for the effect of continuity on the contract of employment, regulation 4(2) directs that all rights, powers, duties, and liabilities of the transferor 'under or in connection with' the employment contracts of the transferring employees transfer across to the transferee. Our understanding of the operation of regulation 4(2) is enhanced if we separate the 'duties and liabilities' of the transferor under the employment contract which transfer from the 'rights and powers':

(1) On the 'duties and liabilities' side of the equation, subsequent to a TUPE transfer, the transferor is discharged from all of its obligations under the contracts of employment of the transferring employees from the transfer date.[101] The transferee inherits the employees employed by the transferor immediately before the transfer on the basis of their existing terms and conditions of employment. Since the liability for the discharge of those terms and conditions arises 'under or in connection with [the] contract [of employment of the transferring employees]', it transfers seamlessly across to the transferee who is bound to honour those terms. For example, when a transferee decided to change the salary payment date from the last Thursday to the last day of the calendar month in the case of *Rask and Christensen v ISS Kantineservice A/S*,[102] the ECJ ruled that this was a breach of Article 3 of the Original ARD, notwithstanding that the total sum payable in salary had not changed. This approach is clearly in accordance with the social policy objectives underpinning the statutory provisions, namely that transferring employees should be protected from unapproved contractual variations.

It would not be stretching matters to say that the post-transfer environment may cause friction in employment relations, particularly where the terms and conditions of the transferring employees are less favourable than those of the existing staff of the transferee. The Court of Appeal considered this issue in *Jackson v Computershare*.[103] It held that a transferring employee was disentitled from parity of terms in such circumstances.[104] The requirement that the transferee must honour the terms and conditions of the transferring employees may also lead to practical difficulties. Regulation 4(2) does not specifically address the status of provisions of the contracts of employment of transferring employees which confer benefits based on the annual turnover, annual profit, share price, or overall performance of the transferor, e.g. performance-related bonuses, share options, profit-sharing schemes, etc. Such contractual provisions can be extremely problematic, since the transferee can exert no control over the turnover, net profit, share price, etc. of the transferor. It would appear to flout common sense to expect the transferee to pay bonuses or other remuneration to the transferring employees in such circumstances. In *MITIE Management Services Ltd v French*,[105] Maurice Kay J in the EAT propounded the 'substantial equivalence' test in order to cater for the difficulties engendered by such contractual provisions. This test places the onus on the transferee to ensure that the transferring employees are entitled to participate in benefits which are substantially equivalent to their contractual benefits, duly stripped of the features which make it unjust, absurd, or impossible for the transferee to meet them. To that extent, the test in *MITIE Management Ltd v French* ensures that the contractual rights of the transferring employees are safeguarded by a suitable exchange of provision insofar as that is possible.

---

[101] *Berg and Busschers v Besselsen* [1990] ICR 396.   [102] [1993] IRLR 133.   [103] [2008] ICR 341.

[104] We consider the opposite situation, i.e. where the terms of the transferring employees are more advantageous than the existing staff of the transferee and the transferee attempts to harmonize them, in section 19.3.3.

[105] [2002] ICR 1395. See also *Unicorn Consultancy Services Ltd v Westbrook* [2000] IRLR 80.

The protection afforded by regulation 4(2) of TUPE is not restricted to con-tractual benefits. It has been held that the tortious liability of transferors in negli-gence will transfer to the transferee on the ground that the transferring employee's claim for personal injury at work arises in connection with the contract of employ-ment.[106] On the same grounds, the Court of Appeal decided that liability for breach of statutory duty will transfer to the transferee.[107] Further, both the transferor and transferee will be statutorily liable on a joint and several basis to pay compensation under regulation 15 where the transferor fails to inform and consult appropriate representatives of the transferring employees under regulation 13.[108] Likewise, as we noted in section 19.1.2, the transferee will assume responsibility for outstand-ing legal claims against the transferor in respect of any act or omission of the transferor prior to the completion of the transfer by virtue of regulation 4(2)(b). The effect of this provision is that the transferee will be liable to meet successful discrimination, equal pay, or harassment[109] claims in the employment tribunal or the courts, even though they are attributable to something done by the transferor prior to the transfer date.[110]

Subsequent to the transfer, any collective agreement which has been concluded between the transferor and a recognized trade union is treated as if it was made by or on behalf of the transferee with that trade union and the transferee will be responsi-ble for meeting its terms.[111] A related issue is whether a transferee is bound to comply with periodic post-transfer modifications to a collective agreement which have been struck by the transferor and a trade union. Where the contract of employment of a transferring employee provides that his/her terms and conditions of employment will be in accordance with that collective agreement, as negotiated from time to time, this gives rise to a difficult question where the transferee has no relationship with the relevant trade union. It may seem outlandish to compel a transferee to abide by post-transfer changes to the original collective agreement to which it was not a party. The question is whether a 'static' or 'dynamic' approach should be taken. The former would relieve the transferee of the obligation to meet the post-transfer variations of the collective agreement agreed by the transferor and the trade union, whereas the latter would oblige the transferee to honour such changes.[112] This issue was resolved in *Alemo-Herron v Parkwood Leisure Ltd*.[113] The CJEU rejected the dynamic interpretation on the basis that the transferee had no power to participate in the negotiating process for the new terms of the collective agreement and that to compel it to honour such renegotiated terms in such circumstances would amount to an unjustifiable interference in the transferee's freedom to run a business. As such, the dynamic approach was rejected on the basis that it would infringe the transferee's fundamental right to conduct a business under Article 16 of the EU Charter of Fun-damental Rights.[114] Regulation 4A of TUPE has now codified the decision of the CJEU in *Alemo-Herron*.

---

[106] *Taylor v Serviceteam Ltd* [1998] PIQR P201; *Martin v Lancashire County Council* [2001] ICR 197.
[107] *Martin v Lancashire County Council* [2001] ICR 197.
[108] TUPE, regulation 15(9).
[109] See *Vernon v Azure Support Services* (UKEAT/0192/13/SM, 7 November 2014).
[110] *DJM International Ltd v Nicholas* [1996] ICR 214; *Sodexo Ltd v Gutridge* [2009] ICR 1486.
[111] TUPE, regulation 5.
[112] See the decision of the ECJ in *Werhof v Freeway Traffic Systems GmbH* [2006] IRLR 400, which adopted the static interpretation; cf. *Whent v T Cartledge Ltd* [1997] IRLR 153, in which the EAT took the dynamic approach.
[113] [2013] ICR 1116. See also *Deveci v Scandinavian Airlines System Denmark-Norway-Sweden* [2015] IRLR 138 for a similar decision by the EFTA court and *Asklepios Kliniken Langen-Seligenstadt GmbH v Felja* [2017] IRLR 653.

However, not all of the liabilities of the transferor are conveyed to the transferee. For example, criminal liabilities are excluded by regulation 4(6) of TUPE, as are the liabilities of a transferor in respect of the payment of protective awards for a failure to inform and consult appropriate representatives of employees potentially affected by collective redundancies under Chapter II of Part IV of the Trade Union and Labour Relations (Consolidation) Act 1992 ('TULRCA').[115] Likewise, occupational pension scheme liabilities do not go across to the transferee in terms of regulation 10.[116]

(2) Turning to the 'rights and powers' side of the equation of regulation 4(2) of TUPE, it has been held that the transferor's rights to an indemnity against an insurance company under an employers' liability insurance policy transferred to the transferee in a personal injury claim.[117] Moreover, the rights of the transferor under restrictive covenants will transfer.[118] However, it has been held that a transferee will not be entitled to avail itself of the rights and powers of a transferor under a mobility clause where the geographical area within which the transferring employee could be required to work was restricted.[119]

The next logical issue to consider is who the transferee will inherit in connection with the TUPE transfer. Regulation 4(1) provides for the preservation of the continuity of employment of 'any person employed by the transferor and assigned to the organized grouping of resources or employees that is subject to the relevant transfer'. This is supplemented by regulation 4(3):

Regulation 4 *Effect of relevant transfer on contracts of employment*

(3) Any reference in paragraph (1) to a person employed by the transferor and assigned to the organised grouping of resources or employees that is subject to a relevant transfer, is a reference to a person so employed immediately before the transfer, or who would have been so employed if he had not been dismissed [for the sole or principal reason of the transfer], including, where the transfer is effected by a series of two or more transactions, a person so employed and assigned or who would have been so employed and assigned immediately before any of those transactions.

---

[114] Pronounced on 7 December 2000 in Nice (OJ 2000 C364/1) and a second time in Strasbourg on 12 December 2007 (OJ 2007 C303/1) and also published in OJ 2010 C83/389. For detailed consideration of this decision, see J. Prassl, 'Freedom of Contract as a General Principle of EU Law? Transfers of Undertakings and the Protection of Employer Rights in EU Labour Law: Case C-426/11 *Alemo-Herron and Others v Parkwood Leisure Ltd*' (2013) 42 *Industrial Law Journal* 434.

[115] *Angus Jowett & Co. Ltd v NUTGW* [1985] ICR 646. See Chapter 20, section 20.5. This is on the basis that protective awards do not arise in connection with an employer's duties and liabilities under the contracts of employment of the transferring employees.

[116] However, regulation 10(2) provides that this exception does not apply to 'provisions of an occupational pension scheme which do not relate to benefits for old age, invalidity or survivors'. For example, in *Beckmann v Dynamco Whicheloe Macfarlane Ltd* [2003] ICR 50 (see also *Martin v South Bank University* [2004] ICR 1234; *Proctor & Gamble Co. v Svenska Cellulusa Aktiebolaget SKA* [2012] IRLR 733), early retirement benefits and benefits intended to enhance the conditions of such retirement were payable on the dismissal of employees who had reached a certain age, rather than on the occurrence of 'old age'. The ECJ held that these early retirement benefits were dependent on the occurrence of dismissal and so were not included within the occupational pension scheme liabilities exemption. The end result was that liability for them transferred across to the transferee.

[117] *Martin v Lancashire County Council* [2001] ICR 197.

[118] *Morris Angel & Son Ltd v Hollande* [1993] ICR 71; *Marcroft v Heartland (Midlands) Ltd* [2011] IRLR 599.

[119] *Tapere v South London and Maudsley NHS Trust* [2009] ICR 1563.

The inclusion of the words 'who would have been so employed if he had not been dismissed [for the sole or principal reason of the transfer]' in the statutory provision effectively codifies the decision of the House of Lords in *Litster v Forth Dry Dock Engineering Co. Ltd (in receivership)*.[120] These words remove the possibility of transferors evading the protections afforded to transferring employees by simply dismissing them a few hours or days before the transfer. If we turn to the word 'assigned', this is defined in regulation 2 of TUPE as 'assigned other than on a temporary basis'.[121]

At this juncture, it is opportune to cast our mind back to the common law authority of *Nokes v Doncaster Amalgamated Collieries Ltd*.[122] Whilst the preservation of a transferring employee's continuity of employment post-transfer in terms of regulation 4(1) of TUPE displaces the employee's common law freedom to choose with whom he/she contracts, his/her ability to object to the transfer of his/her employment is specifically recognized and protected by regulation 4(7) and (8).[123] In fact, it has been held that an employee's objection could be valid notwithstanding that it was made after the transfer,[124] but where an employee objects then continues to work for the transferee post-transfer, the courts and tribunals will apply an objective test to treat that objection as ineffective.[125] Regulation 4(7) and (8) are reflective of the decision of the ECJ in *Katsikas v Konstantinidis*.[126] Here, the Court ruled that it was for each of the Member States to determine the legal consequences of an employee's objection. Regulation 4(8) of TUPE provides that the employee's objection terminates the employee's contract of employment, but he/she is not treated as dismissed. This is not particularly satisfactory from the perspective of the employee, since he/she will:

(1) be unable to remain in the employment of the transferor if that is his/her wish;

(2) have no right of redress against the transferee;[127] and

(3) have no grounds for compensation for wrongful or unfair dismissal.

However, there are exceptions where compensation may be claimed. In *Humphreys v Chancellor, Master and Scholars of the University of Oxford*,[128] it was held that the employee may be entitled to compensation for (constructive or actual) wrongful or unfair dismissal (and so regulation 4(8) will be inapplicable) against the transferor. This is on

---

[120] [1990] 1 AC 546. See the contrasting decisions in *G4S Justice Services (UK) Ltd v Anstey* [2006] IRLR 588 and *Bangura v Southern Cross Healthcare Group plc* (UKEAT/0432/12/RN, 12 March 2013) which consider the situation where an employee dismissed by the transferor before the transfer lodges an appeal against dismissal.

[121] The breadth of the word 'assigned' was particularly important in the case of *Marcroft v Heartland (Midlands) Ltd* [2011] IRLR 599. Here, a transferee sought to enforce restraints in restrictive covenants contained within the contract of employment of a transferring employee. The employee claimed that those restraints did not apply since he had handed in notice of termination of his contract of employment and had been put on garden leave by the transferee. His argument ran that he was, therefore, 'assigned on a temporary basis' to the transferee and regulation 4(1) and (3) did not apply. However, Mummery LJ, in the Court of Appeal, rejected the employee's submissions, and held 'that it cannot be right, in principle, that an employee is automatically assigned on a temporary basis, thereby losing the protection of TUPE, simply as a result of handing in his notice': [2011] IRLR 599, 603.

[122] [1940] AC 1014.

[123] For an overview of the employee's right to object, see J. McMullen, 'The "Right" to Object to Transfer of Employment under TUPE' (2008) 37 *Industrial Law Journal* 169; P. Davies, 'Transfers Again: Contracting out and the Employee's Option' (1993) 22 *Industrial Law Journal* 151; and P. Davies, 'Opting out of Transfers' (1996) 25 *Industrial Law Journal* 247.

[124] *New ISG Ltd v Vernon* [2008] ICR 319. This was the case since it was not until after the transfer had occurred that the transferring employees learned of the identity of the transferee.

[125] *Capita v Health Solutions v McLean* [2008] IRLR 595.   [126] [1993] IRLR 179.

[127] However, see *NHS Direct Trust v Gunn* [2015] IRLR 799 for circumstances where it will be possible to raise legal proceedings against the transferee after an employee objected.

[128] [2000] ICR 405. See also *Tapere v South London and Maudsley NHS Trust* [2009] ICR 1563; *Abellio London Ltd v Musse* [2012] IRLR 360.

the ground that the 'substantial change' requirements of regulation 4(9) and (10) have been satisfied:

Regulation 4 Effect of relevant transfer on contracts of employment

(9) Subject to regulation 9, where a relevant transfer involves or would involve a substantial change in working conditions to the material detriment[129] of a person whose contract of employment is or would be transferred under paragraph (1), such an employee may treat the contract of employment as having been terminated, and the employee shall be treated for any purpose as having been dismissed by the employer.

(10) No damages shall be payable by an employer as a result of a dismissal falling within paragraph (9) in respect of any failure by the employer to pay wages to an employee in respect of a notice period which the employee has failed to work.

Rather bizarrely, where employees claim for wrongful dismissal against the transferor under regulation 4(9), regulation 4(10) deprives them of the right to be paid in respect of the notice period, therefore somewhat negating the efficacy of the provisions.[130]

19.3.2 The status of variations to the contract of employment

We referred to the fact that a transferee will often harbour a desire to harmonize the terms and conditions of employment of the transferring employees with those of its existing workforce subsequent to the transfer. It is not unusual for the transferring employees to enjoy more favourable terms than the existing staff. In order to maintain harmony in post-transfer employment relations, and no doubt also for commercial reasons, the question of contractual variations will inevitably have to be addressed. There are two provisions which must be considered in these circumstances.

(1) Regulation 4(11) provides:

Regulation 4 Effect of relevant transfer on contracts of employment

(11) Paragraphs (1), (7), (8) and (9) are without prejudice to any right of an employee arising apart from these Regulations to terminate his contract of employment without notice in acceptance of a repudiatory breach of contract by his employer.

Regulation 4(11) of TUPE is particularly relevant where the transferor makes substantial variations to the terms and conditions of employment of the transferring employees. In such circumstances, a transferring employee will be entitled to treat him/herself as constructively dismissed by the transferor where those variations are so substantially detrimental that they amount to a repudiatory breach of contract by the transferor. It has been held that the liability under regulation 4(11) for constructive dismissal, whether wrongful or unfair, will not pass to the transferee.[131]

---

[129] In *Cetinsoy v London United Busways Ltd* (UKEAT/0042/14/LA, 23 May 2014), a transfer entailed a change of location of the place of work and it was held that this did not constitute a fundamental breach of contract or a substantial change in working conditions to an employee's material detriment.

[130] Regulation 4(10) appears to conflict with the decision of the ECJ in *Mirja Juuri v Fazer Amica Oy* (C-296/07) [2009] 1 CMLR 902. Here, it was suggested that Member States must ensure that an employee is entitled to the payment of salary and other benefits relating to his/her notice period under the contract of employment where he/she claims that there has been a wrongful or unfair dismissal owing to substantial changes in working conditions to his/her material detriment.

[131] *Humphreys v Chancellor, Master and Scholars of the University of Oxford* [2000] ICR 405.

(2) The most significant set of statutory provisions which impinge on variations are found in regulation 4(4), (5), (5A), (5B), and (5C) of TUPE. Subject to various exceptions applicable

(a) in the context of insolvency sales under regulation 9,[132]

(b) where the variation is agreed and for an economic, technical, or organizational ('ETO') reason entailing changes in the workforce,[133]

(c) where the terms of the employment contract expressly permit transfer-related or post-transfer variations,[134] e.g. pursuant to a 'mobility' or 'flexibility' clause,[135] or

(d) where a term of the employment contract is derived from a collective agreement and the contractual variation (i) takes effect more than one year after the date of the transfer and (ii) results in a contract which is overall no less favourable to the employee,[136]

regulation 4(4), (5), (5A), (5B), and (5C) effectively precludes transfer-related or post-transfer modifications of the terms of the contracts of employment of the transferring employees. These provisions are designed to ensure that transferring employees are not penalized post-transfer by being placed on terms and conditions of employment which are inferior to those contained in their pre-transfer employment contract:

Regulation 4 *Effect of relevant transfer on contracts of employment*

(4) Subject to regulation 9, any purported variation of a contract of employment that is, or will be, transferred by paragraph (1), is void if the sole or principal reason for the variation is the transfer.

(5) Paragraph (4) does not prevent a variation to the contract of employment if—

(a) the sole or principal reason for the variation is an [ETO] reason entailing changes in the workforce, provided that the employer and employee agree that variation; or

(b) the terms of that contract permit the employer to make such a variation.

(5A) In paragraph (5) the expression 'changes in the workforce' includes a change to the place where employees are employed by the employer to carry on the business of the employer or to carry out work of a particular kind for the employer (and the reference to such a place has the same meaning as in section 139 of the [ERA]).

(5B) Paragraph (4) does not apply in respect of a variation of contract of employment in so far as it varies a term or condition incorporated from a collective agreement, provided that—

(a) the variation of the contract takes effect on a date more than one year[137] after the date of the transfer; and

(b) following that variation, the rights and obligations in the employee's contract, when considered together, are no less favourable to the employee than those which applied immediately before the variation.

(5C) Paragraphs (5) and (5B) do not affect any rule of law as to whether a contract of employment is effectively varied.

Regulation 4(4) and (5) of TUPE reflects the decision of the ECJ in the seminal cases of *Foreningen af Arbejdsledere I Danmark v Daddy's Dance Hall A/S*[138] and *Rask and Christensen v ISS Kantineservice A/S*,[139] and of the House of Lords in *Wilson v St Helens Borough*

---

[132] See section 19.3.4.   [133] TUPE, regulation 4(5)(a).   [134] TUPE, regulation 4(5)(b).
[135] For examples of these clauses, see Chapter 7, section 7.2.1.   [136] TUPE, regulation 4(5B).
[137] See *Unionen v Almega Tjansteforbunden ISS Facility Services AB* [2017] ICR 909.
[138] [1988] IRLR 315.   [139] [1993] IRLR 133.

Council.[140] In these cases, it was held that a variation of a transferring employee's terms and conditions of employment, which is attributable to the transfer and which is not an ETO reason, is of no legal effect, even though the employee is no worse off overall when the terms of the contract are looked at as a package.[141] Indeed, in the case of *Credit Suisse First Boston (Europe) Ltd v Lister*,[142] subsequent to a TUPE transfer, the transferring employees had agreed with the transferee to the alteration of the terms of their contract to include restrictive covenants which came into play subsequent to the termination of the contracts of employment of the transferring employees. Notwithstanding the fact that the transferring employees had agreed to the restrictive covenants in return for cash payments and free shares, they were held to amount to an unlawful variation for the reason of the transfer and invalid. The outcome was that the employees could escape the operation of the post-termination restraints.

A number of observations can be made in relation to the terms of regulation 4(4), (5), (5A), (5B), and (5C), as follows:

(1) A transferring employee would appear to be denied the benefit of a transfer-related or post-transfer variation which is entirely positive. Subject to the specific exceptions prescribed, the wording of regulation 4(4) and (5) of TUPE renders any transfer-related or post-transfer changes null and void. However, that was not the approach adopted by the Court of Appeal in *Power v Regent Security Services Ltd*.[143] Instead, Mummery LJ referred to the departmental guidance on TUPE issued by the Department for Business Enterprise and Regulatory Reform in March 2007,[144] which stipulated that 'changes to terms and conditions agreed by the parties that are entirely positive are not prevented'.[145] His Lordship also seemed to say that this approach was consistent with the aims of the ARD, i.e. that '[a]n employee's rights on a transfer are not being safeguarded [as the ARD requires] if he/she is prevented from taking the benefit of a term that was agreed with the transferee on or after the transfer'.[146]

(2) Regulation 4(4) and (5) of TUPE would appear to prevent the employee from cherry-picking the most favourable terms from his/her old or new contract of employment, since it explicitly provides for the nullity of any contractual variation for the reason of the transfer. However, serious doubt was also cast on such an interpretation by the Court of Appeal in the case of *Power v Regent Security Services Ltd*,[147] which concerned the interpretation of regulation 5 of TUPE 1981; there is no equivalent provision in TUPE. Here, an employee's pre-transfer employment contract stipulated

---

[140] [1999] 2 AC 52. See J. McMullen, 'TUPE: Waiver of Employment Rights and Contract Changes after *Wilson*' (1999) 28 *Industrial Law Journal* 76.

[141] There is an argument that the decision in *Daddy's Dance Hall* was merely an authority for the proposition that a transferring employee should not be entitled to *waive* his/her rights under the pre-transfer terms and conditions of employment and that subsequent cases have unjustifiably extended that proposition to post-transfer consensual *variations* of terms and conditions of employment: see J. McMullen, 'TUPE: Waiver of Employment Rights and Contract Changes after *Wilson*' (1999) 28 *Industrial Law Journal* 76, 82–4.   [142] [1999] ICR 794.

[143] [2007] EWCA Civ 1188, [2008] ICR 442. For an analysis of the earlier EAT decision in this case, see C. Wynn-Evans, 'The Ongoing Saga of TUPE and Contractual Variations' (2007) 36 *Industrial Law Journal* 480.

[144] See now the January 2014 version of this document entitled *Employment Rights on the Transfer of an Undertaking: A Guide to the 2006 TUPE Regulations (as amended by the Collective Redundancies and Transfer of Undertakings (Protection of Employment) (Amendment) Regulations 2014) for Employees, Employers and Representatives*, available at https://www.gov.uk/government/uploads/system/uploads/attachment_data/file/275252/bis-14–502-employment-rights-on-the-transfer-of-an-undertaking.pdf at page 21 (last visited 22 October 2017).   [145] [2008] ICR 442, 445F per Mummery LJ.

[146] [2008] ICR 442, 449H per Mummery LJ. Contrast this decision with *Credit Suisse First Boston (Europe) Ltd v Lister* [1999] ICR 794.

[147] [2007] EWCA Civ 1188, [2008] ICR 442. For an analysis of the earlier EAT decision in this case, see C. Wynn-Evans, 'The Ongoing Saga of TUPE and Contractual Variations' (2007) 36 *Industrial Law Journal* 480.

that his contractual retiring age was 60. Subsequent to the transfer, the retiring age was increased to the age of 65 and the question was whether the employee had no option but to rely on the pre-transfer contractual retiring age. The Court held that the employee had no power to waive his right to the pre-transfer retiring age of 60, but that he had also obtained an *additional right* to continue working if he wished up to the age of 65. TUPE did not prevent the employee from choosing from both retiring ages and, therefore, the employee had the best of both worlds. In fact, Mummery LJ opined that there was nothing in regulation 4 of TUPE which would preclude the same construction he had reached in respect of regulation 5 of TUPE 1981 when he stated, '[the provisions in TUPE] are not materially different on the particular point raised [in this case]'.[148]

(3) The provisions of regulation 4(4), (5), (5A), (5B), and (5C) do not function to deprive all transfer-related contractual modifications of legal effect, admitting of no derogation. There are a number of ways in which an employer may avoid the operation of regulation 4(4).

    (a) The employer may establish that there is no causal link between the relevant transfer and the contractual variation. Of course, logic dictates that the longer the period from the date of the relevant transfer to the date of the variation, the more likely that supervening events may furnish a reason for the change. However, this avenue is fraught with difficulty for transferees, since in the case of *Taylor v Connex South Eastern Ltd*[149] the EAT took the view that the mere passage of time without more does not in itself constitute a weakening to the point of dissolution of the chain of causation. Here, it was held that it is a question of fact for an employment tribunal to determine whether the effluxion of a period of time has been sufficient to break the chain of causation in any given case. Therefore, there is no 'magic' period of time after which the transferee can consider itself 'safe'.[150]

    (b) Regulation 4(5)(a) and (5A) recognizes the validity of a transfer-related variation where it is for an ETO reason entailing changes in the workforce. The scope of the ETO reason will be addressed in further detail in section 19.3.3.

    (c) Transfer-related variations made in the context of insolvency sales under regulation 9 will be valid.[151]

    (d) Where the terms of the employment contract expressly permit transfer-related or post-transfer variations,[152] e.g. pursuant to a 'mobility' or 'flexibility' clause,[153] these will be treated as valid.

    (e) Where a term of the employment contract is derived from a collective agreement and the contractual variation (i) takes effect more than one year after the date of the transfer and (ii) results in a contract which is overall no less favourable to the employee, regulation 4(5B) directs that the transfer-related or post-transfer modification will be valid.[154]

---

[148] [2008] ICR 442, 445A–B per Mummery LJ.

[149] [2001] Emp LR 72 (EAT). See also *Smith v Trustees of Brooklands College* (UKEAT/0128/11/ZT, 5 September 2011).

[150] In *Smith v Trustees of Brooklands College* (UKEAT/0128/11/ZT, 5 September 2011), it was held that a period of two years and four months was sufficient to sever any causal link, whereas in *Taylor*, even after the period of two years, the variation was deemed to be for the reason of the transfer. See also *Delahaye v Ministre de la Fonction Publique et de la Réforme Administrative* [2005] IRLR 61. In *Enterprise Managed Services Ltd v Dance* (UKEAT/0200/11/DM, 21 September 2011), it was held that if the transferee was subjectively motivated by an intention to vary the contractual terms of a transferring employee in order to increase productivity, rather than purely for reasons of harmonization of contractual terms, this will be sufficient to show that the reason was not the transfer. In such an event, the variation will be effective.

[151] See section 19.3.4.   [152] TUPE, regulation 4(5)(b).

[153] For examples of these clauses, see Chapter 7, section 7.2.1.   [154] TUPE, regulation 4(5B).

(f) Finally, the transferor or transferee can circumvent the applicability of regulation 4(4) by simply dismissing and re-engaging the transferring employees on the new terms and conditions. Whilst superficially attractive, this is by no means an effective solution, since, in the lion's share of cases, the transferor and/or transferee will be liable under regulation 7 to pay compensation in respect of what is treated as an automatically unfair dismissal[155] for the purposes of Part X of the ERA.[156]

19.3.3 The status of dismissals

Regulation 7 of TUPE clarifies the legal effect of a dismissal of a transferring employee for the reason of a TUPE transfer:

> **Regulation 7 Dismissal of employee because of relevant transfer**
>
> (1) Where either before or after a relevant transfer, any employee of the transferor or transferee is dismissed, that employee is to be treated for the purposes of Part [X] of the [ERA] (unfair dismissal) as unfairly dismissed if the sole or principal reason for the dismissal is the transfer.

The rule in regulation 7 of TUPE, that a dismissal for the reason of the TUPE transfer amounts to an automatically unfair dismissal,[157] links in neatly with the prescription in regulation 4(1) that a TUPE transfer itself cannot constitute a dismissal or a repudiatory breach of contract of employment of the transferring employees. However, a question which is not addressed by regulation 7 is whether a transferring employee is entitled to have a court declare that his/her dismissal is null and void. If so, is the employee entitled to continue in employment with the transferee on the basis of his/her pre-transfer terms and conditions?

■ *Wilson v St Helens Borough Council* **[1999] 2 AC 52, 78A–85D**

> *Lord Slynn of Hadley:*
>
> [The terms of regulation 7 of TUPE] seem to me to point to the dismissal being effective and not a nullity. If there is no dismissal there cannot be compensation for unfair dismissal. It is because the dismissal is effective that provision is made for it to be treated as unfair for the purposes of awarding compensation under employment legislation . . . It follows in my opinion that under the Regulations the dismissals are not rendered nullities; nor is there an automatic obligation on the part of the transferee to continue to employ—to find work for—the employees who have been dismissed . . . In my opinion, the overriding emphasis in the [ECJ]'s judgments is that the existing rights of employees are to be safeguarded if there is a transfer. That means no more and no less than that the employee can look to the transferee to perform those obligations which the employee could have enforced against the transferor. The employer, be he transferor or transferee, cannot use the transfer as a justification for dismissal, but if he does dismiss it is a question for national law as to what those rights are. As I have already said, in English law there would as a general rule be no order for specific performance. The claim would be for damages for wrongful dismissal or for statutory rights including, it is true, reinstatement or re-engagement where applicable . . . But neither the Regulations nor the [Original ARD] nor the jurisprudence of the court create a Community law right to continue in

---

[155] See Chapter 16, section 16.2.4.2, for a list of the automatically unfair dismissals prescribed by statute.

[156] The transferor and transferee would only be able to avoid liability if they were able to show that the dismissal was for an ETO reason or for a reason which was not the transfer.

[157] See Chapter 16, section 16.2.4.2, for a list of the automatically unfair dismissals prescribed by statute.

employment which does not exist under national law . . . Where the transferee does not take on the employees who are dismissed on transfer the dismissal is not a nullity though the contractual rights formerly available against the transferor remain intact against the transferee. For the latter purpose, an employee dismissed prior to the transfer contrary to article 4(1) [of the Original ARD], i.e. on the basis of the transfer, is to be treated as still in the employment of the transferor at the date of transfer . . . I do not read, however, [the ECJ jurisprudence] as meaning that the transferee is bound actually to take on an employee who has been dismissed, whether because of the transfer or for independent reasons, and to give him the same work as he had before. [I]f he does take on the employee he takes him on the terms of the employment with the transferor, i.e. there is a deemed novation by the two willing parties. If the transferee does not take on the employee because the latter has already been dismissed by the transferor, or because he himself dismisses the employee on the transfer, then he must meet all of the transferor's contractual and statutory obligations unless (a) the employee objects to being employed by the transferee or (b) the or the principal reason for dismissal is an [ETO] reason entailing changes in the workforce when the employee is not to be treated as unfairly dismissed and when for the purposes of [Part X of the ERA] the employee is to be regarded as having been dismissed for a substantial reason justifying the dismissal as fair.

This extract from *Wilson* underscores the fundamental point that dismissals for the reason of the TUPE transfer are valid and effective in law. As such, the dismissed employee has no right to be reinstated or re-engaged by the transferee.

Lord Slynn also makes reference to the so-called 'ETO reason'.[158] This enables a transferor or transferee to dismiss transferring employees for the reason of the transfer without being burdened with liability for an automatically unfair dismissal. Some guidance on the scope of the ETO reason is furnished in regulation 7(2) and (3) of TUPE:

Regulation 7 Dismissal of employee because of relevant transfer

(2)   This paragraph applies where the sole or principal reason for the dismissal is an [ETO] reason entailing changes in the workforce of either the transferor or the transferee before or after a relevant transfer.

(3)   Where paragraph (2) applies—

(a) paragraph (1) does not apply;

(b) without prejudice to the application of section 98(4) of the [ERA] (test of fair dismissal), for the purposes of sections 98(1) and 135 of [the ERA] (reason for dismissal)—

(i)   the dismissal is regarded as having been for redundancy where section 98(2)(c) of [the ERA] applies; or

(ii) in any other case, the dismissal is regarded as having been for a substantial reason of a kind such as to justify the dismissal of an employee holding the position which that employee held.

(3A) In paragraph (2), the expression 'changes in the workforce' includes a change to the place where employees are employed by the employer to carry on the business of the employer or to carry out work of a particular kind for the employer (and the reference to such a place has the same meaning as in section 139 of [the ERA]).[159]

---

[158] As noted in section 19.3.2, transfer-related contractual variations attributable to an ETO reason entailing changes in the workforce are also treated as valid by virtue of regulation 4(5)(a) and (5A) of TUPE.

[159] These provisions came into force on 31 January 2014 by virtue of regulation 8 of the Collective Redundancies and Transfer of Undertakings (Protection of Employment) (Amendment) Regulations 2014 (SI 2014/16).

This extract from regulation 7 highlights the point that ETO dismissals will not be automatically unfair; instead, they will be considered to be fair dismissals for the reason of redundancy[160] or for 'some other substantial reason'.[161] To that extent, the ETO reason would on first reflection appear to be a potentially useful device for a transferor or transferee, who are both entitled to deploy it as a defence.[162] However, an evaluation of the case law reveals that it has been interpreted particularly narrowly by the courts and tribunals. For example, it has been held that the words 'entailing changes in the workforce' impose a requirement upon the transferee to alter the structure of the workforce by modifying the functions which the staff undertake or by reducing the numbers of individuals.[163] As such, if there is no variation in the composition of the workforce, e.g. through a diminution in the numbers required to discharge the function, the ETO defence will not be triggered.[164] The effect is that, in the absence of function-related modifications or reductions in workforce numbers, it will not be possible to invoke the ETO defence.[165] This narrow judicial approach to the ETO defence has served to confine its operation within limited bounds. However, the restrictive interpretation of the ETO defence has been offset to some extent by three particular factors:

(1) it has been held that if a change in the numbers of the workforce leads to alterations in their contractual terms, this may constitute grounds for the invocation of the ETO defence;[166]

(2) it is not wholly necessary that the changes affect the entirety of the workforce and it is sufficient that they apply merely to the transferring employees;[167] and

(3) regulation 7(3A) enables an employer to defend a dismissal for an ETO reason where the transfer entails a change in location.[168]

19.3.4 **The special case of insolvency**

One of the principal policy aims of the UK Parliament in introducing insolvency laws in recent years has been to foster the 'rescue culture'. This is a philosophy which seeks to provide support to businesses and companies in financial distress, and to make them more attractive to potential purchasers. It has been argued that employment protection laws applicable on the transfer of an undertaking operate in direct conflict with the 'rescue culture' by obstructing efficiency-enhancing restructurings and reorganizations which

---

[160] See Chapter 18, section 18.2.2.   [161] See Chapter 16, section 16.2.4.3.5.

[162] *Jules Dethier Equipement v Dassy* [1998] ICR 541.

[163] *Berriman v Delabole Slate Ltd* [1985] ICR 546; *Whitehouse v Chas A Blatchford & Sons Ltd* [2000] ICR 542; *Spaceright Europe Ltd v Baillavoine* [2012] 2 All ER 812; *Osborne v Capita Business Services Ltd* (UKEAT/0048/16/RN, 17 June 2016). It is also a requirement that the reduction in the numbers is designed to continue the business, rather than to make it more attractive to an identified buyer in the context of an insolvency sale: *Spaceright Europe Ltd v Baillavoine* [2012] All ER 812. This impedes the ability of administrators to dismiss for an ETO reason, meaning that liability for such a dismissal will transfer to the transferee. However, where the administrator has no buyer in mind when he/she decides to reduce the workforce, but his/her ultimate objective is to enable the business to carry on trading, this will be sufficient to enable him/her to avail him/herself of the ETO exception: *Kavanagh v Crystal Palace FC (2000) Ltd* [2014] ICR 251, on which, see C. Wynn-Evans, 'TUPE and Mothballs: *Crystal Palace FC Limited and Another v Kavanagh and Others* [2014] IRLR 139, CA' (2014) 43 *Industrial Law Journal* 185.

[164] For example, where the employee's duties are distributed among existing members of staff so that there is no diminution in numbers: *Davies v Droylsden Academy* (UKEAT/0044/16/BA, 11 October 2016).

[165] *Manchester College v Hazel* [2014] ICR 989. For a discussion of *Manchester College*, see J. McMullen, 'TUPE, Variation of Employment Terms, and the ETO Reason' (2014) 43 *Industrial Law Journal* 364.

[166] *Crawford v Swinton Insurance Brokers Ltd* [1990] ICR 85.

[167] *Nationwide Building Society v Benn* [2010] IRLR 922.

[168] This overrules the decision of the EAT in *Abellio London Ltd v Musse* [2012] IRLR 360 and *NSL v Besagni* [2014] ICR 1008.

otherwise may have functioned to preserve employment.[169] However, research conducted by Armour and Deakin prior to the introduction of the current incarnation of the insolvency provisions now found in TUPE suggested that the position was more complex. Armour and Deakin's findings provide support for the proposition that whilst employment protection laws on the transfer of an undertaking constrain 'the scope for destructive reorganizations which generate financial gains for shareholders and managers only by extracting rents from employees and other long-term stakeholders', the pervasiveness of this 'positive effect depend[ed] on the extent to which employment protection rights are adjustable through bargaining, both within and between the different stakeholder groups at, or around the time of, the transfer'.[170] Since the publication of Armour and Deakin's research, regulations 8 and 9 of TUPE now provide for the adjustment of contractual terms of transferring employees in the context of certain insolvency sales. This injects a measure of flexibility into TUPE in order to ensure that more businesses are saved.

The current 'compromise' between the competing policy aims of employment protection and fostering the rescue culture now finds its expression in Article 5 of the ARD and regulations 8 and 9 of TUPE. Regulation 8(7) provides as follows:

Regulation 8 Insolvency

(7) Regulations 4 and 7 do not apply to any relevant transfer where the transferor is the subject of bankruptcy proceedings or any analogous insolvency proceedings which have been instituted with a view to the liquidation of the assets of the transferor and are under the supervision of an insolvency practitioner.

Where regulation 8(7) of TUPE applies,[171] transferring employees are denied protection from dismissal. Furthermore, the relative rights, powers, duties, and liabilities arising under the contracts of employment of the transferring employees are not transferred to the transferee. However, the obligations to inform and consult under regulations 11–16 of TUPE are not affected and remain intact. We can see that regulation 8(7) focuses on the end-result of the relevant insolvency proceedings. Its terms are sufficiently broad to cover the sale of an entity's business and assets where it has formally entered into creditors' voluntary or compulsory liquidation proceedings with the clear intention of terminating the existence of that entity. But why should the safeguards in regulations 4 and 7 be disapplied where the transferor is in liquidation?

■ C. Wynn-Evans, 'TUPE, Administration and the Rescue Culture: *OTG Limited v Barke & Others* and Consolidated Appeals' (2011) 40 *Industrial Law Journal* 451, 452–3

A liquidation has the objective of the disposal of the relevant assets. The collective interests of the employees are seen as best served in such circumstances by disapplying the protection of [TUPE] on the basis that the obligation to take on the entire workforce on the same terms might operate as a disincentive to potential purchasers of the business as a going concern. On this analysis, the

---

[169] H. Collins, 'Transfer of Undertakings and Insolvency' (1989) 18 *Industrial Law Journal* 144, 157–8; S. Frisby, 'TUPE or not TUPE: Employee Protection, Corporate Rescue and One Unholy Mess' (2000) 4 *Company Financial and Insolvency Law Review* 249.

[170] J. Armour and S. Deakin, 'Insolvency and Employment Protection: The Mixed Effects of the Acquired Rights Directive' (2003) 22 *International Review of Law and Economics* 443, 445.

[171] It has been held that regulation 8(7) is only triggered once the relevant insolvency practitioner has been formally appointed: *Ward Brothers (Malton) Ltd v Middleton* (UKEAT/0249/13/RN, 16 October 2013).

risk of the dismissal of some employees and the diminution of terms for others who are retained is preferable to the relevant staff all losing their jobs.

The question whether insolvency processes such as administration, which are governed by Schedule B1 to the Insolvency Act 1986, are included within regulation 8(7) has generated a great deal of debate. The Government's opinion was that regulation 8(7) would not apply in the context of a buy-out from a company in administration and so the protections contained in regulations 4 and 7 would be applicable.[172] The Government's position was endorsed in *Key2Law (Surrey) LLP v De'Antiquis*[173] by the Court of Appeal. The Court of Appeal applied an 'absolute approach' by ruling that administration would never fall within regulation 8(7) of TUPE. As such, it was recognized that the objective of administration differs from that of liquidation, and the requirements of regulations 4 and 7 will always be engaged in the case of administration. The end-result is that pre-transfer employment liabilities are conveyed to transferees where there is a transfer by an administrator. However, in the context of a 'pre-pack' administration, where part of the business and assets of a transferor company in administration is sold to a pre-arranged transferee immediately on the appointment of an insolvency practitioner as an administrator,[174] it is controversial that the protections of regulations 4 and 7 should be engaged where the emphasis is on saving a good business from collapse.[175] Since transferees are bound to take on such pre-transfer liabilities, the danger is that this will discourage the operation of the 'rescue culture'.[176]

Reflection points

1. Do you agree with the approach in *Key2Law* which makes a distinction between liquidation and administration? Bearing in mind the respective objectives of liquidation and administration, is this bifurcation sustainable?

2. If so, on what basis? If not, why not?

3. Now consider the other insolvency proceedings in UK law, such as receivership and company voluntary arrangements ('CVAs') under sections 1–7B of the Insolvency Act 1986, in light of their objectives. Would these processes fall within the scope of regulation 8(7) of TUPE and what would the outcome be?

Regulation 8(1)–(6) of TUPE functions to mitigate some of the factors which disincentivize the rescue of businesses in administration or other non-terminal insolvency proceedings such as a CVA. It does so because administration and other non-terminal insolvency

---

[172] See Department for Business, Innovation and Skills, *Guidance on the Transfer of Undertakings (Protection of Employment) Regulations 2006: Redundancy and Insolvency Payments* (June 2006) 2–3.

[173] [2012] ICR 881. This is also the legal position under EU Law and the ARD: *Federatie Nederlandse Vakvereniging v Smallsteps BV* [2017] IRLR 852.

[174] See K. Creighton-Selvay, 'Pre-packed Administrations: An Empirical Rights Analysis' (2013) 42 *Industrial Law Journal* 85; J. McMullen, 'Re-structuring and TUPE' (2012) 41 *Industrial Law Journal* 358.

[175] See C. Wynn-Evans, 'TUPE, Administration and the Rescue Culture: *OTG Limited v Barke & Others* and Consolidated Appeals' (2011) 40 *Industrial Law Journal* 451, 451–2, for a discussion of the merits and demerits of pre-pack administrations and why they are so controversial.

[176] See the pre-*Key2Law* decision of *Oakland v Wellswood (Yorkshire) Ltd* [2009] IRLR 250, where the EAT applied a 'fact-based' approach whereby it was held that whether regulation 8(7) applies to a particular transfer of a business and assets where the transferor is in administration depends on the intentions of the administrator in each case. This was overruled by *Key2Law*.

proceedings in UK law qualify as 'relevant insolvency proceedings' under regulation 8(6). By virtue of regulation 8(1)–(5), the Secretary of State for Business, Energy and Industrial Strategy is liable to pick up certain debts of the transferor in such circumstances out of the National Insurance Fund:

Regulation 8 Insolvency

(1) If at the time of a relevant transfer the transferor is subject to relevant insolvency proceedings paragraphs (2) to (6) apply.

(2) In this regulation 'relevant employee' means an employee of the transferor—

   (a) whose contract of employment transfers to the transferee by virtue of the operation of these Regulations; or

   (b) whose employment with the transferor is terminated before the time of the relevant transfer in the circumstances described in regulation 7(1).

(3) The relevant statutory scheme specified in paragraph (4)(b) . . . shall apply in the case of a relevant employee irrespective of the fact that the qualifying requirement that the employee's employment has been terminated is not met and for those purposes the date of the transfer shall be treated as the date of the termination and the transferor shall be treated as the employer.

(4) . . . the 'relevant statutory schemes' are—

   (a) Chapter VI of Part XI of the [ERA];

   (b) Part XII of the [ERA].

(5) Regulation 4 shall not operate to transfer liability for the sums payable to the relevant employee under the relevant statutory schemes.

(6) In this regulation 'relevant insolvency proceedings' means insolvency proceedings which have been opened in relation to the transferor not with a view to the liquidation of the assets of the transferor and which are under the supervision of an insolvency practitioner.

Lord Justice Rimer explained the operation of these provisions in *Key2Law (Surrey) LLP v De'Antiquis*:[177]

■ *Key2Law (Surrey) LLP v De'Antiquis* [2012] ICR 881, 888F–889E

Rimer LJ:

The intended workings of regulation 8 are not immediately self-evident but they received a typically luminous explanation from Elias J when President of the Employment Appeal Tribunal. In *Secretary of State for Trade and Industry v Slater* [2008] ICR 54, Elias J explained 'the rationale behind regulation 8' as follows . . .

   [']15. Regulation 8 . . . aims to relieve transferees of the burdens which would otherwise apply in certain defined circumstances.

   16. Essentially this is done in two quite distinct ways. The most extensive exception from the effect of the Regulations is created by regulation 8(7) . . . A narrower exception is carved out where regulation 8(6) applies. This applies to insolvency proceedings where the purpose is *not* with a view to liquidation of assets. This does not altogether exclude, but it does modify, the effects of regulations 4 and 7. It means that the transferee does not pick up all of the liabilities which would otherwise transfer to him . . .

---

[177] [2012] ICR 881.

> 18. Regulation 8(3) has the effect of making the Secretary of State liable for all obligations still outstanding at the date of transfer which are caught by Part XII of [the ERA]. There is a deemed dismissal at that stage for purposes of fixing those liabilities even though there has been no actual dismissal. However, to the extent that the liabilities exceed the statutory limits, liability transfers to the transferee.
>
> 19. Regulation 8(5) has the effect of making the [National Insurance F]und rather than the transferee liable to meet any redundancy liabilities . . . these will typically arise where there are dismissals for redundancy which are not for [ETO] reasons . . . [']

This extract from *Key2Law* clarifies that regulation 8(1)–(6) operates to make the Secretary of State liable for certain classes of employment debts via the National Insurance Fund. The classes of debts covered include the transferor's accrued liabilities in respect of unpaid redundancy payments, six weeks' holiday pay, the basic award for unfair dismissal, eight weeks' arrears of pay (subject to a cap at £508 per week), and pay in lieu of the minimum statutory notice period in section 86 of the ERA (also capped at £508 per week).[178]

An administrator or an insolvency practitioner appointed pursuant to non-terminal insolvency proceedings may also disapply the rule in *Foreningen af Arbejdsledere I Danmark v Daddy's Dance Hall A/S*[179] and *Wilson v St Helens Borough Council*[180] that nullifies any transfer-related variations of the terms and conditions of transferring employees. The relevant provisions are now found in regulation 9 of TUPE as follows:

> **Regulation 9 Variations of contract where transferors are subject to relevant insolvency proceedings**
>
> (1) If at the time of a relevant transfer the transferor is subject to relevant insolvency proceedings these Regulations shall not prevent the transferor or transferee (or an insolvency practitioner) and appropriate representatives of assigned employees agreeing to permitted variations . . .
>
> (7) In this regulation—
>
> 'permitted variation' is a variation to the contract of employment of an assigned employee where—
>
> (a) the sole or principal reason for the variation is the transfer and not a reason referred to in regulation 4(5)(a); and
>
> (b) it is designed to safeguard employment opportunities by ensuring the survival of the undertaking, business or part of the undertaking or business that is the subject of the relevant transfer.
>
> 'relevant insolvency proceedings' has the meaning given to the expression by regulation 8(6).

Regulation 9 of TUPE is motivated by a desire to enable businesses in administration or other non-terminal insolvency proceedings to be made more attractive to prospective purchasers, by allowing administrators to strip out and remove terms and conditions of employment of employees of a transferor which are financially onerous for acquirers

---

[178] The Secretary of State will only be responsible for accrued liabilities, in the sense that it is a requirement that liability for the relevant debts must have crystallized prior to the transfer in order to fall within the State guarantee: *Secretary of State for Business, Innovation and Skills v Dobrucki* (UKEAT/0505/13/JOJ, 3 February 2015). Therefore, when a transferee wrongfully and unfairly dismissed a transferring employee subsequent to the transfer in the case of *Pressure Coolers Ltd v Molloy* [2012] ICR 51, the Secretary of State was not liable for the employee's basic award and notice pay, which passed to the transferee.
[179] [1988] IRLR 315.   [180] [1999] 2 AC 52.

to honour. By permitting such contractual terms to be revised in more business-friendly terms with the agreement of appropriate employee representatives, the aspiration is that purchasers will come forward and be found for good businesses in financial difficulty. Thus, the likelihood increases that businesses in administration will be able to be sold quickly, saving jobs in the long run. The protection for the transferring employees lies in the specific direction that the permitted variation must be 'designed to safeguard employment opportunities by ensuring the survival of the undertaking'. As such, if the objective of the variation is simply to make the business of the transferor in administration more attractive to a purchaser who has no intention of protecting employment opportunities post-transfer, the provisions of regulation 9 will not apply.

Regulation 9(1) of TUPE is extremely unusual in that it explicitly enables the transferor, transferee, administrator, or other insolvency practitioner, where the transferor is in a non-terminal insolvency process, to agree modifications to the contracts of employment of the transferring employees without the latter's consent. So long as those changes are agreed with the appropriate representatives of the transferring employees, they are valid. Regulation 9(2)–(6) defines 'appropriate representatives' in the same way as that applicable in the context of the transferor's statutory duty to inform and consult under regulation 13, namely trade union representatives and employee representatives elected for that purpose or for purposes other than that served by TUPE where they have authority from the transferring employees to agree permitted variations.[181]

 For additional reading on the legal implications of a 'relevant transfer', visit the Online Resources for this book at www.oup.com/uk/cabrelli3e/

19.4 INFORMATION AND CONSULTATION OBLIGATIONS AND OTHER OBLIGATIONS

The final piece of the statutory jigsaw regulating the transfers of undertakings involves the imposition of obligations on transferors to:

(1) inform and consult with trade union or employee representatives about the transfer; and

(2) furnish particular details about the transferring employees to the transferee prior to the transfer.

The information and consultation obligations reflect a conscious policy decision adopted by the European Community in the 1970s to introduce a measure of collectivization into the commercial decision-making processes of corporations in the context of business disposals and acquisitions. This policy is also encountered in other issue-specific and economic contexts, which is a point to which we will return in Chapter 20, when we explore the duties applicable in the context of collective redundancies. Meanwhile, the latter obligation which entails a requirement on transferors to notify transferees about various details concerning transferring employees, was introduced in 2006. It implemented a policy objective of Government which sought to incentivize transferors to consult prior to the transfer.

---

[181] There is a fatal defect in the architecture of regulation 9, since the employees can make a conscious decision to avoid its operation if the transferor does not recognize a trade union and the employees steadfastly refuse to elect employee representatives in accordance with the mechanisms set out in regulation 14: in such a case, there is no room for the transferor, transferee, administrator, or other insolvency practitioner to conclude 'permitted variations'.

19.4.1 Information and consultation obligations

The duty to inform and consult finds its expression in regulations 13–16 of TUPE. The primary obligation to inform is contained in regulation 13(2) and the duty to consult is prescribed in regulation 13(6). We first turn to consider regulation 13(1) and (2):

Regulation 13 Duty to inform and consult representatives

(1) In this regulation and regulations 13A, 14 and 15 references to affected employees, in relation to a relevant transfer, are to any employees of the transferor or the transferee (whether or not assigned to the organised grouping of resources or employees that is the subject of a relevant transfer) who may be affected by the transfer or may be affected by measures taken in connection with it . . .

(2) Long enough before a relevant transfer to enable the employer of any affected employees to consult the appropriate representatives of any affected employees, the employer shall inform those representatives of—

   (a) the fact that the transfer is to take place, the date or proposed date of the transfer and the reasons for it;

   (b) the legal, economic and social implications of the transfer for any affected employees;

   (c) the measures which he envisages he will, in connection with the transfer, take in relation to any affected employees or, if he envisages that no measures will be so taken, that fact; and

(d) if the employer is the transferor, the measures, in connection with the transfer, which he envisages the transferee will take in relation to any affected employees who will become employees of the transferee after the transfer by virtue of regulation 4 or, if he envisages that no measures will be so taken, that fact . . .

A close inspection of the terms of regulation 13(1) and (2) reveals that the obligation to provide the information to the appropriate representatives is not confined to the transferor. The definition of 'affected employees' specifically directs that it includes employees of the transferor or the transferee who may be affected by the transfer or measures adopted in connection with it. As such, the duty to inform is also imposed on the transferee. Indeed, in the case of *UNISON v Somerset County Council*,[182] it was held that the definition of 'affected employees' is not sufficiently broad to cover all those employees of the transferor who might be in a position to apply for a vacancy in the part of the undertaking which has been transferred.

Turning now to the terms of regulation 13(2), we should be clear that it is not only information which the transferor and transferee must divulge to the appropriate representatives. In particular, regulation 13(2)(b), (c), and (d) envisages the transferors and transferees advancing *opinions and views* about the effects of the TUPE transfer and any measures that the transferor or the transferee will put in place in connection with it. In the case of *Royal Mail Group Ltd v Communication Workers Union*,[183] the question arose as to how accurate and true the views expressed by the transferors and transferees must be in order to satisfy the requirements of regulation 13. The Court of Appeal adopted a particularly low threshold by applying a subjective test. Waller LJ held that the transferor's or transferee's opinion of the legal implications of the transfer does not need to be legally accurate or warranted as true in order to satisfy regulation 13(2)(b); so long as the employer had described what it genuinely believed to be the legal, social, and economic implications of the transfer, that would suffice. The effect of this rule is that a transferor or transferee will not be liable for a failure to inform and consult if it

---

[182] [2010] IRLR 207.   [183] [2010] ICR 83.

makes a genuine mistake as to what the legal implications of the transfer may be. Furthermore, in relation to the matters prescribed in regulation 13(2)(c) and (d), namely the measures which the transferors and transferees envisage they will take in connection with the transfer, it was also held that these are matters for the genuine belief of the employers.

The information prescribed in regulation 13(2) of TUPE must be furnished by the transferor to the appropriate representatives of the affected employees prior to the relevant transfer[184] by physical delivery, post, or being posted to the relevant trade union where the appropriate representatives are appointed by the trade union.[185] However, regulation 13(4) imposes certain requirements on the transferee by compelling it to furnish information to the transferor at such a time as will enable the transferor to comply with its duties under regulation 13(2)(d). Furthermore, it has been held that the duty to provide information in regulation 13(2) is engaged irrespective of whether the duty to consult in regulation 13(6) is applicable or not.[186] This interpretation of the interaction between regulation 13(2) and (6) ensures that the appropriate representatives of the transferring affected employees are given some basic information about the fact of the transfer, the reasons for it, and its date of completion as a minimum requirement in all cases of a TUPE transfer, i.e. those in which mandatory consultation is triggered under regulation 13(6) and those in which it is not. It also renders it more certain that any voluntary consultation process instigated by the transferor or transferee is meaningful.

The identity of the appropriate representatives of the affected employees is governed by regulation 13(3) of TUPE. This stipulates that these representatives will be trade union representatives or employee representatives elected for that purpose in terms of the provisions for election in regulation 14, or for purposes other than that served by TUPE where they have authority from the transferring employees to be informed and consulted.[187] If there are no trade union representatives in place, the transferor and transferee are obliged to invite the affected employees to elect employee representatives under regulation 14 for this purpose.[188] However, where the transferor or transferee has invited any affected employees to elect representatives and they fail to do so within a reasonable time, the transferor and transferee are not relieved of their obligations to inform; instead, the information and opinions referred to in regulation 13(2) must be submitted to the affected employees individually.[189] Regulation 13(8) requires the transferor and transferee to afford the appropriate representatives access to any affected employee, as well as accommodation and other facilities as may be appropriate.

The provisions for consultation with the appropriate representatives are set out in regulation 13(6) and (7) of TUPE:

Regulation 13 Duty to inform and consult representatives

(6) An employer of an affected employee who envisages that he will take measures in relation to an affected employee, in connection with the relevant transfer, shall consult the appropriate representatives of that employee with a view to seeking their agreement to the intended measures.

---

[184] If there is no relevant transfer, there can be no breach of regulation 13(2): *I Lab Facilities Ltd v Metcalfe* [2013] IRLR 605.

[185] TUPE, regulation 13(5).   [186] *Cable Realisations Ltd v GMB Northern* [2010] IRLR 42.

[187] For example, representatives of the employees elected for the purposes of information and consultation in respect of the collective redundancy provisions in terms of section 188(1B) of TULRCA, on which see Chapter 20, section 20.3.1.7.

[188] *Howard v Milrise Ltd* [2005] ICR 435.   [189] TUPE, regulation 13(1) and (11).

(7) In the course of those consultations the employer shall—

    (a) consider any representations made by the appropriate representatives; and

    (b) reply to those representations and, if he rejects any of those representations, state his reasons.

Subject to the exception for 'micro-businesses'[190] prescribed in regulation 13A, which applies to transfers taking place after 31 July 2014, both the transferor and transferee are under an obligation to consult with their workforces prior to the transfer. However, this does not extend to imposing an obligation on transferees to consult with appropriate representatives of the transferring employees after the transfer in respect of measures it is proposing to take in relation to them.[191] Regulation 13(6) also clarifies that the 'trigger point' for the commencement of consultation hinges on whether the transferor or transferee 'envisages that he will take measures in relation to an affected employee, in connection with the relevant transfer'. In the case of *Todd v Strain*,[192] Underhill J in the EAT ruled that the word 'measures' in regulation 13(6) of TUPE includes 'any action, step or arrangement' which is 'deliberately done by the transferor over and above what necessarily occurs as a consequence of the transfer itself'.[193] Moreover, it was decided that it is not necessary that the measures be disadvantageous to the affected employees in order to trigger the requirement to consult. Ultimately, in holding that post-transfer changes to payment arrangements with which the employees were familiar triggered the obligation to consult, Underhill J opined that there will be a fine line to be drawn between 'measures' which trigger the consultation obligations and those which do not.

As for the scope of the consultation, regulation 13(6) refers back to the 'intended measures'. Therefore, the logical conclusion which can be drawn is that consultation must be about the relevant actions, steps, or arrangements which the transferor envisages taking and that the process should be conducted 'with a view to seeking . . . agreement'. Thus, it is not necessary that agreement is reached, but merely that the consultation procedure has such agreement as its objective.

It ought to be mentioned that the EU Commission issued a Consultation Paper in April 2015 proposing to strengthen the information and consultation obligations contained in the Collective Redundancies Directive.[194] Its intention is to harmonize the meaning of 'information and consultation' across each of the ARD, the Collective Redundancies Directive,[195] and the Information and Consultation of Employees Directive.[196] In essence, the proposal is to introduce more stringent information and consultation obligations which are in line with the more extensive definitions of 'information and consultation' set out in the Recast European Works Councils Directive.[197] However, at the time of writing, the precise content and nature of the adjustments had not been specified.

Subject to the discretion of the employment tribunal to increase the requisite period on grounds of lack of reasonable practicability, the appropriate representatives or the affected employees[198] have a period of three months from the date of completion of the relevant transfer to present a complaint against the transferor or transferee to the employment tribunal for a breach of the duty to inform and consult.[199] The consequences of

---

[190] This is an employer with fewer than ten employees: regulation 13A(1)(a).

[191] *Amicus v City Building (Glasgow) LLP* [2009] IRLR 253.

[192] [2011] IRLR 11.   [193] *ibid.*, 15.

[194] See EU Commission Consultation Document (Brussels, 10 April 2015, C(2015) 2303 final).

[195] Directive 98/59/EC (OJ 1998 L225/16).   [196] Directive 2002/14/EC (OJ 2002 L80/29).

[197] Directive 2009/38/EC (OJ 2009 L122/28).

[198] TUPE, regulation 15(1) prescribes the circumstances in which employee representatives, trade union representatives, or the affected employees will have standing to present the complaint, as the case may be.

[199] TUPE, regulation 15(2).

the employment tribunal finding that there has been a breach of duty are spelt out in the following provisions of regulations 15 and 16 of TUPE:

Regulation 15 Failure to inform or consult

(7) Where the tribunal finds a complaint against a transferee under paragraph (1) well-founded it shall make a declaration to that effect and may order the transferee to pay appropriate compensation to such descriptions of affected employees as may be specified in the award.

(8) Where the tribunal finds a complaint against a transferor under paragraph (1) well-founded it shall make a declaration to that effect and may—

(a) order the transferor, subject to paragraph (9), to pay appropriate compensation to such descriptions of affected employees as may be specified in the award . . .

(9) The transferee shall be jointly and severally liable with the transferor in respect of compensation payable under sub-paragraph (8)(a) . . .

Regulation 16 Failure to inform or consult: supplemental . . .

(3) 'Appropriate compensation' in regulation 15 means such sum not exceeding thirteen weeks' pay[200] for the employee in question as the tribunal considers just and equitable having regard to the seriousness of the failure of the employer to comply with his duty.

In the case of *Sweetin v Coral Racing*,[201] the EAT decided that tribunals and courts should adopt the same approach as that applied by the Court of Appeal in *Susie Radin v GMB*[202] when they seek to calculate the compensation to be awarded in terms of these provisions. The position in *Susie Radin* is to start with the maximum period of 13 weeks' pay where there has been no information and consultation, and then to apply a discount only if there are mitigating circumstances justifying a reduction to an extent which the tribunal considers appropriate. As such, where there has been a complete failure on the part of the transferor or transferee to inform and consult in terms of regulation 13, the starting point is that an award of 13 weeks' pay should be made. The effect of this rule is that the transferor or transferee will be given some credit for the fact that it has, or they have, engaged in something of an (albeit not a complete) information and consultation process, and the award will be reduced accordingly. For example, in *Todd v Strain*,[203] compensation was fixed at seven weeks' pay where the transferor had completely failed to observe the information and consultation requirements of regulation 13, but had informally provided information to the transferring employees.

19.4.2 Notification obligations

Regulations 11 and 12 of TUPE provide machinery for transferees to attain information from the transferors about the transferring employees within a period of not less than 28 days of the relevant transfer.[204] These provisions are designed to 'help the [transferee] to prepare for the arrival of the transferred employees, and the employees also gain because

---

[200] In *Zaman v Kozee Sleep Products Ltd* [2011] IRLR 196, it was held that there is no cap applicable in respect of the amount of a week's pay. See also TUPE, regulation 16(4), for the calculation date in respect of a week's pay, and J. McMullen, 'An Analysis of the Transfer of Undertakings (Protection of Employment) Regulations 2006' (2006) 35 *Industrial Law Journal* 113, 138, for a general discussion of the issues.   [201] [2006] IRLR 252.

[202] [2004] ICR 893.   [203] [2011] IRLR 11.   [204] TUPE, regulation 11(6).

[the transferee] is made aware of his inherited obligations towards them'.[205] Thus, the transferors and transferees are afforded sufficient incentive to engage in pre-transfer consultation. Regulation 11 provides as follows:

> **Regulation 11 Notification of employee liability information**
>
> (1) The transferor shall notify to the transferee the employee liability information of any person employed by him who is assigned to the organised grouping of resources or employees that is the subject of a relevant transfer—
>
>   (a) in writing; or
>
>   (b) by making it available to him in a readily accessible form.
>
> (2) ... 'employee liability information' means—
>
>   (a) the identity and age of the employee;
>
>   (b) those particulars of employment that an employer is obliged to give to an employee pursuant to section 1 of the [ERA];[206]
>
>   (c) information of any—
>
>   (i) disciplinary procedure taken against an employee;
>
>   (ii) grievance procedure taken by an employee,
>
> within the previous two years, in circumstances where a Code of Practice issued under Part IV of [TULRCA] which relates exclusively or primarily to the resolution of disputes applies;
>
>   (d) information of any court or tribunal case, claim or action—
>
>   (i) brought by an employee against the transferor, within the previous two years;
>
>   (ii) that the transferor has reasonable grounds to believe that an employee may bring against the transferee, arising out of the employee's employment with the transferor; and
>
>   (e) information of any collective agreement which will have effect after the transfer, in its application in relation to the employee, pursuant to regulation 5(a).
>
> (3) Employee liability information shall contain information as at a specified date not more than fourteen days before the date on which the information is notified to the transferee...

Where there is a failure on the part of the transferor to comply with the requirements of regulation 11, regulation 12 states that the transferee may present a complaint to an employment tribunal. However, regulation 11 imposes no liability on a transferee to the employees affected by the transfer, who will have no right to directly sue the transferee.[207] The general rule is that the transferee has a period of three months from the date of the relevant transfer to lodge a complaint under regulation 12. If the employment tribunal finds that the complaint is well-founded, it has the power to make an award of compensation compelling the transferor to pay a sum to the transferee which it considers just and equitable in all the circumstances, having regard to the transferee's loss. Moreover, the

---

[205] See the January 2014 version of this document entitled *Employment Rights on the Transfer of an Undertaking: A Guide to the 2006 TUPE Regulations (as amended by the Collective Redundancies and Transfer of Undertakings (Protection of Employment) (Amendment) Regulations 2014) for Employees, Employers and Representatives*, available at https://www.gov.uk/government/uploads/system/uploads/attachment_data/file/275252/bis-14–502-employment-rights-on-the-transfer-of-an-undertaking.pdf at pages 31–2 (last visited 21 October 2017).

[206] See *Born London Ltd v Spire Production Services Ltd* [2017] IRLR 493 concerning the contractual and non-contractual status of such particulars/terms.

[207] *Allen v Morrisons Facilities Services Ltd* [2014] IRLR 514.

employment tribunal must have regard to the terms of any contract between the transfer-or and the transferee in relation to the sale and acquisition of the business. The minimum threshold of any award of compensation is £500 per employee, unless the employment tribunal considers it just and equitable, in all the circumstances, to award a lesser sum.

19.5 FINAL ASSESSMENT OF TUPE

It is by no stretch of the imagination an exaggeration to say that the provisions of the ARD and TUPE have served to enhance greatly the rights of employees on the transfer of the business and assets of their employer. This is in no small measure attributable to the breadth of the 'service provision change' concept, which was introduced in 2006 in order to inject a degree of certainty into the law by clarifying the circumstances in which TUPE would apply in the context of outsourcing arrangements. As we have noted, the great majority of cases of contracting out, contracting in, changes of service provider, and outsourcing arrangements will qualify as a 'service provision change' given the degree of latitude in the definition of that concept in regulation 3(1) of TUPE. However, at the margins, some uncertainty remains. Further, whilst the introduction of that concept has undoubtedly enhanced transparency and the certainty of application of the protections in TUPE, it has been subjected to a great deal of criticism on the ground that it amounts to the 'gold-plating' of EU case law, which instead requires a more fact-based approach to be pursued in order to ascertain whether TUPE is applicable. For example, the UK Government considered the repeal, or at the very least the stripping back, of the 'service provision change' concept to the basic requirements imposed by the ARD in the context of outsourcing arrangements.[208] However, it ultimately back-pedalled at the last moment and instead decided to retain the concept, subject to a modest degree of modification of the concept.[209] Moreover, it is unlikely that Brexit will herald a change of heart on the part of Government, as the 'service provision change' provisions are a generally ac-cepted feature of employment law and have the appeal of drawing a clear 'bright-line' rule which ensures certainty, and against which parties involved in outsourcing can plan their affairs.

The Government also requested views on the extent to which the provisions of TUPE are generally effective. It is suggested that the principal deficiency in TUPE lies in the lack of transparency regarding the scope of application of the employer's ETO defence at both domestic and European levels. This lacuna generates uncertainty for employers in determining the status of dismissals and contractual variations for the reason of a TUPE transfer. Although case law such as *Crawford v Swinton Insurance Brokers Ltd*[210] and *Nationwide Building Society v Benn*[211] have provided some transparency, uncertainty abounds with regard to the degree of reduction in the workforce required to discharge the function. The reforms introduced by the Government in 2014 have improved the situ-ation somewhat, but they apply only where the transfer entails a change in location.[212] As such, they are limited at best and fail to address how much modification of the function or numbers of employees is needed for the ETO exception to be engaged.

---

[208] See Department for Business, Innovation and Skills, *Call for Evidence: Effectiveness of Transfer of Undertakings (Protection of Employment) Regulations 2006* (November 2011), available at https://www.gov.uk/government/publications/improving-the-transfer-of-undertakings-protection-of-employment-reg-ulations-2006-call-for-evidence at page 11 (last visited 22 October 2017).

[209] Department for Business, Innovation and Skills, *Transfer of Undertakings (Protection of Employ-ment) Regulations 2006: Government Response to Consultation* (September 2013), available at https://www.gov.uk/government/uploads/system/uploads/attachment_data/file/236932/bis-13–1023-transfer-of-undertakings-protection-of-employment-regulations-2006-government-response-to-consultation.pdf   at pages 12–13 (last visited 22 October 2017).

[210] [1990] ICR 85.   [211] [2010] IRLR 922.   [212] See TUPE, regulation 7(3A).

A final point worth highlighting concerns the extent to which the traditional pro-employee attitude of the CJEU to the ARD has been diluted somewhat by its decision in *Alemo-Herron v Parkwood Leisure Ltd*.[213] In *Alemo-Herron*, for the very first time, the CJEU subordinated the socially protective purposes of the ARD in the context of reorganizations to an organization's fundamental right to conduct a business under Article 16 of the EU Charter of Fundamental Rights.[214] There is some purchase in the viewpoint advanced by Syrpis, Novitz, and Prassl that the CJEU's emphasis on the commercial freedoms of commercial companies in *Alemo-Herron* can be read as forming part of a wider trend for it to prioritize economic over social considerations, e.g. its decisions in *Viking*,[215] *Laval*,[216] *Ruffert*,[217] etc.[218] This departure from its traditional socially protective attitude is troubling insofar as it sends a signal that the rights afforded to transferring employees by the ARD must be balanced against the commercial interests of employers and the economic imperatives of the EU treaties. However, so far, the CJEU's slightly less enthusiastic take on the ARD would not appear to have filtered down to the domestic tribunals and courts in their approach to the interpretation of the provisions of TUPE. Nonetheless, if past experience is anything to go by, it may only be a matter of time before the change in the CJEU's stance is picked up by the domestic tribunals and courts and used to rein in the protective effect of TUPE.

---

[213] [2013] ICR 1116. See also *Deveci v Scandinavian Airlines System Denmark-Norway-Sweden* [2015] IRLR 138 for a similar decision by the EFTA court.

[214] Pronounced on 7 December 2000 in Nice (OJ 2000 C364/1) and a second time in Strasbourg on 12 December 2007 (OJ 2007 C303/1) and also published in OJ 2010 C83/389.

[215] *International Transport Workers' Federation v Viking Line ABP* [2008] ICR 741.

[216] *Laval un Partneri Ltd v Svenska Byggnadsarbetareforbundet* [2008] IRLR 160.

[217] *Ruffert v Land Niedersachsen* [2008] IRLR 467.

[218] P. Syrpis and T. Novitz, 'The EU Internal Market and Dometic Labour Law: Looking beyond Autonomy' in A. Bogg, C. Costello, A. C. L. Davies, and J. Prassl (eds), *The Autonomy of Labour Law* (Oxford, Hart Publishing, 2015) 300–2; J. Prassl, 'Freedom of Contract as a General Principle of EU Law? Transfers of Undertakings and the Protection of Employer Rights in EU Labour Law: Case C-426/11 *Alemo-Herron and Others v Parkwood Leisure Ltd*' (2013) 42 *Industrial Law Journal* 434, 441.

CHAPTER TWENTY

COLLECTIVE REDUNDANCIES

20.1 AN INTRODUCTION TO INFORMATION AND CONSULTATION ON COLLECTIVE REDUNDANCIES

In Chapter 19, we were introduced to the idea that the imposition of obligations on employers to inform and consult with trade union or employee representatives is a key component of the statutory regime regulating the transfers of undertakings. The point was also made that those information and consultation obligations represented the manifestation of a policy choice by the European Community in the 1970s in favour of the collectivization of decision-making in certain issue-specific and economic contexts. This policy of favouring obligatory worker participation in key decision-making contexts also extends to collective dismissals and it is this central area to which we turn in this chapter. With these thoughts in mind, we now move on to look at the relevant context to collective dismissals, before we consider in detail the provisions of the Collective Redundancies Directive 98/59/EC[1] ('the Collective Redundancies Directive') and sections 188–198 of the Trade Union and Labour Relations (Consolidation) Act 1992 ('TULRCA').

---

[1] Directive 98/59/EC (OJ 1998 L225/16).

20.1.1 Contextual and historical introduction

In Chapter 18, we examined the issue of redundancy through the lens of the statutory obligations owed by management to those individual employees it is proposing to make redundant. The individual employee's right to a statutory redundancy severance payment and the duties of the employer under the rubric of the individual employee's right not to be unfairly dismissed were discussed within that context. In this chapter, our attention is directed towards collective redundancies, e.g. the large-scale off-loading of labour by an employer. Where such collective redundancies are proposed by an organization, they often give rise to various social, economic, and political implications which have an impact upon that organization, its employees, and the wider public. The social and economic implications of mass redundancies at a particular plant, site, or factory may be potentially devastating for the locality concerned. This may lead to intervention at a political level which results in the generation of alternative proposals in advance of the commencement of the information and consultation obligations under law. For example, when the management of Tata Steel proposed to close its steelworks in Scunthorpe and North Lanarkshire as part of a restructuring initiative in October 2015, concerted political pressure was brought to bear with the objective of compelling it to reconsider its proposals and extend the period of consultation beyond the statutory minimum 45-day period in terms of section 188(1A)(a) of TULRCA.[2] Ultimately, this political intervention was unsuccessful, but such episodes serve to highlight the social and political consequences of collective redundancies and the central role performed by the information and consultation obligations in Chapter II of Part IV of TULRCA. In basic terms, the relevant provisions of TULRCA enjoin an employer to consult with trade union or workers' representatives for a minimum period of 30 days where it is proposing to dismiss between 20 and 99 employees at one establishment within a period of 90 days or less. Where the employer proposes to dismiss 100 or more employees, the minimum period of consultation is increased to 45 days.[3]

The statutory provisions found in Chapter II of Part IV of TULRCA can only be understood by first engaging in a discussion about the rationales for the introduction of their legislative source, namely the original Collective Redundancies Directive.[4] This Directive was a response to a managerial practice which the European Community felt amounted to a distortion of the European single internal market for persons, goods, capital, and services. It is beneficial to construct a hypothetical example in order to flesh out the idea being pursued here.

Hypothetical A

Danny's Demolishers plc ('the Employer') is a large multinational company based in the UK, with five subsidiary companies whose shares it wholly owns in France, Germany, Portugal, Spain, and Belgium. Each of the subsidiaries in France, Germany, Portugal, and Spain has a workforce of 4,000 employees. However, the Belgian subsidiary has a workforce of only 600 employees.

Owing to a European-wide recession in the construction trade, market demand for its services has plummeted. In particular, trade has been hard to come by in France, Germany, Spain, and Portugal, whereas, in contrast, the Belgian subsidiary continues to boast a healthy customer order book. The board of directors of the Employer responds to this development by proposing to make 500 of its employees redundant throughout

---

[2] See http://www.bbc.co.uk/news/uk-england-34580178 (last visited 16 September 2017).
[3] Before 6 April 2013, this period was 90 days.   [4] Directive 75/129/EEC (OJ 1975 L48/29).

Europe. The Employer decides that it is imperative that the costs of implementing the redundancies should be kept to a minimum. Therefore, it instructs a firm of management consultants to report on the best option that it ought to adopt.

The management consultants advance a particular strategy as the optimal decision. This strategy involves instructing the Belgian subsidiary to sack 500 employees. The reason cited for this policy is that Belgian law does not impose any (1) restrictions or conditions on an employer's ability to make its employees redundant or (2) obligations on employers to pay redundancy payments to workers dismissed for economic reasons. This can be contrasted with German, French, Portuguese, and Spanish law where statutory redundancy payments are mandatory and extremely high. Indeed, matters are compounded by the fact that French, Portuguese, and Spanish law preclude employers from dismissing workers unless misconduct can be shown.

In light of that report, the board of directors of the Employer decides to sack the 500 employees in Belgium. That is despite the fact that it is the only subsidiary based in Europe which is profitable.

The scenario set out in Hypothetical A is reflective of what occurred in 1973 in the case of AKZO. Although it was not a case which was reported in the law reports or which came before a court, the details of this case circulated widely throughout Europe in 1973–74 and led to disquiet within the ranks of European policy-makers. Leaving aside the social dimension of the case for the moment, the concern of policy-makers at the European level focused on the implications of the strategy adopted by AKZO for the proper functioning of a European internal market. By permitting Member States to erect legal regimes with minimal redundancy protection, the fear was that this could create disparities in conditions of competition and incentivize transnational enterprises to set up operations in those Member States where the costs of effecting redundancies were at their minimum. Ultimately, there was felt to be a danger that such opportunities for social dumping could generate a 'race to the bottom' in terms of which Member States responded by liberalizing their redundancy protection regimes in order to compete with each other for transnational corporations.[5] European policy-makers perceived the absence of a level playing field in relation to redundancy protection as having the potential to encourage Member States to engage in a process of regulatory competition in the field of redundancy law which could disrupt market integration in Europe.

In the field of European social policy, there are a myriad of potential options which could be adopted to respond to the challenge identified. The potential character of these options becomes apparent if one thinks in terms of the particular issues which policy-makers ought to address as operating at two intersecting levels. For example, if one characterizes the first level as one which enjoins a policy-maker to consider the extent to which the regulatory regime should harmonize collective redundancy laws across the Member States, certain competing policy options begin to rise to the surface:

- Policy-makers could seek to fully harmonize redundancy protection laws across Europe. This option would entail the rigorous approximation of redundancy rules. However, it was rejected as impracticable and as representing a disproportionate interference with the principle of subsidiarity, which lies at the heart of the European project. Subsidiarity

---

[5] Of course, this discussion presupposes that jurisdictions with minimal labour laws have the most efficient labour markets and economies and brings back to mind one of the key debates in labour law today, which we considered in Chapter 1, section 1.2.1, namely the degree to which labour laws do or do not impede the efficiency, flexibility, and dynamism of external labour markets and the wider productive economy.

is the doctrine that Member States should have the competence to legislate in policy areas where the relevant challenges are better dealt with at the level of the Member States. It was felt that the introduction of uniform redundancy protection laws across Europe was unwarranted since that would entail the promulgation of measures which extended beyond simply tackling cross-border challenges (where the European Community more naturally ought to have competence). The thinking was that such a strategy could have unintended and negative consequences for national labour markets.

• Instead, akin to the strategy pursued in many other areas of European social policy, policy-makers decided to fashion a regime which set minimum standards, whilst affording Member States certain options. The result was a 'minimum and partial harmonization' Directive which sought to achieve a balance of economic and social development within Europe through the partial approximation of rules and standards on redundancy. The economic aims would be realized by enacting measures designed to integrate labour markets (the market integration model), whilst erecting a floor of social protection (the social citizenship model) upon which Member States or employers could build. To that extent, the Collective Redundancies Directive combines a mixture of economic and social objectives:

■ F. Dorssemont, 'Case C-55/02, *Commission of the European Communities v Portuguese Republic*, judgment of the Second Chamber of the Court of Justice of 12 October 2004. Case C-188/03, *Imtraud Junk v Wolfgang Kühnel*, judgment of the Second Chamber of the Court of Justice of 27 January 2005' (2006) 43 *Common Market Law Review* 225, 225–8

[The original Collective Redundancies Directive was] adopted on the basis of the former Article 100 EC (now Art. 94 EC).[6] The *legal basis* for adoption recalls a Market Integration Model: divergences between the Member States regarding the level of workers' protection were considered to have a direct effect on the functioning of the internal market[, the third recital to the original Collective Redundancies Directive 75/129 stipulating that 'differences [in the provisions in force in the Member States of the Community concerning the practical arrangements and procedures for redundancies and the measures designed to alleviate the consequences of redundancy for workers] can have a direct effect on the functioning of the common market].' . . .

The [Collective Redundancies Directive] . . . is an interesting example of combining a Market Integration and a Social Citizenship Model. According to the second recital, the [Collective Redundancies Directive] takes into account a *balanced* economic and social development within the Community. The general outlook of both the 1975 and 1998 Collective Redundancies Directives is procedural. The Community legislature sought to harmonize legal provisions relating to workers' involvement (information and consultation) as well as provisions on the public authorities to whom collective redundancies had to be notified.

The Community legislature regulated two distinct legal relations. The *first* concerns the relation between an employer *contemplating* collective redundancies and the workers' representatives. The employer is required to inform and consult workers' representatives 'in good time with a view to reaching an agreement' . . .

The second relation affects the interplay between the employer and the competent public authority. The employer is obliged to inform the authority of the information and consultation process and to notify any projected collective redundancies in writing. The projected collective redundancies shall take effect not earlier than 30 days after the notification. During that period, the

---

⁶ This is now Article 115 of the Treaty on the Functioning of the European Union ('TFEU').

competent public authority is required to 'seek solutions to the problems raised by the projected collective redundancies', though that formula does not seem to impose any obligation for Member States to allow the public authorities to veto the projected collective redundancies. The [Collective Redundancies Directive] does *not* provide any indication that the competent public authority is supposed to assess the appropriate or reasonable character of the projected managerial decision to make workers collectively redundant. In fact, the [Collective Redundancies Directive] does not seem to question the exercise of the managerial prerogative at all. *Whether* and *when* the employer will make his workers collectively redundant is part of his freedom to conduct a business . . .[7]

Two points can be drawn from this extract:

(1) First, as discussed, the Directive sought to achieve a mixture of economic and social objectives through minimum and partial harmonization of the collective redundancy consultation laws of the Member States.[8]

(2) The second point which we can take from the extract can be understood best if we return to the idea of the two intersecting levels we canvassed earlier in this section. For example, one could conceptualize the second level at which certain competing policy measures come into play as requiring policy-makers to address the extent to which the regulatory regime should constrain the prerogative of management to engage in collective dismissals on economic grounds. Two opposing approaches emerge here, which can usefully be committed to the shorthand of 'substantive' versus 'procedural' social protection. These policy options allude to the trend we identified earlier in this book in Chapter 1, section 1.2.1, namely the preference on the part of the legislature and the judiciary to craft labour laws which operate to furnish procedural protection to employees, as opposed to substantive rules which constrain managerial decision-making, or subject it to an exacting intensity of scrutiny. Our discussion in Chapter 18 reached the conclusion that domestic redundancy laws concentrate more on the procedural fairness of individual redundancy dismissals than their substantive fairness. As such, one could perhaps be forgiven for thinking that a scheme designed to regulate collective redundancies might have struck a form of counter-balance by proffering substantive rights to affected employees. However, this would be wide of the mark. This becomes clear when one considers the nature of the original proposals for the Collective Redundancies Directive which were on the table in the early 1970s:

■ **M. R. Freedland, 'Employment Protection: Redundancy Procedures and the EEC' (1976) 5 *Industrial Law Journal* 24, 27**

[W]hen, in November 1972, the Commission presented its draft directive on collective dismissals to the Council, the proposals were of three kinds: (a) for compulsory consultation with workers' representatives about collective dismissals; (b) for compulsory notification of impending redundancies to public authorities; (c) for powers on the part of public authorities to postpone or prohibit dismissals in certain circumstances. The progress from the first draft to the final directive was a long and tortuous one involving extensive disagreements between the Member States both as to the substance of the proposals and as to the extent of the harmonisation re-

---

[7] Writer's annotations appear in square brackets throughout this chapter.
[8] The extent to which harmonization across the Member States has been achieved is debatable, on which, see B. Bercusson, *European Labour Law*, 2nd edition (Cambridge, CUP, 2009) 114–20.

> quirement to be imposed. Suffice it to remark that Britain was in the vanguard of the opposition to that part of the proposals which dealt with powers of public authorities to prohibit dismissals, and in June 1974 effectively placed a temporary veto upon the proposals as a whole. The crucial compromise, necessary to enable a directive to be made, was reached at the meeting of the Council of Social Ministers in December 1974, when it was agreed that it would be optional to Member States whether or not to grant veto powers over collective dismissals to their Departments of Employment.

If proposal (c) set out in this Freedland extract had been chosen, the outcome would have been to provide employees with substantive, rather than procedural, rights: it would have operated to severely limit the decision-making power of management. However, this is not the route which the original Collective Redundancies Directive took or the current Collective Redundancies Directive[9] and Chapter II of Part IV of TULRCA take. Instead, the social citizenship model arm of the Directive was procedural, rather than substantive. As such, it provided minimum and partial harmonization information and consultation rights, rather than legislative intervention with the potential to overturn the substance of managerial resolutions to collectively dismiss the workforce. Furthermore, no power of review was furnished to the courts in respect of the reasons for a closure, the decision to scale down the workforce, or how an employer might choose to organize or manage its personnel. Therefore, unlike collective bargaining, which would operate to affect the sphere of the managerial prerogative by enabling worker representatives to negotiate and *conclude* collective agreements, the Directive strove to offer a measure of social protection at a transnational level. It attempted to do so by constructing a floor of *procedural information and consultation* protection in favour of trade union and workers' representatives upon which Member States or employers could build. Although the European Court of Justice ('ECJ' or 'CJEU') has since stated[10] that the Collective Redundancies Directive does indeed enjoin management to negotiate with workers' representatives, this is little more than a paper tiger, since the negotiations need only be conducted 'with a view to' reaching agreement with management.[11] The end result is a process not too dissimilar to the 'efficiency model' of procedural fairness which we analysed in Chapter 17, section 17.1.1. As such, the information and consultation regime does no more than give management cause to reflect upon the alternatives to collective redundancies and whether its decision was in the enterprise's best interests.

The efficiency model of procedural fairness, inherent within the statutory duty to inform and consult workers' representatives, has been dismissed as ineffective by some commentators. Proponents of this view argue that the absence of substantive controls on redundancies enables employers to simply pay lip service to the Collective Redundancies Directive's aim of requiring employers to consider the suggestions of affected employees and their representatives about the 'ways and means of avoiding collective redundancies or reducing the number of workers affected, and of mitigating the consequences[, including the potential] for redeploying or retraining workers made redundant'.[12] However, empirical research has indicated otherwise, i.e. that employers do genuinely engage in the consultation process and that, in certain cases, proposals put forward by representatives are taken on board by management:

---

[9] Directive 98/59/EC (OJ 1998 L225/16).   [10] *Junk v Kühnel* (C-188/03) [2005] IRLR 310, 314.
[11] Article 2(1) of the Collective Redundancies Directive; section 188(2) of TULRCA.
[12] Article 2(2) of the Collective Redundancies Directive.

■ **M. Hall and P. Edwards, 'Reforming the Statutory Redundancy Consultation Procedure' (1999) 28 *Industrial Law Journal* 299, 312–13**

Much existing research suggests that managerial decision-making over redundancies is little affected by consultation. However, in the cases we looked at, where redundancy consultation was carried out via union representatives, and in the one case where consultation was via specially elected employee representatives, it appears to have been more effective than is sometimes suggested. The law requires there to be consultation about ways of avoiding the dismissals, reducing the number to be dismissed and mitigating the consequences of the dismissals. In practice, the requirement to consult 'about ways of avoiding the dismissals' was not seriously addressed because, in all eight cases, management had reviewed their operations over a period of several months and the key decisions about the basic need for redundancies had been made before the start of the consultation process. Consultation therefore focused on the process of handling job losses, not the principle, but in a number of cases nonetheless 'made a difference' in terms of influencing original managerial proposals, as the following examples show.

At one of the organisations we studied, SecurCo, where redundancies arose when two control centres were merged, the union secured some improvements to the proposed new harmonised terms and conditions, for example protecting the holiday entitlement of one group of staff, while all those selected for redundancy were offered alternative positions with the firm. At another organisation, EngCo, the union was able to defend the established principle of 'last in, first out', and also to shape the definition of how the principle actually worked. It also made some suggestions for reorganisation which were felt to have saved four or five jobs out of 65 that were under threat. Similarly, around 15 out of 80 members of staff due to lose their jobs at Urban College were retained, albeit only for a limited period. At TeleCo, where consultation was carried out via elected employee representatives, the representatives managed to persuade the company to change its initial insistence on selecting for redundancy on merit-based criteria and to allow volunteers. A range of more specific issues such as pension entitlements were also identified and resolved.

Meaningful consultation, albeit on the ways of handling redundancies and not the overall principle, thus took place in several of the organisations. The extent to which representatives could influence the process tended to reflect the context of the redundancies and the nature of managerial objectives. Consultation via union and/or employee representatives is no guarantee that effective discussion takes place but generally provides a structure or forum within which issues can be identified and discussed.

If it is accurate to portray the statutory information and consultation process as one in which the employer does meaningfully engage with, and consider, the proposals of workers' representatives, then the proficiency, skill set, and general quality of the workers' representatives appointed to the task becomes crucial. This point feeds into a wider debate about the extent to which employee representatives appointed or elected under the provisions of section 188(1B)(b)(ii) of TULRCA are truly independent of management and have sufficient strength and credibility to engage in consultations with the employers. A comparison of the statutory provisions on the status of the trade union and employee representatives who are entitled to represent the employees in the statutory information and consultation process reveals that the former must be independent of the employer, but this is not the case for the latter.[13] The absence of any requirement in the statute for the appointed and elected employee representatives to be independent of management has two potential effects, both of which overlap:

• First, the employer is afforded the opportunity to engage in underhand tactics. Such schemes serve to undermine the ability of the employee representatives to engage in effective consultation.

---

[13] Cf. section 188(1B)(a) of TULRCA with section 188(1B)(b)(ii) of of TULRCA.

- The second effect, which is related to the first, is that there is a case for arguing that the domestic law fails to properly implement the decision of the ECJ in *Commission v UK*,[14] i.e. that UK law does not take appropriate measures to ensure that effective information and consultation can take place. To some extent, this argument is diluted insofar as section 189(1) enables an employee to complain to an employment tribunal that the employee representatives were not 'appropriate' or that the balloting and election process was deficient. Nevertheless, this does not deflect from the charge that this modest measure fails to provide the same protection as an 'independence' requirement. As such, there is a case for the argument that it is nothing more than a half-measure insofar as it purports to protect the affected employees from representatives who have been compromised by management.

 For additional reading on the contextual and historical introduction to collective redundancies, visit the Online Resources for this book at www.oup.com/uk/cabrelli3e/

20.2 THE COLLECTIVE REDUNDANCIES DIRECTIVE

In this section, we will briefly consider the key provisions of the Collective Redundancies Directive. In particular, we will focus on the meaning of 'collective redundancies' and discuss the basic obligations of the employer, namely consultation and notification. As already noted, the thinking which underpins the Collective Redundancies Directive is that, where informed and meaningful consultation takes place with workers provisionally selected for redundancy and their representatives, an employer may revisit its original proposal to dismiss. After a period of reflection and the consideration of alternative proposals put forward by the potentially affected employees or their representatives, it may be that the number of redundancies is significantly reduced or the requirement for the redundancies is avoided altogether. Thus, at a theoretical level, the philosophy which is subsequently fleshed out by the Collective Redundancies Directive and Chapter II of Part IV of TULRCA is about reflection and the efficiency of the proposed decision.

In the case of *Rockfon A/S v Specialarbejderforbundet I Danmark, acting for Nielsen*,[15] the ECJ offered an explanation of the other purpose of the Collective Redundancies Directive. In other words, it was designed to introduce a floor of protection at a transnational level in the context of collective redundancies rather than to interfere in the managerial prerogative:

■ *Rockfon A/S v Specialarbejderforbundet I Danmark* [1996] ICR 673, 688B–C

. . . it is sufficient to state that the sole purpose of [the Collective Redundancies Directive] is the partial harmonisation of collective redundancy procedures and that its aim is not to restrict the freedom of undertakings to organise their activities and arrange their personnel departments in the way which they think best suits their needs. Article 1(1)(a) [of the Collective Redundancies Directive] in particular defines 'collective redundancies,' thus determining the scope of the Directive, but lays down no rules relating to the internal organisation of undertakings or the management of their personnel.

One should stress that the Collective Redundancies Directive has no influence on how employers effect redundancies on an individual basis, which falls firmly within the

[14] (Case C-383/92) [1994] ICR 664.   [15] (Case C-449/93) [1996] ICR 673.

province of domestic labour law.[16] From the perspective of the social citizenship model addressed earlier, if one considers that the effect of this passage is that the information and consultation obligations of the employer amount to nothing more than obligations to listen and negotiate—rather than any requirement to reach agreement—with employees, their representatives, and trade unions, the limitations which lurk deep within the collective redundancies regime are soon laid bare. This point was made in the case of *Junk v Kühnel*,[17] where the ECJ stated that 'Article 2 of the [Collective Redundancies Directive] impose[s no more than] an obligation [on the employer] to negotiate'.[18] This duty to negotiate is not the same thing as a duty to collectively bargain with trade unions and conclude collective agreements.[19]

20.2.1 Definition of 'collective redundancies'

The meaning of the term 'collective redundancies' is set out in Article 1(1)(a) of the Collective Redundancies Directive as follows:

Article 1

1. For the purposes of this Directive:

    (a) 'collective redundancies' means dismissals effected by an employer for one or more reasons not related to the individual workers concerned where, according to the choice of the Member States, the number of redundancies is:

    (i) either, over a period of 30 days:

        – at least 10 in establishments normally employing more than 20 and less than 100 workers,
        – at least 10% of the number of workers in establishments normally employing at least 100 but less than 300 workers,
        – at least 30 in establishments normally employing 300 workers or more,

    (ii) or, over a period of 90 days, at least 20, whatever the number of workers normally employed in the establishments in question.

    (b) 'workers' representatives' means the workers' representatives provided for by the laws or practices of the Member States.

    For the purpose of calculating the number of redundancies provided for in the first subparagraph of point (a), terminations of an employment contract which occur on the employer's initiative for one or more reasons not related to the individual workers concerned shall be assimilated to redundancies, provided that there are at least five redundancies.

The employer's information and consultation obligations are triggered when there are 'collective redundancies', and this expression is satisfied where:

(1) there are 'dismissals effected by an employer for one or more reasons not related to the individual workers concerned'; and

(2) either of the thresholds in Article 1(1)(a)(i) or (ii) are engaged in relation to 'workers'.

---

[16] See Chapter 18 for more detail.   [17] [2005] IRLR 310.   [18] *ibid.*, 314.
[19] See P. Davies and M. Freedland, *Labour Law: Text and Materials*, 2nd edition (London, Weidenfeld and Nicholson, 1984) 230 for a classic exposition of the distinction between 'consultation' and the 'negotiation' involved in collective bargaining. See also F. Dorssemont, 'Case C-55/02, *Commission of the European Communities v. Portuguese Republic*, judgment of the Second Chamber of the Court of Justice of 12 October 2004. Case C-188/03, *Imtraud Junk v. Wolfgang Kühnel*, judgment of the Second Chamber of the Court of Justice of 27 January 2005' (2006) 43 *Common Market Law Review* 225, 237–9.

As such, (1) entails a focus on the *individual workers* who have been dismissed, and (2) is the factor which renders those redundancies *collective* in nature.[20] In *Balkaya v Kiesel Abbruch- und Recycling Technik GmbH*,[21] the ECJ ruled that the concept of 'worker' in the Collective Redundancies Directive has a distinctive and independent meaning in EU law, namely that, for a certain period of time, a person performs services for and under the direction of another person, in return for which he/she receives remuneration. It is this criterion which must be taken into account in calculating the number of workers in the establishment, for the purposes of ascertaining whether sufficient numbers of individuals have been made redundant to trigger the information and consultation obligations.

Turning to the meaning of the central term 'dismissals effected by an employer for one or more reasons not related to the individual workers concerned' at (1), these words have also been given an autonomous meaning within European law, which is independent of their meaning in the national domestic laws of the Member States.[22] This point is underscored by the decision of the ECJ in *Commission v Portugal*:

■ *Commission v Portugal* (Case C-55/02) [2004] ECR I-9387, paras 49–60

. . . the concept of 'redundancy', as mentioned in Article 1(1)(a) of [the Collective Redundancies Directive], may not be defined by any reference to the laws of the Member States, but has instead meaning in Community law.

The concept has to be interpreted as including any termination of contract of employment not sought by the worker, and therefore without his consent. It is not necessary that the underlying reasons should reflect the will of the employer.

That interpretation of the concept of 'redundancy' for the purposes of [the Collective Redundancies Directive] follows from the aim pursued by the latter and from the background to the provision at issue. . .

The objectives referred to in [the Collective Redundancies Directive] would be attained only in part if the termination of a contract of employment that was not contingent on the will of the employer were to be excluded from the body of rules laid down by [the Collective Redundancies Directive] . . .

[T]he ninth recital to the preamble to [the Collective Redundancies Directive] and the second paragraph of Article 3(1) thereof make it clear that [the Collective Redundancies Directive] applies, as a rule, also to collective redundancies caused by termination of the establishment's activities as a result of a judicial decision. In that situation, the termination of contracts of employment is the result of circumstances not willed by the employer . . .

[R]edundancies are to be distinguished from terminations of the contract of employment which, on the conditions set out in the last paragraph of Article 1(1) of the Directive, are assimilated to redundancies for want of the worker's consent.[23]

Two points emerge from this *Commission v Portugal* case extract:

(1) The expression 'dismissals effected by an employer for one or more reasons not related to the individual workers concerned' refers to the termination of the contract of employment of an employee.

---

[20] One will note that each Member State of the EU was given a choice between the 30-day and 90-day periods in Article 1(a)(i) and (ii). As will become apparent in section 20.3.1, the UK opted for (ii).

[21] [2015] IRLR 771.

[22] For example, contrast *University College Union v Stirling* [2015] IRLR 573 with *Rabal Cañas v Nexea Gestión Documental* [2015] IRLR 577.

[23] Sourced from BAILII available at http://www.bailii.org/cgi-bin/markup.cgi?doc=/eu/cases/EU-ECJ/2004/C5502.html&query=European+and+commission+and+v+and+portugal&method=boolean (last visited 14 September 2017).

(2) The termination of the employee's contract must not be sought by the employee: it must be without his/her consent. As such, a voluntary resignation is not covered,[24] although a resignation in response to the employer unilaterally varying the employee's contract of employment to the employee's detriment is covered.[25] The termination may be for any kind of reason or reasons, irrespective of the nature of the intention or will of the employer, provided that the reason does not relate 'to the individual worker concerned'. Therefore, the dismissal of an employee for misconduct, incompetence, or incapacity is not covered, since these reasons *do* relate to that individual employee's behaviour or capacities. The implication of the interpretation in *Commission v Portugal*[26] is that the definition includes dismissals owing to the employer's insolvency, the employer's death, or the employer's incapacity. Voluntary early retirement is also included within the scope of these words. This can be contrasted with the definition of 'redundancy' in section 139(1) of the Employment Rights Act 1996 ('ERA').[27] In Chapter 18, we noted that the majority of the case law which considered whether an employee was dismissed for 'redundancy' looked at whether an employer's requirements for work generally, or at a particular location, had ceased or diminished in terms of section 139(1)(b). As such, one must demonstrate a labour surplus and that the employee's dismissal was attributable to that state of affairs. As we noted, in some cases, it was decided that certain dismissals pursuant to an employer's reorganization or restructuring of its commercial operations were not redundancies within the meaning of section 139(1)(b). However, under the definition of the words 'dismissals effected by an employer for one or more reasons not related to the individual workers concerned' in *Commission v Portugal*, a different outcome would be reached. Instead, whether there was or was not a cessation or diminution in the requirements of the employer for labour generally is irrelevant. The key criterion being whether an employee's contract was terminated without his/her consent for a reason that is not related to him/her in particular. The conclusion can be drawn that the definition of 'collective redundancies' in Article 1(1)(a) of the Collective Redundancies Directive is much broader than that found in section 139(1).[28]

20.2.2 Employer's consultation and notification obligations

Article 2(1) and (2) of the Collective Redundancies Directive provides as follows:

> **Article 2**
>
> 1. Where an employer is contemplating collective redundancies, he shall begin consultations with the workers' representatives in good time with a view to reaching an agreement.
>
> 2. These consultations shall, at least, cover ways and means of avoiding collective redundancies or reducing the number of workers affected, and of mitigating the consequences by recourse to accompanying social measures aimed, inter alia, at aid for redeploying or retraining workers made redundant.

It can be seen that the employer's consultation obligations are invoked when it is within its contemplation that collective redundancies will be declared, i.e. where no final decision

---

[24] *Dansk Metalarbejderforbund v H. Nielsen & Sn* (Case C-284/83) [1986] 1 CMLR 91, 99.
[25] In other words, a constructive dismissal: *Pujante Rivera v Gestora Clubs Dir SL* [2016] IRLR 51.
[26] (Case C-55/02) [2004] ECR I-9387.   [27] See Chapter 18, section 18.2.2.2.
[28] See *Commission v UK* (Case C-383/92) [1994] ICR 664.

has yet been taken. Article 2(1) does not define the meaning of the word 'contemplating', and this is a key issue to which we will return in section 20.3.1.4 when we come to analyse section 188(1) of TULRCA. Likewise, we can note from the extract that there is no definition of 'consultations'. However, some indication of the nature and purpose of the consultation is prescribed in Article 2(2). Further guidance is provided by the ECJ in *Junk v Kühnel*,[29] namely that the employer's consultation obligation entails negotiation with trade union representatives or employee representatives without any requirement to reach agreement.

The requirements for employers to furnish information for the purposes of the consultation process are detailed in Article 2(3) of the Collective Redundancies Directive:

Article 2

3. To enable workers' representatives to make constructive proposals, the employers shall in good time during the course of the consultations:

    (a) supply them with all relevant information and

    (b) in any event notify them in writing of:

        (i)   the reasons for the projected redundancies;

        (ii) the number of categories of workers to be made redundant;

        (iii) the number and categories of workers normally employed;

        (iv) the period over which the projected redundancies are to be effected;

        (v)   the criteria proposed for the selection of the workers to be made redundant in so far as national legislation and/or practice confers the power therefor upon the employer;

        (vi) the method for calculating any redundancy payments other than those arising out of national legislation and/or practice.

The employer shall forward to the competent public authority a copy of, at least, the elements of the written communication which are provided for in the first subparagraph, point (b), subpoints (i) to (v).

It is provided in Article 3(1) that the employer must forward to 'the competent public authority' a copy of the elements of communication relating to the matters listed in Article 2(3), at the very least. Moreover, 'the competent public authority' must be informed in writing of any projected collective redundancies, including the following:

- details of the consultations with workers' representatives provided for in Article 2;
- the reasons for the redundancies;
- the number of workers to be made redundant;
- the number of workers normally employed; and
- the period over which the redundancies are to be effected.

With some understanding of the European background in mind, we now turn to the provisions which transpose the Collective Redundancies Directive into UK law. In doing so, we will consider the basic architecture of Chapter II of Part IV of TULRCA and, in particular, with whom and when consultation must take place.

---

[29] [2005] IRLR 310, 314.

20.3 AN INTRODUCTION TO CHAPTER II OF PART IV OF TULRCA

The UK transposed the original Collective Redundancies Directive[30] into UK law in March 1976 when Part IV of the Employment Protection Act 1975 came into force. The provisions regulating collective redundancies are now contained in Chapter II of Part IV of TULRCA.[31] This chapter has been modified five times since 1992, namely by:

(1) section 34 of the Trade Union Reform and Employment Rights Act 1993;

(2) the Collective Redundancies and Transfer of Undertakings (Protection of Employment) (Amendment) Regulations 1995;[32]

(3) the Collective Redundancies and Transfer of Undertakings (Protection of Employment) (Amendment) Regulations 1999;[33]

(4) the Trade Union and Labour Relations (Consolidation) Act 1992 (Amendment) Order 2013;[34] and

(5) the Collective Redundancies and Transfer of Undertakings (Protection of Employment) (Amendment) Regulations 2014.[35]

The reforms in 1995 and 1999 were chiefly introduced in response to the judgment of the ECJ in *Commission v UK*.[36] In that case, the ECJ had held that the UK had not properly implemented the requirements of the Collective Redundancies Directive as it had failed to provide for consultation of workers' representatives where there was no recognized trade union. The 1995 and 1999 Regulations require the employer to consult either appointed or elected representatives of the employees, or representatives of a recognized trade union, in the event of collective redundancies. Meanwhile, the 2013 reforms reduced the period for consultation from 90 to 45 days where the employer is proposing to dismiss 100 or more employees at one establishment within a period of 90 days or less.[37] The opportunity was also taken in 2013 to bring domestic law into conformity with Article 1(2)(a) of the Collective Redundancies Directive, by excluding all employees from the coverage of the consultation obligations who are engaged on fixed-term contracts and have been dismissed at the end of the specific term, the completion of a particular task, or the occurrence or non-occurrence of a specific event laid down in their contracts.[38] However, there are exceptions to this general rule. As such, if the fixed-term contract is terminated early by the employer for the reason of redundancy, or prior to the natural expiry of the specific term, the completion of the particular task, or the occurrence or non-occurrence of the specific event, then the employee will fall within the scope of section 188 of TULRCA.[39] Finally, the reforms introduced on 31 January 2014 amended section 188 of TULRCA to enable prospective transferee employers to undertake collective redundancy consultation with representatives of affected transferring individuals prior to the transfer of the transferor employer's undertaking to the prospective transferee employer in terms of the Transfer of Undertakings (Protection of Employment) Regulations 2006.[40]

---

[30] Directive 75/129/EEC (OJ 1975 L48/29).   [31] Sections 188–198 of the ERA.

[32] SI 1995/2587.   [33] SI 1999/1925.   [34] SI 2013/763.   [35] SI 2014/16.

[36] (Case C-383/92) [1994] ICR 664.

[37] Article 3(1) and (2) of the Trade Union and Labour Relations (Consolidation) Act 1992 (Amendment) Order 2013 (SI 2013/763).

[38] Article 3(1) and (4) of the Trade Union and Labour Relations (Consolidation) Act 1992 (Amendment) Order 2013 introduces a new section 282 of TULRCA to that effect and thus reverses the decision of the Supreme Court in *University College Union v University of Stirling* [2015] IRLR 573.

[39] Section 282(2) of TULRCA.   [40] SI 2006/246.

20.3.1 **The consultation obligation**

The employer's duty to consult is governed by section 188(1) and (1A) of TULRCA as follows:

> **Section 188 Duty of employer to consult representatives**
>
> (1) Where an employer is proposing to dismiss as redundant 20 or more employees at one establishment within a period of 90 days or less, the employer shall consult about the dismissals all the persons who are appropriate representatives of any of the employees who may be affected by the proposed dismissals or may be affected by measures taken in connection with those dismissals.
>
> (1A) The consultation shall begin in good time and in any event—
>
> (a) where the employer is proposing to dismiss 100 or more employees as mentioned in subsection (1), at least 45 days, and
>
> (b) otherwise, at least 30 days, before the first of the dismissals takes effect.

Since the employer's duty is to consult with 'appropriate representatives' for a period of at least 30 days where the employer proposes to make 20 or more employees redundant within a period of 90 days or less, one can see that the UK decided to implement the option in Article 1(1)(a)(ii) of the Collective Redundancies Directive in preference to that contained in Article 1(1)(a)(i).

A number of overlapping issues emerge from these deceptively simplistic words, as follows:

(1) Who are 'affected' 'employees' for these purposes?

(2) What is meant by 'dismiss'?

(3) What is meant by 'redundant'?

(4) What is meant by 'proposing'?

(5) What is an 'establishment'?

(6) Who is the 'employer'?

(7) Who are the 'appropriate representatives'?

(8) What is meant by 'in good time'?

(9) When are the dismissals deemed to 'take effect'?

Each of these matters will now be considered in turn.

20.3.1.1 Affected employees

Section 188 of TULRCA directs that the information and consultation obligations extend to 'employees who may be affected by the proposed dismissals or may be affected by measures taken in connection with those dismissals'. In terms of section 295(1), an employee 'means an individual who has entered into or works under (or, where the employment has ceased, worked under) a contract of employment', and the latter is defined as a contract of service or apprenticeship. Therefore, the individuals covered are restricted, and 'workers' who may be affected by the employer's proposals are not taken into account for the purposes of section 188.[41] Since 'workers'—in terms of the domestic

---

[41] For further details on the distinctions between an 'employee', 'worker', and independent contractor, see Chapters 3 and 4.

conception of that concept—are excluded, it is not entirely outside the realms of possibility that the UK is in non-conformance with EU law, bearing in mind the decision of the ECJ in *Balkaya v Kiesel Abbruch- und Recycling Technik GmbH*.[42] In *Balkaya*, it was held that the concept of 'worker' in the Collective Redundancies Directive has a distinctive and independent meaning in EU law, namely that, for a certain period of time, a person performs services for and under the direction of another person, in return for which he/she receives remuneration. In line with that formulation, the ECJ held that a director of a company and a trainee qualified as 'workers' for the purposes of the Collective Redundancies Directive. Of course, this can be contrasted with the domestic position, whereby a trainee and director are unlikely to be classified as 'workers'.

As noted earlier, section 282(1) goes on to provide that the consultation duty does not apply to employees who are engaged on fixed-term contracts and have been dismissed at the end of the specific term, the completion of the particular task, or the occurrence or non-occurrence of the specific event laid down in their contracts. Moreover, it is expressly provided that Crown servants,[43] members of the armed forces,[44] the police,[45] parliamentary staff,[46] and share fishermen[47] are excluded employees. The ECJ has held that no other categories of employees may be excluded for the purposes of the computation of the staff numbers at a particular 'establishment'.[48] In calculating the number of affected employees, section 188(3) stipulates that an employer must take no account of any employees it has proposed to dismiss in respect of whom consultation has already begun. The overall effect of these provisions is that a not insubstantial amount of individuals providing personal services to an organization are not accounted for in the evaluation of who is an affected 'employee'.

20.3.1.2 The meaning of 'dismissal'

The definition of the words 'dismiss' and 'dismissal' in section 188 of TULRCA differs from the meanings of these terms applicable under Part XI of the ERA[49] for the purposes of determining whether an individual has been dismissed for the reason of redundancy. Section 298 of TULRCA stipulates that 'dismiss', 'dismissal', and 'effective date of termination' must be interpreted in accordance with the definitions within Part X of the ERA.[50] As such, the terms of section 95(1) of the ERA, which are applicable in the context of the unfair dismissal regime, provide the appropriate definition in this context:

Section 95 Circumstances in which an employee is dismissed

(1) an employee is dismissed by his employer if (and, subject to subsection (2), only if)—

  (a) the contract under which he is employed is terminated by the employer (whether with or without notice),

  (b) he is employed under a limited-term contract and that contract terminates by virtue of the limiting event without being renewed under the same contract, or

  (c) the employee terminates the contract under which he is employed (with or without notice) in circumstances in which he is entitled to terminate it without notice by reason of the employer's conduct.

---

[42] [2015] IRLR 771.   [43] Section 273 of TULRCA.   [44] Section 274 of TULRCA.
[45] Section 280 of TULRCA.   [46] Sections 277 and 278 of TULRCA.
[47] Section 284 of TULRCA.
[48] *Confederation Generale Du Travail v Premier Ministre* (Case C-385/05) [2007] 2 CMLR 6.
[49] Sections 135–181 of the ERA. See Chapter 18, section 18.2.1.
[50] Sections 94–134A of the ERA. See Chapter 16, sections 16.2.2 and 16.2.3.

It is arguable that this definition of dismissal is over-inclusive of the minimum require-ments under the Collective Redundancies Directive. To place this argument in its context, one must recall that the ECJ in *Commission v Portugal*[51] construed the word 'dismissal' in Article 1(1)(a) of the Directive to mean a termination of the employee's contract of employment without his consent and which is not sought by the employee concerned. Therefore, a resignation by the employee does not fall within the definition. Section 95(1) (a) of the ERA is compatible with the European framework as it involves the termination of the employee's contract of employment by the employer, which will be without that employee's consent. However, the scope of section 95(1)(b) is more extensive than the formulation adumbrated in *Commission v Portugal*. For instance, section 95(1)(b) seems worded broadly enough to cover the mutually consensual termination of a fixed-term contract, albeit that section 282(1) specifically excludes fixed-term employees from the duty to consult. Meanwhile, section 95(1)(c) involves a particular form of resignation by the employee, i.e. a constructive dismissal which conforms with the interpretation of Ar-ticle 1(1)(a) of the Collective Redundancies Directive in *Pujante Rivera v Gestora Clubs Dir SL*.[52] Here, an employee resigned in response to a unilateral change to his contract of employment by the employer—and the CJEU held that this was a dismissal in terms of the Collective Redundancies Directive.

20.3.1.3 The meaning of 'redundant'

In much the same way as the definition of the word 'dismissal', there is a difference in the meaning of the word 'redundant' in the context of the individual and collective redun-dancy regimes under Parts X and XI of the ERA and TULRCA. The latter prescribes the following for the purposes of collective redundancies:[53]

> **Section 195 Construction of references to dismissal as redundant etc.**
>
> (1) In this Chapter references to dismissal as redundant are references to dismissal for a reason not related to the individual concerned or for a number of reasons all of which are not so related.
>
> (2) For the purposes of any proceedings under this Chapter, where an employee is or is proposed to be dismissed it shall be presumed, unless the contrary is proved, that he is or is proposed to be dismissed as redundant.

In conformity with Article 1(1)(a) of the Collective Redundancies Directive, section 195(1) of TULRCA seeks to ensure that the definitions of 'redundancy' and 'redundan-cies' for the purposes of TULRCA include dismissals of employees owing to the death or insolvency of the employer and for breach of statute or contract, as well as dismissals which are caused by the employer's proposals to restructure or reorganize its commercial operations. As such, we can surmise that the scope of these words is wider than the word 'redundancy' in section 139(1) of the ERA, which hinges on the more limited 'surplus labour' type of analysis. Moreover, it is not restricted to the situation where an em-ployee's contract of employment is terminated for the reason that the employer no longer has any need for that particular individual. It will also cover the situation where the employer dismisses an employee and then re-engages him/her on new terms, e.g. where the employee refuses to accept a proposed variation of the terms of his/her contract of employment.[54] It has also been held by the Supreme Court in *University College Union*

---

[51] (Case C-55/02) [2004] ECR I-9387.   [52] [2016] IRLR 51.
[53] See Chapter 18, section 18.2.2, for the definition in relation to individual redundancies.
[54] *Kelly v Hesley Group Ltd* [2013] IRLR 514.

v University of Stirling[55] that the words 'for a reason not related to the individual concerned' are broad enough to include employees whose fixed-term contracts have come to a natural end, even though Article 1(2)(a) of the Collective Redundancies Directive is clear to the effect that a worker whose fixed-term or limited-term contract has expired will be excluded from the scope of protection.[56] However, as mentioned earlier,[57] since 6 April 2013 fixed-term contracts have been excluded, so the domestic law in the *University College Union* decision only applies to employees with fixed-term contracts whose contracts were terminated prior to that date.[58]

Finally, one should note the statutory presumption of dismissal for the reason of redundancy in terms of section 195(2) of TULRCA, which mirrors the terms of section 163(2) of the ERA.[59] A final point to note is that the ECJ decided in *Junk v Kühnel*[60] that the word 'redundancy' in the Collective Redundancies Directive means the declaration by an employer of its intention to terminate the contract of employment rather than the actual cessation of the employment relationship upon expiry of the period of notice. This is an important point in the context of the evaluation of the point in time at which the employer must commence consultations, which is a point to which we now turn.

20.3.1.4 What is meant by 'proposing'?

The word 'proposing' is of central importance, since it governs the point in time at which the employer is expected to start the consultation process. Therefore, it is the concept upon which the timing of the consultation process essentially hinges. It can be distinguished from the wording in Article 1(1)(a) of the Collective Redundancies Directive, which states that the employer's consultation obligation starts when it is 'contemplating' collective redundancies. In *Re Hartlebury Printers Ltd (in liquidation)*,[61] Morritt J in the EAT was prepared to construe 'contemplating' in a sense which was equivalent to 'proposing'.[62] However, in a number of other cases, it has been asserted that section 188(1) of TULRCA fails to adequately transpose the Collective Redundancies Directive into domestic law on the basis that the word 'contemplates' enjoins an employer to commence consultations earlier in the process than the word 'proposes' does, such are the differences in the dictionary meaning of these words. For example, the most apposite meaning of the word 'contemplate' in this context which is to be found in the *Oxford English Dictionary* is '[t]o have in view as a purpose'; in the case of the word 'propose', it is 'to form an intention or design'. In other words, the former is formed at an earlier stage in the decision-making process than the latter:

■ *MSF v Refuge Assurance plc* [2002] ICR 1365, 1373–9

. . . we see no reason not to give the word 'contemplating' in Directive 75/129 a meaning reflecting a relatively early stage in the decision process, one at which a collective redundancy falling within the meaning of the Directive was no more than a thing which the employer had in view, something he was taking account of as a contingency . . .

---

[55] [2015] IRLR 573.   [56] *Rabal Cañas v Nexea Gestión Documental* [2015] IRLR 577.
[57] See section 20.3.1.1.
[58] See article 3(1) and (4) of the Trade Union and Labour Relations (Consolidation) Act 1992 (Amendment) Order 2013 that introduces a new section 282 of TULRCA to that effect.
[59] Section 163(2) of the ERA provides for a rebuttable presumption that an employee has been dismissed for the reason of redundancy in the context of the statutory right to receive a redundancy payment, on which, see Chapter 18, sections 18.2.2, 18.2.3.1, and 18.2.4.
[60] (Case C-188/03) [2005] 1 CMLR 42.   [61] [1993] 1 All ER 470.
[62] [1993] 1 All ER 470, 478E. That was notwithstanding that he felt unable to do the opposite, i.e. to construe 'proposing' in all of the same senses as 'contemplating'.

[I]n our view, if our construction of the requirements of the Directive is right, then section 188 cannot be made to accord with it without distortion. Pace the *Hartlebury* case, it would distort the section's 'is proposing to dismiss' to make it akin to the Directive's 'is contemplating'. We respectfully adopt Glidewell LJ's view in [*R v British Coal Corpn and Secretary of State for Trade, ex parte Vardy* [1993] ICR 720] that 'proposes' relates to a state of mind which is much more certain and further along the decision-making process than the verb 'contemplate': see also *Association of Pattern Makers & Allied Craftsmen v Kirvin Ltd* [1978] IRLR 318, 320, para 9 and see obiter in *Scotch Premier Meat Ltd v Burns* [2000] IRLR 639, 641, paras 14 and 15. There Lord Johnston giving the judgment of the appeal tribunal inclined to the view that it was extremely difficult if not impossible to construe 'propose' as wide enough to cover 'contemplation'; he added: 'What concerns us is whether the less can include the greater while the opposite is certainly the case.'

Moreover, section 188's predecessor, section 99 of the 1975 Act, which was indistinguishable from section 188 in this respect, has been construed to require that the material that has to be disclosed in writing to the union (section 99(5); section 188(4)) has to be disclosed *before* the consultation begins: see *E Green & Son (Castings) Ltd v Association of Scientific, Technical and Managerial Staffs* [1984] ICR 352, 360. It would, on that basis, distort section 188 were one either to add to it the general obligation to supply information (whether orally or in writing) in good time *during the course* of the consultations that is found in article 2(3)(a) or the requirement to supply information in writing in good time *during the course* of the consultations found in article 2(3)(b). Nor does Directive 75/129 have any equivalent to section 188's inescapable periods of [45] days and 30 days as specified in section 188(1A) . . . all in all, in our judgment section 188 cannot be construed to accord with the Directive.

That being so, but this not being a case where, on that account, the domestic provision can be disapplied by us, we are left with the task of seeing whether the employment tribunal erred in law, that question to be approached on the basis that, on a straightforward construction of the language of section 188, a 'proposal' to dismiss within it emerges, if at all, at a stage later than the 'contemplation' of redundancies. Of the meanings of 'to propose' given by the *Shorter Oxford English Dictionary* perhaps the most fitting in context is 'to lay before another or others as something which one offers to do or wishes to be done'.[63]

However, the decision of the ECJ in *Akavan Erityisalojen Keskusliitto AEK ry v Fujitsu Siemens Computers Oy*[64] functions to limit the extent of the differences between the UK and European positions. Here, it was held that the words 'contemplating collective redundancies' in Article 2 of the Collective Redundancies Directive enjoin an employer to start the consultation procedure once it has made a strategic or commercial decision compelling it to contemplate or to plan for collective redundancies—and not when such a decision is merely in the mind of the employer:

■ *Akavan Erityisalojen Keskusliitto AEK ry v Fujitsu Siemens Computers Oy* [2010] ICR 444, 467–8

. . . as the United Kingdom Government rightly observes, a premature triggering of the obligation to hold consultations could lead to results contrary to the purpose of Directive 98/59, such as restricting the flexibility available to undertakings when restructuring, creating heavier administrative burdens and causing unnecessary uncertainty for workers about the safety of their jobs.

[63] See also *R v British Coal Corp. and Secretary of State for Trade, ex parte Vardy* [1993] ICR 720; *Griffin v South West Water Services Ltd* [1995] IRLR 15. [64] [2010] ICR 444.

Lastly, the raison d'etre and effectiveness of consultations with the workers' representatives pre-suppose that the factors to be taken into account in the course of those consultations have been determined, given that it is impossible to undertake consultations in a manner which is appropriate and consistent with their objectives when there has been no definition of the factors which are of relevance with regard to the collective redundancies contemplated. Those objectives are, under article 2(2) of Directive 98/59, to avoid termination of employment contracts or to reduce the number of workers affected, and to mitigate the consequences: see *Junk v Kühnel* (Case C-188/03) [2005] ECR I-885, para 38. However, where a decision deemed likely to lead to collective redundancies is merely contemplated and where, accordingly, such collective redundancies are only a probability and the relevant factors for the consultations are not known, those objectives cannot be achieved.

On the other hand, it is clear that to draw a link between the requirement to hold consultations arising under article 2 of Directive 98/59 and the adoption of a strategic or commercial decision which makes the collective redundancies of workers necessary may deprive that requirement, in part, of its effectiveness. As is clear from the first sub-paragraph of article 2(2), the consultations must cover, inter alia, the possibility of avoiding or reducing the collective redundancies contemplated. A consultation which began when a decision making such collective redundancies necessary had already been taken could not usefully involve any examination of conceivable alternatives with the aim of avoiding them.

It must therefore be held that, in circumstances such as those of the case in the main proceedings, the consultation procedure must be started by the employer once a strategic or commercial decision compelling him to contemplate or to plan for collective redundancies has been taken.

In those circumstances, the answer to be given to the first question referred is that article 2(1) of Directive 98/59 must be interpreted to mean that the adoption, within a group of undertakings, of strategic decisions or of changes in activities which compel the employer to contemplate or to plan for collective redundancies gives rise to an obligation on that employer to consult with workers' representatives.

The effect of the decision of the ECJ in *Akavan Erityisalojen Keskusliitto AEK ry v Fu-jitsu Siemens Computers Oy* is that the distance between the UK and European criteria of 'proposing' and 'contemplating' may not be as great as was once thought. However, as the Court of Appeal noted in the case of *USA v Nolan*,[65] the reasoning of the ECJ concerning the exact point in time at which consultation must begin is not easy to understand: what did it intend when it stated that the consultation obligations must start when the employer has adopted 'strategic decisions or . . . changes in activities which compel [it] to contemplate or . . . plan for collective redundancies'? Does this trigger the obligation to consult '(i) when the employer is proposing, but has not yet made, a strategic business or operational decision that will foreseeably or inevitably lead to collective redundancies, or (ii) only when that decision has actually been made and he is then proposing consequential redundancies'?[66] In *USA v Nolan*, the US Government made a decision to close the US military base RSA Hythe in Hampshire prior to 13 March 2006 and the workforce at the base were informed of that decision on 24 April 2006. The US Government intimated its decision to close the base to the UK Government on 9 May 2006 and consultations under section 188 of TUL-RCA commenced on 5 June 2006. The issue for resolution was whether the employer's consultation obligation was engaged by a proposed decision on the part of the employer to close the base or whether it arose at a subsequent stage when the commercial decision had been made by the employer and the intention to make the employees redundant had been formed. Lord Justice Rimer in the Court of Appeal felt unable to answer that question

---

[65] [2010] EWCA Civ 1223, [2011] IRLR 40.
[66] *USA v Nolan* [2011] IRLR 40, 49 at para 57 per Rimer LJ.

and decided to refer questions to the ECJ relating to the exact point in time at which the consultation obligations arose.[67] Unfortunately, the ECJ declined to answer the questions on the ground that it lacked jurisdiction to determine the issue: the employees concerned were employed by the armed forces, which is a public administrative body and, as such, fell within the exemption laid down in Article 1(2)(b) of the Collective Redundancies Directive.[68] When the case came before the Court of Appeal again,[69] the issue was whether the domestic provisions in TULRCA implementing the Collective Redundancies Directive went beyond the requirements of EU law, which does not extend to public administrative bodies in terms of Article 1(2)(b). This issue was appealed to the Supreme Court,[70] which gave a positive response to that question, meaning that the USA is subject to the information and consultation obligations under TULRCA notwithstanding the position in EU law. The Supreme Court has now remitted the substantive issue about the precise trigger point for consultation to the Court of Appeal and we can expect an answer at some later date.

E Ivor Hughes Educational Foundation v Morris[71] is a case which demonstrates how tricky it can be to make a judgment call on the most appropriate date to commence consultation. The case concerned the closure of a school and when the obligation to consult had been engaged. The evidence revealed that, on 27 February 2013, a meeting of the governors of the school took place to discuss the serious financial implications of falling student numbers, at which the head teacher was present. The head teacher informed the meeting that the financial position of the school was precarious and put forward options as to how to enable the school to be kept open or turn the position around. Ultimately, these options were not sufficiently concrete to amount to clear solutions and she admitted that the school had reached a position where it was no longer viable if the future intake projections had not improved by April 2013. On 25 April 2013, the head teacher informed the governors that, on the latest projected pupil numbers for the following academic year, there would be a deficit in the order of £250,000. On that basis, the governors then decided to close the school at the end of the summer term of 2013. On one reading of this evidence, no concrete commitment to close the school was made at the meeting on 27 February 2013, since no strategic business or operational decision that would lead to collective redundancies had been made by that point, let alone proposed. Nevertheless, the tribunal and the EAT arrived at the conclusion that the obligation to consult commenced on 27 February 2013 for the reason that a contingent and provisional decision to close the school in April 2013 had been taken at the meeting, namely that unless matters improved by April 2013, the school would have to close.

Prior to the decision of the ECJ in *Junk v Kühnel*,[72] the approach of the tribunals and courts in the UK was to permit an employer to commence consultation after it had served notice of dismissals upon the affected employees.[73] In fact, it was possible for consultations to begin after the affected employees had been dismissed. *Junk v Kühnel* removed this option. The ECJ decided that the event constituting a redundancy consists of a declaration by an employer of its intention to terminate the contract of employment, rather than the actual determination of the employment relationship upon expiry of the period of notice. The effect of this rule is that it is unlawful for an employer to terminate the contracts of employment of employees for the reason of redundancy prior to the conclusion of the consultation procedures. In accordance with the reasoning in *Junk v Kühnel*, in the case of *Leicestershire County Council v Unison*,[74] the EAT ruled that an employer will be 'proposing to dismiss' its employees when it is 'proposing to give notices of dismissal' to

---

[67] [2010] EWCA Civ 1223, [2011] IRLR 40, 48–50.

[68] [2013] ICR 193, 209F–212B. For the transposition of this exemption into UK law, see sections 273 and 274 of TULRCA which exclude Crown employees and members of the armed forces from the coverage of the collective redundancies consultation regime.   [69] [2014] ICR 685.

[70] [2016] AC 463.   [71] [2015] IRLR 696.   [72] [2005] IRLR 310, 314.

[73] *Middlesborough Borough Council v TGWU* [2002] IRLR 332.   [74] [2005] IRLR 920.

those employees. Likewise, in *UK Coal Mining Ltd v NUM (Northumberland Area)*,[75] the EAT held that the consultation process must have been completed in advance of notices of dismissal having been served upon the affected employees. The *Junk v Kühnel* case also decided that any action by an employer to terminate the contracts of employment of employees for the reason of redundancy prior to the conclusion of the consultation procedures will be unlawful under Article 2 of the Collective Redundancies Directive.

A final issue to address concerns the interaction between the employer's purported proposal to dismiss employees and the 20-employee minimum specified in the statute. It has been held that the effect of the words 'proposing to dismiss' is that an employer's statutory obligations will be engaged notwithstanding the fact that it intended to offer some of the employees alternative employment, which, if taken into account, would reduce the number of employees earmarked for redundancy below the figure of 20.[76] Conversely, where the employer makes 17 employees compulsorily redundant and a further three employees volunteer for redundancy, it has been held that the 20-employee threshold in section 188 of TULRCA was satisfied on the ground that the employer had proposed to dismiss 20 or more employees. In both cases, one can detect the adoption of an approach that is protective of the employees.[77]

20.3.1.5 What is an 'establishment'?

It is prescribed that an 'employer' must consult with appropriate representatives where it 'is proposing to dismiss as redundant 20 or more employees *at one establishment* within a period of 90 days or less'.[78] One might expect the terms 'at one establishment' and 'employer' to have been defined in TULRCA or the Collective Redundancies Directive. However, rather surprisingly, they have not. The starting point for our discussion of the relevance of the words 'at one establishment' is the decision of the ECJ in *Rockfon A/S v Specialarbejderforbundet I Danmark, acting for Nielsen:*[79]

■ *Rockfon A/S v Specialarbejderforbundet I Danmark* [1996] ICR 673, 689

The term 'establishment' appearing in Article 1(1)(a) of the [Collective Redundancies Directive] must therefore be interpreted as designating, depending on the circumstances, the unit to which the workers made redundant are assigned to carry out their duties. It is not essential in order for there to be an 'establishment' for the unit in question to be endowed with a management which can independently effect collective redundancies.

That interpretation is supported by the fact that the Commission's initial proposal for a Directive used the term 'undertaking' and that that term was defined in the last sub-paragraph of article 1(1) of the proposal as 'local employment unit.' It appears, however, that the Council decided to replace the term 'undertaking' by the term 'establishment,' which meant that the definition originally contained in the proposal and considered to be superfluous was deleted.

The answer to the second part of the preliminary question must therefore be that the term 'establishment' appearing in article 1(1)(a) of the [Collective Redundancies Directive] must be understood as meaning, depending on the circumstances, the unit to which the workers made redundant are assigned to carry out their duties. It is not essential, in order for there to be an 'establishment,' for the unit in question to be endowed with a management which can independently effect collective redundancies.

---

[75] [2008] ICR 163.   [76] *Hardy v Tourism South East* [2005] IRLR 242.
[77] *Optare Group v Transport & General Workers' Union* [2007] IRLR 931.
[78] Section 188(1) of TULRCA. Writer's emphasis is shown in italics.
[79] (Case C-449/93) [1996] ICR 673.

Two points can be drawn from this extract:

(1) the unit to which the workers (to be made redundant) are assigned will vary from case to case; and

(2) there is no need for a specific layer of management to be in place which is particular to the body of workers whom it is proposed to make redundant. The *Rockfon* case also establishes that the word 'establishment' must be given a European-wide uniform definition.

In the case of *Athinaiki Chartopoïï AE v Panagiotidis*,[80] the ECJ built on the guidance it provided in *Rockfon A/S v Specialarbejderforbundet I Danmark, acting for Nielsen.* Athinaiki Chartopoïï operated three separate paper manufacturing production units in three different locations: a unit for the manufacture of writing paper, printing paper, mechanical pulp, chip-board, and aluminium sulphate, with a staff of 420 people; a second unit for the manufacture of soft kitchen paper, toilet paper, bags, etc.; and a third unit which processed soft paper. Each of the three units operated autonomously, had distinct equipment, and a specialized workforce. A chief production officer made sure that the work was carried out properly. He was also responsible for supervision of the entire operation of the unit's installations and ensured that technical issues were resolved. However, decisions about operating expenditure, the purchase of materials, and the costing of products were taken, on the basis of information forwarded by the units in question, at Athinaiki Chartopoïï's headquarters, where a joint accounts office was set up for salary payment, invoices, and the drawing up of a single balance sheet. When Athinaiki Chartopoïï decided to close the first production unit owing to losses and to dismiss almost all of the workers of that unit, the question was whether that unit amounted to an independent establishment for the purposes of the Collective Redundancies Directive. The ECJ answered this question in the affirmative and took a broad interpretation of the word 'establishment':

■ *Athinaiki Chartopoïï AE v Panagiotidis* (Case C-270/05) [2007] ECR I-1499, paras 25–29

The court has interpreted the concept of 'establishment' in [the Collective Redundancies Directive], in particular in Article 1(1)(a), as designating, depending on the circumstances, the unit to which the workers made redundant are assigned to carry out their duties (*Rockfon*, paragraphs 31 and 32, and case-law cited). In so doing, the Court has defined the term 'establishment' very broadly, in order to limit as far as possible cases of collective redundancies which are not subject to [the Collective Redundancies Directive] because of the legal definition of that term at national level (see, inter alia, Joined Cases C-187/05 to C-190/05 *Agorastoudis and Others* [2006] ECR I-0000, paragraph 37). However, given the general nature of that definition, it cannot by itself be decisive for the appraisal of the specific circumstances of the case at issue in the main proceedings. Thus for the purposes of the application of the [Collective Redundancies Directive], an 'establishment', in the context of an undertaking, may consist of a distinct entity, having a certain degree of permanence and stability, which is assigned to perform one or more given tasks and which has a workforce, technical means and a certain organisational structure allowing for the accomplishment of those tasks. Given that the objective pursued by [the Collective Redundancies Directive] concerns, in particular, the socio-economic effects which collective redundancies may have in a given local context and social environment, the entity in question need not have any legal autonomy, nor need it have economic, financial, administrative or technological autonomy, in order to be regarded as an 'establishment'.

---

[80] (Case C-270/05) [2007] IRLR 284.

> It is, moreover, in this spirit that the Court has held that it is not essential, in order for there to be an 'establishment', for the unit in question to be endowed with a management which can independently effect collective redundancies (*Rockfon*, paragraph 34, and point 2 of the operative part) . . .[81]

A particular question which has vexed the courts is whether a distinct store, site, or unit which is physically distinctive will count as an 'establishment'.[82] In *USDAW v WW Realisation 1 Ltd*,[83] the ECJ gave an affirmative response to that question.[84] The case concerned the collapse of Woolworths and Ethel Austin, two high street stores, which resulted in approximately 30,000 job losses. There was no consultation prior to redundancies in the case of some of the employees who worked at stores with fewer than 20 employees. The argument was made that there was no need to consult employees working at such sub-20 employee stores, since those stores, units, or sites did not constitute an 'establishment'. Ultimately, the ECJ agreed with this argument on the ground that an 'establishment' 'may consist of a distinct entity, having a certain degree of permanence and stability, which is assigned to perform one or more given tasks and which has a workforce, technical means and a certain organisational structure allowing for the accomplishment of those tasks . . . [and that] it is the entity to which the workers made redundant are assigned to carry out their duties that constitutes the "establishment" for the purposes of article 1(1)(a) of the Collective Redundancies Directive'.[85] Together with the decision of the ECJ in *Lyttle v Bluebird UK Bidco 2 Ltd*,[86] *WW Realisation* is authority for the proposition that if the employer is proposing to make 20 or more employees redundant across its business as a whole, then the statutory duty to consult will not be triggered if fewer than 20 employees are made redundant at a particular unit or store to which those employees are assigned in order to perform their work tasks and duties. That is notwithstanding that the employer is proposing to dismiss well in excess of 20 or more employees in aggregate at more than one site/establishment. In light of *WW Realisation*, consider Hypothetical B, which underscores the 'single-site' rather than 'business-wide' approach which is taken to the 'establishment' consultation trigger.

Hypothetical B

One of Danny's Demolishers plc's subsidiaries, namely Danny's Demolishers (Northwest) Ltd ('the Employer') trades from 43 separate units located throughout the northwest of England, consisting of 16 offices, a factory, and 26 depots. It has 2,323 employees at those 43 units. It decides to make 19 employees redundant at each of the 43 geographical locations, i.e. 19 × 43 = 817 employees in total. Despite the fact that employees well in excess of the 20-employee threshold are to be made redundant across the Employer's entire commercial operations, since fewer than 20 employees are affected at each of the 43 sites/units, it is not obliged to collectively consult under section 188(1) of TULRCA.

---

[81] Sourced from Curia website, available at http://curia.europa.eu/juris/liste.jsf?pro=&nat=&oqp=&dates=&lg=&language=en&jur=C%2CT%2CF&cit=none%252CC%252CCJ%252CR%252C2008E%252C%252C%252C%252C%252C%252C%252C%252C%252C%252Ctrue%252Cfalse%252Cfalse&num=c-270%252F05&td=ALL&pcs=O&avg=&page=1&mat=or&jge=&for=&cid=92539 (last visited 14 September 2017).

[82] In *Renfrewshire Council v Educational Institute of Scotland* [2013] ICR 172, a school was treated as a distinct entity so as to qualify as an establishment, since the word 'establishment' connotes a physical presence, rather than in any organizational sense. See also *MSF v Refuge Assurance* [2002] ICR 1365.

[83] [2015] ICR 675.   [84] *ibid.*, 706G–H.   [85] *ibid.*, 704A–D.

[86] [2015] IRLR 577. In light of *WW Realisation* and *Lyttle v Bluebird*, it is unlikely that the result in *Barratt Developments (Bradford) Ltd v UCATT* [1978] ICR 319 remains good law.

20.3.1.6 Who is an 'employer'?

Like the concept of 'establishment', the approach adopted in respect of the interpretation of the word 'employer' is one which follows a distinctly legalistic path. For example, in the case of *E Green & Son (Castings) Ltd v ASTMS*,[87] a proposal was made to make employees redundant who were spread over three different legal entities: 97 employees with one company; 36 with another company; and 24 with the third company. The three companies operated from the same premises, shared the same services, and were subsidiary companies of the same parent company. The personnel director of the parent company was responsible for the employees of each of the three subsidiary companies and the managing director of the parent company took the decision to make the employees redundant at each of the three subsidiaries. The issue was whether the three companies should be treated as one-and-the-same employer, in which case there would be a proposal to dismiss 100 or more employees and so an obligation to consult for at least 90 days[88] in terms of section 188(1) of TULRCA, or whether each of the subsidiaries should be treated separately, in which case the consultation period would be at least 30 days.

The EAT recognized that the 157 employees were linked to 'one establishment',[89] but since they worked for three different employers, it was held that each of the subsidiaries was an employer. Therefore, they each had an obligation to engage in consultations with the affected employees for a minimum of 30 days before the dismissals were to take effect, rather than 90 days.[90] The EAT rejected the argument that the three companies should be treated as one-and-the-same employer; instead, it stated that the focus ought to be on the identity of the party who was the employer of the affected employees under the terms of their contracts of employment.

Some support for the somewhat mechanical approach of the EAT is provided in the decision of the ECJ in *Akavan Erityisalojen Keskusliitto AEK ry v Fujitsu Siemens Computers Oy*.[91] Here, the ECJ recognized that where a decision to make employees redundant is taken by the parent company of a subsidiary, the latter will nonetheless be the 'employer' for the purposes of the consultation obligations:

■ *Akavan Erityisalojen Keskusliitto AEK ry v Fujitsu Siemens Computers Oy*
[2010] ICR 444, 470

Consequently, article 2(1) and the first sub-paragraph of article 2(4) of [the Collective Redundancies Directive] are to be interpreted to the effect that, under those provisions, irrespective of whether collective redundancies are contemplated or projected as a result of a decision of the undertaking which employs the workers concerned or a decision of its parent company, it is always the former which is obliged, as the employer, to start consultations with the representatives of its workers. . .

Where the parent company of a group of undertakings adopts decisions likely to have repercussions on the jobs of workers within that group, it is for the subsidiary whose employees may be affected by redundancies, in its capacity as their employer, to start consultations with the workers' representatives. It is therefore not possible to start such consultations until such time as that subsidiary has been identified.

In addition, with regard to the intended objectives of the consultations, under article 2(2) of [the Collective Redundancies Directive], those consultations are, at least, to cover ways and means

---

[87] [1984] ICR 352.   [88] Please note that the threshold is now 45 days: section 188(1A) of TULRCA.
[89] In light of *WW Realisation* and *Lyttle v Bluebird*, it is very unlikely that this statement remains good law.
[90] Please note that the threshold is now 45 days: section 188(1A) of TULRCA.
[91] [2010] ICR 444. For a critique, see J. Prassl, *The Concept of the Employer* (Oxford, OUP, 2015) 96–105 and 225.

of avoiding collective redundancies or reducing the number of workers affected, and of mitigating the consequences by recourse to accompanying social measures aimed, inter alia, at aid for redeploying or retraining workers made redundant. If a consultation on those matters is to have any meaning, the subsidiary whose employees will be affected by the contemplated collective redundancies must be known.

In those circumstances, the answer to be given to the third and fourth questions referred is that article 2(1) of [the Collective Redundancies Directive], read in conjunction with the first sub-paragraph of article 2(4) of [the Collective Redundancies Directive], must be interpreted to mean that, in the case of a group of undertakings consisting of a parent company and one or more subsidiaries, the obligation to hold consultations with the workers' representatives falls on the subsidiary which has the status of employer only once that subsidiary, within which collective redundancies may be made, has been identified.

The implication of *Akavan* is that if an employer incorporates distinct subsidiary companies and assigns each of them to run sites at different geographical locations (e.g. factories, offices, stores, premises, etc.) where its employees are based, it will be able to avoid collective consultation if it proposes to dismiss 20 or more employees across its business as a whole, but fewer than 20 at each of these locations. As such, like the outcome in Hypothetical B, the 'single-site' rather than 'business-wide' approach is taken to the consultation trigger. Consider Hypothetical C.

Hypothetical C

Danny's Demolishers plc ('the Employer') sets up 43 separate subsidiary companies to run operations at 43 sites, comprising 16 offices, a factory, and 26 depots. There are 2,323 employees in total at those 43 units and each of the employees has contracts of employment with the relevant subsidiary company operating at the site. The Employer's board of directors decides to make 19 employees redundant at each of the 43 geographical locations, i.e. $19 \times 43 = 817$ employees in total. In accordance with the Employer's instructions, each of the 43 subsidiary companies announces to its respective workforces that it is proposing to make 19 employees redundant. As such, there are fewer than 20 employees to be made redundant by each of the employers/subsidiary companies at each of the units. Although there are 817 employees to be dismissed across the Employer's business as a whole, since the 43 groups of 19 employees have different employers, there is no obligation on the Employer or the 43 subsidiary companies to collectively consult under section 188(1) of TULRCA.

A final issue to be stressed is that the nature of the employer is irrelevant for the purposes of the evaluation as to whether an organization is an 'employer' in terms of section 188(1) of TULRCA. For example, in the case of *Commission v Italian Republic*,[92] the fact that an employer was a not-for-profit entity did not relieve it of its obligation to consult. Therefore, charitable bodies, foundations, trade unions, and co-operatives qualify as employers under section 188(1).

---

[92] (Case C-32/03) [2003] ECR I-12063.

20.3.1.7 Who are the 'appropriate representatives'?

The employer has an obligation to consult with 'appropriate representatives' under section 188(1) of TULRCA. The appropriate representatives may be drawn from those employees *who may be affected by the proposed dismissals or the measures taken in connection with those dismissals*, rather than from those whom the employer proposes to dismiss. The aforementioned italicized words clarify that the representatives may be selected from a broad constituency. This may extend to the entire workforce of the employer depending on the extent of the employer's restructuring proposals.

The appropriate representatives may be selected from three particular groups:

Section 188 Duty of employer to consult representatives

(1B) For the purposes of this section the appropriate representatives of any affected employees are—

(a) if the employees are of a description in respect of which an independent trade union is recognised by their employer, representatives of the trade union, or

(b) in any other case, whichever of the following employee representatives the employer chooses:—

   (i) employee representatives appointed or elected by the affected employees otherwise than for the purposes of this section, who (having regard to the purposes for and the method by which they were appointed or elected) have authority from those employees to receive information and to be consulted about the proposed dismissals on their behalf;

   (ii) employee representatives elected by the affected employees, for the purposes of this section, in an election satisfying the requirements of section 188A(1) . . .

Section 196 Construction of references to representatives

(1) For the purposes of this Chapter persons are employee representatives if—

(a) they have been elected by employees for the specific purpose of being consulted by their employer about dismissals proposed by him, or

(b) having been elected or appointed by employees (whether before or after dismissals have been proposed by their employer) otherwise than for that specific purpose, it is appropriate (having regard to the purposes for which they were elected) for the employer to consult them about dismissals proposed by him, and (in either case) they are employed by the employer at the time when they are elected or appointed.

(2) References in this Chapter to representatives of a trade union, in relation to an employer, are to officials or other persons authorised by the trade union to carry on collective bargaining with the employer.

(3) References in this Chapter to affected employees are to employees who may be affected by the proposed dismissals or who may be affected by measures taken in connection with such dismissals.

The representatives referred to in section 188(1B)(a) and (b)(ii) of TULRCA are fairly self-explanatory, i.e. representatives of an independent trade union which is recognized by the employer,[93] and representatives elected by the affected employees in accordance

---

[93] For example, a shop steward or a district union official or, if appropriate, a national or regional official.

with the election and balloting requirements of section 188A(1). The difficulty with the latter 'employee representatives' group is that there is no legal requirement for them to be independent of management, a point we discussed earlier in section 20.1.1. Therefore, there is the danger that the employer can take action which frustrates the effectiveness of these employee representatives, and, for the reasons ventilated, one might argue that section 188(1B)(b)(ii) does not effectively implement the requirements of the Collective Redundancies Directive.

Section 188(1B)(b)(i) of TULRCA, which deals with the third group, demands further explanation. It applies where pre-existing employee representatives have been put in place and covers employee representatives who have been appointed or elected by the affected employees for another purpose, e.g. under the Information and Consultation of Employees Regulations 2004[94] or the Transfers of Undertakings (Protection of Employment) Regulations 2006.[95] However, there is a further requirement for such other representatives to be sufficiently qualified, specified in section 188(1B)(b)(i), which is that, having regard to the purposes for and the method by which they were appointed or elected, they have authority from those employees to receive information and to be consulted about the proposed dismissals on their behalf. In *Kelly v Hesley Group Ltd*,[96] rather than go through the process of arranging for the balloting and election of employee representatives, the employer consulted with an existing non-negotiating body referred to as a joint consultative committee ('JCC'), which had been established to channel the views of staff to management[97] and vice versa. On the ground that the employer had not shifted the burden of proving[98] that the JCC had the authority from the employees to receive information and be consulted in accordance with the requirement in section 188(1B)(b)(i), the EAT reached the decision that the JCC was insufficiently representative of the workforce and, as such, the employer had failed to engage in proper collective consultation.

The procedures for the election of employee representatives are governed by sections 188(7A), (7B), and (7C) and 188A of TULRCA. These provisions are extremely elaborate. Suffice to say that the key principle is that the employer must invite the affected employees to elect representatives, make such 'arrangements' as are reasonably practical to ensure that the election is fair, and must not unreasonably exclude affected employees from standing for election. However, it has been held that there is no requirement for an employer to conduct a ballot where the number of candidates is equivalent to the number of vacancies which existed for elected representatives.[99] Where no employee representatives are elected (for whatever reason), the employer is required to provide each of the affected employees with the information it would otherwise be obliged to provide to the employee representatives.[100]

20.3.1.8 What is meant by 'in good time'?

We have seen that when the employer 'proposes to dismiss' employees for redundancy, this acts as the trigger point for the commencement of consultations with appropriate representatives of the affected employees. Once that point has been reached, section 188(1A) of TULRCA stipulates that consultations must commence 'in good time' and in any event, where the employer is proposing to dismiss 100 or more employees, at least 45 days before the first of the dismissals takes effect or otherwise at least 30 days before the first of the dismissals takes effect, as the case may be. In the case of *Amicus v Nissan Motor Manufacturing (UK) Ltd*,[101] Ansell J provided some guidance as to the meaning of this term as follows:

---

[94] SI 2004/3426.   [95] SI 2006/246.   [96] [2013] IRLR 514.
[97] Rather than negotiate with management.   [98] See section 189 of TULRCA.
[99] *Phillips v Xtera Communications* [2012] ICR 171.   [100] *Howard v Milrise Ltd* [2005] ICR 435.
[101] [2005] All ER (D) 128 (September).

■ *Amicus v Nissan Motor Manufacturing (UK) Ltd* (UKEAT/184/05, 26 July 2005), para 11

> . . . 'good time' means no more and no less than time sufficient for fair consultation to take place working back from the final date which is the first date for dismissal . . . we accept that one cannot adopt a too mechanistic or arithmetical approach to working out what is or is not good time. It will depend on many factors and is essentially a question for a Tribunal. A number of the matters involved will obviously be firstly the numbers of staff and indeed unions to be involved in the process; secondly what is a reasonable time for the union to be able to respond to the proposals and to make counter-suggestion regarding redundancies whilst the proposals are still at a formative stage. Timing will depend on the eventual outcome that is being envisaged how many are to be relocated or redeployed and the ancillary issues involved in association with that redeployment issues such as re housing expenses and if necessary new schooling for children involved. What are the subjects to be discussed within the consultation process? How many meetings are likely to be required to cover that process and as the process develops one has to consider what changes are taking place to the proposals and how those changes will affect the time for consultation and whether the time for consultation thereafter as a result needs to be extended.[102]

Where there is a requirement to hold an election to appoint appropriate representatives, section 188(7A) of TULRCA directs that 'in good time' is to be construed as 'as soon as is reasonably practicable after the election of the representatives'. In the case of *E Green & Son (Castings) Ltd*,[103] further guidance was given on the time periods of 45 days and 30 days referred to in section 188(1A). Here, the EAT opined that these periods are referable to the date on which the first dismissal would take effect if the employer's redundancy proposals were implemented.

20.3.1.9 When are the dismissals deemed to 'take effect'?

Dismissals take effect on the expiry of the period of notice in the notices of dismissal. In line with the jurisprudence of the ECJ in *Junk v Kühnel*,[104] collective consultation must be completed before any affected employee is issued with a notice of dismissal.

20.4 THE NATURE AND EXTENT OF THE STATUTORY INFORMATION AND CONSULTATION OBLIGATIONS

The employer's statutory obligations consist of providing information to, and consulting with, the trade union or employee representatives of the affected employees. We now subject those obligations to closer scrutiny.

20.4.1 Information rights

The information which the employer must disclose in writing to the appropriate employee representatives or trade union representatives is listed in section 188(4) of TULRCA as follows:

---

[102] Sourced from BAILII available at http://www.bailii.org/cgi-bin/markup.cgi?doc=/uk/cases/UKE-AT/2005/0184_05_2607.html&query=nissan+and+motor+and+manufacturing&method=boolean (last visited 17 September 2017).   [103] [1984] ICR 352.
[104] [2005] IRLR 310, 314.

Section 188 Duty of employer to consult representatives

(4) For the purposes of the consultation the employer shall disclose in writing to the appropriate representatives—

(a) the reasons for his proposals,

(b) the number and description of employees whom it is proposed to dismiss as redundant,

(c) the total number of employees of any such description employed by the employer at the establishment in question,

(d) the proposed method of selecting the employees who may be dismissed,

(e) the proposed method of carrying out the dismissals, with due regard to any agreed procedure, including the period over which the dismissals are to take effect,

(f) the proposed method of calculating the amount of any redundancy payments to be made (otherwise than in compliance with an obligation imposed by or by virtue of any enactment) to employees who may be dismissed,

(g) the number of agency workers working temporarily for and under the supervision and direction of the employer,

(h) the parts of the employer's undertaking on which those agency workers are working, and

(i) the type of work those agency workers are carrying out.

Where an employer furnishes such information pursuant to a prior intention to make employees redundant, which is dropped or deferred subsequent to consultation with the appropriate representatives, the employer must submit such information afresh if it then decides to reopen the possibility of collective redundancies. As such, its subsequent decision to reopen is not treated as relating to the same employees and the same prospective redundancies.[105] Such information must be furnished to each of the appropriate representatives by being delivered to them or sent by post to an address notified by them to the employer, or (in the case of a trade union representative) sent by post to the trade union at its head or main office address.[106] The employer's duty includes co-operating with the appropriate representatives by providing all such information during the process of consultation. In the case of *Lancaster University v University College Union*,[107] it was held that the service of a list with the names of employees on fixed-term contracts whom the employer proposed to make redundant marked 'for consultation purposes' amounted to a breach of section 188 of TULRCA. Such a list failed to furnish the trade union representatives with sufficient background information to (1) challenge the selection process, or (2) engage in consultation with the employer with a view to reaching agreement.

The employer has a defence where it is unable to comply with its obligations under this section:

Section 188 Duty of employer to consult representatives

(7) If in any case there are special circumstances which render it not reasonably practicable for the employer to comply with a requirement of subsection (1A), (2) or (4) [of section 188 of TULRCA], the employer shall take all such steps towards compliance with that requirement

---

[105] *Vauxhall Motors Ltd v Transport and General Workers' Union* [2006] IRLR 674. The employer will also have to comply with the consultation obligations in such a case.

[106] Section 188(5) of TULRCA.   [107] [2011] IRLR 4.

as are reasonably practicable in those circumstances. Where the decision leading to the proposed dismissals is that of a person controlling the employer (directly or indirectly), a failure on the part of that person to provide information to the employer shall not constitute special circumstances rendering it not reasonably practicable for the employer to comply with such a requirement . . .

Section 189 Complaint and protective award

(6) If on a complaint under this section a question arises—

   (a) whether there were special circumstances which rendered it not reasonably practicable for the employer to comply with any requirement of section 188, or

   (b) whether he took all such steps towards compliance with that requirement as were reasonably practicable in those circumstances, it is for the employer to show that there were and that he did.[108]

It will only be in exceptional, uncommon, or out of the ordinary[109] circumstances that an employer will be able to take advantage of this relaxation in section 188(7) of TULRCA and very detailed evidence will be needed to convince a tribunal or court that such relief should be given.[110] For example, where an employer has not applied its mind to whether consultation ought to have taken place because it was unaware at the time that it ought to engage in consultation, it will be unable to avail itself of the 'special circumstances' defence, since the focus of sections 188(7) and 189(6) is on the actual events which occurred and whether those events rendered it not reasonably practicable for the employer to consult.[111] Circumstances will be 'special' where the employer is able to show that something exceptional or out of the ordinary has occurred, such that it is not reasonably practicable to consult the union or employee representatives, e.g. the destruction of a plant, site, or factory,[112] or a general trading boycott. Although the sudden withdrawal of supplies from a main supplier may amount to special circumstances, the need to make staff redundant in rapid response to the sudden decision of a contractor to reduce the amount of work required of the employer will not so qualify.[113] Without more, it is unlikely that compliance with the UK Takeover Code[114] will amount to a 'special circumstance' excusing the employer from complying with its information (and consultation) obligations.[115] This, of course, is particularly relevant to employers whose shares and securities have been listed by the UK Listing Authority, e.g. on the London Stock Exchange or some other financial exchange.

---

[108] On section 189(6) of TULRCA, see *Iron and Steel Trades Confederation v ASW Holdings plc (in administrative receivership)* [2005] All ER (D) 174 (October).

[109] *Bakers' Union v Clarks of Hove Ltd* [1978] 1 WLR 1207, 1215H per Geoffrey Lane LJ.

[110] *UK Coal Mining Ltd v NUM (Northumberland Area)* [2008] ICR 163.

[111] *E Ivor Hughes Educational Foundation v Morris* [2015] IRLR 696.

[112] *Bakers' Union v Clarks of Hove Ltd* [1978] 1 WLR 1207, 1215 per Geoffrey Lane LJ; *Re Hartlebury Printers Ltd (in liquidation)* [1993] 1 All ER 470, 479–80 per Morritt J.

[113] *Shanahan Engineering Ltd v Unite the Union* [2010] All ER (D) 108 (March).

[114] The Takeover Code, available at http://www.thetakeoverpanel.org.uk/wp-content/uploads/2008/11/code.pdf (last visited 17 September 2017).

[115] *MSF v Refuge Assurance* [2002] ICR 1365, 1382A–C per Lindsay J. An employer will be subject to the Takeover Code where its securities are traded on a regulated market or other exchanges such as the Alternative Investment Market, on which, see A3–A4 of the Takeover Code.

An obvious question to ask is whether an employer who has entered into a formal insolvency process will be entitled to plead 'special circumstances'. In the case of *Bakers' Union v Clarks of Hove Ltd*,[116] the Court of Appeal held that the sudden insolvency of an employer leading to dismissals did not amount to 'special circumstances'.[117] Likewise, where an employer entered into administration in *Re Hartlebury Printers Ltd (in liquidation)*,[118] this was held to be insufficient to constitute 'special circumstances'. These cases can be contrasted with *USDAW v Leancut Bacon (in liquidation)*.[119] Here, where the employer's bankers withdrew credit facilities and the employer entered into receivership, this was deemed to be sufficient to amount to 'special circumstances'. Therefore, there is no hard-and-fast rule of thumb that the insolvency of the employer will amount to 'special circumstances'; instead, account must be taken of the nature and outcome of the relevant insolvency process, as well as all of the circumstances of the case.[120] This is confirmed in the ACAS booklet *Handling Large-Scale (Collective) Redundancies*.[121]

20.4.2 Consultation rights

When we examined the obligations of employers under the unfair dismissal legislation in Chapter 18, we noted that consultation with the individual employees provisionally selected for redundancy was a key element of that process. In *Williams v Compair Maxam Ltd*,[122] Browne-Wilkinson J underscored the importance of consultation with trade unions where the workforce was unionized. We also noted that this consultation obligation had evolved over time to include duties on management to consult individually. The statutory consultation obligations under section 188(2) of TULRCA operate in parallel with those individual consultation obligations. The statutory consultation obligation is set out in the following terms:

Section 188 Duty of employer to consult representatives

(2) The consultation shall include consultation about ways of—

   (a) avoiding the dismissals,

   (b) reducing the numbers of employees to be dismissed, and

   (c) mitigating the consequences of the dismissals, and shall be undertaken by the employer with a view to reaching agreement with the appropriate representatives.

The employer is under an obligation to consult on each of these mandatory factors. Consultation is more than simply offering the appropriate representatives the opportunity to discuss such matters with management, or matters of concern to the employees; rather, it is a process whereby the appropriate representatives seek to reach an agreement with management.[123] An employer is precluded from being excused performance of these consultation obligations on the ground that they would be futile or utterly useless in the circumstances,[124] i.e. there is no rule akin to that of *Polkey v A. E. Dayton Services Ltd*.[125] However, in much the same way as the information

---

[116] [1978] 1 WLR 1207.   [117] *ibid*., 1215 per Geoffrey Lane LJ.
[118] [1992] ICR 559.   [119] [1981] IRLR 295.
[120] *Re Huddersfield Fine Worsteds Ltd* [2006] ICR 205, 209H–210A per Neuberger LJ.
[121] See http://www.acas.org.uk/index.aspx?articleid=4547 at pages 25–6 (last visited 17 September 2017).
[122] [1982] ICR 156, 162–7.   [123] *Kelly v Hesley Group Ltd* [2013] IRLR 514.
[124] *Middlesbrough Borough Council v TGWU* [2002] IRLR 332, 338 per Clark J; *Susie Radin Ltd v GMB* [2004] ICR 893, 906H–907A per Gibson LJ.   [125] [1988] AC 344.

obligations under section 188(4) of TULRCA, an employer will be relieved of liability for a failure to consult under section 188(2) if it can demonstrate that there are special circumstances which render it not reasonably practicable for the employer to comply with such obligations.[126] The construction of the expression 'special circumstances' is identical to that adopted in the context of the employer's information obligations under section 188(4).[127]

A current matter of controversy is whether the employer is required to consult with the representatives about the commercial rationales for the proposed collective redundancies as part of the statutory exercise. For example, in the case of *R v British Coal Corp. and Secretary of State for Trade, ex parte Vardy*,[128] Lord Glidewell made the *obiter* comment that the statutory provisions do not require consultation about the reason for redundancy, including whether or not a plant should close.[129] Instead, consultation should be about *how* the employer should carry out the proposed redundancies which management have deemed to be necessary. This interpretation was followed by the EAT in *Middlesbrough Borough Council v Transport and General Workers' Union*[130] and *Securicor Omega Express Ltd v GMB*.[131] However, in the case of *UK Coal Mining Ltd v NUM (Northumberland Area)*,[132] the EAT adopted a diametrically opposite approach. The case concerned consultations about the proposed closure of a coal pit owing to an inrush of water at the coal face. A question arose as to whether the employer also ought to have consulted about the commercial reasons for the closure:

■ *UK Coal Mining Ltd v NUM (Northumberland Area)* [2008] ICR 163, 184

But the obligation to consult over avoiding the proposed redundancies inevitably involves engaging with the reasons for the dismissals, and that in turn requires consultation over the reasons for the closure. Strictly, of course, it is the proposed dismissals that are the subject of consultation, and not the closure itself. Accordingly, if an employer planned a closure but believed that redundancies would none the less be avoided, there would be no need to consult over the closure decision itself, at least not pursuant to the obligations under [TULRCA] . . . In the context of a closure, that is likely to be a very exceptional case. Where closure and dismissals are inextricably interlinked, the duty to consult over the reasons arises . . .

We also accept that in substance there is no distinction in practice in this case at least between the closure and the dismissals. Indeed, if anything it could be said that the closure followed the dismissals, rather than the dismissals following the closure since the labour costs were a significant cause of the economic problems. It is artificial to treat the closure as the reason for the dismissals. The true reason was the economic difficulties facing the employers. [Counsel for the employers] accepted that if the decision had been to make cost savings by, say, making half the workers redundant, then the employers would in principle have had to open up consultations about possible ways of avoiding those redundancies. There is no logic in treating the proposed dismissal of the whole workforce, resulting in a closure, any differently. In each case the factors causing the dismissals are economic; the only difference lies in the proportion of the workforce whom it is proposed to dismiss.

---

[126] Section 188(7) of TULRCA.

[127] It should be pointed out that it has been held that an employer may be obliged to continue to perform its statutory consultation obligations under section 188(1) and (2) of TULRCA, notwithstanding the fact that it has been excused of the statutory requirement to inform the representatives under section 188(4) on the basis of 'special circumstances': *Shanahan Engineering Ltd v Unite the Union* [2010] All ER (D) 108 (March).   [128] [1993] ICR 720.

[129] *ibid.*, 752.   [130] [2002] IRLR 332.   [131] [2004] IRLR 9.   [132] [2008] ICR 163.

The EAT based its decision on the premise that Article 2(1) of the Collective Redundancies Directive requires consultation to begin when the employer contemplates measures or changes affecting the activity as a consequence of which a need for collective redundancies is to be expected. It also held that if the employer plans the closure of a site, but is of the view that redundancies would be avoided, there would be no requirement to consult over the commercial reasons and decision to close itself, at least not pursuant to section 188(2) of TULRCA.

However, in the case of *USA v Nolan*,[133] the Court of Appeal heard argument from the employer that this part of the decision of the EAT in *UK Coal Mining Ltd v NUM (Northumberland Area)* could not survive in light of the reasoning of the ECJ in *Akavan Erityisalojen Keskusliitto AEK ry v Fujitsu Siemens Computers Oy*.[134] The employer's argument was that *Akavan* had ruled that the obligation to consult only arose after the employer proposed to close a workplace, which would lead to redundancies, at the point when it had definitively made such a decision and formed an intention to dismiss the employees. Therefore, since the decision to close had been taken, it was not logically possible that the consultation exercise should involve an evaluation of the commercial rationales for the closure. The Court of Appeal felt that it was not in a position to find for or against the employer's argument, since the judgment of the ECJ was unclear. Hence it stated that it required further guidance as to the point in time at which the consultation obligation commenced and the nature of that obligation, and so made a reference to the ECJ. However, the ECJ declined jurisdiction[135] and, as such, this legal point remains undecided.

Furthermore, at present, it is not wholly clear if there is a duty imposed upon an employer to engage with the reasons for the proposed redundancies in a 'non-closure' case. A final point to make here is that the employer must meaningfully engage with the appropriate representatives 'with a view to reaching agreement' in terms of section 188(2) of TULRCA. It should be stressed that this is not the same thing as obliging the employer to 'reach agreement' with the appropriate representatives. So long as the employer is able to show that it took on board and dealt with the suggestions of the representatives on each of the matters listed in section 188(2) and other matters of concern to the employees,[136] it will have discharged its duty. This is the case even though the employer ultimately decides to reject the alternative proposals or representations of the representatives.[137]

There are two final points worth stressing. First, the EU Commission issued a Consultation Paper in April 2015 proposing to strengthen the information and consultation obligations contained in the Collective Redundancies Directive.[138] Its intention is to harmonize the meaning of 'information and consultation' across each of the Collective Redundancies Directive, the Acquired Rights Directive ('the ARD'),[139] and the Information and Consultation of Employees Directive ('I&C Directive').[140] In essence, the proposal is to introduce more stringent information and consultation obligations which are in line with the more extensive definitions of 'information and consultation' set out in the Recast European Works Councils Directive ('Recast EWC Directive').[141] However, at the time of writing, the precise content and nature of the adjustments had not been specified, and of course, whether the UK will be affected by any EU law reform will depend much on the negotiation package regarding the post-Brexit position. In addition, in April 2015,

---

[133] [2011] IRLR 40.   [134] [2010] ICR 444.   [135] [2013] ICR 193.

[136] See *Kelly v Hesley Group Ltd* [2013] IRLR 514.

[137] *Junk v Kühnel* (Case C-188/03) [2005] IRLR 310.

[138] See EU Commission Consultation Document (Brussels, 10 April 2015, C(2015) 2303 final).

[139] Council Directive 2001/23/EC of 12 March 2001 on the approximation of the laws of the Member States relating to the safeguarding of employees' rights, in the event of transfers of undertakings, businesses or parts of undertakings, or businesses (OJ 2001 L82/16).

[140] Directive 2002/14/EC (OJ 2002 L80/29).   [141] Directive 2009/38/EC (OJ 2009 L122/28).

the Department for Business, Innovation and Skills issued a call for evidence on the back of the publication of a parliamentary report into the collapse of City Link and the failure of that employer to consult with its redundant employees. In particular, the call focused on the effect of pre-packaged administrations and insolvency generally on the statutory consultation obligations and whether the existing law had created a financial incentive for employers not to engage in the consultation process.[142] The Insolvency Services examined the responses to the call for evidence in a publication summarizing the responses of consultees in November 2015. It concluded by stating that the UK Government will conduct further work on the issue but since then, little progress has been made.[143]

Reflection points

1. In your opinion, do you believe that it is satisfactory that an employer must consult with the workers' representatives about the commercial reasons for the collective redundancies? Did the EAT make an error in coming to this view in *UK Coal Mining Ltd v NUM (Northumberland Area)*?

2. Is it ever possible to divorce the consultation about the collective redundancies from consultation about the commercial rationales for collective redundancies?

20.5 THE PROTECTIVE AWARD AND NOTIFICATION REQUIREMENT

Where the employer fails to comply with the statutory information and consultation procedures in section 188 of TULRCA, the consequences are twofold.

(1) An employee, trade union, or employee representative may present a complaint to an employment tribunal under section 189(1), alleging a failure to (a) follow the relevant information and consultation procedures, or (b) arrange the election of appropriate representatives. The burden of proving the contrary falls on the employer under section 189(1B). However, it should be stressed that it is by no means the case that an affected employee has an automatic right to present a complaint to an employment tribunal under section 189(1)(a)–(d), since much depends on the nature of the claim being pursued. The italicized words in the following extract from section 189 determine when an employee representative, trade union, or the affected employee may present a complaint, and in what circumstances:

Section 189 Complaint and protective award

(1) Where an employer has failed to comply with a requirement of section 188 or section 188A, a complaint may be presented to an employment tribunal on that ground—

    (a) in the case of *a failure relating to the election of employee representatives*, by any of the affected employees or by any of the employees who have been dismissed as redundant;

---

[142] See https://www.gov.uk/government/consultations/collective-redundancy-consultation-for-employers-facing-insolvency (last visited 17 September 2017).

[143] See https://www.gov.uk/government/uploads/system/uploads/attachment_data/file/478683/summary_of_responses_-_combined_17–11–15.pdf (last visited 17 September 2017).

> (b) in the case of *any other failure relating to employee representatives*, by any of the employee representatives to whom the failure related,
>
> (c) *in the case of failure relating to representatives of a trade union*, by the trade union, and
>
> (d) *in any other case*, by any of the affected employees or by any of the employees who have been dismissed as redundant . . .
>
> (2) If the tribunal finds the complaint well-founded it shall make a declaration to that effect and may also make a protective award.

Two points emerge from this extract.

- First, it is primarily employee representatives and the relevant trade union that will have the right to present a claim, rather than any affected employee.

- Secondly, the statutory provision carefully prescribes the identity of the parties who are empowered to present a complaint and in what circumstances. For example, in the case of *TGWU v Brauer Coley*,[144] protective awards were made in favour of affected employees who were members of a trade union recognized by the employer. There were other employees in respect of whom the trade union was not recognized and the trade union representatives sought to have the tribunal make a protective award in respect of those other employees. However, the EAT refused on the ground that the trade union representatives had no right to claim in relation to those employees, since they were not of a description in respect of which the trade union was recognized by the employer. Instead, those other employees would have to make a claim under section 189(1) (a) or (d) of TULRCA, as the case may be.[145] Moreover, in the case of *Independent Insurance Co. Ltd v Aspinall*,[146] it was held that if an affected employee makes a claim under section 189(1), he/she is limited to making a claim for a protective award in respect of him/herself. Therefore, an affected employee is not entitled to claim a protective award for other employees similarly affected by the collective redundancies; only a complaint brought by the employee or trade union representatives will be entitled to proceed on that basis, since those representatives are the only parties upon whom the statute confers representative rights. One can argue that this is a further deficiency in the effectiveness of the legislation from the perspective of the social citizenship model, since the affected employees will be deprived of any machinery to enforce their right to a protective award if employee representatives lack sufficient incentive or resources to raise proceedings on their behalf.

(2) Turning now to the second implication of management failure to observe the requirements of the statutory information and consultation regime, one must look to the provisions of section 189(2) of TULRCA. Here, it is provided that if the employment tribunal finds the complaint to be well-founded, it must make a declaration to that effect and make a protective award. Section 188(8) and the decision of the High Court in the case of *Griffin v South West Water Services Ltd*[147] both demonstrate that the protective award is the exclusive sanction available for a breach of the provisions of sections 188 and 188A. Therefore, an injunction/interdict restraining the employer from effecting the collective redundancies is not competent. Although not explicitly decided in *Griffin v South West Water Services Ltd*, the same reasoning would apply to preclude (a) a claim for breach of statutory duty or (b) a tribunal or court from

---

[144] [2007] ICR 226.

[145] For a similar approach on the part of the Court of Appeal, see *Northgate HR Ltd v Mercy* [2008] ICR 410.

[146] [2011] ICR 1234.

[147] [1995] IRLR 15, 34–5 per Blackburne J.

declaring the redundancies to be null and void. However, judicial review of the employer's conduct may be possible depending on the status of the employer, which may enjoin a court to grant an injunction/interdict.[148]

20.5.1 Nature and extent of the protective award

Section 189(3) and (4) of TULRCA provides guidance on the nature and extent of the protective award as follows:

Section 189 Complaint and protective award

(3) A protective award is an award in respect of one or more descriptions of employees—

   (a) who have been dismissed as redundant, or whom it is proposed to dismiss as redundant, and

   (b) in respect of whose dismissal or proposed dismissal the employer has failed to comply with a requirement of section 188, ordering the employer to pay remuneration for the protected period.

(4) The protected period—

   (a) begins with the date on which the first of the dismissals to which the complaint relates takes effect, or the date of the award, whichever is the earlier, and

   (b) is of such length as the tribunal determines to be just and equitable in all the circumstances having regard to the seriousness of the employer's default in complying with any requirement of section 188; but shall not exceed 90 days.

Hence the maximum protective award payable to an affected employee is 90 days' actual pay (without any statutory maximum cap, since section 227 of the ERA does not apply to a protective award) for each affected employee. Additionally, it must be fixed at a length which an employment tribunal considers to be 'just and equitable in all the circumstances having regard to the seriousness of the employer's default in complying with any requirement of section 188'. The tribunals and courts have considered two particular aspects of the protective award in line with that definition:

(1) whether the protective award is intended to (a) compensate the employee for the employer's failure to properly inform and consult or (b) punish the employer for such a failure; and

(2) guidance has been provided as to how the 'just and equitable' criterion ought to be applied to fix the level of the award in individual cases.

20.5.2 The protective award: compensatory or punitive?

In the case of *Susie Radin v GMB*,[149] the Court of Appeal held that the purpose of a protective award is to punish the employer rather than to compensate an affected employee. Thus, it is designed to act as a deterrent and to dissuade the employer from

---

[148] *R v British Coal Corp. and Secretary of State for Trade, ex parte Vardy* [1993] ICR 720.
[149] [2004] ICR 893. See also *Shields Automotive v Langdon* (UKEAT/0059/12/BI, 21 March 2013); *AEI Cables v GMB* (UKEAT/0375/12/LA, 5 April 2013).

failing to follow its statutory obligations. This represented a departure from the previous case law, which had characterized the protective award as one designed to compensate the affected employees for the lack of consultation.[150] Since the award is punitive, the Court ruled that, in fixing the amount of the award, a proper approach where there had been no consultation is to start with the maximum period and reduce it only if there are mitigating circumstances justifying a reduction to an extent which the tribunal considers appropriate. It makes no difference that an employer may be unable to pay or is insolvent by the time the protective award is made. The case of *Smith v Cherry Lewis Ltd*[151] is an authority for the proposition that the tribunal should focus on the seriousness of the employer's default in failing to comply with its statutory duty of consultation, not on its ability to pay. It also decided that the level of the protective award should be judged at the point in time when the failure to consult occurred, rather than at some later date, e.g. the date on which the redundancies were effected or the date on which the complaint was presented to the employment tribunal.

20.5.3 The protective award: 'just and equitable'?

Another issue which must be addressed is the correlation between what is 'just and equitable' and the level at which the protective award is fixed. In *Susie Radin v GMB*,[152] the Court of Appeal furnished the following guidance which should be applied by employment tribunals and lower courts:

- the seriousness of the employer's non-compliance is important;

- the employer's default will vary in seriousness from the technical to a total failure to provide any of the statutory information or undertake any consultation, and where there has been no consultation, the likely consequence is that the maximum protective award of 90 days' actual pay will be made against the employer;[153] and

- whether the employer's failure was deliberate and calculated will be relevant, as will the availability of legal advice to the employer on their obligations under TULRCA.

As such, the link between the protected period was decoupled from the consultation period, which had been the approach adopted by the tribunals and courts before. Two issues which go to the heart of the question of the seriousness of the employer's breach are (1) the nature of the mitigating circumstances, including the extent of any information and consultation undertaken by the employer, and (2) the state of mind of the employer. For example, the protective award will be reduced to reflect the following mitigating factors:

- the extent of any non-co-operation on the part of the trade union or employee representatives;[154]

- the extent of any consultation which did take place, e.g. if some consultation has taken place, the starting point for compensation for a failure to inform and consult is not the maximum protective award of 90 days' actual pay sanctioned in *Susie Radin*;[155]

- whether continuing to trade would give rise to the risk of wrongful trading by the directors of the employer;[156]

---

[150] *Spillers-French (Holdings) Ltd v Union of Shop, Distributive and Allied Workers* [1980] ICR 31.
[151] [2005] IRLR 86.   [152] [2004] ICR 893.
[153] *E Ivor Hughes Educational Foundation v Morris* [2015] IRLR 696.
[154] *GMB v Lambeth Service Team Ltd* [2005] All ER (D) 153 (July).
[155] *London Borough of Barnet v Unison* (UKEAT/0191/13/RN, 19 December 2013).
[156] *AEI Cables v GMB* (UKEAT/0375/12/LA, 5 April 2013).

- whether the union acquiesced to the negligible consultation that did take place;[157] and
- whether the breaches of the statutory procedure are merely technical or minor.[158]

As such, the employer will be given credit for having undertaken some consultation or having elicited a desire or shown a willingness to consult.[159] This is consistent with the statement in *Amicus v GBS Tooling Ltd (in administration)*[160] that the tribunals have a wide discretion in determining what is 'just and equitable' in the circumstances. In particular, Burton J took into account mitigating circumstances which pre-dated the point at which the employer's proposal to make redundancies had crystallized. Here, the employer had become insolvent, and the union had been kept informed of the situation and that redundancies were likely prior to the onset of that insolvency. Burton J made a distinction between employers who had the deliberate intention of being secretive and those who had failed to inform and consult through negligence or misguidedness. Therefore, in determining the materiality of the employer's breach, the subjective intentions or motives of the employer will be relevant, as will the impact and effect of that breach.

In *Amicus v GBS Tooling Ltd (in administration)*, the employer had become insolvent and entered into the insolvency process which is known as 'administration'. One of the purposes of administration is to rescue the employer as a going concern if possible,[161] but more often than not a company will emerge from administration only to be wound up pursuant to liquidation. One question which has arisen is whether an administrator or liquidator will be liable to pay the protective award to the employees. In *Re Huddersfield Fine Worsteds Ltd*,[162] Neuberger LJ, in the Court of Appeal, held that where an administrator adopts the contracts of employment of the affected employees, protective awards payable to those employees do not have priority over the expenses of an administration. As such, administrators will not be liable for these sums.[163] In contrast, in *Day v Haine*,[164] the Court of Appeal held that protective awards were provable debts in the liquidation of the employer and so were preferential debts payable in priority to unsecured creditors of the employer.[165] The effect of that decision is that the employees will rank as preferred unsecured creditors in the liquidation of the employer and the funds which the liquidator has attained in order to pay creditors of the employer will be available to the affected employees to meet their protective awards.

20.5.4 Who has the right to be paid a protective award?

The persons who are entitled to claim a protective award are governed by section 189(1) and (2) of TULRCA, which we considered earlier. Meanwhile sections 190 and 191 delineate the nature of the affected employee's entitlement and the circumstances in which an affected employee will forfeit his/her right to a protective award:

---

[157] *Lancaster University v University College Union* [2011] IRLR 4.

[158] *Shields Automotive v Langdon* (UKEAT/0059/12/BI, 21 March 2013).

[159] For example, see *Leicestershire County Council v Unison* [2006] IRLR 810 where the protective award was reduced to ten days.   [160] [2005] IRLR 683.

[161] Paragraph 3(1)(a) of Schedule B1 to the Insolvency Act 1986.

[162] [2005] EWCA Civ 1072, [2006] ICR 205.

[163] See also *Unite the Union v Nortel Networks UK Ltd* [2010] IRLR 1042 on the differences in the treatment of protective awards and other sums in the administration of a corporate employer.

[164] [2008] EWCA Civ 626, [2008] ICR 1102.

[165] If the Court of Appeal had not reached that decision, the Secretary of State for Business, Energy and Industrial Strategy (i.e. the taxpayer) would have been liable to foot the bill of protective awards in terms of section 182 of the ERA.

Section 190 Entitlement under protective award

(1) Where an employment tribunal has made a protective award, every employee of a description to which the award relates is entitled, subject to the following provisions and to section 191, to be paid remuneration by his employer for the protected period.

(2) The rate of remuneration payable is a week's pay for each week of the period; and remuneration in respect of a period less than one week shall be calculated by reducing proportionately the amount of a week's pay . . .

(4) An employee is not entitled to remuneration under a protective award in respect of a period during which he is employed by the employer unless he would be entitled to be paid by the employer in respect of that period—

(a) by virtue of his contract of employment, or

(b) by virtue of sections 87 to 91 of the Employment Rights Act 1996 (rights of employee in period of notice), if that period fell within the period of notice required to be given by section 86(1) of that Act.

Section 191 Termination of employment during protected period

(1) Where the employee is employed by the employer during the protected period and—

(a) he is fairly dismissed by his employer otherwise than as redundant, or

(b) he unreasonably terminates the contract of employment, then, subject to the following provisions, he is not entitled to remuneration under the protective award in respect of any period during which but for that dismissal or termination he would have been employed.

(2) If an employer makes an employee an offer (whether in writing or not and whether before or after the ending of his employment under the previous contract) to renew his contract of employment, or to re-engage him under a new contract, so that the renewal or re-engagement would take effect before or during the protected period, and either—

(a) the provisions of the contract as renewed, or of the new contract, as to the capacity and place in which he would be employed, and as to the other terms and conditions of his employment, would not differ from the corresponding provisions of the previous contract, or

(b) the offer constitutes an offer of suitable employment in relation to the employee, the following subsections have effect.

(3) If the employee unreasonably refuses the offer, he is not entitled to remuneration under the protective award in respect of a period during which but for that refusal he would have been employed.

On its face, section 190(4) precludes an employee from being paid a protective award in circumstances in which he/she is employed by the employer during any part of the protected period. However, in *Cranswick Country Foods plc v Beall*,[166] the EAT stressed that it must be shown that the employees working during that period are not being paid under their contract of employment or in respect of the period of statutory notice under section 86 of the ERA. The EAT approached section 190(4) on the basis that it conferred the right to be paid a protective award in favour of those employees who had worked throughout the protected period but were subsequently dismissed. As such, this case yields the point that section 190(4) of TULRCA was designed to deal with the position of individuals who

---

[166] [2007] ICR 691.

continue to be employed during the protected period but are not being paid for some reason, such as that they are on long-term sickness leave or unpaid long-term leave of absence.

20.5.5 Notification requirements

It will be recalled that Article 3(1) of the Collective Redundancies Directive stipulates that the employer must forward to 'the competent public authority' details of the consultations with workers' representatives, the reasons for the redundancies, the number of workers to be made redundant, and other relevant matters. This is reflected in section 193 of TULRCA, which provides the following:

Section 193 Duty of employer to notify Secretary of State of certain redundancies

(1) An employer proposing to dismiss as redundant 100 or more employees at one establishment within a period of 90 days or less shall notify the Secretary of State, in writing, of his proposal—

   (a) before giving notice to terminate an employee's contract of employment in respect of any of those dismissals, and

   (b) at least 45 days before the first of those dismissals takes effect.

(2) An employer proposing to dismiss as redundant 20 or more employees at one establishment within such a period shall notify the Secretary of State, in writing, of his proposal—

   (a) before giving notice to terminate an employee's contract of employment in respect of any of those dismissals, and

   (b) at least 30 days before the first of those dismissals takes effect . . .

(4) A notice under this section shall—

   (a) be given to the Secretary of State by delivery to him or by sending it by post to him, at such address as the Secretary of State may direct in relation to the establishment where the employees proposed to be dismissed are employed,

   (b) where there are representatives to be consulted under section 188, identify them and state the date when consultation with them under that section began,

   (c) be in such form and contain such particulars, in addition to those required by paragraph (b), as the Secretary of State may direct.

(5) After receiving a notice under this section from an employer the Secretary of State may by written notice require the employer to give him such further information as may be specified in the notice.

(6) Where there are representatives to be consulted under section 188 the employer shall give to each of them a copy of any notice given under subsection (1) or (2) . . .

Although section 193 of TULRCA stipulates that notice must be given to the Secretary of State for Business, Energy and Industrial Strategy, in fact the notice must be delivered to the Insolvency Service,[167] by completing a Form HR1.[168] The basic pattern is that 30 days' prior notice must be given to the Insolvency Service where the employer proposes to dismiss for redundancy between 20 and 99 employees at one establishment[169] within a period

---

[167] See http://www.bis.gov.uk/insolvency (last visited 17 September 2017).

[168] See https://www.gov.uk/government/uploads/system/uploads/attachment_data/file/504957/NEW_HR1__2_.pdf (last visited 17 September 2017).

[169] It is currently unclear whether the words 'at one establishment' are to be interpreted in conformity with *USDAW v WW Realisation 1 Ltd* [2015] IRLR 577; see section 20.3.1.5.

of 90 days or less. The notification period is extended to 45 days where the employer's proposal is to dismiss 100 or more employees for redundancy at one establishment within the same period. The failure to observe the prescribed statutory notification will result in the employer being liable to criminal sanctions and relevant officers of the employer may be held personally liable.[170] A failure to file an HR1 form prior to the commencement of consultation with employee representatives will now attract unlimited fines.

> ### Reflection point
>
> Do you agree with the legal position that the protective award is intended to punish the employer who fails to comply with the statutory information and consultation requirements rather than to compensate the employees for the employer's failure to consult? Is there any difference?

 For additional reading on the information and consultation obligations, the protective award, and the notification requirement, visit the Online Resources for this book at www.oup.com/uk/cabrelli3e/

20.6 FINAL ASSESSMENT

From the perspective of the social citizenship model, which is said to underpin the Collective Redundancies Directive, it may be concluded that the overall effectiveness of the regime designed to regulate collective redundancies is modest at best. Throughout the discussion in this chapter, we have identified a number of areas in which the provisions of the Collective Redundancies Directive and the domestic law in TULRCA are deficient insofar as they purport to advance the social protection of employees in the context of collective redundancies. For example, neither an employee nor the State has the right to prevent proposed collective redundancies or question the rationales for the lay-offs with the employer as part of the information and consultation procedure. The bare minimum expectation imposed on the employer is to attempt to reach agreement with employee representatives, rather than actually reach any agreement. From the perspective of the employer, the statutory information and consultation requirements amount to a trade-off between the untrammelled power of management to direct and reduce its labour force as it requires, on the one hand, and the costs of a protective award in the event of non-compliance, on the other. Although the protective award is punitive, rather than compensatory in nature, the 90-day pay maximum and the relative willingness of the courts[171] to reduce it in response to the efforts at consultation taken by the employer serve to demonstrate that it is little more than a nuisance to the employer, as opposed to a real disincentive to the pursuit of collective redundancies. In fact, the significance of EU regulatory intervention in the field of collective redundancies lies more in the challenges which it presented to the single channel model of worker representation in the UK than anything it might offer in terms of meaningful social protection to employees earmarked for redundancy. This issue of a break with 'single channel' is a matter which we will address in Chapter A of the Online Resources when we consider the role of employee engagement and participation in the workplace.

---

[170] Section 194 of TULRCA.
[171] For example, see the credit given to the employer in *Amicus v GBS Tooling Ltd (in administration)* [2005] IRLR 683; and *Leicestershire County Council v Unison* [2006] IRLR 810.

ONLINE RESOURCES CHAPTER A

INFORMATION, CONSULTATION, PARTICIPATION, AND INSOLVENCY

This chapter evaluates the degree to which employment law facilitates worker participation in corporate decision-making and confers rights upon workers to be informed and consulted about developments in their employer's business and strategic operations, at both cross-border and national levels. The chapter presents arguments advanced in favour of worker participation, before going on to note how the scope of application of workers' rights of participation, information, and consultation has expanded over the years—partially in response to the decline in collective bargaining and the power of the trade unions in the UK over the past 40 years or so. Finally, the rights of employees where their employer becomes insolvent or enters into an insolvency process are examined.

PART VIII
COLLECTIVE LABOUR LAW

ONLINE RESOURCES CHAPTER B

INTRODUCTION TO TRADE UNIONS, STATUS, LISTING, AND INDEPENDENCE, AND MEMBERS' RIGHTS AND PROTECTION

The function, constitution, status, listing, and independence of trade unions are explored in this chapter. Moreover, the freedom of collective association and the role of trade unions in workplace representation are analysed. The chapter moves on to an exploration of the rights of members vis-à-vis their unions and the protection of trade union members in employment.

ONLINE RESOURCES CHAPTER C

RECOGNITION OF TRADE UNIONS, COLLECTIVE BARGAINING, AND INDUSTRIAL DEMOCRACY

The examination of the statutory machinery for the recognition of trade unions are explored in this chapter. The purpose of recognition and the rights of recognized trade unions are elaborated upon, before the chapter goes on to look at the role and effectiveness of collective bargaining within an industrial democratic framework. Finally, the status of collective agreements is considered.

ONLINE RESOURCES CHAPTER D

INDUSTRIAL ACTION AND STATUTORY IMMUNITIES

This chapter examines the law of trade disputes and industrial action in the UK, i.e. the law which regulates action taken by members of a trade union which imposes restrictions upon employers when collective relations between the employer and the workforce have broken down. The position is analysed in the context of the legality of industrial action in European law and under the European Convention on Human Rights.

■ GLOSSARY

ACAS the Advisory, Conciliation and Arbitration Service.

Additional adoption leave additional statutory leave available to parents of adopted children.

Additional maternity leave additional statutory leave available to mothers of children.

Adoption leave statutory leave available to parents of adopted children.

Appeal hearing hearing at which an employee appeals a decision of an employer, e.g. a decision to dismiss the employee or to reject a grievance raised by the employee.

Atypical working a working relationship from which at least one of the following six variables is missing (a) a full-time contract (b) with a single employer (c) for an indefinite period of time to (d) perform personal services (e) at the employer's premises, (f) irrespective of whether the employer has sufficient work to provide the employee or not.

Automatic theory of termination the theory that posits that the contract of employment automatically comes to an end when the employer or employee commits a repudiatory breach of the contract of employment.

Basic award the award comprising an element of the compensation available to an employee if he/she is successful in establishing that he/she has been unfairly dismissed under Part X of the Employment Rights Act 1996 ('ERA'). The maximum basic award is currently £15,240, but usually changes each year.

Burden of proof the onus of proving or disproving disputes, facts, or evidence in a case in court or the tribunal.

Business transfer the transfer, sale, or exchange of the assets and business of a legal person A to a legal person B or legal persons.

'But for' test the test for establishing direct discrimination in a 'criterion' case, namely (a) that there is a difference in sex, age, race, etc. between the claimant A (or a person with whom the claimant A is associated) and the comparator B and (b) that the evidence shows that A was treated less favourably than B.

CAC the Central Arbitration Committee.

Certification Officer an independent officer appointed by the Secretary of State after consultation with ACAS, whose principal function is to maintain a list of trade unions and employers' associations in terms of sections 2 and 123 of the Trade Union and Labour Relations (Consolidation) Act 1992 ('TULRCA'), and to evaluate whether a trade union ought to be considered 'independent' under section 6 of TULRCA.

CJEU the Court of Justice of the European Union.

Codes of practice codes issued under statutory authority such as the ACAS Code of Practice 1 on Disciplinary and Grievance Procedures, and the Codes of Practice on Employment and Equal Pay, both promulgated by the EHRC.

Collective agreement any agreement or arrangement made by or on behalf of one or more trade unions and one or more employers or employers' associations and relating to one or more of the following matters:

(a) terms and conditions of employment, or the physical conditions in which any workers are required to work;
(b) engagement or non-engagement, or termination or suspension of employment or the duties of employment, of one or more workers;
(c) allocation of work or the duties of employment between workers or groups of workers;
(d) matters of discipline;
(e) a worker's membership or non-membership of a trade union;
(f) facilities for officials of trade unions; and
(g) machinery for negotiation or consultation, and other procedures, relating to any of the above matters, including the recognition by employers or employers'

associations of the right of a trade union to represent workers in such negotiation or consultation or in the carrying out of such procedures.

Collective bargaining negotiations relating to or connected with the conclusion of any agreement or arrangement made by or on behalf of one or more trade unions and one or more employers or employers' associations and relating to one or more of the following matters:

(a) terms and conditions of employment, or the physical conditions in which any workers are required to work;

(b) engagement or non-engagement, or termination or suspension of employment or the duties of employment, of one or more workers;

(c) allocation of work or the duties of employment between workers or groups of workers;

(d) matters of discipline;

(e) a worker's membership or non-membership of a trade union;

(f) facilities for officials of trade unions; and

(g) machinery for negotiation or consultation, and other procedures, relating to any of the above matters, including the recognition by employers or employers' associations of the right of a trade union to represent workers in such negotiation or consultation or in the carrying out of such procedures.

Collective labour law the labour laws regulating the constitution, status, listing, independence, and recognition of trade unions, the relationship between trade union members and their trade union, the protection of trade union members in employment, the statutory recognition or derecognition of trade unions by employers, the regulation of collective bargaining, and the law of industrial action, on which see Chapters B, C, and D of the Online Resources.

Collective laissez-faire the British approach to the regulation of industrial relations, involving the promotion of collective bargaining as the preferred means of setting terms and conditions of employment and of settling industrial disputes. Rather than intervening directly in employment relations by conferring statutory rights upon individual employees, successive British Governments left it to trade unions and employers to negotiate the rules that would govern working lives and production in a framework which operated autonomously and independently from the State.

Collective redundancies dismissals effected by an employer for one or more reasons not related to the individual workers concerned where, according to the choice of the Member States, the number of redundancies is either:

(a) over a period of 30 days:
  (i) at least ten in establishments normally employing more than 20 and fewer than 100 workers,
  (ii) at least 10 per cent of the number of workers in establishments normally employing at least 100 but fewer than 300 workers,
  (iii) at least 30 in establishments normally employing 300 workers or more, or
(b) over a period of 90 days, at least 20, whatever the number of workers normally employed in the establishments in question.

Common law the principles and rules, embodied in case law rather than legislative enactments, that have been developed and interpreted over the centuries by the judiciary in the common law courts.

Compensatory award the award comprising an element of the compensation available to an employee if he/she is successful in establishing that he/she has been unfairly dismissed under Part X of the ERA. The maximum compensatory award is currently the lower of £83,682 or 12 months' wages/salary of the employee, but usually changes each year.

Compulsory maternity leave statutory leave from work granted to mothers of children during the two-week period commencing with the date of childbirth.

Confidential information information belonging to the employer of a confidential nature, usually including secret processes, policies, information, and trade secrets.

Constructive dismissal a situation where the employee terminates the contract of employment (with or without notice) in circumstances in which he/she is entitled to terminate it without notice by reason of the employer's conduct. The employer's conduct must amount to a repudiatory breach of the contract of employment.

Consultation a meeting or conference at which advice is given or views are exchanged.

Continuous employment the period of employment of an employee calculated for statutory purposes in accordance with sections 210–219 of the ERA.

Contract for services a contract agreed between an individual service provider and a recipient of those services whereby the former agrees to perform work provided by the latter in return for the payment of a fee by the latter for a definite or indefinite period of time. The contract may be express or implied, and if it is express, agreed orally or in writing.

Contract of employment a contract of service or apprenticeship.

Contract of service a contract agreed between an employee and employer whereby the former agrees to perform work provided by the latter in return for remuneration for a definite or indefinite period of time. The contract may be express or implied, and if it is express, agreed orally or in writing.

Control test one of the tests applied to determine whether an individual providing personal services to a third party is an employee, which asks whether the employer has a sufficient degree of power to decide how the thing is to be done by the individual, the way in which it is to be done by the individual, the means to be employed by the individual in doing it, and the time when and the place where it is to be done by the individual.

Corrective justice a conception of justice enjoining one party to make good, i.e. 'correct', the loss or harm suffered by another party as a result of a wrong inflicted by the former on the latter.

Custom and practice of the workplace implicit understandings of the employee and employer which develop over time and crystallize into workplace rules, becoming legally binding.

Declaration of rights a declaration as to the rights of the employee and the employer in relation to the matters to which certain dis-crimination proceedings relate under section 124(2)(a) of the Equality Act 2010 ('EA').

Decollectivization the process whereby the number of employees covered by collective agreements in workplaces diminishes over time.

Deunionization the process whereby the number of employees who are members of a trade union diminishes over time.

Direct discrimination the situation where, because of a protected characteristic, an employer A treats an employee B less favourably than A treats others or would treat others.

Disciplinary hearing a hearing held as part of an employer's disciplinary procedure.

Disciplinary procedure a procedure, policy, or process adopted by an employer to be applied in circumstances in which an employee of the employer is subject to disciplinary proceedings.

Discrimination arising from disability the situation where an employer A treats an employee B unfavourably, because of something arising in consequence of B's disability, and which A cannot show to be a proportionate means of achieving a legitimate aim.

Discrimination by association the situation where an employee A is treated by his/her employer B less favourably than C because of a protected characteristic relating to D, where D is a person associated with A.

Discrimination by perception the situation where an employee A is treated by his/her employer B less favourably than C because of a protected characteristic which B perceives A to have, but A does not actually have.

Dismissal the actual or constructive termination of the employee's contract of employment (with or without notice) by the employer.

Distributive justice a model of justice which seeks to redistribute resources, wealth, power, and opportunities away from a group A in society that is structurally advantaged or over-represented towards a structurally disadvantaged or under-represented group B in society.

Dominant purpose test one of the tests applied to determine whether an individual is working under a 'worker' contract or a 'contract personally to do work'. The question is whether the obligation of personal service is the dominant purpose of the contract entered into between the individual service provider and the third party.

Dual-channel system of representation a model of worker representation whereby worker representation functions are differentiated and then divided between separate worker representation structures, such as trade unions, on the one hand, and works councils, on the other.

Duty to make reasonable adjustments the obligation imposed on employers under sections 20–22 of the EA to make reasonable adjustments for disabled employees where such employees suffer a substantial disadvantage in comparison with persons who are not disabled, in relation to the application of a provision criterion or practice, a physical feature of the workplace, or the absence of an auxiliary aid.

EAT the Employment Appeal Tribunal.

ECJ the European Court of Justice.

Economic dismissal a situation where an employee is dismissed for economic reasons having no connection with the employee's conduct, performance, competence, capability, etc., i.e. a redundancy situation.

Economic torts the torts of intimidation, inducement to commit a breach of contract, causing loss to a third party by unlawful means, and conspiracy.

Economic/business reality test one of the tests applied to determine whether an individual providing personal services to a third party is an employee, which asks whether the performance of the work was undertaken by the individual in business on his/her own account having assumed a sufficient level of financial risk.

ECtHR the European Court of Human Rights.

Effective date of termination a statutory concept that identifies the date of termination of an employee's contract of employment under section 97 of the ERA.

EHRC the Equality and Human Rights Commission.

Elective theory of termination the theory that posits that the contract of employment does not automatically come to an end when the employer or employee commits a repudiatory breach of the contract of employment, but only when that repudiatory breach is accepted by the innocent party.

Employee an individual providing personal services to a third party who has entered into or works under a contract of employment.

Employment judge a legally qualified judge in an employment tribunal.

Enhanced redundancy package a package made available by the employer to employees who are made redundant that is more generous than that available under the statutory scheme.

Enhanced redundancy payment a contractually agreed payment made under an enhanced redundancy package that is made available by the employer to employees who are made redundant that is more generous than that available under the statutory scheme.

ET an employment tribunal.

EUCFR the European Union Charter of Fundamental Rights pronounced on 7 December 2000 in Nice (OJ 2000 C364/1) and a second time in Strasbourg on 12 December 2007 (OJ 2007 C303/1) and also published in OJ 2010 C83/389.

European Works Councils works councils established under the Transnational Information and Consultation of Employees Regulations 1999.

Express term (in the contract of employment) contractual terms agreed between an employer and employee orally or in writing.

Fair and proper procedure a disciplinary procedure, policy, or process adopted by an employer and applied in circumstances in which an employee of the employer is subject to disciplinary proceedings, which meets the requirements of (1) the Code of Practice 1 on Disciplinary and Grievance Procedures issued by ACAS and (2) unfair dismissal law.

Fiduciary a person who is subject to fiduciary obligations, usually someone who has had trust reposed in them by a third party.

'First in, first out' ('FIFO') a selection criterion whereby the employees with the greatest length of service are prioritized for redundancy.

Fixed-term contract a contract of employment where the employment under the contract is not intended to be permanent and provision is made in the contract for it to terminate by virtue of a limiting event, namely (a) in the case of a contract for a fixed-term, the expiry of the term, (b) in the case of a contract made in contemplation of the performance of a specific task, the performance of the task, and (c) in the case of a contract which provides for its termination on the occurrence of an event (or the failure of an event to occur), the occurrence of the event (or the failure of the event to occur).

Fixed-term work work performed by an individual working under a fixed-term contract.

Flexibility clause an express term in a contract of employment empowering an employer to compel an employee to adapt his job responsibilities to those newly prescribed by the employer.

Formal equality a model whereby a group A that is deemed to be alike to a group B is treated in the same way as group B, i.e. consistently, and no less favourably than group B.

Freedom of contract doctrine the doctrine embraced by the common law that contracting parties are free to agree the terms of their contract, subject to the law, which will be upheld by the State in a court of law.

Frustration termination of the contract of employment where supervening events render it impossible for the employee and employer to perform their respective contractual obligations.

'Function' test one of the historical tests applied by the law to determine whether an employee had been made redundant under the ERA, namely whether the actual work done by the employee on a daily basis ceased to exist.

Functional flexibility the policy adopted by employers whereby they demand that employees regularly retrain and reskill themselves to adapt to new technological innovations and methods and patterns of work in the employer's workplace.

Garden leave clause an express term of the contract of employment empowering the employer to instruct the employee not to attend work during the period of notice of termination of the latter's employment.

Gender pay gap the percentage gap in pay between female and male workers.

Gig economy an environment in which temporary positions are common and organizations contract with independent workers for short-term or on-demand engagements, involving individuals selling their services to buyers who are matched together via a technologically intermediated interface, such as an app or internet platform operated and co-ordinated by companies such as Uber, Deliveroo, etc.

Grievance procedure a procedure, policy, or process adopted by an employer to be applied in circumstances in which an employee raises a complaint against the employer or employees employed by the employer.

Harassment unwanted conduct by A relating to a protected characteristic which has the purpose or effect of (a) violating an employee B's dignity or (b) creating an intimidating, hostile, degrading, humiliating, or offensive environment for employee B.

Illegality a common law doctrine which posits that a contract is void from the outset on the ground of public policy.

ILO the International Labour Organization.

Implied contractual term of mutual trust and confidence the implied term of the contract of employment which enjoins neither party to the contract, without reasonable and proper cause, to conduct itself in a manner calculated or likely to destroy or seriously damage the relationship of confidence and trust between employer and employee.

Implied term in fact a term of a contract of employment which is implied because it is necessary to do so in order to give business efficacy to the contract of employment agreed between an employee and employer.

Implied term in law a term implied into a particular class or type of contract, such as a contract of employment, based on 'necessity', i.e. because it is a 'necessary incident' of the employment relationship based on 'wider considerations' or 'general considerations' of policy.

Implied terms of the employment contract an implied term in law of the contract of employment prescribed by the common law.

Imposed terms terms inserted into a particular class or type of contract, such as a contract of employment, by virtue of statute, e.g. the 'sex equality' clause inserted into all contracts of employment pursuant to section 66 of the EA.

Indirect discrimination the situation where an employer A applies to an employee B a provision, criterion, or practice in relation to a protected characteristic of B which:

(a) puts, or would put, persons with whom B shares the protected characteristic at a particular disadvantage when compared with persons with whom B does not share the protected characteristic;

(b) puts, or would put, B at that particular disadvantage; and

(c) A cannot show to be a proportionate means of achieving a legitimate aim.

Individual employment law the common law and statutory provisions that regulate the individual contract of employment.

Industrial action strike action, 'work to rule' action, and picketing.

Industrial relations relations between the management of an industrial enterprise and its employees.

Inequality of bargaining power the situation where party A has the upper hand in negotiations with party B owing to a power imbalance in favour of A.

Injunction/interdict a court order by which an individual is restrained from performing a particular act. An interdict is the equivalent of an injunction in Scots law.

Insolvency process liquidation, receivership, administration, sequestration (in Scotland), or bankruptcy (in England and Wales).

Insolvent in terms of section 123(1)(e) and (2) of the Insolvency Act 1986, a company is deemed to be insolvent where it is unable to pay its debts as they fall due or its liabilities exceed its assets.

Integration test one of the tests applied to determine whether an individual providing personal services to a third party is an employee or a worker, which asks whether the individual was an integral part of the business or organization of the putative employer.

Job evaluation study a study undertaken with a view to evaluating, in terms of the demands made on a person by reference to factors such as effort, skill, and decision-making, the jobs to be done by some or all of the workers in an undertaking or group of undertakings.

'Job package'/'contract' test one of the historical tests applied by the law to determine whether an employee had been made redundant under the ERA, namely whether the work which the employee was contractually obliged to perform had ceased to exist.

Judicial review a procedure in English administrative law by which the courts in England and Wales supervise the exercise of public power on the application of an individual.

Labour market flexibility the managerial demand for flexible labour, usually contracted on the basis of an atypical working relationship, such as zero-hours contract workers, casual workers, home workers, agency workers, etc.

'Last in, first out' ('LIFO') a criterion historically applied by employers to decide the employees who would be made redundant, whereby the employees with the shortest length of service would be selected for redundancy.

Like work a test for establishing whether a claimant is entitled to an equal pay claim.

Managerial prerogative the employer's general power to assign tasks and functions to the employee and to direct and allocate methods and patterns of working as it sees fit.

Material factor an employer's defence to an equal pay claim.

Maternity leave statutory leave available to mothers of children.

Maternity pay statutory pay paid to an employee when she is on maternity leave.

Mobility clause an express term in a contract of employment empowering an employer to transfer an employee from one place of work to another.

Mutuality of obligation test one of the tests applied to determine whether an individual providing personal services to a third party is an employee, which asks whether there is on ongoing commitment on the part of the employer to provide a reasonable and minimum amount of work to the employee in the future and pay for it, and a corresponding obligation imposed on the employee to perform that reasonable and minimum amount of work when offered in the future.

Neoliberal philosophy the philosophy which seeks to limit State interference in the conduct and practices of the individual, entailing a guarantee of freedom from State coercion.

Occupational requirements exception the provisions in Schedule 9 to the EA which prescribe where it is legal to lawfully commit direct or indirect discrimination in the workplace.

Ordinary adoption leave a period of statutory leave available to parents of adopted children.

Ordinary maternity leave a period of statutory leave available to mothers of children.

Parental leave statutory leave available to parents of children.

Part-time work work performed by an individual on a part-time basis.

Paternity leave statutory leave available to fathers and partners or civil partners of mothers of children.

Personal service one of the tests applied to determine whether an individual providing personal services to a third party is an employee, which asks whether the individual is contractually obliged to provide the service to the third party on a personal basis without substitution.

Pool for redundancy the body of employees against whom selection criteria will be applied as a means of deciding who will be made redundant.

Positive action the situation where persons falling within group A are treated more favourably than persons falling within group B, where groups A and B are of equal merit and group A has experienced, and experiences, structural barriers, disadvantages or under-representation in the workplace, and group B has not and does not.

Positive discrimination preferential, or more favourable, treatment of a particular group A or constituency A in the workplace.

Protected characteristics sex, race, age, disability, gender reassignment, marriage and civil partnership, pregnancy and maternity, religion or belief, and sexual orientation.

Protective awards awards of compensation to an employee of up to 90 days' pay for a failure of an employer to comply with the provisions of section 188 or 188A of TUL-RCA.

'Reason why' test the test for establishing direct discrimination, namely (a) that there is a difference in sex, age, race, etc. between the claimant A (or a person with whom the claimant A is associated) and the comparator B, (b) that the evidence shows that A was treated less favourably than B, and (c) the factor which influenced the alleged discriminator/employer to act in the way that it did was the reason of sex, age, race, etc.

Redundant/redundancy where the dismissal of an employee is wholly or mainly attributable to:

(a) the fact that his/her employer has ceased or intends to cease—
   (i) to carry on the business for the purposes of which the employee was employed by him/her, or
   (ii) to carry on that business in the place where the employee was so employed; or
(b) the fact that the requirements of that business—
   (i) for employees to carry out work of a particular kind, or
   (ii) for employees to carry out work of a particular kind in the place where the employee was employed by the employer,

have ceased or diminished or are expected to cease or diminish.

Re-engagement a remedy available to an employee who has succeeded in his/her unfair dismissal claim, whereby the employee is entitled to re-employment with the employer in suitable and comparable employment.

Reinstatement a remedy available to an employee who has succeeded in his/her unfair dismissal claim, whereby the employee is entitled to re-employment with the employer in his/her old job.

Reorganization the organization or reorganization of an employer's business according to scientific principles of management in order to increase efficiency, often involving the redeployment or redundancy of staff.

Repudiatory breach of the contract of employment a breach of the contract of employment going to the root of that contract, or conduct which demonstrates that the employer no longer intends to be bound by one or more of the essential terms of the contract, entitling the employee to treat him/herself as discharged from any further performance.

Restrictive covenant/clauses in restraint of trade a non-compete covenant, non-solicitation of customers covenant, and/or a non-solicitation of employees covenant.

Right to appeal an employee's right to appeal a decision to dismiss him/her or reject his/her grievance under an employer's disciplinary procedure or grievance procedure.

Right to request flexible working the statutory right to request to work flexibly under section 80F of the ERA.

Right to take time off work to deal with dependants the statutory right to take time off work to deal with emergencies with dependants under section 57A of the ERA.

Selection criteria the factors to be applied to the pool for redundancy as a means of deciding who will be made redundant.

Service provision change a situation in which—

(a) activities cease to be carried out by a person ('a client') on his/her own behalf and are carried out instead by another person on the client's behalf ('a contractor'),

(b) activities cease to be carried out by a contractor on a client's behalf (whether or not those activities had previously been carried out by the client on his/her own behalf) and are carried out instead by another person ('a subsequent contractor') on the client's behalf, or

(c) activities cease to be carried out by a contractor or a subsequent contractor on a client's behalf (whether or not those activities had previously been carried out by the client on his/her own behalf) and are carried out instead by the client on his/her own behalf, and in which the following conditions are satisfied:

(i) immediately before the service provision change—

(A) there is an organized grouping of employees situated in the UK which has as its principal purpose the carrying out of the activities concerned on behalf of the client,

(B) the client intends that the activities will, following the service provision change, be carried out by the transferee other than in connection with a single specific event or task of short-term duration, and

(ii) the activities concerned do not consist wholly or mainly of the supply of goods for the client's use.

Sex equality clause a statutorily imposed term of the contract of employment under Chapter 3 of Part 5 of the EA.

Sexual harassment unwanted conduct of a sexual nature by A which has the purpose or effect of (a) violating an employee B's dignity or (b) creating an intimidating, hostile, degrading, humiliating, or offensive environment for employee B.

Sham test the test established by *Autoclenz Ltd v Belcher* which enables a court to override the terms of a purported commercial contract for services and instead characterize it as a contract of employment. or a 'worker' contract

Shared parental leave a form of 'leave transfer' from the mother of a child to the father/partner, enabling leave to be taken simultaneously by the mother and the father of the child, and regulated in terms of the Shared Parental Leave Regulations 2014, the Statutory Shared Parental Pay (General) Regulations 2014, and the Maternity and Adoption

Leave (Curtailment of Statutory Rights to Leave) Regulations 2014.

Single-channel system of representation a model of worker representation whereby worker representation functions are monopolized by, and channelled exclusively through, trade unions.

Statutory immunities from liability in tort the immunities from liability in respect of the economic torts prescribed in Part V of TULRCA.

Statutory redundancy payment a statutory payment which must be made to an employee who has been dismissed by reason of redundancy and has been continuously employed for a period of not less than two years ending with the date on which the last of the four or more weeks before the service of the notice of intention to claim a statutory redundancy payment came to an end.

Subordination one of the tests applied to determine whether an individual is working under a 'contract personally to do work'. The question is whether the individual is subordinate to the hirer of his/her labour in the sense of some subservience to the direction of the hirer in return for the receipt of remuneration.

Substantive equality a model of equality in which the interests of a group A are preferred over those of group B, where group A has experienced, and experiences, structural barriers, disadvantages, or under-representation in the workplace, and group B has not and does not.

Summary dismissal the situation where an employer, being entitled to terminate an employee's contract of employment without notice by reason of the employee's conduct, terminates it either (a) without notice, (b) by giving shorter notice than that which, in the absence of conduct entitling the employer to terminate the contract without notice, the employer would be required to give to terminate the contract, or (c) by giving notice which includes, or is accompanied by, a statement in writing that the employer would, by reason of the employee's conduct, be entitled to terminate the contract without notice.

Suspension clause an express term of the contract of employment empowering the employer to suspend the employment contract for a particular reason or reasons.

TFEU the Treaty on the Functioning of the European Union.

Trade secret a secret process, invention, technology, information, procedure, policy, or technique owned by an employer.

Trade union an organization (whether temporary or permanent):

(a) which consists wholly or mainly of workers of one or more descriptions and whose principal purposes include the regulation of relations between workers of that description or those descriptions and employers or employers' associations, or

(b) which consists wholly or mainly of—

   (i) constituent or affiliated organizations which fulfil the conditions in paragraph (a) (or themselves consist wholly or mainly of constituent or affiliated organizations which fulfil those conditions), or

   (ii) representatives of such constituent or affiliated organizations, and whose principal purposes include the regulation of relations between workers and employers or between workers and employers' associations, or the regulation of relations between its constituent or affiliated organizations.

Two-tier labour force a labour force where some of those working are employees working on the basis of a permanent contract of employment and others are working on the basis of some other atypical work contract which does not attract the benefit of common law and statutory employment rights.

Unfair dismissal the dismissal of an employee which is unfair in terms of Part X of the ERA.

Unilateral variation clause an express term in a contract of employment empowering an employer to vary the terms of the contract of employment without the consent of the employee.

Vicarious liability the doctrine whereby an employer A is held liable to third party C for the torts committed by its employee B against C in the course of B's employment.

Victimization the situation where the employer subjects an employee to a detriment as a result of the employee performing one of the following acts:

(a) the employee brings proceedings under the EA;

(b) the employee gives evidence or information in connection with proceedings under the EA;

(c) the employee does any other thing for the purposes of or in connection with the EA; or

(d) the employee makes an allegation (whether or not express) that the employer or another person has contravened the EA.

Wage protection legislation provisions protecting the wages of workers in Parts II and III of the ERA.

Wage-work bargain the basic agreement between the employer and the employee, in terms of which the employer provides a reasonable and minimum amount of work and pays for it and the employee performs the reasonable and minimum amount of work offered by the employer.

Wages councils statutory bodies comprising representatives of employees and employers, established by the Wages Councils Acts 1945, 1969, and 1979 which prescribed minimum remuneration for particular sectors of the economy or industries only. The wages councils were the statutory successors of the Edwardian trade boards and were abolished in the 1990s.

Work of equal value a test for establishing whether a claimant is entitled to an equal pay claim.

Work rated as equivalent a test for establishing whether a claimant is entitled to an equal pay claim.

Work-life balance the balance in an individual's life between time spent in the workplace and time spent outside the workplace.

Workers individuals who have entered into or work under (a) a contract of employment, or (b) any other contract whereby the individual undertakes to do or perform personally any work or services for another party to the contract whose status is not by virtue of the contract that of a client or customer of any profession or business undertaking carried on by the individual.

Wrongful dismissal an outright/summary or constructive dismissal of an employee by an employer in repudiatory breach of the contract of employment.

Zero-hours contract a contract of employment or other worker's contract under which (a) the undertaking to do or perform work or services is an undertaking to do so conditionally on the employer making work or services available to the worker, and (b) there is no certainty that any such work or services will be made available to the worker.

■ INDEX